BLACK LAMB AND GREY FALCON

REBECCA WEST (1892–1983) was the adopted
name of Cecily Isabel Fairfield, born in County Kerry
of a Scottish mother and an Anglo-Irish journalist
father.

Her writing career encompassed poetry, criticism,
fiction and political commentary, but began with journalism supporting the suffragette movement. In 1912
she wrote as outspoken review of H. G. Wells' book,
Marriage, which led to a love-affair that lasted ten
turbulent years and gave them a son, Anthony West.
It was during this period that Rebecca West developed into a writer of considerable skill and depth. Her
first novel, *The Return of the Soldier* (1918), describes
the homecoming of a shell-shocked soldier and was
followed by seven others: *The Judge* (1922), *The Strange
Necessity* (1928), *Harriet Hume* (1929), *The Thinking
Reed* (1936), *The Fountain Overflows* (1956) and *The
Birds Fall Down* (1966). Her last, *Cousin Rosamund*
(1988), was unfinished. *Black Lamb and Grey Falcon*
(1941) is widely regarded as West's magnum opus.

GEOFF DYER's many books include *But Beautiful*
(winner of the Somerset Maugham Prize), *Out of
Sheer Rage* (a finalist for the US National Book Critics
Circle Award), *Yoga for People Who Can't Be Bothered
To Do It* (winner of the WH Smith Best Travel Book
Award) and most recently *The Ongoing Moment*
(winner of the ICP Infinity Award for Writing on
Photography). He recently received the E. M. Forster
Award from the American Academy of Arts and
Letters.

REBECCA WEST

Black Lamb and Grey Falcon

A JOURNEY THROUGH

YUGOSLAVIA

Introduced by Geoff Dyer

CANONGATE

Edinburgh · London

First published in Great Britain in 1942
by Macmillan London Ltd

First published as a Canongate Classic in 1993
by Canongate Press Ltd, Edinburgh

This edition first published by Canongate Books Ltd,
14 High Street, Edinburgh, EH1 1TE

British Library Cataloguing-in-Publication Data
A catalogue record for this book is available on
request from the British Library

1 84195 787 9 (10-digit ISBN)
978 1 84195 787 6 (13-digit ISBN)

The publishers gratefully acknowledge subsidy
from the Scottish Arts Council towards the
publication of this title

Printed and bound in Great Britain by
Clays Ltd, St Ives plc

www.canongate.co.uk

TO MY FRIENDS IN YUGOSLAVIA,
WHO ARE NOW ALL DEAD OR ENSLAVED

Καὶ τὴν ποθεινὴν πατρίδα παράσχου αὐτοῖς,
Παραδείσου πάλιν ποιῶν πολίτας αὐτούς.

Grant to them the Fatherland of their desire,
and make them again citizens of Paradise.

Note on Pronunciation

The spelling of Yugoslavian names presents a serious problem. The Serbo-Croat language is spoken in all parts of Yugoslavia described in this book; but to write it the Serbs use the Cyrillic alphabet (which is much the same as the Russian, but simpler) and the Croats use the Latin alphabet. Most foreign writers on Yugoslavia follow the Croatian spelling, but this is not satisfactory. The Cyrillic alphabet is designed to give a perfect phonetic rendering of the Slav group of languages, and provides characters for several consonants which other groups lack. The Latin alphabet can only represent these consonants by clapping accents on other consonants which bear some resemblance to them; and the Croatian usage still further confuses the English eye by using 'c' to represent not 's' and 'k' but 'ts,' and 'j' for 'y.' I have found that in practice the casual English reader is baffled by this unfamiliar use of what looks familiar and is apt to pass over names without grasping them clearly. I have therefore done my best to transliterate all Yugoslavian names into forms most likely to convey the sound of them to English ears. Cetinje is written here as Tsetinye, Jajce as Yaitse, Peč as Petch, Šestinje as Shestinye. Kosovo I have written Kossovo, though the Serbo-Croat language uses no double consonants, because we take them as a sign that the preceding vowel is short.

This is a rough and ready method, and at certain points it has broken down. The Cyrillic alphabet provides special characters for representing liquid consonants; the Latin alphabet can only indicate these by adding 'j' to the consonant, and this is extremely confusing at the end of a word. In pronouncing 'Senj' the speaker says 'Sen,' then starts to says a 'y' sound, and stops half-way. The English reader, seeing 'Senj,' pronounces it 'Senge' to rhyme with 'Penge.' But the spelling 'Seny' makes him pronounce it as a disyllable; and if the suggestion of the Royal Geographical Society is adopted and the word is spelled 'Sen" ' he is apt for some strange reason to interpret this sign as a Scotch 'ch.' I have therefore regarded the problem as insoluble, and have left such words spelt in the Croatian fashion, with the hope that readers will take the presence of the letter 'j' as warning that there are dark phonetic doings afoot. In 'Bitolj,' I may add, the 'l' has almost entirely disappeared, having only a short 'y' sound.

I have also given up any attempt to transliterate 'Sarajevo' or 'Skoplje.' For one thing 'Sarajevo' is a tragically familiar form; and for another, it is not a pure Slav word, and has the Turkish word '*saraï*,' a fortress, embedded in it, with a result hardly to be conveyed by any but a most uncouth spelling. It is pronounced something like 'Sa-raï-ye-vo,' with a faint accent on the second syllable, and a short 'e.' As for 'Skoplje,' the one way one must not pronounce it is the way the English reader will certainly pronounce it if it is spelt 'Skoplye.' The 'o' is short, and all the letters after it are combined into a single sound. I have committed another irregularity by putting an 'e' into the word 'Tsrna,' so often found in place-names. This makes it easier for the English reader to grasp that the vowel sound in the rolled 'r' comes before it and not after.

R. W.

Contents

Introduction

THE AUTHOR OF GUIDE BOOKS SHOULD HAVE NO ARTISTIC personality. Entirely at the mercy of the place being written about, he or she is ideally an anonymous conduit of reliable information about bus times, places to stay and museum opening hours. At the other end of the spectrum, in his book *Fiction*, photographer Michael Ackerman claims that 'places do not exist. A place is just my idea of it'.[1]

Literary travel writing thrives between the extremes represented by the travel guide and the solipsistic Ackerman. The best travel writers may be of only limited reliability when it comes to bus times, but they express timeless truths about the buses of a given country – or at least about their relationship with those buses. Take D. H. Lawrence, whose responsiveness to places was both instantaneous and profound. Editors and publishers were keenly aware of this gift and Lawrence was eager to turn it to financial advantage.

When Rebecca West visited Norman Douglas in Florence in 1921 he joked that although Lawrence had been in town only a few hours he was probably already hammering out an article, 'vehemently and exhaustively describing the temperament of the people'.[2] To West this seemed 'obviously a silly thing to do', but Douglas was right: they turned up at Lawrence's hotel to find him doing just that. At the time West thought that Lawrence did not know enough about Florence 'to make his views of real value'. It was only after his death that she appreciated that Lawrence 'was writing about the state of his own soul at that moment' and could only do so in symbolic terms. For this purpose 'the city of Florence was as good a symbol as any other'.[3]

West wrote this in 1931. She had not yet made the first of the trips to Yugoslavia which would form the basis of *Black Lamb and Grey Falcon*, but the importance of this realisation for her own *magnum opus* is considerable. Indeed, relative to the size of the finished book, her experience of Yugoslavia was pretty skimpy. As Edith Durham, a noted authority on the Balkans, bitchily put it at the time, 'The novelist Miss West has written an immense book on the strength of one pleasure trip to Yugoslavia, but with no previous knowledge of land or people.'[4] For the record, Miss West had made three trips to Yugoslavia: the first, at the invitation of the British Council, to give lectures in the spring of 1936; a second with her husband, Henry Andrews, in the spring of 1937; the third in early summer of the following year. Initially she had hoped quickly to write 'a snap book'; four months after the second trip this potentially profitable venture had grown into a 'wretched, complicated book that won't interest anybody'.[5]

In the course of researching its 'long and complicated history' [p.1089] West learned and clarified her ideas about Yugoslavia – and about much else besides. To paraphrase Italo Calvino's comment on *The Ruin of Kasch* by Roberto Calasso, *Black Lamb and Grey Falcon* takes up two subjects: the first is Yugoslavia, and the second is everything else. By the time it was published – in two volumes totalling half a million words – West was some-what at a loss to discover why she had been moved 'in 1936 to devote five years of my life, at great financial sacrifice and to the utter exhaustion of my mind and body, to take an inven-tory of a country down to its last vest-button, in a form insane from any ordinary artistic or commercial point of view'.[6] As the 'mass of [her] material' swelled and changed so this 'inven-tory' became an immense and immensely complicated picture not simply of her *own* soul but that of Europe on the brink of the Second World War. The result, which she feared 'hardly anyone will read by reason of its length' [p.773], is one of the supreme masterpieces of the twentieth century.

Like the book itself, its reputation is rather odd. West is considered a major British writer. If she is not regarded as a writer quite of the first rank, that is largely because so much of the work on which her reputation should rest is tacitly consid-ered secondary to the form in which greatness is expected to manifest itself, namely the novel. As a novelist West is clearly less important than Lawrence, James Joyce (whose genius, in *Ulysses*, was to have 'invented a form and exhausted its possi-bilities at the same time'[7]) or E. M. Forster ('a self-indulgent old liberal with hardly a brain in his head'.[8]) Her best work is scattered among reportage, journalism and travel – the kind of things traditionally regarded as sidelines or distractions. The success of *Black Lamb and Grey Falcon* is due in no small part to the ingenuity with which she contains this tendency to dispersal by *giving it free rein.* The book is manifestly a work of literature but since literature in English (at least as far as prose is concerned) is synonymous with the novel – with an agreed-upon *form* of writing rather than a certain *quality* of writing – it is tacitly removed from the company in which it belongs. (When I mentioned to a novelist friend that I was writing this introduction she asked if the book was *set* in Yugoslavia; it was assumed to be a novel.) Palpably inferior works – novels – sit far more securely on the literary syllabus than an awkward tome whose identifying quality is a refusal to fit. In danger of dislodging other volumes from the top canonical shelf – or, more radically, of bringing the whole shelf crashing down – *Black Lamb and Grey Falcon* topples from its rightful place and is tacitly stocked in a lower, less prominent but safer place.

Even some commentators who claim the book as a master-piece have little to say about *why* it is one. In *Abroad*, Paul Fussell's highly-regarded survey of 'British literary travelling between the wars', West, unlike Waugh, Lawrence or Greene, does not get a chapter-compartment to herself and her book receives a mention more or less in passing. Victoria Glendinning, in her biography of West, has no doubt that *Black Lamb and Grey Falcon* is 'the central book of her life . . . the work in which Rebecca West formulated her views on religion, ethics, art, myth and gender'.[9] Beyond that, she has almost nothing to say about it. Is the book doomed to repel attempts to articulate the awe that it inspires?

To try to make good this lack let's begin, uncontentiously, by observing that it is a key book about Yugoslavia. I read it in 1993 after visiting Serbia (for the British Council, as it happens) to learn about Yugoslavia – or ex-Yugoslavia, as it had by then become. The book had been reissued a few years earlier in response to the outbreak of a conflict West had, in some ways, foreseen. In the Prologue West remembers herself 'peering' at old film footage of the king of Yugoslavia, 'like an old woman reading the tea-leaves in her cup' [p.15]. The book's prophetic quality is hinted at as early as page 10, when West writes that 'it is the habit of the people, whenever an old man misman-ages his business so that it falls to pieces as soon as he dies, to say, "Ah, So-and-so was a marvel! He kept things together so long as he was alive, and look what happens now he has gone!"' I can still remember how weirdly disorientating it was to read this in 1993 when the blaze of contemporary events was fierce

enough to make one wonder if she was writing not about Franz
Josef, but Tito. Much later in the book, in Kosovo, West's chauffeur, Dragutin, grabs a Croat boy by the ear and says with a
mixture of irony and threat, 'We'll kill you all some day.' [p.904]
Even in my own minuscule experience of Serbia and Montenegro
there have been many times when the scene unfolding before
my eyes seemed to have been faithfully enacted from the pages
of *Black Lamb and Grey Falcon*. As a book about Yugoslavia,
then, it is of 'extraordinary usefulness' as a kind of metaphysical *Lonely Planet* that never requires updating.[10] (As West herself
observed, 'sometimes it is necessary for us to know where we
are in eternity as well as in time'. [p.825]) The book's practical
worth is nicely suggested by the journalist Robert Kaplan, who
remembers taking the book with him everywhere in Yugoslavia.
'I would rather have lost my passport and money than my
heavily thumbed and annotated copy of *Black Lamb and Grey
Falcon*.'[11]

If you are not in – or interested in – the Balkan peninsula,
the number of pages devoted to the history of the region can
seem off-putting. Except this is history as it might have been
written by Ryszard Kapuściński or Gabriel García Márquez.[12]
Take the extraordinary scene from Sarajevo in 1914 when, shortly
before his assassination, Archduke Franz Ferdinand finds the
reception hall he is standing in crammed with the half-million
beasts he has killed (by his own estimation) in his career as a
hunter:

> One can conceive the space of this room stuffed all the way
> up to the crimson and gold vaults and stalactites with the
> furred and feathered ghosts, set close, because there were so
> many of them: stags with the air between their antlers stuffed
> with woodcock, quail, pheasant, partridge, capercailzie, and
> the like; boars standing bristling flank to flank, the breadth
> under their broad bellies packed with layer upon layer of hares
> and rabbits. Their animal eyes, clear and dark as water, would
> brightly watch the approach of their slayer to an end that
> exactly resembled their own. [pp.335–336]

When Susan Sontag directed Beckett's *Waiting for Godot* in
Sarajevo during the siege it was widely felt that what was
happening on stage offered some kind of absurdist commentary on events beyond the theatre. In a café in Mostar – a place
which became stitched into international consciousness in the

same way as Sarajevo – a comparable fable had unfolded before West's eyes in the 1930s:

> Young officers moved rhythmically through the beams of white light that poured down upon the acid green of the billiard-tables, and the billiard balls gave out their sound of stoical shock. There was immanent the Balkan feeling of a shiftless yet just doom. It seemed possible that someone might come into the room, perhaps a man who would hang up his fez, and explain, in terms just comprehensible enough to make it certain they were not nonsensical, that all the people at the tables must stay there until the two officers who were playing billiards at the moment had played a million games, and that by the result their eternal fates would be decided; and that this would be accepted, and people would sit there quietly waiting and reading the newspapers. [p.289]

West's intention was 'to show the past side by side with the present it created' [p.1089] and part of her achievement is to reveal how even an apparently ahistorical sensation – the scent of a plucked flower, say – is saturated with the smell of the past. Geography and history, to make the same point rather more sweepingly, cannot always be distinguished from one another – hence the way that certain places 'imprint the same stamp on whatever inhabitants history brings them, even if conquest spills out one population and pours in another wholly different in race and philosophy'[p.747]. Impatient readers tempted to skip the historical bits are taking a big risk because the past – the narrative history – can melt into the immediate present with zero notice. The most spectacular instance comes after a lengthy disquisition – a bit too long, I was thinking – on events in Prishtina during the reign of Stephen Dushan in the fourteenth century. After twenty pages or so we learn of his death:

> In the forty-ninth year of his life, at a village so obscure that it is not now to be identified, he died, in great pain, as if he had been poisoned. Because of his death many disagreeable things happened. For example, we sat in Prishtina, our elbows on a tablecloth stained brown and puce, with chicken drumsticks on our plates meagre as sparrow-bones, and there came towards us a man and a woman; and the woman was carrying on her back the better part of a plough. [p.894]

Wow-ee! Isn't that the boldest jump-cut – the most daring time-shift, the most outrageous deduction – ever? And West does not stop there. The sight of this man and woman prompts her to return to one of the major themes of the book, the vexed relations between men and women.

> Any area of unrestricted masculinism, where the women are made to do all the work and are refused the right to use their wills, is in fact disgusting, not so much because of the effect on the women, who are always taught something by the work they do, but because of the nullification of the men. [p.895]

And West does not stop there either – she loops this vision back to the death of Stephen Dushan before leaving the table to go to 'a lavatory of the Turkish kind':

> The dark hole in the floor, and something hieratic in the propor-tions of the place made it seem as if dung, having been expelled by man, had set itself up as a new and hostile and magically powerful element that could cover the whole earth with dark ooze and sickly humidity . . . I felt as if the place were soiling me with filth which I would never be able to wash off because it was stronger in its essence than mere mild soap and water. [p.896][13]

And West does not stop there either . . . Let's loop back for a moment. The book's inexhaustible capacity for self-fuelling discussion, for examining the implications of everything that it touches upon, is central to West's structural and stylistic method. Any conclusions she draws are tied to the process (a key word in the book) by which they are being teased out. Something catches West's attention; the incident – a Mozart symphony coming on the radio in a restaurant on page 507, say – is conveyed with vivid immediacy. As West articulates and processes this experience, she takes us on a discursive journey into the furthest reaches of speculative thought before returning us to the exact spot or occasion from which we started. Franz Ferdinand's assassin, Princip, is in this way the active representative of the author's own purpose: 'He offered himself wholly to each event in order that he might learn in full what revelation it had to make about the nature of the universe.' [p.378]

How, with this in mind, could *Black Lamb and Grey Falcon* have been anything other than a vast book? Even enthusiastic readers of Robert Fisk's *The Great War for Civilisation* are likely to feel that its impressive bulk is due solely to accumulation, to the mass of material contained in it. *Black Lamb and Grey Falcon* earns its size *as a work of art*. Like W. H. Auden in his 'Letter to Lord Byron' (1936), West needed 'a form that's large enough to swim in'.[14] The scale of its conception is imprinted internally in its syntax and composition. Ostensibly convenient and alluring, the edited selection offered in *The Essential Rebecca West* feels like an aesthetic violation. There is, in fact, something inappropriate about reducing such a book to its essentials. I suspect that some of the passages that most delight me are, by the kind of limiting definition West repeatedly decries, the bits that might be considered *in*essential. I don't want to diminish the importance of *Black Lamb and Grey Falcon* as a book about Yugoslavia; it is predicated on 'a coincidence between the natural forms and colours of the western and southern parts of Yugoslavia and the innate forms and colours of [West's] imagination' [p.1088], but while many of the parts I value have their origin *in* they are not unique *to* that part of the world. A few examples from hundreds: the 'erotic panic' of a horse which 'rolls the eyes not only in fear but in enjoyment, that seeks to be soothed with an appetite revealing that it plainly knows soothing to be possible, and pursues what it declares it dreads' [p.71]; the woman who had 'the beauty of a Burne-Jones, the same air of having rubbed holes in her lovely cheeks with her clenched knuckles' [p.58]; the Muslims for whom 'the reward for total abstinence from alcohol seems, illogically enough, to be the capacity for becoming intoxicated without it' [p.649].

Black Lamb and Grey Falcon is digressive and meandering – you never know what's going to happen next – but this is not to say that it is shapeless. It may sprawl – it *is* sprawling – but remember, for a start, how what is offered as an account of a single journey has in fact been stitched seamlessly together from three separate trips. Over time we have grown familiar with the complex organisation of works like *Bleak House* or *Ulysses*; in contemporary fiction we admire the intricate interweaving of plot, character and themes in the novels of Ian McEwan. Making different demands on the reader's expectations of order, *Black Lamb and Grey Falcon* has the unity and fluidity of a sustained improvisation in prose. As with a saxophonist or trumpeter the controlling factor, the thing that allows West to range so widely without ever losing her way, is *tone*. The book's bold demonstration of the way that tone can take over some of the load-bearing work of structure is crucial to its innovatory importance. Within an overall constancy of tone West moves easily between registers. She can be witty: 'The visit had been extraordinarily pleasant, though it had been nothing at all, and least of all a visit' [p.750]. She can be playful:

> Then why did we not bring the book?' asked my husband. 'Well, it weighs just over a stone,' I said. 'I weighed it once on the bathroom scales.' 'Why did you do that?' asked my husband. 'Because it occurred to me one day that I knew the weight of nothing except myself and joints of meat,' I said, 'and I just picked that up to give me an idea of something else.' [p.140]

She can be lyrical ('As we drew nearer the shore the water under the keel was pale emerald where the diving sunlight had found sand' [p.222] and fantastical at the same time:

> Beyond the bridge the river widened out into a curd of yellow water-lilies, edged with a streak of mirror at each bank, in which willow trees, standing above their exact reflections, amazed us by their shrill green and cat-o'-thousand tails forms; they were like static fireworks. [p.1037]

As happens when she dismisses a woman she meets in a hotel in Bosnia, West can be abusive and intemperate: 'she was cruelty; she was filth' [p.438]. Most surprising of all in a book of such length, West has the gift of brevity: 'We fell again through Swissish country' [p.296]; 'A naked range as black as night, its high ridge starred with snow' [p.734]; 'the first heavy pennies of rain' [p.510].

The progress of this introduction is in danger of being impeded by the quantity of superlatives it has already had to take on board but room must be made, ultimately, for a brief consideration of West's thought. A few years after *Black Lamb and Grey Falcon* was published West sat down to consider a proposal from her American editor, Ben Huebsch, that she write a book on the British Empire. It was something she would like to have done, but 'except for the fancy bits on religion and metaphysics that I would throw in in my demented way', she decided, there was nothing new she could contribute to such a study.[15] It is, of course, these 'demented' bits that make *Black Lamb and Grey Falcon* a great book of ideas. In the Epilogue

West comments on the way that, in her teens, Ibsen 'corrected the chief flaw in English literature, which is a failure to recognise the dynamism of ideas'. With characteristic vehemence she later decided that 'Ibsen cried out for ideas for the same reason that men call out for water, because he had not got any' [p.1086]. To say that West has them by the gallon is an understatement. *Black Lamb and Grey Falcon* is, along with everything else, a great flood of ideas. As with Lawrence, it is impossible to say where sensation stops and cogitation begins. Observation and metaphysics, thought and responsiveness to 'the visibility of life' [p.235], are all the time flowing into each other.

The book's biggest idea is also its simplest, so simple that it should be no more than a preference 'for the agreeable over the disagreeable'. The problem is that

> only part of us is sane: only part of us loves pleasure and the longer day of happiness, wants to live to our nineties and die in peace, in a house that we built, that shall shelter those who come after us. The other half of us is nearly mad. It prefers the disagreeable to the agreeable, loves pain and its darker night despair, and wants to die in a catastrophe that will set back life to its beginnings and leave nothing of our house save its blackened foundations. [p.1102]

As West wrote this, Europe was hurtling towards just such a catastrophe; in 1993, when I first read *Black Lamb and Grey Falcon*, TV screens were full of images of the blackened foundations of houses in the very places she had described. West had enough of the disagreeable in her nature to realise that an affirmation of the agreeable is part of an ongoing personal and political struggle. Her faith in this idea is echoed by Auden in the commentary appended to his sonnet sequence *In Time of War* (published in 1938 while West was immersed in writing her book):

> It's better to be sane than mad, or liked than dreaded;
> It's better to sit down to nice meals than to nasty;
> It's better to sleep two than single; it's better to be happy.[16]

In both cases the modesty of the conclusion is proof of its wisdom – and vice versa. *Black Lamb and Grey Falcon* is a vast, ambitious and complex book which repeatedly stresses the kinship between homely and universal truths. By making a cake for friends, West insists, 'one is striking a low note on a scale that is struck higher up by Beethoven and Mozart'. In Montenegro West encounters a woman who is trying to understand the many hard things that have befallen her. The meeting persuades West that if 'during the next million generations there is but one human being born in every generation who will not cease to inquire into the nature of his fate, even while it strips and bludgeons him, some day we shall read the riddle of our universe' [p1013]. And if, once or twice a century, a book like this appears the wait will be only a fraction as long.

Geoff Dyer, 2006

[1] *Fiction*, Michael Ackerman, Keyahoff Verlag, Munich, 2001 (unpaginated).

[2] 'Elegy', *The Essential Rebecca West*, Penguin, Harmondsworth, 1978, p.388.

[3] *ibid.* p.392.

[4] Quoted in *Inventing Ruritania* by Vesna Goldsworthy, Yale University Press, New Haven, 1998, p.176.

[5] Quoted in *Rebecca West: Saga of the Century* by Carl Rollyson, Hodder and Stoughton, London, 1995, p.161.

[6] *Selected Letters of Rebecca West*, edited by Bonnie Kime Scott, Yale, New Haven, 2000, p.169.

[7] *Selected Letters*, p. 327

[8] *Selected Letters*, p. 440.

[9] *Rebecca West: A Life*, Weidenfeld & Nicolson, London, 1987, p.154.

[10] *Selected Letters*, p.169.

[11] *Balkan Ghosts*, St. Martin's Press, New York, 1993, p.8. For the most up-to-date examination of *Black Lamb and Grey Falcon*'s continuing value as 'a source of information' and as 'a work of literature' see Tony White's *Another Fool in the Balkans: In the Footsteps of Rebecca West*. As White himself concedes, the sub-title is somewhat superfluous since 'any writer visiting the former Yugoslavia is following in the footsteps Rebecca West'. [Cadogan Guides, London, 2006, p49].

[12] Understandably, then, *Black Lamb and Grey Falcon* sits no more reliably in 'History' than it does in 'Literature'. A. J. P. Taylor admired the book but considered its author 'a strange mixture of penetration and wrong-headedness'. Inaccuracies notwithstanding, West believed that she had provided 'a complete explanation of the course of history'. Quoted by Rollyson, p.182 and p.174, respectively.

[13] cf Don DeLillo's description of 'the terminal shithouse of the Peloponnese' in *The Names*: 'The walls were splattered with shit, the bowl was clogged, there was shit on the floor, on the toilet seat, on the fixtures and pipes. An inch of exhausted piss lay collected around the base of the toilet, a minor swamp in the general wreckage and mess. In the chill wind, the soft sweet

rain, this doleful shed was another plane of experience. It had a history, a reek of squatting armies, centuries of war, plunder, siege, blood feuds. I stood five feet from the bowl to urinate, tip-toed. How strange that people used this place, still. It was like an offering to Death, to stand there directing my stream toward that porcelain hole.' [Harvester Press, Brighton, 1983, p.183-4].

[14] *The English Auden*, edited by Edward Mendelson, Faber, London, 1977, p.172.

[15] *Selected Letters*, p.181.

[16] *The English Auden*, p.269.

J'exige un vrai bonheur, un vrai amour, une vraie contrée où le soleil alterne avec la lune, où les saisons se déroulent en ordre, où de vrais arbres portent de vrais fruits, où de vrais poissons habitent les rivières, et de vrais oiseaux le ciel, où la vraie neige découvre de vraies fleurs, où tout sort est vrai, vrai, véritable. J'en ai assez de cette lumière morne, de ces campagnes stériles, sans jour, sans nuit, où ne survivent que les bêtes féroces et rapaces, où les lois de la nature ne fonctionnent plus.

JEAN COCTEAU: *Les Chevaliers de la Table Ronde*

Fluellen: I think it is in Macedon where Alexander is born. I tell you, captain, if you look in the maps of the 'orld, I warrant you sall find, in the comparisons between Macedon and Monmouth, that the situations, look you, is both alike. There is a river in Macedon; and there is also moreover a river at Monmouth: it is called Wye at Monmouth; but it is out of my brains what is the name of the other river; but 'tis all one, 'tis alike as my fingers is to my fingers, and there is salmons in both.

SHAKESPEARE: *King Henry the Fifth*

Prologue

I RAISED MYSELF ON MY ELBOW AND CALLED THROUGH THE open door into the other wagon-lit:

'My dear, I know I have inconvenienced you terribly by making you take your holiday now, and I know you did not really want to come to Yugoslavia at all. But when you get there you will see why it was so important that we should make this journey, and that we should make it now, at Easter. It will all be quite clear, once we are in Yugoslavia.'

There was, however, no reply. My husband had gone to sleep. It was perhaps as well. I could not have gone on to justify my certainty that this train was taking us to a land where everything was comprehensible, where the mode of life was so honest that it put an end to perplexity. I lay back in the darkness and marvelled that I should be feeling about Yugoslavia as if it were my mother country, for this was 1937, and I had never seen the place till 1936. Indeed, I could remember the first time I ever spoke the name 'Yugoslavia' and that was only two and a half years before, on October the ninth, 1934.

It was in a London nursing-home. I had had an operation, in the new miraculous way. One morning a nurse had come in and given me an injection, as gently as might be, and had made a little joke which was not very good but served its purpose of taking the chill off the difficult moment. Then I picked up my book and read that sonnet by Joachim du Bellay which begins *'Heureux qui, comme Ulysse, a fait un beau voyage.'* I said to myself, 'That is one of the most beautiful poems in the world,' and I rolled over in my bed, still thinking that it was one of the most beautiful poems in the world, and found that the electric light was burning and there was a new nurse standing at the end of my bed. Twelve hours had passed in that moment. They had taken me upstairs to a room far above the roofs of London, and had cut me about for three hours and a half, and had brought me down again, and now I was merely sleepy, and not at all sick, and still half-rooted in my pleasure in the poem, still listening to a voice speaking through the ages, with barest economy that somehow is the most lavish melody: *'Et en quelle saison Revoiray-je*

I

le clos de ma pauvre maison, Qui m'est une province, et beaucoup d'avantage.'

I had been told beforehand that it would all be quite easy; but before an operation the unconscious, which is really a shocking old fool, envisages surgery as it was in the Stone Age, and I had been very much afraid. I rebuked myself for not having observed that the universe was becoming beneficent at a great rate. But it was not yet wholly so. My operation wound left me an illusion that I had a load of ice strapped to my body. So, to distract me, I had a radio brought into my room, and for the first time I realized how uninteresting life could be and how perverse human appetite. After I had listened to some talks and variety programmes, I would not have been surprised to hear that there are householders who make arrangements with the local authorities not to empty their dustbins but to fill them. Nevertheless there was always good music provided by some station or other at any time in the day, and I learned to swing like a trapeze artist from programme to programme in search of it.

But one evening I turned the wrong knob and found music of a kind other than I sought, the music that is above earth, that lives in the thunderclouds and rolls in human ears and sometimes deafens them without betraying the path of its melodic line. I heard the announcer relate how the King of Yugoslavia had been assassinated in the streets of Marseille that morning. We had passed into another phase of the mystery we are enacting here on earth, and I knew that it might be agonizing. The rags and tags of knowledge that we all have about us told me what foreign power had done this thing. It appeared to me inevitable that war must follow, and indeed it must have done, had not the Yugoslavian Government exercised an iron control on its population, then and thereafter, and abstained from the smallest provocative action against its enemies. That forbearance, which is one of the most extraordinary feats of statesmanship performed in post-war Europe, I could not be expected to foresee. So I imagined myself widowed and childless, which was another instance of the archaic outlook of the unconscious, for I knew that in the next war we women would have scarcely any need to fear bereavement, since air raids unpreceded by declaration of war would send us and our loved ones to the next world in the breachless unity of scrambled eggs. That thought did not then occur to me, so I rang for my nurse, and when she came I cried to her, 'Switch on the telephone! I must speak to my husband at once. A most terrible thing has happened. The King of Yugoslavia has been assassinated.' 'Oh, dear!' she replied. 'Did you know him?' 'No,' I said. 'Then why,' she asked, 'do you think it's so terrible?'

Her question made me remember that the word 'idiot' comes from a Greek root meaning private person. Idiocy is the female defect: intent on their private lives, women follow their fate through a darkness deep as that cast by malformed cells in the brain. It is no worse than the male defect, which is lunacy: they are so obsessed by public affairs that they see the world as by moonlight, which shows the outlines of every object but not the details indicative of their nature. I said, 'Well, you know, assassinations lead to other things!' 'Do they?' she asked. 'Do they not!' I sighed, for when I came to look back on it my life had been punctuated by the slaughter of royalties, by the shouting of newsboys who have run down the streets to tell me that someone has used a lethal weapon to turn over a new leaf in the book of history. I remember when I was five years old looking upward at my mother and her cousin, who were standing side by side and looking down at a newspaper laid on a table in a circle of gaslight, the folds in their white pouched blouses and long black skirts kept as still by their consternation as if they were carved in stone. 'There was the Empress Elizabeth of Austria,' I said to the nurse, thirty-six years later. 'She was very beautiful, wasn't she?' she asked. 'One of the most beautiful women who ever lived,' I said. 'But wasn't she mad?' she asked. 'Perhaps,' I said, 'perhaps, but only a little, and at the end. She was certainly brilliantly clever. Before she was thirty she had given proof of greatness.' 'How?' she asked. To her increasing distress I told her, for I know quite a lot of Habsburg history, until I saw how bored she was and let her go and leave me in darkness that was now patterned by the lovely triangle of Elizabeth's face.

How great she was! In her early pictures she wears the same look of fiery sullenness we see in the young Napoleon: she knows that within her there is a spring of life and she is afraid that the world will not let it flow forth and do its fructifying work. In her later pictures she wears a look that was never on the face of Napoleon. The world had not let the spring flow forth and it had turned to bitterness. But she was not without achievements of the finest sort, of a sort, indeed, that Napoleon never equalled. When she was sixteen she came, a Wittelsbach from the country bumpkin court of Munich, to marry the young Emperor of Austria and be the governing prisoner of the court of Vienna, which was the court of courts since the French Revolution had annulled the Tuileries and Versailles. The change would have made many women into nothing. But five years later she made a tour of Lombardy and Venetia at Franz Josef's side which was in many ways a miracle. It was, in the first place, a miracle of courage, because he and his officials had made these provinces loathe them for their brutality and inefficiency. The young girl sat with unbowed head in theatres that became silent as the grave at her coming, that were black with mourning worn to insult her, and she walked unperturbed through streets that emptied before her as if she were the plague. But when she came face to face with any Italians there occurred to her always the right word and gesture by which she uncovered her nature and pled: 'Look, I am the Empress, but I am not evil. Forgive me and my husband and Austria for the evil we have done you, and let us love one another and work for peace between us.'

It was useless, of course. Her successes were immediately annulled by the arrests and floggings carried out by the Habsburg officials. It was inevitable that the two provinces should be absorbed in the new kingdom of Italy. But Elizabeth's sweetness had not been merely automatic, she had been thinking like a liberal and like an Empress. She knew there was a real link between Austria and Hungary, and that it was being strained by misgovernment. So the next year she made a journey through Hungary, which was also a matter of courage, for it was almost as gravely disaffected as Lombardy and Venetia, and afterwards she learned Hungarian, though it is one of the most difficult of languages, cultivated the friendship of many important Hungarians, and acquainted herself with the nature of the concessions desired by Hungary. Her plans fell into abeyance when she parted from Franz Josef and travelled for five years. But in 1866 Austria was defeated by the Prussians, and she came back to console her husband, and then she induced him to create the Dual Monarchy and give autonomy to Hungary. It was by this device alone that the Austro-Hungarian Empire was able to survive into the twentieth century, and both the idea and the driving force behind the execution belonged to Elizabeth. That was statesmanship. Nothing of Napoleon's making lasted so long, nor was made so nobly.

Elizabeth should have gone on and medicined some of the other sores that were poisoning the Empire. She should have solved the problem of the Slav populations under Habsburg rule. The Slavs were a people, quarrelsome, courageous, artistic, intellectual, and profoundly perplexing to all other peoples, who came from Asia into the Balkan Peninsula early in the Christian era and were Christianized by Byzantine influence. Thereafter they founded violent and magnificent kingdoms of infinite promise in Bulgaria,

Serbia, and Bosnia, but these were overthrown when the Turks invaded Europe in the fourteenth century, and all were enslaved except the Slavs on the western borders of the Peninsula. These lived under the wing of the great powers, of Venice and Austria and Hungary, which was a doubtful privilege, since they were used as helots and as man-power to be spent without thrift against the Turks. Now all of these were under the Austro-Hungarian Empire, the Czechs and the Croats, and the Slovenes and the Slovaks and the Dalmatians; and they were alike treated oppressively, largely because the German-Austrians felt a violent, instinctive loathing of all Slavs and particularly of the Czechs, whose great intelligence and ability made them dangerous competitors in the labour market. Moreover, Serbia and Bulgaria had thrown off the Turkish yoke during the nineteenth century and had established themselves as free states, and the reactionary parties in Austria and Hungary feared that if their Slav populations were given liberty they would seek union with Serbia under Russian protection. Therefore they harried the Slavs as much as they could, by all possible economic and social penalties, tried with especial venom to destroy their languages, and created for themselves an increasing amount of internal disorder which all sane men saw to carry a threat of disruption. It might have saved the Empire altogether, it might have averted the war of 1914, if Elizabeth had dealt with the Slavs as she dealt with the Hungarians. But after thirty she did no more work for the Empire.

Her work stopped because her marriage, which was the medium for her work, ceased to be tolerable. It appears probable, from the evidence we have, that Elizabeth could not reconcile herself to a certain paradox which often appears in the lives of very feminine women. She knew that certain virtues are understood to be desirable in women: beauty, tenderness, grace, house-pride, the power to bear and rear children. She believed that she possessed some of these virtues and that her husband loved her for it. Indeed, he seemed to have given definite proof that he loved her by marrying her against the will of his mother, the Archduchess Sophie. And she thought that because he loved her he must be her friend. In that she was artless. Her husband, like many other human beings, was divided between the love of life and the love of death. His love of life made him love Elizabeth. His love of death made him love his abominable mother, and give her an authority over Elizabeth which she horribly misused.

The Archduchess Sophie is a figure of universal significance. She was the kind of woman whom men respect for no other reason than

that she is lethal, whom a male cor.mittee will appoint to the post of
hospital matron. She had none of the womanly virtues. Especially
did she lack tenderness. There is no record of her ever having said
a gentle word to the girl of sixteen whom her son brought home
to endure this troublesome greatness, and she arranged for the
Archbishop who performed their marriage ceremony to address an
insulting homily to the bride, bidding her remember that she was a
nobody who had been called to a great position, and try to do her
best. In politics she was practised in every kind of folly that most
affronted the girl's instinctive wisdom. She was always thrusting
the blunt muzzle of her stupidity into conclaves of state, treading
down intelligent debate as a beast treads down the grass at a gate
into mud, undermining the foundations of the Empire by insisting
that everybody possible should be opposed and hurt. She was
personally responsible for some very ugly persecutions: one of her
victims was the peasant philosopher Konrad Deubler. She was also
a great slut. She had done nothing to reform the medievalism of the
Austrian Palaces. It was the middle of the nineteenth century when
Elizabeth came to Vienna, but both at the Winter Palace and the
Summer Palace, at the Hofburg and Schönbrunn, was she expected
to perform her excretory functions at a commode behind a screen in
a passage which was patrolled by a sentry. The Archduchess Sophie
saw to it that the evil she did should live after her by snatching
Elizabeth's children away from her and allowing her no part in
their upbringing. One little girl died in her care, attended by a
doctor whom Elizabeth thought old-fashioned and incompetent;
and the unhappy character of the Crown Prince Rudolf, restless,
undisciplined, tactless, and insatiable, bears witness to her inability
to look after their minds.

After Franz Josef had lost Elizabeth by putting this inferior over
her and proving that love is not necessarily kind, he showed her
endless kindness and indulgence, financing her wanderings and her
castle-buildings with great good temper and receiving her gladly
when she came home; and it seems she had no ill-feeling against
him. She introduced the actress, Katherina Schratt, into his life
very much as a woman might put flowers into a room she felt
to be dreary. But she must have hated him as the Habsburg of
Habsburgs, the centre of the imbecile system, when on January
the thirtieth, 1889, Rudolf was found dead in his shooting-box
at Mayerling beside the body of a girl of seventeen named Marie
Vetsera. This event still remains a mystery. Marie Vetsera had
been his mistress for a year and it is usually supposed that he
and she had agreed to die together because Franz Josef had

demanded they should part. But this is very hard to believe. Marie Vetsera was a very fat and plain little girl, bouncing with a vulgar ardour stimulated by improper French novels, which had already led her into an affair with an English officer in Egypt; and it seems unlikely that Rudolf, who was a man of many love-affairs, should have thought her of supreme value after a year's possession, particularly considering that he had spent the night before he went to Mayerling with an actress to whom he had long been attached. It would seem much more probable that he had taken his life or (which is possible if his farewell notes were forged) been murdered as a result of troubles arising from his political opinions.

Of these we know a great deal, because he wrote a great number of articles for anonymous publication in the *Neues Wiener Tageblatt* and an even greater number of letters to its editor, a gifted Jew named Moritz Szeps. These show that he was a fervent liberal and loathed the Habsburg system. He loathed the expanding militarism of Germany, and prophesied that a German alliance would mean the destruction of Austria, body and soul; and he revered France with its deeply rooted culture and democratic tradition. He was enraged by anti-Semitism and wrote one of his most forcible articles against a gang of aristocrats who after a drunken orgy had gone round the Ghetto of Prague smashing windows, and had been let off scot free by the police. He was scandalized by the corruption of the banks and law-courts, and by the lack of integrity among high officials and politicians, and most of all by the Austro-Hungarian Empire. 'As a simple onlooker,' he wrote, 'I am curious to know how such an old and tough organism as the Austrian Empire can last so long without cracking at the joints and breaking into pieces.' Particularly was he eager to deal with the Slav problem, which had now grown even more complicated. Bosnia and Herzegovina had driven out the Turks and had been cheated of the freedom they had thus won by the Treaty of Berlin, which had given the Austro-Hungarian Empire the right to occupy and administer them. This had enraged the Slavs and given Serbia a grievance, so it was held by reactionaries to be all the more necessary to defend Austrian and Hungarian privileges. Rudolf had shown what he felt early in his career: when Franz Josef had appointed him colonel he had chosen to be attached to a Czech regiment with middle-class officers which was then stationed in Prague.

Whatever the explanation of Mayerling it must have raised Elizabeth's impatience with Vienna to loathing. The situation was unmitigated waste and ruin. She had never achieved a happy relationship with her son, although there was a strong intellectual sympathy between them, because of the early alienating influence of the Archduchess Sophie, and the Habsburgs had spoiled what they had not let her save. Rudolf had been forced for dynastic reasons into a marriage with a tedious Belgian princess, an acidulated child with golden hair, small eyes, and the conservative opinions one would expect from a very old member of the Carlton Club. She was literally a child; at the time of her wedding she had not yet shown the signs of womanhood. Owing to a slip in the enormously complicated domestic machinery of the Habsburgs she and her young bridegroom, who was only twenty-two, had been sent for their honeymoon to a remote castle which had been left servantless and unprepared. This ill-begun marriage had gone from bad to worse, and both husband and wife tortured and were tortured in turn. But it was the Habsburg situation, not merely the specific wrongs the Habsburgs brought on Rudolf, that was his ruin. Chamberlains fussed, spies scribbled, the police bullied and nagged, everybody knew where everybody else was at every moment of the day; Franz Josef rose at four each morning and worked on official papers for twelve or fourteen hours; and not a minute's thought was given to correcting the evils that were undermining the foundations of the Empire. Rudolf, as any intelligent member of the family must have done, tried to remedy this. Either he made some too ambitious plan and was detected and killed himself or was killed, or from discouragement he soused himself with brandy till it seemed proper to die for a plump little hoyden of seventeen. Now he lay dead, and the Austro-Hungarian Empire was without a direct or satisfactory heir.

Elizabeth lived nine years after her son's death, as drearily as any other of the unemployed. Then, perhaps as a punishment for having turned her back on the Slav problem, the key to Eastern Europe, a Western problem slew her. For the newspaper my mother and her cousin spread in the gaslight was wrong when it said that the man who killed her, Luccheni, was a madman. It is true that he said that he had killed Elizabeth because he had vowed to kill the first royal person he could find, and that he had gone to Évian to stab the Duke of Orléans but had missed him and had come back to Geneva to get Elizabeth instead; and this is an insane avowal, for no benefit whatsoever could be derived by anybody from the death of either of these people. But for all that Luccheni was not mad. Many people are unable to say what they mean only because they have not been given an adequate vocabulary by their environment; and their apparently meaningless remarks may be inspired by a sane enough consciousness of real facts.

There is a phase of ancient history which ought never to be forgotten by those who wish to understand their fellow-men. In Africa during the fourth century a great many Christians joined a body of schismatics known as the Donatists who were wrecking the Church by maintaining that only sacraments administered by a righteous priest were valid, and that a number of contemporary priests had proved themselves unrighteous by showing cowardice during the persecutions of Diocletian. They raved: for according to the Church Christ is the real dispenser of the sacraments, and it is inconceivable that a relationship prescribed by Him could break down through the personality of the mediator, and in many cases the tales were scandalmongering. But though these people raved they were not mad. They were making the only noises they knew to express the misery inflicted on them by the economic collapse of the Western Roman Empire. Since there was no economic literature there was no vocabulary suitable to their misery, so they had to use the vocabulary given them by the Church; and they screamed nonsense about the sacraments because they very sensibly recognized that the Western Roman Empire was going to die, and so were they.

It was so with Luccheni. He performed his meaningless act out of his consciousness of what is perhaps the most real distress of our age. He was an Italian born in Paris of parents forced to emigrate by their poverty and trodden down into an alien criminal class: that is to say, he belonged to an urban population for which the existing forms of government made no provision, which wandered often workless and always traditionless, without power to control its destiny. It was indeed most appropriate that he should register his discontent by killing Elizabeth, for Vienna is the archetype of the great city which breeds such a population. Its luxury was financed by an exploited peasant class bled so white that it was ready to send its boys into the factories and the girls into service on any terms. The beggars in the streets of Vienna, who, the innocent suppose, were put there by the Treaty of St. Germain, are descendants of an army as old as the nineteenth century. Luccheni said with his stiletto to the symbol of power, 'Hey, what are you going to do with me?' He made no suggestions, but cannot be blamed for it. It was the essence of his case against society that it had left him unfit to offer suggestions, unable to form thoughts or design actions other than the crudest and most violent. He lived many years in prison, almost until his like had found a vocabulary and a name for themselves and had astonished the world with the farce of Fascism.

So Elizabeth died, with a terrible ease. All her life her corsets had deformed and impeded her beautiful body, but they did not protect her from the assassin's stiletto. That cut clean through to her heart. Even so her imperial rank had insulated her from emotional and intellectual achievement, but freely admitted sorrow. And it would not leave her alone after her death. She had expressed in her will a solemn desire to be buried in the Isle of Corfu, but for all that Franz Josef had her laid in the Habsburg vault at the Capuchin church of Vienna, fifteenth in the row of Empresses. The Habsburgs did not restrict themselves to the fields of the living in the exercise of their passion for preventing people from doing what they liked. Rudolf also asked that he might not be buried among his ancestors, but he had to yield up his skeleton; and the Prime Minister himself, Count Taaffe, called on Marie Vetsera's mother and asked her not to pray beside her daughter's grave, and received many police reports on her refusal to abandon this practice, which seems innocent enough even from the point of view of the court, since the whole of Vienna already knew how the girl had died. This was the kind of matter the Austrian Secret Police could handle. In the more important matter of keeping royal personages alive they were not nearly so successful.

After that Austria became a quiet place in Western eyes. Proust has pointed out that if one goes on performing any action, however banal, long enough, it automatically becomes 'wonderful': a simple walk down a hundred yards of village street is 'wonderful' if it is made every Sunday by an old lady of eighty. Franz Josef had for so long risen from his camp bed at four o'clock in the morning and worked twelve or fourteen hours on his official papers that he was recognized as one of the most 'wonderful' of sovereigns, almost as 'wonderful' as Queen Victoria, though he had shown no signs of losing in age the obstinacy and lack of imagination that made him see it as his duty to preserve his court as a morgue of etiquette and his Empire as a top-heavy anachronism. He was certain of universal acclamation not only during his life but after his death, for it is the habit of the people, whenever an old man mismanages his business so that it falls to pieces as soon as he dies, to say, 'Ah, So-and-so was a marvel! He kept things together so long as he was alive, and look what happens now he has gone!' It was true that there was already shaping in his court a disaster that was to consume us all; but this did not appear to English eyes, largely because Austria was visited before the war only by our upper classes, who in no country noticed anything but horses, and Austrian horses were good.

The next time the red light of violence shone out it seemed of no importance, an irrelevant horror. When I was ten years old, on June the eleventh, 1903, Alexander Obrenovitch, King of Serbia, and his wife Draga were murdered in the Palace at Belgrade, and their naked bodies thrown out of their bedroom into the garden. The Queen's two brothers and two Ministers were also killed. The murder was the work of a number of Army officers, none of whom was then known outside Serbia, and the main characters were not interesting. Alexander was a flabby young man with pince-nez who had a taste for clumsy experiments in absolutism, and his wife, who strangely enough belonged to the same type as Marie Vetsera, though she had in her youth been far more beautiful, was understood to have the disadvantages of being disreputable, having an ambitious family, and lying under the suspicion of having tried to palm off a borrowed baby as an heir to the throne. There can be no question that these people were regarded with terrified apprehension by the Serbians, who had freed themselves from the Turk not a hundred years before and knew that their independence was perpetually threatened by the great powers. The crime lingered in my mind only because of its nightmare touches. The conspirators blew open the door of the Palace with a dynamite cartridge which fused the electric lights, and they stumbled about blaspheming in the darkness, passing into a frenzy of cruelty that was half terror. The King and Queen hid in a secret cupboard in their bedroom for two hours, listening to the searchers grow cold, then warm, then cold again, then warm, and at last hot, and burning hot. The weakly King was hard to kill: when they threw him from the balcony they thought him doubly dead from bullet wounds and sword slashes, but the fingers of his right hand clasped the railing and had to be cut off before he fell to the ground, where the fingers of his left hand clutched the grass. Though it was June, rain fell on the naked bodies in the early morning as they lay among the flowers. The whole of Europe was revolted. Edward VII withdrew his Minister and most of the great powers followed his example.

That murder was just a half-tone square, dimly figured with horror, at the back of my mind: a Police News poster or the front page of a tabloid, seen years ago. But now I realize that when Alexander and Draga fell from that balcony the whole of the modern world fell with them. It took some time to reach the ground and break its neck, but its fall started then. For this is not a strictly moral universe, and it is not true that it is useless to kill a tyrant because a worse man takes his place. It has never been more effectively disproved than by the successor of Alexander Obrenovitch. Peter Karageorgevitch came to the throne under every possible disadvantage. He was close on sixty and had never seen Serbia since he left it with his exiled father at the age of fourteen; he had been brought up at Geneva under the influence of Swiss liberalism and had later become an officer in the French Army; he had no experience of statecraft, and he was a man of modest and retiring personality and simple manners, who had settled down happily at Geneva, to supervise the education of his three motherless children and pursue mildly bookish interests. It appears to be true that though he had told the conspirators of his readiness to accept the Serbian throne if Alexander Obrenovitch vacated it, he had had no idea that they proposed to do anything more violent than force an abdication; after all, his favourite author was John Stuart Mill. The Karageorgevitch belief in the sacredness of the dynasty brought him back to Belgrade, but it might have been safely wagered that he would need all the support he could get to stay there. He was entirely surrounded by the conspirators whose crime he abhorred, and he could not dismiss them, because in sober fact they numbered amongst them some of the ablest and most public-spirited men in Serbia; and with these fierce critics all about him perfectly capable of doing what they had done before, he had to keep order in a new and expanding country, vexed with innumerable internal and external difficulties.

But Peter Karageorgevitch was a great king. Slowly and soberly he proved himself one of the finest liberal statesmen in Europe, and later, in the Balkan wars which drove the Turk out of Macedonia and Old Serbia, he proved himself a magnificent soldier. Never was there worse luck for Europe. Austria, with far more territory than she could properly administer, wanted more and had formed her Drang nach Osten, her Hasten to the East policy. Now the formidable new military state of Serbia was in her way, and might even join with Russia to attack her. Now, too, all the Slav peoples of the Empire were seething with discontent because the free Serbians were doing so well, and the German-Austrians hated them more than ever. The situation had been further complicated since Rudolf's day because the Empire had affronted Slav feeling by giving up the pretence that Bosnia and Herzegovina were provinces which she merely occupied and administered, and formally annexing them. This made many Slavs address appeals to Serbia, which, as was natural in a young country, sometimes answered boastfully.

The situation was further complicated by the character of the man who had succeeded Rudolf as the heir to the Imperial Crown, the Archduke Franz Ferdinand of Este. This unlovable melancholic had upset all sections of the people by his proposals, drafted and expressed without the slightest trace of statesmanship, to make a tripartite monarchy of the Empire, by forming the Slavs into a separate kingdom. The reactionaries felt this was merely an expression of his bitter hostility towards the Emperor and his conservatism; the Slavs were unimpressed and declared they would rather be free, like Serbia. The reaction of Austria to this new situation was extravagant fear. The Austrian Chief of General Staff, Conrad von Hötzendorf, was speaking for many of his countrymen and most of his class when he ceaselessly urged that a preventive war should be waged against Serbia before she became more capable of self-defence. He and his kind would not have felt this if Alexander Obrenovitch had not been murdered and given place to a better man, who made a strong and orderly Serbia.

Then on June the twenty-eighth, 1914, the Austro-Hungarian Government allowed Franz Ferdinand to go to Bosnia in his capacity of Inspector-General of the Army to conduct manoeuvres on the Serbian frontier. It was strange that he should wish to do this, and that they should allow him, for that is St. Vitus's Day, the anniversary of the battle of Kossovo in 1389, the defeat of the Serbs by the Turks which meant five hundred years of enslavement. That defeat had been wiped out in the Balkan War by the recapture of Kossovo, and it was not tactful to remind the Serbs that some of their people were still enslaved by a foreign power. But Franz Ferdinand had his wish and then paid a visit to Sarajevo, the Bosnian capital, where the police gave him quite insufficient protection, though they had been warned that attempts were to be made on his life. A Bosnian Serb named Princip, who deeply resented Austro-Hungarian misrule, was able without any difficulty to shoot him as he drove along the street, and accidentally killed his wife as well. It must be noted that he was a Serb and not a Serbian. A Croat is a Catholic member and a Serb an Orthodox member of a Slav people that lies widely distributed south of the Danube, between the Adriatic and Bulgaria, and north of the Greek mountains. A Serbian is a subject of the kingdom of Serbia, and might be a Croat, just as a Croatian-born inhabitant of the old Austrian province of Croatia might be a Serb. But Princip had brought his revolver from Belgrade, and though he had been given it by a private individual and not by the Government, the Austro-Hungarian Empire used this as a pretext to declare war on Serbia. Other powers took sides and the Great War started.

Of that assassination I remember nothing at all. Every detail of Elizabeth's death is clear in my mind, of the Belgrade massacre I keep a blurred image, but I cannot recall reading anything about the Sarajevo *attentat* or hearing anyone speak of it. I was then very busy being an idiot, being a private person, and I had enough on my hands. But my idiocy was like my anaesthetic. During the blankness it dispensed I was cut about and felt nothing, but it could not annul the consequences. The pain came afterwards.

So, that evening in 1934, I lay in bed and looked at my radio fearfully, though it had nothing more to say that was relevant, and later on the telephone talked to my husband, as one does in times of crisis if one is happily married, asking him questions which one knows quite well neither he nor anyone else can answer and deriving great comfort from what he says. I was really frightened, for all these earlier killings had either hastened doom towards me or prefigured it. If Rudolf had not died he might have solved the Slav problem of the Austro-Hungarian Empire and restrained its imperialist ambition, and there might have been no war. If Alexander Obrenovitch had not been killed Serbia might never have been strong enough to excite the Empire's jealousy and fear, and there might have been no war. The killing of Franz Ferdinand was war itself. And the death of Elizabeth had shown me the scourge of the world after the war, Luccheni, Fascism, the rule of the dispossessed class that claims its rights and cannot conceive them save in terms of empty violence, of killing, taking, suppressing.

And now there was another killing. Again it was in the South-East of Europe, where was the source of all the other deaths. That seemed to me strange, in 1934, because the Slav problem then seemed to have been satisfactorily settled by the war. The Czechs and the Slovaks had their pleasant democratic state, which was working well enough except for the complaints of the Sudeten Germans who under the Habsburgs had been pampered with privileges paid for by their Slav neighbours. The Slovenes and the Croats and the Dalmatians and the Montenegrins were now united in the kingdom of the South Slavs, which is what Yugoslavia means; and though the Slovenes and Croats and the Dalmatians were separated in spirit from the Serbs by their Catholicism and the Montenegrins hankered after their lost independence, the state had seemed to be finding its balance. But here was another murder, another threat that man was going to deliver himself up to pain, was going to serve death instead of life.

A few days later my husband told me that he had seen a news film which had shown with extraordinary detail the actual death of the King of Yugoslavia, and as soon as I could leave the nursing-home

I went and saw it. I had to go to a private projection room, for by that time it had been withdrawn from the ordinary cinemas, and I took the opportunity to have it run over several times, while I peered at it like an old woman reading the tea-leaves in her cup. First there was the Yugoslavian warship sliding into the harbour of Marseille, which I know very well. Behind it was that vast suspension bridge which always troubles me because it reminds me that in this mechanized age I am as little able to understand my environment as any primitive woman who thinks that a waterfall is inhabited by a spirit, and indeed less so, for her opinion might from a poetical point of view be correct. I know enough to be aware that this bridge cannot have been spun by a vast steel spider out of its entrails, but no other explanation seems to me as plausible, and I have not the faintest notion of its use. But the man who comes down the gangway of the ship and travels on the tender to the quay, him I can understand, for he is something that is not new. Always the people have had the idea of the leader, and sometimes a man is born who embodies this idea.

His face is sucked too close to the bone by sickness to be tranquil or even handsome, and it would at any time have suggested a dry pedantry, unnatural in a man not far advanced in the forties. But he looks like a great man, which is not to say that he is a good man or a wise man, but is to say that he has that historic quality which comes from intense concentration on an important subject. What he is thinking of is noble, to judge from the homage he pays it with his eyes, and it governs him entirely. He does not relapse into it when the other world fails to interest him; rather does he relapse into noticing what is about him when for a moment his interior communion fails him. But he is not abstracted, he is paying due respect to the meeting between France and Yugoslavia. Indeed he is bringing to the official occasion a naïve earnestness. When Monsieur Barthou, the French Foreign Minister, comes and greets him, it is as if a jolly priest, fully at ease in his orders, stands before the altar beside a tortured mystical layman. Sometimes, too, he shows by a turn of the head, by a dilation of the pinched nostrils, that some aspect of the scene has pleased him.

About all his reactions there is that jerky quickness which comes of long vigilance. It was natural. He had been a soldier from boyhood, and since the Great War he had perpetually been threatened with death from within, by tuberculosis, and with death from without, by assassination at the hand of Croats or Macedonians who wanted independence instead of union with Serbia. But it is not fear that is his preoccupation. That, certainly, is Yugoslavia. He has the

look of one of those men who claim that they rule by divine right
whether they be kings or presidents, because their minds curve
protectively over their countries with the inclusiveness of the sky.
When one sees President Roosevelt one is sure that he is thinking
about America; sometimes his thought may be soft and loose, but
it is always dedicated to the same service. Those who saw Lenin
say that he was always thinking of Russia; even when his thought
was hard and tight it knew the same dedication. In our own King
George V we recognized that piety.

Now King Alexander is driving down the familiar streets,
curiously unguarded, in a curiously antique car. It can be seen
from his attempt to make his stiff hand supple, from a careless
flash of his careful black eyes, it can be seen that he is taking the
cheers of the crowd with a childish seriousness. It is touching, like
a girl putting full faith in the compliments that are paid to her at
a ball. Then his preoccupation veils his brows and desiccates his
lips. He is thinking of Yugoslavia again, with the nostalgia of an
author who has been interrupted in writing his new book. He
might be thinking, '*Heureux qui, comme Ulysse, a fait un beau
voyage.* . . .' But then the camera leaves him. It recedes. The
sound-track records a change, a swelling astonishment, in the
voice of the crowd. We see a man jumping on the footboard of
the car, a soldier swinging a sword, a revolver in the hand of
another, a straw hat lying on the ground, a crowd that jumps
up and down, up and down, smashing something flat with its
arms, kicking something flat with its feet, till there is seen on the
pavement a pulp covered with garments. A lad in a sweater dodges
before his captors, his defiant face unmarked by fear, although his
body expresses the very last extreme of fear by a creeping, writhing
motion. A view of the whole street shows people dashed about as by
a tangible wind of death.

The camera returns to the car and we see the King. He is lying
almost flat on his back on the seat, and he is as I was after the
anaæthetic. He does not know that anything has happened, he is
still half rooted in the pleasure of his own nostalgia. He might be
asking, '*Et en quelle saison Revoiray-je le clos de ma pauvre maison,
Qui m'est une province, et beaucoup d'avantage?*' It is certain that he
is dying, because he is the centre of a manifestation which would
not happen unless the living had been shocked out of their reserve
by the presence of death. Innumerable hands are caressing him.
Hands are coming from everywhere, over the back of the car,
over the sides, through the windows, to caress the dying King,
and they are supremely kind. They are far kinder than faces can

be, for faces are Marthas, burdened with many cares because of
their close connexion with the mind, but these hands express the
mindless sympathy of living flesh for flesh that is about to die, the
pure physical basis for pity. They are men's hands, but they move
tenderly as the hands of women fondling their babies, they stroke
his cheek as if they were washing it with kindness. Suddenly his
nostalgia goes from him. His pedantry relaxes. He is at peace, he
need not guard against death any more.

Then the camera shows an official running wildly down a street
in top hat and frock-coat, demonstrating the special ridiculousness
of middle-aged men, who have the sagging, anxious faces and
protruding bellies appropriate to pregnancies, but bring forth
nothing. It would be a superb ending for a comic film. Then
we see again the warship and the harbour, where the President
of the Republic stands with many men around him, who are all
as naïvely earnest as only one man was when that ship first came
into the harbour. Now there is no jolly priest confident that he has
the sacred mysteries well in hand: Barthou by now was also dead.
All these men look as the King looked at his coming, as if there lay
behind the surface of things a reality which at any moment might
manifest itself as a eucharist to be partaken of not by individuals,
but by nations. The coffin containing the man through which
this terrible sacrament has been dispensed to France is carried
on board, and the warship takes it away from these people, who
stand in a vast circle, rigid with horror and reverence. They are
intensely surprised that the eucharist was of this nature, but the
King of Yugoslavia had always thought it might be so.

I could not understand this event, no matter how often I saw this
picture. I knew, of course, how and why the murder had happened.
Luccheni has got on well in the world. When he killed Elizabeth,
over forty years ago, he had to do his own work in the world, he
had to travel humbly about Switzerland in search of his victims,
he had but one little two-edged dagger as tool for his crime, and
he had to pay the penalty. But now Luccheni is Mussolini, and
the improvement in his circumstances can be measured by the
increase in the magnitude of his crime. In Elizabeth the insecure
and traditionless town-dweller struck down the symbol of power,
but his modern representative has struck down power itself by
assuming itself and degrading its essence. His offence is not that he
has virtually deposed his king, for kings and presidents who cannot
hold their office lose thereby the title to their kingdoms and republics. His offence is that he made himself dictator without binding
himself by any of the contractual obligations which civilized man

has imposed on his rulers in all creditable phases of history and which give power a soul to be saved. This cancellation of process in government leaves it an empty violence that must perpetually and at any cost outdo itself, for it has no alternative idea and hence no alternative activity. The long servitude in the slums has left this kind of barbarian without any knowledge of what man does when he ceases to be violent, except for a few uncomprehending glimpses of material prosperity. He therefore can conceive of no outlet for his energies other than the creation of social services which artificially and unnaturally spread this material prosperity among the population, in small doses that keep them happy and dependent; and, for his second string, there is the performance of fantasias on the single theme of brute force. All forms of compulsion are practised on any element within the state that is resistant or is even suspected of retaining consciousness of its difference from the dominating party; and all living beings outside the state are conceived as enemies, to be hated and abused, and in ideal conditions to be robbed and murdered. This aggressiveness leads obviously to the establishment of immense armed forces, and furtively to incessant experimentation with methods of injuring the outer world other than the traditional procedure of warfare.

These methods, as time went on and Mussolini developed his foreign policy, included camps where Croats and Macedonians who objected to incorporation with Yugoslavia, or who were simply rogues, were trained as terrorists in the use of bombs and small arms and financed to use the results of that training in raids on Yugoslavia in the alleged service of their separatist campaigns. There could be no more convincing proof of the evil wrought on our civilization by the great cities and their spawn, for in not one state in pre-war Europe could there have been found any such example of an institution designed to teach the citizens of another state to murder their rulers. The existence of these camps and the necessity felt by human beings to practise any art they have learned explain the assassination of King Alexander without properly conveying its indecency. For Italy instructed her satellite, Hungary, to follow her example, and a notorious camp was established near the Yugoslav-Hungarian border at Yanka Puszta. Honour often seems a highly artificial convention, but life in any level of society where it has been abandoned astonishes by its tortuousness. When the Italians sent assassins from their training camps to murder the King, they went to great pains to make it appear that his murderers came from Yanka Puszta, even inducing a Macedonian assassin who had been associated with the Hungarian camp to come to Marseille and be killed, so that his dead body could be exhibited as proof of the conspirators' origin. It is a measure of the inevitable frivolity of a state governed by Fascist philosophy that the crime was entirely wasted and was committed only because of a monstrous miscalculation. Mussolini had believed that with the King's death the country would fall to pieces and be an easy prey to a foreign invader. But if Croat discontent had been a thousand times more bitter than it was, it would still have remained true that people prefer to kill their tyrants for themselves; and actually the murder shocked Yugoslavia into a unity it had not known before. So there was not war; there was nothing except the accomplishment of a further stage in the infiltration of peace with the depravity of war, which threatens now to make the two hardly distinguishable.

But the other participator in the event remained profoundly mysterious. At each showing of the film it could be seen more plainly that he had not been surprised by his own murder. He had not merely known of it as a factual possibility, he had realized it imaginatively in its full force as an event. But in this matter he seemed more intelligent than his own intelligence. Men of action often take an obstinate pride in their own limitations, and so, too, do invalids; and his face hinted that he, being both sick and soldierly, had combined the two forms of fault. All that I could read of his reign confirmed this indication and showed him as inflexible and slow. Yet there was in him this great wisdom, which brought him to the hour of his death sustained by a just estimate of what it is to die, and by certain magnificent conceptions such as kingliness and patriotism. It would be an enigma were it not that an individual had other ways of acquiring wisdom than through his own intellectual equipment. He can derive it, as it were, through the pores from the culture of his race. Perhaps this peculiar wisdom, which appeared on the screen as definitely as the peculiar sanity of Françoise Rosay or the peculiar narcissism of Garbo, was drawn by the King of Yugoslavia from the kingdom of Yugoslavia, from the South Slavs.

As to that I could form no opinion, for I knew nothing about the South Slavs, nor had I come across anybody who was acquainted with them. I was only aware that they formed part of the Balkan people, who had played a curious role in the history of British benevolence before the war and for some time after it. They had been, till they severally won their independences at various times in the nineteenth and twentieth centuries, the Christian subjects of the Turkish or Ottoman Empire, which had kept them in the greatest misery by incompetent administration and very cunningly set each section of them at odds with all the others, so that they could never rise in united rebellion. Hence each people was perpetually making charges of inhumanity against all its neighbours. The Serb, for example, raised his bitterest complaint against the Turk, but was also ready to accuse the Greeks, the Bulgarians, the Vlachs, and the Albanians of every crime under the sun. English persons, therefore, of humanitarian and reformist disposition constantly went out to the Balkan Peninsula to see who was in fact ill-treating whom, and, being by the very nature of their perfectionist faith unable to accept the horrid hypothesis that everybody was ill-treating everybody else, all came back with a pet Balkan people established in their hearts as suffering and innocent, eternally the massacree and never the massacrer. The same sort of person, devoted to good works and austerities, who is traditionally supposed to keep a cat and a parrot, often set up on the hearth the image of the Albanian or the Bulgarian or the Serbian or the Macedonian Greek people, which had all the force and blandness of pious fantasy. The Bulgarians as preferred by the Buxton brothers, and the Albanians as championed by Miss Durham, strongly resembled Sir Joshua Reynolds's picture of the Infant Samuel.

But often it appeared that the Balkans had forced piety to work on some very queer material. To hear Balkan-fanciers talk about each other's Infant Samuel was to think of some painter not at all like Sir Joshua Reynolds, say Hieronymus Bosch. The cats and parrots must often have been startled. In 1912 there was a dispute, extravagantly inappropriate to those who took part in it, as to whether Mr Prochaska, the Austrian Consul in a town named Prizren, had or had not been castrated by the Serbs. Mr. Prochaska, an unusually conscientious public servant, furthered his country's anti-Serbian policy by allowing it to be supposed that he had. Miss Durham, born in 1863, the daughter of a Fellow of the Royal College of Surgeons, a pupil at Bedford College, and an exhibitor at the Royal Institute of Painters in Water-colours, who had been led by her humanitarian passion to spend nearly all her life in the Balkans and was strongly anti-Serbian, made the astonishing statement that a party of Serbian officers whom she had met at a railway station had informed her that they themselves had operated on Mr Prochaska. It is interesting to speculate on what the Fellow of the Royal College of Surgeons or the staff of Bedford College would have thought of this announcement. The controversy raged until Professor Seton-Watson, who had no favourite among the Balkan peoples, but was strongly anti-Austrian, stated that he had himself had access to a confidential account from Mr Prochaska, which made it clear that the operation had not been performed at all. In no other circumstances could one imagine that gentle and elevated character receiving communications which afforded that kind of information. No other cause espoused by liberals so completely swept them off their feet by its own violence. The problems of India and Africa never produced anything like the jungle of savage pamphlets that sprang up in the footsteps of the Liberals who visited Turkey in Europe under the inspiration of Gladstone.

Violence was, indeed, all I knew of the Balkans: all I knew of the South Slavs. I derived the knowledge from memories of my earliest interest in Liberalism, of leaves fallen from this jungle of pamphlets, tied up with string in the dustiest corners of junk-shops, and later from the prejudices of the French, who use the word '*Balkan*' as a term of abuse, meaning a *rastaquouère* type of barbarian. In Paris, awakened in a hotel bedroom by the insufficiently private life of my neighbours, I have heard the sound of three slashing slaps and a woman's voice crying through sobs, '*Balkan! Balkan!*' Once in Nice, as I sat eating langouste outside a little restaurant down by the harbour, there were some shots, a sailor lurched out of the next-door bar, and the proprietress ran after him, shouting, '*Balkan! Balkan!*' He had emptied his revolver into the mirror behind the bar. And now I was faced with the immense nobility of the King in the film, who was certainly *Balkan, Balkan*, but who met violence with an imaginative realization which is its very opposite, which absorbs it into the experience it aims at destroying. But I must have been wholly mistaken in my acceptance of the popular legend regarding the Balkans, for if the South Slavs had been truly violent they would not have been hated first by the Austrians, who worshipped violence in an imperialist form, and later by the Fascists, who worship violence in a totalitarian form. Yet it was impossible to think of the Balkans for one moment as gentle and lamb-like, for assuredly Alexander and Draga Obrenovitch and Franz Ferdinand and his wife had none of them died in their beds. I had to admit that I quite simply and flatly knew nothing at all about the south-eastern corner of Europe; and since there proceeds steadily from that place a stream of events which are a source of danger to me, which indeed for four years threatened my safety and during that time deprived me for ever of many benefits, that is to say I know nothing of my own destiny.

That is a calamity. Pascal wrote: 'Man is but a reed, the most feeble thing in nature; but he is a thinking reed. The entire universe need not arm itself to crush him. A vapour, a drop of water, suffices to kill him. But if the universe were to crush him, man would still be more noble than that which killed him, because he knows that he dies and the advantage which the universe has over him; the universe knows nothing of this.' In these words he writes the sole prescription for a distinguished humanity. We must learn to know the nature of the advantage which the universe has over us, which in my case seems to lie in the Balkan Peninsula. It was only two or three days distant, yet I had never troubled to go that short journey which might explain to me how I shall die, and why. While I was marvelling at my inertia, I was asked to go to Yugoslavia to give some lectures in different towns before universities and English clubs, and this I did in the spring of 1936.

It was unfortunate that at the end of my journey I went to Greece and was stung by a sand-fly and got dengue fever, which is also known, and justly so, as breakbone fever. On the way back I had to rest in a *Kurhaus* outside Vienna, and there they thought me so ill that my husband came out to fetch me home. He found me weeping in my bedroom, though this is a town governed by its flowers, and as it was May the purple and white lilacs were as thick along the streets as people watching for a procession, and the chestnut trees were holding their candles to the windows of the upper rooms. I was well enough to be out, but I was sitting in a chair with a heap of coarse linen dresses flung over my knees and feet. I showed them to my husband one by one, saying in remorse, 'Look what I have let them do!' They were dresses which I had bought from the peasants in Macedonia, and the Austrian doctor who was treating me had made me have them disinfected, though they were quite clean. But the nurse who took them away had forgotten what was to be done with them, and instead of putting them under the lamp she had given them to the washerwoman, who had put them in strong soak. They were ruined. Dyes that had been fixed for twenty years had run and now defiled the good grain of the stuff; stitches that had made a clean-cut austere design were now sordid smears. Even if I could have gone back immediately and bought new ones, which in my weakness I wanted to do, I would have it on my conscience that I had not properly protected the work of these women which should have been kept as a testimony, which was a part of what the King had known as he lay dying.

'You must not think me stupid,' I said to my husband; 'you cannot understand why I think these dresses important; you have not been there.' 'Is it so wonderful there?' he asked. 'It is more wonderful than I can tell you,' I answered. 'But how?' he said. I could not tell him at all clearly. I said, 'Well, there is everything there. Except what we have. But that seems very little.' 'Do you mean that the English have very little,' he asked, 'or the whole of the West?' 'The whole of the West,' I said, 'here too.' He looked at the butter-yellow baroque houses between the chestnut trees and laughed. 'Beethoven and Mozart and Schubert wrote quite a lot of music in this town,' he said. 'But they were none of them happy,' I objected. 'In Yugoslavia,' suggested my husband, smiling, 'everybody is happy.' 'No, no,' I said, 'not at all, but . . .' The thing I wanted to tell him could not be told, however, because it was manifold and nothing like what one is accustomed to communicate by words. I stumbled on, 'Really, we are not as rich in the West as we think we are. Or, rather, there is much we have not got which the people in the Balkans have got in quantity. To look at them you would think they had nothing. The people who made these dresses looked as if they had nothing at all. But if these imbeciles here had not spoiled this embroidery you would see that whoever did it had more than we have.' I saw the blue lake of Ochrid, the mosques of Sarajevo, the walled town of Korchula, and it appeared possible that I was unable to find words for what I wanted to say because it was not true. I am never sure of the reality of what I see, if I have seen it only once; I know that until it has firmly established its objective existence by impressing my senses and my memory, I am capable of conscripting it into the service of a private dream. In a panic I said, 'I must go back to Yugoslavia, this time next year, in the spring, for Easter.'

Journey

Journey

WE SPENT THE NIGHT AT SALZBURG, AND IN THE MORNING WE had time to visit the house where Mozart was born, and look at his little spinet, which has keys that are brown and white instead of white and black. There the boy sat, pleased by its prettiness and pleased by the sounds he drew from it, while there encircled him the rage of his father at this tiresome, weak, philandering son he had begotten, who would make no proper use of his gifts; and further back still the indifference of his contemporaries, which was to kill him; and further back still, so far away as to be of no use to him, our important love for him. That was something we human beings did not do very well. Then we went down to the railway station and waited some hours for the train to Zagreb, the capital of Croatia. When it at last arrived, I found myself in the midst of what is to me the mystery of mysteries. For it had left Berlin the night before and was crammed with unhappy-looking German tourists, all taking advantage of the pact by which they could take a substantial sum out of the country provided they were going to Yugoslavia; and I cannot understand the proceedings of Germans. All Central Europe seems to me to be enacting a fantasy which I cannot interpret.

The carriages were so crowded that we could find only one free seat in a first-class compartment, which I took, while my husband sat down in a seat which a young man had just left to go to the restaurant car for lunch. The other people in the compartment were an elderly business man and his wife, both well on in the fifties, and a manufacturer and his wife, socially superior to the others and fifteen to twenty years younger. The elderly business man and his wife, like nearly everybody else on the train, were hideous; the woman had a body like a sow, and the man was flabby and pasty. The manufacturer was very much better-looking, with a direct laughing eye, but he was certainly two stone overweight, and his wife had been sharpened to a dark keen prettiness by some Hungarian strain. The business man's wife kept leaving her seat and running up and down the corridor in a state of great distress, lamenting that she and her husband had no Austrian schillings and therefore could not get a meal in the restaurant car. Her

27

distress was so marked that we assumed that they had eaten nothing for many hours, and we gave her a packet of chocolate and some biscuits, which she ate very quickly with an abstracted air. Between mouthfuls she explained that they were travelling to a Dalmatian island because her husband had been very ill with a nervous disorder affecting the stomach which made him unable to make decisions. She pointed a bitten bar of chocolate at him and said, 'Yes, he can't make up his mind about anything! If you say, "Do you want to go or do you want to stay?" he doesn't know.' Grieving and faithful love shone in her eyes. My husband was very sympathetic, and said that he himself had nervous trouble of some sort. He even alleged, to my surprise, that he had passed through a similar period of not knowing his own mind. Sunshine, he said, he had found the only cure.

But as she spoke her eyes shifted over my husband's shoulders and she cried, 'Ah, now we are among beautiful mountains! *Wunderbar! Fabelhaft! Ach*, these must be the Dolomites!' 'No, these are not the Dolomites,' said my husband, 'this is the valley that runs up to Bad Gastein,' and he told her that in the sixteenth century this had been a district of great wealth and culture, because it had been a gold-mining centre. He pointed out the town of Hof Gastein and described the beautiful Gothic tombs of mineowners in the church there, which are covered with carvings representing stages of the mining process. Everybody in the carriage listened to this with sudden, proud, exclamatory delight; it was as if they were children, and my husband were reading them a legend out of a book about their glorious past. They seemed to derive a special pious pleasure from the contemplation of the Gothic; and they were also enraptured by the perfection of my husband's German.

'But it is real German German!' they said, as if they were complimenting him on being good as well as clever. Suddenly the manufacturer said to him, 'But have you really got first-class tickets?' My husband said in surprise, 'Yes, of course we have; here they are.' Then the manufacturer said, 'Then you can keep the seat where you are sitting, for the young man who had it has only a second-class ticket!' The others all eagerly agreed. 'Yes, yes,' they said, 'certainly you must stay where you are, for he has only a second-class ticket!' The business man's wife jumped up and stopped a passing ticket-collector and told him about it with great passion and many defensive gestures towards us, and he too became excited and sympathetic. He promised that, as lunch was now finished and people were coming back from the restaurant car, he would wait for the young man and eject him. It was just then that the business man's wife noticed that we were rising into the snowfields at the head of the pass and cried out in rapture. This too was *wunderbar* and *fabelhaft*, and the whole carriage was caught up into a warm lyrical ecstasy. Snow, apparently, was certified in the philosophy as a legitimate object for delight, like the Gothic. For this I liked them enormously. Not only was it an embryonic emotion which, fully developed and shorn of its sentimentality, would produce great music of the Beethoven and Brahms and Mahler type, but it afforded an agreeable contrast to the element I most dislike. If anyone in a railway carriage full of English people should express great enjoyment of the scenery through which the train was passing, his companions would feel an irresistible impulse not only to refrain from joining him in his pleasure, but to persuade themselves that there was something despicable and repellent in that scenery. No conceivable virtue can proceed from the development of this characteristic.

At the height of this collective rhapsody the young man with the second-class ticket came back. He had been there for a minute or two before anybody, even the ticket-collector, noticed his presence. He was standing in the middle of the compartment, not even understanding that his seat had been taken, as my husband was at the window, when the business man's wife became aware of him. 'Oho-o-o-o!' she cried with frightful significance; and everybody turned on him with such vehemence that he stood stock-still with amazement, and the ticket-collector had to pull him by the sleeve and tell him to take his luggage and be gone. The vehemence of all four Germans was so intense that we took it for granted that it must be due to some other reason than concern for our comfort, and supposed the explanation lay in the young man's race and personality, for he was Latin and epicene. His oval olive face was meek with his acceptance of the obligation to please, and he wore with a demure coquetry a suit, a shirt, a tie, socks, gloves, and a hat all in the colours of coffee-and-cream of various strengths. The labels on his suitcase suggested he was either an actor or a dancer, and indeed his slender body was as unnaturally compressed by exercise as by a corset. Under this joint attack he stood quite still with his head down and his body relaxed, not in indifference, but rather because his physical training had taught him to loosen his muscles when he was struck so that he should fall light. There was an air of practice about him, as if he were thoroughly used to being the object of official hostility, and a kind of passive, not very noble fortitude; he was quite sure he would survive this, and would be able to walk away unhurt. We were distressed, but could not believe we were responsible, since the feeling of the Germans was so passionate; and indeed this young man was so different from them that it was conceivable they felt as hippopotami at the Zoo might feel if a cheetah were introduced into their cage.

By the time he had left us the train was drawing in to Bad Gastein. The business man's wife was upset because she could get nothing to eat there. The trolleys carrying chocolate and coffee and oranges and sandwiches were busy with another train when we arrived, and they started on our train too late to arrive at our carriage. She said that she did not mind so much for herself as for her husband. He had had nothing since breakfast at Munich except some sausages and coffee at Passau and some ham sandwiches at Salzburg. As he had also eaten some of the chocolate and biscuits we had given her, it seemed to us he had not done so badly for a man with a gastric ailment. Then silence fell on her, and she sat down and dangled her short legs while we went through the very long tunnel under the Hohe Tauern mountains. This tunnel represents no real frontier. They were still in Austria, and they had left Germany early that morning. Yet when we came out on the other side all the four Germans began to talk quickly and freely, as if they no longer feared something. The manufacturer and his wife told us that they were going to Hertseg Novi, a village on the South Dalmatian coast, to bathe. They said he was tired out by various difficulties which had arisen in the management of his business during the last few months. At that the business man put his forehead down on his hand and groaned. Then they all laughed at their own distress; and they all began to tell each other how badly they had needed this holiday they were taking, and what *pension* terms they were going to pay, and by what date they had to be back in Germany, and to discuss where they were allowed to go as tourists and how much money they would have been allowed if they had gone to other countries and in what form they would have had to take it. The regulations which bound them were obviously of an inconvenient intricacy, for they frequently disputed as to the details; and indeed they frequently uttered expressions of despair at the way they were hemmed in and harried.

They talked like that for a long time. Then somebody came and told the business man's wife that she could, after all, have a meal in the restaurant car. She ran out in a great hurry, and the rest of us all fell silent. I read for a time and then slept, and woke up just as the train was running into Villach, which is a lovely little Austrian town set on a river. At Villach the business man's wife

was overjoyed to find she could buy some sausages for herself and
her husband. All through the journey she was eating voraciously,
running after food down the corridor, coming back munching
something, her mouth and bust powdered with crumbs. But there
was nothing so voluptuous as greed about all this eating. She was
simply stoking herself with food to keep her nerves going, as ill
and tired people drink. Actually she was an extremely pleasant and
appealing person: she was all goodness and kindness, and she loved
her husband very much. She took great pleasure in bringing him
all this food, and she liked pointing out to him anything beautiful
that we were passing. When she had got him to give his attention
to it, she looked no more at the beautiful thing but only at his face.
When we were going by the very beautiful Wörther See, which
lay under the hills, veiled by their shadows and the dusk so that
one could attribute to it just the kind of beauty one prefers, she
made him look at it, looked at him looking at it, and then turned
to us and said, 'You cannot think what troubles he has had!' We
made sympathetic noises, and the business man began to grumble
away at his ease. It appeared that he owned an apartment house
in Berlin, and had for six months been struggling with a wholly
unforeseen and inexplicable demand for extra taxes on it. He
did not allege that the tax was unjust. He seemed to think that
the demand was legal enough, but that the relevant law was so
complicated, and was so capriciously interpreted by the Nazi
courts, that he had been unable to foresee how much he would
be asked for, and was still quite at a loss to calculate what might
be exacted in the future. He had also had a great deal of trouble
dealing with some undesirable tenants, whose conduct had caused
frequent complaints from other tenants, but who were members of
the Nazi Party. He left it ambiguous whether he had tried to evict
the undesirable tenants and had been foiled by the Nazis, or if he
had been too frightened even to try to get redress.

At that the manufacturer and his wife sighed, and said that they
could understand. The man spoke with a great deal of reticence
and obviously did not want to give away exactly what his business
was, lest he get into difficulties; but he said with great resentment
that the Nazis had put a director into his company who knew
nothing and was simply a Party man in line for a job. He added,
however, that what he really minded was the unforeseeable taxes.
He laughed at the absurdity of it all, for he was a brave and
jolly man; but the mere fact that he stopped giving us details
of his worries, when he was obviously extremely expansive by
temperament, showed that his spirit was deeply troubled. Soon

he fell silent and put his arm round his wife. The two had an air of being united by a great passion, an unusual physical sympathy, and also by a common endurance of stress and strain, to a degree which would have seemed more natural in far older people. To cheer him up the wife told us funny stories about some consequences of *Hitlerismus*. She described how the hairdresser's assistant who had always waved her hair for her had one morning greeted her with tears, and told her that she was afraid she would never be able to attend to her again, because she was afraid she had failed in the examination which she had to pass for the right to practise her craft. She had said to the girl, 'But I am sure you will pass your examination, for you are so very good at your work.' But the girl had answered, 'Yes, I am good at my work! Shampooing can I do, and water-waving can I do, and marcelling can I do, and oil massage can I do, and hair-dyeing can I do, but keep from mixing up Göring's and Goebbels's birthday, that can I not do.' They all laughed at this, and then again fell silent.

The business man said, 'But all the young people, they are solid for Hitler. For them all is done.'

The others said, '*Ja, das ist so!*' and the business woman began, 'Yes, our sons,' and then stopped.

They were all of them falling to pieces under the emotional and intellectual strain laid on them by their Government, poor Laocoöns strangled by red tape. It was obvious that by getting the population into this state the Nazis had guaranteed the continuance of their system; for none of these people could have given any effective support to any rival party that wanted to seize power, and indeed their affairs, which were thoroughly typical, were in such an inextricable state of confusion that no sane party would now wish to take over the government, since it would certainly see nothing but failure ahead. Their misery seemed to have abolished every possible future for them. I reflected that if a train were filled with the citizens of the Western Roman Empire in the fourth century they would have made much the same complaints. The reforms of Diocletian and Constantine created a condition of exorbitant and unforeseeable taxes, of privileged officials, of a complicated civil administration that made endless demands on its subjects and gave them very little security in return. The Western Romans were put out of their pain by the invasion of the Goths. But these people could not hope for any such release. It was like the story of the man who went to Dr. Abernethy, complaining of hopeless melancholy, and was advised to go and see the famous clown, Grimaldi. 'I am Grimaldi,' he said. These men and women, incapable of making decisions or enforcing a condition where they could make them, were the Goths.

It was dark when we crossed the Yugoslavian frontier. Handsome young soldiers in olive uniforms with faces sealed by the flatness of cheekbones asked us questions softly, insistently, without interest. As we steamed out of the station, the manufacturer said with a rolling laugh, 'Well, we'll have no more good food till we're back here again. The food in Yugoslavia is terrible.' '*Ach*, so we have heard,' wailed the business man's wife, 'and what shall I do with my poor man! There is nothing good at all, is there?' This seemed to me extremely funny, for food in Yugoslavia has a Slav superbness. They cook lamb and sucking-pig as well as anywhere in the world, have a lot of freshwater fish and broil it straight out of the streams, use their vegetables young enough, have many dark and rich romantic soups, and understand that seasoning should be pungent rather than hot. I said, 'You needn't worry at all. Yugoslavian food is very good.' The manufacturer laughed and shook his head. 'No, I was there in the war and it was terrible.' 'Perhaps it was at that time,' I said, 'but I was there last year, and I found it admirable.' They all shook their heads at me, smiling, and seemed a little embarrassed. I perceived they felt that English food was so far inferior to German that my opinion on the subject could not be worth having, and that I was rather simple and ingenuous not to realize this. 'I understand,' ventured my husband, 'that there are very good trout.' '*Ach*, no!' laughed the manufacturer, waving his great hand. 'They call them trout, but they are something quite different; they are not like our good German trout.' They all sat, nodding and rocking, entranced by a vision of the warm goodness of German life, the warm goodness of German food, and of German superiority to all non-German barbarity.

A little while later my husband and I went and had dinner in the wagon-restaurant, which was Yugoslavian and extremely good. When we came back the business man was telling how, sitting at his desk in his office just after the war, he had seen the bodies of three men fall past his windows, Spartacist snipers who had been on his roof and had been picked off by Government troops; how he had been ruined in the inflation, and had even sold his dog for food; how he had made a fortune again, by the refinancing of a prosperous industry, but had never enjoyed it because he had always been afraid of Bolshevism, and had worried himself ill finding the best ways of tying it up safely; and now he was afraid. He had spent the last twenty-three years in a state of continuous

terror. He had been afraid of the Allies; he had been afraid of
the Spartacists; he had been afraid of financial catastrophe; he
had been afraid of the Communists; and now he was afraid of
the Nazis.

Sighing deeply, he said, evidently referring to something about
which he had not spoken, 'The worst of life under the Nazis is
that the private citizen hasn't any liberty, but the officials haven't
any authority either.' It was curious that such a sharply critical
phrase should have been coined by one whose attitude was so
purely passive; for he had spoken of all the forces that had
tormented him as if they could not have been opposed, any more
than thunder or lightning. He seemed, indeed, quite unpolitically
minded. When he complained of the inflation, my husband tried
to console him by saying that the sufferings he and others had
undergone at that time may have been severe, but they had at
least been of immense service to Germany; that Helfferich had
been justified in his heroic plan, since it had wiped out the internal
debt and cleared the ground for enterprising people to make a new
and triumphant industrialism. But the business man, though he
had himself actually been one of those enterprising men, did not
show any interest in the idea. He seemed quite unused to regarding
anything that the state did as having a cause or any but the most
immediate effect.

Just then I happened to see the name of a station at which
we were stopping, and I asked my husband to look it up in a
time-table he had in his pocket, so that we might know how
late we were. And it turned out that we were very late indeed,
nearly two hours. When my husband spoke of this all the Germans
showed the greatest consternation. They realized that this meant
they would almost certainly get into Zagreb too late to catch the
connexion which would take them the twelve hours' journey to
Split, on the Dalmatian coast, and in that case they would have
to spend the night at Zagreb. It was not easy to see why they were
so greatly distressed. Both couples were staying in Yugoslavia for
some weeks and the loss of a day could not mean much to them;
and they could draw as they liked on their dinars in the morning.
The business man's wife was adding another agony to the strain
of the situation. For it was still just possible that we might get to
Zagreb in time to bundle into the Split train, and she was not sure
if she ought to do that, as her husband was so tired. The necessity
for making a decision on this plan caused her real anguish; she sat
wringing her poor red hands. To us it seemed the obvious thing
that they should simply make up their minds to stay the night, but

it was not at all obvious to them. She looked so miserable that we gave her some biscuits, which she crammed into her mouth exactly like an exhausted person taking a pull of brandy. The other two had decided to stay at Zagreb, but they were hardly in a better state. Consciousness of their own fatigue had rushed upon them; they were amazed at it, they groaned and complained.

I realized again that I would never understand the German people. The misery of these travellers was purely amazing. It was perplexing that they should have been surprised by the lateness of the train. The journey from Berlin to Zagreb is something like thirty hours, and no sensible person would expect a minor train to be on time on such a route in winter, particularly as a great part of it runs through the mountains. It also seemed to me odd that the business man's wife should take it as an unforeseen horror that her husband, who had been seriously ill and was not yet recovered, should be tired after sitting up in a railway carriage for a day and a night. Also, if she had such an appetite why had she not brought a tin of biscuits and some ham? And how was it that these two men, who had successfully conducted commercial and industrial enterprises of some importance, were so utterly incompetent in the conduct of a simple journey? As I watched them in complete mystification, yet another consideration came to horrify them. 'And what the hotels in Zagreb will be like!' said the manufacturer. 'Pig-sties! Pig-sties!' 'Oh, my poor husband!' moaned the business man's wife. 'To think he is to be uncomfortable when he is so ill!' I objected that the hotels in Zagreb were excellent; that I myself had stayed in an old-fashioned hotel which was extremely comfortable and that there was a new and huge hotel that was positively American in its luxury. But they would not listen to me. 'But why are you going to Yugoslavia if you think it is all so terrible?' I asked. 'Ah,' said the manufacturer, 'we are going to the Adriatic coast where there are many German tourists and for that reason the hotels are good.'

Then came a climactic mystification. There came along the first Yugoslavian ticket-collector, a red-faced, ugly, amiable Croat. The Germans all held out their tickets, and lo and behold! They were all second-class. My husband and I gaped in bewilderment. It made the campaign they had conducted against the young man in coffee-and-cream clothes completely incomprehensible and not at all pleasing. If they had been nasty people it would have been natural enough; but they were not at all nasty, they loved each other, tranquillity, snow, and their national history. Nevertheless they were unabashed by the disclosure of what my husband and

I considered the most monstrous perfidy. I realized that if I had said to them, 'You had that young man turned out of the carriage because he had a second-class ticket,' they would have nodded and said, 'Yes,' and if I had gone on and said, 'But you yourselves have only second-class tickets,' they would not have seen that the second statement had any bearing on the first; and I cannot picture to myself the mental life of people who cannot perceive that connexion.

But as we gaped we were plunged into yet another mystification. The Croat ticket-collector told the Germans that they must pay the difference between the first-class and the second-class fares from the frontier. It amounted to very little, to only a few marks a head. The Germans protested, on the ground that not enough second-class carriages had been provided in Berlin, but the Croat explained that that was not his business, nor the Yugoslavian Railway Company's. The German authorities made up the train, and it was their fault if it were not properly constituted. The Yugoslavian Railway Company simply accepted the train, and on its line passengers must pay for the seats they occupied. At that the manufacturer winked at him and held out a hand to him with a bribe in it. The Croat was so poor, his hand curved for it in spite of himself. But he explained that he could not settle it that way, because an inspector might come along, and he would lose his job, for on this matter the company was really strict. The manufacturer persisted, smiling. I nearly bounced out of my seat, for the ticket-collector was so poor that he was grinning with desire for the money, while his eyebrows were going up in fear. It was not fair to tempt him to take this risk. I also wondered how these people, who were sure that Yugoslavia was a land of barbarians, dared put themselves on the wrong side of the law within a few hours of crossing the frontier.

As I wondered, the ticket-collector suddenly lost his temper. His red face became violet, he began to shout. The Germans showed no resentment and simply began to get the money together; yet if anybody had shouted at me like that, I should have shouted back, no matter how much in the wrong I was. In this they showed a marked superiority over me. But in their efforts to make payment they became again flatly incomprehensible. They could pay it in marks, and the amount was much less than the marks they had been allowed to take out of the country, and had in fact taken. Nevertheless they had great difficulty in paying, for the incredible reason that not one of them knew exactly where his money was. They had to turn out pockets and bags and purses, they had to give each other change, they had to do reckonings and correct each other, and they groaned all the time at this inconvenience which was entirely their own fault.

I got up and went out into the corridor. It was disconcerting to be rushing through the night with this carriageful of unhappy muddlers, who were so nice and so incomprehensible, and so apparently doomed to disaster of a kind so special that it was impossible for anybody not of their blood to imagine how it could be averted. It added to their eerie quality that on paper these people would seem the most practical and sensible people. Their businesses were, I am sure, most efficiently conducted. But this only meant that since the Industrial Revolution capitalism has grooved society with a number of deep slots along which most human beings can roll smoothly to a fixed destination. When a man takes charge of a factory the factory takes charge of him, if he opens an office it falls into a place in a network that extends over the whole world and so long as he obeys the general trend he will not meet any obvious disaster; but he may be unable to meet the calls that daily life outside this specialist area makes on judgment and initiative. These people fell into that category. Their helplessness was the greater because they had plainly a special talent for obedience. In the routine level of commerce and industry they must have known a success which must have made their failure in all other phases of their being embittering and strange. Now that capitalism was passing into a decadent phase and many of the grooves along which they had rolled so happily were worn down to nothing, they were broken and beaten, and their ability to choose the broad outlines of their daily lives, to make political decisions, was now less than it had been originally. It was inevitable that the children of such muddlers, who would themselves be muddlers, would support any system which offered them new opportunities for profitable obedience, which would pattern society with new grooves in place of the old, and would never be warned by any instinct for competence and self-preservation if that system was leading to universal disaster. I tried to tell myself that these people in the carriage were not of importance, and were not typical, but I knew that I lied. These were exactly like all Aryan Germans I had ever known; and there were sixty millions of them in the middle of Europe.

'This is Zagreb!' cried the Germans, and took all their luggage down from the racks. Then they broke into excessive cries of exasperation and distress because it was not Zagreb, it was Zagreb-Sava, a suburb three or four miles out of the main town. I leaned out of the window. Rain was falling heavily, and the mud shone between the railway tracks. An elderly man, his thin body clad in a tight-fitting, flimsy overcoat, trotted along beside the train, crying softly, 'Anna! Anna! Anna!' He held an open umbrella not over himself but at arm's length. He had not brought it for himself, but for the beloved woman he was calling. He did not lose hope when he found her nowhere in all the long train, but turned and trotted all the way back, calling still with anxious sweetness, 'Anna! Anna! Anna!' When the train steamed out he was trotting along it for a third time, holding his umbrella still further away from him. A ray of light from an electric standard shone on his white hair, on the dome of his umbrella, which was streaked with several rents, and on the strong spears of the driving rain. I was among people I could understand.

Croatia

Zagreb I

THEY WERE WAITING IN THE RAIN ON THE PLATFORM OF THE real Zagreb, our three friends. There was Constantine, the poet, a Serb, that is to say a Slav member of the Orthodox Church, from Serbia. There was Valetta, a lecturer in mathematics at Zagreb University, a Croat, that is to say a Slav member of the Roman Catholic Church, from Dalmatia. There was Marko Gregorievitch, the critic and journalist, a Croat from Croatia. They were all different sizes and shapes, in body and mind.

Constantine is short and fat, with a head like the best-known satyr in the Louvre, and an air of vine-leaves about the brow, though he drinks little. He is perpetually drunk on what comes out of his mouth, not what goes into it. He talks incessantly. In the morning he comes out of his bedroom in the middle of a sentence; and at night he backs into it, so that he can just finish one more sentence. Automatically he makes silencing gestures while he speaks, just in case somebody should take it into his head to interrupt. Nearly all his talk is good, and sometimes it runs along in a coloured shadow show, like Heine's *Florentine Nights*, and sometimes it crystallizes into a little story the essence of hope or love or regret, like a Heine lyric. Of all human beings I have ever met he is the most like Heine: and since Heine was the most Jewish of writers it follows that Constantine is Jew as well as Serb. His father was a Jewish doctor of revolutionary sympathies, who fled from Russian Poland about fifty years ago and settled in a rich provincial town in Serbia and became one of the leaders of the medical profession, which has always been more advanced there than one might have supposed. His mother was also Polish Jewish, and was a famous musician. He is by adoption only, yet quite completely, a Serb. He fought in the Great War very gallantly, for he is a man of great physical courage, and to him Serbian history is his history, his life is a part of the life of the Serbian people. He is now a Government official; but that is not the reason why he believes in Yugoslavia. To him a state of Serbs, Slovenes, and Croats, controlled by a

41

central government in Belgrade, is a necessity if these peoples
are to maintain themselves against Italian and Central European
pressure on the west, and Bulgarian pressure, which might become
in effect Central European pressure, on the east.

Valetta comes from a Dalmatian town which was settled by the
Greeks some hundreds of years before Christ, and he has the strong
delicacy and the morning freshness of an archaic statue. They like
him everywhere he goes, Paris and London and Berlin and Vienna,
but he is hall-marked as a Slav, because his charm is not associated
with any of those defects that commonly go with it in other races. He
might suddenly stop smiling and clench his long hands, and offer
himself up to martyrdom for an idea. He is anti-Yugoslavian; he is
a federalist and believes in an autonomous Croatia.

Gregorievitch looks like Pluto in the Mickey Mouse films. His
face is grooved with grief at the trouble and lack of gratitude he
has encountered while defending certain fixed and noble standards
in a chaotic world. His long body is like Pluto's in its extensibility.
As he sits in his armchair, resentment at what he conceives to be
a remediable injustice will draw him inches nearer to the ceiling,
despair at an inevitable wrong will crumple him up like a concertina.
Yugoslavia is the Mickey Mouse this Pluto serves. He is ten years
older than Constantine, who is forty-six, and thirty years older
than Valetta. This means that for sixteen years before the war
he was an active revolutionary, fighting against the Hungarians
for the right of Croats to govern themselves and to use their own
language. In order that the Croats might be united with their free
brother Slavs the Serbs, he endured poverty and imprisonment and
exile. Therefore Yugoslavia is to him the Kingdom of Heaven on
earth. Who speaks more lightly of it spits on those sixteen years of
sorrow, who raises his hand against it violates the Slav sacrament.
So to him Constantine, who was still a student in Paris when the
Great War broke out, and who had been born a free Serb, seems
impious in the way he takes Yugoslavia for granted. There is the
difference between them that there was between the Christians of
the first three centuries, who fought for their faith when it seemed
a lost cause, and the Christians of the fourth century, who fought
for it when it was victorious.

And to Gregorievitch, Valetta is quite simply a traitor. He is
more than an individual who has gone astray, he is the very
essence of treachery incarnate. Youth should uphold the banner
of the right against unjust authority, and should practise that form
of obedience to God which is rebellion against tyranny; and it seems
to Gregorievitch that Valetta is betraying that ideal, for to him

Yugoslavia represents a supreme gesture of defiance against the tyranny of the Austro-Hungarian Empire. Only a sorcerer could make him realize that the Austro-Hungarian Empire ceased to be when Valetta was six years old, and that he has never known any other symbol of unjust authority except Yugoslavia.

They are standing in the rain, and they are all different and they are all the same. They greet us warmly, and in their hearts they cannot greet each other, and they dislike us a little because it is to meet us that they are standing beside their enemies in the rain. We are their friends, but we are made from another substance. The rich passions of Constantine, the intense, graceful, selected joys and sorrows of Valetta, and Gregorievitch's gloomy Great Danish nobility are all cut from the same primary stuff, though in very dissimilar shapes. Sitting in our hotel room, drinking wine, they showed their unity of origin. A door opens, they twitch and swivel their heads, and the movement is the same. When these enemies advance on each other, they must move at the same tempo.

My husband has not met any of them before. I see him transfixed by their strangeness. He listens amazed to Constantine's beautiful French, which has preserved in it all the butterfly brilliances of his youth, when he was one of Bergson's favourite students, and was making his musical studies with Wanda Landowska. He falls under the spell of Constantine. He strains forward to hear the perfect phrase that is bound to come when Constantine's eyes catch the light, and each of his tight black curls spins on his head, and his lips shoot out horizontally, and his hands grope in the air before him as if he were unloosing the neckcloth of the strangling truth. Now Constantine was talking of Bergson and saying that it was to miss the very essence in him to regard him only as a philosopher. He was a magician who had taken philosophy as his subject matter. He did not analyse phenomena, he uttered incantations that invoked understanding. 'We students,' said Constantine, 'we were not the pupils of a great professor, we were the sorcerer's apprentices. We did strange things that are not in most academic courses. On Sundays we would talk together in the forest of Fontainebleau, all day long sometimes, reconstituting his lectures by pooling our memories. For, you see, in his class-room it was not possible to take notes. If we bent our heads for one moment to take down a point, we missed an organic phrase, and the rest of the lecture appeared incomprehensible. That shows he was a magician. For what is the essential of a spell? That if one word is left out it is no longer a spell. I was able to recognize that at once, for in my town, which is Shabats, there were three houses in a row, and in one house lived my father who was the greatest doctor in our country, and in the next there lived a priest who was the greatest saint in my country, and in the next there lived an old woman who was the greatest witch in my country, and when I was a little boy I lived in the first of these houses and I went as I would into the other two, for the holy man and the witch liked me very much, and I tell you in each of these houses there was magic, so I know all about it as most men do not.'

A line of light ran along the dark map of Europe we all of us hold in our minds; at one end a Serbian town, unknown to me as Ur, peopled with the personnel of fairy-tales, and at the other end the familiar idea of Bergson. My husband, I could see, was enraptured. He loves to learn what he did not know before. But in a minute I could see that he was not so happy. Valetta had said that he was making plans for our pleasure in Yugoslavia, and that he hoped that we would be able to go up into the snow mountains, particularly if we liked winter sports. My husband said he was very fond of Switzerland, and how he enjoyed going over there when he was tired and handing himself over to the care of the guides. 'Yes, the guides are so good for us, who are over-civilized,' said Constantine. 'They refresh us immensely, when we are with them. For they succeed at every point where we fail. We can be responsible for what we love, our families and our countries, and the causes we think just, but where we do not love we cannot muster the necessary attention. That is just what the guides do, with such a wealth of attention that it amounts to nothing comparable to our attention at all, to a mystical apprehension of the whole universe.

'I will give you,' he said, 'an example. I made once a most beautiful journey in Italy with my wife. She is a German, you know, and she worships Goethe, so this was a pilgrimage. We went to see where he had lived in Venice and Rome, and she was so delighted, you cannot believe, delighted deep in herself, so that her intuition told her many things. "That is the house where he lived!" she cried in Venice, jumping up and down in the gondola, and it was so. At length we came to Naples, and we took a guide and went up Vesuvius, because Goethe went up Vesuvius. Do you remember the passage where he says he was on the edge of a little crater, and he slipped? That was much in my wife's mind, and suddenly it was given to her to know by intuition that a certain little crater we saw was that same one where Goethe had slipped, so before we could stop it she ran down to it. I saw, of course, that she might be killed at any moment, so I ran after her. But so did the guide, though she was nothing to him. And then came the evidence of this mystic apprehension which is given by the constant vigilance of a guide's life. Just then this crater began to erupt, and the lava burst out here and there and here. But always the guide knew where it was coming, and took us to the left or the right, wherever it was not. Sometimes there was barely time for us to be there for more than a second; that was proved afterwards because the soles of our shoes were scorched. For three-quarters of an hour we ran thus up and down, from right to left and from left to right, before we could get to safety; and I was immensely happy the whole time because the guide was doing something I could not have done, which it is good to do!'

During the telling of this story my husband's eyes rested on me with an expression of alarm. It was apparent from Constantine's tone that nothing in the story had struck him as odd except the devotion of the guide to his charges. 'Are not her friends very dotty?' he was plainly asking himself. 'Is this how she wants to live?' But the conversation took a businesslike turn, and we were called on to consider our plans. We must meet So-and-so and Such-and-such, of course. It became obvious from certain reticences that the strained relations between Croats and Serbs were making themselves felt over our plans. For So-and-so, it appeared, would not meet Such-and-such, and that, it could be deduced, was the reason. Suddenly such reticences were blown away by a very explicit wrangle about Y., the editor of a certain newspaper. 'Oh, you should meet him, he would interest you,' said Valetta. 'Yes, he has a very remarkable mind,' admitted Constantine. 'No,' exploded Gregorievitch. They squabbled for a time in Serbian. Then Gregorievitch shrugged his shoulders and said to us, with heavy lightness, 'Y. is not an honest man, that is all!' 'He is perfectly honest,' said Valetta coldly. 'Gregorievitch, you are an impossibilist,' said Constantine mildly. 'Let our English guests judge,' said Pluto grimly.

It appeared that one day some years before, Pluto had rung up Y. and reminded him that next week was the centenary of a certain Croat poet, and asked him if he would like an article on him. Y. said that he would, and Pluto sent an article four columns long, including two quotations concerning liberty. But the article had to be submitted to the censor, who at that particular time and in that particular place happened to be Pluto. He sent it back to Y. cut by a column and a half, including both quotations. Then, if we would believe it, Y. had rung up Pluto on the telephone and been most abusive, and never since then had he accepted one single article from Pluto. 'Surely,' said Pluto, immensely tall and grey and wrinkled, 'he must have seen that I had to do what I did. To be true to myself as a critic I had to write the article as I did. But to be true to myself as a censor, I had to cut it as I did. In which capacity did he hope that I would betray my ideals?' As he related this anecdote his spectacles shone with the steady glare of a strong man justly enraged.

But that story I could understand. It proceeds not, as might be thought, from incoherence but from a very high and too rigid sense of order. There lingers here a survival of an old attitude towards status that the whole world held, in days which were perhaps happier. Now, we think that if a man takes an office, he will modify it according to what he is as a man, according to his temperament and official standards. But then it was taken for granted that a man would modify his temperament and his ethical standards according to his office, provided it were of any real importance. In the third and fourth centuries Christian congregations were constantly insisting on electing people as bishops who were unwilling to accept the office, perhaps for some such valid reason as that they were not even Christians, but who seemed to have the ability necessary for the semi-magisterial duties of the episcopacy. Sometimes these men were so reluctant that the congregations were obliged to kidnap them and ordain them forcibly. But once they were installed as bishops, they often performed their duties admirably. They had a sense of social structure, they were aware that bishops, who had by then taken over most of the civil administration that the crumbling Roman Empire could no longer handle, must work well if society was not to fall to pieces. Even so Gregorievitch must have been conscious, all his life, of the social value of patriotic poets and, for the last unhappy twenty years, of censors. Therefore it seemed to him that he must do his best in both capacities, not that he should modify his performances to uphold the consistence of his personality. That I could perfectly understand; but it was so late I did not feel able to explain it to my husband, whom I saw, when I forced open my eyelids, undressing slowly, with his eyes set pensively on the window-curtains, wondering what strange city they were going to disclose next day.

Zagreb II

But the morning showed us that Zagreb was not a strange city at all. It has the warm and comfortable appearance of a town that has been well aired. People have been living there in physical, though not political, comfort for a thousand years. Moreover it is full of those vast toast-coloured buildings, barracks and law courts and municipal offices, which are an invariable sign of past occupancy by the Austro-Hungarian Empire; and that always means enthusiastic ingestion combined with lack of exercise in pleasant surroundings, the happy consumption of coffee and whipped cream and sweet cakes at little tables under chestnut trees. But it has its own quality. It has no grand river, it is built up to no climax; the hill the old town stands on is what the eighteenth century used to call 'a moderate elevation.' It has few very fine buildings except the Gothic Cathedral, and that has been forced to wear an ugly nineteenth-century overcoat. But Zagreb makes from its featureless handsomeness something that pleases like a Schubert song, a delight that begins quietly and never definitely ends. We believed we were being annoyed by the rain that first morning we walked out into it, but eventually we recognized we were as happy as if we had been walking in sunshine through a really beautiful city. It has, moreover, the endearing characteristic, noticeable in many French towns, of remaining a small town when it is in fact quite large. A hundred and fifty thousand people live in Zagreb, but from the way gossips stand in the street it is plain that everybody knows who is going to have a baby and when. This is a lovely spiritual victory over urbanization.

There was a wide market-place, where under red and white umbrellas peasants stood sturdy and square on their feet, and amazed us by their faces, which are as mobile and sensitive as if they were the most cultivated townspeople. The women wore, and were the first to do so I have ever seen anywhere in the world, neither skirt nor trousers, but two broad aprons, one covering the front part of the body and one the back, and overlapping at the sides, and underneath showed very brave red woollen stockings. They gave the sense of the very opposite of what we mean by the word 'peasant' when we use it in a derogatory sense, thinking of women made doltish by repeated pregnancies and a lifetime spent in the service of oafs in villages that swim in mud to the thresholds

47

every winter. This costume was evolved by women who could stride along if they were eight months gone with child, and who would dance in the mud if they felt like it, no matter what any oaf said.

They lived under no favour, however. They all spoke some German, so we were able to ask the prices of what they sold; and we could have bought a sackful of fruit and vegetables, all of the finest, for the equivalent of two shillings: a fifth of what it would have fetched in a Western city. This meant desperate, pinching poverty, for the manufactured goods in the shops are marked at nearly Western prices. But they looked gallant, and nobody spoke of poverty, nobody begged. It was a sign that we were out of Central Europe, for in a German and Austrian town where the people were twice as well off as these they would have perpetually complained. But there were signs that we were near Central Europe. There were stalls covered with fine embroidered handkerchiefs and table linen, which was all of it superbly executed, for Slav women have a captive devil in their flying fingers to work wonders for them. But the design was horrible. It was not like the designs I had seen in other parts of Yugoslavia, in Serbia and Macedonia; it was not even as good as the designs on the dresses of the peasant women who were standing by the stalls, inferior though they were. It was severely naturalistic, and attempted to represent fruit and flowers, and it followed the tradition of Victorian Berlin woolwork. In other words, it showed German influence.

I felt impatient. I was getting no exhilaration out of being here, such as I had hoped for in coming to Yugoslavia. For a rest I went and stood on the steps of the statue in the middle of the square. Looking at the inscription I saw that it was a statue of the Croat patriot, Yellatchitch, and I reflected that if the Croats had not succeeded in cheering me up they had other achievements to their credit. For this is one of the strangest statues in the world. It represents Yellatchitch as leading his troops on horseback and brandishing a sword in the direction of Budapest, in which direction he had indeed led them to victory against the Hungarians in 1848; and this is not a new statue erected since Croatia was liberated from Hungary. It stood in the market-place, commemorating a Hungarian defeat, in the days when Hungary was master of Croatia, and the explanation does not lie in Hungarian magnanimity. It takes the whole of Croatian history to solve the mystery.

The Croats were originally a Slav tribe who were invited by the Emperor Heraclius to free the Dalmatian coast and the Croatian hinterland from the Avars, one of the most noxious pillaging hordes who operated from a centre on the Danube far and wide: they

created an early currency crisis by collecting immense tributes in
gold, year after year, from all surrounding peoples. That was well
on into the decadence of the Western Roman Empire, in the seventh
century. They then stayed on as vassals of the Empire, and when its
power dissolved they declared themselves independent; and they
had their own kings who acknowledged the suzerainty of the Pope.
Very little is known about them in those days, except that they were
not a barbarous people, but had inherited much of the elaborate
Byzantine ritual. The last of their kings was crowned about the time
of the Norman Conquest. He left no kin, and civil war followed
among the Croat nobles. For the sake of peace they recognized
as their sovereign Coloman, King of Hungary, who asserted the
triple claim of conquest, election, and inheritance; the last was
doubtful, but the other two were fair enough. It is a thing to be
noted, the age of legalism in these parts. It is our weakness to think
that distant people became civilized when we looked at them, that
in their yesterdays they were brutish.

Coloman was crowned *Rex Hungariæ Croatiæ atque Dalmatiæ*.
For two centuries the two kingdoms led an independent and
co-equal existence under the same crown. Their peoples were not
likely to assimilate. They were racially unrelated: the Hungarians
or Magyars are a people of far Asiatic origin, akin to the Finns, the
Bulgars, and the Turks, and the Croats are Slav, akin to the Serbs,
the Russians, the Poles, and the Czechs. Neither is meek; each is
passionately attached to his own language; and the Hungarians are
fierce and warlike romantics whereas the Croats are fierce and
warlike intellectuals. Nothing could make them sympathetic, but
their position in Central Europe made the close alliance of a dual
monarchy desirable. But it was not cast-iron. In the fourteenth
century Coloman's line died out, and the Croats would not accept
the king elected by the Hungarians but crowned their own choice in
Zagreb Cathedral, and the union was restored only after six years,
when the Hungarians accepted the Croat King. But the son of that
King was Louis the Great, and he was predominantly Hungarian in
blood, and more in feeling. The Croats had to take a second place.

Many of us think that monarchy is more stable than a republican
form of government, and that there is a special whimsicality about
modern democracies. We forget that stable monarchies are the signs
of genius of an order at least as rare in government as in literature
or music, or of stable history. Monarchy without these conditions is
whimsical to the point of mania. The stock was not fruitful as among
commoners, perhaps because princesses were snatched as brides
before puberty lest others make the useful alliance first; and in no

rank does stock breed true and merit follow merit. If on a king's death he should leave an idiot heir or none, the nobles would send, perhaps far away, to a man whose fame lay in violence, in order to avoid war among themselves. He would rule them with the coldness of an alien, and it might be that in his loins there was working this genetic treachery, to leave them masterless at his death. He was in any case sure to be afflicted with the special malady of kings, which was poverty; the reluctance we feel about paying income tax is only the modern expression of a human incapacity to see the justice of providing for corporate expenses which is as old as the species itself. Here his alien blood made itself felt. Terrified of his insecure position in a strange land, he asked little of the nobles and came down like a scourge on the peasants, and was tempted to plunder them beyond need and without mercy. That is to say, he demanded certain sums from the nobles and made no provisions for social justice which prevented the nobles from wringing them out of the peasants and keeping their private treasures intact. There was the still graver danger that the king's alien blood would let him make contracts to their disadvantage with foreign powers. This danger was very grave indeed. For though there is a popular belief that negotiations to take the place of warfare are a modern invention, nothing could be further from the truth. The Middle Ages were always ready to lay down the sword and sign an agreement, preferably for a cash payment. An alien king was always particularly likely to sell a slice of his lands and people for a sum that would shore up his authority.

It is not comfortable to be an inhabitant of this globe. It never has been, except for brief periods. The Croats have been peculiarly uncomfortable. Louis the Great was a Frenchman, one of the house of Anjou; he married Elizabeth, a Slav, the daughter of a Bosnian king. When Louis died he left two daughters, and nearly all Hungary and Dalmatia recognized as their queen the elder, Mary, who was to govern under the regency of her mother. But certain Croatian and Hungarian barons were against her, and called to the throne her father's cousin, King Charles of Naples. It is to be noted that these Croatian barons were a strange and ungodly lot, with so little care for their people and, indeed, so little resemblance to them that they might be guessed to be alien. This whole territory had been devastated again and again by Asiatic invaders, and it is supposed that many of these nobles were the descendants of various roving brigands, men of power, who had seized land from the exhausted population as the invaders receded; some of them were certainly by origin Italian, German, and Goth, and in some cases themselves

Asiatic. King Charles was crowned King of Hungary and Croatia, and four years afterwards was assassinated by the widow Elizabeth. He was succeeded by his son, Ladislas, a fantastical adventurer. He was faced by Elizabeth and her daughter, Mary, and her betrothed, another alien, Sigismond of Luxembourg, a son of the Emperor Charles of Germany, for whom they desired the crown. Thereafter for fifty years the country agonized under these aliens, who were, however, inevitable at this phase of history. The people screamed with pain. They were tortured, imprisoned, famined; and their national soul was violated. Ladislas, though he had never been crowned, sold Dalmatia to the Republic of Venice for a hundred thousand ducats; and though Sigismond was eventually crowned, he was never in a position to assert his legal rights and recover his possessions. This meant that an enormous number of warlike, thriftless, bucolic intellectuals fell under the control of a community of merchants; and that the Croats of Croatia were thereafter the more helpless against Hungary by this division from their Dalmatian brothers.

Sigismond bore the Croats a grudge, because certain of their nobles had aided Ladislas against him. There was then and thereafter no separate coronation for Croatia. She had to be satisfied with a separate *diploma inaugurale*, a document setting forth the king's oath to his subjects and the privileges he intended to give them. But it is to be observed that she had to be satisfied. Dismembered as she was, she still had enough military power to make her able to bargain. Only as time went on these things mattered less. From the south-east the Turks pressed on and on. In 1453 they took Constantinople. In 1468 they were threatening the Dalmatian coast. Thereafter the Croats and the Hungarians were engaged in a perpetual guerrilla warfare to defend their lands. In 1526 the Hungarians fought the Turks in the battle of Mohacs, without calling on the Croats for aid, out of pride and political cantankerousness among the nobles. They were beaten and the King killed. Now Croatia was quite alone. It had to fall back on Austria, which was then governed by Ferdinand of Habsburg, and it offered him the throne on a hereditary basis.

The Germans have always hated the Slavs. More than that, they have always acted hatefully towards them. Now the Croats began to learn this lesson. Croatia was ruined economically, because the Turks were to its north-east, its east, and its south-east, so the Croats were at Austria's mercy. Austria used her power to turn them into the famous Military Confines, where the whole male population between the ages of sixteen and sixty were treated as a standing army to defend the Austrian Empire. They were given certain privileges which were chiefly legal fictions; but for the very reason that they were isolated from the rest of Europe they lingered in the legalistic Middle Ages and enjoyed these fictions. They were sunk in wretched poverty. At the end of the sixteenth century there was a peasants' rising, which was suppressed with the greatest cruelty conceivable. The leader was killed at a mock coronation. The crown set on his head was of white-hot iron. Thereafter, between Austrian tyranny and Turkish raids, the Croats lived submissively, until 1670, when a number of the Croat nobles formed a conspiracy against the Habsburgs. It is curious to observe that these aliens, noted before for their indifference to the interests of their people, had in the years of misfortune grown truly nationalist. They were discovered and beheaded; and their lands were given to Austrian and Italian families, to whom the peasants were simply brute beasts for exploitation.

Meanwhile there developed among the Croats one of the most peculiar passions known in history: a burning, indestructible devotion to the Habsburgs. Because of the historic union with Hungary they sent their Ban, which is to say their Governor, to sit in the Hungarian Diet, while it sat in exile and when it sat again in Budapest, after the Turks had been driven out. But they had their independence; they ratified separate treaties, and nobody said them nay. They used this power to put the Habsburgs firmly on the throne. When Charles VI had no son he put forward the Pragmatic Sanction, which declared that the house of Habsburg could inherit through the female line, and gave the succession to his daughter Maria Theresa. If this had been resisted by the highly militarized state of Croatia other parts of the Empire might have followed suit; but the Croats eagerly accepted. They received a characteristic return. The aristocracy of Hungary was lawless and disobedient, after a hundred and fifty years of demoralization under Turkish rule. Maria Theresa tore up the constitution to please them, and put Croatia under them as a slave state: not as *regnum socium*, not as a companion state, but as *partes adnexæ*, annexed territory. Since the Croatian nobles had been destroyed there was now nobody to lead a revolt. The imported aristocracy felt a far greater kinship with the Hungarians of their own class than with the peasants on their lands.

So the eighteenth century went by with the Croats enslaved by Hungary, and their passion for Austria idiotically stable. The increasing incapacity of the Habsburgs led to the crisis of 1848. Among other follies Francis I and Metternich had the unhappy idea of closing the Hungarian Diet for fourteen years, an oppressive act which had raised Hungarian national feeling to fever point. It oddly happened that inherent in Hungarian nationalism was a contempt and loathing for all nationalist sentiments felt by any other people in all conceivable circumstances. This is proved by their extraordinary attitude to the language issue. It infuriated them that they should be forced to speak German and should not be allowed to speak their own language, Magyar; but they were revolted by the idea that any of their neighbours, the Croats, Serbs, or Slovaks, should speak their own language, or indeed anything but Magyar. The famous Hungarian patriot, Lajos Kossuth, showed vehemence on this point that was simply not sane, considering he had not one drop of Hungarian blood in his veins and was purely Slovak. When he took charge of the Nationalist Party he announced it as part of his programme to destroy the identity of Croatia. He declared he would suppress the Croatian language by the sword, and introduced an electoral bill which omitted the name of Croatia and described her departments as Hungarian counties.

The Croats showed their love and trust in Austria once more. They sent a deputation to Vienna to ask the Emperor Ferdinand for divorce from Hungary and direct subordination to the Habsburgs, and to suggest that a young officer named Yellatchitch should be appointed Ban of Croatia. The Emperor behaved with the fluttering inefficiency of the German tourists on the train. He was on the eve of a cataclysm in European history. He was surrounded by revolutionary Viennese, by discontented Czechs, by disloyal Hungarians; the only faithful subjects within sight were the Croats. But he hesitated to grant the deputation its requests, and indeed would have refused them had it not been that certain persons in court circles had taken a liking to Yellatchitch. After Yellatchitch was appointed he spent six months in organizing anti-Hungarian feeling throughout Croatia, and then in September 1848 he marched across the frontier at the head of fifty thousand Croat soldiers and defeated a Hungarian army that was hurrying to Austria to aid the Viennese revolutionaries against the Habsburgs. Nobody has ever said that the Hungarians were not magnificent fighters, but this time the Croats were at least as good, and they had the advantage of meeting an adversary under an insane leader. They did not even have to go on holding the Hungarians at bay, for Kossuth was inspired to the supreme idiocy of formally announcing that the Habsburgs were deposed and that he was ruler of Hungary. Up till then the programme of the revolutionaries had simply been autonomy within the Austrian Empire. This extension meant that

Russia felt bound to intervene. Those who fear Bolshevist Russia because of its interventions in the affairs of other countries, which are so insignificant that they have never been rewarded with success, forget that Tsarist Russia carried foreign intervention to a pitch that has never been equalled by any other power, except the modern Fascist states, and that she held it as her right to defend the dynastic principle wherever it was threatened. Kossuth's proclamation meant that the Tsar immediately poured a hundred and eighty thousand Russians into Hungary. By summer-time in 1849 Kossuth was a fugitive in Turkey.

Yellatchitch and the Croats had saved the Austrian Empire. They got exactly nothing for this service, except this statue which stands in Zagreb market-square. The Habsburgs were still suicidal. They were bent on procuring the dissolution of their Empire, on raping time and begetting on her the Sarajevo assassination. Instead of giving the Croats the autonomy they demanded they now made them wholly subject to the central government, and they freed them from Magyarization to inflict on them the equal brutality of Germanization. And then, ultimately, they practised on them the supreme treachery. When the Dual Monarchy was framed to placate Hungary, the Croats were handed over to the Hungarians as their chattels. I do not know of any nastier act than this in history.[1] It has a kind of lowness that is sometimes exhibited in the sexual affairs of very vulgar and shameless people: a man leaves his wife and induces a girl to become his mistress, then is reconciled to his wife and to please her exposes the girl to some public humiliation. But, all the same, Austria did not forget 1848 and Lajos Kossuth. It left the statue there, just as a reminder. So the Croat helots stood and touched their caps to their Hungarian masters in the shadow of the memorial of the Croat General who led them to victory against a Hungarian army. That is the strangest episode of sovereignty I have ever chanced upon in any land.

Well, what did all this story mean to the people in Croatia, the people I was looking at, the people who had been selling me things? I had come to Yugoslavia because I knew that the past has made the present, and I wanted to see how the process works. Let me start now. It is plain that it means an amount of human pain, arranged in an unbroken continuity appalling to any person cradled in the security of the English or American past. Were I to go down into the market-place, armed with the powers of witchcraft, and take a peasant by the shoulders and whisper to him, 'In your lifetime,

---

[1] It must be remembered that this journal was written in 1937.

have you known peace?' wait for his answer, shake his shoulders and transform him into his father, and ask him the same question, and transform him in his turn to his father, I would never hear the word 'Yes,' if I carried my questioning of the dead back for a thousand years. I would always hear, 'No, there was fear, there were our enemies without, our rulers within, there was prison, there was torture, there was violent death.'

And they had no compensation in their history, for that never once formed a historic legend of any splendid magnitude. It was a record of individual heroism that no nation could surpass, but it had never shaped itself into an indestructible image of triumph that could be turned to as an escape from present failure. The Croats have always been superb soldiers; but their greatest achievements have been merged in the general triumphs of the armies of the Habsburgs, who were at pains that they should never be extricated and distinguished, and their courage and endurance were shown most prodigious in engagements with the Turks which were too numerous and too indecisive to be named in history or even preserved with any vividness in local tradition. The only outstanding military victory to their credit was the rout of the Hungarians commemorated by Yellatchitch's statue, and this might as well have been a defeat. Again we must go for an analogy to the sexual affairs of individuals. As we grow older and see the ends of stories as well as their beginnings, we realize that to the people who take part in them it is almost of greater importance that they should be stories, that they should form a recognizable pattern, than that they should be happy or tragic. The men and women who are withered by their fates, who go down to death reluctantly but without noticeable regrets for life, are not those who have lost their mates prematurely or by perfidy, or who have lost battles or fallen from early promise in circumstances of public shame, but those who have been jilted or were the victims of impotent lovers, who have never been summoned to command or been given any opportunity for success or failure. Art is not a plaything, but a necessity, and its essence, form, is not a decorative adjustment, but a cup into which life can be poured and lifted to the lips and be tasted. If one's own existence has no form, if its events do not come handily to mind and disclose their significance, we feel about ourselves as if we were reading a bad book. We can all of us judge the truth of this, for hardly any of us manage to avoid some periods when the main theme of our lives is obscured by details, when we involve ourselves with persons who are insufficiently characterized; and it is possibly true not only of individuals, but of nations. What would England be like if it had not its immense Valhalla of kings and heroes, if it had not its Elizabethan and its Victorian ages, its thousands of incidents which come up in the mind, simple as icons and as miraculous in their suggestion that what England has been it can be again, now and for ever? What would the United States be like if it had not those reservoirs of triumphant will-power, the historical facts of the War of Independence, of the giant American statesmen, and of the pioneering progress into the West, which every American citizen has at his mental command and into which he can plunge for revivification at any minute? To have a difficult history makes, perhaps, a people who are bound to be difficult in any conditions, lacking these means of refreshment. 'But perhaps,' said my husband, 'it does not matter very much.'

Zagreb III

But it matters. He saw, before we went to bed that night, that what happened to these people matters a great deal. As we stood on the steps of the statue there came towards us Constantine, treading delicately among the pigeons that cover all the pavement in the market-square where there are not stalls. He brought his brows together in censure of two of these pigeons which, in spite of the whirling traffic all around them, had felt the necessity to love. '*Ah, les Croates!*' he murmured, shaking his head; and as we laughed he went on, 'And I can see that you two also are thinking of committing a misdemeanour of taste. Not so gross, but still a misdemeanour. You are thinking of going up to look at the Old Town, and that is quite wrong. Up there are villas and palaces, which must not be seen in the morning. In the evening, when the dusk is sentimental, we shall go and peer through the gateways and you shall see colonnades and pediments more remote than those of Rome, because they are built in the neo-classical style that was the mode in Vienna a hundred to a hundred and fifty years ago, and you shall see our little Slav contribution, for in the walled garden before the house we will see iron chairs and tables with nobody sitting at them, and you will recognize at a glance that the person who is not sitting there is straight out of Turgeniev. You cannot look at Austria as it was the day before yesterday, at us Slavs as we were yesterday, by broad daylight. It is like the pigeons. But come to the Cathedral, which is so beautiful that you may see it now or any other time.'

So we went up the steep street into the Cathedral Square, and looked for a time at the Archbishop's palace, with its squat round towers under their candle-extinguisher tops, and then went through the Cathedral's nineteenth-century false front into the dark and stony plant forms of the Gothic interior. It has been cut about as by a country dressmaker, but it has kept the meditative integrity of darkness considering light, the mathematical aspiration for something above mathematics, which had been the core of its original design, and at that moment it housed the same intense faith that had built it. This was Easter Eve; the great cross had been taken down from the altar and lay propped up before the step, the livid and wounded Christ wincing in the light of the candles set at His feet. It was guarded by two soldiers in the olive uniform

57

of the Yugoslavian Army, who leaned on their rifles as if this was a dead king of earth lying in state. As I looked at them, admiring the unity enjoyed by a state which fights and believes it has a moral right to fight, and would give up either fighting or religion if it felt the two inconsistent, I saw that they were moved by a deep emotion. Their lips were drawn outward from their clenched teeth, they were green as if they were seasick. 'Are they tired? Do they have to guard the cross for a long time?' I asked cautiously. 'No,' said Constantine, 'not for more than an hour or two. Then others come.' 'Then they are really looking like that,' I pressed, 'because it is a great thing for them to guard the dead Christ?' 'Certainly,' he replied. 'The Croats are such Catholics as you never did see, not in France, not in Italy; and I think you ask that question because you do not understand the Slavs. If we did not feel intensely about guarding the dead Christ we should not put our soldiers to do it, and indeed they would not do it if we put them there, they would go away and do something else. The custom would have died if it had not meant a great deal to us.' For a long time we watched the wincing Christ and the two boys with bowed heads, who swayed very slightly backwards and forwards, backwards and forwards, like candle-flame in a room where the air is nearly still. I had not been wrong. In Yugoslavia there was an intensity of feeling that was not only of immense and exhilarating force, but had an honourable origin, proceeding from realist passion, from whole belief.

We were to learn after that something about the intellectual level of Croatia. In a restaurant beside the Cathedral people awaited us for lunch: a poet and playwright, author of dramas much larger than life, larger even than art, which make *Othello* seem plotless and light-minded, who looks like Mr Pickwick, and his wife, who had the beauty of a Burne-Jones, the same air of having rubbed holes in her lovely cheeks with her clenched knuckles. They looked up at us absently, said that they had found the poems of Vaughan the Silurist in an anthology of English poems and thought him one of the greatest poets, and, while ordering us an immense meal of which goose-liver and apple sauce were the centrepiece, threw over us the net of an extremely complicated conversation about literature. 'We think,' said the playwright, 'that the greatest writers of recent times are Joseph Conrad, Maxim Gorki, and Jack London.' We blenched. We thought that in fact these people could have no taste, if they could think both Vaughan and Jack London great. We were wrong. The playwright was actually a real poet, and he did not expect anything but poetic forms to satisfy the highest canons of art. Writers like Shaw and Wells and Péguy and Gide did not seem to him artists at all: they wrote down what one talks in cafés, which is quite a good thing to do if the talk is good enough, but is not serious, because it deals with something as common and renewable as sweat. But pure narration was a form of great importance, because it gathered together experiences that could be assimilated by others of poetic talent and transmuted into higher forms; and he liked Conrad and Jack London and Maxim Gorki because they were collecting experiences which were rare, which they had investigated thoroughly by undergoing them themselves, and which they had tested with an abnormal sensitiveness. But the playwright and his wife had been wondering whether Conrad was not in a class alone, because of the feeling of true tragedy that ran through his works. It never blossomed into poetry, but was it not so definitely the proper subject matter of poetry that he might claim to be, so to speak, on the commissariat of the poetic army?

'No,' said my husband suddenly, 'Conrad has no sense of tragedy at all, but only of the inevitable, and for him the inevitable was never the fulfilment of a principle such as the Greek *ananke*, but a *déroulement* of the consequences of an event.' An example of this, he said, is the story 'Duel' in *A Set of Six*, in which the original event is commonplace, bringing no principle whatsoever into play, and the inevitable consequences are so far-reaching that they are almost ludicrous. But there is no factor involved that might come into operation, that indeed must come into operation so generally in human affairs that as we identify it we feel as if a new phase of our destiny has been revealed to us. The playwright's wife said that this was true but irrelevant. To her there was a sense of tragedy implied in Conrad's work not by factual statement but by the rhythm of his language. 'Tchk! Tchk!' said Constantine. 'A great symphony must have its themes as well as the emotional colour given by its orchestration. And listen . . .' He said the sense of inevitability in a work of art should be quite different from the scientific conception of causality, for if art were creative then each stage must be new, must have something over and above what was contained in the previous stages, and the connexion between the first and the last must be creative in the Bergsonian sense. He added that it is to give this creativeness its chance to create what is at once unpredictable and inevitable that an artist must never interfere with his characters to make them prove a moral point, because this is to force them down the path of the predictable. 'Yes, that is what Tolstoy is always doing,' said the playwright, 'and all the same he convinces us he is a great artist.' 'I feel he is not a great artist,' I said, 'I feel he might have been the greatest of all artists, but instead chose to be the second greatest of renegades after Judas.' 'I, too!' said the poet, who had just sat down at the table. 'I, too!'

The bottles thick about us, we stayed in the restaurant till it was five o'clock. We were then discussing Nietzsche's attitude to music. At eight we were back in the same restaurant, dining with an editor leader of the Croat party which is fighting for autonomy under a federal system, and his wife. Valetta was there, but Constantine was not. The editor, though he himself was a Serb by birth, would not have sat down at the same table with an official of the Yugoslavian Government. And Gregorievitch was not there, not only for that reason, but because he would not have sat down at the same table as the editor, whom he regarded as evil incarnate. He had come in for a glass of brandy that evening, and on hearing where we were to spend the evening he had become Pluto dyspeptic, Pluto sunk in greenish gloom, caterpillar-coloured because of the sins of the world. Yet this editor also would have died for the Slav cause, and had indeed undergone imprisonment for its sake before the war. He is still facing grave danger, for he was running his movement from the point of view of an English pre-war liberal, who abhorred all violence, and he not only attacked the Yugoslavian Government for the repressive methods it used against Croatia, but also those Croats who used violence against the Government and who accepted Hungarian and Italian support for terrorism. He does not mind thus risking the loss of his only friends. He is a great gentleman, an intellectual and a moralist, and has carved himself, working against the grain of the wood, into a man of action.

As we talked of the political situation there ran to our table a beautiful young Russian woman, who could be with us only half an hour because she was supervising a play of hers about Pushkin which had been put on at the National Theatre a few nights before and was a failure. She brought the news that this amazing Easter had now produced a blizzard. On her golden hair and perfect skin and lithe body in its black dress snowflakes were melting, her blood running the better for it; and failure was melting on her like a snowflake also, leaving her glowing. 'They are hard on my play!' she cried, choked with the ecstatic laughter of Russian women. '*Ce n'est pas bien, ce n'est pas mal, c'est médiocre!*' The editor, smiling at her beauty and her comet quality, tried to upbraid her for her play. The drama, he said, was a great mystery, one of the most difficult forms of art. All men of genius have tried their hand at a play at some time, and he had read most of them. These people, I realized, could make such universal statements. Both the editor and his wife knew, and knew well, in addition to their native Serbo-Croat, English, French, German, Italian, Russian, Latin, and Greek.

Nearly all these dramas, the editor continued, were bad. The drama demanded concentration on themes which by their very nature tempted to expansion, and only people with a special gift for craftsmanship could handle this problem. And one enormously increased this difficulty if, as she had done, one chose as one's theme a great man, for what could be more obstinately diffused than the soul of a great man? Often, indeed, the soul of a great man refused to be reduced to the terms necessary even for bare comprehension. And especially was this true of Pushkin. Which of us can understand Pushkin? At that the editor and the editor's wife and Valetta and the Russian all began to talk at once, their faces coming close together in a bright square about the middle of the table. The talk had been in French, it swung to Serbo-Croat, it ended in Russian. My husband and I sat tantalized to fury. We knew Pushkin only by translation; we found *Evgenye Onegin* like something between *Don Juan* and Winthrop Mackworth Praed, and we liked his short stories rather less than Nathaniel Hawthorne's; and obviously we are wrong, for because of limitations of language we are debarred from seeing something that is obvious to unsealed eyes as the difference between a mule and a Derby winner.

But the Russian stood up. She had to go back to the theatre to supervise the crowd that in the last scene of the play wept outside Pushkin's house while he was dying. It was plainly the real reason that she was leaving us, and not an excuse. There was nothing more indicative of the high level of culture among these people than their capacity to discuss the work of one amongst them with complete detachment. But before she went she made a last defence. For a short time she had found herself united in experience with Pushkin, and even if that union covered only a small part of Pushkin, it was worth setting down, it might give a clue to the whole of him. Looking past her at her beauty, in the odd way that men do, the editor said, though only to tease her, 'Experience indeed! Are you sure you have enough experience? Do you think you have lived enough to write?' She answered with an air of evasion suggesting that she suspected she might some day have a secret but was too innocent to know what it was, though she was actually a married woman at the end of her twenties, if not in her early thirties: 'I will not argue that, because the connexion between art and life is not as simple as that!' But then her face crinkled into laughter again, 'Sometimes the connexion between art and life is very close! Think of it, there is a woman in the crowd in this last scene whose cries always give a lead to the others and have indeed given the end of the play much of its effect, they are always so sad. The audience cannot hear the words the actors in the crowd are using, they only catch the accent of the whole sentence. And as this woman has caught the very accent of anxious grief, I listened to what she had to say. And she was crying, "Oh, God! Oh, God! Let Pushkin die before the last bus leaves for my suburb!"' She turned from us laughing, but turned back again: 'That's something I don't like! There is a mockery inherent in the art of acting, the players must make everybody weep but themselves; if they don't weep they must jeer inside themselves at the people who do weep!' She shuddered, wishing she had never written the play, never had tried her luck in the theatre, a child who had chosen the wrong birthday treat. She brushed the sadness from her mouth and went away, laughing. This, so far as talk was concerned, was a representative day in Zagreb.

Shestine

'This is a very delightful place,' said my husband the next morning. It was Easter Sunday, and the waiter had brought in on the breakfast-tray dyed Easter eggs as a present from the management, and we were realizing that the day before had been wholly pleasant. 'Of course, Austria did a lot for the place,' said an Englishman, a City friend of my husband's, who was staying in the hotel and had come to have breakfast. 'I suppose so,' said my husband, and then caught himself up. 'No, what am I saying? It cannot be so, for this is not in the remotest degree like Austria. Austrians do sit in cafés for hours, and they talk incessantly, but they have not this raging polyglot intellectual curiosity, they have not this way of turning out universal literature on the floor as if it were a ragbag, which indeed it is, and seeking for a fragment that is probably not there, but is probably part of an arcanum of literature that exists only in their own heads. In cultured Vienna homes they often give parties to hear the works of great writers read aloud: only a few months ago I spent an evening at the house of a Viennese banker, listening to the poems of Wildgans. But it would be impossible to read aloud to a party of Yugoslavs, unless one bound and gagged the guests beforehand.'

There came into the room Constantine and Gregorievitch, who was still a little cold to us because of the company we had kept on the previous night. 'What has Austria done for you?' asked my husband. 'Nothing,' said Constantine; 'it has not the means. What can a country without history do for a people with a glorious history like the Serbs?' 'I was talking of Croatia,' said my husband. Gregorievitch said anxiously, as if he had been detecting himself looking in the mirror, 'The answer stands.' 'But the Austrians have their history,' objected my husband. 'No,' said Gregorievitch, 'we are its history. We Slavs in general, we Croats in particular. The Habsburgs won their victories with Czechs, with Poles, and, above all, with Croats. Without us the Austrians would have no history, and if we had not stood between them and the Turks, Vienna would now be a Moslem city.' The Englishman laughed, as if a tall story that knew its own height had been told. Gregorievitch looked at him as if he had blasphemed. 'Is it a little thing that only yesterday it was decided that Europe should not be Islamized?' he asked. 'What does he mean?' asked the Englishman. 'That the Turks besieged Vienna in 1683 and were turned back,' said my husband, 'and that if they had not been turned back it is possible that they would have swept across all Europe.' 'Is that true?' asked the Englishman. 'Yes,' said my husband. 'But it's not yesterday,' said the Englishman. 'To these people it is,' said my husband, 'and I think they are right. It's uncomfortably recent, the blow would have smashed the whole of our Western culture, and we shouldn't forget that such things happen.' 'But ask them,' said the Englishman, 'if Austria did not do a lot for them in the way of sanitary services.' Gregorievitch looked greenly into the depths of the mirror as if wondering how he showed not signs of gaiety but signs of life under the contamination of these unfastidious English. 'Your friend, who showed no emotion at the thought of the spires of Vienna being replaced by minarets, doubtless would expect us to forgive the Austrians for building oubliettes for our heroes so long as they built us chalets for our necessities. Are you sure,' he said, speaking through his teeth, 'that you really wish to go to hear mass at the village of Shestine? It is perhaps not the kind of expedition that the English find entertaining?'

We drove through a landscape I have often seen in Chinese pictures: wooded hills under snow looked like hedgehogs drenched in icing sugar. On a hill stood a little church, full to the doors, bright inside as a garden, glowing with scarlet and gold and blue and the unique, rough, warm white of homespun, and shaking with song. On the women's heads were red handkerchiefs printed with yellow leaves and peacocks' feathers, their jackets were solidly embroidered with flowers, and under their white skirts were thick red or white woollen stockings. Their men were just as splendid in sheepskin leather jackets with appliqué designs in dyed leathers, linen shirts with fronts embroidered in cross-stitch and fastened with buttons of Maria Theresa dollars or lumps of turquoise matrix, and homespun trousers gathered into elaborate boots. The splendour of these dresses was more impressive because it was not summer. The brocade of a rajah's costume or the silks of an Ascot crowd are within the confines of prudence, because the rajah is going to have a golden umbrella held over him and the Ascot crowd is not far from shelter, but these costumes were made for the winter in a land of unmetalled roads, where snow lay till it melted and mud might be knee-deep, and showed a gorgeous lavishness, for hours and days, and even years had been spent in the stuffs and skins and embroideries which were thus put at the mercy of the bad weather. There was lavishness also in the singing that poured out of these magnificently clad bodies, which indeed transformed the very service. Western church music is almost commonly petitioning and infantile, a sentiment cozening for remedy against sickness or misfortune, combined with a masochist enjoyment in the malady, but this singing spoke of health and fullness.

The men stood on the right of the church and the women on the left. This is the custom also in the Orthodox Church, and it is reasonable enough. At a ceremony which sets out to be the most intense of all contacts with reality, men and women, who see totally different aspects of reality, might as well stand apart. It is inappropriate for them to be mixed as in the unit of the family, where men and women attempt with such notorious difficulty to share their views of reality for social purposes. From this divided congregation came a flood of song which asked for absolutely nothing, which did not ape childhood, which did not pretend that sour is sweet and pain wholesome, but which simply adored. If there be a God who is fount of all goodness, this is the tribute that should logically be paid to Him; if there be only goodness, it is still a logical tribute. And again, the worship, like their costume, was made astonishing by their circumstances. These people, who had neither wealth nor security, nor ever had had them, stood before the Creator, and thought not what they might ask for but what they might give. To be among them was like seeing an orchard laden with apples or a field of ripe wheat, endowed with a human will and using it in accordance with its own richness.

This was not simply due to these people's faith. There are people who hold precisely the same faith whose worship produces an effect of poverty. When Heine said that Amiens Cathedral could have been built only in the past, because the men of that day had convictions, whereas we moderns have only opinions, and something more than opinions are needed for building a cathedral, he put into circulation a half-truth which has done a great deal of harm. It matters supremely what kind of men hold these convictions. This service was impressive because the congregation was composed of people with a unique sort of healthy intensity. At the end we went out and stood at the churchyard gate, and watched the men and women clumping down a lane to the village through the deep snow, with a zest that was the generalized form of the special passion they had exhibited in the church. I had not been wrong about what I had found among the Yugoslavs.

'Are they not beautiful, the costumes of Croatia?' asked Gregorievitch, his very spectacles beaming, his whole appearance made unfamiliar by joy. 'Are they not lovely, the girls who wear them, and are not the young men handsome? And they are very pious.' 'Yes.' I said, 'I have never heard a mass sung more fervently.' 'I do not mean that,' he said irritably, 'I meant pious in their Croat patriotism.' It appeared that the inhabitants of Shestine wore these wonderful clothes not from custom but from a positive and virile choice. They would naturally wear ordinary Western European clothes, as most other peasants round Zagreb do, but they are conscious that the great patriot Anton Starchevitch is buried in the graveyard of their church, and they know that to him everything Croatian was precious. We went and stood by his tomb in the snow, while Gregorievitch, taller than ever before though not erect, hung over its railings like a weeping willow and told us how Starchevitch had founded the Party of the Right, which defied both Austria and Hungary and attempted to negotiate his country back to the position of independence it had enjoyed eight hundred years before. 'It was Starchevitch's motto, "Croatia only needs God and the Croats,"' said Gregorievitch. 'For thirty years when the glamour and wealth and triumphant cruelty of nineteenth-century Hungary might have tempted us young Croats to forget our country, he made us understand that if we forgot the tradition of our race we lost our souls as if by sin.' We were conscious of the second coat that lies about a snow-covered world, the layer of silence; we smelt the wood-smoke from the village below. 'As a child I was taken to see him,' said Gregorievitch, his voice tense as if he were a Welsh evangelist; 'we all drew strength from him.' Constantine, looking very plump and cosy, announced, 'His mother was a Serb.' 'But she had been received at the time of her marriage into the True Church,' said Gregorievitch, frowning.

We moved away, and as Constantine and I stepped into the snow-drifts of the lane we passed three men, dark as any Hindu, carrying drums and trumpets. '*Ohé!* Here are the gipsies,' said Constantine, and we smiled at them, seeing pictures of some farm kitchen crammed with people in dresses brighter than springtime, all preparing with huge laughter to eat mountains of lamb and pig and drink wells of wine. But the men looked at us sullenly, and one said with hatred, 'Yes, we are gipsies.' Both Constantine and I were so startled that we stopped in the snow and gaped at each other, and then walked on in silence. In the eastern parts of Yugoslavia, in Serbia and in Macedonia, the gipsies are proud of being gipsies, and other people, which is to say the peasants, for there are practically none other, honour them for their qualities, for their power of making beautiful music and dancing, which the peasant lacks, and envy them for being exempt from the necessities of toil and order which lie so heavily on the peasant; and this has always been my natural attitude to those who can please as I cannot. It was inconceivable to both Constantine and myself that the gipsies should have thought we held them in contempt or that we should have expressed contempt aloud if we had felt it.

The whole world was less delightful. The snow seemed simply weather, the smell of the wood-smoke gave no pleasure. 'I tell you, Central Europe is too near the Croats,' said Constantine. 'They are good people, very good people, but they are possessed by the West. In Germany and Austria they despise the gipsies. They have several very good reasons. The art of the gipsies commands no respect, for the capitalist system has discredited popular art, and only exploits virtuosos. If I go and play Liszt's scaramoucheries very fast, thump-thump-thump and tweedle-tweedle-tweedle, they will think more of it than the music those three men play, though it is perfectly adapted to certain occasions. Also the gipsies are poor, and the capitalist system despises people who do not acquire goods. Also the West is mad about cleanliness, and the gipsies give dirt its rights, perhaps too liberally. We Serbs are not bourgeois, so none of these reasons make us hate the gipsies, and, believe me, our world is more comfortable.'

I looked back at the gipsies, who were now breasting the hill, huddled under the harsh wind that combed its crest. Life had become infinitely poorer since we left church. The richness of the service had been consonant with an order of society in which peasants and gipsies were on an equal footing and there was therefore no sense of deprivation and need; but here was the threat of a world where everybody was needy, since the moneyed people had no art and the people with art had no money. Something alien and murderous had intruded here into the Slav pattern, and its virtue had gone out of it.

Two Castles

Yes, the German influence was like a shadow on the Croat World. We were to learn that again the next day. Gregorievitch had arranged to take us on Easter Monday into the country, with Constantine and Valetta and some young Croat doctors. It is a sign of the bitterness felt by the Croats against the Serbs that because we were in the company of Constantine and Gregorievitch, who were representatives of the Yugoslavian ideas, very few Croats would meet us: and Valetta, who came to see us because of an existing friendship with me, was slightly embarrassed by the situation, though he concealed it. These Croat doctors were ready to come with us, because it was our intention to visit first a castle belonging to a great Hungarian family who still used it as a residence for a part of the year, and then to go on to another castle, once owned by the same family, but now used as a sanatorium for tuberculosis by a Health Insurance Society. This gave them a professional excuse. But it snowed all through the night of Easter Sunday, and we woke to an Arctic morning, so we telephoned to ask Valetta and these doctors to come all the same and have breakfast, though the expedition would obviously have to be cancelled. They came and proved to be delightful young men, graduates of Zagreb University, with hopes of post-graduate work in Vienna and Berlin and Paris, and we were having a pleasant conversation over our coffee and boiled eggs when the door opened and Gregorievitch came in, and we saw that we had done wrong.

It is of the highest importance that the reader should understand Gregorievitch. If it were not for a small number of Gregorievitches the eastern half of Europe (and perhaps the other half as well) would have been Islamized, the tradition of liberty would have died for ever under the Habsburgs, the Romanoffs, and the Ottoman Empire, and Bolshevism would have become anarchy and not a system which may yet be turned to many uses. His kind has profoundly affected history, and always for the better. Reproachfully his present manifestation said to us, 'Are you not ready yet?' We stared up at him, and my husband asked, 'But is not the weather far too bad?' He answered, 'The sun is not shining, but the countryside will be there all the same, will it not? And the snow is not too deep.' 'Are you sure?' my husband asked doubtfully. 'I am quite sure,' answered Gregorievitch. 'I have rung up a friend of mine, a general who has specialized in mechanical transport, and I have told him the make of our automobiles, and he is of the opinion that we will be able to visit both castles.'

There, as often before and after, Gregorievitch proved that the essential quality of Slavs is not, as might be thought, imagination. He is characteristically, and in an endearing way, a Slav, but he has no imagination at all. He cannot see that the factual elements in an experience combine into more than themselves. He would not, for example, let us go to the theatre at Zagreb. 'No, I will not get you tickets,' he said with a repressed indignation, like a brawl in a crypt, 'I will not let you waste your money in that way. Since you cannot follow Serbo-Croat easily even when it is spoken slowly, and your husband does not understand it at all, what profit can it be for you to go to our theatre?' He envisaged attendance at a play as an attempt to obtain the information which the author has arranged for the characters to impart to the audience by their words and actions; and that the actions could be used as a basis for guesswork to the words, that the appearance of the actors, the inflections of their voices, and the reactions they elicited from the audience, could throw light not only on the play but the culture of which it was a part was beyond his comprehension. So now he conceived of an expedition to the country as being undertaken for the purpose of observing the physical and political geography of the district, and this could obviously be pursued in any climatic conditions save those involving actual physical discomfort. Nevertheless the Slav quality of passion was there, to disconcert the English or American witness, for it existed in a degree which is found among Westerners only in highly imaginative people. As he stood over us, grey and grooved and Plutoish, he palpitated with the violence of his thought, 'These people will go away without seeing the Croatian countryside, and some day they may fail Croatia for the lack of that knowledge.' His love of Croatia was of volcanic ardour; and its fire was not affected by his knowledge that most of the other people who loved Croatia were quite prepared, because he favoured union with the Serbs, to kill him without mercy in any time of crisis.

We rose, abashed, and filed out to the automobiles; and indeed at first the weather was not too bad. We went out of the town in a light drizzle, passing a number of women who were hurrying to market. They wore red kerchiefs on their heads, red shawls and white skirts, and carried red umbrellas in one hand, while with the other they pulled their skirts high over their red woollen stockings, so high that some showed their very clean white drawers of coarse linen edged with elaborate *broderie anglaise*. There was a Breughel-like humour about their movements, as if they were stylizing their own struggles with nature; their faces showed that there was nothing brutish about them. This was very marked among the old women. Slavs grow old more beautifully than the people of other races, for with the years their flesh clings closer to the bone instead of sagging away from it. This ribbon of laughing peasants ran beside us in an unbroken comic strip, right out into the country, where they exercised their humour with extreme good temper, for the automobiles raised fans of liquid mud on each side of them, and everyone we met had to jump some distance into deep snow to keep their clothes dry and clean. But they all made a joke of it. In one village, where the plaster houses were all painted a deep violet which was given great depth and vibrancy by the snow and the grey sky, a lovely young girl laughingly put her umbrella in front of her and mocked us and herself with clownish gestures that were exquisitely graceful and yet very funny.

Then we saw nobody on the roads. The snow began to fall thickly and to lie. People at the door of a cottage smiled, waved, shivered theatrically, and banged the door. We passed through a broad valley paved with the dark glass of floods. In the driving snow a birch wood looked like a company of dancing naked nymphs. Then there was another Chinese landscape of wooded hills furred with snow, that went on for a long time; they were unwinding the whole scroll for us to see. Here and there the scroll was damaged. The painting of the woods stopped abruptly, and we could see nothing but the silk on which the artist worked; the hills were hidden, and there was nothing but the mist. Sometimes it parted and we saw a gross-towered, butter-coloured *Schloss*. They told us what Austrian or Hungarian family had lived there, and what it was now: a textile factory, a canning plant, a convalescent home.

It grew colder. We stopped in a little town and went into the hotel, and warmed ourselves with plum brandy, which is the standard odd-time drink in Yugoslavia. The landlord spoke to us proudly of the place, telling us they had a beautiful memorial to some Croat patriots in the market-place, and that not far away they had found the skeleton of a prehistoric man. We said that we knew how that had happened. The poor man had been taken for a nice drive in the country by Gregorievitch. This delighted Gregorievitch; it was pathetic to see how pleased he was because the young Croats could lay aside their hatred of Yugoslavia and joke with him for a little. He was very happy indeed when, because he had pretended to be aggrieved, we drank another round of plum brandies to his honour. Then we started out again, into hillier country where the snow was still deeper. At the top of a hill our automobile stuck in a snowdrift. Peasants ran out of a cottage near by, shouting with laughter because machinery had made a fool of itself, and dug out the automobile with incredible rapidity. They were doubtless anxious to get back and tell a horse about it.

Thereafter the snow was so thick on the wooded hills that the treetrunks were mere lines and the branches were finer than any lines drawn by a human hand. No detail was visible in the houses of the villages at the base of the hills. They were blocks of soft black shadow edged with the pure white fur of the snow on the roofs. Above the hills there was a layer of mist that drew a dull white smudge between this pure black-and-white world and the dark-grey sky. There was no colour anywhere except certain notes of pale bright gold made by three things. So late was this snowfall that the willows were well on in bud; their branches were too frail to carry any weight of snow, and the buds were too small to be discernible, so each tree was a golden-green phantom against the white earth. There were also certain birds that were flying over the fields, bouncing in the air as if they were thrown by invisible giants at play; their breasts were pale gold. And where the snow had been thickest on the banks of the road it had fallen away in a thick crust, showing primroses. They were the same colour as the birds' breasts. Sometimes the road ran over a stream, and we looked down on the willows at its edge. From this aspect the snow their green-gold branches supported looked like a white body prostrate in woe, an angel that had leaped down in suicide from the ramparts of the sky.

We saw no one. Once a horse, harsh grey against a white field, gave way to that erotic panic peculiar to its species, which rolls the eye not only in fear but enjoyment, that seeks to be soothed with an appetite revealing that it plainly knows soothing to be possible, and pursues what it declares it dreads. It leaped the low hedge and fled along the road before us; and out of a farm on the further side of the field there ran a man, splendid in a sapphire sheepskin jacket, who remembered to close the door behind him as carefully as if it were not merely an extreme of temperature he were shutting out, but an actual destroying element of fire. When he caught the horse and dragged it off the road, our chauffeur shouted our thanks and regrets to him; but he made no answer. He stood still with the horse pressing back its head against his shoulder, in voluptuous exaggeration of its distress, and from the contraction of the man's brows and his lips it could be seen that he was barely conscious of the situation which he was remedying, and could think of nothing

but the intense cold. To the eye the world seemed unified by the
spreading whiteness of the snow, yet actually each horse, even each
person, was shut off from all others in an abnormal privacy by this
pricking, burning icy air.

We passed through a village, still as midnight at midday, and
stoneblind, every door and window closed. 'Think of it,' said
Valetta; 'in all those cottages there are sitting nothing but dukes
and duchesses, barons and baronesses.' The peasants here had
received an emperor handsomely when by the stupidity of his
nobles he had found himself tired and wounded and humpy and
alone after a day's hunting, and he ennobled the whole village
by patents of perfect validity. And a little further on was our
journey's end. We got out of the automobile and found ourselves
at a lodge gateway with extravagant stables behind it, and what
were recognizably 'grounds' beyond, the kind of grounds that
were made in England during the nineteenth century after the
Georgian and Regency schools of landscape gardening, shrubby
and expensive and futile; these sloped to the base of an extremely
steep sugar-loaf hill which had something like Balliol on the top of
it. As we gaped a mist swooped on us and all was suddenly veiled
by the whirling confetti of a gentle snowstorm. Not unnaturally,
nobody was about.

'What can have happened to them all?' asked Gregorievitch. He
went and pounded on the door of the porter's lodge, and when
an astonished face appeared at the upper windows he demanded,
'And where is Nikolai? Why is Nikolai not here to meet us?' 'He
is up at the castle,' said the porter; 'he did not think you would be
coming.' 'Thought we were not coming!' exclaimed Gregorievitch.
'What made him think we were not coming?' It had distressed him
very much to find that Valetta and the Croats and my husband
and I seemed unable to grasp the common-sense point of view
that if one wanted to see a castle one went and saw it, no matter
what the weather, since the castle would certainly be there, no
matter what the weather; but he had excused it because we were
by way of being intellectuals and therefore might be expected to be
a little fanciful. Here, however, were quite simple people who were
talking the same sort of nonsense. He said testily, 'Well, we will go
up and find him for ourselves.' We climbed the sugar-loaf hill by
whimsically contrived paths and stone steps, among fir trees that
were striped black and white like zebras, because of the branches
and the layer of white snow that lay on each of them, while the
porter, who was now invisible to us through the snow, cried up to
the castle, 'Nicolai! Nikolai! They have come!' I was warm because

I was wearing a squirrel coat, but all the men were shaking with cold, and we were all up to our knees in snow. At last we came to a walk running round some ramparts, and Nikolai, who was a very handsome young peasant with golden hair and blue eyes framed by long lashes, dropped the broom with which he had been trying to clear a path for us and ran towards Gregorievitch, crying, 'How brave you are to make such a journey in this weather!' 'Lord above us,' said Gregorievitch, 'what does everybody mean? Open the door, open the door!'

When the door was opened the point of this fierce Arctic journey proved to be its pointlessness. For indeed there was nothing in the castle to match the wildness of the season, of the distraught horses and the wavering birds, of Gregorievitch and his people. A fortress six hundred years old had been encased in a vast building executed in that baronial style which owed so much more to literary than to architectural inspiration, having been begotten by Sir Walter Scott; and though the family which owned it had been unusually intelligent, and free-minded to the point of being Croatian patriots, their riches had brought them under the cultural influence of the Austro-Hungarian Empire. So there were acres of walls covered from floor to ceiling with hunting trophies. These never, in any context, give an impression of fullness. I remembered the story of the old Hungarian count who was heard to mutter as he lay dying, 'And then the Lord will say, "Count, what have you done with your life?" and I shall have to say, "Lord, I have shot a great many animals." Oh, dear! Oh, dear! It doesn't seem enough.' Nobody but the fool despises hunting, which is not only a pleasure of a high degree, but a most valuable form of education in any but a completely mechanized state. Marmont, who was one of Napoleon's most intelligent marshals, explains in his memoirs that he was forced to hunt every day from two o'clock to nightfall from the time he was twelve, and this put him into such perfect training that no ordeal to which he was subjected in all his military career ever disconcerted him. But as a sole offering to the Lord it was not enough, and it might be doubted if this was the right kind of hunting. These trophies spoke of nineteenth-century sport, which was artificial, a matter of reared beasts procured for the guns by peasants, and so essentially sedentary that the characteristic sportsman of the age, commemorated in photographs, had a remarkable paunch.

There was also a clutterment of the most hideous furniture of the sort that was popular in the Austro-Hungarian Empire in the second half of the nineteenth century, walloping stuff bigger than any calculations of use could have suggested, big in accordance with a vulgar idea that bigness is splendid, and afflicted with carving that made even the noble and austere substance of wood ignoble as fluff. It would have been interesting to know where they had put the old furniture that must have been displaced by these horrors. One of the most beautiful exhibitions in Vienna, the Mobiliendepot, in the Mariahilfestrasse, was composed chiefly of the Maria Theresa and Empire furniture which the Emperor Franz Josef and the Empress Elizabeth banished to their attics when they had refurnished their palaces from the best firms in the Tottenham Court Road.

There were also a great many bad pictures of the same era: enormous flushed nudes which would have set a cannibal's mouth watering; immense and static pictures showing what historical events would have looked like if all the personages had been stuffed first; and one of the family had over-indulged in the pleasures of amateur art. She herself had been a woman of enormous energy; a fashionable portrait painter had represented her, full of the uproarious shire-horse vitality common to the women admired by Edward VII, standing in a pink-satin ball dress and lustily smelling a large bouquet of fat roses in a massive crystal vase, apparently about to draw the flowers actually out of the water by her powerful inhalations. This enormous energy had covered yards of the castle walls with pictures of Italian peasant girls holding tambourines, lemon branches, or amphoræ, which exactly represented what is meant by the French word '*niaiserie.*'

There were also some portraits of male members of the family, physically superb, in the white-and-gold uniform of Hungarian generals, solemnized and uplifted by the belief that they had mastered a ritual that served the double purpose of establishing their personal superiority and preserving civilization as they knew it; it was as pathetic to see them here as it would be to go into the garret of a starving family to see the picture of some of its members who had been renowned on the stage as players of kings and emperors. It might be said that though all these things were poor in themselves, they represented a state superior to the barbaric origins of Croatian society. But it was not so, for the family portraits which depicted the generations of the late sixteenth and seventeenth centuries showed people with their heads held high by pride and their features organized by intelligence, set on canvas by artists at least as accomplished and coherent in vision as the painters of our Tudor portraits. They gave documentary proof that German influence had meant nothing but corruption.

The corruption was profound. I left my companions at one point and turned back to a bedroom, to look again from its windows on an enchanting view of a little lake, now a pure sheet of snow, which lay among some groves below the sugar-loaf hill. I found Gregorievitch sitting on the window-sill, with his back to the view, looking about him at the hideous pictures and furniture with a dreamy and absorbed expression. 'It would be very pleasant to live this way,' he said, without envy, but with considerable appetite. This was the first time I had heard him say anything indicating that he had ever conceived living any life other than his own, which had been dedicated to pain and danger and austerity; and I could be sure that it was not the money of the people who lived in the castle, not the great fires that warmed them or the ample meals they ate, it was their refinement that he envied, their access to culture. I had never thought before what mischief a people can suffer from domination by their enemies. This man had lived his whole life to free Croatia from Hungarian rule; he had been seduced into exalting Hungarian values above Croatian values by what was an essential part of his rebellion. He had had to tell himself and other people over and over again that the Hungarians were taking the best of everything and leaving the worst to the Croats, which was indeed true so far as material matters were concerned. But the human mind, if it is framing a life of action, cannot draw fine distinctions. He had ended by believing that the Hungarians had had the best of everything in all respects, and that this world of musty antlers and second-rate pictures and third-rate furniture was superior to the world where peasants sang in church with the extreme discriminating fervour which our poets envy, knowing themselves lost without it, and wore costumes splendid in their obedience to those principles of design which our painters envy, knowing themselves lost without instinctive knowledge of them.

On the way to the sanatorium the party was now more silent. The young men were hungry, we had all of us wet feet, the sky threatened more snow, and the houses were now few and widely scattered. We could understand enough to realize that it was worrying them a little that if the automobiles broke down we should have a long distance to walk before we found shelter. Nobody, however, seemed to blame Gregorievitch. It was felt that he was following his star.

It was not till after an hour and a half that we arrived at the sanatorium, which was a fine baroque castle set on a hill, once owned by the same family which had owned the other castle, but now abandoned because the lands all around it had been taken away and given to peasant tenants under the very vigorous Agrarian

Reform Scheme which the Yugoslavian Government put into effect
after the war. This visit was less of an anticlimax than the other, for
here was the real Slav quality. As we came to the gates a horde of
people rushed out to meet us, and as my husband, who finds one
of his greatest pleasures in inattention, had never grasped that this
castle had been converted into a sanatorium, he believed them to
be the family retainers, and wondered that such state could be kept
up nowadays. But they were only the patients. They rushed out,
men and women and children, all mixed together, some wearing
ordinary Western costume, and some in peasant costume; some
of the men wore the Moslem fez, for the Health Insurance Society
which manages the sanatorium draws its members from all over
Yugoslavia. They looked strangely unlike hospital patients. There
was not the assumption of innocence which is noticeable in all but
the wilder inmates of an English institution, the tramps and the
eccentrics; not the pretence that they like starched sheets as a
boundary to life, that the authority of doctors and nurses is easy
to accept and reasonable in action, that a little larking is the only
departure from hospital routine they could possibly desire, that
they were as Sunday-school children mindful of their teachers.
These people stood there, dark, inquisitive, critical, our equals,
fully adult.

This was, of course, partly due to their racial convictions. Many
of them came from parts of Yugoslavia where there is still no
trace of a class system, where there are only peasants. They had
therefore not the same sense that in going into hospital a worker
placed himself in the hands of his superior, and that he must please
him by seeming undangerous. But also, as it appeared when he
went into the doctor's room, the theory of illness was not the
same as in a Western European hospital. We found there the
superintendent, who was a Serb though long resident in Croatia
and pro-Croat in politics, and his three Croat assistants who all
had an oddly unmedical air to English eyes. I do not mean that
they looked unbusinesslike; on the contrary, each of them had a
sturdy air of competence and even power. But there was in their
minds no vista of shiny hospital corridors, leading to Harley Street
and the peerage, with blameless tailoring and courtesy to patients
and the handling of committees as subsidiary obligations, such as
appears before most English doctors. There was no sense that
medical genius must frustrate its own essential quality, which is
a fierce concentration on the truth about physical problems, by
cultivating self-restraint and a conventional blankness which are
incompatible with any ardent pursuit. These people had an air of

pure positiveness which amounted to contentiousness. They might have been bull-fighters.

They were bull-fighters, of course. The bull was tuberculosis. The formalities of our reception were got over in a minute. Had I been visiting a sanatorium in England cold and with wet feet I would have had to go to the matron's room, and time would have been wasted. Here we shook hands, hurried to the radiators, sat down on them, took off our shoes, and pressed our stocking soles against the warm iron, while the doctors talked their tauromachy around us. Did we know that tuberculosis was the scourge of Southern Slavs? It had to be so, because the country was being rapidly industrialized. Peasants came to the town blankly ignorant of hygiene, drawn by wages that looked high on paper and were in fact far too low to buy proper housing or clothing; and there was still so little hospital treatment that a tuberculosis case was as likely as not to remain untreated and spread infection. And this was not because they were Balkans. They said that with a sudden leap of fire to their eyes, which could be understood by anyone who has heard Germans or Austrians use the adjective '*Balkan*,' with a hawking excess of gross contempt. We English, they said, had had just as much tuberculosis at the beginning of the nineteenth century.

I have acquired, painfully enough, some knowledge of sanatoria; and looking round me as they talked, I could see that in a way this sanatorium was frightful and, in another, most excellent. The first door we opened showed us the anachronistic character of the building in which it had been installed. We stepped suddenly into the opaque darkness, the inconquerable midday chill, of the family chapel, with a gilt and bosomy baroque Virgin and half a dozen cherubs ballooning above the altar, and two of the family gaunt in marble on their tombs. A congregation of nuns, each a neat little core to a great sprawling fruit of black-and-white robes, swivelled round on their knees to see who the intruders might be, and the Mother Superior, with a gesture of hospitality completely in consonance with the air of the presiding Virgin behind the altar, ceased the chanting of the service until we had ended our visit. Such a gesture had probably not been made in Western Europe for three hundred years. I do not believe it is easy to convert to hospital use a seventeenth-century castle built on three stories round an immense courtyard, with immensely high rooms and floors of stone and marble, and to staff it with people so much in accord with that same century that to them everything on the margin of hygiene, the whole context of life in which the phrase of science appears, must have been wholly incomprehensible.

But the place was clean, fantastically clean, clean like a battle-ship. There at least was something that an English hospital authority would have had to approve; perhaps, however, the only thing he could. The patients within doors were shocking to Western theories as they had been when they had met us out of doors on our arrival. They were evidently preoccupied with the imaginative realization of their sickness, and no one was attempting to interfere with them in their pleasure. This was a visiting day; and in what had been the grand drawing-room of the ladies of the castle, a large apartment adorned with sugary, Italianate, late nineteenth-century murals representing the islands of the blest, women sat holding their handkerchiefs to their lips with the plangent pathos of *la dame aux camélias*, and men assumed the sunrise mixed with sunset glamour of the young Keats, while their families made no attempt to distract them from these theatrical impersonations but watched with sympathy, as audiences should. The patients who had no visitors were resting; and when we went into the wards they were lying on their beds, the quilts drawn over their mouths, the open windows showing a firmament unsteadily yet regularly cleft by the changing stripes of snowfall. Shivering, they stared at us, their eyes enormous over the edges of their quilts, enjoying at its most dramatic the sense of the difference between our health and their disease; and indeed in the dark beam of their hypnotic and hypnotized gaze the strangeness of their plight became newly apparent, the paradox of the necessity which obliged them to accept as a saviour the cold which their bodies believed to be an enemy, and to reject as death the warmth which was the known temperature of life. The doctors beside us appeared to take for granted this atmosphere of poetic intensity, and made none of the bouncing gestures, none of the hollow invocations to optimism which in England are perpetually inflicted on any of the sick who show consciousness of their state. The tolerance of these doctors, indeed, was wide. As we passed along a corridor overlooking the courtyard, there trembled, in one of the deep recesses each window made in the thickness of the wall, a shadow that was almost certainly two shadows, fused by a strong preference. 'Yes,' said the superintendent, 'they sometimes fall in love, and it is a very good thing. It sometimes makes all the difference, they get a new appetite for living, and then they do so well.' That was the answer to all our Western scruples. The patients were doing so well. Allowed to cast themselves for great tragic roles, they were experiencing the exhilaration felt by great tragic actors. It was not lack of control, lack of taste, lack of knowledge that accounted for permission of what was not permitted in the West. Rather was it the reverse. Our people could not have handled patients full of the dangerous thoughts of death and love; these people had such resources that they did not need to empty their patients of such freight.

The doctors themselves were living richly. They were enjoying the sense of power which comes to the scientist when he applies his knowledge to a primitive people. They talked of the peasants as of beautiful and vigorous animals that have to be coaxed and trapped and bludgeoned into submitting to the treatment which will keep alive the flame in their bodies without which they will have neither beauty nor vigour. So, of course, do any colonial administrators; but these doctors cared for loveliness with the uncorrupted eye of an unmechanized race, and though they were divided from the patients by the gulf that divides a university graduate from a peasant, that gulf was bridged by the consciousness that they all were Slavs and that their forbears had all been peasants together. Each of these doctors was a magician who was working his spells to save his father and his mother. It is this same situation, I imagine, which is responsible for the peculiar enthusiasm shown by officials engaged in the social services in Soviet Russia. This is often regarded as a specific effect of a Communist regime, but it could certainly be matched all over the Balkans, in all the Baltic provinces that were formerly under the Tsardom, and in Turkey. The old and the new sometimes make an intoxicating fusion. These doctors were enchanted with their X-ray department and their operating theatre where they had a pretty record of successful collapses of the lung, and they were enchanted, too, when they hurried us down the corridors, down a staircase of stone so old that it was black as iron, and through a door of wood so old that it shone as glass, to a vast kitchen, obscure in its great vaulted roof, glowing near the fires which were roaring like the night wind in a forest. At long tables half as thick as tree-trunks, pretty nuns in white robes put the last touches to that state of order which women make twice a day after meals and live only to unmake. The prettiest one of all we found in a store-room half the size of my flat in London, standing by a table covered with the little sweet biscuits made of nuts and meringue and fine pastry which are loved in every Slav country. We caught her eating one. She swallowed it in a gulp, and faced out the men's roar of laughter in the most serene confusion imaginable, smiling, with some tiny crumbs caught in the fair down on her upper lip. It was then that somebody remembered that our dinner was ready for us.

We were taken up to the doctors' mess and set before a further exhibition of antique plenty. There was a river of plum brandy somewhere near, it seemed. Then, to begin with, there was a platter of cold meat such as I never expected to eat in my life again. There was sucking-pig so delicate that it could be spread on bread like butter, and veal and ham and sausage and tongue, all as superb in their austerer way, and slabs of butter and fat cheese. Then there were pancakes, stuffed with chopped steak and mushrooms and chickens' livers, and then spring chicken served with a border of moist and flavoursome rice on a bed of young vegetables, and it appeared that there was also a river of white wine near by. And then there was a compote of quinces, cherries, and peaches, served with a stack of little biscuits, like the one we had found the pretty nun eating. We ate and drank enormously. Valetta said in my ear, 'You really must eat, you know. They will think you dislike their food if you do not. It is our Slav custom to give our guests too much to eat, as a kind of boastfulness, and of course out of good-will, and the guests show how strong they are by eating it. We are really a very primitive people, I am afraid.' I did not complain, and we ate without interruption, save when a nun put her head round the door, and with round eyes cried out an announcement. The superintendent spoke to one of the younger doctors, who took off his coat, rolled up his sleeves, and ran from the room at the double. 'Two of the patients have been talking politics,' explained the superintendent; 'it is not allowed, but sometimes they do it. However it is not really serious, they have no weapons. But go on eating, go on eating. All our food is raised on the land belonging to the sanatorium or round it, and prepared by our good nuns. And mind you, the patients have the same food as you are having. This is a feast for distinguished visitors, of course, but at all times we give them plenty, for it is cheap and we have no need to skimp it.' 'Yes,' said another of the doctors, waving his glass at me, 'we send the patients home five and ten and fifteen kilos heavier.'

Here was the authentic voice of the Slav. These people hold that the way to make life better is to add good things to it, whereas in the West we hold that the way to make life better is to take bad things away from it. With us, a satisfactory hospital patient is one who, for the time being at least, has been castrated of all adult attributes. With us, an acceptable doctor is one with all asperities characteristic of gifted men rubbed down by conformity with social standards to a shining, cornerless blandness. With us, a suitable hospital diet is food from which everything toxic and irritant has been removed, the eunuchized pulp of steamed fish and stewed prunes. Here a patient could be adult, primitive, dusky, defensive;

if he chose to foster a poetic fantasy or personal passion to tide him over his crisis, so much the better. It was the tuberculosis germ that the doctor wanted to alter, not the patient; and that doctor himself might be just like another man, provided he possessed also a fierce intention to cure. To him the best hospital diet would be that which brought the most juices to the mouth; and there was not the obvious flaw in the argument that one might think, for the chicken and the compote were the standard dishes of any nursing-home, but these were good to eat. One of the doctors raised his glass to me; I raised my glass to him, enjoying the communion with this rich world that added instead of subtracting. I thought of the service at Shestine, and its unfamiliar climate. The worshippers in Western countries come before the altar with the desire to subtract from the godhead and themselves; to subtract benefits from the godhead by prayer, to subtract their dangerous adult qualities by affecting childishness. The worshippers at Shestine had come before the altar with a habit of addition, which made them pour out the gift of their adoration on the godhead, which made them add to themselves by imaginative realization the divine qualities which they were contemplating in order to adore. The effect had been of enormous, reassuring natural wealth; and that was what I had found in Yugoslavia on my first visit. I had come on stores of wealth as impressive as the rubies of Golconda or the gold of Klondike, which took every form except actual material wealth. Now the superintendent was proposing the health of my husband and myself, and when he said, 'We are doing our best here, but we are a poor country,' it seemed to me he was being as funny as rich people who talk to their poor relations about the large amount they have to pay in income tax.

'But since they have this Slav abundance here and at Shestine,' I wondered, 'why have I had so little enjoyment of it since I arrived?'

But my attention was caught by a crack that had suddenly begun to fissure the occasion. The superintendent had been telling my husband and me what pleasure he had in welcoming us to Croatia, when Gregorievitch had leaned across the table and corrected him. 'To Yugoslavia,' he said in the accents of a tutor anxious to recall his pupil to truth and accuracy. There fell a silence. 'To Yugoslavia,' he repeated. Severity still lived in his brows, which he brought together by habit. But his eyes were stricken; so does an old dog look when it hopes against hope that the young master will take him out on a walk. After another silence, the superintendent said, 'Yes, I will say that I welcome them to Yugoslavia. Who am I, being a Serb, to refuse this favour to a Croat?' They all laughed kindly at Gregorievitch after that; but there had sounded for an instant the authentic wail of poverty, in its dire extreme, that is caused by a certain kind of politics. Such politics we know very well in Ireland. They grow on a basis of past injustice. A proud people acquire a habit of resistance to foreign oppression, and by the time they have driven out their oppressors they have forgotten that agreement is a pleasure and that a society which has attained tranquillity will be able to pursue many delightful ends. There they continue to wrangle, finding abundant material in the odds and ends of injustices that are left over from the period of tyranny and need to be tidied up in one way or another. Such politics are a leak in the community. Generous passion, pure art, abstract thought, run through it and are lost. There remain only the obstinate solids which cannot be dissolved by argument or love, the rubble of hate and prejudice and malice, which are of no price. The process is never absolute, since in all lands some people are born with the inherent sweetness which closes that leak, but it can exist to a degree that alarms by the threat of privation affecting all the most essential goods of life; and in Croatia I had from time to time felt very poor.

Zagreb IV

There is no end to political disputation in Croatia. None.

Because we were walking near the vegetable market we trod on a mosaic of red and green cabbage leaves, orange peel, and grey stone. I directed the attention of Valetta and Constantine to its beauty, and I even became ecstatic over it; but I could not distract them from their heavy sense of disagreement. I had to admit that the experience I was offering them was perhaps insufficiently interesting, so when I found myself in front of a cage where a grey-and-pink parrot sat before a card index of destinies, I was glad to cry, 'Let us have our fortunes told!' But Constantine and Valetta each looked at the bird with eyes smouldering with hope that the other would have no future whatsoever. So I put in my dinar and the bird picked out a card; and when I gave it to Valetta, he burst out laughing and threw it back to me. 'Oh, wise bird! It says, "You are surrounded by the wrong friends, you must get rid of them at once!"' He waved his cap and went laughing through the crowd. 'Till you have obeyed, it is good-bye!' he cried over his shoulder; and then suddenly grave, lest we should think he had really turned against us, he said, 'And I shall come to see you tonight, about seven.'

They had quarrelled all through lunch. We had spent the morning going round the sights of the town with a Croat lady and Constantine, and over the soup we told Valetta how much we had liked her; and Constantine exploded: 'I did not like her. She is not a true Slav. Did you hear what she told you when you were at the Health Co-operative Society Clinic? She said that all such things were very well looked after in the Austrian times. Yes, and she said it regretfully.' 'Well, it was so,' said Valetta. 'Yes, it was so,' said Constantine, 'but we must not regret it. No true Slav would regret it. That is to say no true human being would say it, for if a true human being is a Slav, he knows that to be a Slav is what is important, for that is the shape which God has given him, and he should keep it. The Austrians sometimes pampered you, and sometimes the Hungarians, so that each should play you off against the others. Benefits you get so are filth, and they spoil your shape as a Slav. It is better to have nearly nothing at all, and be a freeman with your brother Slavs.' He paused, but Valetta was silent and went on eating. 'Do you not think it is better?' Constantine asked him. He nodded slightly. 'Well, if you do not feel that strongly you can feel nothing at all!' said Constantine a little louder. 'Oh, yes, I feel it strongly,' said Valetta, quite softly, and then, more softly still, 'It would be much better for us to be freemen with our brother Slavs.'

For a moment Constantine was satisfied and went on eating. Then he threw down his knife and fork. 'What is that you are saying? It *would* be better . . . You mean it is not so?' 'I mean it is not quite so,' said Valetta. 'How is it not so?' asked Constantine, lowering his head like a bull. Valetta shrugged his shoulders. Constantine collapsed quite suddenly, and asked pathetically, 'But are we not brothers, we Croats and Serbs?' 'Yes,' said Valetta. He was speaking softly, not, as a stranger might have thought, out of guile, but out of intense feeling. He was quite white. 'But in Yugoslavia,' he said painfully, 'it is not so. Or, rather, it is as if the Serbs were the elder brother and we Croats the younger brother, under some law as the English, which gives the elder everything and the younger nothing.' 'Oh, I know what you think!' groaned Constantine. 'You think that all your money goes to Belgrade, and you get hardly anything of it back, and we flood your country with Serb officials, and keep Croats out of all positions of real power. I know it all!'

'You may know it all,' said Valetta, 'but so do we: and it is not a thing we can be expected to overlook.' 'I do not ask you to overlook it,' said Constantine, beginning to roar like a bull, 'I ask you to look at it. You did not have the spending of your money before, when you were under Hungary. All your money was sent to Budapest to landlords or to tax-collectors, and you got some railways, yes, and some hospitals, yes, and some roads, yes, but not costing one-half of your money, and you got also Germanization and Magyarization, you got the violation of your soul. But now you are a part of Yugoslavia, you are a part of the kingdom of the South Slavs, which exists to let you keep your soul, and to guard that kingdom we must have an army and a navy to keep Hungary and Italy in their places, and we must give Serbia many things she did not have because Serbia was fighting the Turk when you were standing safe behind us, and we must do much for Bosnia, because the Hungarians did nothing there, and we must do everything for Macedonia, because the Turks were there till 1912, and we must drain marshes and build schools and make military roads, and it is all for you as well as for us, but you will not see it!'

'Yes, I see it,' said Valetta, 'but if you want to found a strong and civilized Yugoslavia you should have brought the Serb schools up to the Croat level instead of bringing the Croat schools down to Serb level.' 'But now you show you see nothing at all,' wailed Constantine; 'it is a question of money! It is more important that one should have good schools everywhere than that part of the country should have very good schools. A chain is as strong as its weakest link. What good is it to you in Croatia that your boys and girls can read the Hindustani and paint like Raphael if the young men in Macedonia go bang-bang all night at whoever because they do not know anything else to do?' 'We might feel more confidence that our money went to build schools in Macedonia if it did not go through Belgrade,' said Valetta. 'You must forgive us for fearing that a great deal of it sticks in Belgrade.' 'Of course it sticks in Belgrade!' said Constantine, his voice going high, though it is low by nature. 'We must make a capital. We must make a capital for your sake, because you are a South Slav! All Western Europeans despise us because we have a little capital that is not chic. They are wrong, for there is no reason why we should have a big capital, for we are a peasant state. But you must give these people what they want, and they are like children, it is the big shining thing that impresses them. Do you not remember how before the war the Austrian Ministers treated us like dirt, because Vienna is a place of baroque palaces and we had nothing but our poor town that had a Turkish garrison till fifty years ago, though it meant nothing, for at the appointed time we came down on them like a hammer on nutshells?'

'If it were only ministries and hotels that were being built in Belgrade, we Croats might approve,' said Valetta, 'but we understand that there are many private houses which are being built for people who have been connected with politics.' 'It is not true, I swear it is not true,' cried Constantine. 'Are you telling me,' asked Valetta, 'that all Serb officials are honest?' Constantine rocked in his seat. 'I am all for chonesty,' he said, giving the *h* its guttural sound, 'I am a very chonest man.' And that is true: during his life he has had the unquestioned administration of much money, and never has one penny stuck to his fingers. 'And I admit,' he continued heavily, 'that in our Serbia there are sometimes people who are not chonest. But how could we do? There are not enough people in our country to take on the administration, so many of us were killed in the war. Ninety per cent,' he wailed, 'ninety per cent of our university students were killed in the war.' And that, too, I learned afterwards, is true. 'Then why do you not draw on us Croats for officials?' asked Valetta. 'There are many Croats whom nobody in the world would dare to call untrustworthy.' 'But how can we let you Croats be officials?' spluttered Constantine. 'You are not loyal!' 'And how,' asked Valetta, white to the lips, 'can we be expected to be loyal if you always treat us like this?' 'But I am telling you,' grieved Constantine, 'how can we treat you differently till you are loyal?'

It is an absolute deadlock; and the statement of it filled the heart with desolation. Constantine pushed away his plate and said, 'Valetta, I will tell you what is the matter with you.' 'But we can see nothing the matter with either of you,' I intervened. 'After we left you at the Health Co-operative Clinic the Croat lady took us to the Ethnographical Museum. What genius you Slav peoples have! I have never seen such a wealth of design, provoked by all sorts of objects always to perfection. A dress, an Easter egg, a butter-churn.' I knew that my intervention was feeble, but it was the best I could do. I find that this always happens when I try to interrupt Slavs who are quarrelling. They draw all the energy out of the air by the passion of their debate, so that anything outside its orbit can only flutter trivially. 'I will tell you what is the matter with you,' repeated Constantine, silencing me with his hand. 'Here in Croatia you are lawyers as well as soldiers. You have been good lawyers, and you have been lawyers all the time. For eight hundred years you have had your *procès* against Hungary. You have quibbled over phrases in the *diploma inaugurale* of your kings, you have wrangled about the power of your Ban, you have sawed arguments about *regna socia* and *partes adnexæ*, you have chattered like jackdaws over your rights under the Dual Monarchy, you have covered acres of paper discussing the Hungaro-Croatian compromise. And so it is that you are now more lawyers than soldiers, for it is not since the eighteenth century that you have fought the Turks, and you fought against the Magyars only a little time. But now we are making Yugoslavia we must feel not like lawyers but like soldiers, we must feel in a large way about the simple matter of saving our lives. You must cast away all your little rights and say that we have a big right, the right of the Slavs to be together, and we must sacrifice all our rights to protect that great right.'

Valetta shrugged his shoulders once more. 'What have you against that?' roared Constantine. 'I will tell you what is the matter with you. You are an intellectual, you are all intellectuals here in the bad sense. You boast because Zagreb is an old town, but that it is a great pity for you. Everywhere else in Serbia is a new town, and though we have novelists and poets and all, they have now been in no town not more than not one generation.' (This is good Serbian grammar, which piles up its negatives.) 'So what the peasant knows they also know. They know that one must not work against, one must work with. One ploughs the earth that would not be ploughed, certainly, but one falls in with the earth's ideas so much as to sow it with seed in the spring and not in the winter or in the summer. But in the town you do not know that, you can go through life and you can work against all, except the motor car and the railway train and the tram, them you must not charge with your head down, but all other things you can. So you are intellectuals. The false sort that are always in opposition. My God, my God, how easy it is to be an intellectual in opposition to the man of action! He can always be so much cleverer, he can always pick out the little faults. But to make, that is more difficult. So it is easier to be a critic than to be a poet.' He flung down a fork suddenly. 'But I should say it is easier to be a bad critic. To be a good critic you must make sometimes and know how it is in your own self to make well or badly. That is why I am a great critic. I am also a great poet. But you are not poets, you Croats, you do not make. You are always little and clever, you are always in opposition winning points as if it were a game.' He flung himself on his jam pancakes like a hungry lion, then, with his mouth full, roared again, 'All of you in Zagreb are the same. I have been in the cafés every night and the Croats all say to me, "It is disgusting, the trade pact you in Belgrade have made with Italy!" And who are the Croats, who took Italian help to kill our King, who are howling always that your peasants are so poor, to attack us if we swallow our pride and for the sake of getting the peasants a little money make a trade pact with the Italians? *Ach*, in all your little ways you are very terrible.'

For a time Valetta did not answer. It is a considerable part of the Croat argument that Croats do not shout in restaurants and do not speak at all with their mouths full. 'You would say we were well governed here?' he asked presently. 'You would say that nobody is arrested without cause and thrown into prison and treated barbarously? You would say that nobody has been tortured in Croatia since it became Yugoslavia?' He was trembling, and such sick horror passed across his face that I am sure he was recollecting atrocities which he had seen with his own eyes, at which his own bowels had revolted. Constantine nearly cried. 'Ah, God! it is their fault,' he pled, indicating my husband and myself with his thumb. 'These English are hypocrites, they pretend you govern people without using force, because there are many parts of the Empire where they govern only people who want to be governed. It is not necessary to use force in Canada and Australia, so they pretend that there is the general rule, though in India where the people do not want to be governed many people are beaten and imprisoned. And for that I do not blame the English. It must be done if one race has to have power over another; that is why it is wrong for one race to have power over another, and that is why we must have a Yugoslavia, a self-governing kingdom of the South Slavs, and why we should make all possible sacrifices for Yugoslavia.' 'I see the argument,' said Valetta; 'we are to let Serbs torture us Croats, because under Yugoslavia we are not to be tortured by the Italians and Hungarians.' 'Oh, God! Oh, God!' cried Constantine, 'I am glad that I am not a Croat, but a Serb, for though I myself am a very clever man, the Serbs are not a very clever people; that has not been their business, their business has been to drive out the Turks and keep their independence from the Austrians and the Germans, so their strong point is that they can open doors by butting them with their heads. Believe me, in such a position as ours—that is more important. But, my God, my God, do you know what I feel like doing when I talk to you Croats? I feel like rolling up my coat and lying down in the middle of the street, and putting my head on my coat, and saying to the horses and motor cars, "Drive on, I am disgusted." What is so horrible in this conversation is that you are never wrong, but I am always right, and we could go on talking like this for ever, till the clever way you are never wrong brought death upon us.' 'Some have died already,' said Valetta.

Zagreb V

The rest of the afternoon was to prove to us that Constantine was to some extent right, and that the Croat is weakened by Austrian influence as by a profound malady.

When Valetta had left us in front of the parrot's cage, Constantine said, 'Now we must hurry, for we have two things to do this afternoon. We must see the treasury of the Cathedral and then we must go to the dancer who has promised to dance for us in her apartment.' He walked beside us very glumly, looking at the pavement, and then burst out: 'I do not know why you trouble yourself with that young man, he is not of importance, he is quite simply a Croat, a typical Croat.' After a silence we came to the square in front of the Cathedral. He burst out again: 'They do appalling things and they make us do appalling things, these Croats. When God works through the Croats He works terribly. I will tell you what once happened in the war. There was a hill in Serbia that we were fighting for all night with the Austrian troops. Sometimes we had it, and sometimes they had it, and at the end we wholly had it, and when they charged us we cried to them to surrender, and through the night they answered. "The soldiers of the Empire do not surrender," and it was in our own tongue they spoke. So we knew they were our brothers the Croats, and because they were our brothers we knew that they meant it, and so they came against us, and we had to kill them, and in the morning they all lay dead, and they were all our brothers.'

Just then, the face of the Cathedral rose pearly-brown above us. Constantine tiptoed to the sacristan and said that we wanted to see the treasury, and there began a scurrying quest for the key. A sacristan in ordinary breeches and shirt-sleeves was carrying away the tubs of oleanders that had decorated the altar during Easter. His face was pursed with physical effort and an objection to it, and the oleander branches waved about him like the arms of a vegetable Sabine. 'They are a long time seeking the key,' said Constantine wearily, leaning against a pillar and looking up to its high flowering. 'I would not have you think that the Croats are not good people. All Slavs are good people. They were the best soldiers in the Austro-Hungarian Empire. All, all said so, on all the fronts. Hey, what is this?' A priest had come to say that the key had had to be sent for, that it would come soon. He then ran towards a little door through which five or six other people ran constantly during the next quarter of an hour, on errands connected with the finding of the key. 'Now I as a Serb do not think it is as important that the key should be found quickly as you English would do,' said Constantine, 'but I would point out to you that in Zagreb also the key is not found in the quick English tempo. Yet I am sure that here they say to you all day, "We are not as the Serbs in Belgrade, here we are businesslike, we do things as they are done in Vienna,"' And it was true. So they had said to us constantly in the banks and hotels and museums.

At last a priest came with the key in his hand, and took us up a stone staircase to the treasury which had an enormous safe-door, affixed after the theft of a tenth-century ivory diptych, which was discovered some years later in the museum at Cleveland, Ohio. The safe-door took quite a long time to open, it was so very elaborate. Then the priest went in and immediately ran out with a chalice of which he was evidently very proud, though it was not very distinguished late sixteenth-century work. For some reason all Croat priests both in Croatia and Dalmatia have a special liking for dull Renaissance work. Byzantine work they value for its antiquity only, and its lavish use of precious metals, and medieval work they usually despise for its uncouthness. The priest was quite ecstatic about this chalice, which he put down on a little rickety table on the landing outside the treasury, and made us stand and admire it for some time. Then he said that we must see the jewelled mitre of a sixteenth-century bishop, and he showed us into the treasury. After we had looked at the silver we were shown the diptych, which is pleasing but not satisfying, because it lacks spaciousness. The figures are the right hieroglyphics; they could spell out a magic message, but they do not, because they are so crowded it is like a poem printed with the words run together. We were shown also the sham diptych which was substituted by the thief for the real one so that the theft went undetected for some days. This was a surprising story, for though the copy reproduced all the details of the original, it was with such infidelity, such falsity of proportion and value, that the two were quite unlike in effect. It is possible that the copy was carved in some centre of craftsmanship, perhaps in Italy, by somebody who had never seen the original but worked from a photograph.

While we were discussing this the priest uttered a sharp cry and ran out of the room, while Constantine burst into laughter. He explained, 'He has remembered that he has left the chalice on the table outside.' I said, 'But why do you laugh? It is a thing that any of us might have done.' 'But it is not,' said Constantine. 'Your husband would not have done it at all, because he is English. You might or might not have done it, because you are a woman, and so of course you have no very definite personality. But I would have been sure to do it, and the priest was sure to do it. But because I am a Serb I know I am sure to do it, while because he is a Croat he thinks he is like a German or an Englishman and will not do it. Of course I must laugh. It is the same funny thing as about the key.'

When the priest came back he showed us the illuminated Psalters and Bibles; and in one of them we fell on the record of what is always pleasing, a liberal and humanist soul which found perfect satisfaction and a refuge from troubled times in the Church. On the margins of his holy book he painted towns set on bays where it would be good to swim, meadows where spring had smiled four hundred years and was not tired, and rosy nudes with their flesh made sound by much passive exercise. We would have thought that the man who painted so was at ease with the world had we not turned a page and found proof that he was nothing of the kind. With unbroken sweetness but in perplexed misery, he painted a hunter lying asleep in the woods and peopled the glades with his dream. The hunter is spitted before a lively fire by hinds who sniff in the good roasting smell, while hares chase hounds lather-mouthed with fright and cram their limp bodies into baskets, and by every stroke of the brush it is asked, 'What are blue seas and the spring and lovely bodies so long as there are pain and cruelty?' He spoke to us for one second out of the past and instantly returned there, for the priest preferred that we look at his vestments rather than at his books. 'And indeed they are very beautiful,' said Constantine. They were of embroidered damask and stamped velvet, for the most part of Italian provenance, some as old as the sixteenth century. 'But how poor they look!' I said. 'You are hard to please,' he said. 'No, I am not,' I said, 'but compared to the design we saw in the Ethnographical Museum these seem so limited and commonplace.'

I was not flattering Constantine. These designs on the vestments were of that Renaissance kind which, if one sees them in a museum and tries to draw them, distress one by their arbitrariness. They partake neither of naturalism nor of geometrical pattern; they often depict flowers set side by side to make harmonies of colour and united by lines whose unpleasant lack of composition is disguised by those harmonies. The designs in the Slav embroideries are based on sound line, on line that is potent and begets as it moves, so that in copying it the pencil knows no opposition; it is, as Constantine would say, 'working with.' Also the Slav designs have great individuality while keeping loyal to a defined tradition, whereas the Italian designs follow a certain number of defined models. 'You are right,' said Constantine benignly. 'We are a wonderful people. That is why we want to be Slavs and nothing else. All else is too poor for us. But now we must go to the dancer; she is having the accompanist specially for us, so we must not be late.'

The dancer lived on the top floor of a modern apartment house. The blond floor of her practice room shone like a pool under the strong light from the great windows, and though her accompanist had not yet come, she was swaying and circling over it like a bird flying low over the water, as swallows do before rain. She turned at the end of the room and danced back to greet us. She had that vigorous young beauty that seems to carry its keen cold about with it. Her eyes were bright and her cheeks glowed as if she were not really here, as if she were running on her points up the cornices of a snow peak to a fairy ice-palace. She had the most relevant of beauties for her trade, the bird foot that born dancers have, that Nijinsky had to perfection. Before she got to us she stopped and pointed to a gilded laurel wreath that hung on the wall. As she pointed with her right hand her left heel moved a thought backwards, and the result was perfection. I went up and looked at the wreath and found that she had been awarded it at some Berlin dance festival. 'That is why we have come,' said Constantine; 'she won the second prize at the great Folk-Dance Festival. It is a great honour.'

My husband said, 'Please tell her we think her dress most beautiful. Is it a Croatian peasant dress?' '*Ach*, no!' said Constantine. 'But no, my God, I am wrong, it is.' He went down on his knees and looked at the skirt. It was of white linen embroidered with red and white flowers of a very pure design. 'Yes,' he said, 'it is a Croatian peasant girl, but she has adapted it to Western ideas. She has made it much lighter. Well, we shall see. Here comes the accompanist.' We watched the girl's feet move like nothing substantial, like the marks on eddying water. Her skirts flowed round her in rhythms counter to the rhythms of her feet, and, smiling, she held out her hands to invisible partners to share in this dear honourable drunkenness. Out of the air she conjured them till they were nearly visible, frank and hearty fellows that could match her joke with joke, till shyness came and made all more delicate, and for a second all laughter vanished and she inscribed on the air her potentiality for romance. Her head and bosom hung backwards from the stem of her waist like a flower blown backwards, but for fear that this wind blow too strongly she called back the defence of laughter, and romped again.

When she stopped we all applauded; but as soon as she went away to change her dress Constantine said to me, 'It is terrible, is it not?' 'Yes, it is very shocking,' I said, 'but I thought it must be so from her dress.' My husband said, 'I do not know what you mean. It seems to me we have been watching a very accomplished dance of little or no imaginative distinction, but I cannot understand why anybody should consider it as shocking.' 'No, of course you cannot understand, but your wife can, because she has been in Serbia and Macedonia, and she knows how it is natural for a Slav woman to dance. She knows that with us a woman must not dance like this. It does not go with any of our ideas. A woman must not spring about like a man to show how strong she is and she must not laugh like a man to show how happy she is. She has something else to do. She must go round wearing heavy clothes, not light at all, but heavy, heavy clothes, so that she is stiff, like an icon, and her face must mean one thing, like the face of an icon, and when she dances she must move without seeming to move, as if she were an icon held up before the people. It is something you cannot understand, but for us it is right. Many things in our culture accord with it.' 'Is this something that is taken for granted and spoken about, or have you just thought of it?' asked my husband. 'I have just thought of putting it like this,' said Constantine, laughing, 'but that is nothing against it, for I am a demoniac man like Goethe, and my thoughts represent the self-consciousness of nature. But indeed your wife will tell you it is so.' 'Yes,' I said, 'he is right. They shuffle round as if they were dead, but somehow it looks right.'

When the dancer came back she was committing a worse offence against Slav convention. It happens that Lika, which is a district of Dalmatia, in the Karst, that is to say on the bare limestone mountains, breeds a kind of debonair Highlander, rather hard to believe in, so like is he to the kind of figure that a Byron-struck young lady of the early nineteenth century drew in her album. The girl's dress was a principal-boy version of this, a tight bodice and kilt of oatmeal linen, with a multicoloured sporran, and she wore the typical male Lika head-dress, a cap with an orange crown, a black rim, and a black lock of fringe falling over the ear and nape of the neck on the right side. It suited her miraculously, and her legs were the shape of perfection. But the rhythm of her dance was very quick and springing; it was in fact a boy's dance, and she danced it as a girl wanting to emphasize that she was a girl by performing a characteristically male process. She ended standing on the tips of her toes, with her left hand on her hip and her right forefinger touching her chin, her eyebrows raised in coyness; there was never anything less androgynous.

But the attempt to juggle with the two aspects of human sexuality was not the reason why this dance was distressing in its confusion. It was a distress not new to me—I have felt it often in America. I have at times felt suddenly sickened when a coloured dancer I have been watching has used a step or gesture that belongs to 'white' dancing; even if the instant before they had been wriggling in an imitation sexual ecstasy and passed into a dull undulation of the Loie Fuller sort or the chaste muscular bound of a ballet movement, the second seemed more indecent than the first, and I have often experienced the same shock when I have seen white dancers borrow the idiom of coloured dancers. There is nothing unpleasant in the gesture known as 'cherry-picking,' provided it is a Negro or Negress who performs it; the dancer stands with feet apart and knees bent, and stretches the arms upwards while the fingers pull an invisible abundance out of the high air. But it is gross and revolting, a reversion to animalism, when it is performed by a white person. That same feeling of inappropriateness amounting to cultural perversion afflicted me slightly when I saw this girl's first dance, more severely when I saw her second, and to a painful degree in the third, which she did to show us that she could do more than mere folk-dances. It was that cabaret chestnut, the dance of the clockwork doll, which is an imaginative cliché of the stalest sort, never again to be more amusing than the riddle 'When is a door not a door?' And this was the most excruciating rendering of it that I have ever seen. This Croat girl was so noble a creature that when she did a silly thing she looked far sillier than the silly do. At the end of her dance she ran across the shining floor and stood with her bare arm resting on the golden wreath, her reflection broken loveliness at her feet. 'Some day I will make them give me the first prize,' she laughed. 'The poor little one,' said Constantine, 'she should be like an icon, your wife will tell you.'

Zagreb VI

We went up the hill and looked at the archaic statues on the porch of St. Mark's Church, which is a battered old spiritual keep that has been built and rebuilt again and again since the thirteenth century. 'This old square is the heart of the town,' said Constantine. 'Zagreb is the heart of Croatia, and St. Mark's Square is the heart of Zagreb, and I think that only once did it fall, and then to the Tartars, to whom all fell. But now they have renamed it the Square of Stefan Raditch, after the great leader of the Croat Peasant Party, who was shot in the Belgrade Parliament in 1928. Here in Croatia they say we Serbs did it, they say our King Alexander plotted it,' said Constantine, his voice rising to a wail, 'but it is not so. He was shot by a mad Montenegrin deputy whom he had accused of corruption. The Montenegrins are a Homeric people, they do not understand modern life; they think that if a man attacks your honour you kill him, and it is well. But the Croats do not know that, for they will never travel; they have no idea of going any further than Dalmatia. And why would King Alexander want to kill Raditch? He knew very well that if Raditch were killed the Croats would go mad and would make with the Italians and the Hungarians to kill him also. And so they did. And that is a thing to remember when the King is blamed for suspending the constitution. Always King Alexander knew that he would be killed. It is proof of the lack of imagination of all you English liberals that you forget that a man's policy is a little different when he knows he is going to be killed.'

Down in the town we sat and drank chocolate in a café, till Constantine said, 'Come you must go. You must not keep Valetta waiting.' Since he was staying in the same hotel as we were, and he looked tired, I said, 'Come back with us.' But he would not. 'I will come later,' he said, and I am sure he was afraid of meeting Valetta in the lounge and having to admit that Valetta wanted to see us but not him. The Serb, though he seems tough and insensitive, is sometimes childishly hurt by Croat coldness. Some French friends of mine who once attended an international congress of some sort at Zagreb were in the company of a Serb, a middle-aged diplomat, when somebody came into the room with the news that the Croat hospitality committee was not going to ask the Serb delegates to the banquet which was going to terminate the proceedings. The Serb diplomat burst into tears. This story is the sadder because every

Croat, who thinks of the Serb as the gendarme who tortures him, would disbelieve it.

When we got to our hotel we found Valetta waiting for us, and we took him up to our room and drank plum brandy, pleased to see him again though we had seen him so recently. He stood by the window, pulled the curtains apart, and grimaced at the snow that fell aslant between us and the electric standards. 'What a terrible Easter we have given you!' he laughed, and raised his glass to his lips, smiling on us with the radiance that is usually the gift of traitors, but means nothing in him but kindness and good faith. He went on to apologize for the violence with which he had spoken at lunch-time. 'I could not help it,' he said. 'I know that Constantine is a wonderful man, but he is all for Belgrade, and you will understand how we are bound to feel about that. I am so afraid that as you are just passing through the country, you will not see what we Croats have to suffer. Of course everything is better since 1931, when the King gave us back some sort of constitution; and since the King died it has improved still further. But it is still terrible.

'You cannot think,' he said, as we all gathered round the fire with our glasses on our knees, 'what the censorship here is like. Do you know that that little pamphlet about the Dictatorship of the Proletariat, which was a kind of three-cornered debate between Stalin and Shaw and Wells, has been suppressed? Think of the absurdity of it! Of course that hardly matters, for it is imported and it could not be called an epoch-making work, but what does matter is that our own great people are persecuted. You have heard of X. Y.? He is a dramatist, and he is really by far the greatest living writer we have. But he is a Communist. Well, never can we see his plays at our theatre. They simply will not let them be performed. And it matters not only for us, but for him, because he is miserably poor. And he is not allowed to make money any way, for when some people arranged for him to give a lecture here in one of our big halls and had sold all the tickets, the police prevented it twenty-four hours before, on the ground that if there were a riot in the hall they could not undertake to keep order. Now, that is sheer nonsense. We Croats might riot about all sorts of things, but we would not riot because X. Y. was giving a lecture. And really, I am not exaggerating, all this means that the great X. Y. is starving.'

'But wait a minute,' said my husband. 'Is it only the Yugoslavian Government that did not want X. Y. to speak? Is there not a chance that the Croat Clerical Party was also rather anxious that he shouldn't?' Valetta looked uncomfortable. 'Yes, it is so,' he said. 'They would be against any Communist, wouldn't they?' pressed my husband. 'And they would be in favour of a strict censorship, wouldn't they?' 'Yes,' said Valetta. 'Then when you fight for free speech and a free press, you Croats are not only fighting the Serbs, you are also fighting your own Clerical Party?' 'That is so,' agreed Valetta; and he added sadly, 'Our Clerical Party is very violent.' There he was guilty of an understatement. The Croatian Clerical Party is not a force that can easily be regarded as proceeding from God. It is a party with a long pedigree of mischief-makers, for it descends from the nineteenth-century Party of the Right, which was led by Anton Starchevitch, and its successor, the Party of Pure Right, which was led by Dr. Josef Frank. Both these parties were violently bigoted in their pietism, and professed the most vehement antagonism to the Jews (which implied antagonism to liberalism) and to the Orthodox Church (which, as all Serbs are Orthodox, implied antagonism to the Serbs).

There is to be noted, as evidence against the Austro-Hungarian Empire, the neurotic quality of its rebels. It is as if the population were so drugged and depleted that they never raised their voice unless they were stung by some inner exasperation. It has been mentioned that Kossuth, the Magyar patriot and scourge of the Slavs, was himself pure Slovak and had no Magyar blood in his veins. Even so, Starchevitch, who loathed the Serbs, was himself, as Constantine had told us beside his grave, born of a Serb mother, and Dr. Frank, whose anti-Semitism was frenzied, was a Jew. Such Slav patriots as these were meat and drink to the Austro-Hungarian Empire, who hated her Slav subjects. They made it easy for her to rule according to that counsel of Hell, *Divide et impera*. The famous Ban Khuen-Héderváry, whose rule of Croatia was infamously cruel, made a point of granting the Serb minority in Croatia special privileges, so that the Croats would be jealous of them, and there was thus no danger of Serbs and Croats joining together in revolt against Hungarian rule.

The state of mind this produced in the populace can be read in one of the numerous trials that disgraced the Austro-Hungarian Empire so far as Croatia was concerned from the beginning of the twentieth century till the war. This was the famous 'Agram trial' (Agram was the Austrian name for Zagreb) which arraigned fifty-three Serbs of Croatia for conspiracy with the free Serbs of Serbia against the Austro-Hungarian Empire. The charge was flagrant nonsense, cooked up by the Ban, Baron Rauch, a stupid brute, and Count Aehrenthal, the Austrian Foreign Minister, who belonged to the company of Judas and Fouché; but for evidence they never had to turn to Austrians or Magyars. Nearly all the two hundred and seventy witnesses brought by the prosecution, who were nearly all flagrantly perjured, were Croats. They were all willing to swear away the lives of their fellow-Slavs to the authorities they hated; yet there is no difference between Croats and Serbs except their religion.

The Croat Clerical Party, therefore, has always worked with a motive power of anti-Serb hatred, which naturally created its material. The Serbs retorted with as bad as they got, and the Orthodox Church showed no example of tolerance to the Roman Catholics. The greatest of nineteenth-century Slav patriots of the pacific sort, Bishop Strossmayer, once announced his intention of visiting Serbia, and the Serbian Government had to make the shameful confession that it could not guarantee his personal safety. But the greatest stimulus to anti-Serb feeling has lain outside Croatia, in the Roman Catholic Church itself. During the last sixty years or so the Vatican has become more and more Ultramontane, more and more predominantly Italian in personnel; and since the war of 1914 it has become more and more terrified of Communism. Can the Roman Catholic Church really be expected to like Yugoslavia?—to like a state in which Croats, who used to be safely amalgamated with Catholic Austrians and Hungarians, are outnumbered by Orthodox Serbs, who are suspected of having no real feeling of enmity towards Bolshevist Russia?

There are two indications, one small and one massive, of the Roman Catholic attitude to Yugoslavia. In all Slav countries there have been for many years gymnastic societies for young Slavs, called 'Sokols,' or 'The Hawks,' after an original made in Czechoslovakia, where boys and girls are given physical training and instructed in their nationalist tradition and the duties of a patriot. These are, indeed, the models from which the Italian Fascisti copied the Balilla and Avanguardisti. After the war, the Roman Catholic Church started rival societies called 'The Eagles' in both Croatia and Slovenia. It is extremely difficult to see what motive there can have been behind this move except to weaken the state loyalty of the Roman Catholic Yugoslavs; the Church could not possibly fear that the Sokols would interfere with the religious views of their members, for the Czech and Croatian Sokols had always been predominantly Catholic. The more important indication of the pro-Italian and anti-Slav attitude of the Roman Catholic Church is her callousness towards the unhappy Slovenes who were incorporated in Italy under the Peace Treaty. These six hundred thousand people are the worst-treated minority in Europe except the German Tirolese. 'Have bugs a nationality when they

infest a dwelling? That is the historical and moral position of the
Slovenes living within our borders,' once said the *Popolo d'Italia*.
The 1929 Concordat which Pope Pius XI signed with Mussolini did
not adequately protect the religious rights of the Slav minority, and
the Slovenes no longer enjoy the right, which they prized highly,
of using the Slovene liturgy in the churches. The Slav so loves his
language that this was a gesture of hostility to the Slav soul.

It is, therefore, not sensible to trust the Roman Catholic Croat
to like and understand the Orthodox Serb, or even to discourage
the artificial hatred that has been worked up between them in
the past. 'Do you not think, Valetta,' said my husband, 'that the
Belgrade Government knows this, and therefore bargains with
the Church, giving it assistance in its anti-Communist campaign
on condition that it keeps the anti-Serb and Croatian Separatist
Movement within bounds?' Valetta hesitated. 'It may be so,' he
said, his long fingers fiddling with the fringe of a cushion. 'And
there is another thing,' said my husband; 'there is the present
Concordat.'[1] He paused. In 1937 all the Serbian parts of Yugoslavia
were up in arms because the Government had signed a Concordat
with Pope Pius which gave the Roman Catholic Church immense
advantages over the Orthodox Church: in any town where the
Roman Catholics were in an absolute majority over the Serbs all the
schools without exception were to be Roman Catholic; the child of a
Roman Catholic mother and an Orthodox father was to be brought
up as a Roman Catholic even if the mother were received into the
husband's Church; it was to be far easier for Roman Catholic
soldiers to practise their religion than for the Orthodox soldiers,
and so on. The terms were so grossly favourable to the Roman
Catholics that the Government made it very difficult for the Serb
public or for foreigners to obtain the text of the Concordat. 'Yes,'
sighed Valetta, 'this wretched Concordat. We none of us want it
here, in Croatia, you know.'

'Yes, I do not think you Croats want it,' said my husband, 'but
your Church does. And don't you feel that the Church would never
have been able to extort such terms from the Belgrade Government
if it had not been able to trade some favours in return? I suspect
very strongly that it has said to the Belgrade Government, "If you
give us these concessions we will see to it that the Croatian Peasant
Party never seriously menaces the stability of the Yugoslavian

---

[1] This Concordat was abandoned in 1938 because of the fierce opposition of the
Serbs and the lukewarm attitude of the Croats. It was entirely the project of
the Vatican.

state." ' Valetta rocked himself uneasily, 'Oh, surely not, surely not,' he murmured. 'But for what other reason can the Belgrade Government have granted this preposterous Concordat?' pressed my husband. 'I cannot imagine,' said Valetta. 'Oh, I suppose you are right!' He rose and went to the window and drew back the curtains, and looked again on the bright snow that drove out of the darkness through the rays of the street lamps.

'Is it not the tragedy of your situation here,' suggested my husband, 'that you Croats are for the first time discovering that your religion and your race run counter to one another, and that you are able to evade that discovery by putting the blame on the constitution of Yugoslavia? The Croats, like all Slavs, are a democratic and speculative people. You lived for long under the Habsburgs, whom you could blame for every interference with individual liberty. Since the great pro-Croat Strossmayer was a Bishop you could even think of the Roman Catholic Church as the arch-opponent of the Habsburgs, and therefore the protector of liberty. Now the Habsburgs are swept away you should see the Roman Catholic Church as it is: not at all democratic, not at all in favour of speculative thought; far more alarmed by the vaguest threat of social revolution than by any actual oppression, provided it is of monarchical or totalitarian origin, and wholly unsympathetic with any need for free expression but its own. You should proceed to the difficult task of deciding whether you can reconcile yourself to this bias of the Church for the sake of the spiritual benefits it confers upon you. But you are postponing this task by letting the Church throw the blame for all its suppressions of free speech and free press on Belgrade.'

'It is possible that you are right,' said Valetta, coming back and taking his seat by the fire. 'Nothing is ever clear-cut here.' 'Do you never get down to a discussion of first principles?' asked my husband. 'This business of social revolution, how is it regarded by the Croat politicians such as Matchek of the Croat Peasant Party?' 'We never speak of such things, it is too soon,' said Valetta. 'But if they want to become a separate autonomous canton, surely they must have some idea of the kind of society they want to found?' 'No,' answered Valetta, 'it is felt that it would be premature to discuss such things. Oh, I know it is wrong and naïve and foolish, but that is how our people feel.'

That is how they had always felt, the Croat leaders. There lay on the table a wad of papers which was the result of my efforts, practised over some weeks, to discover what opinions had been held by the greatest of Croat leaders, the murdered Stefan Raditch.

Those efforts had been fruitless, except so far as they provided a proof of the essential unity of the Slavs. For Raditch was the spit and image of Tolstoy. He talked nonsense as often as not, but nobody minded; they all listened and felt exalted. It was his habit to speak in parables that were apt to be childish and obscure, and his speeches sometimes lasted for half a day and usually contained matter that was entirely contrary to human experiences; but his audiences adored him as a sage and a saint, and would have died for him. What was peculiarly Croat in him was his appeal to the peasants as a representative of the country as against the town. This was his own invention. Before the war it was possible to meet all the other Croat politicians by frequenting the Zagreb cafés and restaurants, but both Raditch and his brother Anton, who was almost as famous, made it a strict rule never to enter a café or a restaurant. This was to mark themselves off from the bourgeoisie as specifically peasant. This would not have been impressive in any other part of Yugoslavia than Croatia, where alone is there a bourgeoisie which has existed long enough to cut itself off from the peasantry. It would have evoked dislike and impatience in Serbia or Bosnia or Macedonia, where the poorest peasant is accustomed to sit in cafés.

In the minds of his followers Raditch must have sown confusion and little else. He spoke always as if he had a plan by which the Croat peasant was instantly to become prosperous, whereas there is no man in the world, not even Stalin, who would claim to be able to correct in our own time the insane dispensation which pays the food-producer worst of all workers. The only practical step Raditch ever proposed was the abolition of a centralized Yugoslavian Government and the establishment of a federalism which would have left the economic position of the Croat peasant exactly where it was. The rest was a mass of violent inconsistencies. Probably nobody but St Augustine has contradicted himself so often or so violently.

He was pro-Habsburg; at the outbreak of the war he made a superb speech calling on the Croats to defend their Emperor, and his sentiments did not really change after the peace. But he constantly preached that the Croats should form a republic within the kingdom of Yugoslavia, on the grounds that the proletariat was better off in a republic than in a monarchy. Not only was he simultaneously pro-Habsburg and republican, he had friendly correspondence with Lenin and made a triumphal progress through Russia. Though he expressed sympathy with Bolshevist ideas, he had stern race theories, which made him despise many of the inhabitants of the southern parts of Yugoslavia and reproach the Serbs bitterly for admitting to Government posts such people as Vlachs, an ancient and quite respectable shepherd tribe of the Balkans. It is said, however, that he made the visit to Russia not from any ideological motive but because like all Slavs he loved to travel, and though he had lived in Vienna and Berlin and Paris (where he had taken university degrees, for no more than Tolstoy was he a piece of peasantry straight out of the oven) and had visited London and Rome, he had never been in Moscow.

Whatever the reason may have been, the visit did not help him to give a definition to the Croat mind, particularly as shortly afterwards he became a close friend of King Alexander of Yugoslavia, whom he alternately reproached for his interference with Parliamentarianism and urged to establish a military dictatorship. Meanwhile he robbed the Croats of any right to complain that the Serbs refused to let them take any part in the government by ordering the Croat deputies to abstain from taking their seats in the Belgrade Parliament, when the wiser course would have been to leave them as an obstructionist and bargaining body. Some idea of Raditch can be formed by an effort to imagine an Irish politician with Parnell's personal magnetism, who was at one and the same time an agrarian reformer, a Stuart legitimist, a republican, a Communist sympathizer, an advocate of the Aryan race theory, and a close friend of the King of England, to whom he recommended Liberalism and Fascism as he felt like it, and who withdrew the Irish members from St Stephen's while himself constantly visiting London. It is no wonder that his party, even under his successor Matchek, has formed only the vaguest programmes.

'Nothing,' said Valetta, 'has any form here. Movements that seem obvious to me when I am in Paris or London become completely inconceivable when I am here in Zagreb. Here nothing matters except the Croat-Serb situation. And that, I own, never seems to get any further.' 'But this is something very serious,' said my husband, 'for a movement might rush down on you here, say from Germany, and sweep away the Croat-Serb situation and every other opportunity for debate.' 'You are perfectly right,' said Valetta. 'I know it, I know it very well. But I do not think anything can be done.' And of course nothing can be done. A great empire cannot bring freedom by its own decay to those corners in it where a subject people are prevented from discussing the fundamentals of life. The people feel like children turned adrift to fend for themselves when the imperial routine breaks down; and they wander to and fro, given up to instinctive fears and antagonisms and exaltation until reason dares to take control. I had come to Yugoslavia to see what history meant in flesh and blood. I learned now that it might follow, because an empire passed, that a world full of strong men and women and rich food and heady wine might nevertheless seem like a shadow-show: that a man of every excellence might sit by a fire warming his hands in the vain hope of casting out a chill that lived not in the flesh. Valetta is a clean-cut person; he is for gentleness and kindness and fastidiousness against clod-hopping and cruelty and stupidity, and he would make that choice in war as well as in peace, for his nature is not timid. But he must have something defined that it is possible to be gentle and kind and fastidious about. Here, however, there is none, and therefore Valetta seems a little ghostly as he sits by our hearth; and I wonder if Zagreb is not a city without substance, no more solid than the snow-flakes I shall see next time Valetta strolls to the window and pulls the curtain, driving down from the darkness into the light of the street lamps. This is what the consequences of Austrian rule mean to individual Croats.

Zagreb VII

Politics, always politics. In the middle of the night, when there is a rap on our bedroom door, it is politics. 'It may be a telegram,' said my husband, springing up and fumbling for the light. But it was Constantine. 'I am afraid I am late, I am very late. I have been talking in the cafés with these Croats about the political situation of Yugoslavia; someone must tell them, for they are quite impossible. But I must tell you that I will be leaving tomorrow for Belgrade, very early, earlier than you will go to Sushak, for they have telephoned to me and say that I must go back, they need me, for there is no one who works so well as me. I would have left you a note to tell you that, but there was something I must explain to you. I have spoken not such good things of Raditch who was killed and of Matchek who is alive—you had better put on your dressing-gown, for I will be some time explaining this to you—but I want to make you understand that though they are not at all clever men and cannot understand that there must be a Yugoslavia, they are chonest. They would neither of them take money from the Italians and Hungarians. They and their followers would spit on such men as go to be trained in terrorism at the camps in Italy and Hungary. These were quite other men, let me tell you. . . .'

Nevertheless we had woken as early as it was light, and my husband said to me, 'We have never seen Mestrovitch's statue of the great Croat patriot, Bishop Strossmayer; it is in the public garden just outside this hotel. Let us go and look at it now.' So we dressed in the dawn, said 'Excuse me' to the charwomen who were scrubbing the hall, and found the Bishop among the dark bushes and drab laurels of the unilluminated morning. But his beauty, even under the handling of one whose preference for rude strength must have been disconcerted by its delicacy, was a light by itself. Mestrovitch had given up his own individuality and simply reproduced the Bishop's beauty, veiling it with a sense of power, and setting horns in the thick wavy hair, after the manner of Michelangelo's Moses. I would like to know if Mestrovitch ever saw his model: he probably did, for Strossmayer lived until he was ninety in the year 1905.

This dazzling creature had then completed fifty-six years of continuous heroic agitation for the liberation of the Croats and as the fearless denunciator of Austro-Hungarian tyranny. Because of his brilliant performances as a preacher and a scholar he was at thirty-four made the Bishop of Djakovo, a see which included a vast stretch of the Slav-inhabited territory of the Empire; and he immediately declared himself as a passionate pro-Croat. It is an indication of the wrongs suffered by the Croats that the revenues of this bishopric were enormous, though the poverty and ignorance of the peasants were so extreme that they shocked and actually frightened travellers. He amazed everyone by spending these enormous revenues on the Croats. While Hungary was trying to Magyarize the Croats by forbidding them to use their own language, and as far as possible deprived them of all but the most elementary education, he financed a number of secondary schools and seminaries for clerics, where the instructions were given in Serbo-Croat; he endowed many South Slav literary men and philologists, both Croats and Serbs, and, what was most important, he insisted on the rights of the Croats and the Slovenes to use the Slav liturgy instead of the Latin. This last was their ancient privilege, for which they had bargained with Rome at the time of their conversion by Cyril and Methodius in the ninth century, when they were a free people. He founded the University of Zagreb, which was necessary not only for educational reasons but to give the Croats a proper social status; for in the Austro-Hungarian Empire, as in Germany and in the United States, graduation at a university has a class value; it is the mental equivalent of a white collar. Since the Croats had a university they could not be despised as peasants. He was able to raise pro-Slav feeling in the rest of Europe, for he was the friend of many distinguished Frenchmen, and he was the admired correspondent of Lord Acton and Mr Gladstone.

In all this lifelong struggle he had the support of no authority. He stood alone. Though Pope Leo XIII liked and admired him, the Ultramontane Party, which wanted to dye the Church in the Italian colours, loathed him because he was one of the three dissentients who voted against the Doctrine of Papal Infallibility. On this matter he was of the same mind as Lord Acton, but was at odds with his nearer Catholic neighbours. These hated him because he defended the right of the Slavs to have their liturgy said in their own tongue. They also found him lamentably deficient in bigotry. When he sent a telegram of brotherly greetings to the head of the Orthodox Church in Russia on the occasion of the millenary of the Slav apostle Methodius, his fellow-Catholics, particularly the Hungarians, raged against this as an insult to the Holy See. The sense of being part of a universal brotherhood, of being sure of finding a family welcome in the furthest land, is one of the sweetest benefits offered by the Roman Catholic Church to its members. He had none of this enjoyment. He had only to leave his diocese to meet coldness and insolence from those who should have been his brothers.

The Austro-Hungarian Empire could not persecute Strossmayer to his danger. The Croats loved him too well, and it was not safe to have a belt of disaffected Slavs on the border of Serbia, the free Slav state. But it nagged at him incessantly. When he went to open the Slav Academy in Zagreb the streets were thronged with cheering crowds, but the Government forbade all decorations and illuminations. It took him fifteen years to force on Vienna the University of Zagreb; the statutes were not sanctioned till five years after the necessary funds had been collected. During the negotiations which settled the terms on which Croatia was to submit to Hungary, after Hungary had been given a new status by Elizabeth's invention of the Dual Monarchy, Strossmayer was exiled to France. At the height of the trouble over his telegram to the Orthodox Church about Methodius, he was summoned to Sclavonia, a district of Hungary, where the Emperor Franz Josef was attending manoeuvres; and Franz Josef took the opportunity to insult him publicly, though he was then seventy years of age. This was a bitter blow to him, for he loved Austria, and indeed was himself of Austrian stock, and he wished to preserve the Austro-Hungarian Empire by making the Croats loyal and contented instead of rebels who had the right on their side. Again and again he warned the Emperor of the exact point at which his power was going to disintegrate: of Sarajevo. He told him that if the Austrians and Hungarians misgoverned Bosnia they would increase the mass of Slav discontent within the Empire to a weight that no administration could support and the Habsburg power must fall.

But what is marvellous about this career is not only its heroism but its gaiety. Strossmayer was a child of light, exempt from darkness and terror. In person he resembled the slim, long-limbed, and curled Romeo in Delacroix's *Romeo and Juliet*, and the Juliet he embraced was all grace. The accounts given by European celebrities of the visits they had to him read richly. The foreigner arrived after a night journey at a small station, far on the thither side of civilization, and was received by a young priest followed by a servant described as 'a pandour with long moustachios dressed in the uniform of a hussar,' who put him into a victoria drawn by four dappled greys of the Lipizaner strain which is still to be seen in the Spanish Riding School at Vienna. Twenty-two miles they did in two hours and a half, and at the end, near a small market town,

reached a true palace. It was nineteenth-century made, and that
was unfortunate, particularly in these parts. There is a theory that
the decay of taste is somehow linked with the growth of democracy,
but it is completely disproved by the Austro-Hungarian Empire,
which in its last eighty years grew in fervour for absolutism and
for Messrs. Maple of Tottenham Court Road. But there was much
here worthy of any palace. There was a magnificent avenue of Italian
poplars, planted by the Bishop in his young days; there was a superb
park, landscaped by the Bishop himself; there were greenhouses
and winter gardens, the like of which the eastward traveller would
not see again until he had passed through Serbia and Bulgaria and
Roumania and had found his way to the large estates in Russia.

The guest breakfasted by an open window admitting the perfume
of an adjacent acacia grove, on prodigious butter and cream from the
home farm, on Viennese coffee and rolls made of flour sent from
Budapest. Later he was taken to worship in the Cathedral which the
Bishop had built, where peasants proudly wearing Slav costumes
were hearing the Slav liturgy. Then there was the return to the
palace, and a view of the picture gallery, hung with works of art
which Strossmayer had collected in preparation for the museum at
Zagreb. It is an endearing touch that he confessed he was extremely
glad of the imperial opposition which had delayed the foundation of
this museum, so that he had an excuse for keeping these pictures
in his own home. After an excellent midday dinner the Bishop
exhibited his collection of gold and silver crucifixes and chalices of
Slav workmanship, dating from the tenth to the fourteenth century,
pointing out the high level of civilization which they betokened.
Then the Bishop would take the visitor round his home farm. to
see the Lipizaner horses he bred very profitably for the market,
the Swiss cattle he had imported to improve the local stock, and
the model dairy which was used for instructional purposes, and he
would walk with him in his deer park, at one corner of which he had
saved from the axes of the woodcutters a tract of primeval Balkan
forest, within a palisade erected to keep out the wolves which still
ravaged that part of the world. Before supper the visitor took a little
rest. The Bishop sent up to him a few reviews and newspapers: *The
Times, La Revue des Deux Mondes* the *Journal des Economistes, La
Nuova Antologia*, and so on.

After supper, at which the food and drink were again delicious,
there were hours of conversation, exquisite in manner, stirring
in matter. Strossmayer spoke perfect German, Italian, Czech,
Russian, and Serbian, and a peculiarly musical French which
bewitched the ears of Frenchmen; but it was in Latin that he was

most articulate. It was his favourite medium of expression, and all those who heard him use it, even when they were such scholars as the Vatican Council, were amazed by the loveliness he extracted from that not so very sensuous language. About his conversation there seems to have been the clear welling beauty of the first Latin hymns. The early Christians and he alike were possessed by an ardour which was the very quality needed to transcend the peculiar limitations of that tongue. It was an ardour which, in the case of Strossmayer, led to a glorious unfailing charity towards events. He spoke of his beloved Croats, of the victories of their cause, of his friendships with great men, as a lark might sing in mid-air; but of his struggles with Rome and the Habsburgs he spoke with equal joy, as a triumphant athlete might recall his most famous contests. His visitors, who had travelled far to reassure him in his precarious position, went home in a state of reassurance such as they had never known before.

This is not a character in life as we know it: it belongs to the world that hangs before us just so long as the notes of a Mozart aria linger in the ear. According to our dingy habit, which is necessary enough, considering our human condition, we regard him with suspicion, we look for the snake beneath the flower. All of us know what it is to be moon-struck by charmers and to misinterpret their charm as a promise that now, at last, in this enchanting company, life can be lived without precaution, in the laughing exchange of generosities; and all of us have found later that that charm made no promise and meant nothing, absolutely nothing, except perhaps that their mothers' glands worked very well before they were born. Actually such men often cannot understand generosity at all, since the eupeptic quality which is the cause of their charm enables them to live happily without feeling the need for sweetening life by amiable conduct. They often refrain from contemptuous comment on such folly because they have some use for the gifts of the generous, but even then they usually cannot contain their scorn at what seems a crazy looseness, an idiot interference with the efficient mechanism of self-interest. Hence the biographies of charmers are often punctuated by treachery and brutality of a most painful kind. So we wait for the dark passages in Strossmayer's story. But they do not come.

It appears that he turned on the spiritual world the same joyous sensuality with which he chose chalices, Italian pictures, horses, cattle, coffee, and flowers. He rejected brutality as if it were a spavined horse, treachery as if it had been chicory in the coffee. His epicureanism did not fail under its last and supreme obligation, so much more difficult than the harshest vow of abstinence taken by ascetics: he preferred love to hate, and made sacrifices for that preference. The sole companions left to him were the Croats; for them he had forsaken all others. But he never hesitated to oppose the Croat leaders over certain errors tending to malice and persecution, which sprung up here as they are bound to do in every movement of liberation. Though he risked everything to free the Croats from the dominance of the Austro-Hungarian Empire, he would not suffer any attempt to raise hatred among the Slavs against the Austrians or the Hungarian peoples; nor did he ever let ill be spoken of the Emperor Franz Josef. Nor, though he was a most fervent propagandist for the Roman Catholic faith, would he have any hand in the movement to persecute the Orthodox Church which set the Croat against the Serb. He set himself another problem of enormous delicacy in his opposition to anti-Semitism, which was here an inevitable growth, since the feudal system kept the peasants bound to the land and thereby gave the Jews a virtual monopoly of trade and the professions. For thirty-six years, smiling, he dared deny his friends all titbits to feed the beast in their bosoms, and lived in peril of making them his enemies, though he loved friendship above all things. Out of the political confusion of Croatia which makes for the endless embitterment and impoverishment I have described, this creature had derived sweetness and well-being.

'That is one of the most beautiful lives recorded in modern history,' said my husband. We left the lovely statue smiling under the heavy rain.

On the railway station we found the good Gregorievitch and Valetta waiting to say good-bye to us. They stood side by side on the platform, these two enemies, the early morning rain dripping on their turned-up coat collars. Valetta laughed and wriggled as the drops of water trickled down his neck, but Gregorievitch merely bowed beneath the torrents. 'Nothing is as it used to be,' he said stoically; 'even the seasons are changed.' We did not wonder that he correlated his political disappointments with the weather. The previous day we had seen him link them with phenomena fated, it might have been imagined, to be connected with absolutely nothing, to be themselves alone.

We had gone, Constantine and my husband and myself, to take tea with Gregorievitch at his little flat on the hill beyond the Cathedral. His apartment and his family were the work of that God whose creations Tchekov described. Gregorievitch's wife was nearly as tall and quite as thin as he was, and every minute or so she put her hand to her head in a gesture of apprehension so uncontrolled that it disturbed her front hair, which rose in that tangled palisade called a transformation, familiar to us on the brows of nineteenth-century minor royalties, and finally fixed it at an angle of about sixty degrees to her fine and melancholy features. This would have been comic had she not been a creature moulded in nobility, and had it not been probable that that gesture had become a habit in the early days of her marriage, when Gregorievitch was as young as Valetta, and there was a Hungarian Ban in Zagreb, and every knock at the door might mean, and more than once had meant, that police officers had come to arrest him.

There was also a daughter, very short, very plump, very gay, an amazing production for the Gregorievitches. It was as if two very serious authors had set out to collaborate and then had published a limerick. We had heard about her: she wanted to marry a young officer, but could not because Army regulations forbade him to take a bride with a dowry below a certain sum, and the bank in which Gregorievitch had put his savings declared a moratorium. But she laughed a great deal, and wore a dress printed with little yellow flowers. That was not all in the little flat. There was also a small white poodle, which was pretty and neatly clipped, but old and careworn. It barked furiously when we entered; on Sunday afternoon it was evidently accustomed to repose itself and considered visitors a disorderly innovation. Quivering with rage, it watched while we were shown the sitting-room and the little library which opened off it through an arch. These rooms were full of heavy Austrian furniture with stamped leather cushions and embroidered mats, and they were suffused with a curious nostalgia, as if far older people were living in them than was the case. In the library several tables were entirely covered with thousands of typewritten pages: there must have been at least three-quarters of a million words. Gregorievitch told us that this was the typescript of his book on his war experiences, but it was only half finished, and now he had begun to doubt if it was morally justifiable to write it. To make conversation, since everybody was very silent, my husband looked at the bookshelves and seeing that many of the volumes were well worn, said, 'I suppose you love your books very much?' Gregorievitch thought for some time and then said, 'No.' The conversation dropped again.

'Ah! Ah! Ah!' cried Constantine, pointing his forefinger. We all wheeled about and saw that the poodle was relieving itself on the carpet. The poor creature was making the only protest it could concerning its shattered repose; but it must be admitted that the spectacle was extremely obscene, for its froth of white curls over its clipped limbs recalled a ballerina. Gregorievitch and his wife started forward with tragic faces. The dog got up on its hind legs and clung onto Gregorievitch's hand, barking in weak defiance, putting his case about the sacredness of Sunday afternoon. But Gregorievitch inclined from his great height a face of solemn censure, as if it were a child or even a man who were at fault, while his wife beat the poodle with a small stick which had been brought from the hall by the daughter, who was now no longer laughing. Gregorievitch's expression reminded me of the words St. Augustine once addressed to a Donatist bishop whom he was persecuting: 'If you could see the sorrow of my heart and my concern for your salvation, you would perhaps take pity on your own soul.'

The dog was put out into the passage: but the incident could not be considered as ended. There remained in the middle of the carpet the results of its protest. We endeavoured to take the matter lightly, but we found that the Gregorievitches were evidently hurt by our frivolity; it was as if we had chanced to be with them when a son of theirs had returned home drunk or wearing the badge of the Croat Separatist Party, and we had tried to tamper with the horror of the moment by laughter. The atmosphere was tense beyond bearing; so Constantine, who had assumed an air of gravity, walked to the piano in the manner of an official taking charge in an emergency, and played a majestic motet by Bach, which recognizes the fact of tragedy and examines it in the light of an intuitive certainty that the universe will ultimately be found to be reasonable. The Gregorievitches, who had sunk into two armchairs facing each other, sat with their arms and legs immensely extended before them, nodding their heads to the music and showing signs of deriving sober comfort from its message. There entered presently with a brush and dust-pan an elderly servant, in peasant costume, who was grinning from ear to ear at the joke the dog's nature had played on the gentry.

As she proceeded with her task Constantine passed into the calmer and less transcendental music of a Mozart sonata, suitable to the re-establishment of an earthly decorum; and when she left the room he played a brief triumphal passage from Handel and then rose from the piano. Madame Gregorievitch bowed to him, as if to thank him for having handled a social catastrophe with the tact of a true gentleman, and he acknowledged the bow very much as Heine might have done. She then began to converse with me on general topics, on the exceptionally severe weather and its effect on the social festivities of Zagreb. Meanwhile her husband took mine aside, ostensibly to show him a fine print representing the death

of an early Croatian king, but really to murmur in a voice hoarse
with resentment that he had owned both the poodle's father and
grandmother, and that neither of them would ever have dreamed
of behaving in such a way. 'Nothing, man or beast, is as it was.
Our ideals, think what has happened to our ideals . . . what has
happened to our patriots. . . .'

But for dear Valetta it is not all politics. He is a man of letters,
he is a poet. What he could give the world, if there could only be
peace in Croatia! But how is there to be peace in Croatia? It is said by
some that it could be imposed overnight, if the Serbs of Yugoslavia
could nerve themselves to grant federalism on the Swiss model.
That would change the twilit character of Croatian history, it would
give the Croats a sense of having at last won a success, it would give
their national life a proper form. That, however, could never be
a true solution. But supposing Croatia got her independence, and
the peasants found they were still poor, surely, there would be a
movement towards some form of social revolution; and surely then
the bourgeoisie and the conservatives among the peasants would
try to hand their country over to some foreign power, preferably
Nazi or Fascist, for the sake of stability. Surely, too, the Roman
Catholic Church would be pleased enough if Croatia left its union
with Orthodox Yugoslavia. And if that happened there would be
no more peace in Croatia, for either Gregorievitch or Valetta.
They were both true Slavs, and they would neither of them be
able to tolerate foreign domination, firstly because it was foreign,
and secondly because it was Fascist. Suddenly they looked to me
strange and innocent, like King Alexander of Yugoslavia in the
first part of the film, as he was in the boat and on the quay at
Marseille. I pulled down the window so that I could see them
better, my two dear friends who were each other's enemies, who
might yet be united to each other, far more closely than they could
ever be to me, by a common heroic fate. Such a terrible complexity
has been left by the Austro-Hungarian Empire, which some desire
to restore; such a complexity, in which nobody can be right and
nobody can be wrong, and the future cannot be fortunate.

Dalmatia

Sushak

THE TRAIN WENT THROUGH A COUNTRYSIDE DARK WITH floods; and then there was no countryside, but something like an abstract state of ill-being, a mist that made the land invisible but was not visible itself. Then we pulled up to mountains that were deep under new snow. Here trees became curious geometrical erections; white triangles joined each branch-tip to the trunk. I saw one branch break under its burden and fall in a scattery powder of what had wrecked it. Valleys that I had seen in summer-time and knew to be rocky deserts strewn with boulders the size of automobiles were level as lakes and swansdown white. I grumbled at it, for I had wanted my husband to see the crocuses that I had seen the year before lying under the trees like dapples of mauve sunshine, and all the red anemones springing among the lion-coloured stones. I kept on saying, 'It will be all right when we get to Dalmatia, when we come to the coast.' But in the early afternoon we caught sight of the Adriatic across barren, snow-streaked hills, and it looked like one of the bleaker Scottish lochs. Sky and islands and sea alike were bruise-coloured.

Well, I will own it. The grimness of the day was not all to blame. No weather can make the Northern Dalmatian coast look anything but drear. The dreariness is so extreme that it astounds like luxuriance, it gluts the mind with excess of deprivation. The hills are naked. That exclusion of everything but rock that we English see only in a quarry face is here general. It is the landscape. Tracks lead over this naked rock, but it is hard to believe that they lead anywhere; it seems probable that they are traced by desperate men fleeing from barrenness, and doomed to die in barrenness. And indeed these bald hills mean a great deal of desperation. The rainfall sweeps down their slopes in torrents and carries away the soil instead of seeping into it and fertilizing it. The peasants collect what soil they can from the base of the hills and carry it up again and pack it in terraces; but there is not enough soil and the terraces are often swept away by the torrents.

The human animal is not competent. That is the meaning of
the naked Dalmatian hills. For once they were clothed with
woods. These the earliest inhabitants of Dalmatia, the Illyrians
and Romans, axed with an innocent carelessness; and the first Slav
settlers were reckless too, for they came from the inexhaustible
primeval forest of the Balkan Peninsula. Then for three hundred
years, from about the time of the Norman Conquest to 1420, the
Hungarians struggled with the Venetians for the mastery of this
coast, and the nations got no further with their husbandry. Finally
the Venetian Republic established its claim, and thereafter showed
the carelessness that egotistic people show in dealing with other
people's property.

They cut down what was left of the Dalmatian forests to get
timbers for their fleet and piles for their palaces; and they wasted
far more than they used. Venetian administration was extremely
inefficient, and we know not only from Slav complaints but from
the furious accusation of the Republic against its own people that
vast quantities of timber were purloined by minor officials and put
on the market, and that again and again supplies were delivered at
the dockyard so far beyond all naval needs that they had to be let
rot where they lay. After this wholesale denudation it was not easy
to grow the trees again. The north wind, which blows great guns
here in winter, is hard on young plantations; and the peasant as he
got poorer relied more and more on his goat, a vivacious animal
insensible to the importance of afforestation. The poor peasant is
also sometimes a thief, and it is easier to steal a young tree than a
fully grown one. So, for all the Yugoslavian Government can do,
the mainland and the islands gleam like monstrous worked flints.

Bare hills, and young men that shout, both the product of
human incompetence, of misgovernment. That is the immediate
impression given by North Dalmatia. We met our first young man
very soon after we got to Sushak. We strolled for a time round the
port, which has a brown matter-of-fact handsomeness, and then
we drove off to Trsat, a village two or three miles up on the heights
behind Sushak, which is visited by countless thousands every year,
for the sake of the church.

This is not interesting in itself, or even pleasing, except for
a charming triangular piazza in front of it, which is edged by
horse-chestnuts. But it has the supreme claim on the attention
of marking the site where the Holy House, in which the Virgin
Mary and Jesus and St. Joseph lived at Nazareth, rested for three
years and seven months, from the year 1291 to 1294, on its way to
Loretto, where it now is.

This is a story that enchants me. It gives a new meaning to the phrase 'God moves in a mysterious way'; and the picture of the little house floating through space is a lovely example of the nonsensical function of religion, of its power to cheer the soul by propounding that the universe is sometimes freed from the burden of necessity, which inspires all the best miracles. It has often grieved the matter-of-fact. One English priest named Eustace who visited Loretto at the beginning of the nineteenth century wrote that many of the more sensible of his faith were extremely distressed by the story, and 'suppose the holy house to have been a cottage or log building long buried in a pathless forest, and unnoticed in a country turned almost into a desert by a succession of civil wars, invasions and revolutions, during the space of ten or twelve centuries.' It won't do. The place where the Holy House rested at Trsat is a very short distance indeed from the castle where the Frankopan family were living at the time. We must admit that sometimes human beings quite simply lie, and indeed it is necessary that they should, for only so can poets who do not know what poetry is compose their works.

We pushed on to the Frankopan castle, which is the historical equivalent of a stall in the Caledonian Market. It is a huddle of round and square towers, temples and dungeons and dwelling-houses packed within battlements under an excess of plants and creepers due to neglect rather than luxuriousness. The earliest masonry that has been found is Illyrian, and much is Roman, of the time of Julius Cæsar. We climbed a Roman tower to see Sushak lying brown by the blue sea, and the dark ravine that runs up from the town to split a mountain range on the high skyline.

We numbered seven, the little party that was exploring the castle: ourselves, a middle-aged Frenchman and his blonde sopranoish wife, a German honeymoon couple, aggrieved and agonized, as Germans often are nowadays, at contact with foreigners, and a darkly handsome young man, a Dalmatian on holiday from some town further down the coast, who had early detached himself, and was seen only occasionally in the distance, a silhouette on the edge of the round tower after we had left it, or a shadow treading down the brambles at the entrance to the dungeons. We forgot him totally in a great wonder that came upon us when we were looking at the dwelling-house made in the castle by an early nineteenth-century Austrian general of Irish birth, Marshal Nugent. The Nugents had the custom, like the English who live in the West Indies and the early settlers in the southern states, of burying their dead on their premises. But whereas those other exiles buried their dead in their gardens, the Nugents set theirs in niches of the house, above ground, their coffins set upright behind slabs of marble.

That I found puzzling. The only people I have ever heard of as being buried upright are the ancient Irish, whose monotony of mind made them wish to be discovered at the Day of Judgment ready to face their enemies; but the Nugents are English by origin, and never saw Ireland till the days of Queen Elizabeth. But we soon forgot that bewilderment in another. The gardener was telling us that there was buried among the Nugents a stranger, a something that he described in a rapid phrase which we could not at first grasp. Incredulously we repeated his phrase: '*La zia del Signore Bernard Shawa?*' '*Si, signore.*' We still felt a need for verification, and repeated it in other languages: '*La tante de Monsieur Bernard Shaw?*' '*Die Tante von Herrn Bernard Shaw?*' '*Tetka od Gospodina Bernarda Shawa?*' This was the hour for which Olendorff has waited a hundred years. Always the gardener nodded; and there, on the tomb, which indeed had a blue-veined elegance not inappropriate to Bernard Shaw himself, there was carved 'Jane Shaw.' But before we could find out how she came to be there, the dark young man was suddenly amongst us again, shouting at the top of his voice.

He had found, it seemed, a notice behind some creepers, on a wall, stating that the price of admission to the castle was five dinars, and we had all been charged ten. A dinar is about a penny; and I fancy that there was some reasonable explanation of the incident, the tariff had changed. But the young man was terribly enraged. All the resentment that most people feel in their whole lives is not greater than what he felt on this one point. '*Zehn dinar!*' he cried, speaking in German so that we might understand and collaborate with him in fury. '*Zehn dinar ist viel, zehn dinar ist zu teuer, ist viel zu teuer!*' He switched back to Serbo-Croat, so that he could make his accusations against the gardener with the unhampered vigour of a man using his native tongue. 'You are an Austrian!' he screamed at him. 'You are an Italian!' Rage ran through his whole body and out of his tongue. It was plainly an exercised gift, a precious function proudly developed. His gift mastered him, he could not endure the iniquity of this place; he had to leave us. Shouting protests to an invisible person, leaping higher and higher as if to keep in contact with his own soaring cries, he rushed away from us away from the castle of the Frankopans, towards the place where the house of innocence had rested for what appears to have been the insufficient period of three years and seven months.

'Maniac,' said the Frenchman. 'Frightful!' said his wife. 'Savages!' said the German couple. They were wrong. He was simply

the product of Dalmatian history: the conquest of Illyria by
Rome, of Rome by the barbarians; then three hundred years of
conflict between Hungary and Venice; then four hundred years
of oppression by Venice, with the war against Turkey running
concurrently for most of that time; a few years of hope under
France, frustrated by the decay of Napoleon; a hundred years of
muddling misgovernment by Austria. In such a shambles a man
had to shout and rage to survive.

Let me try to understand the plight of this people. Because this
is a story that no Westerner can know of himself, no Englishman,
no American. Let us consider what the Frankopans were. They
are said to have been of Italian origin, to be affiliated with the
Frangipani family of Rome; but that is almost certainly a late
invention. They were typical Dalmatian nobles: of unknown
origin, probably aliens who had come down on the Slavs when
these were exhausted by barbarian invasions, and were themselves
of barbarian blood. Certainly they owed their ascendancy not to
virtue nor to superior culture, but to unusual steadfastness in
seeing that it was always the other man who was beheaded or
tossed from the window or smothered. They lived therefore in
an agony of fear. They were liable to armed attack by Vienna
or Hungary if ever they seemed to be favouring one rather than
the other. Their properties were temptations to pirates. Their
followers, and even their own families, were themselves living
in continual fear, and were therefore apt to buy their safety by
betraying their overlord to his strongest enemy; so overlords
could trust nobody. We know a great deal about one Count Ivan
Frankopan, in the fifteenth century. He was the eldest of nine
sons: the other eight all conspired against him. To protect himself
he used a device common in that age of legalist division: he made
the Venetian Republic his heir. Thus it was not to the advantage
of his brothers, or any other private person, to assassinate him.
But when he seized the fortresses of two of his brothers he found
that they were protected by a similar testamentary precaution; they
had made the Count of Hungary their heir. He fled across the sea
to an island named Krk, which was his. Then he went mad. He
conceived the idea that he must have an infinite amount of money
to save him from disaster. He robbed his peasants of their last coins.
He murdered refugees who landed on his island in flight from the
Turk, for the sake of their little stores. The Venetian Commissioner
was ceded the island by its horrified inhabitants on condition that
he take the poor lunatic away.

The bare hills around the castle told us what followed that:

four centuries of selfish exploitation. Then, with the French occupation, there was hope. The gardener showed us with pride a neat nineteenth-century neo-classical temple, built with the fidelity to antique classicism that does not deceive the eye for an instant, so obvious is it that the builders belonged to a later civilization that had learned to listen to orchestral music and to drink tea from fine cups. There is a cross at the apex of the pediment and two well-bosomed matrons sit on its slopes, one decapitated by an idiot bomb dropped by one of d'Annunzio's planes when he was holding Sushak's neighbour, Fiume. Across the frieze of this temple is written '*Mir Yunaka*,' which I translated to my husband perhaps more often than was absolutely necessary, for I am delighted with my minute knowledge of the Serbian language. Peace to the Heroes, it means. This temple was erected during the French occupation which gave Dalmatia a peace for eight years. Eight years out of all time. No longer.

For in 1806 Napoleon had still much of his youthful genius. It made him take over this territory after he had defeated Austria, and found the two provinces of High and Low Illyria that comprised Croatia, and Dalmatia, and Slovenia, as well as the Slav districts behind Trieste that are now Italian. He had the idea of forming a civilized Slav state, to include in time the Christian provinces of Turkey, which should make South-Eastern Europe stable, pacific, and pro-French. He made Marshal Marmont the Governor of these Illyrian provinces, and it was an excellent appointment. Though Marmont was a self-satisfied prig, he was an extremely competent and honourable man, and he loved Dalmatia. His passion for it was so great that in his memoirs, his style, which was by nature dropsically pompous, romps along like a boy when he writes of his Illyria. He fell in love with the Slavs; he defended them against their Western critics. They were not lazy, he said indignantly, they were hungry. He fed them, and set them to build magnificent roads along the Adriatic, and crowed like a cock over the accomplishment. They were not savages, either, he claimed: they had had no schools, and he built them plenty. When he saw they were fervent in piety, he fostered their religious institutions, though he himself conceived faith as buckram to stiffen the Army Regulations.

Marmont would have spent all his life in paternal service of Dalmatia had his been the will that determined this phase of history. But he could achieve less and less as time went on, and when he resigned in 1811 the commerce of the country was in ruins, the law courts were paralysed by corruption, the people were stripped to the skin by tax-collectors, and there was no sort of civil liberty. For he was only Marmont, a good and just and sensible man whom no one would call great. But none denied the greatness of Napoleon, who was neither good, nor just, nor sensible.

There is a school of historians today who claim with semi-erotic ardour that Napoleon's benevolence and wisdom never failed. It is hard to know how this view can survive a reading of his correspondence with Marmont on the subject of the Illyrian provinces. The style of his letters is curiously frivolous and disagreeable. He addresses Marmont with the provocative mock insolence of a homosexual queen; and there is nothing in the content to redeem this impression. By this time he had forgotten everything about his empire except the crown. He showed complete indifference to the welfare of the French troops he had left in Dalmatia, and refused to sanction the expenditure Marmont insisted was necessary to keep them healthy in this barren coast of extreme weather, and he was completely unresponsive to Marmont's desire to build up a virile and loyal population and bring it into the fold of civilization. As time went on, he ignored Marmont's letters altogether, and his exchequer grudged every halfpenny sent to Dalmatia. Finally, for no other purpose than pure offensiveness, he re-drafted the constitution of the provinces and reduced the post of Governor to a mere prefectship. Marmont could do nothing but resign and go back to the Army. Yet he was a born colonial administrator, and this is one of the rarest forms of genius.

The men Napoleon sent to Dalmatia to replace Marmont prove his odd sluttishness. First was General Bertrand, who was later to share his Emperor's captivity on St. Helena. He deserved it for his treatment of the Dalmatians. To a race of mystics, who had been granted a special revelation of Christianity, because they had had to defend it against Islam, he applied the petty and shallow proscriptions of French eighteenth-century anti-clericalism. On these same mystics, who were also, though the West lacked the scholarship to know it, accomplished jurists, dowered with laws and customs springing from ancient tradition and beautifully adapted to local necessities, he forced the new legislative cure-all, the Code Napoléon. But Bertrand was far better than his successor. Junot, the Duke of Abrantès, brought his career to its only possible climax at the Governor's palace in the delicious Slovenian town of Lyublyana. He gave a state ball, and came down the great marble staircase, under the blazing chandeliers, stark naked and raving mad. But there was yet to come Fouché, the Duke of Otranto: a renegade priest, one of the most pitiless butchers of the Revolution, and in his capacity as the Minister of Police the worst of all traitors, Judas only excepted. He loathed Napoleon yet loved him, was never loyal to him, yet could never bring himself to betray him finally. There was here some nasty coquetry of spirit, some purulent corruption of love. Because his master was by then a beaten man, Fouché came out to Dalmatia in a yeast of loyalty, and indeed was inspired to glorious courage. In this far country, while Napoleon's future crumbled in the West, Fouché acted all day the secure administrator and dawdled through the routine of governorship, and by night worked with frenzy on the plans for evacuation. 'Step by step, therefore, without losses,' writes one of his biographers, 'he withdraws to Venice, bringing away intact or almost intact from the short-lived Illyria, its officials, its funds, and much valuable material.' All very marvellous; but not by any accountancy could it be judged honest to withdraw 'funds and much valuable material' from that hungry country, which had beggared itself saving the West from the Turkish invasion.

I did not wonder that the young man shouted as he ran down the road, shouted as if he must go mad, did not the world at last abandon its bad habit and resolve into mercy, justice, and truth.

Senj

The next morning we woke early, prodigiously early, so that before we embarked on our little steamer we could cross the bridge over the river that leads from Sushak to Fiume. There we found a town that has the quality of a dream, a bad headachy dream. Its original character is rotund and sunburnt and solid, like any pompous southern port, but it has been hacked by treaties into a surrealist form. On a ground plan laid out plainly by sensible architects for sensible people, there is imposed another, quite imbecile, which drives high walls across streets and thereby sets contiguous houses half an hour apart by detour and formality. And at places where no frontiers could possibly be, in the middle of a square, or on a bridge linking the parts of a quay, men in uniform step forward and demand passports, minatory as figures projected into sleep by an uneasy conscience.

'This has meant,' said my husband as we wandered through the impeded city, 'infinite suffering to a lot of people,' and it is true. Because of it many old men have said to their sons, 'We are ruined,' many lawyers have said to widows, 'I am afraid there will be nothing, nothing at all.' All this suffering is due, to a large part, to English inefficiency. The Treaty of London, signed by the Allies and Italy in 1915, was intended as a bribe to induce the Italians to come into the war on the Allied side, and it promised them practically the whole Adriatic seaboard of the Austro-Hungarian Empire and all but one of the Adriatic islands. It was made by Lord Oxford and Lord Grey, and it reflected the greatest discredit on them and on the officials of the Foreign Office. For it handed over to a new foreign yoke the Slav inhabitants of this territory, who were longing to rise in revolt against the Central Powers in support of the Allies; and an Italian occupation of the Adriatic coast was a threat to the safety of Serbia, who of all the Allies had made the most sacrifices. These were good reasons why the Italians should not have Dalmatia, and there were no reasons why they should, for the Italian population was negligible.

Mercifully the Treaty of London was annulled at Versailles, largely through the efforts of Lloyd George and President Wilson. But it had done its work. It had given Italian greed a cue for inordinacy; it started her wheedling and demanding and snatching. So she claimed Fiume on the ground that the inhabitants were

Italian, and proved it by taking a census of the town, excluding one part which housed twenty-five per cent of the population. The Italian Government was discouraged by European opinion from acting on that peculiar proof, but thereafter d'Annunzio marched his volunteers into Fiume, in an adventure which, in mindlessness, violence, and futility exactly matched his deplorable literary works, and plunged it into anarchy and bloodshed. He was made to leave it, but the blackmail had been started. Yugoslavia had to buy peace, and in 1920 she conceded Italy the capital of Dalmatia, Zara, three Dalmatian islands, and the hinterland behind Trieste, and she entered into arrangements concerning Fiume which, in the end, left the port as it is.

All this is embittering history for a woman to contemplate. I will believe that the battle of feminism is over, and that the female has reached a position of equality with the male, when I hear that a country has allowed itself to be turned upside-down and led to the brink of war by its passion for a totally bald woman writer. Years ago, in Florence, I had marvelled over the singular example of male privilege afforded by d'Annunzio. Leaning from a balcony in the Lung' arno I had looked down on a triumphal procession. Bells rang, flags were waved; flowers were thrown, voices swelled in ecstasy; and far below an egg reflected the rays of the May sunshine. Here in Fiume the bald author had been allowed to ruin a city: a bald-headed authoress would never be allowed to build one. Scowling, I went on the little steamer that was taking us and twenty other passengers and as many cattle and sheep southwards to the island of Rab, and we set off in a cold dither of spray.

The bare hills shone like picked bones. I fell asleep, for we had risen at six. Then my husband shook me by the shoulder and said, 'You must come up on deck. This is Senj.' I followed him and stared at the port, which was like many others in Spain and Italy: from the quayside high buttoned-up houses washed in warm colours and two or three campaniles struggled up a hill towards a ruined fortress, the climbing mass girt in by city walls. I groaned, remembering that the climbing mass certified man to be not only incompetent but beastly, that here the great powers had mocked out of their own fullness at another's misery and had shown neither gratitude nor mercy.

Senj was the home of the Uskoks. These are not animals invented by Edward Lear. They were refugees. They were refugees like the Jews and Roman Catholics and liberals driven out by Hitler. They found, as these have done, that when one door closed on them others that should have been open suddenly were not. These were driven out of their homes, out of the fellowship of Christendom, out of the world of virtue, into an accursed microcosm where there was only sin. They were originally Slavs of blameless character who fled before the Turks as they swept over Bulgaria and Serbia and Bosnia, and formed a strange domestic army, consisting of men, women, and children, that fought many effective rearguard actions over a period of many years. Finally they halted at the pass over the Dalmatian mountains, behind the great port of Split, and for five years from 1532 they held back the Turks single-handed. Then suddenly they were told by their Christian neighbours to abandon the position. Venice, which had just signed a pact with Turkey, and was a better friend to her than Christian historians like to remember, convinced Austria that it would be wise to let Turkey have the pass as a measure of appeasement.

Then the Uskoks came down to the coast and settled in this little town of Senj, and performed a remarkable feat. Up till then they had displayed courage and resolution of an unusual order. But they now showed signs of genius. Some of them were from the southern coast of Dalmatia, down by Albania, but most of them were inland men. In any case they can have had few marine officers. But in a short time they had raised themselves to the position of a naval power.

This was not a simple matter of savage daring. The Uskoks had unusual talent for boat-building. They devised special craft to suit the special needs of the Dalmatian coast, which resembled those with which the ancient Illyrians used to vex the Roman fleet: light boats that could navigate the creeks and be drawn up on the beach where there was no harbour. They also developed extraordinary powers of seamanship which enabled them to take advantage of the situation of Senj. Just here the channel between the mainland and the island of Krk widens to ten miles or so, which makes a fairway for the north wind, and it meets another channel that runs past the tail of the island to the open sea, so the seas roar rougher here than elsewhere on the coast. It was so when we came into Senj; a wave larger than any we had met before slapped against the quay. The Uskoks developed a technique of using this hard weather as a shield against their enemies, while they ran through it unperturbed. Therefore they chased the Turkish ships up and down the Adriatic, stripped them, and sank them; and year by year they grew cleverer at the game. This success was amazing, considering they numbered at most two thousand souls. If the Venetian fleet had been directed by men of the quality of the Uskoks the Turks might have been driven out of European waters, which would have meant out of Europe, in the middle of the sixteenth century.

Venice, however, was in her decline, which was really more spiritual than economic. Her tragedies were due to maladministration and indecisive politics rather than to actual lack of means.

She tried to placate Turkey in another way. She stopped attacking her at sea. To the Uskoks this capitulation of the great Christian powers must have seemed the last word in treachery. They had, within the memory of all those among them who were middle-aged or over, been driven from their homes by the Turks in atrocious circumstances; and they had believed that in harrying the Turks they were not only avenging their wrongs but were serving God and His Son. They had often been blessed by the Church for their labours, and Gregory XIII had even given them a large subsidy. But now they were treated as enemies of Christendom, for no other crime than attacking its enemies. And not only were they betrayed in the spirit, they were betrayed in the body. How were they to live? Till then they had provided for themselves, quite legitimately, since the Turks had dispossessed them of all their homes, by booty from Turkish ships. But now all that was over. The Christian powers had no suggestions to make. The plight of a refugee, then as now, provoked the feeling that surely he could get along somehow. There was nothing for the Uskoks to do except defy Venice and Austria, and attack their ships and the Turks' alike.

It seems certain that to see the story of the Uskoks thus is not to flatter them. For nearly thirty years they lived in such a state of legitimate and disciplined warfare that they attacked only Turkish ships. It is not until 1566 that there is the first record of an Uskok attack on a Christian ship. Thereafter, of course, the story is very different. They became gangsters of the sea. They developed all the characteristics of gunmen: a loyalty that went unbroken to the death, unsurpassable courage, brutality, greed, and, oddly enough, thriftlessness. Just as a Chicago racketeer who has made an income of five figures for many years will leave his widow penniless, so the Uskoks, who helped themselves to the richest loot the sea ever carried, always fell into penury if they survived to old age. Also they were looted, as thieves often are, by the honest. It is said that they bribed the very highest Austrian officials, even in the seat of government itself at Graz; and that a Jewish merchant might recognize there on a great lady's breast a jewel which he had seen snatched by a robber's hand on the Adriatic. Because of this traffic, it is alleged, the Austrians did little to restrain the Uskoks after they had become pirates. In any case it is certain that Venetian officials often bought the Uskoks' prizes from them and marketed them at a profit in Venice.

In a very short time the moral confusion of these people was complete. At Christmas and Easter every year there were expeditions financed by the whole of Senj. Everybody, the officials, the soldiers, the private families, the priests and monks, paid their share of the expenses and drew a proportionate share of the booty. The Church received its tithe. This would be funny if murder had not been a necessary part of such expeditions, and if barbarity did not spread from heart to heart as fire runs from tree to tree in a forest in summer. Some of the later exploits of the Uskoks turn the stomach; they would knife a living enemy, tear out his heart, and eat it. Not only did the perpetrators of these acts lose their own souls, but the whole level of Slav morality was debased, for the Dalmatian peasant knew the Uskok's origin and could not blame him. And the infection spread more widely. All the villains of Europe heard that there was good sport to be had in the Adriatic, and the hardier hurried to Senj. It testifies to the unwholesomeness of Renaissance Europe that some of these belonged to the moneyed classes. When a party of Uskoks were hanged in Venice in 1618 nine of them were Englishmen, of whom five were gentlemen in the heraldic sense of the word, and another was a member of one of the noblest families in Great Britain.

It is sometimes very hard to tell the difference between history and the smell of skunk. Both Venice and Austria used the degradation of these men as extra aces in their cheating game. The Austrians pretended to want to suppress them, but rather liked to have them harrying Venice. Venice sacrificed them to her friendship with Turkey, but that friendship was a sham; she never really wept over those Turkish ships. Also she liked to have a legitimate source of grievance against Austria. The insincerity of both parties was proven by their refusal to grant the Uskoks' demand, which was constantly presented during a period of fifty years, that they should be transported to some inland place and given a chance to maintain themselves either by tilling the soil or by performing military duties. Again and again the poor wretches explained that they had no means of living except by piracy, and that they would abandon it at once if they were shown any other way of getting food. But Venice and Austria, though one was still wealthy and the other was becoming wealthier every day, haggled over the terms of each settlement and let it go. Once there was put forward a scheme of selling the forests of pine and beech that in those days still grew round Senj, and using the proceeds to build fortresses on the Austrian frontiers which would be manned by Uskoks. It fell through because neither power would agree to make an initial payment amounting to something like fifty pounds. At the same time the Uskoks were not allowed to go to any country which was prepared to make room for them. They were strictly forbidden to enlist in foreign service. They were shut up in piracy as in jail by powers that affected to feel horror at their crimes.

In the end their problem was settled in the course of an odd war between Austria and Venice, in which the Uskoks were used as a pretext by several people who wanted a fight. This war, which was almost nothing and led to nothing, lasted three years and must have brought an infinity of suffering to the wretched Dalmatian peasant. But, mercifully, as it was supposed to be about the Uskoks, the Peace Treaty had to deal with them. A good many were hanged and beheaded and the rest were transported, as they themselves had requested for fifty years, to the interior. But the method of their transport was apparently unkind. There were no stout fortresses built for them, or hopeful villages, for no certain trace of them can be found. Some say their descendants are to be found on the Alps at the very southern end of Austria; others have thought to recognize them on the slopes of a mountain in North Italy. It is to be feared that their seed was scattered on stony ground. That is sad, for the seed was precious.

We went down to the little dining-saloon and had a good, simple, coarse, well-flavoured luncheon. Opposite us sat a young man, handsome and angry, the very spit and image of the one at Trsat who had cried out to his God about the ten dinars; and indeed they were of the same breed. For this one thrust away his plate as soon as it was brought to him with a gesture of fury. 'This soup is cold!' he shouted, his brows a thick straight line. 'This soup is as cold as the sea!' But he was not shouting at the soup. He was shouting at the Turks, at the Venetians, at the Austrians, at the French, and at the Serbs (if he was a Croat) or at the Croats (if he was a Serb). It was good that he shouted. I respected him for it. In a world where during all time giants had clustered to cheat his race out of all their goods, his forefathers had survived because they had the power to shout, to reject cold soup, death, sentence to piracy, exile on far mountain slopes.

Rab

The sea was green and hard as glass; the crests of the waves were *chevaux de frise* between us and a horizon of pure, very pale-green light, and dark-bronze islands. Our destination, the isle of Rab, lay before us, its mountains bare as Krk, its shores green as spring itself. As we came closer to it my husband said, 'It is only scrub, of course, low woods and scrub.' But a little later he exclaimed, 'Only scrub, indeed! Just smell it! Well, I have heard of this but I never quite believed it.' It was still distant by half a mile or so, but the scent of myrtle and rosemary and thyme was as strong and soothing a delight as sunshine. Through this lovely invisible cloud we rode slowly into the harbour of Rab, and found ourselves in one of the most beautiful cities of the world. It is very little. One can see it all at once, as if it were a single building; and that sight gives a unique pleasure. Imagine finding a place where one heard perpetually a musical phrase which was different every time one moved a few steps, and was always exquisite. At Rab something comparable happens to the sight. The city covers a ridge overlooking the harbour. It is built of stone which is sometimes silver, sometimes at high noon and sunset, rose and golden, and in the shadow sometimes blue and lilac, but is always fixed in restraint by its underlying whiteness. It is dominated by four campaniles, set at irregular intervals along the crest of the ridge. From whatever point one sees it these campaniles fall into a perfect relationship with each other and the city. We sat under a pine tree on the shore and ate oranges, and the city lay before us, making a statement that was not meaningless because it was not made in words. There we undressed and swam out fifty yards, and we stopped and trod water, because the town was making another lovely statement. From every yard of the channel that divides it from its neighbour islands, from every yard of the roads that wind among the inland farms and olive terraces to the bald mountains in the centre of the island, the city can be seen making one of an infinite series of statements. Yet it achieves this expressiveness with the simplest of means: a grey horizontal oblong with four smaller vertical oblongs rising from it. Euclid never spoke more simply.

This island is within sight of the barbarized home of the Frankopans, is set in a sea polluted by the abominations of the Turks and the Uskoks. It is therefore astonishing that there is

nothing accidental about the beauty of Rab; that in the fissure of
this bare land there should be art and elegance of the most refined
and conscious sort. Though Rab is no larger than many villages, it
is a city, a focus of culture, a fantasy made by man when he could
do more with his head and hands than is absolutely necessary for
survival. There is a noble white square by the harbour, where
balconies are supported by tiers of three lions set one upon
another, pride upon pride, and façades are aristocratic in their
very proportions, being broad enough to be impressive yet not
too broad for respect towards neighbouring properties. From this
square streets run up to the ridge of the town or along its base; and
the richness of the doorways and windows and columns makes each
seem a passage in some private magnificence. In one doorway stone
grows as fern fronds above the pilasters, enwreaths with flowers
a coat of arms, and edges the shield above with forms delicate
as wheat-ears. Above another doorway, opening into a cloistered
garden, cupids hold ropes of laurel flowing from a shield and
helmet on which an eagle broods. One cupid holds forth his rope of
laurel with a gesture that expresses the ambition of the Renaissance.
'To humanity be the kingdom, the power, and the glory.' Each of
these doorways has begun to feel the weight of five centuries; in
the first the columns are straddling apart, in the second a stone
has fallen and left a gap through which a flower pokes a scarlet
head. But this shabbiness, which is not at all tainted by dirt, is
very much what a great emperor might permit in the homelier parts
of his palace.

There is the same sense of private magnificence about the Cathedral of Rab. On the ridge there is a little square, with bastions and
cliffs falling deeply to the shore on the further side; between the tall
soldierly flowers of the aloes and the swords of their leaves the eyes
fall on the sea and its scattered islands. Here stands the cathedral
built of rose and white marble in alternate courses, ornamented
with blind arches of a lovely span. It is no bigger than many a
private chapel; and it has an air of not knowing what strangers are.
That was the theory. Without, the horror, the pirate, the Turk;
within, an enclosed community within an enclosed community, a
small city upon an island. One arranges one's house with a certain
lavishness and confidence when one believes that it is going to be
visited only by familiars, and this Cathedral is therefore at once
domestic and elegant. It is Venetian in spirit, which is not to say
that it is actually the work of Venetian hands: our English Norman
and Gothic churches derive from France but were not built by
Frenchmen. It recalls the bone-white architectural backgrounds

of Carpaccio and Bellini, that delicate frame of a world which is at once pious and playful, luxurious and simple-minded. Its interior might have been designed by a maker of masks, who with infinite reverence conceived the high mass as the supreme mask. The stage is set high above the onlookers: six high steps lead up to the choir, where stalls of heraldic pomp indicate that those who sit there are the servants of a great lord, and another flight mounts to the altar, which is sheltered and magnified by a tall baldacchino.

This is a part of an older church, a thousand years old, built in the time of Slav independence. It is one of the utmost elegance imaginable. Its six supporting columns are of fine cipollino marble, and its canopy is carved from one great block of stone, but it is weightless as a candle-flame because of the exquisiteness of its design and execution. Round its six arches are garlands carved more finely than the emblems on the patricians' doorways in the town below, which is as it should be, since this is the palace of the patrician above all patricians. The pyramided roof of the baldacchino is painted a tender red, the vault above it is painted a tender blue, just such colours as grace the festivities of a much later Venice in the paintings of Paolo Veronese. The community that built this Cathedral was so civilized that it could conceive a God who would be pleased not by the howlings of His worshippers and the beating of their breasts, but by their gaiety, by their accomplishment, by their restraint and dignity. At one time the island of Rab paid an annual tribute to the Doge of ten pounds of silk. In this building it paid a tribute of silken elegance to the Doge of Doges.

Because it was noon they came to close the Cathedral. We went out blinking into the sunlight, which for a moment was falling strong between thunderclouds; and a group of women smiled at us and gave us some greetings in Italian, though they were visibly not Italian. For they were completely lacking in Latin facility. They had that flat, unfeigned, obstinate look about the cheekbones, which is the mark of the Slav, and their bodies were unpliable. But they were not of a harsh race that had usurped the home of gentler beings perished through gentleness. These people, and none other, had made Rab. Over the Cathedral doorway the builders had set a Pietà, a Madonna holding her dead son in her arms, and she was as these women. With a stiff spine, with her chin high, she sits and holds a Christ that is dead, truly dead—for if he were not, where would be the occasion for all the excitement?—dead as mutton, dead as the skinned lamb which one of the women was holding like a baby. This Madonna is as sorrowful as sorrow; her son is dead

as death. There is here the fullest acceptance of tragedy, there is
no refusal to recognize the essence of life, there is no attempt to
pretend that the bitter is the sweet. One must not pull wool over
the eyes if one is in danger; for it goes badly with one when the
sword falls unless one has a philosophy which has contemplated
the fact of death.

Above our heads a bell gave out the hour, and I jumped with
surprise. The women laughed indulgently, sleepily; there was a
semblance of noon heat settling down on the city. It was the
Campanile of St. Christopher, the most beautiful of the four towers
of Rab. It is said of the big bell, as it is said of many old ones, that
when it was being cast the citizens came to the foundry and dropped
their gold and silver ornaments into the melting-pot; and certainly
its tone is much mollified for metal; it might be the voice of a dove
that had grown old and great and wise. Leaning back against the
wall of a palace and looking up at the campanile my husband said:
'Look at the thing. It is made on a Euclidean recipe. There are four
stories. On the lowest is a doorway. On the next are on each wall
two windows, each divided by a shaft. On the next there are two
windows, each divided by two columns; on the highest there is
one window divided by three columns; above that is a balustrade
of seventeen columns, every fifth one somewhat stouter. Above is
the spire. How did that man who built this tower seven hundred
years ago know that these severe shapes would affect my eyes as a
chime of joy-bells would affect my ear? He must have been a man of
incredible cunning to make this stony promise of a fluid world, this
geometric revelation of a universe in which there is not an angle.'

Out in the country round the city of Rab there are no revelations.
There is a mystery. It is formulated also in stone, but not in worked
stone, in the terrible naked stone of Dalmatia, in the terrible earth
that here lies shallow and infirm of purpose as dust, and in the
terrible faces of the people, who are all like crucified Christs.
Everywhere there are terraces. High up on the bare mountains
there are olive terraces; in the valleys there are olive terraces; in the
trough of the valleys there are walled fields where an ordinary crop
of springing corn or grass strikes one as an abnormal profusion like
a flood. On these enclosures black figures work frenetically. From
a grey sky reflected light pours down and makes of every terrace
and field a stage on which these black figures play each their special
drama of toil, of frustration, of anguish. As we passed by on the
stony causeway, women looked up at us, from the fields, their faces
furrowed with all known distresses. By their sides lambs skipped
in gaiety and innocence, and goats skipped in gaiety but without

innocence, and at their feet the cyclamens shone mauve; the beasts and flowers seemed fortunate because they are not human, as those who have passed within the breath of a plague and have escaped it. From the olive terraces the men looked down with faces contracted by the greatest effort conceivable; and the trees they stood upon, though the droughts of summer and the salt hurricanes of winter had twisted them to monstrous corkscrews, also seemed fortunate by comparison. Sometimes we met people on these causeways who begged from us without abjectness, without anything but hunger. Their lean hands came straight out before them. Their clothes asked alms louder than they did, making it plain that here were the poorest of creatures, peasants who had not the means to make a peasant costume, to proclaim that in their village they had skill and taste and their own way of looking at things. They wore undifferentiated black rags.

Here, out in the country, the islanders spoke Serbo-Croat; half an hour from the city gates we found peasants who knew only a few words of Italian. These are true, gaunt Slavs, wholly without facility, with that Slav look of being intuitionally aware of the opposite of the state in which they found themselves at the moment, and therefore being more painfully affected by it if it were disagreeable. The poor have at the back of their sunken eyes a shining picture of wealth, the sick know what it is to be sound, and as the unhappy weep the scent of happiness dilates their nostrils. This unfamiliar way of bearing misery gave them a certain unity in our eyes; but there were also marked differences between them, which were terrible because they depended to such a startling degree on the geographical variations, necessarily not very great, which can be observed here within a few hundred yards of each other. That we noticed on our first walk in the island. We followed a stony causeway along the barren lower slopes of a ridge that ran towards an estuary, and there the people who were working on the fields and who begged from us were thin and slow-moving, glaring in misery. Then we came to a village set on firm ground above the estuary, which could draw on the wealth of both the sea and the rich earth among the river's mouth; and here the people were stouter and brisker.

And so it was throughout our walk, rich, poor, rich, poor. Once we found ourselves on the shore of a land-locked bay, broken with a magnificent cliff, round which there was plainly no road at all. We came on an old man in patched clothes sitting under a pine tree watching some goats, on a little headland made into a harbour by a few blocks of stone. He concerned himself in our plight as if he were our host. It was inconceivable that he could have begged from us. There came presently a young fisherman in a rowing-boat, who rowed us across waters that were swimming with the first sunset colours to the village on the other side of the bay, and took his just fare, and would not have taken money for any other cause.

But when we had walked half a mile or so from where we landed we were on barren and wind-swept lands again, and we met an old man, who was like the old man on the headland as one pea and another, and he was begging shamelessly and very pitifully. He had gathered some flowers from the hedgerows and stood there in the dusk on the chance of some tourist coming along, which might justly be called an off-chance, as all the tourists on the island were middle-aged Germans who never moved a mile from the city. All this part was very poor. We met ragged and listless men and women hurrying through the twilight without zest, leaden-footed with hunger. Nevertheless there bloomed suddenly before us the lovely gallant human quality of fantasy, which when necessity binds it down with cords leaps up and exercises its choice where it would have seemed there was nothing to choose, which in destitution dares to prefer this to that and likes its colours bright. We came on a group that was standing lapped in pleasure all across the causeway in front of a young man who was showing off his new suit. They were peering at it and fingering it and exclaiming over it, as well they might, for though it was conventionally tailored in Western fashion it was cut from emerald velveteen. It was the time of dusk when colours liquefy and clot, when in a garden the flowers become at once more solid and more glowing; the suit was a pyre of green flame, about which the black figures pressed insubstantially, yet with ecstatic joy.

The poverty of the island was made plainer still to us the next day. Our first expedition had been over the northern part of the island, which is more or less protected from the north wind by high ground; but this time we walked to the south, where there is no shelter from the blast that rakes the channel between Rab and its neighbour island. Here is a land and a people that are not only grim but desperate. Most of the houses are very large; some of them are almost fortress size, for the customs of land tenure make it convenient for a whole family to live under the same roof, even to several degrees of cousinship. There is something specially terrifying about a house that is very big and very poor, a Knole or Blenheim of misery. At the dark open door of one such home, that seemed to let out blackness rather than let in light, there waited a boy of seven or eight with flowers in his hand for the tourist. My husband thrust down into his pocket, brought up three dinars and one half-dinar, and peered to see what they were. The child shuddered with suspense, broke down, put out his little hand and snatched, and ran into the house. But he had not snatched the four coins. He had snatched just one dinar; his fear had been lest my husband should give him the half-dinar. Later we passed a blind beggar, crouched on a bank with a little girl beside him. To him we gave ten dinars, that is tenpence. The little girl shook him and shouted into his ear and gave him the coin to feel, and then shook him again, furious that he could not realize the miraculous good fortune that had befallen him; but he went on muttering in complaint.

The most heartrending figure we saw was not mendicant. It was a woman, middle-aged and of dignified physique, who was sitting on a stone wall, some distance from the road, in an attitude of despair. When we passed the place on our return, half an hour later, she was still sitting there. And there was here too an outbreak of fantasy, of the human capacity for laughter and wonder and invention. At a fork in the path near by we found a knot of men pausing for gossip, and turning aside from their talk to laugh at the antics of the lambs they were leading to market. They dropped an amused eye on the pale butter-coloured waves in the white lambs' fleeces, the nigger-brown waves in the black lambs' fleeces, on the nearly closed curves the lambs described when they leaped clear off the ground and silly fore-paws dangling from a young and flexible backbone almost met silly hind-paws. These people have not been anæsthetized by loutishness.

The day we left the island we climbed its highest peak. We were led by a well-mannered and intelligent man, whose rags were wretched, though he lived in a huge house and was evidently co-heir to a property of some extent. At the top there was a glory of clean salt air, and intense but unwounding light; for here we are not so far from Greece, where the light is a benediction, and one can go out at noon till near high summer without wearing glasses. Below us lion-coloured islands lay in a dark-blue sea. To the east the mainland raised violet-grey mountains to a dense superior continent of white clouds; to the west the long outer islands lay like the scrolls angels hold up in holy pictures. We leaned on a gate. It was necessary; for the first time I was on a hill where it was impossible to find a place to sit down without inflicting on oneself innumerable sharp wounds. As we rested we tried to account for the state of the island. There is no apparent reason why it should be so poor. There is plenty of fish in this part of the Adriatic, including very good mackerel; there are many parts of the island where oil and wine and corn can be produced, and sheep and swine can be raised. It is said that the population is too lazy to work. There was in the city of Rab a Viennese Jew who managed a photographic store, and he told us that. 'They would rather beg than put their hands to a plough,' he had said, but his spectacles gleamed with smug pleasure as he spoke, and he was expressing nothing but adherence to the disposition of the German subjects of the Austrian Empire to hate and despise all subjects of other races. A Serb doctor who was working in Rab told us that the islanders could not be expected to work on the food they got; and I remembered that Marmont wrote in his memoirs that the laziness of the Dalmatians was notorious, but entirely disappeared when he set them down to build roads on regular and adequate rations.

The reason for the island's melancholy lies not in its present but in its past. It is only now, since the war, since Dalmatia became a part of a Slav state, that it has had a chance to enjoy the proper benefits of its economic endowment; and since then there have been such overwhelming catastrophes in the world market that no community could live without tragic discomfort unless it could fall back on accumulations which it had stored in earlier days. That Rab has never been able to do. Some of the factors which have hindered her have been real acts of God, not to be circumvented by man. She has been ravaged by plague. But for the most part what took the bread out of Rab's mouth was empire. The carelessness and cruelty that infects any power when it governs a people not its own without safeguarding itself by giving the subjects the largest possible amount of autonomy, afflicted this island with hunger and thirst. Venice made it difficult for Dalmatian fishermen to make their profit in the only way it could be made before the day of refrigeration; the poor wretches could not salt their fish, because salt was a state monopoly and was not only extremely expensive but badly distributed. Moreover Venice restricted the building of ships in Dalmatia. It was her definite policy to keep the country poor and dependent. She admitted this very frankly, on one occasion, by ordering the destruction of all the mulberry trees which were grown for feeding silk-worms and all the olive trees. This law she annulled, because the Dalmatians threatened an insurrection, but not until a great many of the mulberry trees had been cut down; and indeed she found herself able to attend to the matter by indirect methods. Almost all Dalmatian goods, except corn, which paid an export duty of ten per cent, had to be sold in Venice at prices fixed by the Venetians; but any power that Venice wanted to propitiate,

Austria, Ancona, Naples, Sicily, or Malta, could come and sell its goods on the Dalmatian coast, an unbalanced arrangement which ultimately led to grave currency difficulties. All these malevolent fiscal interferences created an unproductive army of *douaniers*, which in turn created an unproductive army of smugglers.

This was cause enough that Rab should be poor; but there was a further cause which made her poorer still. It is not at all inappropriate that the men and women on these Dalmatian islands should have faces which recall the crucified Christ. The Venetian Republic did not always fight the Turks with arms. For a very long time they contented themselves with taking the edge off the invaders' attack by the payment of immense bribes to the officials and military staff of the occupied territories. The money for these was not supplied by Venice. It was drawn from the people of Dalmatia. After the fish had rotted, some remained sound; after the corn had paid its ten per cent, and the wool and the wine and the oil had been haggled down in the Venetian market, some of its price returned to the vender. Of this residue the last ducat was extracted to pay the tribute to the Turks. These people of Dalmatia gave the bread out of their mouths to save us of Western Europe from Islam; and it is ironical that so successfully did they protect us that those among us who would be broad-minded, who will in pursuit of that end stretch their minds till they fall apart in idiocy, would blithely tell us that perhaps the Dalmatians need not have gone to that trouble, that an Islamized West could not have been worse than what we are today. Their folly is certified for what it is by the mere sound of the word 'Balkan' with its suggestion of a disorder that defies human virtue and intelligence to accomplish its complete correction. I could confirm that certificate by my own memories: I had only to shut my eyes to smell the dust, the lethargy, the rage and hopelessness of a Macedonian town, once a glory to Europe, that had too long been Turkish. The West has done much that is ill, it is vulgar and superficial and economically sadist; but it has not known that death in life which was suffered by the Christian provinces under the Ottoman Empire. From this the people of Rab had saved me: I should say, are saving me. The woman who sat on the stone wall was in want because the gold which should have been handed down to her had bought my safety from the Turks. Impotent and embarrassed, I stood on the high mountain and looked down on the terraced island where my saviours, small and black as ants, ran here and there, attempting to repair their destiny.

Split I

Split, alone of all cities in Dalmatia, has a Neapolitan air. Except for a few courtyards in its private houses, it does not exhibit the spirit of Venice, which is at once so stately and so materialist, like a proud ghost that has come back to remind men that he failed for a million. It recalls Naples, because it also is a tragic and architecturally magnificent sausage-machine, where a harried people of mixed race have been forced by history to run for centuries through the walls and cellars and sewers of ruined palaces, and have now been evicted by a turn of events into the open day, neat and slick and uniform, taking to modern clothes and manners with the adaptability of oil, though at the same time they are set apart for ever from the rest of the world by the arcana of language and thoughts they learned to share while they scurried for generations close-pressed through the darkness.

Split presents its peculiar circumstances to the traveller the minute he steps ashore. We left the great white liner, the *King Alexander*, that had brought us through the night from Rab, and the history of the place was on our right and our left. On the left was the marine market, where fishing-boats are used for stalls; men who must be a mixture of sailor and retailer bring goods over from the islands, take their boats head-on to the quay, and lay out their wares in little heaps on the prows. Pitiful little heaps they often are, of blemished apples, rags of vegetables, yellowish boards of dried fish, but the men who sell them are not pitiful. They look tough as their own dried fish, and stand by with an air of power and pride. This coast feeds people with other things than food; it grudges them the means of life, but lets them live. On our right was a row of shops, the cafés and rubbisheries which face any port: the houses that rise above them were squeezed between the great Corinthian columns in the outer gallery of Diocletian's palace.

For Split is Diocletian's palace: the palace he built himself in 305, when, after twenty years of imperial office, he abdicated. The town has spread beyond the palace walls, but the core of it still lies within the four gates. Diocletian built it to be within suburban reach of the Roman town of Salonæ, which lies near by on the gentle slopes between the mountains and the coastal plain. The site had already been occupied by a Greek settlement, which was called Aspalaton, from a fragrant shrub still specially abundant here. In the seventh century the Avars, that tribe of barbarian marauders who were to provoke a currency crisis in the Middle Ages because they looted so much gold from Eastern and Central Europe and hoarded it, came down on Dalmatia. They swept down on Salonæ and destroyed it by fire and sword. The greater part of the population was killed, but some had time to flee out to the islands, which gave them the barest refuge. What they suffered in those days from cold and hunger and thirst is still remembered in common legend. In time they crept back to the mainland, and found nothing left more habitable than the ruins of Diocletian's palace. There they made shelters for themselves against the day when there should be peace. They are still there. Peace never came. They were assailed by the Huns, the Hungarians, the Venetians, the Austrians, and some of them would say that with the overcoming of those last enemies they still did not win peace; and during these centuries of strife the palace and the fugitives have established a perfect case of symbiosis. It has housed them, they are now its props. After the war there was a movement to evacuate Split and restore the palace to its ancient magnificence by pulling down the houses that had been wedged in between its walls and columns; but surveyors very soon found out that if they went all Diocletian's work would fall to the ground. The people that go quickly and darkly about the streets have given the stone the help it gave them.

'I would like to go into the palace at once,' said my husband, 'and I greatly wish we could have brought Robert Adam's book of engravings with us.' That thought must occur to many people who go to Split. Adam's book on Diocletian's palace is one of the most entertaining revelations of the origins of our day, pretty in itself and an honour to its author. He came here from Venice in 1757, and made a series of drawings which aimed at showing what the palace had been like at the time of its building, in order to obtain some idea of 'the private edifices of the ancients.' The enterprise took a great deal of perseverance and courage, for all idea of the original plan had been lost centuries before. He had to trace the old walls through the modern buildings, and was often hindered by the suspicions of both the inhabitants and the authorities. The Venetian Governor of the town was quite sure he was a spy and wanted to deport him, but the Commander-in-chief of the Venetian garrison, who happened to be a Scotsman, and one of his Croat officers were sufficiently cultured to recognize Adam for what he was, and they got him permission to carry on his work under the supervision of a soldier.

The indirect results were the best of Georgian architecture, with

its emphasis on space and variety and graceful pomp; often when
we look at a façade in Portman Square or a doorway in Portland
Place, we are looking at Roman Dalmatia. The direct result was
this book of enchanting drawings—some of them engraved by
Bartolozzi—which, though serviceably accurate, are beautiful
examples of the romantic convention's opinion that an artist
should be allowed as much latitude in describing a landscape as
an angler is allowed in describing a fish. The peaks of Dalmatia
are shown as monstrous fencers lunging at the black enemy of
the sky; the Roman cupolas and columns have the supernatural
roundness of a god's attack of mumps; vegetation advances on
ruins like infantry; and peasants in fluent costumes ornament
the foreground with fluent gestures, one poor woman, whom I
specially remember bringing every part of her person into play,
including her bust, in order to sell a fowl to two turbaned
Jews, who like herself are plainly Veronese characters in reduced
circumstances. In the corner of certain drawings are to be seen
Adam himself and his French assistant, Clérisseau, sketching away
in their dashing tricornes and redingotes, very much as one might
imagine the two young men in *Così fan tutte*. It is delightful to find
a book that is a pretty book in the lightest sense, that pleases like a
flower or a sweetmeat, and that is also the foundation for a grave
and noble art which has sheltered and nourished us all our days.

'Yes,' I said to my husband, 'it is disgusting that one cannot
remember pictures and drawings exactly. It would have been
wonderful to have the book by us, and see exactly how the palace
struck a man of two centuries ago, and how it strikes us, who owe
our eye for architecture largely to that man,' 'Then why did we
not bring the book?' asked my husband. 'Well, it weighs just over
a stone,' I said. 'I weighed it once on the bathroom scales.' 'Why did
you do that?' asked my husband. 'Because it occurred to me one day
that I knew the weight of nothing except myself and joints of meat,'
I said, 'and I just picked that up to give me an idea of something
else.' 'Well, well!' said my husband. 'It makes me distrust Fabre
and all other writers on insect life when I realize how mysterious
your proceedings would often seem to a superior being watching
them through a microscope. But tell me, why didn't we bring it,
even if it does weigh a little over a stone? We have a little money to
spare for its transport. It would have given us pleasure. Why didn't
we do it?' 'Well, it would have been no use,' I said; 'we couldn't
have carried anything so heavy as that about the streets.' 'Yes,
we could,' said my husband; 'we could have hired a wheelbarrow
and pushed it about from point to point.' 'But people would have

thought we were mad!' I exclaimed. 'Well, would they?' countered my husband. 'That's just what I'm wondering. In fact, it's what made me pursue the subject. These Slavs think all sorts of things natural that we think odd; nothing seems to worry them so long as it satisfies a real desire. I was wondering if they could take a thing like this in their stride; because after all we feel a real desire to look at Adam's book here.' 'I don't know,' I said, 'but there is Philip Thomson standing in the doorway of our hotel, and we can ask him.'

Philip Thomson teaches English to such inhabitants of Split as wish to learn it. He is a fine-boned, fastidious, observant being, very detached except in his preference for Dalmatia over all other parts of the world, and for Split over all other parts of Dalmatia. We had morning coffee with him, good unnecessary elevenses, in the square outside our hotel, a red stucco copy of a Venetian piazza, with palm trees in it, which is quite a happy effort, and we put the question to him. 'Oh, but they'd think it very odd here, if you went about the streets trundling a book in a wheelbarrow and stopping to look at the pictures in it, very odd indeed,' said Philip. 'You evidently don't understand that here in Split we are very much on parade. We're not a bit like the Serbs, who don't care what they do, who laugh and cry when they feel like it, and turn cartwheels in the street if they want exercise. That's one of the reasons we don't like the Serbs. To us it seems self-evident that a proud man must guard himself from criticism every moment of the day. That's what accounts for the most salient characteristic of the Splitchani, which is a self-flaying satirical humour; better laugh at yourself before anybody else has time to do it. But formality is another result. I suppose it comes of being watched all the time by people who thought they were better than you, the Dalmatians, the Hungarians and the Venetians and the Austrians.'

'But all this,' Philip continued, 'brings to light one very strange thing about Split. Did you notice how I answered you off-hand, as if Split had a perfectly definite character, and I could speak for the whole of its inhabitants? Well, so I could. Yet that's funny, for the old town of Split was a tiny place, really not much more than the palace and a small overflow round its walls, and all this town you see stretching over the surrounding hills and along the coast is new. A very large percentage of the population came here after the war, some to work, some as refugees from the Slav territories which have been given to Italy. Do you see that pretty dark woman who is just crossing the square? She is one of my star pupils and she belongs to a family that left Zara as soon as it was handed over to the Italians, like all the best families of the town. Now Zara has quite a different history, and, from all I hear, quite a different atmosphere. But this woman and her family, and all the others who migrated with her, have been completely absorbed by Split. They are indistinguishable from all the natives, and I have seen them in the process of conversion. It's happened gradually but surely. It's a curious victory for a system of manners that, so far as I can see, has nothing to do with economics. For people here are not rich, yet there is considerable elegance.'

This is, indeed, not a rich city. Later we lunched with Philip in a restaurant which though small was not a mere bistro, which was patronized by handsome and dignified people who were either professional or commercial men. For the sweet course we were given two apiece of palatschinken, those pancakes stuffed with jam which one eats all over Central Europe. The Balkans inherited the recipe from the Byzantines, who ate them under the name of palacountas. We could eat no more than one, for the meal, as almost always in these parts, had been good and abundant. 'Shall I put the palatschinken in paper for the Herrschaft to take home with them?' asked the waiter. We thought not. But the waiter doubted our sincerity. 'Is it because they are strangers,' he asked Philip, 'and do not know that we are always delighted to do this sort of thing for our clients? Down in the new hotels, I fully understand, they would be disagreeable about it, such institutions being, as we know, founded on extravagance and ostentation. But here we are not like that, we know that what God gave us for food was not meant to be wasted, so the Herrschaft need not be shy.' 'I do not think that they are refusing your kind offer because they are shy,' said Philip resourcefully, 'you see they are staying at one of the big hotels, and they will have to dine there anyway, so really the palatschinken would be of very little use to them.'

The waiter accepted this, and went away, but soon came back. 'But if the Herrschaft took them away with them,' he insisted, 'then they would not order a whole dinner. They could just take the soup and a meat dish, and afterwards they could go upstairs and have these instead of dessert.' 'Thank you very much for your kind thought,' said Philip, still not at a loss. 'I think, however, that my friends are *en pension*.' 'But it would be nice,' said the waiter, 'if the lady felt hungry in the night, for her to be able to put out her hand and find a piece of cold palatschinken by her bed.' I shall never think he was right; but his kindly courtesy was something to be remembered, and his sense, not hysterical but quietly passionate, of economy as a prime necessity.

In Diocletian's palace, throughout the ages, a great many very well-mannered people must have learned to draw in their belts very tight upon occasion; and certainly they would be encouraged to be mannerly by their surroundings, which, even today, speak of magnificent decorum.

It is not, of course, remarkable as an example of Roman architecture. It cannot hold a candle to the Baths of Caracalla, or the Forum, or the Palatine. But it makes an extraordinary revelation of the continuity of history. One passes through the gate that is squeezed between the rubbisheries on the quayside straight into antiquity. One stands in the colonnaded courtyard of a fourth-century Roman palace; in front is the entrance to the imperial apartments, to the left is the temple which was Diocletian's mausoleum, now the Cathedral, and to the right is the Temple of Æsculapius, just as a schoolboy learning Latin and as old ladies who used to go to the Royal Academy in the days of Alma Tadema would imagine it. Only the vistas have been filled in with people. Rather less than one-fifth of the population of Split, which numbers forty-four thousand, lives in the nine acres of the palace precincts; but the remaining four-fifths stream through it all day long, because the passages which pierce it from north to south and from east to west are the most convenient ways to the new parts of the town from the harbour. The fifth that lives within the palace packs the sides of these crowded thoroughfares with houses set as closely as cells in a honeycomb, filling every vacant space that was left by Diocletian's architects. One cannot, for example, see the Temple of Æsculapius as one stands in the fine open courtyard as it was intended one should do; the interstices on that side of the peristyle have been blocked by Venetian Gothic buildings, which project balconies on a line with the entablatures of neighbouring columns and open doorways just beside their bases.

Yet there is no sense of disorder or vandalism. It would be as frivolous to object to the adaptations the children of the palace have made to live as it would be to regret that a woman who had reared a large and glorious family had lost her girlish appearance. That is because these adaptations have always been made respectfully. So far as the walls stood they have been allowed to stand; there has been no destruction for the sake of pilfering material for new buildings. It is, therefore, as real an architectural entity, as evident to the eye of the beholder, as the Temple or Gray's Inn. There is only one blot on it, and that is not the work of necessity. In the middle of the peristyle of the imperial apartments, this superb but small open space, there has been placed a statue by Mestrovitch of a fourth-century bishop who won the Slavs the right to use the liturgy in their own tongue. Nobody can say whether it is a good statue or not. The only fact that is observable about it in this position is that it is twenty-four feet high. A more ungodly misfit was never seen. It reduces the architectural proportions of the palace to chaos, for its head is on a level with the colonnades, and the passage in which it stands is only forty feet wide. This is hard on it, for on a low wall near by there lies a black granite sphinx from Egypt, part of the original decorations of the palace, but far older, seventeen hundred years older, of the great age of Egyptian sculpture; and though this is not five feet long its compact perfection makes the statue of the bishop gangling and flimsy, lacking in true mass, like one of those marionettes one may sometimes see through the open door of a warehouse in Nice, kept against next year's carnival.

It cannot be conceived by the traveller why Mestrovitch wanted this statue to be put here, or why the authorities humoured him. If the step was inspired by nationalist sentiment, if it is supposed to represent the triumph of the Slav over Roman domination, nobody present can have known much history. For Diocletian's palace commemorates a time when the Illyrians, the native stock of Dalmatia, whose blood assuredly runs in the veins of most modern Dalmatians, had effective control of the Roman Empire; it commemorates one of the prettiest of time's revenges. Rome destroyed, for perhaps no better reason than that she was an empire and could do it, the ancient civilization of Illyria. But when she later needed sound governors to defend her from barbarian invaders, Illyria gave her thirteen rulers and defenders, of whom only one was a failure. All the others deserved the title they were given, *restitutores orbis*; even though it turned out that the earth as they knew it was not restorable. Of these the two greatest were Diocletian and Constantine; and some would say that Diocletian was the greater of the two.

His mausoleum is exquisitely appropriate to him. It is a domed building, octagonal outside and circular within. It is naughtily designed. Its interior is surrounded by a double row of columns, one on top of the other, which have no functional purpose at all; they do nothing except support their own overelaborate entablatures and capitals, and eat up much valuable space in doing so. Diocletian came to Rome when the rose of the world was overblown, and style forgotten. It must originally have been pitchy dark, for all the windows were made when it was centuries old. Because of this blackness and something flat-footed and Oriental in the design, some have thought that Diocletian did not build it as a temple or as a mausoleum. They have suspected that he, who was first and foremost a soldier and turned by preference to the East, was a follower of the bloody and unspiritual but dramatic religion of Mithraism, the Persian cult which had been adopted by the legionaries, and that here he tried to make a mock cavern, an imitation of the grottoes in which his fellow-soldiers worshipped the god that came out of the Sun. But not only is the building otiose and dank, it is oddly executed. It is full of incongruities such as a lack of accord between capitals and entablatures, which were committed because the architects were using the remains of older buildings as their material, and had to join the pieces as best they could. Diocletian had done much the same for the Roman Empire. He took the remains of a social and political structure and built them into a new and impressive-looking edifice.

In this palace of old oddments put together to look like new, this imperial expert in makeshifts must have had some better moments. His edicts show that he was far too intelligent not to realize that he had not made a very good job of his cobbling. He was a great man wholly worsted by his age. He probably wanted real power, the power to direct one's environment towards a harmonious end, and not fictitious power, the power to order and be obeyed; and he must have known that he had not been able to exercise real power over Rome. It would have been easier for him if what we were told when we were young was true, and that the decay of Rome was due to immorality. Life, however, is never as simple as that, and human beings rarely so potent. There is so little difference between the extent to which any large number of people indulge in sexual intercourse, when they indulge in it without inhibitions and when they indulge in it with inhibitions, that it cannot often be a determining factor in history. The exceptional person may be an ascetic or a debauchee, but the average man finds celibacy and sexual excess equally difficult. All we know of Roman immorality teaches us that absolute power is a poison, and that the Romans, being fundamentally an inartistic people, had a taste for pornography which they often gratified in the description of individuals and families on which that poison had worked.

Had general immorality been the cause of the decay of the Empire, Diocletian could have settled it; he was a good bullying soldier. But the trouble was pervasive and deep-rooted as couch-grass. Rome had been a peasant state, it had passed on to feudal capitalism, the landowners and the great industrialists became tyrants; against this tyranny the bourgeoisie and the proletariat revolted. Then the bourgeoisie became the tyrants. They could bribe the town proletariat with their leavings, but the peasants became their enemies. The army was peasant, for country stock is healthier. Therefore, in the third century, there was bitter strife between the Army and the bourgeoisie. Then came the Illyrian emperors, *restitutores orbis*. Order, it was said, was restored.

But this, the greatest of the Illyrian emperors, must have known that this was not true: that, on the contrary, disorder had been stabilized. His edicts had commanded in the peremptory tone of the parade-ground that every man in the Empire should stay by his post and do his duty, fulfilling this and that public obligation and drawing this and that private reward. There was genius in his plan. But it was a juggler's feat of balancing, no more. It corrected none of the fundamental evils of Roman society. This could hardly be expected, for Diocletian had been born too late to profit by the discussion of first principles which Roman culture had practised in its securer days; he had spent his whole life in struggles against violence which led him to a preoccupation with compulsion. He maintained the Empire in a state of apparent equilibrium for twenty-one years. But the rot went on. The roads fell into ruin. The land was vexed with brigands and the sea with pirates. Agriculture was harried out of existence by demands for taxation in kind and forced labour, and good soil became desert. Prices rose and currency fell; and to keep up the still enormously costly machinery of the central administration the remnants of the moneyed class were skinned by the tax-collector. The invasion of the barbarians was an immediate danger, but only because the Empire was so internally weakened by its economic problems. Of these nobody knew the solution at the beginning of the fourth century, and indeed they have not been solved now, in the middle of the twentieth century.

For some strange reason many have written of Diocletian's resignation of imperial power and retirement to his native Illyria as if it were an unnatural step which required a special explanation. Some of the pious have thought that he was consumed by remorse for his persecution of the Christians, but nothing could be less likely. Immediately after his election as Emperor he had chosen to share his power with an equal and two slightly inferior colleagues, in a system which was known as the Tetrarchy; and it was one of his colleagues, Galerius, who was responsible for what are falsely known as the persecutions of Diocletian. But nothing could be more comprehensible than that he should, just then, have wanted rest and his own country. He was fifty-nine, and had been exceedingly ill for a year; and he had twenty-one years of office behind him. He had had a hard life. He had come from a peasant home to enlist in one of the two Dalmatian legions, and since then he had borne an increasing burden of military and legislative responsibility. Violence must have disgusted such an intelligent man, but he had had to avail himself of it very often. In order to be chosen Cæsar by the military council he had had to whip out his sword and drive it into the breast of a fellow-officer who might have been a rival. So often, indeed, had he had to avail himself of violence that he must have feared he would himself become its victim at the end. A society which is ruled by the sword can never be stable, if only because the sword is always passing from hand to hand, from the ageing to the young.

In the halls of his palace, which must have been extremely cold and sunless, as they were lit only by holes in the roof, he cannot have found the peace he sought. The disorder of the world increased. The members of the Tetrarchy wrangled; some died and were replaced by others not less contentious. They split the Empire between their greeds, and suddenly, improbably, they dipped their fingers into Diocletian's blood. He had a wife called Prisca and a daughter called Valeria, who were very dear to him. Both had become Christians. We know of no protest against this on the part of Diocletian. Valeria's hand he had disposed of in circumstances that bring home the psychological differences between antiquity and the modern world. When he had been chosen as Emperor he had elected to share his power first with Maximian alone, then with two other generals, Galerius and Constantius Chlorus. When these two last were admitted to the sovereign authority, Diocletian adopted Galerius and Maximian adopted Constantius Chlorus, and each adopted father gave his daughter to his adopted son, though this meant that each had to repudiate his existing wife.

The marriage of Valeria must have been sufficiently horrible; for Galerius was a brute whose violence precipitated him from disaster to disaster, and he was bitterly anti-Christian. But she found solace in caring for his illegitimate son, Candidianus, and at last Galerius died, issuing on his deathbed an edict which put an end to the persecution of the Christians. She might have then enjoyed some happiness had she not been left a very rich woman. This made Galerius's successor, Maximin Daia, want to marry her, although he had a wife. When she refused he brought fraudulent legal proceedings against her. All her goods were confiscated, her household was broken up, some of her women friends were killed, and she and the boy Candidianus were sent into exile in the deserts

of Syria. It is only in some special and esoteric sense that women
are the protected sex.

From these dark halls Diocletian appealed for mercy to the man
whom his own invention of the Tetrarchy had raised to power.
He entreated Maximin Daia to allow Valeria to come back to
Aspalaton. He was refused. But later it seemed that Valeria was
safe, for Maximin Daia died, and she and Candidianus were able
to take refuge with another of the four Cæsars, Licinius, who first
received them with a kindliness that was natural enough, since he
owed his advancement to the dead Galerius. It looked as if they
would find permanent safety with him. But suddenly he turned
against them and murdered the boy for no other reason than that
he was a cruel and stupid man and bloodshed was fashionable just
then. Valeria managed to escape in the dress of a plebeian, and
disappeared. To Diocletian, fond father though he was, this may
have brought no special shattering shock. It may have seemed but
one shadow in the progress of a night that was engulfing all. For
Diocletian was receiving letters that were pressing him to visit
Licinius and his ally, the Cæsar Constantine. He excused himself,
pleading illness and old age. The invitations became ominously
insistent. He was in danger of being involved in a dispute among
the Tetrarchs. Sooner or later one side or other would have his
blood. He died, it is thought by self-administered poison, some
time between 313 and 316. The earlier date is to be hoped for;
in that case he would not have heard that in 314 his daughter was
found in hiding at Salonika and there beheaded and thrown into
the sea.

What did Diocletian feel when all this was happening to him?
Agony, of course. It is an emotion that human beings feel far more
often than is admitted; and it is not their fault. History imposes it
on us. There is no use denying the horrible nature of our human
destiny. Diocletian must have felt one kind of agony because he
was a healthy peasant, and his bowels must have slid backwards and
forwards like a snake when he doubted the safety of his daughter;
another because though he had been born a peasant he had been
born a peasant into a civilized world, and faculties developed in
civilization are revolted when they have to apprehend experiences
provided by barbarism; and another because it is always terrible to
advance from particular success to particular success and be faced
at last with general defeat, and he had passed from achievement
to achievement only to see the negation of all his achievements
decreed by impersonal forces which, if he had been truly imperial
and the right object of worship by the common man, he should have

anticipated and forestalled. How did he endure all these agonies? If he went for comfort into the building which was afterwards his mausoleum, and if it was, as some think, the Temple of Jupiter, he can have found little enough. Paganism, when it was not rural and naïvely animist, or urban and a brake applied to the high spirits of success, must have been an empty form, claiming at its most ambitious to provide just that stoicism which an exceptional man might find for himself and recognize as inadequate. If the building was a Mithraic grotto, then he must have looked at the governing sculpture of the god slitting the throat of the bull and he must have said to himself, 'Yes, the world is exactly like that. I know it. Blood flows, and life goes on. But what of it? Is the process not disgusting?' And Mithras would give no answer.

It is possible that Diocletian found his comfort in the secular side of his palace, in its splendour. Some have thought that he built it for the same reason that he had built his baths in Rome, to give work to the vast number of proletarians that were hungry and idle. But these grandiose public works would not have come into Diocletian's mind had he not been in love with magnificence, and indeed he had demonstrated such an infatuation while he was Emperor by his elaboration of court ceremonial. It had grown more and more spectacular during the last century or so, and he gave its gorgeousness a fixed and extreme character. There was more and more difficulty in gaining access to the sacred person of the Emperor, and those who were given this privilege had to bow before him in an act of adoration as due to the holy of holies. The Emperor, who was by then a focus of unresolvable perplexities, stood providing a strongly contrary appearance in vestments stiff with richness and insignia glittering with the known world's finest precious stones and goldsmith's work; and his visitor, even if the same blood ran in his veins, had to kneel down and touch a corner of the robe with his lips.

Diocletian, who had prescribed this ritual, must certainly have derived some consolation from the grandeur of Aspalaton, the great arcaded wall it turned to the Adriatic, its four separate wards, each town size, and its seventeen watch-towers, its plenitude of marble, its colonnades that wait for proud processions, its passages that drive portentously through darkness to the withdrawn abode of greatness. Robes stiff with embroidery help the encased body to ignore its flimsiness; a diadem makes the head forget that it has not yet evolved the needed plan of action. In a palace that lifts the hard core out of the mountains to make a countryside impregnable by wind and rain, it would seem untrue that we can build ourselves no refuge against certain large movements of destiny. But there was a consideration which may have disturbed Diocletian as he tried to sustain himself on Aspalaton. It was not Rome, which he had visited only once, that had given him his conception of magnificence as an aid to the invincibility of government. He had drawn it from Persia, where he had been immensely impressed by the vast palaces and their subtle and evocative ceremonial. But he had visited Persia as an invader, to destroy the Sassanian kings. The symbol that he depended upon he had himself proved invalid.

After his death he remained corporeally in possession of the palace, his tomb resting in the centre of the mausoleum. Thirty years or so later, a woman was put to death for stealing the purple pall from his sarcophagus, a strange, crazy crime, desperate and imaginative, a criticism in which he would by now have concurred, for the walls of the Empire which he had failed to repair had fallen and let a sea of catastrophe wash over his people. The Adriatic was ravaged by Vandal pirates, and Rome had been sacked by the barbarians three times in sixty years; the Huns had devastated the Danube, and Salonæ was crowded with refugees. But this was for the meantime a little ledge of safety, and ordinary life went on and seemed to prove that there was some sense in the idea of building a palace for shelter. Illyria had always been noted for its textiles. There is a statue of the Emperor Augustus in the Capitoline Museum at Rome, which has on its shield the figure of an Illyrian; he is wearing a knee-length tunic, beltless but with sleeves, and ornamented by bands running from the shoulders to the lower hem. This is our first knowledge of the dalmatic. In the third century the Pope ordered that all martyrs should be buried in it, and it is still worn by all deacons and officiating bishops in the Western church, and by English kings at their coronation. No matter what bestial tricks history might be playing, there were always looms at work in Illyria. A considerable corner of Aspalaton was taken up by a large factory, operated by female labour, which turned out uniforms for the Roman Army as well as civilian material.

But other events proved that a palace is no shelter at all. In the middle of the fifth century there arose a Dalmatian of genius, Marcellinus, who served the army loyally on condition that he was allowed to rule Dalmatia as an independent kingdom owing allegiance to the Emperor. It is possible that the Empire might have survived as a federation of such states, modest in extent and governed by men of local ambitions on the old Roman principles of efficiency and public spirit. Marcellinus took up his residence in

Diocletian's palace, and with his courage and wisdom and energy in the defence of his people filled it again with recognizable majesty. But after thirteen years of benign brilliance he went in the service of the Emperor to Sicily, for the purpose of leading an expedition against the Vandals in Africa; and there he was murdered by order of Ricimer, a German general who was one of the barbarians who were destroying Rome from within. They had no use for local potentates who would build up the Empire by raising their territories to military and economic strength; they wanted it as a defenceless field of exploitation for an international army. The last of the *restitutores orbis* had not found safety where he might accomplish his work.

A few years later his nephew, who was called by that name, Julius Nepos, Julius the Nephew, and had ruled Dalmatia in his uncle's place, was called to be Emperor of the West. It was not an encouraging invitation. 'Cocky, cocky, come and be killed.' But since it was issued by the Emperor of the East he did not dare to refuse. He had at once to oust a competitor, whom he consoled for his defeat by making him Bishop of Salonæ; chroniclers with a sense of the picturesque describe him tearing off his rival's imperial insignia and delivering him over to a barber who cut his tonsure and a priest who gave him the episcopal consecration. It was a practical step, since it prevented his rival avenging himself. Julius the Nephew had no chance to show his quality, for he was faced by an infinity of hostile barbarians, within and without the Empire, and he made a fatal error by summoning his Dalmatian Commander-in-chief, Orestes, to govern Gaul. This Orestes was an Illyrian adventurer who had at one time been secretary to Attila the Hun. It can never have been a satisfactory reference. But he had established himself in the Roman order by marrying a patrician's daughter, and he was able to turn on his master and declare his own son Romulus Emperor.

Julius the Nephew went back to Aspalaton and there lived for five years. Meanwhile Orestes was murdered by a barbarian general, Odoacer, who formed a curious plan of supporting the cause of Romulus, whose youth and beauty he much admired, and acting as the power behind the throne. In 480 two Dalmatian counts, Victor and Ovida, one a Romanized Illyrian and the other a barbarian, made their way into Diocletian's palace and treacherously killed Julius. He was the last legitimately elected Emperor of the West. His assassins had been moved by the hope of pleasing Odoacer; the barbarian Ovida wished to make himself King of Dalmatia, and he needed imperial support. But Odoacer was as hostile to regional rulers as the other murderer, Ricimer, and at the end of a punitive war on Dalmatia he killed Ovida with his own hand. Later he himself was killed by Theodoric, King of the Ostrogoths, who after signing a treaty with him invited him to a banquet and then ran him through with a sword, and massacred all his men. Murder. Murder. Murder. Murder.

It was about this time that the sarcophagus of Diocletian disappeared. For about a hundred and seventy years it was visible, firmly planted in the middle of the mausoleum, described by intelligent visitors. Then it suddenly is not there any more. It is suggested that a party of revengeful Christians threw it into the sea; but that is an action comprehensible only in a smouldering minority, and Christianity had been the official religion of the Roman Empire since the time of the Emperor's death. Nor can it be supposed that the sarcophagus was destroyed by the Avar invaders, for they did not reach the coast until a couple of centuries later. Probably the occasion of its disappearance was far less dramatic. The everyday routine of life persisted in Aspalaton, however many barbarians committed murder; in the textile factory the shuttles crossed and recrossed the loom. Without doubt it continued to be necessary that Diocletian's mausoleum should be cleaned and repaired, and it may well have happened that one day the owner of a yard near by said, 'Yes, you can put it down there,' watching it reverently, and wondering that he should be the guardian of such a holy thing. It may be also that the workmen who laid it down did not come back, that there was a threat to the city from land or sea which called them and the authorities who employed them and the owner of the yard himself to the defence. Soon it might be that people would say of the sarcophagus, 'I wonder when they will come and take it back'; but continued unrest may have made it advisable that the treasures of the temples should be kept dispersed. Later it might be that a break in a chain of family confidences, due to violent death or flight or even sudden natural death, would leave the sarcophagus unidentified and only vaguely important. Some day a woman would say of it, 'I really do not know what that is. It is just something that has always been here; and it is full of old things.' She spoke the truth. It was full of old things: the bones of Diocletian the man, the robes of Diocletian the Emperor, the idea of a world order imposed on the peoples by superior people, who were assumed to know because they could act. Aspalaton, the palace of the great Restorer of the Earth, had passed away. It had become Split, a city lived in by common people, who could establish order within the limits of a kitchen or a workshop or a textile factory, but had been monstrously hindered in the exercise of that capacity by the efforts of the superior people who establish world order.

I have no doubt that one day Diocletian's sarcophagus will turn up in the cellars of some old and absent-minded family of Split; and in the cellars of the Dalmatian mind, the foundation on which its present philosophy is built, the old Emperor is to be found also. We in England have an unhistoric attitude to our lives, because every generation has felt excitement over a clear-cut historical novelty, which has given it enough to tell its children and grandchildren without drawing on its father's and grandfather's tales. In all these impressive events the central government has played a part which was, at any rate, not tragically disgraceful, at least so far as our own country is concerned, and was often very creditable. We think of the national organization that controls the public services throughout the country as ambitious on the whole to give the common man every opportunity to exercise his ability for keeping order in his own sphere.

It would not be so, however, if the last clear-cut event in English history had been the departure of the Roman legionaries in 420; and if there had followed a period of internal disorder which the battle of Hastings had perpetuated to our own day, by inaugurating a series of attempts at invasion and settlement by imperialistic Continental powers. Then the idea of the state would seem to us like wine, a delight that must be enjoyed only in moderation lest it lead to drunkenness and violence, uproar and want. We would know that some degree of national organization is necessary, and that dominance is the most exquisite of luxuries, but we would think of kings and statesmen as mischiefmakers whose failure drove us from time to time out of our houses into ditches, to feed on roots and berries. The difference in our attitude can be computed if we try to imagine what our reaction to the word 'queen' would be if we had had no Victoria or Elizabeth, or even Anne, and that Boadicea had had a determining effect on English history.

So it is with the Splitchani, and indeed with all Dalmatians. They are aware of Diocletian's failure to restore the earth, and what it cost them. Therefore their instinct is to brace themselves against any central authority as if it were their enemy. The angry young men run about shouting. But they have Illyrian blood as well as Slav; they are of the same race that produced Diocletian and the other *restitutores orbis*. They are profoundly sensitive to the temptation of power. Therefore they cannot break their preoccupation with the central authority. The young men cannot sit down and get angry about something else. The stranger will be vastly mistaken if he regards this attitude as petulant barbarism. It is an extremely sensible reaction to his experience, and it has helped him to protect his rights under the rule of empires which were indifferent or hostile to him. It might yet be of enormous service to humanity if the world were threatened by an evil domination.

Split II

Diocletian's mausoleum was transformed into a cathedral during the eighth century. It is still obviously a pagan edifice, though the Christians fitted it in the thirteenth century with a good bell-tower, and with fine carved doors that show twenty-eight scenes from the life of Christ, and have gone on filling it with pious objects till it has something of a box-room air. There is a superb pulpit of the same date as the tower and the doors, splendid with winged beasts, and two good fifteenth-century tombs, one showing a Flagellation of Christ, the work of George the Dalmatian, who is alluded to as Georgio Orsini by those who want to show this coast as a Slav wilderness redeemed by Venetian culture, with no other justification than that a son or nephew of his called himself by that name. One can look at nothing in Dalmatia, not even a Flagellation of Christ, without being driven back to the struggle of Slav nationalism. The history of the Cathedral is dominated by it; here was the centre of the movement, which has been for the most part successful, for the use of the Slav liturgy.

There were, however, two ecclesiastics of Split who were of importance to the rest of the world. There was the Archdeacon Thomas of Spalato, in the thirteenth century, who wrote an excellent history of his own times and was the only contemporary foreigner known to have seen St. Francis of Assisi, and heard him preach; and there was the seventeenth-century Archbishop Mark Antony de Dominis, who was typically Slav in being at once an intellectual and incredibly naïve. He came from the city of Rab, from one of its exquisite Gothic palaces. Though he was an archbishop, and added to the mausoleum its present choir, his main interest lay in scientific studies; and he hit on the discovery of the solar spectrum one day while he was saying mass, more than half a century before Newton. Much of Descartes's work is founded on his, and Goethe writes of him in his book on the theory of colour. Unfortunately he became interested in matters of religion, which was a fatal mistake for a Renaissance prelate of his kind. Soon he became convinced of the truth of Protestantism, and through the influence of his friend, Sir Henry Wotton, the author of 'You meaner beauties of the night,' who was then the English Ambassador to Venice, he was appointed Dean of Windsor and Master of the Savoy and Vicar of West Ilsley, up on the Berkshire

downs. He then published a tremendous attack on the Roman
Catholic Church under the title of *De republica ecclesiastica*. But
doubts vexed him, and he came to the conclusion that he was
wrong. In touching abandonment to the Slav belief that people
are not really unreasonable, he went to Rome to talk about it to
the Pope. That Pope died and was succeeded by one less tolerant.
Dominis was thrown into the Castle of St. Angelo and died in its
dungeons. Later the Inquisition tried him for heresy and found
him guilty, so dug up his corpse and burned it together with his
writings.

But though the religious life of Split is obscured by its nationalism in the historical annals, we must remember that much of
human activity goes unrecorded. There is great piety among the
Splitchani. We noted it that night when the Professor came to
dine with us. The Professor is a great Latinist and was the pupil,
assistant, and close friend of Bulitch, the famous scholar who spent
his life working on the antiquities of Split and Salonæ. He is in his
late sixties, but has the charm of extreme youth, for he comes to a
pleasure and hails it happily for what it is without any bitterness
accumulated from past disappointments, and he believes that any
moment the whole process of life may make a slight switch-over
and that everything will be agreeable for ever. His manners would
satisfy the standards of any capital in the world, but at the same
time he is exquisitely, pungently local. 'Thank you, I will have no
lobster,' he said to us. 'I am sure it is excellent, but, like many
of my kind, who have had to renounce robust health along with
the life of action, I have a weak digestion.' He then emptied his
pepper-pot into his soup till its surface became completely black.
'See,' he said, 'how carefully I eat. I never neglect to take plenty of
pepper, since it is excellent for the health. What, did you not know
that? But I assure you, one can hardly live long unless one eats a
great deal of pepper.' I was enchanted; the Abbé Fortis, who made
a tour of the coast in the eighteenth century, expressed amazement
at the enormous quantities of pepper eaten by the Dalmatians, and
their faith in it as a medicament.

Being so much a child of his country, he had of course to speak
of nationalism, and indeed what he said brought home to me more
than anything else the extreme unsuitability, the irksomeness of the
last subjection which the Dalmatians had had to yield to an external
authority. Here was a man who was the exact Adriatic equivalent of
an Oxford don; he would by nature have found all his satisfaction
in the pursuit of learning. But from his youth and through all his
adult years he had been an active member of a party that existed

to organize revolt against the Austrian Government; and there was none of his large and respectable family who had not been as deeply engaged in rebellion as himself. 'One of my brothers,' he told us, 'was very well known as a Dalmatian patriot, for he had trouble that was reported in the newspapers all over Europe. For he was a priest, and the Austrians expelled him from Dalmatia though he had a parish. Still he did not suffer very much from that, for the great Bishop Strossmayer took him under his protection and gave him a parish near Zagreb.

'How fortunate for me all that trouble was!' he exclaimed, beaming. 'For when I was going to the University at Vienna to make my studies Bishop Strossmayer invited me to see him. And that is the most wonderful thing that happened to me in my whole life. It was a very long time ago, for I was then only nineteen years old, but I have forgotten nothing of it. The room seemed bright as an altar at Easter when I went in, but that was not so much because of the chandeliers, which were indeed superb, but because of the company. There was Bishop Strossmayer himself, who was amazing in his handsomeness and elegance, and also there were at least twenty other people, who were all notable, great aristocrats of our race, or scholars, or artists, or foreigners of eminence, or women of superb beauty and great distinction. It is well known that Bishop Strossmayer was deeply respectful to the beauty of women, as to all the beauties of creation.

'But do not think that this was a mere worldly dinner-party. The great man imposed on it his own superiority. First we stood at the table, and he himself said grace in his exquisite Latin, which was Latin as no one else has spoken it, as the angels may speak it. Then we sat down, and as we ate a young priest read us a passage from the Gospel of St John, and then a fable from Æsop. Then the Bishop started the conversation, which, though the party was so large, was nevertheless general and brilliant beyond imagination. It was his own doing, of course, yet it did not seem so. It all appeared to happen quite naturally. It was as if the birds in a wood should start singing and their notes should combine to form utterances of a wisdom unsurpassed by the philosophers. Alas! It is terrible that such a perfect thing should have been, and should be no longer. I suppose all the people who were there are dead, except some of the women; for I was much the youngest man there. But that feeling over what is gone the ancients knew well, and expressed better than we can.' He murmured scraps of Latin verse. It was very characteristically Slav that he said nothing of having been troubled by social embarrassment at this dinner-party. In any other country, a boy of nineteen, not rich, from a provincial town, would have felt timid at a dinner-party given in a capital by one of the most famous men of the time. But Serbs and Croats alike are an intensely democratic people. There are few class distinctions, and Split, being a free and ancient city, would not feel inferior to Zagreb, for all its size and comparative wealth. Nevertheless, perhaps Bishop Strossmayer had his part in the boy's ease.

'I speak foolishly,' said the Professor, when he started to talk again, 'if I imply that the Bishop Strossmayer was an inspiration to me, for, to tell the truth, I have never been inspired. I have committed no great action, nor have I needed to. For the Austrian Government never persecuted us in the grand manner, it never called on us to be heroes, it merely pricked us with pins, and all we had to do was to be gentlemen and philosophers. My worst time was during the war, and that was not so bad.' It appeared that as soon as Austria declared war on Serbia all the men in Split who had shown signs of hostility to the Austrian Government, which is to say all prominent or even respectable citizens, were arrested and sent on tour through Austria and Hungary to be shown off publicly as Serbian prisoners of war. 'I who know German as my own tongue,' said the Professor, 'had to stand there while they described me as an Orthodox priest—that was because of my beard. Certain circumstances concerning that imprisonment were indeed very disagreeable. But let us not remember that, but the good things the war brought us. It brought us our freedom and it brought us many friends. Yes, many English friends. For many English sailors and soldiers came here after the war, and we liked them very much. I suppose you do not know Admiral William Fisher?' 'No,' said my husband, 'but I know his brother, H. A. L. Fisher, the Warden of New College, who is a great historian and one of the most charming people in the world.' 'So is this man! So is this man!' cried the Professor. 'He came here with the fleet several times, and I grew to love him like a brother. I tell you, he is like a hero of old!'

His eyes were glowing. Here, as in Serbia, there is very little effeminacy, and no man puts himself under suspicion by praising another; so one is sometimes aware of a strong current of love running from man to man, from comrade to comrade, from hero to hero. The Professor spoke long of Admiral Fisher, of his solid qualities, his wisdom and patience, and of his lovely lightnesses, his capacity for a gay Homeric cunning, and his tremendous laughter. 'Ah!' he sighed at last, 'I have spoken so much of my friend that without noticing it I have drunk a great deal of red wine. This will not be healthy, unless I drink a lot of black coffee. Is this coffee strong?' 'I am afraid it is,' I said, 'terribly strong.' 'Why are you afraid?' asked the Professor. 'The stronger it is the healthier it is. Did you not know that?'

After the Professor and my husband had talked for a while of their favourite editions of the classics they fell silent; and I said, 'I have asked Philip Thomson to come in afterwards. He could not come to dinner as he had a lesson, but he is coming in at ten. I hope you will like him.' 'I have not met him,' said the Professor, 'but I know him by sight, and I am sure I will like him.' 'Yes, he has a charming, sensitive appearance,' I said. 'It is not that I mean,' said the Professor. 'I am sure I will like him because he is a very pious Catholic. I have noticed that he is most pious in his observances, and during Lent I have gone into my church several times and found him praying like a little child.' And when Philip Thomson came in he greeted him with a special confidential and yet reticent friendliness, as if he knew they had in common certain experiences which, however, cannot be shared.

To start the conversation we talked of what we meant to do in Split before we set off southwards down the coast. 'You really must go up to the park on Mount Marian, that hill below the town,' said Philip; 'it is most beautiful up there among the pines, looking over the sea and the islands.' 'Yes, indeed,' I said. 'I was there last year, and I want to go again. It interested me to see that in Robert Adam's drawings there isn't a tree on the hill, it is just bare rock. I suppose the Austrians planted it.' 'They did not!' cried the Professor, leaping from his chair. 'And shall I tell you who did? I myself, I did it. I found in the archives uncontestable proof that there were once trees on that hill, which were cut down to make Venetian galleys. So I formed the idea that there could be trees there again, and I started a society to do it. Many people thought it was madness and my poor wife received anonymous letters saying that I should be put into a lunatic asylum. But I collected the money, and, believe me, it was Dalmatians who gave it. No, the Austrians did nothing for us, nor the Venetians either. We took the Venetian style of architecture, that is all; and I should not even say that if I were striving to be accurate. It would be more truthful to say that the Venetians and the Dalmatians both drew from the same sources inspiration towards a new movement. . . .'

We were back again at Slav nationalism; but we left it for that permanent and mystical preoccupation which lies deeper in the Dalmatian mind. 'I do not think that the Venetians have left any permanent mark on the life of the people,' said the Professor, 'except perhaps the Venetian habit of blasphemy. Do you not find it dreadful, Mr Thomson, the oaths that one must hear as one walks in the streets of Split?' 'I find it most terrible,' said Philip; 'they use the holy names in a way that makes one clap one's hands over one's ears.' They shook their heads gravely; and I saw the unusual spectacle of a foreigner born to the Catholic faith matching in fervour an English convert. In the Professor I recognized the same Slavic religious passion that had made dark and glowing the voices of the men and women singing mass at Shestine; but it seemed to me that in him it was not only sweetened by the great sweetness of his personality, but also that it was given a special intensity by the long dolorous life of his town, and its reflections upon its tragedy, its refusal to take the sorrow and waste of it at their face value.

It is not to be doubted, as one goes about Split, that this walled city has such a life, far more concentrated than the life of our diffuse Western towns; and that it has been engaged in a continuous effort to find a noble interpretation of its experience through piety. The Professor took us the next morning to the Golden Gate of the palace, which is most recognizably what it was in the days of Diocletian, a very handsome, creeper-hung matter of niches and pillarets and a narrow door, which modern times have pierced with an unending thread of neat and supple Splitchani hurrying down to the harbour. Near this Gate we climbed a stairway, and a door was opened by a nun, who led us up more stairs into a little church built in the thickness of the palace walls. It is about eleven hundred years old, and though it is defaced by hideous *bondieuseries* of the modern Roman Catholic Church, it remains infinitely touching because of its slender stone screen, because of the carvings on that screen which write in shapes as fresh as dew the faith of a people that they have found a beneficent magic to banish the horrors of life. Beside us the nun spoke on and on to the Professor, her voice stilled with amazement, in words that also were as fresh as dew. She was telling him that the Mother Superior of that tiny order which guards this Church of St Martin was growing very old and very sick, but was showing great fortitude. Though she spoke calmly she took nothing for granted; this might have been the first time that pain and fortitude had shown themselves on earth. She was among those who will not suffer any event merely to happen, who must examine it with all the force of the soul and trace its consequences, and seek, against all probability, an explanation of the universe that is as kind as human kindness.

We went, later in the morning, to another church, built in honour of the Virgin Mary actually within one of the gates, over an archway. It is not specially interesting; one has seen its like all over Southern Europe, grey and pliant in its line, a gentle boast that if one has but faith it needs no more than the strength of a lily to withstand life. This, like many of the smaller churches in the Dalmatian towns, belongs to a confraternity; about twenty townsmen sustained it, used it as the centre of their devotions and the means of their charity, and there married their wives and christened their children and were buried. It was shown to us by one of this confraternity, a plasterer, who had left his work to do the Professor this courtesy. Wearing his working clothes, which were streaked with white plaster, he stood still and stiff like a page in a more than royal household, showing subjects the throne-room, the plain transmitter of a tradition which we had recognized earlier that day.

We had recognized it in the Temple of Æsculapius, which lies on the other side of the courtyard from Diocletian's mausoleum and is now the baptistery. This change would not have surprised Diocletian, for the last glimpse that we have of his personal life is his irritation at the refusal of his Christian stone-masons to make him a statue of Æsculapius. There we saw a tenth-century stone slab, roughly carved, which is said by some to represent the adoration of Christ and by others the homage paid to a Croatian king by his subjects. It does not matter which it is. What is important is that the sculptor, wishing to depict magnificence, whether earthly or supernatural, saw it in Byzantine terms. After the Western Roman Empire had collapsed Dalmatia had thirty years of dangerous independence and then fell under the Eastern Empire, under Byzantium. That Empire was a real fusion of Church and State; the Emperor was given absolute power over his subjects only because he professed absolute subjection to God, and the ceremonial of his court was a religious ritual. That slab exists to show that this conception of government by holy ballet deeply impressed the imagination of the governed people, even on its furthermost frontiers.

The devout grace of the workman, which, though it had an instinctive basis, had been borne as far from that by art and discipline as the Guards have been removed in their drill from the primitive emotion of ferocity, proved that the Byzantine tradition had made other signs of vitality than mere diffusion. This man was a Slav. The fair hair, the high cheek-bones, the sea-blue eyes showed it. Byzantium had struck new roots in the race that had come into the Balkans from the mid-Russian plains as pure barbarians, untouched by anything that had happened during the first centuries of the Christian era, and apparently as inaccessible to Christian influence as any race on earth. Without pity, they killed and tortured; without purpose, they burned and laid waste. They came down to the Dalmatian coast on a mission of ruin, in the company of the Huns and Avars. But it happened that the Huns and the Avars turned on and reduced them to slaves, and they rose in revolt. Angry young men ran about shouting. They were heard by the Byzantine Emperor Heraclius, who promised that if they drove the Huns and Avars out of Illyria they might settle the land as vassals of the Empire. He imposed a further condition: that they must adopt Christianity. Who could have foretold that out of this marriage of convenience between the Slav people and the Church would flower a great passion? Who could have foretold that a horde of murderers and marauders would be also addicts to spiritual pursuits and the use of the intellect, believers in magic and the existence of a reality behind appearances, who would perform any ritual and carry on any argument that promised a revelation of the truth? History sometimes acts as madly as heredity, and her most unpredictable performances are often her most glorious.

Salonæ

This was the grimmest Easter; and when the Professor took us up to the remains of the great Roman city, Salonæ, which should be one of the prettiest sights in the whole world, it was nothing of the sort. Its pillars and steps and sarcophagi lie among rich grass and many flowers under the high olive terraces overlooking the sea and its many islands, the very spot which Horace would have liked to visit with a footman carrying a lunch basket behind him. It is one of the disharmonies of history that there is nothing that a Roman poet would have enjoyed more than a Roman ruin, with its obvious picturesqueness and the cue it gives for moralizing. But we could not enjoy it at all, for sharp rain scratched our faces all the four miles we drove from Split, and at Salonæ it grew brutal and we were forced into a little house, all maps and inscriptions, built by the great Bulitch to live in while he was superintending the diggings, and since his death converted into a museum.

We were not alone. The house was packed with little girls, aged from twelve to sixteen, in the care of two or three nuns. They were, like any gathering of their kind in any part of the world, more comfortable to look at than an English girls' school. They were apparently waiting quite calmly to grow up. They expected it, and so did the people looking after them. There was no panic on anybody's part. There were none of the unhappy results which follow the English attempt to make all children look insipid and docile, and show no signs whatsoever that they will ever develop into adults. There were no little girls with poked chins and straight hair, aggressively proud of being plain, nor were there pretty girls making a desperate precocious proclamation of their femininity. But, of course, in a country where there is very little homosexuality it is easy for girls to grow up into womanhood.

But I wondered what the little dears were learning up at Salonæ. I suspected that they were receiving an education with a masculine bias. Indeed, I knew it, for they were being educated by nuns, who are women who have accepted the masculine view of themselves and the universe, who show it by being the only members of their sex who go into fancy dress and wear uniforms as men love to do. I feared that in this particular background they might be instilling into their charges some monstrous male rubbish. It was even possible that they were teaching them the same sort of stuff about

the Romans which I learned when I was at school: panegyrics of
dubious moral value, unsupported by evidence. There is, Heaven
knows, enough to be said in their favour without any sacrifice of
honesty. I can bear witness to it. I was at school in Scotland, and
therefore, owing to the strange dispensations of that country in
regard to the female, learned Latin and no Greek, a silly, lopsided
way of being educated. But even for this one-eyed stance on the
classics I am grateful, though I was slow-witted at learning that
and all other languages, and have forgotten most of what I knew.
It gave me the power to find my way about the Romance languages;
it gave me a sense of the past, a realization that social institutions
such as the law do not happen but are made; it gave, and gives,
me considerable literary rapture. I like a crib, indeed some might
say that I need a crib; but once I have it I enjoy my Latin verse
enormously. To this day I am excited as I read that neatest possible
expression of the wildest possible grief:

Floribus Austrum
Perditus et liquidis immisi fontibus apros.

It also seems to me that the modern mind cannot be fully under-
stood until one has gone back to Latin literature and seen what
European culture was like before it was injected with the ideas of
St. Augustine.

But I regret that to give me this pleasure and information my
teachers should have found it necessary to instruct me, with far
more emphasis than was justified by the facts in their or anybody
else's possession, that the Roman Empire was a vast civilizing force
which spread material and moral well-being all over the ancient
world by its rule. I was taught that this was no mere accident: that
the power to extend their rule by military means sprang from an
intellectual and moral genius that made them able to lay down the
best way of living for the races they subdued. I find these assumptions firmly embedded in the mass of literature written by people
who received a classical education, especially if it had the same Latin
bias as mine, and expressed even more passionately in literature
written by people who have not had any education at all. Every year
I grow more critical of them. We have no real evidence that the peoples on which the Roman Empire imposed its civilization had not
pretty good civilizations of their own, better adapted to local conditions. The Romans said they had not; but posterity might doubt
the existence of our contemporary French and English culture if
the Nazis destroyed all records of them. We may at least suspect
from the geniuses of African stock who appear within the Roman

Empire that when Rome destroyed Carthage, dragging the plough three times through the land, she destroyed her equal or even her superior. The great work by Monsieur Camille Julian on the history of Gaul suggests that when Rome came to France she frustrated the development of a civilization of the first order; and Strzygowski doubts whether she did not bring disorganization to the Germanic tribes. It appears probable from the researches of the last few years, which have discovered codes of law, far from rudimentary, among all the contemporaries of the Romans, even to the nomads, that they might have got on with their social institutions very satisfactorily if they had not been obliged to fight against the external efforts at their betterment. And it seems very probable that Rome was able to conquer foreign territories because she had developed her military genius at the expense of precisely those qualities which would have made her able to rule them. Certainly she lacked them to such an extent that she was unable to work out a satisfactory political and economic policy for Rome itself and perished of that failure.

I am sure of it, those little girls were being taught that they should be proud because Split was the heir to a Roman city. Yet neither I nor anybody else knows whether or not the conquest of Illyria by the Romans was not a major disaster, the very contrary to an extension of civilization. Illyria had its past. It was linked with Greek history, and had a double tie with Macedonia of alternate enmity and alliance. Alexander the Great had Illyrian princesses for his mother and grandmother, and he and his father both fought great campaigns against their country. In the Roman period we know little about Illyria save from Roman sources, but even they suggest a considerable culture. They had an extremely able and heroic queen, Teüta, who was not the sort of monarch that can be raised from a tribe in skins; and while she and her subjects are accused of piracy, examination proves this a reference to efforts, which history would regard as creditable if they had been undertaken by the Romans, to conquer the Adriatic archipelago. It is also brought up against Teüta that she murdered two of three Roman ambassadors who were sent to accuse her people of unmannerly ways at sea. But it is said that these were murdered by brigands outside the Illyrian frontiers; and some heed had better be given to Polybius, a Roman of the Romans, when he explains why the Senate once made war on the Illyrians:

> Since the Romans had expelled Demetrios of Pharos from Illyria they had completely neglected the Adriatic seaboard; and on another hand the Senate wished to avoid at all costs that the

Italians became effeminate during a longstanding peace because it was more than eleven years since the Persian war and the Macedonian Expedition had ended. In undertaking a campaign against the Dalmatians they would reawaken the fighting spirit of the people at the same time that they would give the Illyrians a lesson and would force them to submit to the domination of Rome. Such were the reasons why Rome declared war on the Dalmatians; but the excuse which was given to the other nations was the insolence with which they had treated the ambassadors.

Little girls of Salonæ, try to work out this sum on your fingers. It took Rome two hundred and fifty years of war to bring peace to the Illyrians. Then they had fifty years or so of disturbance, and a hundred years of peace, which I cannot but think they could have procured for themselves, since they had then to take over the government of Rome and provide the long line of Illyrian emperors. They were then precipitated into an abyss of unrest and catastrophe, of which the worst feature, the barbarian invasions, owed its horror largely to Roman expansion. If Italy had been content with herself as a unit and had developed on a solid economic basis, and if Illyria had been allowed to look after her own affairs, they might have put up a far more effective resistance to the invaders. No, the sum does not work out. Remember, when the nuns tell you to beware of the deceptions of men who make love to you, that the mind of man is on the whole less tortuous when he is love-making than at any other time. It is when he speaks of governments and armies that he utters strange and dangerous nonsense to please the bats at the back of his soul. This is all to your disadvantage, for in love-making you might meet him with lies of equal force, but there are few repartees that the female governed can make to the male governors.

Nevertheless, it was sweet for all of us, nuns and the little dears, the Professor and my husband and me, to go out when the rain had stopped and walk among the Roman ruins of Salonæ. Grey and silver were the olive leaves shining in the timid sunlight, dark grey the wet ruins, silver-grey the tall spiked aloes, and blacker than green the cypresses, black the mountains behind us, silver the sea that lay before us, and grey the islands that streaked it; and at our feet storm-battered flowers looked like scraps of magenta paper. The Professor was gay, as birds are after rain. He read us inscriptions, lending them a sweetness that was not in their meaning from the enjoyment of Latinism which had been mellowing in his soul since his youth, and guiding us to the stony stubs and plinths and stairways of temples, baths, churches, the city walls, the city gate, that had been battered less by time than by wars. Again and again this place had been taken and retaken by the Goths and the Huns before the Avars finally smashed it in 639. It is for this reason that the churches in this city have the majesty of a famous battle-field. Here Christianity's austere message that it is better not to be a barbarian, even if victory lies with barbarism, was tested in the actual moment of impact with barbarians, in face of a complete certainty that victory was to be with barbarism. In the baptistery of the Cathedral the chamber round the font still stands. There can still be seen the steps down which the naked men, glistening with the holy oil and reeling with the three days' fast, descended to the holy waters, to be immersed in them three times and lifted out, glorious in the belief that the death that was closing in on them was magically changed to joy and salvation. From the most coldly rationalist point of view it must be pronounced that they were not mistaken. Complete victory was given here to the barbarians; on this spot they followed their nature in all its purity of destructiveness, its zeal of cruelty. But the gentle virtue of the Professor, the dedicated fineness of the plasterer in the confraternity chapel, showed that the stock of the christened men lived still and had not been brutalized.

It was right that the nuns should be trailing the little dears round the site of this miracle of which they formed a part. But I passed one of the nuns and remarked, as I had done before, that the rank and file of the female religious order present an unpleasing appearance because they have assumed the expression of credulity natural and inevitable to men, who find it difficult to live without the help of philosophical systems which far outrun ascertained facts, but wholly unsuitable to women, who are born with a faith in the unrevealed mystery of life and can therefore afford to be sceptics. I feared very much that the nuns' charges would be fed a deal of nonsense along with the bread of truth. They would be taught, for example, to honour those claims of the Church which reflect no reality and spring from certain masculine obsessions of its ecclesiastics: such as its pretension to be unchanging, to have attained in its first years a wisdom about all matters, eternal and temporal, of which it has made a progressive disclosure, never contradicting itself. We are, of course, at liberty to imagine that the Church would be a nobler institution if it knew no alteration; even so it does no harm if we dream that we could all be much happier if our bodies remained for ever young and fair. But these are day-dreams and nothing else, for the Church changes, and we grow old. There was evidence of it, written here on the wet grey stone.

'Look,' said the Professor, 'this is one of our most interesting tombs which is also very touching.' Here a husband had laid to rest his beloved wife; and in the inscription he boasted that he had brought her to his home when she was eighteen and had lived beside her in chastity for thirty-three years. His very grief itself must have been made serene by his consciousness that by their abstinence they had followed the approved Christian course. These were the days when Theodore the Conscript was enraged against paganism because Juno had twelve children. To some this multiplication of divinities might seem as beautiful as the birth of a new constellation, but this Christian it made cry shame on 'a goddess who littered like a sow'; and he died for his opinion, frustrating the intended moderation of the authorities by firing her temple. About this time St. Jerome declared that he valued marriage only because it produced virgins, and advised a widow against remarriage in terms which remind us that he was Dalmatian, and that the inhabitants of this coast have never been noted for understatement. 'The trials of marriage,' he told the Lady Furia, 'you have learned in the married state; you have been surfeited to nausea as though with the flesh of quails. Your mouth has tasted the bitterest of gall, you have voided the sour unwholesome food, you have relieved a heaving stomach. Why would you put into it again something which has already proved harmful to you? The dog is turned to his own vomit again and the washed sow to her wallowing in the mire.' This married pair of Salonæ, eager for salvation, must have believed that they could not be denied some measure of it, since they had allowed themselves to be groomed in barrenness by the Church.

They would have felt amazement had they known that, some few centuries later, the Church would have persecuted them, even to death, for such wedded chastity. For over this coast there was to spread from the hinterland of the Balkan Peninsula the Puritan heresy known as Paulicianism or Patarenism or Bogomilism or Catharism, knowing certain local and temporal variations under these names, but all impassioned over the necessity of disentangling the human spirit from the evilness of matter and convinced that this was immensely facilitated by the practice of virginity. It had the advantage of appealing to that love of the disagreeable which is one of the most unpleasant characteristics of humanity, and it became a serious rival to the orthodox churches, which attacked it not only by reason but by fire and sword. Since it laid such emphasis on virginity, the ecclesiastical authorities came down like wolves on any married pairs whom gossip reported as not availing themselves of their marital privileges. So far was this recognized as a test that a man accused of heresy is said to have brought forward as proof of his orthodoxy that he drank wine and ate meat and swore and lay with his wife. Therefore this couple of Salonæ, had they practised this wedded chastity on the same spot five or six hundred years later, would not have been granted thirty-three years to do it in. They would have had a fate indistinguishable from that of the Christian martyrs whom they revered, but they would have ranked as pagans or lower. Yet even that change in the Church's attitude they might have felt as less confounding than the later change, which would have regarded it as a matter of indifference whether they lived in abstinence or not, provided that they did not prevent the begetting of children in any intercourse they might have. That yawn in the face of their thirty-three years might have seemed worse than martyrdom.

It might have been sad to watch the little dears in their blue coats and straw hats being inducted into male superstition among the sarcophagi on a dampish day; but the Professor took us to a tomb that gave reason for hope that they would suffer no harm, being protected by their own female nature. The Latin of the inscription was so bad that it must have been erected at a time when the ancient world was suffering its last agony. In that hour, when the earth trembled and the columns were falling, a good creature set up this stone in honour of her departed husband. He was so strong, she said, that she had twins some months after he had died, and she had loved him very much. Finally, with a tremendous gesture she put out her arm and drew together two conceptions of the universe to shield him from all dangers, and commended him to the mercy of both Jesus Christ and the Parcæ. She did what she could before the darkness came, acting out of sound sense and good feeling, though with a tendency to idealize virility; and we may suppose that the little dears would do as much, whatever they were taught.

Trogir

The steamer which makes the hour's journey from Split to Trogir was full of Germans, and I wondered more and more at the impossibility of learning the truth. I have been given to understand, partly by what I have read and heard, and partly by parades I have seen in Germany, that Germans are a race of beautiful athletes tense with will, glossy with efficiency, sinister with aggressiveness. The German tourists who had surrounded us in every hotel and on every steamer since we got to Dalmatia were either pear-shaped fat or gangling thin, and in any case wore too much flesh packed on the nape of the neck, and were diffident, confused, highly incompetent as travellers, and not at all unkindly. There was, I suppose, no contradiction here, only proof that Germany has been divided into two nations, a pampered young prætorian guard and the badgered, undernourished, unregarded others. These were the others. But they also were of Hitler's Germany; for the steamer dawdled along the coast from portlet to portlet, and on each landing-stage there were standing a crowd of Dalmatians, tall, lean, upright in pride of body. The tourists stared at them and spoke of them as if they were odd and dangerous animals. The German hatred of the Slav had been revived and reinforced.

Across a milk-white sea, with two silver hydroplanes soaring and dipping to our right and left, we came to the town of Trogir, which covers a minute island, lying close to the coast, in the lee of a larger island. It is one of those golden-brown cities: the colour of rich crumbling shortbread, of butterscotch, of the best pastry, sometimes of good undarkened gravy. It stands naked and leggy, for it is a walled city deprived of its walls. The Saracens levelled them, and the Venetians and the Hungarians would never let them be rebuilt. Now it looks like a plant grown in a flower-pot when the pot is broken but the earth and roots still hang together. On the quay stand Slavized Venetian palaces with haremish lattice-work fixed to screen the stone balconies, to show that here West meets East, brought thus far by Byzantine influence and perpetuated by the proximity of the Turks. Behind them lies a proof that life is often at once mad and consistent, in the manner of dreams. Petronius Arbiter's *Satyricon* lives in the mind long after reading as a fevered progression of flights through a cityful of twisting alleys. Trogir's alleys turn and writhe like entrails. It was in Trogir that the codex of the *Satyricon* was found in 1650. It was not written there, of course. If it had been there would be nothing startling in the resemblance between the work and the town. But it came to light here, after centuries of loss. The appropriateness is as exquisite as the colour of the town, as its spires.

The appropriateness went further still: for Petronius Arbiter was by nature a Puritan, who had he been born in due time would have found himself at home as a Paulician or Patarene or Bogomil or Catharist, or in any other of those heresies which were based on the Persian faith of Manichæism, which held that matter was evil, and sex a particularly evil manifestation of it.

> *Fæda in coitu et brevis voluptas est*
> *Et tædet Veneris statim peractæ.*

Gross and brief is the pleasure of love-making, he says, and consummated passion a shocking bore. He goes on to beg his beloved therefore that they should not mate like mere cattle, but should lie lip to lip and do nothing more, to avoid toil and shame. The meaning of this exhortation lies in *Trimalchio's Supper*, which shows Petronius to have been homosexual and fearful of impotence with women; and perhaps the same explanation lay behind most followers of these heresies. But he rationalized his motives, and so did Trogir. This was an inveterately heretic city.

In its beginning it was a Greek settlement and later a Roman town, and then it was taken over in the Dark Ages by wandering Paulicians. In the twelfth century the town was sacked by the Saracens, and the inhabitants were dispersed among the villages on the mainland. That, however, did not break the tradition of heresy, for when the King of Hungary collected them and resettled them on their island they soon fell under the influence of Catharism, which was sweeping across the Balkan Peninsula from Bulgaria to Bosnia and Herzegovina and the coast. This recurrence is natural enough. Manichæism—for these heresies might as well be grouped together under the name of their parent—represents the natural reaction of the earnest mind to a religion that has aged and hardened and committed the sin against the Holy Ghost, which is to pretend that all is now known, and there can now be laid down a system of rules to guarantee salvation. In its origin it was a reaction against the extreme fatalism of Zoroastrianism, which held that man's destiny was decided by the stars, and that his only duty was to accomplish it in decorum. Passionately Mani created a myth that would show the universe as a field for moral effort: inspired by Christianity as it had passed through the filter of many Oriental minds and by a cosmology invented by an Aramaic astronomer, he imagined that there had been in the beginning of time a kingdom of light and a kingdom of darkness, existing side by side without any commixture, and that these had later been confused, as the result of aggression on the part of the darkness. This was the origin of the present world, which Mani very aptly called The Smudge. It became the duty of all men who were on the side of the light, which was identified with virtue and reason, to recover the particles of light that have become imprisoned in the substance of darkness, which was identified with vice and brutishness.

This is actually an extremely useful conception of life. But Manichæism was handicapped by the strictly literal mind of the founder and his followers, who believed that they were not speaking in allegory but were describing the hard material facts of the universe. When they spoke of the signs of the zodiac as dredges bringing up rescued particles of light to store them in the sun and moon, they meant quite squarely that that is what they thought the constellations were. This literalness turned the daily routine of the faithful into a treasure-hunt, sometimes of an indecorous nature. Excrement was obviously part of the kingdom of darkness, if ever anything was. Hence it became the duty of the Manichæan priests, the 'elect,' to take large doses of purgatives, not furtively. This routine became not only ridiculous but dangerous, as the centuries passed and the ingenious medieval European began to use it to serve that love of the disagreeable which is our most hateful quality. Natural man, uncorrected by education, does not love beauty or pleasure or peace; he does not want to eat and drink and be merry; he is on the whole averse from wine, women, and song. He prefers to fast, to groan in melancholy, and to be sterile. This is easy enough to understand. To feast one must form friendships and spend money, to be merry one must cultivate fortitude and forbearance and wit, to have a wife and children one must assume the heavy obligation of keeping them and the still heavier obligation of loving them. All these are kinds of generosity, and natural man is mean. His meanness seized on the Manichæan routine and exploited it till the whole of an infatuated Europe seemed likely to adopt it, and would doubtless have done so if the Orthodox and Roman Catholic Churches had not hardened their hearts against it and counted no instrument too merciless for use, not even mass murder.

It is our tendency to sympathize with the hunted hare, but much that we read of Western European heretics makes us suspect that here the quarry was less of a hare than a priggish skunk.

In Languedoc there seems to have been some sort of pleasant transmutation of the faith, but for the most part heretical Europe presents us with the horrifying spectacle of countless human beings gladly facing martyrdom for the right to perform cantrips that might have been invented by a mad undertaker. There was a particularly horrible travesty of extreme unction called the 'endura.' Every dying person was asked by the priest whether he wanted to be a confessor or a martyr; if he wanted to be a confessor he remained without food or drink, except for a little water, for three days, and if he wanted to be a martyr a pillow was held over his mouth while certain prayers were recited. If he survived in either case he ranked as a priest. This horrid piece of idiocy was often used as a means of suicide, a practice to which these heretics were much addicted; but as they believed that to suffer torture in dying would relieve them from it in the next world, the real enthusiasts preferred for this purpose to swallow broken glass. The faith also gave encouragement to certain passive methods of murder. The guardians of the sick were urged to extinguish life when death was near; and how this worked out may be deduced from a case in France where a woman subjected her infant grandchild to the endura and then prevented its mother from suckling it till it died. By this necrophily, and a pervasive nastiness about sex, which went so far as to forbid a father to be touched by his own daughter, even if he were very old and she were his nurse, millions were raised to a state of rapture. The whole of modern history could be deduced from the popularity of this heresy in Western Europe: its inner sourness, its preference for hate over love and for war over peace, its courage about dying, its cowardice about living.

This cannot have been the whole truth about these heresies. So inherently noble a vision must have produced some nobility, its own particles of light cannot all have been dissolved. But its achievements were trodden into the dirt by its enemies along with its failures; the Huns and the Avars never made a cleaner job of devastation than the orthodox armies who were sent against the Albigenses and the Catharists, and the heretics in the Balkans were spared such demolition only because of the Turkish occupation, which laid waste their institutions just as thoroughly for quite other reasons. It happens that here in Trogir there is preserved a specimen of Manichæan culture. In the centre of the town a cathedral stands in a flagged square. They began building it in the thirteenth century to replace a cathedral, six hundred years old, which had been burned by the Saracens, and went on for a couple more centuries. It was for long one of the homes of the

Patarene heresy. Its congregation were solidly adepts of the hidden
faith, and so too, at least once in its history, was the bishop who
officiated at its altar. In the porch to the bell-tower of this cathedral
there is a carved portal which is the most massive and pure work
of art produced by Manichæism that I have ever seen. There are,
of course, specimens of heretic architecture in France, but those
were modified by an existing and flourishing French culture. Here
a fresh and vigorous Manichæism has been grafted on a dying and
remote offshoot of Roman and Byzantine culture.

It is the work of a thirteenth-century sculptor called Radovan, or
the Joyous One, and it instantly recalls the novels of Dostoievsky.
There is the same sense of rich, contending disorder changing
oozily from form to form, each one of which the mind strives to
grasp, because if it can but realize its significance there will be not
order, but a hint of coming order. Above the door are many scenes
from the life of Christ, arranged not according to the order of time;
in the beginning He is baptized, in the middle He is crucified, in the
end He is adored by the Wise Men. These scenes are depicted with a
primitive curiosity, but also make a highly cultured admission that
that curiosity cannot be wholly gratified. It is as if the child in the
artist asked, 'What are those funny men doing?' and the subtle man
in him answered, 'I do not know, but I think . . .' On the outer
edge of the door, one to the right and one to the left, stand Adam
and Eve, opinions about our deprived and distorting destiny; and
they stand on a lion and a lioness, which are opinions about the
animal world, and the nature we share with it. In the next column,
in a twined confusion, the sculptor put on record the essence of
the sheep and the stag, the hippopotamus and the centaur, the
mermaid and the apostles; and in the next he shows us the common
man of his time, cutting wood, working leather, making sausages,
killing a pig, bearing arms. But of these earthly types and scenes
the child in the artist asked as eagerly as before, 'What are those
funny men doing?' and the man answered as hesitantly, 'I do not
know, but I think . . .'

There we have an attitude which differentiates Manichæism
sharply from orthodox Christianity. If the common man was
actually interpenetrated with particles of light, or divinity, as
the heretics believed, and if this could be made more or less
difficult to recover by his activities, then each individual and
his calling had to be subjected to the severest analysis possible.
But if the common man has a soul, a recognizable part of himself,
as orthodox Christians believe, which is infected with sin through
the fall of man and can be cleansed again by faith and participation

in the sacraments and adherence to certain ethical standards, then it is necessary not to analyze the individual but to make him follow a programme. This difference corresponds with the difference between Western Europeans and the Slavs, of which many of us receive our first intimations from Dostoievsky. In the West conversation is regarded as a means of either passing the time agreeably or exchanging useful information; among Slavs it is thought to be disgraceful, when a number of people are together, that they should not pool their experience and thus travel further towards the redemption of the world. In the West conduct follows an approved pattern which is departed from by people of weak or headstrong will; but among Slavs a man will try out all kinds of conduct simply to see whether they are of the darkness or of the light. The Slavs, in fact, are given to debate and experiment which to the West seem unnecessary and therefore, since they must involve much that is painful, morbid. This spirit can be recognized also in the curious pressing, exploratory nature of Radovan's imagination.

But there are other resemblances also between Manichæism and Slavism, between Radovan and Dostoievsky. For one, the lack of climax. The orthodox Christian thinks that the story of the universe has revealed itself in a design that would be recognized as pleasing in a work of finite proportions; a number of people, not too great to be remembered, and all easily distinguishable, enact a drama which begins with the Creation, rises to its peak in the Incarnation, is proceeding to its consummation in the Day of Judgment and the coming of the Kingdom of Heaven. The Manichæan believed that an immense crowd of people, often very difficult to distinguish from one another, are engaged in recovering the strayed particles of light, a process which can come to a climax only when it is finished. This is reflected in Radovan's work by a curious levelness of inspiration, a lack of light and shade in his response to his subject; in the Slav's readiness to carry on a conversation for ever, to stay up all night; in Dostoievsky's continuous, unremitting spiritual excitement.

For another resemblance, there is the seeming paradox of a fierce campaign against evil combined with a tolerance of its nature. We cannot understand this in the West, where we assume that sincere hostility to sin must be accompanied by a reluctance to contemplate it and a desire to annihilate it. But according to the Manichæan faith there was no need to take action against darkness except when it enmeshed the light. When the kingdom of darkness was existing side by side with the kingdom of light without any commixture, then it was committing no offence. That attitude can be traced in Radovan's faithful reproduction of life's imperfect forms, in Dostoievsky's choice of abnormality as a subject. And there is yet another resemblance which is particularly apparent in the work of Radovan. The columns he carved with the representations of The Smudge are borne on the shoulders of those who are wholly of the darkness, Jews and Turks and pagans. It is put forward solidly and without sense of any embarrassment that there are those who are predestined to pain, contrary to the principles of human justice. Calvin admitted this with agony, but there is none here; and Dostoievsky never complains against the God who created the disordered universe he describes. This is perhaps because the Manichæans, like the Greeks, did not regard God as the Creator, but as the Arranger, or even as the Divine Substance which had to be arranged.

That the West should be wholly orthodox and not at all Manichæan in its outlook on these matters is the consequence of the zeal of the Roman Catholic Church. Quite simply it physically exterminated all communities who would not abandon the heretic philosophy. But the South-East of Europe was so continuously disturbed, first by civil war and Asiatic invasion and then by the Turkish occupation, that the Eastern Church could not set up an effective machine for the persecution of heretics, even if it had had the temperament to do so. There the outward forms of Manichæism eventually perished, as they were bound to do in time, partly because of the complicated and fantastic nature of its legend and the indecorous and cruel perversions of its ritual; but its philosophy remained, rooted in the popular mind before the Turkish gate closed down between the Balkans and the rest of the world, to travel northwards and influence the new land of Russia, where after several centuries it inspired a generation of giants, to the astonishment of Europe. The Russian novelists of the nineteenth century represented the latest recrudescence of a philosophy that had too much nobility in it ever to perish utterly.

But one wishes one knew how this heresy compared with orthodoxy as a consolation in time of danger: whether the Manichæans of Trogir were as firmly upheld by their faith as the Christians of Salonæ. The Manichæans might claim that it served them better, so far as barbarian invasion was concerned, for they had one of the narrowest escapes from annihilation that is written in all history. The Professor took us on from the Cathedral to see the scene of it. We walked out of the city onto the quay through a gate which still keeps the handsome stone lion of St. Mark that was the sign of Venetian possession, surmounted by the patron saint of Trogir, St. Giovanni Orsini, who was its bishop about the time of the Norman Conquest; he was a remarkable engineer, who was made a saint because he aided the Papacy in its efforts to suppress the Slav liturgy. A bridge crossed a channel hemmed with marble and glazed with the reflection of many cypresses, and joined Trogir to a mainland that showed us a little level paradise under the harsh, bare, limestone hills, where the pepper trees dropped their long green hair over the red walls of villa gardens, and Judas trees showed their stained, uneasy purple flowers through wrought-iron gates. 'You see, it came very near, so near that it could not have come any nearer,' said the Professor.

He spoke of the time in 1241, just after Radovan had started his portal, when the Mongols, seeking to expand the empire made for them by Genghis Khan, conquered Russia and swept across Europe to Hungary, putting King Bela and his nobles to flight. While he vainly petitioned the other Christian powers to help, the invaders swept on towards Vienna and then swung down to Croatia, burning, looting, killing. King Bela tried to stand firm at Zagreb, and sent his Greek wife and their three children to seek safety on the coast. These were ranging in panic between Split and the fortress of Klish, just behind it in the mountains, when the King joined them, frantic with fear. It is doubtful if even our own times can provide anything as hideous as the Mongol invasion, as this dispensing of horrible death by yellow people made terrible as demons by their own unfamiliarity. It is true that the establishment of the Mongol Empire was ultimately an excellent thing for the human spirit, since it made Asiatic culture available to Europe; but as Peer Gynt said, 'Though God is thoughtful for His people, economical, no, that He isn't!'

The King and a tattered, gibbering multitude of nobles and soldiers and priests, bearing with them the body of the saint King Stephen of Hungary, and many holy objects from their churches, trailed up and down the coast. Split received them magnificently, but the King struck away the townsmen's greetings with the fury of a terrified child. The shelter they offered him was useless. They might not know it, but he did. He had seen the Mongols. He demanded a ship to take him out to the islands. Yellow horsemen could not ride the sea. But there was none ready. He shouted his anger and went with his Queen and his train to Trogir, which is within a short distance of many islands. He fled to a neighbouring island, which is still called 'The King's Shelter.' Some of his followers went with him, but enough stayed in Trogir to carpet the place with sleeping men and women when night fell. Worn out by fatigue, by hunger, by fear, they threw themselves down wherever they could: on the floors of all rooms, in every palace and hovel, all over every church, under Radovan's portal, on the flags of the piazza and the alleys, on the quays. Their treasures cast down beside them, they slept. Every boat too was covered with sleeping bodies and upturned faces, and the rocks of every island.

The Mongols came down on the coast. Nothing could stop them. But at the sea they met a check. They had thought the King must be at Klish or Split, and they were repulsed at both. The shelter offered by the Splitchani was not as negligible as the King had thought. The Mongols were used to unlimited space for their operations, and to attack fortifications from a terrain bounded by the sea or sharply broken ground presented them with a new problem. But they found their way to Trogir; and on to this bridge across the channel they sent a herald who cried out in a loud voice the minatory moral nonsense talked by the aggressor in any age: 'Here is the commandment of the Kaïdan, the unconquerable chief of the army: do not uphold the crimes of others, but hand over to us our enemies, lest you be involved in those crimes and perish when you need not.' For the herald himself the delivery of this message must have been the supreme moment of his life, either for perverse joy or for pain. For those who heard him tell us that he spoke in Slav as a Slav. He must have been either a traitor or a prisoner. Either he was dooming his own people, whom he loathed, to their ruin, and his words were sweet as honey in his mouth, or he loved his people, and he found his words bitter as gall.

The guards of Trogir made no answer, for they had been ordered by the King to keep silent. Then we find, which is not common, history following a line to which we are accustomed in our private lives. We have all heard spoken tremendous words which must unchain tragedy, we have all recognized the phrase after which there can be nothing but love and happiness; and afterwards nothing has happened, life goes on precisely the same, there is the vacuum of the anticlimax. But in history the pushed boulder usually falls. In Trogir, however, it was not so. After this tremendous moment, nothing happened. The herald cried out his tremendous message, the guards kept silent; and presently the Mongols went home. It is thought that they were considering whether they should ford or bridge the channel, when they received news that their supreme chief, Ogodai, the son of Genghis Khan, had died in Asia, and that the succession was in dispute. They went back at a trot, just taking time to sack and kill on their way, through Southern Dalmatia, where they burned the lovely city of Kotor, and through Bosnia, Serbia, and Bulgaria. Trogir breathed again. The King returned from his islet, and took his nobles and his armies and his priests and the dead St. Stephen and the holy jewels back to Hungary. But the Queen had to stay in Dalmatia for some time, till her two little daughters, Catarina and Margareta, died of a sickness they had contracted during their flight. Their tombs can be seen in Diocletian's mausoleum at Split.

It is the kind of secret that time takes with it: whether the heretics of Trogir leaned on their faith and found it bore them, in those hours when the Mongol sword hung over their heads. But it can be deduced that in a general way it did them no harm, for they came out of the Middle Ages into the Renaissance strong in art and gallant. The interior of the Cathedral, which is two hundred years later than Radovan's work, has a fine form under its immensely rich vault, cut out of stone that has a warm grey bloom; and there is a baptistery, naughtily overdecorated, but with an exquisite series of panels, in each of which a cherub bearing a torch thrusts his way through ponderous closing doors, ostensibly to illustrate some notion concerning immortality, but more probably because the Renaissance had a liking for fine little boys. And everywhere are small but delicious palaces in the Venetian Gothic style, sweetly compact, covered by elegance as by a creeper, with balconies and trellised windows. There is one such, most lovely, facing the Cathedral, the residence of the Chippitch family. It is the very house where there was found the codex of *The Satyricon*. Here in Trogir it is as if events were caught in the rich architecture like wasps in syrup.

When you go into the courtyard of the Chippitch Palace you will find the figureheads of two old ships, one a delicate victory woman, the other a huge cock. Each was made on a long iron stalk, held in a long iron hand. They are violent in character, as if they were made by desperate men. One was the figurehead of the ship manned and financed by Trogir and commanded by Louis Chippitch at the battle of Lepanto in 1571 and the other belonged to the Turkish ship he captured. He put them there when he came home and they have remained there ever since. Again we were made to realize the debt the West owes the people of this coast. The naval power of the Turks was broken at Lepanto and never was reconstituted. What broke it was a fleet composed of one hundred and fourteen Venetian galleys, a hundred and three Spanish galleys, twelve supplied by the Pope, four supplied by the Duke of Savoy, three from Malta, and seven from the seven Dalmatian towns, although by that time

the coast was ravaged and poverty-stricken. Even devastated Rab
and Krk sent one apiece. And Trogir's contribution also was a
magnificent offering from poverty; for the town was perpetually
forced by the Venetians to give money and supplies as bribes to
the Turkish military and civil officials on the mainland, and it
often knew real need. Not only Rab but Trogir, and indeed every
community on this coast, paid in their gold and then blood for the
security of the West.

Since Trogir created such beauty and achieved such courage
under Venice, the visitor is tempted to believe that foreign dominance was good for Dalmatia. But to think that is to be as
superficial as visitors to an orphanage, who at sight of children with
washed faces doing neat handwork forget the inevitable wrongs
of institutional life. The inhabitants of this coast were looted of
their money and their morals by their alien masters. 'Come into
the Dominican church,' said the Professor, 'and you will see how
savage we were here, how horribly and beautifully savage.' In
that fine church there is a tomb erected by a noble widow to
her murdered husband. Carved as carefully and reverently as any
Madonna in a Pietà, an enraged lioness lifts to Heaven a muzzle
soft and humid with the hope of vengeance. 'It is the vendetta put
into stone,' said the Professor. 'Here the vendetta was a curse as
it was in Corsica, because God has made us a very quarrelsome
people, and the Hungarians and the Venetians encouraged all our
dissensions, so that we should not be a united people and would
therefore be more easy for them to subdue.'

This policy became more formidable in the fifteenth century,
after Trogir had finally become Venetian. Refugees have always
presented a grave problem to the countries that have received them.
The culture they bring with them must clash with the culture they
find established in their new homes. When the Turks overran the
Balkan Peninsula some Bosnian and Herzegovinian landowners
became Moslems and were left in possession of their lands, but
those who clung to their faith fled to Dalmatia. They were pure
feudal lords, of a type that had long disappeared from Western
Europe, and they could not understand the constitution of the
Dalmatian cities, which gave different rights to nobles and citizens,
but on that basis defended them with equal justice. The refugees
could not understand that they must treat with courtesy lawless
men of admittedly inferior social status, and that the nobles also
would be against them if they failed to obey this convention; and
indeed some of the nobles, who were undemocratic and hated the
citizens, were willing to side with the refugees in this. Thus there

arose a great deal of civil strife which time would have corrected if the Venetians had not seen in it an opportunity to obey that evil precept, *Divide et impera*. They secretly backed each party against the others, and refrained from any legislative reform that would have sweetened the situation.

But they went in for simpler misconduct. In the seventeenth century Trogir produced a superb example of the learned gentleman of the Renaissance, Giovanni Lucius, or Yovan Lutchitch, a descendant of one of the same Bosnian refugees. He had studied in Rome and devoted his life to research into Croatian and Dalmatian history. His great work *De Regno Dalmatiæ et Croatiæ* is still a classic: he collected a great many original documents, for though he wrote with patriotic passion he was governed by the love of truth. But one of the feuds that Venice encouraged struck him down. A member of a noble family that had long been political enemies of the Lutchitches, Paolo de Andreis, was himself a historian and was himself engaged on a rival work. Dons will be dons, so he informed the authorities that Lutchitch was searching the archives to prove that the Venetians had violated the ancient constitutions of the Dalmatian cities. Later, when the Venetian Governor-general came to visit Trogir and proposed to quarter himself in the Lutchitch Palace, Yovan Lutchitch excused himself on the ground that his sister was gravely ill; and again Andreis went to the authorities, this time to denounce his rival as a liar. Immediately Lutchitch was thrown into prison among common criminals, while a squad of galley slaves cleared his family out of their palace and the Governor-general took possession of it. Lutchitch himself was about to be bastinadoed, but the Bishop of Trogir saved him by appealing to the power of the Church, and got him permission to take refuge in Rome, where he died after thirty-four years of exile, an extravagant punishment for a patriot.

'We have so greatly needed peace, a little peace,' said the Professor, 'but we have had hardly any. And I will take you now to see a relic of the regime that gave us the fairest promise of it. But I warn you, you will laugh at it, it is not as impressive as it should be.' He took us round the wide hem of the city, the space on its quays where the walls used to stand, to the north end of the island. It did not take us long to get there, for this town is incredibly small: one could walk round it in less than ten minutes. 'Look at it well!' said the Professor, and we gaped, for what we saw was surprising in this land which is precious about its architecture, which will have nothing that is not superb or ethereal or noble. On a patch of waste ground, beside a medieval tower, there stands a little roofless temple raised on a platform of rough-hewn stones, not at all antique, not at all suggestive of sacrifices to the gods, strongly evocative of an afternoon in the park. Almost it is a bandstand. 'Is it not French?' said the Professor. 'So neat, so irreverent to the tragic solemnity of the place and its past, so fundamentally admirable. You see the sea used to wash all round it. It is only since we had a Yugoslavia that there have been drained the marshes along the coast which gave the city malaria, and that has involved deepening the main channel and drawing the sea away from this shore. But when Marshal Marmont built this belvedere it was right out among the waves, and he used to sit there with his officers and play cards when it was very hot. That we find very amusing: it is such a light-minded, pleasure-loving thing to do. And yet Marmont was a hero, a great hero, and the only foreign ruler that was truly good for us. Though we find it hard to forgive our conquerors, we could even find it in our hearts to admit that it would have been a good thing if the French had stayed here longer.'

It is really a very pretty belvedere; and it has the sacred French air of dealing respectfully and moderately with the little things of life that are not sacred. It is better, yes, it is definitely better, than the muzzle of the lioness wetly throbbing towards the scent of blood. That it knows and has put behind it. The sword was declared superseded in the delicious contentment which was housed here between the columns, above the rippling Adriatic. For indeed Marmont must have been extraordinarily happy here, for a time. For one thing, he very greatly disliked his wife, and here he was able to treat her extremely well from a very great distance. For another, he adored the place itself, and he was one of those who like the Slav flavour, who find all other peoples insipid by contrast. And he liked the exercise of independent power, as a colonial governor far from home. 'He was, of course, a very vain man,' said the Professor in a deprecating tone. I wondered why: I have never been able to see why people object to vanity, unless it is associated with blindness to the qualities of others, and it often is not.

But if Marmont was not vain, he was a prig. He must have been very well pleased with himself as he played cards in the belvedere. He was living in accordance with reason and virtue. He might have been very hot, but thanks to this intelligent device he was less hot. He was building up a career, and while many men have had to resort to violence and rapacity to serve their ambition he was at once earning success and disseminating peaceful manners, learning, and hygiene in a land previously barbarian. He did not even compromise his integrity, for he faced quite honestly the moral problem inherent in empire. In his memoirs, which he wrote well for a man of action, he admits that a nation cannot hold alien territories without disingenuous handling of subject populations; he sets down without disguise the plain facts of certain occasions when he found it necessary to play politics and foment misunderstandings among friends in order to establish French authority. It may have happened that, while he waited for a partner to put down a card, he set his eyes on the dancing glass of the Adriatic, or the lion-coloured mountains, trembling like the sea in the heat, and hypnosis made him aware of the question the inner self perpetually asks itself: 'What am I doing, and is it good?' The answer he would have overheard would certainly not have been boastful: it might have been proud of the process in which it was engaged, but it would have been modest regarding the extent of its engagement. The universe was in disorder; its sole offensiveness lay in its disorder. Man having been given, whether by a personal or an impersonal force it hardly mattered, a vision of order, he could correct the universe and regiment it into shining harmony. Marmont had pointed his sword at a bulging plinth and bidden it be straight; he had raised his schoolmaster's rod and a fallen column was again erect. He would have claimed no less, but no more, and would have been happy in an exact accountancy of his limited effort.

But the place held a vaster, darker wisdom. On the edge of the city stands this belvedere with its six frail pillars. In the centre of Trogir stands the Cathedral with its portico sombre with the prophecies of Radovan, with his announcement that there is no hope within man, since he is a fusion of light and darkness, like the universe itself; and that he must work for the liberation of the light and not for the reform of the universe, because the universe is evil, by reason of this fusion, and must pass. This is a hard word, hard with the intolerable hardness of mysticism. It is far harder, far more mystical, than the message of orthodox Christianity. It places on man a tremendous obligation to regard his life as a redemptory act, but at the same time it informs him that he is tainted through and through with the substance of damnation, and that the medium through which alone he can perform this act is equally tainted; and it assumes that this obligation is worth accepting and will in fact be crowned with success, simply because of the nature of the abstractions involved, simply because light is light and therefore to be loved.

That it might be as Radovan thought was confirmed by the

experience of Marmont; his later card games in the belvedere cannot have been happy at all. Napoleon was called by many The Man, and in his manhood he agreed with the Manichæan conception. He was at first a soldier of the light. Marmont must have felt that in working with him he was driving the darkness engendered by the collapsed Revolution out of France, and out of disturbed Europe. He had, indeed, almost no other grounds for liking the association. It is one of the oddest examples of human irrationality that while most of the people who really knew Napoleon well found him unlovable and something of a bore, innumerable people who were not born until long after his death, and have nothing to go upon except the accounts of these familiars, obstinately adore him; and these have blamed Marmont for coldness and ingratitude to him. But as Marmont explains in his memoirs, he had known Napoleon since his early youth and had never really liked him, and he had no reason to feel gratitude to him, for he had earned every step of his military promotion by concrete achievements that would have been similarly rewarded in any army. He worked with him because they both stood for the same ideal of national order.

The darkness suddenly streamed out of Napoleon's soul; the ray had been white, it was black. There was manifest in his relations with his subordinates the same enjoyment of the exciting discord irrelevant to the theme which is familiar enough as a symptom of sexual degeneration, of incapacity for love. Marmont has recorded in his memoirs, with the exquisite accuracy of a perceptive but unimaginative man, the moment when Napoleon sought to slake his appetite on him, to his perturbation and disgust. During the 1809 campaign Marmont returned to headquarters to report after fighting a brilliant and fatiguing engagement and was received by a scowling and soured Napoleon, who grumbled at him for nearly two and a half hours. When he went back to the hovel where he was billeted he flung himself down in an agony of weariness and humiliation, and was reduced to the extreme of bewildered misery because the room began to fill up with more and more people. Suddenly he found that they had come to congratulate him. The two and a half hours of nagging had been Napoleon's way of adding spice to the promotion of Marmont to the rank of marshal: so might a lover, of the sillier sort, pick a quarrel with the beloved before making her or him a present. But Marmont was interested in the art of war, in France, and in the establishment of the international order he thought most favourable to France; and he could not imagine why his promotion from one rank of the army to another, about which there was nothing unnatural, which was according to routine, should be attended by discourtesy and gross disregard for his feelings. He records it with restraint. Napoleon had long been fallen when he wrote. But behind the well-mannered writing sounds a perplexity. If Napoleon thought I was good enough to be marshal, which was pleasant, why couldn't he have been pleasant about it? Marmont would have liked pleasantness everywhere. The light was in him, seeking to establish its kingdom.

When he first went to Dalmatia it must have seemed that the light in him and in Napoleon was working to free itself from the long captivity it had endured in these darkened lands. A strong and peaceful Illyria emerging from the state of war and anarchy that had lasted since nearly the beginning of recorded time would have shone like the moon coming out of a black cloud. There was a time in Napoleon's life when the whole of Europe appeared to be suffering defeat before France only in order to rise again and put on an immortal brightness. But in a few months the prospect changed. It was as if there had been an eclipse; the Manichæans would have recognized its nature. In Napoleon there seemed now to be nothing but darkness. In Marmont's letters he held up to Napoleon his own conception of a radiant Illyria, part of a transfigured Europe, and asked for support in realizing it, in men, in money, in words. But Napoleon turned away, shutting his eyes as if he could no longer bear the light. He ignored all Marmont's requests and replied in letters hot and sticky with roguishness, or did not reply at all.

In the belvedere Marmont must have found it difficult to keep his mind on his cards. In the end, we know, he threw them in and pushed back his chair and strolled away, to leave Dalmatia for ever. There was fault in him too. He was man also, he was a fusion of good and evil, of light and darkness. Therefore he did not want with his wholeness that there should be a victory of light; he preferred that darkness should continue to exist, and this universe, The Smudge, should not pass away. He showed it, and so did all his reasonable kind, by leaving power in the hands of Napoleon, who had long ceased to be reasonable, who was now seeking disgrace as he had earlier sought glory. He went to Spain, he went to Russia, against the advice of his counsellors, for no other purpose than to make a long journey and be benighted at its end. But the change in him excited no horror in the people; rather their passion for him rose to an orgasm, as if this were the climax to which his glory had been but the preparation. The great men for whom humanity feels ecstatic love need not be good, nor even gifted; but they must display this fusion of light and darkness which is the essential human character; they must even promise, by a predominance of darkness, that the universe shall for ever persist in its imperfection.

After Napoleon had safely led back Europe to the limits of frustration it preferred to paradise, nothing happened in Dalmatia for a hundred years. Austrian rule was sheer negativism. The Slavs were raised up in enmity against the Italian-speaking sections, who were either such descendants of the Roman settlers as had never amalgamated with the Slavs, or Venetian immigrants. There was no coherence; very little trade, since the Austrian railway system was designed to encourage the prosperity of Austria and Hungary and leave the Slav territories isolated from the rest of Europe. In Trogir grass grew in the streets and piazzas. But the tradition of its rich civic life was not broken. After the war this town, like many another on the Dalmatian coast, was coveted by the Italians, who one September night in 1919 sent a small party of soldiers to seize it. It should have been defended by eight Yugoslav soldiers, but these had too ingenuously accepted hospitality of some pro-Italians on the previous evening and were all unconscious. So when the inhabitants woke up in the morning they found their town in possession of Italian soldiers. There were, however, only five families that were pro-Italian; and the rest of the population rushed at the invaders and disarmed them with their bare hands. One woman ran at four men in charge of a machine-gun and took it away from them, and many others chased out runaway Italians who had taken refuge in the courtyards of the houses, beating them with their fists and tearing away their helmets and belts. 'I do not tell you their names,' said the Professor, 'because it is a very disagreeable thing for a lady to have to commit such violent acts, and these were not viragoes, they were ladies. But I can assure you that they bore names which have been distinguished in the annals of Trogir for many centuries, and that they were none of them ignorant of their ancestors' achievements.'

It is a very quiet city now: an empty city, for it suffered like Rab from a terrible visitation of the plague, and the population has never replenished itself, because the malaria that raged here till recently caused sterility. But it exists. That is to be noted, for there is a legend all over Europe which leaves not one of its stones standing upon another. Close by the Cathedral there is a loggia which was the ancient hall of justice, undatable because it was built of bits and pieces from the old town which was destroyed by the Saracens and from near-by Roman settlements. It was in ruins during the Austrian occupation, and it was roofed and made decent by the Yugoslav Government. Nevertheless in all anti-Slav circles it has become a symbol of the barbarity of the Yugoslavs, because of a very small defacement. It happened that on the wall behind the stone table at which the judges used to sit there was placed during the late fifteenth century a winged lion of St Mark, surrounded by saints and emblems of justice. Every Dalmatian town bears such a symbol at one place or more, on a wall or a gate, or a public building, and always it is beautiful. The lion is always waved and opulent, and reminds one that it was Bronzino and Paris Bordone who first celebrated the type which we know now, in brass instead of gold, as Mae West. To judge from photographs the lion in the loggia was a specially glorious example of its kind, a *lilium auratum* in stone. While the Austrians were in Dalmatia the wind and the rain beat on this lion, but it was properly sheltered after the Yugoslavs had done their repairs.

It unfortunately happened, however, that about Christmastime in 1932 some young men of Trogir got drunk, and their larger, simpler emotions were liberated. They then remembered that the Italians had tried to steal their city, and had not given up the hope of doing so some day; and they inflicted severe damage on this lion and another at the port gate of the town. They were not utterly destroyed. They still exist, in a quite recognizable form, on the walls of a museum. This was one of those incidents which prove it to be a matter of sheer luck that man does not go on all fours, but it obviously had no other significance. Italy, however, took the opportunity to give an extraordinary exhibition of her intentions towards Dalmatia. There took place all over the country demonstrations against the Yugoslavian Government, organized by two societies which exist for the purpose of such mischief-making, Dalmatia Irredenta and Pro-Dalmatia. Mussolini himself declared that in the mild hooliganism of the intoxicated young men he saw 'the clear expression of a mentality of hate that made no secret of its opposition to Italy. . . . It is a carefully premeditated plan. . . . The responsible parties are to be found among elements of the ruling classes. . . . The lions of Trogir are destroyed, but in their destruction they stand stronger than ever as a living symbol and a certain promise.' To keep the peace the Yugoslavian Government had to eat dirt and, what is worse, harden its tradition of mercilessness towards its own people by suppressing the counter-demonstrations against Italy which naturally took place all over Yugoslavia.

The wickedness and absurdity of Mussolini's proceedings can be estimated if one imagines Great Britain making hostile demonstrations against Ireland because some drunken boys in Cork

had destroyed a couple of Union Jacks that had been left there
during the English occupation. But that does not quite express the
perversity of the Italian attitude, for it must further be remembered
that Trogir had not belonged to Venice for a hundred and forty
years, at which time it would have been impossible for a Roman
or the inhabitant of any other Italian city except Venice to feel
any emotion whatsoever regarding an insult to the lion of St Mark,
except perhaps a lively sympathy. This immense forgery of feeling
led on to a forgery of fact. There spread all over Italy and into
Central Europe, and thence all over the world, a belief that the
inhabitants of Trogir had destroyed all the historic beauties of their
town, and even their entire town. 'What, you went to Trogir?' a
refugee German professor said to me in London, after my first visit
to Dalmatia. 'But it cannot have been worth your while, now that
these barbarous Yugoslavs have levelled everything worth looking
at to the ground. Ah, if you had only visited it, when I did, two
years before the war! You can have no idea how beautiful it was
then!' Medieval Europe was ignorant, it believed in unicorns and
mermaids, it debated how many angels could dance on the point of
a needle. The folly of modern Europe provides us with no agreeable
decorative symbols, it does not lead us to debate on the real fact
of the different planes of existence. It pretends for mean motives
that a city which stands steadily among the moving waters, its old
buildings and its old families as they have been for seven hundred
years, is not.

Split III

My husband was reading to me from Count Voinovitch's *Histoire de Dalmatie* a fairy story that they tell about the Emperor Diocletian all over this coast and Bosnia and Herzegovina and Montenegro. It is a variant of the story we all know about Midas. It seems that he had a ridiculous physical secret which he could keep from all the world except his barber, a little matter of ears like an ass and horns like a ram. So his barbers shaved him but once, and were never heard of again. At last a barber who was the only son of a widow was told that the next day he must shave the Emperor's beard. He was overcome with horror, but his mother told him not to despair, and made him a little cake moistened with her own milk, and said to him, 'While you are shaving the Emperor take a bit of this cake.' When he did so, Diocletian smelt the curious odour of the paste, and asked for a piece of it. He liked it, but found the taste peculiar, and felt he knew it yet could not name it. 'What did your mother use to moisten this cake?' he asked. 'Her own milk,' answered the barber. 'Then we are brothers and I cannot kill you,' said the Emperor. Thereafter the story follows familiar lines: the barber's life is spared, but he is sworn to silence, and he is so inconvenienced by the secret that he murmurs it to a reed, which is made into a flute by the village children and repeats it whenever it is played.

'How characteristic it is of the Slavs to keep on telling this story,' said my husband; 'it is so packed with criticism of the idea of power. The folk imagination that invented it is responsible to the majesty of the Emperor and his usefulness to the community, and it recognizes that he can exercise power and that his subjects can obey him only if there is a convention that he is superhuman, that he has none of the subhuman characteristics which compose humanity. The Emperor must therefore be permitted to commit acts in defence of this convention which would be repulsive if an individual committed them for his private ends. But here nature speaks, through the mother, who is a superb example of the hatefulness of women as Strindberg sees it. She pulls down what men have built up by an appeal to the primitive facts of life which men have agreed to disregard in order that they may transcend them. She proves to the Emperor that after all he is an individual, that the murder he commits for the sake of maintaining a useful convention may be a social act but is also fratricide on a basis of reality. But the story does not give her the victory either, for it gives a warning that, once a breach is made in that convention, it must fall; what the barber knows the village children must know before long, and then there must be anarchy. The story is perfectly balanced; but it shows bias to have preserved it, and that bias would make it very difficult for Slavs ever to settle down under a government, and lead a *rangé* political life.'

'I wonder what the woman really put in the cake,' I said, 'for it requires a great deal of explanation if the widowed mother of a grown-up son should have any milk. But what on earth are our friends doing? It is half-past eight.' For we were in our bedroom, waiting for a lady and her husband, Mr and Mrs X., who were to take us to a charity festival in the town, where there was to be a dance and a cabaret supper, and there we were to meet other friends of ours, Mr and Mrs A., and spend the evening with the four of them. 'Yes, something must have gone wrong,' said my husband, 'for they said they would come at seven.' 'Then let us go downstairs and have dinner,' I demanded. 'No,' said my husband, 'if we do that we will eat a lot at dinner because it is so good, and then we will have to eat more food at the dance, and we are effete Westerners. If you are hungry, it is your own fault for rejecting the waiter's advice, and not keeping that nice cold palatschinken by you.' And indeed it was only a few minutes later that Mr and Mrs X. sent up a message to say that they were in the hall of the hotel, but would be glad if we did not come down but received them in our room, as they wished to speak to us on a private matter.

As soon as they entered, Mrs X., who was an exquisite creature made of moonlight and soot-black shadows, cast from her slimness her heavy coat, which fell from her like a declaration in recitative. Both she and her husband, who was himself exceedingly hand-some, were in a state of excitement that recalled Italian opera. It was tragic yet not painful, it was accomplished and controlled, and yet perfectly sincere. What it was putting forward as important, it in fact felt to be important. They both began by apologizing to us deeply, for having kept us waiting, for not being able to offer us the most intense and comprehensive hospitality possible. But they had found themselves unable to carry out Mr A.'s plan for the evening. Absolutely unable; and it was astonishing that Mr A. could have conceived that it should be otherwise. He would never have put forward such a proposal had he not been exposed to alien influences, had he not just returned from several years in the United States and had his wife not been a Czech. This had, naturally enough, no doubt, made him insensitive to the state of public opinion in Split.

When the X.'s had first received Mr A.'s letter two hours before, they said, warming up nicely, they had looked at each other in horror. For it had presented them with a dilemma. Mr A. would not have put forward his proposal had it not suited our convenience. Was it therefore their duty to overlook the affront it offered to the public opinion of Split in order to fulfil the Dalmatian ideal of hospitality? To decide this they had visited a friend, a judge ninety years old, of a very ancient Splitchani family, who was a connexion of Mr X.'s mother. He had told them that he considered the question immensely delicate, but that he understood we had shown signs of sensibility and it was therefore unlikely we would wish them to violate the feeling of their birthplace. The judge had added that as we were travelling abroad instead of being in England at the time of the Coronation, we were probably members of some party which was in opposition to the Government, and would be the more ready to understand their point of view. So Mr and Mrs X. had gone to see Mr and Mrs A., who had seen their point of view when it was explained to them, and had instantly apologized, but had had to go to the festival all the same, as they had promised to act as judges in some competition; and they had, indeed, framed an alternative plan for the evening which we might perhaps consider, if we were not incensed against hosts who altered their programme of hospitality for the sake of their own honour.

We felt unworthy subject-matter for this excitement, and we realized that there had been some monstrous over-estimation of the delicacy of our sentiments. So might two comfortable toads feel if the later Henry James and Edith Wharton at her subtlest insisted on treating them as equals. 'Let me give you some of the brandy I have brought from London,' said my husband, and I could see that the poor creature was trying to make a claim to some sort of fineness, even though it were other than that which they were ascribing to us. We all sipped brandy with an air of sustaining ourselves during a crisis. Then they went on to explain that Mr A. had forgotten that whereas the charitable festival was being held for the benefit of some fund for supplying the poor with medical attention, it was organized by Dr and Mrs Y., emigrated Jews from Zara, the Dalmatian town which has been handed over to the Italians, who were almost the only prominent pro-Yugoslavians in the town, and who might use this fund in co-operation with institutions which ought to be ignored, because they had been founded by the Government. The charity festival was therefore being boycotted by all the considerable families in Split, of the social level of Mr and Mrs X., or Mr and Mrs A. Other people could take us, if we cared to go. But it was impossible, the X.'s assured us in something like a duet by the early Verdi, impossible that they should do so.

We refrained from warning them that some day they might have something really worth worrying about; and we intimated that, as we had promised a very civil shopkeeper friend of ours to go to this festival, we should prefer to keep our promise. This we did, and enjoyed a spectacle of nice-looking young people performing with graceful awkwardness under the eyes of adoring parents, of which we had seen the like in Exeter, in Edinburgh, and in Cleveland, Ohio. There are a few institutions which are universal, and it is pleasant when one proves to be pretty and innocent. But the organizers, the doctor and his wife, were interesting and pathetic. They seemed outside the Splitchani tradition, not because they were Jews, but because they belonged to that warm and idealistic and intelligent breed of Jew that puts its trust in synthesis and centralization. Always they would assume that hatred and stupidity were peculiar local conditions, which any general government would make its business to correct; and this optimism would be reinformed by their knowledge that there does in fact exist a unifying force, which on the whole is benevolent, in science. They were both learning English, and they beamed as they spoke of it. It appeared to them, much more clearly than it did to me, that they were associating themselves with liberalism. But that was only part of their buoyant Utopianism, which believed that if a large enough number of charity festivals of this kind were held, if enough people studied a language other than their own, if enough vows of tolerance were taken by the state, there would be an end to poverty, war, and misery. I could only hope that, holding such inoffensive views in our offensive age, they might be permitted to die in their beds.

Our four friends, the X.'s and the A.'s, met us in the principal café of the town after the entertainment, and we took an early opportunity to ask them why they and their world were against the Yugoslav state. Their first reply was simply to look very handsome. Their eyes widened, their nostrils dilated. The natural exception was Mrs A., the Czech, who seemed, like ourselves, a little gross by contrast. We were in effect watching racehorses racing, beautiful specialized animals demonstrating their speciality, which was opposition. I had to remind myself that this concentration on opposition had substantially contributed to the saving of Western Europe from Islam. Few of us have as much reason to be thankful to the plainer and blunter virtues as to this cloak-and-sword romanticism that I saw before me; and they themselves owed their very existence to it. Only that had saved them from Rome, from the barbarian invaders, from the Hungarians and Venetians, from the Turks, from the Austrians. But all the same a government which was not seeking to destroy them but to co-operate with them must find this attitude so maddening that it would be not unnatural did it sometimes behave as if it were seeking their destruction.

'Tell me,' said my husband, 'some specific things that you find objectionable about Yugoslavia.' 'Belgrade!' exclaimed Mr and Mrs X. in one voice. 'This country,' Mr X. explained, 'is fantastically and extraordinarily poor. You would not believe how poor the poor people in our city are, how poor nearly all the people in the country outside are. The Government does nothing for us, but they take our taxes and they spend them in Belgrade. They are putting up whole new streets of offices, there is not a Ministry that hasn't a palace for its home. Is that fair, when down here we lack bread?' 'It was a wretched little village before the war,' said Mrs X., 'a pig-town. It made one laugh to see it, particularly if one had been to Zagreb. But now they are turning it into a place like Geneva, with public buildings six and seven stories high, all at our expense.' 'But do you not think that is necessary?' asked my husband. 'For it was because Serbia had such a capital as Belgrade was before the war that the Austrian Foreign Office used to treat the Serb diplomats as if they were farm labourers come up to the great house with an impertinent demand.' 'But the Serbs are not like us,' said Mrs X. vaguely. 'They are not like us, they have not the tradition that we have here in Split. And how can Belgrade ever be such a beautiful town as our Split?'

'I see the problem from a different aspect,' said Mr A., 'because I have been in America for a very long time. It does not shock me so much that Dalmatia should be governed from Belgrade, for I have lived in Milwaukee for many years, and things went very well there, though we were governed from Washington, which was far further away from us than Belgrade is from Split. And I have been to Washington, which is a fine city, and I know it is right that the government of a great country should have impressive buildings. But my case against Belgrade is that it governs badly. Oh, I know there is corruption and graft in American politics, but you have no idea what it is like here. The trouble is not only that, as X. says, the money goes to Belgrade, it's what happens to it when it gets there. It sticks to people's palms in the most disgusting way. There are ever so many people in Belgrade who have made

fortunes, huge fortunes, by peculation. And that's the only activity
in which they ever show any efficiency. For the idiotic muddle of
the administration is beyond belief.'

'It is worse, then, than it was under the Austrians?' asked my
husband. They looked at him in astonishment. 'Not at all,' said
Mr A.; 'the Austrians were not inefficient at all. They were
assassins. Look what they did here with the railways!' They all
broke out into cries of anger and disgust. 'Why, think of it,' said
Mr X., 'the railway stopped outside Split, so as to make sure we
should be nothing of a port.' 'And we could not go to Austria
except through Budapest,' said Mrs X. 'That was the Hungarian
influence, of course,' said Mr A. 'But Austria permitted it,' said
Mr X. 'Permitted it!' cried Mrs A., the Czech. 'Tell me when
those who speak German have not rejoiced in humiliating the
Slavs. And there are people in your country,' she said to us, 'who
are sorry for the German-speaking minorities in Czechoslovakia.
There are beings so charitable that they would get up funds to
provide feeding-bottles for baby alligators.'

But my husband persisted. 'Then you found the Austrians
efficient in what? Assassination only?' 'In that certainly,' said
Mr A., 'but they were also far more efficient than our present
Government in the everyday routine of administration. Take
the case of my family. Several of them have been university
professors. Now, the old ones, who retired under the Austrians,
never had any difficulty in getting their pensions. They drew their
pay, they retired, they filled in papers, they drew the appointed
sum. Nothing could have been simpler. But now there is terrible
disorder. I have an uncle, a professor of mathematics, who retired
months ago. He fulfilled all the requisite formalities, but he has
not yet touched a penny of his pension. The papers have not come
through from Belgrade, for no other reason than sheer muddle.'
'And it is so, too, in my profession,' said Mr X. 'I am a lawyer, it is
the calling of my family, and some of my older relatives are judges.
It is the same with pensions, and appointments, and even dates
for trials, everything that comes from Belgrade. There is endless
bother and muddle. And we are not accustomed to such things in
Split, for here we manage our affairs simply, it may be, but with a
certain distinction.' 'Ah, yes,' said Mrs A., 'if they would leave us
Splitchani to manage our own affairs, that would be all we ask.'

'But there are affairs which are certainly your own, but which
equally you cannot manage,' said my husband. 'You could not
yourselves have got rid of Austria, and you cannot yourselves protect yourselves if she comes back, or if Italy wants to establish the

same domination over you.' They looked at him with preoccupied bright eyes, and said, 'Of course, of course.' 'And though some money must vanish in Belgrade in peculation, since that inevitably happens in every new country,' said my husband, 'a great deal must be spent in legitimate enterprises. There is, after all, Macedonia and Old Serbia. I have not yet been there, but my wife tells me it has been revolutionized since the days when it was Turkish, that she has seen with her own eyes hundreds of miles of good military roads, whole districts of marshes that have been drained and now are no longer malarial, and many schools and hospitals. All that costs money.' 'Yes, there was nothing down there in those parts,' said Mr A. without enthusiasm. 'They are nearly barbarians,' said Mrs X., wrinkling her nose with distaste. 'Have you ever been there?' asked my husband. They shook their heads. Split is two days' easy journey from Old Serbia, three days from the heart of Macedonia. 'It is not easy for us to go to such places,' said Mrs X.; 'here in Split we have a certain tradition, we would not be at home there.'

When we got back to our room in the hotel, my husband said, 'All this is very sad. Men and women have died and lived for the ideal of Yugoslavia, the South Slav state; and here are these very charming people chafing with discontent at the realization of it. And so far as I can see, however bad Belgrade may be, they give it no chance to prove its merits. These people are born and trained rebels. They cry out when they see a government as if it were a poisonous snake, and seize a stick to kill it with, and in that they are not being fanciful. All the governments they have known till now have been, so far as they are concerned, poisonous snakes. But all the same that attitude would be a pity, if they happened to meet a government for once who was not a poisonous snake.

'Moreover, I cannot see how these people can ever fit into a modern state. They are essentially the children of free cities. Because all these towns, even while they were exploited and oppressed so far as their external relations were concerned, possessed charters that gave them great freedom to manage their internal affairs. Under the Hungarian crown the towns enjoyed the same sort of freedom, as of a state within a state, that the City of London enjoyed under Henry the First. Their rights were ceaselessly attacked by Venice, but they managed to defend most of them. They were forced to provide men for the Venetian Army and Navies, and their trade was ruined by the restrictions laid upon it; but they were always to some extent masters at their own firesides. They really cannot conceive of a centralized government at all as otherwise than an evil: and when they got rid of Austria there must have been a childish idea at the back of their minds that they had also got rid of a centralized government, and would return to medieval conditions. Alas! Alas!'

'Look,' I said, 'I am watching three people talking in the square. They are so very picturesque; come and see them.' My husband turned out the light and came and sat beside me on the window-seat. The square was whitewashed with moonlight; the dark shadows took the nineteenth-century Venetian Gothic architecture and by obscuring the detail and emphasizing the general design made it early, authentic, exquisite. On the quay ships slept, as alone among inanimate objects ships can sleep; their lights were dim and dreaming. Between the flaked trunk of a palm tree and the wild-haired shadow of the leaves stood three men of the quick and whippy and secret kind we had seen when we first entered Split, descendants of those who had lived through the angry centuries the lives of rats and mice in the walls of Diocletian's palace. Sometimes we could hear their voices raised in lyrical mockery, and sometimes they made gestures that united them on a platform of heroism and loaded some absent person with ridicule and chains. 'Yes, they are wonderful,' said my husband. 'Though they probably have no noble ideas, they are noble in the intensity of their being, and in the persistency with which they try to identify their standards and the ultimate values of right and wrong. See how they are pretending that behind them, had one but the proper eyesight, could be seen the wings of the hierarchy of angels and the throne itself, and that behind the man they are despising is primeval ooze and chaos. These people are profoundly different from us. They are not at all sentimental, but they are extremely poetic. How they examine everything, and analyse it, and form a judgement on it that engenders a supply of the passion which is their motive power! How I should hate to govern these people who would not accept the idea of government and would insist on examining it, but only as a poet does, from the point of view of his own experience, which is to say that they would reject all sorts of information about it which they ought to consider if they are going to form a just opinion about it.'

We watched the three men till a languor showed in their vehemence. They had laughed so much at the fourth man who was not there that any further mockery would seem an anticlimax. The night was left to the sleeping ships, to the temporary romantic perfection of the Venetian arcades. 'Get into bed,' my husband said, 'and I will read you the other story which Voinovitch says the Dalmatian peasantry tell about the Emperor Diocletian.' It was the prettier of the two. It represents Diocletian's daughter, Valeria, as the victim of her father; not, as in fact she was, as the subject of a good worldly marriage that went maniacally wrong, but with a destiny cut fairy-tale fashion. She had, according to this story, a crowd of suitors, and of these her father chose a prince whom she could not tolerate. So she refused obedience, and upon this her father cast her into one of the dungeons in his palace. But God was on her side. Once a year invisible hands opened the door of her prison, and she travelled through the city clad in cloth of gold, in a shining chariot drawn by winged horses. Her presence was a benediction, and anybody who could stop the chariot and embrace her would be happy all the rest of his life. When Diocletian heard of these visits he sent soldiers to clear the streets, but it could not be done. The people worshipped Valeria and would not be driven away. Then Diocletian decided to kill her. But the walls of her prison melted, and not all his power could discover her. According to this legend, she still lives, and once every hundred years she comes back to her worshippers. It is not known what year of the century she chooses for her visit, but be that as it may, her visit always falls at Christmastide. When they are saying the midnight mass in the Cathedral, a procession of ghosts starts from Salonæ and winds up the road to Split; and at the end the lovely young Valeria rides in her golden coach, still able to give lifelong happiness to all that embrace her. She still, it must be observed, carries on her quarrel with authority. She was at odds with her pagan father, but she does not attend the Christian mass.

'See, this story cuts at the root of the idea of power,' said my husband; 'it denies all necessary sanctions to authority. For power claims to know what life is going to be about and what prescription to offer, and authority claims to be able to enforce that prescription. But the Slav knows, as this story proves, that life, which is to say Valeria, is in essence unpredictable, that she often produces events for which there is no apt prescription, and that she can be as slippery as an eel when wise men attempt to control her; and they know that it is life, not power or authority, that gives us joy, and this often when she is least predictable. Knowing Valeria, they cannot respect Diocletian; yet they produce Diocletian, they are Diocletian, they know perfectly well that power and authority are necessary.'

BOAT

On another great white steamer we glided down the coast to Korchula, and received at one port, and put ashore at another, the older of the two German couples with whom we had travelled from Salzburg to Zagreb. They hastened towards us uttering cries of welcome, excessively glad to see us because their holiday had made them excessively glad about everything. The man no longer looked ill; he seemed bound to his wife by a common novel satisfaction, as if they had been on their honeymoon. 'It is so good here,' they laughed, 'one forgets all one's worries.' There seemed fresh evidence for the malignity of the universe in the sight of these Aryans, blossoming in their temporary exile from Germany, when all over England and France and America so many Jews were mourning for the fatherland in a grief visible as jaundice. Another of Dalmatia's angry young men watched them coldly as they disembarked. 'I am a hotel manager at Hvar,' he said. Hvar is a beautiful town, which lies on an island of the same name. It is noted for the extraordinary sweetness of its air, which is indeed such as might be inhaled over a bed of blossoming roses, and by a perversity rare in the Serbo-Croat tongue it is pronounced 'Whar.' 'Your friends will presently come to me and demand impossible terms. They are a curious people, the Germans. They seem content to travel when we would prefer to stay at home. Where is the pleasure of travelling if you cannot spend freely? Yet these Germans come here and have to count every penny and do not seem at all embarrassed. Now, that is all right if one is a poor student at Zagreb or Vienna, or is ill and has to go to a spa. But for a tourist it seems very undignified.' It had struck me before that there are many resemblances between the Slavs and the Spanish, and this spoke with the very voice of Spain, in its expression of the purse-pride which comes not from wealth but from poverty, in its conception of handsome spending as an inherently good thing, to be indulged in, like truthfulness, even against one's economic interest.

The angry young man scowled down at the marbled blue and white water that rushed by our ship. 'I have read in Jackson's great book on Dalmatia,' said my husband, to soothe him, 'that the inhabitants of the island of Hvar added to their income by making a sweet wine called *prosecco*, by distilling rosemary water, and by making an insecticide from the wild chrysanthemum. Do they still do all those pleasant things?' 'Not to any extent,' answered the young man, his brows enraged. 'Now they cultivate the tourist traffic all summer, and talk politics all winter. Politics and politics and politics, I am sick of politics. Why can we never have any peace? Why must there always be all this conflict?' He was as angry as the young man who had been angry with the gardener at Trsat, or the other who had been angry with the cold soup on the boat to Rab, and it was with them that he felt angry. My husband attempted to comfort him by telling him that in England we were suffering from marked deterioration of political life, and even of national character, because we have no effectual opposition. 'But here there is nothing but disputes and disputes and disputes!' cried the young man.

There had been standing beside us a middle-aged man in expensive clothes, who was holding up his hand to hide the left side of his face. He now pressed forward and made what was evidently a sharp remark to the angry young hotel manager, who turned to us and said gloomily, 'This man, who is a native of Hvar, says that I do wrong to speak to you like this, for it might discourage you from visiting Hvar, and it is certainly the most beautiful place in the world. I hope I have not done that?' The middle-aged man interrupted in German, 'Yes, you must not take what he says too seriously, for though we in Hvar are quarrelsome, as all Slavs are (it is the curse that has been laid upon us), that does not alter its extraordinary beauty. You must not miss visiting us, indeed you must not.' 'We cannot do so now,' said my husband, 'for we have made definite plans to go to Korchula today. But we will try to stop at Hvar on our way back.' 'Yes, that you must do! For, though I do not want to be discourteous to a sister island, and indeed all Dalmatia is glorious country, Korchula has little to show compared to Hvar.' He began to speak of their main street, which is broad and paved with marble and lined with fifteenth-century palaces weathered to warm gold; of the old Venetian arsenal, that had a dry dock for the galleys below and above a theatre, the first theatre to be built in the Balkans, which is still just as it was in the seventeenth century, though the curtains in the boxes are thin as paper; of the Franciscan monastery that stands on a piny headland, with its picture of the Last Supper which is so marvellous that a Rothschild who had been made an English duke had tried to buy it from the monks for as many sovereigns as would cover the canvas; and of the lovely garden that had been made on the hill above the town, by a pupil of our dear Professor at Split, who had wished to emulate his teacher's achievement in planting the woods on Mount Marian, which is as pretty a testimony to the value of humanist education as I know. During his story there sometimes came to him living phrases which made actual the beauty of his home, and then his hand dropped, no longer feeling it urgent to hide the port-wine stain that ravaged the left side of his face from temple to chin; and when the steamer entered Hvar harbour, and it was as he had said, he let his hand drop by his side.

When these new friends had left us and we were out in midchannel, I picked up a guide-book, but soon laid it down again, saying to my husband peevishly, 'This guide-book is written by a member of my sex who is not only imbecile but bedridden. She is wrong about every place we have been to, so wildly wrong that it seems probable that not only can she never have visited any of these particular cities, but that she can have seen no scenery at all, urban or rural.' 'I think,' said my husband, 'that that is perhaps something of an over-statement. In any case there is no need for you to keep your eyes down on any guide-book, you might just as well be looking at the islands, which are really becoming very beautiful now that they support some trees. But I rather suspect that you are nervous about coming to Korchula and do not want to face it until the last moment.' 'Well, neither I do,' I admitted. 'I must own that I am seriously nervous about it, because I can't believe that it had quite the revelatory quality I thought it had last year. You see, I passed it on my way from Split to Dubrovnik last year. I had been asleep on one of the benches on deck, and I woke suddenly to find that we were lying beside the quay of a little walled town which was the same creamy-fawn colour as some mushrooms and some puppies. It covered a low, rounded peninsula and was surmounted by a church tower, rising from it like a pistil from a flower; and its walls girt it so massively that they might have been thought natural cliffs if a specially beautiful lion of St. Mark had not certified them as works of art.

'Standing on the quayside was a crowd which was more male in quantity and in quality than we are accustomed to in Western Europe. There were very few women, and the men were very handsome with broad shoulders and long legs and straight hair, and an air of unashamed satisfaction with their own good looks which one finds only where there is very little homosexuality. The faces of the crowd were turned away from the steamer. They were all staring up a street that ran down the steepness of the town to the quay. Presently there was a hush, all the window-sashes of the quayside houses were thrown up, and the crowd shuffled apart to make a clear avenue to the gangway. Then there came out of the street and along this alley four men carrying a stretcher on which there lay a girl of about sixteen. The air was so still that there could be heard the quick padding of the stretcher-bearers' feet on the dust, and as they left the street its mouth filled up with people who stood gaping after them. This must have been a notorious tragedy in the town, for the girl was extravagantly beautiful, as beautiful as Korchula itself, and she was very ill. The shadows on her face were blue. She was being taken, a sailor said, to a hospital at Dubrovnik, but I am sure not by her own consent. It was evident that she had wholly lost the will to live. Her hands lay lax and open on the magenta coverlet; and as they turned her stretcher round to manoeuvre it onto the gangway, she opened her eyes and looked up at the tall ship in hostility, loathing it because it was something and she wanted nothingness. Behind her the alley closed, the crowd formed into a solid block and stared at us as if we were taking with us a sign and a wonder.

'But the crowd divided again. Another four men hurried along, bearing this time a chair to which there was strapped an old woman, so immensely old that she had nothing to do with the substance of flesh; she seemed to be compounded of glittering intelligence and a substance more than bony, resembling the hard parts of a very aged and gnarled lobster. She looked towards the steamer with an air of unconquerable appetite. It was something, and therefore better than nothingness, which was what she feared. When the stretcher-bearers halted in manoeuvring her up the gangway she rose up in her chair, a twisted hieroglyphic expressing the love of life, and uttered an angry sound she might have used to a mule that was stopping in midstream.

'Now that was something worth while seeing for itself. But it also seemed typical of life in Yugoslavia, in the Balkans, because I had been able to see it. In Western Europe or in America it would have been highly unlikely that I would see an old woman or a young girl who were desperately ill, unless they were my relatives or close friends, and then my interest in them as individuals would distract my attention from their general characteristics. I might have guessed, and indeed had done so, from a great many subtle indications, that the appetite for life comes in eating, though not by any simple process of taste. Experience often causes people to pass an adverse judgment on life, and if they fall ill when they still hold this opinion with the violence of youth they may die of it, should their personalities be vehement enough. But if they live long enough they seem to be governed by a kind of second strength, a secret core of vitality. There is a Finnish word, '*sisu*,' which expresses this ultimate hidden resource in man which will not be worsted, which takes charge when courage goes and consciousness is blackened, which insists on continuing to live no matter what life is worth. This may mean only that the skeleton wishes to keep its accustomed garment of flesh, that the eyeball fears to feel naked without the many-coloured protection of sight; but it might mean that the whole of us knows some argument in favour of life which the mind has not yet apprehended. But the point is that here in Yugoslavia I did not have to poke about among the detritus of commonplace life to find allusions to this process: an old woman and a young girl came out into the street and gave a dramatic rendering of it in the presence of the people. It is that quality of visibility that makes the Balkans so specially enchanting, and it was at Korchula that I had the first intimations of it. So naturally I am alarmed lest I find the town not so beautiful as I had supposed, and life in the Balkans precisely the same as everywhere else.'

Korchula I

We found, however, that I was perfectly right about Korchula. 'And let that be enough for you,' said my husband. 'As for your other demands that from now on every day will be an apocalyptic revelation, I should drop that, if I were you. You might not like it even if you got it.' We were talking as we unpacked in the room we had taken in the hotel on the quay, which is either a converted Venetian palace or built by one accustomed to palaces from birth. A good hotel, it showed that expiatory cleanliness which is found sometimes in southern countries; from early in the morning till late at night, women were on their knees in the corridors as if in prayer, scrubbing and scrubbing, and murmuring to themselves through compressed lips. It was scented with the classic kitchen smell of the Mare Internum, repellent only to the effete, since it asserts that precious plants can live in waterless and soilless country, that even after centuries of strife and misery woman still keeps the spirit to put a pinch of strong flavour in the cook-pot, and that it takes the supreme assault of urban conditions to bring on humanity the curse of a craving for insipidity. Our fellow-guests were a couple of men as floridly grave as wreathed Cæsars, and their two ladies, both in cloaks, who might have been travelling for the same romantic and detective reasons as Donna Anna and Donna Elvira: ornaments of the Sushak wine trade and their wives.

'I will lie down and sleep for half an hour,' I said, looking at the clean coarse sheets, bluish and radiant with prodigious laundering. 'I will sit here and look at the maps,' said my husband, who is much given to that masculine form of auto-hypnosis. But we did neither of these things, for there was a knock at the door and an announcement that two gentlemen of the town, who had received a letter about us from a friend at Split, were waiting for us downstairs. We had no idea who these people might be. My husband imagined mild antiquaries living among the ruins of Korchula like ageing doves; I thought of mildewed Irish squires. We went downstairs and found two handsome men in early middle age telling the hotel-keeper's wife to be sure to cook us a good fish for dinner that night, and give us a certain red wine grown on the island, and it was as if we looked on a Venetian picture come to life, for the heads of all were bowed intently towards the argument, the men's gestures were wide and made from expanded chests, the woman promised them obedience with the droop of her whole body. Of the men one had the great head and full body of a Renaissance cardinal, the other had the rejecting crystal gaze of a Sitwell. They dismissed the hotel-keeper's wife with a National Gallery gesture and turned to welcome us. They told us that they would be pleased to act as our guides in the town, and would start now, if we wished, with any destination we pleased. We expressed our gratitude, and said that we would leave it to them where we should go. The gentleman with the Sitwell gaze then said: 'Perhaps you would like to see our new steam bakery.'

Neither myself nor my husband replied. We both sank into a despondent reverie, wondering why he should think we wanted to see a new steam bakery. We could only suppose that to him we were representatives of a Western civilization that was obsessed with machinery, and perhaps he suspected us of thinking for that reason that in Dalmatia they ate no bread, or only bread prepared in a filthy way. Fortunately the one who looked like a cardinal blanketed the topic by saying, not accurately, 'Ah, but you will have seen many, many steam bakeries; you would like better to see our old churches and palaces.'

We walked along the quay that runs round the point of the little peninsula, following the walls, and then went up a steep little street, close-packed with palaces, which thrust out balconies to one another or were joined by bridges, into the town. We found it like a honeycomb; it was dripping with architectural richness, and it was laid out in an order such as mathematicians admire. But its spirit was riotous, the honey had fermented and turned to mead. The men who accompanied us had fine manners, and only by a phrase or two did they let us gather that they appreciated how beautiful Korchula must seem to us because they had known the great towns of the West, Berlin and Paris, and found them filthy; but they were not exquisites, they were robust. They climbed the steep streets at a great rate, telling us the historic jokes of the town with gusts of laughter, and apologizing for the silence that they shattered by owning that the city had never repopulated itself after the attack of plague in the sixteenth century, that had taken five thousand citizens out of seven thousand. The one that looked like a Renaissance cardinal had a peculiarly rich and rolling laugh, in which there seemed to join amusement at a particular fact with extreme satisfaction with life in general. Bringing us to a small square in front of the Cathedral, which was smoothly paved and therefore had that air of being within the confines of some noble household, he said, 'Here we have always walked and talked, and often we have talked too loud. That is one thing that never changes, our archives are full of the priests' complaints that we talked so loud out here that they could not hear themselves saying mass in the Cathedral.' His laughter rolled. 'Also we played ball,' said the Sitwell; 'they complained of that also.' 'That leads to the story of Jacopo Faganeo,' said the Cardinal. 'He was a seventeenth-century Tuscan priest who was a very great preacher, but a very good companion too. The Admiral in command of the Venetian fleet in the Adriatic got him to take a cruise with him, and when they got here the sailors came ashore, even to the Admiral and his friends, and we townsmen challenged them to a game of ball. Nobody was such a good ballplayer as this priest, so he tucked up his gown and gave a wonderful display, and we all cheered him. But this scandalized our local priests, and when Lent came along they refused to let Father Jacopo preach in the Cathedral, though he was still here with the fleet. However, soon after our Bishop died, and the Admiral, who had the Pope's ear, paid out our priests by getting Father Jacopo appointed to fill his place. And a very good Bishop he was, too.'

Then the square must have rung with laughter, with the laughter of strong men; but it always knew that there was darkness as well as light. Above the ballplayers rose the Cathedral, which is giraffish because of the architect's consciousness that he must work on a minute site, but which owes its strangeness of appearance to the troubled intricacy of the ornamentation, loaded with tragic speculations of the Slav mind. For Korchula, like Trogir, is an intensely Slav town. The degree of the oddity of this ornament can be measured by the sculpture which projects from the gable above the central door and rose window. It is a powerfully realistic bust of a richly decked old woman, not a grotesque, but far too passionate to be, as some suppose, merely the representation of a fourteenth-century Queen of Hungary who gave money to the Church. It has the same Dostoievsky quality as Radovan's work at Trogir. Perhaps it was to exercise this note of metaphysical fantasy that a nineteenth-century bishop made a jigsaw puzzle of the inside of the Cathedral, interchanging the parts and putting in a horrid but matter-of-fact pulpit. But the outside remains enigmatic in its beauty, partly because it looks across the square to the roofless ruin of the palace, wild-eyed with windows whose marble traceries are outlined against the sky, wild-haired with the foliage of trees that had taken root in the angles of the upper story and grew slantwise out of balconies.

'What is that?' said the Cardinal. 'Regrettably enough, it is the home of my family. We burned it to disinfect it, in the sixteenth century, after many of our household had died in the plague, and we have never had the money to rebuild it. But now I will show you another church which you ought to see.' It was at the foot of one of the steep streets, a church where the Gothic was melting into the Renaissance, where the architectural spring was over and the summer was warm and drowsy. These people could look on this summer-time with much more satisfaction than we could, for they knew nothing of the winter-time that had followed it with us, they were unaware of Regent Street. But they were specially pleased with this church for another reason which had nothing to do with architecture. They told us that this church was in the care of a confraternity and began to explain to us what these confraternities were; but when they found out that we already knew, they stopped and said no more. They did not tell us that they themselves belonged to this confraternity; but that was evident. With the ease of men who were showing strangers round their own house they took us up a staircase and over a bridge across an alley into the room where the confraternity kept its records and its treasures. There we all sat down, and they smiled about them, gentle and secret smiles. Here they came for the benefit of magic, and enjoyed a mystical, uplifting version of the pleasures of brotherhood. The room was itself an astonishment. It was hung with a score or so of Byzantine icons, in the true colours of icons, that is to say of flame and smoke; with the true message of icons, that is to say of spirit rising from matter with the precise yet immaterial form of a flame. Of these they said, smiling at their own history, 'You see, we are a very pious people—all of us—even our sailors.' These had, in fact, been looted by good Catholic Korchulans on expeditions that may sometimes have been certified as naval, but were sometimes plainly piratical, from Orthodox shrines. 'People come here and try to buy them,' said the Cardinal lazily, and laughed into his hand, while his awed eye raked them and found them valid magic.

'But some day there will be no question of our being poor people who can be tempted by foreigners to part with their goods,' said the Sitwell. 'Nor will we need the tourist traffic though the money will come in welcome,' said the Cardinal; 'we shall be able to live exactly like other people, on our production, when we have repaired the wrongs that the Venetians and Austrians have done to us. We are not only sailors, we are shipbuilders. But of course we need more wood. We have a lot for Dalmatia, more than you will find on the other islands you have seen, but we still have not enough. Come and see what we are doing about that.' We went from a gate on the landward side of the town, down a superb stone staircase, and we found ourselves in a motor bus full of people who knew our guides and were known by them, who by some miraculous adjustment deferred to them and yet behaved as their equals. It was going to a village on the top of the mountain lying south of Korchula, and we left it as it got to the foothills, to take a path into a pinewood. Soon the Cardinal stopped and laid his hand on the thick trunk of a tall pine and said, 'These trees were planted by my grandfather when he was mayor.' And later, in a further valley he stopped by a slenderer trunk in a lower, thinner wood, and said, 'These trees were planted by my father when he was mayor.' And later still, in the crease of a spur that stretched towards an unmedicined barrenness, dull ochre rock save for the slightly different monotone of the scrub, we came to a plantation of pine saplings, hardly hip-high. 'These are the trees I have planted, now I am mayor,' he said. He stood among them spreading his arms wide above them, laughing lazily. 'Have I not poor spindly children? But they will grow.'

On our way back through the denser pinewoods we came to a terrace, where there were tables and benches for people to sit and eat on their Sunday walks, and because we were tired, having started on our journey in the early morning, we asked if we might rest there for a little. So we sat down on one side of the table, and they on the other, and they told us what they hoped to do for the reafforestation of the island and how the Government had helped them. Then they spoke of how the Venetians had cut down the woods, and how little the Austrians had done to replace them; and as they talked these men, who were essentially aristocrats, assumed the sullenness and shabbiness of conspirators. They muttered bitterly into their fingers, their underlips came forward. Then the Cardinal, suddenly noble once more, looked up at the sky through the trees and cried, 'It is better now, it is still difficult, but the chief offence has been removed; we are free, and the work goes well. Are you rested? Shall we return?'

We went all the way back on foot, first by an inlet edged with prosperous modern villas, belonging to rich Croats, and then by a road that would have seemed dusty if it had not passed a monument that flattered my pride. By a very pretty semicircle of stone seats, conceived in the neo-classical tradition, was a tablet giving thanks to the English troops who occupied the island when the French were driven out, and governed it for two years till the Peace of 1815 handed it over with the rest of Dalmatia to Austria. We English were then a different breed. We could build. We could administer. We gave these islands a democratic institution which they thoroughly enjoyed and followed the French tradition of efficient public works by making good roads and harbours. Now we would build tin huts all over the place, would have been compelled from Downing Street to kick the natives in the face for fear of encouraging revolutionary movements which did not in fact exist, and would have ended up with the evil reputation of oppressors without any of the fruits of oppression.

Something has changed us. The life we lead does not suit us. I knew it a few minutes later when we were back in Korchula, and our guides took us into one of the shipyards on the shore. We went through a yard stacked with wood, that clean, moral substance, and carpeted with shavings, into a shed where three men stood contemplating the unfinished hull of a motor boat. The overlapping timbers were as neat as the feathers on a bird's wing, the shape was neat as a bird in flight. It was a pity that so much beauty should be hidden under the water. Of the three men in front of it, one held up a blueprint very steadily; another held a rule to the boat and made measurements; the other watched and spoke with authority. They were all three beautiful, with thick, straight, fair hair and bronze skins and high cheekbones pulling the flesh up from their large mouths, with broad chests and long legs springing from arched feet. These were men, they could beget children on women, they could shape certain kinds of materials for purposes that made them masters of their worlds. I thought of two kinds of men that the West produces: the cityish kind who wears spectacles without shame, as if they were the sign of quality and not a defect, who is overweight and puffy, who can drive a car but knows no other mastery over material, who presses buttons and turns switches without comprehending the result, who makes money when the market goes up and loses it when the market goes down; the high-nosed young man, who is somebody's secretary or is in the Foreign Office, who has a peevishly amusing voice and is very delicate, who knows a great deal but far from all there is to be known about French pictures. I understand why we cannot build, why we cannot govern, why we bear ourselves without pride in our international relations. It is not that all Englishmen are like that, but that too many of them are like that in our most favoured classes.

It is strange, it is heartrending, to stray into a world where men are still men and women still women. I felt apprehensive many times in Korchula, since I can see no indications that the culture of Dalmatia is going to sweep over the Western world, and I can see many reasons to fear that Western culture will in the long run overwhelm Dalmatia. We crossed the road from the shipyard to call on an elderly woman who lived in a house which, a bourgeois kind of palace, had belonged to her husband's family for four hundred years. We were taken through a finely vaulted passage to the garden, where we stood under a pergola of wistaria and looked up at the tracery of the windows, which were greatly enriched by the salty weathering of the stone to an infinity of fine amber and umber tones; for we had been asked to wait till she had finished some pious business she was performing in the private chapel, which stood, an arched and pointed outhouse, among the crowded flowers, close to a niched wall that sheltered a Triton and a nymph. On the steps of the chapel there lay some candles and a match-box and a packet of washing soda on a sheet of newspaper. For a second I took this as an indication that the family fortunes were in decline, but on reflection I wondered what evidence I had that palaces had ever been neat. All historical memoirs portray a union between the superb and the sluttish; and probably tidiness is a creation of the middle classes, who have had their tendency to bare and purging Protestantism reinforced by their panic-stricken acceptance of the germ theory. Boucher's famous portrait of Madame Pompadour reveals that even she, who was the ideal civil servant, kept her personal possessions lying about on the floor. The homely disorder on the chapel steps was therefore simply a proof that this establishment was not yet a museum.

At length the lady of the house came out of the private chapel, followed by the kitchen smells of piety, not less powerful and classic than the kitchen smells of our hotel. She was elderly, though not old; and it could be seen that she had been very lovely; and immediately she began to flirt with my husband. She knew with absolute realism, and had known it, I am sure, from the first moment when the knowledge became necessary to her, that she was too old for love. But she knew that a repetition of the methods by which she had charmed the hearts and intelligences of the men of her time would give him the same pleasure an enthusiastic theatre-goer would feel if a famous old actress rehearsed for him her celebrated performance of Juliet. Therefore we enjoyed again the gaieties in which her voice and face and body had combined to promise her admirers that not only she but all her life was infinitely and unpredictably agreeable. After there had been a long rally of teasing compliment and mockery, a bell tolled somewhere in the town, and we all stopped to listen. When it ceased there was a silence. My husband breathed

deeply, warmed and satisfied by her aged and now sexless charm
as one might be by a wine so old that all the alcohol had
disappeared, and said, 'It is wonderfully quiet.' She abandoned
her performance and said to him not sentimentally but with an
almost peevish recollection of past enjoyment, as one might say
that in one's youth one had cared greatly for racing but could no
longer get about to the meetings, 'It's too quiet. I liked it when
there were children about, laughing, and then crying, and then
laughing again. That's how it ought to be in a house.' She spoke
with complete confidence, as one who expresses an opinion held
by all the world. A house with children is better than a house
without children. That she assumed to be an axiom, on that she
had founded all her life and pride. It was as if she were a child
herself, a fragile child who had escaped death by a miracle and
was boasting of its invulnerability to all ills. Her life had for
the most part been secure because in her world men had been
proud to be fathers, and had marvelled gratefully at women for
being fine-wrought enough to make the begetting of children an
excitement and sturdy enough to bear them and rear them, and had
thought of the mother of many children as the female equivalent
of a rich man. Because these masculine attitudes had favoured her
feminine activities, her unbroken pride was lovely as the trumpet
of a lily. It might have been different for her if she had been born
into a society where men have either lost their desire for children,
or are prevented from gratifying it by poverty or the fear of war.
There she would have been half hated, and perhaps more than
half, for her sex. Her womb, which here was her talisman, would
have been a source of danger, which might even strike at the very
root of her primal value, and one day make her husband feel that
the delight he had known with her was not worth the price he
must pay for it. It was terrible that this fate, even if it had failed
to engulf her, was certain to annihilate many of her blood, of her
kind, and that the threat was implicit in many statements that she
made without a shadow of apprehension, as when she told us that
her husband and all his forebears had been sea captains, and that
her sons were still of the tradition and not of it, for they were
agents for great steamship lines.

The Cardinal said to me, 'You are looking very tired. Before I
take you to our house to meet my parents, we will go to a café on the
quay, and you can rest.' This seemed to me a peculiar programme,
but it was agreeable enough. As we drank very good strong coffee
the two men talked again of trees: of the possibility of making many
motor boats for the new tourist traffic, of the fishing fleets, of the

wrong Italians had done by seizing the southward island, Lagosta, where the fish are specially plentiful. 'The Slavs all left it when the treaty was known,' said the Sitwell. 'And they have not been able to repopulate it with Italians,' said the Cardinal, 'for they are idiots, worse than the Austrians. Think of it, they wanted to colonize the island with Italian fishermen and they renamed it after an Italian airman who had been killed. Think of doing a silly thing like that, when you're dealing with peasants. It's such a silly townsman's trick.' His great laughter rolled up out of him. 'You're accustomed to deal politically with people in person,' said my husband. 'That is a funny idea, for us. Not by the million, through newspapers and the radio, or by the thousand or hundred in halls, but just in person.' The Cardinal answered modestly, 'One does what one can, in order not to be destroyed. But come and see my father, who is cleverer at it than I am.'

We went back into the town, and had but one more digression. The Cardinal whisked us into a courtyard gorgeous with two balustraded galleries. Because it was an orphanage there projected between the pillarets the grave puppy-snouts of interested infant Slavs, while above them were the draperies and blandness of young nuns. The presence of the Cardinal produced a squealing babble of homage from the orphans, and the wheeling and bowing courtesies of the nuns recalled the evolutions of angels. The institution wailed its disappointment as we left, and the Cardinal hurried us round a corner up another street, into the medievalism of his home.

The courtyard was dark with its own shadows as well as the dusk, and ghostly with the pale light filtering down from the still sunlit upper air, through the gutted palace, burned because of the plague, which formed its fourth side. It looked even more fantastic than we had thought it in the Cathedral square. At a window on its ground floor a tree stood like a woman looking into the courtyard, and on the floors above trees, some of them clothed with blossom which in this uncertain light was the colour of a grey Persian cat, shot forth from the empty sockets of vanished rafters in the attitudes of acrobats seeking the trapeze. The courtyard itself spoke of something even older than this palace, for it was full of carved stone; slabs bearing inscriptions or low reliefs had been let into its walls, and there were set about many statues and fragments of statues, some of which were Roman. It held as well an infinity of growing things, of flowers bursting from a lead cistern and a sarcophagus, full-fleshed leafy plants and bronze-backed ferns, a great many of them in little pots hung on lines of string secured to details of sculpture. We were reminded of

what he had sometimes forgotten during this water-logged spring,
that this was the far South, accustomed to seasons when grass is
a recollected miracle and everything that can be coaxed to grow
in a flowerpot is a token and a comfort. On the other side of
the courtyard, facing the ruin, was another palace, also Venetian
Gothic and of the fifteenth century, but intact. Its great door was
open, and showed a dark room and another beyond it that was
lit by the soft white light of a chandelier. Towards this reserved
and even defensive interior the Cardinal now led us. But I delayed
to admire the richness of a design impressed on the lead cistern,
and he told me, 'Those are the arms of my family. But now we
do not use such cisterns. We have modern methods. See, there is
a great cistern under this courtyard.' He brought down his heel
on the pavement, making a sharp ringing noise that sent a little
bird whirring out of one of the plants back to its home in the
ruined palace. 'Trees and water,' said the Sitwell, 'they are more
precious to us on the island than gold.' 'We will have all we want
of them under Yugoslavia,' said the Cardinal.

We paused again at the door to handle the great knocker, which
was perhaps by Giovanni Bologna: it was a Neptune between two
rear-uplifted dolphins, magnificent whatever hand had made it.
Inside we found the same vein of magnificence, though the
proportions here, as everywhere else in the city, were constrained
by a want of space; and the furniture showed the influence of
nineteenth-century Italy and Austria, which was not without a
chignoned and crinolined elegance, but was coarsened by the
thick materials it employed, the chenille and rep, the plush and
horsehair. In the second room, at a table under the chandelier,
sat a white-haired lady, in her sixties, dressed in a black velvet
gown. From the stateliness of her greeting we understood why
her son had taken us to rest at a café before he brought us into
her house. The social life in this palace was extremely formal, that
is to say we were expected to play our part in a display of the social
art in its highest sense, the art of meeting people with whom one
may have little or nothing in common and distilling the greatest
possible pleasantness out of the contact without forcing an unreal
intimacy. But it was light as air, weightless swordsmanship. The
old lady first addressed herself to me with a maternal air that was
flattering yet not indecently so, as if the gulf of years between us
were greater than it actually was, but not impossibly great. Then,
like the lady in the sea captain's palace, she began to address herself
to my husband for the excellent reason that she was a woman and
he was a man. The performance she gave, however, was probably

not modified by time: for the difference in their social status meant that though all her life she must have taken for granted that her beauty was a beacon before the eyes of men, it must have also been her faith that all its sexual implications, to the remotest, must be private to her immediate family. The sea captain's widow was certainly chaste as snow, but it was probable that many men had looked on her and thought it a pity that she was not their wife; but this lady was to such an extreme degree the wife of her husband, the queen of this palace, that she was withdrawn from even such innocent and respectful forms of desire. She made, therefore, since her career was to be a wife and a mother, an exclusively feminine appeal, but it was remote, ethereal, almost abstract.

When her husband came he proved to be as noble-looking as she was; a slender bearded man, with a wolfish alertness odd in a man of his type. It was like seeing Lord Cecil with the springy gait of a matador. He apologized at once, in Italian, for having spoken to his son in Serbo-Croat as he entered the room. 'I am afraid,' he said, 'we had better converse in Italian, but I hope you will not take it as a proof of the truth of the Italian lie that we are Italian on this coast by race and in language. That is propaganda, and mendacious for that. They have the impudence to deny us our blood and our speech, and they have never minded what lies they told. One of them has even inconvenienced us to the point of having to change our name. It happened that though we are pure Slavs our name originally ended in -*i*, which is not a Slav but an Italian termination, for a surname, for the reason that in the sixteenth century we chose to be known by the Christian name of a member of our family who was a great hero and was killed by the Turks while he was defending Candia. This circumstance, which was to our glory, the Italians attempted to turn to our shame, by pretending that our name proved that we, one of the leading patrician families of Korchula, were of Italian origin. There is no infamy to which they will not stoop.'

At that point a decanter of wine and some little cakes were brought in, and we drank to one another's health. My husband explained what a pleasure it was for us to meet them and to see their historic home. It was strange that when they answered they seemed not more proud of the stone glories of their palace than of the little ferns in the pots on the string lines. 'Once,' said the old gentleman, a gleam coming into his eye, 'I had birds as well as plants in my courtyard.' His son began to laugh, the old lady held her handkerchief to her lips and pouted and shook her head from side to side. 'Very beautiful they looked in their cages, and they sang like angels,' went on the old gentleman severely. 'But my wife did not like having them there. She did not like it at all. And that is why they are not there now. Shall I tell the story, Yelitsa? Shall I tell the story? Yes, I had better tell the story. It is something the like of which they will never have heard; never will they have heard of a woman behaving so wickedly.'

We were evidently being admitted to a favourite family joke. 'Think of it,' he told us with much mock horror, 'we were entertaining a large company of friends in the courtyard on Easter morning, as is our custom. Suddenly my wife rose and began to walk from cage to cage, opening all the doors and saying, "Christ is risen, the whole world is rejoicing, rejoice thou also, bird, and fly away home!" And as it was an assembly, I could not jump up and chastise her, and our friends sat and smiled, thinking this was some graceful pious comedy, suitable for Easter. Did ever a woman play such a trick on her husband? I ask you, sir, did your wife ever play such a trick on you?' Her husband, and indeed all of us, gazed at her in adoration through our laughter, and she shrugged her shoulders and said comfortably, 'Well, birds in cages, that is something I do not like.'

But in no time we were back in the conflict of Dalmatia with history. The old gentleman said to us, 'I think you will enjoy your travels amongst us. But you must make allowances. We are in some respects still barbarous simply because we spent so much of our time defending the West. We fought the Turk, and then we fought the Turk, and then we fought the Turk. For that reason we could not throw off the tyranny of Venice, so that it was able to use us as a deathbed, to use our life as a mattress for its decay. The French were better, but they brought with them their taint of revolution. There were some sad scenes, here and in Trogir especially, where the doctrines of Jacobinism caused revolt. But of your countrymen we have only the happiest recollections. Alas, that the peace treaty of 1815 should have made the mistake of handing us over to the Austrian Empire, that unnecessary organization, which should have ceased to exist after the destruction of the Turks, and which survived only to cultivate grossness and frivolity at the expense of her superior subject races.' 'The Austrians were the worst oppressors of all that we have known,' said his son, 'for Venice was a dying power during much of her reign over us, and had not the energy to conquer our spirit. But Austria felt in excellent health till the beginning of the Great War, and when she kicked us there was plenty of force in the boot.' 'Four generations of us were under Austria,' said his father, 'and always we rebelled against them for that very reason. Not out of their poverty but out of their wealth the Austrians would not plant our ruined forests, would not give us water, and taxed salt, so that our fisheries could not preserve their fish; and they hated those of us who were fortunate but defended the cause of our less fortunate fellow-Slavs.' 'But it is excessively hard on women,' said his wife, addressing me, 'when the men are for ever busying themselves with politics.'

The old gentleman regarded her tenderly. 'My wife pretends to be frivolous,' he said, 'but she is really true to the courageous tradition of Dalmatian womanhood, which indeed has been carried on with peculiar glory in Korchula. In 1571, when we had been abandoned by our cur of a Venetian governor, who ran away to Zara, and all our men were fighting at sea, a garrison of women and children successfully defended the town against the infamous Turkish corsair, Uliz Ali, who by the way was no Turk, but a renegade, simply another of those Italians. I can say that my wife has been a worthy successor to those women, for I have never known her to flinch before danger.' 'Perhaps I do not,' she said, 'but all the same it has sometimes been very boring.' Nevertheless, I could see his view of her was the truth. Her standard expression was one I had seen before, on the faces of women whose husbands had been prewar Russian revolutionaries, or Spanish liberals under Alfonso. The eyebrows were slightly raised, so that the space between them was fairly smooth, and the eyelids were lowered: so people look when they expect at any moment to receive a heavy blow in the face. But her chin was tilted forward, her lips were resolutely curved in a smile: she mocked the giver of the blow before he gave it, and removed her soul to a place where he could not touch it. 'Were you ever frightened?' I asked. 'Again and again I had reason to be, on account of the way my husband behaved,' she replied. 'But I thank God that by the time my sons were men we were safe under Yugoslavia.'

'You hear in her words what Yugoslavia means to us Dalmatians,' said the old gentleman. Then he paused. I felt he was searching for words to say something that had been in his mind since he set eyes on us, and that he found intensely disagreeable. 'I am glad,' he continued, 'that you have come to see our Yugoslavia. But I think you have come to see it too soon. It is what I have fought for all my life, and it is what must be, and, as my wife tells you, it already means a security such as we have never known before, not since the beginning of time. But you must remember what Cavour said: "Now there is an Italy, but we have not yet got Italians." It is so with us. We have the machinery of the state in Yugoslavia, but we have not yet learned how to work it. We have many amongst us who do not understand its possibilities, who are unaware of . . .'—his hands moved in distress—'of what it should be to us Slavs.' He began to speak in a slow, braked tone, of the Croatian discontent, and of the Matchek movement; and it was clear from his son's uneasiness and the muting of his wife's gaiety that this household felt itself still girt by enemies, and that this last encirclement was harder to bear than any of the others, since these enemies were of their own blood. These people had remembered they were Slavs for a thousand years, in spite of the threats of empire, and had believed they could not hate their fellow-Slavs. But now they saw their fellow-Slavs conspiring against Yugoslavia and giving Italy its opportunity to impose itself again as their oppressor, it seemed to them that they must hate them, must exterminate them without pity, as in the past they had exterminated renegades of their race who went over to the Turks.

The old gentleman was saying, 'You will find it hard to believe, but there are those amongst us who are so misguided as to wish to alienate the Croats from our fellow-Slavs, the Serbs; and indeed there are very great differences between us and the Serbs, differences of manners due to the unfortunate circumstance that they suffered what we did not, centuries of enslavement by the Turks. But they are not only brothers, they have given us enormous gifts. I remember that many years ago your admirable Professor Seton-Watson came to stay with me here, and he said to me, "You are insane to think of complete Slav independence, all you can hope for is full rights for the Slavs as citizens within the Austro-Hungarian Empire; it is far too strong for any of the Slav powers." But then he came back early in 1914, just after Serbia had beaten Turkey in the Balkan War, and he said, "Now it is different. When I see what the Serbs have done against Turkey, I am not at all sure that the Serbs and the Czechs and you Croats will not beat the Austro-Hungarian Army." He spoke truly. It was the triumph of the Serbs that gave us hope. I find it therefore disgusting that over a slight affair of manners people should disdain their liberators.' He spoke as a clear-cut man of action, used to making clear-cut decisions, used to arriving at clear-cut computations which are necessary before a compromise can be arranged. Not in a thousand years would he understand the Croatian world, which had been diluted by the German poison, which was a platform of clouds for drifting personalities, Slav in essence but vague in substance, unclimactic in process.

'And this Matchek movement,' cried the old gentleman, 'is

Bolshevist! It is Communist! What is all this nonsense about the necessity for a social revolution? If there is work the people earn wages and benefit. What other economic problem is there beyond this? If we can build up our fisheries and our shipbuilding on Korchula, then our islanders will have plenty of money and have all they want. What more is there to say about it?' He looked at us with the eyes of an old eagle that is keeping up its authority, yet fears that he may be wrong. He knew that what he was saying was not quite right, but he did not know in what it was wrong. We thought that his predicament was due to his age, but when we looked at his son we found precisely the same expression on his face. He said, without his usual authority, 'This is all the work of agitators, such as Mussolini used to be.' He probably alluded to the fact that when Mussolini was a Socialist he once organized a dock strike at Split. The experience of these people was very rich.

But in one respect it was very poor. They laboured, I saw, under many advantages—innate gifts, a traditional discipline which had been so ferociously applied through the centuries to cowards and traitors that courage and loyalty now seemed theirs of birthright, a devotion to public interest which made them almost as sacred as priests. But they laboured under one disadvantage. The ideas of the French Revolution had never been talked out in this part of the world. A touch of the Jacobin fever had reached Dalmatia when it was still under Venice, and had been drastically cured, first by the Venetians and later by the French. The year 1848 had brought a revival of revolutionary ideas to all Europe, but not to Dalmatia and Croatia, because the Hungarian uprising had taken an anti-Slav turn under Kossuth, and the Croats were obliged to offend their racial interests by fighting for the Habsburgs and reaction. Nobody in these parts, therefore, had ever discussed the possibility that the doctrine of Liberty, Equality, and Fraternity might be an admirable prescription to maintain the peace in an expanding industrial civilization. They had no means of understanding those believers in their doctrine who have discovered that it is impossible to guarantee liberty, equality, or fraternity to every member of a community while some members hold economic power over others, and who now demand a redistribution of wealth. This family took all the pother for a modern version of something which as Korchulan patricians they understood quite well: a plebeian revolt. Without a qualm they would resist it, for they knew what the people really wanted, and were doing their best to get it for them as fast as possible. Water, that was what they needed, and trees. Innocent in their misapprehension, bright with charity and public spirit, but puzzled by the noise of some distant riot for which their intimate knowledge of the civic affairs had not prepared them, the father and mother and son sat in the white circle under the chandelier, the darkness in the courtyard beyond now entirely night.

Korchula II

I woke early next morning, and heard Ellen Terry speaking as she had spoken at the Theatre Royal, Edinburgh, when I was a little girl. Her voice had lifted imperiously to cry, 'Kill Claudio!'—a behest not at all offensive since it was essentially just, yet raising certain problems. It was good that somebody should speak up for simple dealing with evil, although no one who knew all, who had comprehended the whole mystery of good and evil, would say it like that. There was perhaps something about the family I had visited last night which had recalled the speaking of those words. I fell asleep again, and was reawakened by the sound of singing, a little rough and wolfish for mere gaiety. When I went to the window there was a crowd of young men standing on the quay, each carrying a bundle. 'They must be conscripts,' said my husband, 'waiting for a steamer to take them to the mainland.' 'Yes,' I said, 'this is the time of year when they start their training. And look, they all look oddly shabby for such clean young men. They are all brisked up to look their best, but at the same time they've all come in their old clothes and left their new ones at home.' 'Let us wash and dress very quickly, and go down and have a look at them as they go on board.'

As we came out of the front door of the hotel, our cups of coffee in our hands, a white steamer came round the peninsula, lovely as a lady and drunk as a lord. She listed deeply landwards, because she already carried a freight of young men, and they had all run to the side to have a look at Korchula. 'It is the steamer come to take the conscripts away,' said a man standing beside us, in English which had been learned in America. 'Yes,' we said. 'They go to do their military service now on the mainland,' he continued. 'Yes,' we said. 'They go now to do their military service for Yugoslavia,' he said, 'but they are good Dalmatians, they are good Croats. Those songs you have heard them singing are all against the Government.' He wore a fixed, almost absent-minded smile that represented derision grown second-nature, having long forgotten its first or any other reason. I remembered something Constantine once told me. 'We Slavs love the terrible,' he said, 'and it happens that when we feel deeply terrible expressions come on our faces. As we love the terrible we keep them there, and they become grins, grimaces, masks that mean nothing. That is one of the things that has happened among the Bolsheviks. Revolution has become a rictus.' It has perhaps gone wrong here also.

As the ship drew nearer we heard that the young men leaning over the rail were singing just these same angrily hopeful songs as the young men on the quay, and by the time she came alongside the quay they were joined in one song. Some of those on the ship could not wait to land until the gang-plank was lowered, and, after shouting for the crowd below to fall back, they jumped from the rails to the quay, their bodies full of a goatish vigour, their faces calm and stubborn and withdrawn. They ran past us and came back in an instant carrying yard-long loaves under their arms, and stood quietly, rapt in the exaltation of having started on a new adventure, behind the young men of Korchula, who were standing more restlessly, the new adventure not having begun for them, and the distress of their families being a disagreeable distraction. Unifying these two groups was this dark overhanging cloud of discontented song. We went inside the hotel and buttered ourselves second rolls, and when we returned the boat had taken aboard its load and started out to sea. She was some hundreds of yards from the shore, more drunken than ever, listing still deeper with her increased freight, which was singing now very loudly and crowding to the rails to wave to the residue of their grieving kin, who were now moving along the quay to the round towers at the end of the peninsula so that they would be able to see her again as she left the bay and went out into the main channel; they walked crabwise, with their heads turned sideways, so that they should not miss one second's sight of their beloveds. They were obviously much moved by that obscure agony of the viscera rather than of the mind, or even of the heart, which afflicts the human being when its young goes from it over water, which St. Augustine described for ever in his *Confessions*, in his description of how his mother Monica grieved when he took sail from Africa to Italy. Presently the ship was gone, and the crowd came back, all walking very quickly and looking downwards and wiping their noses.

We found standing beside us the Cardinal, the Sitwell, and a handsome lady who was the Sitwell's wife. It was a pity so far as we were concerned, but it threw an interesting light on the claims of Italy to Dalmatia, and the real orientation of Dalmatia, that this lady spoke no languages but Serbo-Croatian and Russian, which she had acquired from a teacher who had been at the Tsarina's boarding school in Montenegro. They took us down to a motor boat by the quay, and we went out through a blue and white and windy morning for a trip about the island. Now the city of

Korchula was a goldsmith's toy, a tortoise made of precious metals, sitting on its peninsula as on a show-stand, and we were chugging past a suburb of villas, pink and white like sugar almonds. We passed a headland or two and came to a bay wide enough to be noble, and narrow enough to be owned. On its lip were moor and rock, and behind them olive terraces and almond orchards rose to scrub and bleakness. A track ran up to a high village in a crevice of this bleakness, and the Cardinal, laughing, told us that its inhabitants plagued the central and the local authorities for a better road down to this bay. 'And we say, "But why? You have a perfectly good road down to Korchula!" And they say, "But Korchula is not *our* port. This bay should be *our* port." So you see the little world is the same as the big world, and both are silly.'

In that, and a further bay, we made the boat linger. The green water glittered clean as ice, but gentle. 'Could we buy some land?' we asked. 'Could we build a villa?' It would be a folly. To get there from London would take two nights and two days by rail and steamer, and I do not suppose that either of us would ever be on easy terms with a language we had learned so late. But the sweet wildness of these bays, and the air rich with sun-baked salt and the scent of the scrub, and the view of the small perfect city, made this one of the places where the setting for the drama is drama enough. 'Yes, you could buy it, yes, you could build,' they said. 'But one thing,' said the Cardinal, rather than deceive a stranger, 'one thing you will not have in abundance. That is water. But then you could afford to build yourself a big cistern, and it always rains here in winter. That is the trouble, things work in a circle. People here need water if they are to make money. But because they have no money they cannot build cisterns to store water. So they cannot make any more money. All that, however, we shall settle in time.'

As we set off to the opposite coast, which looked like an island but was the peninsula of Pelyesatch, the Korchulans still talked of water. 'We had a great disappointment,' said the Sitwell. 'Over at Pelyesatch there is a spring of which the inhabitants have no very great need, and it was thought that we could raise enough money to build a pipe-line across this channel to our island. But alas! we discovered at the last moment that from time to time, and especially during droughts, when we would need it most, the spring ran salt.' 'You from England,' said the Cardinal, 'can have no notion of how disappointed we were. Still, we must not complain. When the worst comes to the worst, they send us a ship with a cargo of water down from Split.'

As we drew nearer the shore the water under the keel was pale emerald, where the diving sunlight had found sand. We landed on a little stone quay, where fishermen in a boat with a rust-coloured sail called greetings to our friends, as in the Middle Ages plebeians who were yet free men would have greeted nobles, when the dispensation was working well. We stepped out and walked along the coast by a line of small houses and gardens, and the Cardinal said, 'This is the village where all retired sea captains come to live if they can possibly manage it.' Sea captains are sensible. There was nothing that was not right in this village. There was nothing there which was not quietly guided to perfection by a powerful tradition. Every house was beautiful, and every garden. And they were small, they were not the results of lavish expenditure; and most of them were new, they were not legacies from a deceased perfection.

Even the quite businesslike post-office had an air of lovely decorum. Its path led through a garden which practised a modest and miniature kind of formality, to a small house built of this Dalmatian stone which is homely as cheese and splendid as marble. Within, a cool and clean passage, finely vaulted, was blocked by a high stand of painted iron, proper in every twist of its design, in which were posed flowers that needed special gentleness. A woman, well-mannered and remote, came from the back of the house and talked gravely of some local matter with the Cardinal, while she plucked me a nosegay with precise taste. The people who went by on the road looked like her, the houses we had passed had all been like this. Here man was at ease, he had mastered one part of the business of living so well that it was second nature to him. If we bought that bay over on Korchula we would not know what kind of house to build, we would have to take an infinite amount of thought, and our success would be a matter of hit and miss; and we would have to think of what we wanted our garden to look like. But these people's culture instructed them exactly how best they might live where they must live.

We went next into the garden of a larger and a grander house, which was empty, and from an orange tree the Cardinal broke me a branch laden with both fruit and blossom. 'It belongs,' he said, looking up at its desolation, 'to some Croats, who, poor people, bought it to turn into a hotel without reflecting that they had no money to rebuild it or run it.' Though he was so practical, he spoke of this not unimportant negligence as if it were not blameworthy, as if they had just been afflicted with this lapse of memory as they might with measles or loss of sight. I carried my sceptre of oranges along till we came to a church, a little church, the least of churches, that was dwarfed by a cypress which was a third of its breadth and a quarter taller, and itself was no king of trees. Small as it was, this church was recognizably of a superb tradition, and had big brothers that were cathedrals. We stood on the lawn admiring its tiny grandeur, while the Cardinal, who knew that all things were permitted to him everywhere, went to the bell-tower, which stood separate, and pulled the rope. While its deep note still was a pulse in the air, the Cardinal pointed to the road behind us and said, 'Look! There is something you will not often see nowadays.'

An old gentleman was having his walk, neat and clean, with white mutton-chop whiskers joining the moustaches that ran right across his shining pink face, wearing a short coat and sailorly trousers. He had the air of being a forthright and sensible person, but time was disguising him, for he had checked himself on seeing us from carrying on a conversation with certain phantoms, and age forced him to walk drunkenly. '*Zdravo!*' said the Cardinal, as is the way of Slavs when they meet. 'Flourish!' it means. '*Zdravo,*' the old man answered, as from the other side of an abyss. 'I told you that all retired sea captains wanted to live here. There is one of them; and you may see from his Franz Josef whiskers that he was in the Austrian Navy. I think those side-whiskers on such an old man are the only things coming from Vienna that I really like.' We watched the old man totter on his way, and as he forgot us, he resummoned his phantom friends and continued their argument. 'God pity us,' said the Cardinal. 'Yugoslavia must be, but it is almost certain that because of it there is here and there a good soul who feels like a lost dog.'

The boat took us for a time round the pale emerald waters close to the beach within a stone's throw of these houses and gardens that would have been theatrical in their perfection if they had not been austere. Then we drew further out and saw how above this hem of fertility round the shore olive groves and almond orchards rose in terraces to bluffs naked except for a little scrub, on which rested a plateau with more olives and almonds and a scattered blackness of cypresses and some villages and churches; and above this were the naked peaks, reflecting the noonlight like a mirror. Then fertility died out. Under the bluffs there was now a slope of scrub that sent out a perfume which I could smell in spite of the flowering orange branch upon my knee; and then a thick forest of cypresses, which for all their darkness and chastity of form presented that extravagant appearance that belongs to a profusion of anything that is usually scarce. Then the mountains dropped to a bay, a shoulder of sheer rock, and on the flat shore lay a pleasant town. 'This is Orebitch,' said the Cardinal. 'Look, there is painted all along the pier, 'Hail and welcome to the Adriatic.' It is the greeting the town made to our poor King Alexander when he sailed up this coast on his way to his death at Marseille. He had no time to stop there, so they paid their respects in this way.' We murmured our interest and kept our eyes on that inscription, and not on the other which some daring young man had scratched giant-high on the shoulder of rock above. '*Zhive* Matchek,' it read. Long live Matchek, the enemy of Yugoslavia, the emblem of the economic struggle which awakened no sympathy among our friends, though they could feel kindly for Croats who bought hotels without the money to run them, and for old Austrian naval officers, simply because nothing in their experience had prepared them for it.

Across the channel Korchula's lovely form was minute and mellow gold. We started towards it over a sea that was now brighter emerald, among islets which were scattered pieces of Scotland, rugged points of rock and moor with the large air of the Grampians though hardly paddock-wide. Our boat could slip within a foot or two of them, so deep and calm were the waters. Here was one much visited for the seagulls' eggs. As we chugged past the gulls rose and crossed and recrossed the sky above us, wailing against us who were their Turks, their pirates. At another islet a boat was hauled up on a yard of shingle and three fishermen lay sleeping among the scrub, bottles and empty baskets beside them. One heard our boat and lifted his head. His preoccupied eyes, blinking before the noon, found and recognized us; he raised his hand and said '*Zdravo!*' in an absent voice, and sank back with an air of returning to a more real world. The other two did not wake, but stirred defensively, as if guarding their own sleep.

'They will have been fishing since dawn, the good lads,' said the Sitwell. We passed another and more barren islet which rose to a flat top, not broad. Perhaps five fishermen might have taken their midday rest there. 'Here a famous treaty in our history was signed,' said the Cardinal. Men had scrambled out of boats on to this stony turret, barbarian and jewelled, for this coast was as much addicted to precious stones as to violence. Merchants went from island to island, hawking pearls and emeralds among the nobles, and the number of jewellers in the towns was extraordinary. In Korchula there were at one time thirty-two. After a few more such islets we came on a larger island, Badia, which illustrated the enigmatic quality of Dalmatian life. A monastery stands among its pinewoods, where there had been one for nearly a thousand years, though not the same one. Again and again men have gone there to live the contemplative life, and because it lies by the shore on a flatness hard to defend, and is distant from both Korchula and the mainland, pirates have murdered and looted their altars; and always other monks have come in their stead, to be murdered and looted in their turn. This series of pious tragedies continued until the middle of the nineteenth century. This might be comprehensible, were the place the site of some holy event, or were it some desert supremely appropriate to renunciation of the world and union with the supernatural. But Badia has no story other than this curious mutual persistence of monks and pirates, and the monastery lies as comfortably and unspiritually among its gardens as a Sussex manor-house. The history presents an exactly matched sadism and masochism, equally insane in the pursuit of what it finds its perverse pleasure, and nothing more.

Nuns, finding themselves as unwholesomely situated, would have gone home. That I thought before we landed, and I knew it afterwards. For we walked through the well-husbanded gardens, and round the cloisters, which are a mixture of Venetian Gothic and early Renaissance and conventional classic, yet are handled with such genius that they please as if they were of the purest style, and into the church, where the golden stone of the country makes splendour out of a planish design. There, though this was a Franciscan monastery and a boys' school, a very pretty nun was scrubbing the floor in front of the altar. She sat back on her pleasing little haunches and smiled with proprietary pride while we were shown a wooden cross, brought to Korchula by refugees who had fled here after the Turks had beaten Balkan Christendom at the battle of Kossovo, which showed on each side a realistic Christ in agony, the one manifestly dead, the other manifestly still living. So might a farmer's daughter smile when strangers came to her father's byres to marvel at a two-headed calf. Had she been in charge of the religious establishment when pirates threatened, this and all other holy objects would have been gathered up and stuffed with simple cunning into loads of hay or cabbages and rowed back to safety.

She was sensible. There is nothing precious about this Dalmatian civilization. It rests on a basis of good peasant sense. We left Badia and chugged back to the island of Korchula, to a bay of hills terraced with vineyards and set with fortress-like farms, stocky among their fig and mulberry trees. The roads that joined them ran between thick walls, up great ramps and steps that not all the armies of the world and marching a year could tread down; wine always converts

those who deal in it to the belief that all should be made for time to
gather up into an ultimate perfection. 'On that headland yonder,'
said the Cardinal, pointing to a moory headland, 'was found the
tablet which told us who we Korchulans are. An archæologist
working there last century found an inscription which gave the
names of five hundred Greek colonists who settled there in the
third century before Christ.' 'Was it not a hundred?' asked the
Sitwell. 'That is not important,' said the Cardinal, 'what matters
is that they were Greek. It means that here is a part of ancient
Greece which never was conquered by the Turk, which was never
conquered at all in any way that could conquer ancient Greece.
For in spite of Hungary and Venice and Austria we have, as you
may have noticed, kept ourselves to ourselves.' I listened, smiling
as at a boast, and then forgot to smile. What was ancient Greece
that all the swains adore her? A morning freshness of the body and
soul, that will have none of the dust; so it might be said. That
was not incongruous with much we had seen since we first took
to the water that morning. The claim was perhaps relevant to the
extreme propriety of the sea captain's village, the gracefulness of
the olive orchards and the almond orchards that had been forced on
the mountains, the town of Orebitch and its clear, virile inscription
and counter-inscription, the fisherman on the islet, the peasant
nun scrubbing the golden stone in front of the altar at Badia, the
vineyards and their sturdy forts and redoubts. It was certainly
completely in harmony, that claim, with this last island that we
visited.

'This you must see,' the Sitwell had said; 'there is a great quarry
there, which has given the stone for some of the most beautiful
buildings on our coast. They say the Rector's palace at Dubrovnik
came from here.' We slid by so near that we could see the weed
floating from its rocks, and looked at something that surely could
not be a quarry town. There are certain ugly paradoxes that hold
good in almost every society; for example, the people who satisfy
humanity's most urgent need and grow its food are ill-paid and
enjoy little honour. Another is the scurvy treatment of those who
hew from the earth its stone, which not only gives shelter but
compels those who use it towards decorum; for even the worst
architect finds difficulty in committing certain meannesses of
design when he is working with stone, and it will help him to
fulfil whatever magnificent intentions he may conceive. But in
most quarry villages privation can be seen gaining on man like a
hungry shark; and in France I have visited one where the workers
lived in lightless and waterless holes their hands had broken in the

walls of a medieval castle. But here it was not so. The island was like a temple, the village we saw before us was like an altar in a temple.

The village lay on the shore under a long low hill, riven with quarries and planted with some cypresses. The houses were built in proper shapes that would resist the winter gales but were not grim, that did not deny the existence of spring and summer, in stone that was the colour of edible things, of pale honey, of pie-crust, of certain kinds of melon. Flowers did not merely grow here, they were grown. Nasturtiums printed a gold and scarlet pattern on a wall under a window, vine leaves made an awning over a table outside a house where an open door showed a symmetry of stacked barrels. Some men walked down the street, two and then another group of three. Because they knew our friends and thought them worthy, they raised their hands in salutation, then thought no more of us, receding into their own lives as the fisherman had receded into his sleep. Four children, playing with a goat and its kid, looked backwards over their shoulders for a second, and went back to their play. A woman scrubbing a table in her garden straightened her arm and rested on it, wondering who we might be, and when she had rested enough put aside her curiosity and went on with her work. The houses and the people made a picture of a way of life different from what we know in the West, and not inferior.

My power to convey it is limited; a man cannot describe the life of a fish, a fish cannot describe the life of a man. It would be some guide to ask myself what I would have found on the island if we had not been water-strolling past it on our way back to familiarity but had been cast on it for ever. I would not find literacy, God knows. Nearly one-half the population in Yugoslavia cannot read or write, and I think I know in which half these men and women would find themselves. From the extreme æsthetic sensibility shown in the simple architecture of their houses and the planting of their flowers it could be seen that they had not blunted their eyes on print. Nor would I find clemency. This was no sugar-sweet island of the blest; the eyes of these men and women could be cold as stone if they found one not to be valuable, if they felt the need to be cruel they would give way to it, as they would give way to the need to eat or drink or evacuate. Against what I should lack on this island I should count great pleasure at seeing human beings move about with the propriety of animals, with their muscular ease and their lack of compunction. There was to be included in the propriety the gift, found in the lovelier animals, of keeping clean the pelt and the

lair. At a close gaze it could be seen that not in this quarry village
either had the damnably incongruous poverty been abolished, but
all was clean, all was neat. But not animal was the tranquillity of
these people. They had found some way to moderate the flow of
life so that it did not run to waste, and there was neither excess nor
famine, but a prolongation of delight. At the end of the village a
fisherman sat on a rock with his nets and a lobster-pot at his feet,
his head bent as he worked with a knife on one of his tools. From
the deftness of his movements it could be seen that he must have
performed this action hundreds of times, yet his body was happy
and elastic with interest, as if this were the first time. It was so
with all things on this island. The place had been a quarry for over
a thousand years: it was as if new-built. The hour was past noon;
it was as undimmed as dawn. Some of the men, and a woman who
was sitting between her flowers on the doorstep, were far gone in
years, but there was no staleness in them.

On the last rock of the island, a yard or so from the shore,
stood a boy, the reflected ripple of the water a bright trembling
line across his naked chest. He raised his eyes to us, smiled, waved
his hand, and receded, receded as they all did, to their inner riches.
There passed through my mind a sentence from Humfry Payne's
book on *Archaic Marble Sculpture in the Acropolis*, which, when
I verified it, I found to run: 'Most archaic Attic heads, however
their personality, have the same vivid look—a look expressive of
nothing so much as the plain fact of their own animate existence.
Of an animate existence lifted up, freed from grossness and decay,
by some action taken by the mind, which the rest of the world
cannot practice.' I said to the Cardinal, 'You have a way of
living here that is special, that is particular to you, that must be
defended at all costs.' He answered in a deprecating tone, 'I think
so.' I persisted. 'I do not mean just your architecture and your
tradition of letters, I mean the way the people live.' He answered,
'It is just that. It is our people, the way we live.' We were running
quicker now, past the monastery among its pinewoods, past the
headland where the Greek tablet was found, and could see the
town of Korchula before us. 'I should like,' said the Cardinal,
'you to come back and learn to know our peasants. This business
of politics spoils us in the towns, but somebody has to do it.'

It was at this point, when the town had become a matter of
identifiable streets, that the motor boat stopped and began to spin
round. The Sitwell said, 'We in Korchula are the descendants of a
hundred or perhaps of five hundred Greeks, and we have defended
the West against the Turks, and maybe Marco Polo was one of our

fellow-countrymen, but all the same our motor boats sometimes break down.' The boatman made tinkering sounds in the bowels of the boat, while the green waters showed their strength and drew us out to the wind-crisped channel. 'They will miss the steamer to Dubrovnik,' said the Sitwell. 'Is it of importance,' asked the Cardinal, 'that you should be at Dubrovnik today?' 'Yes,' said my husband. The Cardinal stood up and made a funnel of his hands and hallooed to a rowing-boat that was dawdling in the bright light on the water to our south. Nothing happened, and the Cardinal clicked his tongue against his teeth, and said, 'That family has always been slow in the uptake. Always.' It would have been amusing to ascertain what he meant by always: probably several centuries. But he continued to halloo, and presently the boat moved towards us. It proved to contain two young persons evidently but lately preoccupied with their own emotions: a girl whose hair was some shades lighter than her bronze skin but of the same tint, and a boy who seemed to have been brought back a thousand miles by the Cardinal's cry, though once he knew what was wanted and we had stepped from our boat to his, he bent to his oars with steady vigour, his brows joined in resolution. The girl, who was sucking the stem of a flower, derived a still contentment from the sight of his prowess, which indeed did not seem to surprise her. Behind us, across a widening space of shining milk-white water, the motor boat we had just left had now become a stately national monument, because the Cardinal remained standing upright, looking down on the boatman. He was quite at ease, since he had got us off to our boat, but he was watching this man, not to reprove him for any fault but to judge his quality. From a distance he resembled one of those stout marble columns in the squares of medieval cities from which the city standard used to be flown.

Dubrovnik (Ragusa) I

'Let us wire to Constantine and ask him to meet us earlier in Sarajevo,' I said, lying on the bed in our hotel room. 'I can't bear Dubrovnik.' 'Perhaps you would have liked it better if we had been able to get into one of the hotels nearer the town,' said my husband. 'Indeed I would not,' I said. 'I stayed in one of those hotels for a night last year. They are filled with people who either are on their honeymoon or never had one. And at dinner I looked about me at the tables and saw everywhere half-empty bottles of wine with room-numbers scrawled on the labels, which I think one of the dreariest sights in the world.' 'Yes, indeed,' said my husband, 'it seems to me always when I see them that there has been disobedience of Gottfried Keller's injunction, "*Lass die Augen fassen, was die Wimper hält von dem goldnen Ueberfluss der Welt*," "Let the eyes hold what the eyelids can contain from the golden overflow of the world." But you might have liked it better if we were nearer the town.' 'No,' I said, 'nothing could be lovelier than this.'

We were staying in a hotel down by the harbour of Gruzh, which is two or three miles out of Dubrovnik, or Ragusa as it used to be called until it became part of Yugoslavia. The name was changed, although it is pure Illyrian, because it sounded Italian: not, perhaps, a very good reason. Under the windows were the rigging and funnels of the harbour, and beyond the crowded waters was a hillside covered with villas, which lie among their gardens with an effect of richness not quite explicable by their architecture. The landscape is in fact a palimpsest. This was a suburb of Dubrovnik where the nobles had their summer palaces, buildings in the Venetian Gothic style furnished with treasures from the West and the East, surrounded by terraced flower-gardens and groves and orchards, as lovely as Fiesole or Vallombrosa, for here the Dalmatian coast utterly loses the barrenness which the traveller from the North might have thought its essential quality. These palaces were destroyed in the Napoleonic wars, looted and then burned; and on their foundations, in the nineteenth and twentieth centuries, have been built agreeable but undistinguished villas. But that is not the only confusion left by history on the view. The rounded slope immediately above the harbour is covered by an immense honey-coloured villa, with arcades and terraces and balconies hung with wistaria, and tier upon tier of orange trees and cypresses and chestnuts and olives and palms rising to the crest. It makes the claim of solidity that all Austrian architecture made, but it should have been put up in stucco, like our follies at Bath and Twickenham; for it was built for the Empress Elizabeth, who, of course, in her restlessness and Habsburg terror of the Slavs, went there only once or twice for a few days.

'I like this,' I said, 'as well as anything in Dubrovnik.' 'That can't be true,' said my husband, 'for Dubrovnik is exquisite, perhaps the most exquisite town I have ever seen.' 'Yes,' I said, 'but all the same I don't like it, I find it a unique experiment on the part of the Slav, unique in its nature and unique in its success, and I do not like it. It reminds me of the worst of England.' 'Yes,' said my husband, 'I see that, when one thinks of its history. But let us give it credit for what it looks like, and that too is unique.' He was right indeed, for it is as precious as Venice, and deserves comparison with the Venice of Carpaccio and Bellini, though not of Titian and Tintoretto. It should be visited for the first time when the twilight is about to fall, when it is already dusk under the tall trees that make an avenue to the city walls, though the day is only blanched in the open spaces, on the bridge that runs across the moat to the gate. There, on the threshold, one is arrested by another example of the complexity of history. Over the gate is a bas-relief by Mestrovitch, a figure of a king on a horse, which is a memorial to and a stylized representation of King Peter of Serbia, the father of the assassinated King Alexander, he who succeeded to the throne after the assassination of Draga and her husband. It is an admirable piece of work. It would surprise those who knew Mestrovitch's work only from international exhibitions to see how good it can be when it is produced under nationalist inspiration for a local setting. This relief expresses to perfection the ideal ruler of a peasant state. Its stylization makes, indeed, some reference to the legendary King Marko, who is the hero of all Serbian peasants. This king could groom the horse he rides on, and had bought it for himself at a fair, making no bad bargain; yet he is a true king, for no man would daunt him from doing his duty to his people, either by strength or by riches. It is enormously ironic that this should be set on the walls of a city that was the antithesis of the peasant state, that maintained for centuries the most rigid system of aristocracy and the most narrowly bourgeois ethos imaginable. The incongruity will account for a certain coldness shown towards the Yugoslavian ideal in Dubrovnik; which itself appears ironical when it is considered that after Dubrovnik was destroyed by the great powers no force on earth could have come to its rescue except the peasant state of Serbia.

For an ideal first visit the traveller should go into the city and find the light just faintly blue with dusk in the open space that lies inside the gate, and has for its centre the famous fountain by the fifteenth-century Neapolitan architect Onofrio de la Cava. This is a masterpiece, the size of a small chapel, a domed piece of masonry with fourteen jets of water, each leaping from a sculptured plaque set in the middle of a panel divided by two slender pilasters, into a continuous trough that runs all round the fountain: as useful as any horse-trough, and as lovely and elevating as an altar. On the two steps that raise it from the pavement there always lie some carpets with their sellers gossiping beside them. At this hour all cats are grey and all carpets are beautiful; the colours, fused by the evening, acquire richness. On one side of this square is another of the bland little churches which Dalmatians built so often and so well, a town sister of that we had seen in the village where the retired sea captains lived. At this hour its golden stone gives it an air of enjoying its own private sunset, prolonged after the common one. It has a pretty and secular rose-window which might be the brooch for a bride's bosom. Beside it is a Franciscan convent, with a most definite and sensible Pietà over a late Gothic portal. The Madonna looks as if, had it been in her hands, she would have stopped the whole affair; she is in no degree gloating over the spectacular fate of her son. She is not peasant, she is noble; it is hardly possible to consider her as seducible by the most exalted destiny. Facing these across the square is the old arsenal, its façade pierced by an arch; people walk through it to a garden beyond, where lamps shine among trees, and there is a sound of music. For background there are the huge city walls, good as strength, good as honesty.

Ahead runs the main street of the town, a paved fairway, forbidden to wheeled traffic, lined with comely seventeenth-century houses that have shops on their ground floor. At this time it is the scene of the Corso, an institution which is the heart of social life in every Yugoslavian town, and indeed of nearly all towns and villages in the Balkans. All of the population who have clothing up to the general standard—I have never seen a person in rags and patches join a Corso in a town where good homespun or manufactured textiles are the usual wear, though in poverty-stricken districts I have seen an entire Corso bearing itself with dignity in tatters—join in a procession which walks up and down the main street for an hour or so about sunset. At one moment there is nobody there, just a few people going about the shops or sitting outside cafés; at the next the street is full of all the human beings in the town that feel able to take part in the life of their kind, each one holding up the head and bearing the body so that it may be seen, each one chattering and being a little gayer than in private, each one attempting to establish its individuality. Yet the attempt defeats itself, for this mass of people, moving up and down the length of the street and slowly becoming more and more like each other because of the settling darkness, makes a human being seem no more than a drop of water in a stream. In a stream, moreover, that does not run for ever. The Corso ends as suddenly as it begins. At one instant the vital essence of the town chokes the street with its coursing; the next, the empty pavement is left to the night.

But while it lasts the Corso is life, for what that is worth in this particular corner of the earth; and here, in Dubrovnik, life still has something of the value it must have had in Venice when she was young. A city that had made good bread had learned to make good cake also. A city that had built itself up by good sense and industry had formed a powerful secondary intention of elegance. It is a hundred and thirty years ago that Dubrovnik ceased to exist as a republic, but its buildings are the unaltered cast of its magnificence, its people have still the vivacity of those who possess and can enjoy. Here the urbanity of the Dalmatian cities becomes metropolitan. Follow this Corso and you will find yourself in the same dream that is dreamed by London and Paris and New York; the dream that there is no limit to the distance which man can travel from his base, the cabbage-patch, that there is no pleasure too delicate to be bought by all of us, if the world will but go on getting richer. This is not a dream to be despised; it comes from man's more amiable parts, it is untainted by cruelty, it springs simply from a desire to escape from the horror that is indeed implicit in all man's simpler relationships with the earth. It cannot be realized in a city so great as London or Paris or New York, or even the later Venice; it was perhaps possible to realize it in a city no larger than Dubrovnik, which indeed neither was nor is very far from the cabbage-patches. For on any fine night there are some peasants from the countryside outside the walls who have come to walk in the Corso.

To taste the flavour of this Corso and this city, it is good to turn for a minute from the main street into one of the side streets. They mount steep and narrow to the walls which outline the squarish peninsula on which the city stands; close-pressed lines of houses—left at this hour to sleeping children, the old, and servant-maids—which are rich in carved portals and balconies, and perfumed with the spring. For it took the Industrial Revolution

to make man conceive the obscene idea of a town as nothing but
houses. These carved portals and balconies are twined with flowers
that are black because of the evening but would be scarlet by
day, and behind high walls countless little gardens send out their
sweetness. Back in the main street the people from these houses
and gardens sweep down towards their piazza, past a certain statue
which you may have seen in other towns, perhaps in front of the
Rathaus at Bremen. Such statues are said to represent the hero
Orlando or Roland, who defeated the Saracens: they are the sign
that a city is part of liberal and lawful Christendom. To the left of
the crowd is the Custom House and Mint, in which the history of
their forebears for three centuries is written in three stories. In the
fourteenth century the citizens of the Republic built themselves a
Custom House, just somewhere to take in the parcels; in that age
the hand of man worked right, and the courtyard is perfection.
A hundred years later so many parcels had come in that the
citizens were refined folk and could build a second story for
literary gatherings and social assemblies, as lovely as Venetian
Gothic could make it. Prosperity became complicated and lush,
the next hundred years brought the necessity of establishing a
handsome Mint on the top floor, in the Renaissance style; and
for sheer lavishness they faced the Custom House with a loggia.
Because the people who did this were of the same blood, working
in a civilization that their blood and none other had made, these
different styles are made one by an inner coherence. The building
has a light, fresh, simple charm.

They mill there darkly, the people of Dubrovnik, the buildings
running up above them into that whiteness which hangs above the
earth the instant before the fall of the night, which is disturbed
and dispersed by the coarser whiteness of the electric standards.
The Custom House is faced by the Church of St. Blaise, a great
baroque mass standing on a balustraded platform, like a captive
balloon filled with infinity. In front is an old tower with a huge
toy clock: at the hour, two giant bronze figures of men come out
and beat a bell. The crowd will lift their heads to see them, as their
fathers have done for some hundreds of years. Next to that is the
town café, a noble building, where one eats well, looking on to the
harbour; for we have reached the other side of the peninsula now,
the wind that blows in through the archways is salt. Then to the
right is the Rector's palace, that incomparable building, the special
glory of Dubrovnik, and even of Dalmatia, the work of Michelozzo
Michelozzi the Florentine and George the Dalmatian, known as
Orsini. Simply it consists of a two-storied building, the ground

floor shielded by a loggia of six arches, the upper floor showing eight Gothic windows. It is imperfect: it once had a tower at each end, and these have gone. Nevertheless, its effect is complete and delightful, and, like all masterpieces of architecture, it expresses an opinion about the activities which are going to be carried on under its roof. Chartres is a speculation concerning the nature of God and of holiness. The Belvedere in Vienna is a speculation concerning political power. With its balanced treatment of its masses and the suggestion of fecundity in its springing arches and proliferating capitals, the Rector's palace puts forward an ideal of an ordered and creative society. It is the most explicit building in an amazingly explicit town, that has also an explicit history, with a beginning and an end. It is another example of the visibility of life which is the special character of Yugoslavia, at least so far as those territories which have not been affected by the Teutonic confusion are concerned.

The Corso says, 'This is the city our fathers made.' The city says, 'These are the men and women we have made.' If you should turn aside and go into the café to eat an evening meal, which here should be preferably the *Englische Platte*, an anthology of cold meats chosen by a real scholar of the subject, the implications of this display will keep you busy for the night. There is, of course, the obvious meaning of Dubrovnik. It was quite truly a republic: not a protectorate, but an independent power, the only patch of territory on the whole Dalmatian coast, save for a few unimportant acres near Split, that never fell under the rule of either Hungary or Venice. It was a republic that was a miracle: on this tiny peninsula, which is perhaps half a mile across, was based a great economic empire. From Dubrovnik the caravans started for the overland journey to Constantinople. This was the gateway to the East; and it exploited its position with such commercial and financial and naval genius that its ships were familiar all over the known world, while it owned factories and warehouses in every considerable port of Southern Europe and in some ports of the North, and held huge investments such as mines and quarries in the Balkans. Its history is illuminated by our word 'argosy,' which means nothing more than a vessel from Ragusa. It is as extraordinary as if the city of London were to have carried out the major part of the commercial achievements of the British Empire up to, say, the reign of Henry VII, with no more territory than itself and about three or four hundred square miles in the home counties which it had gradually acquired by conquest and purchase. That is the primary miracle of Dubrovnik; that and its resistance to Turkey, which for century after century coveted the port as the key to the Adriatic and the invasion of Italy, yet could never dare to seize it because of the diplomatic genius of its defenders.

But as one contemplates the town other issues crowd on the mind. First, the appalling lack of accumulation observable in history, the perpetual cancellation of human achievement, which is the work of careless and violent nature. This place owes its foundation to the ferocity of mankind towards its own kind. For Dubrovnik was first settled by fugitives from the Greek city of Epidaurus, which is ten miles further south down the coast, and from the Roman city of Salonæ, when these were destroyed by the barbarians, and was later augmented by Slavs who had come to these parts as members of the barbarian forces. It was then monstrously harried by the still greater ferocity of fire and earthquake. Some of the fires might be ascribed to human agency, for the prosperity of the group—which was due to its fusion of Greek and Roman culture with Slav virility—meant that they were well worth attacking and therefore they had to make their rocky peninsula into a fortress with abundant stores of munitions. They were, therefore, peculiarly subject to fires arising out of gunpowder explosions. The Rector's palace was twice burned down for this reason during twenty-seven years. But such damage was trifling compared to the devastation wrought by earthquakes.

The bland little church beside the domed fountain at the City Gate was built in the sixteenth century as a thanksgiving by those who had been spared from an earthquake which, in a first convulsion, shook down houses that were then valued at five thousand pounds, and then continued as a series of shocks for over eighteen months; and there was apparently an earthquake of some degree in this district every twenty years. But the worst was the catastrophe of 1667. The sea was tilted back from the harbour four times, each time leaving it bone dry, and each time rushing back in a flood-wave which pounded many vessels to pieces against the docks and cliffs. The greater part of the public buildings and many private houses were in ruins, and the Rector of the Republic and five thousand citizens were buried underneath them. Then fire broke out; and later still bands of wolfish peasants from the mountain areas devastated by Venetian misrule and Turkish warfare came down and plundered what was left.

We know, by a curious chance, exactly what we lost in the way of architecture on that occasion. In the baroque church opposite the Rector's palace there is a two-foot-high silver statuette of St. Blaise, who is the patron saint of the city, and he holds in his hand a silver model of Dubrovnik as it was before the earthquake. It shows us the setting for a fairy-tale. In particular it shows the Cathedral, which was built by Richard Cœur de Lion as a thanksgiving for his escape from shipwreck on this coast, as a thirteenth-century building of great beauty and idiosyncrasy, and the main street as a unique expression of commercial pride, a line of houses that were true palaces in their upper parts and shops and offices below. We can deduce also that there was an immense loss of pictures, sculptures, textiles, jewels, and books, which had been drawn by the Republic from West and East during her centuries of successful trading. Indeed, we know of one irreparable loss, so great that we cannot imagine what its marvellous content may have been. There existed in Bosnia a society that was at once barbarous and civilized, an indirect heir to Byzantine civilization and able to fight Rome on doctrinal points as a logic-chopping equal, but savage and murderous. This society was destroyed by the Turk. At the end of the fifteenth century, Catherine, the widow of the last King of Bosnia, murdered by his illegitimate son, who was later himself flayed alive by Mahomet I, fled to Dubrovnik and lived there till she went to Rome to die. Before she left she gave some choral books, richly illustrated and bound, to the monks of the Franciscan monastery, who had a famous library. If these books had survived they would have been a glimpse of a world about which we can now only guess: but the whole library perished.

What is the use of ascribing any catastrophe to nature? Nearly always man's inherent malignity comes in and uses the opportunities it offers to create a graver catastrophe. At this moment the Turks came down on the Republic to plunder its helplessness, though their relationship had till then been friendly. Kara Mustapha, the Turkish Grand Vizier, a demented alcoholic, pretended that the armed resistance the citizens had been forced to put up against the wretched looters from the mountains was in some obscure way an offence against Turkish nationals, and on this pretext and on confused allegations of breach of tariff agreements he demanded the payment of a million ducats, or nearly half a million pounds. He also demanded that the goods of every citizen who had been killed in the earthquake should be handed to the Sublime Porte, the Republic being (he suddenly claimed) a Turkish possession. For fifteen years the Republic had to fight for its rights and keep the aggressors at bay, which it was able to do by using its commercial potency and its diplomatic genius against the Turks when they were already rocking on their feet under the blows of Austria and Hungary. Those were its sole weapons. France, as professed defender of Christianity and order in Europe, should have aided the Republic. But Louis XIV would not lift his little finger to help her, partly because she had been an ally of Spain, partly because the dreary piece of death-in-life, Madame de Maintenon, supreme type of the she-alligator whom men often like and admire, had so inflamed him with pro-Jesuit passion that a mere rumour that the Republican envoy was a Jansenist was enough to make him cancel his mission.

The story of what happened to the four ambassadors who left to plead with the Turkish Government is one of the classic justifications of the human race: almost a promise that there is something to balance its malignity. Caboga and Bucchia were sent to Constantinople to state the independence of the Republic. They were, by a technique familiar to us today, faced with documents admitting that the Republic was a Turkish possession and told with threats and curses that they must sign them. They refused. Dazed and wearied from hours of bullying they still refused, and were thrown into a plague-stricken prison. There they lay for years, sometimes smuggling home dispatches written in their excrement on packing paper. Their colleagues, Bona and Gozzi, went to Sarajevo to make the same statement of independence to the Pasha of Bosnia, and were likewise thrown into captivity. They were dragged behind the Turkish Army on a war it was conducting with Russia on the Danube, and there thrown in irons into the dungeons of a fortress in a malarial district, and told they must remain prisoners until they had signed the documents which Caboga and Bucchia had refused to sign in Constantinople. There Bona died. A Ragusan priest who had settled in the district stood by to give him the last sacrament, but was prevented by the jailers. There is no knowing how many such martyrs might have been demanded of Dubrovnik and furnished by her, had not the Turks then been defeated outside Vienna by John Sobieski, King of Poland. Kara Mustapha was executed, and there was lifted from the Republic a fear as black as any we have felt today.

It is a glorious story, yet a sad one. What humanity could do if it could but have a fair course to run, if fire and pestilence did not gird our steps and earthquakes engulf them, if man did not match his creativeness with evil that casts down and destroys! It can at least be said that Dubrovnik ran well in this obstacle race. But there is not such exaltation in the spectacle when it is considered how she had to train for that victory, both so far as it was commercial and diplomatic in origin. Everywhere in the Dalmatian cities the class struggle was intense. The constitution of the cities provided for the impartial administration of justice, legal and economic, to persons arranged in castes and made to remain there, irrespective of their merits, with the utmost rigid injustice. This was at first due to historical necessity. The first-comers in a settlement, who had the pick of the economic findings and whatever culture was going, might really be acting in the public interest as well as defending their own private ends, when they insisted on reserving to themselves all possible social power and not sharing it with later-comers, who might be barbarians or refugees demoralized by years of savage warfare. But it led to abuses which can be measured by the continual rebellions and the horrible massacres which happened in every city on the coast. In Hvar, for instance, the island where the air is so sweet, the plebeians took oath on a crucifix held by a priest that they would slaughter all the nobles. The Christ on the crucifix bled at the nose, the priest fell dead. Nevertheless the plebeians carried out their plans, and massacred many of the nobles in the Hall of Justice in the presence of the Rector, but were overcome by a punitive expedition of the Venetian fleet and themselves put to death or mutilated.

This caste system never led to such rebellions in Dubrovnik, partly because the economic well-being of the community choked all discontent with cream, partly because they had little chance of succeeding; but it existed in a more stringent form than anywhere else. The population was divided into three classes: the nobles, the commoners, and the workers. The last were utterly without say in the government. They did not vote and they could hold no office. The commoners also had no votes, but might hold certain unimportant offices, though only if appointed by the nobles. The actual power of government was entirely in the hands of the nobles. The body in which sovereignty finally rested was the Grand Council, which consisted of all males over eighteen belonging to families confirmed as noble in the register known as the Golden Book. This Council deputed its executive powers to a Senate of forty-five members who met four times a week and at times of emergency; and they again deputed their powers to a Council of Seven (this had numbered eleven until the earthquake) who exercised judicial power and performed all diplomatic functions, a Council of Three, who acted as a tribune of constitutional law, and a Council of Six, who administered the Exchequer. There were other executive bodies, but this is a rough idea of the anatomy of the Republic. It must be remembered that these classes were separated in all departments of their lives as rigidly as the Hindu castes. No member of any class was permitted to marry into either of the other two classes; if he did so he lost his position in his own class and his children had to take the rank of the inferior parent. Social relations between the classes were unthinkable.

It is interesting that this system should have survived when all real differences in the quality of classes had been levelled by general prosperity, when there might be commoners and even workers who were as rich and as cultured as any noble. It is interesting, too, that it should have survived even when the classes were cleft from within by disputes. When Marmont went to Dubrovnik in 1808 he found that the nobles were divided into two parties, one called the Salamancans and the other the Sorbonnais. These names referred to some controversy arising out of the wars between Charles V of Spain and Francis I of France, a mere matter of two hundred and fifty years before. It had happened that in the earthquake of 1667 a very large proportion of the noble class was destroyed, and it was necessary to restore it to strength by including a number of commoners. These the Salamancans, sympathizers with Spanish absolutism, would not treat as equals; but the Sorbonnais, Francophil and inclined to a comparative liberalism, accepted them fully. It is also a possible factor in the situation that the Sorbonnais had been specially depleted by the earthquake casualties and wanted to keep up their numbers. Be that as it may, the two parties were exactly equal in status and sat together on the Councils, but they had no social relations and did not even greet each other on the streets; and a misalliance between members of the two parties was as serious in its consequences as a misalliance between classes.

But this was far from being the only sop offered by the Republic to that disagreeable appetite, the desire of a human being to feel contempt for another not in fact very different from himself. The commoners in their turn were divided into the confraternities of St Anthony and St Lazarus, who were as rancorous in their relationship as the Salamancans and the Sorbonnais. The survival of this three-class system in spite of these dissensions suggests that it was actually a fusion of long-standing customs, native to the different races which composed the Republic: say a variation of the classical system of aristocracy grafted on some ancient Illyrian organization of which we now know nothing, which pleased the Slav late-comers, though themselves democratic in tendency, because of the solid framework it gave to internal bickerings. 'Whether they agree or do not agree,' an exasperated Roman emperor wrote of the first Slav tribes to appear within the Empire's ken, 'very soon they fall into disturbances among themselves, because they feel a mutual loathing and cannot bear to accommodate one another.'

The system, of course, was far from being merely silly. One

may wonder how it survived; one cannot question the benefits it conferred by surviving. The Republic was surrounded by greedy empires whom she had to keep at arm's length by negotiation lest she perish: first Hungary, then Venice, then Turkey. Foreign affairs were her domestic affairs; and it was necessary that they should be conducted in complete secrecy with enormous discretion. It must never be learned by one empire what had been promised by or to another empire, and none of the greedy pack could be allowed to know the precise amount of the Republic's resources. There was therefore every reason to found a class of governors who were so highly privileged that they would protect the *status quo* of the community at all costs, who could hand on training in the art of diplomacy from father to son, and who were so few in number that it would be easy to detect a case of blabbing. They were very few indeed. In the fifteenth century, when the whole population was certainly to be counted by tens of thousands, there were only thirty-three noble families. These could easily be supervised in all their goings and comings by those who lived in the same confined area.

But it is curious that this ultra-conservative aristocratic government should develop a tendency which is often held to be a characteristic vice of democracy. Dubrovnik dreaded above all things the emergence of dominant personalities. The provisions by which this dread is expressed in the constitution are the chief differences which distinguish it from its obvious Venetian model. The Senate was elected for life, and there you had your small group of hereditary diplomats. But these elections had to be confirmed annually, and infinite precautions were taken lest any Senator should seize excessive power and attempt dictatorship. The Rector wore a superb toga of red silk with a stole of black velvet over the left shoulder, and was preceded in his comings and goings by musicians and twenty palace guards; but he held his office for just one month, and could be re-elected only after intervals of two years; and this brevity of tenure was the result of ever-anxious revision, for the term had originally been three months, had been reduced to two, and was finally brought down to the single month. He was also held prisoner within the palace while he held office, and could leave it only for state appearances, such as his obligatory solemn visit to the Cathedral.

The lesser offices were as subject to restriction. The judiciary and diplomatic Council of Seven was elected afresh every year, and could not be re-elected for another year. The Council of Three, who settled all questions of constitutional law, was also elected for but one year. The Council of Six, who administered the state finances, was elected for three years. There were also certain regulations which prevented the dominance of people of any particular age. The Council of Seven might be of any adult age, but the youngest had to act as Foreign Secretary; but the Council of Three had all to be over fifty. These devices were entirely justified by their success. Only once, and that very early in the history of Dubrovnik, did a noble try to become a dictator; and then he received no support, save from the wholly unrepresented workers, and was forced to suicide. Later, in the seventeenth century, some nobles were seduced by the Duke of Savoy into a conspiracy to seize power, but they were arrested at a masked ball on the last day of Carnival, and executed by general consent of the community.

That terror of the emergent personality is not the only trait of this aristocratic society which recalls its contrary. There is a great deal in the history of Dubrovnik which had its counterpart among our Puritan capitalists. The nobles believed in education even more seriously than was the custom of their kind in other Dalmatian towns, though even there the standard was high: the Venetian Governor of Split is found complaining of young men who came back from their studies at Oxford filled with subversive notions. But they did not, as might have been expected, try to keep learning as a class prerogative. As well as sending their own sons to universities in Italy and France and Spain and England, they built public schools which were open to the children of all three classes. They also created a hospital system which included the first foundling hospital in the whole civilized world, and they were as advanced in their treatment of housing problems. After one of the earlier earthquakes they put in hand a town-planning scheme which considered the interests of the whole community, and their arrangements for a water supply were not only ahead of the time as an engineering project but made an attempt to serve every home.

They also anticipated philanthropists of a much later date and a wholly different social setting in their attitude to the slave-trade. In 1417 they passed what was the first anti-slavery legislation except for our own English laws discouraging the export of human cargo from Bristol. This was no case of damning a sin for which they had no mind, since a great deal of money could be made in the Mediterranean slave-trade, a considerable amount of which had come to certain Republican merchants living further north on the coast; and it must be remembered that, owing to the survival of the feudal system in the Balkans long after it had passed away from the rest of Europe, the state of serfdom was taken for granted by many of the peoples under the Republic's rule or in relationship with her. But the Grand Council passed a law providing that anybody selling a slave should be liable to a heavy fine and six months' imprisonment, 'since it must be held to be base, wicked, and abominable, and contrary to all humanity, and to redound to the great disgrace of our city, that the human form, made after the image and similitude of our Creator, should be turned to mercenary profit, and sold as if it were brute beast.' Fifty years later they tightened up this law and made the punishment harsher, adding the proviso that if a slave-trader could not recover his victims from captivity within a certain period after he had been directed to do so by the authorities, he was to be hanged. All through the next three centuries, until the Mediterranean slave-trade became wholly extinct, it was a favourite form of philanthropy among the wealthy Republicans to buy slaves their freedom.

There were other Whig preferences in Dubrovnik: the right of asylum, for instance, was strictly maintained. When the Turks beat the Serbs at Kossovo in 1389 one of the defeated princes, the despot George Brankovitch, took refuge in Dubrovnik and was hospitably received, though the Republic was an ally of Turkey. When the Sultan Murad II protested and demanded that he should be delivered up, the Senate answered, 'We, men of Ragusa, live only by our faith, and according to that faith we would have sheltered you also, had you fled hither.' But there is a quality familiar to us Westerners not only in the political but in the social life of the Republic. The citizens kept extremely comfortable establishments, with the best of food and drink and furniture, but their luxury was strictly curbed in certain directions. There was never any theatre in Dubrovnik till fifty years after the destruction of the Republic, when one was built by the Austrians. In the fifteenth century, which was a gay enough season for the rest of Europe, Palladius writes: 'To make manifest how great is the severity and diligence of the Ragusans in the bringing up of their children, one thing I will not pass over, that they suffer no artistic exercises to exist in the city but those of literature. And if jousters or acrobats approach they are forthwith cast out lest the youth (which they would keep open for letters or for merchandising) be corrupted by such low exhibitions.'

There must have been many an English family of wealthy bankers and manufacturers in Victorian days who ate vast meals and slept in the best Irish linen and were surrounded by the finest mahogany and the most distinguished works of Mr Leader and Mr Sidney Cooper (and, perhaps, thanks to John Ruskin, some really good

Italian pictures), but who never set foot in a theatre or music-hall or circus. But an even more significant parallel between the Republic and England is to be found in the hobbies of the wealthier citizens. English science owes a great deal to the discoveries of business men, particularly among the Quakers, who took to some form of research as an amusement to fill in their spare time. So was it also in Dubrovnik. The citizens had a certain taste for letters, though chiefly for those exercises which are to literature as topiary is to gardening, such as the composition of classical or Italian verses in an extremely formal style; but their real passion was for mathematics and the physical sciences. They produced many amateurs of these, and some professionals, of whom the most notable was Roger Joseph Boscovitch, a wild Slav version of the French encyclopædists, a mystic, a mathematician and physicist, a poet and diplomat. In his writings and those of his compatriots who followed the same passion, there are pæans to science as the illuminator of the works of God, which have countless analogues in the writings of Englishmen of the same class in the eighteenth and early nineteenth centuries.

But the resemblance does not stop there. There is a certain case to be made against the bourgeois class of Englishmen that developed into the nonconformist liberals who followed Mr Gladstone through his triumphs, and reared their sons to follow Lord Oxford and Mr Lloyd George to the twilight hour of their faith. It might be charged against them that their philanthropy consisted of giving sops to the populace which would make it forget that their masters had seized all the means of production and distribution, and therefore held them in a state of complete economic subjection. It might be charged against them also that they were virtuous only when it suited their pockets, and that while they would welcome Kossuth or Mazzini or any other defender of oppressed people outside the British Empire, they were indifferent to what happened inside it. It might be charged against them that they cared little how much truth there was in the bitter description of our exports to the coloured races, 'Bibles, rum, and rifles,' so long as there was truth in the other saying, 'Trade follows the flag.' There is enough testimony to the virtue of this class to make such charges not worth discussing with any heat of spirit; but there was enough truth in them to make it impossible to regard the accused as an ideal group, and the society which produced them as paradisaical. It is even so with Dubrovnik.

The Republic was extremely pious. She spoke of her Christianity at all times, and in her Golden Book there is a prayer for the magistrates of the Republic which runs: 'O Lord, Father Almighty, who hast chosen this Republic to serve Thee, choose, we beseech Thee, our governors, according to Thy Will and our necessity: that so, fearing Thee and keeping Thy Holy Commandments, they may cherish and direct us in true charity. Amen.' Never was there a city so full of churches and chapels, never was there a people who submitted more loyally to the discipline of the Church. But there was a certain incongruity with this in their foreign policy. Had Dubrovnik the right to pose as a proud and fastidious Catholic power considering her relations with the Ottoman Empire, the devouring enemy of Christendom? The other Dalmatian towns were less complaisant than Venice in their attitude to the Turks, the Republic far more. She never fought the Turk. She paid him tribute, and tribute, and again tribute.

Every year two envoys left the city for Constantinople with their load of golden ducats, which amounted, after several increases, to fifteen thousand. They wore a special dress, known as the uniform of the divan, and had their beards well grown. They placed their affairs in order, embraced their families, attended mass at the Cathedral, and were bidden godspeed by the Rector under the arches of his palace. Then, with their cashier, their barber, numerous secretaries and interpreters, a troop of armed guards, and a priest with a portable altar, they set forth on the fifteen days' journey to the Bosporus. It was not a very dangerous journey, for the caravans of the Republic made it an established trade route. But the envoys had to stay there for twelve months, till the next two envoys arrived and took their place, and the negotiation of subtle business with tyrants of an alien and undecipherable race, while physically at their mercy, was a dangerous task, which was usually performed competently and heroically. This was not, however, the only business they transacted with the Turks. The envoys to Constantinople had also to do a great deal of bribery, for there was a sliding scale of tips which covered every official at the Porte from the lowest to the highest. This burden increased yearly as the Turkish Empire increased in size to the point of unwieldiness, and the local officials became more and more important. As time went on it was almost as necessary to bribe the Sandjakbeg of Herzegovina and the Pasha of Bosnia and their staffs as it was to make the proper payments to the Sublime Porte.

All this would be very well, if Dubrovnik had avowed that she was an independent commercial power in a disadvantageous military and naval position, and that she valued her commerce and independence so highly that she would pay the Turks a great ransom for them. But it is not so pleasing in a power that boasts of being fervent and fastidious in its Christianity. Of course it can be claimed that Dubrovnik was enabled by her relations with the Porte to render enormous services to the Christians within the territories conquered by the Turks; that wherever her mercantile colonies were established—and that included towns all over Bosnia and Serbia and Bulgaria and Wallachia and even Turkey itself—the Christians enjoyed a certain degree of legal protection and religious freedom. But on the other hand the Republic won for herself the right to pay only two or sometimes one and a half per cent on her imports and exports into and out of the Ottoman Empire, while all the rest of the world had to pay five per cent. It is no use. Nothing can make this situation smell quite like the rose. If Dickens had known the facts he might have felt about Dubrovnik as he felt about Mr Chadband; and if Chesterton had attended to them he might have loathed it as much as he loathed cocoa.

Especially is this readiness to rub along with the Turks displeasing in a power which professed to be so fervent and fastidious in its Christianity that it could not let the Orthodox Church set foot within its gates. Theoretically, the Republic upheld religious tolerance. But in practice she treated it as a fair flower that was more admirable if it blossomed on foreign soil. Though Dubrovnik had many visitors, and even some natives, who were members of the Orthodox Church, they were not allowed to have any place of worship within the Republic. It curiously happened that in the eighteenth century this led to serious difficulties with Catherine the Great, when her fleet came to the Mediterranean and Adriatic to tidy up the remains of Turkish sea-power. Her lover Orloff was the Admiral in charge, and he presented the Republic with an agreement defining her neutrality, which included demands for the opening of an Orthodox church for public use in Dubrovnik, and the establishment of a Russian consulate in the city, to protect not only Russians but all members of the Orthodox Church. The second request was granted, the first refused. Jesuit influence, and the Pope himself, were again illustrating the unfailing disposition of the Roman Catholic Church to fight the Orthodox Church with a vehemence which could not have been exceeded if the enemy had represented paganism instead of schism, whatever suffering this campaign might bring to the unhappy peoples of the Balkan Peninsula.

The agreement Russia offered the Republic was in every other regard satisfactory; but for three years an envoy from Dubrovnik argued the point in St Petersburg, and in the end won it, by using the influence of Austria and Poland, and the personal affection that the Prussian Ambassador to Russia happened to feel for the beauty of the city. It is pathetic how these Northerners love the South. In the end, after two more years, Orloff had to sign a treaty with Dubrovnik, by which she exchanged the right to trade in Russian waters for her sanction of the appointment of a Russian consul, who was to protect only Russian subjects, and who might build in his house a private chapel at which his own nationals might worship according to the Orthodox rite. History is looked at through the wrong end of the opera-glasses when it is recorded that the Republican envoy signed the treaty, went straight to Rome, and was given the warmest thanks for the services he and the Republic had rendered the Holy Catholic religion by 'forbidding the construction of a Greek chapel.' Such pettiness is almost grand. Owing to a change in Russia's foreign policy the consul was never appointed, and the Republic permitted instead the building of a tiny chapel in a deserted spot over a mile from the city walls. When, in 1804, the Republic was again asked to grant its Orthodox citizens the free practice of their religion it absolutely refused.

This intolerance led ultimately to the extinction of the Republic. At the Congress of Vienna the Tsar Alexander could have saved it, and the cause of this small defenceless state might well have appealed to his mystic liberalism; but he remembered that the Republic had obstinately affronted his grandmother, and that in order to persecute his own religion, and he withheld his protection. But it would be a mistake to suppose that in the defence of the Papacy the Republic acted out of fidelity to its religious principles and contempt for its worldly interests. It found—and here we find it achieving a feat of economy that has brought on its English prototypes many a reproach—that in serving the one it served the other. When an Austrian commissioner was taking over Dubrovnik after it had been abandoned by the French, he remarked to one of the nobles that he was amazed by the number of religious establishments in the city. The answer was given, 'There is no cause for amazement there. Every one of them was as much good to us as a round-house.' And indeed this was true. The Roman Catholic fervour of this state that lay on the very border of the Orthodox territory guaranteed her the protection of two great powers, Spain and the Papacy. Again there is a smell not of the rose.

This equivocal character of the Republic is worth considering, because it affects an argument frequently used in the course of that soft modern propaganda in favour of Roman Catholicism which gives testimony, not to the merits or demerits of that faith, but to the

woolliness of modern education. It is sometimes put forward that
it is right to join the Roman Catholic Church because it produces
pleasanter and more mellow characters than Protestantism. This,
of course, is a claim that the Church itself would regard with
contempt. The state of mind demanded from a Roman Catholic
is belief that certain historic events occurred in fact as they are
stated to have occurred by the teachers of the Church, and that
the interpretation of life contained in their teachings is literally and
invariably true. If membership in the Church inevitably produced
personalities intolerable to all other human beings, that would
have no bearing on the validity of the faith. But those who do not
understand this make their bad argument worse by an allegation
that Roman Catholicism discourages two undesirable types, the
Puritan and his complicated brother, the hypocritical reformist
capitalist, and that Protestantism encourages them. Yet the Puritan
appears throughout the ages under any form of religion or none,
under paganism and Christianity, orthodox and heretical alike,
under Catholicism and Protestantism, under deism and rational-
ism, and in each case the authorities have sometimes encouraged
and sometimes discouraged him. There is indeed some excuse for
the pretence that Protestantism has had a special affection for the
reformist capitalist, because geographical rather than psychological
conditions have made him a conspicuous figure in the Northern
countries which resisted the Counter-Reformation. But here in
Dubrovnik, here in the Republic of Ragusa, is a complete chapter
of history, with a beginning and an end, which shows that this type
can spring up in a soil completely free from any contamination of
Protestantism, and can enjoy century after century the unqualified
approbation of Rome.

Expedition

I. Tsavtat

THE ROAD RUNS ALONG THE COAST BETWEEN ROCKY BANKS
dripping with the golden hair of broom. The hillside above and
below us was astonishing in its fertility, although even here the
rain was diluting the spring to a quarter of its proper strength.
There was everywhere the sweet-smelling scrub, and thickets of
oleander, and the grey-blue swords of aloes; and on the lower slopes
were olive terraces and lines of cypresses, spurting up with a vitality
strange to see in what is black and not green. Oaks there were—the
name Dubrovnik means a grove of oaks; and where there were some
square yards of level ground there were thick-trunked patriarchal
planes, with branches enough to cover an army of concubines. The
sea looked poverty-stricken, because, being here without islands,
it had no share in this feast served up by the rising sap. There was
presented a vision of facility, of effortless growth as the way to salvation. This coast, in ancient times, was a centre of the cult of Pan.

There were, however, other interesting residents of a supernatural character. Somewhere up in the mountains on this road is the
cave in which Cadmus and his wife suffered their metamorphosis.
They were so distressed by the misfortunes of their children, who
were persecuted by Hera, that they begged the gods to turn them
into snakes. Ovid made a lovely verse of it. When Cadmus had
suffered the change

> . . . *ille suoe lambebat coniugis ora*
> *inque sinus caros, veluti cognosceret, ibat*
> *et dabat amplexus adsuetaque colla petebat.*
> *quisquis adest (aderant comites), terrentur; at illa*
> *lubrica permulcet cristati colla draconis,*
> *et subito duo sunt iunctoque volumine serpunt,*
> *donec in adpositi nemoris subiere latebras,*
> *nunc quoque nec fugiunt hominem nec vulnere lœdunt*
> *quidque prius fuerint, placidi meminere dracones.*[1]

---

[1] 'He licked his wife's face, and crept into her dear familiar breasts, enfolded
her and sought the throat he knew so well. All who were there—for they

It is an apt symbol of the numbness that comes on the broken-hearted. They become wise; they find comfort in old companion-ship; but they lose the old human anatomy, the sensations no longer follow the paths of the nerves, the muscles no longer offer their multifold reaction to the behests of the brain, there is no longer a stout fortress of bones, there is nothing but a long, sliding, writhing sorrow. But what happened to Cadmus was perhaps partly contrived by the presiding deity of the coast, for he was the arch-enemy of Pan, since he invented letters. He made humankind eat of the tree of knowledge; he made joy and sorrow dangerous because he furnished the means of commemorating them, that is to say of analysing them, of being appalled by them.

That was not an end of the strange events on the coast. We learn from St. Jerome's life of St. Hilarion that when (in the fourth century) the holy man went to Epidaurus, which was a town founded by the Greeks not far from here, he found the whole district terrorized by a monster living in a cave near by, who could draw peasants and shepherds to his lair by his breath. It was certainly Cadmus; literature has always found readers. St. Hilarion went to the mouth of the cave and made the sign of the cross and bade the dragon come forth. It obeyed and followed the saint as meekly as might be back to Epidaurus: all literature worth naming is an expression of the desire to be saved. There the saint said to the townspeople, 'Build a pyre'; and when they had done that, he said to the dragon, 'Lie down on that pyre.' It obeyed. The townspeople set the pyre alight, and it lay quietly till it was burned to ashes. Without doubt it was Cadmus, it was literature. It knew that it was not a dragon, it was a phoenix and would rise restored and young from its ashes; it knew that pagan literature was dying and Christian literature was being born.

Since then Epidaurus has changed its name twice. It was destroyed by the barbarians in the seventh century and its popu-lation fled ten miles further north and founded Dubrovnik, or Ragusa. But after a time some stragglers returned to the ruins of the sacked city and built another of a simpler sort, which came to be known as Ragusa Vecchia. Now it is called Tsavtat, which is said to be a Slavonic version of the word '*civitas*.' We stopped there and

---

Cont. had friends with them—shuddered with horror. But she stroked the sleek neck of the crested reptile, and all at once there were two snakes there with intertwining coils, which after a little while glided away into the woods near by. Now, as when they were human, they neither fear men nor wound them and are gentle creatures, who still remember what they were.'

found that the story about St. Hilarion and the dragon was perfectly true. It cannot be doubted. The town lies on a double-humped dromedary of a peninsula, and the road can be seen where the dragon trotted along behind the saint, looking as mild as milk but sustained by its inner knowledge that not only was it to be reborn from the flames, but that those who kindled them were to know something about death on their own account. It was aware that when we visited the scene fifteen hundred years later we should be able to see in our mind's eye the tall villas which it passed on the way to its martyrdom, and the elegant and serious people who held their torches to the pyre; and it knew why. It knew that one day the sailors and crofters would come to live among the ruins of the town and would delve among the burnt and shattered villas and take what they would of sculptures and bas-reliefs to build up their cottage walls, where they can be seen today, flowers in the buttonhole of poverty. It knew that the peasants' spades would one day attack a part of the peninsula which, in the Greek town, had been the jewellers' quarter; and that afterwards intaglios on the hungry breasts and rough fingers of people who had never known what it was to satisfy necessity, would evoke a dead world of elegant and serious ladies and gentlemen, otherwise sunk without trace. 'Lie down,' St. Hilarion was obliged to say to the dragon, 'lie down, and stop laughing.'

Yet even that was not the last event to happen here as it does nowhere else. Two seafaring families of this place became rich and famous shipowners, and just after the war a woman who had been born into the one and had married into the other conceived the desire that Mestrovitch should build a mausoleum for herself, her father, her mother, and her brother. She held long discussions with the sculptor, and then she and her father and her brother all died suddenly, for no very probable medical reason; and the mother had only time to make the final arrangements for the execution of the plan before she joined them. There is something splendid and Slav about this. They had resolved to provoke an analysis of death by their own deaths, and hastened to carry out their resolution.

Mestrovitch made the mausoleum in the form of a Chapel of Our Lady of the Angels, standing among the cypresses in the cemetery on one of the two summits of the peninsula. It is characteristic of him in the uncertainty with which it gropes after forms: there are some terrible errors, such as four boy musician angels who recall the horrid Japaneseries of Aubrey Beardsley. There is no getting over the troublesome facts that the Turkish occupation sterilized South Slav art for five hundred years, and that when it struggled back to creativeness it found itself separated by Philistine Austria from all the artistic achievements that the rest of Europe had been making in the meantime. But there are moments in the Chapel which exquisitely illustrate the theory, the only theory that renders the death of the individual not a source of intolerable grief: the theory that the goodness of God stretches under human destiny like the net below trapeze artists at the circus. The preservation offered is not of a sort that humanity would dare to offer; a father would be lynched if he should do so badly for his son. Yet to die, and to know a meaning in death, is a better destiny than to be saved from dying. This discussion Mestrovitch carries on not by literary suggestion, but as a sculptor should, by use of form.

But this coast belongs to Pan. In this mausoleum Cadmus goes too far, he delves into matters which the natural man would forget and ignore, and he is punished. The sexton in charge of this cemetery, whose work it is to show visitors the tomb, is a cheerful soul who has taken up mortuary interests as if they were football or racing. He has himself tried his hand at sculpture, and his carvings are all excruciating parodies of Mestrovitch, criticisms which none of his enemies have ever surpassed in venom; and, as every artist knows, there are tortures which a dragon dreads far more than the pyre.

II. Perast

From Savtat the road goes inland and passes one of those Dalmatian valleys which cannot be true, which are an obvious Munchausen. In winter they are lakes, not swamps but deep lakes, which can be swum and fished and rowed over in quite sizable boats; I have seen one as long as Derwentwater. In spring an invisible presence pulls out a plug, and the water runs away through the limestone and out to sea by miles of subterranean passages, and instead of Derwentwater there is dry and extremely cultivable land. Thereafter we came back to the sea and the town of Hertseg Novi, where wistaria and fruit blossoms and yellow roses frothed over the severely drawn diagram of military works, to which the Bosnians and the Turks and the Venetians and the Spaniards have all contributed in their time. In the distance we saw, and did not visit because the hour was wrong, the sixteenth-century monastery of St. Savina, where King Alexander of Yugoslavia delivered to himself an intimation of his approaching death. He had visited it many times, but when he went there just before he embarked for France, he did not pull the rope that rings the bell to announce the coming of a guest. He walked past it and rang the passing-bell.

It is to be noted that his very presence there is an indication of some of the difficulties inherent in the State of Yugoslavia. This was the first Orthodox monastery we had yet seen in the whole of our journey through the country. The piety which made him visit it could not have endeared him to his Catholic-Croat subjects in the North and on the coast; and they would not have shared in the passionate interest he felt in the treasures of this church, which comprise some holy objects in the possession of the Nemanyas, the great dynasty that made the Serbian Empire, because those emperors had no historical association with them. Yet if the Karageorges had not been sustained by the Orthodox Church and their pride in their medieval past they could never have driven out the Turks or defended themselves in the Great War or freed their fellow-Slavs from the Austrian yoke. There are, as Metchnikoff said, disharmonies in nature, and probably the greatest of them is our tendency to expect harmony in nature.

We ran along a coast that was pretty in a riverside way, though it was edged with the intended cruelty of naval warfare, with dockyards and out at sea the iron sharks of torpedo-boats and submarines. But then it suddenly became lovely, we were in the Bocca di Cattaro, the Boka Katorska, the winding natural harbour, of which one has read all one's life; and like a Norwegian fjord, it made an effect that was to the ordinary landscape as ballet-dancing is to walking. The channel became wilder in shape as it became milder in surface, it narrowed to a river and widened to a bay, then flung itself away like a shawl and lay cast down between rocks in an unpredictable line. Above us the mountainside was cut with ledges where spring stood at different stages, sometimes showing the clearest green of early woodlands, laced with wild fruit-blossom, sometimes only as the finest haze over winter darkness of tree and soil; and high above all, pricking the roof of the sky at its full height, was the snow-covered peak of Mount Lovchen. But to Norway there was added here the special Dalmatian glory: a great deal of the coast is edged with a line of Venetian Gothic palaces and churches.

The channel drew to its narrowest. Here a King of Hungary once closed it with a chain. We passed a waterfall, which, according to the custom of this limestone country, burst straight from the living rock, and came on Rishan, one of the oldest inhabited towns in the world. It was the capital of old Illyria, the seat of Queen Teüta. It is a little place that has had the breath beaten out of its body, for it has been invaded again and again since the time of the Goths onward, and has suffered also earthquake. It is a grotesque fact that when the Crown Prince Rudolf was taught Croat, the court chose as his tutor not a learned professor from Vienna or Zagreb, or any of the cultivated gentlemen to be found in the Dalmatian cities, but a country squire from this town.[1] Battered though it is, it keeps the exquisite imprint of the coastal taste, and it has something of the hardy quality of the town opposite Korchula where the sea captains lived; nets hang bronze over the golden and lilac stone.

Perast a few miles further along the fjord is finer and larger, with a surrealist touch added to its Venetian Gothic charm. For beside the harbour an unfinished church, hardly more than an open arch, stands in front of a large and completely finished church, in very curious relations to its campanile, like one distracted before a superior, like Ophelia before the Queen; and many of the palaces have been cleft asunder by earthquakes, and

---

[1] I was about to discover the reason for this from a Viennese historian when the Anschluss came, and there was silence.

are inhabited by Judas trees and fig trees and poplars and wistaria vines, which are wildly contortionist, hanging over a richly carved balustrade and forcing an entrance back to the house through a traceried window a story higher. But Perast offers a touch of familiarity to the ear, and to the eye. Its name comes once into the life of Peter the Great, who, in the course of one of his five-year plans, sent sixteen young nobles here to go to sea with the local sea captains to learn the art of navigation. The boys must have blinked at the South, at the sea, at the discipline, all new to them. And set in the bay are two islands, lying two or three hundred yards out, both covered with low buildings, one bare of all but stone, the other guarded by some cypresses. At the second every visitor must feel a startled, baffled stirring of recognition which afterwards they will probably repudiate.

But the recognition is right. This is the island on which Arnold Böcklin based his horrid vision of what happens to Bubbles and His Majesty King Baby when the goblins get them because they don't watch out: '*Die Toteninsel*,' the Isle of Death. But the original is a curious contrast to the picture. The island is as if one met the reverse of a common experience, it is like seeing a photograph which represents a woman as bloated and painted, and finding that she is in fact a sunburned young athlete. It is a chaste, almost mathematical arrangement of austerely shaped stones and trees. A boatman rowed us out, and we found it the most proper and restrained little Benedictine abbey of the twelfth century, ruined, but still coherent. We walked about it for a little, and found some stately tombstones that belonged, the boatman said, to the families that lived in the palaces on the mainland, which we could see lying on the shore and on the hillside among the spring woods. The names on the tombs were all Slav, Venetian though the place seemed to the eye.

But our boatman plainly wished us to make a move, he kept on looking over his shoulder at the other island, and explaining that the baroque church there was very beautiful, and that many miracles had been performed in it. 'He does not like us being here,' I said; 'perhaps there are snakes.' But when we rowed to the other island we found he had wished to take us to it simply because he lived there, and his dog had been wearying for his company. He had been quite right in thinking this important, for it was a unique animal. Its coat, which was of drab tow, struck one as uncoiffed. Apparently dogs must pay some attention to their toilet, since it could be seen at a glance that this one paid none, being preoccupied with holy things. It had fervent sherry-coloured eyes and was the very dog for a miraculous shrine, for it had such a rich capacity for emotional life that it could hardly have retained any critical sense of evidence.

If this dog had a fault, it lay in giving to God's creatures too much of the feelings that it should have reserved for the Creator. It greeted the boatman, who could not have been away from it for more than half an hour, and offered us its friendship, as it might have broken an alabaster box of ointment over our feet and washed them with its hair. It had a baroque excessiveness, perfectly matched to the place where it lived. This island is artificial, banked up round a small rock, and it is covered with a marble pavement, on which there stands a Renaissance church, holy yet swelling its lines like the bosom of a well-nourished female saint. There is a lovely and insane piece of furniture, or masonry, left out on this pavement: a large marble table, upheld by crouching giants. Inside, the church is lined with some Italianate pictures, themselves passable, and set against a background of some two thousand votive tablets, worked in silver, an encyclopædia of the silversmith's art and the moods of the pious. There is among them one large work which is a masterpiece: it is a bas-relief showing the Turks coming down the mountains to attack Perast and being driven back. It is Renaissance work that has been preserved from its own sins by the virility of the people who practised it.

As we left, the dog promised to pray for our own salvation and expressed its intention of lighting a candle before the altar of Our Lady for the safety of its master during his journey to the shore and back. I suggested that we should ease its emotional strain by taking it in the boat with us, but this caused it great distress, and even seemed to shock the boatman. I suppose it had taken a vow not to leave the island. As we rowed away it ran round in circles, barking wildly, its head down, while behind it a totally superfluous archway, the curve of its span as sweet as the drip of syrup from a spoon, framed the grey glass of the sea by the shores of ancient Rishan. I blushed a little for the dog's abandonment, and was glad that no cat was by to sneer. She must have been a thorn in the side of her spiritual adviser.

III. Kotor

There is a city named Dobrota, which is a string of Venetian palaces and churches along the coast, four miles long. It is a city, it is gloriously a city, for it was made so by the Republic on account of its exploits in naval warfare against the Turks. In one of its churches is the turban taken from Hadshi Ibrahim, who fell at Piræus by the swords of two soldiers from this parish. And the place is not dead, though the earthquake struck here also, and the stained purple of the Judas tree appears suddenly between cleft walls. The Yugoslavian Navy and the liners draw many of their crews from Dobrota. The sea gives these places an unending life.

In Kotor, too, there might be death. It was once a great city. It was part of the great medieval Serbian Empire, and after that was destroyed by the Turks it belonged to Hungary and then to Venice, and became superbly rich. The route from Dubrovnik to Constantinople ran through it, and it carried on a caravan trade on its own account, which it combined with sea trade to Italy. There are in the town thirty chapels built, none meanly, by private families. But all this was stopped by Napoleon's attack on foreign trade. That, and the actual fighting he brought down on this unoffending coast, destroyed a gentle and eclectic culture. Later, the rule of Austria paralysed any movement towards recovery. A great many of the mountain tribes about here were irreconcilable, particularly on the hills by Rishan, and Austria policed the coast with a persistent nagging inefficiency that kept it poor and undeveloped and sullen.

It lies at the fjord-head, pressed almost perpendicularly against the barren foothills under the mountains which are scaled by the famous road to Tsetinye; and it is cooped up by military fortifications. Always it is a little cold. The sun shines on it only five hours a day in winter, and summer is not long enough to correct the accumulated chill. A labyrinth of alleys and handkerchief-wide squares leads from beauty to beauty. There is a tenth-century cathedral, rough but with a fine front, two towers joined by a portal that forms an arch. Inside there is a doorway from a ninth-century church that stood on the same site, which is superbly carved; among a design of interlacing strands, like our Celtic borders but of superior rhythm, two devils snatch at two escaping souls; all persons concerned are violent but serene. There is a treasury, untidy as the jewel-case of a rich woman who has become careless of such things through age and trouble, still stuffed, in spite of Napoleon's army and its requisitions: I have never seen such a show of votive arms and legs made in silver, and there were some touching crosses that had been borne hither and thither in the long wars between the Christians and the Turks. And there is a bishop's palace beside it, with good capon lined, and grown with climbing flowers.

Further on among the cold alleys there is a twelfth-century Orthodox church. Here in Kotor there are many Orthodox. It has a tiny separate church within its aisle, a box within a box, a magic within a magic. It reminded me of what I had forgotten, the difference between the dark, hugged mystery of the Eastern Church and the bold explanation proffered by the lit altars of the Western Church. Round an icy corner was a Romanesque church built in the fourteenth century yet adorned with the eagles of pagan Rome. Here there is the crucifix of a suffering Christ, with a crown of real thorns and hair made of shavings, which is ascribed to Michelangelo by a learned monk of the seventeenth century, who must have been a great liar; and here one mounts some steps before a side altar and looks down through glass on the Blessed Osanna, a Montenegrin saint who died nearly four hundred years ago, but keeps about her rags and tatters of skin and bones a look of excited and plaintive sweetness. It is odd how Catholicism and Orthodoxy modify the Slav character. In the Orthodox parts of Yugoslavia they do not believe that it is the part of women to lead consecrated lives though they should be pious, and there are very few convents.

'Nothing ever happens in Kotor,' one would think. We thought it proven by our guide's insistence that on one day of the year, in February, something does happen in Kotor. Then the Guild of Sailors parades the streets in medieval costume, bearing the weapons their ancestors used to fight the Turks, and there is a ceremony at the cathedral, unique, and I believe not strictly permissible, when the relics from the treasury are laid on the altar and are censed alternately by two leading citizens, one Roman Catholic and one Orthodox. We are far from the seats of authority here, and Slavs are individualist. 'Is it still a great show?' we asked doubtfully. 'Surely,' said our guide. 'We have lost our merchants, but we still have our sailors, which is more important.'

It was an agreeable answer to hear from a man who was wearing an overcoat so threadbare that it showed its weft. He proved he meant it by taking us through the Town Gate to the quay, and saying proudly, 'Here are our sailors.' They were walking in the pale evening sunshine, with the mountains behind them curving over the fjord like a blown wave: they were indolent as highbred horses when they are not ridden, and their faces were quietly drunken with stored energy, which they would know how to release should they one day be at Piræus, and a pirate pass them wearing a turban. 'If I had not been born in war-time, so that as a child I had many sicknesses,' said the guide, 'I too should have been a sailor.'

IV. Home by Gruda

Our chauffeur was the son of a Swabian, which is to say a German belonging to one of those families which were settled by Maria Theresa on the lands round the Danube between Budapest and Belgrade, because they had gone out of cultivation during the Turkish occupation and had to be recolonized. His father had come to Dubrovnik before he was born, and he can never have known any other people but Slavs, yet quite obviously Slavs struck him as odd and given to carrying on about life to an excessive degree. He himself, particularly when he spoke in English, attempted to correct the balance by under-statement. Hence, when we approached the village of Gruda, on our way from Dubrovnik to Kotor, he turned his head and said, 'Nice people.' He meant, it proved, that the men and women of this district were undistinguishable in appearance from gods and goddesses. This was one of those strange pockets one finds scattered here and there at vast intervals in the universe, where beauty is the common lot.

'But why,' the chauffeur was asking himself, 'make a fuss about that?' He put the question to himself with a kind of stolid passion, when we passed through the village again on our way home to Dubrovnik, and a group of three young girls, lovely as primroses in a wood, came towards us, laughing and stretching out their hands and crying out, 'Pennies, pennies,' as if they were not only begging but were ridiculing the ideas of beggary and benevolence alike. Since we were on the return journey we knew we had time to waste, and hammered on the glass and made the chauffeur stop. He slowed up under protest. 'They will beg,' he said. 'Why not?' said my husband. They were, indeed, most prettily prepared to do so, for each of them carried a little bouquet of flowers for an excuse.

'Pennies, pennies!' they cried, laughing, while we stared at them and adored them. This was no case of a racial tendency imposing itself on the mass, each germ-cell had made an individual effort at beauty. One was black, one was chestnut, one was ash-blonde; they were alike only in their golden skins, their fine eyebrows, their full yet neat mouths, the straightness of their bodies within their heavy black woollen gowns. 'Have you any pennies, my dear? I have none,' said my husband, full of charitable concern. 'Not one,' I answered, and I turned to the chauffeur. 'Give me three tenpenny pieces,' I said. 'Three tenpenny pieces!' he exclaimed very slowly. 'But you must not give them three tenpenny pieces. Three tenpenny pieces! It is very wrong. They should not beg at all. Begging is disgraceful. And even if it were excusable, three tenpenny pieces is far too much.'

There was much to be said for his point of view. Indeed, he was entirely right and we were wrong. But they were so beautiful, and in spite of their beauty they would be poor all their lives long, and that is an injustice I never can bear. It is the flat violation of a promise. Women are told from the day they are born that they must be beautiful, and if they are ugly everything is withheld from them, and the reason scarcely disguised. It follows therefore that women who are beautiful should want for nothing. 'Please, I would like to give it to them,' I besought the chauffeur, 'just three tenpenny pieces; it's not much for us English with the exchange as it is.'

He did not answer me at once. His nature, which was so profoundly respectful of all social institutions, made him hate to refuse anything to an employer. At last he said, 'I have only one tenpenny piece on me.' As I took it we both knew that we both knew that he lied. Glumly he started the engine again, while the lovely girls stood and laughed and waved good-bye to us, a light rain falling on them, the wet road shining at their feet, the creamy foam of the tamarisk on the bank behind them lighter in the dusk than it is in the day, but the yellow broom darker. 'I wonder how old those girls were,' said my husband, a few miles further on. 'Let's ask the chauffeur. Since he's a native he ought to know.' The chauffeur answered, 'They were perhaps fifteen or sixteen. And if they are encouraged to be impudent when they are so young, what will they be like when they are old?'

Dubrovnik II

The day after our expedition we went to see the treasury of the Cathedral. This is now fairly easy, though it can be seen only once or twice a week at a fixed hour; it is typical of the stagnancy which covered Dalmatia under Austrian rule that before the war it was hardly to be visited, since the clergy took it for granted in that darkened world that a traveller was more likely to be a thief than a sightseer. A visit still takes time, for Dalmatians, like Croatians, sometimes find that difficulty about being at a particular place at a particular hour for a particular purpose which they believe to be characteristic of the Serb. With a crowd of fellow-tourists we sat about for half an hour or more after the prescribed moment, in the great baroque Cathedral, a creamy, handsome, worldly building. Then a priest, not old but already presenting a very prominent stomach, came in with the keys and took us through the safe-doors into the treasury, which is divided down the middle by a low spiked barrier. We waited in a line along this, while the priest went behind it and opened a large number of the cupboards which lined the room from floor to ceiling. He took from them object after object and brought them over to us, carrying them slowly along the barrier so that each of us could see them in detail.

Some of these objects were very beautiful, notably a famous reliquary containing the head of St. Blaise, which is the shape of a skull-cap six inches high and six inches across, and is studded with twenty-four enamel plaques of eleventh-century Byzantine work, austere and intense portraits of the saints. There were some other good Byzantine and Serbo-Byzantine pieces, which the priest seemed to reckon as less interesting than the numerous examples of commonplace Renaissance work in the treasury. Though the Catholic priests in Croatia and Dalmatia are pleasant and well-mannered they have none of that natural taste and aptitude for connoisseurship which are often found in quite simple priests in France and Italy. This one, indeed, felt little tenderness towards the arts. He showed us presently a modern crucifix, highly naturalist but very restrained and touching, which had been made by a young man of the town in his early twenties; and when the stout Swiss woman beside me asked if the sculptor had fulfilled his promise, he replied, 'Ah, no, he died at twenty-four of drink. It's always so, with these artists.' 'Yes, indeed!' agreed the Swiss, and

264

they shrugged their shoulders and nodded darkly, preening their flabbiness in superiority over a race who must necessarily follow a discipline stricter than they could ever have imagined.

But these people believed themselves to be lovers of the arts; presently the priest brought from the cupboards an object which he dandled and beamed upon while he showed it to the spectators, who responded by making the noise that is evoked by the set-piece of a firework display. I stretched my neck but could see nothing more than a silver object, confused in form and broken in surface. When it came to the Swiss woman I could see that it was a basin and ewer which are mentioned in many guide-books as the pearl of this collection. They are said to have been left by a certain archbishop to his nephew in 1470, but a blind and idiot cow could tell at once that they are not so. Such disgraces came later.

Nothing could be more offensive to the eye, to the touch, or to common sense. The basin is strewn inside with extremely realistic fern-leaves and shells, among which are equally realistic eels, lizards, and snails, all enamelled in their natural colours. It has the infinite elaborateness of eczema, and to add the last touch of unpleasantness these animals are loosely fixed to the basin so that they may wobble and give an illusion of movement. Though Dubrovnik is beautiful, and this object was indescribably ugly, my dislike of the second explained to me why I felt doubtful in my appreciation of the first. The town regarded this horror as a masterpiece. That is to say they admired fake art, naturalist art, which copies nature without interpreting it; which believes that to copy is all we can and need do to nature; which is not conscious that we live in an uncomprehended universe, and that it is urgently necessary for sensitive men to look at each phenomenon in turn and find out what it is and what are its relations to the rest of existence. They were unaware of our need for information, they believed that all is known and that on this final knowledge complete and binding rules can be laid down for the guidance of human thought and behaviour. This belief is the snare prepared for the utter damnation of man, for if he accepts it he dies like a brute, in ignorance, and therefore without a step made towards salvation; but it is built into the walls of Dubrovnik, it is the keystone of every arch, the well in every cloister. They surrounded themselves with real art, the art that moves patiently towards discovery and union with reality, because to buy the best was their policy, and they often actually bought the best. But they themselves pretended that they had arrived before they had started, that appearances are reality.

That is why Dubrovnik, lovely as it is, gives the effect of hunger and thirst.

But the priest assumed that I would wish to look long on the basin, and bent towards me over the barricade to put it as close to me as possible; and I learned how far worse than aethetic pain the vulgarer physical sort can be. My right hand was transfixed with agony. I had rested it on the top of one of the spikes in the barricade, and now it was being impaled on the spike by the steady pressure of the priest's immense stomach. I uttered an exclamation, which he took for a sign of intense appreciation evoked by his beautiful basin, and with a benevolent smile he leant still closer, so that I could see the detestable detail more plainly. His stomach came down more heavily on my hand, and my agony mounted to torment. I tried to attract his attention to what was happening by spreading out my fingers and twitching them, but this seemed to make no impression whatsoever on the firm rubbery paunch that was pressing upon them.

This filled me with wonder. It was odd to arrive at middle age and find that one had been wrong about much that one had believed about human anatomy. I tried to speak, but the only words that came into my mind came in an incorrect form which I immediately recognized and rejected, '*Ton ventre, dein Bauch, il tuo ventre, tvoy drob*, I must not say that,' I told myself, 'I must say *votre ventre, Ihr Bauch, il suo ventre, vash drob*.' But at that it still seemed an odd thing to say to a priest before a crowd of people. I found myself, in fact, quite unable to say it, even though I taunted myself with displaying, too late in life, something like the delicacy which made Virginia refuse to swim with Paul from the shipwreck, because she was ashamed of her nudity. I uttered instead a low moan. The priest, certain now that I was a person of extreme sensibility, swayed backwards and then forwards. My husband, even more certain on that point, dug me savagely in the ribs. I uttered a piercing scream.

The priest recoiled, and seemed about to drop the basin, but my pleasure was mitigated by the fear that my husband was going to strangle me. I held out my hand, which was bleeding freely from a wound in the palm. 'Ah, pardon!' said the priest, coming forward bowing and smiling. He was taking it lightly, I thought, considering the importance which is ascribed to like injuries when suffered by the saints. 'But, my dear, what was it?' asked my husband. 'The priest's stomach pressed my hand down on the spike,' I said feebly. 'It can't have done!' exclaimed my husband. 'He would have felt it!' 'No,' I said, 'about that we were both wrong.' 'What was it?' asked the Swiss woman beside me. 'It was the priest's stomach,' I said, imprudently perhaps, but I was beginning to feel very faint.

She looked at me closely, then turned to her husband. He, like everybody else in the room except the priest, who had returned to his cupboards, had his eyes fixed on me. I heard her say, 'She says it was the priest's stomach.' He looked at me under knitted eyebrows, and when he was nudged by his neighbour I heard him answer the inquiry by repeating, 'She says it was the priest's stomach.' I heard that neighbour echo incredulously what he had been told, and then I saw him turn aside and hand it on to his own neighbour. Though the priest came back with the ewer which was the companion to the basin and fully as horrible, containing a bobbing bunch of silver and enamelled grasses, he was never able to collect the attention of his audience again, for they were repeating among themselves, in all their several languages, 'She says it was the priest's stomach.' It seemed unfair that this should make them look not at the priest but at me. 'Let us go,' I said.

Out in the open air I leaned against a pillar and, shaking my hand about to get rid of the pain, I asked my husband if he did not think that there was something characteristic of Dubrovnik, and dishonourable to it, in the importance it ascribed to the basin and the ewer; and we discussed what was perhaps the false finality of the town. But as we spoke we heard from somewhere close by the sound of bagpipes, and though we did not stop talking we began to move in search of the player. 'But the Republic worked,' my husband said, 'you cannot deny that the Republic worked.' 'Yes,' I agreed, 'it worked.' The music drew us across the market-place, which lies just behind the Cathedral, a fine irregular space surrounded by palaces with a robust shop-keeping touch to them, with a flight of steps rising towards the seaward wall of the town, where baroque domes touch the skyline. There were some fiercely handsome peasants in the dark Dalmatian costume sitting with their farm produce at their feet, and some had heard the bagpipes too and were making off to find them. We followed these, and found a crowd standing outside a building with a vaulted roof, that looked as if in the past it had formed part of some ambitious architectural scheme, perhaps a passageway between two state offices. Now it seemed to be used as a stable, for there was horse's dung on the floor; but that would not explain why there was an upturned barrel on the floor, with a penny bottle of ink and a very large scarlet quill-pen lying on a sheet of newspaper spread over the top. Just inside the open doors stood a very old man, dressed in the gold-braided coat and full black trousers of a Bosnian, playing bagpipes that were made of nicely carved pearwood and faded blue cloth. He had put the homespun satchel all peasants carry down on the floor; the place did not belong to him. He played very gravely, his brow contorted as if he were inventing the curious Eastern line of his melody, and his audience listened as gravely, following each turn of that line.

'Look at them,' I said; 'they are Slavs, they believe that the next Messiah may be born at any minute, not of any woman, for that is too obvious a generation, but of any impersonal parent, any incident, any thought. I like them for that faith, and that is why I do not like Dubrovnik, for it is an entirely Slav city, yet it has lost that faith and pretends that there shall be no more Messiahs.' 'But wait a minute,' said my husband; 'look at these people. They are all very poor. They are probably the descendants of the workers, the lowest class of the Republic. That means that they have never exercised power. Do you not think that they may owe to that very fact this faith which you admire, this mystical expectation of a continuous revelation that shall bring man nearer to reality, stage by stage, till there is a consummation which will make all previous stages of knowledge seem folly and ignorance? The other people in Dubrovnik had to exercise power, they had to take the responsibility. Perhaps none can do that unless he is sustained by the belief that he knows all that is to be known, and therefore cannot make any grave mistake. Perhaps this mystical faith is among the sacrifices they make, like their leisure and lightheartedness, in order to do the rest of us the service of governing us.'

'Then it should be admitted that governors are inferior to those whom they govern,' I said, 'for it is the truth that we are not yet acquainted with reality and should spend our lives in search of it.' 'But perhaps you cannot get people to take the responsibility of exercising power unless you persuade the community to flatter them,' said my husband, 'nor does it matter whether the governed are said to be lower or higher than their governors if they have such faces as we see in the crowd, if wisdom can be counted to dwell with the oppressed.' 'But they are hungry,' I said, 'and in the past they were often tortured and ill-used.' 'It is the price they had to pay for the moral superiority of the governed,' said my husband, 'just as lack of mystical faith is the price the governors have to pay for their morally unassailable position as providers of order for the community. I think, my dear, that you hate Dubrovnik because it poses so many questions that neither you nor anybody else can answer.'

Herzegovina

Trebinye

ALL TOURISTS AT DUBROVNIK GO ON WEDNESDAYS OR
Saturdays to the market at Trebinye. It is over the border in
Herzegovina, and it was under a Turkish governor until the
Bosnians and Herzegovinian rebels took it and had their prize
snatched from them by the Austrians in 1878. It is the nearest
town to the Dalmatian coast which exhibits what life was like for
the Slavs who were conquered by the Turks. The route follows
the Tsavtat road for a time, along the slopes that carry their olive
terraces and cypress groves and tiny fields down to the sea with the
order of an English garden. Then it strikes left and mounts to a
gorgeous bleakness, golden with broom and gorse, then to sheer
bleakness, sometimes furrowed by valleys which keep in their very
trough a walled field, preserving what could not be called even a
dell, but rather a dimple, of cultivable earth. On such bare rock
the summer sun must be a hypnotic horror. We were to learn as we
mounted that a rainstorm was there a searching, threshing assault.

When the sky cleared we found ourselves slipping down the side
of a broad and fertile valley, that lay voluptuously under the guard
of a closed circle of mountains, the plump grey-green body of a
substantial river running its whole length between poplars and
birches. We saw the town suddenly in a parting between showers,
handsome and couchant, and like all Turkish towns green with
trees and refined by the minarets of many mosques. These are
among the most pleasing architectural gestures ever made by
urbanity. They do not publicly declare the relationship of man
to God like a Christian tower or spire. They raise a white finger
and say only, 'This is a community of human beings and, look
you, we are not beasts of the field.' I looked up at the mountain
and wondered which gully had seen the military exploits of my
admired Jeanne Merkus.

That, now, was a girl: one of the most engaging figures in the
margin of the nineteenth century, sad proof of what happens to
Jeanne d'Arc if she is unlucky enough not to be burned. She was

born in 1839, in Batavia, her father being Viceroy of the Dutch
East Indies. Her mother came of a clerical Walloon family, and
was the divorced wife of a professor in Leiden University. Jeanne
was sixth in the family of four boys and four girls. When she was
five her father died, and she was brought home to Holland, where
she lived with her mother at Amsterdam and The Hague until she
was nine. Then her mother died and she went to live with an uncle,
a clergyman, who made her into a passionate mystic, entranced in
expectation of the second coming of Christ.

It happened that when she was twenty-one she inherited a
fortune far larger than falls to the lot of most mystics. Her peculiar
faith told her exactly what to do with it. She went to Palestine,
bought the best plot of ground she could find near Jerusalem, and
built a villa for the use of Christ. She lived there for fifteen years,
in perpetual expectation of her divine guest, and conceiving as a
result of her daily life a bitter hatred against the Turks.

When she heard of the Bosnian revolt she packed up and went
to the Balkans, and joined the rebels. She came in contact with
Lyubibratitch, the Herzegovinian chief, and at once joined the
forces in the field, attaching herself to a party of comitadji led by
a French officer. We have little information as to where she fought,
for very little has been written, and nothing in detail, about this
important and shameful episode of European history. We have an
account of her, one winter's night, struggling single-handed to fire
a mine to blow up a Turkish fortress among the mountains when
all the rest of her troop had taken to their heels, and failing because
the dynamite had frozen. It is almost our only glimpse of her as a
campaigner.

Jeanne's more important work lay in the outlay of her fortune,
which she spent to the last penny in buying Krupp munitions for
the rebels. But as soon as the revolt was a proven success the
Austrians came in and took over the country, and in the course
of the invasion she was captured. She was set free and allowed
to live in Dubrovnik, but she eluded the authorities and escaped
over the mountains to Belgrade, where she enlisted in the Serbian
Army. There the whole population held a torch-light serenade
under her window, and she appeared on the balcony with a round
Montenegrin cap on her fair hair.

But there was to be no more fighting. The action of the great
powers had perpetuated an abuse that was not to be corrected till
thirty-five years later, and then at irreparable cost to civilization,
in the Balkan wars and the first World War. There was nothing for
Jeanne to do, and she had no money to contribute to the nationalist

Balkan funds. The Turks had seized the house in Jerusalem which she had prepared for Christ, and, not unnaturally, would pay her no compensation. We find her moving to the French Riviera, where she lived in poverty. Sometimes she went back to Holland to see her family, who regarded her visits with shame and repugnance, because she talked of her outlandish adventures, wore strange comitadji-*cum*-deaconess clothes, smoked big black cigars, and was still a believing Christian of a too ecstatic sort. It is said that once or twice she spoke of her lost spiritual causes before young kinsfolk, who followed them for the rest of their lives. The relatives who remained insensible to her charm carried their insensibility to the extreme degree of letting her live on Church charity at Utrecht for the last years of her life, though they themselves were wealthy. When she died in 1897 they did not pay for her funeral, and afterwards they effaced all records of her existence within their power.

It is important to note that nothing evil was known of Jeanne Merkus. Her purity was never doubted. But she never achieved martyrdom, and the people for whom she offered up her life and possessions were poor and without influence. She therefore, by a series of actions which would have brought her the most supreme honour had she acted in an important Western state as a member of the Roman Catholic Church in the right century, earned a rather ridiculous notoriety that puts her in the class of a pioneer bicyclist or Mrs. Bloomer.

We passed certain coarse cliffs with lawns between which were once Austrian barracks. 'Now I remember something I was told about this place,' I said. 'What was that?' asked my husband. 'Nothing, nothing,' I said. 'I will tell you later.' 'Look, you can see that the Austrians were here,' said my husband; 'there are chestnut trees everywhere.' 'Yes, there's been a lot of coffee with *Schlagobers* drunk under these trees,' I said as we got out of the car at the market-place. We were walking away when our Serbian chauffeur called to us, 'You had better take this man as a guide.' This surprised us, for we had come only to see the peasants in their costumes, and any interesting mosques we could find, and the guide was a miserable little creature who looked quite unable to judge what was of interest and what was not. 'Is it necessary?' asked my husband. 'No,' admitted the chauffeur unhappily, but added, 'This is, however, a very honest man and he speaks German, and it will cost you only tenpence.' He mentioned the sum with a certain cold emphasis, evidently recalling the scene with the three lovely girls of Gruda.

But he was, I think, reacting to the complicated racial situation of Yugoslavia. He was a Swab, and had lived out his life among the Croatians and Dalmatians; and all such Slavs who had never known the misery of Turkish rule harbour an extremely unhappy feeling about the fellow-Slavs of Bosnia and Herzegovina and Macedonia, who have so often suffered a real degradation under their Turkish masters. It is as if the North and East of England and the South Coast were as they are now, and the rest of our country was inhabited by people who had been ground down for centuries by a foreign oppressor to the level of the poor white trash of the southern states or South Africa. Were this so, a man from Brighton might feel acutely embarrassed if he had to take a Frenchman to Bath and admit that the ragged illiterates he saw there were also Englishmen. Different people, of course, show this embarrassment in different ways. If they are the hating kind they quite simply hate their unpresentable relatives. But this chauffeur was a gentle and scrupulous being, and he settled the matter by regarding them as fit objects to be raised up by charity. Doubtless he would give somebody here his mite before he left; and he felt this to be a good opportunity to direct to a useful channel the disposition to wastefulness which he had deplored at Gruda.

The guide turned out to be as we had thought him. It was a poor day for the market. A storm had been ranging over the mountains all night, and as the year was still early and the crops light, most of the peasants had not thought it worth while to get up at dawn and walk the seven or eight miles to Trebinye. There were a few handsome women standing with some vegetables before them, soberly handsome in the same vein as their plain round caps and their dark gathered dresses, gripped by plain belts. We saw a tourist level a camera at two of these. They turned away without haste, without interrupting their grave gossip, and showed the lens their backs. These were very definitely country women. They wore the typical peasant shoes of plaited thongs, and by their movements it could be seen that they were used to walking many miles and they bore themselves as if each wore a heavy invisible crown, which meant, I think, an unending burden of responsibility and fatigue. Yet there were women among them who were to these as they were to town ladies, country women from a remoter country. The eyes of these others were mild yet wild, like the eyes of yoked cattle, their skin rougher with worse weather than the others had seen and harsher struggles with it; and their bodies were ignorant not only of elegance but of neatness, in thick serge coats which were embroidered in designs of great beauty but were coarse in execution, if coarse is used not in the sense of vulgarity but to suggest the archaic, not to say the prehistoric. There was a difference among the men also. Some seemed sturdy and steadfast as the rock, others seemed the rock itself, insensitive, except to the weathering power of the frost and sun.

There were also about the market-place plenty of Moslems, the men wearing the red fez, the women in the black veil and the overall made of a straight wide piece of cotton pulled in at the waist by a drawstring. 'Turks,' said the guide, and he was talking nonsense. Nearly all the Moslems in Yugoslavia except in the extreme south, in Macedonia, are Slavs whose ancestors were converted by the Turks, sometimes in order to keep their properties, sometimes because they were Bogomil heretics and wanted defence against Roman Catholic persecution. This is pre-eminently the case in Bosnia and Herzegovina; the true Turks left at the time of the Austrian occupation. 'Look!' said my husband, and I found that he was enraptured at the sight of the fezes and the veils, for though he had spent some time in Istanbul and Ankara, that had been since the days of the Ataturk and his reforms. 'Do you think the veil adds charm to the female?' I asked. 'Yes, in a way,' he answered; 'they all look like little Aberdeen terriers dressed up to do tricks, with those black muzzles sticking out.' One stopped, and offered to sell him some white silk handkerchiefs of offensive aspect, with tatting at the corners. His taste in linen is classical; she was not fortunate. Nor were any of the six others who sought to sell him such handkerchiefs at various points in Trebinye. 'I don't like their handkerchiefs and I don't like them,' he decided. 'No doubt they're perfectly respectable, but they waggle themselves behind all this concealment with a Naughty Nineties sort of sexuality that reminds me of Ally Sloper and the girls, and the old Romano, and the Pink 'Un and the Pelican.'

This was not the last we were to see of that peculiar quality. After our guide had so far exhausted the possibilities of Trebinye that he was driven to taking us down a street to see a boot-shop and saying reverently, '*Batya*,' we decided we would go back to Dubrovnik. But we changed our minds because a little Moslem boy handed us a leaflet which announced that tourists could visit an old Turkish house in the town, formerly the home of a famous pasha, which was complete with its original furniture and its original library. We found it in the suburbs, standing among gardens where spring was touching off the lilac bushes and the plum trees: a house perhaps a hundred or a hundred and fifty years old. It was a very pleasing example of the Turkish genius for building light and airy country houses that come second only to the work of our own Georgians, and in some ways are superior, since they hold no dark corners, no mean holes for the servants, no rooms too large to heat.

This stood firm and bright and decent, with its projecting upper stories, the windows latticed where the harem had been, and its two lower stories that had their defended Arabian-nights air of goods made fast against robbers. Across a countryish courtyard, almost a farmyard, was the servants' house, where the kitchens and stables were. Down an outer staircase ran a pretty, smiling girl of about sixteen, unveiled but wearing trousers, which here (though not in other parts of Yugoslavia) are worn only by Moslem women. Behind her came an elderly man wearing a fez and a brocade frock-coat. On seeing us the girl broke into welcoming smiles, too profuse for any social circle that recognized any restrictions whatsoever, and left us with a musical comedy gesture. Her trousers were bright pink. 'Turkish girl,' said the man in the frock-coat, in German. 'Then why is she unveiled?' asked my husband. 'She is too young,' said the man in the frock-coat, his voice plump to bursting with implications.

We wavered, our faces turning back to Trebinye. 'Come in, come in,' cried the man in the frock-coat, placing himself between us and Trebinye. 'I will show you all, old Turkish house, where the great pasha kept his harem, all very fine.' He drove us up the stairs, and shepherded us through the main door into a little room, which in its day had been agreeable enough. Pointing at the latticed windows he said richly, 'The harem was here, beautiful Turkish women wearing the beautiful Turkish clothes.' He opened a cupboard and took out a collection of clothes such as may be found in any old-clothes shop in those provinces of Yugoslavia that were formerly occupied by the Turks. 'Very fine, all done by hand,' he said of the gold-braided jackets and embroidered bodices. 'And look, trousers!' He held up before us a garment of white lawn, folded at the ankle into flashy gold cuffs, which can never have been worn by any lady engaged in regular private harem work. 'Transparent,' he said. It was evident that he was affected by a glad pruritis of the mind. Coyly he sprang to another cupboard and brought out a mattress. 'The bed was never left in the room,' he said; 'they took it out when it was needed.' There was unluckily a third cupboard, with a tiled floor and a ewer. 'This was the bathroom, here is where the Turkish lady kept herself clean, all Turkish ladies were very clean and sweet.' He assumed a voluptuous expression, cocked a hip forward and put a hand on it, lifted the ewer upside-down over his head, and held the pose.

Undeterred by our coldness, he ran on to the next room, which was the typical living-room of a Turkish house, bare of all furniture save a bench running along the walls and an ottoman table or two, and ornamented by rugs nailed flat to the wall. I exclaimed in pleasure, for the view from its window was exquisite. The grey-green river we had seen from the heights above the city ran here through meadows deep in long grasses and pale flowers, and turned a mill-wheel; and the first leaves of the silver birches on its brink were as cool to the eye as its waters. Along this river there must have once wandered, if there is any truth in Oriental miniatures, a young prince wearing an ospreyed fez and embroidered garments, very good-looking now though later he would be too fat, carrying a falcon on his wrist and smugly composing a poem about the misery of his love.

'I should be obliged,' said the man in the frock-coat, 'if the well-born lady would kindly pay some attention to me. Surely she could look at the view afterwards.' 'Shall I throw him downstairs?' asked my husband. 'No,' I said, 'I find him enchantingly himself.' It was interesting to see what kind of person would have organized my life had I been unfortunate enough, or indeed attractive enough, to become the inmate of a brothel. So we obeyed him when he sharply demanded that we should sit on the floor, and listened while he described what the service of a formal Turkish dinner was like, betraying his kind with every word, for he took it for granted that we should find all its habits grotesque, and that our point of view was the proper one. 'And now,' he said, rising and giving a mechanical leer at my ankles as I scrambled off the floor, 'I shall show you the harem. There are Turkish girls, beautiful Turkish girls.'

At a window in the passage he paused and pointed out an observation post in the roof of the servants' house. 'A eunuch used to sit there to see who came into the house,' he said. 'A eunuch,' he repeated, with a sense of luxuriance highly inappropriate to the word. He then flung open a door so that we looked into a room and saw three girls who turned towards us, affected horror, and shielded their faces with one hand while with the other they groped frantically but inefficiently for some coloured handkerchiefs that were lying on a table beside them. Meanwhile the custodian had also affected horror and banged the door. 'By God, it is the Pink 'Un and the Pelican,' said my husband. Then the custodian knocked on the door with an air of exaggerated care, and after waiting for a summons he slowly led us in. 'Typical beautiful Turkish girls,' he said. They were not. Instead of wearing the

black veil that hides the whole face, which almost all Yugoslavian
Moslems wear, they wore such handkerchiefs as Christian peasant
women use to cover their hair, but knotted untidily at the back
of the head so that their brows and eyes were bare. 'Now they
are cultivating our beautiful Turkish crafts,' he explained. They
were not. Turkish embroidery and weaving are indeed delicious;
but two of these wenches held in their hands handkerchiefs of the
offensive sort that my husband had rejected in the market-place,
and the third was sitting at a loom on which a carpet which ought
never to have been begun had been a quarter finished.

After we had contemplated them for some time, while they
wriggled on their seats and tittered to express a reaction to my
husband which both he and I, for our different reasons, thought
quite unsuitable, the custodian said, 'Now, we will leave the ladies
by themselves,' and, nodding lecherously at me, led my husband
out of the room. I found this disconcerting but supposed he had
taken my husband away to show him some beautiful Turkish
'feelthy peectures,' in which case they would be back soon enough.
As soon as we were alone the girls took off their veils and showed
that they were not ill-looking, though they were extremely spotty
and had an inordinate number of gold teeth. They suggested that
I should buy some of the offensive handkerchiefs, but I refused.
I meant to ask my husband to give them some money when he
came back.

To pass the time I went over to the girl at the loom and stood
beside her, looking down on her hands, as if I wanted to see how
a carpet was made. But she did nothing, and suddenly I realized
she was angry and embarrassed. She did not know how to weave
a carpet any more than I do; and the girls with the handkerchiefs
did not know how to sew, they were merely holding them with
threaded needles stuck in them. They all began to laugh very loudly
and exchange bitter remarks, and I reflected how sad it is that slight
knowledge of a foreign tongue lets one in not at the front door but at
the back. I have heard poems recited and sermons preached in the
Serbian language which were said to be masterpieces by those who
were in a position to judge, and I have been unable to understand
one word. But I was able to grasp clearly most of what these young
women were saying about me, my husband, my father, and my
mother.

The scene was horrible, because they looked not only truculent,
but unhappy. They were ashamed because I had detected that they
could not sew or weave, for the only women in the Balkans who
cannot handle a needle or a loom are the poorest of the urban

population, who are poorer than any peasant, and cannot get hold of cloth or thread because they have no sheep. The scene was pitiful in itself, and it was pitiful in its implications, if one thought of the fair-mannered and decent Moslem men and women in Trebinye and all over Yugoslavia, sad because they knew themselves dead and buried in their lifetime, coffined in the shell of a perished empire, whose ways these poor wretches were aping and defiling. I could not bear to wait there any longer, so I left them and walked through the house, calling for my husband. The search became disagreeable, for I opened the door of one or two rooms, and found them full of trunks and bundles lying on the bare floor, stuffed with objects but open and unfastened, as if someone here had meditated flight and then given up the plan on finding that the catastrophe which he had hoped to escape was universal.

I called louder, and he answered me from a room by the main door. 'What did he take you away for?' I asked. 'He didn't take me away for anything but to give you the thrilling experience of seeing those wenches unveiled,' said my husband. The custodian came forward and said, 'I have been showing your husband these beautiful Turkish books; they have been in this house for many centuries.' He thrust into my hand a battered copy of the Koran, which fell open at a page bearing a little round label printed with some words in the Cyrillic script. 'Oh, Lord! Oh, Lord,' I said. 'This is the stamp of a Sarajevo second-hand book-shop.' 'Really, this is all too bloody silly,' said my husband; 'it is like charades played by idiot ghosts round their tombs in a cemetery.' We went out into the courtyard, followed by the custodian, who seemed at last to realize that we were not pleased by his entertainment. 'Do they speak Serbian or not?' he asked our guide. 'No, I don't think so,' he was answered. He looked puzzled and decided to assume that life as he knew it was continuing in its usual course. So he gave us the Turkish greeting by raising his hand to his forehead, exposing that national custom to our patronage or derision, he did not care which it was so long as we tipped him, and he said, 'Now you have met a Turkish gentleman and seen how all Turkish gentlemen used to live.' My husband gave him money, and we walked away very quickly. The guide said, 'Were you pleased with the visit? It is interesting, is it not?' My husband asked, 'Who is that man?' 'He used to be the servant of the owner of the house,' said the guide. 'Who is the owner?' my husband asked. 'He is a Moslem baron,' said the guide. 'Once his family was very rich, now he is very poor. He furnished this house and put his servant in charge of it, and I think the money he gets from it is nearly all that he has. He lives far out in the country, where it is very cheap.'

When we were driving out of the town I said, 'I hate the corpses of empires, they stink as nothing else. They stink so badly that I cannot believe that even in life they were healthy.' 'I do not think you can convince mankind,' said my husband, 'that there is not a certain magnificence about a great empire in being.' 'Of course there is,' I admitted, 'but the hideousness outweighs the beauty. You are not, I hope, going to tell me that they impose law on lawless people. Empires live by the violation of law.' Below us now lay the huge Austrian-built barracks, with the paddocks between them, and I remembered again what I had hated to speak of as we drove into Trebinye, when we were out to have an amusing morning. Here the Herzegovinians had found that one empire is very like another, that Austria was no better than Turkey. Between these barracks the Austrian Empire killed eighty people for causes that would have been recognized on no statute book framed by man since the beginning of time.

When the news came in 1914 that the Archduke Franz Ferdinand and his wife had been assassinated by Serb patriots at Sarajevo, the Austrian authorities throughout Bosnia and Herzegovina arrested all the peasants whom they knew to be anti-Austrian in sentiment and imprisoned some and hanged the rest. There was no attempt at finding out whether they had been connected with the assassins, as, in fact, none of them were. Down there on the grass between the barracks the Austrians took as contribution from Trebinye seventy Serbs, including three women, such women as we saw in the market-place. Someone I met in Sarajevo on my first visit to Yugoslavia had had a relative killed there, and had kept photographs of the slaughter which the Yugoslavian Government had found among the Austrian police records. They showed the essential injustice of hanging: the hanged look grotesque, they are not allowed the dignity that belongs to the crucified, although they are enduring as harsh a destiny. The women looked particularly grotesque, with their full skirts; they looked like icons, as Constantine had said Slav women should look when dancing. Most of them wore an expression of astonishment. I remember one priest who was being led through a double line of gibbets to his own; he looked not horrified but simply surprised. That indeed was natural enough, for surprise must have been the predominant emotion of most of the victims. They cannot have expected the crime, for though it was known to a large number of people these were to be found only in a few towns, far away from Trebinye; and when they heard of it they can never have dreamed that they would be connected with it.

'The scene was a typical illustration of the hypocrisy of empires, which pretend to be strong and yet are so weak that they constantly have to defend themselves by destroying individuals of the most pitiable weakness,' I said. 'But an empire,' my husband reminded me, 'can perform certain actions which a single nation never can. The Turks might have stayed for ever in Europe if it had not been for the same combination of forces known as the Austrian Empire.' 'But there was no need for them to combine once the Turks were beaten,' I objected; 'in the nineteenth century the Turks were hopelessly beaten, and the Porte was falling to pieces under the world's eye, yet the Austrians were flogging their peoples to keep them in subjection exactly as if there were a terrifying enemy at their gates.' 'Yes, but by that time there were the Russians,' said my husband. 'Yes, but Tsarist Russia was a rotten state that nobody need have feared,' I said. 'That, oddly enough, is something that no nation ever knows about another,' said my husband; 'it appears to be quite impossible for any nation to discover with any accuracy the state of preparedness for war in another nation. In the last war both Great Britain and Serbia were grossly deceived by their ideas of what support they were going to receive from Russia; and Germany was just as grossly deceived by her ally Austria, who turned out to be as weak as water.' 'But how absurd the behaviour of nations is!' I exclaimed. 'If I ran about compelling people to suffer endless inconveniences by joining with me in a defensive alliance against someone who might conceivably injure me, and never took proper steps to find out if my companions were strong enough to aid me or my enemies strong enough to injure me, I would be considered to be making a fool of myself.' 'But the rules that apply to individuals do not apply to nations,' said my husband; 'the situation is quite different.' And indeed I suppose that I was being, in my female way, an idiot, an excessively private person, like the nurse in the clinic who could not understand my agitation about the assassination of King Alexander of Yugoslavia. But it is just to admit that my husband was indulging his male bent in regard to international affairs, and was being a lunatic.

When we were well on our way back to our hotel at Gruzh, past Dubrovnik and among the lovely terraced gardens of its suburb Larpad, my husband said, 'When we were in that idiot house at Trebinye, which was like *Hamlet* without the Prince of Denmark, a brothel with the sexual intercourse left out, I could not help thinking of that poor chap we came on in that farm over there.'

We had a night or two before walked up to the top of Petka, a pine-covered hill at the edge of the sea, and after seeing the best of the sunset had strolled over the olive groves towards Dubrovnik and dinner. We had missed our path and when the dark fell we were wandering in an orchard beside a farm, obviously very old, and so strongly built that it had a fortress air. The place bore many touches of decay, and the steps between the terraces crumbled under our feet; we took one path and it led us to a lone sheep in a pen, the other brought us to a shut wooden door in a cavern-mouth. We felt our way back to the still mass of the farm, and we heard from an open window the rise and fall of two clear voices, speaking in a rhythm that suggested a sense of style, that recognized the need for restraint, and within that limit could practise the limitless freedom of wit. Both of us assumed that there were living in this house people who would certainly be cosmopolitan and polyglot, perhaps ruined nobles of Dubrovnik, or a family from Zagreb who had found a perfect holiday villa.

We knocked confidently at the door, and prepared to ask the way in German. But the door was opened by a man wearing peasant costume and a fez, and behind, the light of an oil-lamp hung on a wall shone down on a room paved with flagstones, in which a few sacks and barrels lay about in a disorder that suggested not so much carelessness as depression. At the back of the room sat a woman who gracefully turned away her head and put up her hand to hide her face, with a gesture that we were later to see parodied and profaned by the girls in the Turkish house at Trebinye. The man was a tall darkness to us, and he remained quite still when my husband spoke to him in German and Italian. Then I asked him in my bad Serbian how we might get to Dubrovnik, and he told me slowly and courteously that we must go round the corner of the house and follow a landward wall. Then I said '*Sbogom*,' which means 'With God' and is the Serbian good-bye. He echoed it with the least possible touch of irony, and I perceived I had spoken the word with the wrong accent, with a long lift on the first syllable instead of a short fall.

We moved away in the darkness, turned the angle of the house, and found a cobbled path beside the wall. As we stood there a door in the house behind us suddenly opened, and there stood the tall man again. 'Good!' he said, and shut the door. It had been done ostensibly to see that we were on the right path, but really it had been done to startle us, as a child might have done it. It was as if this man who was in his body completely male, completely adult, a true Slav, but had the characteristic fire and chevaleresque manners of the Moslem, had not enough material to work on in this half-ruined farm, and had receded into childishness of a sort one can dimly remember. As one used to sit in the loft and look down on the people passing in the village street, and think, 'They can't see me, I'm sitting here and looking at them and they don't know it; if I threw an apple at their feet they wouldn't guess where it came from,' so he, this tall man sitting in this fortress, had told himself, 'They won't know there is a door there, they will be startled when I open it,' and the empty evening had passed a little quicker for the game.

I said, looking down the slopes towards the sea. 'It was odd a Moslem should be living there. But it is a place that has only recently been resettled. Until the Great War this district was largely left as it was after it had been devastated in the Napoleonic wars. Ah, what a disgusting story that is! See, all day long we have seen evidences of the crimes and follies of empires, and here is evidence of how murderous and imbecile a man can become when he is possessed by the imperial idea.' 'Yes,' said my husband, 'the end of Dubrovnik is one of the worst of stories.'

When France and Russia started fighting after the peace of Pressburg in 1805 Dubrovnik found itself in a pincer between the two armies. The Republic had developed a genius for neutrality throughout the ages, but this was a situation which no negotiation could resolve. The Russians were in Montenegro, and the French were well south of Split. At this point Count Caboga proposed that the inhabitants of Dubrovnik should ask the Sultan to grant them Turkish nationality and to allow them to settle on a Greek island where they would carry on their traditions. The plan was abandoned, because Napoleon's promises of handsome treatment induced them to open their gates. This meant their commercial ruin, for the time, at least, since after that ships from Dubrovnik were laid under an embargo in the ports of all countries which were at war with France. It also meant that the Russian and Montenegrin armies invaded their territory and sacked and burned all the summer palaces in the exquisite suburbs of Larpad and Gruzh, hammering down the wrought-iron gates and marble terraces, beating to earth the rose gardens and oleander groves and orchards, firing the houses themselves and the treasures their owners had accumulated in the last thousand years from the best of East and West. The Russians and Montenegrins acted with special fervour because they believed, owing to a time-lag in popular communication and ignorance of geography, that they were thus defending Christianity against the atheism of the French Revolution.

When Napoleon was victorious the inhabitants of Dubrovnik expected that since they had been his allies they would be compensated for the disasters the alliance had brought on them. But he sent Marshal Marmont to read a decree to the Senate in the Rector's palace, and its first article declared: 'The Republic of Ragusa has ceased to exist.' This action shows that Napoleon was not, as is sometimes pretended, morally superior to the dictators of today. It was an act of Judas. He had won the support of Dubrovnik by promising to recognize its independence. He had proclaimed when he founded the Illyrian provinces that the cause of Slav liberation was dear to him; he now annulled the only independent Slav community in Balkan territory. He defended his wars and aggressions on the ground that he desired to make Europe stable; but when he found a masterpiece of stability under his hand he threw it away and stamped it into the mud.

There is no redeeming feature in this betrayal. Napoleon gave the Republic nothing in exchange for its independence. He abolished its constitution, which turned against him the nobles, from whom he should have drawn his administrators, as the Venetians had always done in the other Adriatic cities. Hence, unadvised, he committed blunder after blunder in Dalmatia. In a hasty effort at reform he repealed the law that a peasant could never own his land but held it as a hereditary tenant, and therefore could never sell it. In this poverty-stricken land this was a catastrophe, for thereafter a peasant's land could be seized for debt. He also applied to the territory the Concordat he had bullied Pius VII into signing, which bribed the Church into becoming an agent of French imperialism, and caused a passionately devout population to feel that its faith was being tampered with for political purposes. This last decree was not made more popular because its execution was in the hands of a civil governor, one Dandolo, a Venetian who was not a member of the patrician family of that name, but the descendant of a Jew who had had a Dandolo as a sponsor at his baptism and had, as was the custom of the time, adopted his name. These errors, combined with the brutal indifference which discouraged Marmont's efforts to develop the country, make it impossible to believe that Napoleon was a genius in 1808. Yet without doubt he was a genius till the turn of the century. It would seem that empire degrades those it uplifts as much as those it holds down in subjection.

ROAD

Because there was a wire from Constantine announcing that he would arrive at Sarajevo the next day, we had to leave Dubrovnik, although it was raining so extravagantly that we saw only little vignettes of the road. An Irish friend went with us part of the way, for we were able to drop him at a farmhouse fifteen miles or so along the coast, where he was lodging. Sometimes he made us jump from the car and peer at a marvel through the downward streams. So we saw the source of the Ombla, which is a real jaw-dropping wonder, a river-mouth without any river. It is one of the outlets of the grey-green waters we had seen running through Trebinye, which suddenly disappear into the earth near that town and reach here after twenty miles of uncharted adventure under the limestone. There is a cliff and a green tree, and between them a gush of water. It stops below a bridge and becomes instantly, without a minute's preparation, a river as wide as the Thames at Kingston, which flows gloriously out to sea between a marge of palaces and churches standing among trees and flowers, in a scene sumptuously, incredibly, operatically romantic.

Our sightseeing made us dripping wet, and we were glad to take shelter for a minute or two in our friend's lodgings and warm ourselves at the fire and meet his very agreeable landlady. While we were there two of her friends dropped in, a man from a village high up on the hills, a woman from a nearer village a good deal lower down the slopes. They had called to pay their respects after the funeral of the landlady's aunt, which had happened a few days before. Our Irish friend told us that the interment had seemed very strange to his eyes, because wood is so scarce and dear there that the old lady had had no coffin at all, and had been bundled up in the best table-cloth. But because stone is so cheap the family vault which received her was like a ducal mausoleum. The man from the upland village went away first, and as the landlady took him out to the door our Irish friend said to the woman from the foothills, 'He seems very nice.' 'Do you think so?' said the woman. Her nose seemed literally to turn up. 'Well, don't you?' asked our friend. 'We-e-e-ell,' said the woman, 'round about here we don't care much for people from that village.' 'Why not?' asked our friend. 'We-e-e-ell, for one thing, you sometimes go up there and you smell cabbage soup, and you say, "That smells good," and they say, "Oh, we're just having cabbage soup."' A pause fell, and our friend inquired,

'Then don't they offer you any?' 'Oh, yes.' 'And isn't it good?'
'It's very good. But, you see, we grow cabbages down here and
they can't up there, and they never buy any from us, and we're
always missing ours. So, really, we don't know what to think.'

Mostar

I was so wearied by the rushing rain that I slept, and woke again in a different country. Our road ran on a ledge between the bare mountains and one of these strange valleys that are wide lakes in winter and dry land by summer. This, in spite of the rain, was draining itself, and trees and hedges floated in a mirror patterned with their own reflections and the rich earth that was starting to thrust itself up through the thinning waters. We came past a great tobacco factory to Metkovitch, a river port like any other, with sea-going ships lying up by the quay, looking too big for their quarters. There we stopped in the hotel for some coffee, and for the first time recognized the fly-blown, dusty, waking dream atmosphere that lingers in Balkan districts where the Turk has been. In this hotel I found the most westward Turkish lavatory I have ever encountered: a hole in the floor with a depression for a foot on each side of it, and a tap that sends water flowing along a groove laid with some relevance to the business in hand. It is efficient enough in a cleanly kept household, but it is disconcerting in its proof that there is more than one way of doing absolutely anything.

Later we travelled in a rough Scottish country, where people walked under crashing rain, unbowed by it. They wore raincoats of black fleeces or thickly woven grasses, a kind of thatch; and some had great hoods of stiffened white linen, that made a narrow alcove for the head and a broad alcove for the shoulders and hung nearly to the waist. These last looked like inquisitors robed for solemn mischief, but none of them were dour. The women and girls were full of laughter, and ran from the mud our wheels threw at them as if it were a game. Moslem graveyards began to preach their lesson of indifference to the dead. The stone stumps, carved with a turban if the commemorated corpse were male and left plain if it were female, stood crooked among the long grasses and the wild irises, which the rain was beating flat. Under a broken Roman arch crouched an old shepherd, shielding his turban, which, being yellow, showed that he had made the pilgrimage to Mecca.

The rain lifted, we were following a broad upland valley and looked over pastures and a broad river at the elegance of a small Moslem town, with its lovely minarets. It was exquisitely planned, its towers refined by the influence of the minarets, its red-roofed houses lying among the plumy foliage of their walled gardens; it was in no way remarkable, there are thousands of Moslem towns like it. We left it unvisited, and went on past an aerodrome with its hangars, past the barracks and the tobacco factory that stand in the outskirts of any considerable Herzegovinian town, and were in Mostar, 'Stari most,' old bridge. Presently we were looking at that bridge, which is falsely said to have been built by the Emperor Trajan, but is of medieval Turkish workmanship. It is one of the most beautiful bridges in the world. A slender arch lies between two round towers, its parapet bent in a shallow angle in the centre.

To look at it is good; to stand on it is as good. Over the grey-green river swoop hundreds of swallows, and on the banks mosques and white houses stand among glades of trees and bushes. The swallows and the glades know nothing of the mosques and houses. The river might be running through unvisited hills instead of a town of twenty thousand inhabitants. There was not an old tin, not a rag of paper to be seen. This was certainly not due to any scavenging service. In the Balkans people are more apt to sit down and look at disorder and discuss its essence than clear it away. It was more likely to be due to the Moslem's love of nature, especially of running water, which would prevent him from desecrating the scene with litter in the first place. I marvelled, as I had done on my previous visit to Yugoslavia, at the contradictory attitudes of the Moslem to such matters.

They build beautiful towns and villages. I know of no country, not even Italy or Spain, where each house in a group will be placed with such invariable taste and such pleasing results for those who look at it and out of it alike. The architectural formula of a Turkish house, with its reticent defensive lower story and its projecting upper story, full of windows, is simple and sensible; and I know nothing neater than its interior. Western housewifery is sluttish compared to that aseptic order. Yet Mostar, till the Austrians came, had no hotels except bug-ridden shacks, and it was hard to get the Moslems to abandon their habit of casually slaughtering animals in the streets. Even now the average Moslem shop is the antithesis of the Moslem house. It is a shabby little hole, often with a glassless front, which must be cold in winter and stifling in summer, and its goods are arranged in fantastic disorder. In a stationer's shop the picture-postcards will have been left in the sun till they are faded, and the exercise-books will be foxed. In a textile shop the bolts of stuff will be stacked in untidy tottering heaps. The only exceptions are the bakeries, where the flat loaves and buns are arranged in charming geometric patterns, and the greengroceries, where there is manifest pleasure in the colour and shape of the vegetables. There are, indeed, evident in all Moslem life co-equal strains of extreme fastidiousness and extreme slovenliness, and it is impossible to predict where or why the one or the other is going to take control. A mosque is the most spick-and-span place of worship in the world; but any attempt to postulate a connexion in the Moslem mind between holiness and cleanliness will break down at the first sight of a mosque which for some reason, perhaps a shifting of the population, is no longer used. It will have been allowed to fall into a squalor that recalls the worst Western slums.

The huge café of our hotel covered the whole ground floor, and had two billiard-tables in the centre. For dinner we ate the trout of the place, which is famous and, we thought, horrible, like fish crossed with slug. But we ate also a superb cheese soufflé. The meal was served with incredible delay, and between the courses we read the newspapers and looked about us. Moslems came in from the streets, exotic in fezes. They hung them up and went to their seats and played draughts and drank black coffee, no longer Moslems, merely men. Young officers moved rhythmically through the beams of white light that poured down upon the acid green of the billiard-tables, and the billiard balls gave out their sound of stoical shock. There was immanent the Balkan feeling of a shiftless yet just doom. It seemed possible that someone might come into the room, perhaps a man who would hang up his fez, and explain, in terms just comprehensible enough to make it certain they were not nonsensical, that all the people at the tables must stay there until the two officers who were playing billiards at that moment had played a million games, and that by the result their eternal fates would be decided; and that this would be accepted, and people would sit there quietly waiting and reading the newspapers.

Here in Mostar the really adventurous part of our journey began. Something that had been present in every breath we drew in Dalmatia and Croatia was absent when we woke the next morning, and dressed and breakfasted with our eyes on the market square beneath our windows. It might be identified as conformity in custom as well as creed. The people we were watching adhered with intensity to certain faiths. They were Moslem, they were Catholic, they were Orthodox. About marriage, about birth, about death, they practised immutable rites, determined by these faiths and the older faiths that lie behind them. But in all other ways they were highly individualistic. Their goings and comings, their eating and drinking, were timed by no communal programme, their choice of destiny might be made on grounds so private as to mean nothing

to any other human being. Such an attitude showed itself in the
crowds below us in a free motion that is the very antithesis in spirit
to what we see when we watch people walking to their work over
London Bridge in the morning. It showed too in their faces, which
always spoke of thought that was never fully shared, of scepticism
and satire and lyricism that felt no deed to have been yet finally
judged.

It showed itself also in their dress. Neither here nor anywhere
else do single individuals dare while sane to dress entirely according
to their whim; and the Moslems keep to their veils and fezes with
a special punctilio, because these mark them out as participants in
the former grandeur of the Ottoman Empire. But here the smallest
village or, in a town, a suburb or even a street, can have its own
fantasy of costume. The men go in less for variations than the
women, for in the classic costume of these parts the male has
found as becoming a dress as has ever been devised for him.
The stiff braided jacket has a look of ceremony, of mastership
about it, and the trousers give the outer line of the leg from the
hip to the ankle and make it seem longer by bagging between the
thighs. But the women presented us with uncountable variations.
We liked two women, grey-haired and harsh-featured, who looked
like Margate landladies discussing the ingenious austerities of the
day's menus, until a boy wheeled away a barrow and we could see
their long full serge bloomers. Other women wore tight bodices
and jackets and baggy trousers, each garment made of a different
sort of printed material, such as we use for country curtains; but
though these wore the Moslem trousers they were Christians, for
their faces were unveiled, and they covered their heads loosely
with what we know as Paisley shawls. The Moslems slid about
black-muzzled, wearing their cotton wrappers, which were usually
striped in coldish colours, greys and slate-blues and substanceless
reds, except for those who wore that costume one sees in Mostar
and not again when one leaves it, unless one's journey takes one
very far: to Turkestan, I have heard it said.

The costume is as stirring to the imagination and as idiotically
unpractical as any I have ever seen. The great point in favour
of Moslem dress in its Yugoslavian form is a convenience in hot
weather, which in these parts is a serious consideration, for even
in Mostar the summer is an affliction. The cotton overall keeps the
hair and the clothes clean, and the veil protects the face from dust
and insects and sunburn. This is not true of the heavy horse-hair
veil worn in the real East, where the accumulation of dust is turned
by the breath of the mouth and nostrils to actual mud, but the light

black veil of voile or cotton does no harm and a great deal of good. There is, however, no such justification for the traditional Mostar costume. It consists of a man's coat, made in black or blue cloth, immensely too large for the woman who is going to wear it. It is cut with a stiff military collar, very high, perhaps as much as eight or ten inches, which is embroidered inside, not outside, with gold thread. It is never worn as a coat. The woman slips it over her, drawing the shoulders above her head, so that the stiff collar falls forward and projects in front of her like a visor, and she can hide her face if she clutches the edges together, so that she need not wear a veil. The sleeves are allowed to hang loose or are stitched together at the back, but nothing can be done with the skirts, which drag on the ground.

We asked the people in the hotel and several tradesmen in Mostar, and a number of Moslems in other places, whether there was any local legend which accounted for this extraordinary garment, for it seemed it must commemorate some occasion when a woman had disguised herself in her husband's coat in order to perform an act of valour. But if there was ever such a legend it has been forgotten. The costume may have some value as a badge of class, for it could be worn with comfort and cleanliness only by a woman of the leisured classes, who need not go out save when she chooses. It would be most inconvenient in wet weather or on rough ground, and a woman could not carry or lead a child while she was wearing it. But perhaps it survives chiefly by its poetic value, by its symbolic references to the sex it clothes.

It has the power of a dream or a work of art that has several interpretations, that explains several aspects of reality at one and the same time. First and most obviously the little woman in the tall man's coat presents the contrast between man and woman at its most simple and playful, as the contrast between heaviness and lightness, between coarseness and fragility, between that which breaks and that which might be broken but is instead preserved and cherished, for the sake of tenderness and joy. It makes man and woman seem as father and daughter. The little girl is wearing her father's coat and laughs at him from the depths of it, she pretends that it is a magic garment and that she is invisible and can hide from him. Its dimensions favour this fantasy. The Herzegovinian is tall, but not such a giant as this coat was made to fit. I am barely five-foot-four and my husband is close on six-foot-two, but when I tried on his overcoat in this fashion the hem was well above my ankles; yet the Mostar garment trails about its wearer's feet.

But it presents the female also in a more sinister light: as the male sees her when he fears her. The dark visor gives her the beak of a bird of prey, and the flash of gold thread within the collar suggests private and ensnaring delights. A torch is put to those fires of the imagination which need for fuel dreams of pain, annihilation, and pleasure. The austere yet lubricious beauty of the coat gives a special and terrifying emphasis to the meaning inherent in all these Eastern styles of costume which hide women's faces. That meaning does not relate directly to sexual matters; it springs from a state of mind more impersonal, even metaphysical, though primitive enough to be sickening. The veil perpetuates and renews a moment when man, being in league with death, like all creatures that must die, hated his kind for living and transmitting life, and hated woman more than himself, because she is the instrument of birth, and put his hand to the floor to find filth and plastered it on her face, to affront the breath of life in her nostrils. There is about all veiled women a sense of melancholy quite incommensurate with the inconveniences they themselves may be suffering. Even when, like the women of Mostar, they seem to be hastening towards secret and luxurious and humorous love-making, they hint of a general surrender to mortality, a futile attempt of the living to renounce life.

Bosnia

Bosnia

ROAD

A MOSLEM WOMAN WALKING BLACK-FACED IN WHITE ROBES among the terraces of a blossoming orchard, her arms full of irises, was the last we saw of the Herzegovinian plains; and our road took us into mountains, at first so gruffly barren, so coarsely rocky that they were almost squalid. Then we followed a lovely rushing river, and the heights were mitigated by spring woods, reddish here with the foliage of young oaks, that ran up to snow peaks. This river received tributaries, after the astonishing custom of this limestone country, as unpolluted gifts straight from the rock face. One strong flood burst into the river at right angles, flush with the surface, an astonishing disturbance. Over the boulders ranged the exuberant hellebore with its pale-green flowers.

But soon the country softened, and the mountains were tamed and bridled by their woodlands and posed as background to sweet small compositions of waterfalls, fruit trees, and green lawns. The expression 'sylvan dell' seemed again to mean something. We looked across a valley to Yablanitsa, the Town of Poplars, which was the pleasure resort of Mostar when the Austrians were here, where their officers went in the heat of the summer for a little gambling and horse-racing. Before its minarets was a plateau covered with fields of young corn in their first pale, strong green, vibrant as a high C from a celestial soprano, and orchards white with cherry and plum. We drove up an avenue of bronze and gold budding ash trees and lovely children dashed out of a school and saluted us as a sign and wonder. We saw other lovely children later, outside a gipsy encampment of tents made with extreme simplicity of pieces of black canvas hung over a bar and tethered to the ground on each side. Our Swabian chauffeur drove at a pace incredible for him, lest we should give them pennies.

A neat village called Little Horse ran like a looped whip round a bridged valley, and we wondered to see in the heart of the country so many urban-looking little cafés where men sat and drank coffee. The road mounted and spring ran backwards like a reversed film; we were among trees that had not yet put out a bud, and from a high pass we looked back at a tremendous circle of snow peaks about whose feet we had run unwitting. We fell again through Swissish country, between banks blond with primroses, into richer country full of stranger people. Gipsies, supple and golden creatures whom the window-curtains of Golders Green had clothed in the colours of the sunrise and the sunset, gave us greetings and laughter; Moslem women walking unveiled towards the road turned their backs until we passed, or if there was a wall near by sought it and flattened their faces against it. We came to a wide valley, flanked with hills that, according to the curious conformation, run not east and west nor north and south but in all directions, so that the view changed every instant and the earth seemed as fluid and restless as the ocean.

'We are quite near Sarajevo,' I said; 'it is at the end of this valley.' Though I was right, we did not arrive there for some time. The main road was under repair and we had to make a detour along a road so bad that the mud spouted higher than the car, and after a mile or so our faces and topcoats were covered with it. This is really an undeveloped country, one cannot come and go yet as one chooses.

Sarajevo I

'Look,' I said, 'the river at Sarajevo runs red. That I think a bit too much. The pathetic fallacy really ought not to play with such painful matters.' 'Yes, it is as blatant as a propagandist poster,' said my husband. We were standing on the bridge over which the Archduke Franz Ferdinand and his wife would have driven on the morning of June the twenty-eighth, 1914, if they had not been shot by a Bosnian named Gavrilo Princip, just as their car was turning off the embankment.

We shuddered and crossed to the other bank, where there was a little park with a café in it. We sat and drank coffee, looking at the *Pyrus Japonica* and the white lilacs that grew all round us, and the people, who were almost as decorative as flowers. At the next table sat a Moslem woman wearing a silk overall striped in lilac and purple and dull blue. Her long narrow hand shot out of its folds to spoon a drop from a glass of water into her coffee-cup; here there is Turkish coffee, which carries its grounds in suspension, and the cold drop precipitates them. Her hand shot out again to hold her veil just high enough to let her other hand carry the cup to her lips. When she was not drinking she sat quite still, the light breeze pressing her black veil against her features. Her stillness was more than the habit of a Western woman, yet the uncovering of her mouth and chin had shown her completely un-Oriental, as luminously fair as any Scandinavian. Further away two Moslem men sat on a bench and talked politics, beating with their fingers on the headlines of a newspaper. Both were tall, raw-boned, bronze-haired, with eyes crackling with sheer blueness: Danish sea captains, perhaps, had they not been wearing the fez.

We noted then, and were to note it again and again as we went about the city, that such sights gave it a special appearance. The costumes which we regard as the distinguishing badge of an Oriental race, proof positive that the European frontier has been crossed, are worn by people far less Oriental in aspect than, say, the Latins; and this makes Sarajevo look like a fancy-dress ball. There is also an air of immense luxury about the town, of unwavering dedication to pleasure, which makes it credible that it would hold a festivity on so extensive and costly a scale. This air is, strictly speaking, a deception, since Sarajevo is stuffed with poverty of a most denuded kind. The standard of living among the working classes is lower than

even in our great Western cities. But there is also a solid foundation
of moderate wealth. The Moslems here scorned trade but they
were landowners, and their descendants hold the remnants of their
fortunes and are now functionaries and professional men. The trade
they rejected fell into the hands of the Christians, who therefore
grew in the towns to be a wealthy and privileged class, completely
out of touch with the oppressed Christian peasants outside the city
walls. There is also a Jewish colony here, descended from a group
who came here from Spain after the expulsory decrees of Ferdinand
and Isabella, and grafted itself on an older group which had been
in the Balkans from time immemorial; it has acquired wealth and
culture. So the town lies full-fed in the trough by the red river, and
rises up the bowl of the blunt-ended valley in happy, open suburbs
where handsome houses stand among their fruit trees. There one
may live very pleasantly, looking down on the minarets of the
hundred mosques of Sarajevo, and the tall poplars that march
the course of the red-running river. The dead here also make for
handsomeness, for acres and acres above these suburbs are given up
to the deliberate carelessness of the Moslem cemeteries, where the
marble posts stick slantwise among uncorrected grass and flowers
and ferns, which grow as cheerfully as in any other meadow.

But the air of luxury in Sarajevo has less to do with material goods
than with the people. They greet delight here with unreluctant and
sturdy appreciation, they are even prudent about it, they will let no
drop of pleasure run to waste. It is good to wear red and gold and
blue and green: the women wear them, and in the Moslem bazaar
that covers several acres of the town with its open-fronted shops
there are handkerchiefs and shawls and printed stuffs which say
'Yes' to the idea of brightness as only the very rich, who can go to
dressmakers who are conscious specialists in the eccentric, dare to
say it in the Western world. Men wash in the marble fountain of the
great mosque facing the bazaar and at the appointed hour prostrate
themselves in prayer, with the most comfortable enjoyment of
coolness and repose and the performance of a routine in good
repute. In the Moslem cookshops they sell the great cartwheel tarts
made of fat leaf-thin pastry stuffed with spinach which presuppose
that no man will be ashamed of his greed and his liking for grease.
The looks the men cast on the veiled women, the gait by which the
women admit that they know they are being looked upon, speak of a
romanticism that can take its time to dream and resolve because it is
the flower of the satisfied flesh. This tradition of tranquil sensuality
is of Moslem origin, and is perhaps still strongest among Moslems,
but also on Jewish and Christian faces can there be recognized this

steady light, which makes it seem as if the Puritans who banish pleasure and libertines who savage her do worse than we had imagined. We had thought of them as destroying harmless beauty: but here we learned to suspect that they throw away an instruction necessary for the mastery of life.

Though Sarajevo has so strong a character it is not old as cities go. It was originally a mining town. Up on the heights there is to be seen a Turkish fortress, reconditioned by the Austrians, and behind it are the old workings of a mine that was once exploited by merchants from Dubrovnik. This is not to say that it had ever any of the casual and reckless character of a modern mining town. In past ages, before it was realized that though minerals seem solid enough their habits make them not more reliable as supports than the rainbow, a mining town would be as sober and confident as any other town built on a hopeful industry. But it was neither big nor powerful when it fell into the hands of the Turks in 1464. The capital of Bosnia was Yaitse, usually but unhelpfully spelt Jajce, about ninety miles or so north in the mountains. But after the conquest Sarajevo became extremely important as a focal point where various human characteristics were demonstrated, one of which was purely a local peculiarity, yet was powerful and appalling on the grandest scale.

It happened that the Manichæan heresy, which had touched Dalmatia and left its mark so deeply on Trogir, had struck even deeper roots in Bosnia, where a sect called the Bogomils had attracted a vast proportion of the people, including both the feudal lords and the peasants. We do not know much about this sect except from their enemies, who were often blatant liars. It is thought from the name 'Bogomil,' which means 'God have mercy' in old Slavonic, and from the behaviour of the surviving remnants of the sect, that they practised the habit of ecstatic prayer, which comes easy to all Slavs; and they adapted the dualism of this heresy to Slav taste. They rejected its Puritanism and incorporated in it a number of pre-Christian beliefs and customs, including such superstitions as the belief in the haunting of certain places by elemental spirits and the practice of gathering herbs at certain times and using them with incantations. They also gave it a Slav character by introducing a political factor. Modern historians suggest that Bogomilism was not so much a heresy as a schism, that it represented the attempt of a strong national party to form a local church which should be independent of either the Roman Catholic or the Orthodox Church.

Whatever Bogomilism was, it satisfied the religious necessities of the mass of Bosnians for nearly two hundred and fifty years, notwithstanding the savage attacks of both the Roman Catholic and the Orthodox Churches. The Roman Catholic Church was the more dangerous of the two. This was not because the Orthodox Church had the advantage in tolerance: the Council of Constantinople laid it down that Bogomils must be burned alive. It was because the political situation in the East became more and more unfavourable to the Orthodox Church, until finally the coming of the Turks ranged them among the objects rather than the inflictors of persecution. The Latin Church had no such mellowing misfortunes; and though for a time it lost its harshness towards heretics, and was, for example, most merciful towards Jews and Arians under the Carlovingians, it was finally urged by popular bigotry and adventurous monarchs to take up the sword against the enemies of the faith.

At the end of the twelfth century we find a King of Dalmatia who wanted to seize Bosnia complaining to the Pope that the province was full of heretics, and appealing to him to get the King of Hungary to expel them. This began a system of interference which was for long wholly unavailing. In 1221 there were none but Bogomil priests in Bosnia, under whom the country was extremely devout. But the zeal of the Church had been fired, and in 1247 the Pope endeavoured to inspire the Archbishop of Bosnia by describing to him how his predecessors had tried to redeem their see by devastating the greater part of it and by killing or carrying away in captivity many thousands of Bosnians. The people, however, remained obstinately Bogomil, and as soon as the attention of the Papacy was diverted elsewhere, as it was during the Waldensian persecutions and the Great Schism, they stood firm in their faith again. Finally it was adopted as the official state religion.

But the Papacy had staked a great deal on Bosnia. It had preached crusade after crusade against the land, with full indulgences, as in the case of crusades to Palestine. It had sent out brigades of missionaries, who had behaved with glorious heroism and had in many cases suffered martyrdom. It had used every form of political pressure on neighbouring monarchs to induce them to invade Bosnia and put it to fire and the sword. It had, by backing Catholic usurpers to the Bosnian throne, caused perpetual disorder within the kingdom and destroyed all possibility of dynastic unity. Now it made one last supreme effort. It supported the Emperor Sigismund of Hungary, who held Croatia and Dalmatia, and who wished to add Bosnia to his kingdom. This was not a step at all likely to promote the cause of order. Sigismund was a flighty adventurer whose indifference to Slav interests was later shown by his surrender of Dalmatia to Venice. But the Pope issued a Bull calling Christendom to a crusade against the Turks, the apostate Arians, and the heretic Bosnians, and the Emperor embarked on a campaign which was sheer vexation to the tortured Slav lands, and scored the success of capturing the Bosnian king. The Bosnians were unimpressed and replaced him by another, also a staunch Bogomil. Later Sigismund sent back the first king, whose claim to the throne was naturally resented by the second. The wretched country was again precipitated into civil war.

This was in 1415. In 1389 the battle of Kossovo had been lost by the Christian Serbs. For twenty-six years the Turks had been digging themselves in over the border of Bosnia. They had already some foothold in the southern part of the kingdom. A child could have seen what was bound to happen. The Turks offered the Bogomils military protection, secure possession of their lands, and full liberty to practise their religion provided they counted themselves as Moslems and not as Christians, and did not attack the forces of the Ottoman Empire. The Bogomils, having been named in a Papal Bull with the Turks as common enemies of Christendom and having suffered invasion in consequence, naturally accepted the offer. Had it not been for the intolerance of the Papacy we would not have had Turkey in Europe for five hundred years. Fifty years later, the folly had been consummated. Bosnia was wholly Turkish, and the Turks had passed on towards Hungary and Central Europe. It is worth while noting that a band of Bogomils who had been driven out of Bosnia by a temporary Catholic king, while their companions had been sent in chains to Rome to be 'benignantly converted,' valiantly defended the Herzegovinian mountains against the Turks for another twenty years.

But the story does not stop there. It was only then that a certain peculiar and awful characteristic of human nature showed itself, as it has since shown itself on one other occasion in history. There is a kind of human being, terrifying above all others, who resist by yielding. Let it be supposed that it is a woman. A man is pleased by her, he makes advances to her, he finds that no woman was ever more compliant. He marvels at the way she allows him to take possession of her and perhaps despises her for it. Then suddenly he finds that his whole life has been conditioned to her, that he has become bodily dependent on her, that he has acquired the habit of living in a house with her, that food is not food unless he eats it with her.

It is at this point that he suddenly realizes that he has not conquered her mind, and that he is not sure if she loves him, or even likes him, or even considers him of great moment. Then it occurs to him as a possibility that she failed to resist him in the first place because simply nothing he could do seemed of the slightest importance. He may even suspect that she let him come into her life because she hated him, and wanted him to expose himself before her so that she could despise him for his weakness. This, since man is a hating rather than a loving animal, may not impossibly be the truth of the situation. There will be an agonizing period when he attempts to find out the truth. But that he will not be able to do, for it is the essence of this woman's character not to uncover her face. He will therefore have to withdraw from the frozen waste in which he finds himself, where there is neither heat nor light nor food nor shelter, but only the fear of an unknown enemy, and he will have to endure the pain of living alone till he can love someone else; or he will have to translate himself into another person, who will be accepted by her, a process that means falsification of the soul. Whichever step he takes, the woman will grow stronger and more serene, though not so strong and serene as she will if he tries the third course of attempting to coerce her.

Twice the Slavs have played the part of this woman in the history of Europe. Once, on the simpler occasion, when the Russians let Napoleon into the core of their country, where he found himself among snow and ashes, his destiny dead. The second time it happened here in Sarajevo. The heretic Bosnian nobles surrendered their country to the Turks in exchange for freedom to keep their religion and their lands, but they were aware that these people were their enemies. There could be no two races more antipathetic than the Slavs, with their infinite capacity for inquiry and speculation, and the Turks, who had no word in their language to express the idea of being interested in anything, and who were therefore content in abandonment to the tropism of a militarist system. This antipathy grew stronger as the Turks began to apply to Bosnia the same severe methods of raising revenue with which they drained all their conquered territories, and the same system of recruiting. For some time after the conquest they began to draw from Bosnia, as from Serbia and Bulgaria and Macedonia, the pick of all the Slav boys, to act as Janizaries, as the Prætorian Guard of the Ottoman Empire. It was the fate of these boys to be brought up ignorant of the names of their families or their birth-places, to be denied later the right to marry or own property, to be nothing but instruments of warfare for the Sultan's use, as inhuman as lances or bombs.

To these exactions the Bosnians submitted. They could do nothing else. But the two Bosnian nobles who had been the first to submit to the Turks came to this mining town and founded a city which was called Bosna Sarai, from the fortress, the *Sarai*, on the heights above it. Here they lived in a pride undiminished by conquest, though adapted to it. It must be remembered that these people would not see themselves as renegades in any shocking sense. The followers of a heresy itself strongly Oriental in tone would not feel that they were abandoning Christianity in practising their worship under Moslem protection, since Mohammed acknowledged the sanctity of Christ, and Moslems had no objection to worshipping in Christian churches. To this day in Sarajevo Moslems make a special point of attending the Church of St. Anthony of Padua every Tuesday evening. The Bosnian Moslems felt that they had won their independence by a concession no greater than they would have made had they submitted to the Roman Catholic Church. So they sat down in their new town, firm in self-respect, and profited by the expanding wealth of their conquerors.

It was then, no doubt, that the town acquired its air of pleasure, for among the Turks at that time voluptuousness knew its splendid holiday. An insight into what its wealth came to be is given us by a catastrophe. When Kara Mustapha, the Vizier who tormented Dubrovnik, was beaten outside Vienna his camp dazzled Europe with a vision of luxury such as it had never seen, such as perhaps it has never known since. His stores were immense; he travelled with twenty thousand head apiece of buffaloes, oxen, camels, and mules, a flock of ten thousand sheep, and a country's crop of corn and sugar and coffee and honey and fat. His camp was the girth of Warsaw, wrote John Sobieski to his wife, and not imaginable by humble Poles. The Vizier's tent—this I know, for I once saw it in Vienna—was a masterpiece of delicate embroidery in many colours. There were also bathrooms flowing with scented waters, gardens with fountains, superb beds, glittering lamps and chandeliers and priceless carpets, and a menagerie containing all manner of birds and beasts and fishes. Before Kara Mustapha fled he decapitated two of his possessions which he thought so beautiful he could not bear the Christian dogs to enjoy them. One was a specially beautiful wife, the other was an ostrich. The scent of that world, luxurious and inclusive, still hangs about the mosques and latticed windows and walled gardens of Sarajevo.

But however sensuous that population might be, it was never supine. Sarajevo, as the seat of the new Moslem nobility, was made the headquarters of the Bosnian Janizaries. These Janizaries, however, singularly failed to carry out the intention of their founders. Their education proved unable to make them forget they were Slavs.

They insisted on speaking Serbian, they made no effort to conceal a racial patriotism, and what was more they insisted on taking wives and acquiring property. Far from inhumanly representing the Ottoman power in opposition to the Bosnian nobles, they were their friends and allies. The Porte found itself unable to alter this state of affairs, because the Janizaries of Constantinople, who were also Slavs, had a lively liking for them and could not be trusted to act against them. It had no other resources, for it had exterminated the leaders of the Bosnian Christians and in any case could hardly raise them up to fight for their oppressors.

Hence there grew up, well within the frontiers of the Ottoman Empire, a Free City, in which the Slavs lived as they liked, according to a constitution they based on Slav law and custom, and defied all interference. It even passed a law by which the Pasha of Bosnia was forbidden to stay more than a night at a time within the city walls. For that one night he was treated as an honoured guest, but the next morning he found himself escorted to the city gates. It was out of the question that the Ottoman Empire should ever make Sarajevo its seat of government. That had to be the smaller town of Travnik, fifty miles away, and even there the Pasha was not his own master. If the Janizaries of Sarajevo complained of him to the Sublime Porte, he was removed. Fantastically, the only right that the Porte insisted on maintaining to prove its power was the appointment of two officials to see that justice was done in disputes between Christians and Moslems; and even then the Commune of Sarajevo could dismiss them once they were appointed. Often the sultans and viziers must have wondered, 'But when did we conquer these people? Alas, how can we have thought we had conquered these people? What would we do not to have conquered these people?'

Things went very well with this mutinous city for centuries. Its independence enabled it to withstand the shock of the blows inflicted on the Turks at Vienna and Belgrade, which meant that they must abandon their intention of dominating Europe. There came a bad day at the end of the seventeenth century, when Prince Eugène of Savoy rode down from Hungary with his cavalry and looked down on the city from a foothill at the end of the valley. Then the Slavs proved their unity in space and time, and the Bosnians rehearsed the trick that the Russians were later to play on Napoleon. The town, Prince Eugène was told, had been abandoned. It lay there, empty, to be taken. Prince Eugène grew thoughtful and advanced no further, though he had been eager to see this outpost of the East, whose atmosphere must have been pleasing to his own type of voluptuousness. He turned round and went back to the Danube at the head of a vast column of Christian refugees whom he took to Austrian territory. Perhaps that retreat made the difference between the fates of Prince Eugène and Napoleon.

After that a century passed and left Sarajevo much as it was, plump in insubordination. Then came the great reforming sultans, Selim III and Mahmud II, who saw that they must rebuild their house if it were not to tumble about their ears. They resolved to reorganize the Janizaries and, when that proved impossible, to disband them. These were by now a completely lawless body exercising supreme authority over all lawfully constituted administrative units. Also the sultans resolved to reform the land and taxation system which made hungry slaves of the peasants. Nothing would have been less pleasing to Sarajevo. The Janizaries and the Bosnian nobility had worked together to maintain unaltered the feudal system which had perished in nearly all other parts of Europe, and the proposal to remove the disabilities of the Christian peasants reawakened a historic feud. The Bosnian Moslem city-dwelling nobles hated these Christian peasants, because they were the descendants of the Catholic and Orthodox barons and their followers who had opened the door to the invader by their intolerance of Bogomilism.

Therefore the Janizaries and the Moslem nobles fought the sultans. The Janizaries refused to be disbanded and when their brothers had been exterminated in Constantinople the prohibited uniform was still to be seen in Sarajevo: the blue pelisse, the embroidered under-coat, the huge towering turban, decorated when the wearer was of the higher ranks with bird-of-paradise plumes, the high leather boots, red and yellow and black according to rank. In time they had to retreat from the town to the fortress on the heights above it, and that too fell later to the troops of the central authority; Bosnian nobles were beheaded, and the Pasha entered into full possession of the city where for four centuries he had been received on sufferance. But after a few months, in July 1828, the Sarajevans took their revenge and, aided by the citizens of a neighbouring town called Visok, broke in and for three days massacred their conquerors. Their victory was so terrible that they were left undisturbed till 1850, and then they were defeated by a Turkish Empire which itself was near to defeat, and was to be drummed out of Bosnia by peasants not thirty years later. At last the two lovers had destroyed each other. But they were famous lovers. This beautiful city speaks always of their preoccupation with one another, of what the Slav, not to be won by any gift, took from the Turk, and still was never won, of the unappeasable hunger with which the Turk longed throughout the centuries to make the Slav subject to him, although the Slav is never subject, not even to himself.

Sarajevo II

We knew we should try to get some sleep before the evening, because Constantine was coming from Belgrade and would want to sit up late and talk. But we hung about too late in the bazaar, watching a queue of men who had lined up to have their fezes ironed. It is an amusing process. In a steamy shop two Moslems were working, each clapping a fez down on a fez-shaped cone heated inside like an old-fashioned flat-iron and then clapping down another cone on it and screwing that down very tight, then releasing the fez with a motherly expression. 'What extremely tidy people the Moslems must be,' said my husband; but added, 'This cannot be normal, however. If it were there would be more shops of this sort. There must be some festival tomorrow. We will ask the people at the hotel.' But we were so tired that we forgot, and slept so late that Constantine had to send us up a message saying he had arrived and was eager to go out to dinner.

When we came downstairs Constantine was standing in the hall, talking to two men, tall and dark and dignified, with the sallow, long-lashed dignity of Sephardim. 'I tell you I have friends everywhere,' he said. 'These are two of my friends, they like me very much. They are Jews from Spain, and they speak beautiful soft Spanish of the time of Ferdinand and Isabella, not the Spanish of today, which is hard and guttural as German. This is Dr Lachan, who is a banker, and Dr Marigan, who is a judge. I think they are both very good men, they move in a sort of ritual way along prescribed paths, and there is nothing ever wrong. Now they will take us to a café where we will eat a little, but it is not for the eating they are taking us there, it is because they have heard there is a girl there who sings the Bosnian songs very well, and it is not for nothing that there are so many mosques in Sarajevo, this is truly the East, and people attach great importance to such things as girls who sing the Bosnian songs, even though they are very serious people.'

The men greeted us with beautiful and formal manners, and we went down the street to the café. It could be seen they liked Constantine half because he is a great poet, half because he is like a funny little dog. But at the door they began to think of us and wonder if they should take us to such a place. 'For us and our wives it is nice,' they said, 'but we are used to it. Perhaps for an English lady it will seem rather strange. There are sometimes dancers . . .

well, there is one now.' A stout woman clad in sequined pink muslin trousers and brassière was standing on a platform revolving her stomach in time to the music of a piano and violin, and as we entered she changed her subject matter and began to revolve her large firm breasts in opposite directions. This gave an effect of hard, mechanical magic; it was as if two cannon-balls were rolling away from each other but were for ever kept contingent by some invisible power of attraction. 'Your wife does not mind?' asked the judge and the banker. 'I think not,' said my husband. As we went down the aisle one of the cannon-balls ceased to revolve, though the other went on rolling quicker than ever, while the woman cried out my name in tones of familiarity and welcome. The judge and the banker showed no signs of having witnessed this greeting. As we sat down I felt embarrassed by their silence and said, in explanation, 'How extraordinary I should come across this woman again.' 'I beg your pardon?' said the judge. 'How extraordinary it is,' I repeated, 'that I should come across this woman again. I met her last year in Macedonia.' 'Oh, it is you that she knows!' exclaimed the judge and the banker, and I perceived that they had thought she was a friend of my husband's.

I was really very glad to see her again. When Constantine and I had been in Skoplje the previous Easter he had taken me to a night club in the Moslem quarter. That form of entertainment which we think of as peculiarly modern Western and profligate was actually far more at home in the ancient and poverty-stricken Near East. In any sizable village in Macedonia I think one would find at least one café where a girl sang and there was music. In Skoplje, which has under seventy thousand inhabitants, there are many such, including a night club almost on a Trocadéro scale. In the little Moslem cabaret we visited there was nobody more opulent than a small shopkeeper, but the performers numbered a male gipsy who sang and played the gusla, a very beautiful Serbian singer, a still more beautiful gipsy girl who sang and danced, and this *danseuse de ventre*, who was called Astra. When Astra came round and rattled the plate at our table I found she was a Salonika Jewess, member of another colony of refugees from Ferdinand and Isabella who still speak Spanish, and I asked her to come and see me the next day at my hotel and give me a lesson in the *danse de ventre*.

She was with me earlier than I had expected, at ten o'clock, wearing a curious coat-frock, of a pattern and inexpert make which at once suggested she had hardly any occasion to be fully dressed, and that she would have liked to be a housewife in a row of houses all exactly alike. The lesson in the *danse de ventre* was not a success. I picked up the movement wonderfully, she said; I had it perfectly, but I could not produce the right effect. '*Voyez-vous, Madame*,' she said, in the slow French she had picked up in a single term at a mission school, '*vous n'avez pas de quoi*.' It is the only time in my life that I have been reproached with undue slenderness; but I suppose Astra herself weighed a hundred and sixty pounds, though she carried no loose flesh like a fat Western woman, but was solid and elastic. After the lesson had failed we sat and talked. She came of a family of musicians. She had a sister who had married an Englishman employed in Salonika, and now lived in Ealing and had two pretty little girls, like dolls they were so pretty, Milly and Lily. It was terrible they were so far away. She herself was a widow, her husband had been a Greek lorry driver who was killed in a road accident after three years of marriage. She had one son, a boy of ten. It was her ambition that he should go to a French school, in her experience there was nothing like French education '*pour faire libre l'esprit*.' In the meantime he was at a Yugoslavian school and doing well, because he was naturally a good and diligent little boy, but she wanted something better for him.

It was very disagreeable, her occupation. She did not state explicitly what it included, but we took it for granted. It was not so bad in Greece or Bulgaria or in the North of Yugoslavia, in all of which places she had often worked, but of late she had got jobs only in South Serbia, in night clubs where the clients were for the most part Turks. She clapped her hand to her brow and shook her head and said, '*Vous ne savez pas, Madame, à quel point les Turcs sont idiots*.' Her complaint, when I investigated it, was just what it sounds. She was distressed because her Turkish visitors had no conversation. Her coat-frock fell back across her knee and showed snow-white cambric underclothing and flesh scrubbed clean as the cleanest cook's kitchen table, and not more sensuous. She was all decency and good sense, and she was pronouncing sound judgment.

The judgment was appalling. The Turks in South Serbia are not like the Slav Moslems of Sarajevo, they are truly Turks. They are Turks who were settled there after the battle of Kossovo, who have remained what the Ataturk would not permit Turks to be any longer. They are what a people must become if it suspends all intellectual life and concentrates on the idea of conquest. It knows victory, but there is a limit to possible victories; what has been gained cannot be maintained, for that requires the use of the intellect, which has been removed. So there is decay, the long humiliation of decay. At one time the forces of Selim and Suleiman covered half a continent with the precise and ferocious ballet of perfect warfare, the sensuality of the sultans and the viziers searched for fresh refinements and made of their discoveries the starting points for further search, fountains played in courtyards and walled gardens where there had been till then austere barbarism. At the end an ageing cabaret dancer, the homely and decent vanishing point of voluptuousness, sits on a bed and says with dreadful justice: '*Vous ne savez pas, Madame, à quel point les Turcs sont idiots.*'

When Astra came to our table later she told me that she hoped to be in Sarajevo for some weeks longer, and that she was happier here than she had been in Skoplje. '*Ici*,' she pronounced, '*les gens sont beaucoup plus cultivés.*' As soon as she had gone I found at my shoulder the Swabian chauffeur from Dubrovnik, whom we had paid off that afternoon. 'Why is that woman talking to you?' he said. He always immensely disconcerted me by his interventions. I was always afraid that if I said to him, 'What business is this of yours?' he would answer, in the loathsome manner of a miracle play, 'I am Reason' or 'I am Conscience,' and that it would be true. So I stammered, 'I know her.' 'You cannot know such a person,' he said. 'Do you mean you have been in some café where she has performed?' 'Yes, yes,' I said, 'it was in Skoplje, and she is a very nice woman, she has a son of whom she is fond.' 'How do you know she has a son?' asked the chauffeur. 'She told me so,' I said. 'You do not have to believe everything that such a person tells you,' said the chauffeur. 'But I am sure it is true,' I exclaimed hotly, 'and I am very sorry for her.' The chauffeur gave me a glance too heavily veiled by respect to be respectful, and then looked at my husband, but sighed, as if to remind himself that he would find no help there. Suddenly he picked up my bag and said, 'I came to say that I had remembered I had forgotten to take that grease-spot out with petrol as I had promised you, so I will take it outside and do it now.' He then bowed, and left me. I thought, 'He is really too conscientious, this is very inconvenient for now I have no powder.' But of course he would not have thought it necessary for me to have any powder.

But my attention was immediately diverted. A very handsome young man had come up to our table in a state of extreme anger; he was even angrier than any of the angry young men in Dalmatia. He evidently knew Constantine and the judge and the banker, but he did not give them any formal greeting. Though his hair was bronze and his eyes crackled with blueness, and he might have been brother to the two Moslems we had seen talking politics in the park that afternoon, he cried out, 'What about the accursed Turks?' The judge and the banker made no reply, but Constantine said, 'Well, it was not I who made them.' The young man insisted, 'But you serve our precious Government, don't you?' 'Yes,' said Constantine, 'for the sake of my country, and perhaps a little for the sake of my soul, I have given up the deep peace of being in opposition.' 'Then perhaps you can explain why your Belgrade gangster politicians have devised this method of insulting us Bosnians,' said the young man. 'We are used,' he said, stretching his arms wide and shouting, 'to their iniquities. We have seen them insulting our brothers the Croats, we have seen them spitting in the faces of all those who love liberty. But usually there is some sense in what they do, they either put money in their pockets or they consolidate their tyranny. But this crazy burlesque can bring them no profit. It can be done for no purpose but to wound the pride of us Bosnians. Will you be polite enough to explain a little why your horde of thugs and thieves have formed this curious intention of paying this unprovoked insult to a people whose part it should be to insult rather than be insulted?'

The judge leaned over to me and whispered, 'It is all right, Madame, they are just talking a little about politics.' 'But what has the Government done to insult Bosnia?' I asked. 'It has arranged,' said the banker, 'that the Turkish Prime Minister and Minister of War, who are in Belgrade discussing our military alliance with them, are to come here tomorrow to be received by the Moslem population.' 'Ah,' said my husband, 'that accounts for all the fezes being ironed. Well, do many people take the visit like this young man?' 'No,' said the banker, 'he is a very extreme young man.' 'I would not say so,' said the judge sadly.

At that moment the young man smashed his fist down on the table and cried into Constantine's face, 'Judas Iscariot! Judas Iscariot!' 'No,' said poor Constantine to his retreating back, 'I am not Judas Iscariot. I have indeed never been quite sure which of the disciples I do resemble, but it is a very sweet little one, the most *mignon* of them all.' He applied himself to the business of eating a line of little pieces of strongly seasoned meat that had been broiled on a skewer; and when he set it down wistfulness was wet in his round black eye. 'All the same I do not like it, what that young man said. It was not agreeable. Dear God, I wish the young would be more agreeable to my generation, for we suffered very much in the war, and if it were not for us they would still be slaves under the Austrians.'

Cautiously the banker said, 'Do you think it is really wise, this visit?' Constantine answered wearily, 'I think it is wise, for our

Prime Minister, Mr Stoyadinovitch, does not do foolish things.'
'But why is it objected to at all?' said my husband. 'That even
I understand a little,' said Constantine, 'for the Turks were our
oppressors and we drove them out, so that we Christians should
be free. And now the heads of the Turkish state are coming by
the consent of our Christian state to see the Moslems who upheld
the oppressors. I see that it must seem a little odd.' 'But how is it
possible,' said my husband, 'that there should be so much feeling
against the Turks when nobody who is not very old can possibly
have had any personal experience of their oppressions?'

The three men looked at my husband as if he were talking great
nonsense. 'Well,' said my husband, 'were not the Turks booted out
of here in 1878?' 'Ah, no, no!' exclaimed the three men. 'You do
not understand,' said Constantine; 'the Turkish Empire went from
here in 1878, but the Slav Moslems remained, and when Austria
took control it was still their holiday. For they were the favourites
of the Austrians, far above the Christians, far above the Serbs or
the Croats.' 'But why was that?' asked my husband. 'It was because
of the principle, *Divide et impera*,' said the banker. It was odd to
hear the phrase from the lips of one of its victims. 'Look, there
were fifty or sixty thousand people in the town,' said the banker.
'There were us, the Jews, who are of two kinds, the Sephardim,
from Spain and Portugal, and the others, the Ashkenazi, who are
from Central Europe and the East, and that is a division. Then
there were the Christian Slavs, who are Croats and Serbs, and
that is a division. But lest we should forget our differences, they
raised up the Moslems, who were a third of the population, to be
their allies against the Christians and the Jews.'

Their faces darkening with the particular sullenness of rebels,
they spoke of their youth, shadowed by the double tyranny of
Austria and the Moslems. To men of their position, for both
came from wealthy and influential families, that tyranny had been
considerably mitigated. It had fallen with a far heavier hand on
the peasants and the inhabitants of the poorer towns, and there it
meant a great deal of imprisonment and flogging, and occasional
executions. But to these people there had been a constant nagging
provocation and a sense of insult. The Moslems were given the
finest schools and colleges, the best posts in the administration
were reserved for them, they were invited to all official functions
and treated as honoured guests, the railway trains were held up
at their hours of prayer. The Turkish land system, which grossly
favoured the Moslems at the extense of the Christians, was carefully
preserved intact by his Catholic Majesty the Emperor Franz Josef.

And it was a special source of bitterness that the Austrians had forced their way into Bosnia after the Slavs had driven out the Turks, on the pretext that they must establish a garrison force to protect the Christians there in case the Turks came back. That they should then humiliate the Christians at the hand of those Moslems who had stayed behind seemed to these men an inflaming piece of hypocrisy which could never be forgotten or forgiven.

They evidently felt this deeply and sincerely, although they themselves were Jewish. The situation was obviously one of great complexity. That was apparent when they likened the Turks to dogs and swine, and spoke the words with more than Western loathing, as the Turks would have done. 'When I went to Berlin to study for my degree,' said the banker, 'I used to feel ashamed because the Germans took me as an equal, and here in my house I was treated as an inferior to men with fezes on their heads, to Orientals.' In that statement too many strands were twisted. Later my husband asked, 'But are the Moslems a sufficiently important and active group for it to matter whether they are encouraged or not?' The lawyer and the banker answered together, 'Oh, certainly,' and Constantine explained, 'Yes, they are very, very clever politicians, much cleverer than we are, for Islam taught them something, let us say it taught them not to run about letting off guns just because one of them had a birthday. Our Government has always to conciliate the Moslems. In the present Cabinet Mr Spaho is the Minister of Transport, and he is a Moslem from this town.' 'A most excellent man,' agreed the judge and banker, beaming. All that they had spoken of for so long in such a steady flow of hatred was forgotten in a glow of local patriotism.

At last it was time to go. 'No, your Mr Stoyadinovitch has not done well,' said the banker finally. 'It is not that we do not like the Moslems. Since the war all things have changed, and we are on excellent terms. But it is not nice when they are picked out by the Government and allowed to receive a ceremonial visit from the representative of the power that crushed us and ground us down into the mud.' We rose, and Astra in her sequins and pink muslin bounced from the platform like a great sorbo-ball to say good-bye. I wanted to give her a present, but remembered that the chauffeur had taken my bag away to clean it, so I told her to come and see me at the hotel next day. As we went out the Swabian chauffeur suddenly reappeared, rising from a table which was concealed by the bushes and creepers which were set about to give the cabaret the appearance of an open-air beer-garden. He handed back my bag with a triumphant smile, and I perceived that he had hidden himself for this very reason, that I should not be able to find him and get my money if I felt a charitable impulse towards my unsuitable friend.

'And please note,' he said, his eyes passing uneasily from my husband to me and then back again, deeply distressed by our lack of sense, 'it would be a good thing to stay indoors tomorrow morning, for the Turkish Prime Minister and War Minister are coming to visit the Moslems and there might be a disturbance. At any rate, it is not for you, there will be great crowds.' He spoke with authority out of the mass of his ideal world, which was almost as solid as if it were real because it had been conceived by his solid mind: a world in which people with money were also reasonable people, who did not give alms to the unworthy and stayed indoors when it was not so safe outdoors. And his blindish-looking eyes begged us to remember that we were English and therefore to refrain from acting like these Slavs.

Sarajevo III

I woke only once from my sleep, and heard the muezzins crying out
to the darkness from the hundred minarets of the city that there is
but one God and Mohammed His prophet. It is a cry that holds
an ultimate sadness, like the hooting of owls and the barking of
foxes in night-time. The muezzins are making that plain statement
of their cosmogony, and the owls and the foxes are obeying the
simplest need for expression; yet their cries, which they intended
to mean so little, prove more conclusively than any argument that
life is an occasion which justifies the hugest expenditure of pity.
I had nearly fallen asleep again when my husband said out of his
dreams, 'Strange, strange.' 'What is strange?' I said. 'That Jewish
banker,' he replied, 'he said so proudly that when he was a student
in Berlin he felt ashamed because he was treated there as an equal
when here he was treated as inferior to the Moslems. I wonder what
he feels about Germany now.'

In the morning we were not late, but Constantine was down
before us, breakfasting in the café. One of the reasons why people
of the Nordic type dislike Constantine is that he is able to do things
out of sheer vitality for which they require moral stimulus. His
good red blood can fetch him out of bed without a moment of
sombre resolution, his vigorous pulse keeps him going without
resort to perseverance. The writings of the early Christian Fathers
show that few things irritated them like a pagan who was in full
possession of the virtues. But though he was vigorous this morning
he was not gay. 'Look at all the flags,' he said, 'it is a great day for
Sarajevo. See how I show you all.' But he spoke glumly.

I suspected that he was secretly of his friends' mind about the
day's doings; and indeed it was not exhilarating to look out of the
café windows and see a stream of passing people, and none of the
men without fezes, all of the women veiled. I do not mind there
being such men and women, but one sees them with a different
eye when they are in a majority and could put at a disadvantage
all those not of their kind. 'I can understand that such a ceremony
as this can revive all sorts of apprehensions,' I said tartlessly. 'We
had better go,' said Constantine, ignoring my remark. 'The party
from Belgrade are not coming to the railway station, they stop the
railway train at a special halt in the middle of the boulevards, near
the museum, and it is quite a way from here.'

For part of the way we took a cab, and then we had to get out and walk. Because Constantine had his Government pass and we were to be present at the reception at the station, we were allowed to go down the middle of the streets, which were entirely lined with veiled women and men wearing fezes. Only a few Christians were to be seen here and there. 'There seem to be a great many Moslems,' I said, after the first two or three hundred yards. The crowd was close-packed and unified by a common aspect. The faces of the men were flattened, almost plastered by an expression of dogged adherence to some standard; they were all turned upwards to one hope. The women were as expressive in their waiting, though their faces were hidden. A light rain was falling on their silk and cotton overalls, but they did not move, and only some of them put up umbrellas, though most of them were carrying them. It was as if they thought of themselves already as participants in a sacred rite. Some of the spectators were arranged in processional order and held small, amateurish, neatly inscribed banners, some of them in Turkish script; and a great many of them carried Yugoslavian flags, very tidily, not waving them but letting them droop. There were many children, all standing straight and good under the rain. I looked at my watch, and I saw that we had been walking between these crowds for ten minutes. There are thirty thousand Moslems in Sarajevo, and I think most of them were there. And they were rapt, hallucinated, intoxicated with an old loyalty, and doubtless ready to know the intoxication of an old hatred.

We came to the halt at the right moment, as the train slid in and stopped. There was a little cheering, and the flags were waved, but it is not much fun cheering somebody inside the tin box of a railway carriage. The crowd waited to make sure. The Moslem Mayor of Sarajevo and his party went forward and greeted the tall and jolly Mr Spaho, the Minister of Transport, and the Yugoslavian Minister of War, General Marits, a giant who wore his strength packed round him in solid masses like a bull. He looked as Göring would like to look. There were faint, polite cheers for them; but the great cheers the crowd had had in its hearts for days were never given. For Mr Spaho and the General were followed, so far as the expectations of the crowd were concerned, by nobody. The two little men in bowlers and trim suits, very dapper and well-shaven, might have been Frenchmen darkened in the colonial service. It took some time for the crowd to realize that they were in fact Ismet Ineunue, the Turkish Prime Minister, and Kazim Ozalip, his War Minister.

Even after the recognition had been established the cheers were not given. No great degree of disguise concealed the disfavour with which these two men in bowler hats looked on the thousands they saw before them, all wearing the fez and veil which their leader the Ataturk made it a crime to wear in Turkey. Their faces were blank yet not unexpressive. So might Englishmen look if, in some corner of the Empire, they had to meet as brothers the inhabitants of a colony that had been miraculously preserved from the action of time and had therefore kept to their road.

The Moslem Mayor read them an address of welcome, of which, naturally, they did not understand one word. This was bound in any case to be a difficult love-affair to conduct, for they knew no Serbian and the Sarajevans knew no Turkish. They had to wait until General Marits had translated it into French; while they were waiting I saw one of them fix his eye on a distant building, wince, and look in the opposite direction. Some past-loving soul had delved in the attics and found the green flag with the crescent, the flag of the old Ottoman Empire, which these men and their leader regarded as the badge of a plague that had been like to destroy their people. The General's translation over, they responded in French better than his, only a little sweeter and more birdlike than the French of France, and stood still, their eyes set on the nearest roof, high enough to save them the sight of this monstrous retrograde profusion of fezes and veils, of red pates and black muzzles, while the General put back into Serbian their all too reasonable remarks. They had told the Moslems of Sarajevo, it seemed, that they felt the utmost enthusiasm for the Yugoslavian idea, and had pointed out that if the South Slavs did not form a unified state the will of the great powers could sweep over the Balkan Peninsula as it chose. They had said not one word of the ancient tie that linked the Bosnian Moslems to the Turks, nor had they made any reference to Islam.

There were civil obeisances, and the two men got into an automobile and drove towards the town. The people did not cheer them. Only those within sight of the railway platform were aware that they were the Turkish Ministers, and even among those were many who could not believe their eyes, who thought that there must have been some breakdown of the arrangements. A little procession of people holding banners that had been ranged behind the crowd at this point wrangled among itself as to whether it should start, delayed too long, and finally tried to force its way into the roadway too late. By that time the crowd had left the pavements and was walking under the drizzle back to the city, slowly and silently, as those who have been sent empty away.

We had seen the end of a story that had taken five hundred years to tell. We had seen the final collapse of the old Ottoman Empire. Under our eyes it had heeled over and fallen to the ground like a lay figure slipping off a chair. But that tragedy was already accomplished. The Ottoman Empire had ceased to suffer long ago. There was a more poignant grief before us. Suppose that such an unconquerable woman as may be compared to the Slav in Bosnia was at last conquered by time, and sent for help to her old lover, and that there answered the call a man bearing her lover's name who was, however, not her lover but his son, and looked on her with cold eyes, seeing her only as the occasion of a shameful passage in his family history; none of us would be able to withhold our pity.

Sarajevo IV

'I am so glad that this is a bad spring,' I said, 'for otherwise I should never have seen snow on the roof of a mosque, and there is something delicious about that incongruity.' 'But it is killing all the plum blossom you like so much to see,' said Constantine, 'and that is a terrible thing, for in Bosnia and Serbia we live a little by our timber and our mines, but mostly by our pigs and our plums. But for you I am glad of the bad weather, for if it had been better you would have wanted to be out on the hills all the time, and as it is you have got to know my friends. Will you not agree that life in this town is specially agreeable?' 'Yes,' said my husband, 'it is all that I hoped for in Istanbul, but never found, partly because I was a stranger, and partly because they are reformists and are trying for excellent motives to uproot their own charm.' 'I have liked it all,' I said, 'except that afternoon when the Turkish Ministers were here and I went to see the mosque in the bazaar. Then I felt as if I had insisted on being present while a total stranger had a tooth out. But that was my fault.'

I had thoughtlessly chosen to see the mosque that afternoon, and had found the whole courtyard full of Moslems who were waiting there because a rumour had spread that the Turkish Ministers were going to visit it. On their faces lay that plastered, flattened look of loyalty to a cause which I had noticed in the crowd at the railway station that morning. But it was mingled now with that stoical obstinacy a child shows when it insists on repeating a disappointing experience, so that it can have no doubt that it really happened. It seemed indecent for a Christian to intrude on them at such a moment, and for a woman too, since the whole Moslem theory of the relationship of the sexes falls to pieces once any man has failed in a wordly matter. I had even hesitated to admire the mellow tiles and fretted arches of the façade or to go into the interior, so like a light and spacious gymnasium for the soul, to see the carpets presented by the pious of three centuries: what have been the recreations of the warrior must seem a shame to him when his weapons have been taken away.

But this was the one time when staying in Sarajevo was not purely agreeable. The visit was, indeed, like being gently embraced by a city, for all classes had borrowed from the Moslem his technique for making life as delightful as might be. Our Jewish friends were strict

319

in their faith but their lives were as relaxed, as obstinately oriented towards the agreeable, as Mohammed would have had his children in time of peace. We went up to visit the banker in his large modern offices, which indeed almost amounted to a sky-scraper, and his welcome was sweet without reserve, and this was not due to mere facility, for he was a very wise man, sometimes almost tongue-tied with the burden of his wisdom, as the old Jewish sages must have been. It was only that till the contrary evidence was produced he preferred to think us as good as any friends he had. He was no fool, he would not reject that evidence if it came; but it had not come.

There were brought in, as we sat, cups of a sweet herbal infusion, as distinct from all other beverages as tea or coffee. We exclaimed in delight, and he told us, 'It is a Turkish drink that we all give to our visitors in our offices in Sarajevo. It is supposed to be an aphrodisiac.' He was amused, but without a snigger, at the custom he followed. 'Think of it,' he said. 'I told that to a German engineer who was here last month, and he went out and bought two kilos of it. An extraordinary people.' He went on to speak of his city, which he saw with the eye of a true lover, as astonished by its beauty as any stranger. That we should see it well he had arranged for two young women relatives of his to take us round the sights, and he produced them forthwith. They were entrancing. For theme they had the free, positive, creative attractiveness of the Slav; their style had been perfected in the harem. They had husbands and loved them, the banker was no more than kin and a friend, and my husband himself would admit that they felt for him only as the courtier speaks it in *As You Like It*, 'Hereafter, in a better world than this, I shall desire more love and knowledge of you.' But though they kept well within the framework of fastidious manners, they reminded the banker and my husband that it must have been very pleasant to keep a covey of darlings in silks and brocades behind latticed windows, who would laugh and scuttle away, though only to an inner chamber where they could be found again after a second's search, and sing and touch the strings of the gusla and mock the male and be overawed by him, and mock again, in an unending, uncriticized process of delight.

I record a wonder. The work of the bank was well done. That, with my cold inner eye that trusts nothing, least of all my own likings, I checked later. The banker was a man of exceptional ability and integrity and he worked hard according to the severest Western standards. But he appeared to keep his appointments with life as well as, and even during, his business engagements. Several times we went out with the two young women, and we always went back to the office and found the hot herbal tea, and coffee served with little squares of Turkish delight on tooth-picks, and much laughter, and a sense of luxurious toys. Once we went in and found half a dozen pictures of Sarajevo, bought by the banker out of his infatuation with the city, stacked on the big sofa and against the walls, and it was as if the caravans had come in from the North with a freight of Frankish art. The two women ran about from one to another of these novelties, they took sides, they became partisans of this picture and intrigued against that. There was an inherent fickleness in their admiration. They would tire of the familiar, but no doubt it is more important for the artist to have the new encouraged.

'What do you think of them?' the banker asked me. I wished he had not. They were the work of a Jewish refugee from Berlin, and though his perception was delicate and his brush subtle, each canvas showed him the child of that spirit which had destroyed him. There was the passion for the thick black line, the Puritan belief that if one pays out strength when making an artistic effort one will create a strong work of art. He had put a cast-iron outline to the tree on his canvas, and because it took vigour to make such an outline, and because cast-iron is an unyielding substance, he believed that the result was virile painting, even though his perception of the tree's form had been infantile in its feebleness. It is the same heresy that expresses itself in the decree that had driven him into exile. Because it is a vigorous act to throw the Jews out of Germany and because it causes pain and disorder, it is taken as a measure of virile statecraft, although its relevance to the troubles of the country could be imagined only by an imbecile.

Something of this I said, and the banker motioned my husband and myself to step with him to the window, leaving the two women to bicker like birds over the pictures. With the grave smile, which could not possibly become laughter, of a sage confessing his own folly, he said, 'I have remembered again and again a foolish thing I said when we first met. I told you that when I went to Berlin as a student I rejoiced as a Jew at being treated as an equal, while I was treated as an inferior here. That must have amused you. It was a piece of naïveté like a man boasting of his friendship with one who has spared no pains to show him that he considers him a fool, a bore, an oaf.' He looked out for a moment on the mosques, on the domes of the old caravanserai among the tiled roofs of the bazaar, on the poplars standing over the city like the golden ghosts of giant Janizaries. 'But it is puzzling, you know, not to be able to look to Germany as one's second home, when it has been that to one all one's life long. But one can come home to one's hearth, and I am fortunate that Sarajevo is mine.'

He went back and stood before the pictures, the young women each taking an arm, one fluting that he must hang the picture of the little Orthodox church over his desk, the other screaming that he must throw it away, he must burn it, he must give it to one-eyed Marko the scavenger. I thought he was promising himself too little. In this office there lingered something of the best of Turkish life; and in his integrity, in his dismissal of the little, in the seriousness which he brought to the interpretation of his experience, there was preserved the best of what a German philosophical training could do for a man of affairs. It seemed to me exquisitely appropriate that the vulgar should call the Jews old-clothes men. Since it is the peculiar madness of us other races to make ourselves magnificent clothes and then run wild and throw them away and daub ourselves with mud, it is well that there should be some old-clothes men about.

These Jews of Sarajevo are indeed an amazing community. I could bring forward as evidence the Bulbul and her mate, the two human beings who more than any others that I have ever met have the right arrangement and comforting significance of a work of art. They were not only husband and wife, they were kin; and this common blood had its own richness and its own discipline, for they came of a family that was considered among orthodox Jews as orthodox Jews are considered by liberal Jews, as the practitioners of an impossibly exacting rule. 'His father,' said Constantine of the Bulbul's mate, who was named Selim, 'was the most hieratic Jew that can ever be. All to him from the rising to the setting of the sun was a ritual, and he was very dominant, he made it so for all the world. I have seen it happen that when Selim was swimming in the sea at Dubrovnik, and he saw his father standing on the beach, and immediately he began to swim in a very hieratic manner, putting his hands out so and so, very slowly, and lifting his head out of the water and looking very gravely down his nose.'

This was credible, for Selim's dignity was magnificent but not pompous, as if it were an inherited garment and its previous wearers had taken the stiffness out of it. He was a very tall man with broad shoulders, broad even for a man of his height. His build suggested the stylized immensity of a god sculpted by a primitive people, and his face also had the quality of sculpture; though his wit and imagination made it mobile, it was at once the tables of the law and the force that shattered them. He had an impressive habit, as we discovered the first night we went out to dinner with him and his wife, of stopping suddenly as he walked along the street when he had thought of something important and staying quite still as he said it. The spot where he halted became Mount Sinai, and in his leisurely and massive authority could be seen the Moses whom Michelangelo had divined but could not, being a Gentile and therefore of divided and contending will, fully create in the strength of his lawfulness.

But the fascination of himself and his wife lay initially in their voices. There is a special music lingering about the tongues of many of these Spanish Jews, but no one else gave it such special performance. Selim had constrained his gift a little out of deference to the Western tenet that a man should not be more beautiful than can be helped and that a certain decent drabness should be the character of all he does, but from his wife's lips that music came in such animal purity that we called her the Bulbul, which is the Persian word for nightingale. Voices like these were the product of an existence built by putting pleasure to pleasure, as houses are built by putting brick to brick. A human being could not speak so unless he or she loved many other sounds—the wind's progress among trees or the subtler passage it makes through grasses; note by note given out by a musical instrument, each note for its own colour; the gurgle of wine pouring from a bottle or water trickling through a marble conduit in a garden—all sorts of sounds that many Westerners do not even hear, so corrupted are they by the tyranny of the intellect, which makes them inattentive to any message to the ear which is without an argument. Listening to her, one might believe humanity to be in its first unspoiled morning hour. Yet she was accomplished, she used her music with skill, and she was wise, her music was played for a good end. She built for grave and innocent purposes on a technique of ingenuity which had been developed in the harem.

The Bulbul was not as Western women. In her beauty she resembled the Persian ladies of the miniatures, whose lustre I had till then thought an artistic convention but could now recognize in her great shining eyes, her wet red lips, her black hair with its white reflections, her dazzling skin. This brightness was like a hard transparent veil varnished on her, wholly protective. Even if someone had touched her, it would not have been she who was touched. Within this protection, she was liquid with generosity. She was continually anxious to give pleasure to her friends, even were they so new and untried as ourselves. If we were in a café and a man passed with a tray of Turkish sweetmeats, her face became tragical till she was sure that she could call him back and give us the chance of tasting them. If we were driving down a street and she saw the first lilies of the valley in a flower shop, she would call on the driver to stop that she might buy us some, with an imperativeness found more usually in selfishness than in altruism. When she had brought us to the café where a famous gipsy musician was singing, she relaxed like a mother who has succeeded in obtaining for her children something she knows they should have. The seasons irked her by the limitations they placed on her generosity: since it was not mid-winter she could not take us up to the villages above Sarajevo for skiing, and since it was not mid-summer she could not open her country house for us. Had one been cruel enough to point out to her that one would have been happier with a million pounds, and that she was not in a position to supply it, she would for a moment or two really have suffered, and even when she realized that she had been teased her good sense would not have been able to prevent her from feeling a slight distress.

Yet there was nothing lax about this woman. Though she lived for pleasure and the dissemination of it, she shone with a chastity as absolute as that radiated by any woman who detested pleasure. She had accepted a mystery. She had realized that to make a field where generosity can fulfil its nature absolutely, without reserve, one must exclude all but one other person, committed to loyalty. That field was marriage. Therefore when she spoke to any man other than her husband she was all to him, mother, sister, friend, nurse, and benefactress, but not a possible mate. She was thus as virginal as any dedicated nun, and that for the sake not of renunciation but of consummation. But her nature was so various that she comprised many opposites. Sometimes she seemed the most idiosyncratic of natures; standing on a balcony high over a street, we looked down on the pavement and saw her walking far below, with a dozen before her and behind her, darkly dressed like herself, and we were able to say at once, 'Look, there is the little Bulbul.' But there were other times when everything she did was so classical, so tried and tested in its validity, that she seemed to have no individuality at all, and to be merely a chalice filled with a rich draught of tradition.

There was, indeed, a great range of human beings to be seen in Sarajevo, all of sorts unknown to us. In Dubrovnik we had visited an antique shop kept by a young man called Hassanovitch, of admirable taste, and my husband had bought me the most beautiful garment I have ever possessed, a ceremonial robe of Persian brocade about a hundred and fifty years old, with little gold trees growing on a background faintly purple as a wine-stain. We bought it in a leisurely way, over several evenings, supported by cups of coffee and slices of Banya Luka cheese, which is rather like

Port Salut, brought in by his little brothers, of which there seemed an inordinate number, all with the acolyte's air of huge quantities of original sin in suspension. He had given us a letter of introduction to his father, the leading antique dealer of Sarajevo, who invited us to his house, a villa up among the high tilted suburbs.

There we sat and enjoyed the crystalline neatness and cleanliness of the prosperous Moslem home, with its divans that run along the wall and take the place of much cumbrous furniture, and its wall decorations of rugs and textiles, which here were gorgeous. We told the father about his son and how much we had admired his shop, and we mentioned too a feature of our visits that had much amused us. Always we had found sitting by the counter a beautiful girl, not the same for more than a few evenings, an English or American or German tourist, who would look at us with the thirsty and wistful eye of a gazelle who intends to come down to the pool and drink as soon as the hippopotami have ceased to muddy the water. The elder Mr Hassanovitch stroked his beard and said in gratified accents, 'And the kitten also catches mice,' and took me to the women's quarters so that I could tell his wife, the mother of his fourteen children. She was an extremely beautiful woman in her middle forties, peace shining from her eyes and kneaded into the texture of her smooth flesh; and she was for me as pathetic as the women of Korchula, who believed that they had earned their happiness because they had passed certain tests of womanhood, and did not realize how fortunate they were in having those tests applied. Like those others, she was unaware that these tests would be irrelevant unless the community felt a need for the functions performed by women, and that infatuation with war or modern industry can make it entirely forgetful of that need.

But our last impression of Mr Hassanovitch was not to be merely of benign domesticity. From the moment of our meeting I had been troubled by a sense of familiarity about his features, and suddenly my husband realized that we had seen his face many times before. When the Archduke Franz Ferdinand and his wife came to the Town Hall of Sarajevo on the morning of June the twenty-eighth, 1914, Mr Hassanovitch was among the guests summoned to meet them for he was already an active Moslem politician, and he is standing to the right of the doorway in a photograph which has often been reproduced, showing the doomed pair going out to their death. That day must have been a blow to him. The contention of our Jewish friends that the Austrians had pampered the Moslems at the expense of the Christians, and had made them zealous supporters, is borne out by the constitution of the assembly shown by that photograph; and other photographs taken that morning show that when Princip was arrested the men in the crowd who are throwing themselves on him are all wearing the fez.

But I think he would have preferred it to the day he had just endured. The friends accompanying us, who knew him well, spoke to him of the visit of the Turkish Ministers, and he answered them with words that were blankly formal, a splendid bandage of his pain and their possible embarrassment at having provoked it. It was surprising that the visit had evidently been as keen a disappointment to such an expert and informed person as it was to the people in the street. Yet I suppose an Irish-American politician would suffer deep pain if time should bring to power in Eire a president who wanted to break with the past and sent an emissary to the States to beg that the old Catholic nationalism should be forgotten; and that he would even shut his eyes to the possibility that it might happen. The analogy was close enough, for here, just as in an Irish ward in an American town, one was aware that the actions and reactions of history had produced a formidable amount of politics. One could feel them operating below the surface like a still in a basement.

But history takes different people differently, even the same history. The Sarajevo market is held on Wednesdays, at the centre of the town near the bazaar, in a straggling open space surrounded by little shops, most of them Moslem pastrycooks', specializing in great cartwheel tarts stuffed with spinach or minced meat. The country folk come in by driblets, beginning as soon as it is fully light, and going on till nine or ten or eleven, for some must walk several hours from their homes: more and more pigeons take refuge on the roofs of the two little kiosks in the market-place. There are sections in the market allotted to various kinds of goods: here there is grain, there wool, more people than one would expect are selling scales, and there are stalls that gratify a medieval appetite for dried fish and meat, which are sold in stinking and sinewy lengths. At one end of the market are stuffs and embroideries which are chiefly horrible machine-made copies of the local needle-work. The Moslem women are always thickest here, but elsewhere you see as many Christians as Moslems, and perhaps more; and these Christians are nearly all of a heroic kind.

The finest are the men, who wear crimson wool scarfs tied round their heads and round their throats. This means that they have come from villages high in the mountains, where the wind blows down from the snows; and sometimes the scarf serves a double purpose, for in many such villages a kind of goitre is endemic. These men count themselves as descendants of the Haiduks, the Christians who after the Ottoman conquest took refuge in the highlands, and came down to the valleys every year on St. George's Day, because by then the trees were green enough to give them cover, and they could harry the Turks by brigandage. They reckon that man can achieve the highest by following the path laid down in the Old Testament. I cannot imagine why Victorian travellers in these regions used to express contempt for the rayas, or Christian peasants, whom they encountered. Any one of these Bosnians could have made a single mouthful of a Victorian traveller, green umbrella and all. They are extremely tall and sinewy, and walk with a rhythmic stride which is not without knowledge of its own grace and power. Their darkness flashes and their cheekbones are high and their moustaches are long over fierce lips. They wear dark homespun jackets, often heavily braided, coloured belts, often crimson like their headgear, the Bosnian breeches that bag between the thighs and outline the hip and flank, and shoes made of leather thongs with upcurving points at the toes. They seem to clang with belligerence as if they wore armour. In every way, I hear, they are formidable. Their women have to wait on them while they eat, must take sound beatings every now and again, work till they drop, even while child-bearing, and walk while their master rides.

Yet, I wonder. Dear God, is nothing ever what it seems? The women of whom this tale is told, and according to all reliable testimony truly told, do not look in the least oppressed. They are handsome and sinewy like their men; but not such handsome women as the men are handsome men. A sheep-breeder of great experience once told me that in no species and variety that he knew were the male and female of equal value in their maleness and femaleness. Where the males were truly male, the females were not so remarkably female, and where the females were truly females the males were not virile. Constantly his theory is confirmed here. The women look heroes rather than heroines, they are raw-boned and their beauty is blocked out too roughly. But I will eat my hat if these women were not free in the spirit. They passed the chief tests I knew. First, they looked happy when they had lost their youth. Here, as in all Balkan markets, there were far more elderly women than girls; and there is one corner of it which is reserved for a line of women all past middle life, who stand on the kerb hawking Bosnian breeches that they have made from their own homespun, and exchange the gossip of their various villages. Among them I did not see any woman whose face was marked by hunger or regret. All looked as if they had known a great deal of pain and hardship, but their experience had led none of them to doubt whether it is worth while to live.

It was quite evident as we watched them that these women had been able to gratify their essential desires. I do not mean simply that they looked as if they had been well mated. Many Latin women who have been married at sixteen and have had numbers of children look swollen and tallowy with frustration. Like all other material experiences, sex has no value other than what the spirit assesses; and the spirit is obstinately influenced in its calculation by its preference for freedom. In some sense these women had never been enslaved. They had that mark of freedom, they had wit. This was not mere guffawing and jeering. These were not bumpkins, they could be seen now and then engaging in the prettiest passages of formality. We watched one of the few young women at the market seek out two of her elders: she raised her smooth face to their old lips and they kissed her on the cheek, she bent down and kissed their hands. It could not have been more graciously done at Versailles; and their wit was of the same pointed, noble kind.

We followed at the skirts of one who was evidently the Voltaire of this world. She was almost a giantess; her greyish red hair straggled about her ears in that untidiness which is dearer than any order, since it shows an infatuated interest in the universe which cannot spare one second for the mere mechanics of existence, and it was tied up in a clean white clout under a shawl passed under her chin and knotted on the top of her head. She wore a green velvet jacket over a dark homespun dress and coarse white linen sleeves, all clean but wild, and strode like a man up and down the market, halting every now and then, when some sight struck her as irresistibly comic. We could see the impact of the jest on her face, breaking its stolidity, as a cast stone shatters the surface of water. The wide mouth gaped in laughter, showing a single tooth. Then a ferment worked in her eyes. She would turn and go to the lower end of the market, and she would put her version of what had amused her to every knot of women she met as she passed to the upper end. I cursed myself because I could not understand one word of what she said. But this much I could hear: each time she made her joke it sounded more pointed, more compact, and drew more laughter. When she came to the upper end of the market and her audience was exhausted, a blankness fell on her and she ranged the stalls restlessly till she found another occasion for her wit.

This was not just a white blackbird. She was distinguished not because she was witty but by the degree of her wit. Later on we found a doorway in a street near by where the women who had sold all their goods lounged and waited for a motor bus. We lounged beside them, looking into the distance as if the expectation of a friend made us deaf; and our ears recorded the authentic pattern, still recognizable although the words could not be understood, of witty talk. These people could pass what the French consider the test of a civilized society: they could practise the art of general conversation. Voice dovetailed into voice without impertinent interruption; there was light and shade, sober judgment was corrected by mocking criticism, and another sober judgment established, and every now and then the cards were swept off the table by a gust of laughter, and the game started afresh.

None of these women could read. When a boy passed by carrying an advertisement of Batya's shoes they had to ask a man they knew to read it for them. They did not suffer any great deprivation thereby. Any writer worth his salt knows that only a small proportion of literature does more than partly compensate people for the damage they have suffered by learning to read. These women were their own artists, and had done well with their material. The folk-songs of the country speak, I believe, of a general perception that is subtle and poetic, and one had only to watch any group carefully for it to declare itself. I kept my eyes for some time on two elderly women who had been intercepted on their way to this club in the doorway by a tall old man, who in his day must have been magnificent even in this land of magnificent men. Waving a staff as if it were a sceptre, he was telling them a dramatic story, and because he was absorbed in his own story the women were not troubling to disguise their expressions. There was something a shade too self-gratulatory in his handsomeness; no doubt he had been the *coq du village* in his day. In their smiles that knowledge glinted, but not too harshly. They had known him all their lives: they knew that thirty years ago he had not been so brave as he said he would be in the affair with the gendarmes at the ford, but they knew that later he had been much braver than he need have been when he faced the Turks in the ruined fortress, they remembered him when the good seasons had made him rich and when the snows and winds had made him poor. They had heard the gossip at the village well pronounce him right on this and wrong over that. They judged him with mercy and justice, which is the sign of a free spirit, and when his story was finished broke into the right laughter, and flattered him by smiling at him as if they were all three young again.

I suspect that women such as these are not truly slaves, but have found a fraudulent method of persuading men to give them support and leave them their spiritual freedom. It is certain that men suffer from a certain timidity, a liability to discouragement which makes them reluctant to go on doing anything once it has been proved that women can do it as well. This was most painfully illustrated during the slump in both Europe and America, where wives found to their amazement that if they found jobs when their husbands lost theirs and took on the burden of keeping the family, they were in no luck at all. For their husbands became either their frenzied enemies or relapsed into an infantile state of dependence and never worked again. If women pretend that they are inferior to men and cannot do their work, and abase themselves by picturesque symbolic rites, such as giving men their food first and waiting on them while they eat, men will go on working and developing their powers to the utmost, and will not bother to interfere with what women are saying and thinking with their admittedly inferior powers.

It is an enormous risk to take. It makes marriage a gamble, since these symbols of abasement always include an abnegation of economic and civil rights, and while a genial husband takes no advantage of them—and that is to say the vast majority of husbands—a malign man will exploit them with the rapacity of the grave. It would also be a futile bargain to make in the modern industrialized world, for it can hold good only where there are no other factors except the equality of women threatening the self-confidence of men. In our own Western civilization man is devitalized by the insecurity of employment and its artificial nature, so he cannot be restored to primitive power by the withdrawal of female rivalry and the woman would not get any reward for her sacrifice. There is in effect no second party to the contract. In the West, moreover, the gambling risks of marriage admit of a greater ruin. A man who is tied to one village and cannot leave his wife without leaving his land is not so dangerous a husband as a man who can step on a train and find employment in another town. But the greatest objection to this artificial abjection is that it is a conscious fraud on the part of women, and life will never be easy until human beings can be honest with one another. Still, in this world of compromises, honour is due to one so far successful that it produces these grimly happy heroes, these women who stride and laugh, obeying the instructions of their own nature and not masculine prescription.

Sarajevo V

One morning we walked down to the river, a brightening day shining down from the skies and up from puddles. A Moslem boy sold us an armful of wet lilac, a pigeon flew up from a bath in a puddle, its wings dispersing watery diamonds. 'Now it is the spring,' said Constantine, 'I think we shall have good weather tomorrow for our trip to Ilidzhe, and better weather the day after for our trip to Yaitse. Yes, I think it will be well. All will be very well.' When he is pleased with his country he walks processionally, like an expectant mother, with his stomach well forward. 'But see what we told you the other night,' he said as we came to the embankment and saw the Town Hall. 'Under the Austrians all was for the Moslems. Look at this building, it is as Moslem as a mosque, yet always since the Turks were driven out of Bosnia the Christians have been two-thirds of the population. So did the Catholic Habsburgs deny their faith.'

Actually it is the Moslems who have most reason to complain of this Town Hall, for their architecture in Sarajevo is exquisite in its restraint and amiability, and even in modern times has been true to that tradition. But this was designed by an Austrian architect, and it is stuffed with beer and sausages down to its toes. It is harshly particoloured and has a lumpish two-storied loggia with crudely fretted arches, and it has little round windows all over it which suggest that it is rich beyond the dreams of avarice in lavatories, and its highly ornamented cornices are Oriental in a pejorative sense. The minaret of the mosque beside it has the air of a cat that watches a dog making a fool of itself.

Within, however, it is very agreeable, and remarkably full of light; and in an office high up we found a tourist bureau, conducted with passion by a man in the beginnings of middle life, a great lover of his city. He dealt us out photographs of it for some time, pausing to gloat over them, but stopped when Constantine said, 'Show these English the room where they held the reception which was the last thing the Archduke Franz Ferdinand and the Archduchess Sophie saw of their fellow-men.' The head of the tourist bureau bowed as if he had received a compliment and led us out into the central lobby, where a young man in a fez, a woman in black bloomers, and an old man and woman undistinguishable from any needy and respectable pair in South Kensington shuffled up the great staircase, while a young man quite like an Englishman save that

331

he was carrying a gusla ran down it. We went into the Council Chamber, not unsuccessful in its effort at Moslem pomp. 'All is Moslem here,' said the head of the tourist bureau, 'and even now that we are Yugoslavian the mayor is always a Moslem, and that is right. Perhaps it helps us by conciliating the Moslems, but even if it did not we ought to do it. For no matter how many Christians we may be here, and no matter what we make of the city—and we are doing wonderful things with it—the genius that formed it in the first place was Moslem, and again Moslem, and again Moslem.'

But the three reception rooms were as libellous as the exterior. They were pedantically yet monstrously decorated in imitation of certain famous buildings of Constantinople, raising domes like gilded honeycomb tripe, pressing down between the vaults polychrome stumps like vast inverted Roman candles. That this was the copy of something gorgeous could be seen; it could also be seen that the copyist had been by blood incapable of comprehending that gorgeousness. Punch-drunk from this architectural assault I lowered my eyes, and the world seemed to reel. And here, it appeared, the world had once actually reeled.

'It was just over here that I stood with my father,' said the head of the tourist bureau. 'My father had been downstairs in the hall among those who received the Archduke and Archduchess, and had seen the Archduke come in, red and choking with rage. Just a little way along the embankment a young man, Chabrinovitch, had thrown a bomb at him and had wounded his aide-de-camp. So when the poor Mayor began to read his address of welcome he shouted out in a thin alto, 'That's all a lot of rot. I come here to pay you a visit, and you throw bombs at me. It's an outrage.' Then the Archduchess spoke to him softly, and he calmed down and said, 'Oh, well, you can go on.' But at the end of the speech there was another scene, because the Archduke had not got his speech, and for a moment the secretary who had it could not be found. Then when it was brought to him he was like a madman, because the manuscript was all spattered with the aide-de-camp's blood.

'But he read the speech, and then came up here with the Archduchess, into this room. My father followed, in such a state of astonishment that he walked over and took my hand and stood beside me, squeezing it very tightly. We all could not take our eyes off the Archduke, but not as you look at the main person in a court spectacle. We could not think of him as a royalty at all, he was so incredibly strange. He was striding quite grotesquely, he was lifting his legs as high as if he were doing the goosestep. I suppose he was trying to show that he was not afraid.

'I tell you, it was not at all like a reception. He was talking with the Military Governor, General Potiorek, jeering at him and taunting him with his failure to preserve order. And we were all silent, not because we were impressed by him, for he was not at all our Bosnian idea of a hero. But we all felt awkward because we knew that when he went out he would certainly be killed. No, it was not a matter of being told. But we knew how the people felt about him and the Austrians, and we knew that if one man had thrown a bomb and failed, another man would throw another bomb and another after that if he should fail. I tell you it gave a very strange feeling to the assembly. Then I remember he went out on the balcony—so—and looked out over Sarajevo. Yes, he stood just where you are standing, and he too put his arm on the balustrade.'

Before the balcony the town rises on the other side of the river, in a gentle slope. Stout urban buildings stand among tall poplars, and above them white villas stand among orchards, and higher still the white cylindrical tombs of the Moslems stick askew in the rough grass like darts impaled on the board. Then fir-woods and bare bluffs meet the skyline. Under Franz Ferdinand's eye the scene must have looked its most enchanting blend of town and country, for though it was June there had been heavy restoring rains. But it is not right to assume that the sight gave him pleasure. He was essentially a Habsburg, that is to say, his blood made him turn always from the natural to the artificial, even when this was more terrifying than anything primitive could be; and this landscape showed him on its heights nature unsubdued and on its slopes nature accepted and extolled. Perhaps Franz Ferdinand felt a patriotic glow at the sight of the immense brewery in the foreground, which was built by the Austrians to supply the needs of their garrison and functionaries. These breweries, which are to be found here and there in Bosnia, throw a light on the aggressive nature of Austrian foreign policy and its sordid consequences. They were founded while this was still Turkish, by speculators whose friends in the Government were aware of Austria's plans for occupation and annexation. They also have their significance in their affront to local resources. It is quite unnecessary to drink beer here, as there is an abundance of cheap and good wine. But what was Austrian was good and what was Slav was bad.

It is unjust to say that Franz Ferdinand had no contact with nature. The room behind him was full of people who were watching him with the impersonal awe evoked by anybody who is about to die; but it may be imagined also as crammed, how closely can be judged only by those who have decided how many angels can dance

on the point of a needle, by the ghosts of the innumerable birds and
beasts who had fallen to his gun. He was a superb shot, and that is
certainly a fine thing for a man to be, proof that he is a good animal,
quick in eye and hand and hardy under weather. But of his gift
Franz Ferdinand made a murderous use. He liked to kill and kill
and kill, unlike men who shoot to get food or who have kept in touch
with the primitive life in which the original purpose of shooting is
remembered. Prodigious figures are given of the game that fell to
the double-barrelled Mannlicher rifles which were specially made
for him. At a boar hunt given by Kaiser Wilhelm sixty boars were
let out, and Franz Ferdinand had the first stand: fifty-nine fell dead,
the sixtieth limped by on three legs. At a Czech castle in one day's
sport he bagged two thousand one hundred and fifty pieces of small
game. Not long before his death he expressed satisfaction because
he had killed his three thousandth stag.

This capacity for butchery he used to express the hatred which
he felt for nearly all the world, which, indeed, it is safe to say, he
bore against the whole world, except his wife and his two children.
He had that sense of being betrayed by life itself which comes to
people who wrestle through long years with a chronic and dangerous
malady; it is strange that both King Alexander of Yugoslavia
and he had fought for half their days against tuberculosis. But
Franz Ferdinand had been embittered by his environment, as
Alexander was not. The indiscipline and brutality of the officials
who controlled the Habsburg court had been specially directed
towards him. It happened that for some years it looked as if Franz
Ferdinand would not recover from his illness, and during the whole
of this time the Department of the Lord High Steward, believing
that he would soon be dead, cut down his expenses to the quick in
order to get the praises of the Emperor Franz Josef for economy.
The poor wretch, penniless in spite of the great art collections Franz
Ferdinand had inherited, was grudged the most modest allowance,
and even his doctor was underpaid and insulted. This maltreatment
had ended when it became obvious that he was going to live, but by
that time his mind was set in a mould of hatred and resentment,
and though he could not shoot his enemies he found some relief in
shooting, it did not matter what.

Franz Ferdinand knew no shame in his exercise of this too simple
mechanism. He was ungracious as only a man can be who has never
conceived the idea of graciousness. There was, for example, his dispute with Count Henkel Donnersmark, the German nobleman who
was a wild young diplomat in Paris before the Franco-Prussian War,
returned there to negotiate the terms of the indemnity, astonished

the world by marrying the cocotte La Païva, and changed into a sober and far-seeing industrialist on the grand scale. This elderly and distinguished person had bought an estate in Silesia, and had made it pay for itself by selling the full-grown timber and replacing it by a careful scheme of reafforestation. This estate he leased to the Archduke at a rent calculated on the assumption that so much game existed on the property and would do so much damage to the saplings. As the Archduke enormously increased the stock of game, and practically no new trees could grow to maturity, the Count very reasonably raised the rent. This the Archduke, who had the wholly whimsical attitude to money often found in royal personages, conceived to be a senseless piece of greed. He gave notice to terminate his lease and decided to punish the landlord by ruining the estate as a sporting property. The remainder of his tenancy he spent in organizing battues which drove all the beasts of the field up to his guns to be slaughtered in such numbers that slaughter lost its meaning, that the boundary between living and dying became obscured, that dazed men forgot that they were killing. But he and his staff found that the forces of life outnumbered them, so he let part of the shoot to a Viennese manufacturer, a man with whom he could not have brought himself to have relations for any other reason, on condition that he pursue the same crusade of extermination. That, however, was still not enough, and the employees of the hunt were set to kill off what was left of the game by any means, abandoning all sporting restraints. Because the forest still twitched with life, because here and there the fern was trodden down and branches stirred by survivors of the massacre, the Archduke suffered several attacks of rage which disgusted all witnesses, being violent as vomiting or colic.

It may be conceived therefore that, even as the game which St Julian Hospitaller had killed as a cruel hunter appeared before him on the night when he was going to accomplish his destiny and become the murderer of his father and mother, so the half million beasts which had fallen to Franz Ferdinand's gun according to his own calculations were present that day in the reception hall at Sarajevo. One can conceive the space of this room stuffed all the way up to the crimson and gold vaults and stalactites with the furred and feathered ghosts, set close, because there were so many of them: stags with the air between their antlers stuffed with woodcock, quail, pheasant, partridge, capercailzie, and the like; boars standing bristling flank to flank, the breadth under their broad bellies packed with layer upon layer of hares and rabbits. Their animal eyes, clear and dark as water, would brightly watch the approach of their slayer to an end that exactly resembled their own. For Franz Ferdinand's greatness as a hunter had depended not only on his pre-eminence as a shot, but on his power of organizing battues. He was specially proud of an improvement he had made in the hunting of hare: his beaters, placed in a pear-shaped formation, drove all the hares towards him so that he was able without effort to exceed the bag of all other guns. Not a beast that fell to him in these battues could have escaped by its own strength or cunning, even if it had been a genius among its kind. The earth and sky were narrowed for it by the beaters to just one spot, the spot where it must die; and so it was with this man. If by some miracle he had been able to turn round and address the people in the room behind him not with his usual aggressiveness and angularity but in terms which would have made him acceptable to them as a suffering fellow-creature, still they could not have saved him. If by some miracle his slow-working and clumsy mind could have become swift and subtle, it could not have shown him a safe road out of Sarajevo. Long ago he himself, and the blood which was in his veins, had placed at their posts the beaters who should drive him down through a narrowing world to the spot where Princip's bullet would find him.

Through Franz Ferdinand's mother, the hollow-eyed Annunziata, he was the grandson of King Bomba of the Sicilies, one of the worst of the Bourbons, an idiot despot who conducted a massacre of his subjects after 1848, and, on being expelled from Naples, retired into a fortress and lived the life of a medieval tyrant right on until the end of the fifties. This ancestry had given Franz Ferdinand tuberculosis, obstinacy, bigotry, a habit of suspicion, hatred of democracy, and an itch for aggression, which, combined with the Habsburg narrowness and indiscipline, made him a human being who could not have hoped to survive had he not been royal. When he went to Egypt to spend the winter for the sake of his lungs it appeared to him necessary, and nobody who knew him would have expected anything else, to insult the Austrian Ambassador. By the time he had passed through his twenties he had made an army of personal enemies, which he constantly increased by his intemperate and uninstructed political hatreds. He hated Hungary, the name of Kossuth made him spit with rage. When receiving a deputation of Slovaks, though they were not a people whom he would naturally have taken into his confidence, he said of the Hungarians, 'It was an act of bad taste on the part of these gentlemen ever to have come to Europe,' which must remain an ace in the history of royal indiscretion.

He had a dream of replacing the Dual Monarchy by a Triune

Monarchy, in which the German and Czech crown lands should form the first part, Hungary the second, and the South Slav group—Croatia, Dalmatia, Bosnia, and Herzegovina—the third. This would have pleased the Croats, and the Croats alone. Most German Austrians would have been infuriated at having to combine with the Czechs and to see the South Slavs treated as their equals; Hungary would have been enraged at losing her power over the South Slavs; and the non-Catholic South Slavs would have justly feared being made the object of Catholic propaganda and would have resented being cut off from their natural ambition of union with the Serbs of Serbia. By this scheme, therefore, he made a host of enemies; and though he came in time to abandon it he could not quickly turn these enemies into friends by making public his change of mind. As he was the heir to the throne, he could announce his policy only by the slow method of communicating it to private individuals.

He abandoned his plan of the Triune Monarchy, moreover, for reasons too delicate to be freely discussed. In 1889, when he was thirty-three, he had paid some duty calls on the Czech home of his cousins, the Archduke Frederick and the Archduchess Isabella, to see if he found one of their many daughters acceptable as his bride. Instead he fell in love with the Archduchess's lady-in-waiting, Sophie Chotek, a woman of thirty-two, noble but destitute. He insisted on marrying her in spite of the agonized objection of the Emperor Franz Josef, who pointed out to him that, according to the Habsburg House Law, the secret law of the Monarchy, a woman of such low birth could not come to the throne as consort of the Emperor.

It was not a question of permission that could be bestowed or withheld, but of a rigid legal fact. If Franz Ferdinand was to marry Sophie Chotek at all he must do it morganatically, and must renounce all rights of succession for the yet unborn children of their marriage; he could no more marry her any other way than a man with a living and undivorced wife can marry a second woman, though the infringement here was of an unpublished dynastic regulation instead of the published law. But some mitigation of this severe judgment came from an unexpected quarter. The younger Kossuth declared that, according to Hungarian law, when the Archduke ascended the throne his wife, no matter what her origin, became Queen of Hungary, and his children must enjoy the full rights of succession. This weakened the vehemence of Franz Ferdinand's loathing for Hungary, though not for individual Hungarians. He still meant to revise the constitutional machinery of the Dual

Monarchy, but he no longer wished to punish the Hungarians quite so harshly as to take away from them the Croats and Slovaks. But this was not a consideration he could publicly name. Nor, for diplomatic reasons, could he confess later that he was becoming more and more fearful of the growing strength of Serbia, and was apprehensive lest a union of South Slav provinces should tempt her ambition and provide her with a unified ally. So, by his promulgation of an unpopular policy, and his inability to announce his abandonment of it, the first beaters were put down to the battue.

His marriage set others at their post. Franz Ferdinand had far too dull a mind to appreciate the need for consistency. That was once visibly demonstrated in relation to his passion for collecting antiques, which he bought eagerly and without discrimination. When he paid a visit to a country church the simple priest boasted to him of a good bargain he had driven with a Jew dealer, who had given him a brand-new altar in exchange for his shabby old one. Immediately Franz Ferdinand sat down and wrote to the Bishop of the diocese asking him to give his clergy an order not to part with Church property. But he was quite amazed when later this order prevented him from carrying out the sacrilegious purchase of a tombstone which he wished to put in his private chapel. He showed a like inconsistency in regard to his marriage. His whole life was based on the privileges that were given to the members of the Habsburg family because the Habsburgs had been preserved in a certain state of genealogical purity which Austria had agreed to consider valuable. He could not understand that, as this purity was the justification of those privileges, they could not be extended to people in whom the Habsburg blood had been polluted. He took it as a personal insult, a bitter, causeless hurt, that his wife and his children should not be given royal honours.

Nor did his inconsistencies end there. Himself a typical product of Habsburg indiscipline, he nevertheless made no allowances when his relatives and the officials of the court reacted to his marriage with a like indiscipline. He had here, indeed, a legitimate object for hatred, in a character as strange as his own. Franz Josef's Chamberlain, Prince Montenuovo, was one of the strangest figures in Europe of our time; a character that Shakespeare decided at the last moment not to use in *King Lear* or *Othello*, and laid by so carelessly that it fell out of art into life. He was a man of exquisite taste and æsthetic courage, who protected the artists of Vienna against the apathy of the court and the imprudence of the bourgeoisie. The Vienna Philharmonic under Mahler was his special pride and care. But he was the son of one of the bastard sons mothered by the wretched

Marie Louise, when, unsustained by the opinion of historians yet unborn that she was and should have been perfectly happy in her forced marriage with Napoleon, she took refuge in the arms of Baron Neipperg. To be the bastard son of a race which was so great that it could make bastardy as noble as legitimacy, but which was great only because its legitimacy was untainted with bastardy, confused this imaginative man with a passionate and poetic and malignant madness. He watched over the rules of Habsburg ceremonial as over a case of poisons which he believed to compose the elixir of life if they were combined in the correct proportions. 'And now for the strychnine,' he must have said, when it became his duty to devise the adjustments made necessary by the presence at the court of a morganatic wife to the heir of the throne. Countess Sophie was excluded altogether from most intimate functions of the Austrian court; she could not accompany her husband to the family receptions or parties given for foreign royalties, or even to the most exclusive kinds of court balls; at the semi-public kind of court balls which she was allowed to attend, her husband had to head the procession with an Archduchess on his arm, while she was forced to walk at the very end, behind the youngest princess. The Emperor did what he could to mitigate the situation by creating her the Duchess of Hohenberg: but the obsessed Montenuovo hovered over her, striving to exacerbate every possible humiliation, never happier than when he could hold her back from entering a court carriage or cutting down to the minimum the salutes and attendants called for by any state occasion.

It is possible that had Franz Ferdinand been a different kind of man he might have evoked a sympathy that would have consoled him and his wife for these hardships: but all his ways were repellent. When his brother, Ferdinand Charles, a gentle soul with literary tastes, doomed to an early death from consumption, fell in love with a woman not of royal rank, Franz Ferdinand was the first to oppose the misalliance and made violent scenes with the invalid. When it was pointed out that he had married for love he answered angrily that there could be no comparison between the two cases, because Sophie Chotek was an aristocrat and his brother's wife was the daughter of a university professor. Such lack of humour, which amounts to a lack of humours in the Elizabethan sense, isolated him from all friends; so instead he created partisans. He had been given, for his Viennese home, the superb palace and park known as the Belvedere, which had been built by Prince Eugène of Savoy. He now made it the centre of what the historian Tschuppik has called a shadow government. He set up a military Chancellery of his own; and presently the

Emperor Franz Josef, who always treated his nephew with an even remarkable degree of tenderness and forbearance, though not with tact, resigned to this his control over the army. But the Chancellery dealt with much more than military matters. Franz Ferdinand attracted every able man in Austria who had been ignored or rejected by the court of Franz Josef, and thanks to the stupidity and bad manners of that court these were not contemptible in quality or inconsiderable in numbers. Helped by Franz Ferdinand to form a running point-by-point opposition to the mild policy of Franz Josef, these men carried into effect his faith in half measures; and they drafted a programme for him which was indiscreetly spoken of as a scheme of reform designed for preventing the dissolution of the Austro-Hungarian Empire, to be applied as soon as Franz Josef was dead and Franz Ferdinand had ascended the throne.

This way of life set still more beaters around him. It automatically roused the animosity of all at the court of Franz Josef, and many of his own partisans became his overt or covert enemies. He became day by day less lovable. His knowledge that he could not leave the royal path of his future to his children made him fanatically mean and grasping, and his manner became more and more overbearing and brutal. He roused in small men small resentments, and, in the minds of the really able men, large distrust. They realized that though he was shrewd enough to see that the Austro-Hungarian Empire was falling to pieces when most of his kind were wholly blind to its decay, he was fundamentally stupid and cruel and saw his problem as merely that of selecting the proper objects for tyranny. Some of them feared a resort to medieval oppression; some feared the damage done to specific interests, particularly in Hungary, which was bound to follow his resettlement of the Empire. Such fears must have gained in intensity when it became evident that Kaiser Wilhelm of Germany was taking more and more interest in Franz Ferdinand, and was visiting him at his country homes and holding long conversations with him on important matters. The last visit of this kind had occurred a fortnight before the Archduke had come to Sarajevo. There is a rumour that on that occasion the Kaiser laid before Franz Ferdinand a plan for remaking the map of Europe. The Austro-Hungarian and German Empires were to be friends, and Franz Ferdinand's eldest son was to become King of a new Poland stretching from the Baltic to the Black Sea, while the second son became King of Bohemia, Hungary, Croatia, and Serbia, and Franz Ferdinand's official heir, his nephew Charles, should be left as King of German Austria. It is certain that Kaiser Wilhelm must, at that moment, have had many important things on his mind, and that it is hardly likely that he would have paid such a visit unless he had something grave to say. It is definitely known that on this occasion Franz Ferdinand expressed bitter hostility to the Hungarian aristocracy. It is also known that these remarks were repeated at the time by the Kaiser to a third person.

The manners of Franz Ferdinand did worse for him than make him enemies. They made him the gangster friends that may become enemies at any moment, with the deadly weapon of a friend's close knowledge. Franz Ferdinand's plainest sign of intelligence was his capacity for recognizing a certain type of unscrupulous ability. He had discovered Aehrenthal, the clever trickster who as Austrian Minister had managed to convert the provisional occupation of Bosnia and Herzegovina into annexation behind the backs of the other great powers in 1907. Since Aehrenthal on his deathbed had recommended Berchtold to succeed him, that incompetent war-monger might also be counted as one of the works of Franz Ferdinand. But an even greater favourite of his was Conrad von Hötzendorf, whom he made the Chief of General Staff. This creature, who was without sense or bowels, fancied himself not only as a great soldier but as a statesman, and would have directed the foreign policy of his country had he been allowed. He was obsessed by the need of preserving the Austro-Hungarian Empire by an offensive against Serbia. 'Lest all our predestined foes, having perfected their armaments should deliver a blow against Austria-Hungary,' he wrote in a memorandum he presented to Franz Josef in 1907 which was followed by many like it, 'we must take the first opportunity of settling accounts with our most vulnerable enemy.' In the intervening seven years this obsession flamed up into a mania. In 1911 Franz Josef, with the definite statements that 'my policy is pacific' and that he would permit no question of an offensive war, obtained Aehrenthal's consent and dismissed Conrad from his post, making him an Inspector-general of the Army. But Franz Ferdinand still stood by him, and so did all the partisans of the Belvedere, who numbered enough industrialists, bankers, journalists, and politicians to make plain the decadence of pre-war Vienna. Berchtold was so much impressed by Conrad that in 1912 he was once more appointed Chief of General Staff. He was preaching the same gospel. 'The way out of our difficulties,' he wrote to Berchtold, 'is to lay Serbia low without fear of consequences.'

But at this time Franz Ferdinand's convictions took a new turn. He was becoming more and more subject to the influence of the German Kaiser, and Germany had no desire at that time for war, particularly with a Balkan pretext. He admired the Germans and thought they probably knew their business. This infuriated Conrad, who thought that Franz Ferdinand ought to persuade Germany to support Austria, so that he could feel confident even if their offensive war against Serbia spread into a general conflagration, which shows that he knew what he was doing. But in 1913 Berchtold had to tell Conrad, 'The Archduke Franz Ferdinand is absolutely against war.' At this Conrad became more and more desperate. His influence over Berchtold had been sufficient to make him refuse to see the Prime Minister of Serbia when he offered to come to Vienna to negotiate a treaty with Austria, covering all possible points of dispute. He persuaded Berchtold, moreover, to withhold all knowledge of this pacific offer from either Franz Josef or Franz Ferdinand. This is the great criminal act which gives us the right to curse Berchtold and Conrad as the true instigators of the World War. But Conrad was no less crude when in 1913 he used a trifling incident on the Dalmatian coast to attempt to get the Emperor Franz Josef to mobilize against Serbia and Montenegro. This coercion Franz Josef, with a firmness remarkable in a man of eighty-seven, quietly resisted, even though Berchtold supported Conrad, and this time Franz Ferdinand was in agreement with the old man.

Shortly after this another incident lowered Conrad's stock still further. Colonel Redl, the Chief of General Staff to the Prague Corps, who had been head of the Austrian espionage service, was found to be a spy in the pay of Russia. He was a homosexual, and had fallen into the hands of blackmailers. He was handed a loaded revolver by a brother officer and left alone to commit suicide. This caused Franz Ferdinand to fly into one of his terrible attacks of rage against Conrad, who had been responsible both for Redl's appointment to the espionage department and for the manner of his death. He was incensed that a homosexual should have been given such a position partly for moral reasons, and partly because of the special liability of such men to blackmail; and it offended his religious convictions that any man should have been forced to commit suicide. This last was hardly a fair charge to bring against Conrad, since the loaded revolver was an established Army convention in the case of shameful offences. But thenceforward the two men were enemies.

There was no doubt about this after the autumn of 1913. At the Army manoeuvres in Bohemia Franz Ferdinand grossly insulted and humiliated his former friend, but refused to accept his resignation. He, however, made it clear that the only reason for the refusal was fear of a bad effect on the public mind. In June

1914 Conrad was eating his heart out in disappointment, bearing a private and public grudge against the man who had disgraced him and who would not engage in the war against Serbia which he himself believed necessary for his country's salvation.

It must be realized that he was a very relentless man. He himself has told of a conversation he had with Berchtold about the unhappy German prince, William of Wied, who was sent to be King of Albania. 'Let us hope there will be no hitch,' said Berchtold. 'But what shall we do if there is?' 'Nothing at all,' said Conrad. 'But what if the prince is assassinated?' asked Berchtold. 'Even then we can do nothing,' said Conrad. 'Somebody else must take the throne in his place. Anybody will suit us as long as he is not under foreign influence.' The conversation is the more grievous when it is understood that they had just refused William of Wied's very reasonable request that he might live on a yacht rather than lodge among his reluctant subjects.

Such enemies surrounded Franz Ferdinand; but it cannot be laid at their door that he had come to Sarajevo on June the twenty-eighth, 1914. This was a day of some personal significance to him. On that date in 1900 he had gone to the Hofburg in the presence of the Emperor and the whole court, and all holders of office, and had, in choking tones, taken the oath to renounce the royal rights of his unborn children. But it was also a day of immense significance for the South Slav people. It is the feast-day of St. Vitus, who is one of those saints who are lucky to find a place in the Christian calendar, since they started life as pagan deities; he was originally Vidd, a Finnish-Ugric deity. It is also the anniversary of the battle of Kossovo, where, five centuries before, the Serbs had lost their empire to the Turk. It had been a day of holy mourning for the Serbian people within the Serbian kingdom and the Austrian Empire, when they had confronted their disgrace and vowed to redeem it, until the year 1912, when Serbia's victory over the Turks at Kumanovo wiped it out. But, since 1913 had still been a time of war, the St. Vitus's Day of 1914 was the first anniversary which might have been celebrated by the Serbs in joy and pride. Franz Ferdinand must have been well aware that he was known as an enemy of Serbia. He must have known that if he went to Bosnia and conducted manoeuvres on the Serbian frontier just before St. Vitus's Day and on the actual anniversary paid a state visit to Sarajevo, he would be understood to be mocking the South Slav world, to be telling them that though the Serbs might have freed themselves from the Turks there were still many Slavs under the Austrian's yoke.

To pay that visit was an act so suicidal that one fumbles the pages of the history books to find if there is not some explanation of his going, if he was not subject to some compulsion. But if ever a man went anywhere of his own free will, Franz Ferdinand went so to Sarajevo. He himself ordered the manœuvres and decided to attend them. The Emperor Franz Josef, in the presence of witnesses, told him that he need not go unless he wished. Yet it appears inconceivable that he should not have known that the whole of Bosnia was seething with revolt, and that almost every schoolboy and student in the province was a member of some revolutionary society. Even if the extraordinary isolation that afflicts royal personages had previously prevented him from sharing this common knowledge, steps were taken to remove his ignorance. But here his temperament intervened on behalf of his own death. The Serbian Government—which by this single act acquitted itself of all moral blame for the assassination—sent its Minister in Vienna to warn Bilinski, the Joint Finance Minister, who was responsible for the civil administration of Bosnia and Herzegovina, that the proposed visit of Franz Ferdinand would enrage many Slavs on both sides of the frontier and might cause consequences which neither Government could control. But Bilinski was an Austrian Pole; Ferdinand loathed all his race, and had bitterly expressed his resentment that any of them were allowed to hold high office. Bilinski was also a close confidant of old Franz Josef and an advocate of a conciliatory policy in the Slav provinces. Thus it happened that, when he conscientiously went to transmit this message, his warnings were received not only with incredulity but in a way that made it both psychologically and materially impossible to repeat them.

Franz Ferdinand never informed in advance either the Austrian or the Hungarian Government of the arrangements he had made with the Army to visit Bosnia, and he seems to have worked earnestly and ingeniously, as people will to get up a bazaar, to insult the civil authorities. When he printed the programme of his journey he sent it to all the Ministries except the Joint Ministry of Finance; and he ordered that no invitations for the ball which he was to give after the manoeuvres outside Sarajevo at Ilidzhe were to be sent to any of the Finance Ministry officials. It is as if a Prince of Wales had travelled through India brutally insulting the Indian Civil Service and the India Office. There was a thoroughly Habsburg reason for this. Since the military authorities were in charge of all the arrangements, it had been easy for Franz Ferdinand to arrange that for the first time on Habsburg territory royal honours would be paid to his wife. This could not have happened without much more discussion if the civil authorities had been involved. The result was final and bloody. Bilinski could not protest against Franz Ferdinand's visit to Sarajevo when he was not sure it was going to take place, considering the indelicate rage with which all his approaches were met. This inability to discuss the visit meant that he could not even supervise the arrangements for policing the streets. With incredible ingenuity, Franz Ferdinand had created a situation in which those whose business it was to protect him could not take one step towards his protection.

When Franz Ferdinand returned from the balcony into the reception room his face became radiant and serene, because he saw before him the final agent of his ruin, the key beater in this battue. His wife had been in an upper room of the Town Hall, meeting a number of ladies belonging to the chief Moslem families of the town, in order that she might condescendingly admire their costumes and manners, as is the habit of barbarians who have conquered an ancient culture; and she had now made the proposal that on the return journey she and her husband should alter their programme by going to the hospital to make inquiries about the officer wounded by Chabrinovitch. Nothing can ever be known about the attitude of this woman to that day's events. She was a woman who could not communicate with her fellow-creatures. We know only of her outer appearance and behaviour. We know that she had an anaphrodisiac and pinched yet heavy face, that in a day when women were bred to look like table-birds she took this convention of amplitude and expressed it with the rigidity of the drill sergeant. We know that she impressed those who knew her as absorbed in snobbish ambitions and petty resentments, and that she had as her chief ingratiating attribute a talent for mimicry, which is often the sport of an unloving and derisive soul.

But we also know that she and Franz Ferdinand felt for each other what cannot be denied to have been a great love. Each found in the other a perpetual assurance that the meaning of life is kind; each gave the other that assurance in terms suited to their changing circumstances and with inexhaustible resourcefulness and good-will; it is believed by those who knew them best that neither of them ever fell from the heights of their relationship and reproached the other for the hardships that their marriage had brought upon them. That is to say that the boar we know as Franz Ferdinand and the small-minded fury we know as Countess Sophie Chotek are not the ultimate truth about these people. These were the pragmatic conceptions of them that those who met them had to use if they were to escape unhurt, but the whole truth about their natures must certainly have been to some degree beautiful.

Even in this field where Sophie Chotek's beauty lay she was dangerous. Like her husband she could see no point in consistency, which is the very mortar of society. Because of her noble birth, she bitterly resented her position as a morganatic wife. It was infamous, she felt, that a Chotek should be treated in this way. It never occurred to her that Choteks had a value only because they had been accorded it by a system which, for reasons that were perfectly valid at the time, accorded the Habsburgs a greater value; and that if those reasons had ceased to be valid and the Habsburgs should no longer be treated as supreme, then the Choteks also had lost their claim to eminence.

Unfortunately she coupled with this inconsistency a severely legalistic mind. It can be done. The English bench has given us examples. She had discovered, and is said to have urged her discovery on Franz Ferdinand, that the oath he had taken to renounce the rights of succession for his children was contrary to crown law. No one can swear an oath which affects the unborn; this is, of course, perfectly just. It did not occur to her that, if the maintenance of the Habsburgs required the taking of unjust oaths, perhaps the Habsburg dynasty would fall to pieces if it were forced to live on the plane of highest justice, and that her children might find themselves again without a throne.

Countess Sophie Chotek must therefore have had her hands full of the complicated hells of the humourless legalist; it must have seemed to her that her environment was always perversely resisting the imposition of a perfect pattern, to her grave personal damage. She had, however, a more poignant personal grief. She believed Franz Ferdinand to be on the point of going mad. It is on record that she hinted to her family lawyer and explicitly informed an intimate friend that in her opinion her husband might at any moment be stricken with some form of mental disorder. This may have been merely part of that corpus of criticism which might be called 'Any Wife to Any Husband.' But there were current many stories which go to show that Franz Ferdinand's violence had for some time been manifest in ways not compatible with sanity. The Czech officials in charge of the imperial train that had brought Franz Ferdinand from Berlin after a visit to the German Emperor reported to the chief of the Czech Separatist Party that when Franz Ferdinand had alighted at his destination they found the upholstery in his compartment cut to pieces by sword thrusts; and in a visit to England he struck those who met him as undisciplined in a way differing in quality and degree from the normal abnormality which comes from high rank.

This woman had therefore a host of enemies without her home, and within it an enemy more terrifying than all the rest. That she was in great distress is proven by a certain difficulty we know to have arisen in her religious life. It was one of the wise provisions of the early Church that the orthodox were not allowed the benefits of communion or confession except at rare intervals. There is obviously a sound and sensible reason for this rule. It cannot be believed that the soul is sufficiently potent to be for ever consummating its union with God, and the forgiveness of sins must lose its reality if it is sought too rapidly for judgment to pronounce soberly on guilt. Moreover limiting the approach to the sacraments prevents them from becoming magical practices, mere snatchings at amulets. By one of the innovations which divide the Roman Catholic Church from the early Church, Pope Leo X removed all these restrictions, and now a devotee can communicate and confess as often as he likes. But the Countess Sophie Chotek availed herself of this permission so extremely often that she was constantly at odds with the Bishop who guided her spiritual life. At their hotel out at Ilidzhe a room had been arranged as a chapel, and that morning she and her husband had attended mass. Not one day could go without invoking the protection of the cross against the disaster which she finally provoked by her proposal that they should visit the wounded aide-de-camp in hospital.

There was a conversation about this proposal which can never be understood. It would be comprehensible only if the speakers had been drunk or living through a long fevered night; but they were sober and, though they were facing horror, they were facing it at ten o'clock on a June morning. Franz Ferdinand actually asked Potiorek if he thought any bombs would be thrown at them during their drive away from the Town Hall. This question is incredibly imbecile. If Potiorek had not known enough to regard the first attack as probable, there was no reason to ascribe any value whatsoever to his opinion on the probability of a second attack. There was one obvious suggestion which it would have been natural for either Franz Ferdinand or Potiorek to make. The streets were quite inadequately guarded, otherwise Chabrinovitch could not have made his attack. Therefore it was advisable that Franz Ferdinand and his wife should remain at the Town Hall until adequate numbers of the seventy thousand troops who were within no great distance of the town were sent for to line the streets. This is a plan which one would have thought would have been instantly brought to the men's minds by the mere fact that they were responsible for the safety of a woman.

But they never suggested anything like it, and Potiorek gave to Franz Ferdinand's astonishing question the astonishing answer that he was sure no second attack would be made. The startling element in this answer is its imprudence, for he must have known that any investigation would bring to light that he had failed to take for Franz Ferdinand any of the precautions that had been taken for Franz Josef on his visit to Sarajevo seven years before, when all strangers had been evacuated from the town, all anti-Austrians confined to their houses, and the streets lined with a double cordon of troops and peppered with detectives. It would be credible only if one knew that Potiorek had received assurances that if anything happened to Franz Ferdinand there would be no investigation afterwards that he need fear. Indeed, it would be easy to suspect that Potiorek deliberately sent Franz Ferdinand to his death, were it not that it must have looked beforehand as if that death must be shared by Potiorek, as they were both riding in the same carriage. It is of course true that Potiorek shared Conrad's belief that a war against Serbia was a sacred necessity, and had written to him on one occasion expressing the desperate opinion that, rather than not have war, he would run the risk of provoking a world war and being defeated in it; and throughout the Bosnian manoeuvres he had been in the company of Conrad, who was still thoroughly disgruntled by his dismissal by Franz Ferdinand. It must have been quite plain to them both that the assassination of Franz Ferdinand by a Bosnian Serb would be a superb excuse for declaring war on Serbia. Still, it is hard to believe that Potiorek would have risked his own life to take Franz Ferdinand's, for he could easily have arranged for the Archduke's assassination when he was walking in the open country. It is also extremely doubtful if any conspirators would have consented to Potiorek risking his life, for his influence and military skill would have been too useful to them to throw away.

Yet there is an incident arising out of this conversation which can only be explained by the existence of entirely relentless treachery somewhere among Franz Ferdinand's entourage. It was agreed that the royal party should, on leaving the Town Hall, follow the route that had been originally announced for only a few hundred yards: they would drive along the quay to the second bridge, and would then follow a new route by keeping straight along the quay to the hospital, instead of turning to the right and going up a side street which led to the principal shopping centre of the town. This had the prime advantage of disappointing any other conspirators who might be waiting in the crowds, after any but the first few hundred yards of the route, and, as Potiorek had also promised that the automobiles should travel at a faster speed, it might have been thought that the Archduke and his wife had a reasonable chance of getting out of Sarajevo alive. So they might, if anybody had given orders to the chauffeur on either of these points. But either Potiorek never gave these orders to any subordinate, or the subordinate to whom he entrusted them never handed them on.

Neither hypothesis is easy to accept. Even allowing for Austrian *Schlamperei*, soldiers and persons in attendance on royalty do not make such mistakes. But though this negligence cannot have been accidental, the part it played in contriving the death of Franz Ferdinand cannot have been foreseen. The Archduke, his wife, and Potiorek left the Town Hall, taking no farewell whatsoever of the municipal officers who lined the staircase, and went on to the quay and got into their automobile. Franz Ferdinand and Sophie are said to have looked stunned and stiff with apprehension. Count Harrach, an Austrian general, jumped on the left running-board and crouched there with drawn sword, ready to defend the royal pair with his life. The procession was headed by an automobile containing the Deputy Mayor and a member of the Bosnian Diet; but by another incredible blunder neither these officials nor their chauffeurs were informed of the change in route. When this first automobile came to the bridge it turned to the right and went up the side street. The chauffeur of the royal car saw this and was therefore utterly bewildered when Potiorek struck him on the shoulder and shouted, 'What are you doing? We're going the wrong way! We must drive straight along the quay.'

Not having been told how supremely important it was to keep going, the puzzled chauffeur stopped dead athwart the corner of the side street and the quay. He came to halt exactly in front of a young Bosnian Serb named Gavrilo Princip, who was one of the members of the same conspiracy as Chabrinovitch. He had failed to draw his revolver on the Archduke during the journey to the Town Hall, and he had come back to make another attempt. As the automobile remained stock-still Princip was able to take steady aim and shoot Franz Ferdinand in the heart. He was not a very good shot, he could never have brought down his quarry if there had not been this failure to give the chauffeur proper instructions. Harrach could do nothing; he was on the left side of the car, Princip on the right. When he saw the stout, stuffed body of the Archduke fall forward he shifted his revolver to take aim at Potiorek. He would have killed him at once had not Sophie thrown herself across the car in one last expression of her great love, and drawn Franz Ferdinand to herself with a movement that brought her across the path of the second bullet. She was already dead when Franz Ferdinand murmured to her, 'Sophie, Sophie, live for our children'; and he died a quarter of an hour later. So was your life and my life mortally wounded, but so was not the life of the Bosnians, who were indeed restored to life by this act of death.

Leaning from the balcony, I said, 'I shall never be able to understand how it happened.' It is not that there are too few facts available, but that there are too many. To begin with, only one murder was committed, yet there were two murders in the story: one was the murder done by Princip, the other was the murder dreamed of by some person or persons in Franz Ferdinand's entourage, and they were not the same. And the character of the event is not stamped with murder but with suicide. Nobody worked to ensure the murder on either side so hard as the people who were murdered. And they, though murdered, are not as pitiable as victims should be. They manifested a mixture of obstinate invocation of disaster and anguished complaint against it which is often associated with unsuccessful crime, with the petty thief in the dock. Yet they were of their time. They could not be blamed for morbidity in a society which adored death, which found joy in contemplating the death of beasts, the death of souls in a rigid social system, the death of peoples under an oppressive empire.

'Many things happened that day,' said the head of the tourist bureau, 'but most clearly I remember the funny thin voice of the Archduke and his marionette strut.' I looked down on the street below and saw one who was not as the Archduke, a tall gaunt man from the mountains with his crimson scarf about his head, walking with a long stride that was the sober dance of strength itself. I said to Constantine, 'Did that sort of man have anything to do with the assassination?' 'Directly, nothing at all,' answered Constantine, 'though indirectly he had everything to do with it. But in fact all of the actual conspirators were peculiarly of Sarajevo, a local product. You will understand better when I have shown you where it all happened. But now we must go back to the tourist bureau, for we cannot leave this gentleman until we have drunk black coffee with him.'

As we walked out of the Town Hall the sunshine was at last warm and the plum blossom in the distant gardens shone as if it were not still wet with melted snow. 'Though the hills rise so sharply,' I said, 'the contours are so soft, to be in this city is like walking inside an opening flower.' 'Everything here is perfect,' said

Constantine; 'and think of it, only since I was a grown man has this
been my town. Until then its beauty was a heartache and a shame to
me, because I was a Serb and Sarajevo was a Slav town in captivity.'
'Come now, come now,' I said, 'by that same reckoning should not
the beauty of New York and Boston be a heartache and shame to
me?' 'Not at all, not at all,' he said, 'for you and the Americans are
not the same people. The air of America is utterly different from
the air of England, and has made Americans even of pure English
blood utterly different from you, even as the air of Russia, which
is not the same as Balkan air, has made our Russian brothers not
at all as we are. But the air of Bosnia is the same as Serbian air,
and these people are almost the same as us, except that they talk
less. Besides, your relatives in America are not being governed by
another race, wholly antipathetic to you both. If the Germans had
taken the United States and you went over there and saw New
England villages being governed on Prussian lines, then you would
sigh that you and the Americans of your race should be together
again.' 'I see that,' I said. I was looking at the great toast-coloured
barracks which the Austrians set on a ledge dominating the town.
They seemed to say, 'All is now known, we can therefore act
without any further discussion': a statement idiotic in itself, and
more so when addressed to the essentially speculative Slav.

'All, I tell you,' said Constantine, 'that is Austrian in Sarajevo
is false to us. Look at this embankment we are walking upon. It
is very nice and straight, but it is nothing like the embankment
we Yugoslavs, Christian or Moslem, would make for a river. We
are very fond of nature as she is, and we do not want to hold up a
ruler and tell her that she must look like that and not stick forward
her bosom or back her bottom. And look, here is the corner where
Princip killed the Archduke, and you see how appropriate it was.
For the young Bosnian came along the little street from the real
Sarajevo where all the streets are narrow and many are winding
and every house belongs to a person, to this esplanade which the
Austrians built, which is one long line and has big houses that
look alike, and seeing an Arch-Austrian he made him go away.
See, there is a tablet on that corner commemorating the deed.'

I had read much abuse of this tablet as a barbarous record
of satisfaction in an accomplished crime. Mr Winston Churchill
remarks in his book on *The Unknown War* (*The Eastern Front*) that
'Princip died in prison, and a monument erected in recent years
by his fellow-countrymen records his infamy and their own.' It
is actually a very modest black tablet, not more than would be
necessary to record the exact spot of the assassination for historical

purposes, and it is placed so high above the street-level that the casual passer-by would not remark it. The inscription runs, 'Here, in this historical place, Gavrilo Princip was the initiator of liberty, on the day of St. Vitus, the 28th of June, 1914.' These words seem to me remarkable in their restraint, considering the bitter hatred that the rule of Austria had aroused in Bosnia. The expression 'initiator of liberty' is justified by its literal truth: the Bosnians and Herzegovinians were in fact enslaved until the end of the war which was provoked by the assassination of the Archduke Franz Ferdinand. To be shocked at a candid statement of this hardly becomes a subject of any of the Western states who connived at the annexation of these territories by Austria.

One must let the person who wears the shoe know where it pinches. It happened that as Constantine and I were looking up at the tablet there passed by one of the most notable men in Yugoslavia, a scholar and a gentleman, known to his peers in all the great cities of Europe. He greeted us and nodded up at the tablet, 'A bad business that.' 'Yes, yes,' said Constantine warily, for they were political enemies, and he dreaded what might come. 'We must have no more of such things, Constantine,' said the other. 'No, no,' said Constantine. 'No more assassinations, Constantine,' the other went on. 'No, no,' said Constantine. 'And no more Croats shot down because they are Croats, Constantine,' rapped out the other. 'But we never do that,' wailed Constantine; 'it is only that accidents must happen in the disorder that these people provoke!' 'Well, there must be no more accidents,' said his friend. But as he turned to go he looked again at the tablet, and his eyes grew sad. 'But God forgive us all!' he said. 'As for that accident, it had to happen.'

I said to Constantine, 'Would he have known Princip, do you think?' But Constantine answered, 'I think not. He was ten years older, and he would only have known a man of Princip's age if their families had been friends, but poor Princip had no family of the sort that had such rich friends. He was just a poor boy come down from the mountains to get his education here in Sarajevo, and he knew nobody but his school-fellows.' That, indeed, is a fact which is of great significance historically: the youth and obscurity of the Sarajevo conspirators. Princip himself was the grandson of an immigrant whose exact origin is unknown, though he was certainly a Slav. This stranger appeared in a village on the borders of Bosnia and Dalmatia at a time when the Moslems of true Turkish stock had been driven out by the Bosnian insurrectionary forces, and occupied one of the houses that had been vacated by the Turks.

There must have been something a little odd about this man, for he wore a curious kind of silver jacket with bells on it, which struck the villagers as strange and gorgeous and which cannot be identified by the experts as forming part of any local costume known in the Balkans. Because of this eccentric garment the villagers gave him the nickname of 'Princip,' which means Prince; and because of that name there sprang up after the assassination a preposterous legend that Princip's father was the illegitimate son of the murdered Prince Rudolf. He was certainly just a peasant, who married a woman of that Homeric people, the Montenegrins, and begot a family in the depths of poverty. When Austria came in and seized Bosnia after it had been cleared of Turks by the Bosnian rebels, it was careful to leave the land tenure system exactly as it had been under the Turks, and the Bosnian peasants continued on starvation level. Of Princip's children one son became a postman, and married a Herzegovinian who seems to have been a woman most remarkable for strength of character. In her barren mountain home she bore nine children, of whom six died, it is believed from maladies arising out of under-nourishment. The other three sons she filled with an ambition to do something in life, and sent them down into the towns to get an education and at the same time to earn money to pay for it. The first became a doctor, the second a tradesman who was chosen at an early age mayor of his town. The third was Gavrilo Princip, who started on his journey under two handicaps. He was physically fragile, and he entered a world distracted with thoughts of revolution and preparations for war.

The two most oppressive autocracies in Europe were working full time to supply themselves and all other European countries with the material of revolution. Russia was producing innumerable authors who dealt in revolutionary thought. The Austrian Empire was producing innumerable men who were capable of any revolutionary act, whether in the interests of military tyranny or popular liberty. The Russian influence came into Bosnia through several channels, some of them most unexpected. For political purposes the Russian imperial family maintained a boarding school for girls at the top of the road from Kotor, in Tsetinye, the capital of Montenegro, where many of the aristocratic families of Dalmatia and Bosnia and Herzegovina and even Croatia sent their daughters to be educated. As all familiar with the perversity of youth would expect, the little dears later put to use the Russian they acquired at that institution to read Stepniak and Kropotkin and Tolstoy. This was but a narrow channel, which served only to gain tolerance among the wealthier classes for the movement which swept through practically the whole of the male youth of the Southern Slavs and set them discussing nihilism, anarchism and state socialism, and experimenting with the technique of terrorism which the advocates of those ideas had developed in Russia.

In this last and least attractive part of their activities the Bosnians show at a disadvantage compared to their Russian brothers during the period immediately before the war: they appear more criminal because they were more moral. Among the Russian revolutionaries there had been growing perplexity and disillusionment ever since 1906, when it was discovered that the people's leader, Father Gapon, owing to the emollient effects of a visit to Monte Carlo, had sold himself to the police as a spy. In 1909 they received a further shock. It was proved that Aseff, the head of the largest and most powerful terrorist organization in Russia, had from the very beginning of his career been a police agent, and though he had successfully arranged the assassination of Plehve, the Minister of the Interior, and the Grand Duke Serge, he had committed the first crime partly because he was a Jew and disliked Plehve's anti-Semitism, and partly because he wanted to strengthen his position in revolutionary circles in order to get a higher salary from the police, and he had committed the second to oblige persons in court circles who had wanted to get rid of the Grand Duke. This made all the sincere revolutionaries realize that their ranks were riddled with treachery, and that if they risked their lives it was probably to save the bacon of a police spy or further a palace intrigue. For this reason terrorism was practically extinct in Russia for some years before the war.

But the Southern Slavs were not traitors. It is true that there existed numbers, indeed vast numbers, of Croats and Serbs and Czechs who attempted to raise funds by selling to the Austro-Hungarian Empire forged evidence that their respective political parties were conspiring with the Serbian Government. But their proceedings were always conducted with the utmost publicity, and their forgeries were so clumsy as to be recognized as such by the most prejudiced court; they presented telegrams, which were supposed to have been delivered, on reception forms instead of transmission forms, and they put forward photographs of patriotic societies' minutes which bore evidence that the original documents must have been over three-foot-three by thirteen inches: a nice size for reproduction but not for a society's minutes. Neither the officials of the Empire nor the Slav nationalists ever took any serious measures against these disturbers of the peace, and they seem to have had such a privileged position of misdoing as is given in some villages to a pilferer, so long as he is sufficiently blatant and modest in his exploits so that he can be frustrated by reasonable care, and the community loses not too much when he scores a success.

But the real traitor and *agent provocateur*, who joined in revolutionary activities for the purpose of betraying his comrades to authority, was rare indeed among the South Slavs, and therefore terrorist organizations could function in confidence. They honeycombed the universities and the schools to an extent which seems surprising, till one remembers that, owing to the poverty of the inhabitants and the defective system of education imposed by the Austrian Empire, the age of the pupils at each stage was two or three years above that which would have been customary in a Western community.

The terrorism of these young men was given a new inspiration in 1912 and 1913 by the Balkan wars in which Serbia beat Turkey and Bulgaria. They saw themselves cutting loose from the decaying corpse of an empire and uniting with a young and triumphant democratic state; and by the multiplication of society upon society and patriotic journal upon patriotic journal they cultivated the idea of freeing themselves by acts of violence directed against their rulers. This, however, did not alter that horrible dispensation by which it is provided that those who most thirstily desire to go on the stage shall be those who have the least talent for acting. The Croats and Serbs are magnificent soldiers; they shoot well and they have hearts like lions. But they are deplorable terrorists. Much more individualist than the Russians, the idea of a secret society was more of a toy to them than a binding force. They were apt to go on long journeys to meet fellow-conspirators for the purpose of discussing an outrage, and on the way home to become interested in some other aspect of the revolutionary movement, such as Tolstoyan pacifism, and leave their bombs in the train. When they maintained their purpose, they frequently lost not their courage but their heads at the crucial moment, perhaps because the most convenient place for such *attentats*, to use the Continental word for a crime directed against the representative of a government, was among crowds in a town, and the young Slav was not used to crowds. He felt, as W. H. Davies put it of himself in urban conditions, 'like a horse near fire.' Such considerations do not operate now. The Great War hardened the nerves of a generation in the dealing out of death, and it trained the following generation with its experience plus the aid of all the money and help certain foreign nations could give them. The Croats and Macedonians trained in Italy and Hungary who killed King Alexander of Yugoslavia represented the highest point of *expertise* in terrorism that man has yet attained.

But in the days before the war the South Slavs were touching and ardent amateurs. Typical of them was young Zheraitch, a handsome Serb boy from a Herzegovinian village, who decided to kill the Emperor Franz Josef when he visited Bosnia and Herzegovina in 1910. With that end in mind he followed the old man from Sarajevo to Mostar, and from Mostar to Ilidzhe, revolver in hand, but never fired a shot. Then he decided to kill the Governor of Bosnia, General Vareshanin, who was specially abhorrent to the Slavs because he was a renegade Croat. He waited on a bridge for the General as he drove to open the Diet of Sarajevo. The boy fired five bullets at him, which all went wide. He kept the sixth to fire at his own forehead. It is said that General Vareshanin got out of his car and walked over to his body and savagely kicked it, a gesture which was bitterly remembered among all young South Slavs. This poor boy was typical of many of his fellows in his failure. In June 1912 another Bosnian tried to kill the Ban of Croatia in the streets of Zagreb, and killed two other people, but not him. In August 1913 a young Croat tried to kill the new Ban of Croatia, but only wounded him. In March 1914 another young Croat was caught in the Opera House at Zagreb just as he was about to shoot the Ban and the Archduke Leopold Salvator. And so on, and so on. The Balkan wars altered this state of affairs to some extent. A great many young Bosnians and Herzegovinians either swam across the river Drina into Serbia, or slipped past the frontier guards on the Montenegrin borders by night, in order to join irregular volunteer bands which served as outposts for the Serbian Army as it invaded Macedonia. All these young men acquired skill and hardihood in the use of weapons. But those who stayed at home were incurably inefficient as assassins.

Princip was not among the young Bosnians who had gone to the Balkan wars. He had soon become weary of the school life of Sarajevo, which was reduced to chaos by the general political discontent of the pupils and their particular discontents with the tendentious curriculum of the Austro-Hungarian education authorities. He took to shutting himself up in his poor room and read enormously of philosophy and politics, undermining his health and nerves by the severity of these undirected studies. Always, of course, he was short of money and ate but little. Finally he felt he had better emigrate to Serbia and start studies at a secondary school at Belgrade, and he took that step in May 1912, when he was barely seventeen. One of his brothers gave him some money, and he had saved much of what he had earned by teaching some little boys; but it must have been a starveling journey. In Belgrade he was extremely happy in his studies, and might have become a contented scholar had not the Balkan War broken out. He immediately volunteered, and was sent down to a training centre in the South of Serbia, and would have made a first-rate soldier if gallantry had been all that was needed. But his deprived body broke down, and he was discharged from the Army.

Princip's humiliation was increased to a painful degree, it is said, because another soldier with whom he was on bad terms grinned when he saw him walking off with his discharge and said, '*Skart,*' throw-out, bad stuff. Though he went back to Belgrade and studied hard and with great success, he was extremely distressed at his failure to render service to the Slav cause and prove his worth as a hero. It happened that in Serbia he had become a close friend of a young printer from Sarajevo called Chabrinovitch, a boy of his own age, who had been banished from Bosnia for five years for the offence of preaching anarchism. Much has been written about this youth which is not too enthusiastic, though it might be described as querulous rather than unfavourable. His companions found something disquieting and annoying about his high spirits and his garrulity, but it must be remembered that those who are very remarkable people, particularly when they are young, often repel more ordinary people by both their laughter and their grief, which seem excessive by the common measure. It is possible that what was odd about Chabrinovitch was simply incipient greatness. But he was also labouring under the handicap of an extremely hostile relationship to his father. In any case he certainly was acceptable as a friend by Princip, and this speaks well for his brains.

They had a number of Sarajevan friends in common, whom they had met at school or in the cafés. Among these was a young schoolmaster called Danilo Ilitch, a neurotic and irascible and extremely unpopular ascetic. He is said to have served in the Serbian Army during the Balkan War, but only as an orderly. From the beginning of 1914 he was engaged in an attempt to form a terrorist organization for the purpose of committing a desperate deed, though nobody, least of all himself, seemed to know exactly what. Among his disciples was a young man called Pushara, who one day cut out of the newspaper a paragraph announcing the intended visit of Franz Ferdinand to Bosnia, and posted it from Sarajevo to Chabrinovitch in Belgrade. It is said by some that he meant merely to intimate that there would be trouble, not that trouble should be made. It is also to be noted that one of his family was said to be an Austrian police spy. If he or somebody connected with him had been acting as an *agent provocateur* they could not have hoped for better success. Chabrinovitch showed the paragraph to Princip, and they decided to return to Sarajevo and kill Franz Ferdinand.

But they needed help. Most of all they needed weapons. First they thought of applying to the Narodna Obrana, the Society of National Defence, for bombs, but their own good sense told them that was impossible. The Narodna Obrana was a respectable society acting openly under Government protection, and even these children, confused by misgovernment to complete callousness, saw that it would have been asking too much to expect it to commit itself to helping in the assassination of a foreign royalty. Moreover they both had had experience of the personalities directing the Narodna Obrana and they knew they were old-fashioned, pious, conservative Serbs of the medieval Serbian pattern, who were more than a little shocked by these Bosnian children who sat up till all hours in cafés and dabbled in free thought. When Chabrinovitch had gone to the society to ask a favour, an old Serbian captain had been gravely shocked by finding the lad in possession of Maupassant's *Bel Ami* and had confiscated it.

It is unfortunate that at this point they met a Bosnian refugee called Tsiganovitch who had heard rumours of their intention and who offered to put them in the way of getting some bombs. He was a member of the secret society known as the 'Black Hand,' or was associated with it. This society had already played a sinister part in the history of Serbia. It was the lineal descendant of the group of officers who had killed King Alexander and Queen Draga and thus exchanged the Obrenovitch dynasty for the Karageorgevitch. The Karageorges, who had played no part in this conspiracy, and had had to accept its results passively, had never resigned themselves to the existence of the group, and were continually at odds with them. The 'Black Hand' was therefore definitely anti-Karageorgevitch and aimed at war with Austria and the establishment of a federated republic of Balkan Slavs. Their leader was a man of undoubted talent but far too picturesque character called Dragutin Dimitriyevitch, known as 'Apis,' who had been for some time the head of the Intelligence Bureau of the Serbian General Staff. He had heard of Ilitch and his group through a Bosnian revolutionary living in Lausanne, Gachinovitch, a boy of twenty-two who had an extraordinary power over all his generation among the South Slavs, particularly among the Bosnians; his post-humous works were edited by Trotsky. It was by his direction that

Chabrinovitch and Princip had been approached by Tsiganovitch, and were later taken in hand, together with another Bosnian boy of nineteen called Grabezh who had just joined them, by an officer called Tankositch, who had been concerned in the murder of King Alexander and Queen Draga.

Tankositch took the boys into some woods and saw how they shot—which was badly, though Princip was better than the others. Finally he fitted them out with bombs, pistols, and some prussic acid to take when their attempts had been made so that they might be sure not to break down and blab in the presence of the police. Then he sent them off to Sarajevo by what was known as the underground route, a route by which persons who might have found difficulty in crossing the frontier, whether for reasons of politics or of contraband, were helped by friendly pro-Slavs. The boys were smuggled through Bosnia by two guards who were under orders from the 'Black Hand,' and with the help of a number of Balkan peasants and tradesmen, who one and all were exceedingly discomfited but dared not refuse assistance to members of a revolutionary body, they got their munitions into Sarajevo.

This journey was completed only by a miracle, such was the inefficiency of the conspirators. Chabrinovitch talked too much. Several times the people on whose good-will they were dependent took fright and were in two minds to denounce the matter to the police, and take the risk of revolutionary vengeance rather than be hanged for complicity, as indeed some of them were. Ilitch was even less competent. He had arranged to fetch the bombs at a certain railway junction, but he fell into a panic and did not keep the appointment. For hours the sugar-box containing the weapons lay in the public waiting-room covered with a coat. The station cat had a comfortable sleep on it. Unfortunately Ilitch recovered his nerve and brought the bombs to his home, where he kept them under the sofa in his bedroom. He had swelled the ranks of those who were to use their arms by some most unsuitable additions. He had enrolled a Moslem called Mehmedbashitch, a peculiar character who had already shown a divided mind towards terrorism. In January 1913 he had gone to Toulouse with a Moslem friend and had visited the wonderful Gachinovitch, the friend of Trotsky. He had received from the leader weapons and poison for the purpose of attempting the life of General Potiorek, the Military Governor of Bosnia, but on the way he and his friend had thought better of it and dropped them out of the carriage window. Ilitch had also enrolled two schoolboys called Chubrilovitch and Popovitch, and gave them revolvers. Neither had ever fired a shot in his life. The few days before the visit of the Archduke Ilitch spent in alternately exhorting this ill-assorted group to show their patriotism by association and imploring them to forget it and disperse. He was himself at one point so overcome by terror that he got into the train and travelled all the way to the town of Brod, a hundred miles away. But he came back, though to the very end he seems at times to have urged Princip, who was living with him, to abandon the *attentat*, and to have expressed grave distrust of Chabrinovitch on the ground that his temperament was not suited to terrorism. It might have been supposed that Franz Ferdinand would never be more safe in his life than he would be on St. Vitus's Day at Sarajevo.

That very nearly came to be true. On the great day Ilitch made up his mind that the assassination should take place after all, and he gave orders for the disposition of the conspirators in the street. They were so naïve that it does not seem to have struck them as odd that he himself proposed to take no part in the *attentat*. They were told to take up their stations at various points on the embankment: first Mehmedbashitch, then Chabrinovitch, then Chubrilovitch, then Popovitch, and after that Princip, at the head of the bridge that now bears his name, with Grabezh facing him across the road. What happened might easily have been foretold. Mehmedbashitch never threw his bomb. Instead he watched the car go by and then ran to the railway station and jumped into a train that was leaving for Montenegro; there he sought the protection of one of the tribes which constituted that nation, with whom his family had friendly connexions, and the tribesmen kept him hidden in their mountain homes. Later he made his way to France, and that was not to be the end of his adventures. He was to be known to Balkan history as a figure hardly less enigmatic than the Man in the Iron Mask. The schoolboy Chubrilovitch had been told that if Mehmedbashitch threw his bomb he was to finish off the work with his revolver, but if Mehmedbashitch failed he was to throw his own bomb. He did nothing. Neither did the other schoolboy, Popovitch. It was impossible for him to use either his bomb or his revolver, for in his excitement he had taken his stand beside a policeman. Chabrinovitch threw his bomb, but high and wide. He then swallowed his dose of prussic acid and jumped off the parapet of the embankment. There, as the prussic acid had no effect on him, he suffered arrest by the police. Princip heard the noise of Chabrinovitch's bomb and thought the work was done, so stood still. When the car went by and he saw that the royal party was still alive, he was dazed with astonishment and walked away to a café, where he sat down and had a cup of coffee and pulled himself together. Grabezh was also deceived by the explosion and let his opportunity go by. Franz Ferdinand would have gone from Sarajevo untouched had it not been for the actions of his staff, who by blunder after blunder contrived that his car should slow down and that he should be presented as a stationary target in front of Princip, the one conspirator of real and mature deliberation, who had finished his cup of coffee and was walking back through the streets, aghast at the failure of himself and his friends, which would expose the country to terrible punishment without having inflicted any loss on authority. At last the bullets had been coaxed out of the reluctant revolver to the bodies of the eager victims.

Sarajevo VI

'Do you see,' said Constantine, 'the last folly of these idiots?' There is a raw edge to the ends of the bridge, an unhemmed look to the masonry on both sides of the road. 'They put up a statue of the Archduke Franz Ferdinand and his wife, not in Vienna, where there was a good deal of expiation to be done to those two, but here, where the most pitiful amongst us could not pity them. As soon as we took the town over after the liberation they were carted away.' They may still be standing in some backyard, intact or cut into queer sculptural joints, cast down among ironically long grass. There was never more convincing proof that we do not make our own destinies, that they are not merely the pattern traced by our characteristics on time as we rush through it, than the way that the destinies of Franz Ferdinand and Sophie Chotek continued to operate after their death. In their lives they had passed from situation to situation which invited ceremonial grandeur and had been insanely deprived of it in a gross ceremonial setting, and it was so when they were in their coffins. They were sent to Vienna, to what might have been hoped was the pure cold cancellation of the tomb. They were, however, immediately caught up and whirled about in a stately and complicated vortex of contumely and hatred that astonished the whole world, even their world, accustomed as it was to hideousness.

The Emperor Franz Josef cannot be blamed for the insolence which was wreaked on the coffins on their arrival in Vienna. A man of eighty-seven whose wife had been assassinated, whose son was either murdered or was a murderer and suicide, cannot be imagined to be other than shattered when he hears of the assassination of his heir and nephew, who was also his enemy, and his wife, who was a shame to his family. The occasion drew from Franz Josef a superb blasphemy: when he heard the news the thought of the morganatic marriage came first to his mind, and he said that God had corrected a wrong which he had been powerless to alter. But the guilt of the funeral arrangements at Vienna must rest on Prince Montenuovo, the Emperor's Chamberlain, who had tormented Franz Ferdinand and Sophie Chotek during their lives by the use of etiquette, and found that by the same weapon he could pursue them after their death.

Nothing but actual insanity can explain Prince Montenuovo's

362

perversion of the funeral arrangements. He was not only a cultured man, he had shown himself at times humane and courageous. In March 1913 he had acted for Franz Josef in his resistance to Conrad's attempt to drag Austria into an unprovoked war with Serbia and Montenegro, and he had performed his duties with great tact and sense and principle. It would have been supposed that such a man, on finding himself charged with the duty of consigning to the grave the bodies of a husband and wife with whom he had been on contentious terms for many years, would feel compelled to a special decorum. Instead he could find no impropriety too wild for any part of the ceremony.

He arranged that the train which brought the bodies home should be delayed so that it arrived at night. It came in horribly spattered by the blood of a railwayman who had been killed at a level crossing. Montenuovo had two initial reverses. He prescribed that the new heir, the Archduke Charles, should not meet the train, but the young man insisted on doing so. He tried also to prevent Sophie Chotek's coffin from lying beside her husband's in the Royal Chapel during the funeral mass, but to that Franz Josef would not consent. But he had several successes. Sophie's coffin was placed on a lower level to signify her lower rank. The full insignia of the Archduke lay on his coffin, on hers were placed the white gloves and black fan of the former lady-in-waiting. No wreath was sent by any member of the imperial family except Stephanie, the widow of the Crown Prince Rudolf, who had long been on atrocious terms with her relatives. The only flowers were a cross of white roses sent by the dead couple's two children, and some wreaths sent by foreign sovereigns. The Emperor Franz Josef attended the service, but immediately afterwards the chapel was closed, in order that the public should have no opportunity to pay their respects to the dead.

Montenuovo attempted to separate the two in their graves. He proposed that Franz Ferdinand should be laid in the Habsburg tomb in the Capuchin church, while his wife's body was sent to the chapel in their castle at Arstetten on the Danube. But to guard against this Franz Ferdinand had left directions that he too was to be buried at Arstetten. Montenuovo bowed to this decision, but announced that his responsibility would end when he had left the coffins at the West Terminus station. The municipal undertaker had to make all arrangements for putting them on the train for Pöchlarn, which was the station for Arstetten, and getting them across the Danube to the castle. But Montenuovo provided that their task was made difficult by holding back the procession from the chapel till late at night. As a protest a hundred members of the highest Hungarian and Austrian nobility appeared in the costumes that would have been the proper wear at an imperial funeral, thrust themselves into the procession, and walked on foot to the station.

The coffins and the mourners travelled on a train that delivered them at Pöchlarn at one o'clock in the morning. They found that the station had not been prepared for the occasion, there were no crape hangings or red carpets. This was extremely shocking to a people obsessed with etiquette and pomp. But they soon had more solid reasons for resentment. The moment when the coffins were laid on the platform was the signal for a blinding and deafening and drenching thunderstorm. The disadvantages of a nocturnal funeral became apparent. Nobody in charge of the proceedings knew the village, so the mourners could not find their way to shelter and had to pack into the little station, impeding the actual business of the funeral. It had been proposed to take the coffins to a neighbouring church for a further part of the religious services, but the hearses could not be loaded in the heavy rain, and indeed the mourners would not have known where to follow them in the darkness. So the bewildered priests consecrated the coffins in the crowded little waiting-room among the time-tables and advertisements of seaside resorts. At last the rain stopped, and a start was made for the castle. But there was still much thunder and lightning, and the sixteen horses that drew the hearses were constantly getting out of control. It was dawn when the cavalcade was brought safely to a quay on the Danube, and in the quietness the horses were coaxed on to the ferry-boat by attendants who had water running down round their feet in streams from their sodden clothing. The mourners, left on the bank to wait their turn, watched the boat with thankfulness. But when it was in the middle of the stream there was a last flash of lightning, a last drum-roll of thunder. The left pole-horse in front of the Archduke's hearse reared, and the back wheels slipped over the edge of the ferry-boat. Till it reached the other side it was a shambles of terrified horses, of men who could hardly muster the strength to cling to the harness, and cried out in fatigue and horror as they struggled, of coffins slipping to the water's edge.

It is strange that it was this scene which made it quite certain that the Sarajevo *attentat* should be followed by a European war. The funeral was witnessed by a great many soldiers and officials and men of influence, and their reaction was excited and not logical. If Franz Ferdinand had been quietly laid to rest according to the custom of his people, many Austrians would have felt sober pity for him for a day, and then remembered his many faults. They would

surely have reflected that he had brought his doom on himself by
the tactlessness and aggressiveness of his visit to the Serbian frontier
at the time of a Serbian festival; and they might also have reflected
that those qualities were characteristic not only of him but of his
family. The proper sequel to the *Walpurgisnacht* obsequies of Franz
Ferdinand would have been the dismissal of Prince Montenuovo,
the drastic revision of the Austrian constitution and reduction of the
influence wielded by the Habsburgs and their court, and an attempt
at the moral rehabilitation of Vienna. But to take any of these steps
Austria would have had to look in the mirror. She preferred instead
to whip herself into a fury of loyalty to Franz Ferdinand's memory.
It was only remembered that he was the enemy of Franz Josef,
who had now shown himself sacrilegious to a corpse who, being a
Habsburg, must have been as sacred as an emperor who was sacred
because he was a Habsburg. It was felt that if Franz Ferdinand had
been at odds with this old man and his court he had probably been
right. Enthusiasm flamed up for the men who had been chosen
by Franz Ferdinand, for Conrad von Hötzendorf and Berchtold,
and for the policy of imperialist aggression that they had jointly
engendered. Again the corpse was outraged; he could not speak
from the grave to say that he had cancelled those preferences, to
protest when these men he had repudiated put forward the policy
he had abandoned and pressed it on the plea of avenging his death.
The whole of Vienna demanded that the pacifism of Franz Josef
should be flouted as an old man's folly and that Austria should
declare war upon Serbia.

The excuse for this declaration of war was the allegation that
the conspirators had been suborned to kill Franz Ferdinand by the
Serbian Government. During the last twenty years, in the mood of
lazy and cynical self-criticism which has afflicted the powers that
were apparently victorious in 1918, it has been often pretended
that there were grounds for that allegation. It has been definitely
stated in many articles and books that the Serbian Government
was aware of the murderous intentions of Princip, Chabrinovitch,
and Grabezh, and itself supplied them with bombs and revolvers
and sent them back to Bosnia. Sometimes it is suggested that
the Russian Government joined with the Serbian Government to
commit this crime.

Not one scrap of evidence exists in support of these allegations.

One of the most celebrated contemporary writers on European
affairs sets down in black and white the complicity of the Serbian
and Russian Governments. I have asked him for his authority. He
has none. A famous modern English historian, not pro-Serb, tells

me that ever since the war he has been looking for some proof of the guilt of Serbia, and has never found it, or any indication that it is to be found.

It is clear, and nothing could be clearer, that certain Serbian individuals supplied the conspirators with encouragement and arms. But this does not mean that the Serbian Government was responsible. If certain Irishmen, quite unconnected with Mr De Valera, should supply Irish-Americans with bombs for the purpose of killing President Roosevelt, and he died, the United States would not therefore declare war on Eire. A connexion between the Irishmen and their Government would have to be established before a *casus belli* would be recognized. But no link whatsoever has been discovered between the Serbian Government and Tsiganovitch and Tankositch, the obscure individuals who had given Princip and Chabrinovitch and Grabezh their bombs. They were, indeed, members of the 'Black Hand,' the secret society which was savagely hostile both to the Karageorge dynasty and the political party then in power. That this hostility was not a fiction is shown by the precautions taken against discovery by the Serbian sentries who helped the conspirators over the frontier.

There are only two reasons which would give ground for suspicion of the Serbian Government. The first is the marks on the bombs, which showed definitely that they had been issued by the Serbian State Arsenal at Kraguyevats. That looks damning, but means nothing. Bombs were distributed in large numbers both to the comitadji and regular troops during the Balkan War, and many soldiers put them by as likely to come in handy in the rough-and-tumble of civil life. A search through the outhouses of many a Serbian farm would disclose a store of them. Tankositch would have had no difficulty in acquiring as many as he liked, without any need for application to the authorities. The other suspicious circumstance is the refusal of several Serbian officials to disclaim responsibility for the crime, and the assumption by others of a certain fore-knowledge of the crime which was first cousin to actual responsibility for it. This can be discounted in view of the peculiar atmosphere of Balkan politics. A century ago no political leader could come forward among the Slavs unless he had distinguished himself in guerrilla warfare against the Turks, warfare which often involved what would be hard to tell from assassination. For this reason politicians of peasant origin, bred in the full Balkan tradition, such as the Serbian Prime Minister, Mr Pashitch, could not feel the same embarrassment at being suspected of complicity in the murder of a national enemy that would have been felt by his English contemporaries, say Mr Balfour or Mr Asquith. After all, an Irish politician would not find a very pressing need to exculpate himself from a charge of having been concerned in the murder of Sir Henry Wilson, so far as the good-will of his constituents was concerned. But no hint of any actual meeting or correspondence by which Mr Pashitch established any contact, however remote, with the conspirators has ever been given; and as any such contact would have involved a reconciliation with those who before and after were his enemies, there must have been go-betweens, but these, in spite of the loquacity of the race, have never declared themselves. There was a Mr Liuba Yovanovitch, Minister of Education under Mr Pashitch, who could not stop writing articles in which he boasted that he and his friends in Belgrade had known for weeks ahead that the conspiracy was hatching in Sarajevo. But unkind researchers have discovered that seven years before he put in exactly the same claim concerning the murder of King Alexander and Queen Draga, and that members of that conspiracy had indignantly brought forward proof that they had nothing to do with him. Mr Yovanovitch, in fact, was the Balkan equivalent of the sort of Englishman who wears an Old Etonian tie without cause.

On the other hand there were overwhelming reasons why the Serbian Government should not have supported this or any other conspiracy. It cannot have wanted war at that particular moment. The Karageorges must have been especially anxious to avoid it. King Peter had just been obliged by chronic ill-health to appoint his son Alexander as his regent and it had not escaped the attention of the Republican Party that the King had had to pass over his eldest son, George, because he was hopelessly insane. Mr Pashitch and his Government can hardly have been more anxious for a war, as their machine was temporarily disorganized by preparations for a general election. Both alike, the royal family and the Ministers, held disquieting knowledge about the Serbian military situation. Their country had emerged from the two Balkan wars victorious but exhausted, without money, transport, or munitions, and with a peasant army that was thoroughly sick of fighting. They can have known no facts to offset those, for none existed. Theoretically they could only rely on the support of France and Russia, and possibly Great Britain, but obviously geography would forbid any of these powers giving her practical aid in the case of an Austrian invasion.

In fact, the Karageorges and the Government knew perfectly well that, if there should be war, they must look forward to an immediate defeat of the most painful sort, for which they could receive compensation only should their allies, whoever they might be, at some uncertain time win a definite victory. But if there should be peace, then the Karageorges and the Government could consolidate the victories they had won in the Balkan wars, develop their conquered territory, and organize their neglected resources. Admittedly Serbia aimed at the ultimate absorption of Bosnia and Herzegovina, Montenegro and the South Slav provinces of the Austro-Hungarian Empire. But this was not the suitable moment. If she attained her aims by this method she would have to pay too heavy a price, as, in fact, she did. No country would choose to realize any ideal at the cost of the destruction of one-third of her population. That she did not so choose is shown by much negative evidence. At the time the murder was committed she had just let her reservists return home after their annual training, her Commander-in-chief was taking a cure at an Austrian spa, and none of the Austrian Slavs who had fought in the Balkan War and returned home were warned to come across the frontier. But the positive evidence is even stronger. When Austria sent her ultimatum to Serbia, which curtly demanded not only the punishment of the Serbians who were connected with the Sarajevo *attentat*, but the installation of Austrian and Hungarian officers in Serbia for the purpose of suppressing Pan-Slavism, Mr Pashitch bowed to all the demands save for a few gross details, and begged that the exceptions he had made should not be treated as refusals but should be referred for arbitration to The Hague Tribunal. There was not one trace of bellicosity in the attitude of Serbia at this point. If she had promoted the Sarajevo *attentat* in order to make war possible, she was very near to throwing her advantage away.

The innocence of the Serbian Government must be admitted by all but the most prejudiced. But guilt lies very heavy on the 'Black Hand.' There is, however, yet another twist in the story here. It seems fairly certain that that guilt was not sustained of full intent. We may doubt that when 'Apis' sent these young men to Bosnia he believed for one moment that they would succeed in their plan of killing Franz Ferdinand. He was just as well aware as the authorities of the military and economic difficulties of his country, and probably wanted war as little as they did. But even if he had been of another mind he would hardly have chosen such agents. The conspirators, when they first attracted his attention, numbered only two weakly boys of nineteen, Princip and Chabrinovitch. He had learned that their only revolutionary connexions in Sarajevo were through Ilitch; and as this information came from Gachinovitch, the exile who knew everything about the unrest in Bosnia, he must have learned at the same time how inexperienced in terrorism Ilitch was. 'Apis' must also have known from his officers that Princip was only a fair shot, and that Chabrinovitch and the third boy who joined them later, Grabezh, could not hit a wall. He must have realized that in such inexpert hands the revolvers would be nearly useless, and the bombs would be no better, for they were not the sort used by the Russian terrorists, which exploded at contact, but the kind used in trench warfare, which had to be hit against a hard object before they were thrown, and then took some seconds to go off. They were extremely difficult to throw in a crowd; any soldier could have guessed that Chabrinovitch would never be able to aim one straight.

Yet 'Apis' could have got any munitions that he wanted by taking a little trouble, and, what is more, he could have got any number of patriotic Bosnians who had been through the Balkan wars and could shoot and throw bombs with professional skill. I myself know a Herzegovinian, a remarkable shot and a seasoned soldier, who placed himself at the disposition of the 'Black Hand' to assassinate any oppressor of the Slav people. '*Dans ces jours-là,*' he says, '*nous étions tous fous.*' His offer was never accepted. It is to be wondered whether 'Apis' was quite the character his contemporaries believed. Much is made of his thirst for blood, and he was certainly involved, though not in any major capacity, in the murder of King Alexander and Queen Draga. But the rest of his reputation is based on his self-confessed participation in plots to murder King Nicholas of Montenegro, King Constantine of Greece, the last German Kaiser, and King Ferdinand of Bulgaria. The first three of these monarchs, however, died in their beds, and the last one is still with us. It is possible that 'Apis' was obsessed by a fantasy of bloodshed and treachery, which he shrunk from translating into fact, partly out of a poetic preference for fantasy over fact, partly out of a very sensible regard for his own skin.

There is, indeed, one circumstance which tells us that the 'Black Hand' took Princip and his friends very lightly indeed. Over and over again we read in the records of these times about boys who took out revolvers or bombs with the intention of killing this or that instrument of Austrian tyranny, but lost heart and returned home without incident. There must have been many more such abortive attempts than are recorded. The 'Black Hand' was the natural body to which such boys would turn with a request for arms; it would be interesting to know how often they had handed out munitions which had never been used. Repetition had, it seems, bred carelessness in classification. For when Princip and Chabrinovitch took the prussic acid which Tsiganovitch and Tankositch had given them, it had no effect on either. It is said vaguely that it had 'gone bad,' but prussic acid is not subject to any such misfortune. In the only form which is easy to obtain, it does not even evaporate quickly. What Tsiganovitch and Tankositch had given the boys was plain water, or something equally innocuous. They would not have made this substitution if they had believed in the effectiveness of the conspiracy. They must have known that if the boys succeeded and were tortured and talked they would have reason for the gravest fears: which, indeed, were realized. 'Apis' was executed by the Serbian Government three years later, after a mysterious trial which is one of the most baffling incidents in Balkan history; nothing is clear about it save that the real offence for which he was punished was his connexion with the Sarajevo *attentat*. Tankositch and Tsiganovitch also paid a heavy price in their obscurer way.

Only one person involved in this business did what he meant to do: Princip believed he ought to kill Franz Ferdinand, and he shot him dead. But everybody else acted contrary to his own will. The dead pair, who had dreamed of empire stretching from the Baltic to the Black Sea, surrendered the small primary power to breathe. If the generals about them had had any hope of procuring victory and the rule of the sword they were to fail to the extraordinary degree of annihilating not only their own army but their own nation. The conspirators wanted to throw their bombs, and could not. Ilitch, whose flesh quailed at the conspirator's lot, was compelled to it by the values of his society, distracted as it was by oppression. In Vienna Montenuovo raised a defence of criminal insolence round the sacred Habsburg stock, and uprooted it from Austrian soil, to lie on the rubbish-heap of exile. There was an exquisite appropriateness in this common fate which fell on all those connected with the events of that St. Vitus's Day; for those who are victims of what is known as St. Vitus's disease suffer an uncontrollable disposition to involuntary motions.

Sarajevo VII

'You must come up to the Orthodox cemetery and see the graves of these poor boys,' said Constantine. 'It is very touching, for a reason that will appear when you see it.' Two days later we made this expedition, with the judge and the banker to guide us. But Constantine could not keep back his dramatic climax until we got there. He felt he had to tell us when we had driven only half-way up the hillside. 'What is so terrible,' he said, 'is that they are there in that grave, the poor little ones, Princip, Chabrinovitch, Grabezh, and three other little ones who were taken with them. They could not be hanged, the law forbade it. Nobody could be hanged in the Austrian Empire under twenty-one. Yet I tell you they are all there, and they certainly did not have time to die of old age, for they were all dead before the end of the war.'

This, indeed, is the worst part of the story. It explains why it has been difficult to establish humane penal methods in countries which formed part of the Austrian Empire, and why minor officials in those succession states often take it for granted that violence is a part of the technique of administration. The sequel to the *attentat* shows how little Bosnians had to congratulate themselves for exchanging Austrian domination for Turkish.

When the Serbian prussic acid failed, both Princip and Chabrinovitch made other attempts at suicide which were frustrated. Princip put his revolver to his temple, and had it snatched away by a busybody. Chabrinovitch jumped into the river and was fished out by the police. He made at that point a remark which has drawn on him much heavy-footed derision from German writers owing to a misunderstanding over a Serb word. A policeman who arrested him said in his evidence at the trial, 'I hit him with my fist, and I said, "Why don't you come on? You are a Serb, aren't you?"' He said that Chabrinovitch answered him in a phrase that has been too literally translated, 'Yes, I am a Serbian hero.' This has been taken by foreign commentators as proof of Chabrinovitch's exalted folly and the inflamed character of Serbian nationalism. But the word '*Yunak*' has a primary meaning of hero and a secondary meaning of militant nationalist. The words the policeman intended to put into Chabrinovitch's mouth were simply 'Yes, I am a Serbian nationalist,' so that he could say that he had then asked, 'Where did you get your gun?' and that he had been answered, 'From

our society.' Chabrinovitch gave a convincing denial that the
conversation, even in this form, ever took place. Thus is the face
of history thickly veiled.

The two youths, beaten to unconsciousness, were taken to
prison; which on the morrow of St. Vitus's Day was as good a
place to be as any in Sarajevo. For there broke out an anti-Slav
riot which in its first impulse destroyed the best hotel in Sarajevo
and the office of a Serb newspaper, and the next day merged
into an organized pogrom of the Serb inhabitants of Sarajevo.
There was, of course, some spontaneous feeling against them.
Many Moslems grieved over the loss of their protector, and a
number of devoutly Catholic Croats regretted their coreligionist
for his piety; it is known that some of these, notably a few Croat
clerical students, joined in the rioting. But General Potiorek had
had to contrive the rest. The bulk of the demonstrators consisted
of very poor Catholics, Jews, and Moslems, many of whom had
come to town to work in the new factories and had fallen into a
pitiful slough of misery. Those unhappy wretches were told by
police agents that if they wanted to burn and loot authority would
hold its hand, and, more than that, that they had better burn and
loot good and hard, lest a misfortune should fall on the town.

This warning was more heavily impressed on the people by the
thousands of troops that had been brought into the town now that
Franz Ferdinand and Sophie Chotek were dead and beyond need of
protection. There were enough of them to line three-deep the long
route by which the coffins passed from the Cathedral to the railway
station. Many of them were Croat and Austrian, and afterwards
they walked about with fixed bayonets, singing anti-Serb songs.
They did not interfere with the rioters. Rather were they apt to
deal harshly with those who were not taking a sufficiently active
part in the riot. It was doubtless easy to take the hint and enjoy
the licence. Human nature is not very nice.

But the full blame for the riot cannot be laid on these helpless victims of coercion. The leading Serb in Sarajevo owned
a house, a hotel, a café, warehouses, and stables, in different
parts of the town. All were visited, and all were methodically
sacked from cellar to roof. Street fighters do not work with
such system. Then those who appeared with pickaxes and slowly
and conscientiously razed to the foundations houses belonging
to the Serbs were not stopped by the authorities. In this way
material damage was inflicted on the town to the amount of two
hundred thousand pounds. So little was the rioting spontaneous
that many Croats and Jews and Moslems risked their lives by

giving shelter to Serbs; but so many lives were lost that the figures were suppressed.

Not a single rioter was jailed nor a single official, military or civil, degraded for failure to keep order. It is not surprising that like riots broke out during the next few days in every provincial town and sizable village where the Croats and Moslems outnumbered the Serbs. This is said to have been a device of General Potiorek to placate the authorities and dissuade them from punishing him for his failure to protect Franz Ferdinand. But it is doubtful if he had any reason to fear punishment, for he was promoted immediately afterwards. Meantime hundreds of schoolboys and students were thrown into prison, and were joined by all eminent Serbs, whether teachers or priests or members of religious or even temperance societies. As soon as war broke out there were appalling massacres; in such a small place as Pali, the winter sports village above Sarajevo, sixty men and women were killed. Wholesale arrests filled the fortresses of Hungary with prisoners, of whom more than half were to die in their dungeons.

The Austrian excuse for this war was self-defence; but it is hard to extend it to cover the riots at Sarajevo. It is carrying self-defence too far to use a pickaxe and demolish the house of the man whom one regards, surely by that time only in theory, as an aggressor. Moreover, already the arrested youths had been interrogated and it must have been suspected by the authorities that the conspiracy might consist of a few isolated people of no importance. Before the provincial riots that suspicion must have become a certainty. For the prisoners had talked quite a lot. They, and those friends of theirs who had been arrested later, had been put to torture. Princip was tied to an oak beam so that he stood tiptoe on the ground. Grabezh was made to kneel on a rolling barrel, so that he continually fell off in a stifling cloud of dust, and was put in a strait-jacket that was pulled in again and again; and shepherd dogs, of the sort that are often terribly strong and savage in Bosnia and Serbia, were let loose in his cell when he was faint with pain and lack of sleep. Chabrinovitch apparently escaped such tortures, because the garrulity of which his friends complained came in useful; from the very beginning he told the police a great deal, and they did not find out till the end of the trial that it was not true. He concocted a very clever story that the Freemasons had ordered the murder of Franz Ferdinand because he was so militant a Catholic, which diverted suspicion from Belgrade. But Ilitch was also arrested, and the threat of torture was enough to make him tell everything. Let him who is without fear cast the first stone; but it meant that all the peasants and tradesmen who had reluctantly helped in the journey from the frontier, all the schoolboys who had chattered with him about revolt at the pastrycook's, joined the conspirators in jail. Some of them, however, would have been arrested in any case, for the Austrian Army had by now crossed the Serbian frontier and seized the customs records, which made them able to trace the route. The conspirators passed a time of waiting before the trial which would have been unutterably terrible to Western prisoners, but which these strange, passionate, yet philosophical children seem to have in a fashion enjoyed, though at one time hope deferred must have made their hearts sicken. In their cells they heard the guns of the Serbian Army as it crossed the Drina, and they expected to be rescued. But the sound of the firing guns grew fainter and died away, and later Serbian prisoners of war were brought into the prison.

On the twelfth of October the trial began. It is typical of the insanity of our world that, ten weeks before this, Austria had declared war on Serbia because of her responsibility for the *attentat*, although these were the first proceedings which made it possible to judge whether that responsibility existed. The trial was for long veiled from common knowledge. Only certain highly official German and Austrian newspapers were allowed to send correspondents. Chabrinovitch, in the course of one of his very intelligent interventions in the trial, talked of the secret sittings of the court, and when the president asked him what he meant, he pointed out that no representatives of the opposition press were present. To this the president made the reply, which is curiously like what we have heard from the Nazis very often since, 'What! According to your ideas, is a court open only when the representatives of the opposition are allowed to come in?' There were naturally no English or French correspondents at that time; and there were apparently no American journalists. None could follow Serbo-Croat, so they took their material from their German colleagues. The most dramatic event of our time was thus completely hidden from us at the time when it most affected us; and it has only been gradually and partially revealed. The official reports were sent to Vienna and there they disappeared. Not till the early twenties was a carbon copy found in Sarajevo. This can be read in a French translation; care should be taken in consulting a German version, for one at least abounds in interpolations and perversions devised in the interest of upholding Chabrinovitch's fabrications about Freemasonry. The only account of it in English is contained in Mr Stephen Graham's admirable novel *St. Vitus' Day*.

It is perhaps for this reason that there are many false ideas abroad today concerning the conspiracy. It is imagined to have been far more formidable than it was. People say, 'You know Franz Ferdinand had no chance, there were seven men in the street to shoot him if Princip failed.' This is what the Moslems in the Town Hall thought, but it is not true. Princip was not the first but the last in the line of assassins, and all the rest had proved themselves unfitted for their job. It is also held that the conspirators were dangerous fanatics of maniacal or at least degenerate type. But actually their behaviour in court was not only completely sane but cheerful and dignified, and their evidence and speeches showed both individual ability and a very high level of culture. Even those who hate violence and narrow passions must admit that the records of the trial open a world which is not displeasing.

It is, of course, disordered. As a schoolboy goes into the dock he is asked according to form whether he has any previous convictions. Yes, he has served a fortnight in prison for having struck a teacher in a political disturbance in a class-room. One peasant, charged with helping the conspirators to dispose of the bombs, wept perpetually. It was the fate of his simple law-abiding sort to be ground between the upper and the nether millstones of an oppressive government and revolutionary societies so desperate that they dared to be almost as oppressive. When they asked him why he had not denounced the party to the police when he saw the bombs, he said, 'But with us one cannot do a thing like that without the permission of the head of the family.' He was sentenced to be hanged, and though his sentence was reduced to twenty years' imprisonment, he died in prison. Other prisoners showed the essential unity of the Slav race by talking like Dostoievsky characters, by falling out of a procession that marched briskly to a temporal measure and settling down to discuss spiritual matters, no more quickly than the slow pulse of eternity. When the president of the court said to one of the schoolboys, 'But you say you're religious . . . that you're a member of the Orthodox Church. Don't you realize that your religion forbids the killing of a man? Is your faith serious or is it on the surface?' the boy thoughtfully answered, 'Yes, it is on the surface.' Another expounded the mysticism of Pan-Slavism, claiming that his nationalism was part of his religion, and his religion was part of his nationalism. How poorly Austria was qualified to bring order into these gifted people's lives—and there was no reason for her presence if she could not—is shown by the shocking muddle of the court procedure. Dates were hardly ever mentioned and topics were brought up as they came into the heads of the lawyers rather than according to any logical programme.

Nobody made any recriminations against Ilitch, though it was apparent he had behaved far from well. Some of the prisoners fought for their lives, but with a certain dignity, and on the whole without sacrifice of their convictions. It is very clear, however, that Princip was in a class apart. Throughout the trial he was always selfless and tranquil, alert to defend and define his ideas but indifferent to personal attacks. He never made a remark throughout the trial that was not sensible and broadminded. It is interesting to note that he declared he had committed his crime as a peasant who resented the poverty the Austrians had brought on his kind.

Chabrinovitch, however, was a very good second, in spite of the unfavourable impression he often made. That impression one can quite understand after one has read the records. At one point he held up the proceedings to make a clever and obscure joke that did not quite come off, of the sort that infuriates stupid people; but it is also clear that he was extremely able. He kept his Freemasonry myth going with remarkable skill; and Princip carried on a debate which the left-wing youth of England and France came to only much later. Chabrinovitch had in the past been a pacifist. Indeed, though a passionate Pan-Serb, he had dissuaded many of his fellow-students from enlisting in Serbia's ranks during the Balkan wars. He was still so much of a pacifist that he was not sure whether his act in attempting the life of Franz Ferdinand had been morally defensible. It was, if it were ever right to use force; but of that he was never fully persuaded. In his speech to the court before it pronounced judgment this point of view was very apparent. He did not ask for mercy, and he quite rightly laid the blame for his crime on the poisoned atmosphere of the oppressed provinces, where every honest man was turned into a rebel, and assassination became a display of virtue. But Princip had always been of the opinion that this was not the time for Bosnians to delve into first principles. He had never been a pacifist, and as a boy had argued coldly and destructively with the Tolstoyan group in Sarajevo. He simply said: 'Anyone who says that the inspiration for this *attentat* came from outside our group is playing with the truth. We originated the idea, and we carried it out. We loved the people. I have nothing to say in my defence.'

The trial went as might have been expected. Consideration of the speeches of the counsel for the defence show that it was very nearly as difficult in Austria for a prisoner charged by the Government to find a lawyer to put his case as it is in Nazi Germany. The Croat lawyer who was defending one prisoner showed the utmost reluctance to plead his cause at all. He began his speech by saying, 'Illustrious tribunal, after all we have heard, it is peculiarly painful for me, as a Croat, to conduct the defence of a Serb.' But there was one counsel, Dr Rudolf Zistler, who bore himself as a hero. With an intrepidity that was doubly admirable considering it was war-time, he pointed out that the continual succession of trials for high treason in the Slav provinces could only be explained by misgovernment; and he raised a vital point, so vital that it is curious he was allowed to finish his speech, by claiming that it was absurd to charge the prisoners with conspiracy to detach Bosnia and Herzegovina from the Austrian Empire, because the legal basis of the annexation of these provinces was unsatisfactory, and in any case the annexation had never been properly ratified. Apparently the first proposition can be disputed, but the second is sound enough. Neither the Austrian nor the Hungarian Parliament ever voted on the necessary Act of Annexation. It was only a technicality, just another piece of *Schlamperei*; but it adds yet one more fantastic touch to the event that Princip had had a legal right to be where he was in Sarajevo, and that Franz Ferdinand had had none.

Nothing, of course, was of any avail. Ilitch, together with a schoolmaster, a retired bioscope exhibitor, the peasant who wept, and one more stoical, who had all played a part in harbouring and transporting the munitions, was sentenced to the gallows, and the first three of them were hanged in Sarajevo four months later. The last two were reprieved and sentenced to imprisonment for twenty years and for life, respectively. Princip, Chabrinovitch, and Grabezh would have been hanged had they not been under twenty-one. As it was they received sentences of twenty years' imprisonment, one day of fast each month, and twenty-four hours in a dungeon on every anniversary of the twenty-eighth of June. The rest of the conspirators were sentenced to terms of imprisonment ranging from life down to three years. These were not excessive sentences. In England Princip would have very rightly been sent to the gallows. Nevertheless, the sequel is not such as can be contemplated without horror and pity. Thirteen conspirators were sent to Austrian prisons. Before the end of the war, which came three and a half years later, nine of them had died in their cells.

How this slow murder was contrived in the case of Princip is known to us, through Slav guards and doctors. He was taken to an eighteenth-century fortress at Theresienstadt between Prague and Dresden. The Austrians would not leave him in Sarajevo because they already saw that the war was not going as they had hoped, and they feared that Bosnia might fall into Serbian hands. He was put in an underground cell filled with the stench of the surrounding marshes, which received the fortress sewage. He was in irons. There was no heating. He had nothing to read. On St Vitus's Day he had sustained a broken rib and a crushed arm which were never given proper medical attention. At Theresienstadt the arm became tuberculous and suppurated, and he contracted a fungoid infection on the body. Three times he tried to commit suicide, but in his cell there lacked the means either of life or of death. In 1917 his forearm became so septic that it had to be amputated. By this time Chabrinovitch and Grabezh were both dead, it is said of tuberculosis. Grabezh at any rate had been a perfectly healthy boy till his arrest. Princip never rallied after his operation. He had been put in a windowless cell, and though he could no longer be handcuffed, since the removal of his arm, his legs were hobbled with heavy chains. In the spring of 1918 he died. He was buried at night, and immense precautions were taken to conceal the spot. But the Austrian Empire had yet to make the last demonstration of *Schlamperei* in connexion with the Sarajevo *attentat*. One of the soldiers who dug the grave was a Slav, and he took careful note of its position; he came forward after the peace and gave his information to the Serbs. They were able to identify the body by its mutilations.

Princip appears to have suffered greatly under his imprisonment, though with courage. In his death, as in everything we hear reported of his life, there was a certain noble integrity of experience. He offered himself wholly to each event in order that he might learn in full what revelation it had to make about the nature of the universe. How little of a demented fanatic he was, what qualities of restraint and deliberation he brought to his part in the *attentat*, is revealed by the testimony of the Czech doctor who befriended him in prison. From the court records one would suppose him to be without personal ties, to be perhaps an orphan, at any rate to be wholly absorbed in politics. Yet to the Czech doctor he spoke perpetually of his dear mother, of his brothers and their children, and of a girl whom he had loved and whom he had hoped to marry, though he had never kissed her.

Chabrinovitch took his punishment differently, and almost certainly a little more happily. It chanced that in prison he had momentary contact with Franz Werfel, the greatest of post-war

Austrian writers, who was working there as hospital orderly. In an essay Werfel has recorded his surprise at finding that the Slav assassin, whom he had imagined as wolfish and demented, should turn out to be this delicate and gentle boy, smiling faintly in his distress. It can be recognized from his account that Chabrinovitch used in prison that quality which annoyed his less-gifted friends, which was the antithesis, or perhaps the supplement, of Princip's single-mindedness. He took all experience that came his way and played with it, discussed it, overstated it, understated it, moaned over it, joked about it, tried out all its intellectual and emotional potentialities. What these youths did was abominable, precisely as abominable as the tyranny they destroyed. Yet it need not be denied that they might have grown to be good men, and perhaps great men, if the Austrian Empire had not crashed down on them in its collapse. But the monstrous frailty of empire involves such losses.

At the cemetery we forgot for a moment why we were there, so beautifully does it lie in the tilted bowl of the town. It is always so in Sarajevo. Because of the intricate contours of its hills it is for ever presenting a new picture, and the mind runs away from life to its setting. And when we had passed the cemetery gates, we forgot again for another reason. Not far away among the tombs there was a new grave, a raw wound in the grass. A wooden cross was at its head, and burning candles were stuck in the broken clay. At the foot of it stood a young officer, his face the colour of tallow. He rocked backwards in his grief, though very slightly, and his mouth worked with prayer. His uniform was extremely neat. Yet once, while we stared at him in shocked distress, he tore open his skirted coat as if he were about to strip; but instantly his hand did up the buttons as if he were a nurse coolly tending his own delirium.

This was a Slav, this is what it is to be a Slav. He was offering himself wholly to his sorrow, he was learning the meaning of death and was not refusing any part of the knowledge; for he knew that experience is the cross man must take up and carry. Not for anything would he have chosen to feel one shade less pain; and if it had been joy he was feeling, he would have permitted himself to feel all possible delight. He knew only that in suffering or rejoicing he must not lose that control of the body which enabled him to be a good soldier and to defend himself and his people, so that they would endure experience along their own path and acquire their own revelation of the universe.

There is no other way of living which promises that man shall ever understand his destiny better than he does, and live less familiarly with evil. Yet to numberless people all over Europe, to numberless people in Great Britain, this man would be loathsome as a leper. It is not pleasant to feel pain, it is the act of a madman to bare the breast to agony. It is not pleasant to admit that we know almost nothing, so little that, for lack of knowledge, our actions are wild and foolish. It is not pleasant to be bound to the task of learning all our days, to be under the obligation to go on learning even though it involves making acquaintance with pain, although we know that we must die still in ignorance. To do these things it is necessary to have faith in what is entirely hidden and unknown, to cast away all the acquisitions and certainties which would ensure a comfortable existence lest they should impede us on a journey which may never be accomplished, which never even offers comfort. Therefore the multitudes in Europe who are not hungry for truth would say: 'Let us kill these Slavs with their dedication to insanity, let us enslave them lest they make all wealth worthless and introduce us at the end to God, who may not be pleasant to meet.'

The judge and the banker said, 'Look, they are here.' Close to the palings of the cemetery, under three stone slabs, lie the conspirators of Sarajevo, those who were hanged and five of those who died in prison; and to them has been joined Zheraitch, the boy who tried to kill the Bosnian Governor General Vareshanin and was kicked as he lay on the ground. The slab in the middle is raised. Underneath it lies the body of Princip. To the left and the right lie the others, the boys on one side and the men on the other, for in this country it is recognized that the difference between old and young is almost as great as that between men and women. The grave is not impressive. It is as if a casual hand had swept them into a stone drawer. There was a battered wreath laid askew on the slabs, and candles flickered in rusty lanterns. This untidiness means nothing. It is the Moslem habit to be truthful about death, to admit that what it leaves of our kind might just as well be abandoned to the process of the earth. Only to those associated with a permanent system, who were holy men or governors or great soldiers, do Moslems raise tombs that are in any sense monuments, and they are more careful to revere these than to keep them in order. After all, a stone with a green stain of weed on it commemorates death more appropriately than polished marble. This attitude is so reasonable that it has spread from the Moslems to the Christians in all territories where they are found side by side. It does not imply insensibility. The officer swaying in front of the cross on the new grave might never be wholly free of his grief till he died, but this did not mean that he would derive any satisfaction at all in making the grave look like part of a garden. And as we stood by the shabby monument an old woman passing along the road outside the cemetery paused, pressed her face against the railings, looked down on the stone slab, and retreated into prayer. Later a young man who was passing by with a cart loaded with vegetables stopped and joined her, his eyes also set in wonder on the grave, his hand also making the sign of the cross on brow and breast, his lips also moving.

On their faces there was none of the bright acclaiming look which shines in the eyes of those who talk of, say, Andreas Hofer. They seemed to be contemplating a mystery, and so they were; for the Sarajevo *attentat* is mysterious as history is mysterious, as life is mysterious. Of all the men swept into this great drawer only one, Princip, had conceived what they were doing as a complete deed. To Chabrinovitch it had been a hypothesis to be used as a basis for experiment; his vision of it came from the brain only, and not from the blood. To some of the others it had been an event interesting to imagine, which would certainly not be allowed to happen by the inertia we all feel in the universe, the resistance life puts up against the human will, particularly if that is making any special effort. To the rest, to the unhappy peasants and tradesmen who found themselves quite involuntarily helping the boys in their journey from the Serbian frontier, it must have seemed as if the troubles of their land had fused into a mindless catastrophe, like plague or famine. But the deed as Princip conceived it never took place. It was entangled from its first minute with another deed, a murder which seems to have been fully conceived by none at all, but which had a terrible existence as a fantasy, because it was dreamed of by men whose whole claim to respect rested on their realistic quality, and who abandoned all restraint when they strayed into the sphere of fantasy. Of these two deeds there was made one so potent that it killed its millions and left all living things in our civilization to some degree disabled. I write of a mystery. For that is the way the deed appears to me, and to all Westerners. But to those who look at it on the soil where it was committed, and to the lands east of that, it seems a holy act of liberation; and among such people are those whom the West would have to admit are wise and civilized.

This event, this Sarajevo *attentat*, was in these inconsistencies an apt symbol of life: which is loose and purposeless, which weaves a close pattern and doggedly pursues its ends, which is unpredictable and illogical, which follows a straight line from cause to effect, which is bad, which is good. It shows that human will can do anything, it shows that accident does everything. It shows that man throws away his peace for a vain cause if he insists on acquiring knowledge, for the more one knows about the *attentat* the more incomprehensible it becomes. It shows also that moral judgment sets itself an impossible task. The soul should choose life. But when the Bosnians chose life, and murdered Franz Ferdinand, they chose death for the French and Germans and English, and if the French and Germans and English had been able to choose life they would have chosen death for the Bosnians. The sum will not add up. It is madness to rack our brains over this sum. But there is nothing else we can do except try to add up this sum. We are nothing but arithmetical functions which exist for that purpose . . . We went out by the new grave where the young officer was trying to add up the sum in the Slav way. A sudden burst of sunshine made the candle-flames sadder than darkness. He swayed so far forward that he had to stay himself by clutching at the cross. His discipline raised him and set him swinging back to his heels again.

Ilidzhe

We were going to see the village outside Sarajevo where the Austrians built a racecourse and where Franz Ferdinand stayed the night before he died. The road was so extravagantly bad that we bounced like balls, and Constantine had a star of mud on his forehead as he told us, 'Sarajevo has a soul like a village, though it is a town. Now, why has a village the sort of soul that it has? Because it is irrigated, because there flow through it rivers of water and rivers of air. If there is water running through a city it is no longer water, it is not clear, it might evoke demonstrations of fastidiousness from a camel; if there is air blowing through the city it cannot be called wind, it loses its force among the houses. So it is with movements in the mind, they become polluted and effete. Religion instead of being an ecstasy and a cosmology becomes ethical, philosophical, penitential. But in Sarajevo,' he continued, as the car lifted itself out of a rut with a movement not to be expected from a machine, credible only in a tiger leaping out of a pit, 'there is a vivifying conception which irrigates the city and makes it fresh like a village. Here Slavs, and a very fine kind of Slav, endowed with great powers of perception and speculation, were confronted with the Turkish Empire at its most magnificent, which is to say Islam at its most magnificent, which is to say Persia at its most magnificent. Its luxury we took, its militarism and its pride, and above all its conception of love. The luxury has gone. The militarism has gone. You saw at the railway station the other morning what had happened to the pride. But the conception of love is still in the city, and it is a wonderful conception, it refreshes and revivifies, it is clean water and strong wind.'

'What is peculiar about this conception of love?' asked my husband, who had just been thrown on his knees to the floor of the car. 'It is,' said Constantine, failing to remove his stomach from the small of my back, 'the conception of love which made us as small boys read the *Arabian Nights* with such attention, so that Grandmamma always said, "How he reads and reads, we must make a priest of him." Is it not extraordinary, by the way, that all over Europe, even in the pudic nurseries of your own country, this should be regarded as a children's book? It is as if our civilization felt fear that it had carried too far its experiment of bringing up children in innocence, but would not admit it, and

called in another race to administer all that knowledge which had
been suppressed, in an exotic and disguised form, so that it could
be passed off as an Eastern talisman engraved with characters
which naturally cannot be read, though they are to be admired
aesthetically.' 'About this conception of love,' said my husband,
struggling up to a seated position and wiping the mud off his
glasses, 'you mean the old crones arriving with messages and
the beautiful women in darkened rooms, and the hiding in jars?'
'Yes, that is it,' said Constantine, 'the old crones, very discreet,
the pursuit of the occasion that demanded faith, the flash of eye
below a veil lifted for only a second, the wave of a scarf from a
lattice, which was at once a promise of beauty and a challenge to
cunning and courage, for there might be a witty ambush hiding
in jars and there might be death from a eunuch's sword. It is too
beautiful.

'Too beautiful!' he repeated, beaming as one cradled in content
though at the moment he was actually suspended in the air. 'It is
a conception of love which demands that it should be sudden and
secret and dangerous. You from the West have no such conception
of love. It seems to you that love must be as slow as the growth of
a plant: a man and woman must come throughout many months to
a full understanding of each other's natures and take serious vows
to fulfil each other's needs. You think also that a man insults a
woman if he wishes to make love to her without delay, and that a
woman is worthless if she gives herself to a man before they have
killed a great part of the calendar. In this there is much truth. I
remember that when I was a young man in Paris, it sometimes
happened that though I had two mistresses there were times when
I went out into the street and took the first woman I met, and it
was because I am in part a barbarian and so I could not wait. That
was nothing. But love can be sudden and quite different from that.
It can be so ecstatic that it can come into full being at a single
encounter, that it needs only that encounter to satisfy the lovers.

'If you offered them a lifetime together you could not offer them
more than the night that follows when the old crone has opened
the door. No, the car is not going to turn over. And when you
come back next year the road will be better. We are a young
country, and we will do all, but we have not yet had the time.
Such love could properly be engendered by a single glance from
the eyes. Indeed it could not claim to be this kind of love, this
ultimate affinity, if the most infinitesimal contact was not enough
to declare it. That is why it must be sudden.

'It must be secret because jealousy is a part of both this sudden love and the other, slow-moving kind. A man who performs the miracle of keeping a woman happy for forty years cannot bear it that on one night during those forty years another man should be necessary for her happiness; and a man who meets a woman once and makes that meeting as fabulous in her memory as a night spent in the moon cannot bear it that he should not be the father of the eleven children whose noses she wipes. Hence these men must not know of each other. We roar like bulls about our honour, but so it is.

'Also this love must be dangerous, or it would not be itself. That is not to say that one does not value a thing unless one has paid a great price for it—that is vulgar. But if a woman did not know that to lift her veil before a stranger was perhaps to die, she might perhaps lift it when she had received no intimation of this great and sudden love: when she was merely barbarian. And indeed neither she nor her lover could fully consummate this kind of love without a sense of peril. They would not shut the eyes of reason and precipitate themselves into the abyss of passion, unless they knew this might be their last chance to experience it or, indeed, anything else.

'It is a more marvellous conception of love, I think, than anything other nations know. The French make love for the sake of life; and so, like living, it often falls to something less than itself, to a little trivial round. The Germans make love for the sake of death; as they like to put off civilian clothes and put on uniform, because there is more chance of being killed, so they like to step out of the safe casual relations of society and let loose the destructive forces of sex. So it was with *Werther* and *Elective Affinities*, and so it was in the years after the war, when they were so promiscuous that sex meant nothing at all. And this is not to speak ill of the French and Germans, for the love of life and the love of death are both necessary things. But this conception unites love of life and death in a single experience. Such lovers are conscious at once of the extremity of danger and that which makes danger most terrible and at the same time most worth challenging.'

'But that is the essence of all adventure,' said my husband, 'and indeed it is the essence of——' 'Yes, yes, what you say is very true,' said Constantine, as he always does when he intends that the person who is talking to him shall talk no more. 'It is this conception of love which gives life to the city of Sarajevo. How far this tradition exists today I cannot tell. But I think that even now old women are sometimes sent with messages that must be

read by only one person, and I think that the plum trees would
not blossom so freely round those little restaurants on the hillside
above the town if some god or goddess had not been placated by
sacrifice.' 'You think,' said my husband, 'the rose never grows
one-half so red.' 'But I am sure,' continued Constantine, 'that
the conception gives the town a special elegance. The men and
women in it have another dimension given to their lives, because
they have kept in their hearts the capacity for this second kind of
love. They are not mutilated by its suppression, and they have
hope. All of them may yet have this revelation, and some of them
have actually had it. I think that is why so many of the women
here have lips and eyes that shine like children's, and why the
men are not bitter or grudging or hurried. A sensuality that is also
a mysticism,' he cried, 'what can a race invent better for itself?
But here is Ilidzhe, here is our marvellous Ilidzhe!' He leaped
in one second from well-buttered reverie to shaking indignation.
'Ilidzhe, our Potemkin village! They built it to show the foreign
visitors how well they had imposed civilization on our barbarism,
just as Potemkin built villages on the steppes to impress the foreign
ambassadors with Russian prosperity, hollow villages that were
built the day before and were pulled down the day after. Come,
look at their civilization, at our barbarity!'

The spa waited for us behind the scrubby, half-forested edge
of a park, and indeed it was not pleasing. In earlier days it had
certainly been better kept; it now looked like any of the other
Yugoslavian spas, which are patronized by the peasants and
small shopkeepers, and showed a certain homely untidiness,
though nothing worse. But the place was unengaging in its
architectural essence. A string of shapeless hotels was joined
by a covered corridor to a central restaurant and pump-room,
a pudding of a place. Every building was smothered in heavy
porches and balustrades and balconies of craftless but elaborate
woodwork. The hotels were all closed at the moment, they did not
open till the heat brought people out of the city; and we strolled
about looking for the proprietor of the Hotel Bosnia, the largest
of the hotels, at which Franz Ferdinand and Sophie Chotek had
spent their last night. 'I think that they have kept the chapel that
was made for their coming,' said Constantine, 'and I know they
keep their room as it was, for I have seen it. It was the suite
reserved always for the royal family and for the governor, and
it was altogether Moslem, but a terrible Moslem. It was like a
place I have seen in your London, when I was there for five days
during the war, called the Kardomah Café: all little inlaid tables

and a clutter of many things, whereas, as you have seen, the chief furniture of a Moslem house is the light. Also I would like you to meet my friend who is the director of the spa, he has a very beautiful wife and her sister, who would like to talk to you about Tennyson's *Idylls of the King*. They read nothing else, they would be Enid and Guinevere.' He waved his arms as if he were wearing long flowing sleeves, and pulled out his neck to its most swanlike. 'But here is a man with keys.'

They fitted, however, only the door of a little shop in the Hotel Bosnia's arcade; but the man was glad to have a talk. 'He says,' said Constantine, 'that they do their best to keep the place neat, but that there is not enough money to do much. Many people come here in summer, but they are not rich, like the nobles who used to come here from Austria and Germany and England to see how beautifully Bosnia was being governed by the Austrian Empire. But he would not have it different, though he has been here since a child and loves the place, for he is a very patriotic Yugoslav. But really it is disgusting, this Ilidzhe. They did nothing for the country, but they built these hotels and the racecourse which I am going to show you presently, and all the grand people came and looked at it and said, "Ah, it is so in Bosnia, all weeded gravel paths and new houses and good beer, it is too good for these cattle of Slavs."' He mimicked the tone of a fine lady, turning his face from side to side and twirling an imaginary open parasol.

The man with the keys had been watching. He suddenly threw down his keys on to the pavement and began to shout straight past us to the horizon: like the young man at Trsat, like the young man on the boat whose soup was cold, like the hotel manager from Hvar. 'Yes, yes,' he cried, 'and they had our men and women brought in to dance the kolo to them, we were for them the natives, the savages, and we had to dance for them as if we were bears at a fair.' He bent and picked up the keys, then remembered something and threw them down again. 'And what they did to us as soldiers! They made us become soldiers, and when a man goes into battle he may be called before his God, and they made us Christians wear the fez! Yes, the fez of the accursed Turks was the headgear of all our four Bosnian regiments!'

He picked up his keys for the second time and led us along the corridor to the railway station, which indeed was very grand, in the manner of Baden-Baden or Marienbad. 'I find this grotesquely unpleasing,' I said. 'I did not bring you here to please you,' said Constantine, 'when I take you to see things that were left by the Turks and the Austrians it is not to please you, it is so that you shall understand. And now, will you please look where I tell you? This station is very untidy, is it not? The paint has gone and there are no flowers growing in wire cages. Will you please look at the chestnut tree that stands in the middle of this piece of gravel outside the station? Do you see that there are growing round it many weeds? Now, I apply a test. If you are saved, if you know what the soul is and what a people is, you will be able to see that that tree is better now, standing among weeds, than it was when it was spick and span; for these weeds are the best we can do, they are all the order we can yet attain in Bosnia, and the spickness and spanness came from another people, and were therefore nothingness, they could not exist here, because they were not part of the national process.' 'There I cannot agree,' I said. 'I do not believe that it was wrong of the English to drain India and abolish suttee, I do not believe that the Pères Blancs did wrong in medicining the sicknesses of Africa.' 'Do I not know such things must be done?' said Constantine. 'We Yugoslavs are stamping out malaria in Macedonia and we are raising up peasants that have been trodden into the mud by the Turks. But it should be done by one's people, never by strangers.' 'Rats,' said my husband; 'if a people have wholly gone under, without a fringe that has kept its independence and its own folk-ways, strangers must butt in and help it get on its feet again. The trouble is that the kind of stranger who likes helping unfortunate people usually does not get leave to set about it unless other members of his group see a military or commercial advantage to be got out of it. But if you mean that the Bosnians had enough force and enough remnants of the old Slav culture to look after themselves once they got the Turks off their necks, and that the Austrians had nothing to give them and had no business here, then I'm with you.' 'Ah, you have said something true and so untidy,' complained Constantine, 'and what I said was not quite true, but so beautifully neat.'

But it was where the racecourse drew its white diagram on the gardeny plains that the irrelevance of the Austrian intervention appeared most apparent. The scene was now enchanting. All over the course sheep and cattle were grazing on the turf, ringing faint little bells as they were pressed on by comfortable, slow-moving greed, or met the active air, not quite a wind, which flowed quietly down the great tawny valley that led back to Sarajevo. Where there was not grass the earth showed red; and the poplars stood like jets of chill green-gold light. Scattered on the plains were the rough white farms and cottages of Christians; and on every slope which promised a fine view there stood a Moslem villa, smoothly and solidly white among the white clouds of its orchard. One such villa stood on a little hill close by the racecourse, as compact a delight as if an enormous deal of spring had been boiled down till it would fill just a little pot, according to the method of making rose-leaf jam.

And the white rails, of course, recalled another delight. I saw a string of horses going like a line of good poetry, under a cloudless morning on Lambourn Downs. I remembered what the author of the Book of Job had said about the horse: 'The glory of his nostrils is terrible. He paweth in the valley, and rejoiceth in his strength. . . . He saith among the trumpets, Ha, ha; and he smelleth the battle afar off, the thunder of the captains, and the shouting. . . .' A pleasure, undoubtedly, but how irrelevant to the starving Bosnian peasant, and how irrelevant, how insolent to Sarajevo. The scenery before me was distressing in its evocation of Austrian society as it was in the time of Franz Josef, as Metternich had foreseen it must become if the Empire was not allowed some measure of freedom. Banality rose from the tomb and stood chattering about the lawns: women with heavy chins and lively untender eyes and blonde frizzes of hair under straw boaters, wearing light blouses and long skirts and broad waistbands, men with the strongly marked expressions of ventriloquists' dummies, with sloping shoulders and ramrod backs. They chattered loudly, with the exaggerated positiveness of those who live in a negative world. They were Catholics who could nourish among them a '*Los von Rom*' movement, they were cosmopolitans who lived by provincial standards, they were bound by etiquette and recognized no discipline, they were the descendants of connoisseurs yet neither produced nor appreciated great art, they sacrificed all civil interests to a military caste that proved as soon as war broke out to be wholly civilian in everything but its splendid and suicidal valour.

These people had come to govern, to change, to civilize such men and women as we had seen in Sarajevo: the Jews with their tradition of fine manners and learning; the Moslems with their houses full of light and their blossoming gardens and dedication to peaceful nature; the old women we had seen in the market-place, whose souls had attained to wit; the men whose long strides were endurance itself, who would know, like our friend with the keys, that an honest man must not dance before tyrants nor go to his God in the fez. These women in blouses and skirts had come as examples of the fashion to those who had worn Persian brocades since West was on visiting terms with East; the ramrod men had come to command such as the officer who had stood swaying by the new grave. The builders of these horrible hotels, of the little covered corridor that looked as if one end of it might have led to the old Druce's Bazaar in Baker Street, had come to Sarajevo, the town of a hundred mosques, to teach and not to learn.

Treboviche

Later that afternoon we drove out of Sarajevo by the road that leads to Treboviche, the mountain which rises too near the town and too steeply to be seen from it. The craned neck can see only its foothills. Half-way up we stopped the automobile and stood on a grassy ledge to see the orchards and villas lying beneath us, all little pots of spring jam, like the villa by the racecourse. On a ledge above us were standing some gipsies, eight or nine girls in jackets and trousers of printed curtain stuffs, and two men who were jumping and gesticulating in front of them, the upturned toes of their leather sandals looking like cockspurs. Something about the gestures of Constantine's plump little arms as he showed us the city brought them tumbling about us. A good many people of the lettered sort recognized Constantine from his caricatures in the papers; but the unlettered see him for what he is with astonishing quickness. He has only to swing an eloquent hand at a street-corner and there are men and women about us looking at him with an expression which sums up the twofold attitude of ordinary folk to the poet: a mixture of amused indulgence, as of a grown-up watching a child at play, and ecstatic expectation, as of a child waiting for a grown-up to tell it a fairy-story. These gipsies ran down the grassy slope and stood about us giggling in a circle of crimson and plum and blue and green and lemon and cinnabar, the wind blowing out their full trousers and making them hug their shawls under the chin. They bring a lovely element into a community which allows them to exist without sinking into squalor. It is as if one could go out and make love to a flower, or have foxes and hares to play music at one's parties.

The higher rocks above the road were pale green with hellebores, and there were primroses and cowslips and cyclamen, and at last the faded mauve flames of crocus. Then we came to the snow, lying thinly on scars and under pinewoods. Where it deepened we left the car and walked past a house which might have been a Swiss chalet, had it not been for the music that someone within was plucking from the strings of a gusla, to a peak shoulder crusted in ice and deep with snow where there was a shadowed seam. About us were the smouldering Bosnian uplands, their heathy heights red with last year's autumn, though in some valleys the first touch of spring had given a spinney or an alp a hard mineral viridity. These heights and valleys run neither north nor south nor west nor east, but in all ways for a mile at a time, so that the landscape turns like a merry-go-round. Beyond these broken and burning highlands lay a wall of amber cloud, and above this rose two unknown ranges, one reflecting on its snows the brightness of an afternoon that was for us already dimmed, the other crimson with an evening that had not yet reached us. Sarajevo we could not see: the valley that runs down from it was a vast couch for a white river, until it twisted and broke and broadened and couched several rivers, which in winding spread their whiteness in mist. Over all the nearer highlands was cast a web of paths joining the villages across the tawny distance; and from some of them, though they were a mile or two away, came sounds of playing children and barking dogs.

Cold, we went back to the chalet and drank warming coffee under the pictures of the boy King and his mother and his murdered father. They are found in every public place in Yugoslavia, even Croatia. I think they are present in anti-Serb territory because they are sold by some charitable society which nobody wishes to refuse, but in other parts, where there lingers the medieval conception of the king as a priest of the people, they have nearly the status of holy pictures. At the back of the room sat a handsome young man playing the gusla and singing, apparently the proprietor, and two very pretty young women, all with that characteristically Slav look which comes from the pulling of the flesh down from the flat cheekbones by the tense pursing of the mouth. On the face of the murdered King there was the same expression, hardened to woodenness by the fear of death coming from assassination without or tuberculosis within.

Constantine drank his coffee, pushed away his cup, and said, 'When you look at things, try to remember them wholly because you have soon to go home to England. I think of a story I heard from a monk of how King Alexander came to see the frescoes in his monastery which contained portraits of our Serbian kings of our old Empire, in the thirteenth century, which are real portraits, mind you. Before one he stood for three-quarters of an hour, looking terribly, as one would look on one's father if he came back from the dead, sucking him with the eyes. The monk asked him if he had a special cult for this king, and he said, "No. For all kings of Serbia must I have a cult. All kings I must understand, in order that the new dynasty be grafted on the old. And this king I must make a special effort to understand, since nothing that is written of him makes him quite clear to me." You see, he was a mystic, and because the channel of his mysticism was Yugoslavia, nobody outside Yugoslavia can understand him.'

He put his elbows on the table and rumpled his little black curls. 'Nobody outside Yugoslavia understands us,' he complained. 'We have a very bad press, particularly with the high-minded people, who hate us because we are mystics and not just intelligent, as they are. *Ach!* that Madame Geneviève Tabouis, how she writes of us in her Paris newspaper! She suspects us of being anti-democratic in our natures, when we Serbs are nothing but democratic, but cannot be because the Italians and the Germans are watching us to say, "Ah, here is Bolshevism, we must come in and save you from it." And really she is not being high-minded when she makes this mistake, she makes it because she hates the Prime Minister, Mr Stoyadinovitch; and it is not that she hates him because he is a bad man, she hates him just because they are opposites. She is little and thin and fine, he is a great big man with a strong chest and much flesh that all comes with him when he moves; she finds all relationships difficult, and all men and women follow him as if he were a great horse; she is noble when she loves her country, and when he loves his country it is as natural as when he sweats; and *en somme* he likes wine and can drink it, all sorts of wine, red wine, white wine, champagne, little wines of our country and great wines of France, and she must drink only a little drop of mineral water from a special spa, and of that she has a special source. So they hate each other, and since she is idealistic and is therefore ashamed that she should hate people for the kind of marrow they have in their spines, she pretends to herself she hates Yugoslavia. And yet she is great in her way. But not so great, my pardon to your wife, my dear sir, who I know is a lady writer also, as Mr Stoyadinovitch.'

I never heard anybody else in Yugoslavia speak well of Stoyadinovitch except Constantine; but Constantine was sincere. He laid his cheek on the table, and drew his folded hands back and forward across his forehead. 'There is something,' I said, 'which has been worrying me ever since I stood by the tomb of the *attentateurs*, and what you said at Ilidzhe this morning has intensified my perplexity. Listen. The predominantly German character of the Habsburg monarchy, and the concessions it had to make to the Hungarians, meant that the Austro-Hungarian Empire oppressed its Slavs and feared the kingdom of Serbia as a dangerous potential ally to these discontented subjects. At the same time there were economic conditions in the Austro-Hungarian Empire which meant that there must be sooner or later a revolt, in which these discontented Slavs would be specially likely to bear the brunt of the fighting. Therefore precisely this war that happened in 1914 was bound to happen sooner or later.' 'But certainly,' said Constantine, 'it had nearly happened in 1912, when Franz Ferdinand's friends all but succeeded in starting a preventive war over Albania.' 'Then it mattered not at all what happened in Sarajevo on June twenty-eighth, 1914,' I said. Constantine was silent for a minute. The man behind us stopped playing his gusla, as if he understood what had been said. Constantine said, 'In a sense you are right. The little ones need not have died. And of the two big ones the poor angry one could have gone on shooting his beasts, and the poor striving one could have continued to strive after the little things the other poor ones did not want her to have. We should have had the World War just the same.' 'What a waste!' I said. 'Well, Sarajevo is the one town I know that could bear with equanimity the discovery that her great moment was a delusion, a folly, a simple extravagance,' said Constantine. 'She would walk by her river, she would sit under the fruit tree in her courtyard, and she would not weep.' But after a pause he added, 'But she is not an imbecile. If she would not weep it is because of her knowledge that we are wrong. By the *attentat* she took the war and made it a private possession of the South Slavs. Behind the veil of our incomprehensible language and behind the veil of lies the Austrians and Hungarians have told about us and our wrongs, the cause of the war—more than that, the reason for the war—is eternally a mystery to the vast majority of the people who took part in it and were martyrized by it. Perhaps that is something for us South Slavs, to know a secret that is hidden from everybody else. I do not know. How I wish,' he said, standing up, 'that we could stay here tonight. There are such honest little rooms upstairs, with coarse clean sheets, and it is so quiet. That is to say there are many noises, but they all have a meaning, it is this bird that cries or that, whereas the noises in a city mean nothing. But if we are going to Yaitse tomorrow we must go down to the town.'

It was not yet dark. As we came down we could still see the cyclamen and the primroses and the cowslips on the banks of the road, looking sweetly melancholy as flowers do when seen by other than full light. When we were half-way down the dusk was deep blue, and we stopped the car when we came to the knoll where we had stood beside the gipsies, in order to look down on the scattered lights of Sarajevo. But our chauffeur called out to us from the car, pointing at the city. 'He is asking you to listen to the bells,' said Constantine. 'They are sounding all over the city, and it is a great

thing for him because when the Turks were here there might be
no church bells. This man's father, or his grandfather, told him
of the time, sixty years ago, when they were not allowed, and he
feels proud that they are there now.'

Travnik

On our way out of Sarajevo the next morning we stopped to buy oranges, and I filled my lap with white violets and cowslips and marigolds; and so we started on a morning's drive through valleys which might have been landscaped by Capability Brown, so prettily were the terraces set and planted, so neat was the line the climbing woodlands drew against the hilltop moor. This is in part due to geological accident, but it is also true that hereabouts man has the neatest of hands. He is extremely poor, but he can work miracles with his restricted materials. We came presently to a little spa called Kiselyak, a very old spa, which was popular, particularly among the Jews, in the Turkish times. I suppose that in the last twenty-five years the mass of people who had stayed there were on the same financial level as those in America who have an income of forty dollars a week or under. The place was as pretty as a musical-comedy set. In the main street there was a long low Park Hotel, plastered white as snow, with a brightly striped mattress taking the air at every window, which it seemed could not have been put there in answer to mere necessity, so gay was the pattern.

To admire it, we left the car, and crossed a little stream to a pinewood where there stood an artlessly built bath-house and drinking-fountains. On the bridge there was an elderly Moslem contemplating the running water. Always, in this part of the world, where there is running water, there is an elderly Moslem contemplating it. He joined our party without intrusiveness, and pointed out to us a café near by, a wooden summerhouse built over the stream in a thicket of willows which he rightly thought particularly pleasing, and then he took us over to the drinking-booths and found a Christian gardener who unlocked them and gave us cups of water. It had a fortifying taste of metal. We strolled along a path through the pinewood and came on a black marble monument from which a gold inscription had been savagely excised. The Moslem and the gardener, who had been following us at a few paces' distance, came forward to tell us that it had been put up to commemorate a victory of the Austrian Army over the Bosnian insurgents. 'Would you rather have things as they are now?' said Constantine. They agreed that they would, and we all sat down on a bench, while I finished my cup of water.

'I want to stay here, I do not want to go on,' I said. 'It is the

Moslem who is making you feel like that,' said Constantine, 'that is the great art of the Moslem; and mind you, that is very interesting, for, look at him, he is a Slav like the gardener, who has it not. It is the Turks and his religion that have taught him to sit and do nothing so very nicely. He would be content to sit here all day, just as we are doing now; and indeed it would be most pleasant, for we would listen to the stream and watch the clouds above the tree-tops, and we would smoke and sometimes we would exchange polite remarks.' We stayed there, just as he said, for nearly half an hour. The feeling was as in one of the delightful households to be found in Bath, where there are beautiful manners and beautiful furniture and a complete sense of detachment from modern agitation. But there was not the anxiety about income tax which usually mars such interiors. The Moslem was as poor as can be, even here: he was in neatly mended rags, his leather sandals were tied up with string.

On our way again, such poverty was all about us. The mosques were no longer built of stone and bricks, but were roughly plastered like farm buildings, with tiled roofs and rickety wooden minarets. But they had still a trace of elegance in their design; and there were fine embroideries on the boleros the women wore over their white linen blouses and dark full trousers, and on the shirts of the black-browed men. With some of these people we could not get on friendly terms. If they were in charge of horses they looked at us with hatred, because the horses invariably began to bolt at the sight of the automobile, however much we slowed down. We sent two hay-carts flying into the ditch. So rarely had these people seen automobiles that they looked at us with dignified rebuke, as at vulgarians who insisted on using an eccentric mode of conveyance which put other travellers to inconvenience. But the people who had no horses to manage looked at us with peculiar respect, since automobiles passed so rarely that it seemed to them certain that my husband and Constantine must be important officials from Belgrade. With a stylized look of sternness the men saluted and stood to attention while we passed. 'Look at their faces,' said Constantine; 'they think that all the time they must die for Yugoslavia, and they cannot understand why we do not ask them to do that, but that now we ask another thing, that they should live and be happy.'

The road climbed to a wide valley, where spring winds were hurrying across wet emerald pastures, and through woods sharply green where winter had left them, and bronze where it still dawdled. Little pink pigs and red foals ran helter-skelter before our coming, and men and women in gorgeous clothes, more richly coloured than in the lower valleys, chased after them, but paused to laugh

and greet us. In the distance loomed mountains, holding on their
ledges huge blocks of monastic buildings. These are among the
few relics of the Austrian occupation other than barracks; it was
here that the Empire made the headquarters of their attempt to
Catholicize the Bosnians who belonged to the Orthodox Church.
The Dominicans and the Franciscans, who had been here for
seven hundred years, were reinforced, not altogether to their own
pleasure, by the Jesuits.

At the base of these mountains we touched it, the town which
for good reason was called by the Turks Travnik, or Grassy-town.
Narrow houses with tall and shapely slanting tiled roofs sit gracefully, like cats on their haunches, among the green gardens of a
garden-like valley. Here, in this well-composed littleness, which
lies snug in the field of the eye, can be enjoyed to perfection
the Moslem counterpoint of the soft horizontal whiteness of fruit
blossom and the hard vertical whiteness of minarets. This town was
the capital of Bosnia for two centuries under the Turks, the seat of
the Pasha from the time that Sarajevo would not have him, and it has
a definite urban distinction, yet it is countrified as junket. 'This is
where the Moslem at Kiselyak would like to have a house,' said my
husband, 'if he ever let himself want anything he did not have.'

We had been invited to luncheon with the father and mother
of the lovely Jewess in Sarajevo whom we called the Bulbul,
and we found their home in an apartment house looking over
the blossoming trench of the valley from the main road, under
a hill crowned with a fortress built by the old Bosnian kings.
We found it, and breathed in our nostrils the odour of another
civilization. Our appearance there caused cries of regret. The
father stood in the shadow of the doorway, a handsome man in his
late fifties, whose likeness I had seen often enough in the Persian
miniatures, gazelle-eyed and full-bodied. In the delicious voice of
the Sephardim, honey-sweet but not cloying, he told us that he was
ashamed to let us in, for we would find nothing worthy of us. He had
thought we meant to call at his factory, which was a couple of miles
outside the town, so he had ordered a real meal, a meal appropriate
to us, to be cooked there, and he had left an explanation that he
could not be with us, as his wife had broken her ankle and till she
was well he would eat all his meals with her. He bowed with shame
that he should have blundered so. But a voice, lovely as his own but
a woman's, cried from the darkened room beyond and bade him
bring the strangers in. It was at once maternal, warm with the desire
to do what could be done to comfort our foreignness, and childlike,
breathless with a desire to handle the new toy.

She lay on a sofa, fluttering up against the downward pull of her injury, as hurt birds do; and she was astonishing in the force of her beauty. She was at least in her late forties, and she was not one of those prodigies unmarked by time, but she was as beautiful, to judge by her effect on the beholder, as the Bulbul. That could not really be so, of course. As a general rule Horace must be right, for reasons connected with the fatty deposits under the skin and the working of the ductless glands, when he writes, '*O matre pulchra filia pulchrior*.' Yet in this case he would have been wrong. He should have ignored his metre and written of '*mater pulchrior pulcherrimoe filioe*,' for there was the more beautiful mother of the most beautiful daughter. The Bulbul was the most perfect example conceivable of the shining Jewish type, but so long as one looked on this woman she seemed lovelier than all other women. Her age was unimportant because it did not mean to her what it means to most Western women: she had never been frustrated, she had always been rewarded for her beautiful body and her beautiful conduct by beautiful gratitude.

My husband and I sat down beside her, smiling as at an unexpected present; and she apologized to us for the poor meal she would have to improvise, and cried over our heads directions to her cook in a voice that floated rather than carried, and then settled to ask us questions which were by Western standards personal, which were extremely sensible if she wished to be able to like us quickly before we left her house. In a painted cage a canary suddenly raised fine-drawn but frantic cheers for the universe, and they checked it with gentle laughter that could not have hurt its feelings. The canary, it seemed, her husband had brought home to divert her while she must lie on the sofa. The room was littered with gifts he had fetched her for that purpose: a carved flute, a piece of brocade, an eighteenth-century book of Italian travel with coloured illustrations, an amber box—a trifle, I should say, for each day she had been kept in the house. Their household rocked gently on a tide of giving and receiving.

They watched us sadly while we ate, uttering coos of regret for the meal that was really worthy of us, waiting uneaten in the factory. But we were not discontented. We were given home-made spaghetti, those eggs called 'Spanish eggs' which are boiled for three days in oil and come out greaseless and silky to the palate, lamb chops from small ethereal lambs who probably had wings, sheep's cheese, pure white and delicately sharp, peaches and quinces foundered in syrup that kept all their summer flavour, and raki, the colourless brandy loved by Slavs. As we ate we told them of our meetings with their daughter in Sarajevo, and they stretched like cats in pride and pleasure, owning that all we said of her was true, and reciting some of her accomplishments that they thought we might not have had the chance to observe. Nothing could have been less like the uneasy smile, the deprecating mumble, which is evoked in an Englishman by praise of his family.

But this was a long way from England. Constantine went on to tell the gossip he had picked up in Sarajevo, and the more ambassadorial gossip he had brought from Belgrade, and while they rewarded his perfect story-telling by perfect listening, I looked about the room. It was certainly provincial; anything that had reached the room from Vienna, Berlin, Paris, or London had taken so long to get there and had been so much modified by the thought of the alien taste for which it was destined that it would be antiquated and bizarre. But built into this room, and inherent in every word and gesture of its owners, was a tradition more limited in its scope than the traditions of Vienna, Berlin, Paris, or London, but within its limits just as ancient and sure and competent. Whatever event these people met they could outface; the witness to that was their deep serenity. They would meet it with a formula compounded of Islam and Judaism. Their whole beings breathed the love of pleasure which is the inspiration of Sarajevo, which was perhaps the great contribution the Turks had to make to culture. But it was stabilized, its object was made other than running water, by the Jewish care for the continuity of the race. It was a fusion that would infuriate the Western moralist, who not only believes but prefers that one should not be able to eat one's cake and have it. I went later to comb my hair and wash my hands in these people's bathroom. A printed frieze of naked nymphs dancing in a forest ran from wall to wall, and several pictures bared the breasts and thighs of obsoletely creamy beauties. Naïvely it was revealed that these people thought of the bath as the uncovering of nakedness, and of nakedness as an instrument of infinite delight. It was the seraglio spirit in its purity; and it was made chaste as snow by the consideration that these people would have offered this flesh of which they so perfectly understood the potentialities to burn like tallow in flame if thereby they might save their dearer flesh, their child.

So one can have it, as the vulgar say, both ways. Indeed one can have a great deal more than one has supposed one could, if only one lives, as these people did, in a constant and loyal state of preference for the agreeable over the disagreeable. It might be thought that nothing could be easier, but that is not the case. We in the West find it almost impossible, and are caught unawares when we meet it in practice. That was brought home to me by this woman's tender gesture of farewell. First she took all the lilacs from a vase beside her sofa and gave them to me, but then felt this was not a sufficient civility. She made me lay down the flowers, and took a scent-bottle from her table and sprinkled my hands with the scent, gently rubbing it into my skin. It was the most gracious farewell imaginable, and the Western world in which I was born would not have approved.

There sounded in my mind's ear the probable comment of a Western woman: 'My dear, it was too ghastly, she seized me by the hands and simply drenched them with some most frightful scent. I couldn't get rid of it for days.' Their fastidiousness would, of course, have been bogus, for the scent was exquisite, a rich yet light derivative from Bulgarian attar of roses. These people were infallible in their judgment on such matters, having been tutored for centuries by their part in the luxury trade between Bosnia and Tsarigrad, as they named Constantinople; and she had assumed that persons of our kind would have a like education and would recognize that this scent was of the first order. She had also assumed that I would like to receive a gift which showed that somebody who had not known me two hours before now liked me. She assumed, in fact, that I too preferred the agreeable to the disagreeable. Remembering the grey ice that forms on an Englishman's face as he is introduced to a stranger, I reflected that she was too audacious in her assumption.

Before we left the town her husband took us for a stroll. A lane wound among the mosques and villas through gardens that held much plum blossom and lilac and irises and, here and there, among the shrubs, the innocent playfulness of witch-balls. Travnik had changed its aspect now, as a town does after one has eaten salt in one of its houses. It is no longer something painted on one's retina, it is third-dimensional, it is a being and a friend or an enemy. We climbed up to the old castle, which is a fortress now, and were met by very grave young soldiers. Slav soldiers look devout and dedicated even when they are drunk; these sober boys, guarding their white town and pale-green valley, were as nuns. There had been an intention of calling on the commandant, but the young soldiers said he was asleep. They looked at us for some time before they told us this, and spoke sadly and with an air of pronouncing judgment; and I think that perhaps they thought that their commandant was a sacred being, and that it would be a profanation to disturb him for the sake of three men not in uniform and a woman no longer young. They bade us good-bye with a worried air, as if they wished they were sure they had done right. All to them was still of great moment.

We followed a little path down a grassy hill, miraculously untainted as glades are on the edge of Moslem towns, to a big pool lying among trees. It was fed by three springs, each bursting from the mauve shelter of a clump of cyclamen. It was dammed by a steep stone wall, broken at one end by a channel through which the waters burst in a grooved sliver that looked to be as solid as crystal. We admired it for a long time as if it were a matter of great importance; and then we went down to the main road and found a café which had settled itself in snug melancholy at the corner of a Moslem graveyard, near by the pompous canopied tombs of a couple of pashas.

There we sat and drank black coffee and ate Turkish delight on toothpicks, while a gentle wind stirred the flowering trees that met above the table, and set the grasses waving round a prostrate pillar which had fallen by one of the pashas' tombs. There strolled up and sat down some of those mysterious impoverished and dignified Moslems who seem to have no visible means of support, but some quite effective invisible means. They watched us without embarrassment; we were unembarrassed; and the men talked of country pastimes. Here, the Bulbul's father said, was real game for shooting in winter.

There is deep snow here in winter-time, it seems; and the beasts come down from the heights and loiter hungrily on the outskirts of the town. A friend of his had sauntered a few yards out of his garden, his gun loaded with pellets. He paused to look at a black bush that had miraculously escaped the snow. It stood up and was a bear, a lurch away. His friend raised his gun and shot. The pellets found the bear's brain through the eye, he staggered, charged blindly, and fell dead. He himself had been driving down to his factory one November afternoon when he saw a pack of wolves rushing down the mountain on a herd of goats. He stopped his car and watched. They came straight down like the water we had seen rushing down by the dam. They leaped on the goats and ate what they wanted. He had heard the goats' bones cracking, as loud, he said, as gunshots. When the wolves had eaten their fill they rushed up the mountain again, dragging what was left of the goats. It took only five minutes, he thought, from the time he first saw them till they passed out of sight.

He pointed up to the mountains. 'It is only in winter you see them,' he said, 'but all the same they are up there, waiting for us

and the goats.' We looked in wonder at the heights that professed
the stark innocence of stone, that was honeycombed with the
stumbling weighty hostility of bears, the incorporated rapacity of
wolves. And as we lowered our eyes we saw that we were ourselves
being regarded with as much wonder by other eyes, which also
were speculating what the sterile order of our appearance might
conceal. A gaunt peasant woman with hair light and straight and
stiff as hay and a mouth wide as a door had stopped in the roadway
at the sight of us. She was so grand, so acidulated, so utterly at
a disadvantage before almost anyone in the civilized world, and
so utterly unaware of being at a disadvantage at all, that I made
Constantine ask her to let herself be photographed. She whinnied
with delight, and arranged herself before the camera with her chin
forward, her arms crossed, her weight on her heels, acting a man's
pride; I think nothing in her life had ever suggested to her that
there is a woman's kind of pride.

She was poor. Dear God, she was poor. She was poor as the
people in Rab. Her sleeveless white serge coat, her linen blouse,
the coarse kerchief she had twisted round her head, were stained
with age. The wool of the embroidery on her coat was broken so
that here and there the pattern was a mere fuzz. Garments of this
sort have a long life. To be in this state they must have been worn by
more than one generation. She had probably never had new clothes
in all her days. This was not the most important aspect of her. There
were others which were triumphant. It could be seen that she was
a wit, a stoic, a heroine. But for all that it was painful to look at
her, because she was deformed by the slavery of her ancestors as
she might have been by rheumatism. The deep pits round her eyes
and behind her nostrils, the bluish grooves running down her neck,
spoke of an accumulated deprivation, an amassed poverty, handed
down like her ruined clothes from those who were called rayas, the
ransomed ones, the Christian serfs who had to buy the right to live.
To some in Bosnia the East gave, from some it took away.

Yaitse (Jajce) I

Beyond Travnik the road rose through slashing rain to a high pass, beset before and behind with violet clouds, rent and repaired in the same instant by the scissors of lightning. The open faces of the primroses were pulpy under the storm, the green bells of the hellebore were flattened against the rocks. In the valley beyond we ran into a high blue cave of stillness and sunshine, and came on a tumbledown village, shabby and muddy and paintless and charming, called Vakuf. '*Vakuf*' is a Turkish word meaning religious property; I have never heard anything that made me more positively anxious not to study Turkish than the news that the plural of this word is '*Evkaf.*' It is called by that name because the land hereabouts was given by pious Moslems to provide for the maintenance of mosques and charitable institutions, and some hundreds of the labourers that tilled it lived in this village. Under the Austro-Hungarian Empire these properties were specially nursed, and the labourers given preferential treatment. They were, indeed, the only agricultural workers whose position was in any way better under the Austrians than it had been under the Turks. Nowadays the property is well looked after by the Moslem Political Party, but the village has fallen into that state of gentle disorder rather than actual squalor, which is characteristic of Ottoman remains in Bosnia.

The violent rains had set the main street awash with mud, and we saw nobody but an old man with the white twist in his turban that denotes the Moslem priest, tiptoeing across the morass, with the air of a disgusted cat, to a rickety wooden mosque. He looked agreeable; but the town was irritating to the female eye, with its projecting upper stories where the rotting latticed harem windows are ready to fall out of their rotten casements. It is impudent of men to keep women as luxuries unless they have the power to guarantee them the framework of luxury. If men ask women to give up for their sake the life of the market-place they must promise that they will bring to the harem all that is best in the market-place; that, as all intelligent Moslems have admitted, is the only understanding on which the harem can be anything but a field of male sexual gluttony and cantankerousness. But if they fail to keep that ambitious promise, which there was indeed no obligation to make, they should surrender the system and let women go back to freedom and get what they can. A harem window with a hole boarded up and a lattice tied by a rag to its casement is a sign of the shabby failure that has broken faith with others, like a stranded touring company.

After Vakuf we passed through a valley that was like a Chinese landscape, with woods leaning to one another across deep vertical abysses; and suddenly we found ourselves at the waterfall which is the chief glory of Yaitse. That town stands on a hill, divided by a deep trench from a wide mountain covered by forests and villages, and a river rushes down from the town and leaps a hundred feet into a river that runs along the trench. The chauffeur and Constantine ran about the brink uttering cries. All South Slavs regard water as a sacred substance, and a waterfall is half-way to the incarnation of a god. My husband and I went a stroll, hobbling over the slippery stones, to see the smooth lap and the foaming skirts of the waters from a distance, and when we looked back we saw that Constantine had taken a seat on a rock; and by the waving of his little short arms and the rolling of his curly black bullet head we knew that near him a bird was fluttering over the falls, exulting in the coolness, in the blows the spray struck on its almost weightless body, in the challenge that was made to its wing-courage. From the turn of his plump wrists and the circles described by his short neck, we knew it beyond a doubt. His hands and his head told us too when the wind swung out the fall from the cliff and it floated like a blown scarf, and what delicious fear was felt by the bird. Constantine is a true poet. He knows all about things he knows nothing about.

We heard laughter. On the mountainside beyond the river three peasant girls were taking a walk, in bright dresses which showed a trace of Turkish elegance, which recalled that the word used for 'well-to-do' in this district means literally 'velvet-clad,' and Constantine's bird-ballet had caught their eye. They had huddled into a giggling group and watched him for some minutes, then burst into teasing cries, and waved their arms and rolled their heads in parody. Then when Constantine stood up and roared at them in mock rage, they squealed in mock fear, and fled along the path, across a flowery field, into a glade, and again across a field. In alarm the birds that had been fluttering through the spray flew out into the void of the abyss and divided to the right and left. The three girls took hands and laughed over their shoulders, louder than ever, with their heads thrown back, and entered a deep wood, and were not seen again. Constantine slumped forward, his head on his knees, and seemed to sleep.

When it grew cold we roused him, and walked slowly towards the town under flowering trees. The word '*Yaitse*' (or '*Jajce*') means either little egg or, in poetry, groin, or testicle. I am unable to say what sort of poetry. The town is extravagantly beautiful. It stands on an oval hill that is like an egg stuck on the plateau above the river, and its houses and gardens mount over the rounded slope to a gigantic fortress; and it has the shining and easy look of a land where there is enough water. There is a royal look to it, which is natural enough, for it was the seat of the Bosnian kings, and an obstinacy about the wholemeal masonry of the city walls and the fortifications which is also natural enough, for it resisted the Turks for a painful century and in 1878 met the Austrians with dogged, suicidal opposition. Now it has a look of well-being, which is partly a bequest from the colony of wealthy Turkish merchants who settled here, and partly a sign that, what with pigs and plums and a bit of carpet-weaving and leather-working, things here are not going so badly nowadays.

The Austrians tried to direct their tourist traffic here, and that is why Yaitse owns an immense old-fashioned hotel with a Tirolean air. When I saw the high bed with gleaming sheets, so suggestive of ice-axes and early rising, I would willingly have lain down and gone to sleep, but already Constantine, who is never tired, had found a guide. This was a pale and emaciated lad, probably phthisical, for tuberculosis is the scourge of this land. All day long one sees peasants sitting on the ground, even shortly after rain, yet they rarely have rheumatism; but tuberculosis is as murderous as it is in the Western Isles. It seems to be the stuffy nights in the overcrowded houses that do it. The lad was the worse off for being a Christian; he had not that air of being sustained in his poverty by secret spiritual funds that is so noticeable in the poverty-stricken Moslem. Coughing, he led us through the white streets, in front of a fan of children that stared but never begged, to a gardenish patch, where steps led down into the ground.

We found ourselves walking through black corridors and halls, cold with the wet breath of the living rock. Black vaults soared above us, in hard mystery. From a black throne a sacrifice had been decreed, on a black altar it had been offered, in a black sepulchre it had been laid by; and throne and altar and sepulchre were marked with black crescent moons and stars. 'These are the catacombs of the Bogomils,' said the guide. That I believe is not certain; they are probably the funeral crypt of some noble Bosnian family, stripped of its skeletons by the Turks. But they revealed the imaginative bent which would find hermetic belief attractive. This subterranean palace came as near as matter could to realizing the fantasy, dear to childhood and never quite forgotten, of a temple excavated from the ebony night, where priests swathed and silent, though putatively *basso profundo*, inducted the neophyte by torchlight, through vast pillared galleries dominated by monolithic gods, to the inmost and blackest sanctuary, where, by bodiless whisper or by magic rite brightly enacted against the darkness, The Secret was revealed.

I felt agreeably stimulated. 'This ought to be a setting for a wonderful play,' I thought; but it would not develop past the image of the pale and powerful Master of Mysteries, sitting on his black throne and thundering his awful judgment. I could think of no event that would seem adequate as cause for pallor extreme enough to equal the blackness of the living rock, and I was forced to ask myself why, if this Master of Mysteries was so powerful, he had to do his work downstairs. I remembered that when Mozart wrote *The Magic Flute* in exploitation of our love for the crypto-cavern and the solemn symbol, he and his librettist had finally to turn their backs on the unresolved plot and go home whistling with their hands in their pockets. I remembered, too, that this strand of fancy had at first been identified with Christianity, but swung loose when Christianity became respectable and a church was as much a state building as a mint or a law-court. Then it identified itself with heresy; and, when religious tolerance had spread over Europe and heresy became dissent, it adopted political unrest and revolution as its field. Thus it happened that the secret societies of Europe, particularly those which had been formed in the universities, were responsible for '48. Now I was faced with a material expression of this fantasy, and realized my own inability to use it as a stepping-stone to any new imaginative position; I could see how it was that '48 led merely to '49, and to '50, and to all the other flat and doleful years; and how it was that left-wing movements, which are so often tinged with romanticism, fade away after the initial drama of their seizure of power.

'Come,' said Constantine, 'there are so many things to be seen in Yaitse, you cannot wait. There are two friends of mine who run a chemical factory here, you shall meet them tomorrow, and they have uncovered an altar of Mithras near here on the hillside, which I think you should see.' As we came out of the crypt we saw that the afternoon had nearly become evening. There was a grape-bloom on the light, and the little children who were waiting for us cast their giants of shadows on the cobbles. We went on through the lanes till we found an orchard, opened a gate in the palings, and followed a path to the shed. Inside it was quite dark, and the guide gave us candles. We raised them, and the light met the god of light.

It was the standard sculptured altar of Mithras. A winged young man, wearing a Phrygian helmet, his cloak blown out by the wind, sits on the back of a foundering bull, his left knee on its croup, his right leg stretched down by its flank so that his booted foot presses down on its hoof. With his left hand he grips its nostrils and pulls its head back, and with his right he is plunging a knife into its neck just above the shoulder. Mithras is not an Apollo, but a stocky divine butcher, and his divinity lies solely in his competence, which outdoes that of ordinary butchers. This is the supreme moment in his career. He so causes the earth. From the blood and marrow that ran forth from the bull's wound was engendered the vine and the wheat, the seed emitted by him in his agony was illuminated by the moon and yeasted into the several sorts of animal, while his soul was headed off by Mithras's dog, who had hunted down his body, and was brought into the after-world to be guardian god of the herds, and give his kind the safety he himself had lost.

The bas-relief is enormously impressive. It explains why this religion exerted such influence that it is often said to have just barely failed to supplant Christianity. That is an over-statement. It had no following among the common people, its shrines are never found save where there were stationed the soldiers and functionaries of the Roman Empire, and it generally excluded women from its worship. But it was the cherished cult of the official classes, that is to say the only stable and happy people in the dying state; and it must have had some of the dynamic force of Christianity, because it had so much of its content. The Christians hated it not only because it offered a formidable rivalry but because this sacrificial killing of the bull was like a parody of the crucifixion; and that was not the only uncomfortable resemblance between the two faiths. Tertullian says that 'the devil, whose work it is to pervert the truth, invents idolatrous mysteries to imitate the realities of the divine sacraments. . . . If my memory does not fail me he marks his own soldiers with the sign of Mithras on their foreheads, commemorates an offering of bread, introduces a mock resurrection, and with the sword opens the way to the crown.' He was also annoyed because virginity was practised by certain followers of Mithras. There is no pleasing some people.

But Mithraism has its own and individual attraction. Power, which is perhaps the most immediately attractive concept we know, is its subject matter. Mithras is the Lord of Hosts, the God of Victory, he who sends down on kings and princes the radiance that means success. This slaughter of the bull is a fantasy of the power that never runs to waste, that can convert defeat itself to an extreme refreshment. Mithras conquers the bull, which is to say, the power of mind and body conquers the power of the body alone. But it is not tolerable that any power of whatever sort should be wasted, particularly in the primitive and satisfying image of the bull, so there is invented a magic that makes him the source of all vegetable and animal life at a moment which it then becomes trivial to consider as his death. He even destroys death as he dies, for as the guardian god of the herds he guarantees the continued existence of his powerful species. Power rushes through this legend like the waterfall of Yaitse, falling from a high place but rising victoriously unhurt, to irrigate and give life.

It was so dark that even by candlelight one could see little: but the best way to see sculpture is not with the eyes but with the finger-tips. I mounted on the plinth and ran my hands over the god and the bull. Strength welled out of the carving. The grip of the god's legs on the bull recalled all the pleasure to be derived from balance, riding and rock-climbing and skiing; the hilt of the dagger all but tingled, the bull's throat was tense with the emerging life. My hands passed on from the central tableau. Right and left were the torch-bearers, one holding his torch uplifted, as symbol of dawn and spring and birth, the other letting it droop, as symbol of dusk and winter and death. How did this faith alter the morning? How did it improve the evening? What explanation of birth could it furnish, what mitigation of death? My finger-tips could not find the answer.

The central tableau showed that power was glorious and the cause of all; but all must be caused by power, for power is the name given to what causes all. That is to say, the central tableau proves that $x = x = x$. There are no other terms involved which can be added or subtracted or multiplied. The imagination came to a dead stop, as it had done in the crypt which we had just left. I remembered that there had been tacked on to the Asiatic elements in Mithraism a system something like Freemasonry, which put the faithful through initiatory ceremonies and made them in succession Ravens, Occults, Soldiers, Lions, Persians, Runners of the Sun, and Fathers. Each rank had its sacred mask, legacy from the tradition of more primitive cults. But when one had put on one's Lion's Head and walked about in procession, what did one do? One went home. So Mithraism waned, defended by martyrs who died as nobly as any Christians, and Christianity triumphed, by virtue of its complexity, which gives the imagination unlimited material.

We went through the fruit trees, their blossom rosy now with evening, and climbed to the heights of the town, between high houses with steep tiled roofs, new churches, and old mosques. Women, often veiled, leaned over balconies, out of suddenly opened casements; little dogs, harlequined with the indications of a dozen breeds, ran out of neat little gardens and bade us draw and deliver. We came at last to the fortress that lifts a broad breast of wall and two hunched shoulders of strong towers on the summit of the hill. This was built by the Bosnian kings, who were warmed by a reflection of Byzantine culture, and it was occupied for centuries by the Turks; but, with the irrelevance scenery sometimes displays, its interior is a perfect expression of French romanticism. As we walked round the broad turfed battlements we looked on rough mountains that a fading scarlet and gold sunset clothed with a purple heather made of light; and from the town below came the virile and stoical cries of Slav children. But within the enceinte all was black and white and grey, grace and melancholy.

It contained a deeply sunken park, such as might have surrounded a château in France. In it there were several stone buildings fallen into stately disrepair in the manner of the ruins in a Hubert Robert picture; there was a long cypress avenue, appropriate for the parting of lovers, divided either by the knowledge that one or both must die of a decline, or by the appearance of the ghost of a nun; and there were lawns on which ballet-girls in tarlatan should have been dancing to the music of Chopin. It evoked all sorts of emotion based on absence. As the colour faded from the sky, and it became a pale vault of crystal set with stars blurred with brightness as by tears, and the woods lay dark as mourning on the grey mountains, it was as if the park beneath had carried its point and imposed its style on its surroundings. The moon was high and shed on these lawns and cypresses and ruins that white bloom, that finer frost, that comes before the moonlight. We felt an aching tenderness, which was a kind of contentment; Constantine began to speak of the days when he was a student under Bergson, as he always did when he was deeply moved.

But the mind pricked on, as in the black crypt and before the Mithraic altar, to use this scene as a point of departure for the imagination. And again I found no journey could be made. A ruin is ruined, nothing of major importance can be housed in it. If the two lovers were consumed by a fatal illness, that was the end of them. If the ghost of a nun appeared she would perhaps reveal a secret, such as the position of the grave of her child, which would be rendered completely unimportant by the fact that she was a ghost,

since the existence of an after-life would make everything in this life
of trifling importance; or she would disappear, which would leave
matters precisely as they had been. The dancers would sometime
have to stop dancing, to retreat on their slowly shuddering points
into the shadow of the cypresses, until the undulating farewells of
their arms were no longer moonlit. None of the component parts
of this lovely vision admitted of development. Better men than I
am had felt it. The romantics are always hard put to it to begin
their stories, to find a reason for the solitude and woe of their
characters; that is why so often they introduce the motive of incest,
a crime only really popular among the feeble-minded, and open
to the objection that after a few generations the race would die
of boredom, each family being restricted to a single hereditary
hearth. And the romantics can never finish their stories; they go
bankrupt and put the plot in the hands of death, the receiver, who
winds it up with a compulsory funeral.

We went back to a hotel, pausing to blink through the night at
a kind of shop window in a church, a glass coffin let into the wall,
where there lies the last Bosnian king, a usurper and persecutor, yet
honoured because he was a Slav ruler and not a Turk. For half an hour
I lay on the steep and shining bed in my room, and then came down
to eat the largest dinner I have eaten since I was a little girl. There
was chicken soup, and a huge bowl of little crimson crayfish, and
very good trout, and a pile of palatschinken, pancakes stuffed with
jam like those at Split which the waiter had tried to make me lay up
against the hungers of the night, and some excellent Dalmatian wine. I
said to Constantine something of what I had felt at the sights of Yaitse,
and he answered: 'Yes, it is strange that there are sensations quite
delightful which are nevertheless not stimuli; that there are spectacles
which make us shiver with pleasure of a quite refined and intricate
sort and yet do not open any avenue along which our minds, which
are like old soldiers, and like to march because that is their business,
can travel. And listen, I will tell you, it is very sad, for we need more
avenues. Since some of the avenues that our minds can march down
very happily are bad places for us to go.

'Let me tell you a story of Yaitse. This was a great place to the
Turks. For them it was the key to Central Europe, and so for
many years they would have it. For seven years it was defended
by a Bosnian general, Peter Keglevitch, and at last he came to the
end. He knew that if there was another attack he could not meet
it. Just then he heard that the Turkish troops had left their camp
and were massing in one of the ravines to make a surprise sally
on the fortress with ladders. So he sent a spy over to talk with

the Turks and tell them that he had seen they had gone from
their camp, and had been very glad, and had told all his soldiers,
'Now you may laugh and be glad, for the enemy has gone far away,
and you may sing and drink and sleep, and tomorrow, which is
St. George's Day, your women and girls may go out as usual,
to the mountains in the morning according to our custom and
wash their faces in the dew and dance and sing.' But the Turks
were doubtful, and they lay in wait at dawn, and they saw all the
women and girls of Yaitse come out of their houses in their most
beautiful clothes, and go down the steep streets to the lawns and
terraces beyond the river, yes, where those most impudent ones
were this afternoon. There they washed their dear little faces in
the dew, and then some struck the strings of the gusla, and others
sang, and others joined their hands and danced the kolo. Poor little
ones, their fingers must have been very cold, and I do not know
if they sang very well, for each of them had a knife hidden in her
bosom, to use if her plan miscarried.

'Then, when the Turks heard them singing and saw them
dancing they thought that what the spy had said must be true,
and the fortress would be like a ripe fruit in their hands. But
since they were always like wolves for women, they left their
ladders and they ran down to rape the poor little ones before
they started looting and killing in the town. When they were in
the woodlands and marshes down by the river the Christians rose
from their ambush and destroyed them. And the little ones who
had been so brave went back to the city they had saved, and for
a few more years they were not slaves.

'Now, that is a story that will send the mind marching on,
particularly if it belongs to a good and simple man or woman.
Peter Keglevitch was a cunning man, and it is right to be cunning,
that the Turks and such evil ones may be destroyed. The little ones
were very brave, and to save their city and their faith they risked
all; and it is right to be brave, because there is always evil. And it
is all so beautiful; for the little ones were lovely as they sang and
danced, and they were trusted by their Slav men, so that there
must have been an honourable love between them, and the desire
of the Turks makes us think of other things of which we would be
ashamed and which are nevertheless very exciting and agreeable.
And St. George's Day is a most beautiful feast, and our mountains
are very beautiful, and Yaitse is the most beautiful town. And so
a man can give himself great pleasure in telling himself that story,
and he can imagine all sorts of like happenings, with himself as
Peter Keglevitch, with all the loveliest little ones being brave for

his sake, and all his enemies lying dead in the marshes, with water over the face; and on that he can build up a philosophy which is very simple but is a real thing; it makes a man's life mean more than it did before he held it. Now, will you tell me what in peace is so easy for a simple man to think about as this scene of war? So do not despise my people when they cannot settle down to freedom, when they are like those people on the road of whom I said to you, "They think all the time they must die for Yugoslavia, and they cannot understand why we do not ask them to do that but another thing, that they should live and be happy." You have seen that all sorts of avenues our artists and thinkers have started lead nowhere at all, are not avenues but clumps of trees where it is pleasant to rest a minute or two in the heat of the day, groves into which one can go, but out of which one must come. You will find that we Serbs are not so. We are simpler, and we have not had so many artists and thinkers, but we have something of our own to think about, which is war, but a little more than war, for it is noble, which war need not necessarily be. And from it our minds can go on many adventures. But you must go to bed now, you look tired.'

Yaitse (Jajce) II

'You must wake up at once,' said my husband. But it was not next morning. The room was flooded with moonlight, and my watch told me that I had been in bed only half an hour. 'Get up and dress,' my husband urged me, 'there is a female dentist downstairs.' In his hand I noticed he held a glass of plum brandy. 'She has a voice like running water,' he continued, 'and she says she will sing us the Bosnian songs, which in this region are particularly beautiful.' 'What is all this about?' I asked coldly. 'She is the sister of Chabrinovitch, the boy who made the first attempt on Franz Ferdinand's life, and then threw himself into the river. She is the wife of the medical officer here and practises herself. Somebody in Sarajevo wrote and told her we were coming. Come down quickly. I must go back to her, Constantine is telephoning to his bureau in Belgrade, and she is all alone.'

He left me with such an air of extreme punctiliousness that I was not surprised when I came downstairs to find a very attractive woman. She was not young, she was not to any pyrotechnic degree beautiful, but she was an enchanting blend of robustness and sensitiveness. She possessed the usual foundation of Slav beauty, lovely head bones. Her skin was bright, her eyes answered for her before her lips had time, and she had one of those liquid and speeding voices that will never age; when she is eighty it will sound as if she were an unfatigued and hopeful girl. In pretty German she said that she had come to take us to her house, where we could drink coffee and meet her husband, and so we went out into the moonlit town.

She was a little shy of us, since Constantine was still telephoning and we had to go alone. Like a foal she ran ahead, on the excuse that she knew the way; but kindness drew her back as we were going up an alley. 'You would like to see,' she said, and pointed to a small window in a white wall. We had already remarked a sound of chanting, and we found that we were looking into a mosque, where about a hundred Moslems were attending their evening rite. Through the dim light we could see their arms stretch up in aspiration, and then whack down till their whole bodies were bowed and their foreheads touched the floor in an obeisance that was controlled and military, that had no tinge of private emotion about it. The sound of their worship twanged like a bow. They rose again, relaxed, and we thought the prayer must be over; but again they strained up tautly, and again they beat the floor. It looked as if it were healthy and invigorating to perform, like good physical jerks, which, indeed, the Moslem rite incorporates to a greater degree than any other liturgy of the great religions. Five times during the day a Moslem must say prayer, and during these prayers he must throw up his arms and then get down to the ground anything from seven to thirteen times. As the average man likes taking physical exercise but has to be forced into it by some external power, this routine probably accounts for part of the popularity of Islam. We watched till a fezed head turned towards us. It was strange to eavesdrop on a performance so firmly based on self-confidence of success and solidarity with the big battalion, and feel diffident, not because one was on the side of failure and the beaten battalion, but because the final issue of the battle had been not as was expected. We went on to an apartment house that stood several stories high in the shadow of the fortress, and were taken into a home that recorded a triumph, which perhaps belonged truly to yesterday, but had certainly not been completely annulled by today.

It was a room that could be found anywhere in Europe. It had light distempered walls and a polished floor laid with simple rugs; it was hung with pictures in the modern style, bright with strong colours; the furniture was of good wood, squarely cut by living hands; there was a bowl of fruit on the sideboard; there were many books on the shelves and tables, by such writers as Shaw and Wells, Aldous Huxley and Ernest Hemingway, Thomas Mann and Romain Rolland and Gorky. This sort of room means the same sort of thing wherever it is, in London or Paris, Madrid or Vienna, Oslo or Florence. It implies a need that has been much blown upon since the last war ended and reaction got its chance; but it certifies that its owners possess honourable attributes. They have a passion for cleanliness, a strong sense of duty, a tenderness for little children that counter-balances the threat made to young life by the growth of the town, a distaste for violence, a courageous readiness to criticize authority if it is abusing its function. Such a room implies, of course, certain faults in its owners. They are apt to be doctrinaire, to believe that life is far simpler than it is, and that it can be immediately reduced to order by the application of certain liberal principles, which assume that man is really amenable to reason, even in matters relating to sex and race. They are also inclined to be sceptical about the past and credulous towards the present; they will believe any fool who tells them to fill themselves

with some contorted form of cereal and despise the ancient word
that recommends wine and flesh. These are, however, slight faults,
easily corrected by experience, compared to the dirt and irrespon-
sibility, violence and carelessness towards children, cowardice and
slavishness, on which these people wage war.

Only the malign bigot hates such rooms. Even those who believe
that there is more in life than such people grant must admit that
these rooms are worthy temples to subsidiary gods. There are those
who sourly remark that Bolshevism was made in such rooms. It
is not true. The Russian exiles who were responsible for that sat
on unmade beds in flats as untidy as Versailles or any medieval
castle. They were the powerful people who never tidy up, who
only happened for the moment to be out of power. But those who
live in these swept and garnished rooms wish only to serve. In the
hereafter they shall be saved when all the rest of us are damned.

It could be seen that the doctor husband was of salvation, like his
wife: his handsome face spoke of kindliness, discipline, and hope.
They gave us coffee, and we told them of the beauty of our journey,
and they told us how homesick they had been when they had to
leave Bosnia to take their training at the University in Belgrade,
and how happy they had been to come back and practise here.
They spoke of their work with a sternness which seemed strange
in people who are in their own country, which we hear only from
colonists and missionaries in Africa or Asia. But they were in
the position of colonists and missionaries, because Austria left
Bosnians in the position of Africans or Asiatics. 'They did nothing
for us,' said the doctor, 'nothing, in all the thirty-six years they
were here. You can test it. Look for the buildings they left behind
them. You will find a great many barracks, some tourist hotels,
and a few—pitifully few—schools. No hospitals. No reservoirs.
No houses for the people.' They told us that when they had left
Bosnia after the war to study in Serbia they had been astonished
at the superior lot of the Serbian peasant. His country had been
sacked and invaded, but nevertheless he was better fed and better
clad than his Bosnian brother. 'Liberation meant to us,' said the
dentist, 'release from being robbed.' I thought grimly of the many
books written by English travellers between 1805 and 1914 which
stoutly maintained that the Bosnians and Herzegovinians were so
much better off, first under Turkey and then under Austria,
than the free Serbs. It would be pleasant if this could be proved
quite unconnected with the circumstance that the Turks and the
Austrians knew how to entertain a Western visitor, while the free
Serbs lacked the money and experience.

At length Constantine came in, and they greeted him affection-ately. After we had drunk the ceremonial round of coffee that was brought in for him, he spoke to the dentist in Serb and she turned to us with a face suddenly flushed, the eyes and mouth happy and desperate, as in a memory of a love-affair that had been unfortunate but glorious. 'Constantine says I am to tell you about my brother,' she said. 'But the story is so long, and it is so difficult for foreigners to realize. This will help you to understand some of it.' She took from the book-case an album of photographs of the *attentat* that had been sent to her after the war by the Chief of Police at Sarajevo, and spread it out before us, and then walked up and down, her hands over her face, quivering in that lovely nervousness which, save when her sense of duty was organizing her, governed her being. Most of the photographs we had seen before; they showed the streets of Sarajevo, with the two poor stuffed and swollen victims being pushed on to their deaths, and the frail and maladroit assassins laying hold of the lightning for one minute, and then falling into the power of the people in the streets, who on this day looked so much more robust and autonomous than either the victims or the assassins that they might have belonged to a different race. But there were in addition some ghastly pictures of the terror that followed the assassination, when, long before any inquiry into the crime, hundreds of Bosnian peasants who had barely heard of it were put to death. There were some particularly ghastly pictures of men who had never known anything but injustice, misgovernment by the Turks and Austrians, poverty, and this undeserved death, and were now saying in grim pride with their wry necks and stretched bodies, 'Nevertheless I am I.' There were also pictures of some peasant women who hung from the gallows-tree rigid as saints on icons among their many skirts. There were several photographs of the fields round the barracks at various towns where these mass-executions took place, each showing the summer day thronged as if there were a garden-party going on, with the difference that every single face was marked with the extremity of agony or brutality. The interest and strangeness of the pictures were so great that I swung loose from what I was and for a moment looked about me, lost as one is sometimes when one wakes in a train or in an unfamiliar hotel; it might have been that we were all dead and that I was looking at some records of the death-struggle of our race.

Coming close to me, the dentist cried, in that voice which was delicious even when what she said was acutely painful, 'But we have no record of the worst part, of what happened to him in prison. That should be known, for if such things happen it is not right that they should not be known. But it is dreadful to me to wonder what he did suffer, for you cannot think how delicate and fragile he was, my little brother. He was so—fine. If it had not been for the oppression never would he have done anything violent. So it was easy for them to kill him in prison.' I asked, 'Is it true, what they say, that he was bound to die, because before he went into prison he had tuberculosis?' 'No, no, no,' she protested, 'never did he have anything of the sort before they got hold of him, never!' Then, correcting her impulsiveness by a lovely effort of self-discipline, she explained, 'I have asked myself again and again, in the light of my medical training, if he suffered from anything of the sort, and quite honestly I do not think so, I cannot remember any definite symptoms at all. He was not robust, and he had a tendency to catarrh and bronchitis, but really there was nothing more than that. But it is the habit of our people to say when they see a boy or girl who is thin and weakly, "He looks consumptive," and the Austrians took advantage of that to excuse themselves.'

It has always interested me to know what happens after the great moments in history to the women associated by natural ties to the actors. I would like to know what St. Monica had to do after her son, St Augustine, heard the child in the garden say, '*Tolle lege, tolle lege*,' and was converted to Christianity; how she treated with the family of the little heiress whom St. Augustine was then obliged to jilt, how she dismissed the concubine with whom he had been passing the difficult time of his engagement, how she gave up the lease of the house in Milan. These are the things you are never told. I said to the dentist, 'Tell me what happened to you and your mother after the *attentat*.' She said, 'You cannot think how terrible it was for my poor mother. She knew nothing of politics, she had been married when she was a young girl, she had had many children, my father was a very stern man who would hardly let her speak and never spoke to her save to order her and scold her, she was quite dazed. Then suddenly this happened! Her eldest child tried to kill the Archduke and his wife—apart from anything else, she felt it was too grand for us, it could not happen. Then, that same evening, they came and arrested my father, and it was as if the end of the world had come, she had not known what it was to be without a man, without her father or her husband. I was no use to her. I was a girl, and indeed I was only fifteen. She was like a terrified animal. But then the next morning a neighbour climbed into her back garden and said, "Come, you must escape, a mob is coming to kill you," and she and I had to take the five children that were younger than me and my brother, and get them down the back garden and out through another house into the street beyond where another friend sheltered us. As we got clear we heard the mob wrecking our home. Then she was very brave. But for long she simply could not understand what had happened. Nothing in her life had prepared her for it.

'Later on, before she died, she saw that my brother had been very brave and had done something that history demanded, but at first it was only a disgrace and a disaster. You see, for long she was stunned by the terrible things that happened to us. We were taken with many other Bosnians to an internment camp in Hungary, and she and I had to earn money by working all day as laundresses, but even so my little brother and sisters were always hungry, and so were we, and many people died all round us. It was like Hell, and we grieved for my poor brother Nedyelyko, for we did not know what had happened to him, and even now, beyond the fact that he is dead, we do not know. Then at the end of the war it was still terrible, for one day they simply came to us and turned us loose, drove us out of the camp with no money and nowhere to go, and no clear idea of what had happened, and we were so weak and foolish and confused with suffering. That was a nightmare. Then, when we had found my father, we settled down again and all lived together in the same house. But it was not for long, she was a dying woman, and she lived only a year or two. I will show you a photo that we had taken of her on her deathbed only a few days before she died.'

The dentist rose to fetch it, and Constantine said to me, prepared to hate me if I was unsympathetic, 'It is the habit of our people to take photographs of their beloveds not only at weddings and at christenings, but in death too, we do not reject them in their pain.' It marked a real division between our kinds. I could not imagine any English person I knew having had this photograph taken, or preserving it if by chance it had been taken, or showing it to a stranger. The mother's face was propped up against pillows, emaciated and twisted by her disease, which I imagine must have been cancer, like the petal of a flower that is about to die; her eyes reviewed her life and these circumstances that were bringing it to an end, and were amazed by them. The children's faces, pressing in about her sharp shoulders and her shrunken bosom, mirrored on their health the image of their mother's disease and were amazed by her amazement. But no part of their grief was being rejected by them, it was running through them in a powerful tide, it was adding to their power. Constantine need not have been alarmed, I felt this difference between his people and mine as a proof of our inferiority. To be afraid of sorrow is to be afraid of joy also; since we do not take photographs of our deathbeds, it is hardly worth the trouble to take photographs of our weddings and christenings. 'Think of it,' said the dentist, 'there is such a sad and funny thing I remember about that photograph! We sent for the photographer and gathered round the bed; and afterwards we found that my father was hurt because we had not told him that the photographer was coming and he could not be included in the picture. It did not occur to him that to us he was the instrument of her martyrdom, that we would have thought it as odd to have him in a picture of her agony as it would be for the wife of a shepherd who has been fatally mauled by a wolf to include the animal in a last photograph of him. It showed how innocent he was in his severity, how it was all part of a role he had chosen and stuck to because he had not the sensitiveness to realize the consequences.'

'This is what he was like,' said the doctor, who had been turning over the portfolio out of which his wife had taken her mother's picture. He handed us a photograph of a man in peasant costume, with a face as completely 'made-up' by an aggressive expression as Mussolini's, standing in a defiant pose in front of some banners bearing Serbian inscriptions of a patriotic nature. 'He was a very stern Bosnian patriotic man,' said Constantine; 'see, these are the banners of his secret nationalist society. *Es musste mit ihm immer trotzen sein, immer trotzen.*' The dentist picked it up, looked at it for a minute as intently as if she had never seen it before, shook her head and put it down. 'In the house, never a gentle word,' she said. She buried her face in her hands, but began to laugh 'I can think of things that seemed terrible to me at the time, but now they seem funny. There was the time when I was chosen to recite for my class at the school prize-giving.' 'Yes,' said the doctor, 'tell them that, it always makes me laugh!' 'Yes, please do,' we said.

'It was when we still lived at Trebinye,' said the dentist, 'and already my brother and I were very ambitious, we meant to be educated, so I worked very hard, and I was top of my class. Therefore I was chosen to say a recitation at the prize-giving which was a great affair, all the functionaries came to it and even some of the officers and their wives, to say nothing of all the townspeople. But, of course, I was miserable when I heard that I was chosen, because I knew that all the other little girls who were chosen to recite for their class would have pretty new dresses and light shoes and stockings for the occasion, and I knew I would have nothing. We had nothing, none of us, never. We had

only to ask for something and Father immediately felt that made
it a duty to refuse it, lest we become spoilt and self-indulgent. It
was no good asking our mother to speak for us. That would make
it doubly certain we should not get what we wanted, he would then
want to prove that he was master in his own house.

'But I began to see he was proud I had been chosen. I found
out that he was taking about with him the local newspaper in
which the choice of pupils was announced and showing it to his
friends. So very, very timidly I approached him. I was not honest.
Usually I was honest with him, however much he beat me. But this
time—ah, I wanted so much a little soft, fine dress! So I went and
I told him how I wanted a new dress and new shoes, and I thought
I should have them, because the Austrians and Hungarians would
be there and they would sneer at me as a Serb, if I was in my old
clothes. And that impressed him. "Yes," he said, "I see it, you must
have a new dress, and new shoes, and new stockings. It must be
done." I shall never forget how my heart leaped up when I heard
him say this.

'But I had not reckoned it was still my father who said I could
have these things, and therefore it followed that they could not
possibly be the things which I wanted and which would give me
pleasure. The poor dear man began to think of these shoes and
these stockings and this dress as expressions of his *Weltanschauung*.
He became very smiling and mysterious, he treated me as if he
were about to confer some benefit on me which I was not old
enough to understand as yet, but which would astonish me when
I came to full knowledge of it. Then at last a day came, just before
the prize-giving, when he took me out to see what he had been
preparing for me. We went to a bootmaker who had already made
for me a pair of boots, immensely large for me so that I should not
grow out of them, made so strongly that if I had walked through
a flood I should have come out with dry feet, cut out of leather
so tough and thick that it might have been from an elephant or
a rhinoceros. For weeks he had been inquiring which cobbler in
Trebinye made the stoutest footwear, used the most invincible
leather. I put them on, saying in my heart, "This cannot be true."

'Then he took me to a tailor who tried on me a dress that was
as incredibly horrible as my boots. For weeks the poor man had
been going about the drapers' shops, in search of material that was
strongest, that would never wear out. He had found out something
with which one could build a battleship, I cannot tell you what it
was like. It hardly went into folds. This had been made into a dress
for me by a tailor, who had been chosen because he was an old man

who made no concessions to modern taste and cut clothes as the people in the hill villages wore them, more like the cloths you put on horses and cattle. By the instructions of my father he had made my dress far too big for me, so that I should not grow out of it for years, and it even had deep hems, that felt like planks, so that the skirt would be long enough for me when I was a grown woman. It had even great insets in the bodice, for the days when my bosom should develop, that stuck out like capes.

'I cannot tell you what I felt like as I had this horror tried on me. But it was only a day or two before the prize-giving; and if there had been weeks and months before it happened, I still could have done nothing. For never had I seen my father in such a good humour, and this terrified me. I felt that interference in this state would lead to something so horrible that it could not be faced. My brother was very kind to me about it and I wept in his arms, but my mother was no use to me, because she was so dazed by my father, she said nothing but "Hush, hush, you must not anger him!" So on the day of the prize-giving I crept into my school weeping. All my teachers and my school-fellows were very kind to me; they understood at once, for my father was well known for his severity. But the time came for me to speak my recitation, and then I had to stump on the platform in these horrible new boots that would have been suitable for a peasant working in one of our flooded valleys. I was scarlet, and with reason, for I must have been the most ridiculous sight in the world, less like a little girl than a fortress. But I stood there, and it seemed to me that this was just another battle in the endless war that I would have to carry on with my father all my life if I wanted to do anything, so I began my recitation as well as I could.

'I believe the audience was very kind. But I really knew nothing of what was happening, for I was caught up into an extraordinary state. I felt as if my mind was gagged, as if there was a bar preventing my feelings flowing in the natural direction, which was of course, for a child in such a situation, hatred. What was holding me back was the sight of my father in the audience. He was sitting far back, of course, because naturally as a patriotic Serb he would not sit in front where the Austrian and Hungarian functionaries would sit, but he sat in the front of the seats where the townspeople were, because he was much respected. So I could see him distinctly, and I could see that his face was alight as I had never seen it before, with a sense that at last, just for once in his troubled life, everything was going well, his daughter had wanted something sensible, and he had granted her desire, and added more to it, so that from then on he might be sure of getting more of that gratitude and obedience he craved. I could not love him, but I could not hate him. Oh, the poor dear, the poor dear!'

She burst into distressed and loving laughter; and her fingers, as if without her own knowledge, turned over the photograph of her mother, laying it with its face down, as if to protect the dead woman from the ancient enemy whose personality was being evoked by these memories. 'My father had so many funny ways,' she went on. 'You have perhaps noticed how greatly our people, however poor they are, love to be photographed. It was so with him also. Whenever things seemed to be going well he wanted to take us all to the photographer's and be photographed in the midst of his children. But then when he quarrelled with any of us he would go round the house cutting our photographs out of the groups. But he would never destroy them; perhaps he was too much of a peasant, with primitive ideas of magic, and to burn the images of his children or to throw them into a waste-paper basket would have seemed too much like killing them. He kept them in a box, and when he took us back into favour he would paste them back into the group, so that some of our photographs presented a most extraordinary appearance. I would see one day that my little sister had gone, and then she would be back, and then she would be pasted in again—oh dear, oh dear, the poor man!'

Again she laughed into her hands; and again her husband said, a smile on his sane and handsome face, 'It was extraordinary how it had never occurred to him that family life might be conducted agreeably. Once in Belgrade, long after the war, he came in and found me sitting in the café we frequented, and he asked me where my wife was. I said, 'I had an appointment to meet her here at six and she has not come yet.' He said, 'But it is already half-past. Tonight you must box her ears for this.' Then I said, 'But I married your daughter precisely because I know that she would never keep me waiting except for a very good reason, and in any case I am quite happy sitting here reading my papers and drinking my coffee, and furthermore I do not like striking women, particularly when I love them. So why should I give your daughter a box on the ears?' That horrified him. If I had said something really nasty, something really cruel and base, I could not have upset him more. He felt I was striking at the foundations of society.'

'Yet, do you know,' said the dentist, 'in his last years he accepted everything. He used to talk of my whole life, of my profession, and even of my marriage as if it were something for which he had worked and planned.' 'Yes, indeed,' said the doctor, 'some months

before he died we went out and had a meal alone together as my
wife was away, and he said to me, "Well, you know you have reason
to thank me. I have brought my daughter up so that she is a good
sensible girl, not just interested in foolishness as so many women
are, and now you have a wife with a professional standing you can
be proud of, whom you can treat as an equal."' 'Now what do you
think of that?' said the dentist happily. But her face changed. She
held up her forefinger. 'Is not that one of my little ones?' 'Yes,'
said the doctor, 'I believe I heard a cry a minute ago, but I was
not sure.' 'You might have told me,' said the dentist, in a tone that
was a little sister to reproach. 'Would you care to see our babies?'
she asked me, and as we went along the passage she explained to
me, 'They are not really our babies. My sister, the very lovely one
who has her head against my mother's shoulder in that photograph
I showed you, married and had four children, and recently died.
So, as her husband has to live in the town and has to work very,
very hard, we have adopted them.'

The children were lying in two beds in a large room, with their
four bright heads pointing to the four quarters of the compass.
The little one had her feet right up on the pillow and her head
down on her sister's stomach. They stirred and fretted a little
as the dentist turned on the light, but they had the more than
animal, the almost vegetable serenity, of well-kept children, which
Tennyson described when he wrote of 'babes like tumbled fruit in
grass.' As the dentist put them right way up and tucked them in,
she laughed; and she said, after she put out the light and we were
tiptoeing along the passage, 'It is such a joke, you know, to have
a ready-made family like this. To have the four children, that is
grave and wonderful, but to have all of a sudden four little
toothbrushes, and four little pairs of bedroom slippers and four
little dressing-gowns, it is all like a fairy-story.' She came back into
the living-room much more placid than when she had left it. 'Now
you will hear some Bosnian songs,' she said, her voice soaring as if
it were glad that her mind were giving it liberty to sing.

Yaitse (Jajce) III

When I awoke and saw the sun a pale-green blaze in the tree-tops below our windows, my husband was already awake and pensive, lying with his knees up and his hands clasped behind his head. 'That was interesting last night,' he said. 'She loved her brother, but still to her the important person was the brow-beating father. She had to talk of him because he seemed to her the prime cause of everything in the house, and even the Sarajevo *attentat* seemed to her simply a consequence of him.' 'I remember there is an odd passage in the trial which shows that her brother was of the same opinion. Here, pass it, it is lying on the chair.' I saw, for we had taken with us Mousset's French translation of the court proceedings. 'Yes,' I said, 'it is right at the end. The father makes a few dreary contentious appearances in the evidence of other people, bullying, raging, having his son shut up in the police station because he had offended a pro-Austrian servant in their house and had refused to apologize, and so on. Then at the end they read a deposition made by the father, notably certain passages significant as regarding the father's opinion of the son. He complained of his children's ingratitude, and he expressed the hope that they in their turn might be treated in the same way by their own children.' I thought of the plump children I had seen the night before, deep in their contented sleep in the airy bedroom, and shuddered on behalf of the dead. 'The president of the court asked Chabrinovitch, "Do you see what an ungrateful son you are?" and Chabrinovitch made rather an astonishing answer. He said, "I do not wish to accuse my father, but if I had been better brought up, I would not be seated on this bench." It was an odd thing for a man to say whose case it was that, granted the annexation of Bosnia, it was inevitable that he and his friends should murder the Archduke. It is the fashion now to sneer at Freud, but nobody else could have predicted that in the mind of Chabrinovitch his revolt against his father and his revolt against the representative of the Habsburgs would seem one and the same, so that when a question was put to him in court that associated the two revolts, he answered not with the reason of an adult, but with the excuse of a defiant child. How exactly this bears out the psychoanalytic theory that they who attack the heads of states are not acting as a result of impersonal political theory so much as out of the desire to resolve emotional disturbances set up by childish resentment against their parents!'

425

'But wait a minute, wait a minute,' said my husband. 'I have just thought of something very curious. It has just occurred to me, does not Seton-Watson say in his book *Sarajevo* that Chabrinovitch was the son of a Bosnian Serb who was a spy in the service of the Austro-Hungarian Government?' 'Why, so he did!' I exclaimed. 'And now I come to think of it, Stephen Graham says so, too, in *St. Vitus' Day.*' 'This is most extraordinary,' said my husband, 'for Seton-Watson is never wrong, he is in himself a standard for Greenwich time.' 'And Stephen Graham may slip now and then, but in all essential matters he is in his own vague way precise,' I said. 'Yet all the same this cannot be true,' said my husband; 'this girl was talking under the influence of a memory so intense that it was acting on her like a hypnotic drug, I do not think she could have lied even if she had wanted to do so. And she never mentioned it; on the contrary she mentioned several things that were inconsistent with it, and she showed us that photograph of her father standing among the banners of a Serb patriotic society, which if he were a police spy would be a piece of Judas treachery such as the sister of Chabrinovitch could not bear to keep in her home, much less show to strangers.'

'No, indeed,' I said, 'I do not believe that if she had known him to be a police spy she would have mentioned him to us. But there's something else than that. Chabrinovitch was a youth without reticence, and in the court at Sarajevo he did not care what he said against the Government. If his father had been a Government agent I believe he would have denounced him to the world, just as a young Communist would have denounced his father as a counter-revolutionary. Yet never once in all the pages of Chabrinovitch's evidence, and in any of the countless comments he made on the evidence of other witnesses, did he say, "My father was a traitor to the Slav cause!" He says that he complained that his father hoisted both the Serbian and Austrian flags on his house, but that was not an individual act on the part of his father, it was a matter of conforming to a police regulation, which we know most people in Sarajevo obeyed. But there is no other act of his father's that is denounced by Chabrinovitch.' 'Could they perhaps not have known?' proceeded my husband. 'The dentist at least must have considered the question,' I said, 'for if Seton-Watson and Stephen Graham spread this story it must be because they have heard it on good authority and from several sources. It must have come before her notice some time.' 'It is a mystery,' said my husband; 'but let us get up, once we get downstairs we will find Constantine and probably he will be able to clear up the mystery.'

We found Constantine downstairs having a breakfast which was as admirable as the dinner. 'You have stumbled upon something very intriguing, and very disgusting, and very frightening,' said Constantine, 'and lovely too, because it is the instrument of the martyrdom of a saint. But may I ask you, do you not find the coffee and the bread excellent?' 'Yes, yes,' we said. 'My people know how to live,' he purred, and continued. 'It unfortunately happened that after the war we were all running hither and thither, and we had many other things to do besides write down what we had been doing. So the writing of the history of what happened at Sarajevo fell into the hands of a few who were clever enough to look to the future. Now, because there were no papers, because the reports of the trial were then lost to us, there was nothing for serious historians to work upon, and the field was free to anybody who had been in Bosnia at the time of the *attentat* and had come in contact with the conspirators. One of these was a young man who had certainly known the *attentateurs*, and who had himself been involved in the revolutionary movements of the students. It cannot be denied he has studied the subject very fully, and all foreigners who are writing about the *attentat* come and consult him. But unfortunately it happened that soon after the war this young man met Chabrinovitch's sister and fell madly in love with her. Many men have felt so about her; it is her voice, that makes one feel as if she was a *vila*,' (the Serbian fairy, a kind of wood nymph) 'and would dance with one for ever in the glades. But she could not love him, already she would marry with the doctor whom you saw last night. Long, long this other young man tried to change her heart for him, but it could not be done. So he went away, and then it appeared to him that the whole family of Chabrinovitch was not so wonderful, and he wished to destroy them with his scorn. So in everything he writes and tells, Chabrinovitch seems not such a hero after all. Just a little shade of scorn here, just a little touch of impatience there, and he spoils Chabrinovitch.'

'I recognize that you are telling the truth,' I exclaimed. 'I can see that the descriptions of a jerky, fretful, loquacious, hysterical Chabrinovitch might be a jaundiced view of a vivacious, temperamental, and fluent personality such as his sister.' 'Yes,' said Constantine, 'there has been nothing grossly untrue said about Chabrinovitch, but it has all been made a little nasty and puny, and to this same cause I put down the story that Chabrinovitch's father was a police spy. I do not believe it, for I know that his daughter has heard it, and I know that she is such a good and true woman that she would not deny it unless she had investigated it and found it baseless, and if she had not found it baseless she would never have spoken his name again.'

'What a cruel lie!' I exclaimed. 'Oh, it will not be exactly a lie,' said Constantine. 'I do not think that this man would deliberately tell a lie. But he loved this woman, and because she does not love him he wants to prove that she and everything about her is worthless, and in this state of mind he thinks that facts bear a significance which he would certainly not see in them had he gained what he wanted. Here, I imagine, he has simply misinterpreted some incident, or rather given it greater weight than it merits. Think of Chabrinovitch's father. He was a monstrous egotist, *ein Subjektivist* without limit or restraint; it appeared to him that every part of the universe which was not him had shown the basest treachery by separating itself. We have seen how his children, who as you see from this specimen I have shown you (as I will show you all, all in my country) were really extremely serious, seemed to him ungrateful and unnatural. It is not to be imagined that when he was in a patriotic society, his comrades would not sometimes, and perhaps often, seem to be conspiring against him and their common cause, simply because they disagreed with him on some minute point of policy. It might quite well then happen that as a threat to his comrades he declared that he might leave the whole of them in the lurch and go off, and inform against them at the local police office. This threat may have been taken in earnest by some simple people, who might be misled by subsequent happenings into believing that he had carried it out, though he never did so. Other people, not simple but malevolent, may have spread stories that he had done so; for it cannot be expected that such a man would not make many bitter enemies. Moreover, it may have happened, perhaps just on one occasion, that Chabrinovitch's father may have denounced to the police some man in the Bosnian revolutionary movement whom he thought a danger to it. This is a method that was very often used by the revolutionaries in Russia under the Tsardom, to rid themselves of comrades whom they considered undesirable, on account of indiscretion or some form of indiscipline. Here amongst our people it was very rarely used; but remember this man was an exception, he was a law unto himself, it is just possible that he may have done it. Still, that

he practised any sort of conscious treachery against his fellow-
Serbs, and that he was in receipt of payment from the Austro-
Hungarian authorities, that I do not believe.' 'What a shame
that such a story should be told!' I said. 'No, not a shame,'
said Constantine, 'it is something that could not be helped. For
if a woman does not do a man the little favour of handing him
over her body and her soul, regardless of whether she likes him,
it appears to him the unvarnished truth that she is a leper,
that her father is a hunchback who sold his country, that her
mother was a cripple who nevertheless was a whore. Besides,
I think between this man and Chabrinovitch there was to start
with a little bit of dislike. I think he either gave evidence or
made a deposition, and that Chabrinovitch commented on it
in a way that makes one feel there had been a lack of sympathy —'

But at this point our table was approached by one of those
pale persons in subfusc Western clothes, closely resembling the
minor characters in a Maeterlinck drama, who carry messages in
the Balkan countries. He said something to Constantine which
made him burst into happy exclamations, and gave him a note.
'Drink up your coffee, you English people are always eating,'
cried Constantine. He had been oddly showing his delight at
the note by tearing it up into small pieces. 'My two very good
friends who are chemical manufacturers here are eager to see
me, and they ask us to go down to the Temple of Mithras,
so that they may show it to you more properly, but of course
it is me they want to see, for we were very great friends when
we were young in Russia.' He hurried us out to our car and to
the chemical factory, which stood among the grass and orchards
on the outskirts of the town, incongruously urban, built with a
gratuitous solidity that was considered appropriate to industrial
architecture in Central Europe during the nineteenth century.
But the two managers were not there, and Constantine stood,
in an ecstasy of disappointment, crying, 'But they told me to
come here,' and searching in his pockets for the note he had
received. 'You tore the note up at the hotel,' I said. 'You English
are fantastic,' said Constantine. 'Why should I have done that?'
By good fortune there drove up at the moment a large car,
out of which there bounded, almost vertically, two huge men
who fell upon Constantine and kissed him and smacked his
bottom and cried out lovingly with voices such as loving bears
might have. They paid no attention to my husband and me
for some time, so delighted were they with this reunion with

one whom they had evidently looked on as a little brother, as a fighting cock, and as a magician. They turned to us and cried, 'Such a comrade he was, in Russia! Ah, the good little poet!'

But after a time Constantine told them that we must be moving on soon, and they became flushed with the prospect of half an hour's abandonment to their secret passion, which was archaeology in general, and the Mithraic temple in particular, and with great loping strides they led us along a lane and down a field to the orchard. They came from the most Western Slav territories; one was a Croat, and the other, the taller, came from Slavonia, which used to be in Hungary; but both looked extremely and primitively Slav, as we think Russians ought to be. The taller, indeed, belonged to that order of Russian which looks like a gigantic full-bodied Chinaman. When we got to the orchard it was found that the key to the gate had been left at the factory, but they lifted up their voices and roared like bears in pain, and there came running up the hillside a workman in a beautiful braided plum-coloured peasant costume. When he had learned what was the matter he went away and returned with an axe and proceeded to break down a portion of the wooden fence round the orchard, which was of quite respectable solidity. While he was cutting, there approached us an extremely handsome and venerable old Moslem priest, well suited by the twist of white in his turban that announced his office, who, after greeting the men in our party, joined us, for no comprehensible reason, since he showed a profound indifference to both us and to what we were doing. When the gap was made we all filed through it, except for the Moslem priest. To him the sight of a statue representing the human form was forbidden, so he sat down with his back to the temple on a tree-trunk under a cloud of plum blossom.

It was too plain, the Mithraic mystery, this morning. The night before I had seen with my eyes the outlines and felt with my finger-tips the planes that made a massy hieroglyphic meaning strength. Now I could see the emotional overtones of the design, and its details. The god's face was empty of all but resolution, and resolution is not enough to fill a face; and that the bull's sexual organs were excessive in size would hardly be denied, even by another bull, and the scorpion that attacked them was as gargantuan. Grossness was being grossly murdered, with gross incidentals. No wonder women were not admitted to this worship, for it was distinctively masculine. All women believe that some day something supremely agreeable will happen, and that afterwards the whole of life will be agreeable. All men believe that some day they will do something supremely disagreeable, and that afterwards life will move on so exalted a plane that all considerations of the agreeable and disagreeable will prove petty and superfluous. The female creed has the defect of passivity, but it is surely preferable. There is a certain logic behind it. If a supremely agreeable event occurs it is probable that the human beings within its scope will be sweetened, and that therefore life will be by that much more harmonious. But there is no reason to suppose that a supremely disagreeable event will do anything, except strain and exhaust those who take part in it. It is not true that the vine and the wheat spring from the blood and marrow of a dying bull, the beasts from its sperm. The blood and marrow and sperm of the dead clot and corrupt, and are a stench.

The two giants exhibited this lunatic altar respectfully, because they too were male. But suddenly they caught sight of Constantine, who had climbed on an upturned basket, nosing in the side lines for additional symbols, and at the sight of his Pan-like plumpness they cried out, 'Ah, the good Constantine, he is just the same as ever!' They spread out their arms and called to him, and he came down and let them smack and embrace him all over again. All three began to cry out, 'Do you remember? Do you remember?' I was listening, and was quite unable to profit by it, to a passage of history that is, so far as I know, uncommemorated in Western history, yet is of considerable interest. After the Serbian Army had been driven out of its own country by the German and Austrian invaders and had reached the Adriatic by the famous retreat through Albania, a number of the survivors were sent to Russia. When the Revolution broke out some of these Serbians joined the Whites, and some the Reds. A number who had been in touch with Russian revolutionary propaganda at home played quite conspicuous roles in the Kerensky party. When the Bolsheviks seized power some were killed, and others followed Lenin; but they too were for the most part killed in the next few years. Only a few survive, and those whom one meets have escaped only by luck and preternatural daring.

The three survivors under my eyes were laughing so much that they had to lean against each other to keep on their feet. They felt they owed us an explanation, and the Croat wheezed out between his guffaws, '*Nous étions ensemble tous les trois dans la fortresse de St. Paul et de St. Pierre à Petrograd.*'[1] '*Oui, Madame,*' added the taller one, the Slavonian, '*moi et notre bon petit Constantin, nous étions enfermés dans la même cellule. Et après nous étions condamnés à mort, tous les deux.*'[2] At this point Constantine remembered a joke so rich that he staggered about and caught his breath while he tried to tell it to us. Pointing at the Slavonian, he gasped, '*Figurez-vous, il était deux fois condamné à mort. Deux fois! Deux fois!*'[3] At the thought of it they collapsed and sat down on the ground at the foot of the altar, crying with laughter. At last the Slavonian pulled himself together and said to us apologetically, wiping his eyes, '*Ah, que voulez-vous, Madame? On était jeune.*'[4]

---

[1] 'We were all three together in the fortress of St. Peter and St. Paul at Petrograd.'
[2] 'Yes, Madame, I and our good little Constantine were shut up in the same cell, and afterwards we were condemned to death, both of us.'
[3] 'Just think of it, he was condemned to death twice. Twice! Twice!'
[4] 'You know how it is, Madame! We were only young.'

Yezero

That morning we followed the river of the waterfall some miles towards its source. It filled the trough of a broad and handsome valley, and interrupted itself every half-mile or so with shallow cascades, handsomely laid out in bays and scallops, and shaded by willow-gardens. In the lower reaches of the valley there are strung across these cascades lines of four or five mills, little wooden huts on piles, with a contraption working underneath which is a primitive form of the turbine. 'It is here among my people,' said Constantine in his fat, contented voice, 'that the principle of the turbine was invented, hundreds of years ago.' But the mills stand very high-shouldered nowadays, for some years ago Yaitse was shaken with twenty-three earth tremors, and a landslide altered the course of the river. To please Constantine we stopped the car and went into one of the mills, but lost heart, because there was a beautiful young man lying on the floor under a blanket, who woke up only to give a smile dazzling in its suggestion that we were all accomplices, and closed his eyes again. So we went on our way by the river, widened now into a lake, which held on its rain-grey mirror a bright yet blurred image of the pastoral slopes that rose to the dark upland forest, and which seemed, like so much of Bosnia, almost too carefully landscape-gardened. At the end it split with a flourish into two streams, which were linked together by a village set with flowering trees, its minaret as nicely placed as the flowers on those trees.

Some of its houses spoke, by lovely broken woodwork and tiled roofs fistulated with neglect, of a vital tradition of elegance strangled by poverty; and this was still alive in certain houses which in their decent proportions and their unpretentious ornament, kept trim by cleanliness and new plaster, recalled, strangely enough, some of the more modest and countrified dwellings in Jane Austen's Bath. There were lilacs everywhere, and some tulips. There was nobody about except some lovely children. From the latticed upper story of one of the houses that were rotting among their lilacs there sounded a woman's voice, a deep voice that was not the less wise because it was permeated with the knowledge of pleasure, singing a Bosnian song, full of weariness at some beautiful thing not thoroughly achieved. They became credible, all those Oriental stories of men who faced death for the sake of

433

a woman whom they knew only as a voice singing behind a harem window. Later, standing on a bridge, watching water clear as air comb straight the green weeds on the piers, we heard another such voice coming from a trim Christian house, divided from a wooden mosque by a line of poplars. This was more placid and less young, but was still urgent, urgent in its desire to bring out beauty from the throat, urgent to state a problem in music. Both these women made exquisite, exciting use of a certain feature peculiar to these Balkan songs. Between each musical sentence there is a long, long pause. It is as if the speaker put her point, and then the universe confronted her with its silence, with the reality she wants to alter by proving her point. Are you quite sure, it asks, that you are right? Are you quite sure it is not worth while being right about this thing? Then the melodic line gathers itself up and tries again to convert the inert mass of the silence by the intensity of its argument.

In an inn by the river we drank coffee. A gendarme came to see who the strangers might be, a huge old soldier with one eye missing and fierce grey moustaches. 'Well, how goes it, old moustachioed one?' asked Constantine, laying his arm about the old man's shoulders. Something in the turn of his words gave credit to the old man as a soldier and a rebel and a descendant of the Haiduks, and he blushed and laughed with pleasure. The innkeeper's son, a pleasant boy in his teens, made himself agreeable by showing us the brown trout and the big crayfish wriggling in the floating box of their reserve. On the opposite bank was a prosperous Moslem house, bright as a Christmas present just off the tree, with a garden where the plants grew with a decorative precision we expect only from cut flowers in a florist's vase. It possessed a pavilion on the water's edge, and I was reminded, for the second time, of Jane Austen's Bath. Such little seemly shelters for those who love coolness and shade and the power to look out and not be looked at may be found on the banks of the Avon and on the park walls of great houses, where the traffic goes by. Indeed Bath and the surrounding country, with its towns that may be small but could not be taken for bumpkinish villages, and its enjoyment of private yet not greedy delights, such as walled gardens, is the most Moslem part of England that I know.

A veiled woman had flitted in, her puny shoulders rounded by the weight of something she carried under her overall. There was a murmuring with the innkeeper's wife in a corner, the veiled woman flitted off again, carrying herself straighter. There had been left for our inspection three boleros which a woman in the village, of a fine family now poverty-stricken, wished to sell. We laid them out on a

bench and were abashed to see the value, for the price was a pound.
All were of velvet, dark rose, soft scarlet, purple, and they were
sewn so thickly with gold braid that the velvet appeared only as
a steady factor behind the design which sprung and thrust and
never lost its vital purpose in mere incrustation. Into the purple
jacket some woman had put great cunning. Purple and gold are
heavy matters, so she had placed here and there, by threes and
sixes, tiny buttons of lavender and rose, always in a manner that
lightened the burden on the eye, sometimes together, sometimes
apart. 'The woman who did this might still be alive in the village,'
I said. 'I see they are old, but perhaps she sewed the jacket when
she was very young.' But I was wrong, for it was lined with an early
nineteenth-century chintz. 'How maddening that a person like that
should have been swept away by time,' I said; 'but her work I shall
save, I shall take that home and show it to people, and they will all
like it, and I will leave it in my will to someone who will like it, and
so it will be rescued from the past.' 'Of that you cannot be sure,'
said Constantine, 'the past takes enormous mouthfuls. There may
come a day when nobody will think that bolero beautiful, when it
will seem simply tedious, or ludicrous, or even evil to those who lift
it from the rag-bag.

'You are thinking that there are standards which do not change.
But I will tell you a story of the town we have just left, of Yaitse,
which will prove to you that objects which are beautiful and even
sacred in the eyes of a whole people may lose their value in quite
a few generations. When Bosnia fell to the Turks many of the
Franciscan monks stayed where they were, but one house in Yaitse
fled to the coast and set sail for Venice. They fled in order to save
the dear treasure of their church, which was the body of St Luke.
It had been given to them by a daughter of George Brankovitch, the
despot of Serbia, who had redeemed it for thirty thousand ducats
from the Turks when they had seized it in Epirus. But when the
poor Franciscans came to Venice, all was not well for them, and they
were attacked as if they were pagans and had brought with them a
false god. For there was already another body of St Luke in Italy;
some Benedictines at Padua had him already, and had had him for
three hundred years, and he was the object of an impassioned cult
of the people.

'The Yaitsean Franciscans had to defend their title at a trial before
the Papal Legate at Venice which lasted three months. At the end
the Papal Legate said, "It is right what you say, your treasure is
the true St Luke." But always the Franciscans were kept very poor
and very unhappy, for the Paduans tried again and again to get the

judgment reversed. At that I cannot wonder, for they had a strong point in their favour. Their body was headless, the Yaitsean Luke was whole, he had all; but about 580 the Emperor Tiberius had given St. Gregory the head of St. Luke, which was still in the Vatican, and which was still shown to the people as his true head even after the Papal Legate had pronounced that the whole body from Yaitse was the true St. Luke. No doubt he was in a position where he found it difficult to be logical, for another church in Rome had long been curing the sick by an arm of St. Luke, which was now certainly the third.

'There is nobody today to whom that story would not seem absurd, except very simple people, too simple people, idiots. Those who believe in the power of relics and who are solemn will beg you not to talk of such things, not to recall how the stupidities of our ancestors made foolish a beautiful thing. But most people, whether they are believing or not, will only laugh. But the people of five hundred years ago did not see anything ridiculous in a dead man with two heads and three arms, all working miracles; and they did not feel suspicious because many monks made much money out of such dead men. They saw something else, which made them add a head and a head and make it one head, and two arms and one arm, and make it two arms, and we do not know what that something was. For me, I hate it when I read history and I see that now there is nothing where once there was something. It shows me that man has been eating food which has done him no good, which has passed out of him undigested.'

ROAD

A man fishing from a boat in the middle of the lake stood up and with wide sleeves waved what looked like a greeting; but he must have been a supernatural being in control of the elements, and very disagreeable in disposition, for at that moment a rage of rains broke on us. We saw nothing of our road till, at Vakuf, Christian women wearing woven aprons of bright winy colours, Moslem men with fezes, Moslem women with black muzzles, stood in mud during a moment's sunshine, marketing tiny piles of vegetables, lean and hungry livestock. Then it rained again, and we saw as little of the new road we took when we turned aside at Vakuf, save once when we left the car and stood by a thicket of blackthorn that climbed over great tombs resting on stone platforms. They are said to house the Bogomil dead, and they have the massive and severe quality which belongs to all manifestations of their heresy. But the blackthorn, polished silver in a sudden outpouring of sunshine, redeemed them. Then we came on a town that lay on the flat of a plain with the tedium of a military station which strategy has dumped where natural man would never halt. 'This,' said Constantine, 'was an important garrison in Austrian days.'

It was time for the midday meal, and we stopped at the hotel, which was quite big. We went into a dining-room where a surprisingly large number of people, including a good many military officers, were sitting at a small table and eating in a silence broken only by furtive whispers. I thought that they had perhaps come to the town to attend the funeral of some great personage, and after we sat down I asked Constantine if this could be the case, but he answered as softly, 'No, I think there must be some generals here.' And it was so. Presently four officers, of whom two were generals, rose from a table and went out; as soon as they had passed through the door conversation soared and filled the upper air, noisy as a flock of London pigeons. Our wine was given us long before our food, and proved to be very palatable, red and sweetish, not like any French wine but quite good. We were wondering where it came from, for its name gave no indication, when we received a visit by the landlady. I found her suddenly, leaning over the back of my chair, an elderly Jewess, with a chestnut wig, rapidly undulant in her cringing. We asked her about the wine, and she answered, 'It is from Hungary.' 'What?' said Constantine. 'But it cannot be from Hungary, it is too cheap; it cannot have had any duty paid on it, it must be from Yugoslavia.' 'No,' she said, 'it is from Hungary, it is from the Voivodina.'

Somebody called her away, and she left, with a gait so conditioned by continual cringing that even between tables she bowed from right to left and pressed her clasped hands forward in objectless obeisances. Constantine said, 'But why does she call the Voivodina Hungary? It has been ours since the war, it is the centre of Banat. She must have some reason to hold to the old Austrian days.' We then thought for some time of nothing but our food, which was excellent, not in the Balkan but in the Central European way. There was vegetable soup without paprika, lamb stew of a Viennese type, and superb Apfelstrudel. But while we were eating it the Jewess came back and wavered about us, and my husband said to her, 'What beautiful German cooking you are giving us, and what beautiful German you speak. May I ask where you learned your German?' 'It is my native language,' she said, and explained that she had been born in a certain town on the borders of Austria and Hungary. 'But I have been here for fifty-two years. Fifty-two years, my dear,' she repeated coquettishly, and slowly drew her hand down my arm with the rancid tenderness of the procuress. There could be felt the iron hand in the dirty velvet glove. It was sickening to reflect how often in those fifty-two years she must have brought to the exigencies of brothel life all they needed. One could see her wiping up the vomit of drunkenness, striking some soft white body into the required posture and conducting some forcible examination in search of venereal disease, jerking a frightened child by the arm and telling her not to whimper, carrying basins and perhaps performing direct services in the matter of hopeless and murderous abortions. 'I am glad you drink my poor wine. I am glad you eat my little bit of an Apfelstrudel,' she carnied, and bowed backwards to the door. 'Yes,' said Constantine, 'you are perfectly right. I expect she came here when she was a little girl of sixteen or so, to be with the officers. I think she must have been very beautiful. And then as she got older she managed a house. So the Austrians spread culture among us barbaric Slavs. So she would hunger always for her dear Austrians, and say that the Voivodina is in Hungary.'

As he spoke the old woman came back, followed by an elderly man, a middle-aged man, and two women in their late thirties or early forties, who sat down at a table near us. We had come late, and by this time the dining-room was nearly empty, so she and her family were having their meal. The elderly man was evidently her brother and the others her children, but they were malevolent parodies of her. In the stock that had produced her vigour some poison had been working which had spared only herself. Her features, which in her heyday must have had a Semiramic richness and decision, were in these others splayed into Oriental rubbish. Heaps of bone, they carried long stooping bodies on uncertain feet that turned out at obtuse angles. It was apparent when the meal was brought to them that the parody had been carried to a cruel height. They could not eat properly. Often the soup missed their mouths and ran down their chins into their plates. As the landlady sat at the head of the table, lifting the good soup she had made to her lips with a steady hand, looking on them with weary and tender eyes, and occasionally indicating some dropped food with a word or a proffered napkin, it appeared that to herself her life might seem like the triumphant bearing of a cross, a moral victory of which she might be proud. It was a point not to be denied too hastily. Nevertheless, she was cruelty; she was filth.

Sarajevo VIII

We were at a party at the Bulbul's. She had a house on the quay by the river, not far from the corner where Franz Ferdinand was killed, a modern house which owed its handsomeness to the Turkish tradition, for it was full of light and clear of unnecessary furniture, and in the large reception room on the first floor there was a raised dais by the windows, running right across the floor, which is a common and charming feature of Moslem houses. What furniture there was was the best obtainable of its kind, but that kind is not good. There is no fine European furniture in the Balkans except a few baroque pieces in Croatia and Dalmatia. It is a contrast with the North of Europe, where the wealthy Danish and Swedish merchants and Russian landowners spread the knowledge of Chippendale and Sheraton right across the Baltic. The Turkish domination cut the Balkans off from that or any other European artistic tradition; and when the Balkan peoples came in contact with it, it was through the intervention of Central Europe, where there has never been any good furniture except the baroque and the Biedermeier, which were based entirely on fantasy rather than on sound principles of design and thus could found no school of cabinet-making. Taste degenerated more rapidly in Austria during the nineteenth century than in any other country, with the possible exception of Russia, so she imposed on the Balkans a corrupt fashion in these matters. A bookcase and a sideboard made by a man who knows nothing of what the masters of his craft have discovered in the past are apt to be merely large boxes; and if that man believes that quantity can be a substitute for quality, those boxes are apt to be very big and clumsy indeed.

But the little Bulbul had bought the best furniture that this dispensation produces, and her carpets and hangings were all beautiful in the Oriental style; and there was in every clean and sunlit square inch of the house a sense of housewifery that was conscientious yet leisurely, inspired not by irritable dislike of dirt but through sensuous preference for cleanliness. She herself was unhurried, in a crisp dress that made her edible beauty cool without chill, like the flesh of a melon. Her husband was gracious and sculptural, gentle, even soft, and yet immovable, imperishable, as a granite monolith might be that was carved in the likeness of a tender and amiable god. They had other guests, his sister and her son, who was studying science at Zagreb; in each of them giant liquid eyes and a purposeful scimitar slimness transmitted the Sarajevo tradition of prodigious good looks. It is the misfortune of the Jews that there are kinds of Jews who repel by their ugliness, and the repulsion these cause is not counterbalanced by the other kinds who are beautiful, because they are too beautiful, because their glorious beauty disconcerts the mean and puny element in the Gentile nature, at its worst among the English, which cannot stand up to anything abundant or generous, which thinks duck too rich and Chambertin too heavy, and goes to ugly places for its holidays and wears drab clothes. Many Gentiles, very many English, might have come out of this room hating the people inside for no other reason than their physical perfection.

The talk, also, might have been too good for a Western visitor. The artist among these people so far as talking was concerned was Constantine, who could exploit his own brilliance with the ancient cunning of the Oriental story-teller; but everybody in the room knew how to support the star; they not only understood what he was saying, they knew the play, they could give him his cues. Such conversation demanded attention, discrimination, appreciation, all forms of expenditure which we Westerners, being mean, are apt to grudge. But, indeed, the main objection an English person might have felt against this gathering was its accomplishment and its lack of shame at showing it. When we rose from the table we went into the sunlit room with the dais, and drank coffee which had had an egg beaten into it so that its black bitterness should be mitigated more subtly than by milk, and then, as the saying goes, we had a little music. A little music!

The Bulbul took up her gusla and, in a voice exquisitely and deliberately moderate, she sang many Bosnian songs. She did not sing them like the women in Yezero, for she was not Slav and she had not made that acceptance of tragedy that is the basis of Slav life. It was as if she were repeating in a garden what she had heard the wild Slavs wailing outside the walls. Mischievously she sang a love-song with her eyes fixed on my husband's face, because it is the custom of the country to sing such songs looking steadfastly into the beloved's face. Everybody laughed because it was understood that an Englishman would find this embarrassing, but he acquitted himself gallantly, and they clapped him on the back and told him they thought him a good fellow. This too recalled Jane Austen's Bath; such a pleasantry might have enlivened a drawing-room in the Crescent.

Presently the Bulbul put her gusla in her husband's hands and said, 'Now you,' and with adoring eyes she turned to her guests and explained, 'I sing and sing well, but he not only sings, he has a voice.' It was true. He had a voice like drowsy thunder, forged by a god only half awake. He sang a Serbian song, longer than most, about the pasha of the town where Constantine was born, Shabats. He was a drunkard and a gambler: the song suggests a mind dazed, as one has seen people in the modern world, at casinos and over card-tables, by a certain amount of alcohol and the ecstatic contemplation of number, divided from any substance. He had played away his fortune; he sat penniless in the shell of his splendour. He suffered like a morphinomaniac deprived of his drug because he could not gamble, so with the leisurely heartlessness of the drunkard he ordered that his mother be taken down to the slave-market and sold as a servant. But his wife, who was young and beautiful and noble, came and, with the even greater leisureliness of the heart-broken, told him that she must be sent to the slave-market and sold instead of his mother; for there is disgrace and there is disgrace, and one must choose the lesser. The song presents ruin in a framework of decorum, it takes up the melancholy of drunkenness and the coldness of long-standing vice and examines them as if they were curiously coloured flowers.

But in a later song he paused, smiled, repeated the last phrase, and sang a phrase from a song by Schumann which was like a translation of the other into its different idiom. The science student ran to the piano, and everybody joined in snatches of Schumann's songs. They went on well with 'The Two Grenadiers,' with Constantine in the middle of the room, acting it as well as singing it, until he spread out his arms and thundered, '*Mein Kaiser, mein Kaiser gefangen*,' and the foolish little white dog which was the Bulbul's only apparent weakness woke up in its basket and leapt forward barking, anxious to lend any help that was needed. They laughed; they were not ashamed to laugh, laughter is agreeable, and they had come here to enjoy agreeable things together. Then they began to sing again, but this time in mockery, pursuing German romanticism from lyric to lyric, passing from 'Myrtillen und Rosen' to 'Poor Peter.' Constantine, very stout and very red with lunch and happiness, and still accompanied by the kindly and questioning dog, enacted poor Peter. ('*Der arme Peter wankt vorbei, Gar langsam, leichenblass und scheu.*')[1] In spite of all their clowning they were singing their four parts exquisitely, and their parody was a serious criticism of the romantic spirit. But Constantine put up a

---

[1] 'Poor Peter totters slowly by, pale as a corpse, and full of fear.'

prohibitory hand and said, 'Enough. Now let us restore ourselves
by contact with the genius of the great Nordic One. Are we not all
Aryans?' And they passed into a compost of scenes from the *Ring*,
which went very well considering that Constantine was singing the
character of Carmen. Why Carmen? They knew. It was because
Nietzsche in a famous passage expressed a belief that what Wagner
needed was an infusion of the spirit of Bizet. Therefore in this
performance of the *Ring* Siegfried and Brünhilde were sustained
through their troubles by the companionship of the gipsy, and
'Yo-ho-eo' mingled with the 'Habañera.' Such musical virtuosity
and such rich literary allusiveness is, in my experience, rarely the
sequel of English lunch-parties.

There came into the room as we applauded, quiet-footed and with
his perpetual air of gentle cheerfulness about all particular issues
and melancholy about our general state, our friend the banker,
whom we had not seen for some days. The Bulbul detached herself
from the singers for a moment and came to have her hand kissed,
and stood by us for a little till they haled her back, and she left us
with the prettiest smile of real regret thrown over her shoulder,
though she was glad to sing again. I think her idea of perfect
happiness would have been to find herself simultaneously feeding
every mouth in the universe with sugar plums. The banker watched
his friends with a smile for a moment or two, and then asked us how
we had enjoyed our trip through Bosnia. I said, 'It was beautiful
beyond anything. Travnik was lovely and Yaitse better still. But
best of all I liked the sister of Chabrinovitch.' 'You are like the dwarf
in the fairy-tale who declared, "Dearer to me than any treasure is
something human,"' he said. 'I am sure you are right, you will
not see better than her in any journey. She is truly noble.' I spoke
also of Yezero and the jackets, of Vakuf and the women with the
wine-coloured aprons, and lastly of the terrible old woman at the
inn where we had eaten. 'You are quite right,' he said, 'she would
be what you suppose. Indeed, I think I have heard of this woman.
I will speak to you now of things that you will not read about in
any of the books that were written by English travellers who visited
Bosnia while the Austrians were here.' 'Which, if I may say so, were
not very intelligent,' I agreed. I had that morning been reading one
which I thought imbecile. The author had circulated in fatuous
ecstasy among the Austrian and Hungarian officials, congratulating
them on having introduced the mulberry tree, which had been a
most prominent feature of the Bosnian landscape under the Turk,
and congratulating the Governor's wife, 'called, not unjustly, the
"Queen of Bosnia,"' on teaching handicrafts to such women as

had made the purple bolero at Yezero. 'You see, we were not an easy people to govern any time in the occupation before or after the annexation. The soldiers were all paid as if they were on active service, and the functionaries also were given specially high salaries. This meant that a great many camp-followers came down to our country to batten on these men who had plenty of money and no natural ways of spending it. It had something of the atmosphere of the Klondike rush. And there were many, many prostitutes among these, and of these many were Hungarians, not that they are a people lacking in virtue, but that the land system left many of the peasants so poor that they had to send their daughters out to service in the world or see them starve. So it happens that for us Hungarian is the language of gallantry, even as French is in London.'

He paused. The singers had stopped their opera, and were singing old favourites. 'Let us sing "Wow—wow—wow—,"' said Constantine, and nobody could for a moment fail to realize that he meant 'Ay, ay, ay.' 'The fault,' continued the banker, 'is not with these women, who are often exceedingly kind and good, and achieve every kind of moral victory that they are permitted, but with the Austro-Hungarian Empire, which, although pretentiously Roman Catholic, violated all Catholic counsels of chastity by itself organizing a system of brothels in our country, which could not be excused on the grounds of the necessities of the troops. Certainly the brothels they opened in Sarajevo were far in excess of the requirements of the garrison and the functionaries. There were five very large expensive ones, which were known as The Red Star, The Blue Star, The Green Star, and so on, and two for the common soldiers, The Five Matches and The Last Groschen. It was a wicked thing to do to our town, for before that we had not such things. We Jews have our traditional morality, which was then undisturbed. The Serbs and Croats are a chaste, patriarchal people; where a man will kill any other man who has taken the virtue of his wife or daughter there must be a harsh kind of purity. All cases where our codes broke down were met by the gipsies, whose part it is alone among the nations of the world to exorcise dishonour. But we had never known prostitution, and there is something extremely exciting to a young man in the knowledge that he can acquire the enjoyment of a beautiful girl by payment of a small sum. To many of us, also, the furniture of the brothels was a revelation of Western luxury. Those who did not belong to families who had been wealthy for a long time had never seen big mirrors before, or gold chairs covered with red velvet, and they were profoundly impressed. I am afraid that his Catholic Majesty the Emperor Franz Josef did not sin only against purity when he organized these brothels; he committed also the sin of conspiring for the souls of others. For I am sure the intention was to corrupt all the young men of Sarajevo so that our nationalist spirit should be killed and Bosnia should be easy to govern. But this would not be only a political move; the thought of the corruption would in itself be delicious, for the Austrian hates the Slav, every German hates the Slav, with an appetite that simple death, simple oppression cannot satisfy.'

He added, 'But I wonder if you can understand how mighty hatred can be. I think you English do not, for you have long been so fortunate that nobody else's hatred could touch you, and you had yourselves no reason to hate anybody. Let me point out to you that in your journey to Travnik and Yaitse there was one thing you did not see. You saw nothing of the kingdom of Bosnia. You saw a few fortresses, and perhaps a church or two, and probably the funeral vaults of the Vakchitch family. There is nothing else to see. Yet once the Doge of Venice wrote to the Pope, "Under our eyes the richest kingdom of the world is burning!" and he meant Bosnia. Conquest can swallow all. The Turks consumed Bosnia. The Austrians did what they could to consume that little which remained, but they then had weak mouths. But sometimes I fear lest some of their blood have grown strong jaws like the Turks.'

Serbia

Serbia

TRAIN

WE LEFT SARAJEVO IN THE EARLY MORNING, PICKING OUR way over the peasants who were sleeping all over the floor of the station. Nothing we believe about peasants in the West is true. We are taught to think of them as stolid, almost physically rooted to the soil, and averse from the artificial. Nothing could be less true, for the peasant loves to travel, and travels more happily by train than on horseback. In old Spain I first remarked it. At the junctions trains used to stand packed as they are in the English Midlands, where there are myriad commercial occasions to set people travelling; but these had nobody in them except peasants who can have had the slenderest material motives to leave their homes. In the account of the Sarajevo trial the mobility of the prisoners and the witnesses is far greater than that of anybody in England below the more prosperous middle classes. Now that the country is self-governing and there are fewer restrictions, every train and motor omnibus is stuffed with people amiable with enjoyment, as if they were going to a Cup Tie, but with no Cup Tie whatsoever in view.

The journey out of Sarajevo is characteristic, leisurely and evasive and lovely. The train starts at the bottom of the bowl in which the city lies, and winds round it and comes out at a nick in the rim. There is a high station at the nick, and there one looks down for the last time on the hundred minarets, the white houses, and the green flames of the poplars. Thereafter the train travels through a Swiss country of alps and pinewoods, with here and there a minaretted village, until it goes into a long wooded gorge, which has one superb moment. Where two rivers meet they thunder down on each side of a great rock that has been sharpened by ages of their force to a razor-edged prow. Sometimes we looked at the scenery and sometimes we slept, and often we listened to Constantine, who throughout our entire journey, which lasted

447

thirteen hours, talked either to us or some of the other passengers. The first time I was in Yugoslavia Constantine took me down to Macedonia so that I could give a broadcast about it, and when we arrived at Skoplje I thought I would have to run away, because he had talked to me the whole time during the journey from Belgrade, which had lasted for twelve hours, and I had felt obliged to listen. Now I know that in conversation Constantine is like a professional tennis-player, who does not expect amateurs to stand up to his mastery for long, who expects to have to play to relays, so sometimes I did not listen to him, until I caught one of the formulas which I know introduce his best stories.

'When you are in Belgrade,' said he to my husband, 'you will meet my wife. My wife she is a German. She was very, very beautiful, and she is of a very old German family, and they did not wish her to marry me, so I rapted her from them in an aeroplane. And for long they would not be good with me, and I was not always very fortunate in the efforts I made to win them. You see, my mother-in-law she is the widow of a Lutheran pastor, and I know well that is a different religion from mine, but I think there are only two Christian religions in Europe, and one is the Orthodox Church and the other is the Roman Catholic Church. Now I know that my mother-in-law is not an Orthodox, for one of the things that disgusts her with me is that I am Orthodox, so it seems to me that to be Lutheran is to be some kind of Catholic. Perhaps a Catholic that lets his pastor be married. So one day my wife and I are staying with my mother-in-law among the mountains, and my mother-in-law and I are having breakfast on the balcony, before my wife has come down, and there is sunshine, and the coffee is so good, and there are many flowers, and I am so happy that I say to myself, "Now is the time to make myself pleasant to the old lady," so I say to her that I see in the papers that the Pope is ill, and that I am sorry, because I think very well of the Pope, and I give her instances of all the things that have made me think the Pope is a good and wise man. I point to the snow peaks in the distance, and I say that to climb such heights is a great achievement, and so often had done the Pope, for he is a great mountaineer; and from that I pass on to the Papal Edicts, and praise their wisdom and discretion. And my mother-in-law says nothing to me, but that does not surprise me, because often I talk all, and others not at all. But then my wife comes down and my mother-in-law stands up and cries to her, "Look at the savage you have married, that sits there and on such a beautiful morning praises in my very face the Pope, who is the devil!"'

'And from her side the efforts to be friends with me are often not very good, though in time she came to like me. It is so with the white beer. Do you know white beer? It is the last of all that is *fade* in the world, and it is adored by the *petite bourgeoisie* in Germany. They go to the beer-gardens in the woods and by the lakes and with their little eyes they look at the beauties of their Germany, and they drink white beer, which is the most silly thing you can drink, for it does not taste of anything and cannot make you drunk. It is just like the life of the *petit bourgeois* in liquid form, but it is gross in its nothingness, so that some of them who have shame do not like it, and order raspberry syrup to add to it. But there are those who are not ashamed of being *fade* and they would not spoil it with a flavour, and they order "*ein Weisses mit ohne* . . ." *Mit ohne, mit ohne*, could you have anything that is better for the soul of the *petite bourgeoisie* that is asked what it wants and says, "I want it with without." That is to be lost, to be damned beyond all recovery, and yet there they are very happy, they sit in their beer-gardens and ask for *mit ohne*. It is altogether delicious, it is one of those discords in the universe that remind us how beautifully God works when He works to be nasty. Once I said this in front of the mother-in-law, and do you know ever after she gives me to drink this horrible white beer. And my wife has tried to tell her she should not do so, and my mother-in-law says, "You are foolish, I have heard him say he likes very much *mit ohne*," and my wife she says, "No, you have it wrong, it is the expression *mit ohne* he likes," and my mother-in-law says, "How can you say such nonsense, why should he be pleased when people say they will have white beer without raspberry syrup?" And to that there is nothing to be said, so I must drink white beer, though I am a Serb and therefore not a *petit bourgeois*, but a lord and a peasant.'

We were passing through lumber country, by a river on which we saw the lumbermen steering great rafts of logs over the rapids. 'Some day you must travel so,' said Constantine, 'in the calm places you will hear the men singing so wonderfully.' We passed through Vishegrad, a lumber town with many stacks of new logs and old houses, with minarets and a wide brown bridge over which there rode on a pack-horse a Moslem who must have been very old, or from the far south, for alone of all Bosnian Moslems I have ever seen he wore the head-dress which preceded the fez among the Turks, the turban. Then I slept a little and woke up in a little town where there was not a minaret, where there was no more trace of Islam than there would be in a Sussex village. We were, in fact, in Serbia. We went and stood on the platform and breathed the air, which was now Serbian air. It is as different from Bosnian air as in Scotland the Lowland air differs from Highland air; it is drier and, as they say of pastry, shorter. Anybody who does not know that it is one pleasure to fill the lungs up at Yaitse or Loch Etive and another to fill them down at Belgrade or the Lammermuir Hills must be one of those creatures with defective sensoria, who cannot tell the difference between one kind of water and another. On the platform a ceremony was going on, for there was travelling on our train an officer, a light-haired boy in his twenties, who had once been in the garrison of this town, and had afterwards been moved south and was returning northward to take up some new and more exalted duty. The people of the town had heard beforehand that he would be passing through and had gathered with their children to congratulate him on his promotion. It could be grasped, chiefly from their cheering when the train arrived and left, that they had liked him very much; but when he was standing in front of them he and they alike were transfixed with shyness, evidently arising from the sense of sacredness of military glory, for from what they said it appeared that he had reached a rank extraordinary for so young a man. He was extremely touching as he stood before them solemn with honour, his compact body whittled down from broad shoulders to a slim waist and lean haunches by discipline and exercise. He had one of those Slav faces that puzzle the Westerner, for he had the stern eyes and brows and cheekbones with which we expect hard, thin lips, but his mouth was full and sensitive. I liked the look of him as he stood there in his neat, olive uniform; I liked the faces of the children lifted to him, tranced by the thought of his austere and defensive destiny. There are better things in life than fighting, but they are better only if their doers could have fought had they chosen.

'My town is Shabats,' said Constantine, and I listened, for all his best tales begin with those words. 'In Shabats we were all of us quite truly people. There were not many people who spoke alike and looked alike as there are in Paris and in London and in Berlin. We were all of us ourselves and different. I think it was that we were all equal and so we could not lift ourselves up by trying to look like a class that was of good repute. We could only be remarkable by following our own qualities to the furthest. So it is in all Serbian towns, so it was most of all in Shabats, because we are a proud town, we have always gone our own way. When old King Peter came to visit Shabats he spoke to a peasant and asked if he did well, and the peasant said he did very well, thanks to the trade in pigs and smuggling. We do not at all care, yet we care much. The peasant would tell the King he smuggled and broke his law, but he would die for the King. In the war we were a very brave town. The French decorated us as they decorated Verdun.

'I would like to take you to see Shabats. But it is not as it was. I mean I do not know it now. You might not be disappointed by a visit, but I should be, because I should not be able to introduce you to all the people that were there when I was young, and that now are dead. Some of them were so very nice, and so very strange. There was an old man that I was very fond of, yes, and I loved his wife too. He had made something of a fortune out of making Army clothing, and he made it honestly, for he was a good, patriotic man, and did not cheat the poor soldiers. So with his money he could follow his mania, which was for the new thing, for Science, for the machine, for the artificial, the modern. You may not remember it, for I think it came earlier with you than with us, but there was some time ago a rage for such things. It was partly due to your H. G. Wells and his imitators, and it was partly due to our ideas about America, which we then believed to be entirely covered with sky-scrapers and factories. I had it myself a little, which is how I became friendly with the old man, for I spoke of such things before him and after that he used to send for me sometimes to come to his home and eat, because he had been to Belgrade, or Novi Sad, and had brought back a tin of vegetables or fruit, so I used to sit down with him and his wife in the midst of the country which grows the best fruit and vegetables in the world and we used to smack our lips over some pulpy asparagus and turnipy peaches from California, and talk of the way the world was going to be saved when we all lived in underground cities and ate preserved food and had babies artificially germinated in tanks and lived for ever.

'I was only a boy then and I grew out of it, but the old man was firm in the faith, and his wife, who, I think, never believed in it at all but who loved him very dearly, followed him. I have said he was very rich, and so he was able to have the first sewing-machine in our town, and then the first gramophone, and then the first motor car, which, as we then had no roads for motoring, was of no use to him, but sent him into ecstasy. But there were many other objects on which he gratified his passion, far more than you would believe. His house was full of them. He had many very odd clocks; one I remember very well, the dial of which was quite hidden, which told the time only by throwing figures of light on the ceiling, which was all very well in the dark, but cannot have been much use to my friends, who always went to bed early and slept like dogs till the sunrise. He also fitted his house with a water-closet, which he was always changing for a newer pattern. Some of these water-closets were very strange, and I have never in my life seen anything like them since, and I cannot imagine what ideas were in the inventors' minds. In some kinds one had to go so and so, and why in a water-closet should one go so and so? Surely that is the one place in the world where a man knows quite simply what he has to do. The clothes of my friends were very strange also. He would not wear peasant costume, of course, but as soon as he had adopted Western costume, he rebelled against that also, and he had ties that fastened with snappers and trousers that were made in one with a waistcoat. But he was worse about his wife's dress. He made her wear knickerbockers under her skirts which our women used not to do, and which for some reason shocked them. Trousers they knew from the Turks, and skirts they knew, but trousers under the skirts, that they thought not decent. And when he heard of brassières, those too he sent for, and made his wife wear them, and as she was an old peasant woman, very stout, they had to be enormously enlarged, and even then they remained clearly to be seen, never quite accommodated to her person. And he was so proud of having everything modern that he could not help telling people that she was like an American woman, and was wearing knickerbockers and brassières, and then the poor thing grew scarlet and suffered very terribly, for our women are modest. But she endured it all, for she loved him very much.

'I know how she loved him, for I became involved in her heart. You know that young men are very callous, and when I had got out of my boyhood it no longer seemed to be glorious to eat tinned vegetables, and I laughed at my old friend behind my hand. When I came from Paris after my first year at the Sorbonne, I went to see them and out of wickedness I began to tell them preposterous stories of new machines which did not really exist. Some of them might have existed, indeed some of them have come to exist since then. I remember I told them an American had discovered a system by which houses and trains were always kept at the same temperature, no matter what the weather is like outside. It is air-conditioning, it is now quite true, but then it was a lie. And I went on so, telling more and more absurd stories, until I said, "And of course I was forgetting, there is the artificial woman that was invented by the celebrated surgeon Dr. Martel. That is quite wonderful." And my old friend said to me, "An artificial woman? What is that? A woman that is artificial! For God's sake! Tell us all about it!" So I went on and on, telling many things that were not at all true, and that were not honest, and my friend listened with his eyes growing great, and then I looked at his wife and her eyes were great too, and they were full of pain. Then my old friend said to me, "But you must get me one, you must get me an artificial woman!" He could afford all, you see, and I realized she had known that he was going to say that, and that she was terribly sad, because she knew that she was his real wife and that she would not be able to keep him from an artificial mistress. So I said it was not ready yet, that Dr. Martel was working on it to improve it, and that it could not be bought, and then I sweated hard to tell him something that would make him forget it, and drank more plum brandy, and I pretended to be drunk. But before I left he came round to my house and he told me to bring him back an artificial woman, that he did not care at all how much it cost, and that he would sell all he had to be possessed of such a marvel.

'So it was every time I came back from Paris on my holidays. I would go to their house and he would talk of other things for a time, but only as a little boy who has been well brought up, and knows that he must talk to the uncle for a little while before he asks, "And did you not forget my toy train?" But sooner or later he would say, "Now about the artificial woman. Is she ready yet?" And I would shake my head and say, "No, she is not yet ready." Then I would see his wife's face grow so happy and young and soft. She had him a little longer. Then I would explain that Dr. Martel was a very conscientious man, and a very great surgeon, and that such men like to work very slowly and perfectly. And then I would put my hand up so that she would not hear, and I would tell him some story that would not be very decent, of how the artificial woman had broken down under experiment, but the old man would listen with his eyes right out of his head, and she would go away to the kitchen and she would fetch me the best of her best, some special preserve or a piece of sucking-pig that she had meant to keep for the priest, because I said that the artificial woman was not yet ready. And I saw that she was getting very fond of me, like a mother for her son, and I grieved, for I did not like to have brought this sorrow to her by a silly joke. I felt very ashamed when she came to see me at a time when the cold wind had made me bad with my lungs, and it was as if I should go like my sister, who had died when she was sixteen, and I said to her, "Aunt, you are too good to me. I have done nothing for you," and she answered with tears in her eyes, "But you have been as good to me as a son. Do you think I am so simple that I do not know the artificial woman must long ago be finished, with such a clever man

as you say working on it? You tell my husband that it is not so only
because you know that I could not bear to have such a creature in
my house." There was nothing at all that I could say. I could not
confess to her that I had been a monkey without making it plain
to her that her husband had been an ass. As many people in the
town laughed at him, and she was more aware of it than he was
and hated them on his account, I could not admit that I had been
of their party, she would have felt betrayed. So I could do nothing
but kiss her hand and tell her that always, always I would protect
her heart from the artificial woman.

'The last year of my studies was the last year before the war,
and then I did not come back for my holidays at all, I was studying
too hard philosophy under Bergson and the piano under Wanda
Landowska, and then for years I was a soldier and all people were
swept away, and it did not seem to matter to ask how or where
they were. So it was not till years after that I heard what had
happened to my two old friends. It is a terrible story to me, not
only because I had a sort of love for them, but because it is typical
of us Slavs. We are a light people, full of *légèreté* till it becomes
heavy as lead, and then we jump into the river for no reason, and
if our *légèreté* had not grown heavy as lead one would say for the
sake of sport, but that has altered the case. Do you remember,
no, we none of us can remember it, but we all have read of it,
that at the end of the century people believed that something had
happened to humanity and that we were all decadent and that we
were all going to commit suicide? *Fin de siècle*, the very phrase
means that. Everything takes a long time to reach this country
and this talk arrived here very late, in 1913, and in the meantime
it had been translated into German and it had become heavy, and
morbid, and to be feared. It came to this poor silly old man and
he learned that the most modern thing to do was to kill yourself,
and so he did it. He became very melancholy for a time, working
at it as other old men work at learning chess, and then went into
his stable and hanged himself, to be modern, to have an artificial
death instead of a natural. I think he was probably sure that there
was immortality, for though he believed he was a freethinker I
do not believe it ever crossed his mind that he would not live
after death. And soon after his wife also hanged herself, but I
do not think there was anything modern about her reasons, they
could not have been more ancient. In Shabats many strange things
happened, very many strange things indeed, but I think that of all
of them not nothing was not never more sad.'

I slept, and woke up into a world of mirrors. They stretched away on each side of the railway, the hedges breathing on them with their narrow images. We were passing through the floods that every year afflict the basin of the Danube and its tributaries, and to me, who love water and in my heart cannot believe that many waters can be anything but pleasure heaped upon pleasure, there came a period of time, perhaps twenty minutes or half an hour, of pure delight. During this period I remained half asleep, sometimes seeing these floods before me quite clearly yet with an entranced eye that was not reminded by them of anything I had learned of death and devastation since my infancy, sometimes falling back into sleep and retaining the scene before my mind's eye with the added fantasy and unnameable significance of landscapes admired in dreams. The scene was in fact if not actually unearthly, at least unfamiliar, in aspect, because of the peculiar quality of the twilight. Light was leaving the land, but not clarity. For some reason, perhaps because there was a moon shining where we could not see it, the flooded fields continued to reflect their hedges and any height and village on their edge as clearly as when it had been full day; and though the dusk was heavier each time I opened my eyes I could still see a band of tender blue flowers which grew beside the railway. By mere reiteration of their beauty these flowers achieved a meaning beyond it and more profound, which, at any rate when I was asleep, seemed to be immensely important though quite undefined and undefinable, like the sense of revelation effected by certain refrains in English poetry, such as 'the bailey beareth the bell away.'

But presently the floods were blotted out from me, as thoroughly as if a vast hand had stretched from the sky and scattered earth on the waters till first they were mud and then land. Then Constantine came back into the compartment after an absence I had not noted, his face purplish, his black eyes hot and wet, his hands and his voice and his bobbing black curls lodging a complaint against fate. He sat down on the feet of my husband, who till then had been asleep, and he said, 'On this train I have found the girl who was the first real love of my life. She was of my town, she was of Shabats, and we went to school together, and when we grew to the age of such things, which among us Serbs is not late, we were all for one another. And now she is not young any more, she is not beautiful, she has more little lines under her eyes even than you have, but it can be seen that she was very beautiful indeed, and that she is still very fine, very fine in the way that our women sometimes are, in the way that my mother is fine, very good for her husband, very good for her children, and something strong beyond. You know my mother was a very great pianist. It seems to me it would have been very well for me if I had made this girl my wife before the war and had come back to her, for I had terrible times when I came back from the war and it would have been good if I had had a grand woman like this to stand by me. But she would not have me; though we had been sweethearts for two years I knew that when I left Shabats to go to the Sorbonne she was glad to see that I am going, and all the way to Paris I was glad that it looked very well and as it should be, and I the man was leaving her the woman and going to a far place and having new adventures, because I knew that was how it was not and that she was tired of me. Never did I write to her because I was afraid she would not answer.

'But now when I saw her here on the train I knew that it was a pity it was so, and I said to her, "Why did you treat me so? When I was young I was very handsome and my father was very rich and already you knew I was a poet and would be a great man, for always I was a *Wunderkind*, but you did not want me, though I think that once you loved me. What had you?" At first she would not tell me, but I asked her for a long time, and then she said, "Well, if you trouble me so for so long a time, I will tell you. There is too much of you! You talk more than anybody else, when you play the piano it is more than when any other person plays the piano, when you love it is more than anybody else can make, it is all too much, too much, too much!" Now, that I cannot understand. I talk interesting things, for I have seen many interesting things, not one man in a hundred has seen so many interesting things, your husband has not seen so many interesting things. And I play the piano very well, also when I love with great delicacy of heart, and in passion I am a great experience for any woman. And you must ask my dear wife if I am not a kind man to my family, if I do not do all for my little sons. Now, all these things are good things, how can I do them too much? And I am sure that at first she loved me, and when she saw me here in this train she was so glad to see me that her eyes shone in ecstasy. Why then did she become weary and let me go to Paris with all things finished between us? Why does she now become cross and tell me there is too much of me? Why have I so many enemies, when I would only do what is good with people, and when I would ask nothing but to be gentle and happy? I will go back and ask her, for she cannot have meant just what she said, for it was not sensible, and she is a very fine sensible woman.'

When he had gone my husband sighed, and said, 'Good old

Constantine. Now in all my life I have never got on a train and met a woman I used to love. Indeed, the nearest I have ever come to it was once going down to Norfolk when I met my old matron at Uppingham. That was indeed quite agreeable. But really, I prefer it that way. It seems to me that the proper place for the beloved is the terminus, not the train.' 'I am, however, travelling with you on this occasion,' I reminded him. 'Yes, my dear, so you are,' he said, closing his eyes.

I myself slept after a time; and when I awoke he was still asleep and it was night, and a conductor was telling me that we were near Belgrade. We packed our books and collected our baggage and went to look for Constantine. He had fallen asleep in the corner of another compartment, and was now sitting half awake, running his hand through his tight black curls and smiling up at the lamp in the roof. There was no sign of the first woman he had ever loved, and he said, 'As I woke up I thought of a beautiful thing that happened to me when I was a student in Paris. Bergson had spoken in one of his lectures of Pico della Mirandola who was a great philosopher in the Renaissance but now he is very hidden. I do not suppose you will ever have heard of him because you are a banker, and your wife naturally not. He did not say we must read him, he just spoke of him in one little phrase, as if he had turned a diamond ring on his finger. But the next morning I went to the library of the Sorbonne and I found this book and I was sitting reading it, and Bergson came to work in the library, as he did very often, and he passed by me, and he bent down to see what book I had. And when he saw what it was he smiled and laid his hand so on my head. So, I will show you.' Passing his plump hand over his tight black curls, he achieved a gesture of real beauty. 'That happened to me, nothing can take it away from me. I am a poor man, I have many enemies, but I was in Paris at that time, which was an impossible glory, and so Bergson did to me.' He sat with his heels resting on the floor and his toes turned up, and his black eyes winking and twinkling. He was indestructibly, eternally happy.

The railway station at Belgrade is like any big railway station anywhere. It was odd to step back from a world where everything had its strong local flavour into scenes which were familiar precisely because they were so flavourless, so international in the pejorative sense of the word. In the colourless light descending its vaults there waited Constantine's wife, Gerda, a stout middle-aged woman, typically German in appearance, with fair hair abundant but formless, and grey eyes so light and clear that they looked

almost blind, vacant niches made to house enthusiasms. She wore
a grey coat and skirt and a small hat of German fashion, and among
the dark hurrying people she stood as if drawing contentment from
her own character, from her advantageous difference. When we
got out of the train Constantine ran to her and hugged her, and
she smiled over his shoulder at us in resigned amusement. Then
she greeted me, and my husband was introduced to her, and it
might have been a tea-party in Hamburg or Berlin, with the same
proud stress on a note which nobody not German can define. It is
not magnificence; the slightest touch of the grand manner would
be regarded as absurd. It is not simplicity; massive elaboration is
required in furniture, in dress, in food. It is not the moderation
of the French bourgeoise, for that is based on craftsmanship,
on a sense that to handle material satisfactorily one must keep
one's wits about one and work coolly and steadily; these people
at such tea-parties have no sense of dedication to the practical and
financial problems of a household, they have an air of regarding it
as an ideal that by handsome expenditure they should buy the right
to be waited upon. Yet there is nothing wild, nothing extreme,
about them or Gerda, only aims that are respected by the mass,
such as continuity and sobriety. There is a positive element, even
impressive in its positiveness, that welds these negatives into a
dynamic whole; but I have no idea what it is.

We stood still together while Constantine and my husband
looked for a lost suitcase, in an amiable yet uneasy silence. She
took my book from my hand, looked at the title, and handed it
back to me with a little shake of the head and a smile, full of
compassionate contempt. It was a book called *The Healing Ritual*,
by Patience Kemp, a study of the folk-medicine of the Balkan
Slavs, which traced the prescriptions and practices it described
back to early Christianity, to pre-Christian mythology, and to
the culture of Byzantium and Greece and the Orient. Puzzled by
Gerda's expression, for it seemed to me a most admirable book,
I asked, 'Have you read it?' 'No,' she said, smiling and shaking
her head again, 'but I do not believe it. I am not a *Mystik*.' 'But
it is not that sort of book at all,' I said, 'it is by a graduate of the
School of Slavonic Studies, who is also a trained anthropologist,
and she has travelled all over the country collecting legends and
customs and analysing them.' Gerda continued to smile, bathed
in satisfaction at the thought of her superiority to Miss Kemp in
her poetic fantasy, to me in my credulity. 'But it is a work of great
learning,' I insisted. Miss Kemp could obviously look after herself
and I did not care what Gerda thought of my intelligence, but there

seemed to me something against nature in judging a book without having read it and in sticking to that judgment in spite of positive assurances from someone who had read it. 'It is published by a firm called Faber,' I continued; 'they do not publish books such as you imagine this to be.' She turned away so that she stood at right angles to me, her smile soared up above us: I could see her spirit, buoyed up by a sense of the folly of myself, of Miss Kemp, of Messrs. Faber, mounting and expanding till it filled the high vaults of the railway station. Unconstrained by any sense of reality, there was no reason why it should not.

Belgrade I

When we were having breakfast in our bedroom a chambermaid came in about some business, one of those pale women with dark hair who even in daylight look as if one were seeing them by moonlight, and we recognized each other and talked affectionately. It was Angela, a Slovene, who had been very kind to me when I was ill in this hotel with dengue fever last year. She was the gentlest and sweetest of women and for that reason had developed a most peculiar form of hysteria. Perhaps because of her experience as a tiny child in the war she was a true xenophobe, she could not imagine anything more disgusting than a member of another race than her own. But she did not like to feel anything but love for her fellow-creatures, so she transformed her loathing for them into a belief that they exude powerful and most unpleasant odours. This belief made her life as a chambermaid an extraordinary olfactory adventure, for to this hotel there came people of all nationalities. She staggered from room to room on her round of duties, almost in need of a gas-mask when she came to making the beds. Her political convictions led her to think very poorly of the Bulgarians, the Italians, and the Greeks, and therefore it appeared to her that these people smelt like manure-heaps, like the area round a gasometer, like a tanner's yard. Particularly was this so with the Greeks. When she spoke of her daily work in the suite then occupied by a wealthy young Greek merchant her face assumed a look of poignant physical apprehension, as if she were a miner talking of the firedamp which might provoke a disaster. The Hungarians seemed to her to have a strong smell, which, however, was not unpleasant, only extremely different from the smell a human being ought to exhale. But the Germans and Austrians were definitely very gross in her nostrils, and the French smelt wicked and puzzling, as I imagine a chemist's shop might to a country woman who knew the uses of hardly any of the articles it exhibited.

About the natives of countries more remote she knew less, so she smelt less, and about such people as the Swedes and Finns her nose invented what were to full odours as suspicions are to certainties. To test her, I told her that I was not truly English, but half Scottish and half Anglo-Irish. This distracted her, because she had never heard of the Scottish or Irish, and while she was won to Scotland by my explanation of the resemblance between the Scottish and the Bosnians, it rightly seemed to her that to be Anglo-Irish was to be like an Austrian or Hungarian landowner among the Slovenes or Croats, or to be a Turkish landowner among the conquered Slavs. She would cry out as she made my bed, 'I have it, I know what you smell like,' and it would always be something valuable but ambiguous, not universally appreciated, such as some unusual herb, some rarely used kind of wood. But there would be some strain of pleasantness in the comparison, due to her belief that the Scottish resembled the Bosnians. And no matter how I and other borderline cases smelt, her toil was not repellent, since the foul miasma given out by the foreign guests of the hotel was exorcized and exquisitely replaced by the fragrance, stronger than that of rosery or herb garden because it was imaginary, which hung about the rooms occupied by Croats, Serbs, and Slovenes.

'I feel happier about your illness now that I have been here and seen that the hotel is very good, and that the people are so very friendly,' said my husband, 'but it looked terrible when I read in the papers before I had got your letter that you were ill in a hotel in Belgrade. I thought of Belgrade then as the Viennese talk of it, as the end of the earth, a barbarian village.' 'I am sorry I tried to keep it from you,' I said, 'but after all I too had a shock when I read of my illness in the paper. For it said that I was in the care of two doctors: but there were three gentlemen coming in every day and baring my bosom and laying their heads against my heart, and I had hoped they were all members of the medical profession. On the whole I have never been more happily ill than I was here. When my temperature was very high and I really felt wretched, Angela and two other chambermaids and a waiter came and stood at the end of my bed and cried nearly the whole afternoon. Also my nurse cried a lot. I liked it enormously.' 'But you always say you hate scenes,' said my husband. 'So I do, when I am well, there are so many other things to do,' I answered; 'but when I am ill it is the only incident that can cheer and reach me under the blankets. And really it is sensible to show emotion at serious illness. Death is a tragedy. It may be transmuted to something else the next minute, but till then it is a divorce from the sun and the spring. I also maintain that it would have been a tragedy for myself and for a few other people if I died in my early forties, so it was quite logical for susceptible people to burst into tears at such a prospect and neglect the bells that their more robust clients were pressing. I am quite sure that it must be more exhilarating to die in a cottage full of people bewailing the prospect of losing one and the pathos of one's destruction than to lie in a nursing-home with everybody pretending that the most sensational moment of one's life is not happening.'

'I see that,' said my husband, 'but you must remember that if people behaved like that they would not be able to bear the strain of patiently nursing the victims of long illness.' 'That is what is called taking the long view,' I said, 'and I do not believe it is so superior to the short view as is supposed. I remember once going a walk in Greece with two Englishwomen, one of them the enchanting Dilys Powell, to see a marble lion that lies somewhere near the foot of Mount Hymettus, when from a long way off we had seen some peasants about their business of repainting and cleaning a little church that had been erected to commemorate the feat of a Christian saint, who had turned to marble this lion (which was in fact archaic and many centuries older than any Christian). Suddenly one of their number who was walking away from the church towards a farm stopped in horror, just where the grass grew long at the edge of the road, looked down, and cried out to his companions, who also looked down, and then also cried out. Some went down on their knees on the ground, others ran back to the church and returned carrying things. When we got there we found that the first peasant had stopped because he had come on an old man who had fallen in a faint by the roadside, from hunger and thirst and weariness. He was, as one of the peasants explained to us, one of "those without corn," a peasant who for some reason has no land and must tramp the country seeking to be employed by others. The English ladies might find it difficult to believe, he said, speaking with embarrassment, that such people existed, since we were from a rich country, but in a poor country like Greece there were some of them. This I found extremely embarrassing. But I forgot that, in my pleasure in the delightful kindness they were showing the old man, the way they were folding coats and cloaks to make a bed for him, and holding up to his mouth bottles of wine and pieces of bread, and crying out what a shame it was that he should have to be wandering on such a day and without food.

'Then one of my companions said, "Yes, they are like this, very kind to people in trouble at first, but they are like children, they soon get tired. So-and-so of the British colony in Athens was taken ill with fever when he was walking in the mountains, and some peasants took him in and looked after him with extraordinary care for a few days, and then they simply turned him out.' I felt a jar at that, for it seemed to me that here was a difference between primitive and civilized practice, which was, on the whole, to the advantage of the primitive. For there are more short illnesses than long, at least in circumstances where one is obliged to be dependent on strangers; and sympathy seems to me more necessary for acute pains than for chronic suffering, which gives one time to muster one's defences. That, indeed, is something about which I feel bitterly. Twice it happened to me, before I married you, that people who were close friends of mine wrote inquiring how I was and what my plans were, and I had to write back to them telling that an extraordinary calamity had befallen me, something almost as extraordinary as that a wicked stepmother had sent me out into the woods in winter with instructions not to come back till I had gathered a basket of wild strawberries, and infinitely agonizing as well. On neither occasion did I receive any answer: and when I met my friends afterwards each told me that she had been so appalled by my news that she had not been able to find adequate words of sympathy, but that I was not to think she was anything but my friend and would be till death. And indeed both women are still my friends. It, however, only gives me a modified pleasure, it presents me with the knowledge that two people know me very well and enjoy my society but are not inspired by that to do anything to save me when I am almost dying of loneliness and misery, and that this unexhilarating relationship is likely to persist during my lifetime. It seems to me it would have been much better for me if I had had someone who would have cried out and said it was a shame that I should be so unhappy, as the peasants did when they found the old man by the roadside.'

My husband said, 'I wonder. I wonder very much indeed. This has all something to do with economics.' 'What on earth?' I said derisively. 'I am moved, and your friends were moved, by fear of exceeding emotion,' he explained, 'and I believe it is because Western people always regard their emotion exactly as they do their material wealth. Now in a highly artificial capitalist society such as we live in, one's money comes to one piece by piece, and if one spends it one might not be able to replace it, because the circumstances in which one made it may not be repeated, and in any case it takes a long time to store up capital, so that considering the shortness of life a piece of extravagance may never be corrected. But a peasant's material wealth comes from the soil; he therefore knows that if he is wasteful one year the summer and autumn will bring him replenishment, and even the hazard of drought and frost and flood does not amount to anything so threatening as the immense discrepancy between capital and income, the enormous amount that has to be saved for a competency. So even a rich and lavish man may be more uneasy in his mind about expenditure than a very poor and economical peasant. And I fancy that therefore all of us in the Western world know an instinct to skimp our emotional expenditure which the peasant has not. It is true therefore that my feeling that Angela and the waiters and the nurses were doing something wrong in crying round your bed has no logical basis at all, and is a stupid transference and confusion.' 'Yet there are practical conveniences,' I said, 'because in towns we could not cry out and wail and weep as one could in a village. Think how strangers to Paris feel it the most frightening of towns instead of the least, simply because Parisians quarrel and grieve exactly as they would if they were the inhabitants of some hamlet of thirty houses, and the cries echo back from the tall houses and the pavements, exaggerated to the intensity of Hell.'

The telephone rang and my husband answered it. Putting it down, he said, 'Constantine's wife is coming up to see us.' I sat down at the dressing-table and began to powder my face, but my eye was caught by the view from the window. Belgrade straggles over a ridge between the Danube and its tributary the Sava, and the Hotel of the Serbian King is high on that ridge, so between the blocks of the flats and houses on the opposite side of the street I looked at the flat plate of the floods. The waiter who had come to take away our breakfast tray followed the line of my eye and said, 'Yes, it is unfortunate, you will be able to have no fresh caviare, for while the river is high they cannot get it.' My husband exclaimed, 'What, do you get caviare here?' 'You had better ask,' the waiter replied, 'where else can you get it? It is well known that Serbian caviare is the best in the world.'

When he had gone we rejoiced at this patriotic remark and I at last remembered to show my husband a verse I found quoted in a book by a Serbian author called Mitchitch:

> *Le ciel serbe est couleur d'azur*
> *Au dedans est assis un vrai dieu serbe*
> *Entouré des anges serbes aux voix pures*
> *Qui chantent la gloire de leur race superbe.*

We were laughing over this when Gerda came in, and we repeated it to her. She smiled and said, 'So you have got over your liking for the Serbs?' 'Not at all,' I said. 'But it is stupid to be like that,' she said, 'you cannot like people who are stupid.' 'Yes, we can,' said my husband, with an air of quietly asserting our rights.

It did not seem possible to carry on this conversation on fruitful

lines, so we spoke of other things; and presently, according to a
charming German custom, she rose from her seat and shook hands
with me in thanks for a handbag I had sent her from London some
time before. Then we showed her some things we had bought
in Bosnia, a Persian tile picture of a prince on his white horse,
delicately holding out a fruit to a bird that delicately received it
with his beak, in the most delicate of landscapes, and my coat of
cloth of gold; and it was all very agreeable. We were lifted for a
moment into that state of specifically German contentment that I
had remarked in Gerda at the station, in which my husband was
perfectly at ease, from sheer habit, since he had lived so much in
Germany, but in which I am acutely uncomfortable, as I do not
understand its basis and I feared I might put my foot through it
at any moment. Its basis, on this occasion I think, was a sense
that we were a group of the elect, connoisseurs of objects which
many people would not at all appreciate, and able at the minute to
command leisure for our enjoyment. She looked happy and much
younger, and I remembered Constantine's boasting of her beauty.
Suddenly I remembered friendship and how beautiful it is, in a
way that is difficult in London or any capital where one suffers
from an excess of relationships, and I realized that it was probably
a great comfort for this German woman, so far from home, to talk
with my husband, whose German is like a German's and of her
own kind, for he learned it in Hamburg and she was of Bremen.

These thoughts made me say, next time there was a pause,
'It was very pleasant in Sarajevo to see how many friends
Constantine had, and how much they loved him.' But Gerda
made no answer. My husband thought she had not heard, and
began to enumerate the families and individuals we had met in
Bosnia, and the affectionate things they had said of Constantine
to us. She remained perfectly impassive, so impassive that it
seemed as if she was perhaps hiding some painful emotion; and
my husband, afraid lest she had some idea that these friends of
Constantine's were not friendly to her, said, 'And those who had
met you spoke very regretfully because they had not seen more of
you.' He told her truthfully that the Bulbul's father and mother,
who had entertained Gerda at Travnik when Constantine and she
came to Bosnia on their honeymoon, had asked after her with a
special warmth. Gerda shrugged her shoulders and said, 'I cannot
remember them.' 'What a pity!' I exclaimed, 'they are such a
wonderful pair,' but before I could say very much about them
she interrupted me, by asking coldly and wearily as if I had been
talking for a long time about something I should have known

would bore her, 'It is twelve years ago since I saw these people, how can I possibly be interested in them?' Impatiently she made arrangements that we should visit her for tea that afternoon, and soon after rose and left.

'I do not understand that,' said my husband later, as we walked out of the hotel towards the park that lies beside it, the Kalemegdan, which is the special glory of Belgrade and indeed one of the most beautiful parks in the world. 'Usually a wife or husband is delighted, if only for superficial and worldly reasons, when the other partner has many friends. Unless of course there is hatred between them. Do you think Gerda perhaps really hates Constantine?' 'I do not know,' I said. 'Constantine thinks that she adores him. She certainly gives you the impression she would adore her husband if she could, and Constantine certainly adores her.' 'I have it!' exclaimed my husband. 'Most of the people I mentioned were Jews. What an odd, what an allusive thing it is to be a German nowadays.' 'It is like asthma,' I said. 'Suddenly they begin to strangle spiritually, and you have to remember it is because they are allergic to Jews. But there is more than that to it. She was happy with us, together we formed a group of people who were like the groups who are approved in her own country. Suddenly by talking of Constantine's friends we deserted the camp and went over to the enemy, we took sides with the Jews and the Slavs who are constantly afflicting her with their strangeness, who make up the bitterness of her exile.' 'Yes, but it is a pity she does not fit her emotions better into the framework of society,' said my husband, 'for surely she would bring no other accusation against the Jews and the Slavs than that they do not fit into the framework of society. But it does not matter, she is probably a very nice woman and has many good points.'

But now we were in the park, and its charm was separating us from everything outside it, as good parks should do. We went through an area which is common to all parks, no matter where they may be, where nurses watch their children play among lilac bushes and little ponds and the busts of the departed nearly great, whose living prototypes sit beside the nurses on the benches, writing, or reading in books taken out of shiny leather portfolios. Then there is a finely laid-out flower garden, with a tremendous and very beautiful statue to the French who died in Yugoslavia during the Great War, by Mestrovitch, showing a figure bathing in a sea of courage. Many people might like it taken away and replaced by a gentler marble. But the pleasantness of this park is such an innovation that it has hardly earned the right to put all grimness from its gates. For this is the old fortress of Belgrade, which till the end of the Great War knew peace only as a dream.

Ever since there were men in this region this promontory must have meant life to those that held it, death to those that lost it. Its prow juts out between the two great rivers and looks eastward over the great Pannonian Plain (superb words, the flattest I know) that spreads across Hungary towards Central Europe. Behind it is the security of broken country and forest. Here, certainly not to begin at the beginning, the Illyrians made a stand against the Romans and were driven out. Here the Romans made a stand against the Huns and the Avars, and were driven out. Here the Slavs joined the Huns and were oppressed by them, and for a brief space enjoyed peace under the Byzantines, but were submerged by the Hungarians, until war between Byzantium and Hungary brought a victorious Greek army to the foot of this rock. Then the Serbs came, and knew imperial glory under the Nemanya dynasty; here the petty Serbian kings who had failed to uphold that glory made their last stand before the Turks. But the Hungarians, with typical Christian frivolity, claimed it for nearly a hundred years, harrying the Serbs so that they could not beat back the Turkish army. Hence Belgrade fell to Suleiman the Great in 1521. The Hungarians paid their scot five years later, when the Turks beat them at Mohacs and kept them in servitude for a hundred and fifty years. Then the tide turned, the maniac Vizier Kara Mustapha was defeated outside Vienna and brought to this very place to be strangled. Then in 1688 the Austrians swept them out and took the fortress, but lost it two years later, and it was not retaken till Prince Eugène of Savoy came down on it in 1717.

So far the history of Belgrade, like many other passages in the life of Europe, makes one wonder what the human race has lost by its habit of bleeding itself like a mad medieval surgeon. But it may be that not much has been wasted which we miss. Those that are preserved to unfold the buds of their being often produce very repulsive blossoms. In 1739 by a hideously treacherous agreement the Austrians handed Belgrade and its Serb inhabitants to Turkey. This was, however, not such a calamity for the Serbs as appears, for they had been so oppressively governed by the Austrians that many had already fled into Turkish territory, though the treatment they received there could be described not as good, but better.

In 1792, however, the Austrians conferred some benefits on the Serbs by a treaty which they had designed simply for their own security. They arranged that no Janizaries should be admitted to the garrison of Belgrade or any other Serbian town. This was to save the Austrians from a frontier that could immediately become aggressive in time of war, it virtually imposed a no-man's-land. But to the Serbs it meant liberation from the unchecked tyranny of the dominant military caste. In the next few years the Belgrade Pashalik became happy and prosperous under Hadji Mustapha Pasha, one of the few Turks who ever showed signs of a talent for colonial administration. He was so much beloved by his Christians that he was known as 'the Mother of Serbs,' an odd title for an intensely military people to bestow on the bearded representative of another. But there was a shift in palace politics far away in Constantinople, and the treaty was annulled. The Janizaries came back. They stole by fraud into this fortress, murdered the wise Hadji Mustapha, and set up a looting, murdering, raping tyranny over the countryside.

It was against them that Karageorge, Black George, the founder of the dynasty, a pig-farmer of genius, led his revolt in 1804. He besieged this fortress and it was handed over to him in 1806. He freed his whole country down to Parachin and Krushevats, in 1810. But when Serbia became the ally of Russia against Turkey in 1813, she was betrayed by Russian incompetence, and the Turks came back to Belgrade. They took a terrible revenge for Karageorge's revolt. They massacred all the men who were not quick enough to take refuge in the Shumadiya, as it is called, the Wooded Place, the country lying south of Belgrade which formed most of the old kingdom of Serbia; and they sold many of the women and children into slavery. But later another Serbian leader arose, one Milosh Obrenovitch, and he induced Russia to support him in a revolt against the Ottoman Empire. It was successful. It was too successful. Russia had not wanted Serbia to be free, but to be absorbed into the Tsardom. But the Serbs had shown such mettle that Belgrade could not be mistaken for anything but the capital of a free Serbia. She was therefore cheated out of the victory she had earned. To prevent her from being too free she was forced to let a garrison of Turkish troops remain in Belgrade fortress.

This led to incidents. It could not have been otherwise. And the great powers were always there to turn them, sometimes out of greed and baseness, sometimes out of sheer idiocy, into wounds and humiliations. Their guilt can be judged from the conduct of the English in June 1862. One evening in that month two Turkish soldiers sitting at a fountain fell into a dispute with a Serbian youth and killed him. In the subsequent disorder a Serbian policeman was killed and another wounded. This started a race riot which lasted all night. The Serbian Cabinet and the foreign consuls and the Turkish Pasha joined together to take measures to stop it, and peace was believed to be restored when the garrison of the fortress suddenly opened fire on Belgrade. For four hours the unhappy town was bombarded. Not until the foreign consuls took the courageous step of pitching their tents on the glacis between the town and the fortress were the guns silenced. After this the British Foreign Office took a step memorable in its imbecility. Lord John Russell, without making any inquiries whatsoever, decided that the incident had occurred because the Serbians had violated their treaty obligations to Turkey, and he put forward the strange decision that Austria should invade Serbia. Fortunately Austria perceived that she could not choose a more dangerous moment, and sent no troops. It is a relief to remember that four years later English influence induced the Porte to withdraw from Serbia altogether. Foreign students of our politics must be puzzled to find that this change in attitude was due to the substitution of a Conservative for a Liberal Government.

But this withdrawal did not yet bring peace to the fortress. In front of it lay Hungary and Austria, greedy for it. Behind it lay Russia, greedy for it. Both wanted to snatch the Balkans from the hands of the dying Ottoman Empire. When the young Serbian state tried to placate Austria, Russia raged. In its rage it financed the Bulgars to turn against the Serbs, filling them with hopes of Balkan ascendancy which have ever since complicated and embittered the international situation. Later the great powers met at the Congress of Berlin and gave Bosnia and Herzegovina to the Austrian Empire, and thereby left Serbia helpless and humiliated. In 1905 Serbia resisted Austrian commercial aggression by a tariff war which was known as 'the pig war,' and formed a customs Anschluss with the Bulgars. So Austria's hatred for Serbia grew day by day, till in 1914 Princip's bullet acted as a catalytic to Central European passions, and the Austrian monitors bombarded the fortress from the Danube. In 1915 it was occupied by Austrian troops, not to be freed until 1918. Now its ramparts and glacis shelter in their mellow bluish-rose brickwork a sequence of little flower-gardens, which stuff the old ravelins and redoubts with pansies and tulips and forget-me-nots. It is the prettiest and most courageous piece of optimism I know: but for all that I think the Yugoslavs wise to have Mestrovitch's statue by, to remind them of the imbecile ferocity of their kind.

There is another statue by Mestrovitch in Kalemegdan. It is the war memorial of Yugoslavia itself, the glorious naked figure. It can be seen only imperfectly, it stands on the very top of a column, at the prow of the promontory, high up above the waters, which it faces; on the park it turns its back, and that is all the observer can see. This is not according to the intention of the sculptor, nor is it a sacrifice made to symbolism, though it is very apt that the Yugoslavian military spirit should look out in vigilance and warning towards Hungary and Austria. It happens that the statue is recognizably male, so the municipality of Belgrade refused to set it up in the streets of the town, on the ground that it would offend female modesty. But the Serb is not only a peasant in prudery, he is an artist, he has some knowledge of handicrafts, so he saw that it was natural for a man cutting out the shape of a man to cut out the true shape of a man; the councillors felt therefore no Puritan hatred of the statue, and their peasant thrift told them that it would be wicked waste to throw away a statue well carved in expensive material by an acknowledged master. So up it went, buttocks to the fore.

And beautiful it looked, outlined against the landscape, which lay under the floods as a human being in a bath; the face of the land, its trees and houses, were above the water, but the body was wholly submerged. These floods were even threatening the low platform that lies below the slope which drops, purple with lilacs, from the prow of Kalemegdan. But the low grey barracks down there were still occupied; on the nacreous surface of an exercise-ground there walked in twos and threes a number of soldiers wearing round Cossack caps and long fullskirted coats opening over scarlet breeches. The scene had the air of the beginning of a ballet, because each body was so tautly sprung in its trained perfection. There were two dovecotes in the compound, one a pleasant faded jade-green, the other earth-brown. Sometimes some soldiers would halt underneath one of these cotes and cry out or clap their hands so that the doves whirred out and travelled a low arc to a corrugated iron roof. But for the most part these young men strolled about talking with a peculiar intensity that was untinged by homosexuality but spoke of male friendships more acute and adventurous than anything we know in the West. To look at them was to understand the military conspiracies that have been the special difficulty of Serbia during the last fifty years.

By now the surface of the floods was hacked into choppy waves, which became a coarse trembling silver where the sunlight pierced the grey-violet clouds. We shuddered and took refuge in the fortress. It is immense. It is shaped by the Oriental tradition which obliged a ruler to symbolize his greatness by the size of

his habitation. Some of it the Yugoslav Government has not yet
had time or money to take in hand. A labyrinth of corridors and
cells is as the Turks left it seventy years ago; but in other parts
there are arsenals, barracks, offices, tennis-courts, and a museum
which holds, as a grisly and suspicious exhibit, the automobile
in which King Alexander was assassinated at Marseille. It is not
to be comprehended why the French authorities let it leave the
country. It is an old-fashioned vehicle—seven years old in 1934
and clumsily refitted with new coachwork after a smash—which
had actually been used for the transport of better-class criminals.
The French chauffeur is known to have protested against being
made to drive a king in such a piece of old iron. It is right that the
automobile should be in Belgrade, for it beautifully symbolizes the
way the Western powers have dealt with the Balkans. There also,
in the landward ramparts, is a charming zoo of the Whipsnade
sort. Grey skies bring out the colour of flowers and animals: a lion
and lioness drinking at a stream shone like topazes. But it was no
use, the day was growing colder, we went back to our hotel.

Belgrade II

We ate too large a lunch, as is apt to be one's habit in Belgrade, if one is man enough to stand up to peasant food made luxurious by urban lavishness of supply and a Turkish tradition of subtle and positive flavour. The soups and stews and risottos here are as good as any I know. And the people at the tables round about one come from the same kitchen: rich feeding, not too digestible, but not at all insipid. Some of them, indeed, are definitely indigestible, beings of ambiguous life, never engaged in any enterprise that is crystalline in quality. It is said that Belgrade is the centre of the European spy system, and it may be that some of these people are spies. One about whom such a doubt might be harboured came up to me while we were eating our chicken liver risotto, an Italian whom I had last seen at a night club in Vienna. I remembered our meeting because of his answer to my inquiry as to what he was doing in Austria. 'I come from Spain, but I have never good fortune,' he said. 'I hoped to bring here a bull-fight, but the bull, he will not come.' This did not, of course, refer to a startling example of animal sagacity, but to the change noticeable in the attitude of the customs officials as the animal passed from territories where bull-fighting is done to where it is not. The unhappy beast had started on its journey as a symbol of life, glorious in the prospect of meeting a sacrificial death, and ended it as something like a fallen girl, to be rescued by bloodless humanitarians. Today when I asked the Italian a like question about his presence he made a more optimistic answer. 'I am about to take up very, very great concessions,' he said. 'A pyrites mine in Bosnia.' 'But,' I thought, 'the pyrites, he will not come.'

This man was an adventurer for the reason that most Westerners turn adventurers: he was too weak and silly to fit into the grooves of ordinary life, to be accepted in the company of the really important business men, the industrialists and financiers who would take up the concessions in Bosnia if they were worth anything, and who are also to be seen lunching at this hotel. But the native Yugoslavs who are offering them their country's resources over the table seem also to be adventurers, though for another reason. They would deviate from the strict pathway drawn by business necessity not because they were too negative but too positive for daily life. They are robust men who speak and laugh

472

and eat and drink a great deal, so that by early middle life they have the lined faces of actors and are full-bodied. The vitality of these Yugoslavs to be seen at midday in this or any other big Belgrade hotel is in astounding contrast to any English gathering of the sort. Englishmen, if they happen to be physically dynamic, usually disclaim it by their manners. These Yugoslavs have never had an ache or pain in their lives. Yet all the historical factors involved should by rights have produced an opposite effect; for all the Yugoslavs over forty must have taken part in a military campaign of the most appalling nature, and all adults who were below that age had undergone as boys privations and dangers such as never threatened French or English or German children.

I could understand why English diplomats, too often the most delicate of a delicate class, hated being *en poste* among the Balkan peoples; but I could guess also at another reason why they should hate it. These Yugoslavs were not only very well, they were certain in any circumstances to act vigorously; and it would be impossible to foresee what form that action would take. In the Yugoslavian villages one felt certain of the peasants' vigour and the predictability of their conduct. They might be intensely individual in their emotions and their expression of them, but they would follow a tested tradition. Here one had no such certainty. These men in the hotel dining-room were not united by the acceptance of any common formula. This gave them the alien and enigmatic character of wild animals: the lion and lioness, drinking at the stream in the Kalemegdan were not more sealed from one in their feeling and thinking than these jolly, healthy men. I asked myself in vain, 'What will they do?' And I asked myself also the more important question, 'What would they feel that they could not do?' I remembered what English people who had lived in the Balkans had told me of dishonesty and punctilio, of grossness and delicacy, avarice and handsomeness, co-existent in the same person, of statesmen who had practised extremes in patriotism and in peculation not at different times in their career but on the same day, of brutality that took torture and bloodshed in its stride and suddenly turned to the tenderest charity. Surely this meant that not only I, but the Yugoslavs, were unable to answer the question. They were not yet familiar with the circumstances of urban life. It could hardly be otherwise, since thirty-five years ago there was not a town in Serbia the size of Rockford, Illinois. The Yugoslavs could not be blamed, therefore, if they had not worked out a tradition of conduct to fit those circumstances.

Urban life takes a deal of learning. We saw further evidence

of that when we went out to see the procession of children that
always on this day, April the twenty-fourth, marches through the
street along the ridge of Belgrade, to receive the blessing of the
Patriarch at the Cathedral, which is near the park. We took up
our places near the central square among a mob of infatuated
parents, and languidly kind big brothers and sisters who were
too old to walk in the procession, and bubbling and dancing little
brothers and sisters who were too young, and had for the most
part been given balloons for compensation. There was a great
deal of apprehension about, for every child had had new clothes
bought for this occasion, and this worst of springs ranged drably
overhead, sometimes spilling great heavy pennies of rain; and the
procession was forty minutes late.

All that was forgotten, however, every time one of the children
in the crowd lost grip of its balloon, and we all saw it rise slowly,
as if debating the advantages of freedom, over the wide trench of
the cleared street. Then we all laughed, and laughed louder when,
as usually happened, since the wind was short of breath, the balloon
wobbled and fell on the heads of the crowd on the other side of the
road, and was fetched back by its baby owner. There was one such
recovery which caused great amusement. A red balloon was blown
higher than any of the others, as high as the first-floor windows,
and then travelled across the street very slowly, with jerks and
hesitations, while its owner, a little boy in a sky-blue serge coat,
staggered exactly beneath it, his anxious body expressing all the
consternation a man might feel when the stock market is breaking.
'It's going. It's gone. No, it isn't. See, it's going to be all right.
No, there isn't a chance.' The puce-faced old soldier who held
the line in front of us shook and heaved, producing laughter from
some place one would never keep it unless one was in the habit
of packing things away as safely as possible. Three schoolgirls who
had been stiff in adolescent affectation laughed as comfortably as
if they were women already.

But in spite of all this good-humour the occasion was not as
pretty as we had hoped, because the little children were so
remarkably fragile and pasty-faced. 'It is perhaps because they
have been waiting so long in the cold,' suggested my husband.
But that was not the reason, for the children who were walking
briskly in the procession were just as pallid and dull of eye and
hair. 'I cannot understand it!' I said. 'Why should the Serbs,
who are so superbly healthy when they grow up, be such weakly
children?' A Frenchwoman standing beside us in the crowd said
primly, with that air of having put in her thumb and taken out

a plum which we in England have not used with ease since the days of Maria Edgeworth, 'It is because they keep their children indoors all winter. You would not believe how little they understand the importance of giving the little ones plenty of air and exercise.' After a moment's complacent pause, she added, 'And vegetables too. That is another thing of which they are ignorant. The children are given enormous quantities of meat, and some salad, yes, but green vegetables they hardly eat at all.'

That was to say, in fact, that the Serbs had not mastered the technique of bringing up children in town, which indeed is hard enough to learn so far as winter is concerned. For in the country a peasant's child must go out into the cold, whatever the day be like, to help with the crops or the livestock. It gets air and exercise without ever having the need for them propounded. But a great deal of information has to be stated and realized before a man and woman living in town see that it is their duty to commit the obvious unkindness of sending a child out into the cold for no reason at all. The matter of food is perhaps not so urgent as the Frenchwoman alleged; for it is said that the paprika, with which the Serb flavours his soups and his stews, compensates for the lack of green vegetables. But the excess of meat is also a real injury to the child, which it is very hard for its parents to avoid inflicting. For in the country a peasant can eat a great deal of meat and profit by it, and it is not easy for him when he comes to town to realize that this source of his strength has suddenly become a danger to him.

They are learning a new technique, and the conditions of their education are not ideal. 'What a calamity it is that the Serbs consider it of such importance to have a great capital,' I said to my husband; 'think of all the new ministries, and look at these poor teachers.' 'Unfortunately the Serbs are perfectly right,' said my husband. 'The old prewar Belgrade was in no way discreditable to any Serbs except those who five hundred and fifty years ago were beaten on the field of Kossovo, and let the Turks stream north. But it was always being brought up against her in every German or Austrian or French or English book on the Balkans, and it was perpetually alluded to by diplomats. But I agree with you, these teachers are a most unhappy sight.' For just as remarkable as the pallor and fragility of the children was the neediness of the schoolmasters and schoolmistresses who were in charge of them.

They bore themselves with dignity, and their faces were for the most part thoughtful and dedicated. This was to be expected, for the profession of teacher offers not the steady job which the peasant longs for above all else when he leaves the soil, but has a special heroic prestige. Before the Balkan wars all the young bloods of both sexes with a turn for letters took teaching diplomas and went down to Old Serbia and Macedonia, which were still Turkish provinces. The great powers had forced Turkey to permit the establishment of schools with foreign staffs for the benefit of the Christians among their subjects; but the result was hardly what could have been expected from such a benevolent intervention. No area since the world began can have been at once so highly educated and so wildly uncivilized. Macedonia was important to all Europe, because a power that got a foothold there had a chance of falling heir, by actual occupation or by economic influence, to the territories of the dying Ottoman Empire. So the land was covered with schools staffed by nationalist propagandists, who, when they hailed from the neighbouring Balkan powers, took their duties with more than normal pedagogic ferocity. Macedonia had a large population of Christian Slavs, who were mainly of Serb or Bulgarian or Greek character, though they often exchanged characters if they shifted or their districts fell under different domination. Serbia and Bulgaria and Greece therefore all founded schools which aimed at making the Macedonian infants into Serbs or Bulgars or Greeks who could be counted on to demand the transfer of the province to whatever state had secured their adherence. Quite a number of the schoolmasters and schoolmistresses in these competitive establishments were shot, or were not shot only because they shot first. This situation was not wholly ended by the war. Until a few years ago the I.M.R.O. or Internal Macedonian Revolutionary Organization, which wished to take Macedonia from Yugoslavia and make it Bulgarian, often attacked Yugoslav schools and murdered the staff, and yet many Serbian teachers volunteered to put in some years of duty in the South before they settled down at home. So the teacher in Yugoslavia is often a hero and fanatic as well as a servant of the mind; but as they walked along the Belgrade streets it could easily be seen that none of them had quite enough to eat or warm enough clothing or handsome lodgings or all the books they needed.

It must be admitted that this city, with its starved professional classes, its lavish governmental display, and its pullulation of an exploiting class, sometimes presents an unattractive appearance. I did not like Belgrade that evening when I sat in the hotel lounge and watched the bar fill up with high-coloured, thick-necked, stocky little men whose black moustaches were lustreless as apes' hair. There had been some sort of conference upstairs in a private room, with two foreign visitors, one pale and featureless and round, like an enormous Dutch cheese, the other a Jew as Hitler sees Jews. I think the dreams raised at that conference would never be realized in all their rosiness. No party was going to be left, as the others hoped, with the horns and the hooves as his share of the carcass. But everybody would do pretty well, except the general public here and in the rest of Europe, which was going to provide the carcass. And the rest of Europe can look after itself. It has had its opportunities, and if it has never used them to tidy up its financial system, so much the worse for it. The heavier offence is against Yugoslavia, a new country that has to make its body and soul.

The extent of the damage that is done to the state by these financial and industrial adventurers is not easy to compute. I do not believe that it is nearly so much in terms of money as the Yugoslavs outside Belgrade allege. The great fortunes in Yugoslavia come from shipping and timber, and are as legitimate as such riches are in England or America. For the rest, there are only sporadic and unimpressive evidences of wealth, however gained. There may be some large villas in Belgrade whose owners could not explain how they came to be able to build them; but then there are very few large villas in Belgrade. Nor are there many large cars, or expensive restaurants, or jewellers, or furriers. It looks to me as if all the city's speculators absorb a much smaller proportion of their country's goods than England and the United States cede as a matter of course to the City and to Wall Street. But to a community of peasants it may well seem that such rewards for the middleman are altogether exorbitant; and indeed the political consequences of such a privateering strain in society are altogether disastrous for a new country.

If the politicians of a state are dominated by ideas, then few parties form. There are certain natural classifications which establish themselves: those who are for repression and those who are for freedom, those who are for the townpeople and those who are for the peasants, those who are for the army and those who are for finance and industry, and so on. Sometimes these groups stand sharply defined and sometimes they coalesce into fewer and larger groups. But there is only a limited number of such classifications, and of the combinations that can be formed from them. But if there are a thousand financiers and industrialists in a country, they can, especially when they are Slavs, turn political life into a multiplicity of small slippery bodies like a school of white-bait. In the ten years after the granting of the Yugoslavian constitution in 1921 twenty-five different governments held office. There is nothing more necessary for the country than a steady agrarian policy; there have been as many as five Ministers of Agriculture in thirteen months.

It was to end this gangsterish tumult that King Alexander took the disastrous step of proclaiming a dictatorship in 1929. This introduced what seemed to be a change for the better, but most Yugoslavs would say that it produced no change at all, for it ultimately put into the saddle Stoyadinovitch, who was hated throughout the length and breadth of the country. That hatred was extraordinarily widespread. I have literally never heard any Yugoslav, except Constantine and a very simple-minded judge from a Dalmatian town, express admiration for him. He was hated chiefly because he was said to be a tyrant and enemy of freedom. He was said to have suppressed freedom of speech and freedom of the press by throwing his opponents into jail, where they were often starved and beaten. It is extremely difficult to weigh the justice of these accusations. It must be conceded at once that if a man is imprisoned in Yugoslavia he is likely to be maltreated. A bad penal tradition has been inherited both from Turkey and from Austria. I have known a most enlightened Serb official who had had the greatest difficulty in persuading his subordinates that it was not good form to use torture for the purpose of extracting confessions. It added to the complexity of the situation that when they were not torturing their prisoners they would treat them with a fatherly kindness unknown in our Western prisons.

Whether Stoyadinovitch imprisoned many people or not was hard for a stranger to tell. My impression was that the regime was far more indulgent than German Nazism or Italian Fascism. I have heard malcontents loudly abuse the government freely when sitting in a café or by an open window giving on a lane, and I have often received through the ordinary post letters in which my Yugoslav friends abused the Prime Minister and signed their names. I have been told several stories of atrocities which on investigation turned out to be either completely untrue or exaggerated. For example, I was told in Croatia of a Croat who had been exiled to a Macedonian town and was forced to report to the gendarmerie every two hours; but a pro-Croat anti-Government Macedonian living in that town could not trace him, and had never heard of anybody undergoing that peculiar punishment. I was also told of a man who had been given a long term of imprisonment for having abused Stoyadinovitch to his companion as they sat at dinner in a restaurant; but actually the magistrate had done no more than advise him not to talk so loud next time.

But sometimes the hand of Stoyadinovitch fell very heavily indeed. It sometimes fell vexatiously on the intellectuals. I have known of a provincial lawyer of the highest character who was sent to prison for two months for treasonable conversation on the evidence of an ignoble personage who had before the war been an Austrian spy in Belgrade. The real damage done to the intellectuals lay not in the number of such cases or the severity of the sentences but in the insecurity arising from the knowledge that they could happen at all. But I believe that the hand fell with a murderous heaviness on the working classes. An English friend of mine once came on a tragic party of young men being sent down from a Bosnian manufacturing town to Sarajevo by a night train. All were in irons. The gendarmes told him that they were Communists. I expect they were nothing of the sort. Real Marxian Communism is rare in Yugoslavia, for it is not attractive to a nation of peasant proprietors and the Comintern wastes little time and energy in this field, but the word is extended to cover the mildest of left activities. These young men had probably done nothing worse than try to form a trade union. It was against such as these, I believe, that the Stoyadinovitch regime brought up its full forces.

Consideration of this bias brought one to the reason that the more serious-minded among the Yugoslavs gave for their hatred of Stoyadinovitch. They knew that their abominable prison system could not be reformed in a moment, they knew that they were often difficult and ungracious under government. But they could not forgive him for representing the thick-necked, plundering little men in the bar. Those men were his allies, and they were united against the rest of Yugoslavia. They were against the peasants, against the starving schoolmasters, against the workmen who had been brought to town and poverty like lambs to the slaughter.

It is plausible, yet I do not think it is true. Certainly Stoyadinovitch represented the financial and industrial interests of Belgrade, but he may not have meant to be his country's enemy. I have known Englishmen and Frenchmen who have done business with him, and they all received honest, even handsome treatment at his hands, which seemed to be part of a certain Augustan attitude, hardly consonant with carelessness for his country's interest. The truth was, I suspect, that he was astonishingly naïve, and that his naïveté was cut to an old-fashioned pattern. The clue to that was supplied every evening to anybody who would listen to it by the radio. The Yugoslavian news bulletins had in 1937 certain peculiarities. There was very little given out about the boy King and his mother, Queen Mariya: there was far more to be heard about the Regent, Prince Paul, and his family. This was a great mistake. I believe that it was the result of a very proper desire to give young King Peter some sort of unpublicized boyhood, but it was misinterpreted by the rural and provincial population who considered it was a sign that Prince Paul was ambitious and might wish to usurp the throne. But there was never nearly so much about any member of the royal family as there was about Mr Stoyadinovitch. I have never turned on the radio in Yugoslavia without hearing a full account of everything the Prime Minister had done on the previous day, delivered in accents that would have been appropriate had he been a Commander-in-chief that had just driven an invading army over the frontier.

That might be taken as just another manifestation of the sham Cæsarism which is a commonplace of our age; and, indeed, towards the end of Stoyadinovitch's regime he had the unhappy notion of packing his meetings with youths who chanted, in a concert that was most uncharacteristic of the Slav, '*Vodyu! Vodyu! Vodyu!*' as it might be, '*Führer! Führer! Führer!*' But there was a difference. Here we had a relic of the pre-Cæsarean age that has passed from the rest of Europe. 'Mr Stoyadinovitch,' Constantine once said to me, 'admires capitalism.' 'Admires capitalism?' I echoed. 'Why, how can he do that? Capitalism is an attempt at solving the problem of how man shall get a steady living off an earth that does not care a jot for him, and it may be said, until some Communist state has worked out its theory with better results than Russia, that we know of none more successful. But surely it is nothing like as good as what we want for ourselves, surely it can only be regarded with disappointment, not admiration.' 'So you think,' said Constantine, 'but so does not Mr Stoyadinovitch. He knows that we are a poor country, since the Turks have taken all for five centuries, and he thinks it would be beautiful if much foreign money came here and bred more money, and if we had many factories such as they have in America, splendid white palaces full of machinery so intricate that when it moves it is like symphonies being played in steel, pouring out new and clean things for our people, pouring out golden streams of wages that all could be bought.' 'But sometimes money does not breed,' I said, 'sometimes it dies in childbirth, and the community is left with a whole lot of corpses on hand. And as for such factories, they may look like palaces but the people who work inside could never be taken for princes and princesses, and the stream of wages, which is golden in the same sense that the Danube is blue, often washes them back in the evenings to filthy slums.' 'You are a woman, you want all to be pretty,' said Constantine, 'you do not see the beauty of ruthlessness, and as for money, Mr Stoyadinovitch is a very clever man. He would see that there are no depressions as there have been in America.'

There is something here, touching in its inexperience, which is very different from Fascism or Nazism. Mussolini and Hitler came to power because they offered the victims of capitalism a promise of relief by a magical rite of regimentation. But this is an innocent who does not know that such victims can ever be numerous enough to exercise a determining force in society. He thinks of them as failures, as weak and impotent, and so they may be in their personal lives; but if they form a seething and desperate mass they may develop a dynamic power surpassing that engendered by success. Under this delusion he conducts himself with an extraordinary imprudence. He does not understand that it is wise to allow as many of the failures as possible to convert themselves by organization to something more like success, and so he fails—and in this he resembles many members of the propertied classes both in England and in America—to understand that trade unionism is not a disintegrating but a stabilizing force.

How should such men as these in the bar know otherwise? When the Industrial Revolution had dawned on the Western powers, the Serbs were Turkish slaves; to this day eighty-seven per cent of Yugoslavs are agricultural workers; Leskovats is called the Manchester of Yugoslavia and is no such thing, but a pleasant good-weathered little town of under twenty thousand inhabitants who have no difficulty in keeping their faces clean; never has Belgrade known a time when, from the uplifting windows of sky-scraper hotels it does not possess, ruined bankers dropped like the gentle dew from heaven upon the place beneath. It may be asked why these adventurers might not have learned of the inconveniences of capitalism from books and newspapers. Certain mistakes the printed word never kept anyone from committing. *Manon Lescaut* never deterred a man from loving a whore, no ageing woman sent away a young lover because she had read *Bel Ami*. There exists a mountain of economic publications which prove that in our modern world of shrinking markets and increasing production it would be impossible to found John Company; the Germans plan to draw such wealth from colonial expansion.

I felt a rush of dislike towards the men in the bar who were instruments of this error. I detected in them a strong physical resemblance to certain types found in Western cities during the last century, to pictures representing the financial adventurers who dominated Paris under the Second Empire, to the photographs of City men which can be seen in the illustrated papers of the nineties, named as founders of enterprises not now extant. Idiotically, they were not only copying a system that was far from ideal, they were themselves imitating those who had proved incapable of grasping such success as the system offers. I could imagine the hotel making the same error. It would repudiate its good fat risottos, its stews would be guiltless of the spreading red oil of paprika, it would employ chambermaids who would not howl by the beds of ailing clients and whose muzzles would not twitch in animal certainty before a Greek, in doubt before a Finn. It would not then resemble a good French hotel, it would become international, a tethered wagon-lit, like the large Spanish hotels.

Belgrade, I thought, had made the same error. It had till recently been a Balkan village. That has its character, of resistance, of determined survival, of martyred penury. This was a very sacred Balkan village; the promontory on which it stood had been sanctified by the blood of men who had died making the simple demand that, since their kind had been created, it might have leave to live. Modern Belgrade has striped that promontory with streets that had already been built elsewhere much better. I felt a sudden abatement of my infatuation for Yugoslavia. I had been enchanted on my first visit with the lovely nature and artifice of Bosnia, and I had recognized in Macedonia a uniquely beautiful life of the people. When the Macedonians loved or sang or worshipped God or watched their sheep, they brought to the business in hand poetic minds that would not believe in appearances and probed them for reality, that possessed as a birthright that quality which Keats believed to be above all others in forming a 'Man of Achievement, especially in Literature, and which Shakespeare possessed so enormously.' 'Negative Capability,' he called it, and it made a man 'capable of being in uncertainties, doubts, without any irritable reaching after fact and reason.' But Macedonia had been under the Ottoman Empire until 1913; it had till then been stabilized by Turkish misgovernment in precisely those medieval conditions which had existed when it was isolated by its defeat at Kossovo in 1389. Macedonia should perhaps be looked on as a museum not typical of the life outside it. It had had only twenty-five years of contact with the modern world. Serbia had known no such seclusion. It was liberated in 1815. For a century it had been exposed to the peculiar poisons of the nineteenth century. I had perhaps come a long way to see a sunset which was fading under my eyes before a night of dirty weather.

But some of this threatened degeneration was still a long way from consummation. This hotel may have longed to slip off its robust character and emulate the Savoy and the Crillon and the Plaza; but its attempt was not well under way as yet. A newcomer had arrived in the bar; the stocky little men were now greeting with cries of love and trust another of the kind who would have betrayed them for about the sum that would have made them betray him, lifting their glasses to him and slapping him on the back with the exaggeration of children playing the game 'In the Manner of the Word.' That I might have seen in London or Paris or New York. But in none of those great cities have I seen hotel doors slowly swing open to admit, unhurried and at ease, a peasant holding a black lamb in his arms. He took up his place beside the news-stand where they sold *Pravda* and *Politika*, the *Continental Daily Mail*, *Paris Soir*, the *New York Herald Tribune*. He was a well-built young man with straight fair hair, high cheekbones, and a look of clear sight. His suit was in the Western fashion, but he wore also a sheepskin jacket, a round black cap, and leather sandals with upturned toes; and to his ready-made shirt his mother had added some embroidery. He looked about him as if in search of someone. Twice he went to the door of the bar and peered at the faces of the stocky little men, so it was plain that he was waiting for one of their kind; and indeed the middle class in Yugoslavia is so near to its peasant origin that any of them might have had such a cousin or nephew. But the one he sought was not there, so he went back to his place by the news-stand. He stood still as a Byzantine king in a fresco, while the black lamb twisted and writhed in the firm cradle of his arms, its eyes sometimes catching the light as it turned and shining like small luminous plates.

Topola

As arranged, we called the next morning at Constantine's house ready to go with Gerda to see the half-finished Monument to the Unknown Soldier on the hill of Avala, twelve miles from Belgrade, and the Karageorgevitch Mausoleum on the hill of Oplenats. The expedition began badly. Gerda opened the door in trim, fresh clothes and was formally welcoming us in the hall when Constantine's old mother slipped in. Her mouth had suddenly watered for some kind of food, so she had tied a kerchief round her head and gone along to the market in her wrapper and slippers, and she had hoped to get back into the house without anybody being the wiser. But here we all were, being *hochwohlgeboren* in the passage. So Gerda looked at the floor with the air of blushing for shame, though her skin did not in fact show any alteration at all, and the poor old mother hung her Beethovenish head. This was all quite wrong, for she was really a magnificent pianist, and Balzac's dressing-gown is the one garment all artists have in common. One cannot create without a little sluttishness packed away somewhere. Neatness and order are delicious in themselves, but permissible only to the surgeon or the nurse. Schiller knew that when he kept rotting apples in his writing-desk, and opened the drawer when he needed inspiration, so that he could look on their brownness, inhale the breath of over-ripeness.

But Gerda had not been able to coerce Constantine. Shamelessly he called us into his study, and we found him fat and round and curly in his candy-striped pyjamas and dressing-gown, with little bouquets of black hair showing between his jacket buttons. 'Ah, she is your girl too,' said my husband, pointing to the photograph over Constantine's desk, which represented the Ludovisi triptych of Venus rising from the foam. 'And why not?' said Constantine. 'She is perfect, for what she is and what she is not. There is nothing in her pose of patriotism or propaganda or philosophy or religion, simply she says, "I am rising to delight."' His little fat hands paddled in the air, lifting him through the same tide as Venus, to the same sweet enamoured air. He, who is one of the ugliest of human beings, knows intuitively all that it is to be the goddess of beauty. 'That sculpture is the very opposite of the frescoes that you have seen in South Serbia, that your husband will see in the mosaic copies that King Alexander made for the mausoleum at Oplenats.

484

For there is no delight, it is all patriotism and propaganda and philosophy and religion, but all the same there is rising, there is floating, there is an ecstasy, but it is a terrible one.' His mouth was full of bread and coffee, but his hands paddled, and he rose up a beam of white light to a light that was whiter.

'You are an intelligent man, though you are a banker,' he said to my husband, 'so you will make no error at Oplenats, you will take these mosaics as an indication of what you will see in Macedonia, in South Serbia, not for themselves. All the Macedonian frescoes are painted, and these have been copied in mosaic. A painted fresco is a painted fresco and a mosaic fresco is a mosaic fresco, and a fresco that is meant to be painted and is worked in mosaic is a mongrel, and mongrels should be gay little dogs, not very large works of art. I suffered the tortures of the damned when I was in Germany and must arrange all for our King with the German manufacturer of mosaics, but I must own it was not only because of my artistic conscience, it was also because the manufacturer was the slowest man in the world. A tall, fat man he was with a great beard, and he spoke so . . . and so . . . and so . . . and once I could not help myself; I cried out, "*Mein Herr*, will you not speak a little faster, for I have many things to do," and he answered, very angrily, but still very slowly, "No, I cannot speak fast, for in the mosaic business we do all things very slowly, we make for eternity." But you will see what he made. I am not sure that it was for eternity, I think it was only for ever, which is not at all the same.'

On the porch he said, 'It is fine weather, and it will be fine weather tomorrow, I am so glad that tomorrow we go to the Frushka Gora. That I have not told you about: there are some old monasteries of our people on some hills by the Danube, that are called the Frushka Gora, that is the Frankish Hills; they are very pretty in themselves, and they explain Belgrade and all that you will see today.' So we drove off along the boulevards, which were crowded with leisurely people, for it was Sunday, and even those who had come to the market were taking it easy. For the same reason there were boys lolling at the open windows of the University Students' Hostel, in the lovely cat-like laziness only possible to highly exercised youth. From one window a boy, darker and more fiery than the rest, was leaning forward and making a burlesque harangue to a laughing group, who raised their hands and cried in mock-hatred, 'Long live Stoyadinovitch!' Of such are the students whom the newspapers often describe as Communists, and a number of them would claim that title. Yet to Westerners nothing could be less accurate. These people are peasants who have in a sense enjoyed an unusual amount of class freedom. They were serfs only to the Turks, who were alien conquerors, and have not for centuries been subordinate to large landowners of their own blood, so they find it natural to criticize such of themselves as set up to be governors. Since they are South Slavs, they have never had a Peter the Great or Catherine the Great to teach them obedience to a centralized power. If they were to rebel against the Government they would act in small independent groups, as Princip and Chabrinovitch did, they would never joyously become subordinate atoms in a vast Marxist system. When they say they are Communists they mean that they are for the country against the town, for the village against Belgrade, for the peasant against the industrialist; and for that reason they one and all loathed Stoyadinovitch.

We were out of Belgrade, we were driving to the dark cone of distant Avala across a rolling countryside that was the spit and image of Lowland Scotland, though richer to the eye by reason of the redness of the earth. It bears signs of comfortable peasant proprietorship, and there came into my mind the verdict my Provençal cook had passed on a certain village on the Côte des Maures: '*C'est un bon pays; personne n'est riche là-bas mais tout le monde a des biens.*' Fairer words cannot be spoken of a country, in my opinion; and I felt in great good humour. So, too, I was delighted to find, did Gerda. Her face was serene and she was making conventional German small-talk with my husband, and she was plainly passing through a specifically German experience which has always struck me as charming. Its simplest form is often displayed in old-fashioned German children's books. Little girls arrive in a coach at a Cologne hotel, with their hearts singing like birds within them: 'Our papa,' rises their carol, 'is a Herr Geheimrath from Hanover, our mamma is everything a Frau Geheimrath should be, we are two well-behaved little girls, wearing beautiful new travelling ulsters, and we are going to see the Rhineland, which everybody knows is one of the most beautiful sights in the world, and all, all is heavenly.' Neither the French nor the English ever get quite the same naïve, unpresumptuous joy in what one is and what one does, when both are unremarkable. We may rejoice in what we do, but we are too Augustinian not to detest what we are, or not to pretend such detestation. It pleased me enormously that Gerda was saying to herself as she drove along, 'I come of an old family of Lutheran pastors, I am the wife of a Yugoslavian official, I am accompanying an Englishman, a cultured person and graduate of

Oxford University and a banker, and his wife, who is a writer, and we are going to see two interesting *Denkmals*, and it is a fine day.'

The road swung round and round the cone of Avala, running between woodlands, green with their first leaves and bronze with buds and carpeted with blue periwinkles. We got out and climbed to the summit over the unfinished gauntness of the engineering construction which is to support the vast Mestrovitch memorial. At the very top we halted, embarrassed by an unusual view of the fighting male. On the descending slope beyond stood two rows of soldiers, one facing the other, every man of them holding in his hand something that flashed. An officer cried out a word of command, which roared from his throat like a spell designed for the instant precipitation of an ocean of blood. The soldiers raised to their lips the things that flashed, which were tin mugs, and we heard a strange sound which might have been made by birds singing underground. Then the officer cried out for atrocity again, and a jet of liquid, silver in the sunlight, spurted from each soldier's lips. They were doing gargling drill against influenza. They saw us, but showed no signs of self-consciousness. If the Serbian heroes of old had been ordered by their Tsars to gargle in front of female tourists they would have obeyed. Military service appears to be the only thing that makes a Slav calm. The difference between the students we had seen at the windows of the University Hostel and these soldiers was that which might be remarked in France between the girl pupils of a *lycée*, gadding and gossiping their way home through the streets of a provincial town, and the still and stylized products of an extremely expensive convent school.

We went down the hill again and paused beside a model of the Mestrovitch memorial which was mounted on a truck. The roof of the tomb is to be supported by immense calm caryatides, Serbian peasant women, the mothers of these calm boys. We looked at the existing memorial, which is rough and small, cut by some simple mason, and out of curiosity I put my head into a little hut beside it. I wished I had not. It housed the wreaths that had been laid on the memorial by various official bodies. Through its gloom immortelles and ribbons lettered with gold and striped with crude national colours emitted the nostril-stopping smell of dust. By reason of the words spelled out by gold letters and the combinations of the national colours, the spectacle was horrifying. These wreaths were displeasing in any case because they were official, and had been ordered by preoccupied functionaries and supplied as articles of commerce for a minor state occasion that would provoke no wave of real feeling in the people, but their provenance reminded one that the quality of Balkan history, and indeed of all history, is disgusting.

One wreath had been given by Nazi Germany, which had now absorbed the body of Austria, and which had been absorbed by the spirit of Austria; Vienna is speaking again, through Hitler as through Lueger and Schoenerer and Conrad von Hötzendorf, a message of self-infatuation and a quiver of hatreds for all but the chosen Teutonic people, the most poisonous being dedicated to the Slav. Another had been given by Italy, who had incessantly harried Dalmatia by her greed, who gave the assassins of King Alexander arms and the knowledge how to use them. It was a kind of filthy buffoonery almost unmatched in private life which had made these powers lay their wreaths on a grave sacred to a people whom they meant to send to its grave as soon as possible. It was an indictment of man that this people was forced to stand by when their enemies came to defile their holy place, simply because no political arrangement has been discovered which annuls the dangers arising out of Yugoslavia's proximity to Central Europe and Italy.

I became filled with feminist rage. I would have liked to deface the model of Mestrovitch's monument, which represented peasant women without contrition. Since men are liberated from the toil of childbirth and child-rearing, they might reasonably be expected to provide an environment which would give children the possibility to survive and test the potentialities of humanity. The degree of failure to realize that expectation revealed in this disgusting little room could not be matched by women unless ninety per cent of all births were miscarriages. Gerda, however, liked the wreaths. 'Our father is a Herr Geheimrath. . . .' I put out my hand and touched the Italian offering, and murmured my distaste, but Gerda only wrinkled her nose and laughed slyly, like a little girl who sees something that her nurse has told her is dirty.

We drove away from Avala by a pleasant road that runs among water-meadows where willows mark the constant stream, and orchards with plump foliage smothering the last of the blossom, and vineyards naked and unpromising as graveyards, with their poles stripped bare for spring. Like the Pas de Calais, this Serbian countryside presents inconsistently neat cultivations and sluttish villages. The villages here are very large, for except in the neighbourhood of the big towns there are no scattered farmsteads. Wherever the peasant's land may be he lives in the village and drives his livestock home at night and out again in the morning. This custom proved its convenience during the Turkish occupation, for it enabled the Christians to put up a combined defence against night raids by irregular troops or bandits, but it had its origin further back than that. The basis of the Slav social system was the *Zadruga*, the family whose members shared equally in the labours and profits of a jointly owned estate, which was governed by an elected Elder, who was usually the oldest man in the group but might sometimes be a younger man who had shown exceptional ability, or might even be a woman. The Elder and his wife lived in a central house and the others inhabited either rooms joined to it or adjacent houses. The *Zadruga* naturally split up when the number of descendants began to press too heavily on the resources of the estate, but it usually included at least three generations and often numbered a hundred persons or more. The dreary identification between country life and solitude has therefore never depressed Serbia as it has other lands; and even quite insignificant villages run long main streets down a hill and over a stream and up the hill on the other side, where the cultivators of the trim orchards and vineyards loll outside tumbledown cafés, looking anything but trim themselves.

They were, indeed, not out to look trim. Ferocity was this district's line. They would have preferred to curdle the blood, just a little, by their manifest kinship with the Haiduks, with the great chief Karageorge himself. For we were already on the stage where that first liberator of Serbia had unveiled his violence and power. At a turn of the road we stopped to see the place where Karageorge was one day riding with his herdsmen behind his swine, just after the Janizaries had come back to power and murdered the pro-Serb Mustapha Pasha and were massacring every important Serb that they could find. Through the dust he saw the flashing weapons of a party of Turkish soldiers and without an instant's hesitation he and his herdsmen turned their horses' heads into the oak forests that bordered the road, leaving the swine to take care of themselves. Later we came to the village where Karageorge had met with two Serbian chiefs and five hundred of the rank and file, and had been chosen their Commander-in-chief in the first insurrection of 1804. This moody and valiant giant, who was no mere springing tiger but possessed real military genius, did not wish to accept that office, for curious reasons which have been reported for us by an actual witness. He said, 'I want to go with you, but not before you,' and when they pressed him for a reason he told them, 'For one thing, you've not learned soldiering, and because of that, after some days, you will surrender to the Turks, then you know what will happen! And for another, if I accepted I certainly would do much not to your liking. If one of you were taken in the smallest treachery—the least faltering—I would kill him, hang him, punish him in the most fearful manner.'

This was not a mere threat of disciplinary firmness; it was a confessional allusion to the violences which he had already committed under the stress of patriotism. Years before, when he was a youth, he had taken part in an uprising and had had to flee with his stepfather and their cattle towards the Austrian frontier. But when they came to the river Sava his stepfather's nerve failed him, and he announced he would turn back and seek pardon from the Turks. Karageorge did not believe that he would receive anything from the Turks but torture, so in desperation he took out his pistol and shot the old man dead. Then he went on to the next village and asked the headman to give the corpse burial, and left him all his cattle in payment. That Karageorge should at the moment of being chosen leader by his people have referred to their characteristic faults and his own, not in comfortable tones of conventional modesty but with an unimpassioned accuracy, is characteristically Slav. But East can meet West. The house where the three chiefs met has been pulled down and replaced by a towered school, closely resembling a small suburban public library.

We passed by a spa almost as unlike Bath or Vichy or Baden-Baden as the spa we had seen in Bosnia: no fine ladies and gentlemen were here in search of undefined recuperation, peasants were striding down a chestnut avenue towards the spring, solemnly conscious of what they expected its waters to do to their bowels, solemnly conscious of what their forefathers had known, that in water there are gods. There was a solid yet naïve *Kurhaus*, built by somebody who had gone to the West to see how these things were done, and had gaped at his model as well as studying. Since it was Sunday there were little boys offering trays of scones and rolls, for the Serbs love breadstuffs almost as much as the Scots; and others were selling miniature leather sandals of the type worn throughout Yugoslavia, with the upturned toe, which is useless though appropriate as a symbol of the *x* which is added to the usual human characteristics in the Slav. The evaluation of that *x* became an increasingly interesting problem as we drove along the lanes into Karageorge's village, Topola (which is one of the two Serb words for poplar), for there

his kind stood in the mud, all with these cockspur points to their
sandals, all with that Slav mystery heavy on their dark forelocks,
across their scowling brows, hanging round a playground that
had been Karageorge's stableyard. The main street took us to a
village green, running uphill alongside a church with dome and
walls battered and pitted with rifle-fire, and a galleried farmhouse
that had been Karageorge's home and now bore the emblems of a
Sokol headquarters. On a seat beneath some trees sat two parent
wolves, an old man and woman, their ferocity silvered down to
gentle and amiable dignity, emitting fire from the nostrils only
now and then, finely dressed in the sheepskin and embroidered
homespun of peasant costume. The unknown quantity was not
what one might have thought, for mere lawlessness and savagery
do not age in majesty, with accumulated goods about them.

An old man came and took us into the church, which was full
of the dark magic of the Orthodox rite, and told us that here
Karageorge had come to take communion, and here his bones
had rested ever since they had been laid there several years after
his death, till they had been moved to the great new mausoleum
on the hill of Oplenats half a mile away. 'Where had they been
in the meantime?' I asked. 'In the ground,' said the old man, 'in
a valley not far from here. He had come back from exile after
Obrenovitch had become the leader of the Serbs, and Obrenovitch
sent a man to kill him, that he might placate the Sultan by sending
him his head. But later Obrenovitch's wife grew alarmed, because
one of the children in her family grew ill, and she had the bones
of Karageorge dug up and sent back to us here.' Behind us in
the darkness Gerda tittered. We turned in surprise and found her
looking surprisingly fair. 'They are such savages,' she explained.
The old man gazed at her perplexed, as if she might perhaps be
ill or unhappy, and went on slowly with doubtful, kindly glances
at her, to show us the screen that divides the whole altar from the
church, the iconostasis. It was carved with artless sculptures of
holy stories seen through peasant eyes, after the fashion of the
fourteenth century, although the wood was new. 'They were
carved for us by three brothers,' he said, 'descendants of the
three brothers who did the famous iconostasis and pulpit at the
Church of the Holy Saviour in Skoplje, two hundred years ago.
They have carried on the craft from father to son. Eight years
they lived here, making this screen. Now they have been for many
years at Nish, working on a screen that will be greater than this,
but not more beautiful. For the Karageorgevitches they did their
best.' He opened the royal door in the iconostasis, that opens on

the altar, and his face folded with grief. 'Here once God gave us
a great mercy. When our King Alexander went to Bulgaria we
said mass here day and night during all the three days he was in
Sofia, and although there are many Bulgarians who hate us and
have evil hearts, nothing happened to him, he came back to us in
safety. But, God forgive us, when he went to France we did not say
mass for him at all, for we thought he was among friends.' Again
history emitted its stench, which was here particularly noisome.
Nothing a wolf can do is quite so unpleasant as what can be done
to a wolf in zoos and circuses, by those who are assumed not to
be wolfish, to be the civilized curators of wolfdom.

Before we got back into the car we stood for a minute on
the green, looking at the fierce little church, at the fierce little
farmhouse out of which some fierce boys were issuing, fresh from
gymnastic exercises dynamized by patriotic fury, at the fierce and
handsome ancients on the seat. 'Now I see the truth of the old
saying that there are more ways of killing a cat than by choking
it with cream,' said my husband. 'Observe that in Bosnia the
Slavs did choke the Turk with cream, they glutted him with their
wholesale conversions and kept him outside of Sarajevo. But here
cream just did not come into the question. The Serbs fought the
Turks, and then they fought them, and then they fought them.
What we see in these people is the normal expression to be looked
for in a fighting army that has just come out of the trenches after
a long hand-to-hand fight, and thinks it may yet be ambushed.'
But later, as we walked to the mausoleum where it lifts its white
cupolas in a wooded park, as we passed under the dry grainy gold
of its mosaic vaults, he said, 'This, however, is something else.
Has it anything to do with these people, this extraordinary place?
Or is it just a fantasy of these Karageorgevitches?'

The church, which is dedicated to St George, is quite new, and
externally it is very beautiful. Fidelity to the Byzantine tradition
is responsible for quite a number of very ugly small churches, for
its reliance on pure form shows up any defects in the way of bad
machine cutting and ugly stone; but it automatically imposes a
certain majesty and restraint on a church which is given good
material and skilled workmanship. Oplenats was built by old
King Peter in 1912, but it was reduced to ruins during the Great
War. In 1922 King Alexander rebuilt it, and added two features
which had, apparently, not been in his father's mind when he
originally planned it. King Alexander brought up the bones of
Karageorge from the village church at Topola, and buried them
under a plain block of marble in the right apse: that is to say, beside

the royal throne which stands in any Orthodox church of dignity, which is here an impressive matter of green marble surmounted by a white-and-gold eagle. The only other Karageorgevitch whom King Alexander thought worthy to be buried in the church itself, and not in the crypt, was King Peter, who lies under another plain block of marble in the left apse. This indicates a critical attitude which ruling monarchs do not usually adopt towards their dynasty: for there was another Karageorgevitch ruler, Alexander the son of Karageorge, but he was not a success.

The other contribution of King Alexander was the mosaics; King Peter planned no other decoration than the shot-riddled regimental banners, borne in the Balkan wars and the Great War, which hang from the marble pillars. These mosaics are indeed at first extremely disconcerting in their artistic impropriety. It is not mere pedantry to object to mosaic as a medium for copying painted frescoes, for the eye is perpetually distracted by its failure to find the conditions which the original design was framed to satisfy. These frescoes are Byzantine in origin: their proper title in the histories of art is Serbo-Byzantine. The flame-like forms that should have been fixed in appropriate tenuity by colours flame-like in their smoothness and transparency were falsified in their absence because they were represented in a material opaque and heterogeneous as sand. The man who ordered these mosaics to be made must have been lacking in any fine æsthetic perception. But they compose an extremely ably prepared encyclopædia of medieval Serbian art. Looking up at them one can say, 'That Dormition of the Virgin comes from Grachanitsa, that sequence of the life of St George comes from Dechani, that Flight into Egypt from Petch,' and without receiving the intense pleasure which is given by the actual sight of these works of art, one is afforded useful information as to what sort of pleasure that is going to be.

'But why did this man want to hold up an encyclopædia of medieval Serbian art over his family vault?' asked my husband. 'It seems to me as if an English king should build a mausoleum full of allusions to Richard Cœur de Lion.' 'Well, that is all the remote past they have,' I said, 'and they came straight out of that glory into the misery of Turkish conquest.' 'But is there any real continuity between the medieval Serbian Empire and these Serbs?' asked my husband. 'Of course there is,' I said; 'you will see that once you get away from Belgrade.' 'But these frescoes are so beautiful,' said my husband, 'this is a true legacy from Byzantium. It is too patently sensitive for the great period of Byzantine art, but there is the right hieratic quality, the true desire to arrange all things in an order that shall disclose a relationship between the lowest and the highest, even God Himself.' Then a thought struck him. 'But where are these Serbo-Byzantine frescoes?' he asked. 'In monasteries,' I said, 'some in Serbia; some of the most beautiful are in Studenitsa and Mileshevo and Zhitcha, but many are in Old Serbia and in South Serbia.' 'All on strictly Serb territory,' said my husband, 'so this building with its enormously costly mosaics can mean nothing whatsoever to any Croatians or Dalmatians or Slovenes. Yet it is the mausoleum of their King, and superbly appropriate to him. I see that though Yugoslavia is a necessity it is not a predestined harmony.'

We went towards the crypt where King Alexander himself is buried, but the beauty of one of the frescoes caught my husband back. 'But you never told me of this extraordinary thing,' said my husband. 'Here is a man whom I know only as a Balkan king with an unfortunate tendency to dictatorship. He appears to have conceived a gloriously poetic idea, such as only the greatest men of the world have ever had. He recovered the ancient lands of his people in the Balkan wars and tried—what was it Constantine once said?—'to graft his dynasty' on the stock of their ancient emperors so that what was dead lived again. It is quite a different idea from mere conquest. Those frescoes say to his people, 'This is what you were, so this is what you are.' But, tell me, was it anything more than a pedagogic fancy? Can those toughs we have seen outside really respond to such an idea?' 'I am not sure,' I said, 'but I think he got it from them.' 'Nonsense,' said my husband. 'I refuse to believe that those young ruffians fret for lack of the Byzantine frescoes their ancestors enjoyed in the fourteenth century.' 'Well, I assure you they knew they had lost something,' I said, 'they all know by heart a lot of poetry.' 'They do not look as if they did,' said my husband. 'Oh, not Arthur Hugh Clough,' I said, with a bitterness that referred to an attempt made by my husband to read me a poem by that writer which he had declared was tolerable, 'but they know thousands of lines of folk-poetry about the defeat of the Serbs at Kossovo, and it gives an impression of a great civilization. I know that they tested the patients in the Serbian military hospitals during the war to see how many knew it, and it was something like ninety per cent.' 'Maybe,' said my husband.

In the crypt lamps hanging above the tombs illumined long arcades. Mosaics on the walls and vaults shook with a feeble pulse in this uncertain light. There are numbers of Karageorgevitch dead lying here, and though it is only a hundred and twenty years since

Karageorge died, not a few have lain here for many times the length of their lives. This family, though so potent, was physically fragile. There are children, lads, young wives in their twenties, their names all trembling with that suggestion of weakness, headache, fever, which is given by tremulous lamplight. A stronger brightness was shed by the candles which blazed in an iron stand beside the grave of King Alexander, which lies at the altar end of the crypt, under slabs of onyx. Half a dozen men and women were lighting fresh candles and putting them in the stand, were crossing themselves and murmuring and kneeling and bringing their roughness down to kiss the shining onyx; such passion, I have heard, is shown by Lenin's tomb. The King lies beside his mother, as his will directed: she died of tuberculosis when he was fifteen months old. In this crypt, the foundation of this immense mass of marble erected to a parricide by his descendants, the core of this countryside on which defensive resentments grew like thick forests, all was plaintive and wistful, tender and nostalgic.

Franzstal

Above us the day was blue and golden, as it had rarely been during this lachrymose spring. Around us it may have been so also, but we did not know. We were shut up in the courtyard of an inn. There was nothing remarkable about this courtyard. It was quite large; the rooms round it had a certain cosy quality, not at all Slav, as if they were built for a congestion which would not be at all contentious, but warm and animal and agreeable; on a line across the courtyard hung scarlet blankets and white sheets and towels embroidered in red cross-stitch; in flower-beds running by the walls primroses and tulips grew with an amusing stiffness. All that was worth seeing there could be seen in ten seconds.

Nor was this inn set in an interesting place. Outside there was a village consisting of one very broad and muddy street, lined with one storied houses and shops. Sometimes a light cart passed, drawn by a mare with her foal running alongside, harnessed outside the poles; so do they accustom horses to the traffic from the beginning. Sometimes a herd of dirty and ill-tailored pigs roamed by, apparently free from all governance. There was really no reason to pay a visit to such a village, particularly on a Monday afternoon, when none of the population was visible to display such interesting characteristics as they possessed.

Nor was it for the food that we had come to this inn. On the table in front of the four of us, Gerda, Constantine, my husband, and myself, there were stacked platefuls of long undulant sausages that can never have been good specimens of their kind, that were particularly unpleasant at the moment, for they were neither quite warm nor quite cold. The liver sausage was peculiarly horrible, and left a layer of grease on the lips and palate.

My husband and I were not even there because we had made a mistake, and had been deceived by our ignorance of the country into believing that this village was interesting. We had not wished to come at all. It had been announced to us that we should. The evening before, on our return from Topola, we had been sitting at dinner in our hotel, uneasily discussing Gerda. During the day's expedition she had shown that she was disappointed with us. When we showed admiration or curiosity about Serbian things she behaved as if we were letting her down and betraying some standards which we should have held in common: as an exceptionally stupid Englishman might behave in India to tourists who showed an interest in native art or philosophy. 'But she is worse than that,' said my husband. 'She said something to me this afternoon when you were making a sketch of the church at Topola which seemed to me profoundly shocking. She told me that the Serbs hold that the Austrians had no right to bombard Belgrade, as it was an unfortified town, and I could not understand whether this was just an attitude of the people or a serious opinion of informed men. So I asked, 'Does your husband think so?' She gave a queer, sly smile and said, 'Yes, he would say so, but then he is a good official.' That seemed to me the most utterly undisciplined and disloyal thing that the foreign-born wife of an official could possibly say.' It was then that a waiter came to announce a telephone call from Constantine. When my husband came back he said, 'Constantine tells me we will not be going to the Frushka Gora tomorrow, but the day after. Tomorrow he wants us to go and have lunch at a place called Franzstal.' 'Franzstal? Why Franzstal?' I said. 'It is a suburb inhabited by the Swabs, the Germans who were settled here by Maria Theresa to colonize the lands that had been neglected by the Turks. But we will not see them if we go there by day, they will all be out at work in Belgrade or in the fields. Is there anything specially interesting there?' 'That is what I asked Constantine,' said my husband, 'but he only said, as one who is doing his best, that the Swab girls wore from ten to twenty petticoats.'

Next day we learned that the second part of our conversation was explained by the first, as we crossed the Danube and found our way to Zemun, which used to be the first town over the Hungarian frontier, and is now remarkable only for its enormous population of storks. Gerda wore an expression of sleepy satisfaction which increased as we drew nearer to Franzstal. Now, as she sat at this table in the courtyard, eating her tepid sausages, her face was soft with complete contentment. Constantine watched her and broke into a tender laugh. 'Is it not extraordinary, the patriotism of Germans?' he asked us. 'My wife is quite happy, because this little village is quite German and she feels she is surrounded by what is German.' It was difficult to make a helpful response. I am fond of England myself, but I trust that if I lived in Rome I would not insist that some French or German visitors who happened to be in my power should cancel a trip to Tivoli or Frascati in order to spend the day in an English tea-room. 'Would you believe it,' continued Constantine fondly, 'she would not consent to be my wife until I had admitted to her that Charlemagne was a German.

They are like rocks, these Germans.' A silence fell. My husband
and I were both reflecting that in the Nazis' opinion Charlemagne
was not a German but an oppressor of Germans. Since we dared
not make a frivolous comment and could not make a serious one,
our eyes grew vacant. Above us the misused day was glorious.
We heard doors banging in the inn, somewhere a parrot began to
scream. A girl in bunchy skirts came into the courtyard, put down
a ewer, and pulled up an iron plate in the paving and drew herself
some water from a well. 'Look,' said poor Constantine timidly,
'she is wearing very many petticoats, it might be as many as ten
or twenty.'

Frushka Gora

We stood in the disordered rooms of some sort of society called
'The Serbian Queen Bee,' and I had difficulty in fixing my
attention on Constantine and the officials of the society as they
explained to us precisely what it was. We had started at seven from
Belgrade and had travelled for two hours to Novi Sad, a journey
which might have been pleasant, for the train ran beside the
hallucinatory landscape of the misted Danube floods, but which
was not, because it became apparent that Gerda had decided to
detest us. Every word and movement of hers, and even in some
mysterious way her complete inaction, implied that she was noble,
patient, industrious, modest, and self-effacing, whereas we were
materialist, unstable, idle, extravagant, and aggressive. She was at
that moment standing in the corner of the room behind the men
who were talking to me, silently exuding this libellous charade.

The town, I understood they were telling me, had been founded
by the Patriarch Arsenius III at the end of the seventeenth century.
When the Serbians revolted against the Turks in 1689 and failed,
the Emperor Leopold of Austria offered them asylum on his
territories, with full rights of religious worship and a certain degree
of self-government. There were already a number of Serb settlers
there who had been introduced by the Turks when Hungary was
theirs. The Patriarch accepted the offer and led across the Danube
thirty thousand Serbian families, from all parts of the land, as far
south as Macedonia and Old Serbia. Some of them had settled here
in Neuestadt, as it had been called. A good many of them had fled
back to Turkish territory, for the Emperor broke his promises, and
the Austrians and Hungarians bled them white with financial and
military levies and forbade them the use of the Orthodox rite. Only
for a little time, under Maria Theresa's liberal son, the Emperor
Joseph, did the refugee Serbs enjoy honest treatment. But they
never forgot their language and their culture, and in 1823 they
founded this literary society, 'The Serbian Queen Bee.' It was
unfortunate that we had come to visit its headquarters just when it
had been handed over to the house painter, they said anxiously.

We could get some idea of what the society had preserved, we
replied; and pulled out some of the pictures that were stacked
against the wall. We came again and again on typical portraits of
the sort that pullulated on the whole of nineteenth-century Europe

except France, where there were too many good eighteenth-century portrait-painters for artlessness to take the country by storm. Men who were nothing but moustaches and sloping shoulders, women who were nothing but smoothly parted coiffures and stiffly caged bodices, had their Slav characteristics contracted down to a liverish look. 'They did not migrate here,' murmured my husband, 'until three hundred years after the destruction of the Serbo-Byzantine civilization. I expect the continuity was quite thoroughly broken, and that King Alexander was simply a doctrinaire acting on nationalist——' His voice broke. 'Theory,' he added, uncertainly. He had turned to the light a Byzantine Madonna, vast-eyed, rigid in the climax of an exalted rhythm. The Serbs had, indeed, not lost all their baggage on their way here.

'I will show you all,' said Constantine, 'all I will show you. Therefore we must hurry, for I will show you the Patriarchate at Karlovtsi, which has been the headquarters of the Serbian Church since the great migration of Arsenius, before we go to the monasteries of the Frushka Gora.' So we soon left this town, which was very agreeable and recalled my own Edinburgh in its trim consciousness of its own distinction. Our road took us into pretty country, green and rolling, at the river's edge. Once we paused at a church that had the remarried look of a building that has changed its faith. It had been a mosque during the hundred and fifty years the Turks held Hungary; it has since the early eighteenth century been a Roman Catholic Church. The clublike atmosphere of a mosque still hung round it: it had a wide terrace overlooking the waters, where there should have been sitting impassive and contented men in fezes, drawing on some immense secret fund of leisure. We stood there for a moment, soothed by the miles of water, pale as light itself, on which stranded willows impressed dark emblems, garlands and true-lover's knots and cat's-cradles. We went back to our contest with mud, with the dark Central European ooze that is never completely mastered save by a drought so extreme as to be a still greater affliction, that rose now in thick waves before our wheels, that kept the upper hand even in the main street of Karlovtsi, though that was a handsome little town.

The Patriarchate was a nineteenth-century stone palace, built in the Byzantine style with Austrian solidity, rich in arch and balcony. We went up a flight of steps to the florid entrance and rang the bell, and looked round us at the gardens, which were very ornate in the formal style, with many flower-beds laid out in intricate shapes and surrounded with low box hedges, and numbers of lilac bushes bearing peculiarly heavy purple flowers. The door did not open. We rang the bell again, we knocked with our fists, we went back to the car and sounded the hooter. Nothing happened, so we went into the gardens, Constantine clapping his hands and crying 'Holla! Holla!' to the unresponsive palace. The gardens were mystifying, inside the beautifully tended box hedges the flower-beds were choked with weeds, a single garden chair, made of white painted wire in the Victorian fashion, was set quite alone on a wide gravel space, with an air of deluded sociability, as if it had gone mad and thought that there were about it many other garden chairs. Children came in from the street and followed us about. We could find no gardener, and the only door we could find opened into a large room with stone shelves used for storing an immense quantity of jam. We had given up all hope of entering, and had paused to inhale the scent of the prodigious purple lilacs, when an old man carrying an orange came out of a door we had not seen and told us that the Patriarch was in Belgrade, but there were some priests working at the printing-press near by, and he would fetch us one of them.

There came to us a tall monk, nobly beautiful, wearing a cloak of complicated design and majestic effect: all the garments worn in the Eastern Church are inherited from Byzantium and recall its glory. He had perfect manners, and was warm in his greeting to Constantine and Gerda, but his eyes lay on us with a certain coldness and reproach. I was surprised at this, for I had always found Orthodox ecclesiastics disposed to treat English people as if they were members of the same Church; but I supposed that here, at headquarters, they might be stricter in their interpretation of schism and heresy. But he was courteous, and told us that he would take us over the Patriarchate, and would like also to show us the printing-press, in which he took a special interest as he was head of Propaganda.

It lay behind the gardens, in a no-man's-land of alleys and outhouses, countryish and clean, with here and there more of those prodigious lilacs, and little streams running down to the Danube. From a courtyard filled with green light by a gnarled old fruit tree we went into a dusty office, where an old priest and a young one sat at rickety desks furnished with ink-wells and pens and blotting-paper that all belonged to the very dawn of stationery. Pamphlets of artless appearance, incompetently tied up in bales, were lying about not in disarray but in only amateurish array. We went down a step or two to the composing-room, where a man stood before the sloping trays and set up print in the fantastic Old

Slavonic type used in Orthodox missals and in no secular writings
whatsoever. We went up a step or two into a room where young
girls bound the pamphlets, not very skilfully but most devoutly.
Then in another room, either two steps up or two steps down but
certainly not on the same level, we found a lovely twisted old man,
deformed by the upward spiral of his spirit, as El Greco loved to
paint his holy kind. He fed the printing machine with sheets as
if he had to school himself to remember that the poor mindless
thing could do its sacred work only at a certain pace. We might
have been visiting the office of some small, fantastic cult carried
on by a few pure and obstinate and unworldly people in some
English town. Indeed, I know a shop in a Sussex village, owned
by a sect which believes that the way to please God is by ritual
water-drinking, which was the precise analogue of this modest and
fanatic establishment. Yet this was the analogue of a printing-press
owned by the Church of England and housed by the Archbishop
of Canterbury in the grounds of Lambeth Palace.

We had still to wait for some minutes before the front door of
the Patriarchate, though the priest had gone through the kitchen
to send up a servant to open it. Then it slowly swung open, and
a withered little major-domo looked out at us. It seemed to me
that he pursed his lips when he saw my husband and myself.
'Good morning,' said Constantine, stepping inside, 'and how is
life going with you?' '*Polako, polako*,' answered the little man, that
is, 'Only so-so.' 'Why, he speaks like a Russian,' said Constantine,
and talked to him for a little. 'Yes,' he said, 'he was a Russian
officer, and he is very pious and he would like to be a monk, but
he has a wife, so they have made him major-domo here.' He was
at least somewhere which might have reminded him of his home. I
have never been to Russia, but I have visited states which formed
part of Tsarist Russia, Finland and Estonia and Latvia, and I am
familiar with villas that have belonged to rich Russians in France
and Italy and Germany, and I can recognize a certain complex of
decoration and architecture as Romanoff and nothing else.

It has elements that can be matched in other countries. Something like it can be seen in the older mansions built by the
nineteenth-century barons on Riverside Drive and in the Middle
West and the West; there is the same profusion of busy and
perforate woodwork in the interior. There is a suggestion also
of the photograph-frames and boxes made of shells which are
to be bought at English seaside towns; and they recall also
the presents that people give each other in German provincial
shops, such as umbrellas with pink marble tops cut into stags'

heads. There is a suggestion, in fact, of every kind of bad taste known to Western civilization, down to the most naïve and the most plebeian; and there is a curious absence of any trace of the classical and moderating influence which France has exercised on the rest of Europe, though it has suffered the gilt infection spread by the Roi Soleil. Yet there is also from time to time the revelation of a taste so superb that it puts the West to shame. There is here a passion which is the root of our love for beauty, and therefore of our effort for art; the passion for beautiful substances, for coloured gems, for shining stone, for silver and gold and crystal. There is not only this basis for art, there is art, there is a creative imagination that conceives vast and simple visions, as a nomad would see them, who, lifting his eyes from the plains, looks on the huge procession of the clouds. There is also a feeling for craft; this nomad was accustomed to pick up soft metal and twist it into the semblance of horses and wild beasts, shapes he could criticize, since he rode the one and hunted the other, so much that he knew their bodies as his own.

We are perhaps looking not at a manifestation of bad taste at all, but at the bewilderment of a powerful person with perfect taste who has been suddenly transported from a world in which there are only a few materials, and those in a pure state, to be shaped by that taste or ignored, into another world, crammed with small manufactured objects, the product of other people's tastes, which are so different from his that he cannot form any just estimate of their value. The powerful Russian people were kept from Western art by the Tartar occupation. They have never made full contact with it. This is no more than a giant's stupendous innocence; yet it is also a giant's stupendous vulgarity. He has resolved his doubts in too many cases by consideration of the money value of objects, or of the standards of people who may be of rank but who are historically ridiculous. But he is a giant, and it is something to be above the dwarfish ordinary stature.

There was, indeed, one room in the Patriarchate that was magnificent, a conference chamber with a superb throne and crimson curtains which might have been taken from one of the finest Viennese palaces, but was derived from a larger and more dramatic inspiration. The rest was faintly bizarre and sometimes that not faintly. We sat down in a small drawing-room, while Constantine talked to the priest and the major-domo; and I remarked that the furniture was not what would have been found in an English archbishop's palace. It was a suite made from black wood, including chairs and tables and bookcases, all decorated with gilt carvings, three or four inches long, representing women nude to the waist, with their breasts strongly defined. They were placed prominently on the pilasters of the bookcases, on the central legs of the round tables, on the arms of the chairs. They were a proof, of course, of the attitude of the Orthodox Church regarding sexual matters, which it takes without excitement, and I am sure nobody had ever cast on them a pornographic eye. But for all that they were naïvely chosen as ornaments for an ecclesiastical home.

'But why,' I said to Constantine, 'are both the priest and the major-domo looking at me and my husband as if they hated us?' 'Oh, it is nothing personal,' said Constantine, 'but they both hate the English.' 'Ha, ha, ha!' said Gerda, laughing like somebody acting in an all-star revival of Sheridan. 'That I suppose you find very odd, that anybody should hate the English.' 'But what do they know about the English?' asked my husband. 'The old officer hates very much the English,' explained Constantine, 'because he says that it was Sir George Buchanan who started the Russian Revolution.' We had to think for a minute before we remembered that Sir George Buchanan had been our Ambassador at St Petersburg in 1917. 'But does he not think that perhaps Kerensky and Lenin had a little to do with it?' asked my husband. When it was put to him the major-domo shook his head and emitted an impatient flood of liquid consonants. 'He says,' translated Constantine, 'that that is nonsense. How could unimportant people like Kerensky and Lenin do anything like starting a revolution? It must have been someone of real influence like Sir George Buchanan.'

'Now, ask the priest why he hates the English,' I said. 'It is because he believes that Lloyd George could have saved the Romanoff dynasty,' said Constantine, 'but I do not understand what he means.' 'I know what he means,' I said; 'he has heard the story that the Bolsheviks would have allowed the Tsar and Tsarina and their family to come to England, and Lloyd George would not let them. But you can tell him that there was not a word of truth in that story, that Lloyd George's worst enemies have never been able to confirm it. The Bolsheviks never offered to turn the poor souls over to us and there is no shred of evidence that they would ever have done so if they had been asked.' But the priest only shook his head, his beautiful brown eyes showing him as inaccessible to argument as if he were a stag. 'It is no use talking to these good people,' said Constantine, 'for this house is all for White Russia. The Patriarch is mad against the Bolsheviks, and he thinks that all European problems would be solved and that we would enter a Golden Age if only the Romanoffs were restored, and he cannot see why England has not done it.' I thought apprehensively of the stacks of pamphlets in the printing-press, with their rough biscuit-coloured paper and their pale sticky type, and I wondered what astonishing information they gave out when they were designed, as they sometimes are, to instruct the Orthodox laity in political matters.

But before we left for the Frushka Gora, the priest in the grand cloak would have us see the Patriarchate church, which is next door to the palace; and once we were there all the ineffectiveness and artlessness that we had seen, the clutching at broken toys and the kindergarten assurance that life was simple when it was in fact most complicated, fell into its place and appeared legitimate. In the white-and-gold theatre of a baroque church the students of the theological seminary attached to the Patriarchate were assisting at a Lenten mass. The priests passed in and out of the royal door in the great iconostasis, which framed in gilt the richness of the holy pictures. As they came and went there could be seen for an instant the shining glory of the altar, so sacred that it must be hidden lest the people look at it so long that they forget its nature, as those who stare at the sun see in time not the source of light but a black circle. The students' voices affirmed the glory of the hidden altar, and declared what it is that makes the adorable, what loveliness is and harmony. The unfolding of the rite brought us all down on our knees in true prostration, with the forehead bent to the floor. 'It is only necessary to do this during Holy Week,' gasped Constantine apologetically in my ear. 'I am so very sorry.' He thought that English dignity would be affronted by the necessity to adopt this attitude. But there could have been nothing more agreeable than to be given the opportunity to join in this ceremony, which, if nothing in the Christian legend were true, would still be uplifting and fortifying, since it proclaims that certain elements in experience are supremely beautiful, and that we should grudge them nothing of our love and service. It inoculated man against his constant and disgusting madness, his preference for the disagreeable over the agreeable. Here was the unique accomplishment of the Eastern Church. It was the child of Byzantium, a civilization which had preferred the visual arts to literature, and had been divided from the intellectualized West by a widening gulf for fifteen hundred years. It was therefore not tempted to use the doctrines of the primitive Church as the foundation of a philosophical and ethical system unbridled in its claim to read the thoughts of God; and it devoted all its forces to the achievement of the mass, the communal form of art which might enable man from time to time to apprehend why it is believed that there may be a God. In view of the perfection of this achievement, the ecclesiastics of the Eastern Church should be forgiven if they show the incompetence in practical matters and the lack of general information which we take for granted in painters and musicians. They are keeping their own order, we cannot blame them if they do not keep ours.

The Frushka Gora, that is to say the Frankish Hills, which are called by that name for a historical reason incapable of interesting anybody, lie to the south of the Danube; and we had to drive across the range to find the monasteries founded by the seventeenth-century migrants, for they lie scattered on the southern slopes, looking back towards Siberia. Once we were over the crest we found ourselves in the most entrancing rounded hills, clothed with woods now golden rather than green with the springtime, which ran down to vast green and purple plains, patterned with shadows shed by a tremendous cloudscape, slowly sailing now on its way to Asia. We stopped to eat at a hotel high above a valley that fell in a golden spiral to the plains; and it should have been agreeable, for this is a centre for walking-tours, and we had around us many young people, probably teachers freed from their duty because it was near Easter, and there is nothing so pretty as the enjoyment people get out of simple outings in countries that have been liberated by the Great War. It is so in all the Habsburg succession states, and it is so in the Baltic provinces that once were Russia, Finland and Estonia and Latvia. But we did not enjoy our outing so much as we might have, because Gerda had been on the wrong side of the peace treaties.

Constantine was saying, 'And much, much did we Serbs owe to those Serbs who were in Hungary, who were able to bring here the bodies of their kings and their treasure and keep alive their culture,' when Gerda crossly interrupted him. 'But why were the Serbs allowed to stay here?' 'It is not a question of being allowed to stay here,' said Constantine, 'they were invited here by the Austrian Empire.' 'Nonsense,' said Gerda; 'one does not invite people to come and live in one's country.' 'But sometimes one does,' said Constantine; 'the Austrian Emperor wanted the Serb soldiers to protect his lands against the Turks, so in exchange he promised them homes.' 'But if the Austrians gave the Serbs homes then it was most ungrateful for the Yugoslavs to turn the Hungarians out of this part of the country,' said Gerda, 'it should still be a part of Hungary.' 'But we owe nothing to Hungary, for they broke all their promises to the Serbs,' said Constantine, 'and since the Austro-Hungarian Empire has ceased to exist and we reconstituted it according to the principle of self-determination and there were more Slavs here than any other people, this certainly had to become Yugoslavia.'

To change the subject Constantine went on, 'But there are Slavs everywhere, God help the world. You have the Wends in Germany, many of them, and some distinguished ones, for the great Lessing was a Wend. They are Slavs.' 'But surely none of them remember that,' said my husband. 'Indeed they do,' said Constantine; 'there was a Wendish separatist movement before the war and for some time after the war, with its headquarters in Saxony. I know that well, for in 1913 I went with a friend to stay in Dresden, and when we described ourselves as Serbs the hotel porter would not have it at all. He said, "I know what you mean, and I have sympathy with all who stand with their race, but you will get me into trouble with the police if you say you are Serbs," and he would hardly believe it when he looked at our passports and saw that there was a country called Serbia.' 'But if all the Wends are Slavs,' said Gerda, 'why do we not send them out of Germany into the Slav countries, and give the land that they are taking up to true Germans?' 'Then the Slavs,' I said, 'might begin to think about sending back into Germany all the German colonists that live in places like Franzstal.' 'Why, so they might,' said Gerda, looking miserable, since an obstacle had arisen in the way of her ideal programme for making Europe clean and pure and Germanic by coercion and expulsion. She said in Serbian to her husband, 'How this woman lacks tact.' 'I know, my dear,' he answered gently, 'but do not mind it, enjoy the scenery.'

She could not. Her eyes filled with angry tears, the lower part of her face became podgy with sullenness. We none of us knew what to say or do, but just at that moment someone turned on the radio and the restaurant was flooded with a symphony by Mozart, and we all forgot Gerda. Constantine began to hum the theme, and his plump little hands followed the flight of Mozart's spirit as at Yaitse they had followed the motion of the bird at the waterfall. We all drew on the comfort which is given out by the major works of Mozart, which is as real and material as the warmth given by a glass of brandy, and I wondered, seeing its efficacy, what its nature might be. It is in part, no doubt, the work of the technical trick by which Mozart eliminates the idea of haste from life. His airs could not lag as they make their journey through the listener's attention; they are not the right shape for loitering. But it is as true that they

never rush, they are never headlong or helterskelter, they splash
no mud, they raise no dust. It is, indeed, inadequate to call the
means of creating such an effect a mere technical device. For it
changes the content of the work in which it is used, it presents
a vision of a world where man is no longer the harassed victim
of time but accepts its discipline and establishes a harmony with
it. This is not a little thing, for our struggle with time is one
of the most distressing of our fundamental conflicts; it holds us
back from the achievement and comprehension that should be
the justification of our life. How heavily this struggle weighs
on us may be judged from certain of our preferences. Whatever
our belief in the supernatural may be, we all feel that Christ was
something that St Paul was not; and it is impossible to imagine
Christ hurrying, while it is impossible to imagine St Paul doing
anything else.

But that was not all there was in the music; it was not merely
the indication of a heavenly mode. The movement closed. It was
manifest that an argument too subtle and profound to be put into
words—for music can deal with more than literature—had been
stated and had been resolved in some true conclusion. If those
of us who listened should encounter the circumstances which
provoke this argument we would know the answer, we would not
have to agonize to find it for ourselves if we had been sensitive
enough to recognize it. But as the eardrums were taken over
by the ordinary sounds of a restaurant, by chatter and clatter,
it became apparent how little as well as how much the music had
done for us. A particular problem had been solved for us, but in
a way that made it completely unserviceable to those millions of
people who do not like music, and that indeed was not as clear
to all of us as it should have been if we were to get on with the
business of living. To comprehend this solution we had all had to
learn to listen to music for years, and when we wanted to recall
it in time of need we had to exercise both our memories and our
powers of interpretation. A tool should not make such demands
on those that handle it. And of such solutions Mozart had found
only a number, which was large when one considered how great
the genius required for their finding, but small compared to the
number of problems that vex mankind; and he was unique in his
powers, none has excelled him. Art covers not even a corner of
life, only a knot or two here and there, far apart and without
relation to the pattern. How could we hope that it would ever
bring order and beauty to the whole of that vast and intractable
fabric, that sail flapping in the contrary winds of the universe? Yet

the music had promised us, as it welled forth from the magic box in the wall over our heads, that all should yet be well with us, that sometime our life should be as lovely as itself. But perhaps no such promise had been given; perhaps it was only true that had a human voice spoken in such tones it would have been to express tender and protective love. If the musician used them in the course of his composition it might be only because he found they fitted in some entertaining arrangement of the scale.

At a point on the plains there was now heaped up a drift of dark cloud; and through this there ran a shaft of lightning. A storm was on us, and it was in alternate blackness and greenish crystal light that we began our journey to four of the monasteries of the Frushka Gora, a journey which was astonishing in the directness of its contact with the past. It was as if one should drive along the South Downs, turning off the main road and following by-roads in to the downlands at Sullington and Washington and Steyning, and should find buildings where persons involved in the tragedy of Richard II had but newly cast aside their garments in mourning, where the sound of their weeping was hardly stilled. It made for a strangeness which immediately caught the eye that all these monasteries, so far from Byzantium, are built in the Byzantine fashion, with the quarters for the monks or nuns and pilgrims built in a square round and open space with the church in the middle. Though some have been burned down and rebuilt in the style of the Austrian baroque, they keep to the original ground plan, and cannot be confused with anything of recent or Western inspiration.

The first monastery we visited had been rebuilt in Austrian fashion. It raised above its quadrangle roofs a cupola as ornate as a piece of white coral, dazzling now in the strange stormlight against an inky sky; and it lay among orchards, their tree-trunks ghostly with spray. It might have been in the Helenenthal, an hour from Vienna. But within we found that the Eastern idea was still in government, that a wall had been built before the altar to damn the flow of light, to store up a reservoir of darkness where mystery could engender its sacred power. It possessed some relics of a saint, a Herzegovinian soldier who had wandered hither and thither fighting against the Turk, first under a Serbian despot and then under a Hungarian king. The legend ran that the Turks took the town where he was buried and were terrified because rays of light proceeded from his grave, and went to their emir, who was overcome at finding who the dead man had been and gave his body to the monks of this monastery. For this emir was a renegade who

had been taken prisoner by the Turks and had bought his life by
renouncing his faith; and he was not only a Herzegovinian, he
was actually kin to the dead man. The news of this wonder came
to the Saint's widow, who was a refugee in Germany, and she
sought out this monastery, in defiance of the Turks, and became
a hermit near by, till she died and was buried here, near to her
husband.

This might have happened yesterday, indeed it might have
happened today, for the monastery is in the care of White
Russian nuns, wearing a melancholy head-dress of a close black
cap fitting over a black veil that falls about the shoulders, and
still preoccupied by the distress of their exile. It was hard to
keep their misfortunes distinct in our minds from those of the
founders of the monastery, and indeed others had failed to do
so. Constantine halted by a grave in the quadrangle to tell me
that it housed an abbess who had been stricken down during the
seventeenth-century migration; and two young novices who were
standing by, girls who had been born after their parents' flight
from their fatherland and had been drawn here by an inborn
Tsarist nostalgia, exclaimed in surprise. They had thought her
one of their own community who had died on her way from
Russia.

The black sky was pressing lower, the cloisters gleamed at us
through an untimely dusk. Constantine thought that if we were to
be storm-bound it had better be in a monastery where there was
more to see, and we hurried back to the car under the first heavy
pennies of rain. Thunder and lightning broke on us as we ran into
Krushedol, another monastery which has been burned and given
an Austrian exterior while keeping its ancient core. But this was
older than the others. When the leader of the Slav forces at the
battle of Kossovo, the Tsar Lazar, was killed on the field, the rags
of his power were inherited by his kin, and there was one unhappy
heir, named Stephen, whose fate was lamentable even for that age.
His father, forced to seal a treaty by giving the Sultan Murad his
daughter as a bride, sent his son to bear her company; but in
time the Sultan fell into war with his wife's father and put out the
young man's eyes lest he should take up arms in the fight. In his
private darkness he reeled across the Balkan Peninsula, sometimes
a captive dragged from prison to prison, then, released, back to
his father's camp on the Danube, then away with his father again
to wander in exile. His father died; his two brothers, one blinded
like himself by the Sultan, engaged in fratricidal war; his mother
also died, it is thought of poison; his blind brother fled and

became a monk on Mount Athos; his victorious brother died. Though this dead usurper had named an heir, a party of the nobles took Stephen, and, spinning him round as in the game of blind-man's-buff, made him declare himself Despot of Serbia. The Serbians, seeing themselves threatened with civil war in the face of their Hungarian and Turkish enemies, rushed on him and sent him out of their land, bound and under guard. Again he stumbled about the Balkan Peninsula, sometimes pushed back into Serbia by his heartless supporters and beaten out again by his reluctant subjects, always preserving his gentle, patient fortitude. At one time he seemed to find a lasting refuge in Albania, where the great hero Skanderbeg took a great liking to him and gave him his own daughter, the Duchess Angelina, for wife. But the Turks came to Albania also, and the blind man was homeless again, and was in Italy when death took him. Then his widow and his two sons, now penniless, started to wander afresh, and Hungarian charity maintained them here. One of the sons became a priest, and he founded this monastery, and in time all three of them were laid in the same tomb before the altar. In the dark church, that blazed with light because of the profligate but mellow gilding on the iconostasis, we were shown the Duchess Angelina's narrow and elegant hand, black and mummified, loaded with the inalienable rings of her rank.

But there was other royalty here. Under a round red stone on the floor was buried King Milan Obrenovitch, the king who was so little of a success that he was forced to abdicate in 1889. Who wandered almost as much as Stephen, but on more comfortable routes, from Belgrade to Vienna and Paris, harried not by the Turks without but by the Turk within. Nor was his grave all we saw of him at Krushedol. There is a memorial to him in the church wall, erected by the Emperor Franz Josef. 'Why not?' said Constantine. 'Milan was all for Austria, he governed our country as an Austrian dependency.' Later, in the treasury, which was not in the church but in the monastery, a flash of lightning dispersed the unnatural dusk and showed us the contorted trees of the wind-flogged woods outside, and inside a medley of Byzantine church vestments, medieval chalices and crosses, ancient manuscripts, and the cups and saucers, prettily painted with pale flowers in the Slav fashion, the silver teapots and coffee-pots, the wine-glasses and decanters, of King Milan's last establishment. These had been sent here by the Emperor Franz Josef, to whom, by an act of testamentary whimsy, King Milan had left the entire contents of his home.

'It would be, quite simply, that he would hardly notice to whom he left them, so long as it was not to his wife, Natalia,' said Constantine. 'Is she buried here?' I asked. 'No, not at all,' said Constantine. The negative he used sounded delightful in this connexion. 'She is not dead, she is living in Paris, very poor.[1] Only the other day the Government was obliged to prevent a German company from making a film about the Obrenovitches and she wrote a letter about it.' 'And she will never be buried here,' said the Abbot, a grave person who had been a priest and had become a monk ten years ago, after the death of his beloved wife. 'That is, unless she is granted the light before she dies, for she was converted to Roman Catholicism about thirty years ago. It was a strange thing to do, for our people had been kind to her, and had taken her part when her husband dealt wickedly with her.'

In another room there was arranged all the furniture from King Milan's drawing-room; a salon of the eighties sat there in its stuffy and shiny richness, and from its walls there stared the portraits of the doomed family—King Milan, with the wide cat-grin of a tormented buffoon, the excessively, grossly beautiful Queen Natalia, their fat son Alexander, who was like his father in resembling a cat, though this time the cat had been doctored, and Queen Draga, who was so prosaic that even now, when we can recognize her expression as fear and know what she feared, her face remains completely uninteresting. 'Our Mrs Simpson,' said Constantine, pointing to her picture. 'Yes! yes! Our Mrs Simpson,' cried the Abbot, going into fits of laughter. There was also King Milan's bedroom, furnished in rosewood, and more portraits of these unhappy people, preserved in tragedy like flies in amber.

Before we went away I went into the treasury again to take a last look at the embroideries and caught sight of two photographs which showed Serb peasants and soldiers and priests walking through the snow, with expressions of extreme anguish, bringing the body of King Milan to his grave. 'But how could they feel so passionately about Milan Obrenovitch?' I asked Constantine. 'He had done ill by his country and ill in his personal life. I noticed that even the Abbot spoke of him as behaving wickedly.' 'It does not matter what Milan Obrenovitch was in himself,' said Constantine. 'He was our first-crowned king after the Turkish conquest. When we were free our power flamed like a torch in the hands of our Emperor Stephen Dushan, but afterwards it grew dim, and in the poor wretch who was the husband of the Duchess

---

[1] Queen Natalia died in a convent in Paris in May 1941.

Angelina it guttered and went out. The dead torch was lit again by Karageorge, and it grew bright in the hand of his successor, Prince Michael Obrenovitch, and when Milan made himself King its light grew steady, though his was not the hand that was to bear it, and it was the same torch that our ancient dynasty of the Nemanyas had carried. So why should we care what else he had done? It was not Milan but their king whom these Serbs were following through the snow, it was the incarnation of Serbian power.'

When the storm had lifted we drove out again on the plains, now lying under a purged and crystal air, in which all things were more than visible, in which each blade piercing the rich spring earth could be seen for miles in its green sharpness, in which the pools outside the villages carried not reflections but solid paintings of the blue sky and silver clouds. Then we turned back to the range of downs and entered it by a little valley, which presently ran into a cache of apple orchards, a lovely coomb as sweet as anything Devonshire or Normandy can show. Behind a white wall shielded by fruit trees and Judas trees we found a monastery enclosing an astonishing church, that had been built after the emigration had done its work on the migrated craftsmen's imagination; it was a fusion, lovely but miscegenic, of the Byzantine and the baroque styles, of fourteenth-century Eastern and seventeenth-century Western styles. While we gaped there came up to us a Russian monk, a young man who, like the nuns we had seen at the first monastery, must have been born after his parents had left Russia. He was beautiful, with the eyes seen only in Russians so far as I know, which look dangerous as naked lights carried on the stage, by reason of their extraordinary lambency. He told us with smiling remoteness that the Abbot was away; and we were disappointed, for the Abbot is a Pribitchevitch, one of a family that has been dominant in this Serb colony ever since the migration, and is the brother of a famous democratic politician who died in exile during the dictatorship of King Alexander. 'That is a pity,' said Constantine; 'however, we can still show these English people what is interesting here.' 'But there is nothing interesting here,' said the Russian monk, 'we have only the body of a Serbian emperor.' He spoke without insolence, his remark proceeded from a complete failure to form any sort of relationship with his surroundings, however hospitable they might have been, which is characteristic of a certain kind of White Russian *émigré*.

We said that we found that interesting enough; and he went with us into the exquisite mongrel church, and we found it glowing and beautiful within. There were two handsome girls on step-ladders cleaning the windows, and they clattered down and followed us, smiling in welcome and at the same time murmuring in piety, as we went towards the sarcophagus of the Emperor. The Russian monk lifted its lid and showed us the body under a square of tarnished cloth of silver, but would not uncover it for us. He shrugged his shoulders and said that it was only done on the Emperor's day; he would have seemed on a par with a girl in a milliner's shop refusing to take a hat out of the window had it not been quite plain that, while he was flagrantly frivolous, religious ecstasy was not only within the range of his experience, it was never very far from him. But the two girls behind us sighed deeply in their disappointment.

'This is Urosh, the son of Stephen Dushan,' said Constantine; 'he was a poor weakling, and lost all his father's empire in a few years.' 'Yet he is venerated,' I said. 'But certainly,' said Constantine. 'But do the people who venerate him know what he did?' I asked. 'Do these girls, for instance, know that he destroyed the Serbian Empire and paved the way to Kossovo?' 'Well, I would not say they could pass an examination in the facts,' said Constantine, 'but certainly they know that he was weak and he failed. That, however, is not of the smallest importance. He was of our ancient dynasty, he was a Nemanya, and the Nemanyas were sacred. Not only were they the instruments of our national power, they have a religious significance to us. Some of them are described on their graves as "*saintement né*," born in sanctity; and this Urosh, though he was quite simply killed by a usurper of his secular power, is called by our Church the martyr. This is not mere nationalist piety. It is due to the historical fact that the Nemanyas simultaneously enforced on us Serbs Christianity and unity. We were Christians before, of course, but we had not a living church of our own. Then this extraordinary family of little, little princelings from an obscure village below Montenegro on the Adriatic came and did in a few years as much as Rome has done for any state in centuries. The first Nemanya to rule Serbia, Stephen Nemanya, became a monk, when he abdicated in favour of his son Stephen, and is known as St Simeon, and he is a true saint: the oil from his grave at Studenitsa does many miracles; and one of his sons became our St Sava, and was a monk on Mount Athos, and left his monastery when his brother's throne seemed insecure and organized Serbia into such a close-knit fabric of church and state that, though the heirs of the throne were incompetent for sixty years afterwards, nothing could unravel it. But as well as a statesman Sava was a saint, and was a pilgrim and visited the monks of Thebaid. And his brother, too, King Stephen II, he also was a saint. When he lay dying he sent for St Sava to make him a monk, but St Sava came too late; but God vouchsafed that he should be raised from the dead to take his vows as a monk and so his corpse stood up and was consecrated. I tell you no people could be expected to forget the identification between saint and king, between religion and nationalism, which was made by our early history.'

'Good-bye,' said the Russian monk at the gateway, 'the Abbot will be sorry not to have seen you, particularly as you are English. He has gone to the post-office now to complain because some English books have not arrived; I think they were sent to him by something called the Left Book Club.' We left the hills and went back into the plains, which were again threatened by storm, and then returned to the hills by another valley, which was astounding in its likeness to a corner in the Wiltshire downs. Twisted thorn trees guard austere channels of turf; but the hillside that closed our road was broken by the fine-drawn iron-mongery of a pithead, and we came into a mining village, as monotonous as such are in every country and continent, but here radiant with whitewash. Among its right angles we got lost, and stopped to ask our way to the Vrdnik monastery from a group of boys. One of them got on the footboards to guide us, and brought us down to a morass in the middle of the village, which we had to skirt carefully, for it was involved with a railway line. 'Look up, look up,' said the boy, pointing up to the hillside before us, 'there stands Vrdnik, see how great its walls are, see how rich it is, with all its vineyards and orchards.' As we walked up a gold-green avenue of poplars to the gateway he told us that he was going to be a monk, and so were all the boys with whom he had been walking when we found him. 'Why is that?' asked Constantine. 'Did your mothers promise you to God when you were born?' 'No, no,' he said. 'It is our own idea. We love this monastery, we come to it whenever we can and we are always happy here, and we want to serve it all our lives.'

Vrdnik is larger than the other monasteries, which is natural, since its unique possessions attract many pilgrims; and because of the wealth drawn from these pilgrimages the large two-storied quadrangle is in good repair, handsomely whitewashed, and laid out like a garden with plum trees and Japanese quinces. The church is also different from the others. It seems to reject the Byzantine prescription that magic must be made in darkness.

Direct light shines on the gilded iconostasis and on the multicoloured thrones, and shines back amber from the polished marble pavement. It can be so, for there is no need to manufacture magic here. That already exists in the coffin lying before the iconostasis, which contains the body of the Tsar Lazar who fell at Kossovo.

He lies in a robe of faded red and gold brocade. A dark cloth hides his head and the gap between it and his shoulders. His mummified brown hands, nearly black, are crossed above his loins, still wearing the bright rings of his rank. His dwindled feet have been thrust into modern stockings, and over them have been pulled soft medieval boots of blue silk interwoven with a gold thread. He is shrunken beyond belief; his hip-bones and his shoulders raise the brocade in sharp points. He is piteous as a knot of men standing at a street-corner in Jarrow or a Welsh mining town. Like them he means failure, the disappointment of hopes, the waste of powers. He means death also, but that is not so important. Who would resent death if it came when all hopes had been realized and all powers turned to use? There is an ideal point at which the fulfilment of life must pass into the acceptance of death. But defeat is defeat, and bitter; not only for the sake of pride, but because it blunts the sword of the will, which is the sole instrument man has been given to protect himself from the hostile universe and to impose on it his vision of redemption. When this man met defeat it was not only he whose will was frustrated, it was a whole people, a whole faith, a wide movement of the human spirit. This is told by the splendid rings on the Tsar Lazar's black and leathery hands; and the refinement of the pomp which presents him in his death, the beauty and gravity of the enfolding ritual, show the worth of what was destroyed with him. I put out a finger and stroked those hard dry hands, that had been nerveless for five hundred years. It is written here that the lot of man is pitiful, since the odds are against him, and he can command the success he deserves only if an infinite number of circumstances work in his favour; and existence shows no trace of such a bias.

In a dark and cramped treasury are some untidy ancient manuscripts, on which a Tauchnitz edition of *The Hound of the Baskervilles* has curiously intruded, and certain possessions of the Tsar Lazar: the icon on which he swore his nobles to loyalty before the battle, the beaker from which he drank, the model of one of his cities. There is no reason to doubt that any of these are genuine. The Turks let Lazar's widow take his corpse and all his private treasures, and in the course of time she placed them in the monastery of Ravanitsa, which he himself had founded, in Serbia, far south of Belgrade on the way to Nish. It was often attacked and damaged by the Turks, and the migrants of 1683 took away its relics and built this new monastery, which for this reason is often also called Ravanitsa, to house them. I went down on my knees to peer at the precious objects through the glass case of the cupboard. The icon was damaged but enormously beautiful: in the background was a soaring close-pressed assembly of saints, conceived by an imagination disciplined and formalized by experience of ceremonial. There was also a panel of velvet, once crimson, now maroon, which was embroidered in silver-gilt thread with words, many words, a prayer, a poem.

It was sewn by the Princess Euphemia, the widow of a Serbian prince killed by the Turks, who had found refuge at the court of the Tsar Lazar. After Lazar had fallen at Kossovo she went with his widow Militza to the monastery of Lyubostinya, where they both became nuns. She was an embroideress of great genius. Two of the most famous pieces of early embroidery in Europe are her work: the curtain for the sanctuary doors in the church of Hilandar, the Serbian monastery on Mount Athos, and a cloth for laying on the altar during Lent, now in the monastery of Putna in Roumania. In the silence of the monastery she worked a pall to cover the severed head of the Tsar Lazar, and on it she wrote him a letter with her needle.

'You were brought up among all the good things of this earth, O Prince Lazar, O new-made martyr,' she begins. 'The power of the Lord made you strong and famous among all the kings of the world. You ruled over the land of your fathers and in all right ways did you give happiness to the Christian folk who were laid in your hands. In courage and piety did you go out to do battle against the snake Murad, the enemy of God's church, because your heart could not bear to see the hosts of Ismail ruling in Christian lands. You were determined that if you failed you would quit this crumbling fortress of earthly power and, red in your own blood, be one with the hosts of the Heavenly King.

'You had both your desires fulfilled. You slew the snake and you won from God the martyr's crown. So do not now forget your beloved children, who are left desolate by your death, while you are enjoying the everlasting delights of Heaven. Many troubles and sufferings have fallen on your beloved children, and their lives are passed in sorrow, for the sons of Ismail rule over them, and we sorely need your help. Therefore we beg you to pray the Ruler of Mankind for your beloved children and all who serve them in love and faith. For your children are girt about with many ills, and have forgotten, O martyr, your goodness to them. But though you have quitted this life, you know the troubles and sufferings of your children, and since you are a martyr, you can take certain freedoms with the Lord.

'So bow your knee before the Heavenly King who bestowed on you the martyr's crown; beg Him that your beloved children may live long and be happy and do His will; beg Him that the Orthodox Church may stand firm in the land of our fathers; beg Him, who is the Conqueror of All, that He give your beloved sons, Prince Stephen and Prince Vuk, the victory over all their enemies, seen and unseen. If the Lord gives us His help, we shall give you praise and thanks for it. Gather together the company of your fellows, the Holy Martyrs, and with them pray to the God that glorified you. Call St George, rouse St Demetrius, persuade the saintly Theodores, take with you St Mercurius and St Procopius; forget not the forty martyrs of Sebaste, in which town your beloved sons, Prince Stephen and Prince Vuk, are now vassals in the army of the Sultan. Pray that they may be given help from God, come, you, too, to our aid, wherever you may be.

'Look on my humble offerings and magnify them with your regard, for the praise I offer is not worthy of you, but is only the little that I can do. But as you, my dear Ruler and Holy Martyr, were ever generous of temporal and passing things, how much more freely so will you give us of those great and everlasting things which you have received from God. You abundantly gave me what my body needed when I came to you as a stranger in exile, and now I pray you both that you will save me and that you will calm the wild storm in my soul and in my body. Euphemia offers this from her heart, O blessed saint!'

Belgrade III

What has made modern Belgrade, though no one could guess it by looking at the town, is a conscious attempt to restore the glories of the medieval Serbian Empire. The nostalgic frescoes of Oplenats truly reveal the dominating fantasy not only of the Karageorgevitches but of the Serbian people. The memory of the Nemanyas and their wealth and culture was kept alive among the peasants, partly by the Orthodox Church, which very properly never ceased to remind them that they had once formed a free and Christian state, and also by the national ballads. These poems are not quite so artless as they seem. They were composed by the Serbs, more or less collectively, quite a century after the battle of Kossovo, on the model of the *chansons de geste*, which reached the Balkan Peninsula through Dalmatia at a very early date. Thereafter the full force of the artistic genius of the nation, denied all other outlet, poured into this medium; and the late eighteenth century, which marked the decline of folk-song in the West, here brought it new strength, for the nationalist and liberal ideas popularized by the French Revolution found their perfect expression ready-made in the laments of this enslaved people. The Serbs who took part in the first rising against the Turks in 1804 were, therefore, nothing like primitives who were simply revolting against an immediate injustice. That revolt they were making; but also they were the heirs of a highly developed civilization, which they intended from the first to create anew.

It is possible that the monasteries of the Frushka Gora, the blackened body of the Tsar Lazar, exerted a direct influence on this rising. Karageorge, after the flight from Serbia during which he killed his stepfather, joined the Austrian Army; and though he deserted for a time and became a Haiduk in the mountains, because he believed that he was unfairly neglected in a distribution of medals, he ultimately rejoined his regiment and was accepted by his colonel, who was greatly impressed by his personality, and got him employment after the end of the Turco-Austrian War as a forest ranger in the Frushka Gora. He was there for some years before the mildness of the new Pasha of Belgrade, Hadji Mustapha, 'the Mother of Serbia,' tempted him to return to Serbia. He had therefore an ideological experience which is not conveyed in the usual description of him as a swine-herd;

and indeed even his material circumstances are not what the term
suggests. He was a dealer in swine on such a large scale that his
income was probably equivalent to about a thousand pounds a
year at the time when he was chosen as the Commandant of
Serbia. Though the common lot of the Christian inhabitants of
the Ottoman provinces was poverty-stricken, a certain number
of exceptions enjoyed quite a handsome degree of prosperity;
and according to the usual paradox of revolutions it was these
exceptions and not the oppressed multitude who revolted.

It is not clear why the Serbs chose Karageorge for this office.
He was over forty. Though he had served in the Austrian Army
he does not seem to have won any particular distinction. He was
of definitely unstable temperament: he was subject to fits of
abstraction that lasted for days, and to gusts of violence caused
by flimsy suspicion. But he had a superb physique. He was tall
even for a race of tall men, with burning eyes, wild coal-black
hair, a face that was still handsome though deeply scared, and a
strange vibrant voice. He was a born warrior, and war was the
breath of life in his nostrils. More than all else he liked to take
part in a cavalry charge, spring from his horse at the climactic
moment, and use his rifle in close combat; he shot with his left
hand because his right had been smashed to pieces in one of his
early campaigns. He had the prestige of high courage, and also
that other strange, almost mystical prestige which is accorded to
a wealthy man who renounces the more obvious enjoyments that
his money might buy. It was the habit of these prosperous Serb
rebels to practise a certain imitation of the Turkish pashas, to dress
in silks and use gold harness and chased arms, and keep a certain
degree of state in their homes. Karageorge dressed and lived and
worked with his hand like a peasant.

These were intimations of a certain distinction, but not of
the degree or kind which Karageorge afterwards manifested. He
showed himself for nine years as one of the most remarkable men
in European history. He was brilliant not only as a fighting soldier
but as a strategist; his use of his forces to harass an enemy that
outnumbered them sometimes by three to one is among the most
amazing triumphs of military genius, and it is the more amazing
since he had seen the inside of no staff college. He was also a
skilful diplomatist, both in dealing with his own people, whom
he had to educate in the primal idea of unity, and in playing off
Austria and Russia against Turkey without compromising Serbian
independence. In the task of setting up some sort of governmental
system to oust Turkish maladministration he acted like a farseeing

statesman. There, indeed, he showed the first and most unexpected qualities of his genius.

It was evident that the strong individualities of the rebels threatened the country with another form of the anarchy they were seeking to correct. There was every possibility that it might be split up under regional military chiefs, who would wrangle among themselves and reduce the Balkan Christians to the same state of disunity that had left them helpless before the Turks four hundred years before. To control this situation Karageorge founded a Skupshtina or Parliament, of Chiefs, which met each New Year to settle all military matters, tactical, strategic, political, financial, and disciplinary. But this was obviously not a complete government, and shortly after a visit of certain Serbian chiefs to the Tsar led to the formation of another body. In the course of their journey they went to Kharkov, in Poland, and there they met a lawyer named Filipovitch, who was a native of Novi Sad, a descendant of the seventeenth-century Serb migrants. He suggested that he should accompany them home and found a legislative and judicial system in Serbia. They agreed, and took him back with them to Karageorge, who, loyal to the influences of the Frushka Gora, made him welcome and told him to get on with the job.

Filipovitch then sat down and drafted a constitution for the Serbian state. He invented a Soviet, or Council, of twelve persons elected and paid by different districts to manage the general affairs of the country. He inaugurated it, and became its Secretary. There is extant the correspondence in which he made financial provision for the Army by selling the houses and land owned by Turks in Serbian territory, fixed the taxes, organized a system of magistrates, and instructed the Soviet delegates in the exact nature of their rights while warning them against corruption. He also promulgated a legal code based on the Code Napoléon. It is difficult to think of any man in all history who undertook a more comprehensive labour single-handed; and it is interesting to find that Filipovitch was never a vociferous patriot. He appears to have accepted the post largely to escape the climate of Kharkov, which he found extremely disagreeable. But he had a truly legalist mind, in the highest sense, and he delighted in the task of imposing order on a disorderly society for order's sake; and it is quite apparent that that delight found a response in Karageorge's very different nature.

He supported Filipovitch enthusiastically in his educational schemes, which were ambitious. Till that time the only schools in Serbia were held in the monasteries, and attendance at them involved great inconvenience, for the monks could not afford to house pupils who did not help in the cultivation of their lands, and a scanty education took several years. The Soviet was instructed by Filipovitch to found an elementary school in every big town, and a secondary school of ambitious curriculum in Belgrade. This greatly pleased Karageorge, for though he himself could not read or write he was a great believer in education, and he was always impressing on his followers, who were for the most part as illiterate as himself, the advantages of having all business recorded in writing.

Even after Filipovitch's premature death Karageorge continued to work on his high plans. It became obvious as time went on that the Senate did not counterbalance the Skupshtina as had been hoped. The power of the rebel chiefs was, in fact, the only real power in the land, and soon it controlled the Soviet indirectly just as it directly controlled the Skupshtina. They seemed likely not only to split up the country so that it would be helpless before external aggression, but also to become greedy and oppressive despots not to be distinguished from the Turkish pashas. Karageorge met this threat by deposing two of the most powerful chiefs, and by using his prestige as national Commandant to dominate the Soviet and force on it regard for the interests of the whole people. He took this attitude partly, no doubt, because the democratic tradition of the Slavs was working in him, but chiefly because he knew as a soldier the importance of national unity to a country perpetually threatened by foreign dominance.

Karageorge kept at his task with unremitting grimness; and indeed he must have seemed a grim figure, for the essence of his struggle was austerity. He was fighting against the Turks, the practitioners of pagan luxury; and in the first part of his struggle he engaged those among the Turks who were the most skilful in that practice, the rebellious Janizaries who had given Sarajevo its intoxicating air of pleasure, and were rebelling against the reformist Sultan Selim because he was endeavouring to brace them to a new and Spartan dispensation. One of his followers has left us an account of a night the Serbian Army spent during the campaign of 1805 on the heights above the town of Parachin, which was occupied by the Turks. When the trenches had been dug and Karageorge had inspected them and seen that all was prepared for the morrow's battle, he sat down on a cannon and asked his officers if there was any plum brandy about. They fetched him a flask of plum brandy and some corn-pone, and he drank and passed the flask to them, and shared the corn-pone out. They looked down on Parachin, which was blazing with light in the darkness below. It seemed almost to be in flames, such was the brightness. Light was streaming out from the Pasha's palace, and they could hear the sound of pipes and flutes and drums. One of Karageorge's suite, a man who was called Stephen the Scribe and was kept simply as a secretary, being notoriously no good as a soldier, looked down on the town and said, 'Do let me fire off this gun at the Turks!' Karageorge laughed at him, but he went on begging. 'Do let me take one shot—just one—at the palace!' Karageorge jeered, 'But you might kill the Pasha!' 'Well, why not?' asked Stephen the Scribe. 'Well,' said Karageorge, 'you mustn't do that. You might make his children orphans, and they'd have nobody to buy them shoes, and then they might catch cold running round barefoot and die of fever.' But Stephen the Scribe teased him till he got his way, and very unskilfully pointed the gun and fired it. The ball cut through the air like lightning, and went straight for the Pasha's palace. In one instant the flutes and pipes and drums came to a stop, the lights went out, and there was darkness and silence. Very often Karageorge's rebellion must have seemed just such a murderous cannon-ball, that put an end to brightness and music, and established the night.

His end was not to be deduced from his beginning. After a time the war he had to conduct changed its form. The Serbs had begun their insurrection to rid themselves of the Dahis, the rebel Janizaries who had set themselves up as independent despots in defiance of the Sultan; but when they had beheaded the four chiefs they began to dream of freeing themselves from Turkey. Indeed, the treachery with which the Sultans treated them in spite of their services made them realize this as a necessity. This raised a problem which differed from year to year according to the situation of Europe. When Napoleon defeated Austria and the Turks were harried by Britain and Russia, then Serbia had reason for hope. But Napoleon's star waned, Russia was a preoccupied and often disloyal ally, and Turkey was reorganized by the great Sultan Mohammed II. Finally in 1813 a Serbian army of fifty thousand faced an army of treble that number. Defeat was certain, but the Serbians knew what it was to be outnumbered and could quite well have put up enough resistance to gain them a negotiated peace, had not Karageorge, quite simply and shamefully, run away. He fell back, when he should have been bringing up reinforcements to support a harassed body of troops who were making a magnificent stand before the main Turkish army. His officers suddenly found he had deserted them without a word of explanation. For a time he wandered about the country, and then fled over the Danube back to Novi Sad and the Frushka Gora.

Nobody knows the reason for Karageorge's conduct. He never published any justification of it. Till then his worst enemies had never charged him with cowardice or lack of care for his country. It is possible that fatigue had released that unstable element which had caused his early fits of melancholy and abstraction. His family life had been tragic. The murder of his stepfather had not been the only act of violence which he had been obliged to commit against his family. He had a ne'er-do-well brother who had crowned his career by committing rape. This was an offence which was regarded as being at least as serious as murder; it was so often committed by Moslems on Christians that for a Christian to rape a Christian was not only a sexual crime, it had a renegade flavour. So Karageorge ordered his brother to be hanged at the door of his house, and forbade his mother to mourn her son. This was the appointed procedure, and there was nothing remarkable about it, but the relationship of brother and brother among Slavs is peculiarly close, and even if his individual sensibility was calloused his racial self must have been appalled.

He had also led as extravagantly busy a life as, say, Napoleon, if one takes his illiteracy into account and considers what it would mean to be Commander-in-chief and Prime Minister under that handicap; and he was now fifty-one. He had added to his routine considerable demands on his detective capacities and a perpetual burden of apprehension. He had all the time to scan the rebel chiefs who were the medium through which he had to work, and judge whether they were loyal or disloyal, and if the latter, decide when he had best strike against them. Again and again he had to smother conspiracies, not only to save himself, but to protect the state. It would be no wonder if after nine years of this hagridden life he should forget his nature and sink into apathy. But it is perhaps also relevant that the dominant figure of the Kossovo legend which shaped him as all other Serbians was the Tsar Lazar, who was not victorious, who did not preserve his people, who lay a blackened and much-travelled mummy in the exile of the Frushka Gora. That dominance perhaps explains why the Serbs always respect Karageorge as the founder of their liberty, withdrawing no part of their homage because of his failure.

There is a yet a pendant to this mysterious eclipse of a great man. Four years later Karageorge returned to Serbia. Since the country was then ruled by Milosh Obrenovitch, his deadly enemy, who hated him because he suspected him of the murder of his half-brother, he cannot but have anticipated that he would meet his death. And the trip proves to be even more suicidal than it appears at first sight if his ostensible reason for returning is examined. Though the Greeks were, like the Serbs, in revolt against the Turks, the Serbs had never trusted them. Since the Turks had abolished the Serbian Patriarchate and put the Serbs under Greek priests there were too many old scores about to make for a successful alliance. Karageorge knew this and during his domination of Serbia he had for this reason held his country free of all entanglements with the Greek rebels. But in 1817, at a time when Milosh Obrenovitch was engaged in the most delicate negotiations with the Sultan, Karageorge came back to Serbia as an agent of the Greek revolutionary society, the Ethniké Hetairia, to induce the Serbians to stage a rising at the same time as a Greek revolt. He must have known that Milosh Obrenovitch would have to silence him, not for his own interest but for the sake of the country. He must have known how Milosh Obrenovitch was likely to silence him. He was killed by an unknown assassin while he lay asleep in a cave.

But that suicidal streak was not peculiar to him. It showed, against all expectation, in Milosh Obrenovitch also, though the two men were utterly different in character. His palace still stands in Belgrade; it is a Turkish house, with a projecting upper story, full of air and light with many water conduits. In Belgrade there may be seen, on the first floor of the Museum of Prince Paul, the robes worn by him and his wife. Richer far than the gear of the Karageorges, which is shown alongside, they might have been worn by a Turkish pasha and the flower of his harem. And indeed he gave his audiences like a pasha, seated crosslegged on silk cushions, wearing the turban. Milosh had his eye set on the quality that Karageorge had seemed likely to drive out of Serbia, the luxury and pleasure which had made Sarajevo, which had lit the lights at Parachin. He meant not to expel it but to transfer it from the possession of the Moslems to the Christians.

He was capable of arranging the transference. He had only to follow where Karageorge led, but he brought genius to his following. When Karageorge fled across the Danube in 1813, and most of the chiefs who had owned him as leader fled into exile like lost sheep, Milosh stood his ground and calmly awaited the horror which he knew would burst on the country once the Turks returned. There was a preliminary massacre, with impalements and mutilations and roastings on spits; then there was systematic banditry, the worst of it under a legalistic guise. All sorts of Turks appeared, passing themselves off as landowners and merchants driven out by the rebel Serbs, who claimed land and wealth which had certainly never been theirs; and all those claims were allowed. The Serb population was beggared.

Milosh waited by, smiling and bland. He ingratiated himself with Suleiman, the new Pasha of Belgrade, who had been wounded by him on the battlefield and therefore respected him, and who trusted him because of his known enmity to Karageorge. Suleiman made him Governor of three large districts, and he repaid this honour by apparent subjection of the most absolute kind. He constantly exhorted the Serbians to lay down their arms and think no more of resistance to the Turks. When some rebels collected in one of his own districts, he went at once and persuaded them to surrender on a promise from Suleiman that they should be pardoned. That promise was broken. One hundred and fifty of them were beheaded, and nearly forty impaled; and Milosh himself was sent to Belgrade and kept in captivity. He bribed his way out. The resources on which all these rebels could draw were far larger than the modern reader would imagine. He returned to his home and found the people frantic with rage and terror, persuaded that there was again about to be a general massacre. Then he judged it well to act, and he put himself at their head. In six months he had driven out the Turks.

It must be owned that Milosh never faced such huge odds as Karageorge, and that he gained one of his most inexplicable victories because the Turkish Commander made a sudden flight, just as inexplicable as Karageorge's great defection. But Milosh showed military genius of the same impressive order as his rival, and later he showed himself a far greater diplomat and, by one supremely important act, at least as great a statesman. After his victory he made a technical avowal of subjection to the Sultan and then sat down to negotiate the independence of his country, with infinite guile and patience. He knew just how to play on Turkey's fear of Russia; and he never let himself forget that, in actual fact, it would not be easy for the Russian Army to come to Serbia's aid. He threatened to adhere to one or other of the great powers when Turkey was at ease in her foreign relations, but when she was perturbed he proffered the most soothing assurances of neutrality. He had an infallible nose for the right moment to bribe a pasha or roll a threatening eye on a vizier. It took him eighteen years to wring Serbian independence from the Porte, when not a soul in Europe had thought the Porte would give way to him till the Turkish Empire had dissolved. True, it was not complete independence that he gained. Turkey insisted on her right to garrison certain towns, notably Belgrade, and refused to promise not to poke her nose into Serbian affairs. But it was practical independence. Turkish officials and regular and irregular troops no longer roamed at large in the land.

Milosh's supreme act of statesmanship followed that victory. The Treaty of Adrianople which gave Serbia its effective freedom, burdened only by a few irksome but not serious restrictions, also handed over to Milosh extensive crown lands. He might have distributed them as baksheesh to his followers and founded a large class of landowners on whose power he could have relied. Instead he gave the lands to the people as small-holdings, and guaranteed Serbia as a peasant state, thereby giving her her happiness and her distinctive genius. This great service, as the culmination of a career so full of military and diplomatic gifts to his country, might have made him the most beloved ruler in Europe, had he not seen to it that his fame was far otherwise. He had for years been practising a highly offensive and unnecessary despotism. He was certainly responsible for the death of two of his political opponents; and even if a light hand with murder was not to be harshly judged on territory demoralized by Turkish occupation, there was no excuse for seizing a fellow-Serb's house and fields without a shadow of justification, or forcing peasants to labour for him at his will, or enclosing common forestland as pasture for his own swine.

As he became more and more powerful, he behaved with more and more fantastic improbity. It might have sobered him that the Sultan had appointed him first Prince of Serbia; but it only seemed to intoxicate him. He made his subjects pay their Turkish tribute in Austrian currency, but forwarded it in Turkish currency and pocketed the difference. He insisted on his right to punish his officers by beating. He enraged his subjects by establishing a monopoly on salt, a commodity which was scarce in Serbia and had to be imported from Wallachia, and by investing his ill-gotten profits in a Wallachian estate, to which he proposed to retire if he was deposed. This, surely, was putting the words into the people's mouth. He had a remarkable wife, Princess Lyubitsa, who had in her youth stood beside many a battlefield and urged on the warriors with heroic invective, who cooked her husband's meals and waited on him at table all her days, who was reputed to chastise any lady who caught her husband's eye with such terrible effect that some had been known to die. It is fairly plain that his absolutism made her think he had gone mad, and that she begged his friends to warn him that he was running his head into a noose.

But the noose was where he wanted his head to be. In 1838 a constitution was thrust upon him, in the course of a farce played out by the great powers. Russia and Turkey believed that if Serbia had a constitution they could in practice guarantee and interpret it; so the Tsar Nicholas and the Sultan Mohammed, the two great despots of Europe, forced constitutionalism on Serbia. Hence Palmerston and Louis Philippe, the two apostles of liberalism and Parliamentary control, found themselves forced to urge Milosh to become an absolute monarch. The fuss seems quite nonsensical; why it should be easier for an external power to influence a constitutional monarch than an absolute one is not clear, and the whole dispute was probably conjured up by some silly young man in one of the foreign offices. But Russia and Turkey won, and a constitution was presented to the delighted Serbian people.

Milosh refused to execute it. He tried, indeed, to suppress it altogether, but the opposition knew of it. A group of determined men gathered under a chief called Vutchitch, who had been one of Milosh's bravest and most devoted aides till his loyalty had been broken by the cruel and imbecile caprices of his master. One day they surrounded Milosh's house and sent away his guards of honour, and also those who were detailed to wait on the Princess Lyubitsa. She went to her husband to be by his side, and when he saw her he said, 'Well, you see it was no use your siding with my enemies. They have taken away your guard of honour too.' She burst into tears.

There was a long discussion concerning Milosh's fate. Some of the chiefs maintained that he should be put to death for the sake of national peace and unity. But he was the first prince Serbia had had since Kossovo, and the profound, even superstitious sense of dynasty which had been inherited by these Serbians made them regard him as by that token sacred. They decided he must abdicate in favour of his eldest son Milan, and go into exile. When they told Milosh he said, 'If they no longer desire to have me, it is well, I will not intrude on them,' and he signed the deed of abdication. Two days after, he crossed the Sava to Austrian territory. Many people, even Vutchitch, wept to see him. Nevertheless Vutchitch flung a stone into the river and cried out to Milosh, 'When this stone floats you will come back to Serbia.' 'I shall die as Serbia's ruler,' answered Milosh, and the boatmen rowed on, bearing him to his strange, imbecile, unsanctified renunciation.

Belgrade IV

The action of Vutchitch and his followers in accepting Milosh's princedom as hereditary was more bizarre, more a matter of totem and taboo, than appears. For his heir was totally unsuited to be a ruler, at least at that moment. Always delicate, he was now so ill that he could not be told of his father's fall, and he died after some weeks without ever having learned that he was Prince of Serbia. His younger brother, Michael, was still a boy, and his accession involved the inconveniences bound to arise out of the appointment of counsellors who were practically regents. Quite suddenly Turkey insisted on appointing these counsellors, and named Vutchitch and a chief called Petronievitch, who was on good terms with the Turk and was strongly anti-Milosh. The Serbians disliked these counsellors because they were named by Turkey and held Turkish sympathies; Michael resented their existence because he wished to govern by himself, and had a personal grudge against them for their hostility to his father. A further complication existed because a conspiracy to remove Michael from the throne was being organized in an unexpected quarter. The other members of the Obrenovitch family marshalled themselves against him with a unity that sprang from an unusual and fascinating diversity of opinion. Two of Milosh's brothers had remained in Serbia; one of these was all in favour of deposing Michael because he himself had not been made a cabinet minister, another wanted to expel his nephew because he thought the boy would make a mess of it and one fine day all Obrenovitches would be massacred. And abroad the Princess Lyubitsa was deeply involved in the conspiracy, for the reason that, if there had to be shooting, she preferred her husband rather than her son to be the target.

The boy met this complicated situation with spirit. Actually he had inherited all his father's genius and brought a much better character to the using of it. He faced the pestilential Vutchitch, who had rebelled against Milosh with courage and patriotic passion, but now discounted that achievement by showing that rebellion was his only reaction to every circumstance; and he drove him into exile. But this very spirit raised the suspicions of the peasants, particularly as about that time it became necessary to depreciate Serbian currency and to raise the taxes, which Vutchitch had disingenuously lowered when he drove out Milosh in order to make the step popular. They feared that he was going to rob them of their money and their rights as impudently as his father, and when Vutchitch returned to Serbia in the guise of a defender of the constitution they took up arms and followed him. Michael knew Vutchitch was inspired by the Sultan and went out to fight him, confident that he would free his country from the last traces of Turkish suzerainty, and that his people must applaud him for it. He was amazed when the deluded peasants followed Vutchitch, and his own army, itself disaffected, ran away. With a certain significant dignity, he disbanded such of his troops as remained loyal and sent home all peasants who had come from the provinces to support him, and passed over to Austrian territory. It is one of the paradoxes of Balkan history that though the Serbians who rejected Michael were moved by ignorance and stupidity and negativism, later events proved they were performing an enormous service to their country.

Vutchitch then entered Belgrade in triumph and was acclaimed as 'Leader of the Nation,' but his profound instinct against simplicity prevented him from putting himself forward as Prince. It seemed good to him, for what reason it cannot be imagined, to force on the Skupshtina Alexander Karageorgevitch, the son of Karageorge, a man of thirty-six, upright and sensible and not contentious, but not impressive in personality. This set in motion the strange oscillation of Serbian sovereignty between the Obrenovitches and the Karageorgevitches which has been so misconceived in the West. It has been thought of as a sanguinary conflict between the two families. Even H. W. Temperley writes in his *History of Serbia*, 'For a century the ghastly struggle was continued by the partisans of both houses, until the last living Obrenovitch was assassinated in our own day'; and elsewhere he deplores 'this terrible blood feud.' But in actual fact when Milosh Obrenovitch murdered Karageorge he committed the last crime that either family was to inflict on the other. Only one Karageorgevitch was ever to die by violence, and that was King Alexander of Yugoslavia; and he can hardly have been killed at Marseille by an Obrenovitch, for by then the breed was extinct. Two Obrenovitches died by violence, but there is no evidence that any Karageorgevitch was responsible. One Karageorgevitch was deposed and one Obrenovitch was forced to abdicate, but in neither case could the other family be blamed. Indeed the abdicating Obrenovitch handed over his throne to his son.

It may be doubted whether there was any effective enmity between the families till late in the second half of the nineteenth century. Certainly there was little at this time. Milosh Obrenovitch had persuaded Karageorge's widow that he was guiltless of her husband's death; and at his invitation she had brought her children back from Hungary to Serbia, and had accepted a pension to keep them. During the reign of young Prince Michael, Alexander Karageorgevitch had cheerfully and loyally acted as the boy's Adjutant. He certainly did not rise to princedom by any attacks he had made on the Obrenovitches, and it needed no effort on their part to account for his expulsion seventeen years later in 1859. His reign began tediously with a great deal of hubbub caused by Russia and Turkey. Dynastic Russia was shocked because Serbia had cast aside a hereditary prince and thought that she ought to have been consulted. Turkey had already recognized Alexander and told Russia so. In the end Russia grumpily consented to recognize Alexander, though only after he had been chosen by a free election, on condition that the abominable Vutchitch and his colleague Petronievitch, both pro-Turks, were sent into exile. Vutchitch had therefore gained nothing by his continual intrigues and mischief-making. But when these excitements settled down it was only to disclose a situation in which Alexander's failure was inevitable.

The historians call him weak. It would be far more true to say that in his reign Serbia discovered its weakness. It had come to life again not as a great empire, but as a small nation; and it was to learn, what was to become tragically clear in the twentieth century, that modern conditions make the independence of a small nation a bad joke. In 1848 Alexander and Serbia suffered a deep and inevitable humiliation. The Magyars of Hungary rose against the Austrian Government; and as their nationalist movement, under the leadership of the renegade Slav Kossuth, showed the most bitter hostility to all Slavs, the Serbs of Novi Sad and the Frushka Gora made haste to revolt against Hungary. It was then that the Croats took the same resolve and marched into Hungary under Yellatchitch. It was a shame and an agony to the Serbians that their brothers, the descendants of the seventeenth-century migrants, the guardians of the blackened body of the Tsar Lazar, should be in danger, and that they should not go to help them. But Russia would not have it so, lest Austria should defeat the Slavs and draw a conquered Serbia into her orbit. So Alexander Karageorgevitch had to sit with folded hands while the Danubian Serbs fought for life and lost. Twelve thousand Serbian volunteers went to their aid, but Serbia as a state had to behave like a coward.

Six years later it again seemed to his people that he had humiliated them. The Crimean War broke out and Serbia longed to take sides with Russia against Turkey. Serbia's incubus, Vutchitch, who had been exiled as pro-Turk and anti-Russian, had now got back to the country as anti-Turk and pro-Russian, and he persuaded the country to elect him as Prime Minister. Needless to say, he did nothing whatsoever to further its cause. He was a pure negativist. A Turkish army advanced towards Serbia on the south and an Austrian army confronted her across the river at Belgrade. Again Alexander had to remain inactive and frustrate national feeling.

The peasants could not understand that he was bowing to the inevitable. They only saw that he did not resist their ancient enemy, Turkey, and that he had shown complete subservience to Austria, whom they now hated almost as much as Turkey, and quite rightly. For though the Serbs of Novi Sad had helped Austria to defeat the Magyar revolt, Franz Josef had betrayed them as he betrayed the Croats who had shown him a like loyalty. He had after a few years handed them back to the Hungarians, who were now taking their revenge by a merciless process of Magyarization, which denied the Serbs their language, their religion, and their culture. The infuriated Serbians lost patience, and, needless to say, Vutchitch skipped forward to organize their discontent, and there was a conspiracy of Senators to murder Alexander. It failed, but it was made unnecessary by a meeting of the Skupshtina, which without a dissentient called on him to resign and demanded the recall of Milosh Obrenovitch.

Alexander Karageorgevitch obeyed without a shadow of resistance, and Milosh returned with his son Michael. The old man was now seventy-eight years of age, and the records show that he thoroughly enjoyed the day of his return. The Austrians refused to let him cross the river in their steamers, so he came over in a rowing-boat, just as on that day when he told Vutchitch that he would die the ruler of Serbia. On landing he made a deft speech which made it quite clear that he intended to disregard the Turkish pretension that the princedom of Serbia was not to be hereditary. 'My only care,' he said to the cheering crowds, 'will be to make you happy, you and your children, whom I love as well as my only son, the heir to your throne, Prince Michael.' That established the issue so firmly that the Turks could hardly care to dispute it. The old man then took up the routine where he had laid it down twenty years before, with all his characteristic zest. It is impossible not to feel pleasure in recording that one of his first actions was to throw Vutchitch into prison. There, very shortly, he died. The Turks wished to examine his body, but Milosh explained that it was better that they should not.

His reign lasted only twenty months, during which he gave himself great amusement and pleased his people by using his old insolent skill in diplomacy to inflict some important defeats on the Turks. It is as well that he ruled so short a time, for he had nothing to offer but that skill. If he had lived longer he must have been faced by that hard fact, the helplessness of the small nation, which had vanquished Alexander Karageorgevitch, and he must have been vanquished too, for he had no resources to meet it. But it was very different with his son Michael, who on his accession to the throne showed how well the tricksters and simpletons responsible for his exile in 1842 had worked for their country. For he had spent the intervening years in improving his education and visiting the Western capitals of Europe, in pursuit of the definite end of fitting himself for monarchy. The specific problem before him was the transformation of a medieval state into a state which would be modern enough to defend itself against modern empires. He attacked it with a genius that never failed until his death.

First, Michael gave Serbia internal order. He impressed on it the conception of law as a code planned to respect the rights of all which must be obeyed by all. No longer was the ruler to bring his enemies before judges who touched their hats and gave the desired sentence. He and all his subjects had to face a blindfold justice. He reorganized the political constitution, laying it down that the members of the Soviet were no longer to be responsible to the Sultan but to their own national authority, and that the Soviet was to be subordinate to the democratic Skupshtina. He also took a powerful step towards the establishment of order by setting up a regular army under French instructors. Till then the Serbian military forces had been a synthesis of private armies led by chiefs who submitted only fitfully to the discipline of a central command, and were always favourable material for a meddler like Vutchitch. This Michael did against the violent opposition of Austria, who wanted to annex Serbia, Turkey, who wanted to recover her, and Great Britain, who was Turcophile. Only Russia and France befriended her.

Second, he drove the Turks out of Serbia. For they were still in the fortresses of the principal towns. Two years after his accession there occurred the famous incident when the population of Belgrade were not unnaturally moved to demonstrations at the murder of two Serbians by two Turks, and the Pasha in command of Kalemegdan fortress thought fit to bombard the open town for five hours, until he was forcibly restrained by the foreign consuls. Michael was able to use this to prove just how intolerable it was for a vigorous and developing country to have to submit to these fantastical vestiges of an ill-regulated authority, and to represent the outrage in terms comprehensible to the Western powers. He followed this up by sending his beautiful and able wife, Julia Hunyadi, to London to influence British public opinion, which she was able to do through Cobden and Palmerston. Soon he had Great Britain, France, Russia, and even Austria lined up behind him in his demand that the Turks should withdraw their garrison; and he showed his father's diplomatic skill by making the demand in terms that enabled Turkey to grant it without lack of dignity.

Third, he found a new foreign policy. He knew he was his father's son and better, and that he could get everything he wanted from the great powers by wheedling and threatening. But that was not enough, for he knew it would hold good only so long as the empires were in a state of quiescence. When they should be moved by a real need for expansion his guile would be unavailing, they would sweep down on his little principality like robbers on a child. For that, however, his period of exile had suggested a remedy. After he had lost his throne in his boyhood he had first gone to live with his father among the Serbs of Hungary. He had visited the shrines of the Frushka Gora and had seen the relics of his people's ancient glory. Among the Serb scholars of Novi Sad and Budapest and Vienna he had learned how real these glories had been, how certainly the medieval Serbian Empire had been begotten by Byzantine civilization, and how near it had come to being heir and transmitter of that civilization, prevented only by the coming of the Turks. He learned enough to know that in the past the struggle for power in the Balkans had swung from east to west, and from west to east, and victory had rested now with the Serbs, now with the Bulgarians. The Bulgarians were a people of other than Slav origin, being akin to the Turks and Hungarians and Finns, but they were interpenetrated with Slav blood and spoke a Slav language. Now they had another bond with the Serbs, they had been conquered by the Turks; and they were still enslaved. Michael believed that it would be a glorious thing to unite the South Slav peoples. The independent state of Montenegro would certainly be his ally; and since he could not join hands with the Croatians and Dalmatians and Hungarian Serbs, because they were under the vigorous tyranny of the Austro-Hungarian Empire, it would perhaps be wiser to link up with the Bulgarians, who would be more accessible than the others because of the inefficiency of the

Turkish administration, and for the same reason more eager for
emancipating friends. Then again should there be a vast area,
solidly Slav, magnificently free.

This dream, which was born of poetic and historical imagination,
was immediately expanded by Michael's practical sense. Why
should not past and present experience of Turkish oppression
bind together small states, even though they were not Slav, into an
effective union that should destroy the Turk? He planned a Balkan
League that should join Serbia and Montenegro with Greece, which
indeed was full of Slav blood, and Roumania, and should receive
the Bulgarians, the Bosnians and Herzegovinians, the Macedonians
and the Hungarian Serbs, as soon as these revolted against their
oppressors. He actually came to an understanding with Greece and
Roumania, and sent Serbian propagandists to work among all the
enslaved Slav peoples, while he increased his military strength at
home. A check was sharply applied to his plan when England
and France, with incredible fatuity, joined Austria-Hungary in
rebuking him. It is difficult to imagine why they did this, for a
young and prosperous Balkan League able to defend itself must
have been a most powerful factor for European peace. The Great
War of 1914 could never have happened if Austria had had on
her east a solid wall of people able to protect themselves, and
had therefore had to accept her limitations. But so it was, and
Michael had to neglect obvious opportunities for fulfilling his
programme. He was about to fill in the time by revising his
constitution and making it more democratic when, on the tenth
of June 1868, he went for a walk in the Topchider, the delightful
park outside Belgrade that looks across the river Sava at the town
on its great ridge of rock. He was accompanied by his cousin and
her daughter Katarina, a lame girl of brilliant intellect, with whom,
it is said, he was in love, but whom he could not marry because the
kinship was within the degree prohibited by the Orthodox Church.
He had some time before been divorced, for reasons which are
still mysterious, from his Hungarian wife, Julia Hunyadi, who
subsequently married the Duke of Ahremberg and died in Vienna
fifty-one years later, in 1919. Three men came up to the party and
attacked all three with knives. Katarina was wounded, her mother
and Prince Michael were killed. Again the Great War was brought
nearer to us, another wall between us and that catastrophe was
pulled down.

It has been alleged that this assassination was the work of
Alexander Karageorgevitch, and indeed he was tried *in absentia*
by a Serbian court and condemned. But no evidence was called

which was worth a straw. It is not easy to believe that this man, who was now sixty-one, and who had never been ambitious and was completely aware of his own unpopularity, decided to kill his successor, whom he knew to be adored by his people, and reclaim the throne at a time when a vast and exacting programme had been begun and would have to be triumphantly accomplished by any prince who wanted to save his neck. It is still more difficult to believe that Alexander Karageorgevitch arranged the assassination yet took no steps to seize the power of the murdered man, and, indeed, never left his estate in Hungary before or after the crime.

Alexander followed this up by an even stranger omission. Michael's marriage had been childless, and the Serbian Cabinet was forced into proclaiming as ruler young Milan, a boy of thirteen, the grandson of one of Milosh's brothers. The relationship was uninspiring in its remoteness, and indeed there were suspicions that it was actually nonexistent. But Alexander Karageorgevitch never appeared to take advantage of the countless opportunities offered him or any other malcontent during the boy's minority. The assassins may have called themselves partisans of the Karageorgevitches; and the Karageorgevitches certainly had partisans. Everybody at odds with Michael's administration, which was far too efficient to satisfy everybody, used to take trips to see Alexander Karageorgevitch and grumble over endless black coffees. But they were most likely to do this if they were old and remembered the good old days of corruption. The assassins of Michael Obrenovitch were young and vigorous; they were known to have relations with the Austrian police, and it was Austria who profited by Michael's death.

Belgrade V

Every Slav heart grieved at Michael's death; and apparently the powers that are not to be seen were also perturbed. At noon on the ninth of June 1868, a peasant called Mata, or Matthew, ran through the streets of a town called Uzhitse crying out: 'Brothers! Brothers! Rise up and save our Prince! They are cruelly murdering him! Look, they are slashing him with *yataghans*! Look, look, the blood! Help him, help him!' The police thought he had gone mad and arrested him; but his position looked more serious when next day there reached Uzhitse the news that Michael had been stabbed to death in Topchider. Matthew was examined by the Mayor on the assumption that he must have been concerned in the conspiracy; but he was able to prove that nothing was less probable, and the whole countryside came forward to bear witness that he was a seer and often foretold events that had not yet happened or were happening far away. The Mayor then told Mata to say what he saw of the future, and had a secretary to take it down in writing; and he was so impressed that he sent the notes up to the Minister of the Interior. The Minister also was impressed. He ordered Matthew to be brought to Belgrade, and for some days the man sat in a room in the Foreign Office dictating to an official. The notes were filed in the archives, and only disclosed gradually to persons connected with the court or Cabinet. But the notes taken by the Mayor of Uzhitse were not so well guarded. They became common knowledge and were finally published and sold all over the country.

Mata foresaw all of Balkan history for the next fifty years. He said: 'Michael will be succeeded by a child, and for a time the country will be governed by three Regents. When he comes of age all will go ill. He is clever but unstable, and he will be a torment to Serbia, which will know nothing of peace or security so long as he is on the throne. He will lead several wars, will enlarge the country; and will be more than a Prince, he will be a King. But there will always be trouble. Finally he will abdicate and die in exile before he is old. He will leave but one son, born of a detested wife. This son will mean even more suffering to Serbia. His rule will plunge the country into disorder, and he too will make a disastrous marriage. Before the thirtieth year he will be dead, and his family will die with him. Another family will come to reign in Serbia; but the new

King will disappear after three years and then there will be agony unspeakable for our people. There will be revolts and bloodshed, and then a foreign power will invade our country. That foreign power will torture us. There will come such sad and hard times that those who are living will say when they pass a churchyard, "O graves, open that we may lie down and rest. Oh, how happy are you who have died and are saved from our troubles and misfortunes!" But a better time will come. . . .'

He said other things, not yet fulfilled, which explain why nowadays one cannot buy the prophecies of Mata of Krema. It is no wonder that those who are threatened by them are apprehensive, for all that he said of Milan and his son came true. Milan was an unqualified disaster to his country. It is possible that he was not an Obrenovitch at all. His mother was a noble and beautiful and indecorous Roumanian, and there was some doubt as to whether his father also was not Roumanian, and the Obrenovitches in no way involved. When Milan was presented to the Skupshtina on coming of age, one of the deputies stayed in his seat and explained that he did not intend to rise till he had seen the young man's birth certificate. In any case, even had Milan been an Obrenovitch his upbringing would have prevented him from behaving like one. Their courage and vitality and craft were theirs only because they had lived the life of peasant soldiers. But Milan spent his childhood in not quite the best palace hotels of Paris and Vienna and Belgrade and Bucharest, alternately petted and neglected by parents who detested each other. Although it must have been realized how likely it was that he should succeed Michael, nobody seems to have regarded his education as a matter of any importance. He grew up with no virtue except an extreme aesthetic sensibility, which would have been revolted could he have caught sight of himself. In mind and body he was the perfect *rastaquouère*.

His marriage was indeed as disastrous as Mata had foretold. When he was nineteen, while his Ministers were negotiating with St Petersburg to secure him the hand of a young Russian princess, he announced his engagement to Mademoiselle Natalia Keshko, the daughter of a Russian colonel belonging to the lesser ranks of the Moldavian nobility, who was a strange mixture of Slav and Roumanian and Levantine. As the couple left the Cathedral after their wedding a thunderstorm broke over Belgrade and the horses of the state carriage reared and bolted. The omen was not excessive. Natalia was a detestable child, and cruel to the child she had married. When he showed her the peculiar best of himself she answered with a sneer. Because he once heard her say she liked lilies of the valley he had a whole field planted with them, which is a gesture a *rastaquouère* might make if stirred to his depths. When he took her to see them at the perfect moment of their flowering she was puzzled and annoyed by this extravagance. A whole field of lilies of the valley! This coldness she manifested in all phases of their common life. Violently aphrodisiac in appearance, with the immense liquid leaf-shaped eyes and the voluptuous smoothness of the ideal odalisque, she bore within her the conventionality of the kind of Russian provincial society that is described in some of Tolstoy and much of Tchekov, and she deeply resented her husband's passion. They had but one child, Alexander, born when its father was twenty-one and its mother twenty. Thereafter Milan took a mistress, an ugly and intelligent Levantine Greek ten years older than himself, who was perhaps a Russian agent. Natalia, who was at once narrow and loose, knew no restraint in her public resentment of this situation, particularly when this mistress gave birth to a son. Belgrade was startled and shocked by the public brawls of their Prince and his wife. These were not peasant manners, but they were not fine manners either.

As a ruler Milan was not less a failure than as a husband. When the Bosnians and Herzegovinians revolted against Turkey he marched against the Turks from the north while Prince Nicholas of Montenegro marched on them from the south-west. Prince Nicholas made a brilliant success, and wrung an advantageous peace treaty out of them. Milan failed, and had to be saved from disaster by Russian intervention. That started a movement in Serbia for the dethronement of Milan in favour of Prince Nicholas, which soon lost its vigour owing to the flaws that were evident in the Montenegrin's character whenever he stopped fighting; and it started a much more lively and lasting movement in favour of recalling Peter Karageorgevitch, who had fought with the Bosnian rebels and shown himself remarkable as a soldier and as a man. It is hard to blame Milan either for his defeat or for the steps he took to remedy it. He was only twenty-one when he led out his troops against Turkey; and in a modern and orderly state genius has no chance to be precocious. If he had lived in the Old Serbia of Karageorge and Milosh he would have been fighting since he was fifteen or sixteen, and would have known that to keep his throne he had to placate or outwit a dozen wily old chiefs, and in either case earn their respect as well. That was the training Michael Obrenovitch had had; it was ironic that it had enabled him to sweep away such barbaric conditions, which as it proved were apparently necessary to equip a Serbian ruler, his heir not excepted, for the difficult task of modernizing his state.

A later campaign against the Turks was more satisfactory. But at treaty-making Milan was pitifully incompetent. He let the Treaty of San Stefano, which was signed between the Russians and Turks in 1878, take a form which inevitably was to destroy Michael Obrenovitch's dream of a union of the South Slavs for many years and perhaps for ever; for he did not prevent Russia's giving her vassal state, Bulgaria, extended boundaries to which not only the Serbs but the Greeks could legitimately object. The Balkan League was split in three before it was founded. Then came the infamous Congress of Berlin, which was called for no other reason than to frame a treaty which should deprive the democratic Slavs of their freedom and thrust them into subjection under the imperialism of Turkey and Austria-Hungary. Without the Balkan League to use as a counter Milan was utterly helpless, he was back in the position of poor Alexander Karageorgevitch.

It is not to be wondered at that in 1881 Milan signed a secret convention with Austria which handed over his country to be an Austrian dependency. He promised not to make any effort to redeem the Bosnians and Herzegovinians, in return for a vague promise of support for a war, which he was not likely ever to declare, against the Turks in Macedonia, and he agreed to submit his policy day by day to Austrian control. The Austrian military attaché in Belgrade used to call at the palace and give Milan his orders. It is suspected that Milan received, directly or indirectly, financial recompense for this treachery. This increased the dishonour of the transaction; but it would be superficial to take it as proof that Milan's motives were simply mercenary. There can be no doubt that he was chiefly moved by his sense that the great aggressive empires of Turkey, Russia, and Austria made it impossible for him to give his country that independence which it thought it his duty to guarantee.

A year after Milan sold his country down the river, down the Danube, he proclaimed himself King, and had himself anointed in the ancient church of Zhitcha, where all the Nemanyan dynasty had been crowned. It is a crimson church which stands among land like the fairest parts of the Lake District, solemnly dedicated to its royal ritual. A new door was pierced in the wall for each king to come to his coronation, and on his going out it was bricked up again. The people were not placated by Milan's elevation. He was notoriously given to drunkenness, he was spendthrift to the point of mania, his relations with his wife were already scandalous;

and owing to his secret convention with Austria-Hungary his political conduct looked like the caprice of a lunatic. Most of his Ministers and all of the public had no idea of the agreement, and they were therefore completely mystified when, as constantly happened, their King suddenly abandoned a project which he had fully approved and which was indeed plainly in the interests of Serbia, or when he put forward a plan which appeared meaningless because its context was known only in the Ballplatz. It is typical of Austrian *Schlamperei* that those who gave Milan his orders took no trouble whatsoever to make them such as he could obey without coming to loggerheads with his people. In 1883 certain districts rose in rebellion which was savagely suppressed.

When little Alexander was nine years old his father and mother separated with the utmost indecency. Their venomous hatred and bad manners were such as Strindberg describes in his play *Divorce*. Natalia on one occasion abominably kidnapped the child and took him to Wiesbaden, and Milan equally abominably had him brought back by the German police. The only respite in these brawls was due to Milan's imbecile declaration of war against Bulgaria, which led to a disgraceful defeat in 1886. By 1888 Milan had exhausted all other means of persecuting his wife and conceived the idea that he must divorce her, though he had no grounds whatsoever, for she was entirely virtuous. He persuaded the Serbian Primate to regard as precedents certain cases of Russian Tsars who had been divorced by simple edicts of the Metropolitans. This deeply shocked his people, who now knew that their king was a thoroughly bad lot. His treasury was incessantly faced with cheques he had cashed in nearly every capital in Europe and with dunning letters from money-lenders; and his military defeat meant even more in a Balkan country than it would have in the West. It was apparent that even if Milan was contented with the situation his backers were not. In January 1890 he tried placating his subjects by giving them a liberal constitution, but three months afterwards, abruptly and without explanation, he abdicated in favour of his son, who was only twelve years old. It is probable that the new constitution and the abdication were Austrian attempts at coping with the steadily increasing interest that Serbia felt in the sober personality of Peter Karageorgevitch, who would certainly never be amenable to foreign influence if he ascended the throne.

The boy Alexander ruled until his majority, through three Regents, two of whom were military men known as 'the tarnished generals' since certain unlucky incidents in the war against

Bulgaria, while the third was a political boss who had always been
Milan's henchman. They were hardly ideal substitutes for a father
and a mother, as they very soon had to be. For Milan insisted when
he left his son in their care that he should never be allowed to see his
mother or hold any communication with her. This was probably
not purely an act of domestic hatred. The quarrels between the
two seem, particularly towards the end of their dreadful marriage,
to have had some sort of political basis. Natalia was strongly
Russophile, and it is probable that she found out the existence of
the secret convention with Austria. Indeed some of her recorded
utterances make it almost certain that she had. It may be that Milan
feared she would impart this knowledge to the boy before he had
the discretion to realize its full consequences.

Whatever the cause of this prohibition, Natalia turned it to the
vulgarest account. She came to Belgrade and used to stand with
her face pressed against the gates, looking up at the windows to
see her adored son, whom she had done little or nothing to protect.
She took a house near by and hung from a balcony when the young
King went by on his daily drive. She also distributed secretly to
the foreign newspaper correspondents information damaging to
Serbia which she had learned in her position as Queen. Finally the
Regents rushed through Parliament a bill providing that neither
King Milan nor Queen Natalia should be allowed to reside even
temporarily in Serbia. The inclusion of both parents enabled the
Regents to avoid the accusation of partiality; and indeed they were
probably feeling none too fond of Milan, who had been sent abroad
with a handsome allowance but was running up enormous debts in
Paris and Vienna. Once the Act was passed the Government asked
Natalia to leave Belgrade, and when she refused they sent a police
commissioner and his men to put her on a Danube steamer. She
locked her door and the men had to climb over the roof to get
into her house. They drove her away in a cab, and her beautiful
grief inspired a mob of young men to make an attempt at rescue.
After several of them had been killed and many wounded, she
addressed the mob and begged them to disperse, declaring that
to prevent any more of this dreadful bloodshed she would leave
Belgrade at once.

When Alexander was seventeen, and a weak-kneed, stout,
spectacled boy, he asked the Regents and the principal Ministers
of the Cabinet to dine with him at the palace. They came to
dinner in high spirits, for they were all Liberals, which is to
say in this confusing country that they were not liberals at all,
but Tammany politicians with a great deal more machine than

ideology, and they had just pulled off a smart manoeuvre against the Radicals, who here are not radicals at all but anti-Western, nationalist, democrat conservatives who base their programme on the ancient Slav communist tendencies growing out of the Zadruga system. But before they had finished dining the palace aide-de-camp entered and spoke in a low voice to the boy, who nodded, rose to his feet, and said, 'Gentlemen, it is announced to all the garrisons in Serbia, to all the authorities, and to the people, and I announce it here to you, that I declare myself of full age, and that I now take the government of the country into my own hands. I thank you, my Regents, for your services, of which I now relieve you. I thank you also, gentlemen of the Cabinet, for your services, of which you are relieved also. You will not be allowed to leave this palace tonight. You can remain here as my guests, but if not, then as my prisoners.'

For a second the men were silent, then they jumped up and hurried round the table towards the boy, crying out threats and protests. The aide-de-camp drew his sword and stopped them, then went silently to the folding doors on one side of the room and threw them open. Bayonets glittered on the rifles of a company of soldiers. 'I leave you in charge of Lieutenant-colonel Tyirich, whose orders you will have implicitly to obey, while I go to give the oath of fidelity to the Army,' said the King, and he left the hall. Next morning the Regents and the Ministers were released, and went home through streets placarded with royal proclamations stating that King Alexander had watched the illegal actions of the Liberal Government, and feared that if they had been suffered to continue the country would drift into civil war, and therefore had declared himself of age and taken the reins of power into his hands. The people came out of their houses, read the proclamation, ran back and hung out their flags, and then rushed to the courtyard before the palace to cheer the Obrenovitch who after all had shown himself an Obrenovitch.

There is but one explanation of this incident and the anticlimax that followed it; there can be only one reason why Alexander made this superb gesture and then never another, why he afterwards only acted as if he wished to surpass his father in caprice and cruelty towards his subjects. The clue is given by an utterance he made concerning this secret convention with Austria, and by certain of his actions which are apparently conflicting. There seems to be no doubt that later he spoke of his father's signature to the convention as 'an act of treason.' At the time of his *coup d'état* he called the nationalist, democratic, anti-Western radicals to power. But only a year later he illegally removed the radicals from power, and later he annulled the constitutional reforms of the past twenty years, suppressed the freedom of speech and freedom of the press, and governed with the Parliamentary help of an insignificant pro-Austrian party called the Progressives. Yet all this time Alexander was on the most affectionate terms with his mother, Natalia, who was pro-Radical and pro-Russian, and he frequently left the country to spend holidays with her, which were apparently not marred by any differences of opinion. Finally, to the country's amazement and rage, he recalled his father from his scandalous life abroad and made him Commander-in-chief. This was not altogether a disaster. Milan was far from being a fool. In between his orgies in Paris he had acquired a superb collection of pictures by the yet unrecognized masters of the nineteenth century; some of the finest Cézannes once belonged to him. And though he had not been a successful general on the field, his sense of style made him an excellent organizer of a peace-time army. But he took his fun in persecuting the Radicals and pro-Russians, many of whom he did to death. Serbia had never sunk lower since its foundation as a state.

These incidents fall into a comprehensible pattern if certain assumptions are made for which there is some independent evidence. It happened that in 1892 a copy of the secret convention had fallen into the hands of a Serbian nationalist and patriot, Prince Lazarovitch Hrbelianovitch, a descendant of the Tsar Lazar, and he had communicated it to the European press. Its existence was explicitly denied, both by the Serbian Regents and by the Austro-Hungarian Empire through the Parliaments of both Vienna and Budapest. If Alexander had discovered, perhaps by some secret communication from Natalia, that the convention indeed existed, it might well be that his young idealism revolted and he decided to appear before his country as their deliverer from the hidden tyrant. That would explain why he drove out his Regents and assumed power a year before the proper time, and why he favoured the anti-Austrian Radicals. But his first conversation with the Austrian Minister would show him the reality of the fear that had paralysed Alexander Karageorgevitch and disintegrated his own father. He was probably told that any public disclosure and repudiation of the convention would be treated as an unfriendly act by Austria and would be followed by an invasion, or by his murder and replacement by a Karageorgevitch. The boy, sobered, would try to compromise. He would keep silent about the convention, but he would continue his support of the Radicals. Austrian pressure slowly increased. Every year that Alexander reigned without disclosing the convention to his people put him in a worse position to assert his independence. He could not turn to his country and demand its support in his war against the foreign oppressor when it could be proved that he had for long been acting as the oppressor's agent. So he was forced backwards along a dark corridor, a pistol at his breast, to meet an unknown and horrid end, till suddenly he stopped. He struck the pistol away from the hand that held it, careless whether it might be picked up again or not. He had fallen in love with a woman who was Serbian and pro-Russian.

Belgrade VI

By now the Serbians were deeply unhappy. They were a people who had lived by a tradition that had never failed them for five hundred years, that had never let them forget how much fairer than all the conquering might of Islam their Christian knightliness had been. They had lived by St Sava and Stephen Dushan, by the King Marko and the Tsar Lazar. But Milan and Alexander Obrenovitch, who were perhaps not Obrenovitches at all, nor even Serbians, and who were entirely and essentially nineteenth-century, to such a degree that they both might have been minor characters in Proust, cannot possibly have been even faintly interested in these medieval personages. Milan was infatuated with the modern West, and he had surrounded himself with people who shared his infatuation and expressed it in ways less admirable than the purchase of Cézannes. His favourite Foreign Minister, Chedomil Miyatovitch, who supported him in the signature of the secret convention with Austria, once wrote a book on Serbia in which he speaks very ill of the Serbian Church. In shocked accents he tells how he took some 'distinguished English gentlemen' to an ancient monastery and found there the Bishop of Nish, who bade him tell his friends 'that it would be much better if, instead of sending us Bibles, they were to send us some guns and cannons.' This was an answer which, of course, might have come from any bishop of the early Church. Leave to us the instruction of the people, it says, and help us to wage war against the heathen that sell the baptized into captivity. There were many such captives over the Serbian frontiers, in the hands of the Turks, not possibly to be redeemed until there was again a strong Christian power in the Balkans. Men like Miyatovitch wanted the Serbians to lay aside this grandiose subject matter which their destiny had given them for their genius to work upon; and instead they offered them, as an alternative, to be clean and briskly bureaucratic and capitalist like the West. It was as if the *Mayflower* and Red Indians and George Washington and the pioneer West were taken from the United States, and there was nothing left but the Bronx and Park Avenue.

The Serbian tradition was not killed. The Serbians did not forget the field of Kossovo. Simply they felt that every day Kossovo was desecrated by the indifference of the father and son who governed them in this curious unconstitutional partnership. They were also conscious, though they did not openly admit it, that they could not even flatter themselves that they were really governed by this pair. It is impossible that the interpretation of Alexander's capricious and terrified despotism should have escaped a people so subtle, so politically experienced, and so suspicious. But to admit it would have involved recognition that Serbia could never be independent, that though it had freed itself from Turkey now it must fall under the tutelage of Austria or Russia: and that was to insult the Tsar Lazar, to leave the defeat of Kossovo unredeemed for ever. The Serbians became moody, hallucinated, creative; and the real persecution they suffered at the hands of the anti-Russian and anti-Radical agents sent out by Milan tinged their fantasies with a certain colour, a certain brooding, cryptic violence.

When Alexander Obrenovitch was a little boy he and his tutor had often walked in the Royal Park outside Belgrade with an American newspaper correspondent named Stephen Bonsal and an English military attaché named Douglas Dawson, who was later to be the Controller of the Household of King George V. One day the two foreigners talked of the delights of swimming in the Danube, and they were shocked to find that the little boy could not swim. So they found him a pool among the trees, and in spite of the tutor's protests they gave him his first swimming lesson. They were distressed to see how badly the boy stripped. He was misshapen and top-heavy, with clumsy shoulders and long arms, meagre loins and thighs, and knock-knees. As soon as he could cross the pool, which was about thirty feet wide, he said proudly to his unhappy tutor, 'Now you need not worry about telling the Regents that I am being given swimming lessons by these gentlemen, who are my friends. You can tell them that the King can swim.'

Alexander never lost his delight in swimming. When he visited his mother at her home in Biarritz, as he did regularly after his dismissal of the Regents, he spent much of his time in the sea or lying on the sands in the sunshine. One of his companions was Queen Natalia's chief lady-in-waiting, a very pretty widow, ten years older than himself, named Draga Mashin. With her, as time went on, he fell deeply in love. She was the first woman in whom he had shown any interest. His reluctance to marry and his distaste for feminine society had led it to be generally believed that he was physiologically defective. But some time between the years 1894 and 1897 his passion for her became so overwhelming that he forced his way into her bedroom at night. She, however, took him by the shoulders, turned him out, and locked the door. This is regarded by her enemies as proof of her subtle guile, but according to the King's own account she used a degree of muscular strength far greater than a designing woman would risk. Alexander came near to being in a position where he could say, 'Perhaps you were right to dissemble your love, but why did you kick me downstairs?'

After this the story becomes obscure. Some time in the autumn of 1897 Queen Natalia discovered a letter from Alexander to Draga, and flew into a rage most curious in a middle-aged woman of great social experience. It is not clear why she was angry with Draga, who, however indiscreet she had been to evoke the letter, had answered it with the extreme discretion of staying where she was instead of going to Belgrade. But Natalia at once dismissed Draga, turned her out of the house, and sat down to write to all her friends that her lady-in-waiting had behaved to her like a traitress and a wanton. This at once threw Draga on her own resources, which amounted to about a hundred pounds a year, and closed to her the only circle where she might have found fresh employment. She was therefore obliged to return to her family in Belgrade. Queen Natalia, in fact, had made inevitable the relationship which she affected to loathe. For this reason some have suspected her of finding an ingenious device for planting a pro-Russian agent in her son's court and looking as if she were doing no such thing. But the suspicion is unfounded, for she evidently conceived a real resentment against her son, and never saw him again. There is no reason to see anything here but the tropisms of a stupid and vulgar woman.

It is hard to imagine a life more complicated than young Alexander's in the winter of 1897. His father, to whom he had become more attached since his quarrel with his mother, and who had only lately returned to the country as Commander-in-chief, had already begun to embarrass him as a Serbian patriot by pro-Austrian activities. Alexander went for a holiday to Merano, where Draga was staying, though she was still, according to his later and convincing accounts, not yet his mistress; and there he was visited by the Russian diplomat Isvolsky, then *en poste* in Bavaria, who fully realized the extent to which he was anti-Austrian and might become pro-Russian, and reported to his superiors that, although Draga had caused a breach between the young King and his pro-Russian mother, she was herself a pro-Russian influence. It seems probable that he arranged for certain transactions to be carried on through the mediation of Draga, in order to shield them from the observation of Alexander's father. This extreme intricacy of relationship was just what might have stirred the interest and sympathy of the Serbian people, but it had to be kept secret. So Alexander and Draga went back to Belgrade, to all appearances in the excessively simple characters of a tyrannous king and his venal mistress.

It is still not known when the reality came to correspond with the popular belief. Alexander declared it was three years after the night when she had turned him out of her bedroom at Biarritz, but that scene may have occurred any time between 1894 and 1897. It is possible that she did not surrender to him till long after her return to Belgrade, perhaps only a short time before their marriage in the summer of 1900. But the people had no reason to guess at the unexpected purity of their relationship. Draga lived in a pretty little house near the palace in a style which was plainly not within the reach of her own resources, and she was constantly visited by the King. They naturally concluded that she was his mistress; but the feeling aroused by their conclusion was not natural. Before long she was hated as few women since the beginning of time, as no cruel mother, as no murderess, has ever been loathed. I have heard of a Serbian scholar, born beyond the Danube, in Hungary, whose great work was crowned by the Belgrade Academy. Though he was a passionate patriot and free Serbia was sacred soil to him, he would not come to claim his honour. To him Belgrade was utterly polluted by the presence of Draga.

All over Europe spread this campaign of defamation; when the King married her not a country but looked down its nose. She was supposed to be a woman of low origin who had led a vicious life, and this impression was confirmed by the current photographs of her, which showed a bloated face, coarsening around the jaw. But there are other things than dissipation that thicken the features. Tears, for example. Certainly the first part of the story was not true, for she was by birth the equal of the Obrenovitches. Her grandfather, Nikola Lunyevitza, was a friend of Milosh Obrenovitch, a very prosperous cattle-breeder, who had ruined himself financing the rebellions against the Turks. Her more immediate antecedents had been painful, but quite respectable. Her father had died in a lunatic asylum, but till he went mad he had been an efficient and popular Prefect of Shabats. His collapse had left a large family poorly provided for, and Draga, who was one of the elder children, married at seventeen a mining engineer and civil servant. He was himself a worthless and depraved person, but he came of a quite successful family; his father was a noted doctor and one of his brothers had risen high in the Army.

There is an overwhelming consensus of opinion that there is no defence possible in the second part of the story. It is still held by the mass of people today in Serbia that she unquestionably had had many lovers before Alexander, and that she might fairly be called a woman of loose life. Though it is always rash to challenge such unanimous certainties, the student must wonder where and when Draga Mashin was able to live loosely. She was born in 1866. She married her husband some time before her eighteenth birthday in 1884. He immediately fell ill with a disorder due to alcoholism, and she nursed him, except during periods when she had to flee from his ill-treatment, till his death in 1885. When she became a widow she was left badly off, but not so badly off that she could not buy food and shelter; and her unfortunate position attracted the attention of Queen Natalia, who had her taught foreign languages and prepared for her duties as a lady-in-waiting. She was so constantly in attendance at the palace during this time that it was rumoured she was King Milan's mistress, although in fact King Milan hated her. In 1889 she began to travel about with Queen Natalia, and from 1890 lived under her roof at Biarritz. Her bad reputation can be taken as deserved only if it is accepted that from 1885 to 1889, between the ages of nineteen and twenty-three, she conducted herself so licentiously in Belgrade that it was still remembered in 1897. But Queen Natalia was chaster than snow, she was as chaste as sleet, and she was no more likely than Queen Victoria to have a woman of damaged reputation as her personal attendant. She was also noted for knowing everything that went on in Belgrade. If there existed in 1885 stories about Draga so rich and strange that they survived eight years of absence, it seems odd that Queen Natalia never heard them. It seems odder still that a young woman who had spent her youth in the arms of innumerable lovers should at the age of twenty-three be willing to take up her quarters for the rest of her life in what was virtually the nunnery of Queen Natalia's court, particularly when she was so beautiful that she could have set up as a cocotte in any capital of Europe.

There are discrepancies here which cannot be reconciled. We may be warned by the puerility of the case against her. Vladan Georgevitch, the Jewish scoundrel who was Progressivist Prime Minister and specialized in terrorism, theft of state papers, and blackmail, was driven to denouncing her for lending one of his family an immoral book by a Russian Nihilist: it was Mr. Gladstone's favourite, the *Journal* of Marie Bashkirtseff. It seems as if it might be wiser to pay heed to the curiously sober and lethargic expression noticeable even in the earliest photographs of Draga, and accept their indication that a woman who has known at the age of nineteen what it is to have an insane father and an alcoholic husband may develop a certain caution about the exploration of life. Her bad reputation had probably two sources: one limited though effective in a highly important sphere, the other unconfined as a comet, the poetry in the heart of the people, catching fire from a fiery destiny.

It has already been said that Draga Mashin had a brother-in-law in the Army: Colonel Alexander Mashin. He and most of his family hated her. It is hard to believe that this hatred can have been justified. A girl of seventeen cannot have offended greatly against a husband, much older than herself, who during their brief year of married life was suffering from the effects of alcoholic excess. It is likely that this emotion sprung from the reluctance of obstinate people to humble themselves before a stranger to whom one of their kind has done an injury. To Colonel Mashin this hatred was bound to seem justified when she became Alexander's mistress, for he was a partisan of the Karageorgevitches, though he had also received great kindness from King Milan. There is no doubt that Colonel Mashin, who was a good soldier and very popular in the Army, widely disseminated his sincere belief that she was abominable.

For the rest, the people hated Alexander Obrenovitch because he had taken from them their dream of avenging Kossovo, because he had destroyed the integrity of their free state, because he was laying low the representatives of their ancient ways, because he was vulgarizing their style, their austere Byzantine splendour, which made their men gaunt and minatory, their women still and patient, like the ancient kings and holy personages in the frescoes. Because the woman a man loves is in a sense his soul, or at any rate the answer to the call it makes, they thought of Draga as Alexander's soul, and therefore their enemy, and therefore utterly evil, as all of us in our simplicity conceive our enemies.

It is certain that she was aware of the people's hatred and was full of fear. It looks as if, with a not unnatural cynicism, she thought that her lover's passion would pass and that she would then be free. It is said that he gave her twenty thousand pounds; and it is probable that she hoped to spend the rest of her life quietly in some French watering-place, where there was a casino at the end of an esplanade planted with palms, and pink villas with jalousies. This vision might well seem heavenly, for Balkan politics were thickening round her to a nightmare. In February 1899 the Austrian influence in the court, of which the chief representative was King Milan, insisted on a suspension of relations with Russia. In July of the same year King Milan was driving from the Belgrade fortress to the palace when a young man stepped forward and fired a revolver at him. The assassin was a revolutionary Russophile Bosnian. Like all his kind save Princip, he missed. King Milan used the event as a pretext for throwing many of his personal and political enemies into jail, but he, and several of the Ministers who were in the best position to form an opinion, believed that it was his son Alexander who had employed the assassin.

It is not easy to visualize family life as it was lived in the palace at Belgrade during this period. However, calm was apparently restored, and Alexander shuffled along quietly enough under instructions from Vienna until March 1900, when Count Goluchowsky, the Austrian Foreign Minister, was unfortunately inspired to send him a peremptory demand that he should marry a German princess without delay. This was typical of the extraordinary incompetence which the Austro-Hungarian Empire always showed in its dealings with Serbia. It was notorious that Alexander was still passionately in love with his mistress, and as he was not yet twenty-four years of age there was no reason whatsoever to hurry him into marriage. But Alexander's Ministers obeyed the orders from Vienna and extracted from him a promise that he would marry before the year was out. They lacked the sound common sense of the Chief of the Belgrade Police, a simple peasant who believed that Draga owed her power over Alexander to magic potions. When he heard of the promise he blurted out, 'Here, what's this? We all know that this creature has bewitched the King so thoroughly that he firmly believes that he couldn't even be a husband to another woman. If he has promised you to marry within the year, he means to marry Draga Mashin.'

He was right. On July the eighth Alexander announced to the world his intention of marrying his mistress. He chose a moment when both his father and his Prime Minister were on holiday in different parts of the Continent. As he had taken the precaution of ordering them to be supplied with different code books, they wasted a great deal of time after hearing the news in sending each other incomprehensible messages. But at home he had immediately to face a flood of opposition not to be deflected by such easy means. We know how he met it in one case. He addressed one of his Ministers in terms which were drawn from the common language of lovers, which we may even recognize as having been used in our own times by other lips.

'You know, Vukashin,' he said, 'that I have had neither child-hood nor youth like other men. . . . I have never had any ambition, not even the ambition to reign as a King. I wear the crown, not because I love it, but because it is my duty to do so. You must have noticed that yourself. . . . . There now exists a woman whom I love more than anyone or anything in this world, the only woman with whom I can be perfectly happy, and only then can I consecrate my whole life to the interests of the people if she becomes my wife. In the whole world there is only one woman who can make me forget the bitterness of my past life, and make me feel happy. This woman has been hitherto my good angel, who gave me strength to bear patiently all that I had to bear. That woman is—Madame Draga, the daughter of Panta Lunyevitza. . . . . I am inflexibly resolved to marry her. Don't insult me by attacks on her. . . . She is a pure and honourable woman, and only her enemies speak badly of her. . . . Only after she received proof that without her and her love I could not live, did she sacrifice herself to me. Yes, I am passionately in love with her, and without her I cannot live. There is now no power on earth which could prevent my marrying Draga, whatever the consequences may be. I would prefer to give up my crown and live with Draga, on an income of three hundred and sixty pounds a year, than have the throne and an apanage of forty-eight thousand pounds a year. I knew that my marriage with her would meet with extraordinary difficulties, therefore I have surrendered myself to her, body and soul, and therefore I have made it impossible for her to leave me. You ought to know that she persistently refused to become Queen. I alone know what difficulties I have had to gain her consent. And now, after I have at last broken down her resistance, you come and make difficulties! Have you no pity for me? Do you wish to force me to go away for ever? Because you ought to realize that if I cannot marry Draga as King, I will leave Serbia for ever, and marry her as a private individual.'

His Ministers were unmoved by his eloquence. The whole country was filled by the news of the approaching marriage, by a black horror such as they would not have felt at a threat of invasion by the Turks. On the day the King proclaimed his betrothal to his people the Cabinet resigned, and sent two of their number to Draga Mashin with the message that she must leave the country without delay. It was in their minds that if she refused she must be kidnapped; and it must have been in her mind that her life was no longer safe. She consented at once to their demand, but she not unnaturally asked if she might not wait till her maid had packed up her clothes and papers, provided that meanwhile she went to a friend's house where the King would not be likely to seek her. Once she had her possessions, she said, she would gladly cross the river to Hungary. To this the two Ministers agreed.

But it was then that her tragic origins put out a hand to drag her down to her doom. She had two younger brothers who were Army officers. Both seem to have inherited the mental instability of their father. They were flighty, garrulous, arrogant, extremely indiscreet, and not at all abashed by their sister's curious position. There is no doubt that their behaviour had contributed largely to Draga's unpopularity. It was unfortunate that that very morning the worse of the two was with his sister, and that as she got into her carriage she whispered to him the name of the friend with whom she was going to take shelter while her maid packed for her. This was a natural enough precaution for one who knew herself to be in danger of kidnapping or death. It was not natural for her brother to give this name to the King when he called on his mistress two hours later. He drove at once to Draga's hiding-place and brought her home in his own carriage, and there and then put on her finger a diamond engagement ring, and left her under a strong armed guard.

For four days the capital was in a turmoil. It is indicative of the curious standards of this people that deputation after deputation visited the palace, urging the King not to marry the woman whom he adored, on the ground that she was old, his mistress, and of depraved habits, and that they were permitted to depart in impunity. This is not what one would have expected in a country where freedom of speech and the press had long been violated. But the Slavs are so inherently democratic that even under an autocracy there was an admitted right for the common man to discuss his ruler's affairs once they entered a phase of supreme importance. These deputations went away and formed various schemes for meeting the situation. Some wanted King Milan to be recalled and put in his son's place, others wanted Peter Karageorgevitch, others reverted to the original plan of exiling Draga, with the added precaution of putting Alexander under arrest till she was out of the country. There was no question but that the Army was to prevent the marriage by a rebellion. It only remained to settle how they were to do it.

Without any doubt a plan would have been devised which would have found general support, but on the fifth day an announcement was issued which hamstrung all opposition to the King's marriage. The Tsar Nicholas declared his approval of the engagement and sent an emissary to congratulate not only Alexander but Draga. More than that, the Tsar expressed his readiness to be 'Kum' at their wedding; the Kum is the chief witness, who plays a more important part in a marriage celebrated according to the Orthodox rite than any equivalent figure we know in the West, who is as it were the godparent of the marital tie. The enemies of Alexander were almost all pro-Russian. They could no longer oppose him now that he was obviously transferring his allegiance from Austria to Russia; and the marriage showed in quite a different light now that the Tsar was going to lend it his spiritual authority. A silence fell on Belgrade, not the less profound because it proceeded from bewilderment rather than from satisfaction. It had some chance to settle, for King Milan never returned to Serbia. The Continental press published a letter which he was supposed to have sent his son concerning his marriage, but which appears to have been written for journalistic use; and he helped the Austrian authorities in a campaign of libel against Belgrade. His son directed his generals that if his father attempted to re-enter Serbia he was to be shot like a mad dog. But this scene, which would indeed have been not at all a surprising climax to the family life of the Obrenovitches, was rendered impossible by Milan's death in Vienna in 1901. Nothing could have been more ironical than that his corpse and household possessions should have been sent to Krushedol on the Frushka Gora, among the holy Serbian things which had never interested him. But it can well be understood why the Emperor Franz Josef sent them there. 'Put them with the rest of the Slav rubbish,' he may have said. For Milan had failed in his duty of keeping Serbia as an Austrian dependency, and henceforth he and all Serbs were hateful and worthless in Habsburg eyes.

But the silence in Belgrade broke. The public loathing of Draga had to find words to lift its corroding bitterness out of the heart. There is no indication that Draga was not an admirable wife to Alexander. She seems always to have treated him with an ungrudging maternal tenderness. There is no record of her having sided with the world against him by showing consciousness of his lack of dignity or physical repulsiveness. But though certain Ministers recognized her virtues this did not improve her popularity, for there were other counteracting forces. There was a mysterious event which touched the primitive instincts of the people. It was commonly believed that Draga was sterile as a result of a surgical operation. This does not seem probable. If she had had such an operation while she was in France it seems unlikely that anybody would hear about it except her immediate family, who would hardly have broadcast it. This was the nineteenth century, in Belgrade as anywhere else. But it is still more unlikely that it was performed before she went to France, for it is rarely required by very young women. It is a little difficult to believe that if it had ever been performed Draga would have ventured to announce shortly after her marriage that she was expecting a child, for the doctors and the nurses who had attended on her would have become potential dangers, threatening even her life. Furthermore, a famous French gynæcologist examined her and confirmed her opinion. Careless as fashionable doctors become, it is hard to imagine one failing to notice that an expectant mother lacked a womb; and it is not likely that he would have accepted a bribe, or that Alexander, who was in difficulties with his exchequer, could have raised one.

In the spring of 1901 there were rumours that Draga had been mistaken or had lied. The Tsar of Russia offered to lend the court two of his own physicians. Because he had been Kum at the wedding he would have had to be godparent to the first child, and it is possible that he had heard the gossip from Belgrade, thought he had been rash in backing the unpopular pair, and wanted to keep clear of any dubious proceedings. These two Russian doctors declared that Draga was not pregnant, but they explained clearly enough that this was not the result of a surgical operation but of a malady that might necessitate one. They also explicitly stated that the symptoms of this malady might easily have misled Draga into believing herself pregnant, and that the French gynæcologist's diagnosis might have been justified at the time when it was made.

The mischief was done. The people's mind was nursing an image that it always likes to hate and dandle in its hatred, the woman who is death, who is a whore and barren. They were moved to new folk-lore by this story, which troubled them by allusions to all sorts of dangers specially feared by the blood, to threats against kingship, to pollution of the race. Before long it was believed that Draga had been frustrated by the Tsar in an attempt to palm off as heir to the throne a child belonging to a sister of hers named Petrovitch. It is quite true that Madame Petrovitch was pregnant; and it may be true that in panic, finding her own hopes of pregnancy were false, Draga had thought of a 'warming-pan baby.' If that were so, only those who have never felt fear can blame her. Her situation was daily made more perilous by the conduct of her wretched brothers, who were certainly insane. The Serbian habit of expressing high spirits by discharging firearms into the air has alarmed many travellers, but these two young men indulged in it in a manner that alarmed even the Serbians. They also insisted that when they entered a café or restaurant the band should play the national anthem. If they did not start the rumour that one or other of them was to be adopted as heir to the throne, they at least behaved in a way that supported it and made it seem the beginning of anarchy.

From Draga's photographs it can be seen that she grew rapidly stout, old, wooden. A hostile newspaper published a serial written round the prophecies of Mata of Krema, and she brooded on the fate that had been foretold for her. She must have been aware, for she was not a fool, that her husband's reign was a tragic catastrophe. The change from dependence on Austria had done Serbia no whit of good. If Austria gave Alexander bad advice Russia gave him none at all, and that was worse, for though he had been on the throne ten years he had no knowledge of how to govern independently. The constitutional routine that steadied Russian absolutism was utterly unknown to him. For too long he had defended his crown and his very existence by alternate cringing and terrorism, and he could conceive no other procedure.

In 1901 he promulgated a new and democratic constitution, and almost immediately quarrelled with the Radicals whom the country elected to work it. Very soon he swept it out of existence and appointed a military dictatorship under General Tsintsar-Markovitch. The task of the Government was not to be performed. The finances of the country were in ruins, largely through the rogueries of Milan. The Army and Government officials were irregularly paid. Graft tainted every service. Nobody's liberty was safe. And both interior and foreign policy, owing to the long period of Austrian tutelage and Alexander's inability to profit by its termination, presented a completely bewildering spectacle to the people.

In April 1903 rioters were shot down in the streets of Belgrade. In May there was a General Election, with all returns grossly falsified by the Government. On the night of June the eleventh General Tsintsar-Markovitch went to King Alexander and told him that he could no longer face the task of ruling the country when the people were so solidly against him. This news distressed and angered the King, and he covered him with bitter abuse. But later he became calmer and admitted the reasonableness of the resignation, and asked only that his Prime Minister should carry on in office till a successor could be found. About ten o'clock the interview ended, and the King and Queen committed a last imprudence. Every evening a military band played in the gardens in front of the palace, while the crowds walked to and fro. The King and Queen went out on a balcony and sat there surrounded by Draga's sisters, including the one who was supposed to have assisted her in a plot to foist a false heir on the throne, and her two insanely ambitious brothers. Through the gathering darkness the people looked at the royal party with hatred that was strangling in its intensity, that had need to come to a climax. Meanwhile Tsintsar-Markovitch had gone to his home and sat up talking to his wife over a glass of wine. There were two reasons why they did not go to bed. Their eldest daughter, a girl of twenty-one, was married to a young officer named Milkovitch, who was that night on guard at the palace, and she was expected to give birth to her first child at any moment at her own home, which was in a neighbouring house. Also both Tsintsar-Markovitch and his wife felt sorrow over his resignation, and concern lest it should lead to royal disfavour.

In the cafés and garden-restaurants the usual summer crowds were sitting listening to the gipsy bands and watching the fireflies among the trees. There stands by Kalemegdan Park a hotel called the 'Serbian Crown,' which is distinguished by a certain romantic, haunted grace, as if the shutters had been flung back by ghosts keeping trysts made in a past and more passionate age. It has a long veranda which on warm nights is thrown open to the air, and there, on this night of June the eleventh, which was the anniversary of the murder of Prince Michael Obrenovitch thirty-five years before, sat a party of officers who attracted a great deal of attention. One of them was 'Apis,' Dragutin Dimitriyevitch, who ten years later was to give out guns and bombs to the lads from Sarajevo who wanted to kill Franz Ferdinand. They were drinking an enormous amount of plum brandy, and they called repeatedly for the tune which was played in honour of the Queen when she appeared in public, 'Queen Draga's Kolo.' Once at least they got up and danced the kolo, the Serbian national dance, forming a circle with their arms on each other's shoulders and their feet shuffling in an intricate rhythm. It was not extraordinary that they should dance the kolo. To this day soldiers will do that at any minute, outside their barracks or when they have to wait in a public place, say at a railway station. But it was extraordinary that these officers should dance Queen Draga's kolo, considering her unpopularity. It was explained for many of the onlookers by their drunkenness. A number of them were visibly drunk by eleven o'clock.

Shortly after that hour they left and walked towards the palace. They were joined by certain other parties of officers who had been spending their evening at various cafés and the Officers' Club. Some of them also were flushed and riotous, but some were quite sober and well able to play their appointed parts in the conspiracy. One of these was Draga's brother-in-law, Colonel Mashin. His motive in leading these soldiers against the palace may be taken as largely base. He had received large gifts of money from King Milan, who had often sent him on interesting missions; with exquisite inappropriateness he had been one of Serbia's representatives at The Hague International Peace Conference of 1899. All these benefits had stopped at the marriage of Alexander and Draga, when Milan left the country to die. This must have inflamed to fever-point his resentment against Draga for her failure to appreciate his brother's delirium tremens. Of Mashin nothing noble has ever been disclosed. But other leaders of the conspiracy were of a quite different sort. One lived to be a great man, of proven courage and wisdom, incorruptible in a time of temptation, never forgetful of his peasant origin, and always loyal to the peasants. His family speak of him as selfless, austere to himself, and tender with all others. Their followers also were of different qualities. Some were going to the palace in the expectation of murder and loot. Others went to demand the abdication of Alexander and to promise him and his wife a safe conduct over the frontiers on condition he did not name either of the Lunyevitza brothers as his successor. And of the eighty-six conspirators twenty-six had come up that day from scattered garrisons in answer to telegrams from Mashin telling them to get leave on any pretext and hurry to Belgrade, and were still not quite sure what was going to happen.

From the restaurant some went to the barracks of certain regiments to keep them from leaving for the defence of the palace when the alarm was given. Others went to the palace and gave the previously arranged signal, which was to bring them the King's equerry to open the outer door and lead them to the royal bedroom. But he had already repented of his consent to the conspiracy and had reacted to repentance in the manner of a Dostoievsky character. He had not betrayed his comrades to the King, he had simply sat in a chair in the entrance-hall and drunk himself into a state of unconsciousness, so that he would be unable to hear them when they came. Eventually they had to explode the locked door with a dynamite cartridge. This gave the alarm inside the palace and out. The King's aide-de-camp ran to the telephone but found the wires cut. Then the electric lights went out, either because the system had been damaged by the explosion or, some say, because the aide-de-camp turned off the central switch. Outside some gendarmes ran out of the neighbouring police station, saw a mob in the street, and began to fire. But what they thought was a mob was the Sixth Regiment, who had been brought out of barracks by one of the conspirators, and the soldiers answered fire. For a quarter of an hour there was a battle, but then the lie which had brought the Sixth Regiment to the palace spread to the police. They were told that King Alexander

was turning Queen Draga out of the palace and that they had been
sent for to keep peace in the town while she and her family were sent
off to the frontier; and at once they ceased action. The same lie had
disarmed the palace guard. All stood silent, bemused, cataleptic,
because of their hatred of this woman.

The King's equerry was shocked out of his drunken sleep and
staggered to the door. The conspirators cried out that he had
betrayed them and 'Apis' shot him dead. There is no record that
this inveterate plotter of *attentats*, who dreamed all his life long of
murdering crowned heads, ever killed anyone with his own hands
except this dazed and unimportant man. Terrified, with the din
of the street-fighting in their ears, they sent over to the house
of a doctor near by and asked for candles. Since the doctor was
told the story of Draga's expulsion, he gladly gave them. With
these feeble lights the conspirators hurried into the palace, not
knowing how long they had left for their work, and blundered
about amongst the shifting shadows and the litter of furniture.
The palace was a fine example of the school of interior decoration
to which the dynasties of Europe seem irresistibly drawn, and they
had to find their way among objects including many bead *portières*,
a huge black bear that someone had shot during the Bulgarian War,
marble fountains removed from old Turkish palaces, an immense
number of occasional tables covered with bric-à-brac, tom-toms,
and Turkish hookahs. They stumbled about, knocking things
over, and tried to find their way to the royal bedroom. Sometimes
enemies detached themselves from the shadows, loyal members of
the palace guard, who were instantly killed. One was Milkovitch,
husband of Tsintsar-Markovitch's eldest daughter, who was that
night in childbirth.

Concerning these loyalists a divergence of opinion soon appeared.
Some were merely for overpowering the King and Queen, others
were for outright murder and did it. There must have been a certain
amount of mutual distrust among the conspirators themselves by
the time they struggled through the darkness to the royal bedroom
and found that the King and Queen had gone. There was no
question but that they had just left, for the bed was still warm, and
a French novel had been thrown down on the bed-table, open and
face-down. Now the conspirators had reason to feel real fear. If the
King had got away and roused those soldiers who were still faithful,
they would all lose their lives. They ordered the aide-de-camp,
whom they had wounded in the shooting downstairs, to be brought
upstairs and they questioned him. Though he was weak and in pain
he lied glibly and sensibly to gain time. First he persuaded them to

go down and search the cellars, which they did for an hour. When they were satisfied that there was nobody there they ran upstairs and ransacked the rooms again, some holding candles while the others drew their swords and poked them under sofas and pierced curtains with them, and beat them on the walls to detect secret doors. Their situation was becoming more and more desperate.

Meanwhile two officers had been sent with a company of soldiers to the house of Tsintsar-Markovitch. When they knocked at the door the General and his wife thought a messenger had come from their daughter's house. But owing to the conversation that they had been having about the results of his resignation, he was not surprised and he received them courteously and tranquilly. The senior officer told him that they had been sent to place him under arrest in his own house until it was time for him to go to the palace to hand over the seals of office. The General still showed no surprise and treated them as soldiers doing their duty, bidding them sit down while he gave them cigarettes. They smoked for a while. The senior officer showed signs of agitation which puzzled his junior, who did not know that they had been sent to kill the General. After a time the General rose and said, 'I will go and order some coffee,' and as soon as he turned his back on his guests the senior officer lifted his revolver and shot him three times. The assassin stood in great distress, crying out that he had been ordered to do this thing, while the junior officer knelt down and took the dying man in his arms. 'Your Majesty, Your Majesty,' Tsintsar-Markovitch said with his last breath, 'I have been faithful to you. I did not deserve that you should do this thing to me.' And in this error he died.

At the palace, King Alexander and Queen Draga were hiding in a little room that opened off their bedroom, scarcely more than a wardrobe, where her dresses were hung and her maid did her sewing and ironing. There had been a secret passage specially built by King Milan to meet just such an occasion as this, but Alexander had scornfully had it bricked up. The door to this wardrobe room was covered by the same wallpaper as the bedroom walls, and it completely deceived the conspirators, perhaps because they searched by candlelight. The King and Queen kept silent till they heard their enemies question their aide-de-camp and then go stumbling down to the cellars. Then the King went to the window and cried to the soldiers whom he saw dimly standing about in the gardens about the palace. But they were all some way off, and he was leaning from a dark window, and they had been told that the officers of the palace guard were protecting their King against a conspiracy started by Draga and her family. They stood silent and immovable. The hatred of Draga had become a wandering spell, an enchantment that played about the city, sealing the mouths and paralysing the bodies of all its inhabitants.

The royal pair seem to have given up the attempt to save themselves for a time and to have tried to clothe themselves decently. The King was wearing trousers and a red silk shirt, and Draga had found lying about a pair of white silk stays, a petticoat, and yellow stockings. She did not dare to open a cupboard to get out a dress, for fear of making a noise, and they were in darkness. Their torture lasted for about two hours. Then the Queen, who was standing at the window, saw an officer come into the gardens just below, and recognized him by his walk as the Commander of the Royal Guard. She leaned out and cried to him, 'Come and save your King! He is in danger!' The Commander halted, looked up, and made sure that it was she. He raised his revolver and fired at her: or rather at the Austrian Empire, at our evil earth, at our polluted species, at sin. A wide shot, for she was in fact none of these things. It was no wonder he missed her.

This Commander went round to the entrance-hall and found the conspirators, with their drawn swords in their hands, wrangling with the dying aide-de-camp, who was on the point of persuading them to search another building near by. He told them that he had seen the Queen at a window near the royal bedroom. They ran back to it at once, but still could not find the wardrobe room. An axe was fetched from a woodshed in the palace courtyard, and one of the officers struck the walls till he came on the door. It was locked, and there is no evidence whether it was broken open or whether the King and Queen unbolted it under promise of safety. All that is known is that at the last they stood in their bedroom, the flabby spectacled young man and the stout and bloated middle-aged woman, fantastically dressed, and faced a group of officers whose shaking hands held guttering candles and drawn swords and revolvers.

Mashin was there, but so was a leader of the highest character. This man asked the King if he would abdicate, and was answered with the bitterest words a son ever spoke. 'No; I am not King Milan, I am not to be overawed by a handful of officers.' Then all the revolvers in the room fired at once, and Alexander fell into Draga's arms. He cried, 'Mito! Mito! How could you do this thing to me?' Mito was the familiar name of Tsintsar-Markovitch. Alexander died in the belief that he had been assassinated by order of the man who had died an hour before, in the belief that he had been assassinated by order of Alexander. Then the revolvers fired again, and Draga dropped to the floor. A madness came on most of the men in the room. They stripped the bodies and hacked them with their swords, gashing the faces, opening their bellies. Some of them who did not run amuck shouted to them that they must all go away now that the deed was done, now that partisans of the King and Queen might come in and arrest them. This, however, did not do anything to restore decency to the scene. For with a dreadful sanity the men who had been stripping and slashing tumbled the naked corpses out of the window into the gardens below. This was sound common sense and guaranteed their own safety, for it showed that both King and Queen were dead and there was now no one to protect or be protected by, since there were no Obrenovitches left to succeed to the throne. But it added another indecency to the scene. Alexander's arms had always been much more developed than the rest of his body; and as there was a spark of life in him he clung to the balcony with one hand as he went over, and an officer had to sever his fingers with a sword before he would let go. When he had been cast down on the lawn his other hand closed on some blades of grass.

The morning broke; and although it was June some rain fell about four o'clock. That brought the Russian Minister out of his Legation, which looked across a chestnut avenue at the palace. He had been watching the tragedy all night through the slits in his shutters. Though he could certainly have taken steps to rescue the King and Queen, he had intervened neither then nor when he had been informed of the conspiracy, which had happened two or three days earlier. For a great number of people had known of it beforehand. Mr. Miyatovitch, who was then Serbian Minister in London, received a full description of it at a spiritualist séance held by Mr. W. T. Stead three months before. The medium, Mrs. Burchell, had visualized the scene with singular fidelity. Such at least was the opinion of everybody present who came from Finsbury Park, though a gentleman from Hounslow heard nothing. Other persons, however, received intimations later and from more materialistic sources. The Austrian Government knew of it, and certain movements of troops on its frontiers could be explained only by that foreknowledge. But it would not issue a warning to Alexander, its enemy. And the Russian Legation would not issue a warning to its highly unsatisfactory friend, who was so

unpopular, so awkward, and, above all, so unlucky. But there is
a point at which a gentleman must draw the line. Entering the
garden, the Russian Minister went up to the officers who were
standing about and pointed to the corpses. 'For God's sake,' he
said, 'carry them into the palace. Do not leave them here in the
rain exposed to the gaze of the public.' This sentence may well be
preserved as a symbol of the kind and degree in which the great
powers have acted as a civilizing influence in the Balkans.

Belgrade VII

Thereafter the city blossomed like the rose. Serbia was young again, it was refreshed, it tossed its head and threw off its sleep and faced the morning in its strength, because Draga was dead, because the bad woman had been killed. The actual ills that Alexander Obrenovitch had committed, or at any rate consented to, the imprisonments and floggings, the corruption and fraud, were quickly forgotten. For long the people have spoken as if he had been murdered because he was Draga's husband, and as if his murder were secondary to hers, and as if the murders were purgations of a plague, which was nothing but Draga.

This is a mystery. For Draga was insignificant. She is one of the most negative people who appear in history. At no point in her career does she seem to have said or done anything that could be remembered five minutes later. She represents prose in its defective sense, in its limitation to factual statement, in its lack of evocation and illumination. Her enemies found it difficult to make a case against her, because she provided them with no material from which any deduction could be made; and for the same reason her friends could build up no defence. When she went into a room she did nothing that was noble and nothing that was base, she stood up if standing was good, and she sat down if sitting was better. No man except Alexander seems to have loved her, and although a few women felt a protective kindness towards her they do not talk of her as in any way interesting.

Such a woman could not have committed a great crime, and indeed she never was accused of any. To plan the substitution of an heir to the throne would have been disgraceful, had she ever truly done so; but that can be left on one side, for Serbia's hatred of Draga was mature before she ever became Queen. It was ostensibly based on the immorality of her life as a young widow in Belgrade; and let us visualize exactly what that meant if it were real. A beautiful and dull young woman lived in a small room somewhere in Belgrade; on the walls there would be hung many family photographs and a poor bright rug or two, and on the wooden floor there would be one or two others of these poor rugs. There would come to her sometimes men who would perhaps be comely and young like herself, for she was not so poor as to need to take lovers against her inclination. There would follow some

565

conversation, agonizing in its banality had one had to listen to it, but not criminal, not threatening to anyone's peace or life. It would not be unnatural if the couple soon abandoned the use of words, and turned to embraces, which would as like as not be purely animal in inspiration. Then, if the worst of what the Queen's enemies said was true, they went into another room, in which there was a bed, and lay down on it. Once they were there nature limited them to the performance of a certain number of movements which except to the neurotic are not abhorrent, which some people find agreeable and others disagreeable, which by common consent have to be judged ethically solely by their results, since they themselves carry hardly any but a momentary and sensational significance.

Now, this is admittedly not what one would hope to find in the past of a royal personage. A queen should know only the love that lasts, as a king should know only the courage that never fails. But it must be reiterated that Draga was hated before there was any probability that she should become Queen: and that makes the power of the scene over the popular imagination remarkable. It might have led to the birth of an illegitimate child, but it did not. It might have led to the transmission of venereal disease, but it did not. Still, the potentiality shadows it. But even so it is extraordinary that the Serbs should have been distraught and frenzied by a scene that was darkened by only the shadow of horror when they were so familiar with scenes that were black with its substance. They were used to murder, to the bullet that sped from the forest branches, to the rope that strangled the captive who the next day would be pronounced a suicide. They were used to the fraudulent trial, the lying witnesses, the bribed judge, the undeserved imprisonment, and the thieving fine. Yet it was Draga who sent their blood rushing to blind their eyes, who made them draw their swords in a completely supererogatory murder. For there was no reason whatsoever to kill Draga. Alexander it would perhaps have been impossible to leave alive, for his obstinacy and his sense of grandiose destiny would have made him cling to power if it meant wrecking his country's peace. But Draga could safely have been put on a train and sent off to spend the rest of her days between Passy and Nice. There was no reason at all why the conspirators should have spent that night of panic in the palace staggering about among the occasional tables and the bead *portières*, accumulating damnable guilt.

But it would be fatuous to deny the dynamic effect of the deed. There was at first the movement towards demoralization that would have been expected. The conspirators murdered not only the King and Queen and the Prime Minister, but also the Minister of War, and Draga's two brothers. These two young men were brought to the barracks of the regiment and confronted by the Commander of the Royal Guard, the same who had shot at Draga from her garden. 'Their Majesties are now dead,' he said to them with ferocious irony. 'The moment has come for your Royal Highnesses to command. Do not hesitate. We are your faithful subjects. Pray give your orders. But if I may presume to advise you, you will not ask for more than a glass of water and a cigarette.' They were then taken out into a courtyard and shot by a firing-party commanded by Lieutenant Tankositch, the friend of 'Apis,' who eleven years later was to aid him in giving arms to Princip and his friends for the Sarajevo *attentat*. After such a blood bath there was bound to be disorder and there was some looting of the palace and the houses of the murdered Ministers. But in a day the Army was brought to heel, and the business of government was competently carried on. A provisional Government was formed, and after a peculiar religious service, of a kind not prescribed in any missal, attended by the Ministers and conspirators, a deputation set off to Geneva to offer the throne to Peter Karageorgevitch.

It is incontestable that Peter Karageorgevitch had known nothing about the murders before hand. His worst enemies never seriously alleged that he had been consulted, and several of the conspirators admitted that they never dared tell him. He was a man of fifty-seven, with an upright character and a complete incapacity for pliancy, and they were well aware that had he known of their intentions he would have stiffly denounced them to the proper authorities. For a royal pretender he had had a curious career. He was the grandson of the great Karageorge and the son of the Alexander Karageorgevitch who had ruled without zest from 1842 to 1858. Because of his father's democratic principles he had been brought up as much like a peasant child as possible, and had gone out from the palace to the national school every morning. At the time of his father's abdication he was sent to a boarding-school in Geneva, which was singularly successful in marking him for life. To the end of his days there was grafted on the essential Serb in him an industrious, conscientious, Puritan Swiss. He spent his holidays on his father's estate in Transylvanian Hungary and learned the elements of farming; but he elected to become a soldier, and at seventeen went to France and passed through the Military Academies of Saint-Cyr and Metz. He fought in the Franco-Prussian War, and was wounded and decorated, and laid the foundations of the rheumatism that was to cripple him in later life by swimming the Loire in midwinter to escape capture. We have an odd vignette of him bursting into a house in a French town one quiet evening during the campaign, explaining that he had heard from the streets the tones of a harmonium and begging that he might be allowed to play on it. He then spent a happy hour wheezing out Serbian national airs.

He remained inveterately serious and simple. It is doubtful whether he ever learned that a harmonium is not chic. But the rest of his family established itself in Paris and could have taught him that the right thing was a grand piano covered with a Japanese embroidery. His younger brother, Arsenius, became a dashing Russian officer, and later a well-known boulevardier; of his young cousins, Alexis and Bozhidar, much can be read in Marie Bashkirtseff's *Journal*. Indeed, one of the most interesting exhibits in Prince Paul's Museum at Belgrade, though it has some fine Corots and Degases and Van Goghs and Matisses, is a charming picture by Marie of the bearded young Bozhidar, leaning from a balcony threaded with orange nasturtiums, looking down on a Paris silvery with autumn. This boy grew to be a water-colourist of some merit and wrote several Loti-like books about travel in the East which consisted almost entirely of colour-adjectives; he was a close friend of Sarah Bernhardt, and was in much demand for masquerades because of his capacity for Arielesque gaiety. Alexis and he both spent money like water on highly amusing and refined objects. They were conspicuously not what would be expected of the grandchildren of a Serb pig-breeder and rebel chief. But all the genes characteristic of Karageorge seemed to have been transmitted in almost uncomfortable purity to Peter.

He spent some time in France after he left the Army, and studied the elements of law and social science. It was at this time that he translated John Stuart Mill's *Essay on Liberty* into Serbian. In 1875 he went to Bosnia and fought in the revolt against Turkey, and was unremittingly in command of a company of comitadji throughout the whole three years of the campaign. After the settlement he went to Serbia, not to advocate his claim to the throne but to see his native country again. He was soon expelled by the police. Five years later he went to Montenegro to help Prince Nicholas reorganize his army, and married one of his daughters. In 1889 his wife died of consumption, leaving him with three children, two boys and a girl. By this time he had taken an intense dislike to his father-in-law, whom he rightly considered dishonest and dishonourable, so he moved with his family to Geneva.

There he lived in great poverty. There was barely enough money to feed the family, and some people in Switzerland believe that Peter added to his income by some such work as the copying of legal documents. He also took his full share in his family responsibilities. He had taken furnished rooms, and an elderly cousin acted as nurse to the children, but there were three of them, and presently four; for his brother Arsenius had married in Russia a member of the plebeian but wealthy family of Demidoff, and they had separated, leaving a little boy (now Prince Paul) without a home. Peter brought them up with a tender, anxious, austere care. He gave them their first lessons, and he watched over their manners and morals with an unrelenting eye. A Serb and a Swiss, he thought that one must be a soldier, and that one must be good. The training that this faith brought on the four children is not altogether agreeable to contemplate. They were all over-worked. They had to attend the ordinary Swiss elementary school during the day, which was supposed to be a whole-time education, and in the evening they had to learn the Serbian language and history and literature from a Serbian governess and their father. They were also subjected to ferocious discipline. In 1896 their mother's sister Helen married the Crown Prince of Italy, and invited the children, of whom she was very fond, to the wedding at Rome. The little daughter was not allowed to go because her marks at school had been bad.

But he was kind and loving. To understand his severity towards his children it must be remembered that he intensely disapproved of his own family. He thought Arsenius might probably be saved in so far as he was a good soldier, but his Swiss side found much to disapprove of in his brother considered as a dashing Russian officer and the divorced husband of Aurora Demidoff. As for Bozhidar and Alexis, he thought they were degeneration itself. Alexis had married a very rich American lady, and to please her had tried to get Peter to stand back and let him assume the role of pretender, pointing out that he at least had the money to finance his claim. This had struck Peter as a most unholy proposal, and he coldly continued to instruct his children in the legend of Kossovo and deprive them of their meals if they were not in time for them, trusting that by such means he would prevent them from resembling their relatives. But it could not escape his notice that his elder son, George, showed undoubted signs of the unstable charm which he disliked in Alexis and Bozhidar, and, what was perhaps more serious, the moody violence that had darkened the genius of Karageorge.

It was perhaps for this reason that in 1898 Peter accepted an offer made by the Tsar to receive all three of his children in St Petersburg, give them the freedom of the palaces, and educate them at the best Russian schools. It is certain that his liberal tendencies would have been better pleased if the children had been educated in Switzerland or France; but he could no longer face the responsibility of bringing them up on scanty food, in uncomfortable lodgings, and without advice, when there was this handsome alternative. But though this improved his family's lot it initiated a most uncomfortable routine for him. The little Paul could not at first be taken to Russia for reasons connected with his parents' troubles, and he remained in Geneva under the care of Prince Peter and his cousin till later. But Prince Peter had to take care that his children remained good Serbs and were not Russified, so he visited them in Russia in the holidays, travelling as cheaply as possible. These journeys were not wasted. His second son, Alexander, remained curiously impervious to Romanoff luxury, practised his father's frugality and chastity, and cultivated Serb circles in St. Petersburg. The Roman virtue of this man was real, and had its emanations.

The news of the Belgrade murders must have been unspeakably disgusting to Peter Karageorgevitch. He had never supported his claim to the Serbian throne by the most faintly dubious action. He had announced that he believed himself to be the rightful ruler of Serbia and that he was willing to take up the sceptre whenever the Serbian people demanded it; and there he had left it. Now he was faced with what is the nastiest thing in the world from an Army officer's point of view: an Army conspiracy. He was faced with what is the next nastiest thing from a soldier's point of view: the slaughter of unarmed civilians. Also one victim had been a woman, and there had been a great deal of drunkenness. It must have been the bitterest moment in his life when he went to his café to read the morning newspapers and found them black with this blot on his country, which—as it must have struck him after the first second's shock—was also a blot on his own name. When the Skupshtina elected him King he was faced with one of the most unpleasant dilemmas that has ever faced a decent man. He knew that if he accepted the throne the whole world would suspect him of complicity in the murders, he would be ostracized by all other reigning sovereigns, and he would be in the deadliest personal danger, since mutiny is no exception to the rule that the appetite grows by what it feeds on. But he knew that Serbia needed a good king and that there was nobody else likely to rule well except himself. He knew too that there were many people in Serbia who trusted him to save them from misgovernment. It is also possible that the Tsar had given his children their education on the understanding that he would go to Belgrade when the opportunity served and protect the country from the Austrian devourer of the Obrenovitches.

When the twenty-four delegates from the Skupshtina arrived in Geneva and offered Peter Karageorgevitch the Serbian crown, he stiffly accepted. Without temporizing, without waiting till European excitement had subsided, he took the train to Belgrade and got there thirteen days after the assassination. By that time all powers except Austria and Russia had withdrawn their diplomatic representatives as a mark of scorn. Peter greeted his people with a gravity which made it plain that it was for him to approve them rather than for them to approve him. His first legislative act was to remove the censorship on the foreign press. No newspapers from abroad were to be seized or blacked. 'Serbia,' said Peter, without explaining himself further, 'shall henceforth know what other countries think of it.'

His immediate problem was how to deal with the regicides. He never dealt with them in the complete and clear-cut way suggested by the over-zealous apologists of the Karageorgevitches. It is said in one history that he removed them all within three years. This is not true. Peter recognized that there were differences in guilt among the conspirators, and that some were high-minded men who had conceived the crime out of public spirit and had never intended it to be so bloody. Even under strong foreign pressure he refused to expel these men from office. One was the famous General Mishitch, who showed himself a great soldier in the Balkan wars and still greater in the World War. But others he recognized as base and sooner or later excluded from official favour: Mashin was one. And Peter would not persecute those who denounced the crime. When he was reviewing a regiment four months after his arrival a lieutenant left the ranks and shouted in his face that the blood of Alexander was still crying out for vengeance; the young man was removed from the Army but was not otherwise punished. Soon the baser regicides banded together to protect themselves, and in 1907 they assassinated the head of the anti-regicide group. Peter used that assassination, in conjunction with an Austrian attempt to eject him and give the Serbian throne to an Anglo-German, to sober public opinion. He told his people that if they insisted on behaving like wild beasts they must expect to be caged and put in charge of a keeper. But he himself was well aware that though he had thereby cleansed public opinion he had not succeeded in rounding up all the conspirators of dangerous character. Chief among these was Dragutin Dimitriyevitch, who was protected by the extraordinary personal fascination which made him a popular figure in the Army.

But the question of the regicides mattered far less than can be supposed. Incredible as it may seem, it was dwarfed by the astonishing achievements of which the people, refreshed by their sacrifice of Draga, found themselves easily and happily capable. Peter began a programme of reforms in the simplest, most Genevese spirit. When his major-domo came to him on the day of his arrival to inquire what sort of menus he preferred, he exclaimed, 'Menus! Menus! I have no time for menus! Never speak of such things to me again.' He can indeed have had very little time, for he started to reform Serbia on foot and by hand. He would walk without military escort to a hospital, and if he found all the doctors out, as was not unlikely to happen in those Arcadian days, he wrote in the visitors' book, 'King Peter has been here.' He would visit a school, and if he found the children playing and the teachers gloomily discussing their grievances, he wrote on the blackboard, 'King Peter has been here.' He went on, however, to deal with the grievance which most afflicted doctors and teachers, and indeed many civil servants and soldiers in Serbia, and explained a great deal of disordered conduct: he saw that they were paid regularly. Swiss honesty, which in the place of its origin sometimes seems too much of a good thing, affected the Serbians, after thirty-five years of Milan and Alexander, as picturesque and exotic. It was to them what their national costume is to us. They stood gaping, while by continuous probity Peter brought his own state to financial order and even won the respect of international financiers. Alexander had been unable to raise a loan in Vienna even by pledging the entire railway system of Servia, but Peter was cheerfully lent nine times the sum his predecessor had vainly importuned.

The Serbs rose to their dawn. They followed him along the new path that Serbia had not trodden for five hundred years, to the world where success, and golden, luxuriant success at that, was won not only by the sword but by the plough, the loom, the pen, the brush, the balance. For the first time since the Turkish conquest the lost civilization of Byzantium showed signs of revival, and at last it seemed as if the monotonous reciprocal process of tyranny and resistance were to be displaced by a truly polymorphous life. The Serbians spread their wings, they soared up to the sun. When Austria saw them it was enraged. It contrived a snare to get Serbia back under its tutelage. When King Peter reorganized his army, under the commandership of his brother, Arsenius Karageorgevitch, he proposed to buy some big guns from France; he also arranged a customs agreement of a most brotherly sort with Bulgaria. Vienna rapped him sharply over the knuckles.

The agreement with Bulgaria must be cancelled, and the guns must be ordered from Austria. King Peter refused; so did his Prime Minister, Nicholas Pashitch, the Lloyd George of Serbia, a crafty idealist; so did the intoxicated Serbians. 'The Obrenovitches are gone, the Karageorgevitches are here, we are no longer slaves,' they said.

Austria then declared economic warfare on the Serbians. It looked as if it must conquer, and that easily. Serbia had only one industry, pig-breeding, and there was nothing simpler than raising the tariff against their livestock to prohibitive heights. That killed at one blow nine-tenths of their trade. However, the Serbians tightened their belts, and very soon found new markets in France, Egypt, and even England, while the price of meat mounted to preposterous heights in Austria. The 'pig war' lingered on for five years, from 1905 to 1910. As its failure became manifest, Austria made it clear she had not accepted defeat. In 1908 the abominable Aehrenthal chose to annex Bosnia and Herzegovina; which, once annexed, were a threat to every state between Austria and the Black Sea. It meant that the Habsburgs, having failed to subdue Serbia by economic warfare, meant some day to settle the score by the use of arms. Again the Serbians spread their wings and soared up to the sun. 'If there is Austria,' they said, 'there is also Russia. We have no need to cringe before any state; we are a strong people whose strength will buy us allies.' And this indeed was true, now that they had a king who could not be bought and would not let his Ministers sell themselves.

This moment must have found King Peter at his happiest and his most sorrowful. The contrast between the disorganized and dishonoured Serbia which he had taken over from the Obrenovitches and the proud and virile state which was now making its own terms with the great power was, indeed, the sign of one of the most dramatic personal achievements in modern history. But it is quite possible that he was not altogether pleased by the company his triumph had brought on him. He had had to accept Russian upbringing for his children in his days of exile; now he had to accept Russian protection for his subjects. But the democratic Serb, the liberal Swiss, the translator of John Stuart Mill's *Essay on Liberty*, could not but disapprove of Russian absolutism; his frugality must have been repelled by the luxury of the Romanoffs; and he knew that the South Slavs had every reason to fear the Russian movement known as Pan-Slavism. That had become evident in the seventies, when the Turks had tried to kill Greek and Serb influence in Macedonia by founding of the Bulgarian Exarchate, which was to make the government of the Macedonian churches independent of the Greek Patriarchate. This Exarchate was inevitably anti-Serb, as Serbs wanted self-government for their own churches; and Russia lent her support to the Exarchate, because it feared the Austro-Hungarian Empire and its dominance of Serbia and therefore wished to have no Serbs in Macedonia. Hence it put up the money for Bulgarian churches, schools, and newspapers, which had no other object than to turn Serbs into Bulgarians. In fact Russia had, in the name of Pan-Slavism, destroyed the unity between the Serbs and the Bulgarians which was necessary if the South Slavs were ever to maintain themselves against the Turks and the Austrians. Later Russia sometimes retrieved her position, but she often backslid. This was no stable ally of the sort that King Peter, King Rock, would have chosen.

He had another and more personal sorrow. His elder son, the Crown Prince George, took a prominent part in politics and became the leader and idol of the violent pro-war party. Of his charm and courage and ability there was no doubt; and he was even sound in judgment. When the rest of Europe still held blind faith in the efficiency of the Austrian Army he predicted its collapse under the first prolonged strain. But the fantastic strain in him which had grieved his father in the old days at Geneva was flowering into a monstrosity not to be ignored. King Peter could not deal with him in the summary manner that would have been best; his popularity with the Army, and particularly among those officers who had formed the more disreputable part of the regicidal conspirators, would have made it dangerous to seclude him. But in 1909 he fell into trouble. He killed his valet in an attack of rage. The most charitable account has it that he found the man reading his letters and kicked him downstairs with no intention of inflicting on him any serious injury. The King then inflexibly required that the Crown Prince should resign his claim to the succession in favour of his brother Alexander, though he felt obliged to let him retain his commission in the Army. It has been said by envenomed critics of the dynasty that this was the result of Alexander's intrigues; but he was then a silent boy of twenty-one, who was still a student at the Military Academy in St. Petersburg, and had paid only a few brief visits to Serbia during the six years since his father's accession. King Peter, who was now sixty-five, cannot have been altogether certain of the quality of the boy he now recalled from Russia to help him against his internal and external enemies.

Now destiny took charge of his kingdom. The Austrian provocation became more and more insolent. In January 1909 there had been a spectacular trial in Zagreb where fifty-three Serb subjects of the Austrian Empire had been charged with conspiring against their country with the connivance of the Serbian Government, and thirty-one of them had been convicted on obviously forged or frivolous evidence. In March 1909 the Austrian Foreign Office handed the official historian of the Habsburg family, one Dr. Friedjung, forged documents which purported to prove the existence of a new conspiracy against the Empire not only directed but financed by certain members of the Serbian Government. King Peter and his Ministers issued a statement roundly calling the Austrians liars, and over fifty Serbian politicians backed up that statement by filing actions for libel against Dr. Friedjung in Vienna. The subsequent trial showed beyond a doubt that all his evidence was fabricated. Smiling, the Serbs went home, and prepared themselves for the war that must come. They believed that it would not come at once. Russia had been greatly annoyed by the annexation of Bosnia, and her annoyance was a fortress wall behind the Serbians, clearly visible to the Austrians.

There was work they could do in the meantime. Macedonia was still unredeemed, a Christian province in the hands of the Ottoman Empire: a hell of misgovernment, that had known no respite for five hundred years, save for a brief period of international control at the beginning of the twentieth century, which had been terminated by the Austro-Hungarian and German Empires for no other reason than the Teutonic hatred of the Slav. It was now in the deeper darkness that follows a false dawn. The Young Turk movement had suddenly swept away the Sultanate, and established a constitution promising liberty to all its subjects of whatever race. Very soon it appeared that the Young Turk was simply the son of the Old Turk, with a Prussian military training, and there was set on foot a ferocious scheme for denationalizing the Macedonian Christians. Serbia and Bulgaria not only abhorred this spectacle from the bottom of their Balkan souls, but were touched by it in their self-interest. If the Austrians were to have an empire stretching to the Black Sea they would first go down the valley of the Vardar through Serbia and get command of the Ægean at Salonika, and Serbia and Bulgaria would be impeded in their resistance to his invasion, because Macedonia, a strip of disordered country in the hands of their enemies, the Turks, would lie between them and their allies, the Greeks. There was no question but they must drive out the Turks; and with that resolution there came to the Serbs an extraordinary happiness. There is nothing like the peculiar gratification which fills us when we find ourselves able to satisfy the claims of reality by enacting a fantasy that has long warmed our imagination. The Serbians, to live in modern Serbia, must realize the poem that was written in the monasteries of the Frushka Gora, that was embodied in the dark body of the Tsar Lazar. They had not to choose whether they would make a day-dream into fact: they were under the necessity of choosing between life with that day-dream and death without it.

There has been no fighting in our time that has had the romantic quality of the Balkan wars that broke out in 1912. The Serbians rode southwards radiant as lovers. The whole West thought them barbarous swash-bucklers, and fools at that, advancing on an enemy who had never been defeated, and had found some magic prescription for undeserved survival. That mattered nothing to these dedicated troops, wrapped in their rich and tragic dream. They were determined to offer themselves to the horrors of war in a barren land where the climate is bearable for only four months in the year, where there were dust-storms and malaria and men who had been turned by art to something more savage than savagery. Those horrors accepted them. The summer burned them, the winter buried them in snow; on the vile Turkish roads their commissariat often broke down for days and they had to live on roots and berries; the wounded and malarial lay contorted among the untender rocks; they suffered atrocities and committed them. But they were not perturbed. In their minds there lay the splendid image of Slav empire, potent in spite of time and defeat, like the Tsar Lazar in his coffin. It can be conceived as filling with a special glory, altogether Byzantine in its rigidity of forms and intense incandescence, the mind of the Crown Prince Alexander, for the Karageorgevitches permitted themselves no other poetry.

In three months the poem had completed itself. By December 1912 the Ottoman Empire, as Europe had known it for six hundred years, had been destroyed. The Serbians and Bulgarians and Greeks laughed in the astonished faces of the West. All should have gone magically well, had it not been that the quality that the West has shown in its dealings with the Balkans was too pervasive and enduring not to tarnish even the purest metal of achievement. It may be remembered that the Slavs had won this same victory once before, in 1876; and had been diddled out of their victory first by Russia's incompetence, which made them sign the unsatisfactory Treaty of San Stefano, and then by the criminal idiocy of all the great powers combined, and of England in particular, which replaced it by the infinitely more mischievous Treaty of Berlin, designed for the maintenance of Turkey in Europe. This had left all sorts of unsettled issues for the Serbians and Bulgarians to quarrel about; and the intrigues it engendered had placed upon the Bulgarian throne in 1887 a being of tortuous impulses and unlovely life called Prince Ferdinand of Saxe-Coburg-Gotha. During his reign he watered and tended corruption as if it were a flower. The disorder of Bulgarian politics, which is often cited as a reproach to the Balkans, was very largely an importation of this detestable princeling. He was always a tool of Austria, although his bias towards treachery makes all statements about his character difficult to frame; and after the Karageorgevitches had freed Serbia from the Austrian yoke he became one of Austria's most useful instruments in its increasingly frenetic anti-Russian and anti-Serbian policy. He had been forced to join with Serbia in the Balkan wars by the will of his people, and indeed his Austrian masters told him that there was no objection against it, provided he was ready to do a Judas-trick at the end. And this he did.

Ferdinand assured the Serbians and the Greeks that he had shifted his allegiance from Austria to Russia, signed pacts with them, and went to war at their side, though not as the most satisfactory ally imaginable. With money and munitions he was extremely stingy, but he was generous to a fault in the manufacture of 'incidents' which faced too simply the problem of rousing public sympathy. A staff of his blackguards distributed bombs among trained bandits who exploded them in mosques, which not unnaturally inspired the infuriated Moslems to rush out and massacre Christians. This pleased neither the Christians who were massacred nor the Serbs and Greeks, who found themselves regarded with suspicion by neutral observers. Such, however, was the melodic line traced by Ferdinand's soul. Then, when the peace came he saw to it that discord between the Serbians and the Bulgarians should be its first result. The Treaty of San Stefano had awarded Bulgaria territory that gave her a position in the Balkans only to be justified if she had been the real liberator of the Peninsula, and the three peoples had gone into the war with a loose understanding that the Treaty might at last be carried into effect if Bulgaria provided that justification. But in that she failed. Ferdinand had mismanaged his gallant army so that they had in fact not even done their share of the fighting; and the decisive battle of the campaign, Kumanovo, had been won by the Serbians alone. It was natural that Serbia should demand some recognition of her special services in the peace treaties, which should take the form of a common frontier with her ally Greece and access to the sea at Salonika. This was an absolute necessity to her existence, as Austria had recently created out of the wreckage of Turkish territory a puppet state of Albania, which was to be an Austrian stronghold that should control Serbia and Greece.

But Ferdinand impudently resisted these reasonable demands. The Judas-trick he had been asked to perform by Austria was the sowing of deep dissension between the Serbians and Bulgarians at the end of the war, if need be by the betrayal of his own subjects' good name. During the summer of 1913, while the peace treaties were being discussed, he spread among his troops all manner of lies about the Serbians. Then on June twenty-eighth, St. Vitus's Day, which was the anniversary of the defeat of the Christians on the field of Kossovo, which was to see the assassination of the Archduke Franz Ferdinand and Sophie Chotek, he issued certain orders which even his own kept Government was not allowed to know. Many Bulgarian officers dined with Serbian officers to celebrate the recovery of Kossovo; when they returned to their trenches they were told that the discovery of a conspiracy made it necessary for them to make a surprise attack on the Serbian regiments in the early morning. This is one of the vilest episodes in Balkan history; and it was not committed by a Slav. It was not a vestige of Balkan medievalism. It cannot be laid at the door of the Turk. It was the fruit of nineteenth-century Teutonism.

But the Serbians, knifed in the back, continued within their dream, to achieve their poem. The powerful magic of that dream, that incantatory poem, blunted the knife. They beat back the Bulgarians. The Greeks, the Turks, the Roumanians, closed in on Ferdinand, who was unperturbed. He believed his time was yet to come. He made a secret pact with the Emperor Franz Josef towards the end of 1913, that he should place all the resources of Bulgaria at the disposal of Austria and Germany, provided he was given a large portion of Serbian and Greek and Roumanian territory if he kept his throne, and a fat pension if his subjects expelled him. He then set to work to thrall Bulgaria to Germany by a loan, to which the assent of Parliament was given during a most peculiar scene. Ferdinand's Prime Minister faced the assembly with a revolver in his hand, but all the same the opposition deputies did considerable damage on the Ministerial Front Bench by using inkstands and books as missiles. The angels must have been greatly perplexed by the determination of European statesmen to civilize the Balkans by sowing them with German princelings; for in Belgrade, the only capital in the Peninsula ruled by a Slav, things were going better. It would be light-minded to deny that the second Balkan War cast for a time a red shadow of barbarism across Serbian life. That treacherous early-morning attack on the trenches, though the guilt lay on the Bulgarian crown and not on the people, engendered a hatred that met atrocity with atrocity; and the first Serbian official who went to settle the newly acquired territories behaved as if they were conquerors and not liberators. But the liberalism of King Peter was quietly attending to these natural inflammations of a national spirit which had suffered war; it is typical of the difficulties of his task and of the infinite incalculabilities of Balkan history that by far his most sagacious aide in dealing with the problem of the tyrannous and dishonest officials in Macedonia was one of the regicides. The tiger, blood on its claws, crossed itself; the golden beast became a golden youth; church and state, love and violence, life and death, were to be fused again as in Byzantium.

Hardly had the transformation been made when it was threatened; and the threat shocked and startled. It was known to all Europe, and to Serbia best of all, that the Central powers were preparing for an aggressive war, but it was not generally expected that they meant to act in 1914. What the intelligence services of the great powers had reported in these years has never yet been published, though this would be far more enlightening than any amount of diplomatic correspondence. But it is said that both France and Russia were for some reason convinced that Germany and Austria would not make war until 1916, and certainly that alone would explain the freedom with which Russia announced to various interested parties in the early months of 1914 that she herself was not ready to fight. So Serbia was in a trance of amazement when Franz Ferdinand and Sophie Chotek were killed at Sarajevo, and it became certain that the enemy was going to use the murder as a pretext for instant attack. There could have been no more hopeless moment. The Serbian peasant army had been fighting since 1912, and every soldier had either already gone home or was homesick. The arsenals were empty of arms, the treasury was empty of money to buy them. There was a difficult internal situation. King Peter was now completely crippled by the rheumatism he had contracted in swimming the Loire to escape capture during the Franco-Prussian War, and only ten days before he had appointed his younger son, Alexander, already recognized as Crown Prince in place of his elder brother George, as Regent; and since George had acquitted himself well in the Balkan wars his partisans were excited and angered. It looked as if the history of resurrected Serbia was to end in the same moment as it began.

Such was the authority of Russia that some Serbs were incredulous. Nicholas Pashitch, the Prime Minister, did not believe that

Austria's outcry was serious, and was half-way to Athens on a visit to Venizelos when he had to be recalled to Belgrade, to deal with Count Berchtold's famous ultimatum. This had been framed in defiance of the report of a high official of the Austrian Foreign Office who had been sent to Sarajevo to investigate the crime and had come to the conclusion that it was 'out of the question' to suppose a connexion between the Serbian Government and the assassins. The ultimatum made eleven demands. The Serbian Government was required:

(1) To admit a policy of incitement to the crime, and publish a confession of this and a promise of future good conduct which should be dictated from Vienna, and both published in the official journal at Belgrade and read to the Serbian Army by King Peter.

(2) To suppress all publications inciting to hatred of Austria-Hungary and directed against her territorial integrity.

(3) To dissolve the Society of National Defence (a perfectly respectable society which had no connexion whatsoever with the crimes), and to suppress all other societies engaged in propaganda against Austria-Hungary.

(4) To eliminate from the Serbian educational system anything which might foment such propaganda.

(5) To dismiss all officers and officials guilty of such propaganda, whose names might be communicated, then or later, by Vienna.

(6) To accept 'the collaboration in Serbia' of Austro-Hungarian officials in suppressing this propaganda.

(7) To open a judicial inquiry concerning those implicated in the crime, and to allow Austro-Hungarian delegates to take part.

(8) To arrest without delay Major Tankositch and Milan Tsiganovitch, the Serbians who had supplied the Sarajevo assassins with arms.

(9) To supervise the Serbian frontier so that no arms and explosives might pass, and to dismiss the customs officials who had helped the assassins.

(10) To give explanations regarding the 'unjustifiable' language used by high Serbian officials after the crime.

(11) To notify Vienna without delay of the execution of all the above measures.

Serbia was given only forty-eight hours to accept or reject this ultimatum.

It was not easy to accept. The fifth and sixth demands meant that Serbia must become a spiritual vassal of the Austrian Empire, in conditions that were bound before long to produce provocative incidents, with a sequel of bloodshed and annexation. Yet the Serbian Government accepted that ultimatum, with only three reservations. It pointed out that the constitution of the country made it impossible to comply with certain of the Austrian demands, such as interference with the freedom of the press, without legislative changes impossible to enact during the time-limit; but it was willing to submit these points to the arbitration of The Hague Tribunal. Pashitch took the humiliating document of his country's submission to the Austrian Legation a few moments before six o'clock on the evening of July the twenty-sixth; though the Legation was a quarter of an hour from the station the Austrian Minister and his staff were in the train on their way to the frontier by half-past six, a sign that the acceptance had been rejected. The three reservations were better than he had hoped; though it would not have mattered if there had been none at all, for the legal adviser of the Austrian Foreign Office had already handed in a memorandum as to how war could be declared on Serbia no matter what her reply to the ultimatum. 'If Serbia announces her acceptance of our demands *en gros*, without any protest, we can still object that she did not within a prescribed time provide proofs that she carried out those provisions which had to be executed "at once" or with all speed, and whose execution she had to notify to us "without delay." '

By such means Serbia was trapped, and the whole of Europe doomed. Count Berchtold and his friend Conrad von Hötzendorf, who were resolved upon hostilities, persuaded the Hungarian Minister, Count Tisza, to withdraw his opposition, and gained the consent of the old Emperor Franz Josef by a totally false statement that Serbian troops had fired on the Austrian garrison of a Danubian port; and the final declaration of war was dispatched on July twenty-eighth. The consequences were clearly foreseen by all these plotters against peace. If Austria attacked Serbia and stretched out its hand to the Black Sea, Russia was bound to intervene; for Russia did not want, for reasons that may seem far from frivolous in view of what has already been written in this volume, to have the Austrian Empire as a neighbour on another front, and it could not like to see Slavs subject to Teutons. Germany must join in on the pretext of aiding Austria, because it had its own appetite for Russian territory, having long hankered after the Baltic, and because it could now find a pretext for attacking France, who was Russia's ally and was showing dangerous signs of having recovered its strength after the defeat of 1870. Immediately millions of people were delivered over to the powers of darkness, and nowhere were those powers more cruel than in Serbia.

Belgrade was at once bombarded. An army of three hundred and fifty thousand men fought a rearguard action, without big guns to answer their enemy's artillery, with so few arms that some regiments had but one rifle to two men. They gave up Belgrade, their only town, their earnest that they were Byzantium reborn materially as well as spiritually, and pressed back, bitter and amazed. But Belgrade did not fall. It was left to be defended by a single division commanded by a colonel, who blew up the iron bridge across the Danube so that it blocked the river against Austrian traffic, and dressed the customs officials and such townsfolk as remained in extemporized uniforms so that Austrian spies reported a large garrison; and by a miracle it remained intact when the Serbian Army turned on its tracks, and, to the world's amazement, sprang at the Austrians' throats and drove them out of the country in less than a month. They even invaded Austrian territory and set foot in Bosnia and Herzegovina and the Serb parts of Hungary, and the Frushka Gora itself.

But the Austrian Empire had numbers. It had at this moment little else; it had so little virtue or wisdom or even common sense that again and again the student must marvel that this was the same state as eighteenth-century Austria. But what it had it used, and it sent back its armies in September. This time they enjoyed a certain disgraceful advantage. During the first invasion they had laid waste the country, pillaging the crops, burning the houses, murdering the civil population: at least three hundred and six women are known to have been executed, as well as many people over eighty and children under five. So the Serbian Army had this time to retreat over a devastated countryside which could give it no food and offered it much discouragement, not diminished by the floods of civilian refugees, some Serbian, some from the Slav parts of the Austro-Hungarian Empire, all hungry and footsore and with tales to tell of the enemy's malign brutality. There might have been panic had it not been for the spirit of the Karageorgevitches and the higher command. King Peter hobbled up to some troops that were wavering under artillery fire to which their army had no answer, and said to them, after the manner of a Homeric general, 'Heroes, you have taken two oaths: one to me, your king, and one to your country. From the first I release you, from the second no man can release you. But if you decide to return to your homes, and if we should be victorious, you shall not be made to suffer.'

They did not go. To lead them General Mishitch, the grave and reluctant regicide whom King Peter had refused to dismiss, now appointed fourteen hundred young students as non-commissioned officers. Of these boys, who before the war had been studying at Belgrade, Vienna, Prague, Berlin, and Paris, one hundred and forty survived the war. Arms came suddenly to this army, sent from England. These men who were so spent that they no longer lived by their experience but by what is known to our common human stock, these boys who had no experience at all and therefore were also thrown back on that same primitive knowledge, alike they forgot the usual prudent opinion that dying is disagreeable, and valued death and life and honour as if they were heroes who had died a thousand years before or gods who were under no necessity to die. They flung themselves again on the Austrians. By the end of December they had retaken Belgrade. They took down the Hungarian flag that had floated above the palace and laid it on the steps of the Cathedral when King Peter went with his generals to the mass of thanksgiving for victory. They had to thank the Lord for a real suspension of natural law; for when the Austrians had withdrawn over the frontiers there remained behind rather more Austrian prisoners of war than there were Serbian soldiers.

It is not known what King Peter thought of the future. In his old age he had become more of a Serb, and the Genevan mark was not so strong as it had been. He was now wholly a warrior king, a Nemanya reborn. But it is said that the Crown Prince Alexander, the pale and pedantic graduate of St Petersburg Military Academy, knew that the victory was no more than a breathing-space, and that there must follow another assault, which would mean defeat. This certainly must have become a growing horror when it was manifest that the country had received a wound deeper than any that could be inflicted by military action. Some of the Austrian troops had come from parts of Galicia where typhus was endemic, and they had brought the germs with them. Where food was scarce, water was polluted, and vast districts were littered with dead men and animals far beyond the power of scavenging, the fever spread. The hospital system, particularly in the recovered Turkish provinces, was utterly unable to cope with this inundation of disease, and indeed it killed a third of all Serbian doctors. There came out several foreign sanitary units, of which Dr Elsie Inglis's Scottish Women's Hospital left an imperishably glorious name. Alexander, himself sickening of an internal malady, spent his days travelling up and down the country organizing a medical service.

In the summer of 1915 Austria approached Serbia with proposals for a separate peace. The Skupshtina rejected them one blazing day, at Nish, and expressed its resolution to continue the war till all Slavs were liberated from the Austrian yoke. This meant that Peter and Alexander and Pashitch had come to believe that the life of their nation was not worth preserving unless the tyrannical power that had threatened them throughout their entire existence were disarmed and disintegrated. They thought it better for the nation to go down into death for a time on the chance they might live again, if France and England and Russia destroyed the might of the Central powers.

In the heat and dust they waited. About them refugees wandered over a famined land; the soldiers who waited by their guns were worn out by three years of fighting in medieval conditions of sanitation and commissariat; and on the near frontiers massed enemies which their Allies, the British and the French, would not allow them to disperse. Incredible as it may seem, though Great Britain and France were fighting Germany, they still accepted the legend that Bulgaria was the most civilized and powerful of the Balkan states, though the only evidence ever adduced for such an estimate was that it is the most Germanized among them; and the Allies formed the curious notion that it would be the easiest thing in the world to persuade the Bulgarians to fight against the Germans in defence of the Serbians, who had beaten and humiliated them only two years before. They therefore forbade the Serbians to attack the Bulgarian armies which were massing on the border, and which could have been easily defeated, and when Serbia asked for a quarter of a million men to repel the impending invasion, they made the astonishing reply that they were arranging for the Bulgarians to supply these troops. This they attempted to do by offering Bulgaria territories which Roumania, Greece, and Serbia had acquired in the Balkan wars. This naturally turned Roumania and Greece against the Allies, and filled the hearts of the Serbians with perplexity and bitterness.

In September the invasion began. By October the Serbian Army, which now numbered a quarter of a million men, was faced with three hundred thousand Austro-German troops, under the great strategist Mackensen, and as many Bulgarians. It was now necessary for the country to die. The soldiers retreated slowly, fighting a rearguard action, leaving the civil population, that is to say their parents, wives, and children, in the night of an oppression that they knew to be frightful. Monks came out of the monasteries and followed the soldiers, carrying on bullock-carts, and on their shoulders where the roads were too bad, the coffined bodies of the medieval Serbian kings, the sacred Nemanyas, which must not be defiled. So was carried King Peter, whose rheumatic limbs were wholly paralysed by the cold of autumn; and so too, before the retreat was long on its way, was Prince Alexander. The internal pain that had vexed him all year grew so fierce that he could no longer ride his horse. Doctors took him into a cottage and he was operated on for appendicitis. Then he was packed in bandages wound close as a shroud, and put on a stretcher and carried in the procession of the troops. It is like some fantastic detail in a Byzantine fresco, improbable, nearly impossible, yet a valid symbol of a truth, that a country which was about to die should bear with it on its journey to death, its kings, living and dead, all prostrate, immobile.

The retreating army made its last stand on the field of Kossovo, where a short time before, in a different dream of the Creator, it had known victory: where the Tsar Lazarevitch had proved that defeat can last five hundred years. Above them circled enemy aeroplanes, evil's newest instrument. After a last rearguard action to shake off the Bulgarians, they turned to the wall of Montenegrin and Albanian mountains that rises between Kossovo and the Adriatic. Rather than face that icy path into exile, many of the soldiers and the civilian refugees turned and fled back towards Serbia and were butchered by the Moslem Albanians, who had been the favoured subjects of the Turks and bitterly resented the Serbian conquests in the Balkan wars. The rest of the Army obeyed the order that they must take this desperate step in the hope that some might survive and be reorganized on the Adriatic shore with the help of the British and French. When they came to the foot of the mountains the weeping gunners destroyed their guns with hand grenades and burning petrol. The motor-drivers drove their cars and lorries up to a corner where the road became a horse-trail on the edge of the precipice, jumped out, and sent them spinning into space. Then all set out on foot to cross the five-thousand-foot peaks that lay between them and the sea. Some took other routes, but on any of the roads their fate was the same. They trudged in mud and snow over the mountain passes, the December wind piercing their ragged uniforms. Many fell dead, some died of hunger. They were passing through one of the poorest parts of Europe, and the inhabitants had little to sell them, and in any case were instructed to withhold what they had by the King of Montenegro, who, though he was Serbia's ally and King Peter's father-in-law, had come to a treacherous understanding with Austria. The Serbians ate the raw flesh of the animals which fell dead by the track, they ate their boots. Some died of dysentery. Some were shot by Albanian snipers. Of the quarter of a million Serbian soldiers, one hundred thousand met such deaths. Of thirty-six thousand boys nearing military age who had joined the retreat to escape the Austrians, over twenty thousand perished on this road. Of fifty thousand Austrian and German prisoners, who had had to follow the Serbians because their own military authorities had refused to exchange them, the greater part never came down from the mountains.

When the survivors reached the coast they found that the Allies again had failed them. The port they arrived at was blocked with shipping sunk by Austrian submarines and it was impossible either to bring them food or to ship them away. They had to trudge southwards, still hungry. Too much of the responsibility for their safety rested on the Italians, who had already signed the Treaty of London, and knew that if the Serbian nation should by a miracle reconstitute itself it would certainly dispute the allocations of Slav territory made by that imbecile document. At last the French and the British settled that the Serbians should be sent to the Greek island of Corfu, since Greece was under obligations to the Allies which not even their diplomacy could wholly annul. Still hungry, they were put on boats to be taken out to the transports. It happened, that when the first boatloads pushed off, not many hours had passed since a food ship had been torpedoed in the channel outside the harbour, and loaves of bread were still floating on the waves. Many of the Serbians had never seen deeper water than a fordable stream, and these jumped out of the boats to wade towards the bread, and sank immediately. Others, who knew the northern rivers or the lakes of Ochrid or Presba, tried to hold back those who wanted to jump, and there were struggles which overturned some of the boats. Thus many were drowned.

On Corfu the Serbian Army fell down and slept. Some never awoke. For quite a long time there was still not enough food, and there was a shortage of fuel. Every night for weeks boats put out to sea weighed down with those who had been too famished and diseased to recover. The others stirred as soon as the spring warmed them, stretched, and looked up into the sunshine, and were again golden and young and victorious, golden and ancient and crafty, as they had been in the Balkan wars. Alexander, restored to health, travelled to Paris, Rome, and London, and urged on the Allies the value of an expeditionary force that would use Salonika as a base and would strike up at the forces the Central powers were maintaining in Serbia. He carried his case, and his troops were drilled, equipped again, inspired again. In summer they embarked for Salonika. A year after they had been driven out of Serbia they were back on

Serbian soil, fighting the Bulgars. In November 1916 they put forth their strength and took Kaimakshalan, the Butter-churn, the mountain that dominates the southern plains of Macedonia and the road to the north, and had been thought impregnable. In effect the Near Eastern campaign was over. But the war was not sufficiently mature in its other theatres to make it safe to harvest the victory, so the Serbian Army sat in Macedonia and waited. In the summer of 1917 the Serbian Government and a committee of South Slavs issued a manifesto proclaiming a 'Kingdom of Serbs, Croats, and Slovenes, a democratic and Parliamentary monarchy under the Karageorgevitch dynasty, giving equality of treatment to the three religions, Orthodox, Catholic, and Mussulman, and in the use of the Latin and Cyrillic alphabets.' They announced, in fact, that the Austro-Hungarian Empire was destroyed and that out of its ruins they were making a kingdom of the South Slavs, such as had inherited the glory of Byzantium eight hundred years before. The poem was now written. In the autumn of 1918 the Serbian armies, as the spear-head of the Allied forces, drove into the enemy forces and scattered the Bulgars back to Bulgaria, the Austrians and Germans back to a land which was no land, which had lost all institutions, even all its characteristics, save that discontent which springs of conceiving poems too formless and violent ever to be written. The more poetic nation was in Belgrade thirteen days before the Armistice.

Belgrade VIII

What sequel to this story would not be an anticlimax? There are heights which the corporate life has never surpassed and which it attains only at rare intervals. It is not so with the personal life, for the mind, in its infinite creativeness, can always transcend any external event. To King Peter, it may be, the war was only prelude to a greater experience. He had taken no part in the campaign of 1918, since by that time he could only hobble. He went to Greece, and did not leave it even when victory was achieved. The state entry into Belgrade took place without him. He lingered where he was till late in 1919, and then went north, but no further than Arandzhlovats, the simple and even shabby spa near the Karageorgevitches' old home at Topola. One day, without warning, he returned to Belgrade, which did not recognize him, for while he was in Greece he had grown a long white beard like a priest's. The Prince Regent and his people welcomed him, and begged him to take up residence in the palace, but that he would not do, for he said it would be wrong, since he was no longer King. It is proof of the strangeness of the Karageorgevitches, and their ambivalent attitude to their own royalty, that Alexander also would not move into the palace, though it was new and comfortable. He made his home in a simple one-storied house in the main street of the town, which he furnished hardly more comfortably than if it had been his staff headquarters in time of war.

Peter went to live in a villa overlooking Topchider, the park where Prince Michael of Serbia was murdered and little Alexander Obrenovitch learned to swim, and he became more and more of a recluse. He was not indifferent to his people; he cut off his beard because they complained that it disguised their beloved King from them. But all his forces were devoted to a relationship which it is hard to imagine. The Karageorgevitches were not now a united family. Alexander was busy forging the new state of Yugoslavia into a reality, and was working all day and half the night. Peter's brother, Arsenius, was not without the strain of frivolity that had made his cousins, Alexis and Bozhidar, such wellknown boulevardiers, and he had returned to Paris, where he was to prove that there are many paths to a serene old age. The son of Arsenius and Aurora Demidoff, Prince Paul, was virtually secretary to the Prince Regent, and worked as hard as his chief.

A cloud had fallen between Peter's only daughter, Yelena, and her relatives. She, having married the Grand Duke Constantine, had been caught up in the Russian Revolution. Her husband had been killed and she had been put in prison, from which she was released only through the intervention of a Serbian officer who had joined the Bolsheviks. On her return to Belgrade it began to be whispered that the Karageorgevitches were greatly angered by some circumstance connected with her flight from Russia. Either they thought, the story ran, that she had accepted her freedom on dishonourable terms or that she had not honourably observed those terms. These were probably fantasies spun by outsiders to explain a quarrel that for insiders had some more prosaic significance. But the fact remains that the Grand Duchess soon left Yugoslavia for ever and settled in Switzerland. There were no others in the family except Peter's elder son, George.

Peter had dispossessed George of his birthright and given his crown to his younger brother; and daily George's mind was growing wilder and more restless. It might have been judged dangerous that the father and son should live together in the quiet villa at Topchider. But they were very happy. Peter treated his son with a gentle devotion which guided him away from tragedy. The old King was no longer what Geneva and France had made him, he had lost the Western sense that a man's life ought to describe a comprehensible pattern. He was not appalled when George laughed or wept louder than was reasonable, or sent a bullet without cause out into the night. If his handsome son's spirit was wandering where it could not be followed, it might be that he too was seeking wisdom. They lived together in perfect love, and when the old man lost his wits and fell mortally ill in the summer of 1921, George upheld him with his patient kindness. At the time of the death the Prince Regent was in Paris, and the news threw him into a state of collapse so complete that his doctor forbade him to travel back to Belgrade for the funeral. So George was his father's chief mourner, and performed his duties with great dignity. Thereafter he was seen no more among ordinary men. Enemies of Alexander say that this was due to fraternal hate, but that is not the opinion of foreigners who came in accidental contact with the elder brother.

Alexander was not permitted by his duties to cultivate the personal life. He must struggle with the external world, so anticlimax was his lot; and he resented it, for he was perhaps the last ruler in the world to be inspired by a Homeric conception of life. The day should always be at the dawn, all men should be heroes, the sword should decide rightly. He found himself, on the contrary, smothered with small mean difficulties. These were the harder to bear because he had foreseen them and would have avoided them if it had not been for the blindness of others. He was unable to proceed with the real business of state-making because, do what he would, he could not secure unity among the Croats and Slovenes and Serbs; but he himself had never wished to include the Croats and Slovenes in his kingdom. He had hoped, at the beginning of the war, not for a Yugoslavia, not for a union of all South Slavs, but for a Greater Serbia that should add to the kingdom of Serbia all the Austro-Hungarian territories in which the majority of the inhabitants were Serbs, that is Slavs who were members of the Orthodox Church. The school of thought to which he belonged rightly considered the difference between the Roman Catholic and the Orthodox Churches so great that it transcended racial or linguistic unity.

It cannot be doubted that this Greater Serbia would have been a far more convenient entity than Yugoslavia, but it could exist only on two conditions: it must be supported on the east by the Russian Empire, and divided on the west from German-speaking countries by Catholic Slav states. In 1917, however, the Tsardom fell in ruins, and of all the Slav subjects of the Austrian Empire the Czechs alone were sufficiently highly organized to convince the peacemakers that they could be entrusted with the governance of an independent state. So Serbia had need of the Catholic Slavs and they had need of her; and the Kingdom of the Serbs, Croats, and Slovenes, as Yugoslavia was then called, became inevitable. But that did not annul the temperamental incompatibilities of the Serbs and the Croats, which faced the King with a sea of troubles.

It is likely that Alexander was the less able to bear these dissensions with equanimity because of the personal tragedy that had befallen him during the war. We now know that while he was a student at the Military Academy in St. Petersburg he had fallen in love with one of the Tsar's daughters, though she was still a schoolgirl. He had mentioned it to his father, who had asked the Tsar if Alexander would be allowed to present himself as a suitor when the girl was of a proper age, and had received an encouraging answer. In January 1914 Mr Pashitch, the Serbian Prime Minister, visited Russia to inquire whether, now that the Balkan wars were over, Alexander might begin his courtship, and the permission was given. It is probable that Alexander would have gone on this errand shortly after he had been declared Regent, had not the war broken out.

We cannot be certain that this courtship would have been

successful, for we know that the Tsar's daughters were allowed to choose for themselves in such matters, and that the Tsarina wished none of them to marry outside Russia. But it is beyond doubt that this was for Alexander a real affair of the heart. He did not merely want to be the husband of one of the Tsar's daughters. He wanted to have this particular daughter as his wife. In March 1917 the news came that the Tsar had abdicated and that he and his family were in the hands of the revolutionaries. Some time in July 1918, while Alexander was in the sweltering heat of the Macedonian plains, all of them were put to death at Ekaterinburg. It seems reasonable to ascribe Alexander's hatred of Bolshevism at least as much to this event as to temperamental bias or political prejudices.

For a very long time no other woman seems to have convinced him that she existed. After his father's death he looked about for a wife, but plainly only for dynastic reasons; and though the Princess Marie of Roumania was very beautiful, he probably chose her rather for her English connexions and her Romanoff blood. But he became devoted to her, and derived very great happiness from his life with her and their three sons. She was indeed an excellent wife for him, as she had inherited from her mother, the famous Queen Marie, a great deal of the fluency and brilliance that he lacked. She liked driving a high-powered automobile over mountains down to the Adriatic, she was fond of flying. She had also an instinct for comfort which was welcome in the Balkans. Between the Karageorgevitches' barbarous and glorious old home at Topola and the tremendous Byzantine assertion of majesty and death at Oplenats there lies, set among orchards and vineyards, a cottage planned by the Queen, where she and Alexander and the children lived the kind of home life, uncultured but civilized and amiable, that Queen Victoria made common form for European royalty. it is as if the Karageorgevitches, usually immersed in the tide of their terrible and splendid experience, had for a moment come to the surface to breathe.

The King had his marriage to console him, and, perhaps, his ambition. For he was still ambitious. He had come a very long way in his thirty-odd years. He had spent his childhood as the son of a pretender almost comic in his destitution, in a poky flat in Geneva, as a youth he had been lifted to a step of the Romanoff throne, and as a young man he had overthrown an imperial dominance that had pressed on his people for five hundred years, and before he was yet a ripe man had driven back another empire, the most formidable of Continental powers, and thereby reincarnated the glory of the Emperor Stephen Dushan. It is said that he meant to travel still further. He would never consent to be crowned. Though he was so resolute that the Karageorgevitch stock should be grafted on the Nemanya dynasty, no fresh door was ever opened for him in the crimson wall of Zhitcha Cathedral and walled up when he left it an anointed king, according to ancient custom. There is reason to suspect that he was postponing the ceremony till he might be crowned not king but emperor, and that of an empire greater than Stephen Dushan ever knew.

Alexander took a great interest in the internal condition of Russia, and he was convinced that the Bolshevik regime would not last more than twenty or thirty years. During this time he hoped to make a Balkan Federation, a real union of South Slavs, which might go in and rescue the North Slavs when Bolshevism had collapsed. Then he would be crowned in Zhitcha as King of Serbia and Emperor of all the Russias.

This dream was not as insane as it sounds to Western readers. The South Slav loves the Russian, White or Red, but he does not think him as efficient as himself, and the task of overthrowing Bolshevism would not seem to him any greater than his conquest of the Turk. Nor was it purely aggressive. The King believed, and was right in his belief, that the Slavs needed to protect themselves against Italy, Hungary, and the German-speaking peoples; and the firmer they were in unity the better. But whatever his plans and their justification, they involved Herculean labours. His heart, however, approved of Herculean labours; what afflicted him beyond bearing was the business which fell to him in the meantime, of settling the small differences of small men.

The primary disease of Yugoslavia was the same that was wasting every European country which had taken part in the war: a shortage of young and middle-aged men. Three-fifths of Serbia's man-power had been lost, and nine-tenths of the university students who had been made non-commissioned officers. The Croats had suffered terribly fighting for the Austrian Empire. It was, as it always is in war, the flowers that had fallen. There were no young and able leaders coming up, the pre-war politicians were worn out with age and responsibility, second-rate adventurers were taking advantage of the dearth of better men to obtain office for the sake of profit, and the distracted rank and file wrangled over these unsatisfactory leaders. The King suffered at all times from the professional soldier's inability to distinguish between an argument and a mutiny; but now he had some real excuse for finding the political controversies of his subjects disquieting.

There was another element in the situation which was common

to all combatant countries at this time; the old liberalism was faced with problems for which it had no solution. Although the King had been tempted in his youth into a flirtation with his brother's Praetorian Guard type of Fascism, he had been educated as an old-fashioned liberal and probably would have remained one had circumstances allowed it. But they did not. It is extremely difficult to maintain the freedom of the press, when that is used by different parties to advocate the assassination of each other's leaders. It is extremely difficult not to throw people into prison without trial if disorder is so great that the law courts dare not convict the most guilty disturbers of the peace. And the King could not discuss his difficulties with his liberal subjects, because he was incapable of understanding intellectuals.

Artists he might have understood better. He had grown up in contemplation of a historic poem, and was passionately fond of music, and his cousin and closest friend, Prince Paul, was a lover of great painting. But with intellectuals he had nothing in common. He could not—and perhaps this was because he was something of an artist—understand why they could not suppress their faculty of criticism in order to follow a common purpose. Underneath the great mountain of Durmitor in Montenegro there lies a dark and glassy lake, mirroring many snow peaks, which are doubly pure in their reflection, with the purity of their own snow, with the purity of its black crystal waters. By this lake the King once camped for thirteen days. To one of the secretaries who brought state papers to his tent he said, his prim voice trembling, 'If those intellectuals in Belgrade could come here and look at this lake as I have done they would not . . . they would not . . .' This is an idiotic remark from the point of view of those intellectuals who were defending the rights of man, who were protesting against innocent people being thrown into prison and the suppression of free speech. But it is not an idiotic remark from the point of view of a man who had realized the vision of the Frushka Gora.

The King was further handicapped by his inability, which was greater than one would have expected in a man of his age, to understand anything at all about the post-war left wing. He thought it sheer wickedness that many of his subjects should sympathize with Bolshevik Russia and that some should join the Communist Party. He asked why the very people who were most shocked if he used force against the Croats, no matter how mildly, should accept the Red massacres without a murmur, and he put the question without the capacity to listen to the answer, for he was thinking of a murdered girl. When he was told that this attitude was part of a revolt against poverty, he replied that there was no need for such a revolt, since people in his kingdom were much better off than they used to be, and if the country were allowed to settle down there was every hope that this might continue. In this he was perfectly accurate, yet quite irrelevant. A man who is hungry is suffering from an absolute discomfort, and cannot be comforted by the statement, or even believe it, that he was often hungrier when he was a boy, and that his father had been hungrier still.

Nor could the King understand why the intellectuals kept on talking about peace. In Belgrade there was once held an exhibition of German pictures which had been selected by a Serbian official in the Yugoslav Legation at Berlin. When the King visited it he made a conscientious inspection of the pictures, and then sent for this official. Instead of congratulating him he coldly censured him for including certain canvases by Käthe Kollwitz which were designed to expose the horrors of warfare. This and other manifestations of his distaste for pacifism were regarded by the left wing as proof of the bloodthirstiness of the man, but in that they were wholly mistaken. Few generals in modern history have experienced the horrors of warfare as fully as he had, and his was not the temperament which intoxicates itself with action. But he believed that it might be necessary again for Yugoslavia to fight for its life, and he therefore saw the discouragement of the fighting spirit as a step towards national suicide. He entirely forgot that it is the proper function of the intellectual to hold up certain moral values before the eyes of the people, even if it is not possible to realize them in action at the moment. But it must be conceded that his situation made that forgetfulness inevitable.

The King was, of course, entirely right in his assumption that Yugoslavia might have to fight for her life. Recent years, by bringing so many ill-favoured personalities to the fore, have made Mussolini seem by contrast genial and almost inoffensive, but we must not forget that he owes that character entirely to contrast. A face which might seem reassuringly normal in a criminal lunatic asylum might repel and terrify in a railway carriage. The part that Mussolini played in Yugoslavian affairs as soon as he had acceded to power was purely evil. He screamed insults at them for their possession of Dalmatia and constantly provoked riots and disorder; but that was the most innocent side of his relations with the country. There were two main centres of disaffection in Yugoslavia, Croatia and Macedonia, and in these Mussolini attempted to establish himself as a murderous enemy of civil peace. In Croatia he found it at first difficult to get a footing, for the rebels were for the most part men of high principle who had their wits about them and knew what happens when the lamb asks the fox for aid against the wolf. But the Macedonians were at once more criminal and more innocent. Their case was pitiful, for it was the result of ancient virtues running to waste in an altered world. The Macedonians, a magnificent people, had prepared the way for the Balkan wars by a perpetual revolt, sometimes open, sometimes covert, against the Turk. This was organized by the Internal Macedonian Revolutionary Organization—known as I.M.R.O.—which was formed in 1893 by Bulgarian Macedonians, bloodthirsty men who were nevertheless great heroes and pitiable victims.

When the Turks were driven out as a result of the Balkan wars Macedonia was divided between Greece, Serbia, and Bulgaria; and Bulgaria greatly resented the terms of the division. Some Bulgars wanted a purely Bulgarian Macedonia; others wanted an independent Macedonia, a dream state which was to be entirely free, though it would have had to be financed and to a large extent repopulated from abroad; others again wanted a federated state, similar to a Swiss canton. All these parties consisted of those who had been revolutionaries all their born days and who could no more have taken to a conforming way of life than an elderly seamstress could become a ballet dancer. They were also subjected to great provocation by the harshness of the Yugoslavs in forcing the many Bulgarian inhabitants of their newly acquired territory to speak Serbian and alter their names to Serbian forms, and the incompetence of many of the Yugoslav officials, which was, indeed, no greater than that which had been shown by the Turks or would have been shown by the Bulgarians, but was none the less (and very naturally) resented. They therefore reconstituted I.M.R.O. as an anti-Yugoslav organization.

In no time they formed a guerrilla army which had its headquarters near the frontier and repeatedly crossed it on raids into Yugoslav Macedonia, burning and looting and killing just as in the old Turkish days. Of the damage done there can be no accurate estimate, for the peasantry was too terrorized to report its losses to the officials; but it is said that over a thousand violent deaths are known to have occurred between the years 1924 and 1934. This reign of horror might have gone unchronicled, for the government of neither Yugoslavia nor Bulgaria wished to publish the shameful inability to keep order, had it not been that passengers on the Athens Express gazed astonished, since they knew that Europe was theoretically at peace, on the unbroken line of barbed wire entanglements, block-houses, redoubts, and searchlight posts which followed the Yugoslav-Bulgarian frontier. Every bridge and tunnel and station was guarded by soldiers in full battle kit; and even so the passenger on the Athens Express sometimes ceased abruptly to gaze and wonder, for I.M.R.O. liked to get bombs aboard the international trains, since explosions were reported in newspapers all over the world, and gave their cause publicity. But if the passenger was spared to continue his thoughts he might well have asked himself how I.M.R.O. could afford to maintain the standing army whose assaults made necessary this vigilant and elaborate defence, for the Macedonian peasantry was notoriously among the poorest in Europe.

There was, indeed, more reason for this question than even the prodigious view from the carriage window. I.M.R.O. published newspapers and pamphlets in Bulgaria and abroad. It maintained propaganda offices in all the Western capitals. It specialized in curious slow-motion assassinations that cost a great deal of money; a member would be sent to a distant place to murder an enemy of the cause and would be ordered not to do it at once, but to live beside him for some months before striking the blow. It also ran an expensive and efficient machine in Sofia which for many years dominated Bulgarian politics; indeed, I.M.R.O. became the Fascist Party of Bulgaria, murdering Stambulisky, the great leader of the Peasant Party, and routing the Communist Party, though that numbered a fourth of the electorate. In this last feat they were aided by the indecisiveness of the General Secretary of the Bulgarian Communist Party, one Dimitrov, later to be famous for his not at all indecisive part in the Reichstag trial. But that and all their other feats cost money. Some of this was given gladly by Macedonian supporters. Some of it was filched from Macedonians, whether supporters or not, by an efficient system of illegal taxation. The tax-collector who, whether he was a believer in a Bulgarian Macedonia or not, had kin in the country whose safety he valued produced two tax demands, one to be paid to the Bulgarian Government, and the other, amounting to ten per cent of the first, to be paid through him to I.M.R.O. But for a great part its funds were provided by Italy.

If Alexander sometimes acted brutally towards the insurgents he saw conspiring with foreign powers against the safety of his people, and towards the intellectuals who showed themselves so blind to the implications of these conspiracies, he cannot be altogether blamed. The situation was too confusing. It cannot have clarified it that no hostile act against a malcontent ever cost the King so dearly as the act of reconciliation he made with his arch-enemy, which seemed for long a great political triumph and was certainly his greatest moral triumph. This was the root of all the troubles that darkened the last six years of his life. From the first the leader of the Croat Peasant Party, Stefan Raditch, had been a thorn in the King's side. Not even Gandhi had a more magnetic effect on his followers, and though he guided them in all sorts of different directions he could claim consistency, for he never took them down a road that did not lead away from Serbia. Before the war he had been anti-Hungarian but fiercely pro-Austrian, with a deep veneration for the Habsburgs, and he had advocated the creation of a triune kingdom comprising Austria, Hungary, and a Greater Croatia which should include a conquered Serbia. After the war he preached an independent Croatia in the form of a republic where no taxes would be collected from peasants, prevented the Croat deputies from going to Belgrade and taking their seats in the Skupshtina, and attacked the Government in terms that, not at all inexplicably, led every now and then to his imprisonment.

In 1923 this situation should have been materially changed. He went to London and Mr Wickham Steed, the former editor of *The Times*, one of the few Englishmen who understood Balkan conditions, urged him to give up his republicanism, and work to shear the Yugoslavian constitution of certain undemocratic features and convert it into a constitutional monarchy on the English pattern. Raditch afterwards said he was convinced. But he omitted to mention this change of heart when he returned to Yugoslavia, and he was imprisoned and his party was declared illegal, largely because he had come back by way of Russia. This punitive action of the King and his Government was unwise and ill-tempered, but was not as silly as it seems. Raditch's own account was that he had called on Lenin to advise him to abandon Bolshevism and set up a peasant republic. It seems certain that he was moved to this trip partly by his love of travel, which was inordinate. But detached observers among the Bolsheviks believed he came to Moscow in order to blackmail Belgrade with the fear of social revolution, and it appears that while there he joined the Peasant International. Once he found himself in prison, however, he sent for his nephew and dictated to him a confession of his belief in the monarchy and the constitution.

Immediately the King was told of this declaration he appointed Raditch Minister of Education and gave ministerial posts to three leading members of his illegal party. It is proof of the strange political nature of the Croats that, though this was the first indication Raditch's followers had received that he had completely changed his programme, they do not seem to have been disconcerted for more than a short time. Raditch went straight from prison to the

King's palace, and there the two enemies sat down, talked for hours, and fell into an instant friendship. This was unbroken for five years. The royal household became very fond of him, and he constantly came to the palace simply as a familiar. He was a fine linguist, and the Queen liked speaking English with him. As his sight was failing she used to take his plate at meal-times and cut up his food for him. The King learned to like him better than he had liked any politician since the war.

In 1928 there fell the catastrophe. The country was in a disturbed state, and complained of many troubles. Some of these were inevitable: it had been necessary to unify the currencies of the country into a single unit, and a certain amount of inflation had followed. Some of these might easily have been avoided: the political parties were perpetually disintegrating into smaller and smaller factions, and this made it almost impossible for any government to maintain itself in power over any period sufficient for effective action. In ten years twenty-one political parties came forward to save Yugoslavia, and there were twenty-five changes of government. Raditch was still a Minister. It must be confessed that he had brought nothing new into political life, and that he had done little to distinguish himself from the Serbian Ministers he had for so long attacked. At this point, though he was theoretically left, he suddenly demanded a military dictatorship. 'Our national army,' he told the King, 'which is our national shrine in its finest form, can perhaps alone provide a generally recognized leader, strong enough to drive away corruption unmercifully, as well as lawlessness, to destroy partisanship in administration, and to overcome the political terrorism which is turning our entire country into a huge penitentiary.' This infuriated alike the political parasites and the sincere democrats of Yugoslavia, and to justify himself he carried on a campaign against corruption, defining the abuses which he thought made a dictatorship imperative, and named their perpetrators.

The baser newspapers called for his blood, desiring quite literally that someone should shed it. But it must be admitted that he himself conducted this campaign with less than perfect wisdom. He was violently provocative in a situation where the most pressing need was calm; and his violence was unrestrained. He was capable of standing up in Parliament and calling his fellow-Ministers swine. It was also unfortunate that the Germanic bias he derived from Austria made him speak contemptuously of all races outside the sphere of German influence. With difficulty, and only under the influence of the King and Queen, he had learned to accept the Serbians, but the remoter peoples of wilder Yugoslavia were hardly better than Negroes seen through the eyes of Southerners. He used the term 'Tsintsar' as an insult, as if it meant a kind of human mongrel, although the Tsintsari are a race of shepherds who have gone respectably about their business on the Macedonian uplands since the days of Byzantium. He was completely insensible to the poetry of the Yugoslavian idea, to the charity that inspired it in spite of its blunders and brutalities. It meant nothing to him, and to most Croats, that people had been rescued from the power of Islam and were restored to Christian civilization in the shelter of this state.

June is not a favourable month in Serbian history. On the twentieth of June 1928 a Montenegrin deputy named Punisha Rachitch, who was among those charged with corruption, entered the Skupshtina and fired five shots from a revolver. With these he killed outright a Croat deputy named Basarichek, a brilliant and beloved man, and Raditch's nephew Paul, he slightly wounded two other Croat deputies, and he mortally wounded Raditch himself. Six weeks afterwards this strange and inconclusive genius died. The King was constantly at his bedside, pale and trembling with grief. The wounded man gripped his hand when the pain was worst. During those weeks there went on a pathetic wrangle, which later events were to make bitterly ironical. 'When you are well,' the King said, 'you must be Prime Minister.' 'No, no,' answered Raditch, 'it must be a general.' He had already picked a general for the job, one Zhikovitch. But the others could see that all such talk was idle, and soon he was taken home to Zagreb to die. On his deathbed he uttered many wishes, which were also to be made bitterly ironical in later years, that none of his followers should seek to avenge his death, and that the Croats and the Serbs were to come to the fullest and most ungrudging reconciliation.

It is almost incredible that King Alexander should have been blamed for Raditch's death. He had much to lose by it and nothing whatsoever to gain. But there was brought up against him what is true enough, that a sinister association binds the name of Karageorgevitch to murder. Prince Michael of Serbia, King Alexander Obrenovitch and Queen Draga, the Archduke Franz Ferdinand and Sophie Chotek, all had been murdered and all had been enemies of the Karageorgevitches. It was also recalled that during the war, at Salonika, the famous 'Apis,' Dragutin Dimitriyevitch, had been found guilty of an attempt on Alexander's life, on what seemed strangely slight evidence, and had been shot. Slavs like telling each other bloodcurdling stories, and in the pleasure of these recitals it was forgotten that Raditch for five years had ceased to be the King's enemy.

All these suspicions of the King were held to be confirmed by the sentence passed on Punisha Rachitch. He was adjudged insane and sent to a lunatic asylum. This was regarded as a ruse adopted to evade the plain duty of exacting the death penalty. But many murders have been committed by rebels, including Croats, who have suffered nothing worse than imprisonment and it is just possible that Punisha Rachitch was insane. He was a man of outstanding ability who, in spite of having studied law in Paris, had remained essentially the chief of a primitive tribe, and he had done valuable work in establishing order on the new Yugoslav-Albanian frontier. This involved a certain amount of savage suppression, for the Albanians and pro-Austrian Montenegrins were raiding Serb villages, murdering travellers, and cutting down telephone wires. The educated comitadji often cracked. They saw more horrors and felt more fear than the subtilized mind can endure. In 1919, when Punisha Rachitch arrested an English captain who was touring the country on the business of an allied commission, his recorded proceedings suggest a certain degree of hallucinated arrogance.

But whether Rachitch was sane or mad hardly mattered; it mattered so much more that in either case it would have been extremely difficult for the King and the Government to inflict on him the death penalty. He was adored by the Montenegrin tribesmen who were his constituents. He was a man of superb physique, which always counts for much among virile communities, and of undoubted courage; and he had a high reputation as a shrewd and impartial judge of local disputes. In the eyes of these tribesmen he must have been perfectly justified in the murder he committed, for Raditch had attacked his honour. If Rachitch had been tried on charges of corruption by a legal tribunal they would have recognized another victory for the new state which was invading their lives and which, whether for better or worse, was proving irresistible. But the Government (of which, it must be remembered, Raditch was a member) never had prosecuted Rachitch. So there was, for the tribesmen, simply an old and familiar situation: two chiefs undermined each other's credit by abuse till the only way of finding the better man was by murder. The Government might be crotchety about such matters as graft, though that seemed unreasonable enough, since the tribesmen accepted the payment of tribute to strong individuals as a natural practice; but when it came to a large classic situation like murder among chiefs it was no use putting up new-fangled ideas. Because of this attitude the execution of Rachitch might have caused serious unrest among the Montenegrins: and here we are faced again with the early, pre-genial Mussolini. He was financing a large number of Montenegrin insurgents in order to further his designs on Albania, and would certainly have used the death of Rachitch to stir up well-armed revolt. It would so greatly have profited the King to tamper with justice and save Rachitch from his proper punishment on a false plea of madness that most people took it for granted that he took that course. There is no possible means, short of the appearance of Punisha Rachitch before an independent medical board, by which we can tell whether this is the case or not.

After that catastrophe nothing went right. The King was left alone on the political stage. The obvious step was to form a Coalition Ministry. It was impossible to appoint a Serb. Since a Roman Catholic had been killed by a member of the Orthodox Church, the whole faith must perform an act of penance. It proved impossible to appoint a Croat, for Raditch's successor, Matchek, and all Croat deputies except a few freaks, withdrew to Zagreb and refused to take their seats again in the Skupshtina. It is hard to understand why they did this. It was contrary to Raditch's wishes; they cannot have thought that they owed it to their loyalty to him to flout the Serbs, for he had been murdered by a Montenegrin, and the Serbs were on notoriously bad terms with the Montenegrins; and had they collaborated with the Serbs at this time they could have extracted from them every concession they wanted short of actual home rule. These were the realities of the situation. But the Croat Peasant Party preferred to react to the baser newspapers, which continued to attack Raditch after his death, and to the Serbian political bosses who inspired them, though with the King against them these had little chance of survival.

There remained only the Slovenes, and their leader, Father Koroshets, was appointed Prime Minister. The Slovenes are a sensible and unexcitable people who had had better opportunities than their compatriots to live at peace. Much of the trouble between the Croats and the Serbs had arisen because their language was identical and Serb officials could be sent to administer Croat territory. But the Slovene tongue differs greatly from Serbo-Croat, and the Slovenes had been left to govern themselves in peace. It is only fair to the Serbs to recognize that the Slovenes are not of the same oppositionist temperament as the Croats and therefore can be trusted with self-government. But the Church had supplied the Slovenes with a leader not up to the standard of his followers. Anton Koroshets had been the confessor of the last Empress of Hungary, Zita, and he represented the sombre and reactionary type of Catholicism cultivated by the Habsburgs. His spirit was therefore blind to the fundamental problems presented by the ancient and the modern world and moved busily in an etiquette-ridden bourgeois nineteenth-century limbo which had no correspondence with reality. This made him a past master of political intrigue, and a calamitous and irritating statesman. It was his imbecile custom to respond to the challenge of troubled times by using manifestos which ascribed all his country's ills to revolutionary movements engendered by Communists, Jews, and Freemasons. But there are very few Communists in Yugoslavia; the Jews are a stable body of traders producing few intellectuals; there are practically no Freemasons in Croatia and Slovenia, and Serbia is the only place in the world where Freemasonry gathers together the forces of reaction. It happened that under Alexander Obrenovitch a pro-Austrian and anti-democratic politician was Grand Master of the Belgrade Lodge and used it as a centre of intrigue with the lodges of Vienna and Budapest, and at that time all masons of progressive sympathies resigned and have never rejoined. All Koroshets's interventions in Yugoslav politics were on this level, and it is not surprising that in this crisis he proved unable to lead the country.

His failure left the King with only one course to follow: to obey Raditch's advice and establish a military dictatorship. In January 1929, after six months' turmoil, he dissolved Parliament, and made General Zhikovitch his Prime Minister, to be responsible to the Crown and not to the deputies. This was a complete breach with the Karageorgevitch tradition, for it involved the infringement of the constitution and the dynasty had always been defenders of constitutionalism. The King, with his narrow and intense concentration on the idea of his royalty, must have known that he had put an axe to the root of his power the minute he decided to exercise it absolutely: and General Zhikovitch could do nothing to repair this injury. It is proof of the essential capriciousness of Raditch's character that he should have advised the King to entrust himself and his country to this obscure man. His respectable but undistinguished military career had brought him no prestige, and, while he had a passion for political intrigue, he was completely ignorant of political principles.

He was, however, a perfect instrument for the King. It is said that Raditch had proposed him as dictator only to expose his inefficiency and emptiness; and such tortuousness can be believed of Raditch. Completely at a loss, Zhikovitch had to obey the King. For a time there was a superficial improvement in Yugoslavian affairs, because the dictatorship put into effect various necessary reforms—many concerning public utilities—which had been held up in the Skupshtina by regional and personal rivalries. In the preceding ten years Parliament had passed only 110 laws. The King and Zhikovitch passed 118 laws and 535 minor decrees in twelve months, and most of these were in accordance with the people's wishes. They also promulgated new penal and civil codes. Then the Nemesis of dictatorship laid its paralysing hand on the King's shoulder. The dictator seizes power, and it is yielded to him, because Parliament has failed to solve certain fundamental problems which are vexing the people. But Parliament has failed in that task only because the human mind has not yet discovered the solution of those problems. Other minor problems can be deliberately left unsolved by individuals, classes, or regions which find that the *status quo* favours their interests. But nobody would be able to suppress the solution of a major problem, such as war or poverty, if only because the existence of an enormously complicated idea—such as the solution of a complicated problem must be—could not be kept a secret, since it must be the product of the spirit of the age acting on a number of intellectually active people. It is not possible that one man alone could have conceived such a solution, because the range of variation in our species is extremely small, particularly at the top of the scale. A dictator might have an idea that was not shared by the village idiot, but it is extremely unlikely that a dictator would have an idea which had not already occurred in some comparable form to an elected assembly of men, some of whom, since the intellect is of some use in competition, must be of intellectual eminence. The chief problems of Yugoslavia were its proverty and the antagonisms felt by sections of the population which had different cultures. When the King had cleared up the arrears of work that could be settled by a firm and legible signature, he looked these problems in the face and realized that he could solve them no better than the Skupshtina.

He made some gallant attempts. To tackle the economic problem, he tried to develop the country's industries, but luck was against him, for the world slump began in the autumn of 1929. In any case Yugoslavia is primarily an agricultural country, and cannot know prosperity until an answer is found to man's world-wide refusal to pay a fair price for the food he eats. He also took steps to heal the antagonisms among his subjects, which showed him a very strange man, pedantic, doctrinaire, morally earnest, intellectually naïve, and, at that moment, desperate and alone. The problem was enormously intricate. It sprang from the inclusion in the same state of two kinds of Slavs: Slavs who were the inheritors of the Byzantine tradition of culture and the primitive Christianity of the Orthodox Church, and had been informed with the tragic conception of life by the defeat of Kossovo and the ensuing five hundred years of slavery; and Slavs who had been incorporated in the Western bourgeois system by Austrian influence and were spiritually governed by the Roman Catholic Church, which owes its tone to a Renaissance unknown to the other Slavs, and were experienced in discomfort but not in tragedy. To reconcile these two elements, which were different as the panther and the lynx, the King enforced certain measures which bring tears to the eyes by their simplicity.

He changed the name of his state from the Kingdom of Serbs, Croats, and Slovenes to Yugoslavia, the country of the South Slavs; and, forbidding the use of the old regional names such as Serbia, Bosnia, and the rest, he cut it up into nine provinces, called after the rivers which ran through them, except for Dalmatia, which was called the Littoral. He forbade the existence of the old regional political parties. Thus he disclosed the innocent hope that if Croatia were called the Savska Banovina the inhabitants would forget that they were Croats, would cease to wish to vote for Matchek, and would learn to respect the Macedonians, since they had become the inhabitants of the Vardarska Banovina; and thus he committed a terrible wrong towards his own people. It was a shameful thing that Serbia, with its glorious history of revolt against the Turks, should cease to be an entity, and that the Serbian regiments which had amazed the world by their heroism should have to send their colours to the museums and march under the new, and as yet meaningless, flag of Yugoslavia. There is no doubt that at this time the King went too far in his desire to conciliate the Croats. He relaxed his devotion to the Orthodox Church, so that he should not seem too alien from his Roman Catholic subjects. He also took a step that was offensive not only to the Serbs but to common sense when he tried to abolish the use of the Cyrillic script in the Serb districts and replace it by the Latin script used by the Croats and in Western Europe. This Cyrillic script has a great historical significance for the Serbs, for it is a modification of the Greek alphabet made by St Cyril and St Methodius for the use of their converts when they came to evangelize the Slavs in the ninth century. But it is also much better suited than the Latin script to render the consonants peculiar to the Slav languages, it is virtually the same that is used in neighbouring Bulgaria, and is almost the same as that used in Russia, and it can be mastered by any intelligent person in a couple of days.

While these measures widened the gulf between the King and his Serb subjects they did not bring him an inch nearer the Croats.

Strangely enough, though it was Raditch himself who had urged the establishment of a military dictatorship, nobody was so hostile to it as his followers. It was then that Italy found an opportunity to get her foot into Croatia and play the same part there that she had played in Macedonia. She had an advantage in finding a willing ally in this enterprise in Hungary, who had lost Croatia and the rich Danubian territory of the Voivodina to Yugoslavia and longed for revenge, but otherwise the soil was more difficult. The Croats had practised a steady policy of resistance to Hungarian rule, but it was mainly passive; and their rulers had not, like the Turks, accustomed them to the idea of murder. Hence the terrorists hired by Italy and Hungary to organize a movement on I.M.R.O. lines had, at first, little success. Neither then nor later did they win over the main body of the Croat Peasant Party, or indeed of any Croat political party. It is said that after a year's work there were not more than thirty active adherents of the new organization; and though it established training camps in Italy and Hungary these could not be filled. At enormous expense agents were sent everywhere where Croats were seeking their fortunes, France, Belgium, South America, the United States, and recruited them with cock-and-bull stories of how the Serbs were massacring their brothers by the thousands. Even this was not too successful, and the Hungarian camp was driven to decoying Yugoslav peasants over the frontier and kidnapping them.

But the Croat terrorists had their successes. They were far from inefficient. They distributed treasonable newspapers and pamphlets all over the world, many most persuasively written. They started an able and unscrupulous propaganda office in Vienna, which wounded the King's feelings bitterly and succeeded in poisoning European opinion; and they practised here no less successfully than on the Bulgarian frontier the art of placing bombs on international trains. This caused the Yugoslavian Government endless trouble. It was usually foreigners who were injured, and that made trouble with their governments; and the foreigners who were not injured showed themselves curiously irritating in their reaction to the measures that were taken for their protection. An English or French liberal, asked to leave his carriage while a police officer searched under the seats and on the racks, was apt to write home attacking the tyranny of the King's regime, and to add comments on the glumness of the searcher, although men are apt to look glum when doing a job that may cost them their lives. There were also, as in Macedonia, constant deliveries of arms to the rebels on a vast scale. Bombs, grenades, rifles, machine-guns, were brought in by smugglers who frequently murdered Yugoslav frontier guards, and were deposited in arsenals from which they were drawn by terrorists, who used them for such purposes as the blowing up of an Orthodox church in Zagreb during a service and the firing of a barracks dormitory full of conscripts.

Nobody came forward to help the King. There was one man, Svetozar Pribitchevitch, the greatest liberal journalist and politician in post-war Yugoslavia, who might have been expected to furnish him with a policy. He was one of a great family, descendants of the emigrants who had been led to Hungary by the holy Arsenius in the seventeenth century, and he had played a fearless part in the movement for Slav independence within the Austro-Hungarian Empire. All he had to suggest was, however, that the King should abdicate and the kingdom be converted into a republic. This was, in fact, an impractical suggestion. The Orthodox Church gave the King a stable position as the God-appointed head of the state in the minds of his Serb subjects; and no possible president had emerged from the Yugoslavian politics of that time who could have supplied by his own qualities any substitute for even that amount of unifying force. But the King reacted to the blunder with an excessive rage. Pribitchevitch's newspaper was suppressed and he was placed under arrest in his own home. Later he became ill and the Yugoslavs were humiliated by a request from President Masaryk that he might be allowed to harbour the rebel in Czechoslovakia.

Everybody failed him. Zhikovitch resigned, hurting the King intolerably by a frank admission that together they had made a great mess of Yugoslavia. Father Koroshets demanded home rule for the Croats and the Slovenes, and again the King showed excessive rage, and ordered him to be interned in Dalmatia. There was some excuse for his resentment. Koroshets had always been treated handsomely by Yugoslavia, and his famous respect for institutions, which was the card with which he always trumped the democratic ace, might well have been extended to the Karageorgevitch dynasty. Then Matchek, Raditch's successor, put in a claim for the Croat right of self-determination, and was arrested and sentenced to three years' imprisonment. At this both Croats and Serbs were outraged, but the King was implacable. It must be remembered in his defence that these programmes were completely unfeasible. The Catholic Slavs of the kingdom, who numbered five and a half million, had no sort of chance of maintaining their existence as an independent state. Inevitably some would have been absorbed by Italy and others by Hungary, and we have the spectacle of the four hundred thousand Slovenes at present in Italy and the memory of what the Croats and

Serbs of the Voivodina suffered from Hungarian oppression before the war, to tell us exactly what such absorption would mean. These annexations would not only have meant misery for the annexed but would have brought enemy powers up to the hearthstone of the Serbian people, who would have been as badly off as they were in the middle of the nineteenth century. There remained the solution of federation. But it is asking a great deal of a sovereign to apply that to a region which has lent itself to insurrection financed and organized by a hostile foreign power.

So the King dealt with Croatia by the light of his own wisdom, which proved insufficient. He could not send an army to deal with the unrest. It would have ruined the national prestige to have admitted the existence of civil war, and indeed the actual state of affairs was a good deal short of that. Many people travelled through Croatia at this time without observing any disruption, and the bulk of the population never ran any physical risks whatsoever. So instead of soldiers the Government sent Serbian or pro-Serb gendarmerie, who without any doubt treated the Croats with hideous brutality. There were many reasons for this. For one, they were sincere believers in the Yugoslav idea, and thought that Slavs who wanted to desert their brother Slavs and forgather with non-Slavs were very wicked people, who would be the better for a beating. For another, the Croats met them with a hostility that terrified them, strangers as they were and far away from home, and they felt justified in using any methods that would disarm their enemies. It must be remembered that when they came to grips with the terrorists financed by Italy they were dealing with men who habitually practised mutilation and had been known to torture a man for three days before they killed him. Since a Serbian policeman in Croatia was faced with many different types of Croat dissidents and usually had no means of distinguishing between them, it is not surprising that very often mild and inoffensive liberals were subjected to treatment that would have been appropriate, and then only according to Mosaic law, when applied to professional assassins and torturers. This meant that a great many people, some of whom were entirely innocent, were beaten and ill-treated in Croatian police stations.

Yet another reason for the brutality of the police lay in the difficulty of maintaining discipline in a police force, which is always less easy to control than an army, since it works in smaller and more scattered groups. No order could be issued in Belgrade which would make it certain that Belgrade's orders were being obeyed in Croatia. There was also, as a disturbing factor, the appalling police tradition which lingered in a form that was bad enough in all territories which had once been Habsburg, and in a far worse form in all territories which had been Turkish. The police were regarded as a body that had to get results satisfactory to the supreme power in the state, and that had better not be questioned by lower powers on how it got those results lest it take its revenge. This encouraged a spirit of enterprise that was usually regrettable in its manifestations; that was notably regrettable in Croatia when the police themselves started murdering Croatian politicians whose removal they thought likely to facilitate their tasks, and organized bands of gangsters called *chetnitsi* who went about assaulting Croat patriots and breaking up their meetings as they themselves could not do in uniform for fear of being reported to the highest authorities.

It would be easy to exaggerate the extent of this situation. Atrocities did not happen everywhere, or every day. It would not be easy to exaggerate the degree to which Raditch and Matchek, by the mindlessness and emotionalism of their leadership and their failure to turn the political situation to their advantage, were responsible for the suffering of their followers. But it was a detestable situation, and though the King did not hear the whole truth about it, owing to the independence of the police, he heard at least enough to make him realize that the policy of suppression was a mistake, and that he must make another attempt at a policy of reconciliation, since even if that failed it would smell better than the other. But he was strangely obstinate in his persistence. It has been suggested that there was an international explanation for his obstinacy, and that he had mistaken the personal affection felt for him by Sir Nevile Henderson, then British Minister in Belgrade, for approval of his political actions. According to this story he made the pathetic error of believing that his dictatorship won him favour in English eyes and was worth maintaining if for that reason alone.

Every independent mind in Croatia was now anti-Serb, and had been thrown into the arms of the foreign terrorists. In September 1931 the King had had the unhappy idea of proclaiming a new constitution which virtually annulled the principle of popular representation. A Senate was established with eighty-seven members, no less than forty-one of whom were to be nominated by the King. Ministers were responsible to the King and not to Parliament, and were to be nominated by the King. The ballot was no longer secret and voluntary, but open and obligatory. With a free Parliament thus abolished, and freedom of speech and freedom of the press long ago become mere memories, the Croats had to take what means they could to defend themselves by secret arming and appeals to foreign opinion. This was precisely what Mussolini had designed, yet the King showed no signs of retraction.

He had lost the Croats, and he had not kept the Serbs. The new constitution struck the Serbians as an act horrible in itself, since democracy is as essential a part of their social structure as Christianity or agriculture, and doubly horrible because it had been perpetrated by a Karageorgevitch. A man who worked for many years with the King on a scheme for developing the education of the recovered territories, and who greatly loved him, told me that when he went to see him at the palace during this time he could hardly speak to him. 'My voice kept on breaking, I could do nothing but stare at him, as if I were asking him, "Is it really you who have done this thing?" And though he must have noticed my distress and was, I think, quite fond of me, he said nothing about it, but went on talking, pleasantly and calmly, like a teacher who has upset a child by doing something which it cannot understand and which she cannot yet explain to it.' It is possible that there was an explanation. The King told certain people that he intended to give his country a constitution which would actually be more democratic than any previous one, as soon as circumstances convinced him that this step could be taken in safety, and he seems to have spoken as if he meant what he said. Though there are no grounds for supposing him to be a lover of democracy for its own sake, there are none for supposing him to have hated it. What seem political principles in a country which has established its right to existence may seem expedients in a country where the nationalist issue has not yet been settled. The King may have believed that democracy had its value as a national and dynastic tradition, and might well be restored when he had gathered the results of his foreign policy, and had built so strong a wall of peace on his threatened frontiers that he could afford a measure of internal conflict.

For the King was far more successful in settling his affairs abroad than at home. In the international sphere his naïveté did not betray him but inspired him. It sent him forward to offer his hand to ancient enemies, whose surprise disarmed them, so that they found the friendliness in them awakening and answering. He laid the foundations of a most necessary structure that might have subserved the peace not only of his people but of all Europe when he repudiated the hostility between Bulgaria and Yugoslavia that had been encouraged by Russia and envenomed by King Ferdinand. Here he was helped by the recent decline in the fortunes of I.M.R.O. This body had virtually lost its cause in Macedonia, because the Yugoslavian administration was rapidly improving, and the Yugoslav Macedonians, who are no fools, saw that they might live far from disagreeably if only they were not harried by perpetual guerrilla attacks and forced to pay extortionate illegal taxes. This is not to say that the Bulgarians in Yugoslav Macedonia gave up their desire that the territory in which they lived should be handed over to Bulgaria. Many have never been reconciled to Yugoslav rule. But most of them grew heartily sick of I.M.R.O., and joined their Serb neighbours in picking up rifles whenever a raiding party appeared and giving as good as they got.

I.M.R.O., thus repulsed, then turned its whole attention to its work in Bulgaria, where it had for long fulfilled the functions of a Fascist Party, and strengthened that party till it was a state within the state. Its financial resources were enormous, for it had foreign aid and levied illegal taxes on Bulgarian Macedonia as in Yugoslavian Macedonia; from the tobacco industry alone it raised over a million pounds in six years. But its chief resource was its ruthlessness, which, as time went on, made Bulgarian political life into a shambles. Sofia, which is a city full of delightful people, beautiful and extravagantly literate, lay in the power of a savage gang as if enslaved by sorcerers, and stared glassily at the assassinations that occurred nearly every day in the open streets. The whole of life was infected with fear and squalor. No shops could open without paying a tax to I.M.R.O., and all had to supply its followers with goods on the production of an official requisition. Every hotel-keeper had to reserve five rooms for I.M.R.O., two on the first floor for the leaders, three on higher levels for the rank and file. An ancient heroism took on itself the likeness of Al Capone. King Boris of Bulgaria, and indeed most Bulgarians, were deeply ashamed. Because I.M.R.O. had no hold on its followers other than its claim to liberate Yugoslavian Macedonia, King Boris decided to spike the movement's guns by declaring a new and unalterable policy of friendship with Yugoslavia. Henceforward the parasite state would have to fight its host to keep its life. The plundered peasants and shopkeepers, to say nothing of the tobacco industry, were deeply sensible of the conveniences offered by the friendship, even though they may have felt no sentimental attachment for Yugoslavia whatsoever. The leaders of I.M.R.O. were executed, imprisoned, or driven to flight, while their followers were beaten and disbanded; and Bulgaria turned towards a more normal way of life.

This reconciliation would not have been possible without King Alexander's eager acceptance of King Boris's advances. He did much to sweeten Bulgarian feeling by his visits to Sofia and Varna, which, indeed, were among the most fearless acts recorded of any sovereign. All the Balkan peoples like a man with courage. And when King Boris delayed to give proper diplomatic expression to the new friendship, owing to the influence of Italy on some Bulgarian politicians and the tropism of lifelong hatreds in others, King Alexander paid other visits that were designed to hurry him up. It was his aim to keep Italy at bay by uniting his neighbour states into a bloc resolved to keep the South-East of Europe inviolate. He went to Constantinople to see Mustapha Kemal, who smiled at him with eyes which revealed that the Balkans had once more played their trick on the Turk, and had been conquered only to rule; for those eyes were blue, and Ataturk, like some sultans, several viziers, and the flower of the Janizaries, was at least half Slav. He went to Greece, and set going negotiations that were ultimately consummated, in spite of the peculiarly unconcordant character of Greek politicians. Greece, Turkey, and Yugoslavia signed the Balkan Pact in 1933, and once Bulgaria found herself one against three she changed her mind and joined them in 1934.

But even these achievements cannot have convinced King Alexander that the world was as pleasant as he had believed it to be twenty years before, when he was a young man, at the end of the Balkan War: as pleasant as it must be if it is worth while lavishing on it the luxury of poetry, of such dreams as the vision of the Frushka Gora. It was not only that the path of his successes must inevitably lead him to a pact with Soviet Russia. That Mustapha Kemal had told him; and he could see that the support of Russia, no matter whether it was White or Red, was absolutely necessary to the Balkans if they were to make a stand against Western aggression. But there were more disagreeable aspects of his situation than that, which must have struck him at the very beginning of his diplomatic pilgrimage and made him conscious that certain glories had left the world, that nothing was now simple in shape and bright like a sword.

His very first meeting with the King of Bulgaria showed a certain dimming of the monarchic tradition, a certain muting of martial music as it had been heard through history. It happened that in 1930 King Boris had married Princess Giovanna of Italy, who was cousin to King Alexander, as their mothers had been sister princesses of Montenegro. The first meeting of the kings had to take place timidly, under the shelter of this cousinly relationship. It was represented that, on a return journey to Sofia from Paris and London, Queen Giovanna was overcome by her sense that blood was thicker than water, and felt that she must see King Alexander, whom in fact she cannot possibly have laid eyes upon since 1913 when he was twenty-five and she was six. In response King Alexander came down to the railway station and drank coffee with them in a waiting-room, specially decorated in the gloomy fashion habitual on such occasions, during the hour's halt the Orient Express always made at Belgrade. There had been some dealings between the two countries, but King Boris had not dared to make the more definite overtures which would have justified King Alexander in proposing a visit to the palace. But once they were all standing on the platform Queen Giovanna forced the diplomatic pace by kissing King Alexander as if she really meant it, putting her arms on his shoulders as if there were a strong good-will between them all which might do great things for them if they let it. King Alexander was stirred out of his usual formality into responsiveness, and in the waiting-room they talked and laughed together with the warmth of real loyalty. But there was defiance in their laughter. This meeting sprang from the revolt of one of the Italian royal family against Mussolini. Three heirs to the blood of kings were conspiring, not without trepidation, to give the people peace in spite of a blacksmith's son.

Such a spectacle could not have been imagined by the priests and emperors of Byzantium, nor by the Nemanyan kings, nor even by the Serbian peasants who raised Karageorge and Milosh Obrenovitch to be princes over them. Surely, they would have said, a king must be all-powerful; others might snatch his sceptre, but so long as he held it power was his. And surely, they and their subjects would have agreed, the people would never give birth to its own enemy. But now there was a new factor to confound all their certainties. There were two sorts of people. There was the people as it had been since the beginning of time, that worked in the villages, small towns, and capitals. But there was also a new people, begotten by the new towns which the industrial and financial developments of the nineteenth century had raised all over Europe: towns so vast and intricate that, in coping with the problems of their own organization, they lost all relationship to the country round them, so that even though they were called capitals they were not, for a head should have some connexion with its body; towns planned in the biological interest of only the rich, and careless of the souls and bodies of the poor. The new sort of people have been defrauded of their racial tradition, they enjoyed no inheritance of wisdom; brought up without gardens, to work on machines, all but a few lacked the education which is given by craftsmanship; and they needed this wisdom and this education as never before, because they were living in conditions of unprecedented frustration and insecurity. A man without tradition and craft is lost, and book learning is of little help to him, for he lacks the shrewdness to winnow what he reads.

Some among this new people, by a miracle that may be called grace, resist all these assaults on their stock, and are as the best of the old people. But there are those who succumb, never ripen, and are infantile, and so react to their frustration and necessity, as infants react to hunger, by screaming and beating out at what is nearest. One such, named Luccheni, had killed Elizabeth of Austria in 1898. But his kind had grown in power since then. This is not to say that they had become wiser, or had discovered a formula that would medicine their distress; it was only that there were more of them, and that, conscious of their numbers, they had learned to scream orders as well as complaints. So when King Alexander, having achieved the Balkan *entente*, visited France to discuss the new power's future relationship, he was struck down at Marseille not by a hungry vagrant, but by a ruler who was in a position to tyrannize over the royal blood of his country as he had tyrannized over its peasants and workmen. A form of government had arisen which was far more disgusting than any of the governments of the immediate past, though they had been nasty enough. The great powers had perpetuated Balkan misery by the Treaty of Berlin. They had been responsible for many ugly deaths in high places—Prince Michael of Serbia had been killed by Austrian conspiracy, Queen Draga and King Alexander Obrenovitch might have lived to old age had it not been for Austrian intrigue, Franz Ferdinand and Sophie Chotek were doomed by Austrian maladministration. They had been responsible for many ugly births in low places: Luccheni and Mussolini would never have come to be in a just economic system. But at least they knew when they had sinned that there was sin, at least they were aware that there was good and there was evil. But this the new rulers of the world did not know. 'Violence,' said Mussolini in the unmistakable accents of moral imbecility, 'is profoundly moral, more moral than compromises and transactions.' Time had rolled backward. It seemed likely that man was to lose his knowledge that it is wiser being good than bad, it is safer being meek than fierce, it is fitter being sane than mad. He was not only ignoring the Sermon on the Mount, he was forgetting what the Psalmist had known. And since these things are true it was certain that, once man had forgotten them, he would be obliged, with pains that must be immense, to rediscover them.

Belgrade knows all this, and looks forward to her future with apprehension. For, to tell the truth, it is a mournful city. Even in spring, when the young lovers walk among the flowers in

Kalemegdan, and their elders sit in the restaurants talking politics with a new and rosy vehemence, because their nostrils are filled with the savour of roasting lamb and piglet, its underlying mood is an autumnal doubtfulness. The winter is going to be very long and hard. Is it going to be worth while living through it for the sake of what lies beyond? And those who wonder are not ignorant of what winter is, nor are they cowards. This mood is one of the deep traces left on the capital by Alexander Karageorgevitch's personality. It is still his city. If one of the medieval Serbians who painted the frescoes in the monasteries came to life and covered a wall with Belgrade, he would certainly show the murdered king floating on his bier above the city; and if the picture were to be a valid symbol it would show the King's tenacious and reserved face changed by doubtfulness, its reserve breaking to betray a doubt whether its tenacity had been of any avail.

Each Serbian ruler has proved something by his reign. More than once it was proved by this curious sovereignty, newer than the United States and as old as Byzantium, that a small state could defeat a vast empire; always it was proved that it is terrible, even in victory, to be a small state among great empires. It was given to Alexander to give new proof of these arguments, and to prove others also. By the expansion of his state beyond the limits of his people's culture, Serbia had been forced into guilt. It was, evidently, a moral necessity that small peoples should form small states, and the price exacted for the defence of morality looked to be more than men's bodies can afford to pay. This the King had known well as he drove stiffly through the streets of Belgrade. A dictator himself, he was the first ruler in Europe to learn how inimical dictatorship must be to all true order. He knows it still better as he floats over the city on his bier. For his murder went virtually unpunished. France hardly dared to try his assassins, and the League of Nations murmured timid words of censure, such as would offend no one.

Belgrade IX

We grew eager to leave Belgrade, and start on the trip we were to take with Constantine through Macedonia and Old Serbia, though nothing unpleasant was happening to us here. There were indeed two disconcerting moments when we turned a corner too smartly and came on Constantine and Gerda in complete emotional disarray, Gerda weeping in disregard of the passers' frank Slav stares, Constantine red with misery. But we had taken it for granted that Constantine's life would cover the whole range of oddity, and would be painfully odd as well as pleasantly odd, so we were hardly even surprised. It was no personal experience that depressed us in the city, but the pervading air of anticlimax. Nothing real had happened here since King Alexander died. That was indeed more of a miracle than an anticlimax. His murderers had put him out of the way in order that the country should be left without a head and would be unable to defend itself when it was attacked, yet the attack was never made.

This inaction is still mysterious, though there are one or two obvious factors which must have recommended it. The first was the reaction of Yugoslavia to the King's death. It was not split asunder, but on the contrary drew closer in a unity it had not known since King Peter's abdication. Every part of the country, even Croatia, abandoned itself to grief. No state not fallen into animal sloth can lose its head, whether that be king or president, without some amount of visceral anguish, and the Slavs, being analytical, knew that though Alexander had committed many harsh and foolish acts he had been fundamentally the priest of his people. There are not only good men and bad men, there are bad good men and there are good bad men. A bad good man complies in each individual act with accepted ethical standards, but his whole life describes a pattern that cannot be pleasing to God. A good bad man may commit all manner of faults and crimes, but at bottom he lets nothing come before the duty of subjecting experience to the highest law; and the Yugoslavs knew that King Alexander belonged to this order. They were aware that though he had sent too many of them to prison, he had sought to give Yugoslavia an honourable destiny that would preserve its genius. So there was no revolt of the Croats, and the foreign royalties and statesmen who followed the King's bier through the streets of

Belgrade were amazed by the strange, soft sound of a whole city weeping.

The other factor that preserved Yugoslavia from the long-planned assault was the secret attitude of the great powers, which was more audacious than their public showing. Immediately after the assassination the British Mediterranean Fleet took up its position in the Adriatic; and it is possible that the French found out more than they were meant to about the crime, and that they were able to demand a *quid pro quo* for erecting the scaffolding of obfuscation that surrounded the trial of the murderers at Aix-en-Provence. That their policy preserved peace at the moment does not exculpate it, for a war then would have been far less dangerous than later; and meanwhile every totalitarian ruffian in Europe rejoiced to see one of their kind strike down a foreign king in peace-time and go scot-free, and all honest men lost heart.

Here in Belgrade that shadow did not lift by an inch. For all the vehemence and intelligence of life it was at a deadlock. There were plenty of people daring to think, but no one acted, except perhaps the group of financial and industrial adventurers who are supposed to be represented by Stoyadinovitch, who 'admire' capitalism, who are inspired by the myth that the capitalism which is dying all over Europe will revive for their benefit. Error often stimulates the organism more violently than the truth, as cancer produces a more spectacular reaction in its host than the healthy cell. Those who had truer foundations to their thought were simply waiting for their scepticism to be resolved. They used to draw their strength from France and England and Russia. But they were so deeply shocked by the failure of France and England to speak honestly before the League of Nations concerning King Alexander's murder that they no longer thought of those two countries, they only wondered. They could not derive any refreshment from us in the West till we should give them new proof of our value. They still thought much of Russia, but not as they did when the Balkans were perpetually fecundated by Russian mysticism or revolutionary theory, for Russia was by then so remote behind its Chinese wall of exclusiveness and secretiveness, it was like thinking of Paradise, or, as it may seem to others, of Hell.

Sometimes it seemed as if their inactivity was in part due to the mythic quality of the popular imagination. It is as if the people were saying to themselves, 'A state must have a head, but we have none till our king is a man, so we cannot live like a state, we must hold our peace till young Peter can rule us.' That is a wise enough decision; but where the popular mind holds too firmly to its primitive entertainments, its first fairy-tales, it strikes into folly. King Alexander left three Regents to rule Yugoslavia till his son came to maturity: his cousin Prince Paul, his doctor, and the Governor of Croatia (himself a Croat), with a general in reserve. None of the non-royal Regents was outstanding in character or influence, so if they wished to oppose Prince Paul it would have been impossible. The country felt, therefore, that Prince Paul exerted the only effective power under the Regency; and this was probably true. So far as strangers could see, he had acquitted himself very creditably within the limits set by his distaste for his position. For he had an exclusive interest in art which is very odd in a pure Slav, and it is generally known that he would far rather have led the life of a connoisseur in Florence than be tied to a tedious administrative job in almost pictureless Belgrade. Perhaps because of this desire to be doing something else somewhere else, perhaps because of the prudence which enabled him in the past to live calmly among the disturbed Karageorgevitches, he always responded to the forces working in Yugoslavia rather than governed them. He was amiable to Stoyadinovitch, and bowed and smiled to all the powers that Stoyadinovitch led up to him, even to Italy and Germany.

This was not at all a foolish policy for a man who knows himself not naturally a ruler, in an extravagantly perilous time of history. But the myth-making mind of the people saw him as the Regent of the fairy-stories, the Uncle of the Babes in the Wood, who longs to usurp his charge's throne, who is in sympathy with usurpers at their crassest, with Mussolini and Hitler. There was ascribed to him a savage spirit of reaction, fired from an anti-Bolshevism that regrets the Romanoffs and is loyal to the Demidoffs. Yet it seems unlikely that a lover of Western painting, whose law of life is obviously taste, should have felt such passionate nostalgia for the Philistine court of Nicholas III, and the circumstances of the separation between Arsenius Karageorgevitch and Aurora Demidoff must have forbidden the unity that a son might normally feel with his mother's family. From all appearances Prince Paul's political ideas are derived not from Russia but from the upper-and middle-class England he learned to know when he was at Oxford. This is not to say that they were ideally applicable to the Balkan situation, but their inapplicability was of a different sort from Tsarist obscurantism. There were no times when the liberalism of Belgrade failed to be inspiring, for it is a robust tree with roots deep in the nature of the Slav race; but there were times when it seemed as if this Liberalism could never come into effective action again, because it had broken from the peasant tradition of sound sense and preferred those urban opinions which are only clever guesses.

'But you will see that all must go well here,' I said to my husband, as I sat in front of my dressing-table in the hotel bedroom, putting on my hat to go out to tea with Gerda and Constantine, 'as soon as we get to Macedonia. You will see that there is a Balkan genius so strong that its peoples can never perish, that they can take refuge from material death, and even intellectual or moral death, in its spiritual life.' 'That seems so strange to me,' said my husband, 'when I have all my life heard of Macedonia as a symbol of age-long misgovernment and ruin. I used to hear of it when I was a child, as a place where men butchered other men, whom they should have thought of as their brothers.' 'But that was not age-long,' I said. 'I remember that too. We heard our elders talking of the squalid disputes in Macedonia when we were somewhere about nine or ten, and I realize now that it was after the Mürzsteg agreement between Turkey and the great powers was signed in 1903. That was a terrible business. It provided for the policing of Macedonia by military forces sent out by the great powers, and it was drawn up by the Austro-Hungarian and Russian Foreign Ministers, Goluchowski and Lansdorff, at one of Franz Josef's hunting lodges. It happened that Goluchowski, who was a clever man, loved shooting above all things, and that Lansdorff, who was a stupid man, loved writing above all things. So Goluchowski went out with his gun every day and all day, and left Lansdorff to draft the agreement. Apparently he came back too tired to read it, and apparently all the other diplomats in Europe were equally fond of shooting, for they all passed an imbecile clause by which it was announced that as soon as Macedonia could be restored to order the Turkish administrative districts were to be delimited anew so that they might correspond with ethnographical districts. This automatically provoked civil war of the bloodiest character. For this clause terrified the Bulgars, Serbs, and Greeks in Macedonia, who knew that there are hardly any districts which are ethnographically pure in that part of the world, and saw themselves handed over to whatever race was in the majority, by however small a figure. Each group therefore attacked both the others, and killed off as many of them as possible, with the object of reducing them to unquestionable minorities. This went on for three years, till an Englishwoman called Lady Grogan visited Macedonia and informed the Foreign Office of the reason for the massacres, and the great powers drowsily collected themselves and withdrew the clause. But, of course, there had been endless pain and misery for five centuries before. It is astonishing that there should be anything waiting for us in Macedonia, but last time I was there I had the impression that there was more there than anywhere else.'

We started early for our tea-party, because we wanted to visit the Prince Paul Museum and have a last look at the pictures and antiquities with which the Regent had filled one wing of the New Palace on the main street. Some he himself had collected, others were the remains of a collection which the Serbian state had gathered since 1842 but which was pillaged and damaged in the war. There were a lovely gold vessel found in Macedonia, relic of a pre-Mycenæan civilization not recorded in history, some beautiful gold work and enamels from Byzantium and medieval Serbia, some robes and furniture and arms of the earlier Karageorgevitches and Obrenovitches; some bad paintings by the Germans and Austrians, some very good paintings by the French and goodish paintings by the English, and some Slav paintings that had little individuality and were echoes of the German and Austrian and French work; and some Slav sculpture that had great individuality, but was contorted with its struggle to lay hold of a sound tradition. The serene certainty of the medieval work and the uncertainty of the modern work might have been distressing had we not recognized some friends who were manifesting the continuity of Serbian national life, which would doubtless make itself felt in time. During our stay in Belgrade we had sometimes visited a café for wine and hot spiced sausages towards mid-night, and there had listened to the singing of two Roumanian sisters, fine girls, plump as table birds, who had a habit of putting their heads together and smiling widely, just as Phyllis and Zena Dare used to be photographed in my childhood. The night before, we had watched a young man, neatly dressed and confident yet manifestly no townsman, probably the son of the wealthiest peasant in some big village, fall under the charms of both these sisters, with a perfect impartiality which struck us as psychologically curious, but which was apparently accepted by the two girls without resentment. We had no doubt that his passion for them was of a practical nature; but here in the museum we found the three, in front of some medieval icons and reliquaries, and the young man was explaining to the two girls, with violent gestures and proud cries, that the first King of the Nemanyas was the father of St. Simeon, who had founded the monastery of Hilander on Mount Athos. They appeared to be interested and impressed.

When we came to Constantine's house he opened the door to us, a happy little Buddha, as he always is when he is dispensing hospitality, and Gerda waited for us behind her tea-table, composed and gracious in a neat grey silk dress, with not a trace of tears. The two children played about the table, miraculous little creatures, since they reconciled and yet obstinately maintained apart the different elements in them. They can flash a glance which is at once German in its romantic activism, Jewish in its shrewd and swift calculation of probabilities, and Slav in its analytic penetration. They have an amusing coolness, of which I learned the very first time I ever met Constantine. I was taken to call on him at his office in connexion with the work I was doing on my first visit to Yugoslavia, so late in the morning that to finish our discussion we had to lunch together. So Constantine telephoned to his house and said, 'Is that you, my little son? Tell your mother that I will not be home to lunch because I have run away with an Englishwoman.' Sitting at the opposite side of the table, I heard the child's reply in the unknown language, cold as ice-water. 'Do you think,' he asked, 'that the Englishwoman has any stamps?' That was the older boy, but the younger also had an air of being seriously aware of the necessity for imposing form on the extravagances of nature; and it could be seen, now the whole family was united, that they regarded Constantine and his mother as conduits of that extravagance. They were sage about this opinion. They were willing to admit that the prodigiousness of the pair was beneficent and entertaining, but they would not blind themselves to its need for control.

I grieved a little at their attitude, knowing them wrong, with an error that they had inherited from Gerda, with her Western tradition. Constantine may need control, owing to his circumstances, the most unfavourable of which is his surrender to the West; but Constantine's mother has shown herself able to endure so much that there can be no question of better adapting her to life. In her youth her beauty, which must have been superb, presented her with a gifted and loving husband, her son Constantine, and a daughter. Just before the war the scourge of the Balkans, tuberculosis, took the daughter. Then her husband and son went to the war; her husband died of typhus, and her son was sent to Russia and disappeared. Meantime her home was occupied by the Germans, she was without means, and though she found work as a nurse that ended with the war, she nearly starved till life became more normal and she succeeded in getting pupils for music lessons; and even then she was in misery, for not until three years after the peace did she hear that Constantine still lived. All this might conceivably have been borne by a peasant woman, disciplined from birth to silence under frustration. But this woman was a musician, an interpretative artist, whose discipline was all directed towards the public demonstration of what she felt. What might have been expected was that she would feel a transcendent kind of grief and die of it, a special death that would have been a fulfilment. But here she was, her face certainly tortured, but not so much because of her sufferings as because of the impossibility of finding out the exact truth about humanity, which is to say, the impossibility of finding a stable foundation for artistic endeavour.

'Then you can tell me something!' she exclaimed, when we told her that since I had last seen her we had been to Canada. 'Is it possible that Scriabin is really the favourite musician of all Canadians?' We replied that nothing we had seen of Montreal and Toronto had prepared us for this conclusion. 'For myself, I cannot really believe it,' she explained, 'but there came to Belgrade this winter a Canadian professor, and he assured me that in his country the favourite composer of all was not Beethoven or Mozart or Wagner but Scriabin, and that there existed a great society to popularize his works, called the Scriabin Society. But it is not possible, for Scriabin himself would have admitted that if he was anybody's *favourite* composer that person would not have been able to appreciate him. A people which ate lobster and champagne at every meal could never claim to be *fins gourmets* of lobster and champagne. Also, Scriabin is too *difficult.*' Her fingers stood up, stiffly apart, each registering discomfiture before a technical problem. 'Not enough people could play him, not enough people could listen to him, to become truly familiar with him. Besides, how absurd to think of a great country, largely covered with snow, many of whose inhabitants earn their living trapping wild animals, having Scriabin as its favourite composer.'

'Yes, Mamma,' said Constantine, 'but are you not forgetting that Scriabin himself was the child of a great country covered with snow, where there was a good deal of trapping wild animals?' 'Yes, yes,' said the old lady, 'but I do not believe that in the whole of Russia you would find one man who would claim that Scriabin was the favourite composer of Russians!' 'But, perhaps, Mamma,' said Constantine, 'it is a different sort of animal that they trap in Canada.' 'A different sort of animal? But what would that matter?' exclaimed his mother in stupefaction, knitting her fine mind against this puzzle till she saw Constantine winking at us, and then she cried out, laughing, 'Ah, wait till you are old, you will see what it is like when everybody mocks you, even your poor little idiot son!'

Very soon we had an idea that Gerda thought that this was not the proper way to entertain us. She thought the less of us for liking this wild talk about music, which could not really be of any value, because it made no references to the Ideal or the History of Music. It would have been better if we had made statements about specific musical occasions and had evoked them from her, and had thus established our common enjoyment of culture: if we had, for example, spoken of hearing a Beethoven symphony in Toronto or Montreal, and had asked her where she had heard it. She spoke presently of her surroundings as lacking precisely that kind of sophistication, when the conversation turned to food and the amount of cooking that was done in Yugoslavian households. Contemptuously she told us that when a Serbian family expected guests to tea, the housewife would put herself about to bake cakes and biscuits; but, as we would see, she said with a shrug of the shoulders, indicating the food on her table, which had been obviously bought from a shop, she was not so. Her cool tone drew a picture of how she would like to dispense hospitality. One would go down, well dressed, with a full purse, and all one's debts paid, to Kranzler if one lived in Berlin, to Dehmel if one lived in Vienna, to Gerbeaud if one lived in Budapest, and would greet the assistant, who would be very respectful because of one's credit, and would choose exquisite pastries and *petits fours*, which would not only be delightful when crushed against one's friends' palates, but would also be recognizably from Kranzler, or from Dehmel, or from Gerbeaud.

She was assuming that my husband and I would share her feeling, that we would be with her in upholding this cool, powerful, unhurried ideal against the Serbian barbarians who liked a woman to get hot over a stove, as if she could not afford to pay other women to work for her, which indeed was probably the case. It would have been difficult for us to explain how wrong we thought her. We like the Apfelkuchen of Kranzler, we have never gone to Vienna without buying the Nusstorte of Dehmel, we have shamefully been late for a friend's lunch in Budapest for the reason that we had turned into Gerbeaud's to eat meringues filled with cream and strawberries. But we knew that when one goes into a shop and buys a cake one gets nothing but a cake, which may be very good, but is only a cake; whereas if one goes into the kitchen and makes a cake because some people one respects and probably likes are coming to eat at one's table, one is striking a low note on a scale that is struck higher up by Beethoven and Mozart. We believed it better to create than to pay. In fact, England had had a bourgeoisie long before Germany, and we had found out that the bourgeois loses more than he gains by giving up the use of his own hands; but there is no wider gulf in the universe than yawns between those on the hither and thither side of vital experience.

As Gerda spoke Constantine watched her with slightly excessive approval, nodding and smiling. He so obviously meant to reassure her and to recommend her to us that there came back to us the spectacle they had twice presented to us lately in the streets of Belgrade, dishevelled and disunited. It was astonishing to think that between such scenes these people should enjoy the glowing contentment with each other which now warmed this room; but of course there are millions of kinds of happy marriages. Only when we rose to go and Constantine told us that he would walk a little way back with us did we see that he was smiling not only at her but at us, and that his smile bore the same relation to a real smile as false teeth do to real teeth; it performed the function of indicating good-will, but the organism had failed in its normal spontaneous action. I could feel him still smiling through the darkness, as we strolled away from the cache of simple streets in which his pretty little house found itself, into the boulevard where grey concrete cakes of institutions and ministries shone with a blindish brightness behind the electric standards. When we came to the centre of the town, and looked across a circus where people were hurrying in and out of the yellow-lit cafés, at the slow and dark yet gay procession of the corso, he said, still with this undue facial cheerfulness, with the corners of his mouth turned up, 'I must go back now.' But he did not take the hand my husband offered him, but stared across the street at the Corso. Two gipsies, lean and dark as Sikhs, with red rags tied round their heads, padded past, wheeling a handcart in which there lay a bundle. It stirred, it sat up, it was an elderly and beautiful woman in richly coloured garments who looked at us with wild eyes that filled with solemn recognition, who swept out her arm in the gesture of a prophet, and cried out some words in Roumanian, which twanged with the spirit of revelation. For a second it seemed a supreme calamity that we could not understand her. But she softened, and fell back, and was a bundle again; she was simply drunk. Constantine said absently, as if his soul were entirely with the march of the Corso, 'You know, my wife has made up her mind to come with us to Macedonia.'

I stood transfixed with horror. Tears began to run down my cheeks. Macedonia was the most beautiful place that I had ever seen in my life, I had looked forward to showing it to my husband, and now we were to be accompanied by this disagreeable woman who liked neither of us. It was like having to take a censorious enemy on one's honeymoon. Not only was this proposal an outrage to a reasonable sentiment, it raised endless practical difficulties. The cars and cabs we could rely on in Macedonia would be small, too small for four, though comfortable enough for three. Gerda would have to be our guest, as Constantine was to be, and the relationship between host and guest is not easy for people who feel a strong mutual antipathy. And her contempt for everything Slav and non-German would be at its most peevish in Macedonia, which is the most Slav part of Yugoslavia, and which is not only non-German but non-Occidental, being strongly Byzantine and even Asiatic. 'But she will not like it!' I exclaimed. 'So I have told her many, many times!' wailed Constantine. My husband bent down over him, his spectacles shining with a light that looked menacing, that was in fact panic-stricken. 'Your wife cannot come with us,' he said. 'But she will, she will!' cried Constantine. 'All night she cries, because I will not take her, and I get no sleep. And she says she will suicide herself if I go without her! And I cannot let you go alone, for my Ministry wishes me to go with you! I tell you, she must come with us!' And he turned and left us, walking very fast. My husband and I stood staring at each other, feeling like the people in Kafka's books who are sentenced by an invisible and nameless authority for some unnamed sin to a fantastic and ineluctable punishment. It was not a thing that happens to one in adult life, being obliged to go on a journey with someone whom one dislikes and who has no sort of hold over one, sentimental or patriotic or economic.

So, at eight o'clock on the morning of Good Friday (according to the Orthodox calendar) the four of us started for Macedonia from Belgrade station. My husband and I had driven down from the hotel, past a corner of Kalemegdan Park that drops a steep bank towards the river, claret-coloured with tamarisk bloom. The early light lay as a happy presence on the wide grey floods round the city, and it shone on the Obrenovitch villa on the hill-top, which, like all Turkish villas, was exquisitely appropriate to everything freshest in nature, to spring and the morning. At the station we found that Gerda and Constantine had not arrived, and we sat down at the café on the platform and ate beautiful Palestinian oranges, their flesh gleaming like golden crystal. There appeared presently a young doctor of philosophy, a colleague of Constantine's, with whom I had had some official business, who came to say good-bye and bring me a bunch of red roses. He sat down with us and had some coffee, and we talked until it became evident that Constantine and Gerda were very late indeed, and we began to walk up and down, alarmed and exasperated.

They came at the last possible moment, and we had to jump into the train just as it went, the doctor of philosophy handing up the roses to the window after we had started. My husband and I busied ourselves packing away our baggage and putting out cushions and books, for we were to be nearly twelve hours in the train. But soon we became aware that Gerda was standing quite still, looking down at the roses with a resentful expression, and Constantine, with his arm round her, was attempting to console her. 'Yes, it is very bad,' he was saying, 'certainly he should have brought you flowers also.' My husband and I stared at him aghast, for it was obvious that the yong doctor had come down to give me the roses as an impersonal and official act, and that he had refrained from bringing any to Gerda for the precise reason that she had some personal value for him. 'But I am afraid,' said Constantine, 'that this young man really does not know how to behave so well as I had hoped, for look, these are not the flowers he should have given our friend.' '*Nein, ganz gewiss nicht!*' agreed Gerda hotly, and they gazed down at the roses, shaking their heads.

'Tell me,' said Constantine, turning to my husband, 'what sort of flowers would it be considered right in your country for a man to give to a lady whom he does not know very well when he sees her off at a station?' My husband guffawed and said, 'In our country he would go to a florist and ask for some nice flowers.' Gerda looked disgusted, sat down, and stared out of the window. Constantine said in shocked and bewildered accents, '*O! Il y a des règles!*' 'What are they?' asked my husband, laughing coarsely. From Constantine's explanations I learned that it was not by ill luck that I had been dogged through Central Europe by carnations, which I detest; I had brought them on myself by my marriage to a banker. Pains had been taken, which I had never perceived, to keep me from getting above myself, for it was ruled that the flowers which I received on my arrival in a town, and during my stay in it, should be modest. 'It is only on departure,' said Constantine, 'that the bouquet should be really large. And there remains the question of colour, which is what disturbs us at this moment. There are certain colors, particularly in roses, which are purely personal, which are not suitable for gifts of ceremony. It is here that our young friend has offended. These roses are nearly crimson.' My husband turned to me with an air of suspicion, but Constantine did not laugh. There was doubt in his eyes, as if he were wondering whether his wife were not right, and he had greatly exaggerated the degree of our refinement.

The lovely Serbian country, here like a fusion of Lowland

Scotland and New England, with many willows rising golden green, and meadows white with daisies, and nymphean woods, ran past us for some hours. Then there was the call for lunch, and we went along to the restaurant car, to eat one of those pungent and homely meals that are served on the Balkan trains. As we sat down, a middle-aged man in a grey lounge suit stood up in his place and shouted at an elderly man in a braided purple peasant costume who went on with his meal. 'It is nothing,' said the waiter who was taking our order; 'they are only two members of Parliament.' 'Yes,' said Constantine, 'the one in peasant costume in a well-known supporter of Mr. Stoyadinovitch, and the other is an opposition man.' At this point the opposition man bent down to look at his opponent's plate, straightened himself, and cried, 'I see you are eating an enormous amount of fish. No wonder you take no interest in measures for controlling the floods, I suppose you like floods because they bring us quantities of fish.' He then sat down, but sprang up immediately to shout, 'If you don't make better roads we in our banovina will become separatists. We've got a fine regiment, and one will be enough, for only the riff-raff of the Army would march for your lot.' That was the end, and we all went on with our meal.

As we went back along the corridor a man ran out of his carriage and grasped Constantine by both hands. 'Look at him well,' said Constantine, 'he is a typical old Serbian patriotic man.' He was short and thickset, overweight but nimble, with a great deal of coarse black hair on his head and face. 'See, he has not a grey hair on his head,' Constantine went on, 'and he is nearly an old man. I will get him to come and sit with us, for he likes me very much, and you can observe him.' He remained with us for quite a time, bouncing up and down on his seat, as he passionately attacked the Stoyadinovitch Government, not for its reaction, but for its innovations. 'The country has gone to the dogs,' he cried, 'now that there are so many non-Serbs in the Army! Think of it, there are Croat colonels. A Croat colonel, that is something ridiculous to think of, like a woman preacher! I tell you, the Croats are spoiled for ever by the Austrian influence, they are like fallen women, they cannot be raised.' Every now and then he stopped to show my husband and myself some point in the landscape, which he thought strangers should not miss. 'They look good people,' he said of us; but sighed and added gloomily, 'But after all they are from the West, they're Europeans, no doubt they are in sympathy with this horrible age when everything is questioned.'

'Of course he is not at home in the present,' Constantine

explained to us, 'he is one of our medieval heroes reborn.' Though he was very rich and he had much to see to in his own district, all his youth he used to rush backwards and forwards between his home and Macedonia, where he was a comitadji and killed many Turks. He fought like a lion in the Balkan wars and the Great War, and after the peace he was made Ban of South Serbia (which is the administrative title of Macedonia) as a reward. 'But,' said Constantine, 'his ideas were not modern enough for his position. He was splendidly brave, of course, and that was a great qualification, for there could not have been a more dangerous job, what with the I.M.R.O. and the wild Montenegrins and the Albanians. But in other ways he was too simple and too large, too Homeric. He wished to remake Macedonia as it had been five hundred years ago, and whenever he saw a ruined church or a castle that had belonged to the Serbs and had been destroyed by the Turks, he would take Turks and Moslem Albanians away from where they lived until he had enough labour to rebuild them, and then he made them work under armed guards. And when people said, 'But you must not do that,' he answered, 'But why not? They knocked them down, didn't they?'

'But King Alexander was very kind about it, and though he did not keep him there for long, since these things will now not do, he gave him other work that he could do better. And now this man is very happy building many churches, since he is very pious, and the Church and the state to him are one. He aims to make more foundations than our medieval King Milutin, who built thirty-seven monasteries.' He bent across and asked the patriot what his record was, and the old man stroked his coal-black moustache with a flourish and announced, 'Forty-six.' 'The one he loves most,' said Constantine, 'is a chapel near the field of Kossovo, where he has really let himself go. It cost two hundred pounds, and it is ornamented with frescoes, which gratify him in an old quarrel he has with the Church. You see, our medieval kings, the Nemanyas, were recognized as saints, except for the one who was a flagrant sinner and defied the Church, who was that same Milutin who built the thirty-seven monasteries. They were saints because they were heads of a theocratic society on the Byzantine model, and because they defended Christianity against the pagan Turks. So he cannot see why Karageorge and the Karageorgevitches, who also united the Church and state and who actually drove out the Turks, should not be recognized as saints too. But of course the Church of today will have nothing to do with such an idea, they think it is profane, and they tell him not to be so impious. However, down there his chapel is far away from everywhere, so he has had frescoes painted showing Karageorge himself, and Alexander Karageorgevitch and old King Peter, yes, and King Alexander, all with immense haloes like golden soup-plates. He had quite a well-known artist to paint them, and he knew it was wrong and did not want to do it, but this one roared at him like a bull, and snatched so at his belt as if he were finding his pistol, and the artist said, 'Oh, certainly they shall be saints, they shall all be saints!' Then when the Patriarch came down to consecrate the chapel this one covered all the frescoes that showed the new royal saints with banners, and all went well. But his mother, who is very *dévote*, she spends many hours lying on the floors of chapels praying these sins of his will be forgiven.'

'Now tell your friends that we are coming to the heart of Serbia,' the patriot bade Constantine. 'This town we are coming into is Kraguyevats,' Constantine explained, 'and it was the big town of the Shumadiya, that is to say the wooded district, where the most Serbian Serbs came from, the ones that were foremost in the revolt against the Turks. Now there are great munition works here.' 'Tell them to look over there at the memorial to King Alexander,' said the patriot; 'it is a good thing for foreigners to see, it makes him quite stout and broad as a king should be, though God knows the poor man was thin as a student. But now make them look out of the other window, for God's sake.' 'Why?' asked Constantine. 'If they do that they won't see the memorial to the Serbian dead.' 'That's just what I am hoping,' said the patriot. 'But why?' asked Constantine again. 'The figure of the Serbian mother is considered very fine.' 'It's just that figure I don't want them to see,' insisted the other. 'Serbian women have got good breasts, this creature they have put up looks like a toothpick.' 'Never would he think of a woman's breasts except from a patriotic point of view,' explained Constantine. 'His country is all to him. He is as pure as a good monk.'

A little further on he got out at his own station. A peasant in a sheep-skin jacket, a much younger man, was waiting for him and took his baggage, and watched him as he said good-bye to us, with a loving and loyal and condescending smile. 'I am glad to be back!' cried the patriot. 'This is a beautiful part of the country, you know! Some day you must all come and see me!' He smiled up at his local sky, and looked into the branches of one of the lindens that grew all along the platform, and was convulsed with pride. 'These lindens!

Fine, aren't they? I planted them all ten years ago!' 'Ten? It is not possible!' exclaimed Constantine. 'You must mean twenty!' 'No, I mean ten,' said the patriot, and turned to his servant. 'It is not more than ten years since I planted these trees, is it, Sasha?' 'It is twenty-two,' said Sasha. 'Sasha, you are a fool and the son of a fool!' cried the patriot. 'It is twenty-two years since you planted these trees!' the peasant answered, his voice rising. 'How can that be so,' the patriot screamed, 'when——' The train moved on and we re-established ourselves for another long session. 'Would you not like to sit in this corner?' I asked Gerda. 'I think you will see most from the window on this side.' 'That would be interesting, no doubt,' said Gerda, 'if one had the slightest intention of looking out of the window.' The train ran on into the afternoon, into the evening, into the night, into Macedonia.

Macedonia

Skoplje I

I BEHAVED LIKE A PROFESSIONAL GUIDE AS WE HURRIED OUT of the station, waving my hand to indicate the wealth that lay behind the darkness. The station lies in the new part of Skoplje, at the end of the main street, which resembles some hundred yards cut out of a secondary shopping centre in an English industrial town, saving the dimness of its lighting, the cobbles, and the lack of automobiles, and gives the same impression that the scalp of the years has become dandruffed with undistinguished manufactured goods. But behind the station a tableland was Atlas to a sky marbled with moonlit clouds, and about us there was warm air and the scent of lilacs, and the sound of playing and singing, the astringent sound of Macedonian playing and singing, from the little cafés hidden away in side streets and courtyards. And an event was imposing on the city a rhythm, an excitement. Little fiacres with two horses were clattering over the cobbles, people were hurrying along on clattering heels, all in the same direction. 'Look, they are all going to the church for the Easter ceremony,' said Constantine; 'we must just deposit our luggage in the hotel and start out again, if we are not to miss it, for it is nearly midnight.' 'I am afraid that I will have to get some other shoes,' I said, for one heel of the pair I was wearing had come off as I got out of the train. 'But meantime you can tell them to get us a fiacre.'

But when we came downstairs again they had done nothing. In the lounge Gerda was sitting quite still, dazed in contemplation of my inconsiderateness as an antique monk of Mount Athos in contemplation of his navel, and Constantine was nervously agreeing with the strictures she had made before she passed into full ecstasy. The boy who might have fetched us a fiacre was now doing something else, so we had to go back to the station, and there we found only one, which was falling to pieces. It would have been just possible for three, but for four it was dangerous misery. We rattled down the main street to the square leading to the bridge over the Vardar, and my husband turned to crane his neck in

633

wonder at the unique architectural horror which defiled that spot. It regrettably happened that the Yugoslavs, in their joy at turning out the Turks and becoming the masters of Macedonia, pulled down the beautiful mosque that had stood for three centuries in this commanding position, and replaced it by an Officers' Club which is one of the most hideous buildings in the whole of Europe. It is built of turnip-coloured cement and looks like a cross between a fish-kettle and a mausoleum, say the tomb of a very large cod. As my husband received the shock of this building's outline he nearly fell out on the cobbles, and I cried out, 'This is a horrible fiacre!' 'We might have got a better one,' said Gerda, 'if we had been a little earlier.'

It seemed to me for a minute that there was going to be no Easter, that Gerda had annulled it, and that we were to be left with nothing but a scramble and fuss on our hands. But now we were on the bridge, in the cold air that blows off the Vardar, which carries with it the snake-like chill of those rivers which grow big quite soon after they leave the snow mountains. On the black waters the embankment lamps made shuddering pools of golden oil; behind them the new houses, simple and artless yet shaped by a good tradition of living, made un-Western shapes against the darkness; very high above the town the bright windows of a fortress shone where one had expected the stars. We turned off the bridge on to the embankment. The river rushed beside us, above us the flocks of silver clouds rushed over the black firmament, on the pavement shuffled a crowd, so close-set that they could no longer hurry, the night making their clothes darker and their faces lighter than they would be by day, before them going the happy sound of festival chatter, pressing towards the church with the sightseeing greed that is the peculiar charm of an Eastern congregation. They might have been going to see the elephants. We stepped from our fiacre and joined them, shuffled with them down a side street, and found ourselves facing a church that looked like neither a church nor a circus, but an opulent two-storied farm building.

Even within it had its oddities. It was built about a hundred years ago, when the sultans were showing a certain indulgence to the Christians and were letting them put up churches, though usually this permission was useless unless they bribed the local pashas; and its builders were four brothers who had learned their craft working as stonemasons all over the Balkans and in Italy. The chief of them was said to have been unable to read or write, and their work has indeed a strange air of combined culture and illiteracy. There was here a competent yet childish handling of highly developed forms which, profoundly disparate, were forcibly unified by a mind that knew nothing of their origins and therefore not all of their essences. A Byzantine dome suddenly hollowed the flat roof of an immensely high Italian basilica; in its upper shadows Asian galleries guarded their secrets with pierced screens; on the right and the left of the church were two great carved chairs, one for the king and one for the bishop, suggesting a rude Ravenna; a pulpit had been perched at a great height, because the eye of the Balkan builder had been accustomed to the mimbar, the pulpit in the mosque, which is always at the top of a long stairway, steep as a ladder; and here and there were forthright and sensible hinged windows of clear glass set in iron frames, such as one might have seen in a farmhouse.

In this strange building, now full of a deep twilight, stood many people, waiting, holding unlit tapers in their hands. The iconostasis, which is the characteristic architectural feature of the Eastern Church, the screen before the altar, is here a wall surmounted by a cross, a fortification defending the ever-threatened holy things; its height, made gorgeous by icons and gilt carvings, was in this dusk a shadowy richness. The silver plates that are laid over the haloes and hands of the people represented in the icons glimmered like moonlight. Here and there a lamp burned dimly in the chandeliers that hung low from the roof; and a weak light came from the candles on the table in the middle of the church, where the dead Christ lay in the likeness of an embroidered cloth. Most of the people had already paid their respects to this symbol, and were standing still in their places, the men to the right, the women to the left, so far as the elders were concerned, though the younger people often broke this rule. There is a step running round the edge of the church, so that there was a line of people behind the others and raised above them, which gave a handsomeness to the scene, a superfluity of grace; it might have been so ordered in the chapel of a great palace, by an emperor. But even now many people still pressed about the table to greet the body of Christ. The holy table was painted blue-green with some flowers here and there, and it had a canopy rising to a battered trellis canopy; some eighteenth-century bedsteads look so. It was curtained with machine-made lace, and on the embroidered cloth lay a heavy volume of the Gospels and some coins, none of them of great value, which the congregation had left there. Old men whose faces were scored by hard work and poverty as by actual wounds; young men sleek as seals in Western clothes; old women with grey plaits hanging to their waist, in white serge coats covered with black embroideries which were beginning to break away from the stuff, because they had stitched them when they were young and it was too long ago; young girls, who had flowers in the hair yet were rolled into the wintry thickness of sheepskins, and others who were dressed as they are in Palmers Green or Rochester, New York: all these came and looked down on the embroidered cloth, and were tranced in sorrow. They stooped and kissed it with that unquestioning worship which every woman wants to feel for the man whom she loves, but which, should she be able to feel it for him, is more likely to bring their relationship to a painful end than any disagreeable action she might commit against him. It was strange to recognize this kind of worship performed by men as well as women, and not to have to fear that it would arouse resentment and caprice in its object.

There passed to the table a young woman with a round face almost stupid with sweetness, who was wearing the Debar head-dress, which I think one of the most beautiful garments in the world: a handkerchief of fine linen, scattered with a few circles of solid red or rose embroidery, in which there is inscribed, as if to hide it from the public note, a cross, often of crimson or purple. Every woman sews it according to her own vision, but it is always a masterpiece, a sublime symbol of a persecuted but gorgeous religion. As she bent over the table I twitched at my husband's sleeve and said, 'Look, she is from Debar,' and he repeated, nodding his head, 'Yes, she is from Debar,' and I marvelled at his amiability, for I had never told him anything about Debar. Then, suddenly, the full crash of the Easter ritual was upon us. In an instant the procession of priests came through the door in the iconostasis, there was the gentle lion roar of hymns sung by men of a faith which has never exacted celibacy from its priests nor pacifism from its congregations, and flames had run from wick to wick of the tapers in our hands, till the whole church was a field of gentle primrose fires.

This is the supreme moment of Easter, when the priests lift up the embroidered cloth from the table, take it out into the open air, and walk round the church three times at the head of the congregation, all carrying their lighted tapers and singing a hymn proclaiming that Christ has risen. Constantine and I had walked in this procession when we had come to Skoplje the year before, and I had wanted to do it again. It is the very consummation of the picturesque, with the flowerlike yellow brightness of the tapers, the coldness of the starlight and moonlight, the glittering crosses and vestments of the priests, the dark people leaning from the lit windows of the houses in the square, which seem themselves to waver with the pulse of the advancing and receding lights and shadows. But there is here more than that, there is true Easter, the recognition of the difference between winter and summer, between cold and heat, between darkness and light, between death and life, between minus and plus. Something important which passes unnoticed because it is continually experienced is felt again in its real importance. But now we could not join the procession, for we had been at the iconostasis end of the church when it started, and it had accomplished its three circuits before we reached the door. When the Metropolitan who was at the head of the priests halted in the doorway to make his sermon, we were in the antechamber, called the narthex, which runs across the front of any Byzantine church, which here was specially large and secular, because the architects were accustomed to the great porches of mosques, where Moslems are accustomed to sit and gossip and settle business and talk politics.

I was extremely frightened as we stood there, for I thought it possible that a number of people, packed together and constantly stirring in their discomfort and all holding lighted tapers, might set themselves on fire. But I forgot my alarm, because I was standing opposite a peasant woman sitting on a window ledge who was the very essence of Macedonia, who was exactly what I had come back to see. She was the age that all Macedonian women seem to become as soon as they cease to be girls: a weather-beaten fifty. There was a dark cloth about her hair and shoulders, and in its folds, and in her noble bones and pain-grooved flesh, she was like many Byzantine Madonnas to be seen in frescoes and mosaics. In her rough hand she mothered her taper, looking down on its flame as if it were a young living thing; and on the sleeve of her russet sheepskin jacket there showed an embroidery of stylized red and black trees which derived recognizably from a pattern designed for elegant Persian women two thousand years before. There was the miracle of Macedonia, made visible before our eyes.

This woman had suffered more than most other human beings, she and her forebears. A competent observer of this countryside has said that every single person born in it before the Great War (and quite a number who were born after it) has faced the prospect of violent death at least once in his or her life. She had been born during the calamitous end of Turkish maladministration, with its cycles of insurrection and massacre, and its social chaos. If her own village had not been murdered, she had certainly heard of many that had, and had never had any guarantee that hers would not some day share the same fate. Then, in her maturity, had come the Balkan wars and the Great War, with a cholera and typhus epidemic in between. Later had come I.M.R.O.; and there was always extreme poverty. She had had far less of anything, of personal possessions, of security, of care in childbirth, than any Western woman can imagine. But she had two possessions which any Western woman might envy. She had strength, the terrible stony strength of Macedonia; she was begotten and born of stocks who could mock all bullets save those which went through the heart, who could outlive the winters when they were driven into the mountains, who could survive malaria and plague, who could reach old age on a diet of bread and paprika. And cupped in her destitution as in the hollow of a boulder there are the last drops of the Byzantine tradition.

With our minds we all know what Byzantium was. We are aware that the Eastern continuance of the Roman Empire was a supremely beautiful civilization. It was imperfect because it was almost totally ignorant of economics, and the people were distraught with hungry discontents which they could not name. We know that by the Golden Horn the waning empire developed a court ceremonial, which the earlier emperors had borrowed from Asia, until it made all those who watched it wise about the symbols of spiritual things that can be expressed by sight and sound. The Church itself learned from its partner the State, and raised the Mass to a supreme masterpiece of communal art; and the people, saturated with ritual impressions of the idea of God and of the Emperor, who was by theory the Viceroy of God, produced an art that is unique in its nobility, that in its architecture and painting and mosaics and metal-work and textiles found a calligraphy for the expression of man's graver experiences which makes all other arts seem a little naïve or gross. We know that these achievements were not technical tricks but were signs of a real spiritual process, for the Byzantines were able to live in dignity and decency for four centuries in the knowledge that they were doomed, that one day they would be destroyed root and branch by the merciless Turks. They were not merely stoical in that shadow; they continued to live in the fullness of life, to create, even, in the very last phase of their doom, to the point of pushing out the shoots of a new school of painting.

All this we know with our minds, and with our minds only. But this woman knew it with all her being, because she knew nothing else. It was the medium in which she existed. Turkish misrule had deprived her of all benefit from Western culture;

all she had had to feed on was the sweetness spilled from the overturned cup of Constantinople. Therefore she was Byzantine in all her ways, and in her substance. When she took up her needle it instinctively pricked the linen in Byzantine designs, and she had the Byzantine idea that one must decorate, always decorate, richly decorate. As she sat there she was stiff, it might almost be said carpeted, in the work of her own hands. The stiffness was not an accidental effect of her materials, it was a symbol of her beliefs about society. She believed that people who are to be respected practise a more stately bearing than those who are of no account; her own back was straight, she did not smile too easily. Therefore she found nothing tedious in the ritual of her Church. She could have sat for long hours as she was then, nursing her taper in quiet contentment, watching grave and slow-moving priests evoke the idea of magnificence, and induce the mood of adoration which is due to the supremely magnificent. She was not gaping at a peepshow, she was not merely passing the time. She was possessed by the same passion that had often astounded the relief workers who came here at the beginning of the century to fight the famine that always followed the suppression of the Christian revolts. Again and again, in villages which had fallen under Turkish disfavour and were therefore subject without cease to murder and arson and pillage, they urged inhabitants to emigrate to Serbia and Bulgaria; and the peasants always answered that that might be the wisest course, but that they could not desert their churches. This was not superstition. Before the altars, the offshoot of Byzantinism had passed the same test as its parent; it had prevented doom from becoming degradation. This woman's face was unresentful, exalted, sensitive to her sorrows yet preoccupied by that which she perceived to be more important, magnificence and its adoration.

Now the Metropolitan was at the door, a gorgeous figure, not only because his vestments were bright with gold thread, and his high mitre and pastoral staff and the cross on his breast glittered with jewels. There is inherent dignity in the lines of a costume that has incorporated the philosopher's mantle of the ancients, the Roman consul's scarf, and the tunic and gauntlets of the Byzantine Emperor. In a rich voice the Metropolitan announced that Christ had risen, and from the faces above the primrose flames came sharp cries of belief. Then he uttered a prayer or repeated a passage from the Gospels, I was not sure which, and went on to deliver an address which compared the resurrection of Christ and the liberation of Christian Macedonia from the Turks by Serbia twenty-five years before. It was, in fact, straight Yugoslavian propaganda, and most of it could have easily been delivered from a political platform.

It was only our modernity that was shocked. This was not an innovation, but a continuance of the ancient tradition of the Church. 'As the body politic, like the human body, is composed of parts and members, so the most important and the most vital parts are the Emperor and the Patriarch,' wrote a Byzantine theologian; 'in the same way that the peace and happiness of the human being depends on the harmony of body and soul, so in the polity there must be perfect agreement between the Emperor and the priesthood.' Since the Orthodox Church does not pretend to be anything but a religion, since it does not claim to be in possession of the final truth about philosophy and ethics and political science, this does not raise such difficulties as it would in the West. The Orthodox Church conceived, and still conceives, that its chief business is magic, the evocation by ritual of the spiritual experiences most necessary to man. It has also the duty of laying down a general pattern of moral behaviour. If the civil authority assists at the ritual and accepts this pattern it has a right to demand the support of the ecclesiastical authority, and the ecclesiastical authority has a right to give it, save when its own sphere is invaded. It will, in fact, support the civil authority politically if the civil authority does not meddle in theology. This is an attitude that is bound to be adopted by any state church, and that involves no difficulties in the case of a church which does not claim final wisdom on profane subjects as well as divine.

The Orthodox Church did not renounce that claim by choice. The renunciation was forced on it by the troubled character of Byzantine history. One can claim final wisdom on a subject to the degree that life as regards that subject is predictable. Now life in Europe has never been orderly for more than a few years at a time and in a limited area; but in the West it has been orderly enough, if only in the homogeneity of its disorder, to allow clever men to lay down principles that they could safely claim to be eternal, since they afforded useful bases for action and thought during some considerable period of time. In the East of Europe it has not been so. Continual and astonishing were its historical convulsions. The Byzantine Empire, which suffered invasion by blood-thirsty and pitiless fellow-Christians who had come to redeem the tomb of Christ in Jerusalem and stopped to taste the more immediately delectable pleasure of looting Constantinople, and which knew itself certain to be invaded by Asiatics as inaccessible to appeal as the personages in a nightmare, could not prophesy. Hence its genius turned away from speculative thought to art, and its Church preserved its dogma without developing it and concentrated its forces on the glory of the Mass, which gave a magic protection against evils that were unknown as well as those that were known. Thereby it brought on itself the criticisms that it was sterile and archaic in teaching and an arcanum of superstition; but it could not have served its people better in their special tribulation.

For these historical reasons nobody in the congregation was shocked because the Metropolitan's sermon was a speech in support of the Government; and I am sure also, since the circumstances of Balkan life have forbidden any intertwining of religious and pacifist sentiment, that nobody was shocked because the Metropolitan had in his young days been a comitadji. The comitadji who waged guerrilla warfare against the Turks in Macedonia before the war covered a wide range of character. Some were highly disciplined, courageous, and ascetic men, often from good families in the freed Slav countries, who harried the Turkish troops, particularly those sent to punish Christian villages, and who held unofficial courts to correct the collapse of the legal system in the Turkish provinces. Others were fanatics who were happy in massacring the Turks but even happier when they were purging the movement of suspected traitors. Others were robust nationalists, to whom the proceedings seemed a natural way of spirited living. Others were blackguards who were in the business because they enjoyed murder and banditry. All intermediate shades of character were fully represented. This made it difficult for the Western student to form a clear opinion about Near Eastern politics; it also made it difficult, very difficult, for a Macedonian peasant who saw a band of armed men approaching his village.

The Metropolitan had, in point of fact, belonged to one of the most admirable among these bands; but if he had been careless about the choice of his companions it would not have troubled the peasant woman who was nursing her taper and gazing at him in thankfulness over its glow. He was a good magician. He knew how to wear the garments, how to speak the words, how to make the obeisances, that gave her the beautiful experience of loving a flawless being. He was a magician, and, what was a great marvel to her, he was not her enemy. For two centuries her people had been under the horrible necessity of seeking this magic, which was their sole consolation, from agents who, in the intervals of dispensing it to them, contrived their ruin and death. In the eighteenth century the Church fell into the power of the phanariots, the wealthy Greeks, who established themselves in Constantinople and worked hand in glove with the Turks; not least joyfully when their Moslem masters set them on the Slavs though they themselves retained their Christianity. They persuaded the Sultan to put the whole of the Balkan Church under the power of the Patriarchate of Constantinople, an institution which they kept in their pocket. They then turned the Church into an elaborate fiscal system for fleecing the Slavs, by exacting enormous fees for the performance of all religious functions, even stripping the peasants of their last farthing as a charge for saying prayers for the dead. They not only robbed their congregations of their material possessions, they strove to deprive them of their most treasured immaterial possession, their racial identity. There were always a number of Slavs so devout that they insisted upon becoming priests; if these were not prepared to forget that they were Serb or Bulgar, and play traitor to their own blood, they were enlisted as the servants of the Greek clergy, and if they displeased their masters they were beaten during divine service before silent congregations of their own people. There was also a ruthless campaign against the speaking of the Serbian and Bulgarian languages, and an attempt to enforce the use of Greek over the whole of Macedonia, instead of the small Southern district to which it had long been limited.

But as the nineteenth century progressed the Ottoman Turks began to conceive a great fear of the Greeks, some of whom had already achieved independence in the kingdom of Greece; and the unrest of the Serbs and Bulgars grew with every decade. So the Sultan worked out a new application of the fiendish rule *Divide et impera*, and in 1870 he appointed a Bulgarian exarch to rule over the churches of Bulgaria and Macedonia. The term exarch shows the curious persistence of the Byzantine tradition in these parts. It was originally used by the Eastern emperors to denote a viceroy; the Exarch of Ravenna was the governor who represented their power in Italy. But it exemplifies the degradation which the Byzantine tradition had suffered in Turkish hands that it is hard to define the ecclesiastical office to which the name was given in modern times, and it seems indeed to have held a different meaning at different times. In this case it meant the patriarch of this province, appointed to fulfil a political mission but with uncertain guarantee of support against the opponents of his mission. The situation can be grasped if we imagine the British Government sending out an archbishop to Australia to carry on his ecclesiastical duties, and also to compel the Irish and the Scottish to lose their identities and become English patriots, while at the same time doing nothing to prevent the existing Scottish and

Irish religions and political organizations from opposing him. The Sultan did not recall the Greek priests who were already in Macedonia, and they fought savagely to retain their power. As the Serbs naturally found Bulgar control of their Church no more admirable than Greek they too were up in arms. Thus, at the cost of all peace and gentleness in a community of over half a million people, the Ottoman Empire preserved itself from the risks arising out of a union between its Greek and Serb and Bulgar subjects.

This horrible confusion of religion and bloodshed persisted till the end of the Balkan wars. The woman sitting on the window ledge was certainly not too young to remember a certain Greek Archbishop of a Macedonian diocese to the south of Skoplje, whose hatred of the Slavs in his spiritual care was indeed spiritual, since it could hardly be satisfied by anything he could do to their bodies. Once he commissioned a band of assassins to murder a Bulgarian leader who was lying wounded in a hideaway. They were successful. As proof they cut off his head and took it back to the Archiepiscopal Palace, where the Archbishop received it and paid them well. It offered an unpleasing appearance, as a bullet had smashed the jaw. Nevertheless he had it photographed and hung an enlargement on the wall of the room where he received his flock, so that they might take a lesson. Many a woman, such as this one, sensitive and exalted, could never hear the proclamation that Christ had risen except from the lips of this atrocious enemy of her kind. The Archbishop was a man of extreme personal beauty and the graduate of a Western university. At the thought of this unpleasing incongruity, one of a million omens that the world is not simple, not consistent, and often not agreeable, my hand shook and my taper shivered.

The Metropolitan was still speaking, it was becoming enormously hot, and the heat was laden with the smell of honey, for it is ordained that all tapers used in churches must be made of beeswax. There came back to me the fear of fire which I had felt earlier in the service, and this was accompanied by a revulsion from the horror of history, and a dread that it might really be witless enough to repeat itself. Fire spreads, and the substances it inflames put up no defence, burn, and become ashes. Human beings love to inflict pain on their fellow-creatures, and the species yields to its perverse appetite, allowing vast tragedies to happen and endure for centuries, people to agonize and become extinct. The pleasantness of life which is so strong when it manifests itself that it is tempting to regard it as the characteristic and even determinant quality of the universe, is of no real avail. I could be burnt to death in this church, though the air smelt of honey. In moonlight, by fountains where roses grew and nightingales sang, all less tangible and superior beauty could be beaten down into earth, not to emerge itself again until freed by another Creation. I let myself feel these fears to their extreme, with a certain sense of luxury, for facing me was this Macedonian woman, who could, better than anybody else I had ever met, give me an assurance on these points. There was nothing over-positive in her statement. One can shout at the top of one's voice the information that the 11.15 for Brighton leaves from platform 6, but subtler news has to be whispered, for the reason that to drag knowledge of reality over the threshold of consciousness is an exhausting task, whether it is performed by art or by experience. She made no spectacular declaration that man is to be saved; simply her attitude assumed that this Easter would end with no more fatality than any other Easter she had known, and her body, wasted yet proud in its coarse and magnificent clothes, proclaimed that death may last five hundred years yet not be death.

Skoplje II

Before we went down to breakfast my husband called me to look out of the lavatory window. The part of Skoplje behind the hotel exhibits a form of urban economy which I find it hard to understand: in paved gardens crammed with lilac bushes and fig trees, all now bobbing under heavy rain, stand new and trim little houses, each alongside a hovel where a craftsman, who seems to have nothing to do with the house-owner, exercises his skill on the top of rickety stairs under sagging roofs of red-brown tiles. These stucco houses are designed in a vein of pleasantly vapid romanticism. Minnie Mouse might well have chosen one for her first home with Mickey, for they bristle with towers and loggias and a great many silly little balconies, on which she could be discovered by Mr Disney's lens, watering flowers and singing a tender lyric in that voice which is the very distillation of imbecile sweetness.

On the pavement, under one such balcony, lay a Turk, a Moslem of true Turkish blood, as most of the Moslems are, here in Macedonia. He was in rags, his head was covered with the imperfect memory of a fez, the upturned points of his sandals had broken off. The shelter of the balcony afforded him enough dry pavement for his body, and there he stretched himself, looking out at the rain, and slowly eating something, with a notable economy of effort. He was resting his elbow on the doorstep, so that he had to lift his hand not nearly so far as one would suppose to raise the food to his bearded mouth. 'I never saw quite such a hopeless proposition,' said my husband. 'I see he is a Turk, he has that indestructibly handsome air, but he is so unlike the Turks I have seen in the Ataturk's Turkey.' 'Poor man,' I said, 'he is the residue of residues. The Turkish population in Skoplje, which used to be called Üskub, was increased in the seventies by the Turks who left Bosnia when the Austrians occupied it. The Slav Moslems stayed, and a few Turkish Moslems of the better sort, who could cope with Western ways. Probably a large number of these Turks never found a place to fit into here, for this was already a contracting society. Then there has been a further winnowing since the war, by the repatriation of all the Balkan Turks who were willing to face life under the reforms of the Ataturk. But, all the same, I like this man.' 'Yes,' said my husband, 'this is not lethargy we are regarding, it is an

645

immense capacity for pleasure, which is being exercised in difficult circumstances.'

We went down to breakfast and sat at a table by the window, drinking coffee full of the sweet broken curds of sheep's milk, eating the peculiarly excellent rolls that Moslems bake, and enjoying the show of Skoplje. This is one of the best spectacles I have ever enjoyed, and it is due to the presence of the Turk. There are about seventy-five thousand inhabitants of the town, of whom over ten thousand are Turks who gave the town its colour in the first place. There are fewer minarets than there are in Sarajevo, but they are potent. And because there is so strong a Christian element in the town, there are constant dramatic disclosures of the essences of Christianity and Islam, each being shown up by its opposite. Soon there came past the window some Albanians, to begin the revelation. Though I had my back to them I knew they were on their way, for a look of fatherly concern on my husband's face told me that he had just caught sight of his first Albanian. 'They are not really coming down,' I said. No Westerner ever sees an Albanian for the first time without thinking that the poor man's trousers are just about to drop off. They are cut in a straight line across the loins, well below the hip-bone, and have no visible means of support; and to make matters psychologically worse they are of white or biscuit homespun heavily embroidered with black wool in designs that make a stately reference to the essential points of male anatomy. The occasion could not seem more grave, especially as there is often a bunch of uncontrolled shirt bulging between the waistcoat and these trousers. Nothing, however, happens. The little white skull-caps they all wear, which have an air of second-rank haloes, of commoners' aureoles, suggest that there may perhaps be a miraculous element involved. There is of course a partial explanation in the stiffness of the material, which, where it is reinforced by embroidery, must be nearly as stiff as a boned corset. But all the same the cause of the phenomenon lies in the Albanian nature. There is something about the Moslem Albanians which would make them take chances with their national costume: it is as if they had not eaten of the tree of good or of evil, as if they were unalloyed by the seriousness that Christianity adds to the soft metal of human nature. A lovely facile charm hangs about them, comes to dazzling crystallization in their smiles.

The group of Albanians who had startled my husband passed, and were followed by some of their antithesis, women from the villages on Skopska Tserna Gora (the Black Mountain of Skoplje). The tragic majesty of their appearance, which is unmitigated by beauty, and hardly ever put to the slight test of a smile, is consonant with the history of their breed. These villages were never fully conquered by the Turk during the five hundred years of the Turkish occupation, they murdered most of the Turkish landowners who tried to settle amongst them, and an unending tale of tax-collectors, and they dourly clung to their Christian tradition. They wear the most dignified and beautiful dresses of any in the Balkans, gowns of coarse linen embroidered with black wool in designs using the Christian symbols, which are at once abstract (being entirely unrepresentational) and charged with passionate feeling. Their wide sleeves are thick as carpets with solid black embroideries, stitched in small squares, with often a touch of deep clear blue, which gives the effect of an inner light burning in the heart of darkness. Such garments, worn by grim women whose appearance announces that they would not do a number of things possible to less noble natures, have an effect of splendid storm, of symphonic music, and make no suggestion of facility or charm.

The contrast is presented by the town itself, as we saw when we went on for a stroll after our breakfast, as soon as Gerda and Constantine had joined us. We crossed the bridge over the Vardar, which was brownish with the late rains. To the left we looked past a screen of willows at the foot of the cliff on which the garrison fortress stands, on the site of a castle built by the famous Serbian Tsar Stephen Dushan, and we saw the snow mountains from which the river derived its cold breath. To the right there ran along the embankments lines of new dwellings, offices, and public buildings, interspersed with the hovels that are the tide-marks of the Ottoman Empire; and behind was the old town of Skoplje, which has an inveterately country quality, because terraces of rough farm land and orchard fall headlong into the heart of it from the landward side of the fortress. This was a town as the West knows it, exhausting, however picturesque it might be, because of the fret of effort. We took a road that ran uphill into the Turkish quarter, and knew a different sort of town.

Sarajevo is a Moslem, but not a Turkish town: a fantasia on Oriental themes worked out by a Slav population. Here in Skoplje we saw what the Oriental himself does with Oriental themes. Gone was the sense of form; we were faced with an essential discontinuity. It was explicit in the shops. They are at once neat and slovenly, they have been organized by minds that attack any enterprise with brilliance and fluency and then flag. A shopkeeper spends incredible ingenuity in displaying articles of only one or two kinds, and will put the most appetizing of them along side others that have been unsaleable not for mere months but actual decades. In one shop playing-cards of exquisite seventeenth-century design were displayed beside boxes of candles that had once been coloured and fluted, that were now merely stained and collapsed, and that bore a date-stamp of 1921. There is at work also a love of bright colours, which never passes on to the natural development of modifying them and fitting them into designs, but monotonously presents them in their crude state; there are windows piled with skeins of silks, more lustrous than our shamefaced Western yarns have dared to be for many years, and to be bought only in white, yolk-of-egg yellow, Prussian blue, and Jezebel scarlet. Yet, in their very triviality, these shops afforded delight. I never made a more agreeable purchase than a halfpenny cone of roasted nubs of sweet corn. The shop sold nothing else: they lay in great scented golden heaps, through which there ran a ghostly crepitance as soon as one grain was touched. The owner must have heard it a million million times; it still amused him.

But this lack of psychological staying-power has, perhaps, a physiological basis. I realized that in the slight disappointment I felt at our visit, since the quarter was not so vivacious as I had remembered it on my last visit. Now some veiled women were padding by, some bearded men were sitting in cafés as good as veiled by their expressions, which announced a restriction to the pure field of sensationalism utterly outside the comprehension of the Western mind, which can hardly conceive of existence apart from the practice of analysis and synthesis. But before, these streets had been like a scene in an operetta. It had seemed probable that tenor strains might proceed from the young baker, ox-eyed and plumpish, but shapely, who leaned over his long trays of loaves and covered them with linen cloths crossed with delicious lines of reds and blues, and that the black wisps of women bargaining behind those veils might turn out to be the ballet and coalesce in some dance gaily admitting their equivoque of concealing and proclaiming their sex. But I had made my earlier visits at seven and eight in the morning, and now it was eleven, and I had noticed before that the Turks cannot keep abreast the twenty-four hours anything like so well as Westerners. The afternoon finds its vitality clouded; the evening is sluggish; and at night one crosses the Vardar from the new town, where any number of Slavs are sitting in the restaurants, talking politics, drinking wine, eating spiced sausages, and listening to music, into darkened streets where there are bursts of singing from a few shuttered cafés, and, for the rest, houses fast asleep.

The Turks, I fancy, are a people who tire easily. When they are wildly excited, as they often are by militarist ardour and religious fanaticism, they cannot be fatigued; the reward for total abstinence from alcohol seems, illogically enough, to be the capacity for becoming intoxicated without it. But in ordinary life they seem subject to a languor that comes on in the day far too soon after dawn, and in a man's life far too soon after youth. The young Turk, as one sees him with his friends in the café or in a park, is a laughing and active creature, but after thirty-five he acquires a stolidity which might be mistaken for the outward sign of wisdom, were it not that it is impossible for so many to be in possession of that rare quality. He is given to a gesture that claims to express deliberation, that is actually an indefinite postponement of thought; and as he makes it his hand, even if he be scarcely middle-aged, looks sapless and old. It may be that the breakdown of the Turkish administration was not only a matter of political incompetence but resulted from a prevalent physical disability affecting men precisely at an age when they would be given the most responsible administrative posts.

But, if the morning glory had left the quarter, there was much still to delight us. I remember someone who took drugs once attempting to explain to me the charm of the habit, by saying, 'You know, one gives oneself an injection and I do not know how it is, but one spends a delightful day. Nothing happens, but somehow every tiny incident of the routine is interesting and enjoyable. If one is sitting in an armchair and someone comes in to lay a tray on the table, one watches the action as if it were a most exquisite miming, and the simplest remark, a "Hello, are you there?" on the telephone, sounds like an epigram.' The East is said to have the same effect as drugs on those who frequent it, and certainly this town, which was so much next door to the East that one was as good as through the door, exercised that same power of making the ordinary delicious. We turned aside into the garden of a mosque, not an extraordinary building, save for the light cast on the cross-currents of Balkan culture by the contrast between its ancient and fine design and the white crudity of its substance. It was a famous sixteenth-century mosque which had been allowed to fall into ruins by the Turks of the Ottoman Empire, fanatical yet far too indolent to defend their sacred places; and it had been restored by a Yugoslav official, a Herzegovinian Moslem, who had fought against the Turks in the Balkan wars because he was a Slav patriot, was now a freethinker, and was inspired to this act of architectural piety by aesthetic passions engendered in him no further east than Paris, where he had taken a degree in Oriental studies. Everybody in the garden of this not extraordinary mosque was behaving in the most ordinary way. At the fountain before it some young men were washing; two prosperous middle-aged men were sitting on the domed and pillared white porch, and talking not more dramatically than two Londoners at a club window; round the corner some older and poorer men were sitting on the grass by the tomb of a saint, wagging their beards in a conversation, portentous yet as light in weight as could well be, like the conversation in a morning train from an English suburb. There was no formulable reason why these people should afford a ravishing spectacle, but so they did. It was perhaps because irritability was absent from their world. To watch one's kind and find no trace of this disease, which in the West is so prevalent that it might be mistaken for a sign of life, was like looking in a mirror and seeing one's skin unlined as a baby's. We ourselves fell into the serene mood of the place and sat there for longer than we meant.

But there was a view: the garden was built on a terrace high above the domes and minarets and russet roofs of Skoplje, and showed us the green hills surrounding the town, spiked with the white toothpicks of nameless Moslem graves, and the bare blue mountains beyond, shadowed violet by the passing clouds. Our Western conscientiousness made us go to look at this view from the best advantage and we went to the wall of the garden, where we forgot our purpose, for the hills fell steeply to a street where people of a wild and harlequin sort were leading an entertaining life. A load of hay had been flung up against the wall of one house, and was munched by three ponies, raw-boned and flea-bitten. Another house, which had a square of periwinkle blue affixed on its white front for no particular reason, had a mistress who was evidently an indefatigable but eccentric housewife: through its door there flew every few minutes a jet of water from an emptied basin, discharged with the extreme of shrewishness. Outside another house sat a pretty woman and two pretty girls, smiling and bright-eyed in perpetual pleasure, cooking something on a tiny brazier and drinking from an amphora they passed from one to another. One had a kerchief, one a jacket, one trousers, of bright, rich, shallow red. Soon they noticed that we were watching them, and cried out to us and waved their long narrow hands; and presently, as if to show off their treasures, one of the girls ran into the house and came out laughing, holding up a baby for our admiration, naked and kicking and lustrous brown.

This was Slav sensuousness, European sensuousness, quite unlike its Turkish, its Asiatic analogue. At the first stimulus from the outside it had refused to confine itself to mere blandness, it insisted on involving itself with material which, though it certainly can evoke pleasure, can unleash tragedy also. The woman who took her child in her arms was raising trains of thought that could lead far beyond the fields of pleasantness, that referred to the pain of childbirth, the aching inadequacy of love, which cannot keep safe what it loves, the threat of estrangement and death. She would have been safer if she had continued to sit with her friends laughing at little things beside the small flame of the brazier, and drinking cool water out of the amphora, and that is what the true Turk would have done. All over this city of two natures there is demonstrated the contrast between Christian imprudence, immoderation, audacity in search of delight, and the Turkish thrifty limitation to the small cell where anything not delightful cannot enter. We saw an illustration of it that first morning, arising out of the attitude of common men to roses.

We owed the lesson to our intention of visiting the great caravanserai which lies among the little Moslem houses, where the diplomats and merchants stayed on their way from Dubrovnik to Constantinople, a superb memorial of the Ozymandian sort, too huge as a whole and in every part to have been dictated by necessity, with its full-bodied arcades round its marble courtyard, and its inordinate thickness of mulberry-coloured brick. Beside it are its baths, long grass growing like hair from its domes, with a poppy here and there. But there was no way through the hoarding across its Arabian Nights gateway, and when small boys in fezes told us that the key could be found in a cottage down an alley, they were perpetrating what seemed to them an exquisite witticism at the expense of the stranger. This little pavilion standing among lawns hemmed in with lilac bushes and rose trees, which should have been the home of a virtuous young girl supporting herself by her needle, was in fact a police station. We looked through the open casements and saw, not Gretchen at her spinning-wheel, but five gendarmes sitting at table, one purple-faced and mountainous, others with the fine seams of their uniforms running down to tough and slender waists, but all iron-jawed and far too large for the low room. A ray of sunshine showed the red glaze of paprika on their plates and a pink wine oily in their glasses, and shone through one sprung petal of a crimson rose in a little tin cup. They sprang to their feet as we looked in at the window, and came out of a door that was not high enough for any of them, so that they all straightened up as they greeted us, like genial pterodactyls. They explained that for some final reason the caravanserai was closed, and led us back through the gardens with official but unimpassioned courtesy, which suddenly glowed into a warmer emotion when Constantine, in saying good-bye, complimented them on their roses.

Immediately all the gendarmes uttered cries of delight and began to strip roses from the bushes, and pressed them into our hands, giving the men rather more than to Gerda and myself. 'Are these flowers not more pure than the snows of the mountain?' demanded the purple-faced one, tenderly taking some clusters from a white rambler. Then an idea struck him and he cried an order towards the little house in the voice peculiar to sergeant-majors all the world over. It brought out the gendarmerie servant, a young woman who looked robust but tired, carrying the tea-cup containing the rose we had seen on the table. 'This,' he said, pressing the flower into Constantine's hands with the air of one who pretends for politeness' sake that he gives little but who knows well that he gives much, 'this we think the most perfect bloom we have yet had from our garden this spring.'

Later we saw a rose of that same sort, or as like as makes no matter, in the hand of a butcher sitting outside his shop. He was a modish young man who wore his fez at an angle, and was distinctly handsome in spite of a measure of cosy Oriental plumpness. But that is always less deterrent than our Western obesity; while we put on weight because of some defect in our organization, some fault in our digestive or glandular systems, Orientals seem to grow stout because they are fond of their food and their food grows fond of them, and it and they elect to live together in a happy symbiosis. This young man's rounded cheeks and dimpled hands suggested a tranquil and unregretted union with mounds of rice ashine with fat, and soup-platefuls of such Turkish sweets as hot butter-scotch. He was doubtless thinking of his approaching dinner, and he had a right to take his ease, for behind him what was left of his wares was arranged with as much taste as the flowers in a Fifth Avenue florist's. It was surprising, in view of that exquisite neatness, that he showed no emotion when his shop was entered by an extravagantly dirty old Albanian, who set about pinching all the meat between his finger and thumb. The prepossession of the West that a person who is neat will also be clean breaks down at every corner in the East. So the young butcher had nothing to distract him from the perfume and colour of the rose, which he slowly twirled between his fingers, and sometimes slowly raised to his dilating nostrils. He was so well justified, so thoroughly wise, in his enjoyment. If a turn of earth's wheel had brought a moment when it was foolish or dangerous to enjoy a rose it would have fallen through his fingers to the dust.

But the purple-faced gendarme who had cried out his demand for perfection to the house, his iron-jawed men who had run about from bush to bush, they had committed themselves to their roses. They would have worked with sweat and without dignity to grow them. If there had arrived a person of influence who did not share their liking for them they would have disputed their point with him. It must be owned that they were lacking in repose and in discretion.

Skoplje III

Skoplje reveals a difference between the Slav and the Turk, the European and the Asiatic, at every turn of the street, and as we went about on our sightseeing it revealed hardly fewer differences between Gerda and ourselves. There was, some time before lunch, a painful scene in a seventeenth-century church we visited, which is in itself an amusing consequence of racial differences. It is sunk deeply in the earth, because it was built in the days of Moslem fanaticism, when all churches must be set underground. That ordinance had been the fine flower of Turkish spite, for the Turk loves light and makes his mosque a setting for it, but it wholly missed its mark, for the Christians liked their churches dark, as good hatching-places for magic. Indeed, they still like them so, for a couple of women and an old man who were shuffling about from icon to icon in the darkness explained to Constantine that they had a special devotion to this church because of its mystery. Rocking and murmuring, they led us to its chief treasure, which was an iconostasis intricately carved with scenes from the Bible by three brothers, ancestors of the craftsmen who made the screen we had seen in the little church of Topola. This work is Byzantine in its recognition of the moral obligation to decorate, as extensively and intensively as possible, yet in its spirit it is purely peasant. When Abraham sets about sacrificing his son the boy stands in stockish obedience, as sons do in a good patriarchal society, and when the angel prevents him he looks up in exasperation like a farmer interrupted in a heavy job; and the angel's wings were plainly copied from a bird killed for the table, which was probably already inside the sculptor when he settled down to the secondary task of imitating the feathers. Gerda was irritated by this carving, both as a bourgeois and as an intellectual. 'This is not serious art,' she said, and went to the back of the church. There we found her when we came to leave, lighting a candle before a fourteenth-century icon of the Virgin Mary, which in its dim presentiment of worn melancholy was yet precise and radiant. My husband and I exclaimed in admiration, and Gerda said with extreme bitterness, 'Now, I suppose, it will go to the British Museum.'

I took it for granted that her attitude could be explained by certain factors we already knew: she disliked my husband and myself, both as individuals and as representatives of one of the powers which had conquered Germany, and she regarded us as traitors to the bourgeoisie. But after lunch we perceived that her distress proceeded from roots deep in her philosophy, of which we had not yet been made fully aware. Skoplje, which had that morning at every turn of the street illuminated a difference between the Slavs and the Turks in their way of taking pleasure, now revealed a difference between Gerda on the one hand and the Slavs and the Turks and us on the other, which touched a more fundamental problem: whether pleasure has any value.

We started the afternoon standing on the embankment watching the Easter Sunday procession which was making its way along the other embankment facing us on the opposite side of the river and would presently cross a bridge and pass us on its way to the Cathedral. The sun was striking gloriously through the storm clouds on the cross and the vestments of the Metropolitan and the clergy who headed the long line of townspeople and peasants, and it lit up the crocus-coloured kerchiefs that many of the women were wearing on their heads. A gipsy girl so liked the show that, once it had gone by her, she jumped on the embankment and raced along to a point nearer the bridge to see it again, her rose coloured trousers ballooning in the wind and casting a blurred image on the waters below. But the crowd near by were as entertaining as the procession itself. There was a group of formidable old men from some mountain village, each with the eye and lope of a wolf, and all with tender pink rosebuds embroidered on their woollen socks. There were some superb women whose fine and bitter faces were unveiled, and therefore must be Christian, yet wore the Turkish trousers, and strode along in a gait that knew nothing of Islam or, indeed, of Christianity but remembered a primitive matriarchy. There was a group of Tsintsari (or Vlachs) at a street corner sitting on their haunches, feet flat on the ground, buttocks on their heels, chins in a line with their knees, all steady as rocks, and playing with amber rosaries as they gossiped. But most strange of all to Western eyes was a detachment of men, in black uniforms, carrying rifles and wearing cartridge belts, waiting to join the procession under the leadership of a magnificent old man who carried the standard the comitadji always used in the old Turkish days, a black flag printed with a white skull and cross-bones. These seemed at first an odd addition to an Easter Day procession, until one remembered the logical consequences of a nationalist church, and the complete lack of any association between Christianity and pacifism in these people's minds. But I was puzzled by the youth of many of the men in the detachment, which made it quite impossible for them to have fought against the Turks. They were, I suppose, Macedonian Serbs who had aided in the suppression of I.M.R.O. But nobody knew for certain, not even the friend of Constantine's who had just joined us, a professor of ethnology in the University of Skoplje. 'I cannot understand it,' he said, 'for the comitadji have long been disbanded.'

I asked no more, for now the procession was mounting to the crown of the bridge, the cross-bearer was immense against the sky, and the Metropolitan with his tall veiled mitre was still more immense. As they turned the corner of the embankment and came towards us, each squatting Tsintsar rose upright in a single movement with the ease of a stretching cat. Gerda said into my ear, 'Do not believe a word of what these people say to you. Of course there are still comitadji, the only difference is that they are now called chetnichi. They kill and beat people as they like. All these Yugoslavs are lying to you all the time. I said to the Professor, "But why do you tell them there are no more comitadji?" and he answered, "They are foreigners, it is better that they should think so." '

There was nothing to be said. Of course I knew about the chetnichi. I had in my handbag at that moment a pamphlet concerning the doings of these Apache Fascists in the Voivodina. It had never occurred to me that such an institution as the comitadji should not, when the legitimate need for it had ceased to exist, survive in a disagreeable and degenerate form. I knew that in America the guerrilla forces which had fought so well in the Civil War had not been easy to disband, and that the wilder members of them had become roving adventurers who had progressively deteriorating progeny in Jesse James, the St Louis gangsters, and the bootleggers and hi-jackers of Prohibition. I had not thought that it could be otherwise in the Balkans; and in any case it seemed to me that I, who am English by origin and of French sympathy, had little right to despise Yugoslavia for her chetnichi when England and France, with far less excuse, had their British Fascists and their *Camelots du Roi*, and that a German, whose fatherland was ruled by the Nazis, had far less right to exercise her fastidiousness. I could not answer truthfully for the sake of politeness so I meant to answer evasively; but I met Gerda's eyes and saw that she was blind to everything before her, to the procession, to the crowd, to Skoplje. Instead of sight there was the working of a cloudy opacity that wanted to precipitate contempt and violence, and whatever I said would have been turned to its gratification.

The procession reached us, the Metropolitan halted and shook hands with the old comitadji, and the skull and cross-bones took its place among the religious banners. We saw them move towards the Cathedral, and we started to saunter along the embankment, while the Professor gossiped about the holiday-makers around us. He showed us some peasants from the villages down on the Greek border, who could neither read nor write, but got the silly fellows who have gone to the bother of learning such stuff to tell them the commodity prices on the foreign exchanges, and on that information they very cunningly calculated what crops to sow. He showed us also a superb being, like a Cossack in a Russian ballet, who went strutting by in a wide-skirted coat made from the wool of a brown sheep. This, he told us, was a wealthy Tsintsar, a true nomad, who moved with his herds between summer and winter pastures and hoarded all his wealth, according to the classic nomadic fashion, in the form of necklaces and bracelets worn by his womenfolk. And he hurried us across the road to see a family of gipsies who were clearly natives of fairyland. Only there could a father and mother still shapely as gazelles and bloomed with youth have eight children; only there could they have arrayed their coffee-brown beauty, which fastidious nostrils, secretive lips, and eyes like prune-whip made refined and romantic, in garments of chrome yellow, cinnabar, emerald, royal blue, and vermilion, which were so clean that they made the very sunlight seem a little tarnished. Never have I seen a group so ritually, orgiastically unsullied. 'They are Gunpowder gipsies,' said the Professor; 'we call them that because they used to find saltpetre for the Turkish Army, and they are renowned for their cleanliness and their beauty.' 'But they are like Hindus!' I exclaimed. 'They might be from the Mogul court.' 'They are something of that sort,' said the Professor; 'when Gandhi's private secretary came here he could make himself understood to our gipsies in Tamil. We think that they are the descendants of some conquered Indian people who fled out of Asia after some unrecorded catastrophe in the Middle Ages, and certainly these Gunpowder gipsies represent the ruling castes. But come, let me take you to our gipsy quarter, you are sure to be interested.' 'All, all is in Yugoslavia,' said Constantine, glowing happily and trotting beside the tall Professor.

We went up the steep hill to the Moslem quarter, passing the cabaret where I had first met Astra, the stomach dancer whom we had seen at Sarajevo. Outside it were sitting three of the singers: a great distended blonde and two dark girls with that beauty which those who have not got it think must bring its owners all they wish, but which actually seems to have a commercial value just enough to bring them into the sphere of commerce. They blinked into the sunlight, turning their faces from side to side, their hands tucked into the bosoms of their cotton dressing-gowns which were faded and stringy with washing and re-washing. About all Slav life which touches on prostitution there is a strange lustral and expiatory cleanliness. We passed the sunken church we had visited that morning and the mosque garden, and came now on poorer and smaller houses. Suddenly we stopped, because a crowd of laughing people ran out of an alley and came to a halt just in front of us, turning their backs on us and forming a circle. They rocked from side to side, holding their hips and shouting with joy, while there staggered out of the alley, holding himself very stiffly, a gendarme who was very drunk. He was greenish, he held a wavering hand before his eyes to shield them from the sunlight; it could be seen that for him his riding-boots were at the other end of the earth, his dead face muttered. Somebody cried out something from the back of the crowd, and a shout of laughter went up; and he found that he could not put down the foot that he had raised. His other foot wobbled, and it seemed that he must fall. But just then there came out of a cottage a woman with an ageing and compassionate face, who went to him and caught him round his hourglass waist with an arm shrouded in a rose-coloured scarf. The crowd turned about, and walked off, as if the incident had now changed its character and was no longer amusing. She led him into a yard behind a house, and when we looked back a few paces further on, we saw her through a wide gap in a wall, pressing down his rigid body with long fine hands till he knelt, and then bringing his head forward by the temples so that he could be sick, all with a great piety of movement.

'It is here,' said the Professor, just after that, 'here is our gipsy quarter.' From a rise in the road we looked down on a colony of one-storied houses that lay, a sharply distinct entity, on a spit of sand running for a quarter of a mile or so into the green fields surrounding Skoplje. The houses were whitewashed and many were decorated with simple stylized paintings of trees, some dark blue, some mustard yellow. We had a clear view along one or two narrow alleys running down from the high road into this quarter, and we saw a number of people, all gaily dressed in window-curtain material, sitting on the pavements with an air of comfort and even formality, and looking up with intelligent but not impertinent curiosity into the faces of others who were hurrying by, swift and preternaturally sure-footed, never stumbling over those at their feet. They were all of them extremely Hindu in appearance, but their behaviour showed such a strange ease, such a lack of the constraints that are characteristic of every conceivable society, that the scene seemed illusionary, a stereoscopic presentation of a panel from a painted screen 'Look, are they not exotic and wonderful?' said the Professor proudly. 'There are two thousand houses here, which means ten thousand gipsies.' 'Yes,' said Gerda, her voice hoarse with indignation, 'that there are thousands of them I can easily see, but the question is, why are they allowed?' 'Why are they allowed?' repeated the Professor. 'I don't understand.' 'Yes, why have you allowed them to come here?' persisted Gerda. 'But, Gospodja, they have always been here,' said the Professor, 'they have always been in this district, for six hundred years at least, and most of these people have been actually settled here in Skoplje since the time of the Balkan wars.' 'They should be driven out,' said Gerda, trembling with rage. She pointed at six children who were making mud pies outside a cottage just beneath us, under the care of a grandmother who had the delicate profile of an elderly Maharanee. 'Look at them! They should be driven out!'

The Maharanee, who would have been well able to defend her own, heard the vehement accent and turned on us the veiled eyes of a hawk. 'Now it might be agreeable to go to the gipsies' corso,' said the Professor hastily. 'But there,' he added, 'I must leave you, for I have another engagement.' Every evening the Slavs of Skoplje who are of the modern world, the functionaries and the professional men, walk up and down the High Street that leads from the station to the chief bridge over the Vardar, and the Slavs who are of the old world, the artisans and the peasants, walk up and down a section of the embankment. But the Moslems and the gipsies have their corso at this end of the town, on the top of a hill, where there is a French war cemetery, crammed with the flimsy little wooden crosses that make them so much more pathetic than any other burial-places. There is such an effort to make the crosses pretty, with the white paint and the touches of the tricolour, and they are so pitifully cheap, and the reason for the need of cheapness is so plainly the enormous number required. On the edge of this cemetery, fringed with beds of purple iris, there runs a promenade from which a hillside of grass and fruit trees drops steeply to the Vardar river, winding silver among its golden poplars and willows. An immense prospect looks over a broad valley at mountains, so well watered by springs that their pastures are like emeralds and their ploughed fields like rubies, and beyond them to a wall of snow peaks. Along this promenade walk many Moslem men, mostly youths, since their elders prefer to stroke their beards in the mosque gardens, some Moslem women, who usually come to sit in black clutches of three or four in the grass under the fruit trees, and many gipsies, men, women, and children, who pass through the more stolid Moslem crowds with the slippery brilliance of fish. The gipsy women, though most of them are Moslem, go unveiled, which is an extreme example of the position their kind has won for itself as professionally free from ordinary social obligations; and this means that a thread of beauty, never troubling because never marked by profundity, runs through the crowd.

As we came to this promenade through the afternoon, that was still violet with the threat of storm and gilt with spring sunlight, we heard the throbbing of a drum that announces a kolo, a communal dance. Looking down towards the river, we saw that on a little knoll projecting from the hillside some soldiers were dancing the kolo in a circle of young men in civilian clothes, a knot of olive and black against the distant poplars and willows and silver waters. But there was another drum throbbing somewhere and we found it at the end of the promenade, where the ground fell away and there was nothing but a little plateau, wide enough for twenty or thirty people, on the edge of a cliff; and there the gipsies were dancing a kolo. Because they were Moslems and Easter was no festival of theirs, the girls were in everyday dress, and this was fortunate; for their best clothes are usually made of artificial silk brocades, which shine with a horrid yellowish lustre, destructive to the subtle loveliness of their complexions. They were wearing window-curtain material that had been steeped in sunlight and rain till every crude colour was its own fair spectre, and the prevailing note was a light, soft, plum purple; so their skins showed honey-gold, and their lips pale carnation. On the intricate rhythm of the music these girls and their boys floated like seaweed on the tide, just not quite freely, just tenuously attached to the solid universe. Their linked hands, which they raised higher than is the custom of kolo dancers, pulsed in the air, bigger than butterflies but more ethereal than birds.

Gerda said, 'You like it?' I murmured, 'Of course, of course.' Beautiful boys and girls were dancing in the open air, wearing clothes lovely as flowers, against a background of snow peaks, trees palely incandescent with spring, and shining waters. Who on earth would not like it? Gerda said, 'I do not like it. See, I have lit a cigarette. I must smoke here to disinfect myself. When I see these people I feel I am not in Europe.' I said nothing; it would have been so natural to say, 'I wish to God that were so.' She went on, 'Why do you like these people? How can you possibly like them? Do you not see that they are dirty and stupid?' I looked at them again and marvelled at their bodies, which were as economical as a line of poetry. As I looked the music changed its rhythm, but it took none of these bodies at a disadvantage; they hovered for a minute, then received the new measure into their muscles and their blood, and were at one with it. I said, 'They have something we have not got.' And I meant to add, 'A kind of nervous integrity, of muscular wisdom.' But Gerda said savagely, rooting out the double happiness of despising the gipsies and despising me, 'You think that merely because you do not know these people. You are mystical about them, you think they have occult knowledge; I know what you think.'

She did not. Gipsies are, in all but their appearance, particularly what I do not like. I am told that these at Skoplje are the most admirable of their kind, reasonably honest and wholly innocent of the charge, laid against all other Balkan gipsies, of stealing Christian children and deforming them so that they make appealing beggars. But I am cold towards them all, largely because they are the embodiment of that detestable attribute, facility. They never make music of their own, but they take the music of whatever country they happen to be in, play it so slickly that they become the recognized musician caste, and then turn music into a mere titillation of the ear, a pleasant accompaniment to an evening's drunkenness. There is no design in anything they do. On my previous visit to Skoplje I had attended their grand annual festivity, a whole day's picnicking in the huge football stadium just outside the town; and for the first five minutes I thought I had never seen a more gorgeous spectacle. After that I spent half an hour speculating if I found it more bearable seen with my sun-glasses or without. By normal vision the atrocious smear of lustre from the coarse fabrics they preferred spread a smear of grease over the scene; though the dark lenses removed this they thereby exposed the monotony of pattern, the scamped craftsmanship, the lack of embroidery. Then I went home, understanding what the Scandinavians meant to express when they made their troll-women hollow. A human being ought not to be too light, its experience should silt up inside it and give it weight and substance. But, all the same, when gipsies are so beautiful and do beautiful things I experience the reaction that all normal people give to beauty; and I would not that it were otherwise, for like the Slav and the Turk I value delight. But Gerda, intent on something other than delight, insisted, 'It is because you are a foreigner, you do not understand these people. You think they are wonderful. But you are from the north, you should see that they are nothing but dirty and uncivilized savages, who ought not to be in Europe at all.'

I began to walk away from the kolo, which I could no longer enjoy, partly because I thought the gipsies might notice Gerda's undisguised disapproval of them, and I made my way towards Constantine and my husband, who were going across some broken ground back to the high road from Skoplje. But Gerda hurried along beside me, saying, 'I do not understand you, you go on saying what a beautiful country this is, and you must know perfectly well that there is no order here, no culture, but only a mish-mash of different peoples who are all quite primitive and low. Why do you do that?' I said wearily, 'But it's precisely because there are so many different peoples that Yugoslavia is so interesting. So many of these peoples have remarkable qualities, and it is fascinating to see whether they can be organized into an orderly state.' 'How can you make an orderly state out of so many peoples?' she asked. 'They should all be driven out.' I quickened my steps, and soon we came level with Constantine and my husband. At once Gerda began to reproach Constantine angrily for the repulsiveness of the gipsies, and for the shameful compliancy of his country in harbouring them. We stepped on to the high road in broken order, just in front of an old man who was on his way into Skoplje. He was plainly very poor. Indeed I do not think that in all my life I have ever seen anybody poorer. His coat and breeches were so much patched that it was hard to say whether either had originally been black or brown, and the patches had themselves been patched; and his broken sandals were bound with rags but, even so, showed his bare feet. He had been greatly injured by his poverty. He leaned heavily on his staff, and he mumbled sadly through his beard to the ground. Gerda walked up to him and stood in front of him so that he had to stop, and then turned to us. 'Look!' she cried, pointing to his tattered clothes and his broken sandals and laughing, 'if a great producer like Reinhardt had tried to invent a figure of misery he could not have thought of anything so dreadful!' I said to my husband, 'I cannot bear this,' and he answered, 'No, you must cheer up, some day she will do this to somebody who will hit her, and hit her hard.' Constantine betrayed all his sweetness of character out of loyalty to Gerda, and joined in her laughter; but she rejected this sacrifice and made an angry gesture at him. 'Your Yugoslavia ought to do something with all these horrible people!' she said, and they went ahead of us loudly quarrelling over the gipsies and the poor. I turned round and saw the old man staring after us in stupefaction.

The road ran now between barracks that stood in gardens full of fruit trees, lilac bushes, beds of purple and white iris. Soldiers were sitting at tables among these flowers, some playing cards, some singing songs to the sound of the gusla, but very softly because it was now the evening, and it had been a holiday, and everyone was tired. At one table a young soldier sat between two peasants, his parents; he was looking at them reverently because they were his father and mother, they were looking at him reverently because he was their son and a soldier. On a balcony some soldiers were going through a burlesque of drill. We walked on, and the road came out on the naked hills, and we looked over the turf to the ruins of an aqueduct which was pre-Byzantine, which was built when the Roman Empire was still governed from Rome. But the first stars were shining over the mountains, and dusk was already in the valleys, so we turned back, and saw the soldiers at the tables rising and stretching themselves and yawning, gathering up the dealt cards, picking up their guslas and going on with their songs without an accompaniment, because a bugle was calling. As we drew near the gipsy quarter we heard its polyphonic voice across the fields and saw a bonfire on its outskirts with dancing figures black between us and the flames. Nearer Skoplje still, where there was a steep embankment sloping to a little stream, we passed the old man whom Gerda had used for purposes of racial demonstration, who was sitting on the grass in the cold twilight and, with an air of shame, which increased when he saw us, was washing his feet.

Matka

After a ten-mile drive from Skoplje we arrived at the little monastery which is called Matka, or the Mother, because it is kind to
barren women though it is dedicated to St Andrew. I was a little
disappointed because last year it had been painted Reckitts blue
and what is known in Scotland as sweetie pink, but this year it was
plain white. 'I thought we would have a change,' the priest said. It
is hard to imagine such a radical change being applied to, say, the
parish church of Steeple Ashton without some letters being written
to *The Times*. We looked over the monastery, which was typical of
its kind. There is the outer gate, the orchard and paddock, and then
the enclosure containing the church and the priest's little house and
a building with a stable underneath and a staircase running up to a
gallery with guest rooms opening off it. It was in fact something of
a religious centre, something of a fortress where Christians could
forgather without being sniped at by the Moslems, and something
of a country club where the peasants could have their bean-feasts
and be sure of decent company. This last purpose the monasteries
still subserve: many people came out to Matka from Skoplje to have
lunch in the orchard. We told the priest, who was a handsome and
intelligent young Serbian, that we would do the same, after we had
been to see another monastery a mile or so away.

Our path ran towards a mountain gorge along a river-bank that
was torn by the rawness of some engineering enterprise; on a
wooden platform by the water we saw a score or so of white-capped
Albanians, flung down in sleep. We passed through a little makeshift village, plainly built for workmen, which ended in a pretty
house with a well-kept garden, where a handsome family were
eating their midday meal. '*Priyatno*,' called Constantine, using
the Serbian equivalent for *bon appetit*. '*Priyatno*,' they answered
in chorus, the children chirping like little birds. The road became a
rough path overhung by rock, the river a torrent running far below,
the valley a narrow gorge penetrating densely wooded hills rising
to barren peaks. On a broad ledge under dripping cliffs, here hung
with purple flowers, among wind-swept trees that leaned laterally
over the abyss, we found the little monastery. It was minute and
in poor repair, but it had kept its frescoes. A bar of sunlight
struck through a gap in the wall and lay on the anguished figure
of the Virgin Mary lifting Christ down from the Cross, like a

finger laid by nature on the corrupt spot which the animal world has contracted by its development of consciousness: its liability to grief. Bitter what consciousness brings us, yet bitter beyond anything the loss of it; that the painter showed us in the figure of Christ, which was typically Serbo-Byzantine. In too many Western pictures Christ looks as if He were wholly dying, and as if He were making an unmanly fuss over it considering his foreknowledge of the Resurrection. But in all these Macedonian frescoes death is shown working on the body that is bound to the spirit of Christ, wringing the breath out of the lungs as a laundress wrings water out of a shirt, taking the power out of the muscles and nerves like a dentist drawing a tooth whose roots drive down through the whole body. There is demonstrated that separateness of the flesh which Proust once noted, in a passage which describes how we think in our youth that our bodies are identical with ourselves, and have the same interests, but discover later in life that they are heartless companions who have been accidentally yoked with us, and who are as likely as not in our extreme sickness or old age to treat us with less mercy than we would have received at the hands of the worst bandits.

'Are they not beautiful, these frescoes?' Constantine said to my husband. 'You will see that in all these Serbo-Byzantine works the feeling is terribly deep. It is ecstatic, yet far deeper than mere ecstasy, far deeper than Western art when it becomes excited, as in the case of Matthias Grünewald.' 'What is that?' asked Gerda, who had been quite quiet all the morning. 'You are not going to tell me that the man who painted these wretched daubs and smears was greater than our wonderful Matthias Grünewald?' 'No, no,' said poor Constantine, 'I only said that here was a different feeling.' 'Then what is the use of comparing them?' said Gerda. 'I know you did it for only one purpose, to prove that everything here is finer than in Germany.' We left them in the monastery to settle this disagreement, and went a little way along a path that led to the head of a gorge, but it was slimy with recent rains, and we turned back. 'Oh, God, I am so tired of this!' my husband said. 'It is all very well for you to say that some day somebody will hit her,' I said, 'but when will it begin?'

Constantine and Gerda were ready to go when we got back, but it was evident as they walked in front of us that he was still making every effort to placate her. 'It is horrid,' I said, 'to see him being specially nice to her because she has been specially nasty.' 'He is preposterously good to her,' said my husband, 'but why is it that Jews like Germans so much, when Germans do not like Jews? You know, they were very happy in Germany until Hitler came; and I honestly believe that if you gave Constantine the chance of getting rid of Gerda, he would not take it, not only because he is a faithful soul and she is the mother of his children, but because he really likes her society.' 'I believe Constantine is moved by prestige,' I said. 'Most Western culture comes to the Slavs and to the Jews of Central and Eastern Europe through Germany and Austria, and so they respect everything German and Austrian, and are left with an uneasy suspicion that if Germans and Austrians despise the Slavs and the Jews there must be something in it.' 'What you are saying is frightful,' said my husband, 'for it means that there is no hope for Europe unless in a multiplication of nationalisms of the most narrow and fanatical sort. For obviously Slavs and Jews cannot counteract this influence except by believing themselves rather more wonderful than the truth can guarantee, by professing the most extreme Zionism or Pan-Slavism.'

In front of us Constantine and Gerda had stopped, just above the tangle of engineering works by the river. When we came up Constantine said, 'I would like to see what is going on here, for it seems to me that it may be something very interesting. For we are doing the most wonderful things here in Macedonia. If the Italians and Americans had done them the whole world would be clapping their hands.' This is a boast for which there is a good deal of foundation. Until the war Skoplje was a dust-heap surrounded by malarial marshes, and most of the towns in the province were as unhealthy. Now many people brought up in Serbia or Hungary live here all the year round, with at most the months of July and August on holiday, and keep their health and spirits. This is the result of much competent engineering, often planned with genius. 'So let us go down,' said Constantine, and we started to look for a path. But before we could find it, a man with grey hair and burning black eyes hurried out to us from the house where we had seen the family eating in the arbour. Yes, we might see the works, indeed we must see them, for he was in charge of them and he could tell us that they were going to result in a hydro-electric plant such as the world could never have dreamed would be set up in Macedonia, that had been the wash-pot of the Turks, a large hydro-electric plant, a huge one, a colossal one; in default of another adjective, his hands fluttered across the sun as he explained its vastness. 'A pride,' he called over his shoulder as he led the way down the hillside, 'a great pride for Yugoslavia!' Talk of an angel, as the vulgar say; we had been talking of nationalism.

There was a ladder to drop down; and we stood in the river-bed, drained now of its water, so that a dam might be built. Here it had been wholly overhung, so it was as if we stood in a cavern. Above us was the gleaming nudity of the rocks uncovered now for the first time since prehistoric days, and sculptured here and there by the eddying waters into whorls like casts of gigantic muscular arms; and in wooden galleries pinned to the rock face Albanians were working by the light of lamps that gave their white skull-caps and clothes a soft moth-wing brightness. From them proceeded the ringing sounds and the sudden flares of riveting. It was entrancing to contemplate the state of their minds, which knew nothing at all between the primitive and hydro-electricity. The man with grey hair and burning black eyes was pouring into our ears explanations of which we could not understand one single word, since it is the flaw in the state of mind of our sort—hardly indeed preferable to that of the Albanians—that we know nothing whatever of the mechanical means which condition our lives at every turn, when Constantine interrupted to ask him if he employed only Albanians. The man with grey hair glared at us out of the terrible sober drunkenness of fanaticism, which is punished by no deterrent headache, expelled by no purging sickness. 'Why do you call them Albanians?' he cried. 'Now all are Yugoslavs!' In the dusk his eyes were flames.

I grieved. It is notorious that many of the Albanians who became Yugoslavs under the Peace Treaty consented to the change with the utmost reluctance, and that the Government was obliged to adopt an extremely stern policy against them. I use the word 'obliged' because I do not believe that any government in the history of the world has ever conducted such an enterprise as the pacification of Macedonia without resorting to ferocity. But I suspected the manager of being one of those bigots who would keep up this severity after the time for it had passed. However, he went on to say, 'I do indeed try to employ this particular kind of Yugoslav, because they are such excellent fellows. That foreman over there, you cannot believe how good he is, how loyal, how careful of the work and his workmen. I feel to him as if he were my brother.' I had seen this happening before in Macedonia; the irresistible charm of the Albanians works on all other Slavs, on the most hard-hearted patriots sent down from the north, and the ancient grudge is forgotten. Men are wiser than they mean to be, and very different from what they think they are. Looking round the echoing cavern, before we left it, the grey-haired man said, 'It was hard to get the river-bed dry for the building of the dam, for there were many springs gushing out of the rock. Many wonderful

springs,' he repeated reverently, speaking more like a Serb, born
with an inherited instinct for water worship, than like an expert on
hydro-electricity.

When we were at the top of the shaft again we said good-bye
to him, and the parting was deeply emotional on the part of the
grey-haired man and Constantine. 'You have done a heavy work
for Yugoslavia!' cried Constantine, shaking both his hands. 'What
work is heavy if it is done for Yugoslavia?' answered the other.
When we went on our way Constantine was still hopping and
jumping with excitement and cried out, 'Is it not wonderful what
difficulties we have surmounted? And think what it will mean when
it is finished! The whole of the valley down to Skoplje shall be full of
light, and there will be many factories, and we will be rich, rich, like
Manchester and America.' 'Really,' said Gerda, 'one would think
you had done it yourself.' 'Well, did I not do a little of it myself?'
shouted Constantine. 'Did I not fight in the Great War, and was I
not terribly wounded? Did I not so buy Macedonia with my blood?
And shall I not then be glad because it is no longer the desert and
shambles it was under the Turks?' Gerda shrugged her shoulders
and walked on with an air of cool good sense. Constantine threw
himself in her path so that she should not go on, demanding, 'Do
you laugh at your husband because he has paid a price of blood for
his country?' My husband said, in a voice which suggested that he
was also willing to pay a price of blood, 'I think it is time we had
lunch.'

In the paddock a table had been laid for us under an apple tree,
now in the last days of its flowering time, and the priest sat waiting
for us there. At another table there was a party of young men who
were getting drunk, not hastily or greedily, but slowly and gently.
The apple blossom was drifting down on our table at about the
same pace. One of them was already quite drunk and was lying
asleep on the grass, covered by a blanket. The priest had filled our
glasses with some wine of the Macedonian sort which is good to
drink but which tastes hardly at all of grapes, which might just as
well be distilled from pears or quinces, and had set out some good
rough bread and a plate of dyed Easter eggs. The priest pressed us
to eat the eggs so warmly that I thought they must be all we were to
have for lunch, and I took two. But there came some sheep's cheese,
which, when it is fresh and not too salt, is as bland to the palate as its
shining whiteness is to the eye. 'Oh, there is more to come,' said the
priest, when I made my inquiries. 'We have good food here, thank
God, though we do not get such good fish as easily as we used to
do before they started building the dam. But it is wonderful the

snares the devil lays for us. It was through that fish that my poor old predecessor got into such trouble, you know.'

'What was that story, now? I've never quite got the rights and wrongs of it,' said Constantine, who had of course never heard of it till that moment. 'Well, the root of the trouble was that our fish was simply the best in the neighbourhood and we were famous for it,' said the priest. 'So when Mr Yeftitch, who was Prime Minister before Mr Stoyadinovitch, came to stay with the Metropolitan at Skoplje, the Metropolitan was very anxious to give him the best entertainment he could, so he sent a hundred and twenty dinars to the old priest who was here then, and told him to send back as much fish as he could. But the old priest was too old to fish for himself, so he asked a peasant to do it for him. And the peasant was full of the honour of the occasion, and said, 'Here is a matter of a Prime Minister from Belgrade and the Metropolitan, I must do the best that I can,' so he got a stick of dynamite, for though he knew it was unlawful he did not think there would be any question of law when a Prime Minister and a Metropolitan wanted a good dinner. So he got an immense load of fish, and he took it to the old priest, and the old priest said, 'What have you done?' But he was a very honest old priest, and he felt that the Metropolitan had paid for this fish, so he sent it to him, but as it went into the town the customs officers saw it and said, 'But what is this great load?' And they were answered, 'Fish for the Metropolitan!' So the police went to the Metropolitan, and said, 'But you must not dynamite fish, even though you are the Metropolitan.' So he said, 'But I have not dynamited fish,' and when the matter was explained he was very angry with the old priest. And as the police did not believe the Metropolitan, and as the Metropolitan did not believe the old priest, I do not think the matter was ever made quite clear to everybody, though it will be in Heaven.'

There came then a tureen of very strong chicken soup, which we ate with great pleasure, while the young men at the other table sang a melancholy folk-song very, very slowly. It was as if they had put their arms round the neck of the emotion of unrequited love and were leaning on her while, preoccupied with her sadness, she led them to the end of the song. In the middle of it one of them realized that the music was in charge of them and that they were not in charge of it, and he sang a few notes with the force and decision of a sergeant-major. This aroused the man who was lying on the grass, and he threw the blanket back from his face. A flower petal fell on his face, which was clouded with a look of caution and guile until he recognized what it was. After the effort of bringing his hand up to his face to brush it away, his eyes closed again, but a sheepdog that was nosing around the paddock came and sniffed him, and ran away before he had time to push it away. He began to feel that too much was happening to him, he sat up, he cast away his blanket and revealed that he was in acrobat's clothes, in a striped vest and shorts. Angrily he stared about him, saw his friends, and shook his head, grieved at their condition. Alone he must assert control over this universe which was getting out of hand. He rolled over and began to perform athletic feats, to lie on his abdomen and slowly lift his chest and his knees from the ground, to bend backwards and make a bridge with his hands and his feet.

There was admirable cold lamb next, and the sheepdog came for the bones. 'It is a good dog, a very good dog,' said the priest. 'He is wonderful with the wolves. Last winter my servant called to me when I was in church and told me she had seen him outside the wall fighting with two wolves, and one he had hurt so that it ran howling into the hills, and the other one had turned tail and had run down the valley with him after it. And I went after him, because he is a very good dog, and I found he had chased the wolf for three kilometres till he came to a village where a peasant shot the wolf. I had this dog as a puppy from an old woman they called Aunt Persa in these parts, and he has something of her nature. She was a comitadji, just like a man, and she had three husbands, and all she killed because they were not politically sound. One would go with the Turks, and one would go with the Bulgars though he was a Serb because there were so many Bulgars in the village that he felt safer so, and one would go with the Greeks. She was a nurse in the Balkan wars, but she fought as much as she nursed, and she was wounded many times. Then when she was too old to marry or to fight she became a nun and lived as a hermit in a monastery up in the mountains here, that is a thousand years old. She made a very good nun.' I remembered Pausanias and his sensible opinion that the worshippers at a lonely temple who were always losing their priestesses through rape and flight should choose a woman, old in years, who had had enough of the company of men. 'I used to go up and see her, and one day she gave me this puppy which her dog had had. But now she is dead, and the monastery is deserted. Last summer I went up to see how it might be, and the porch had fallen in, and in the paddock I saw twelve wolves. They would not have been there if Aunt Persa had still been alive.'

There came yet another dish, a curious and admirable mixture of trout and chicken. Our distended stomachs thanked God it was the last. When the priest had stopped piling our plates he sat with his chin cupped in his hand and his elbows on the table, enjoying the rosy pleasantness of the early afternoon. Behind us the drunken young men at the table confided themselves to another song which they sang so slowly that to all intents and purposes it ceased to have a tune, but simply reserved the atmosphere for its melancholy. The acrobat was now standing on his head with an uncanny air of permanence. 'I would like,' said the priest, looking up at the grey peak which dominates this valley, 'to have a huge flagstaff planted in the rock up there, to fly the hugest Yugoslavian flag ever made.' He cast a defiant glance at us. 'I suppose your European friends will despise me for that wish. I said the same thing to a French doctor who was here last summer, and he said, "If you were a Catholic priest you would want to set there an enormous statue of the Virgin Mary, but because you are an Orthodox priest you want to put up a huge national flag," and I think he meant it as a reproach. But I said to him, "You speak as one who does not know that this country was not for the Virgin Mary until our flag had flown here." ' The acrobat quivered, collapsed on the grass, and instantly fell asleep, and his friends began to sing 'John Brown's Body.' 'It is an old song of our comitadji,' explained the priest.

Skoplje's Black Mountain

On our way from Matka we stopped at the ruined mosque which is a landmark on the eastward road out of Skoplje. It is a small and lovely thing, with a tomb almost as large as itself beside it, and it suffers gracefully the growth of long grass and yellow flowers on its crumbling cupola. Within, a score of ravens sat immobile on the iron grilles of the glassless window, dark against the outer sunshine. I clapped my hands and they flew out, and a score more dropped from the vault of the cupola, and hovered a second, croaking a complaint, before they too went out into the light. We heard music, and when we went out we found a concert was taking place on the grass between the mosque and the road, for a gipsy band, trudging its way to a village for the Easter Monday celebrations, had stopped for a moment to play to some holiday-makers in a cart. A man in the cart leaned forward as we approached, and threw a coin on to the tilted forehead of the gipsy who was playing the horn, and a roar of laughter went up. The gipsy was careful not to shift his head as he went on playing, so that the coin continued to stick where it was. This seemed to me most exciting, because I had read that it was a favourite diversion at the feasts of the Byzantines to throw coins on the faces and bodies of courtesans who were singing and dancing, and see how long the women could go on with the performance without letting them drop; and as the gipsy played he was smirking and waving his eyelashes in a classic imitation of a courtesan. Actually it seems, apart from its historical interest, an unamusing habit, with an alarming implication that the Byzantines liked a pork-like richness of physique in their women. I even prefer the allied habit that Christians cultivate all over the Near East of throwing coins at certain icons and attaching great importance to the length of time they remain without falling. This is of course irreverent, though not more so than, say, Pascal's wager.

We took a road across the wide valley, through fields of young corn that were edged by the first poppies, and bumped up to the range of hills that is known as the Skopska Tserna Gora, the Black Mountain of Skoplje. There are a group of eight villages on it, of which only a couple are Bulgarian in feeling; all the rest are strongly Serb. They are famous for the dour and fierce character of the inhabitants and the beautiful embroideries worked by the women: the thick, dark, tragic embroideries we had seen some passers-by wearing when we were breakfasting the previous day. They are very large villages. It is an odd circumstance that the disadvantageous political conditions of the Balkans produced an indubitable social benefit in keeping the villages large and compact. As the farmers feared raids from the Turkish troops and all the numerous armed forces begotten by the maladministration, they built houses side by side in some convenient spot and went out to their fields in the morning with their livestock, and brought it back at night; so the most discouraging features of agricultural life, as we know them in England and America, the loneliness of the women and the development of eccentricities due to isolation, are not present in the Balkans.

We came to the first village, a huddle of white houses with darkbrown roofs wedged in a valley rich with poplars, and found a great square choked with peasants watching their young men and women dance the kolo. They were certainly enjoying themselves, yet the effect was not joyful. The young people were wearing clothes covered with the most beautiful designs being invented in any part of the world today, masterpieces of abstract art, yet the effect was not of beauty. They were dancing, and yet the effect was not ecstatic. There was a profoundly depressing element in the scene, which was, quite simply, the women. The men were handsome, but nobody could have got a moment's pleasure from looking at any of the women. I have never seen a plainer-looking lot. This was partly because they were wearing head-dresses and clothes heavy enough to wear down the strength of a bullock. Where a good tradition has not kept the women's head-dresses to simple embroidered scarfs and kerchiefs, as in Debar and some other districts, they become shapeless piles of assorted haberdashery, mixed up with coins and cords and false hair and flowers; and I have never seen any more cumbersome than those of the Skopska Tserna Gora. Their bodies were padded with gowns of the coarse Macedonian linen which is said to be so thick that worms cannot gnaw through a shroud of it; over these they wore sleeveless coats made of rough serge, and many oddments in the way of aprons and belts, and sometimes sheep-skin jackets over these. From the strained expressions on these women's faces it was quite plain that they were suffering the same nervous and muscular inconvenience that we would if we were obliged to go about all day wearing our bed-clothes applied to our persons.

But such head-dresses, such clothes, do not come into existence by chance. They are usually imposed by a society that has formed neurotic ideas about women's bodies and wants to insult them and drive them into hiding, and it is impossible for women to be happy in such a society. The pattern traced by the kolo confirmed that these women were the victims of such social persecution. One's first impression was that the kolo was very lively, and so it was, but only so far as the first half of it was concerned. That half was composed of men, who leaped and twirled high in the air, in the happiest abandonment to the rhythm of the gipsy band; the second half, which was composed of women, shuffled along with their heels never leaving the ground and not a muscle of face or body answering to the music. It is true that Slav women never dance in the same way as men, since the feminine ideal is the stiff and stylized Virgin of the icons, and they therefore prefer to posture rather than to trip, but this was a stockishness surprising to find anywhere but among the inorganic or the dead. It was exhibited still more grossly in the second village we visited, where they danced the kolo on a patch of sloping grassland beside a willow-hung stream. There it was as if the first part of the kolo were a broken-backed snake, the first half rearing and twisting in liveliness, the second half a limp length dragging on the ground.

It was strange, for the women who sewed these embroideries were plainly not lacking in the capacity for excitement. It must be that these women are not allowed to dance, and it could be read in their sullen, colourless faces that there was not much they were allowed to do. I remembered then that I had heard it said in Skoplje that on the Skopska Tserna Gora wives are so harshly treated by their husbands that if they are left widows nothing will induce them to remarry. No degree of privation could approach in horror that masculine tyranny. I also remembered a curious conversation I once had with a young woman who had washed and waved my hair in a shop at Skoplje. She was in her early twenties, she was pregnant with her second child, she rose at five and did the housework and got her elder child ready for the day, and then she worked at the coiffeur's from half-past eight in the morning till half-past seven at night, with a midday interval which she spent in cooking and serving her husband's dinner. On her Sundays she did the family laundry and made clothes. When I told her that this seemed to me a hard life she laughed heartily and said that it was nothing to what she would have had to do if she had stayed at the village where she was born, in the Skopska Tserna Gora. The men, she said with great bitterness, left all the work they could to the women, even if it were far beyond their physical strength.

At the third village we saw more than the dancing. The car we were in was flying the Government flag, because Constantine had borrowed it from the Ban of the province; and it happened that the people here were not only fanatically pro-Serb but wanted something from the authorities. So they broke into cheers as we got out of the car, an action I always dislike, as it never fails to mean that I have been mistaken for someone else. But still Constantine was a Government official, and this was enough for them, so after the young people had danced a kolo for us we were taken to the house of three handsome elderly brothers, who were the chief men of the village. It was the usual Balkan house, with a stable for the livestock on the ground floor and an outside staircase leading up to a balcony off which open the living-rooms. The men put out on the balcony a long table and two benches, covered with rugs. Several other important men of the village came in and were introduced to us, and we all sat down and drank musty red wine, and ate sheep's cheese and hard-boiled eggs, which the brothers shelled for us with their own hands. We were joined by the wife of the eldest brother, a woman of about forty, wearing a dress on which the Persian design of the moon tree was adapted to a Christian purpose, with her healthy and well-mannered youngest child in her arms; and I think other women were listening and whispering behind a half-open door.

When we had eaten and drunk, the men, who were all of dignified bearing and decisive manner, began to instruct Constantine in the message he was to take back to the authorities. It was cool and logical. Yes, it was true that they were having great trouble with another village, grave trouble. It was true that three men had been killed and one wounded. But it was no use sending gendarmes with instructions to keep order, for the trouble was about something, and it would not cease until that something was settled. It was not merely that the other village was Bulgarian: there was a real conflict of interest concerning the water rights; and, as they all realized by now, the dispute had gone on for so many generations and there had been so much ill-feeling engendered that it would go on for ever if some independent person did not intervene and arbitrate. So would the Government please send a commission to look into the matter at once? They had already sent a request for it, but they knew theirs would only be one among innumerable petitions from villages, and would probably not be dealt with for years, or at least months, and this matter was urgent. It ought to take precedence of requests for better roads or lighting, because as long as it was not settled there would be clashes, and there was certain to be more loss of life. So would Constantine please inform the proper people?

He said that he would; and indeed the next day he did. Then these men of the Skopska Tserna Gora went on to talk of other matters. 'And you?' they said. 'We can put our house in order if you put your house in order up in Belgrade. Are you doing that? Sometimes we doubt it.' They said that they saw the economic necessity of the pact with Italy, but they did not believe that it could mean much. 'Those people have worked against us here in our own country, they have spent money like water raising up Macedonians against their brothers, they put bombs in the hands of those who killed our King. Why should they suddenly be our friends? They will steal all they can from us. It is a pity that anything should be done which will make our young men forget that they are enemies and that we must be ready to defend our country against them.' But they were still more perturbed by the pact with Bulgaria. 'It is impossible,' they said, 'to make peace with the Bulgarians. They are our *non-brothers*.' Then the woman with the child in her arms spoke, and all the men fell silent. 'I have seen with my own eyes my brother and my brother's son killed by Bulgarians,' she said, and the statement was even stronger that it sounds to Western ears, because of the special tie that exists between Serb brothers and sisters. 'They killed them without mercy, as if they were not Christians but Turks.' The words came down like a hammer. She closed her lips in a straight line, and the men began to speak again, urging the implacability of their enemies and its everlasting quality.

It was horrible to hear these primitive people speak with such savagery, and to realize that they were savage not because they were primitive but because they had been deliberately corrupted by the Great Powers. The prime cause of Macedonian violence is, of course, five hundred years of misgovernment by the Ottoman Empire. But it would never have assumed its recent extreme and internecine character had it not been for England's support of the Ottoman Empire when it would have fallen apart if it had been left to itself; had it not been for the artificial Bulgarization of the Macedonian Serbs which was carried on, generation after generation, on money supplied by the Tsardom; had it not been for the Austrian Empire, which was so ambitious in its *Drang nach Osten* that it created by reaction a Serbian chauvinism which made Serbs not the most ideal administrators of a province far from unanimous in its desire to be administered; had it not been that Italy had perverted the Macedonian Revolutionary Organization by finance and villainous tutelage. What I saw was not the darkness of these dark men's hearts, as a hostile traveller might have imagined, but the announcement of their legitimate determination to defend the tables and benches we sat on, the musty wine and the hard-boiled eggs and the sheep's cheese, the woman and her child, the breath in their bodies, from the criminal intentions of the silly-clever in great cities, who fancied that the rape of these might secure them some advantage.

As we drove away, my husband said to Constantine, 'Those were magnificent people. They had form, they had style. They were not at all overawed because you came from a big town, and they need not have been, because they knew what was necessary in town or country, to think clearly and put clear thoughts into clear words.' 'Certainly they were magnificent people,' said Constantine, 'they are what the Serbs were before the battle of Kossovo, they have maintained themselves in these hills for five hundred years without giving up what they have. Never were the Turks able to settle here, which they would have liked to do, for nature is everything to them, and it is very beautiful here. But when they came it was well with them only for a few days, and then they died. These men of the Skopska Tserna Gora, they could not be conquered.'

Later I said, 'It was strange how they all fell silent when that woman spoke; they behaved as if they had a great respect for her. Yet the women outside had the air of downtrodden drudges. . . .' But it was easy to see what happened. This was a situation common enough among individuals and among races. There is an attitude of contempt for women in general, a pretence that women are worthless, even though the fullest advantage is taken of their worth. At times that advantage is taken in circumstances so spectacular that it cannot afterwards be repudiated. The woman in the house of the three brothers had plainly proved her quality by some act of courage or cunning in the face of the enemy which could not be forgotten. Yet the general attitude of men to women was still maintained. All the women in the village were treated as if courage or cunning on their part was inconceivable, as if they were lucky to be used as beasts of burden. This cannot have been agreeable, even to the woman who had established herself as an exception. If all Englishmen were compelled by a taboo to be treated as inferiors by all female beings over the age of fourteen, forbidden to move or speak freely in their presence, and obliged to perform all menial duties without thanks, an Englishman who happened to have won the V.C. would still not find life enjoyable.

Yet it has to be recognized that these men of the Skopska Tserna Gora could not be conquered. We must admit here a process that at one and the same time makes life possible and intolerable for women. If there is one certain difference between the sexes it is that men lack all sense of objective reality and have a purely pragmatic attitude to knowledge. A fact does not begin to be for a man until he has calculated its probable usefulness to him. If he thinks it will serve his purposes, then he will recognize it; but if it is unwelcome to him, then he will deny it. This means that he is not sure of the existence of his own soul, for nothing is more debatable for any of us than whether it is a good or a bad thing that our souls should have come to be. That life is preferable to death is a conviction firmly held by our bowels and muscles, but the mind has never convincingly proved it to the mind. Women, however, do not greatly trouble about this, since we have been born and we shall die, and even if the essence of our existence should be evil there is at least a term set to it. Therefore, women feel they can allow themselves to enjoy the material framework of existence for what it is worth. With men it cannot be so. Full of uncertainty, they sweat with fear lest all be for the worst. Hence the dichotomy that has been often observed in homes for the aged: the old women, even those who in their time have known prosperity, do not greatly distress themselves because in their last days they must eat the bread of charity, and they accept what pleasure can be drawn from sunny weather, a warm fire, a bag of sweets; but the old men are perpetually enraged.

Therefore men must be reassured, hour by hour, day by day. They must snatch every aid they can in their lifelong fight against seen and unseen adversaries. It would comfort them enormously if they knew that they were stronger than others. But what others? It would seem obvious to answer, their enemies. But little comfort can be derived from them, for sooner or later comes the battle, to settle the value, never satisfactorily: for an enemy that defeats is plainly superior, in some sense, and an enemy that is defeated appears so contemptible that it is no comfort to be above him. There are, however, exquisitely convenient, all women. It need only be pretended that men's physical superiority is the outward sign of a universal superiority, and at a stroke they can say of half the world's population, 'I am better than that.' The declaration is the more exalting because that half includes the people on whom the man who makes it had been the most dependent, even the person through whom he received his life.

If the community is threatened by any real danger, and only a few fortunate communities are not, women will be fools if they do not accept that declaration without dispute. For the physical superiority of men and their freedom from maternity make them the natural defenders of the community, and if they can derive strength from belief in the inferiority of women, it is better to let them have it. The trouble is that too often the strength so derived proves inadequate for the task in hand. The women in the Skopska Tserna Gora were repaid for their subordination by a certain mitigation of their lot, which is proved real enough when it is compared with the darker misery of the women on the plains below, who suffered far worse at the hands of the Turks, but which was far from giving them security in any ordinary sense of the word. Intense and lifelong discomfort seems an excessive price to pay for this; and they might easily have gone on working out this inequitable contract till doomsday, since their menfolk were never able to liberate their community from the Turks until they were aided by the Serbians, who were outside their sexual transaction. In far worse case were the Turkish women in Macedonia, who received nothing in return for their subordination except the destruction of their community.

Even when the men of the community derive an adequate amount of strength from the suppression of their women, the situation is ultimately unsatisfactory; for it undoes itself, to the confusion of both parties. When men are successful in defending their community they engender a condition of general peace, in which people attempt to live by reason. Then women use their full capacities of mind and body, not because they want to prove their equality with men, for that is a point in which it is difficult to feel interest for more than a minute or two unless one has an unusually competitive mind, but because in such use lies pleasure. In such a world the young woman and the young man dash together out of adolescence into adult life like a couple of colts. But presently the woman looks round and sees that the man is not with her. He is some considerable distance behind her, not feeling very well. There has been drained from him the strength which his forefathers derived from the subjection of women; and the woman is amazed, because tradition has taught her that to be a man is to be strong. There is no known remedy for this disharmony. As yet it seems that no present she can make him out of her liberty can compensate him for his loss of what he gained from her slavery. The disagreeable consequences of this are without end, and perhaps it may be counted the worst that there never can be a society where men are men and women are women, that humanity never reveals the whole of itself at one time. Until there is achieved a settled condition of world peace hard to foresee anywhere nearer than the distant future it will always be more necessary that the revelation should be male. Therefore it will perhaps be reasonable till the end of all time within imaginable scope, to follow the ancient custom and rejoice when a boy is born and to weep for a girl. But there are degrees in the female tragedy. It is our tendency nowadays to deplore as worse than all others the woes of the woman whom modern capitalism allows to earn her own living but deprives of a husband and children, since the wage-slave is an uneager lover and a worse provider. But nowhere have I seen such settled and hopeless despair, such resentment doubled by its knowledge that it might not express itself, as on the faces of the women of the Skopska Tserna Gora.

A Convent Somewhere below
the Skopska Tserna Gora

It is said that many have been cured of madness by drinking of the spring in the orchard of this convent, and I do not doubt it, for this is a very pleasant place, and I fancy that in Macedonia, as in the rest of the world, the mad are usually those who have been surfeited with the unpleasant. We met the fat old Abbess in the poplar avenue, and she said, 'I am so glad that you have come back to see us again,' and there was written in her eye, 'now that I have a rare, an inestimable, and sacred treasure to show you, far more precious than any icon or holy spring,' for she was infatuated with the child she led by the hand. She took us up into her parlour and a nun was sent to bring us brandy and sugar and water, and she explained how she came to have this unique treasure in her possession. The child's mother was a French schoolmistress at Bitolj, and had sent her there to make a good convalescence after scarlet fever and diphtheria, a story which explained much that had been puzzling, for indeed this was the plainest little girl one could well imagine, a spindly little girl, an Indian-famine little girl.

'You must recite, my dear,' said the Abbess, 'you must recite to the foreigners and the gentleman from Belgrade.' She could not bear us to go home without seeing the prettiest thing we should ever see. So after the child had stood on one leg and then on the other, and had pleated the edge of her petticoat till she was told she should not, she repeated a Serbian hymn and sang a French song all about *les fleurs* and *la nature*, in the classic treble of the infant French voice, in the voice that René Clair gave to the morning glories in *Á Nous la Liberté*. When she had finished she stood on the point of her sharp little nose in the immense slopes of the Abbess's bosom.

By now the young nun had come back with the brandy and the sugar and water, and she stood with her arms akimbo and her chin forward, adoring the child. 'Who is that bishop with the very fine head?' said my husband as he drank, nodding at a photograph on the wall. I had asked the very same question when I was here for the first time the year before, and she had looked at the photograph

and had said, 'He is the Metropolitan who received me into the
Church, he was burned alive by the Bulgarians,' and her eyes had
darkened. She had talked of the dead man for a long time. This
time she said the same words, but her eyes did not darken, they
went back to the child at once, and she said, 'We have been here
twenty-six years, never have we had a child here before, it is such
a joy as I could not have believed.' Perhaps the cock crowed, but
it was in Paradise.

Bardovtsi

One wet evening I saw a gentleman wearing a fez come out of one of the Minnie Mouse houses in the new town of Skoplje and with a deep sigh, as if to him the world seemed more obstinately rainy than it does to the rest of us, open his umbrella and set himself to picking his way among the puddles. 'That is the Pasha of Bardovtsi,' said my friend; 'there are no pashas now, but that is what he would be if there were any, and he is not anything else, so that is what we call him. But you must go to Bardovtsi, it is quite close, and nobody lives there now, and you ought to see what a pasha's palace was like.' So one afternoon we borrowed a car from the Governor and drove out to a point in the valley under the Skopska Tserna Gora, where there was a thickly wooded village, and many people walking through air throbbing with distant music towards a festival, in white clothes and tall fantastic head-dress, dappled by sunlight falling through the leaves. We came at last on a patch of grassland and a great wall, set with watch-towers at either end, in which there was a ramshackle door in a lordly gateway. But it was locked, and when our chauffeur beat on it there was no answer. He crossed the grassland to a farm and called up to the balcony, but there was silence. Everybody we had seen had been walking away from the village.

Our chauffeur became very angry. He was a handsome and passionate young man who had never been denied anything in his life. He battered at the door till it appeared about to split, and then it was slowly opened by an old man carrying a scythe, his hand cupping his ear. Behind him an acre of long grass shook its ears, and we saw beyond it the cool prudence, the lovely common sense, of a Turkish country house, as they built them a hundred to a hundred and fifty years ago. The Turks and the Georgian English have known better than anyone how to build a place where civilized man can enjoy nature. The old man with the scythe said we could go where we liked, he had only bought the hay rights and was getting the grass in because the young people had to go to the kolo. 'Yes,' he said with a chuckle, 'they have to go to the kolo, but all the same they know no way of keeping off the rain.'

This acre of grass was one of three paddocks which lay within the great wall, themselves divided by walls. We went to the door on the left, stamping our feet as we went, for fear there were snakes, and looked over more long grass to a solid profligacy of richly coloured bricks such as the Turks loved. There was stabling there for sixty horses, housing for an army of retainers. We went back to the house, a black stork screaming suddenly above our heads. But we could not go in. As we opened the door we saw that the staircase in the hall was barred, and for good reason. A host of ravens fled from the glassless windows, and when some lumps of masonry fell from a ceiling somewhere too many unseen living things scuttled and rustled on the floors where we must walk for real comfort of the mind. We were able only to look through the dimness and see that all the proportions were wise, that it must have been light without flimsiness, and firm without heaviness, and that in the heat the coolness must have been stored here as in a reservoir. Then we went to the wall on the right and through a gateway, and saw a house, only a little less large, that had been the harem. There also we startled many ravens, but it was still safe to enter it, and we went up the stairs to that delicious landing-room which is the special invention of Turkish architecture, where one sits in the freshness of the first story and can look down the well of the staircase and see who is coming in and out of the rooms on the ground floor. It is the spirit of harem intrigue insisting that, to make the game more sporting, all the cards shall be laid on the table straight away. This room was decorated in the curious Turkish Regency style that is so inexplicable. It is hard to imagine why at the end of the eighteenth century, and at the beginning of the nineteenth, when the Turks were still the fiercest of military peoples, they had the houses decorated with paintings which recall the Regency style, not as it was in its own age (which would not be surprising, for some of our eighteenth-century men were terrible as any Turks) but as it is rendered in pastiche by Mr Rex Whistler. There were on these walls pictures of Constantinople and the Bosporus, framed with the most affected of swags and segregated by comic mock pilasters, which were not even Strawberry Hill, which were painted by somebody who seemed to be saying, 'How amusing it was when people thought it amusing to paint in this way.' We went through the other rooms delicately, and we found that there were bathrooms and water-closets, several of them, such as there cannot have been in a single house in England or France or America at that time.

We were wandering entranced in a world of delicate, clean people, surrounded by refined fragilities, when the chauffeur followed us upstairs. He had not joined us before because he had been catching a pigeon, which now fluttered between his two hands. There is a veil between the animal world and those of us who dwell in towns, but there was none to him. Wherever we were, he saw the animals as quickly as he saw the human beings who were present, the stoat or the lizard or the swallow fledgling; and to the animals he must have seemed a god, so swiftly did he stretch out his hand to caress those he favoured and kill those in his disfavour. He looked round him and said 'Ah, the old pig! The old pig of a Turk! Twenty-five women he had here, the old woman says.' He tried to say no more but his rage was too great. He whirled his joined hands round in a circle, the pigeon rattling its startled wings inside them, and began to shout. He was a Serbian from Nish, where they drove out the Turks only a little over sixty years ago. 'And there were many of our Christian women that were brought here! And they would not have children by our women! Our women they made to have abortions! They cut our women to pieces!' Ravens of specially lethargic disposition fled croaking to the light. '*Aïde, aïde*, out of it!' he cried, clattering down the stairs.

The old man stood resting on his scythe. He was proud that we had come to see the palace. It had belonged to Avzi Pasha, he said, and he watched for our faces to lighten. Avzi Pasha, he repeated. But nobody knows anything of him today for there are fewer archives here than there were in Bosnia. To a generation's conflict with a government, to a personality whose virtues and vices made half a dozen countrysides smile or weep, there is often no clue except some crumpled pieces of paper, mostly referring to religious properties. Avzi Pasha, the old man told us, had been a very rich man, a very great man, he had been so great—he waved his feeble arm—that he had even sent his own army against the Sultan in Tsarigrad. But that did not serve, of course. Till the Sultan fell before the armies of the world he did not fall. Avzi Pasha was driven out, but there was another pasha here, and yet another, and they were all grand, but then the land was made free, and there were no more pashas, and the palace was as we saw it.

His voice grumbled as he said it, and I thought he might perhaps be regretting that the palace was not as it had been. I said, 'Will you ask him if it is better now with him than it was then?' It had been only age and a day's mowing that had made his voice drag. He threw down his scythe at our feet, he joined his hands and shook his head, and laughed at the simplicity of the question. 'In those days,' he said, 'we did not know the harvest as a time of joy, half the crops went straight away to the Pasha, but then the tax-collectors came back, and they came back, and they came back, and they said, "This is for him also. It is another tax." We never knew how little we had.' I thought of the Germans on the train from Salzburg. 'If only we could tell what we had to pay . . .' It is that, apparently, and not the single great injustices, the rape of the beloved to the harem or the concentration camp, but the steady drain on what one earns, on what should be one's own if there is justice in earth, or Heaven, that cannot be borne.

Again the chauffeur began to shout. 'And the stables! The beautiful stables! The people had to fetch all the stones from a quarry five miles away for nothing!' 'The harvest was not a time of joy,' repeated the old man. 'Never did I think,' said my husband, 'that I should hear a man speak of the Revolt of the Pashas as a thing his people remembered; I will give him fifty dinars.' When the old man saw the coin he gaped at it, and bent down and kissed my husband's hand. 'Would anybody on the Skopska Tserna Gora kiss my husband's hand if he gave them money?' I asked the chauffeur. 'No,' he said, 'but they were in the mountains and these people were on the flat lands. They were defenceless against the Turks.'

Neresi

In a cab drawn by two horses named 'Balkan' and 'Gangster' we trotted out of Skoplje through market gardens where tomatoes and paprikas glowed their different reds, and climbed a road up the hill behind Skoplje that is called the 'Watery One' because of its many springs. The cab was hardly a cab, the road was hardly a road, and the cabman was a man of irrational pride, which we wounded afresh each time we got out of the cab because it was about to fall over the edge of a ravine. There is a lot of emotion loose about the Balkans which has lost its legitimate employment now that the Turks have been expelled. But it was pleasant to walk along the hedges and sometimes pick the flowers, and sometimes look back and see the snow mountains framed between the apple blossom and the green-gold popular trees, and watch the Moslem girls, who with an air of panic working in their faces, whisked their veils over the face when they saw Constantine and my husband, who, on the contrary, were talking about Bernard Berenson. Also there was good conversation with strangers, as there always is when Constantine is there. An old Moslem was sitting on a rock beside a field of corn under a hawthorn tree, and as he was breathing very heavily, Constantine stopped and asked, 'Are you ill, friend?' 'No,' said the Moslem, 'but I am old and I cannot walk as far as I used to do.' Constantine said, 'Well, this is a very pleasant place to rest.' 'That is why I chose it,' said the Moslem. 'I pressed on, though I was breathless, till I came to this rock. For since I am so old that my soul must soon leave my body, I look at nature as much as I can.'

When we came to Neresi it was as I had remembered it, a rustic monastery, as homely as a Byzantine church can possibly be, a thing that might be a farmhouse, as it stands in a paddock, had it not been that there appear in it domes that are plainly bubbles blown by the breath of God. From the fountain at the corner of the paddock children drew water, dressed in their best for a kolo; the plum tree that nuzzles a corner of the church was in full flower; a small dog was chasing its fleas and in its infant folly transferred itself constantly from spot to spot as if hoping to find one specially suited to the pursuit. All was well in this world, and there came out of the priest's house the little priest whom I find one of the most sympathetic characters in Yugoslavia.

He is a tiny creature without sin. His eyes, which shine out of a

687

tangle of eyebrows and wrinkles and beard, are more than bright,
they are unstained light. He is an exile, for a tenuous and exquisite
cause. He is a Russian monk, but he was not one of those who fled
from the Bolsheviks; he belonged to the great monastery on the
island on Lake Ladoga, which is on the borders of Finland and
Russia and exists to this day. He left this beloved place, where he
had been since his early boyhood, to live in a lonely village, where
there are more Moslems than Christians, in a climate that to his
northern blood is abominable, because he would not consent to
the adoption of the modern calendar. There had been a great many
disputes in the monastery itself as to whether they should adhere
to the old Church calendar, which is a fortnight after the ordinary
world calendar, as the Orthodox Church in some respects still does
in Yugoslavia, or should keep the modern world calendar. These
disputes became so violent that the Finnish Government, a cool
body mainly Lutheran in its origins, lost patience and bade the
monks adopt the modern calendar or leave the monastery. So, for
that and no other reason, did the little creature leave all that was
dear to him.

Nothing, indeed, is more reasonable in the terms of his type of
mysticism. On a certain day you will look up to heaven and think
of the Mother of God as she was at the moment of the annunciation
and she will bend down and accept your thoughts and lift them up
in her heavenly sphere. What is the good of it all if you start looking
up and sending her your thoughts on quite another day from that on
which she has bent down to accept them? He felt as if he was being
condemned to a lifetime of imbecile and heartrending activity, just
as one would if every day one were forced to go to a railway terminus
and wait for some beloved person who had in fact arrived at that
station a fortnight before. I like such literal mysticism. It shows
a desire to embrace the adored spiritual object and hug it till it
passes into enjoyment of the boon of material existence, which is
proof of a nature that would be kind and warm, and that would
prefer the agreeable to the disagreeable. I think of the little man as
of the old anthropomorphist heretic hermit, who was told that he
must cease to believe that God was a person with a human body,
having arms and legs and eyes and ears, and must worship him as
a spirit, and who went away with tears, repeating the text, 'They
have taken away my Lord, and I know not where they have laid
him.' As it is easier to love an abstraction than a material person,
since an abstraction demands no daily sacrifices, has no slippers to
warm, and needs no hot supper, this was to his credit as a human
being, though not as a theologian.

We talked to the little man, and asked him how time went, and he said it went well, but he grieved, as he had when I saw him before, at the lack of fish. At Lake Ladoga he had eaten fish nearly every day, wonderful fish straight out of the water, and there was none in this village. Also he was used to tea, and here they drank coffee and the tea was not good. We asked him if he were not lonely, and he said, 'On the whole, no, for there is God.' Then we were joined by the owner of the fleabitten dog, an elderly woman who had come here from near Belgrade because all her family, all her five sons and daughters, had chosen to give their lives to their country here. She was quite elderly; most and perhaps all of her children must have made this decision before the war, when it meant self-condemnation to an indefinite sojourn in an insanitary Hell with considerable chances of sudden death. My husband and I wondered if we would perhaps find ourselves moved by some extraordinary reason to go to die where we were not born; but as both these people were sitting smiling so happily into the sunshine, to find an answer seemed not so vital as one might suppose.

Presently we went into the church and saw the frescoes, which are being uncovered very slowly, to wean the peasants from the late eighteenth-century peasant frescoes which had been painted over them, for the peasants like these much better than the old ones, and indeed they are extremely attractive. They show tight, round, pink little people chubbily doing quite entertaining things, as you see them represented in the paintings on the merry-go-rounds and advertising boards of French fairs, and exploited in the pictures of Marc Chagall and his kind; and it would be a pity to destroy them if they were not covering fine medieval frescoes. When my husband saw the older frescoes I could see that he was a little disappointed, and at last he said, 'But these are not like the Byzantine frescoes I have seen, they are not so stylized, they are almost representational, indeed they are very representational.'

It is, of course, quite true, though I have doubted whether we are right in considering Byzantine frescoes highly stylized since, on my first visit to Yugoslavia, I went through the Sandjak of Novi Pazar, which is the most medieval part of the country and saw peasants slowly move from pose to pose distorted by conscious dignity which made them exactly like certain personages over the altars of Ravenna and Rome. But the Serbo-Byzantine frescoes are unquestionably more naturalistic and far more literary. In looking at some of these at Neresi there came back to me the phrase of Bourget, '*la végétation touffue de King Lear,*' they are so packed with ideas. One presents in another form the theme treated by the painter of the fresco in the little monastery in the gorge; it shows the terribly explicit death of Christ's body, Joseph of Arimathea is climbing a ladder to take Christ down from the Cross, and his feet as they grip the rungs are the feet of a living man, while Christ's feet are utterly dead. Another shows an elderly woman lifting a beautiful astonished face at the spectacle of the raising of Lazarus: it pays homage to the ungrudging heart, it declares that a miracle consists of more than a wonderful act, it requires people who are willing to admit that something wonderful has been done. Another shows an Apostle hastening to the Eucharist, with the speed of a wish.

But there is another which is extraordinary beyond belief because not only does it look like a painting by Blake, it actually illustrates a poem by Blake. It shows the infant Christ being washed by a woman who is a fury. Of that same child, of that same woman, Blake wrote:

> And if the Babe is born a boy
> He's given to a Woman Old
> Who nails him down upon a rock,
> Catches his shrieks in cups of gold.
>
> She binds iron thorns around his head,
> She pierces both his hands and feet,
> She cuts his heart out at his side,
> To make it feel both cold and heat.
>
> Her fingers number every nerve,
> Just as a miser counts his gold;
> She lives upon his shrieks and cries,
> And she grows young as he grows old.

It is all in the fresco at Neresi. The fingers number every nerve of the infant Christ, just as a miser counts his gold; that is spoken of by the tense, tough muscles of her arms, the compulsive fingers, terrible, seen through the waters of the bath as marine tentacles. She is catching his shrieks in cups of gold; that is to say, she is looking down with awe on what she is so freely handling. She is binding iron around his head, she is piercing both his hands and feet, she is cutting his heart out at his side, because she is naming him in her mind the Christ, to whom these things are to happen. It is not possible that that verse and this fresco should not have been the work of the same mind. Yet the verse was written one hundred and fifty years ago by a home-keeping Cockney and the fresco was painted eight hundred years ago by an unknown Slav. Two things which should be together, which illumine each other, had strayed far apart, only to be joined for a minute or two at rare intervals in the attention of casual visitors. It was to counter this rangy quality in the universe that the little monk had desired to maintain contact between his devotions and their objects. His shining eyes showed a faith that, bidden, would have happily accepted more exacting tasks.

ROAD

We had had a number of bad evenings with Gerda. She was not easy in the daytime. A number of expeditions had been darkened, it seemed without cause, till I discovered that when we jumped out of the car, as we were sure to do quite often, to see a view or a flower or a kolo, I sometimes got in and sat on the right, which was where, she strongly felt, she ought to sit since she was the wife of a Government official. But over our evening meals she was at her worst, for it was then, after the business of sightseeing was over, that she was able to cultivate her ingenuity. Before Constantine came down she would try to correct any pleasant impressions of the country we might have received during the day. She would tell us, 'You do not understand how horrible this country is. You think it is grand when they talk of Serbian pioneers. You do not know what that means. Everybody who goes into the Civil Service and wants to get a good post must volunteer to work here in Macedonia for three years. That is abominable. I knew a woman doctor and she came down here, and they made her go to the smallest mountain villages and teach the people about health and the care of children and it was terrible, the peasants were just like animals, so filthy and stupid. Do you call that right to make an educated woman of good family do that?' 'But if one acquires territory that is not fully developed one must do that sort of thing,' said my husband. 'One is bound to have trouble and loss until it is done. We have had to do exactly the same thing in India.' 'You have done exactly the same thing in India?' repeated Gerda. 'Yes, there are many English people in India who spend their lives doing such work among the natives, both missionaries and civil servants.' Then, as Constantine took his place at the table, she said to him in Serbian, 'Here our friend is telling us that the English do all sorts of philanthropic work among the natives in India. It is wonderful what hypocrites they are.'

She robbed Constantine's talk of all its quality. It is his habit, a harmless one, to begin a reminiscence, which is probably true and interesting, with a generalization based on it which is unsound but arresting. It is his way of saying, 'Wake up! Wake up!' and nobody minds. Once at dinner he put down his wineglass and announced, 'I do not think, but I know, I absolutely know, that most men do not die a natural death but are poisoned by their wives.' Now my husband knew, and I knew, and Constantine knew that such a statement was stark nonsense, but we also knew that it was the prelude to a good story. But my husband said, 'Indeed?' And I said, 'Do you really think so?' and Constantine began to tell us how after he had worked for some time in Russia as an official under the Bolsheviks, to save his life, he could bear it no longer and he decided to escape. First he had to lose his identity and this he did by picking up a gipsy girl and travelling with her for two months from fair to fair as a palmist, till he got down to the Roumanian border. Again and again while he was reading women's hands they asked him if he could supply them with poison for the purpose of murdering their husbands. Nature, it is well known, always supplies its own antidote, and if it is natural for men to feel superior to women it is also natural for women to feed them with henbane when this superiority is carried past a joke. This story is borne out by the number of people who have been tried in Hungary during recent years for supplying poison to peasant women. Whatever Constantine wished to tell us in this connexion we did not hear, for Gerda said crisply, 'Dear me, I am glad that I am in the company of clever people who can believe such things as that most women poison their husbands.' 'But it is true,' began poor Constantine. 'Is it?' said Gerda. 'I am only a simple woman, and I do not write books, but such things seem to me too foolish.' There was then a wrangle in Serbian which left Constantine red and silent.

On all the occasions when Gerda had thus tied a tourniquet round the conversation, she would sit and watch me thoughtfully, making remarks in Serbian of which I could usually catch the meaning, which had always the same subject matter and style. 'They must be very rich. Those two rings of hers must be worth a lot. But of course he is a typical English business man. Good God, how rich the English are!' 'But how stupid she is, how stupid! She cannot possibly be a good writer. But of course there is no culture in England.' These remarks I did not translate to my husband, but sometimes she could not bear him not to know that she was being rude to me, and she would say something uncivil in German, and sometimes her rage against us would flood her face with crimson.

After we had been to the theatre to see Yovanovna, an actress who was an old friend of Constantine's, play the leading part in a classic Serbian play, she was so melancholy with her hatred of us and England, so flushed and heavy with it, as one might be with the advent of a cold or influenza, that I went to bed early rather than have supper. Presently my husband came in and sat on my bed, and faced me with the air of one making a confession. 'My dear,' he said, 'I am in the position of one who has gone into voluntary bankruptcy and still finds himself liable to imprisonment for debt. Tonight I thought Gerda so intolerable that I made up my mind to get rid of her. Good God, why should we not have this holiday? All this last year, when we were going through that terrible time with your aunt and my uncle dying, we promised ourselves we would have this short time together, doing nothing but seeing new things and being quiet. Why should we have this woman who hates us tying herself round our necks? Besides, how do we know when she will not mortally offend some of the people that we meet? So I suddenly made up my mind at supper that I would stand it no longer. After all, we can go to Ochrid alone, and we can see what is to be seen, without Constantine. It will be less delightful, for he is the most entertaining companion in the world, but it can be done. I said therefore over the supper-table, "There will be too many of us in the car tomorrow." I disliked the sound of my own voice intensely as I said it, but I set my teeth, and went on, determined to behave just as badly as she does. "Three and all our luggage will be just as much as the car will carry. Your wife, Constantine, must travel by the motor bus to Ochrid, since you certainly must accompany us if we are to visit the monastery of Yovan Bigorski." I believed that they would be silent for a moment and that Constantine would say, "I am sorry, this arrangement will not suit me. My wife and I will be obliged to go to Belgrade tomorrow morning." But there was a moment's silence and then they agreed. Now, I have behaved just as badly as she does, but I have gained absolutely nothing by it.' I cared less than he did for the depressing moral aspect of the situation. I simply said, 'I believe we shall have to go about with Gerda for the whole of the rest of our lives.'

So the next morning we had an uneasy breakfast, and Gerda left by the eight o'clock bus, telling us bravely that she did not mind. We sat at a table in the street, drinking coffee and sheep's milk until the Ban's car came. A French journalist who was staying in the town delayed a moment to ask me whether I knew the works of Millet on the Serbo-Byzantine frescoes, bought some lilac from a passing boy and laid it on my table. Constantine, away for the moment to buy stamps, and my husband, away for the moment to buy tooth-paste, each met the same boy and had the same idea. An old Turk stood by and watched the increase of the purple heap on my table and over his face spread the thought, 'These people are fond of lilac. They buy lilac. Since they have bought so much they might buy more.' So we saw him go down a side street and look up at a small wall over which some lilac was bobbing from someone else's garden. There was a little negotiation with a barrel drawn from a neighbouring yard, and then the ragged old legs shinned up the wall, a ragged turban and a lean old forearm worked among the branches. He brought back a very respectable armful, considering his age and the circumstances. It seemed hardly possible not to buy it.

A woman with a handsome face worn with suffering but not ascetic, showing a mouthful of gold teeth, stopped and greeted Constantine with pleasure, and I remembered it was one of the chambermaids where Constantine and I had stayed last year. She was glad to see us and showed it in a curiously fantastic and highfalutin way; and I remembered what Constantine had told me about her and the little blonde Slovene who was the other chambermaid. He had said, 'Today my blind would not go up so I called them in to see it. But it was not serious, it was only that some plaster had fallen between it and the wall, nothing was broken. So I said to the chambermaid, "Nothing is bad so long as it is unbroken," and she said, looking a little wicked at me, "Nothing is unbroken in these sinful days." And then they both laughed a great deal, and they looked at my pyjamas, and said how gay they are, and if I wear such gay pyjamas when I am alone, how very gay they must be when I have a companion, and I say, "It is not the pyjamas that make the gaiety when one has a companion!" and at that they were so delighted that they ran out of the room, and then they ran back again and laughed some more, and then they ran out again. And now they like me very much, for that conversation represents something wonderful to them, it was a high-water mark of delicacy that they will perhaps never touch again. For they never talk to anybody about anything else than these matters, because they have nothing else to talk about to people who are strangers, who cannot talk about local things. But usually they have to talk about them to people who make jokes that are too bad, who are rude to them, who cannot be counted on not suddenly to show their teeth and become brutal. But I did not say a rude word, I was elegant with them. I am kind. So months after, years after, they will say to each other, "Do you remember the gentleman who came from Belgrade with the English lady, and who talked to us in that wonderful, witty, drawing-room way?" And it will be just that which I said to them.' And here was proof that Constantine was right.

The handsome young chauffeur, whose name was Dragutin, said farewell to his wife, a slender dark child who looked like one of the Russian ballet, by chance heel-bound. We rushed through the broad valley, past the ruined mosque, past poppies and poplars and the last fruit blossom, to the town of Tetovo, which stands among many apple orchards. It is famous for those apples; there are songs about them; you may know that the hem of the hyperbolic East has touched here when you are told that some of them are so fine that they are transparent and that when you peel them you can see the pips at the core. We went out and drank black coffee at a coffee-house in a dusty market-place, and the bald-headed man who kept it came up with a tray of cakes and said, 'Did you expect to see Dobosch Torte here? Did you expect to see Pozony here? Did you expect to see Nusstorte here?' and we said that we had not, and he said, 'I will explain to you how this has happened. Once upon a time I had a very large bakery in Skoplje. I had many men working for me, and I backed the bill of a friend of mine for two hundred thousand dinars, and he ran away. So I had to sell all I had and start here afresh, and in a place that my wife hates, for she is a very cultivated lady, she comes from the north of the Danube. I have had to labour for five years like a convict, to face life with a clean forehead, and it is not even that I was foolish, for I was bound to back his bill, since in my beginning he had backed mine.' He made us take some cakes for our journey, and a piece of sucking-pig. 'For nowhere,' he said, 'will you find cakes as good as mine and there are few sucking-pigs like this. The whole of it weighed only eight pounds, and it is like butter.' He mentioned food only objectively, but nothing is more certain than that he was a very greedy man. It was good to think that he had this consolation, living in such a remote place, in undeserved ruin, with a very cultivated lady.

On the outskirts of Tetovo we passed a mosque on the edge of a river which had a strange and dissolute air, for it was covered with paintings in the same Moslem Regency style as the harem in the Pasha's palace at Bardovtsi. Not an inch but had its diamond centred with a lozenge or a star, all in the most coquettish, interior decorator's polychrome. It languished in the midst of a sturdy Oriental wall, with square openings in it barred by wooden grilles, very fierce and very rustic. Rain had begun to fall but this mosque

was so curious a thing, so inappropriate in its contrast to its builders,
that we sent a boy for the key and waited for it, though he was
long in coming. On the other side of the river were ruins of a
Turkish bath; about us faultlessly proportioned Turkish houses
slightly projected their upper stories; a little way off the house of
a Turkish merchant, painted periwinkle blue, stood in a garden
great enough to be called a park, lovely enough to be called by
the Midi name for a garden, *un paradoux*. Not a dog barked. The
quarter was tonguetied with decay.

When the key came we entered into an astonishing scene, for
every inch of the mosque inside was painted with fripperies in
this amusing and self-consciously amused style. There was a frieze
of tiny little views, of palaces on the Bosporus with ships neatly
placed in the middle of the sound, of walled gardens with playing
fountains and trees mingling their branches as in agreement, and
on the ceiling were circles containing posies or views of buildings,
Persian in origin but as remote from their origin as is London of
today, though they were all that nearer. The vaulting under the
galleries was painted with roses which proved that there must be
a Turkish expression meaning 'too divine.' It was like being inside
a building made of a lot of enormous tea-trays put together, the
very most whimsical tea-trays that the gift department of Messrs.
Fortnum & Mason would wish to provide. In this erection a fierce
people had met to worship their militant prophet. I understand
nothing, nothing at all.

Out of Tetovo we drove along a road between wide marshes
trenched with yellow irises, lying between high hills where green
terraces climbed to a blue barrenness, streaked by snow. Presently
we came on the motor bus, which had broken down. We uncomfortably felt it our duty to stand by till it recovered. Gerda was
standing with a Turkish woman in her late thirties, in widow's
weeds, who was fat in the curious way of beautiful middle-aged
Turkish women. She did not look like one fat woman, she looked
like a cluster of beautiful women loosely attached to a common
centre, and she was multiplied again by her excess of widow's
weeds, which were enough for the bereaved of a small town.
Her smile advertised sweetness under a thick layer of powder,
like Turkish delight. She was, she said, the widow of a Belgrade
actor, going home to see his parents at Debar. The bus started and
we went ahead of it to Gostivar, which is another town shaped by
the Turkish luxury that has departed. About the market square,
which was edged with rickety shops and characterless cafés and
one Regency Moslem house that might have been a summer-house

designed in our day for a lady of title by some international epicene, men walked about holding squealing lambs in their arms. We left the town and climbed up the mountainside to the pass, and saw how the comitadji were able to carry on their warfare, for we saw for the first time the Macedonian beechwoods and limewoods, leafy and stunted and dense. Under their green mantle an army could have its being and be invisible a quarter of a mile away. We stopped on the heights to look down at Gostivar, now a pool of russet roofs dripping across the river to a lower shelf, with minarets and poplars planted by it cunningly, and at the valley that drives broadly back to Tetovo between snow-brindled mountains to the ultimate pure white peaks. Dragutin left his car and at once cried out, as if hailing a fellow-soldier, and pointed his hand straight above him. An eagle soared above us with a chicken in its claws. We went on and came to the pass, a marshy stretch where there was still winter, and the trees and bushes were bare. Cattle and horses grazed, and they were ornery; it is an American word but it was made for Balkan beasts. On the wetter patches storks stood on one leg, all facing one way.

At an inn on which a stork sat immensely and superbly, as if not knowing that it was an inn, but thinking of it simply as what it sat on, we had a meal of excellent fish. Then the bus drove up, and Gerda came in. My husband, who was transfixed with horror at this turn his device had taken, plied her with fish and bread and wine, and asked her if she had had a comfortable journey. 'Yes,' she said, 'several people have asked me why I am travelling by bus when my husband and friends are travelling in a car, but I have explained that these are English guests and they had to have the most comfortable seats.' My husband ceased to offer her anything at all, he retired into himself and suffered.

Gerda ate in silence for a time and then she addressed herself to Constantine. 'The Turkish widow,' she said, 'asked me if I had been to see Yovanovna, and I said that I had. She asked me if I considered her attractive, and I said yes, quite attractive. And then she said, but Yovanovna is more than quite attractive, she is very attractive. She must be, for she has had so many lovers. Then the woman asked me if I had ever heard of the famous poet called Constantine, and I said I had, and she said that all the world knew that he had been Yovanovna's lover for many years.' After a moment Constantine said sadly, '*Ach*, what a wicked woman to say that to somebody she has just met in a bus!'

Just then the conductor put his head in at the door and said that he had lost time on the road, and he must start again at once. Gerda rose and went, and Constantine followed her. 'But the Turkish widow must have recognized Constantine!' I exclaimed. 'Her husband was an actor and for years Constantine was a dramatic critic, and anyway everybody knows him from the caricatures.' 'Of course the Turkish widow knew him,' said my husband, 'but what on earth can Gerda have been saying to the Turkish widow to make her land such a good one as that?' At this moment Constantine returned. He sat down and ate sucking-pig very pensively. 'I have a very strong impression,' he said, 'that my wife would have liked to say something very disagreeable to me, but could not find what to say.'

The road fell from the pass through a rocky gorge, sordid at first with rockfalls, which widened out into the valley that I had remembered as one of the loveliest things I had ever seen, where steep hillsides, far apart enough to be seen, fell again and again into the shapes that Earth would take if she found pleasure in herself and what she grows. Voluptuously the beechwoods stretch up to the snow, the grasslands down to the streams, the crags with their poplars and ashes come forward like the elbows of a yawning woman. There is a village on these hillsides which I think the most beautiful I have ever seen, anywhere in the world. It is called the Sorrowing Women, a name which, in a countryside where tragedy has till now been the common lot, must mark some ghastly happening. White houses, bluish white, all built tall, like towers, and yet like houses, with grey-brown roofs, stand on a ledge below the snow and beechwoods, and around them grow ashes and poplars and below a lawn falls to the river. There is one minaret. A path winds down through the lawn. The village has a unity like a person, one is disappointed that it cannot speak, that one cannot enter into any relation with it, that one must go away and leave it.

A few miles further on was a monastery that I had to visit for a special purpose. It was no hardship. The view from the monastery, which lies high, is one of the best in Europe, taking the eye the whole journey from the snowfields to the springing corn, over sculptured earth that it seems must have been composed with joy. Also the Abbot is one of the most completely created human beings I have ever met. When we went into the galleried courtyard he was coming down the staircase from the upper story, having heard our automobile as it wound its way up the hairpin bends through the limes. We knew he was on his way, because a servant standing in the courtyard looked up at the staircase and made a gesture such as might be used by an actor in a Shakespearean historical drama to

announce the entrance of a king; and indeed the old man presented
a royal though equivocal appearance, his face shining with a double
light of majesty and cunning. He knew Constantine well, and gave
him a comradely greeting, because he was a Government official.
He himself had been appointed to this important monastery because
he had been an active pro-Serb propagandist in Macedonia before
the war and could be trusted afterwards to persuade to conformity
such Albanians and Bulgarians as were open to persuasion, and
to assist the authorities in dealing with the others. He faintly
remembered me from my previous visit, and it crossed his mind
that my husband and I might be persons of consequence, since we
were accompanied on our travels by a Government official, and a
child could have detected him resolving to impress us and charm
us. But also the thought of the vastness of the earth, and the great
affairs that link and divide its several parts, made his mind stretch
like a tiger ardent for the hunt, because he knew his aptness for
such business.

We were taken up to the parlour, which was very clean and
handsome, like the whole monastery. It had been a pilgrimage
much beloved by various neighbouring towns which had been
prosperous under the Turks because of their craftsmen, particularly
in the eighteenth century, so the church and the monastery have
been richly built and maintained. The servant brought us the usual
coffee and some wine which the Abbot, though he was sparkling
with good-will, poured out for us without any marked air of
generosity, for which I respected him all the more. I had seen
him roll his eye round us and come to the perfectly sound judgment
that my husband and I were too Western to enjoy drinking wine in
the afternoon, and he very sensibly regretted that he had to waste
his good wine in this ceremonial libation. Then we settled down
to a talk about international politics. He expressed confidence in
England as the only country which had remained great after the
war, partly because he wanted to please us, but partly because he
had collected a certain amount of evidence, some of it true and some
of it false, which seemed to him to prove our unique distinction.
The part that Mussolini had played in financing and organizing
Macedonian disorder made him regard Italy as a debauched and
debauching brawler; and he had an insight into Hitler that came
from his knowledge of the comitadji. He recognized that Hitler was
one of those who preferred to send out others to fight rather than to
fight himself, and that the Nazis were the kind of rebels who forget
that the aim of any rebellion should be to establish order. 'They
are unrulers, Hitler and Mussolini,' he said. A sudden thunder

working in his eye, he said, 'I am sure that Hitler does not believe in God'; and he added, after a minute, as if someone had objected that perhaps there was no God, 'Well, what will a man like that believe in if he does not believe in God? Nothing good, it is certain.' I think that in a single second he had boxed the compass, and passed from religious passion to scepticism and back again to faith, though now of a more prudential sort.

I noticed all this through a haze of pleasure caused by the man's immense animal vigour, and his twinkling charm, which was effective even when it was realized to be voluntary. His disingenuousness failed to repel for the same reason that made it transparently obvious. It was dictated by some active but superficial force in the foreground of his mind; but a fundamental sincerity, of the inflexible though not consciously moral sort found in true artists, watched what he was doing with absolute justice. All his intellectual processes were of a hard ability, beautiful to watch, but it was surprising to find that they were sometimes frustrated by his lack of knowledge. 'France,' he said, 'is utterly decadent. It must be so, for she is atheist and Communist.' 'But indeed you are mistaken!' I exclaimed. 'I know France well, and the country is full of life, a sound and sober and vigorous life.' 'If it interests you,' said my husband, 'French literature has not for long been so generally inspired by the religious spirit as it is today; and France is not Communist but democratic.' 'But democracy is an evil thing,' said the Abbot, assuming a sublime expression of prophetic wisdom, 'it is always the beginning of Communism.' To hurry past this occasion for disagreement he began to talk about Mr Gladstone and all that he had done for the South Slavs in their struggle with the Turks. This is a subject about which I never feel at ease, for I am not sure that Mr Gladstone would have retained his enthusiasm for the Balkan Christians if he had really known them. Their eagerness not to be more sinned against than sinning if they could possibly help it, which was actually a most healthy reaction to their lot, might have repelled his ethical austerity. But I forgot my embarrassment in wondering whether the Abbot knew that Mr Gladstone had been a leader of a democratic party. The answer was, of course, that he did not. His life had been spent in a continuous struggle for power, which had given him no time to pursue knowledge that was not of immediate use to him; and indeed such a pursuit would have been enormously difficult in his deprived and harried environment. But his poetic gift of intuitive apprehension, which was great, warned him how much there was to be known, and how intoxicating it would be to experience such contact with reality; and that perhaps accounted for his restlessness, his ambiguity, the perpetual splitting and refusion of his personality.

The Abbot showed us the church, which was very rich, with a gorgeously carved iconostasis and some ancient treasure; and as he closed the door he said to Constantine, 'Of course the English have no real religious instinct, but they approve of religion because it holds society together.' He wagged his beard gravely, infatuated with his dream that it is negotiation which makes the world go round. As we crossed the courtyard he halted and called angrily to his servant, pointing to a broken jar that lay among its oil on the cobbles. My eye was caught by the grime on his hand, and I could no longer contain my curiosity. I asked Constantine, 'How is it that the Abbot is himself dirty when the monastery is so clean, and he obviously has a passion for order?' He answered, 'He does it to be popular, because the older peasants think that a priest ought to be dirty if he is a really holy man,' answered Constantine; 'it is all the same to him, he would be clean if they wanted it.' 'What does she want to know?' asked the Abbot. 'She is wondering what you were before you were a monk,' invented Constantine. The Abbot glittered with his memories. 'I was all,' he said.

He took us out on a gallery that overhung the famous view. Under snow ridges the woods were a bronze and red mist, and lower down were green and shone like wet paint; then came the wide bosom of the terraced hillside, with its scattered villages white among their fruit trees and poplars. 'How I would love to walk on that long snow ridge!' exclaimed my husband. 'The Englishman says he would like to be up there on the snow,' said Constantine, 'I believe he does that sort of thing in Switzerland.' 'Tell him I have been there many times,' said the Abbot, 'there is not a peak in these parts I have not climbed.' He looked at them, snorting with the aerial voluptuousness of the mountaineer, and his pectoral cross stirred on his cassock and gave out brilliance from its jewels. 'That is a fine cross,' said Constantine, and there followed a conversation from which it emerged, though at first not at all clearly, that it was a kind of cross which could be worn only by a monk on whom the Patriarch had conferred a certain honour, and that the Abbot had earned that honour the previous year, by inspiring some peasants in the neighbourhood to rebuild a ruined monastery; but that the cross was not a new possession, since he had bought it years before, when he had first taken orders, in the anticipation of rising to great heights in the Church. He admitted it with a certain reluctance, as if he knew ambition was too strong in him, but went on to say that what he must do next was to reconvert certain Serb villages which in the last years of Turkish oppression had become Moslem and taken to speaking Albanian. He pointed to a village on the hillside opposite. 'You see the minaret? It means nothing. Five years ago I made them see reason, and they turned the mosque into a church.' There was the *expertise* of Tammany about him.

Before we left Constantine told us that the pious peasant women of the district gave the monastery garments which they had worked to be sold to visitors from other parts of the country, who found the regional designs a novelty; and I asked, 'May we buy some?' 'That I am sure you can do,' answered Constantine, 'but I think he will charge you a great deal.' When the Abbot heard what we wanted he opened a large cupboard, which was stuffed with these offerings, picked from here and from there, and spread what he had taken on the floor. This choice betrayed his characteristic dualism. It was made with an infallible taste, with the most profound wisdom about beauty; as I satisfied myself later, he had brought us out the best of his store. But his movements showed a certain contempt for the garments he handled and for us. It was evident that with his intellect he despised beauty, perhaps because of the incalculability which makes it useless to ambition. He watched us with real and radiant charm as well as a sneer while we put by a pair of woollen stockings knitted in a brilliant flower pattern, an apron woven in crimsons and purples, and a Debar head-dress of fine white linen embroidered in colours with crosses inscribed within circles.

As we turned over the heap to make some other purchases Dragutin put his head round the door and said, 'I have come to see what all of you are doing, for it is time we were on our way to Ochrid, if we are to get there before dark.' It could be seen from the greeting the Abbot gave him that they were on terms which were familiar but not good. As Dragutin was a strong pro-Yugoslav and had taken part in the guerrilla war against I.M.R.O. in this very district, he had probably often visited this monastery; and in the discontent there was between them one saw the sag of the *Führerprinzip*, the tendency of all leaders to sit about between performances among their followers, accepting their praise until the weaker of them become sycophants and sending them on inglorious errands until the more villainous of them become parasites, hardening against the nobler of them because of their unamenability, and sometimes reacting in fury against the basely amenable because of the treachery to the first high hopes of the cause. There had evidently been a matter of favours rescinded, or of services withheld, and perhaps a combination of both. 'You have chosen well,' said Dragutin, looking at the garments on the floor. Without the slightest self-consciousness, since he was a manly young Serb, he coiffed his head with the Debar kerchief and tied the apron round his waist, and looked as much like a beautiful young girl as he could. 'Do not our women dress themselves handsomely?' he asked in pride.

The Abbot watched him closely. He was pleased because young Yugoslavs were so upstanding and so decent, displeased because of the recollection of some offence against authority, which half of him admitted to have been justified. Moved by the desire to be friends again with this brave and honest young man, he turned back to the cupboard, groped for a minute or two, and took out a long linen sash, dyed red. 'For you,' he said to Dragutin; but his duplicity, which as always was quite transparent, revealed that in his heart there passed the words, 'I must make this young man feel liking for me again, it is not safe to have him as an enemy.' 'Ha, ha, I'm in luck!' cried Dragutin, stripping off his kerchief and the apron, and winding the sash round and round his slim waist in bullfighter fashion. But he did not really forgive, and I had an impulse to be carping and resentful. The Abbot had made us as dualist as himself. For while we were criticizing him our sense of his superiority overarched us like a sort of fatherhood. Dragutin and I alike would have been amazed if his courage or his cunning had failed, and in time of danger we would run into the palm of his hand. We knew quite well that he cared for nothing but an idea, and that his heart regarded his own ambition without approval. If his ways were tortuous, those of nature are not less so, as the geneticist and the chemist know them. To reject this man was to reject life, though to accept him wholly would have been to doom life to be what it is for ever.

Before we left the Abbot thanked me again for the gift I had brought him, which was a signed photograph of Mr Lloyd George, a statesman for whom he felt a passionate devotion, and who had sent it with sympathetic good-will. Dragutin could not stop talking about him for long after we had driven away. 'Did you have enough of him?' he asked. 'A good priest he is not. Bad priests there are in our Church, and good priests, and I know which he is. Once I went up to that monastery and I said, "Father, I am hungry. What have you got to give me to eat?" and he said, "Nothing." But I knew where to look, and there I found a most beautiful little chicken, and I ate it all up. The Abbot came in as I was finishing it, and he was very angry. He said, "Dragutin, you are a bad man," and I said,

"No, I am not a bad man, but I *was* a hungry man." ' It is not easy
to imagine this exchange taking place between a rural dean and a
chauffeur in England. But in Orthodox Yugoslavia a monastery is
still what it was in primitive times and under the Turks, a church
where a Christian can pray, a place where he can picnic with his
friends, a refuge where he can ask for a meal and a bed. Anybody
can go to a monastery and sleep and eat there for three days. Not
only in theory but in a considerable measure of fact the Church is
a socialist institution.

'I bet,' said Dragutin, as the road wound along between two
walls covered with the spilling greenness of limewoods, on which
villages rested like white birds with spread wings, 'that the Abbot
did not give you his best wine. That he keeps for the good of his
own soul.' 'But we did not want his best wine,' said Constantine.
Dragutin thought for a long time and said, 'That's not the point.
A priest should want to give you his best wine, whether you want
it or not.' Now we came out on a rougher valley, where the river
ran strongly, into a smell of sulphur that became a reek and, at a
point where hot springs fell to it over a cliff, a suffocation. 'They're
fine baths,' said Dragutin, 'and you can stay at the hotel beside
the falls for ten dinars a day.' 'Tenpence a day! How can that
be?' asked Constantine. 'Oh, easy enough,' said Dragutin, 'here
a hotel-keeper can buy a lamb for twenty dinars, feed his guests,
and sell the skin for ten dinars. *Yai!* The ways I could make money
if I had nine lives!'

The valley broadened to wide Biblical plains, stretching to distant
mountains that were of no colour and all colours. The ground we
looked on was sodden with blood and tears, for we were drawing
near the Albanian frontier, and there are few parts of the world
that have known more politically induced sorrow. Here the Turks
fostered disorder, lest their subjects unite against them, and here
after the war Albanians and Bulgarians fought against incorporation
in Yugoslavia and had to be subdued by force. There was no help for
it, since the Yugoslavs had to hold this district if they were to defend
themselves against Italy. But to say that the conflict was inevitable
is not to deny that it was hideous. This land, by a familiar irony,
is astonishing in its beauty. Not even Greece is lovelier than this
corner of Macedonia. Now a violet storm massed low on the far
Albanian mountains, and on the green plains at their feet walked
light, light that was pouring through a hole in the dark sky, but
not as a ray, as a cloud, not bounded yet definite, a formless being
which was very present, as like God as anything we may see. It is
a land made for the exhibition of mysteries, this Macedonia. Here

is made manifest a chief element in human disappointment, the discrepancy between our lives and their framework. The earth is a stage exquisitely set; too often destiny will not let us act on it, or forces us to perform a hideous melodrama. Our amazement is set forth here in Macedonia in these tragically sculptured mountains and forests, in the white village called the Sorrowing Women, in the maintained light that walked as God on the fields where hatreds are like poppies among the corn.

Constantine cried as we took a road to the right, 'Where are you taking us, Dragutin? This is not the way to Ochrid.' 'No,' answered Dragutin, 'but it is the road to Debar, and they must see Debar, of which it was said, "If Constantinople is burned down Debar can build it up again," Debar which is now in Yugoslavia.' 'Perhaps you are right,' said Constantine, 'also it seems to me that I once drank wine in Debar, and that it was good. We may perhaps find a bottle.' 'I think you must have been young and happy when you drank it,' said Dragutin, 'for the wine here is not very good. But we can try it.' Low on the hillside facing the plains and the Albanian mountains, lay our Debar: a double town, its white houses collected in an upper pool and a lower one, its minarets and its poplars placed so that the heart contracted, and it became an anguish to think that one would not be able to recollect perfectly its perfection. Within the town we found an elegance that made the luxury of Tetovo and Gostivar seem mere fumbling, and we perceived that this place had been the subject of a miracle for which all artists would pray, though they might be much relieved if their prayers were not answered. In the early Middle Ages it was famous for its craftsmen, for its goldsmiths and its silversmiths, its woodcarvers and weavers and embroiderers; and when the Turks came against them they were lost only to be saved, for they were immured with their tradition at its height. They were thus protected for five centuries from the grossness which infected their fellow-workmen in the West when life became commercial and ideas confused. I could not find out whether metal-work of the highest order was still carried on in Debar, but up till the Balkan wars it had craftsmen who could work gold and silver in the Byzantine manner. All over the Balkans there are to be found on altars Debar crosses, which enclose minute and living sculptures of the life of Christ in filigree which is not trivial, which has the playful vital purpose of tendrils. Some of the men who made these have been dead since the fourteenth century, others still live.

All the city breathes of instruction by a gifted past. At least one out of every three women wears the Debar head-dress, and of these

white veils spotted with scarlet or crimson circles inscribed with
crosses in purple or some other shade of red, almost none fails to
be a masterpiece of abstract design. It is not written that men or
groups should achieve such perfection by the first efforts of their
eyes and hands; it is the fruit of more failures than are within the
scope of one generation. And this tradition is visible not only in
the special talents of the town but in its general air of urbanity.
It lies on the wild frontiers of Albania, and through the streets
run the cold torrents shed by the snows of the peaks above, where
generation after generation of men whom tyranny had turned to
wolves lurked and raided, yet here the people moved as the citizens
of great cities should but do not, treading neatly on fine narrow
feet, carrying their heads neither too high nor too low, not staring
at the stranger and coldly lowering their eyes should he stare. They
walked between houses worthy of them, which spoke of good living
as proudly as any Georgian mansion, but with the voice of ghosts,
for the roofs were buckling and the windows broken and boarded,
and the wild grasses grew long in their gardens. There lay on this
lovely town the shadow of ruin which must deepen, which could
never pass. It was not conceivable that history could take any turn
which should restore Debar to prosperity. Its beauty was the spilled
sweetness from a cup that had been overturned, utterly emptied,
and shattered. On the plains the light walked no more, and the
green hills round the town, pricked askew with the white tombs
of the careless Moslem dead, seemed to be saying a final word.
In a country where death devoured that which most deserved to
live, the Abbot's lechery for life, his determination to defend it by
cunning could be seen as precious.

Ochrid I

Ochrid is a very long way from London. One gets into a train in London at two o'clock in the afternoon and all the next day one crosses Italy or Austria, and on the morning of the second day one is in Belgrade. Even if one stays in the Athens Express one cannot be in Skoplje before five that afternoon. There one must spend the night, and start early in the morning to reach Ochrid in the late afternoon. It is also a fact that not one in a million Englishmen has been to Ochrid. What happened when we arrived at the hotel on Lake Ochrid, therefore, was unfair. We found Gerda talking to a manageress, one of those strange polyglots who seem to have been brought up in some alley where several civilizations put out their ash-cans, since only bits and pieces have come their way, never the real meat. She showed some interest when she heard we were English. An Englishman had come to the hotel only the other day. Did we know Professor So-and-so? Yes, we knew that ornament of the British academic world. He had liked Ochrid trout, all the world like Ochrid trout, we would like Ochrid trout, but first would we like a risotto of crayfish, such as the Professor had also liked? Yes, we thought we would. And were we really married, or did we want two rooms with a communicating door, like Professor So-and-so and his young secretary? 'My God,' said my husband, with deep emotion, 'if I had a son I would tell him this story several times a year.'

I had remembered this hotel at Ochrid, so strange, like the word 'hotel' acted by children in a charade, and this year it seemed stranger. We were the only guests, and the restaurant was not open nor the electric light connected, so Constantine and Gerda and my husband and I ate a dinner which was superb by any standards, which was as good as the *filet de sole* in Brussels, in a bedroom where four beds were made up, lit by a profligacy of candles stuck in bottles, with the wine cooling in the wash-basin. When Dragutin came for next morning's orders the sight enchanted him and he stood gripping the door-posts and shouting with laughter. 'Thus well lived the Turks!' he said.

In the morning I woke late and found my husband standing beside me and the room full of the smell of new bread. It is one of the peculiarities of Ochrid that, though it is a very poor town, all day long little boys run about with trays of delicious rolls made from fine white flour. We went out and ate them with our coffee, sitting under a tree on the lakeside promenade outside the hotel. But it was bleak. It was with politeness that my husband looked across the bay at the old town, which lies tortoise-wise on a cape, under a hill crowned with a ruined fortress, built by Byzantines and Slavs and Normans and Turks on a Roman foundation. I had told him that it was one of the most interesting towns in Europe, a city which could, like Assisi, claim to be not wholly built by hands. It was a huddle of discoloured houses under a low sky that seemed to have sunk so low that it had been muddied. The hills, which I had remembered as austere sculptures, were now earth that, when earth's capacity for loutishness became exhausted, became scrub-covered rock. The opposite coast of the lake, which is Albania, could not be seen at all, and the water was dead as a pond in a public park.

I said, 'We can see nothing of the place today; this is the sort of thing that Mrs Eddy, probably quite correctly, ascribed to "malicious animal magnetism," but it will be all right when we get to the church where Bishop Nikolai is preaching. Then we will see the genius of the people. He stirs them and they betray what they are. I dare say that those who know them would laugh at me and tell me that the inhabitants are as mean and stupid as people are everywhere, but the truth is that when they are together in a church they show a power to accept life as it is and to glory in it which I have never seen equalled. I hope we start soon to find him.' For I knew, indeed we had timed our journey by reason of our knowledge, that the Bishop Nikolai, who was Bishop of Zhitcha and of Ochrid, was now visiting his second diocese for a week.

But we did not start. Now that Constantine was with Gerda he had lost his innate personality, even down to the simplest and most instinctive ways of dealing with practical matters. She interrupted his exuberant stories, she pruned every expression of what was probably himself, and he submitted; and presently he timidly offered her something he hoped she would find more acceptable, which was an impersonation of what a German would conceive that a Jew who was a Slav by adoption and a poet would be. He was by nature a shouter and a snatcher, who would smash peace into a thousand fragments and then laugh at what he had shouted and give back what he had snatched, but as I had first known him he carried himself precisely enough from point to point of his life. He could rise early if need be, he was punctual, he never lost anything. Now he ran about like a Jewish comedian, yelling questions and not waiting for the answer, losing things, being too late, being too early. He had also developed an embarrassing habit of telling endless stories of himself in the character of a buffoon, a fool who had torn up valuable share certificates in a rage at the dishonesty of the company's directors, who had lost the chance of a valuable appointment through making some tactless remark. This pleased Gerda, and so it pleased him.

It was their kind of happiness, and we would ordinarily have had no objection to it; it was something that Molière might have invented. But it made our morning's search for Bishop Nikolai into a painful fugue, which was reminiscent of a nightmare or the hallucinations of a persecution mania, or sometimes even a miracle play in which our party was playing the roles of the less admirable abstractions. The old town of Ochrid on its hill is stuck as thickly with churches as a pomander with cloves, and there are several churches in the new town that lies flat on the lake shore. The Bishop was going from church to church celebrating services all the morning, and we followed, but we never arrived in time. Every time we were told which church the Bishop was visiting at that moment we were delayed by some buffoonery on the part of Constantine, an insistence on checking the information by making inquiries from some startled person who knew nothing relevant, a sudden desire to buy tooth-paste or a book on fortune-telling, and we got to the church only to meet a crowd walking away from it quickly and with glowing faces, not as if they were in a hurry to reach anywhere, but rather as if some excitement had sent the blood rushing through their veins. There was nothing for us to do except to return to a café in the central square and drink more coffee until the time came for the re-enactment of this scene, which as the morning went on became more and more certainly to our fatigued minds a proof of superior displeasure, of our own unworthiness. It was a great relief to my husband and me when, about lunch-time, it was learned that the Bishop had left the town for a monastery twenty miles distant, and would not be back until the next day.

We spent the rest of the day in the narrow streets of the old town, looking at its lovely seventeenth-century and eighteenth-century houses, which have all their own fine faces, their own complexions, and furtively enjoying the quality of the people. In every part of the world one condition of human life dominates the stage. In the United States the stranger has to get his eye in before he can see anybody but beautiful young girls; in England handsome middle-aged men are the most visible ingredients of society; and here in Ochrid the conspicuous personages are slender old ladies with shapely heads, feline spines that are straight without being rigid, fine hands and feet, and a composure that sharply rather than placidly repulses recognition of all in life that is not noble. A more aristocratic type can hardly be conceived, although there was no suggestion of abstinence from anything but the roughest form of labour. It was not that these old duchesses could not sew and cook and sweep, it was that Ochrid had a long past. Before it was Byzantine it was within the sphere of the lost Illyrian empire, it had been a Greek city, and in its beginnings it had formed part of the settlement of a pre-Mycenaean civilization. That is to say that for thousands of years there have been gentlefolk here, people who preferred harmony to disharmony, and were capable of sacrificing their immediate impulses to this preference. The tenuous thread of civilization that here and there is woven into history never showed itself in prettier patterns than these distinguished old ladies, in whom not the smallest bone is barbarous.

But the most exciting aspect of Ochrid relates to its more recent past, to events divided from us by a mere eleven hundred years. As the Slav tribes fell under the influence of Byzantium a considerable number of them were baptized but they were first converted to Christianity in mass by the Greek brothers, Cyril and Methodius, who translated part of the gospels into Slavonic languages about the year 870; and their mission was carried to Ochrid by their followers, Clement and Gorazd and Naum. That is what it says in the books. But what does that mean? How did these events look and sound and smell? That can be learned on the top of the hill at Ochrid, in the Church of Sveti Kliment, and the other churches up there which were built in that age. According to Serbo-Byzantine fashion they crouch low in the earth, outbuildings for housing something that should not be where people live, something that needs to be kept in the dark. Doubtless in those early days there were converts who went into the blackness of these churches hoping to find new gods like those they had worshipped in their heathen days, but bloodier. Such worship is commemorated in certain Balkan churches, which to this day are ill to enter, being manifestly bad ju-ju. But shadow is also a sensible prescription for good magic, and Christianity as a religion of darkness has its advantages over our Western conception of Christianity as a religion of light.

I remembered as I stood in the Church of Sveti Kliment what a cloak-and-suit manufacturer once said to me when he was showing me his factory on Long Island: 'Yes, it's a beautiful factory, sure it's a beautiful factory, and I'm proud of it. But I wish I hadn't built it. When I get a rush order I can't make my girls work in these big airy rooms the way they did in the little dark place we had down town. They used to get in a fever down there, their fingers used to fly. Up here you can't get them excited.' Though the domes of Sveti Kliment are bubbles the porch is of extravagant clumsiness, approached by squat steps and pressed by a wide flat roof, which is utterly unecclesiastical and might be proper in a cow-byre, and is supported by thick and brutal columns. Within the porch is a wide ante-room which is used as a lumber-room, full of spare chairs, ornate candles for festival use, broken models of other churches. Almost every Orthodox church looks as if the removal men have been at work on it, and that they have been inefficient. Beyond is another darker antechamber, where those sat in the early days of the Church who were not yet baptized or who were penitents; and beyond, darkest of all, is the church, a black pit where men could stand close-pressed and chanting, falling into trance, rising into ecstasy, as they stared at the door in the iconostasis, which sometimes opened and showed them the priests in dazzling robes, handling the holy things by the blaze of candlelight that is to the darkness what the adorable nature of God is to humanity.

It is a valid religious process; and it is the one that these people to this day prefer. Further down the hill is the Church of Heavenly Wisdom, of Sveta Sophia, which was built, it is said, at the same time as the Hagia Sophia of Constantinople and was restored by the Nemanyas. It is a glorious building, the size, I should think, of Steeple Ashton parish church, a superb composition of humble, competent brickwork achieving majesty by its sound domes and arches. It is decorated with some magnificent frescoes of the Nemanya age, one showing an angry angel bending over earth in rage against the polluted substance of those who are not angels, and another showing the death of the Virgin, where sorrowing figures drip like rain down the wall behind the horizontal body of a woman who is giving herself without reserve but with astonishment to the experience of pain, knowing it to be necessary. That the building should be now Christian is a victory, since the Turks used it as a mosque for five hundred years. But the church is full of light. It is built according to the Byzantine and not according to the Serbo-Byzantine fashion, and has no iconostasis but only a low barrier to divide the congregation from the priest. A makeshift iconostasis of chintz and paper and laths has been run up, but it is of no avail. Light stands like a priest over all other priests under the vaults that were raised high to cast out shadow. And this church is unbeloved. A fierce old nun keeps it fanatically clean and would give her life to defend it. But it is not the object of any general devotion. All the other churches in Ochrid have their devotees who can worship happily nowhere else and who speak of them with a passion which has something animal in it, something that one can imagine a beast feeling for its accustomed lair. But though Sveta Sophia was originally the Cathedral, the honour has been taken from it and given to the small dark Sveti Kliment; and nobody gives money or labour to mend the roof which is a sieve.

We left this rejected loveliness, and walked on through the town by a track which followed the top of a cliff beside the lake and took us at last to a church standing on a promontory covered with pale-yellow flowers. This I remembered well, for it was the Church of Sveti Yovan, of St John, where I had learned for the first time the peculiar quality of Eastern Christianity, that is dark and not light, and unkempt as only the lost are in the West. When I had been here with Constantine the year before he had heard that this church was having its annual feast, and that Bishop Nikolai was holding the service. So we took a rowing-boat from the hotel and travelled over the milk-white water, while the morning sun discovered green terraces high on the black Albanian mountains and touched the snow peaks till they shone a glistening buff, and on the nearest coast picked out the painted houses of Ochrid till the town was bright as a posy of pale flowers. As we came nearer to the promontory we heard a sound of voices, not as if they were speaking anything, but just speaking, as bees hum; and I saw that all the ground about the church, and all the tracks that led to it, were covered with people. They were right out on the edge of the promontory, where the rock fell in a sharp overhang, and it seemed as if at any moment some of them must fall into the water. There were also many people in boats who were rowing round and round the promontary, never going very far from it, who were singing ecstatically.

Our boat drew ashore. We climbed a flight of steps that ran upward through the yellow flowers, under bending fig trees; and on the cliff I found myself in the midst of a Derby Day crowd. They were talking and laughing and quarrelling and feeding babies, and among them ran boys with trays of rolls and cakes and fritters, and men selling sweet drinks. They sat or stood or lay in the grass as they would, and they were all dressed in their best clothes, though not all of them were clean. Some were pressing into the church, struggling and jostling in the porch, and others were pushing and being pushed through animal reek in the cave of darkness maintained by the low walls and doors in spite of the sunlight outside. There swaying together, sweating together, with their elbows in each other's bellies and their breaths on each other's napes, were people who had been lifted into a special state by their adoration of the brightness which shone extravagantly behind the iconostasis. After I had overcome the first difficulty of adapting myself to a kind of behaviour to which I was not accustomed, I found I liked the spectacle extremely.

The congregation had realized what people in the West usually do not know: that the state of mind suitable for conducting the practical affairs of daily life is not suitable for discovering the ultimate meaning of life. They were allowing themselves to become drunken with exaltation in order that they should receive more knowledge than they could learn by reason; and the Church which was dispensing this supernatural knowledge was not falling into the damnable heresy of pretending that this knowledge is final, that all is now known. The service was clear of the superficial ethical prescription, inspired by a superstitious regard for prosperity, which makes Western religion so often a set of by-laws tinged emotionally with smugness. Had the Eastern Church in the Balkans wished to commit this error, it has been prevented by history. For centuries it would have found it difficult to find a body of the fortunate sufficiently large to say with authority, 'Be like us, be clean in person and abstinent from sin, for of such is the kingdom of Heaven.' There were too few fortunate Christians, save among the phanariots, who had sold at least the better part of their souls; and the unfortunate were too poor to be clean, and were chaste perforce, since their women had to be enclosed in patriarchal houses against the rape of enemies, and could not wholly abstain from murder, since only by blood could they defend themselves against the infidel. The Church had therefore to concentrate on the Mass, on reiterations of the first meaning of Christianity. It had to repeat over and over again that goodness is adorable and that there is an evil part in man which hates it, that there was once a poor man born of a poor woman who was perfectly good and was therefore murdered by evil men, and in his defeat was victorious, since it is far better to be crucified than to crucify, while his murderers were conquered beyond the imagination of conquerors; and that this did not happen once and far away, but is repeated every day in all hearts.

So the crowd in the church waited and rejoiced, while the deep voices of the singing priests and the candles behind the iconostasis evoked for them the goodness they had murdered, and comforted them by showing that it had not perished for ever. The superb performance of the Mass, a masterpiece which has been more thoroughly rehearsed than any other work of art, rose to its climax and ceased in its own efficacy. Goodness was so completely evoked that it could no longer be confined, and must break forth to pervade the universe; and with it there poured into the open the priests and the congregation. They blinked their eyes, having become accustomed to the shadows and the candlelight. The sunshine must have seemed to them an incendiarism of the air, committed by the radiance that had rushed out from the iconostasis. Bishop Nikolai, a huge man made more huge by his veiled mitre, stood blindly in the strong light, gripping his great pastoral staff as a warrior might grip a weapon when it was difficult for him to see. The people surged forward to kiss his ring, having forgotten in the intoxication of the darkness what they might have remembered if they had stayed sober in broad day, that he was clean and they were dirty, that he was lettered and they could not read. They cried aloud in their gratitude to this magician who had brewed the holy mystery for them behind the screen and had made the saving principle visible and real as brightness. The people rowing on the lake, hearing the cries of those on the cliff, leaned on their oars, and gave themselves up to their singing. The flat brilliant waters trembled, and the snow peaks glittered. It was as if joy had permeated the whole earth.

Ochrid II

We sat for a time by the Church of Sveti Yovan. There were no yellow flowers any more, but a great deal of small purple stock. Presently the lake became a savage green and it grew cold, and we climbed a hill to the fortress, which is no more than a wall encircling the summit, girt with olive orchards and country houses built in the Turkish style, now wistful in decay. We let Constantine and Gerda go on ahead and trespassed among the fruit trees of the loveliest of all these houses, which, with its pale plaster, its grey and crumbling woodwork, was like a ghost, not nearly as substantial as the blossom round it. But a violent storm opened above us like a flower, and we hurried down towards the hotel. We had not got far, however, when Constantine and Gerda called to us from a garden. They were sitting at a table under an acacia tree with a dozen people, and they said, 'Come in, it is the birthday of the man who lives here, and they want us all to drink a glass of wine.'

There came forward to welcome us a young man who looked like a great many Londoners, who might have been the office wag in a small City business, and his wife, who was lovely but too thin and too pallid. There is a great deal of anaemia among Yugoslavian women. We sat down at a table, and they gave us a great deal of wine, very quickly, and even more food. There was a tart filled with spinach, exquisite yoghourt, and a wonderful sweet made of flour drawn fine as coconut and flavoured with orange and chopped nuts. The husband explained that he had made all these himself, since he was a pastrycook, and deserved no credit, for his family had been pastrycooks since time out of mind, 'as many of our people are,' he said, 'for we are Bulgarians.' He said that he had three brothers away working abroad. 'Where are they?' asked Constantine. There was a pause. We had been in the town over twelve hours, and of course everybody knew that he was a Government official. 'One in Australia and two in Bulgaria,' said the pastrycook. These were evidently not only Bulgarians, but Bulgarian adherents, who kept up the connexion with the country of their allegiance.

Just then it came on to rain, and the feast had to be moved into the house. There was a fat man, a chauffeur, who turned this into an entertainment by carrying in the dishes in the manner of various local dignitaries. In the house we found the owner's mother, who

715

was one of the slender handsome old ladies for which Ochrid is so remarkable. We found that the refinement of her type was not a mere matter of appearance: she had fine manners, she knew certain things well, and she could express herself with perfect precision. The room where we sat was curiously like a Turkish room, with a wooden bench covered with cushions running along each side of the room, some rugs hung on the walls, and no other furniture. This was surprising, as the whole family was so definitely not of Oriental type, and the young people, who were all wearing Western clothes, could have been taken for English or French. The pastrycook's wife started showing us the embroideries she had done for the house, which were infinitely distressing; she had inherited the national dexterity of the Macedonian woman, but she had employed it on the most frightful designs that could ever be found in an art needlework shop in Brighton. It is an odd thing that when these women drop the Byzantine tradition of design, even though they have been themselves inventing interesting variations of it, they show no discrimination and will copy with delight the crudest naturalist representations of fruit and flowers in vile colours on drab backgrounds; yet it cannot be said that they are without taste, for they often make themselves the most beautiful dresses in the Western style. Just then Dragutin turned up with the car, for he had already learned in a café in the centre of the town where we were, and thought it was a long way for us to walk home in the rain. But the pastrycook would not let us leave yet, so my husband drove back to the hotel, to fetch a box of sweets we had brought on the chance of such an occasion as this.

When my husband had gone the old mother showed me a photograph of her son who was in Australia, and the girl he had just married, who was a luscious Jewess. The fat chauffeur seized the photograph and held it out at arm's length, rocking himself from side to side and making smacking noises. Another picture showed the young couple surrounded by their friends at their wedding reception. 'The dear girl,' said the old mother, 'he is going to bring her back here in a few years' time.' The mind started back at the thought of the tragedy this statement might foretell. The girl and her friends looked pleasant people but plainly they were dominated by manufactured goods; they would set an immense value on their automobiles, their radios, their refrigerators, and the cinema, and it might be that they could not exist apart from command over machines. It was odd that the degree to which the girl would be able to understand this distinctively Christian home would depend on the degree to which she had remained distinctively Jewish. If she had maintained that link with tradition she might realize the nature of this home, with its hearthstone founded on the past.

The mother brought out yet another photograph, this one showing the son standing with the rest of the staff in the restaurant where he worked, and they asked Constantine to translate the inscription that was painted on the wall. They were evidently puzzled when he had spoken, and made some speculations about the ascetic and exalted character of Australians, which seemed to me unfounded; and I found that Constantine had rendered 'Cleanliness is our motto' as 'Purity is our creed.' Then the mother said that her son wanted her to go to Australia, but she would not go. She said she had heard that in these big towns people had no neighbours, that actually people might live on one story of a building and not know the people on the others. That was dreadful, you couldn't even say it was like the animals, it was quite a new sort of wickedness. But she had done something about it: she had written to the son in Australia and the sons in Sofia and told them that she would come to see them if they sent the money, and they sent it, and she put it in the bank. Otherwise they would have spent it, and they'd be glad of it some day, for the absurd wages that young people got nowadays couldn't go on for ever. *Pourvu que cela dure*, Letizia Bonaparte used to say.

By this time I was becoming anxious because my husband had not returned, for the hotel was only five minutes away, and it was possible that Dragutin had for once been too clever about racing up and down these cobbled alleys. They noticed my distress, and one of the men went out to see if he could find the automobile. The old lady went to the window and said, 'Look, there are some gipsies going up to the fortress. That's funny. I don't know why they would go up there this afternoon. They were all up there yesterday; they go up there every year on that date, because a gipsy was once buried inside the fortress that day. And the odd thing is the poor silly things don't know who it was. I've asked them again and again, and they just say, "Oh, he was one of us, and a great chief, but we don't remember his name, for it was all a long time ago." ' I thought she was giving this information in a forced manner, and I saw that it was to distract the attention of Gerda and myself from what was going on at the other end of the room. There Constantine was standing with the husband and his friends opposite a frame containing several photographs which was hanging on the wall, oddly high. The young men were whispering into his ear and shielding their mouths with their hands, and he had assumed the expression of an indulgent man of the world.

Soon afterwards the wife came in with a fresh bottle of wine, and I used the social movements this caused as an excuse to edge up to the frame. It contained several photographs marked Lille and Anvers and Bruxelles, all but one representing a young man of the year 1900, with a bowler hat and a short tightly waisted coat and a thick tie and waggish trousers, a rude but spirited imitation of the Boni de Castellane 'Oh, what a cad I am' pattern. The exception, which was marked Lille, showed a woman with a Roman nose and a bust of like minatory curve, and a chignon like a brick. Constantine said to me, 'The man was the old lady's brother, who went to be a pastrycook in Belgium and France; the woman was his mistress. It is the great shame and glory of this family that they had an uncle who had a French mistress, and the old lady sometimes says she will take her photograph out of the frame and burn it. But that is how the frame was sent to them, and he is dead, and the mistress is dead also, and so she does not like to make away with it, and indeed they all feel that there is something strange and gay about it.'

A little while afterwards I went to the window and looked out in vain, and said, 'I wish I knew what had happened to my husband!' At that the young wife exclaimed, 'Now this is very curious! Haven't you always heard that English wives were very cold to their husbands? But just see, she's anxious, she's really very anxious about him.' 'Well,' said the old mother, 'he looks a very good man, I'm sure he'll be a kind husband, and don't tell me there's any part of the world where women don't like kind husbands.' Then the friend who had gone out to look for my husband came running in, clapping his hands and crying joyfully. 'He is safe, thanks to God he is safe, but there has been an accident!' The company responded to this announcement with a handsome interest, and listened with cries to his account of how the car had fallen into a ditch and had had to be dragged out by oxen. When my husband came in with the sweets he was greeted as one returned from death, and another bottle of wine was opened. When the exclamations died down the fat chauffeur looked at us over his glass, sighed sentimentally, and said, 'Yes, they're fond of each other all right, look how close they are sitting and they aren't young either.'

Ochrid III

The next morning we woke late and breakfasted under the ash trees by the lake, in the best day this spring had yet given us. The lake was blue and feathered by a light wind, and the red fallow fields and the green pastures were mirrored so indistinctly that they formed a changing abstract pattern, lovely to watch. The mountains on the far shore were a hazy silver, but near at hand all was sharp-cut. Across the bay every house in old Ochrid showed its individual distinction, which was often of the slightest nature, lying in the curve in a pediment, the thrust of a bracket that held up a projecting upper story, but was always as important, in its architectural sphere, as the length of Cleopatra's nose. Time went on, and the hour approached when we should go to the service conducted by Bishop Nikolai. We had made the extremest efforts to inform ourselves exactly when and where this was to take place. We had even taken the precaution, on leaving the pastrycook's agreeable party, to go to the church, which was small but filled with the idea of magnificence, and was strangely set in a pretty cottagey garden full of lilacs and irises, on a road running down from the fortress, and there Dragutin had sought among the neighbouring houses for the sacristan, from whom he had learned beyond all possibility of doubt that the Mass was to be celebrated the next day at half-past nine. But at twenty-five-past nine Constantine and Gerda were not ready, and when we knocked on his door he said that it was all right, the service did not begin till ten. We corrected the impression and went downstairs again and sat in the automobile.

At a quarter to ten Dragutin left the wheel and ran into the hotel, adopting the methods of one trying to make geese leave an outhouse, waving his arms and shouting, 'Aïde! aïde!' (This means 'Come on' or 'Go out,' and indeed any movement which is sought to be imposed by one person on another.) Five minutes later he hustled out Constantine and Gerda, and at ten we were where we had often been before, driving against a tide of glowing worshippers, hurrying away from their refreshment. But the urgency had gone from these people, they were standing about and gossiping. I burst into tears and said to my husband, 'You will never see Bishop Nikolai, and it is ridiculous, because there is no reason why you should not, and you ought to see him, because he is what these people like.' 'But you shall see him,' said Dragutin. He jumped out and spoke to a passing priest, jumped back and swung round the automobile till it headed for the alleys of the old town again, and brought us to a spot which in that town of delicate desolation was singularly bald in its decay. We got out and stood on a ledge; below us a long untended garden ran down to some houses that were mere lath and plaster, and above us, beside a house which had lost its whole façade and had grimly replaced it with a sheet of rusted iron, was the mouth of an alley that rose to a plot of waste ground. A few steps up this alley was a doorway, and Dragutin said, 'Go in there and you will find the Bishop, the church is having its feast.' I went in and found an unkempt garden before a small and battered church, full of people who were all looking at the loggia in front of it. There was Bishop Nikolai at the head of a table laid for a meal, where some priests and a nun, a man in uniform, and several men and women in ordinary clothes were sitting, all with their faces turned towards him. I was surprised that the feast of a church should be a real feast, where there was eating and drinking.

Bishop Nikolai stood up and welcomed us, and I knew that he was not at all glad to see us. I was aware that he did not like Constantine and that he was not sure of me, that he thought I might turn and rend any situation at which he permitted me to be present by some Western treachery. I did not greatly care what he thought of me, for I was too greatly interested in him, and any personal relations between us could not aid my interest, for I could get everything out of him that I could ever get by watching him. He struck me now, as when I had seen him for the first time in the previous year, as the most remarkable human being I have ever met, not because he was wise or good, for I have still no idea to what degree he is either, but because he was the supreme magician. He had command over the means of making magic, in his great personal beauty, which was of the lion's kind, and in the thundering murmur of his voice, which by its double quality, grand and yet guttural, suggests that he could speak to gods and men and beasts. He had full knowledge of what comfort men seek in magic, and how they long to learn that defeat is not defeat and that love is serviceable. He had a warm knowledge of how magic can prove this up to the hilt. He had a cold knowledge, which he would not share with any living thing, of the limited avail of magic, and how its victories cannot be won on the material battlefield where man longs to see them. He was so apt for magic that had it not existed he could have invented it. He saw all earth as its expression. When he greeted our undesired party, when he turned to command order in the mob of peasants and children and beggars that filled the garden and looked over the walls from outside, there was a blindish and blocked look in his eyes, as if he asked himself, 'Of what incantation is this the end? What is the rite we are now performing? Is this white magic or black?'

He bade us take seats at the table, and I looked round and saw some people whom I had met at Ochrid on the first visit. There was the Abbot of the Monastery of Sveti Naum, which lies at the other end of the lake: an old man with a face infinitely fastidious, yet wholly without peevishness, a Macedonian who was a priest under the Turks and lived all his youth and manhood under the threat of sudden death and yet remained uninfected by the idea of violence; and there was a red-haired priest who sings marvellously, like a bull with a golden roar, and laughs like a bull with a golden nature, and who is much in request in Ochrid for christenings and weddings. Others were new: among them a schoolmistress who had been a Serbian pioneer here long before the Balkan wars, a jolly old soul; an immense officer of the gendarmerie, a Montenegrin, like all Montenegrins sealed in the perfection of his virility, as doubtless the Homeric heroes were; a functionary who was in charge of the Works Department of Ochrid, a dark and active man, one of those enigmatic beings who fill such posts, facing the modern world with a peasant strength and a peasant reticence, so that the stranger cannot grasp the way of it.

We all began to eat. The crowd in the garden bought rolls from pedlars, and ice-cream cones from a barrow that was standing under the church steps. We at the table had cold lamb, hard-boiled eggs, sheep's cheese, cold fried fish, unleavened bread and young garlic, which is like a richer and larger spring onion. The Bishop said to my husband, with hatred of Western Europe's hatred of the Balkans in his voice, 'This is something you English do not eat, but we are an Eastern people, and all Eastern peoples must have it.' He gave me a hard-boiled egg and took one himself, and made me strike his at the same time that he struck mine. 'The one that cracks the other's egg shall be the master,' he said. It was to amuse the people and to give himself a moment's liberty not to think, for he was heavy with fatigue. Ever since Easter he had been going from church to church, carrying on the sorcery of these long services, and offering himself as a target for the trust of the people. He had to go on to some other church, and soon he let the crowd see that he must before long dismiss them.

They grieved at it, they gobbled up their rolls and ice-cream

cones or threw them on the ground and crushed forward to the
table. Bishop Nikolai stood up and cried, 'Christ is risen!' and
they answered, 'Indeed He is risen!' Three times he spoke and
they answered, and then they stretched out their hands and he
gave them eggs from a great bowl in front of him. This was pure
magic. They cried out as if it were talismans and not eggs that
they asked for; and the Bishop gave out the eggs with an air of
generosity that was purely impersonal, as if he were the conduit
for a force greater than himself. When there were no more eggs in
the bowl the people wailed as if there were to be no more children
born into the world, and when more eggs were found elsewhere
on the table the exultation was as if there were to be no more
death. There was a group of little boys standing by the Bishop,
who wailed and cheered with the passion of their elders, but had
to wait until the last, since they were children. To these Gerda
now began to distribute eggs from a bowl that was near her.

This was the moment that we all fear when we are little, the
moment when some breach of decorum would put an event into
a shape so disgusting that nobody who saw it could bear to go
on living. Later we learn to disbelieve in this moment, so many
of the prescriptions laid on our infant mind are nonsense, but we
are wrong. The word 'shocking' has a meaning. There are things
that shock, other than crimes. We did not feel any special shame
at Gerda's action because we had come to the feast with her, we
had not got to that yet, it was to come later. For the moment
we simply participated in the staring horror that was shown by
everybody at the table. The children to whom she held out the
eggs took them awkwardly, not knowing what else to do, and
then withdrew their attention from her, like animals turning from
one of their kind who is sick. Bishop Nikolai, turning towards her
and dropping his eyes as if he were looking at her through his
lids, was like Prospero, letting by in silence one of his creature's
faults. But Gerda felt in the bowl for another egg and was about
to hold it out to the children, when my husband said to her, 'You
cannot do that.' She hesitated, then drew back the corners of her
mouth in an insincere imitation of a motherly smile, and said,
quite untruly, 'But some of the children were crying.' Her hand
went back to the bowl, and it was not certain what she would
do, or what Bishop Nikolai would do, when a distraction came
to save us.

Through the doorway from the alley a beggar came into the
garden. He was old and in rags and very filthy, and it could
be judged he was blind, for he was tapping his way with a

staff, and his eyes gleamed like dead fish. He stopped and asked that he should be led to the Bishop, and half a dozen people busied themselves in bringing him up to the table. Once there he said some words of greeting to the Bishop, threw back his sightless head and shuddered, laid his foul hands on my husband's shoulders to steady himself, then stood upright and burst into song. 'I do not know who this man is,' said the red-haired priest in my ear, 'he is not of Ochrid. And this hymn he is singing is very old.' That it might well have been, for it proceeded from the classic age of faith, before the corruption of masochism had crept in, before the idea of the atonement had turned worship into barter. It adored; it did not try to earn salvation by adoring; it adored what it had destroyed, and felt anguish at the destruction, and rejoiced because death had been cheated and the destroyed one lived. Again the sunshine seemed part of a liberated radiance.

He ceased, crossed himself with a gesture not of self-congratulation but of abandonment, and the Bishop called him to the table, gave him his blessing, and filled his hands with bread and lamb and garlic and eggs. He went away and sat on the grass under a fig tree and ate his meal, licking the meat off the bones very happily, and we all talked easily at the table. 'There used to be many beggars like this in the old days,' they told us. 'It was believed that when a man became blind it must be because God wished him not to see but to think, and that it was his duty to leave his home and go where the spirit called, living on what people gave him. But now there is doubt everywhere and nobody thinks of such things.' The occasion was entirely restored. At length Bishop Nikolai made a speech proposing the civil servant as president of the church council for the coming year, a speech full of gentle little jokes, and led the children's cheers for him. Then he made a civil reference to my husband and myself, expressing pleasure that people should come all the way from England to Ochrid; and I found the pale old Abbot of Sveti Naum standing by me, like a courteous ghost, holding out an egg in his thin hand. 'He says,' translated the Bishop whose English is beautiful, as befits one who once preached in St Paul's Cathedral, 'that he is giving you this to take to your parish priest, as a symbol that the Anglican Church and the Orthodox Church are united in the risen Christ, not the buried Christ, but the Christ who lives for ever. Have you got a parish priest?' he inquired very doubtfully. I said, truthfully, but perhaps evasively, 'I will take it to my cousin, who is priest of a church that was built when the Anglican Church and the Orthodox Church were one,' and I tied up the egg in my handkerchief. Bishop Nikolai watched my fingers absently, his hands tightening on the edge of the table, ready to take his weight when he rose.

Then the moment which had been averted returned. Constantine got on his feet and began to make a speech. I do not know what he said, but the Bishop was Prospero again, this time a wearied and infuriated Prospero who had at last lost patience with his creatures. He raised his great head and emitted a look the like of which I had not seen, as of a god ordering that the sun should eclipse the moon and thereafter do its work. But Constantine was not affected, because he was engaged in an enterprise that was itself not without grandeur. For Gerda's monstrous action had denied the validity of magic, and had asserted that an egg given by a human hand must be the same as an egg given by any other human hand; and there had come to annul her action an action, as extraordinary, and indeed more extraordinary, since an ecstasy of well-being is more difficult to come by than a convulsion of pain, and the blind beggar had made his declaration that magic keeps all its promises. So Gerda had been forgotten, and indeed forgiven. But out of loyalty to the strange land where they had lived together, in isolation from the common custom, Constantine was committing again what she had committed, in order that it should stand in spite of the exquisite correction it had received; and he performed this action in the way that would give her pleasure, on a lower plane than hers. When she had given away the eggs it had been with a certain dignity, as if she were the competent mother of a family; but he was now the Jewish comedian. He stood up in clothes crumpled with travel before these people, who were not used to short and stout Jews that jump about and are voluble, who know only the tall and hawk-like Jews that move quietly and are silent, and before their wondering gaze he waved his little arms and spoke so fast and loud that a speck of foam showed on his lower lip. The Bishop could not support the spectacle. He surged out of his chair and, looming about the small Constantine, bade the children give three cheers for him. But when they had finished Constantine went on speaking. The Bishop filled his glass, pouring the wine so wildly that the cloth round it was purpled, and stretched out his huge arm over the table, in front of Constantine's flushed and shining face, and drank a toast to the company. Even then Constantine still went on speaking, so utterly fixed was he in his double intention, which every moment disclosed a more dreadful beauty, to uphold Gerda in her attack on the world, and to uphold her in her contempt for him. The Bishop beat down his glass on the table, said his farewells with a stateliness that was the calm at the heart of a storm, thrust back his chair so that it fell into the hands of the children behind him, and strode out of the garden, the crowd shuffling after him. Soon there was nothing to be seen but the trodden grass. We were left standing at the table, the other guests looking at us curiously.

Ochrid IV

Gerda and Constantine looked quietly happy. 'I did not make too much of my speech,' said Constantine, 'but this is Bishop Nikolai's stamping ground, he must be allowed to do all the shining here. I was thinking that now your husband has seen the Bishop it would be a good thing if we went to the little monastery where we went with the poet last year. It has a very pretty view and it would be a good end to such a nice morning.' I thought it was an excellent idea, for we certainly had to go somewhere, we could not stay where we were, and I remembered the monastery as a pleasant place in the hills behind Ochrid. We had gone there with a young poet of the town to find a place where he could read Constantine his verses without all his friends looking on, but it had not proved very suitable for this. A little dog in the cloisters belonging to a nun had howled incessantly because his mistress had gone into the town to do some shopping; and the priest, a sturdy old man of seventy with ten children, of whom either six or seven, he said, were sons, was distressed by the proceedings. He kept on muttering, 'Verses, tut, tut! It's all right to make up a song in one's head; but to write it down, you can't tell me that's not a waste of time.' The old man was relieved when the poetry-reading was finished and he could take us down to the village and introduce us to his mother, who was sitting on the edge of a fountain with several companions of her own age.

Macedonia makes one doubt many things that one has previously believed, and in nothing is it more unsettling than in its numbers of immensely aged people. They must be old, though probably not as old as they say, but still very old, because one finds them living in the same house with five generations of their descendants. Yet Macedonians have shocking teeth. It is possible that dentists are such deceptions as Solomon said that strange women were, that our puritanism has persuaded us to go to the dentists because the drill hurts, and that what we need today is more dental caries.

But when we got to the monastery the priest and his family had gone, and there was a new priest, a man in his late twenties from Debar, sensitive and a little sad, obviously not robust, and wearing spectacles with very strong lenses. He took us into the church and showed us the frescoes, which were very bad modern peasant stuff; there was a Last Judgment which represented the saved as fitted with hard little haloes like boiled eggs, the apotheosis of the good egg. We looked at Ochrid, lying beyond the green and crimson plains against the white silk of the lake, and then we would have gone away had it not been that the priest was so gently eager for us to stay. We did not want to eat for we had already had both breakfast and the church meal, which had comprised really a great deal of wine and lamb and fish and eggs and garlic, and it was not yet noon; but he hurried away with a shining face and got us some wine and sheep's cheese and eggs, and took us up to his room to eat them. The room was bitterly poor. The mattress of his bed was laid not on a bedstead but on timber trestles, the towels were poor wisps of cotton, and there were no rugs on the floor and no books. He sat and smiled at us and asked questions about life outside Macedonia, of which he seemed to know very little. He spoke with something that was not quite curiosity, that was more tactile; the effect was as if a very gentle blind person were running his finger-tips over one's features.

Suddenly his face fell and we heard the clattering of feet coming up the wooden staircase, very fast. He put down his wineglass and drew his hand across his forehead. The door was thrown open and a nun hurried in, a woman of about fifty-five or sixty. She said, 'Thank God you're still here,' and sat down on the priest's bed and asked who we all were, panting for breath and fanning herself. 'Well, well,' she said, the second Constantine had finished introducing us, 'you're all very interesting people, but I've had an interesting life, you can't say I haven't, you wait till you hear it.' The priest uttered a low sound expressive of agony and fatigue. 'I am a Serbian,' she began after she had taken a full breath, 'I come of a very rich family of the Shumadiya, and I was married very young, naturally enough, for I was very beautiful and everybody in the world wanted to marry me. I was early left the childless widow of the eldest of four rich brothers, and all of them loved me very much, all my family and my husband's brothers, I was their darling and I had everything a woman could want. So I was proud and I was beautiful, I was very beautiful.' I said to my husband, 'But this woman has never been beautiful.' My husband said in choked tones as if he were making a grave accusation, 'She is like a milkman's horse.'

'And,' said the nun, 'I was very coquettish. See, I had one flaw in my beauty'—she tilted up her tall nun's hat to show us what it was—'I had a very high forehead. People used to say to me, 'You have the brow of a professor,' and I used to weep all night because I had this one fault, and then I took to covering it with curls, with little, little, fine curls which took hours to make. And I sang, and I danced, and I was cruel with those who loved me, and so the time passed. But once I dreamed—I dreamed a most wonderful dream.' She caught her breath and stared in front of her. The priest made a gesture which made me recall those lines in which Coleridge fixed for ever the feelings of those who listen to a long tale when they want to do something else:

> The Wedding Guest here beat his breast,
> For he heard the loud bassoon.

But she continued. We were as fresh blood in the vampire's mouth.

In her dream, she told us, the Mother of God had appeared before her, holding a most beautiful child, which she had put into her arms. She had felt the weight and warmth of the child as she held it and experienced a most wonderful glow of joy; and when she woke up she could not believe that it had not really happened. She was worried by this dream, and had told everybody about it, but nobody could tell her what it meant, though once her mother had said to her, 'I believe that dream means that you will have this child, but it will not be yours, it will be called by another name.' Some years passed and she went to a Christian Belief meeting and heard a young theological student make a speech, and as he spoke she had to grip her seat to prevent herself from falling unconscious on the floor, for she recognized him as the child of her dreams grown into a man. At once she sought him out, and as he was an orphan she adopted him as her son. Soon she found a rich girl for him to marry, and then there was trouble. He would not marry this heiress, for he had fallen in love with a poor girl, who was not only poor, but tuberculous.

'I was very angry,' said the nun, 'but then a priest in a monastery said to me, 'Your son will marry the girl he loves, but it will last only three days,' so after that I did not work against his marriage, though I made him promise that he would not sleep with her, for fear he should get tuberculosis.' Then, three days after they were married, the girl had fallen dead in her husband's arms while they were standing together by a window. The nun's attitude to this happening was that of a fisherman who pulls in his line and finds a very large fish on the end of it. A short while afterwards, while she was in Albania, staying with a friend, she had heard that the bereaved boy had announced his intention of becoming a monk, so she and the friend had immediately started for Belgrade and tried to prevent him.

At this point in the story the nun stamped on the floor to show just how hard she had tried to prevent him; and the poor young priest went and looked out of the window, pressing his forehead against the glass. But it had been no use, she continued, her adopted son said that he had promised his wife that if she died he would become a monk. So she had said that she would become a nun, and had done so. And her friend from Albania had been so impressed by the proceedings that she also had become a nun. 'Not,' said this nun, 'that that was much sacrifice, for she was over sixty and not at all good-looking. But I, who was young and beautiful and had everything, I was now to live on nothing, on what people gave me, on what my dog might have had when I was rich. Now did you ever hear such a story in your life?'

One rarely had, for it was purely nihilist. It disclosed no amiable characteristics on the part of the teller, it seemed to consist solely of a capacity for obsession; it disclosed no sense of anybody else's characteristics, the other persons were faceless puppets, though certainly as she went on one had a curious fancy that the theological student talked to his adopted mother downward from the branches of a tree. 'Did your English friends ever hear such a story?' gleefully demanded the nun, looking into our faces and slapping us on the back. 'Now you must come and see my room.' Over her bed hung an immensely enlarged photograph of herself when young, which showed that she had indeed never been beautiful, that my husband had been right, she had always had the long-faced vivacity of not the best sort of horse. She must have rushed through life stamping and shouting and adopting people who were not of her kind and adopting careers for which she had no vocation, and preventing life from forming a coherent pattern.

We went back to the priest's room for a little while but it was useless. She sat and talked, her bony hand twitching on her lap with a desire for activity which had no relation to those movements which actually produce any result, to the movements one makes in playing a musical instrument or writing; and the priest watched her in a silence he would not have broken even if she had let him. He would have to live with this woman in this small monastery which was at least five miles from the town till his ecclesiatical superiors removed him.

When we got into the automobile Constantine turned to us and beamed. 'There is our true Slav mysticism,' he said, 'I am glad that you are not to leave Yugoslavia without seeing something of that side of our lives.' 'Yes,' said Gerda, 'she is like someone in Tolstoy.'

Afternoon at Struga

On returning to our hotel we found to our considerable distress
that because we had pleased the staff in some way there was
being prepared for us a specially fine fish risotto; this made our
fourth meal during the last four hours. We ate in falsely smiling
gratitude under the ash trees by the lake, and then sat in a state of
distension, trying to dilute ourselves with coffee. There minced by
a slim old woman with gallantly dyed brown hair puffed forward
and pinned down into a kind of cap, and a high net collar held to
her lean neck by whalebones, picking her steps and swinging her
reticule in reference to some standard of gentility that was obsolete
and ridiculous, though she was not to be ridiculed, so poignant was
her grief, her gallantry. I said, 'That might be a Russian general's
widow in a story by Tchekov,' and lo, it was a Russian general's
widow, who played the piano in a café down the street.

This set us wrangling about the Russian writers. My husband
and I said we liked Dostoievsky and Turgeniev the best. My
husband said that *The Possessed* seemed to him to cover every
possible eventuality in moral life, and a great many of the particular
eventualities of historical life which we were likely to face, and that
in Turgeniev he found something that reminded him of Greek
literature but without enough of effort or desire to make him feel
that this was the world he knew. I said that I made my choice
because all writers wanted to write the book that Dostoievsky had
written in the Inquisitor's Dream in *The Brothers Karamazov*, and
because all writers knew that all books should be written like *On
the Eve*. But Constantine said, 'No, you are wrong, Tolstoy was
the greatest of them all.' This I found hard to bear; for surely
Tolstoy is the figure that condemns nineteenth-century Europe,
which never would have been awed by him if it had not lost touch
with its own tradition. Otherwise it would have recognized that
everything Tolstoy ever said that was worth saying had been said
far better by St Augustine and various Fathers and heretics of the
Early Church, who carried the argument far beyond the scope of
his intellect. 'But he was a great man, he was a great personality,'
said Constantine. 'I remember reading that a Japanese had once
come to see Tolstoy at Yasnaya Polyana, and, seeing him, had
gone straight back to Japan, in order that nothing might diminish
the intensity of his impression, though he had always longed to

see Europe.' 'But what was his impression, and what happened to him afterwards?' I asked, really wanting to know. 'What does that matter?' said Constantine. 'It is a question of——' His hand reverently described a huge empty circle. There opened a vision of a world without content, where great men spoke and said nothing, where the followers listened and trembled and learned nothing, and existence was never transformed into life.

Dragutin strolled towards us along the edge of the lake, throwing in stones. He called out, 'If we're going to spend the night at the Monastery of Sveti Naum we needn't start till five. Why don't we go and spend the afternoon at Struga, the famous Struga?' He began to sing the special song of Struga, which says that of all towns in the world it is the prettiest, which indeed is somewhere near the truth, as we had noted when we stopped there on our way from Skoplje. 'Yes, let us do that,' said my husband, and the others would not, so we went off alone.

It is an enchanting little place, white and clean like a peeled almond. It straddles the river Drin, which runs out of Lake Ochrid as much brighter than water as crystal is than glass, and its houses are white and periwinkle blue, and everywhere there are poplars and willows and acacias. It is only a country town, it does not bear the stamp of a great culture like Ochrid, but it is pretty, pretty enough to eat, and the minutes pass like seconds if one stands on the bridge and looks at this extravagantly clear water running under the piers, visible just to a point sufficient to give pleasure to the eye.

We walked about the town for a time and came on the church, with many people standing about in the churchyard and a multi-tude of gipsies sitting on the walls. Bishop Nikolai, they said, was holding a service inside, and there were sounds of ecstatic singing. We were told that when he came out with the procession the gipsies would get up and go into the church and worship silently, and then go home. They would not dream of going into the church while the house-dwelling Christians were still about. This confirmed my feeling of dislike for the gipsies, it was such a Puccini thing to do. But we had to linger for a few moments, for though they were all wearing Western clothes they had chosen them with such a valiant appetite for colour, laying orange by royal blue, scarlet by emerald, dun by saffron-yellow, that they outshone the most elaborate peasant costume, though there was not a garment amongst them which could not have been bought in Oxford Street.

'Let us go and see the eels,' clamoured Dragutin, 'let us go and see the eels.' So at last we went to see the fisheries, where they catch eels in a pen of hurdles sunk in the unbelievably clear river. The fishers drew two out of the crystal water, themselves black crystal, and bound them together, alongside but with the head of one to the tail of the other, so that they could wriggle in the long grass under our inspection without getting a chance of liberty. Dragutin cried out in pleasure at this device. He was always happy when there were animals about, just as people who have a great deal of the child in them are happy with children, and when he saw men exercising control over animals he used to cheer heartily but without malice, as a schoolboy might cheer if he saw a wrestler from his own house overcoming one from another house. 'And look,' he said, pointing over the water-meadow to some wooden bungalows standing under poplars in long grass among many little canals, 'there's the biological station. They've got a museum there, where you can see all the birds and beasts to be found in the district; you can go in if you like.'

We left him playing with the eels. He liked living things, he said. But he would have recognized a brother in the old custodian who took us round the curious building, like a houseboat turned to scientific purposes, where stuffed animals, eagles and wolves, bears and wild cats, boars and snakes, stared glassily through a green dusk. He had precisely the same attitude towards animals. There was to him no greater division between himself and the beasts than there is between Serbs and Greeks, Bulgarians and Turks. When my husband said, 'But this is an enormous wild boar,' he explained that, in the no-man's-land between Yugoslavia and Albania, no hunting is allowed in the forests, and the wild boars take refuge there and grow fat on the acorns and chestnuts; and he grumbled, '*Dort leben sie sebr gut*,' just as a Cockney might say of the Lord Mayor of London and his aldermen, 'Turtle soup and port they 'ave, they don't live like us pore men.'

He was glad that most of his charges were where they were, out of mischief, neatly stuffed, preserved for eternity by camphor balls in highly polished glass cases; but over one he mourned. This was a two-headed calf which was strangely lovely in form, it was like a design made for a bracket by the Adam brothers; its body had the modest sacrificial grace of all calves, and it was a shock to find that of the two heads which branched like candelabra one was lovely, but one was hideous, as that other seen in a distorting glass. 'It was perfectly made,' lamented the old man, 'it was perfectly made.' 'Did it live after its birth?' asked my husband. 'Did it live!' he exclaimed. 'It lived for two days, and it should be alive today had it not been for its nature.' 'For its nature?' repeated my husband.

'Yes, its nature. For the peasant who owned it brought it here to our great doctors as soon as it was born, and here it did well. I tell you, it was perfectly made. But for two days did the beautiful head open its mouth and drink the milk we gave it, and when it came to the throat, then did the ugly head hawk and spit it out. Not one drop got down to its poor stomach, and so it died.' To have two heads, one that looks to the right and another that looks to the left, one that is carved by grace and another that is not, the one that wishes to live and the other that does not: this was an experience not wholly unknown to human beings. As we pressed our faces against the case, peering through the green dusk, our reflections were superimposed on the calf, and it would not have been surprising if it had moved nearer the glass to see us better.

Sveti Naum

Sveti naum lies an hour's drive from Ochrid, at the opposite end of the lake. On clear days you may see it across the waters, shining white on a small Gibraltar of dark rock. The road runs to it along the lakeside, over mountains covered with sweet-scented scrub and golden broom, and down to a fishing village with its bronze nets drying on high poles by the shore. When we passed, the young people were sitting about in the late afternoon glow, in particularly exotic peasant costumes which took the mind to Persia, with an air of being very pleasant with one another; and Dragutin said that the village was noted not only for its violent political life but for the tender consideration the men showed towards the women. 'Some of the people have been to America,' he explained, 'and they come back like that.' Then the mountains become fierce again, and as Biblical as the plains round Debar. A naked range as black as night, its high ridge starred with snow, lay to the left, and on the right, across the lapis-blue lake, the Albanian mountains were a darker blue veiled with white clouds, all in forms stern as justice. Then the road dropped to the mercy of the flatlands round Sveti Naum, and the traveller must be conscious thereafter that he has come to a place which is remarkable in a much simpler, more fundamental way than we are accustomed to note in the modern world.

The road to the monastery runs between steep meadows and becomes an avenue of tall poplars on the landward side and stout willows on the lakeward side, growing from smooth and springy turf. There is water on both sides of this avenue. The lake is always near at hand on the right, shining between the trees, and at the end of the avenue we crossed a bridge over a river which flows from a lake on the left, a small and more light-minded lake, prettily reflecting an island hung with willows. When one first comes to Sveti Naum one simply thinks, 'Why, there is water everywhere.' But the situation is more unusual than that, for in many parts of the world dry land is only a figure of speech. Here one finds oneself saying, 'But the trees and the flowers and the grass in this place have never been thirsty, and the air has never been dusty,' and there is a eupeptic air about the scene, as if the earth had here attained a physiological balance in this matter of moisture rarely to be found elsewhere. And this is no illusion. Beyond the range of black rock on the left lies the Lake of Prespa, which covers about a hundred and twenty square miles, lies five hundred feet higher than Lake Ochrid, and has no visible outlet. Its waters percolate through the base of this range and arrive at these flatlands in a spread network that forms a perfect natural irrigation system, so that it emits refreshment to the eye, the nostril, the skin.

Crouching on the massive black rock, of which one face drops down to the great lake, the monastery is curiously deformed by a concrete tower livid in colour and vile in design. It was put up to commemorate the thousandth year of the foundation. It was Bishop Nikolai who let it be built thus, and he has been bitterly criticized for it. His defence is that the monks and the congregation wanted it to be so, and that it was no business of his to earn the approval of the museums. A pier runs out into the lake, and the road turns away and mounts a steep stone causeway, and under an arch enters the paddock that nearly always surrounds a monastery. This is larger than most, for it covers five or six acres of grassy hillside. Round it are some extremely beautiful farm buildings, probably some hundred years old, with wide tiled roofs propped up by wooden pillars, and loggias undercut by arches, which have about them a distant memory of Greek architecture. Swine, and some horses, an imperial and poppy-wattled turkey, and two peacocks crop the grass, and there are some tall and spreading trees. This paddock has its history. Under the Turks fairs were held here, and the Christian merchants and peasants from different parts of the country would meet, the worn threads of Byzantine culture held a little longer, and sometimes insurrection was plotted.

We passed under an arch and were in the small square formed by the monastery buildings. They are a mixed lot, put up at various times since the fourteenth century, which are painted different colours, some white, some grey, some red, for no other reason than that the monks happened to be given these paints. At one point there are no buildings, and a terrace looks down on the wide face of the lake. The air up here is cooled by the breath of the water. In the centre of this square is the tenth-century Church of Sveti Naum. It is dark and low, its stone walls are brown save where they are plastered white, and its two cupolas, one of which is taller than the other, are of red and white brick, very old, very dim in colour; and it is roofed with red-brown tiles. In shape it is like a locomotive. It stands above the cobbles of the square on a platform of earth, walled up with stone. On one side of the church there grows a lilac tree, which bears very large purple flowers, on the other a fig tree. By the fig tree are some poles on which they dry the monastery fishingnets.

There was nobody about when we arrived but one of the more mystical monks, an old man like a long white-pointed flame, to whom we were nothing, who was probably not sure whether we were among the living or the dead. So we went straight into the church, which is the supreme example of the Serbo-Byzantine architecture that burrows to find its God. It is small, it might be the lair of a few great beasts. There are a few narrow windows and most of them are slits in the cupolas. If it were not for the candles burning in front of the icons the dark outer church and the darker inner church would be hardly more distinguishable than the walls of dungeons. The gilded iconostasis here shines only with a dim coppery gleam. There is a curious smell here, strong yet clean; the two squat columns which divide the churches are based on the living rocks. A low door leads from this darkness to a small darker place, where there is the tomb of Sveti Naum. A tin lamp with red and blue glass shows the great marble box, its top covered by a piece of striped white and gold cloth, poorish in quality, and greasy where too many of the faithful have rested their heads; the Scriptures lie on it too, a pair of thick volumes in artless silver bindings, and a common wooden cross, and a collection-box sealed with pink wax; propped against the wall are four icons, all veiled with machine-made lace and one festooned with cotton roses; there are several bundles of clothes, gifts to the monastery which are laid up for a time and then sold; and cast face down among this precious rubbish, in an attitude of despair, was a man in the cap and apron of a scullion.

On a fresco above the tomb was a portrait of Sveti Naum, almost certainly painted by someone who knew him. He was the successor to Sveti Kliment, the first Christian missionary to be sent by Cyril and Methodius into these parts, and he had to bring not peace but a sword, since none of the persons involved had yet heard of peace. He looks a warrior. Throughout these thousand years nobody has ever dared to touch the stern eyes of his portrait, and this means much; for it is near the ground, and it was the unpious habit of Turks to shoot out the eyes of Christian saints in frescoes, and the pious habit of peasants to scratch them out and soak the plaster to make a lotion for failing sight. His sternness, and the black strength of the church, have been claimed as a refuge by the Macedonian peasant from his ultimate terror; and it illuminates the horror of history in these parts that this is not failure of courage but loss of sanity. Travellers who visited the country in the old days were astonished at the amount of madness, often directly traceable to some act of war such as the burning of a village, and sometimes to the severity of peasant life. This monastery is a hospital for the miraculous treatment of such cases. They are brought here and fed and housed and prayed over by this tomb for forty days. No doubt this scullion was one of the melancholics.

We left the monastery and went down the hill to the bridge over the river between the two lakes, for I wanted my husband to see the wonder of it. This river, the Drin, is clear like no other river, it is visible only to the point that it can give pleasure to the eye. It is, in fact, the same river that we had seen at Struga. It has its source in certain springs that flow unmixed into the lesser, willow-hung lake, which is mere water like any other lake; it declares its peculiar shining rapture as it runs under the bridge; it dives into Lake Ochrid like a person, and like a person is not confused with that in which it swims; and twenty miles away it leaves the lake still itself, to be clearly identified, absolutely unlike any other river. As the sun set behind the range of black rock the air became as remarkable as this water in its transparence, its cleanliness, its fluidity. We put our elbows on the parapet and looked out towards the lake, and found our knees were touching something sculptured. It was a slab carved with a ram and a ewe copulating, obviously the relic of some fertility cult. When the first Christian Slavs built their churches they often incorporated into the buildings such remnants of the pagan faiths that had been cultivated on the sites. This was remarkable for its prosaic quality: the ram looked like a rate-payer, the ewe had an air of routine modesty. A fertility cult, in the hands of dull people, must have been duller than any modern form of religion. We heard from the palely glowing land the baaing of sheep, the sweet cracked beat of their bells, and, finally, the sound of a voice, darkened by a saintly shadow, of invitation calling a name again and again. In an orchard that itself looked spectral in the twilight by reason of the whitewash on the tree-trunks, there walked the delicate old Abbot, his red sash as strange as a bright colour worn by a phantom; and presently his call was heard and there ran to him a peasant in a sheepskin coat. The Abbot pointed up to the branches of a tree, and the peasant registered surprise and distress. Then a handsome boy galloped by on a pony, saddled with wood and bridled with rope, and they cried out that he must stop. He rode to them among the fruit trees, and they pointed out to him whatever it was that had distressed them in the tree-top. He stared up, blurted out an answer that apparently proved their distress to be the result of a comical mistake, and they all broke into laughter. The pale glow over the land grew golden.

On our return to the monastery courtyard we found a monk

whom I had met on my previous visit, sitting with two of the
lunatics and singing them airs from *Madame Butterfly*. This monk
is a Serb from Novi Sad, who is called the Doctor because he had
been a medical student for two or three years before he took his
vows. It is said that he took them because he himself was cured
of a mental disorder by Sveti Naum. He is a charming person,
with a face that is at once extremely animal, as if he could find
his way by scent, and extremely mild, as if he were purged of
aggressiveness and all the baser instincts, and he has a beautiful
baritone voice, rich with detached sensuousness. It is delightful
to be with him, though it is not easy to get in touch with him, for
the Austro-Hungarian Empire did not, as is often falsely alleged,
open the Western world to its peoples by teaching them German;
Novi Sad was in Hungary and its children were taught not German
but Hungarian. He works very hard, for he sings at most of the
services; he alone receives all guests who visit the monastery, and
he takes his share of looking after the lunatics, but he has a skin as
smooth as a child's and the charm of an indolent man.

The lunatics bore testimony to his power in dealing with them by
sinking back into their woe as soon as he turned his attention from
them. They kept on starting at the church where all their hopes
were centred. This was the antithesis of the Byzantine practice of
blinding people by making them look at a bright light; they were
trying to get back their inner sight by keeping their eyes on the
darkness. Both of them were so mad that nobody could have seen
them without noticing their condition. One, a young girl in a cheap
cloth coat with a goat-skin collar, was perhaps a shop-assistant from
some small town; she was wearing bedroom slippers, and a hole
in her stocking showed her bare heel. The other was a superbly
handsome man in his thirties, with the long hair and the beard of
a priest, who was dressed, like his companion, in Western clothes,
but with an extreme carelessness; his socks were bright yellow, and
he wore curious strap-shoes like a child's. They were very different.
Of the girl one could say quite simply, 'She would not be mad if
someone had not been so cruel to her,' as simply as one might say,
'That face would not be bruised if someone had not struck it.' But
in the man there worked an elemental distress, peculiar to himself,
which might have vexed him had he never known any but himself,
or only the loving. He was in the predicament of the two-headed
calf, part of his soul was spitting out nourishment it needed.

There was something shocking to a Western mind in the disorder
of their dress. But when I looked back to the time of my life when I
was most miserable I realized that it would have been a great relief

to have let everything about me, including my clothes, express that misery; and it indicated no callousness on the part of their guardians, for some of the monks are so rapt in ecstasy that they notice nothing material, and the others had been brought up in Turkish Macedonia, where a ragged garment was more normal than a whole one in many Christian homes. It was not at all terrible to be with these people, and indeed their condition seemed far from being the worst that can be feared, when we were joined by a young man who was staying in the monastery, not as a lunatic but as a tourist. Small and whippy, wearing curious knickerbockers of Central European pattern, he sat whistling and trimming his nails with a penknife, and was none the more acceptable for having his wits about him. He seemed to find the time pass slowly, as indeed it must in an Orthodox monastery if one is not interested in Orthodox monasteries, and from his lack of response to the conversation it appeared that he was not.

When it drew near the dinner hour the Doctor sent the two lunatics into their refectory, asked the four of us to come with him into the guest-house, and said good-night to the young man, who gave him a nod which was affable in an exceedingly unsuitable way, which would have looked more appropriate over the rim of a glass of beer. The Doctor answered with a smile that was not without reserves. The rest of us went with him up the stairs that led to the gallery, here walled in though it is open in most monasteries, where the visitors are given *slatko*, the ceremonial offering of sugar or jam and glasses of cold water, and where the guests who stay overnight are given their meals. We were given plum brandy, and then shown into our bare little rooms, with the narrow beds and the tin basins. The windows looked out on the lake, which was now silver under a horizon of black clouds. Over the black range on our right a Niagara of radiant white mist was pouring, and some light, of unimaginable provenance, crept low along the ground and turned the trees to a hard emerald green. On the left the Albanian mountains were a deep violet, and below them the lights of villages shone on the water's edge. 'Those lights that are quite near, that are almost at our feet,' said the Doctor, 'that too is an Albanian village. We are right on the frontier here. Indeed we were once actually in Albania, as a result of the first peace settlement. But this was a pilgrimage place for so many who lived in Yugoslavia that the frontier had to be corrected. Still, it will go hard with us if Italy ever strikes at Yugoslavia through Albania.'

At dinner the Doctor sang a long grace in his beautiful and untroubled voice, and sat down to eat with us. We had little appetite, though the food was grown on the rich farmlands of the monastery and was well cooked by a lunatic who had been only uncertainly cured by Sveti Naum and had begged to be allowed to stay near the shrine so that he could resort to it at need; it was our fifth meal that day. But the Doctor ate well, for the day of an Orthodox monk is long and trying. The brothers rise between three and four and breakfast at eight, after the long service, and they have a midday meal at half-past twelve; but they do not have their supper until eight or later, though some of them have had another long service in the afternoon. As the Doctor sat drowsily over his coffee, Constantine said to him, 'Who was the little one in knickerbockers who was sitting down in the courtyard with the lunatics?' The Doctor answered, 'We do not know, but he comes here now and then.' Constantine asked, 'Does he say why he comes?' 'He says he likes the monastery,' said the Doctor, with no great conviction. 'What does he say he is?' asked Constantine. 'He has a Yugoslav passport,' said the Doctor. 'But I think he talks a little like a Saxon, a Saxon perhaps not of Saxony, but of Transylvania,' said Constantine.

A pause fell, and we all drank more wine. 'I am sad,' said the Doctor, 'because I am very happy here, and I may have to leave. I could not be happier, for I like showing guests the monastery, since in a way it is the most wonderful place in the world, and I like working with the lunatics, for many of them are made sound. That is a great joy to me, for my only sorrow on becoming a monk was that I could not be a doctor, and here I find myself helping with cures such as no doctor could ever work. But Bishop Nikolai says that perhaps he will move me to Zhitcha.' Zhitcha is the seat of Bishop Nikolai's other diocese, it is the rose-red monastery where all the Serb kings are crowned, not a hundred miles south of Belgrade. 'Why so?' asked Constantine. 'He says,' replied the Doctor, 'that in Zhitcha, which is an administrative centre, he has need of a modern man, as I am, but that here in Sveti Naum there is a living tradition which can safely be taken care of by the traditionalists. Besides he is making it a rule to have none but Macedonian monks in Macedonian monasteries, and there is no reason why I should be an exception.' He sighed deeply, but added, 'It is a wise rule, for many reasons, even for the sake of Sveti Naum itself. There might come those who did not understand the place and the peasants.'

There was much in what he said, though the rule was probably first conceived as a sop to the Macedonian patriots. The Doctor was a unique personality, who moved in a world of essences and remarked little of the material except its simpler pleasantnesses, such as the feeling of cleanliness. But most men who had been brought up within the orbit of Belgrade and Zagreb would be infected with Western ideas regarding the importance of material possessions and a written culture. When the Abbot and the peasant and the boy had been talking in the orchard that evening they had been divided by differences of age and function, which summed up to considerable differences in authority; but there could be no idea of a fundamental inequality declared at birth, because the Abbot had probably come from a peasant home. There could be nothing more horrible than the idea of a priest coming to this place to treat lunatics and giving them, even if inadvertently, their first knowledge of a class system, thus betraying to them that they were at a disadvantage of which they were previously unaware. Its horror makes one realize that, however inevitable a class system may be in a complicated capitalist state, it must be a cruel burden on the human mind. It would also be horrible if, in a country where a certain proportion of the people must needs be ragged and dirty, those in mental distress should have to go for comfort to a priest who associated the idea of worth with whole and clean garments. There is a like therapeutic threat in the Western incapacity for appreciating a culture which is not dominated by literature, which makes Serb and Croat residents in Macedonia who have graduated in the universities of Berlin, Vienna, and Paris completely blind to the beauty of the peasants' costumes and dances and rituals and certain that they are barbaric. This blindness is indeed a more serious therapeutic threat than the other. There was published some years ago a book by an English doctor about his life as a superintendent in a lunatic asylum for African natives, in which he described how his work had been profitless until he had laid hold on their culture, and had mastered their myths and basic ideas. If this were true in the case of a primitive race, it must be even more so in the case of a people governed by the phantom of a complex culture.

It might be thought that none of these considerations could apply to a shrine, where the cure offered is miraculous, and therefore ought to be conceived to be as simple as a poultice, cold and in reverse action, the patient being clapped on a marble tomb and the supernatural left to take its course. But the cure is in fact far more complicated. It depends on bringing the patients, in as receptive a state of mind as possible, under the influence of Sveti Naum himself, that is to say under the influence of a personality which has been perpetuated by word-of-mouth tradition and by the style of a building. And here too Western influence might be disastrous, for that personality has an exquisite appropriateness to Macedonia as well as to sanity. A grim man, Sveti Naum was not vanquished when he fought among these rocks with the wild men who would be heathen; he passed thereby a Macedonian test. He knew that nothing was too abominable to happen on this earth, but that probably all could be borne if one fought a soldierly campaign, numbering the enemy and recognizing their kind, and drawing on all available forces, of which the mightiest was magical. It would have been a pity if the perpetuation of this message had been left to a Western sentimentalist, who would have represented Sveti Naum as a kind man who kissed the place and made it well, or a Western euphorist who would falsely claim that events were never horrible if properly regarded.

The character of Sveti Naum, or of the tradition that has formed round his name, is so definite that each time I have slept in the monastery it has affected my dreams, making them bleak yet not at all distressful presentations of what was not to be altered for the better in my life, from which I woke refreshed. But the next day my wakening was late. I heard the clanging of the great bell, which announced the last phase of the long morning service, washed in cold water, looking across the lake at a shining world, dressed, ran across the courtyard, where a peacock was preening its tail in a pool of sunlight, and went in, or, as it seemed, down, into the dark church. There in the candlelight were my husband and Gerda and Constantine and Dragutin, two old nuns and a hunchback young one, the two lunatics we had met in the courtyard, and a third, a young peasant girl, who was accompanied by her mother.

The Doctor, with an acolyte standing by him, a lad in a torn coat with his socks in folds above his ankles, was reading the lesson; and when he had finished the royal door in the iconostasis opened and there came out a priest dressed in crimson and gold, who stood waiting, in the space that is left between the congregation and the iconostasis, where there is a circle of white stone with a black star inscribed in it. One of the old nuns led forward the girl in the cloth coat, and she dropped on all fours in front of him. Opening his bearded mouth to make way for a deep-lunged prayer, he swung a censer backwards and forwards over her. Her crouching body made a pitiful hieroglyphic of which the interpretation was very plain. Had the conception of sex been revised in the human mind, so that men are kind to those who give them pleasure, she would not have been mad. But the dark vault and massive pillars of the church about us, the stern and ornate iconostasis, announced the unlikelihood of such a change, and the inveterate inharmoniousness of life. In her place the bearded man crouched down and was censed. He flung himself at the priest's feet with the greatest eagerness, but once he knelt he would have nothing of the rite, he shifted from knee to knee, raised and lowered his head. Here was the source of life's disharmony, of such conceptions as had driven the girl mad. Here was the two-headed calf again, that would drink the milk with one head and spit it out with the other and so must die. Last came the peasant girl, who swung round as she got to the priest and turned her back on him, showing a pretty face, prettily tied up in a white kerchief. She was an idiot, and laughter shook her even when she crouched before the priest. Her mother, who was not old but was dried up by excessive grief as if she had been smoked like a ham, was by her side when she rose, and slewed her round to face the altar. Whispering, she pushed up the girl's hand towards her forehead, and there was achieved a clumsy sign of the cross. The mother must have laboured for years to teach her such a complicated movement.

The priest went back through the royal door, and the Doctor sang another passage from the Mass. The idiot wearied and strayed from her mother, who was standing with her eyes shut in prayer, and spent a little time feeling the fluffy texture of my angora dress. Then she lost interest and stared ahead of her, and saw the back of her mother's head, round under a black kerchief. She put out her hand and began to finger it with an embryonic kind of love; the mother turned a patient face and drew her daughter back to her. Then the priest came out again from the iconostasis and stood holding a bowl full of the sacramental bread, the small flat loaves. The nuns took theirs avidly and happily, the girl in the cloth coat took hers as if it might perhaps be what she really wanted, the bearded man went up eagerly and then turned aside and began to straighten the tangled fringe of the shelf on the iconostasis where the icons stand, the idiot girl came back laughing, with crumbs on her mouth, which her mother brushed away. There was a prayer of thanksgiving, and suddenly the magic was over. The nuns and the priests hurried out of the church about their business, the lunatics sauntered out as if for them all clocks had stopped.

While we were breakfasting in the gallery on coffee and milk and the sweet black bread they bake here from their own corn, I said to Constantine, 'I wish you would ask the Doctor if they cure all kinds of madness alike.' He answered, 'No, he will not like you to ask that. And it is not necessary, for I can tell you what his answer will be. He will say that the mercy of God works on all people that seek it,' and went on with his coffee. I said, 'Please ask him,' but he would not until I had tried to put the question in my stumbling Serbian. The Doctor gave a bright, furtive smile, like a hound thinking of the ways of the fox, and answered, 'There are some cases of madness which can be cured by Sveti Naum, and some for which God apparently reserves another way. Neuroses we can cure. Many, many neurotics have I seen go from here sane men. And of psychotics I have seen some cured here, more, I think I can say, than are cured elsewhere, for I think that in the asylums they do not claim to cure dementia praecox, and that I have seen happen here several times. But where there is something organic, there we can do nothing. But I should not put it like that, for this condition may be altered tomorrow. Also I should be careful to point out that there must be a monastery somewhere where such things are cured. All I can really say is that here we cure other things.' He said that he thought the girl in the cloth coat would probably be completely cured, but he was doubtful about the bearded man, and that he did not expect that they would be able to do anything for the girl with the white handkerchief.

This ruling on the general types and the particular cases is very much the opinion that an alienist trained in modern Western methods would have passed, except for the optimistic prognosis concerning the psychotics; but the Doctor was speaking entirely according to his own experience and the tradition of the monastery, for his medical education had stopped short of any such advanced studies. In fact, there has somehow been worked out in this monastery a system of psychotherapy which is roughly comparable to that recommended by modern medical science, and which certainly achieves some degree of success. This is not unnatural. The patients come to the monastery for forty days, which is the length of a good holiday, and are given wholesome food, of a more varied kind than they have in their houses, which are in the poorest cases limited to bread and paprika, and they are housed with more privacy. For many of them it is the first break in a life of continuous overwork, and for quite a number of women it is an escape from male tyranny. They are also the exclusive objects of the attention of a number of priests, who are the most important kind of people they know, which must be restorative to their self-esteem; and the effect of the ceremony in church that we had just seen must be overwhelming. These people are used to the Mass, they have often stood in church and known that behind the iconostasis the priests are celebrating the holy mysteries. Sometimes the curtain above the door is drawn back and they see them in a blaze of light, like to the saints and kings of old time shown in the frescoes and icons with their gorgeous garments and their long hair; sometimes they come out to dispense the sacramental bread, the most holy of substances. And suddenly it appears that they can come out for no other purpose than to help one's darkened brain.

After breakfast we went to look at the springs which feed the lesser lake. On the way out we went into the church, to have another taste of its powerful and astringent quality. But we did not stop, for at the tomb of Sveti Naum a priest was reading some form of exorcism over a peasant girl, whose mother stood by with her hands folded across her apron front in an attitude of despair. The girl was sitting on the floor with some sort of embroidered liturgical cloth on her head, staring not at all sadly ahead of her with immense black eyes sunk in a white face. In the sickly slenderness of her wrists and ankles, in the jaunty perversity of her expression, she recalled some young ephebe of Paris in the nineteen-twenties, some idol with feet of cocaine, dear to Jean Cocteau and his circle. As we went out of the monastery a terrific avian hullabaloo broke out in the archway over our heads, and we saw that the rafters were thick with the family life of swallows, which was being threatened by a malign pigeon; but this disorder was speedily righted by a lean old monk who ran out of the kitchen with a long pole, making fierce movements while he uttered mild exhortations, appealing to its better side. Outside, the landscape was as under a special blessing because it was so well watered. Its grass and trees shone with the radiance of youth, of perfect health.

We followed a path that ran round the lesser lake. Its centre was calm: across it a line of poplars were reflected exactly in their ash-white wood and gold-green leaf. But the edge trembles perpetually, for here the waters of Lake Prespa burst out from the imprisoning rock in two hundred separate springs, the sources of the river Drin. Each has its own rhythm; some are quick, some are slow, some beat like a pulse, all are clear as crystal. 'How strange that they should both be at Sveti Naum,' said my husband, 'this little church which is the blackest and heaviest thing I have ever seen, this expanse of water which is the lightest, brightest thing I have ever seen.' One spring bubbled up, transparent as air, in a stone basin set among long grass in a roofless chapel; at our coming huge bronze and emerald frogs dived from the grass into the basin. We found another in a basin set in the open, and sat there for a time. Above us, on a hillside stained magenta with wild stock, munched a herd of goats; one kid, grey and delicate, lay sleeping near us, shining and lax like a skein of silk. I put out my hand and it fell

on the most poetical of wild flowers, the grape hyacinth. We saw
Dragutin, whose religious attitude to water we had often noticed
before, reverently walking along the path by the lake, keeping his
eyes on it and often standing still.

When the morning had worn on, we found a path back through
the orchard where we had seen the Abbot and the peasants, and
came back to the bridge over the Drin. Our knees against the ram
and ewe, we leaned over and watched a mill-wheel turning under
a grey tower that is said to be as old as the monastery, a thousand
years or so, and is homely and majestic in the manner of its time.
The brightness of the river was not to be believed. We saw Dragutin
coming along the avenue of poplars and willows, and pausing for
a gossip with the shepherd of a brown and white flock that was
grazing on the cushiony turf under the trees. Presently he came up
and, after pouring into my hand a stream of round white stones he
had found somewhere, leaned over the bridge with us. As I played
with the stones they reminded me of the sacramental loaves in the
church, and there came back to me a poetic moment in the service
I had witnessed on my previous visit to Sveti Naum. At a certain
point in the afternoon service a nun went into the centre of the
church, where there is a circle of white stone inscribed with a black
star on the floor, and put there a rickety little table covered with
a white crocheted mat, such as one might see in seaside lodgings.
Then the priest in crimson and gold had come out carrying a plate
of sacramental loaves and laid it on the table. Then he walked round
the table, pointing towards the loaves a long cross with a lit candle
fixed to the top of its upright arm, where Christ's head must have
rested, and halting at north and south and east and west to chant a
spell. This rite strongly evoked the death of Christ, the radiance of
goodness, the sin of murdering it, and the cancellation of this sin by
the consent of goodness to live again, that those who ate the bread
must have felt that they were swallowing a substance like Christ,
that they were absorbing goodness.

Here in Sveti Naum magic can be worked. The mind accepts it.
That is to say, this is one of the places in the world which, by their
material conformation emphasized by the results of the labours
to which they have inspired their inhabitants, have a symbolic
meaning. The existence of such places is one of the determining
factors in history, and most of the great cities are among them.
The shape of the earth around them, the mountains that uphold
them or the plains that leave them open to their enemies, the
rivers and seas or barrenness about them, recommend certain
philosophies. These are never stated, but the people live or die

by them: so do we sometimes go about all day depressed or exalted by a dream which we do not remember. The proof lies in the power of these places to imprint the same stamp on whatever inhabitants history brings them, even if conquest spills out one population and pours in another wholly different in race and philosophy. Whatever blood finds itself in Constantinople feels an obligation to cultivate an immensely elaborate magnificence under the weight of which it grows fatigued and slatternly; whatever faith finds itself in Rome becomes gluttonous of universal dominion; whether imperialism or communism is in Moscow it sits behind locked doors and balks at shadows.

The argument here, in Sveti Naum, which has been recognized for a thousand years, is a persuasion towards sanity; a belief that life, painful as it is, is not too painful for the endurance of the mind, and is indeed essentially delightful. It presents that argument in a series of symbols. There is the circle of water, which is a natural substance like the rock of the mountains. There is the other lake, far less in size, which is also of common water, of rain that falls from dark clouds and runs down the hillsides, but which receives other water of a brighter sort, derived from the springs that flow from a distant mountain. This other water flows as a river through that lake and the great lake, immersed in them yet always distinct, and leaves them with its nature unchanged. There is, besides these lakes and these springs and this river, a circle of green earth, where the grass and the trees grow tall without experience of drought and the herds browse and are never hungry; and besides this circle of earth, which is the extreme of fertility, is a small circle of rock, the concentrated extreme of barrenness. On this rock there has been built a square of squat, dark, strong buildings. In the centre is the strongest, squattest, darkest of them all. This building is divided into two parts; in the one there are light and people who can by singing and ritual evoke the thoughts and feelings which are to human beings as water is to the grass and trees and turf, in the other there are darkness and people who need this refreshment.

This is a picture of man's life. The difference between the mountains and the lake is as the difference between nature and man. The difference between the lakes and the river which runs through them is as the difference between man's bodily life, of the kind which he shares with the animals, and the life of his mind. There is the difference between the green earth and the barren rock, the difference between life when it goes well and when it goes ill. There is the monastery as example that man is not powerless when life goes ill, that he can assemble sounds and colours and actions into patterns which make spells and evocations, which persuade the universe to give up the antidote it holds against its poison. It is not pretended in any part of Sveti Naum that this revelation is made with facility. Even here truth does not grow on every bush. Bread does not become of like substance to goodness until it is laid on a little table in the centre of the church, over a circle of white stone inscribed by a black star, until it is enchanted by songs from the four points of the compass, and indicated by flame. It is the character of art and thought never to be easy. Nor is it pretended in any part of Sveti Naum that the revelation is complete, that all is now known. If the place makes a claim it is only that here for a mile or two earth corresponds with reality, which this correspondence shows not to be disagreeable.

Ochrid V

On our way back to lunch we went into the chapel of Sveti Naum and found the sexton holding to the tomb a child of seven or so with a large head and a tiny hydrocephalous body, and calling over its shoulder to its mother, 'Now you kneel down and start praying.' But she continued to walk up and down, wringing her hands. She had a handsome face, though if one had seen her working in a field one might have thought her brutish; and probably she was, in some respects. She turned to my husband and cried, 'But what am I to say? You've been educated, you must know what I ought to say!' 'Don't talk to the gentleman,' said the sexton, 'talk to God.' 'But that's just what I don't know how to do,' she complained. 'I don't know what to say to God about this, there's so much to say; I don't know where to begin, it's such a strange thing to have happened.' I thought again how malicious fate had been in choosing people with minds like this to be governed for five centuries by the Turks, who are so destitute of speculative instinct that they have no word for 'interesting' in their language.

Just then the Doctor monk and Constantine came in and announced that we must go and have lunch as quickly as we could and hurry back to Ochrid, because Bishop Nikolai wished us to go to his palace that afternoon. We were extremely embarrassed by this, because we knew this invitation could only be a courteous acknowledgment of some money which my husband had given to one of the priests in Ochrid for his church. But nothing could have been less possible than to refuse this invitation. Gerda and Constantine naturally saw no reason why we should not accept, and though Dragutin showed us that he did, he made it plain also that it was no use resisting. In this place such an invitation was a royal command. So at three o'clock our automobile climbed the heights of the old town, which looked brilliant yet rigid under the heavy crystal of the afternoon heat, and we paid a visit which the East attended to in its own way, preventing it from being what was intended, but making it an unexpected delight.

It was entirely unlike a visit to an English episcopal palace. In a steep alley, behind a paintless door, we found a neatly tumbledown house and garden. So farms look where the folks have much to do and little money but mean well. On the long grass in the garden a boy wearing a school cap played with a mongrel puppy, and a beggar slept face downwards. We went up from an entrance hall which had once been a stable and was not greatly altered, by a rickety staircase, to the Bishop's office, where four men sat and talked, two in peasant dress, two in Western dress. The Bishop, we were told, had not yet returned from a midday service some miles away. So we settled down to wait in a pleasant sleepy coolness. The room was exquisite; the wooden ceiling and a moulded recess, delicately carved and surrounded with plaster leaves, were of the properest imaginable proportions. For a time we leaned from the window and looked at the lake, which was now blinding white and seemed to rise in the middle, like a plate piled high with light, and at the hillside, where the strong sunshine lay on the earth that is crimson in the morning and evening hours and made it seem a pinkish breath blown on the rock; we looked down on the roof of Sveta Sophia, which even to the bird's eye reveals the elegance of its mass, the appropriateness of this tribute paid by an emperor to his heavenly peer; we looked at the shiny black buds of an ash-tree that sheltered the sleeping beggar.

Three-quarters of an hour passed. They brought us black coffee, but the afternoon was drowsy and we sank back in our chairs. Bees circled round a vase of lilacs on the table, an old priest talked politics with Constantine, the four men talked of a dispute about land in a village near Struga. I looked at the delicious ceiling and wondered to what period it belonged. It might have been early seventeenth-century work, but one can never be sure about what was done here after the Turkish conquest, for time stood still, and an isolated district would go on century after century repeating an idiom that had long perished in the rest of Europe. I ceased to care, I woke after an hour, and a servant brought us another round of black coffee, this time with a piece of Turkish delight on a toothpick in each saucer, because the Bishop was so very late. A tortoiseshell cat strolled in, and was told by the old priest that it had no business there, but so civilly that it jumped up on his lap and curled itself into a closed circle. Then the servant came in and told us that a telephone message had come to say that the Bishop's automobile had had a breakdown far away, and that there was no use waiting longer.

We went down the alleys into the main street of Ochrid in an afternoon that was already cooler, that had begun to breathe freely again. The visit had been extraordinarily pleasant, though it had been nothing at all, and least of all a visit. Constantine and Gerda had gone on ahead, and we dawdled, feeling charmed by everything. It happened that this was one of the several times in the day when the little boys come from the bakeries with trays of rolls, and my husband bought two of the kind we specially liked, little sticks of bread so fine that it was nearly pastry, dusted with poppy seeds, and we went into the big café near the lake and ordered coffee and milk to drink with them. It must be admitted that this was sheer voluptuousness, for we were neither hungry nor thirsty, but surely it was of the mildest conceivable sort. Only a very small insect could have called it an orgy. Yet when Constantine and Gerda came into the café and sat down beside us, she said to him, 'These people are always eating and drinking. I wonder if all English people are such gluttons.' As she spoke she picked up my roll and began to eat it.

This mattered little, for just then the little boys with the trays came into the café and my husband bought me another, but there followed a conversation which was excessively disagreeable in its imbecility. The waiter asked me if I was an American, and when I told him that I was not but had often visited America, he asked me if I had ever been to Dallas, Texas, where his brother was a pastrycook. I said that I had once been there, and that it was full of very good-looking people, and we talked a little. As he turned away, Gerda said, 'Since you know America, I wonder if you know how American women do their hair?' 'How they do their hair?' I repeated. 'Why, like other women I should have said, but they spend more time on it.' 'No, no,' said Constantine, 'this is something very curious, you should hear it if you do not know about it. It is the way they keep their hair in order between their visits to the coiffeur.' 'But they have no special way,' I said, 'they all have permanent waves, and many of them wear hairnets, many more than European women do.' 'No, they do not have permanent waves,' said Gerda, 'but every night they screw up their hair into little curls with toilet paper. That is what an American lady did with whom I travelled on a Danube steamboat, and she told me that all American woman did the same.' 'There, is that not strange,' said Constantine, 'you have been to America and she has not, and yet she knows something about the Americans that you do not.' 'Wherever she went,' Gerda told him in Serbian, 'she would see nothing. I tell you, she is a fool.' 'I suppose this is the kind of conversation one will have in Hell,' said my husband. 'One can't do anything with it, it's so silly,' I said. 'I wish to God I thought it was from all points of view,' said my husband, 'but I think it is a part of something rather large. It is the kind of conversation a Roman woman might have had it she had been travelling with a Carthaginian woman in the third century before Christ. Eat up your roll and we will go. By God, she has eaten the second one too.'

But just then there came up to us a lawyer of the town, whose home I had visited with Constantine the year before, who had heard that we were in the café and had hurried down to say that his wife would be glad to see us. I was pleased to go, for she was a woman of special heroic quality, who as a beautiful young girl had come here in the old Turkish days, to teach in a Serbian school, knowing that this was a Bulgarian district and therefore bitterly hostile to Serbs, but believing that it was Bulgarian only because of the propaganda of the Russians. She is a Demeter, her hair is still thick and yellow though she is not young, her voice is rich like clotted cream, and she has a 'green finger'; flowers from her garden filled the vases, special in colour and perfume, and the *slatko* she gave us was not only unusually abundant, including quince and cherries and plums, but was all made of the fruits from her orchard, which were bigger than any others we had seen.

She had wished to see us half from quiet, abounding hospitality, and half from a measure of loneliness and despondency, arising from political origins. She realized, like all the finer people we met, that with all his faults Constantine was a passionate patriot, and she had wanted his sympathy. They had a long talk about local politics in Serbian, which Constantine supposed I could not understand but which I was able to follow. She and her husband were grieved because the feeling of the town was still so pro-Bulgarian. They were even doubtful whether, if a plebiscite were taken, Ochrid would opt to be incorporated with Yugoslavia or Bulgaria. They were downcast about this, not chauvinist. It must be remembered that when the Serbians were attacked by the Austro-Hungarian Empire and the Bulgarians joined their assailants all Serbs thought of them as traitors to their Slav blood, and that there were incidents in the war which poisoned this issue. There is a white column on the hillside not far from Ochrid which catches the eye from a long way off but which is never visited; it commemorates four hundred Serbians who stopped here on the 1915 retreat, being sick and starved and weary, and were shot down by the local Bulgars. Also the Serbs of Ochrid, including this woman, were interned in Bulgaria during the war and were dealt with untenderly. She was heartbroken because Macedonians of Bulgar sympathies should not have been united to the Serbs by twenty years of what seemed to her not at all harsh treatment, and that they should not have recognized that the tyranny which threatened them from without was far greater than any restrictions they had to fear from within.

'I cannot understand them,' she mourned; 'if Italy conquers us there is an end to all liberty for all of us, for Serbs and Bulgars, for Yugoslavia and Bulgaria.'

As if to comfort herself with the fruitfulness of the earth, which stands by man in spite of his political errors, she went out of the room, and came back with a brood of week-old chickens in an apron. She tipped them out over a writing-table, and let them cheep and perk among the inkwells and the blotters, smiling though her brows were still joined by worry. Then there was a knock at the door and it appeared that, as sometimes suddenly happens to travellers, we had been received by the social soul of the town. The old schoolmistress who had been at the feast in the church had sent along to say that she knew the lawyer and his wife were coming along to her *Slava*, and that it would be pleasant if she brought the foreigners along with her too. This was delightful, if only for the light it cast on the town's intelligence service, but I was also enchanted at the opportunity of seeing a *Slava* (the word means 'Holy'), which is the distinctive social custom of the Serbs. It looks like a birthday on a very generous scale; all day the family keeps open house and offers food and drink and amiability to all friends and acquaintances and even passing strangers. But it is an inherited date, which never varies from generation to generation, and it is said to be the anniversary of the day on which the ancestor of the family who first forsook his paganism received baptism. This is plausible. One of the constituents of the feast is a dish of boiled wheat, like our frumenty, which is called by a word meaning 'something killed by a knife for a sacrifice.' The inference is that the new-made Christians were told that they need not kill beasts at the altar of their new god, but could eat a dish of wheat instead. That we came too late to see, but we were given some of the *Slava* cake, which also makes some reference to conversion. It is a very large and extremely rich cake of wheat-flour sweetened with honey, almost like a cold pudding, and historians have traced its connexion with fertility cults; but it has to be made in a mould marked with the name of Jesus Christ, and it has to be blessed by a priest who eats the first slice.

Constantine had gone back to the hotel, to telephone his office in Belgrade; but Gerda and my husband and I went with the lawyer and his wife, and joined a circle of people, numbering about twelve, who sat round the old schoolmistress's bright, bare room. She was obviously very happy simply in the act of entertaining, no matter whom she entertained, and told us stories of her career as a spy during the last war. The first time she had even seen the sea, that was, and she was frightened enough anyway, but the ship she was on had to go and be torpedoed. Still it had all been great fun, and she only hoped the young people would have as good a time as she had had. Every five minutes two pretty little girls in their early teens, who were her adopted daughters, carried round trays covered with little cakes and conserved fruits and glasses of wine. Presently an old peasant woman, who was the grandmother of one of the little girls, came in and was given a chair of honour. Supping her wine, she asked the lawyer about a case in which he had lately taken part. A Christian and a Moslem, it seemed, had combined in a small job of highway robbery and had quarrelled over the division of the spoil, at which point a second Christian had come in and had helped the Moslem murder the first in return for a small share. The second Christian had confessed, and he and the Moslem had been sentenced to fifteen years.

Everybody became very animated, and it was evident that the case had caused a stir in the neighbourhood. This struck me as an extraordinary testimonial to the work of Yugoslavia in Macedonia, since under the Turks highway robbery was so common that a man never travelled unless he had money enough to engage an armed escort. There was evidently a great divergence of opinion about the sentences. The old peasant woman said she had heard endless discussions about this in her village, and she simply didn't know what to think about it, so she wanted to hear what people who could read and write thought. The school-mistress, who had been brought up in an established Serbian town, said, 'No doubt about it at all, they should both have been hanged,' but the lawyer, who had been born and brought up in Macedonia, disagreed. It turned out, however, that he was doubtful about the confession. I guessed that there was some suspicion that the police might have resorted to the third degree, a practice which had been firmly implanted in this part of the country by the Turks, and which even the most conscientious administrators find it difficult to extirpate. But the lawyer went on to say that, as for the robbery part of the charge, he did not think that that should have been punished so heavily, for after all it was a rich man whom they had waylaid, and all wealth was stolen from someone. The old schoolmistress said, 'Oh, shucks! That sort of thing can be gone into on the Day of Judgment, but here below it is better to leave it alone, and take it that in the meantime a man can't have what isn't his.' The lawyer said that that was all very well, and that is a rule we live by now, but he thought we must try for something better. 'Oh, you two are always trying for something better, I know you do, and I love you for it, but this Auntie,' said the schoolmistress, tapping herself on the chest, 'this Auntie can't rise to it.' So the lawyer and his wife laughed and kissed her good-bye, and we left with them.

As we walked back to the hotel by the darkening lake, I said to Gerda, 'Thank you very much for translating what they said for us,' and she replied, 'It is all very well my translating it, but did you understand it? Do you realize what horrible people they are? They are all Marxists.' My husband said, 'What do you mean? What they were saying has nothing to do with Marxism. It sounded more as if the lawyer and his wife were old-fashioned Christian Socialists, but they might not even be that, they might be simply humanitarians.' Gerda repeated, her face heavy with hatred, 'They are all Marxists.'

ROAD

Gerda drove with us from Ochrid to Bitolj, for it is a journey of only a few hours, and there could be no pretence that it meant prolonged discomfort if she joined us. Constantine sat beside Dragutin, who gave him some very good gossip. 'You'll never guess who I saw walking down by the lake yesterday evening. The Kostitches, those people who have got that big draper's shop at Skoplje and another at Bitolj and another at Kossovska Mitrovitsa. They must be staying down here, she's got a sister married to a functionary here. They're nice people and made of money, they've got dinars the way other people have lice. But they've one trouble, they haven't got any children. It worries them terribly. They feel, and of course there's sense in it, that there's no good having all that money if they've nobody to leave it to. They're always in and out of the church praying about it, and they've spent a fortune on doctors. Well, if old Kostitch would give me a good dinner and a hundred dinars, she would have a boy all right. I know money shouldn't come into that sort of thing, but he's a rich man and would never miss it. However, I think she's a poor creature. He once sent her alone to Vienna to see a doctor, and a sensible woman would have done something else than see a doctor, but I know the maidservant of her best friend, and she says she didn't. But here, we must stop, there's something we ought to see.'

He made us walk to a slope where the red earth was bare and blasted, and showed us a tiny pot-hole, with as much steam as comes from the spout of a kettle, when it is first boiling. 'That's a volcano, that is,' he said, 'and though it's small it works. Any poor beast that comes near it—pouf! he's dead.' I did not believe a word of it, and then I looked down and saw beside my foot the shrunken body of a hedge-hog, cut down in the flower of such sins as a hedgehog may have. It was Dragutin's day, the earth behaved as he saw it. For when we got to the top of the pass the car suddenly leaped forward and then stopped, and he jumped out and ran back on our tracks. He returned very sadly, saying, 'I thought I had killed a snake, but it isn't there.' A little later, the car made the same sickening leap again, and this time the snake was maimed, and was easily finished off with a heavy spanner brought down on its head and its heart. 'Look at the black lattice on its back,' he said, gloating over its carcass, 'that shows it's a really dangerous snake, kills in half an hour; there's a lot of them about here.' I asked Constantine, 'Do many people die of snake-bite here?' He tried to do his best for Macedonia. 'Not nearly so many as in Bosnia. In Bosnia very many people die of snake-bite. But,' he added patriotically, remembering that Bosnia also was in Yugoslavia, 'they are not really very many.'

After that the road dropped to broad red plains planted with corn and vines, and brought us to the dull town of Resan, which has the air characteristic of towns on southern plains of having been pressed flat by the heavy thumb of the heat. It is historically remarkable on two counts: in 1903 it was the scene of a magnificently courageous rising of the Christians against the Turks, and here Mustapha Kemal first formed his idea of the Young Turk movement and spread it among his fellow-officers. We sat down in the central square and drank coffee and a man came up and spoke to us in American. He was a man of about forty-five, who had been in Chicago for ten years and had recently returned here on some family errand. We asked him if he could remember anything of the 1903 insurrection, and he said he could. He had wakened out of his sleep and had run out into the street, and seen the sky all red over the Turkish barracks. Then there had followed a terrible time, and he and many other boys had never seen their fathers again. We were then interrupted by the approach of George, the Statesman's Despair.

George, it appeared, had been in America for five years, ending in 1928. He had worked in Detroit and had made fifty dollars a week. He had had to come back to do his military service, and could not get readmitted to the United States. 'But I want plenty to go back,' he said, 'America fine country, nopoty outtawork, nopoty poor.' We suggested that he might find a difference if he went back now. 'No,' he said, 'you don't know Tetroit. Nopoty there poor, nopoty outtawork.' The man from Chicago began to scream at him and wave his arms. We had evidently stumbled into a dispute that had, I suppose, gone on in this dreary little town for years. He turned to us and shouted, 'I keep on tellin' this guy there's been a depression!' 'Nother thing,' continued George, 'there's no taxes in America. Nopoty heard of such a ting. No army, neither.' The man from Chicago held his head and groaned. My husband and I left them to it, and went off to gape at the Officers' Club which the Ataturk made the centre of his conspiracy. It is a white square house, which has a strange and fateful look because the big balcony that used to run across the first story has been taken away, and the brackets that once supported it project like gallows-heads, and the glass door that led on to it now opens on nothingness. Beside it a tumble-down house, that must have been a pretty villa in the great garrison days, lies strangled in its lilacs.

At the café we found Gerda eating bread and kaymak, which is a substitute for butter much nicer than sounds possible, made by boiling milk down to skin and compressing the skins. It was an innocent action, but she felt it ran counter to her pretensions of asceticism, and she explained, 'I would not be eating this as a rule, but when I saw Dragutin killing the snake I felt so upset that I had to have something to eat. Did that not strike you as a barbarous thing to do?' When she had finished we made a detour and left the Bitolj road to have a look at Lake Prespa, which nobody I know of has ever visited except Edward Lear of the limericks, who mildly penetrated to its shores so long ago as eighteen-fifty, in pursuit of subjects for his pretty and oddly sensible water-colours We came to it by a chain of villages where life must be ghastly in the winter winds and ghastlier still in the summer heat, but which were full of lively-eyed people. We stopped to laugh at two water buffaloes lying with consequential expressions in a stream too shallow for them while nimble boys and girls, all with skins of rose and gold and some with gentian eyes, splashed them with the water. Beyond marshes where storks and pelicans stood among tall white grasses, we found the lake. hyacinth-blue among mountains that were no colour at all, that were simply the colour of light which has met something hard and can go no further. It is as beautiful as Lake Ochrid, but not magical, not sacred. An authentic miracle is worked on the water at Sveti Naum.

On the far shores woods fell steeply to the water, and nearer they made a small green blur on the deep blue waters. 'On that island,' said Constantine, 'was the palace of the Bulgarian Emperor Samuel, he who had a mighty Balkan Empire in the tenth century, and was defeated by the Byzantine Emperor Basil known as the

Bulgar killer, though to modern ideas he did worse than kill. He took fifteen thousand Bulgarians captive, and all he blinded, save one in every hundred, to whom he left one eye, so that they might guide the rest home to their Emperor. And when he saw his army all blind he could no more, for he was a true emperor, though he was a Bulgarian, and he died.' 'Can we go to the island?' I asked. 'It is not fortunate,' said Constantine, 'there the frontiers of Greece and Albania and Yugoslavia all meet, and there are many soldiers all jealous of the honour of their countries and with nothing to do, and so they would shoot, and also there are on the island many enormous snakes.' So we walked about on a little headland high above the lake, where there were many flowering bushes and deep springy turf, and we breathed the unbreathed air and saw the untarnished light. 'Glory be to God!' said Dragutin, jumping up and down. 'It's as good as asphalt, this turf.' 'Listen,' said Constantine, 'he is in his soul a chauffeur, he speaks in chauffeur's images, he sees a chauffeur's world. It is like the play a Frenchman wrote, a play which was supposed to be written by a dog for dogs, and began with the direction, "*Le rideau se lève sur un os.*" ' 'And glory be to God!' cried Dragutin. 'These herbs smell good! Lie down and roll on it! That's the way to enjoy it!' So we all threw ourselves down and rolled; and a shepherd came by and watched us, nodding and smiling. 'Yes, it's good,' he said, 'but you ought to come here in July or August, it smells even better then.'

Bitolj I

We lingered so long beside the lake that we had to have lunch at Resan instead of going on to Bitolj. In this meagre little town we had a better lunch than I have ever been given in an English cathedral town, with good chicken soup, lamb and paprika stew, and excellent yoghourt. Because my husband and I were contented Gerda became flushed with anger, and began to complain to Constantine in Serbian. 'These people,' she said, 'haven't had the decency to ask me to go on to Petch. They'll expect you to go on with them, you're useful to them, and I can go home to Belgrade by myself, that's what they expect.' It was true that we had not asked her to go on to Petch. We had felt under no obligation to prolong the torment of the last fortnight, during which she had never expressed any emotion towards us milder than hatred. My husband and I strolled out of the restaurant into the street, and in a stationer's shop, where I bought a magenta tin pencil-sharpener that sharpens one side of a pencil better than any other I have ever possessed, he said, 'We must tell poor Constantine that we can go to Petch quite well without him. We cannot tolerate this any longer.' And when we got back to the automobile this was precisely what Constantine told us. 'I will give you introductions to a functionary I know there,' he said, 'and I will go home with my wife, I have been away for long enough.'

We mounted to a pass between bare mountains that as we approached was exactly spanned by a rainbow, and stopped on its height to see the deep bluebell line of Lake Prespa for the last time. Dragutin pointed to a purple cloud that dragged twisted veils across a grey-green sky, one cloud out of many such, and said, 'Thunder!' A minute later, in that very cloud, a sword flashed. He enjoyed the storm, singing a Wagnerian chant as he drove, but it ended in pelting rain, and we had to drive past fields of wild narcissus without picking any. He paused once to point out very respectfully a village where all the men went to America to work in automobile factories and then came back to buy land. 'Dodges they have made, and Buicks, and Chevrolets, yes, and Lincolns,' he said, his voice full of what Wordsworth described as natural piety. Then we followed the trough of a valley about which we all used to read in the last war; for Bitolj is Monastir. This valley and these mountains were occupied by German and Austrian troops, joining with their allies the Bulgarians in the East against the Greeks. Here innumerable men of all these armies were killed and died of wounds and fever; and to those who were spared Monastir and Macedonia are names standing quite simply for torture.

Yet Bitolj is one of the fairest of all cities. It lies at the valley mouth and spills out into wide plains, shading itself with poplar groves; and till full summer there are snow peaks to be seen beyond the plains. It is one of those cities which prove to our amazement that we Westerners have never even begun to understand what town-planning means. Thirty-five thousand people live in it, yet from every point of the compass it looks like a garden, and there is no part of it so congested or squalid that it would be unpleasant to live in it. The hovels here are hovels, but they are accidents, they mean that somebody has been unfortunate and lost his money or his wits. Its commercial quarter is delicious: two lines of neat shops like boxes run on each side of a little river in the shade of acacia avenues. There is no town I know where an open door more invariably discloses a sensuous and crafty garden; and the cats—I apply here a serious test of civilization—are plump and unapprehensive. The women, even the poorest shop-assistants, dress with simple elegance which would be respected by such dressmakers as Alix and Maggy Rouff, and the whole population is kind without intrusion. This was the Turkish capital of Macedonia, and there is visible an urban tradition of immense antiquity.

But I have a special reason for feeling tender towards Bitolj. It is the only place I have ever visited where the whole community rose to defend me. When I was here with Constantine we were walking down the new High Street, deep in conversation, when a miserable old Moslem woman, like all her kind veiled and swathed in black, tottered out of a doorway to beg of me. I gave her a two-dinar piece. We went back to the hotel and drank coffee; and when I came out a miserable old Moslem woman tottered forward to beg of me. I gave her a dinar. We then crossed the river into the old town and were bargaining with a Jewish dealer in embroideries when a miserable old Moslem woman tottered forward to beg of me. I gave her a two-dinar piece. I returned to the new town and was about to enter the hotel when a miserable old Moslem woman tottered forward to beg of me. I was about to give her a two-dinar piece when a large number of people rushed forward to stay my hand. Though I had had no idea that anybody was taking the slightest interest in my doings, much less following me, they were in a position to tell me that each time it had been the same old Moslem woman, and that to catch me a fourth time she had bargained with a cab-driver to take her the short drive across the bridge at the fee of half a dinar. This last touch seemed to the population to introduce a sordid element into the transaction which did their town no credit.

It was distressing that I could only repay the good-will by seeming to agree with them, although I have never liked a beggar so well as that spirited old lady, just as I have never liked a waiter so well as one in a café on the edge of the river who also would not have been approved by the public-spirited population of Bitolj. It was a small café, patronized only by young men who kept their hats on, pushed well down over their ears, while they drank coffee and played *moulin* with an air of cheating. It was inappropriately decorated by reproductions of Royal Academy pictures in which the courtiers of Louis XV were represented as perpetually testing their very tight white satin knee-breeches in the minuet. When Constantine put down a ten-dinar piece for our coffee, for which he should have been given eight dinars change, the waiter's hand flickered over it for an instant, and he said innocently, 'Funny thing, I thought there was a ten-dinar piece there. Did you pick it up again?' I suppose that if I had been looking at his hand I would have seen nothing, but I was staring past him at one of the Royal Academy pictures and the corner of my eye saw the coin run up his palm into the cuff. He was quite amiable when he was asked to send it down again.

Bitolj has, in fact, a great deal of that amusing rascally parasitism which is a part of the Arabian Nights atmosphere; and in the past it must have been an Arabian Nights city. There is a proof of the Turkish wealth the town held in the fabulously extravagant marble tombs that fill the Moslem graveyards with colossal wedding cakes; and there were then many very rich Greeks sitting by the fountains in their shady gardens, and some very rich Jews. But it suffered a great deal of material damage in the war, and still more some years later from an accidental explosion which accounted for many of the wrecked houses one can see all over the town. People who can see no good in Yugoslavia complain bitterly that she has ruined Bitolj by making Skoplje the administrative capital of the province; but it is hard to see how she could have been expected to keep as a capital a town that was only on a branch railway line and within a few miles of a frontier, when Skoplje was on a main line and nearly a hundred miles from the frontier. Still, Bitolj should have a future as a tourist centre, for when the acacias are out it is a fantastically lovely city, veiled in white flowers and sweet scent. There is a café on a hill-top outside the town which is in the centre of an acacia wood, and it is an exquisite pleasure to sit there on the evening of a hot day and watch the sunset discovering the fourteen minarets of the city and lengthening the poplar shadows on the plains.

Because of rich memories I was eager to go out and show my husband the sights of the town as soon as we had put our luggage in the hotel. But I was not sure that all was going to work well when I met Constantine in the corridor and he said, 'Yes, I think we must go out, we will go out with you. I will make my wife a pleasure by taking her to see the German war memorial.' The German war memorial at Bitolj is one of the most monstrous indecencies that has ever been perpetuated. They invaded Serbia and looted and burned their way through it and then planted themselves on these hills and murdered Macedonia with their guns, till they were beaten out by the superior merit of the Allies. It has seemed good to them to bury their dead on the top of a hill where their guns were mounted for the martyrdom of the city, and to build a wall round it which gives it the likeness of a fortress. Nothing could say more plainly that they have no regret for what they did there, and intend to come back and do it all over again as soon as they are given a chance. It is the only war cemetery I have ever seen that is offensive; and it is doubly offensive, for it insults both the country where it stands and the unhappy soldiers who are crammed pell-mell inside it, without a single record of their names or their regiments. There could be nothing more disagreeable than to accompany Gerda on a visit to this unfortunate symbol of her race, but there was no help for it, as at that moment she came out of her room and said, 'I am so glad that after all we are finding time to look at the poor dead soldiers from my country; I had thought that you would not give me that pleasure, and of course you must decide where we are to go, not I.'

When I got downstairs my husband had already got into the automobile and was sitting beside Dragutin, so I could not warn him where we were going. Ordinarily he would have been a sympathetic visitor to a German war memorial; from his earliest childhood his life had been divided between Germany and England, and there might well lie in one of the graves some boy he had known at kindergarten in Hamburg. But this is not an ordinary war memorial, and his reactions to it were as mine. When he got out of the automobile he looked up the steep hillside and exclaimed, 'But what's this?' I hastened to his side and said, 'The German war memorial.' He answered 'Nonsense! It's some sort of fortress.' I hurried him on in front of Constantine and Gerda, explaining the unfortunate outing to which we had been committed, and we reached the top some time before they did.

My husband gaped at the building, which is quite simply a high circular wall, entered by a slit of a door in a low squat tower. 'But it is nothing but a fortress dominating the town of Bitolj!' exclaimed my husband. 'And what an odd cemetery, because it is immensely massive yet so small that it can hold hardly any soldiers.' 'There are three thousand of them,' I said, 'packed into a small circle and covered with a kind of heath that was brought from Sweden, I do not know why.' 'Poor devils!' said my husband. We tried the door but it was shut. 'It does not matter,' I said, 'there is nothing there, only a black marble coffin, carved with the names and arms of the German states, standing just inside the door, and on the ceiling above it is a mosaic of an eagle with its wings outstretched.' 'But this is not at all German,' said my husband; 'think of the intense family feeling in German life, of the affection that is shown all over a German graveyard. But what is least pleasing is its insult to this country, for it makes a threat of return. Well, here they are, we shall say no more.'

We walked round the memorial, looking up at the snow mountains towards Lake Prespa, looking down at the deliberate loveliness of Bitolj, and when we had made the circuit we found Constantine and Gerda standing at the entrance. 'It is most beautiful,' she was saying, 'it is a most worthy memorial.' Then she turned to us and said, 'Why do you say nothing about it? You don't like it. I looked up from below and I saw you standing here and looking at it with your English coldness. I suppose you think it ridiculous that Germans should have a war cemetery, we ought to be buried like beasts.' 'No, no,' said my husband, 'we were only saying that we did not like it so well as that really beautiful German war cemetery outside Belgrade.' 'That we thought more beautiful than any we had ever seen in France,' I added. 'I was not speaking to you,' said Gerda, and turned back to my husband. 'And why do you not like this cemetery so well?' she cried. 'Why not?' 'Oh, God!' said my husband, suddenly despairing. 'I don't like it because it pays no sort of respect to the individuals who are buried in it and because it is a tactless reminder of the past to an invaded people.'

Gerda threw up her arms and shouted to the sky, 'Now he has insulted my people! He has insulted my whole people! It ought to be published in the newspapers that English people say such things, just to show what sort of people they are. But we Germans don't do such things, because we are too kind, and we want to be friends with England! But think of it, here I am, far from my home, and he insults my blood, the German blood!' Her face was crimson and she was weeping. Slowly and heavily she began to run down the hill. Below her a checker-board of green and crimson hills tilted towards the wooded mountains, on a straight road beside a winding river cattle and carts trod slowly among jets of sunlit mud, the well-bred town sat white under its red roofs among its shady gardens. We saw Dragutin, who was standing beside the car, look up, catch sight of her, and fold his arms, tilting his head on one side. Constantine breathed, 'The Germans are all like this. They are a terrible people.' My husband said, 'Nonsense, many Germans are not a bit like this,' and then, being an exceedingly polite man, stopped in great embarrassment, since what he had been going to say must obviously have been something like, 'Your wife is indeed terrible, but that's because she's herself, not because she's German.' Instead he said, 'I am very sorry that I have offended your wife.' Constantine said miserably, 'Oh, it is all right, everybody knows that you English cannot help being tactless,' and began to walk downhill, kicking the stones in front of him, like an unhappy child.

'Oh, why did you say it?' I complained, as wives should not, while we followed him. 'God knows I was making the most hideous faces at you.' 'I could not help it,' my husband said. 'I knew that she would go on and on insulting both of us till she got the truth out of me, so I let her have it. But how disgusting it all is! To create a scene over a war cemetery! Over a lot of dead boys! It is worse than the Bishop's feast.' 'It is all part of the same thing,' I said. 'Religion and death are not so important as being a German, nothing must exist except Germanity.' When we came to the foot of the hill, Dragutin was sitting at the wheel with a discreet expression and Gerda was walking round and round the automobile. My husband went up to her and said, 'I am sorry that I offended you,' but she flung away from him, crying, 'Do you suppose that words can heal the wound you have dealt me! How can you expect me to tolerate hearing the German people being called tactless?' She said to Dragutin, 'Open the door, I am going to sit beside you,' but paused to tell us, 'And this car in which you can hardly bear me to travel, you will be more comfortable in it henceforward, because I am going back to Belgrade. I cannot stay any longer with people who insult me and my people.'

Dragutin asked for no orders, and we were too shaken to realize that we had given him none. He drove us through the town to the ruins of Heracleia, the Roman city which lay a mile or so beyond it on the Via Egnatia, the Roman road that ran from the Adriatic through Albania to Salonika and Constantinople. Its excavations are at a stage that can interest only dogs and archaeologists, and my husband and I went and sat for a few minutes in the Orthodox cemetery, which straggles over the hillside near by. I have a deep attachment to this cemetery, for it was here that I realized Macedonia to be the bridge between our age and the past. I saw a peasant woman sitting on a grave under the trees with a dish of wheat and milk on her lap, the sunlight dappling the white kerchief on her head. Another peasant woman came by, who must have been from another village, for her dress was different. I think they were total strangers. They greeted each other, and the woman with the dish held it out to the new-comer and gave her a spoon, and she took some sups of it. To me it was an enchantment; for when St Monica came to Milan over fifteen hundred years ago, to be with her gifted and difficult son, St Augustine, she went to eat her food on the Christian graves and was hurt because the sexton reproved her for offering sups to other people on the same errand, as she had been wont to do in Africa. That protocol-loving saint, Ambrose, had forbidden the practice because it was too like picnicking for his type of mind. To see these women gently munching to the glory of God was like finding that I could walk into the past as into another room.

I had liked it, too, on that first visit, when our guide had looked over the plains towards the town and had said, 'Look, there's a funeral coming. But it's only someone old.' 'How can you tell that?' I had asked. 'There are so few people following the hearse, and they walk so slowly,' the guide explained. 'When somebody young dies then the whole town thinks it a pity and comes to the funeral. Look, here is the tomb of Anastasia Petrovitch. She was only twenty and you can see from the photograph on her cross how beautiful she was. Everybody in Bitolj turned out for her, the road from the town was still black with people when she had been carried into the chapel. But when old people die, it is natural, and nobody cares except a few other old people.' And presently the hearse and the procession arrived, and truly enough all the mourners were old. We went with them into the chapel and held lit tapers in its darkness and heard the unfalsified grief of the Orthodox Church office for the dead. 'What a parting is this, my brethren! What a lament is made of this happening! Come then, embrace him who is still for a little while with us. He is to be handed over to the grave, he is to be covered by stone, to dwell in the shadows, and to be buried with the dead. All of us, his kin and his friends, are to be separated from him. Let us pray the Lord to grant him rest.'

We saw Constantine coming along the woodland path, through

the leopard patches of shadow and sunlight. 'There is one thing,' I said to my husband, 'you were awful, unspeakably awful, not to have held your tongue by the German cemetery, but at least we have got rid of Gerda.' 'There you are wrong,' said my husband. 'I am not,' I said. 'Did you not hear her say that she would go to Belgrade tomorrow rather than stay with people who have insulted her?' 'I heard her,' said my husband, 'but she will not keep her word. Think of it, tomorrow we are going up Kaimakshalan, the mountain where the Serbs drove out the Bulgarians and won the decisive battle of the Eastern Campaign. It is evidently a pleasant expedition. She will certainly stay for it, and she will certainly be no more agreeable. But at Skoplje, if you and I have to get up in the middle of the night and go away in secret, this thing must end.' When Constantine got to us he was beaming. 'Now you will see that my wife is really a very sweet woman,' he said, 'she has said that to please you she wills that we all go now to the French war cemetery.' In embarrassment, therefore, we drove to what is one of the most affecting places in the world. It lies out on the plains among flat fields edged with willows and poplars, and it is a forest of flimsy little wooden crosses painted red, white and blue, each with a name or number, and each with its rose tree. It must have cost as little as such a cemetery could cost, and it must be a comfort to the kin of the dead to see that they lie so neatly and apart. There are seven thousand of them, and they have not yet stopped coming, for the shepherds still find skeletons up in the mountains and bring them down next time they go to market. Thus had Gérard Michel just returned to the plains after twenty-three years. He had been tied up in a linen bag, and it could not be believed how pitifully light he was in the hand. When we set him down in the little outhouse where he awaited a priest and the grave-digger and went out into the open air, that seemed now to smell more strongly of life than is commonly noticeable, the snow peaks were red in the sunset, and every cross had its long slanting shadow. 'Think,' said Gerda, as we looked on the wide field of graves, 'think of all these people dying for a lot of Slavs.'

Kaimakshalan

'Today we go to see where my people saved civilization,' said Constantine, halting at the table where we were breakfasting in the sun, three red roses in his hand, 'today we go to see where Serbia won the war for all you other peoples. I have been to buy a little flower for my wife, because she is very sweet this morning; she is in such a good humour that she has said she will stay today and go to Kaimakshalan with us.' When he had gone I said, 'We must make the best of it,' and my husband said, 'I wonder if there is anything we can do to rob the day of its horror.' 'There is,' I said, 'the hotel people say that they can only give us sucking-pig or lamb paprikasch for the picnic lunch, and she has told us she does not like either. Let us give her that glass of tongue we have been keeping for an emergency.' 'Yes, that looks a friendly offering,' said my husband, 'we will produce it on the picnic ground, for she may be embarrassed when we first meet.' In this he was wrong, for Gerda, when she came down, showed no sign of knowing that any unusual situation needed to be bridged.

Our drive took us over the plains, past earth-coloured villages and through lands cut into extraordinarily small divisions, mere tastes of fields, which were marked off by animals' skulls mounted on posts. We saw fifteen people ploughing on what looked to us to be no more than five acres of ground. Some nomads passed us, taking their herds of cattle and horses and sheep from the winter to the summer pastures. On one village green a party of gipsy women sat with their brilliant aprons thrown over their heads, silently rocking to and fro; some of their men, we were told, had been fetched up to the Town Hall for a breach of the law. Over the Greek border we saw villages of white square houses, shining like loaf sugar, built for the refugees the Turks drove out of Smyrna. We came at last to a little house, like any other village house, set on an insignificant little hill, which was the headquarters of King Peter and Prince Alexander during the Macedonian campaign. It has two rooms and a little garden full of irises. We walked uneasily about it, because the imagination can do nothing with what happened here. It is too strange. Here King Peter and Prince Alexander sat and looked at an amphitheatre of low hills before a wall of mountains and reflected that who took the peak called Kaimakshalan, which is to say the Buttertub, dominated the plains, and that it must be taken, though it could not be taken. Their performance of this impossible task puts them among the great men of the world; and the other event which came to pass in this cottage also puts them in some prodigious category, but it is not known what. The Salonika conspiracy proves that history has no authority, because there are secrets of the first importance that can be kept, and motives so complicated that they cannot be discovered by guess-work.

It was here that in 1917 Alexander ordered the arrest of a number of people, including 'Apis' (Dragutin Dimitriyevitch), and Tankositch and Tsiganovitch, the two minor members of the 'Black Hand' who gave Princip the arms for the Sarajevo *attentat*, and Mehmedbashitch, the Moslem boy who failed to throw his bomb at Franz Ferdinand and then rushed to the station and took train for Montenegro. They were charged with conspiring against Alexander's life. 'Apis' and the Black Handers were sentenced to death and shot; and Mehmedbashitch was condemned to twenty years' imprisonment. Not one soul in the length and breadth of the Balkans believes that they were guilty; and it is now an offence against the law for a private person to possess a report of the trial. It cannot be mentioned in a newspaper and would not be mentioned in a speech, and I have met intelligent young university graduates who had never heard of it.

The commonest explanation of this mystery is Byzantine in flavour. It is said that Alexander had lost heart and become convinced that he would have to sue for a separate peace from the Central European powers, and that he therefore wanted to be able to say, 'Yes, the people who conspired to assassinate Franz Ferdinand were shocking scoundrels, but they had nothing to do with me. In fact, they later tried to assassinate me also.' And if when he said this the conspirators were already dead or in prison, he would be saved the embarrassment of being asked by the Central European powers to hand them over, which he could not have done without alienating his people. This theory is supported by some words repeated to me by a German friend of mine as having been uttered some years ago by a Serbian in Berlin. This man, who was an ex-officer and had been for many years in exile, said to him, 'Yes, I would like to be back in Serbia, but "Apis" was my chief, and "Apis" warned me that I must fly at once, because they meant to kill all our group, and only "Apis" was going to stay, because he himself thought it would be for the good of our country if he died.' My German friend had no idea of the event to which these words referred, and had remembered them only for their odd Slav suicidal spirit. The complicity they attribute to 'Apis' is not at all incompatible with his character as we know it, dominated as it was by an obsession with violent death unleashing historical crises.

Yet that solution is not satisfactory. I have met a Moslem Herzegovinian, now middle-aged, who was an intimate friend of Mehmedbashitch, and he tells a story which compels belief that there were yet other elements controlling Alexander's action. He had a command in the Salonika campaign, and one day after the trial he received a smuggled letter from Mehmedbashitch asking him to go and see him in a Serbian prison on a Greek island. He contrived a visit to him and found the boy in a pitiable state of anguish and bewilderment. He had been arrested in France, and before he went back to Greece the French had treated him not only as if he were guilty of a serious crime, but had made repeated efforts to compel him to confess something, he did not know what. Now, it is obvious that the French cannot have been sympathetic accomplices in a scheme by which the Serbian royal family was attempting to make a separate peace. Nor can the Serbian authorities, who knew that the charge which was going to be made against Mehmedbashitch was false, have pressed the French to obtain a confession from him. But the mystery did not stop there. Now that the Serbian authorities had had him tried and sentenced for conspiracy to murder Alexander, he was still being asked to confess to something. The Herzegovinian had no doubt that Mehmedbashitch was not only innocent of conspiracy to murder, but was also ignorant of the matter, whatever it was, to which he was expected to confess. He was a worthy but unimpressive youth of no importance, in whom people in charge of dangerous enterprises would be most unlikely to confide. When the Herzegovinian returned to the front he went to Alexander and told him that in his opinion Mehmedbashitch was being badly and foolishly treated. He did this without fear, because he had a record of honourable service to the Serbian cause. It is odd that a monarch should be suspected of putting his subjects to death and imprisoning them on false charges, and at the same time should be trusted to respect a young officer who had shown fidelity to the national ideal. Alexander listened to him intently and then put to him a series of questions which he found completely incomprehensible. 'I am sure he had something in his mind,' he said, 'but I have no idea what it was, and he was very unhappy about it; he was desperate and very angry.' A short time afterwards, and apparently in consequence of this conversation, Mehmedbashitch was released, and is still living in Sarajevo, a carpenter with a marked disinclination to discuss politics.

There is no hypothesis that fits these facts into a recognizable pattern. Sometimes it seems to me possible that they relate to a story of which rumours are heard, though now only faintly, in Sarajevo. There were obviously two crimes committed against Franz Ferdinand: one active, by Princip and his associates, one passive, by the royal guards who did not guard. It is said that yet a third had been prepared, and that there were people in Sarajevo on that St. Vitus's Day who had expected the guilt to be theirs. Nobody will state quite clearly who is supposed to have inspired these people, but the guess would be that it was an Austrian influence too malignant to remain passive. It might be that this is correct, but that there had also been involved as cat's-paw some indiscreet foreign personage, capable of being tempted to this rashness by an ambition that had been inflamed by frustration. If the assassination should turn out to have fruitful consequences he might have made a bid for power which, backed by the army, might have come near to success. This is simply guess-work. But it has the recommendation of explaining why Alexander should feel an intense interest in the crime of Sarajevo long after it had been an accomplished fact. It must be remembered that Alexander, like the rest of the world, had never seen the records of the trial and therefore would not be aware that Mehmedbashitch was a mediocrity with the most tenuous connexion with the crime. This makes the mystery more impenetrable by historic method, for Alexander was probably working on totally false clues. He was also one of the most secretive men that ever filled high places. Among the purple irises I thought of the long shelves of university libraries, their striation under lofty vaults, the reflected light that shines from historians' spectacles, and I laughed.

Thereafter our road ran up into the mountains, where the Black Drin, a river which many British and French soldiers will recall with loathing, tumbles between bouldered hills. Then grass banks, studded with cowslips, rose to beechwoods, and later we came to firwoods carpeted with yellow pansies, violets, and very large forget-me-nots. These flowers gave one less pleasure than we could have believed because of Gerda's effort to discover why Kaimakshalan was famous. Constantine explained that the Germans and Bulgarians had held the mountain, and had fortified it with heavy artillery and machine-guns, and that the Serbians had climbed up the mountains and taken the fortifications. 'But,' objected Gerda, 'if the Germans and the Bulgarians were up there with machine-guns, why did they let you Serbians get up there?' Constantine said, 'Well, that is just the point, they couldn't prevent us.' She asked, 'But how did you get up?' He answered, 'We climbed up, we walked up.' 'Nonsense,' she said, 'a man cannot climb up a mountain where people are shooting machine-guns down on him.' Constantine answered—and it sounds so well in German that I will leave it in that tongue—'*So dachten die Deutschen und so dachten die Bulgaren, aber so dachten nicht der König Alexander und die Serben!*'

After a pause Gerda asked, 'Were there mostly Germans here or mostly Bulgarians?' He answered, 'Mostly Bulgarians.' 'Ah, now I understand!' she explained exultantly. 'That explains it all. It was treachery. The Bulgarians betrayed the Germans to you Serbs.' 'I think it was not so,' said Constantine wearily, 'the Bulgarians hated us then and for long after.' 'Nonsense!' said Gerda. 'You were all Slavs, you would combine against our German blood. It was treachery. The Bulgarians betrayed the Germans to you. Of course people could not climb up a mountain if other people were shooting down on them, and the answer simply is that they did not shoot. But in any case, how did the Serbs come to be here? I thought they had been driven out through Albania to the sea. How did they manage to get back here again?' 'They came through Greece,' Constantine replied. 'Oh, through Greece, did they!' creid Gerda. 'And yet you dare complain of the Germans for going through Belgium into France!' 'But Belgium was neutral and Greece was our ally!' squealed Constantine. 'I suppose to you and the English that makes a great difference,' said Gerda ironically.

But now the high mountains took us into their peace. We left the automobile on the bare highlands just below the snow, where there was a village of chalets, sightless with their shuttered windows. The nomads who come here in the summer and make cheese had not yet dared come up, so late was the spring. We trod on turf drab with the long hardship of ill weather, but starred with the hard blue light of glory-of-the-snow and the effete mauve flame of the mountain crocus, and looked up at the long ridge of snow, five miles long, that is furrowed by a pilgrim's way to the church on the high peak. There could be no question of going there without proper climbing boots, but we followed the track as far as we could go, the crystal air making us all happy. Gerda became contented, and was pleasant to Constantine. We glacised down a slope and found a boulder surrounded by a sudden affluence of pansies growing sheer from the surrounding snow, and sat on it, staring down at the battlefield that tilted forward to the plains, seamed with deep valleys sunk in firwoods. The joy of the mountains is real, because it is of the blood and the muscles, where life has its ultimate stand,

and yet it is false. Everything that I saw or heard as I sat on the boulder pleased me, yet the battlefield below me proved that I had been born into an age too uncertain about fundamental ideas for continued existence to be easy.

Yes, the proof was there. Surely there are certain things about a battlefield which can be taken for granted by everybody; the first being that if men fought well there for a worthy object they proved themselves valuable human beings. How can it not be so? There are objects which are worth fighting for: the fate of the Slavs under the Turks proved it once and for all. That non-resistance paralyses the aggressor is a lie: otherwise the Jews of Germany would all be very well today. A race that has not good soldiers must be enslaved by any neighbouring race that has them: a race that has not the soldierly characteristics of courage and discipline cannot in later ages refuse to fight unnecessary wars and insist on proceeding with the work of civilization. If ever peace is to be imposed on the world it will only be because a large number of men who could have taken part in the drill display by the Guards or Marines or at the Royal Tournament turn that strength and precision to the service of life.

This I believe to be true, in spite of the obvious defects of many professional soldiers, which afflict them surely not because they are soldiers, but because they are professional. It is doubtful whether army officers of high rank are more limited or unsound in their general ideas than lawyers or doctors of an equivalent degree of specialization. It is in any case unlikely that a soldier would hold as silly ideas about any sphere of civilian activity as vast numbers of civilians would hold about this battlefield. To countless thousands, even millions of people in England and America, the slopes of Kaimakshalan would have no meaning whatsoever except as a place where a lot of people had perished ingloriously, as they might have in a railway accident, because they were stupid enough to get mixed up in a fight. Many Americans, owing to their inexperience of aggression, sincerely believe that all wars are planned by armament manufacturers and that no people ever suffers any real maltreatment at the hands of another. They would not credit the simple fact that the Germans and Austrians and Bulgarians had invaded Serbia with the intention of murdering the inhabitants and seizing their property. Not having been educated to accept the possibility of such an act by the contemplation of a large area where the Turks had certainly done this very thing to the Balkans, and had gone on doing it for five centuries, they feel that this must be a fable

spread by Vickers or Skoda. There has also been in America a wave
of cynicism, entirely mindless, destitute of all content, save 'Oh,
yeah' and 'So what,' which, by a strange twist, results in a bland
acceptance of the whole universe that has never been surpassed by
Christian Scientists. An automatic scepticism regarding stories of
atrocities leads to a rosy belief that every member of an invading
army behaves with the courtesy of a cinema theatre usher. The
Serbs must have been mistaken in believing that the Germans
and the Austrians passed through village after village, wrecking
houses, smashing the furniture, emptying corn and pouring wine
and oil into the mud, and trampling on the icons. Any peasant in
the invaded countries over thirty can tell you that it was so, but
innumerable Americans, over and under thirty, can tell you that it
was not so. This battlefield was therefore to them an area of pure
nonsense, discreditable to the human race.

And so it is to some extent to many English intellectuals. If the
Serbs had done something . . . something . . . something, they
need not have fought. So one feels, when one is young, on hearing
that a friend has to have a dangerous operation for cancer. Surely if
she had not eaten meat, if she had not eaten salt, she need not have
had cancer; and by inference one need not have cancer oneself. Yet
cancer exists, and has a thousand ways of establishing itself in the
body; and there is no end to the ways one country may make life
intolerable for another. But let us not think of it any more, let
us pretend that operations are unnecessary, let every battlefield
seem a place of prodigious idiocy. Of this battlefield, indeed, we
need never think, for it is so far away. What is Kaimakshalan? A
mountain in Macedonia, but where is Macedonia since the Peace
Treaty? This part of it is called South Serbia. And where is that,
in Czechoslovakia, or in Bulgaria? And what has happened there?
The answer is too long, as long indeed, as this book, which hardly
anybody will read by reason of its length. Here is the calamity of our
modern life, we cannot know all the things which it is necessary for
our survival that we should know. This battlefield is deprived of its
essence in the minds of men, because of their fears and ignorances;
it cannot even establish itself as a fact, because it is crowded out
by a plethora of facts.

Dragutin followed us up the track, making as he went little
posies for Gerda and myself. 'I feel a fool in this holy place,' he
said, 'because I was too young to be in the war.' 'Yes, indeed, the
place is holy,' said Constantine. 'If we could only bring a thousand
Croats up here and show them how liberty is won.' 'Yes, yes,' said
Dragutin, bursting into laughter, 'show them how liberty is won,

and then hang the lot of them.' He meant the Croats no actual harm; nothing would have been further from his mind than that he would offer any physical violence to a Croat, but such was his lively and telling way of referring to the political differences that rive Yugoslavia. 'But you can't sit up here all day,' he said, 'holy place or not, I have driven you enough to know that that won't do for you instead of your dinner.'

We ate at a tourist hut ten miles or so down the mountainside, very Swiss among the pinewoods, save for the soldiers' graves in a clearing across the road. Two young soldiers who were in charge of the hut came out and set up a trestle table for us, and I laid out the food. Gerda did not help, and I thought this was because she was happy sitting in the sunshine that came through the cold air all light and no heat, a bodiless excitement. But she was still in the grip of her obscure misery, and when we gave her the tongue she asked grimly, 'What is this?' Weakly I explained, 'We thought you might like this, as you said you cannot eat sucking-pig and paprikasch.' To this she answered, 'It is not that I cannot eat sucking-pig and paprikasch, but I do not see why I should eat them all the time.' She then drew the tongue towards her and cut herself a helping without reluctance. Because my husband held the plate steady for her, her face crumpled up with racial hatred too irrational to find words.

On the step of the automobile Dragutin sat and ate his lunch between the two young soldiers, who had the dutiful and dedicated look I have noticed so often in Yugoslav conscripts. His lunch was, as always, ascetic and chosen in accordance with the principles of sympathetic magic: he liked lean meat and rough black bread and paprika, and he regarded as weakening all soft and slippery things like butter and kaymak and sardines. 'Hey, did you ever hear the like of this!' he called to us. 'These two say that they know it is a great honour to be the guardians of Kaymakchalan, and they are content in the daytime, but it's terrible in the night, because they hear the dead soldiers calling for their mothers.' 'What do they say?' asked Constantine. 'They say, "*Yao matke! Yao matke!*"' one young soldier told us. The words mean Alas, mother! 'And of course the others, the Germans and the Bulgarians, say it in their own languages,' added the other. They both shuddered and went on eating with the solemnity of young calves at a haybox.

I had always wondered whether people who have a primitive attitude towards fighting, who regard it as a necessary and noble activity, were perhaps spared the full realization of the piteousness of death in battle. Now I knew, and life was by so much the more disagreeable; and I had a further testimony to the fatuousness of such pacifism as points out the unpleasantness of war as if people had never noticed it before. I regretted the amateurishness of much in modern thought, but realized that this was only proof of the recalcitrance of the material on which thought must work. On my journey home I felt unequal to sharing the vision of Dragutin which constantly pierced to the primordial disharmony of life which I would have liked to forget. Driving down through the colourless yet radiant hills he came to a stop that we might see in the sky above us an angry monogram which was an eagle fighting with a stork. Later we got out and drank from a spring that leaped out of a rock to join the Black Drin, and Dragutin shot out a finger at an emerald lizard a foot long that leaped through the grass between my feet. 'It is poisonous,' said Dragutin. 'It is not,' said Constantine, but I knew he was only being patriotic. Back in my seat, I fled from this dangerous universe into sleep.

I woke and found that the automobile had broken down beside a fountain, and that Dragutin was tinkering with the engine under the appreciative eyes of three superb women in magnificently embroidered robes, each of whom was carrying a blue-enamelled tin jug with queenly grace. The lot of all the beautiful women who go down to the waters in romantic lands has been irradiated as by sunshine at the passing of the amphora and the coming of enamelware. Dimly I heard Dragutin tell them that the car had broken down because we had passed a priest riding on a donkey, and the queens splutter into laughter. I slept again, and when I woke we were near the outskirts of Bitolj, and I looked across a patch of grass to a little house that stood in a vineyard, with a porch of vine-clad poles, and a flimsy iron balcony under its upper windows. 'Stop the car!' I said. 'Stop the car!'

I had reason; for on the balcony stood a man dressed in shining grey garments who was announcing his intention to address the plains by a gesture of supreme authority. The proud stance of his body showed that he had dug the truth out of the earth where it lay under the roots of the rock. The force of his right arm showed that he had drawn fire from heaven, so that he might weld this truth into our life, which thus shall not perish with our bodies. The long shadows lay bound to the plains, the mountains' bleakness was explored by the harsh horizontal beams of the falling sun; they, and the men and beasts who laboured on them to no clear purpose, would know their deliverance so soon as they had heard him. Near by there squatted on the grass beside the roadside two wretched veiled women, faceless bundles of dust-coloured rags, probably Moslem divorced wives of the sort, more pitiable than the beggars of the towns, who hang about the fields and stretch out their hands to the peasants. It seemed as if they must spring up and throw aside their veils never to beg again as soon as he had spoken.

But he would never speak. He was a scarecrow dressed in rags which had been plastered in mud to give them solidity against the winter, and he had been stored on the balcony till it was time to put him out among the fruiting vines. His authority was an exhalation from a bundle of straw, as the murmured promise of salvation from the Roumanian gipsy in the central square of Belgrade had been an exhalation from the action of alcohol on her tissues. The soul can be uplifted, it can be seduced into seeing an end to its misery and believing that all has been planned for its good from the beginning, by a chance concatenation of matter that in fact means nothing and explains nothing, that is simply itself. So potent was the argument of the scarecrow to the eye that it made for incredulity regarding all other exaltations. It might be that the Mozart symphony which had issued what I had taken to be a proof of beauty from the restaurant radio on the Frushka Gora was not in a different category from the scarecrow's gesture and the gipsy's promise, but only at the other end of the scale, and that it proved nothing save that flesh has a wider range than straw, and that there is a subtler drunkenness than comes of wine.

Bitolj II

The scarecrow was a true citizen of Bitolj, for the town constantly
presents pictures so strange that the mind can take them only as
symbols, though they never disclose their significance. As the
dusk fell we went out for a stroll under the acacia trees by the
river, and looked into the shops, which were little bright caves
in the darkness. At the great mosque, whose swelling cupola and
towering minaret and lovely plaster decoration speak of delicacy
and power, of a clean hand holding a sword, we stared through
a wrought iron gate and saw a procession of grave and beautiful
elderly men passing under the acacias to the porch, their fezes
shining as crowns of mystery because the evening glow caught
the white bands which betokened them to be Moslem priests.
We were halted by the second and really affecting German war
memorial: a carillon in an old tower which twice a day rings out
'*Ich hatt' einen Kameraden, einen bessern findst du nicht,*' evoking
pictures of golden-haired boys dying thirsty and fevered in this
land which is cruel even for the hardy brown amongst us. We
hung behind a Jew of the tall hawk-like kind and his wife who
wore a close cap rimmed with gold sequins and a purple gown of
seventeenth-century Spanish fashion; and we saw them go softly,
murmuring Spanish, into a home refined almost to decadence in its
contempt for the exuberant and its concentration on propriety. We
left this peepshow only because we had risen early and were to rise
early again, and on the way home a final emblem and mystery was
disclosed to us and not explained. The sound of passionate speech
made us look through a doorway, and there in a warehouse, with
sacks of grain lying on the floor and ropes hanging down in loops
from the rafters, under an oil-lamp stuck in the wall, a man leaned
on a broken column of classical appearance, entirely inappropriate
to the place, and addressed three men as if he were preaching them
a gospel. They looked at him with grave and pursuivant anxiety,
for each word he spoke was taking him farther away from them.
One man began to stir uneasily, and it could not be told whether
he was going to surrender to the speaker and throw himself at his
feet, or rebel against him and strike him. But as we watched our
attention was distracted by the rhythm of a sleeper's breathing,
close at hand. We looked about and found that a man in peasant
dress with a mountaineer's round fur cap was standing just beside

us, leaning against the hinged frame of the door, fast asleep. He was a giant, perhaps seven feet tall.

The day gave us other mysteries, though of a more prosaic sort. As we had motored into the town from Resan I had seen a tumbledown mosque with some very elaborate tombs in white marble carved in the Moslem Regency style which I find so enchanting and so surprising; and we went there in the early morning to take some photographs. For half an hour or so we scrambled over the rough ground and through the long grasses, among tombs which, if they were mere columns, were leaning drunkenly to right or left, and if they were solid erections were burst asunder by bushes which, like the poppies and cornflowers beside them, derived rich colour and profligate growth from the uncoffined dead. The monuments were well worth a film or two. They had apparently been produced by a pastrycook under the influence of Persian art. Such sugary little scrolls and swags, such sissy little flowers in pots, such coy little etchings of swords on the soldiers' tombs, so much valid accomplishment lavished on invalid objects. There is here a double paradox. This is so odd a form of art to have sprung up among a military people, and so odd a form of art to be treated with such wild negligence. When an elderly lady makes an exquisitely hem-stitched handkerchief or a beautifully embroidered baby's gown it is not suffered by her or those to whom she gives them that they should go into the rag-bag; and even less is this the case when it is not a female but an ephebe who is responsible for the craftsmanship. Yet it seems to be no protection whatsoever to an object in Moslem possession that it precisely accords with Moslem taste.

But this was not the only paradox to be detected at this mosque. Two veiled women came out of the mosque to see what we were doing, bundles of dusty blackness, who were caretakers, with the difference that it was evidently not expected that they were to take any care of the place. They took us in to see it, and it was inside as it was outside. I think that nowhere in England or America would there be a plot of ground so disordered as this graveyard, unless it were the garden of a home inhabited by a lunatic; and the mosque itself was used as a store by the peasants who farmed the neighbouring land. They had piled hurdles and coops and hoes between several wooden tombs which must have belonged to men of great eminence, for they were painted green, which is the Prophet's colour, and were surmounted by little globes on which there hung rotting kerchiefs which had originally been laid there by pious hands. The plaster had fallen from the walls in thick scabs, but had left two frescoes intact, one a landscape of ochre palaces among blue trees, another a whimsey of bluish curtains caught back with rose-coloured bows that might have been the work of any Madison Avenue decorator. As we looked at them the plank cracked under my feet, and there was a sickening turmoil below. From a hole in the floor on the other side of the room a rat scurried to the open, holding a nameless white object in its mouth.

It seemed incredible that in a city full of Moslems half a dozen pious workmen should not have joined together to put in order a place that had obviously been a centre of worship for many honourable families; and the place seemed to imply the decadence of a pithless people until we went out, and saw through an open door the home of the caretakers which was formed by partitioning off a space from the porch of the mosque. It was impossible to imagine a room that spoke more clearly of an established civilization, a society which took it for granted that to live in cleanliness and order is agreeable. The bare boards were ferociously clean, along the wall a bench made of old packing-cases was covered with cushions of hues chosen by an educated taste, and on the walls were pieces of rugs which, though they were stitched and faded, at least alluded to the finest aesthetic traditions of the East. On a little inlaid table stood a brightly polished ceremonial coffee-set and a little loom, where a fine linen towel was being woven in an exquisite design. 'Good God,' said my husband, 'one can never be sure of anything in this country.'

It was market day. When we got back to Bitolj peasants from the mountains and the plains were sitting on the low walls that edge the river embankments, facing the shops, with their goods in little heaps at their feet. First of all the men sit in a line, with bundles of onions and garlic and baskets of early strawberries and tangled masses of hens tied together; and then the women sit with their lesser goods before them, basins of eggs and little handfuls of spinach and clusters of dark-red paprika, the sunshine pouring through the acacia branches and lying in bright diamonds on the white kerchiefs they wear on their heads. The goods brought by some of the women are so trifling that it can hardly be doubted they come to market not so much for commerce as for gossip, which is as animated here as it was in Sarajevo. When my husband photographed some of them and got involved with a donkey which poked its head over his shoulder, they all laughed and joked with us, quick in speaking and in taking up other speakers' points.

While we were playing with a goat and its kid a man in an offensive suit came up and asked us in American what on earth we were doing in such an uninteresting town as Bitolj. He himself was a Macedonian, but he had early emigrated to Toronto, and was a shoemaker there, and had come back just for a holiday, and he thought this a Godorful place. We spoke to him of America, but after the fashion of his kind he knew nothing of it except cheap automobiles, road-houses, and radios. It cannot be too firmly stated that the average man who emigrates from one of the more primitive countries to America is lost to European civilization without being gained by American civilization. The subsequent generations he begets may acclimatize themselves to the new tradition, but the state of vacuity in the mind of the man who actually makes the transition cannot be exaggerated. He is removed from the economic Hell with which Europe punishes the people who perform the function most necessary to its survival and grow its food for it, and he is lifted to what is for him the economic paradise with which America rewards the people who help it to get into debt by making unnecessary manufactured goods. Therefore his primary needs are so astonishingly well satisfied that he believes himself contented; but he forgets everything that his own people have learned about birth and love and death. This would have happened to him just the same, of course, if he had emigrated to any really big city in Europe which was thoroughly remote from his tradition; but he is much more likely to go to America.

The state of idiocy which this transition had induced in this particular man can be judged from the fact that he winked at us, jerked his thumb over his shoulder, and said, 'Going to the Paris Exhibition, hey?' To get away from him we left the cattle market, and joined a small crowd centred round two men sitting at a table, who were all looking at a white pack-horse that was being led up and down. 'I think this is the market where they sell the goods of the peasants who cannot pay their taxes,' said Constantine. 'If that is so, let us buy the white horse and give it back to its owner,' said my husband. Constantine danced with joy. If he had been left a fortune he could not have been more pleased. 'Do you mean it?' he asked. 'Do you really mean it?' 'Yes, I think it would be an agreeable thing to do,' said my husband.

Constantine bounced through the crowd, crying to the officials, 'Stop! Stop!' as if he had ridden with Dirck and Joris from Ghent. He gave something to the occasion quite beyond our power. The officials acted up to him and received the news with great pleasure, and when they had ascertained that it would cost my husband three hundred dinars, which is about six dollars, and made sure that he would go to this outlay, they announced the news to the people round them, who behaved like a stage crowd, turning to each other and making gestures of surprise. The main person concerned turned out not to be there. The owner of the horse, his friends assured us, was running round Bitolj trying to find a moneylender who would let him have the money without security. But the details of the gift were not settled quickly, for the officials had to draw up a deed of gift, by which my husband returned the horse to the owner, and before he had signed it there was a scuffle at the back of the crowd and the people near me said, 'Here he is! Here he is!' I turned and saw a bearded man wearing a round fur cap and tawny homespuns, but I thought they must be mistaken, for he was showing no signs of pleasure, and was indeed baring his teeth in fury and lifting a club as if to strike a little group of people who had just been assuring us that they were the owner's friends.

'That cannot be he,' I said, but a fattish young man in a saxe-blue sweater answered, 'Indeed it is, but he does not yet understand. Are you Americans?' 'No,' I said, 'we are English.' 'English or American, you have done a good deed,' he said sententiously, 'but I hoped you were Americans, for I love America very much.' 'So do I,' I said. 'Are you going back soon?' 'No,' he answered; 'when I was in America I made a big mistake. All my people here have been smugglers, father and son. Before the war we were smugglers at Riyeka on the borders of Montenegro and Turkey, and since the war here in Bitolj, for the Greek frontier is very close. So when I went to America I thought that smuggling was there as it is with us, wrong but not very wrong, and I used to take liquor in over the Canadian border on a truck, and I did not think nothing of it. Then one day there was a bit of shooting and I was sent up for a stretch. But what I do not like is that afterwards I was deported. It is terrible,' he said, as if he were singing a folk-song, 'to be deported by a country which you love.' He became scarlet, his eyes filled with tears. I found myself saying sympathetically, 'Never mind, never mind, lots of my friends have been deported,' though this is not true.

Gulping down his sorrow, the young man said, 'But here is the owner of the horse; now he understands what you have done, and he wishes to thank you.' 'But what did he think at first that we had done?' 'When you looked at him before,' explained the young man, 'he was saying to his friends that they had done ill by him in letting you buy the horse, for anybody could see from the clothes of you and your husband that you would want an excessive rate of interest for the money you had lent him. He took your husband for a kind of moneylender we have here who have no homes and grow exceedingly rich by travelling from market to market and getting peasants into their power. He meant no harm. It is a mistake that anybody might have made.' My husband said sadly, 'We have been taken for itinerant moneylenders, my dear, and you have committed yourself to the curious statement that many of your friends have been deported from the United States. I think it is perhaps time that we left this town.' But now the owner of the horse was standing in front of us, wringing my husband's hand and sputtering gratitude out of a mouth full of long white wolfish teeth. 'But what is he talking?' asked my husband. 'Surely it is not Serbian. Perhaps he is a Greek.' 'No, he is not talking Greek,' I said, 'he is talking tough baby. Listen.' 'Gee, I am really grateful to you,' he was saying. 'This will bring me luck, it sure will, and I'll say it ought to bring you luck too. Now won't you let me treat you to jus' a little whisky? No? Not just a shot?' At my elbow the shoemaker from Toronto had appeared. 'Is it true that you have bought this man's horse back for him?' he asked. 'For crying out loud, why did you do it? Why did you do it?'

When we had left the crowd, no single member of which asked us for money, though it was proved that we had enough to be generous and some of them had probably not enough to eat, we went back towards the town and came by chance on a little street where a number of women, and women only, were sitting on the kerb. 'They are selling dresses,' I said with delight, and so they were: new dresses for such peasant women as had come into the town to work and had neither the homespun cloth nor the leisure to make their own clothes and were still shy of Western attire, and old clothes that had such fine embroidery on them that they would be worn again. All these dresses were of the standard Slav pattern. They were made of white or cream homespun linen and were embroidered lavishly on the hems and sleeves and more sparingly around the neck. Nearly all of these were serious works of art. That will not be believed by those who know only the commercial peasant art of Central Europe. The cross-stitched blouse of Austria and Hungary is tatty and ill-bred, rightly regarded by the aristocrat and the highbrow as vulgar and by the proletarian as funny. It fails because the themes of peasant art are so profound and its technique so intricate that it requires a deliberation hardly to be found elsewhere than in peasant life or in the sphere of scholarly and dedicated people not in the least likely to make blouses. Women distracted by the incoherent interests of the modern town, or working at the rate necessary to make a living anywhere in the orbit of a modern town, will not have the experience to form the judgements about life which lie behind most of these embroideries, nor the time to practise the stitches and discover the principles of form and colour which make them strike the eye with the unity of flowers. A precisely similar process of degeneration can be seen in Tin Pan Alley, where the themes that are dealt with by folk-song and by the lyric poets are swallowed by shallow people in a hurry and immediately regurgitated in a repulsive condition.

But these old women, who looked at once hearty and tragic, who were able to grin broadly because early and profuse weeping had made their faces unusually mobile, were dealing in uncorrupted merchandise. All the embroidery had a meaning. The first I picked up had a gay little border to its hem, a line of suns with rays, half an inch across, with trees in between them and stars dancing above them. The suns had black centres and rays, and their circumferences were alternately orange and green, and the trees were alternately green and blue, and the stars were green and blue and brown. The design stood on a black line of stitching, under which were two broken lines of stitches in all these colours, and then there was a corded edge oversewn with buttonhole stitches in black, deep blue, light blue, crimson, green, and purple, with the black predominating so that there was an effect of darkness stirring with the colours of creation. But the little suns and trees and stars would not take creation too seriously, it was as if fun was being poked at it. This significance was no fancy of our own, for the woman who sold it to me and her friends smiled as they spread it out for us, and looked grave as they showed us one that was my second choice. On this some woman with a different temperament had given up her mind to thought of the majestic persistence of nature and its untender character, and had fixed on the linen a number of dark upright trees, breaking into aloof flowers, harbouring indifferent birds. The design was so highly stylized as never to tempt the eye to mere gaping by its representation of fact; it refused to let the trees be more than the symbols of a mood.

I found yet another design that was purely abstract. Bars and squares of black with raised designs and touches of purple in the solid background depicted no natural object whatsoever, yet evoked certain exaltations. It appears doubtful whether Tolstoy ever saw a peasant. In the imbecile work *What Is Art?* he asserts that peasants appreciate only pictures which inculcate a moral lesson, such as, for example, a picture of a woman giving food to a beggar boy, and that only a person perverted by luxury can care for art which was created without a specific didactic aim. If he had put his head out of his window and looked at his own village, he would have seen—for embroidery of this kind is done, with varying degrees of merit, all the way up Eastern Europe from the Black Sea to the Baltic—that peasants, more than any other class in the modern community, persistently produce and appreciate art which is simply the presentation of pleasing forms. It was not improbably because Tolstoy was a bad man that he wished art to do nothing but tell him how to be good, and perhaps these peasant women can permit themselves their free and undidactic art because their moral lives are firmly rooted. They had been trodden into the dust by the Turks, condemned to hunger for food and to thirst for blood, but they had never forgotten the idea of magnificence, which is a valuable moral idea, for it implies that the duty of man is to make a superfluity beyond that which satisfies his animal needs and turn it to splendid uses. I bought here a wedding dress perhaps twenty or thirty years old. It was a composite of eight garments, a fine chemise, a linen dress embroidered round the hem and sleeves till it was almost too heavy to be worn, a purple velvet waistcoat braided with silver, a sequin plastron to be worn over the womb as a feminine equivalent to a cod-piece, and a gauze veil embroidered in purple and gold. It was a memory of Byzantium and the Serbian Empire; solemnly it put sequins where the emperors and empresses had worn precious stones, it made of its wool and its flax and what it could buy from the pedlar something that dazzled the eyes a little as the Byzantine brocades had dazzled them much. Even so in the folk-songs of these parts do they sing with nostalgia of gold and silver, not as wealth, not as mintable material, but as glory to be used for shining ornament.

That they should remember glory, after they had been condemned for so long to be inglorious, is not to be taken for granted, as an achievement within the power of any in their place. A tradition is not a material entity that can survive apart from any human agency. It can live only by a people's power to grasp its structure, and to answer to the warmth of its fires. The Churches of Asia became extinct not because Islam threatened them with its sword, but because they were not philosophers enough to be interested in its doctrine nor lovers enough to be infatuated with the lovable throughout long centuries and in isolation. But these Macedonians had liked to love as they had been taught by the apostles who had come to them from Byzantium, they had liked the lesson taught by the emperors that to wear purple and fine linen encourages human beings to differentiate themselves in all ways from the beasts, they had liked, even inordinately, the habit taught them by Byzantine art of examining life as they lived it and inquiring into their destiny as it overtook them; and since they had still their needles they turned to and managed to compress those strong likings into these small reflective and hieratic designs.

The old women were pleased at our enthusiasm. They are of course not fully conscious of the part their embroideries play in the preservation of their ancient culture: when an Englishwoman plays a sonata by Purcell she is not likely to feel that she is maintaining English musical tradition. Yet these women are certainly aware that they are about some special business when they sew. I am told by an Englishwoman who has collected such embroideries for twenty years and knows their makers well that it is an esoteric craft, those who are expert in it do not give away their mystery. Many of the themes which often reappear in the designs have names and symbolic meanings which are not confided to strangers, and a woman will sometimes refuse to discuss the embroidery she has worked on a garment made for her own use. When they marry they make caps for their bridegrooms and about these they are always resolutely reserved. Here is, indeed, another proof of the impossibility of history. There cannot be taken an inventory of time's contents when some among the most precious are locked away in inaccessible parts and lose their essence when they are moved to any place where they are likely to be examined carefully, when their owners are ignorant of parts of their nature and keep secret such knowledge of them as they have.

I bought several dresses and jackets and hung them over my husband's obliging arm while I sought for more; and he would not let me take any of them from him when we turned homeward towards our hotel. We stopped as we came to the bridge over the river, and looked for the last time at the lovely line of women sitting in the shadow of the white acacia trees, their veiled heads dappled with sunlight. 'We must come back again,' I said, 'again and again to the end of our lives.' 'Yes, indeed we must,' said my husband, 'but just see what is happening here.' A couple of peasant women had stopped and were turning over the dresses on his arm with some expressions of approval. 'Well, they evidently think we've got good taste,' he said complacently. But they began to name a sum, first in Serbian, and then, as we made no response, in Greek and in Vlach; and Constantine, who was still glowing with happiness over the business of the white horse, now became happier still. 'They think that you are carrying those dresses over your arm because you are trying to sell them,' he cried joyfully. 'Do you see, they cannot conceive a state of affairs in which a husband would carry anything for his wife, and the only people they know who wear Western clothes and concern themselves at all with peasant things are shopkeepers, and so they do not realize at all that you are English and very grand, no, not at all.' 'My dear,' said my husband, 'it is not twelve o'clock in the day and we have already been mistaken for itinerant moneylenders and second-hand clothes dealers. But I think that the curious statement you made about all your friends having been deported will do us the most harm in the end. Who in the world will they think we are? Mr and Mrs Al Capone *en vacances?* But doubtless Bitolj will turn it all to favour and to prettiness.'

ROAD

Sometimes a country will for days keep its secrets from a traveller, showing him nothing but its surfaces, its grass, its trees, the outside of its houses. Then suddenly it will throw him a key and tell him to go where he likes and see what he can. That afternoon and evening Macedonia passed into such a confidential mood regarding her Serbs and Bulgars. Our instruction began while Constantine was seeing Gerda off to Skoplje by the one o'clock train; she was to stay there another night, and then return to Belgrade. We spent this last half-hour in a café that lies among thick acacia woods in a little hill a mile or so outside the town. It was a holiday and there were many young students from the gymnasium (which is here what the English call a secondary and Americans a high school) sitting about in the darkness cast by the dense white flowers, some of them strumming on guslas. Presently one of them saw that my husband had dropped his matchbox and came to pick it up. 'Are you Germans?' he asked. 'No, but I speak German,' answered my husband. 'You are doing business here, or travelling for pleasure?' the boy went on. 'For pleasure. My wife came here a year ago, and she liked it so much that she insisted on bringing me here.'

The boy nodded gravely, 'Without doubt Macedonia is the most beautiful place in the world. But of course tourists are very rare here, because the Government does nothing to bring them. All, all goes for Dalmatia, the Government spends all its money there and has none for us. Look at the huge hotels they have there, and what we have here.' 'The ones here are quite good enough for us,' said my husband, 'but in any case I don't think Macedonia can ever compete with Dalmatia as a tourist centre, because it takes too long to get here. It takes us English only a little over twenty-four hours to get to the Adriatic, and about three days to Ochrid.' 'They should make a road so that you can come directly here from the Adriatic,' said the boy obstinately. 'But that nobody has done since the Romans,' said my husband. 'Why cannot it be done now?' he asked firmly. 'They had certain advantages,' said my husband wearily; 'the route from the Adriatic to Macedonia ran through exclusively Roman territory, whereas there is now another country named Albania which is involved. Also they employed slave labour, which made it much easier.'

After a pause the boy said, 'Did we but belong to Bulgaria, as we ought to considering we are all Bulgarians, it would be done and well done.' He looked with dreamy eyes at the snow peaks, and sighed. 'You cannot think what a shame it is that we do not belong to Bulgaria, and that we should be linked with Yugoslavia, for Yugoslavia is a poor country and Bulgaria is very rich.' 'I do not think,' said my husband, 'that Bulgaria is a very rich country. I do not think that Yugoslavia is a rich country, but I am sure that Bulgaria is not richer. And I am a banker, and I should know such things.' 'But everybody lives very well in Bulgaria,' sulked the boy. Then a new flame drove through him. 'And why will they not let us go to Bulgaria as we will! All of us have relatives there, and they will not let us go to see them. I have an uncle who has a factory for making sweets in Sofia, and they will not give me a passport when I want to visit him.' 'That I think idiotic of the Yugoslavian Government, unless you mean to do it a mischief,' said my husband, 'and I know that all over Yugoslavia you will find Croats and Serbs and Montenegrins who think the same, and some day they will help you to alter such things.' 'The Croats and Serbs!' scoffed the boy. 'They would never let us have our freedom! And if there were any good Croats and Serbs, which I doubt, how could they get their will done in Belgrade? That is a disgusting city. They are all Tziganes there. If Yugoslavia is a decent country, why is their capital so full of corruption?'

'A new country,' said my husband, 'may have a corrupt capital without being corrupt itself. When America was already a great and noble country its politicians were extremely venal, and Washington was full of what you would call Tziganes. That only means that political machinery does not spring up of itself, and that it has to be manufactured at precisely the moment when the best of the population is tempted away by the more adventurous work of exploiting its resources, so naturally the slimy and parasitic second-raters get hold of the government first. That will all straighten itself out later. As soon, in fact, as you and your friends combine with the Croats and Serbs and all the people in the country who care about decency and toleration.' 'We have begun,' said the boy proudly, 'these are my special friends, sitting on the bank round the young man with the gusla. We are in correspondence with such groups in Ochrid and in Prilep and in Veles. But naturally they are all Bulgarians.'

'Are you going to a university?' said my husband. 'Yes,' he said, 'I am going to Germany to study engineering next year. The Germans are very good people, they were with Bulgaria in the last war; some day Hitler will join with her again and they will fight Yugoslavia and give us back our freedom. Then we will have our rights. Do you realize that none of us here are allowed to join the Communist Party?' 'I am afraid,' said my husband, 'that if you think that Hitler is going to fight Yugoslavia for the purpose of getting you and your friends the right to join the Communist Party you will be very much disappointed. But do many of you want to be Communists?' 'No,' said the boy, 'it does not seem to have anything to do with us, things are so different here. We are more interested in the roots of things. We discuss all the most important subjects and we are not trammelled by our parents' prejudices. Myself, for instance, I am convinced that Jesus Christ was not a divine person but a philosopher, and a very great one. Indeed I think that Jesus Christ and Socrates were perhaps the greatest philosophers that have ever been.' He paused and nodded his head several times, very gravely, staring under knit brows at the distant snow peaks. 'And also,' he added, 'we of our group do not let our sisters use any make-up.'

When we left him he said, 'I wish you had met my mother, she is a very remarkable woman. I do not say that simply because she is my mother, for I think family feeling is old-fashioned and ridiculous. But she has proven her worth by her patriotic work for Bulgaria. When she was a young girl and life was very dangerous, she went to Struga.' She had, in fact, been the opposite number to the yellow-haired woman we had seen in Ochrid who had shown us her chickens; and I am sure that she was equally heroic, for this boy, though at present a juggins, had the makings of a superb creature. 'How are you going to Skoplje?' asked the boy. 'By Veles? Ah, how I wish I could go with you, for in Veles there lives——, a lawyer who is a great Bulgarian patriot. We read of him in the Serbian newspapers, which attack him shamefully. Later we will go to see him, though no doubt the police will persecute us afterwards. Well, good-bye, I am much obliged to you for our conversation. I always like to improve myself by talking with men and women of the world.'

We drove out of Bitolj through plains covered with flowers, with clover and buttercups and tall daisies, and a kind of meadowsweet slimmer than ours, past a brown pool full of buffaloes lying like pieces of meat in a stew, and were met by death on one of its most idiotic missions. The dogs of Macedonia are for the most part a handsome and heroic breed, reared to be ferocious for very good reasons. In the days of brigandage they had to protect their masters' crops and herds by day, and at night warn the household of raiders. They see so few automobiles that they never learn what they are, and see them as animals of a rare and formidable sort which have to be headed off their master's property like any others. On the way to Prilep a heavy white dog, thickly furred as a chow, held firm to this mistaken notion of our nature and ran by us barking with a most likeable gallantry. A hole in the road sent us swerving towards the field it guarded, and it fulfilled its duty as it saw it. It went for the automobile's bonnet as for the head of a hostile animal. We saw its white body fly through the air and fall among the standing corn, a good twenty yards away. It was a mere stupid lump when it flew through the air, it dropped as if it had never lived. One could not help but weep. 'So must many Serbs have died who thought they must attack the Bulgars,' said my husband, 'so must many Bulgars who thought they must attack the Serbs.'

Prilep lay on the plains before us, under a range of hills castellated with outcrops of rock; before we could enter it we drew to the side of the road to let pass a train of shaggy fierce-eyed nomads, hurrying along on heavily laden pack-horses on their way up to the chalets on Kaimakshalan for the summer's cheese-making. When we were crossing the market-place of Prilep, which is an agreeable country town struggling with heat and dust, we heard someone calling Constantine's name, and saw a man in a tight black suit running towards us. 'Get in, my friend,' said Constantine, 'I am taking these English to the monastery of Prince Marko, and I will drop you here on our way back.' He appeared to be a Serbian official in charge of the education of the town, and he was stuffed fuller with grievances than any human being I have ever seen. As soon as he sat down beside Constantine a jet of complaint burst from him, not a weak little whining trickle but a great spout, sent out under heavy pressure, worthy of the principal fountain in a public park. 'He isn't letting up at all,' said my husband, 'and in a minute he will cry. What on earth is the matter with him?' 'He talks of some difficulty in administration,' said Constantine hastily and without candour. The poor man was still at it when we left the car and walked up a steep incline towards Prince Marko's monastery, and my husband said, 'I wish I knew what was worrying him, he's got such a nice, pig-headed, earnest face.' 'He certainly is carrying on,' I said, 'and at such a rate that Constantine has not been able to get in a word edgeways for some minutes. Is this a record?' 'But, good Lord, do you know what he is saying?' asked my husband. 'Listen! Listen! it is most extraordinary.' The man in tight black clothes had stopped on the edge of the platform in front of the church, and was jumping up and down in front of an immense and burning panorama of plains and mountains and sky, and looking far hotter than any of them, and shaking his fist at some absent object of his hatred. 'Yes,' I said, 'it is perfectly true; he appears to be saying, "Lord Buxton! Lord Buxton!" Now I know what it is. Lord Buxton is a pro-Bulgarian, and this poor man is a Serbian official who is complaining that the Bulgarians here do not appreciate his ministrations, and that they are encouraged in insubordination by such foreign sympathizers.'

My husband polished his glasses and looked again at the man in tight black clothes. 'How absurd this is,' he said, 'because this is just the kind of man a Buxton would like, a good and noble prig.' I rushed Constantine's defences by saying, 'What have the Bulgarians been doing to your friend, and how does Lord Buxton come into it?' He squeaked back, 'Lord Buxton came here, with a secretary who like himself was very foolish, and they come only to see what Bulgaria tells them to see and never to see what Yugoslavia is doing here, which as you know is well and very well, and he cannot think why men who are English as Mr Gladstone was should be on the side of movements that are financed by the Italians and that devil Mussolini, and they say we are very harsh against them, and it is no wonder if we were at one time, for they were bad with us, and they put us in danger and we had many things to do, and now how is it when he cannot punish youths for spitting in the classroom without them telling him they will call on Lord Buxton.' 'How surprised our essentially liberal Lord Buxton would be to find himself considered as an ally of Fascism and a bulwark of the spitting habit,' said my husband. 'And how certain it is that all this man says is true! It has the muddled and disappointing quality of life.' At this point the man in tight black clothes recalled our presence and was seized by the memory of something that he ought to do. He pointed at an archway and called out a few passionate words to Constantine, keeping his eyes on us the while. 'My friend wishes you to notice,' said Constantine, 'how the Bulgarians painted the Bulgarian colours on this archway during the war, though this is the monastery of Prince Marko, and it is certainly a Serbian monument. Also he wished me to show you how they defaced certain Serbian frescoes and inscriptions.' 'Good God,' said my husband, 'it is as if we went on chewing over the Wars of the Roses. But I suppose we might if we had been enslaved since and now had to start afresh. Still, that makes it no less of a bore.'

That is very true of all disputes between the Serbs and the Bulgars that are based on historical grounds. Both parties, and this applies not to old professors but to the man in the street, start with the preposterous idea that when the Turks were driven out of the Balkans the frontiers recognized when they came in should be re-established, in spite of the lapse of five centuries, and then they are not loyal to it. The frontiers demanded by the extremists on both sides are those which their peoples touched only at the moments of their greatest expansion, and they had to be withdrawn afterwards because they could not be properly defended. The ideal Bulgaria which the Bulgarians lust for, and nearly obtained through the Russian-drafted Treaty of San Stefano in 1878, actually existed only during the lifetimes of the Tsar Simeon, who died in the tenth century, and of the Tsar Samuel, who died about a hundred years later. The Serbs are as irritating when they regard their Tsar Dushan not only as an inspiration but as a map-maker, for his empire had fallen to pieces in the thirty-five years between his death and the defeat at Kossovo. The only considerations which should determine the drawing of Balkan frontiers are the rights of the peoples to self-government and the modifications of that right to which they must submit in order to keep the peninsula as a whole free from the banditry of the great powers. But the historical approach gratifies the pedantic side of the Slav, and so it has never been abandoned.

I forgot the man in tight black clothes in another matter of antiquity at that moment, for the Abbot and two monks had come out of the monastery to greet us. The Abbot, who was a Serbian of the best type of pioneer who comes down to Macedonia to work in the Church or medicine or education, greeted us with great warmth, not so much for our own sakes, I think, as because we were not the two monks. These were Russians, and they exhibited to an intense degree that detachment from their surroundings which is characteristic of the White exiles in Yugoslavia, and which has always struck me as unpleasing, except in the case of the little monk from Finland at Neresi. They are certainly unworldly, but only because of a superficiality so extreme that it cannot lay hold even of the surface of things. They had an air of being here only because they had missed all the trains in the world. The Abbot took us up into the gallery used for the entertainment of guests and gave us *slatko*, and immediately I was faced with an object which solved a riddle that had been vexing me for some time. The riddle lay in the character of Prince Marko, the Serbian hero who is the subject of many folk-songs. He was a real personage, the son of a fourteenth-century Serbian king and himself Prince of Prilep, but he is also a legend, a symbol of the extrovert, and therefore dear to a people that swings back and forth between extroversion and introversion, and knows quite well which is the pleasanter extreme. He was prodigiously strong, he carried for weapon a mace weighing sixty pounds of iron, thirty pounds of silver, and nine pounds of gold. His horse, Piebald, was the fleetest in the world and understood the human tongue; and from one side of its saddle swung the mace and from the other a counterweight of red wine in a skin, for Marko was a hard drinker though he was never drunk. He was a great fighter and chivalrous. When he killed Moossa Arbanassa, the Albanian rebel, he wept and said, 'Alas, alas to me, may the gracious God forgive me that I killed a far better knight than I am,' and took the severed head and rode back with it to Constantinople and flung it at the feet of the Sultan. When the Sultan started back in alarm Marko cried, 'Since you sprang away from Moossa's head now he is dead, I wonder what you would have done if you had met him when he was alive?'

It must be noted that it was for the Sultan that Marko killed Moossa Arbanassa. That is a reflection of the historical truth. Marko was defeated by the Turks and though he kept his prince-dom of Prilep it was as the Sultan's vassal; and he was obliged to fight against the Christians. This he did not take robustly, but, it appears, sadly and scrupulously. It is told of him that, before the battle of Rovine in Roumania in 1399, he said, 'I pray God to give the victory to the Christians, even if I have to pay for it with my own blood.' And that prayer was answered. Yet it is told of him with equal conviction that one morning he was riding along a road when Piebald stumbled and shed tears; and when he wondered at this portent a fairy who was his adopted sister announced to him that as he was now three hundred years old he must die. So he killed Piebald, for the horse had been his for a hundred and sixty years, and they could not well be parted now, and gave him a fine funeral. Then he threw his mace over the mountains to the sea, shouting, 'When that mace comes up from the sea then such a one as I am may again appear on earth,' and, lying down on the green grass, gave himself to the most cheerful death recorded in literature.

The discrepancy between these two accounts of his death is paralleled in various accounts of his life. It is not as if the one version were written by somebody who stuck to the facts and the other by somebody who either did not know the facts or preferred to use fantasy and was determined to make a story of it, but as if they were written about two different people quite unlike in character. One ballad represents him as drawing on himself his father's curse by refusing to bear false witness and support his claim that the Tsar Stephen Dushan had left him his empire. Another represents him as a captive in pagan hands, gaining his freedom by promising to marry the daughter of the Saracen prince who holds him, on condition that she steal her father's keys and let him out. But once they are on their way to Christian lands he realizes he cannot keep his promise, she is too black, too queer, too outlandish, and he kills her. 'Too bad,' he says, with a little sincerity, but with confidence in his power of forgetfulness. One of the two personalities disclosed in these poems has a sensitive conscience. The other has none.

In the gallery I saw, built into the wall, a carving representing a round and jolly rogue, stark naked, riding a very large horse. 'Where does that come from?' I asked. The Abbot said, 'It was part of the original church here, which was built just before the time of Prince Marko, and was pulled down in the eighteenth century to make room for the one that is standing now, and they put it in this building, which was built about the same time. But I am told that we should not have it here, for the little man was a god who was worshipped here in pre-Christian times.' And so it was. It was the Thracian Rider, a deity worshipped all over ancient Thrace and Macedonia, whom some think to be a form of Rhesus, the hero of whom Homer wrote. He had a long lease of life, for the Roman legionaries of Thracian origin went on worshipping him, and his shrines are found wherever the legions went, and in Rome itself. You may find several sculptures representing him in the Budapest Museum. The mystery of Prince Marko was solved. There had been two similar processes and a synthesis of the results. The cult of the Thracian Rider was practised in Prilep, and was driven underground by Christianity; but it never left the hearts of the people, who in this uncomfortable life liked to think of a comfortable immortal, happy as eternity is long, unacquainted with pain. Even so, when Prince Marko was lowered from power to vassalhood he too never left the hearts of the people, who under the yoke of the Turk liked to think of the milder yoke of this reflective Christian prince. Therefore the two became fused in the common mind, the happy god, the sad mortal, and the imagination of folk-song followed now one strain and now another in this entanglement of opposites.

When we went down the hillside, the man in tight black clothes running before us to show us a cliff where the Bulgarians had defaced a fresco portraying a Serbian king, we saw below us Dragutin standing by the car in an attitude of deep depression. 'He is in bad humour,' said Constantine, 'we will find that he has been worsted in some conflict with an animal.' And when we got to him he mournfully told us that he had seen a very big snake among the stones and had let it get away. He did not recover his spirits till our road took us to a mountain called Babuna, covered with low beechwoods which for time out of mind had sheltered rebels. Here the first Bogomils, the Manichæan heretics, had taken refuge, establishing themselves for so long that they gave the place its name; for they were then called Babuni; and here the Haiduks and the comitadji had hidden, all through the Turkish occupation. 'Rebels gave this place its name,' said Constantine, 'and it gave its name to one of our greatest rebels. For all our Serbian comitadji, who worked for the liberation of Macedonia, took false names, lest some time their kinsmen should have to pass through Turkish territory; and the most gifted of them, who sheltered among these woods for much of his life, called himself Babunsky.' Dragutin gave out a round-mouthed roar of homage as he heard the name.

About us Macedonia changed into what I think is its highest state of beauty, though many travellers call it dreary. It is certainly bare, merely stippled with trees in the valleys, and veined rarely by rivers; but it is superbly sculptured. In passing through it one receives a very pure apprehension of majestic form. Sometimes we passed fields of opium poppies, with their cool, large, positive beauty, their fleshy green leaves and stalks, their pure white and austere purple flowers; and sometimes mosaics of water, divided by fine lines of mud, and just pierced with the sharpest, highest, most vibrant green imaginable, an F-sharp-in-alt green. Dragutin shook his fist at them. 'It is rice,' said Constantine; 'the Government wants to stop it, for it causes terrible malaria, but we cannot, for the people are terribly poor, and rice pays them better than anything else.' In the late afternoon we came to what is the second greatest pleasure I have ever derived from the nose. The greatest is to be enjoyed driving through the Midi in the dark at the time of the vintage, when farmers have laid the pressed wine-skins as manure on the fields outside the town, and there rises through the warm night an ether of drunkenness, potent yet delicate, winier than any wine. Here in Macedonia I learned that honey is not so successful as one believes, that no bee ever realizes its full intention, and that the perfumer is a clumsy bungler who never cracks the fragile crib he covets, by approaching a town built in the Turkish manner, with a multitude of little gardens, at a time when the sun had been working for many hours on the acacia trees. The air was more than scented, it was flavoured, it was dense with the essence of flowers.

It was Veles that we were approaching, a town that a great many people admire on their way to Athens: its elegant dilapidated Turkish houses, painted in refined colours, hang on each side of a rocky gorge cleft by the rushing Vardar. We racketed through the narrow streets to the heights of the town, inconveniencing the inhabitants not so much as might be expected, for it seemed to them that we were doing something very dashing and courageous, and they smiled at us as if we were swashbuckling cavaliers. We came to a great church that stood on the hillside, so high that it enjoyed the day while the evening clouded the town beneath, among lawns and stone terraces and giant planes, abundantly watered by the stream from a fountain. It had the same strange aspect as the Cathedral at Skoplje, of forms handled with competence but without comprehension, and indeed it had been built by the same four brothers. There was an Italian Gothic apse which revealed their command over their craft and their ignorance of it. They had copied it from buildings they had seen when they were working in Italy as stone-masons, but as they knew nothing of the forms that lay between it and its remotest ancestry they had missed its essential quality. Its handsomeness looked blind. Inside it was full of profounder incongruities, admitting elements that were discordant not only from the point of view of architecture but as matters of religion and culture. Here too the pulpit was like a mimbar in a mosque, the preacher climbed extremely steep steps and spoke to the congregation from high under the rafters; and there were immensely broad galleries, completely Islamic in tone, in which there were separate chapels for the women, and great tables and benches set aside for social occasions. The proportions of the place were wildly wrong. The architect had believed that if a church was built unusually high in proportion to its base it would look majestic instead of leggy. But the error was magnificent, and the handling of its stone, particularly the marble, made comprehensible the terror the Turks felt before of the Slav subjects, the terror that made them never rest in their efforts to geld them by famine and massacre.

Two priests came to us over the green lawns through the golden afternoon, clean and handsome men. One said, 'We are so glad you have come to see our church, nobody visits it, and surely it is very beautiful. It looks very rich, as rich as the church at Bitolj; but Veles was never rich like Bitolj, it was only that all the Christians in the town gave what they could, and all the Christians in the villages around for many miles.' And the other said, 'Is it not wonderful that the Turks thought they were insulting us when they made our fathers build their church outside the town, and that it meant that we have the most beautiful site in Veles, and that all the mosques are below our feet?' 'Sit down on the bench,' said the other, 'and I will bring you *slatko*, for here in this fountain we have the most beautiful water, cold and lively as a living thing.' They sat beside us while we drank, and said, 'And we have a precious grave here. Have you seen it? There it is, the white marble one by the cobbles. It is only to see that grave that people come here on week-days, and often they turn back without seeing our church. But still we are very pleased they should come and reverence that sacred stone.' 'Who lies there?' 'Babunsky the comitadji,' said the priest.

'Babunsky!' breathed Constantine. As we followed him down the cobbles we passed Dragutin, who was standing by the fountain, communing with his water-god. 'Did you know Babunsky was buried here?' Constantine asked him. 'Was I not at his funeral?' answered Dragutin. We all stood before the headstone on which it was written that beneath it lay Yovan Babunsky, 1878–1920. 'But I saw him not long before he died,' said Constantine, 'and he looked far older than that.' 'So he did,' said the older of the two priests. 'I knew him well when I was young, and what you say is true. But who could wonder? How many nights of his life did he sleep in a bed? How many days did he eat no food but the berries from the bushes? And he was wounded many times, and often fell sick with fear. All this our Serbian brother did for our sake, that Macedonia should be free.'

In Veles our automobile developed a fault, and Dragutin had to tinker with its innards for half an hour or so. Constantine fell asleep in the back seat, and my husband and I strolled through the dusk about the town, which was just coming to life again after the heat of the day, not to work, but to stretch itself and enjoy the full knowledge that soon it would sleep again. We lingered before some little shops, tiny caves of flimsy woodwork, with their minute stocks, that amounted to perhaps a hundred jugs, or twenty rolls of cloth, or a few basins of yoghourt and rice porridge. We turned a corner into a street where the shops were larger and more Western in their merchandise. I noticed that several of them were not shops at all, but lawyers' offices. Here there was a chemist, there a lawyer, here a draper. 'How amusing it would be if we found Charles Russell or Sir William Jowitt in between Heppell's and the Burma Ruby Company in the Strand,' I said; and we stood for a moment watching one of these lawyers seeing a client to the door of his shop, at first out of curiosity, and then out of friendliness, for the lawyer was a finely made man, with an air of noble destiny about him. He would always be overapprehensive, but only about others; for himself he would show a gentle, stately carelessness. When he had been left alone he remained standing at his threshold for a little, looking out in the darkness, as if he knew that in the end it must take all, but showing only the faintest melancholy.

As he closed the glass door I looked at the name on his sign; and I clutched my husband's sleeve. 'Look! Look!' I said. 'This is the lawyer of Veles whom the schoolboy in Bitolj told us was such a Bulgarian patriot! Let us go and talk to him and find out what the situation really is, for he is sure to speak French or German, and it would be most interesting, for I believe this is a centre of Bulgarian agitation.' When we went into the office the lawyer looked up with unhurried vigilance and dismissed a servant who was in the room, telling her to bring us black coffee. As soon as she had gone, my husband explained why we had come. 'The boy said you had done great things for the Bulgarian cause,' he ended, 'and said that he and his friends hoped to come and see you.' The lawyer smiled. 'He was a good boy, I expect,' he said, 'full of courage, full of heart.' 'Yes,' we said. 'I could weep at what you have told me,' he said. He spoke a slow, old-fashioned French that was a very suitable medium for his gentle and precise personality. 'Yes, I could weep. For you see, I am not a Bulgarian patriot. I am not even a Bulgarian. I can be quite sure about that, for when I was a child I saw my father, who was a Serbian schoolmaster in a village between here and Prilep, murdered by Bulgarians because he was not of their blood.'

He made an anxious deprecating gesture. 'But I try to remember that only as a grief and not as a wrong, for I should be a great fool if I did not admit that had he been a Bulgarian schoolmaster it might easily have happened that he was murdered by the Serbs. But there is another reason why I try to think of my father as having died, and not as having been killed. I believe it is time we stopped thinking of such little things as whether we are Serbs or Bulgars. I believe we should rather realize with a new seriousness that we are all human beings and that every human being needs freedom and justice as much as he needs air to breathe and food to eat. In fact, I am an opponent of the present Yugoslav Government. I am not at all the friend of Monsieur Stoyadinovitch. And that is how the confusion that has brought you to me has arisen. For the official press, in an effort to discredit me, has started a legend that I am a Bulgarian who is working against Serbian interests. There could not be a blacker lie.' I gaped, seeing at work the some process that had united Prince Marko and Rhesus. 'But do not be distressed,' he said kindly. 'I shall think more kindly of the lie now it has given me the pleasure of your visit. Will you take some Turkish delight with your coffee?'

Skoplje

It did not seem possible that Gerda had said good-bye to us. That, literally, was all she had said. She had extended her hand and had uttered the single word 'good-bye,' its starkness unpalliated by any acknowledgment that she had been our guest for a fortnight. It seemed to me that she might have said something, for she had had great fun at dinner the night before, being rude to me with a peculiar virtuosity, using pettiness as if it were a mighty club. While Constantine saw her off on the Belgrade train we sat outside the hotel and drank iced beer, and felt weak but contented, like fever patients whose temperature has at last fallen. My husband bought some guelder roses from an Albanian, laid them on the table, contemplated them for some moments, and said:

'Gerda has no sense of process. That is what is the matter with Gerda. She wants the result without doing any of the work that goes to make it. She wants to enjoy the position of a wife without going to the trouble of making a real marriage, without admiring her husband for his good qualities, without practising loyal discretion regarding his bad qualities, without respecting those of his gods which are not hers. She wants to enjoy motherhood without taking care of her children, without training them in good manners or giving them a calm atmosphere. She wants to be our friend, to be so close to us in friendship that we will ask her to travel about the country with us, but she does not make the slightest effort to like us, or even to conceal that she dislikes us. She is angry when you are paid such little respect as comes your way because you are a well-known writer, she feels it ought to come to her also, though she has never written any books. She is angry because we have some money. She feels that it might just as well belong to her. That our possession of this money has something to do with my work in the City and my family's work in Burma never occurs to her. For her the money might as easily have been attached to her as to us by a movement as simple as that which pastes a label on a trunk. As she has no sense of what goes to bring people love, or friendship, or distinction, or wealth, it seems to her that the whole world is enjoying undeserved benefits; and in a universe where all is arbitrary it might just as well happen that the injustice was pushed a little further and that all these benefits were taken from other people, leaving them nothing, and transferred to her, giving her

799

everything. Given the premiss that the universe is purely arbitrary, that there is no causality at work anywhere, there is nothing absurd in that proposal.

'This is the conqueror's point of view. It was the Turks' point of view in all their aggressive periods. Everybody who is not Gerda is to Gerda "a dog of an infidel," to be treated without mercy. If she could get hold of our money by killing us, and would not be punished for it, I think she would do it, not out of cruelty, but out of blankness. Since she denies the reality of process, she would only envisage our death, which would be a great convenience to her, and not our dying, which would be a great inconvenience to us. She has shut herself off from the possibility of feeling mercy, since pain is a process and not a result. This will give her a great advantage in any conflict with more sensitive people, and indeed it is not her only advantage. Her nature gives her a firm foundation for her life that many a better woman lacks. Constantine is not less but more devoted as a husband because she is a bad wife to him. All his humility says, "If she thinks so little of me, is there perhaps some lack in me?" All his affection says, "Since she is so desperately hungry, what can I give her?" And, needless to say, her children are devoted to her. It is the impulse of children to do whatever their parents do not. If their parents bend to them, they turn away; if their parents turn away, they bend to them.

'In her wider relationships also she is very happy. To begin with, nobody who is not like Gerda can believe how bad Gerda is. We did not, at the beginning; and if we told people the story of what Gerda has been to us on this trip in anything like the concentrated terms in which one usually tells a story we would see a doubt pass over their faces. "They must have been tactless with her," "They cannot have made her properly welcome," is what they would think to themselves. That she invited herself to be our guest and then continuously insulted us is not a proposition acceptable to the mind, which rightly sees that there is no hope for humanity if it can bring itself to behave like that. If we established the truth of our story they would grasp at excuses for her, would plead that she was an alien in a strange land, that her experiences as a young girl in the war had made her neurotic, that she had been given an inferiority complex by the Treaty of Versailles.

'These things may be true; but it is also true that to recognize them is dangerous. It weakens the resistance that should be made against Gerda. For there is no way to be safe from her except to treat her as if she were, finally and exclusively, a threat to existence. Look how she has defeated us. You love Macedonia more than any other country you have ever visited. Sveti Naum is to you a place apart; you wanted to take me there. We have made that journey. We have made it in the company of an enemy who tormented us not only by her atrocious behaviour to us but by behaving atrociously to other people whom we liked when she was with us. This has clouded our vision of the country, it has angered us and weakened us. When Constantine said to us, "My wife wishes to come to Macedonia with us," we should not merely have said, "We do not think that will be a success, we would rather she did not come," we should have said, "We dislike your wife extremely, we dislike the way she speaks against you and Yugoslavia, we will not travel with her, and if she turns up at the train we will take our luggage out of it." But we could not. We did not believe that she could go on being as bad as she had been; we were sorry for her because she was a German who loved her country and had committed herself to living in the Balkans; we have been elaborately trained from our infancy not to express frankly our detestation of others. So she got what she wanted, and she is still getting what she wanted. Do not think she is going to Belgrade because we did not want her to go to Petch: she is going, quite simply, because she thinks it would be more pleasant to go back to her children.

'Gerda, in fact, is irresistible. It is therefore of enormous importance to calculate how many Gerdas there are in the world, and whether they are likely to combine for any purpose. Gerda is, of course, not characteristically German. Think of Gustav and Georg and Brigitte and the ——s! They could not, to save their lives, behave as she has done. But you can, perhaps, think of some English people who are like her.' 'There was a gymnastic teacher at my school who was as insensitive and aggressive as that, and once I went to tea at the home of one of my school friends, and her family seemed to me as bad,' I said, 'and then I once met some Americans who were like that, and then at home Lady——and Lady——and Mrs——seem to me much the same, with only a little more skill in dissembling it.' 'And I know a Jew who belongs to the same order,' said my husband. 'In fact this type appears anywhere and everywhere, though probably much more densely in some areas than others. It seems to me that it appears wherever people are subject to two conditions. The first condition is that they should have lost sight of the importance of process; that they have forgotten that everything which is not natural is artificial and that artifice is painful and difficult; that they should be able to look at a loaf of bread and not realize that miracles of endurance and ingenuity had to be performed before the wheat grew, and the mill ground, and the oven baked. This condition can be brought about by several causes: one is successful imperialism, where the conquering people has the loaf built for it from the wheat ear up by its conquered subjects; another is modern machine civilization, where a small but influential proportion of the population lives in towns in such artificial conditions that a loaf of bread comes to them in a cellophane wrapper with its origins as unvisualized as the begetting and birth of a friend's baby. The other condition is that people should have acquired a terror of losing the results of process, which are all they know about; they must be afraid that everything artificial is going to disappear, and they are going to be thrown back on the natural; they must foresee with a shudder a day when there will be no miraculous loaf born in its virginity of cellophane, and they will have to eat grass.

'Now, these conditions obtained in the case of the Turks when they became nuisances in the Balkan Peninsula. At first their wars were inspired not by fanaticism or greed to enslave foreign populations but by legitimate enough desires for political and commercial security. They became cruel and tyrannous only when they were glutted by the conquest of Mohammed the Conqueror and Selim and Suleiman the Magnificent, and when the emergence of Russia and the successful opposition of Central Europe and Venice made them afraid of losing the fruits of those victories. They had never learned the art of prosperity in peacetime, they were not economically productive. Neither, oddly enough, is Germany, in spite of her enormous energy and resources. Gerda is bourgeoise and town-bred. She is proud because her family are all professional men; it is of importance to her that she cannot bake a loaf, she likes to buy her cakes in a shop. Her theory of her own social value depends on her being able to put down money and buy results of processes without being concerned in the processes themselves. And she is enormously afraid that she will not be able to go on doing this. The war made her afraid; the depression has made her still more afraid. It does not occur to her that what she and her kind must do is to reorganize the process of state life till there is some sort of guarantee of a certain amount of artificial goods for all of us. It does not occur to her that she had better learn to bake bread instead of buy it, for since her social value depends on her not doing so, she regards this as a sentence of death. Therefore she wants to take results that belong to other people: she wants to bone everybody else's loaf.

'Those conditions apply to too many people all over the world to

make me regard Gerda as isolated. She is an international phenomenon. But all the same I think that there may be enough Gerdas
concentrated in separate areas to make her in effect a nationalist
phenomenon. She probably exists in sufficient numbers in Central
Europe to make it an aggressive and, indeed, irresistible power. She
was, after all, the determining element in the Austro-Hungarian
Empire all through the nineteenth century. The parasite city of
Vienna, spoiled by its share of the luxury the Austrian and
Hungarian nobles wrung out of their peasantry, and terrified
by the signs of economic insecurity, howled all the time to be
given other people's loaves. Think how furiously they demanded
that they should be given preference over the Czechs in seeking
employment, that they should not have to pass such difficult
examinations as the Czechs for entrance to the Civil Service. It
must have disgusted a proud German like Bismarck, who was an
aristocrat, a rounded man who repudiated nothing of life and knew
the peasant's role as well as his own, and who was not afraid. But
Gerda would have thought the agitation most natural.

'Let us admit it, for a little while the whole of our world may
belong to Gerda. She will snatch it out of hands too well-bred
and compassionate and astonished to defend it. What we must
remember is that she will not be able to keep it. For her contempt
for the process makes her unable to conduct any process. You
remember how when we met her at the station at Belgrade she
expressed an opinion on the book you held in your hand, *The
Healing Ritual*, which was sheer nonsense, because she had not
read the book; she imagined she could judge it by her knowledge
of the bare fact of its existence. You saw at Ochrid how she
had not the faintest idea of what Communism is and how it is
distinguished from Social Democracy, though she was once a
Communist herself; she had obviously never thought of making
any effort to find out what was the creed behind the church she
had joined simply because it was large and many other people had
joined it before her. You can conquer a country on this principle.
To go up in an aeroplane and drop bombs is a simple use of an
elaborate process that has already been developed. But you cannot
administer a country on this principle. Do you remember what
Sir Charles Eliot said in his book, *Turkey in Europe*, about the
peculiar hollowness of the Ottoman Empire? Here was this great
entity acquired by Turkish military genius in its full force and
retained by its remnants, and within it no process of any degree
of complication or difficulty. In warfare they had the advantage
of what Eliot calls "that special instinct for discipline and order

which has unfortunately nothing to do with good government, but surely makes every man render implicit obedience to his military or official superior." The rest of life they faced with such a blank ignorance of what was needed to secure productiveness and continuity that they were quite contented with their failure. They did not know how to live a comfortable life in their houses: they never learned to protect themselves against the rigour of winter. They liked the country and agricultural life, but they would work only land so fat that it hardly needed to be worked. Their commerce and financing and administration had to be done by foreigners; many of their generals and admirals were Italians and Poles and other European renegades; and many of the most capable grand viziers were Arabs or Albanians or Slavs. They never developed any economic programme other than the confiscation of money from their subjects without repayment. Nor did the Turks ever feel that the nations who could work land and handle business and husband the resources of their countries were using logical means to obtain desirable ends. What is it Eliot says? "The Turk regards them as conjurors who can perform a variety of tricks, which may be, according to circumstances, useful, amusing, or dangerous; but for all Christendom he has a brutal, unreasoning contempt—the contempt of the sword for everything that can be cut."

'I think we can very easily imagine a state engendered by Gerdas falling into such an attitude. The problem is how long the part of the world conquered by Gerda's state will bear with its inefficiency. That inefficiency, mind you, is not a mere prediction of mine. It has already appeared. Consider the disastrous history of Austrian and German banking since the war, which is not to be explained by anything except the sheer inability of bankers of Gerda's kind to realize that banking is a process in which due regard has to be paid all the time to the laws of causality. True, the Ottoman Empire was able to survive in spite of its inefficiency more than five hundred years after it came to Europe. But it had certain advantages Gerda's empire will not have. It had Islam behind it, a religion that was already seven hundred years old, a religion that had not only justified but was identified with militarism. Now Gerda cannot use Christianity to unify her peoples, because it is in essence against aggression and on the side of mercy; she may invent a new religion of a pagan kind, but she won't be able to get it into the blood of the people in time. Young men may rush into battle shouting the names of gods who have been run up on a sewing machine the night before last, but such gods will not comfort those who mourn the young men when the battle goes ill.

'The Turks also had the advantage of facing the Slavs, a people who had known order or peace or unity only intermittently during three centuries and whose religion, unlike Islam, divided rather than united its followers, first by the separation of the Western and the Eastern Churches, and secondly by the exploitation of sectarian differences by the great powers. Gerda will not have that advantage either. Today everybody in Europe knows at first hand or at good second hand of the blessings brought by peace and order, and nearly all of them realize that unity is at least a useful instrument, and, if Protestantism has done much harm by making religion identical with ethical effort of a limited kind, it has done a great deal of good by putting down in black and white the ideas of Christianity, and showing us what life will lose if we abandon them. Remember it will not be to anybody's advantage to keep Gerda's empire in existence. Turkey in Europe was an advantage to England, who wanted a weak power at that end of the Mediterranean to keep out any strong power that might have inconvenient ambitions; it held back the Austrian Empire on its way to the Black Sea, and the Russian Empire from its Pan-Slavist dream and its itch for Constantinople. But Gerda's empire will serve no such purpose. It will be an object of fear and nothing else.

'For this reason I believe that Gerda's empire cannot last long. But while it lasts it will be terrible. And what it leaves when it passes will also be terrible. For we cannot hope for anything but a succession of struggles for leadership among men whose minds will have been unfitted for leadership by the existence of tyranny and the rupture of European tradition, until, slowly and painfully, the nations re-emerge, civilization re-emerges. No wonder that when you came to Macedonia you were fascinated. You were looking in the magic crystal and seeing our future. Oh, I do not wish to exaggerate. It is possible that the full tragedy of Gerda's assault on those who are not Gerda will not be fully enacted, that only seventy or sixty or fifty per cent of the potential evils of the situation will be realized. But the Turks are here, for Gerda is here, and Europe is in her soul Macedonia. If Europeans have not the virtues of the Macedonian peasant, our life is lost, and we are the greenfly on the rose tree that has been torn up and thrown on the rubbish-heap. All that we are and do means nothing, all that our ancestors were and did means nothing, unless we are naturally the equals of the peasant women on the Skopska Tserna Gora and in Bitolj, whose fingers never forget the pattern that an ancient culture had created as symbols for what it had discovered regarding life and death.'

My husband said these things while we drank our beer, while we
took a little walk by the embankment and watched the carters take
their horses into mid-stream of the lowered river, while we lunched
off paprika stew and yoghourt, and later, in our bedroom, while
I sat by the window and mended the clothes that had just been
brought back to us by a gipsy laundress dressed in saffron and
ultramarine. We were resting because tomorrow was St George's
Day, and that evening we were motoring out with some Serbian
friends of ours, a Bosnian Moslem and his wife, a Serbian from
Novi Sad, Mehmed and Militsa, to see some of the rites that are
carried on in the villages during the eve of the festival. They are
all fertility rites, magic remedies against the curse of barrenness
that lies on Macedonia, partly because of the malaria and partly
because of the overwork of the women and the lack of care for
child-bearing women. Constantine was not going with us, for he
had to dine with a Government official in the town. We had not
the least idea what the night was going to be like; it hung before
us like a dark blue curtain which, we knew, would disclose a
beautiful pattern when we came to examine it. I was vaguely
displeased by what my husband said; I complained, 'I cannot bear
this, it sounds as if I would die before things are tidied up.' My
husband said, 'But certainly you will die before things are tidied
up! You must realize that or you are bound to become unhappy and
embittered.' 'It is, of course, not of the slightest importance that we
should have the satisfaction of seeing the world at rights before we
die,' I murmured, feeling about in the work-basket for the darker
beige darning silk, and then I burst out laughing, because I knew
that for all we were saying there lived in both our hearts a bright
idiot hope, 'In five years it will be all right. . . . Well, in ten years,
then . . .'

There was a tap at the door and Constantine came into the room.
He looked tired but liberated. 'The chambermaid,' he said, looking
down the passage, 'is of the Gretchen type. But how different would
Faust have been if the Gretchen Faust and Mephistopheles met
at the well, had been an experienced chambermaid.' 'Well, that
is probably what the play needs,' I said, for I love to torment
Constantine about Goethe, 'for God knows Nietzsche was right
when he said it was a thin and empty little story.' 'Here is a
telegram for your poor husband,' said Constantine, sitting down.
'The chambermaid is not unlike a *petite femme* in Paris who played
a great part in the lives of us Serb students in Paris just before
the war. She was called Blanche la Vache and we found her
enormously sympathetic. It was to her, I remember, that we

owed enlightenment on a matter that had greatly perplexed us. How was it, we wondered, when we went to the *petites femmes* they always knew at once that we were not German, we were not Swiss, we were not Italians, we were not Russians, but quite simply Serbs? So at a favourable moment I put the question to Blanche la Vache and she answered me at once, like a good honest girl. 'It is because,' she said, 'you have the pants that fasten not with buttons but with a cord, like the pyjamas, and all women know that it is only in the Balkans that such are worn.' So I ran back to my comrades and told them, and then what a waste there was! For we rushed out and bought new pants of the European fashion, and threw away those we had brought from home, and of course our good Serbian mothers had sent us to Paris with a dozen of everything.' 'Alas, my dear,' said my husband, 'this is a telegram from Berlin telling me to expect a telephone call this evening. I shall not be able to go with you and Militsa and Mehmed tonight. What a pity! But I will go and have tea with them and see you off. Not for anything would I miss seeing Militsa and Mehmed.'

I did not doubt that he was disappointed, for these friends of ours are at once intoxicating and reassuring. Once I showed Denis Saurat, who is one of the wisest of men, a letter I had received from Militsa. 'She writes from Skoplje, I see,' he said. 'Really, we are all much safer than we suppose. If there are twenty people like this woman scattered between here and China, civilization will not perish.' Militsa was born in Novi Sad when it was Hungarian: that is to say, she is a descendant of one of the thirty-seven thousand families who were led into Austrian territory by the Patriarch Arsenius in 1690 because they could no longer support the tyranny of the Turk. Her father was a dashing figure of the nineteenth century, who had studied medicine in Vienna and became the star of a students' corps, was later an officer in the Russian Army, and ended as a famous man of letters who translated *Faust* into Serbian. Militsa takes in person after his mother, who was a Greek, probably of the true and ancient stock, for she has the same fine and small-boned good looks as some people I have known who were of unquestioned descent from Byzantine families, and she inherited her father's intellectual powers. From her childhood she has known Serbian, German, Hungarian, Latin, and Greek, and later she learned English, French, and Italian. She has studied profoundly the literatures of all these languages; I have rarely met anyone, English or American, who was better acquainted with the English poets. She has taken her doctorate in philosophy, has written much on Plato, and is now tracing the influence of

the Cabbalists on the Bishop-King Peter II of Montenegro, who
was a great mystic poet. She herself writes poetry, in which her
exquisite sensitiveness explores the whole universe in obedience
to the instructions of her ambitious intellect. She talks with the
brilliance of a firefly, but her flight is not wandering, it is a
swift passage from one logically determined point to another. And
besides these things she is what other women spend all their lives
in being. She inherits the medieval tradition of housewifery which
persisted very strongly among the Serbs of Novi Sad; and she is
a devoted daughter to her widowed mother, and a loving wife to
Mehmed.

Mehmed is a Herzegovinian Moslem, a descendant of one of
the Slav landowners who became Moslem in the sixteenth century
rather than abandon the Bogomil heresy. His father was an *imam*,
a Moslem priest, and he was very pious when he was a boy. It
was his ambition then to win the tittle of *bafiz*, which is given
to a man who knows the Koran by heart, but he had only
mastered half of it when he was caught up into the tide of
the Bosnian and Herzegovinian nationalist movement. He was
the leading spirit in the Mostar counterpart of the revolutionary
cell in Sarajevo to which Princip belonged. For a summer he
worked as a comitadji in Macedonia, and later joined the Serbian
Army during the Balkan wars. After that he went to study law in
Vienna and became a leader of the disaffected Slav students of
Austrian nationality. At the outbreak of war in 1914 he escaped to
Belgrade and fought with the Serbian Army. He was in a position
to know how little the Serbian Government had wanted war at
that time, for he found himself fighting in battle after battle that
would have been a decisive victory had he and his comrades not
been hamstrung by lack of munitions. He took part in the retreat
through Albania, and in Corfu was invalided out of the army.
Still a boy, he had behind him five years of almost continuous
military service, irregular and regular. He spent the rest of the
war years taking a degree in Oriental studies in the Sorbonne, and
is a scholar of Turkish, Arabic, Persian, and Sanskrit. After the
peace he returned to Herzegovina, and, without making an effort
to protect his own interests, assisted in the land scheme which
broke up the big estates belonging to the Moslem landowners and
distributed it among the peasants. Through all the intricacies of
post-war Yugoslavian politics, in spite of the temptations they have
offered to passion and acquisitiveness, he has urged the importance
to the state of fundamental virtue, of honest administration, and
of justice towards all races and classes. In fact, experiences which

should have turned him into a wolf have left him unchangeably mild and inflexibly merciful. He was suffered the shipwreck of his political ambitions during the last years, for under the dictatorship of Stoyadinovitch all such democrats as he have been driven out of politics. But he is still unembittered, laughter is always rolling up from the depths of his full-bodied Bosnian handsomeness.

Militsa and Mehmed have a special value to me not only because of what they are, but because of where they are. Twice I passed through Skoplje before I stopped there. After the first time I said to some people in Athens, 'I saw from the train a place called Skoplje which has a most beautiful fortress. Would it be worth while going there?' They were anti-Slav and answered, 'Worth while going to Skoplje? What an idea! It is just a dreary little provincial town; there's nothing there at all, not an intelligent person.' So the second time I went through the town, on my way back to Belgrade, I looked out at it and conceived it as full only with emptiness. My eye travelled over its roofs and I thought of dull rooms underneath them, with dull people eating and drinking and sleeping, with only the drabbest connective tissue of being to bind these functions together into a day. And all the time there was the flat on the Vardar embankment, lovely with old furniture brought from Novi Sad that told of the best in the Austro-Hungarian Empire, that spoke of the Vienna of Mozart and Schubert, and there were Militsa and Mehmed, always in motion, yet always steady. Militsa runs from room to room, from the library to the kitchen, from the kitchen to her bedroom, to find out what Shelley said of Chatterton, to see if there are any bubbles rising in the last lot of preserved peaches, to try on a hat she has bought from the Polish milliner in the High Street; Mehmed sits in conference with a group of grave old Moslem priests, so old that the white bands round their fezes have become blue with many years' washing, and after they have said their slow ceremonial farewells he rushes downstairs to the garden to play with his gun-dogs, and is back again in no time to give restraining advice to some university students who have called to tell him about a meditated demonstration against Mr Stoyadinovitch, Yet these two are steady as pillars. They are pillars supporting that invisible house which we must have to shelter us if we are not to be blown away by the winds of nature. Now, when I go through a town of which I know nothing, a town which appears to be a waste land of uniform streets wholly without quality, I look on it in wonder and hope, since it may hold a Mehmed, a Militsa.

St George's Eve: I

When I arrived at the apartment of Mehmed and Militsa to go with them on a tour round the country to see the various rites that are carried on during St George's Eve, I found her receiving a call from two ladies, and while Mehmed and Constantine and my husband talked politics I listened to them discussing a friend of theirs who had roused Skoplje's suspicions by going to Belgrade for a prolonged visit without her husband. 'I think indeed that this is just foolish talk,' said Militsa. 'Yelena has not left her husband for another man, she is always a little discontented because her husband gives her no freedom, and she wants a little time to be alone and enjoy the poetry of life.' 'That may be so,' said one of the ladies, 'but if all she wanted was a little time to be alone and enjoy the poetry of life, it seems funny that she went all the way out to Mrs Popovitch's new house a week before she left to borrow a copy of *Die Dame* that had some pretty nightdresses in it.' They soon left and we turned from tea to rakia, and Militsa stood for a time discussing neo-Thomism with my husband in an attitude she often adopts when engaged in intellectual conversation. She stands by the tea-table with her old wolf-hound some feet away, and a glass of rakia in her hand, and every now and then she raises the glass and whips it down so that a lash of liquid flies through the air, and the dog leaps forward and swallows it in mid-air. 'We must start,' said Mehmed. 'That is not the philosophic air I breathe easily,' said Militsa, 'and religion is for me not there at all. But I have never found it for me anywhere but in Greece, in the days when God was not considered creator, when He was allowed to be divine and free from the responsibility of the universe.' '*Whee!*' went the rakia. 'Woof, woof!' went the dog. 'We must start,' said Mehmed. 'I will be ready in a minute,' said Militsa, and took the last drop of rakia herself. She looked at her husband and mine and nodded approvingly. 'Alas for poor Yelena,' she said, 'her husband is very fat, he has always been too fat, and her lover in Belgrade is quite an old man.'

At last in a cold grey evening we three drove off to see St George at work. This was a more diverse spectacle than one would have supposed. St George, who is the very same that is the patron saint of England, is a mysterious and beneficent figure who is trusted to confer fertility for reasons that are now completely hidden.

Pope Gelasius, as early as the fifth century, tactfully referred to him as one of those saints 'whose names are justly reverenced among men, but whose actions are known only to God.' Gibbon's description of him as a villainous Army contractor is nonsense; he was confusing him with a rascally bishop called George of Laodicea. The other story that he was a Roman officer martyred during the persecutions of Diocletian has, in the opinion of scholars, no better foundation. But they believe that he really existed, and that he was probably martyred about forty miles east of Constantinople some time during the third century. He was apparently a virtuous and heroic person who had some extraordinary adventure with a wild beast that made him the Christian equivalent of Perseus in the popular mind. Whatever this adventure was, it must have taken the form of a powerful intervention on behalf of life, for his legends represent him as raising the dead, saving cities from destroying armies, making planks burst into leaf, and causing milk instead of blood to run from the severed head of a martyr. He himself was three times put to death, being once cut in pieces, once buried deep in the earth, and once consumed by fire, and was three times brought back to life. In Macedonia he is said to cure barrenness of women and of lands, both by the Christians and the Moslems; for since he had three hundred years' start of Mohammed he was not to be dug out of the popular mind.

We saw some of his work as soon as we left the house. We had crossed the bridge and were driving along the enbankment, and Militsa was saying, 'In that house with the flowers in the balcony lives the girl who was Miss Yugoslavia some years ago, and it is a great misfortune for her, because to marry well one must be correct and not do such things as enter beauty contests, and she is quite a good girl, so now she is unmarried and very poor,' when I saw that a stream of veiled women dressed in black was passing along the pavement beside the river. It was as if the string of a black necklace had broken and the beads were all rolling the same way. 'Yes,' said Mehmed, 'always on St George's Eve they come along to this part of the embankment where these poplars are, and they stand and look down into the river.' That is all they were doing: standing like flimsy black pillars and looking over the low stone wall at the rushing Vardar. It was the most attenuated rite I have ever seen, the most etiolated ceremony; it was within a hair's breadth of not happening at all. Of course, if one cannot show one's face, if one is swaddled by clothing till free movement is impossible, if negation is presented as one's guiding physical principle, this is the most one can do. The custom obviously bore some relation

to the nature worship which is the basic religion of the peoples in
this part, with its special preference for water. But it had none of
the therapeutic properties of worship, it gave the worshippers none
of the release that comes from expressing reverence by a vigorous
movement or unusual action, nor did it give any sense of contact
with magic forces. They were merely allowed to approach the idea
of worship and apprehend it dimly, as they apprehend the outer
world through their veils. 'Why do they come to this particular part
of the embankment?' I asked Mehmed, but he did not know. Yet
I think he was fully acquainted with all the local superstitions held
by male Moslems.

Soon we took to a bad road that lurched among the bare uplands
at the feet of the mountains. It was as if one left the road in the valley
that runs from Lewes to Newhaven and tried one's luck over the
fields and downs. Beautiful children in fantastic dresses watched
us staggering from side to side of the rutted track, courteous old
men in white kilts shouted advice over bleak pastures. Someone
was leaning against a stunted tree and piping. After two hours or
so we came to a great farm that glimmered whitish through the
twilight, among the leggy trunks of a young orchard, and Mehmed
said, 'This is where we are going to stay, though the owner does not
yet know it.' I felt shy at being an unannounced guest; I strolled
nervously in the garden, dipping my nose to the huge flowers of
the lilac bushes that were black in the twilight. Then a voice spoke
from the house in beautiful English, English that would have been
considered remarkably beautiful even if it had been an Englishman
who had spoken it, and a handsome man with fair hair, square
shoulders, and a narrow waist came out and welcomed me. He
looked like a certain type of Russian officer, but his face was more
distracted, being aware of all sorts of alternatives to the actions for
which his body was so perfectly shaped. In the porch there stood
his wife, a lovely girl in her middle twenties, and her mother, a
still lovely woman with silver hair, who were talking to Militsa
and Mehmed with that candid appreciation of their friend's charm
which makes Slav life so agreeable.

The perfect note for a visit had been struck at once; but when our
host heard that we had come to see the rites of St George practised in
the neighbourhood he started up and said that we must go at once,
for if we left the journey till full darkness it would be impossible to
make the journey there and back before midnight. We got back into
the car, and with him as our guide we bounced along a dirt-track
till we came to a cross-roads with some hovels glimmering through
the darkness. 'It is here, the Tekiya,' said our host. 'Yes, this is the

Bektashi village,' said Mehmed, 'I recognize it, I have been here before.' I had not before shown any great curiosity as to what we were to see that night, for the reason that I had always found it a waste of time to try to imagine beforehand anything that Yugoslavia was going to offer me. But I knew that Tekiya was the Turkish word for a sanctuary and that the Bektashi were an order of dervishes, that is to say monks who exist to supply the element of mysticism which is lacking in Orthodox Islam. This particular order was founded by a native of Bukhara named Haji Bektash about six hundred years ago, and it was the special cult of the Janizaries, who spread it all over the Balkan Peninsula. It is said to preach an ecstatic pantheism, and to pronounce the elect free to follow their own inspirations regarding mortality. I stepped out of the car into the kind of twilight that is as dazzling as brilliant sunshine. The white houses glared through what was otherwise thick darkness, the last light shone like polished steel from pools in a road that could only be deduced. Towards us came some men in fezes, their teeth and the whites of their eyes flashing through the dusk. They greeted us with the easy and indifferent manners of the Moslem villager, always so much more like a city dweller in his superficial contacts than his Slav neighbour, who is more profoundly hospitable and indomitably inquisitive, and they led us to a little house that looked like any other. It disturbed me, as I stumbled towards it through the palpitating dusk, and made travel seem a vain thing, that I could no more have deduced that it was a Moslem sanctuary by looking at it than I had been able to deduce Militsa and Mehmed by looking at Skoplje.

Within, it was a square room with a wooden vaulted ceiling, imperfectly lit by a few candles set in iron brackets waist-high on the plastered walls. Our tremendous amazed shadows looked down on a tall black stone standing in the middle of the room, about seven feet high. There was a small flat stone laid across the top of it; it might have been wearing a mortar-board. A string was tied round it, and from this hung flimsy strips of cloth, and beside it lay a collection box. Soon our massive, clear-cut, stolid shadows were brushed across by more delicate shades, and four veiled women were among us. Four times there was the fall of a coin in the collecting-box, four times a black body pressed itself against the black stone, four times black sleeves spread widely and arms stretched as far as possible round its cold girth. 'Tonight if a woman wishes while she embraces this stone,' one of the men explained to us, 'and her fingers meet, then her wish shall be granted.' 'Is that really what they believe?' I asked, and Mehmed and our host confirmed it. Yet it was quite obvious that that was not what the women believed. They were quite unperturbed when their fingers failed to meet, and indeed I do not think I have seen half a dozen women in my life with arms long enough to make the circuit of this stone. The men's mistake was only more evidence of the pitiful furtiveness of the Moslem woman's life, which necessarily defends secrets almost unthreatened by the curiosity of the male.

The women's belief, it could be seen by watching them, lay in the degree of effort they put into the embrace; they must put all their strength, all their passion, into stretching as far as possible, and take to themselves all they could of the stone. Then they must give it their extreme of homage, by raising their veils to bare their lips and kissing it in adoration that makes no reserves. It struck on the mind like a chord and its resolution, this gesture of ultimate greed followed by the gesture of ultimate charity and abnegation. Each woman then receded, fluttering backwards and bringing her whispered prayer to an end by drawing her finger-tips down her face and bosom. They drew tremulously together and then our crasser shadows were along the walls, though none of us actually saw them go. It might be thought that these veiled women who had come to seek from a stone the power to perform a universal animal function for the benefit of those who treated them without honour, who were so repressed that they had to dilute to as near to nothingness as might be even such a negative gesture as leaving a room, would be undifferentiated female stuff, mere specimens of mother ooze. Yet these four had actually disclosed their nature to the room and its shadows, and each of these natures was highly individual; from each pair of sleeves had issued a pair of hands that was unique as souls are. One pair was ageing and had come near to losing hope; one pair was young but grasped the stone desperately, as if in agony lest hope might go; one pair grasped the stone as desperately but with an agony that would last five minutes, or even less, if she saw something to make her laugh; and one pair made the gesture with conscientious exactitude and no urgency, and would, I think, have been happier joining the Orthodox Moslems of Skoplje in their unsubstantial rite down by the river than in this Bektashi traffic with mystery.

As we went out three other veiled women slipped past us into the holy room. They would come all night on this mission, from all villages and towns where the Bektashi order had its adherents, within an orbit of many miles. We drove on through the pulsing and tumbled darkness dispensed by a sky where thick clouds rode under strong star-light. 'Now we are going to the tomb of St. George,' said

Militsa. 'There too are many women who want children. Tell me, what did you wish for?' For we had both kissed the stone. The Moslems had suggested it with a courtesy which meant, I think, that because this was a woman's rite they did not feel it to be truly sacred. 'For myself,' said Militsa, 'I wished for something really terribly drastic politically.' I would not have given a penny for Mr Stoyadinovitch's life if the stone was functioning according to repute.

On a little hillside we saw a glimmer of murky brightness and headed for it. We stepped out into a patch of Derby Day, and saw what one might see on Epsom Downs on the eve of the race, when the gipsies are settling in. On a grassy common people were sitting about, eating and drinking and talking as if there had not yet been established in their minds the convention that associates night with sleep. If one shut one's eyes the hubble-bubble sounded astonished, as if an elementary form of consciousness were expressing its amazement that it should not be still unconscious. A gipsy band thrummed and snorted; lemonade sellers cried their livid yellow ware; the gallery of a house overlooking the common was filled with white light, and many heads and shoulders showed black against it. We took a path up the hillside to a little chapel and joined the crowd that pressed into it. It was a new little chapel, not interesting. At first nothing took my eye save a number of very vividly coloured woollen stockings, knitted in elaborate abstract patterns, which were hanging on the icons and on a rope before the altar. But the crowd bore me forward and I saw in the centre of the floor a cross, and about it a thickening of human stuff. 'The cross is over the tomb of St. George,' whispered Militsa, 'and look, oh, look! It is not to be believed! This is the Greek rite of incubation, this is how the Greeks lay all night on the altar of Apollo, so that they could dream themselves into the minds of the gods and know their futures.'

Round the cross lay a heap of women in ritual trance, their eyes closed, their breasts rising and falling in the long rhythm of sleep. They lay head to heel, athwart and alongside, one with a shoulder on another's knee, another with a foot in someone's face, tangled and still like a knot of snakes under a stone in winter-time. It seemed to me their sleep was real. Their slow breathing, the lumpiness of their bodies, the anguished, concentrated sealing of their eyes by their lids made me myself feel drowsy. I yawned as I looked down on the face of one woman who had devoted herself to sleep, who had dedicated herself to sleep, who had dropped herself into the depths of sleep as a stone might be dropped down a well She had pillowed her head on her arm; and on the sleeve of her sheepskin jacket beside her roughened brow there was embroidered an arch and a tree, the rustic descendant of a delicate Persian design. We were among the shards of a civilization, the withered husks of a culture. How had this rite contracted! The Greeks had desired to know the future, to acquaint themselves with the majestic minds of the gods. These women's demand on the future was limited to a period of nine months, and the aid they sought lay in a being so remote as to be characterless save for the murmured rumour of beneficence. Nevertheless the rite was splendid even in its ruin. The life that had filled these women was of the wrong sort and did not engender new life, therefore they had poured it forth, they had emptied themselves utterly, and they had lain themselves down in a holy place to be filled again with another sort of life, so strong that it could reproduce itself. This was an act of faith, very commendable in people who had so little reason to feel faith, who had received so little assurance that existence was worthy of continuance.

As we left the chapel we saw an old peasant woman with a group of friends round her, who held out her hands to two younger women and kissed them on both cheeks. 'Take a look at her,' said our host, 'it was she who saw in a dream that there was a coffin buried on this hillside, and that the body inside it was St. George.' We tried to see her face through the darkness, but the night was too thick, and we could not learn whether she bore the stigmata of the visionary or of the simpleton. As we passed the apse of the chapel on our way downhill a man went by carrying an electric torch, and its beam showed us that one of the windows was barred with strands of wool, wound from side to side and attached to pieces of wood and metal that had been driven into the wall. 'That they do too, the women who want children,' said our host; 'it must be wool they have spun themselves.' On the common a large part of the crowd was gathered round some men and women sitting in a ditch who were having a quarrel, which was curiously pedantic in tone, although they had to shout to drown the gipsy bands and the venders. They put their cases in long deliberate speeches, which the others then criticized, often with a peevish joy in their own phrases familiar to those who have visited Oxford. Suddenly one of the women in the party took off her sheepskin jacket, threw it on the ground, flung herself down on it, and began to weep; and the scene lost its intensity and broke into sympathetic movements round her sobbing body.

The automobile was not ready, and my host and I walked down our road in the darkness. I said. 'How beautifully you speak English,' and he answered, 'Well, I was at Eton. Has Militsa not told you the ridiculous story? I went there by such a roundabout route.' But Militsa had told me nothing save that his father had been a great general, distinguished both in the Balkan wars and in the Great War of 1914. As this man talked, I realized that I had heard of this general before, as one of the regicides who slew Alexander Obrenovitch and Draga. He himself, he said, had been sent at the age of ten from Serbia to study at the Imperial Military College in St. Petersburg, and had stayed there till he was sixteen. After the Revolution he had escaped over the Urals as one of a small detachment of troops, and in Siberia, after the death of the two officers originally in charge, he became their leader. He took them safely to Vladivostok, sailed back by the United States to Europe, and at Nice was re-united to his family, who had for long mourned him as dead. Then he was sent to London, and soon was summoned to the War Office. In the waiting-room he found amusement in playing noughts and crosses against himself to find out whether he was going to be sent to France or to Salonika. But the officer who saw him said, 'We think it would be good if you went to Eton for a year.' It was as if Leif Ericson, back from America, were sent to school. He was indignant, but came to love Eton; and as the war was over when he had finished his year, he went to Cambridge as an agricultural student, so that he could farm this tract of Macedonia which was given to his father in reward for his services. So now he was trying to repair the curse of sterility laid on the land by the Turk, and he was playing his part in politics, obstinately re-stating the Slav's fundamental preference for democracy. As he talked it became apparent that his air was muted and indirect because he had read extraordinary things on the last page of history which had been turned over. He would not be surprised at anything he might read on the next, and he would not, indeed, be surprised if some page was not turned over but torn out of the book.

On our return we were given an immense dish of bacon and eggs, a huge Swiss roll, sheep's cheese, home-made bread and strong wine. Afterwards, while the others talked, I looked round at the pictures on the living-room wall. There was, according to the custom in old-fashioned Serb houses, the usual gallery of small prints, about six inches by four, hung in a group, that showed the Karageorgevitches and the Obrenovitches: a composite nationalist icon. My host came over to see what I was looking at, and lifted some off the wall so that I could look at them in the full lamplight. 'Here is one of Karageorge that I do not like,' he said, 'it makes him look like Hitler. He cannot have looked like Hitler, for he was large and finely built and trained in manly exercises. But I dislike it that our people should have liked a picture of our leader which makes him look a fanatic, a dervish. I want all such things not to be, I want man to be reasonable.'

Most of the other pictures on the wall were photographs of my host's father, the great general, a small fine-boned man with the expression of pure and docile submission to rule so noticeable in any body of young Serbian soldiers, which in his later photographs had grown to a stare of mystical contemplation. There was one picture that showed him sitting in a pinewood with the murdered King Alexander, who for once looked easy and happy, his mouth made of two lips and not a compression making a signal to give strength to the distressed will. 'My father was a most wonderful man,' said my host, and stopped and sighed. The strongest of our beloveds, once they are dead, seem too fragile to be spoken of to strangers. 'But this is the photograph I like best, it is my father with his mother, who was a peasant.'

Byzantine art is hardly stylized at all. This woman, sitting with a white cloth about her head, in a rigid armament of stuffs, exercised the enormous authority and suffered the enormous grief of the Madonnas. She was the officer of earth, she had brought her children into its broad prison, and her face showed how well she knew what bitter bread they would eat in captivity. Her nose was prominent, a fleshless ridge of bone as it is in many frescoes, and her cheeks were hollow. Such women have to suckle their children too long, because the kings and magi of the world have never yet been ready to take them over at their weaning and give them a liberal diet from the fields, such women all their lives eat only when their husbands and sons have had enough; so they are spare. If she had found life so meanly disposed, why did she condemn her children to suffer it? She could not tell us; but on that point she is inflexible. And her son honours her for this indefensible insistence. He stands by her in reverence, but his slimness and strength and lightness of bearing, even the dedicated fervour in his eyes, so different from her solidity, show a revolt against her decree. He will escape from life, from the prison to which she was delivered him, not directly into death, but into a new kind of life, contrary to the instincts. So he will interfere with natural growth by subjecting himself to unnatural discipline and putting himself to impossible tasks, such as the upsetting of kings and the overthrowal of empires. The fertility for which women were asking the gods everywhere in the dark night over Macedonia was not as simple a gift as they supposed. They were begging for the proper conduct of a period of nine months and a chance to ripen its fruits;

they would obtain the bloodstained eternity of human history. My host put the photographs back on the wall and said, 'I wonder what pictures will hang here when my two little children, who are now sleeping upstairs, are as old as we are.' He came back and sat by the lamp, his head on his hand, and spoke of Mussolini in the West and Hitler in the North. It was clear that he knew that perhaps no other picture would hang on these walls, that these pictures in front of us might some day be brought to the ground with the slash of a bayonet and die under the hot tide of their own glass when the smoke rose from the burning walls. Alone of all these women in the night Militsa had asked for something 'really terribly drastic politically,' trying to protect them and their children with a brilliant thought, an Ariel to aid the Madonna.

St. George's Eve: II

Because we were going to see a ceremony that took place on a stone at Ovche Polye, that is to say the Sheep's Field, an upland plateau some miles away, we got up at half-past five and set off in a grey morning. A cold wind moved about the hillside, marbling the fields of young wheat; and along the lanes peasants on pack-horses, nodding with drowsiness, jogged back from the chapel of St. George's tomb, their cloaks about them. We took to the good road that runs south beside the Vardar down a gorge to Veles, under steep grassy hillsides splashed here and there with fields of deep-blue flowers and thickets of wild roses. As we got nearer the town, we saw that there were people encamped on the brow of each hill, eating and drinking and confronting the morning. Men stood up and drank wine out of bottles, looking at the whiteness above the mountain-tops.

'How beautiful are these rites,' said Militsa, 'that make people adore the common thing, that say to all, "You shall have the fresh eye of the poet, you shall never take beauty for granted"!' 'Yes,' said Mehmed, 'I am down here in an automobile, because I am a lazy fellow, but I am up there with them in spirit, for I know what the morning means. You know, I should be dead. I should have died twenty-three years ago in prison. For on June the twenty-eighth, 1914, I was walking in Vienna with my cousin, who was, like me, a Herzegovinian nationalist, and we came into the Ring, and we saw that everybody was very excited, and we heard something about Serbs and the heir to the throne being killed. We thought it was our Serbian Crown Prince who had been killed, so we were very sad, and we sat down in a café and had a drink. Then a news-boy came by and I bought a paper, and I saw that it was Franz Ferdinand who had been killed by a Serb, and I got up and said, 'Come, we must escape to Serbia, for now the end of all has come. Let us hurry for the train.' But he would not come with me, because he knew how awful the war was going to be and he did not want to admit that it was bound to happen. So I argued with him till I pulled out my watch and saw that I was going to miss the train, so I took to my heels and just caught it. My cousin was arrested that night, and so would I have been if I had stayed; and my cousin died in prison, and I do not think that the Austrians would have been very careful to keep me alive. When I think of that, I feel

what those people up there are feeling. Ouf! The day, just as a
day, is good.'

As we drew towards Veles we passed a gipsy family trudging
homewards, the young daughter in immense balloon trousers of
bright pink satin; a primitive cart with some people dressed in black
and white, profiline and impassive as Egyptians, from a far village,
probably in the Bitolj district; a cart of more modern fashion driven
by a plump and handsome young woman in Western clothes, who,
on seeing Militsa, threw down her reins and shouted for us to stop.
She was a Serbian who had been coached by Militsa in Latin for
her science preliminary in Belgrade some years before, had later
married a Macedonian politician, and now ran a chemist's shop in
a hill town above Veles.

'Why did you not tell me you were coming?' she reproached
them. 'I am going to the *Slava* of a friend who lives on the other
side of Skoplje, but heaven knows I would have liked far better to
stay at home and entertain you. For today I take a holiday, and
indeed I have a right to it. I am always on my feet from morning till
night before St. George's Day.' 'Why is that?' asked Militsa. 'Oh,
all these women who go to the monasteries to ask for children buy
powder and rouge and lipstick to get themselves up for the outing,'
said the chemist, 'they come in all day. But where are you going?'
'We are going to the stone in the Sheep's Field,' said Militsa. 'Oh,
you will like that, if you are not too late,' said the chemist, 'but I
think you will be late if you do not hurry. It is a very interesting
rite, and I think there is something in it, to judge from my own
case. I went there two years ago, because it was nearly five years
since Marko and I had been married and we had no children, and
I did the easiest thing you can do there, which is to climb up on to
the stone and throw a jar down on the ground to break it. Three
times I threw down my jar, and it would not break, and still I
have no children. I will not keep you any longer, for all the people
will be gone unless you make haste.'   The road then mounted, we
saw in the distance Veles lying like a mosaic, cracked across by the
gorge of the Vardar, and we left the road for a hillside track that
climbed a pass between two summits black with people saluting
the morning, and took us into the Sheep's Field. Here we entered
quite a new kind of landscape. It is a wide sea of pastures and arable
land, rising and falling in gentle waves within a haven of blue-grey
mountains. Under a grey sky this place would be featureless, in a
Macedonian summer it must be a hardly visible trough of heat.
But this was spring, and the morning was pearly, there was a mild
wind and soft sunshine, and all forms and colours in the scene were

revealed in their essence. The earth on this upland plain is a delicate red, not so crimson as in the lowlands. Young wheat never looks so green as when it grows from such soil, and where it carries no crop it is transparent and nacreous, because of the powdered limestone which sprays it with the insubstantial conspicuousness of a comet's tail. Of the surrounding hills one stood alone, magnificent in sharp austerity of cliff and pyramid; it is called 'the witness of God.' As the sun rose higher there was manifest in the valley a light that was like Greek light, a steady radiance which stood like a divine person between the earth and the sky, and was the most important content of the horizon, more important than anything on the ground.

The road we followed became a casual assembly of ruts that persisted across the Field for something like ten miles. We saw, near and far, a few bleak white villages, but we touched none of them, save where we crossed a spindly railway by the side of two preposterously large buildings, one a gendarmerie, the other a combined station and post-office. The Sheep's Field was the subject of an unfortunate experiment in land settlement which was among the early mistakes of the new Yugoslav state after the war. It planted some unhappy families from the North on this highly unsuitable site without the necessary equipment and governed them ill, being entirely inexperienced in the arts and sciences of colonization. On the other side of this railway line we began to come on groups of peasants, the women glorious even from far off because of the soft blaze of their multi-coloured aprons. All were walking slowly, and though they looked quite good-humoured it was obvious that they were very tired. Some carts passed us too, and in these people were lying fast asleep. On the sheepskin jacket of one sleeping woman I saw, as we bumped slowly by, the same Persian pattern I had noted on the sleeve of the woman in trance on the tomb of St George.

It became apparent that we were approaching some focal point, which was not a village. The track was running along the crest of one of the land-waves, and though this was not very high it gave us an advantage over the countryside for several miles. We could see a number of people, perhaps twenty in all, who were travelling in every direction away from some spot on the next crest, a spot which was still not to be discovered by the eye. Some of these people were walking, some were in carts, some of them rode on pack-horses; and there passed close by us a party of dark and slender young horsemen, galloping over the pastures on better mounts than I had yet seen in Macedonia, with a gay confidence and a legendary quality that showed them to be the elegants of some isolated and archaic community. 'But they are all going away!' exclaimed Militsa. Her husband called out to one of the horsemen, 'Are we right for the stone, for the Cowherd's Rock, and are we too late?' The young man reined up his horse with a flourish and trotted towards us, making a courteous gesture with a hand gloved in purple. In a flute-like voice, sweeter than is usual among Europeans, he answered, 'Yes, go on, you will see it in a minute or two; you cannot be mistaken, for it is the only stone on the Sheep's Field, and there are still some people there.'

Our car left the track and struggled up a stretch of pasture till it could go no further. When we got out we were so near the rock that we could see its colour. It was a flat-topped rock, uneven in shape, rising to something like six feet above the ground, and it was red-brown and gleaming, for it was entirely covered with the blood of the beasts that had been sacrificed on it during the night. A dozen men were sitting or lying at the foot of the rock, most of them wearing the fez; and one man was very carefully laying a little child on a rug not far away. The grass we walked on from the car was trodden and muddied and littered with paper, and as we came nearer the rock we had to pick our way among a number of bleeding cocks' heads. The spectacle was extremely disgusting. The colour of spilt blood is not properly a colour, it is in itself discoloured, it is a visible display of putrescence. In every crevice of the red-brown rock there had been stuck wax candles, which now hung down in a limp fringe of greasy yellow tails, smeared with blood. Strands of wool, some of them dyed red or pink, had been wound round the rock and were now daubed with this grease and blood. A great many jars had been thrown down from the rock and lay in shards among the cocks' heads on the trodden grass. Though there was nothing faecal to be seen, the effect was of an ill-kept earth closet.

It would have been pleasant to turn round and run back to the car and drive away as quickly as possible, but the place had enormous authority. It was the body of our death, it was the seed of the sin that is in us, it was the forge where the sword was wrought that shall slay us. When it had at last been made visible before the eyes as it is—for we are all brought up among disguised presentations of it—it would have been foolish not to stay for a little while and contemplate it. I noticed that the man who had been settling the child on the rug was now walking round the rock with a black lamb struggling in his arms. He was a young gipsy, of the kind called Gunpowder gipsies, because they used to collect saltpetre for the Turkish Army, who are famous for their beauty, their cleanliness, their fine clothes. This young man had the features and bearing of an Indian prince, and a dark golden skin which was dull as if it had been powdered yet exhaled a soft light. His fine linen shirt was snow-white under his close-fitting jacket, his elegant breeches ended in soft leather boots, high to the knee, and he wore a round cap of fine fur which made it probable that his name was Camaralzaman. He made the circle three times and stopped, then bent and kissed the greasy blood-stained rock. Then he lifted up the lamb, and a man standing on the rock took it from him. It looked to me as if this man held the lamb in a grip that anaesthetized it, for it did not struggle any more and lay still at his feet without making a sound or a movement.

Now the gipsy fetched the child from the rug and brought it to the rock. It was a little girl of eighteen months or so, dressed in very clean white clothes. Her white bonnet was embroidered in designs of the Byzantine tradition in deep brown thread, and was tied with a satin bow of a particularly plangent sky-blue. Her father handed her up to another man who was standing on the rock, and then climbed up himself and set her down tenderly on as clean a place as he could find for her among the filth. Now the man who was holding the lamb took it to the edge of the rock and drew a knife across its throat. A jet of blood spurted out and fell red and shining on the browner blood that had been shed before. The gipsy had caught some on his fingers, and with this he made a circle on the child's forehead. Then he got down again and went round the rock another three times, carrying another black lamb. 'He is doing this,' a bearded Moslem standing by explained, 'because his wife got this child by coming here and giving a lamb, and all children that are got from the rock must be brought back and marked with the sign of the rock.' The gipsy kissed the rock again and handed up the lamb, and climbed to the sacrificial platform, and again the sacrifice was offered; but this time he not only marked the child with the circle but caught some of the blood in a little glass bottle. Then he carried her back to the rug, and the man with the knife laid the carcasses of the lambs, which were still faintly smoking at the throat, on the grass, among the shards and the cocks's heads. Under the opening glory of the morning the stench from the rock mounted more strongly and became sickening.

The man with the knife and his friends gathered round us and told us of the virtue of the place. Many women had got children by giving cocks and lambs to the rock. One woman who had come all the way from Prilep had had a child after she had lived in barren marriage for fifteen years. But it was foolish to doubt the efficacy of making sacrifices to the rock, for people would not go on doing it if it were not efficacious, and they had done it for a very long time, for hundreds of years. They should, of course, have said thousands. Their proof, which should have been valid if man were a reasonable animal, was therefore stronger than they supposed. The men who told us these things were good animals, with bright eyes and long limbs and good bones. They were also intelligent. Their remarks on the stone were based on insufficient information, but were logical enough, and when they went on to talk of matters less mysterious than fertility, such as their experiences in the last war, they showed considerable good sense and powers of observation. One spoke a little English, another spoke fluent French; two or three seemed to follow skilled trades. But what they were doing at the rock was abominable.

All I had seen the night before was not discreditable to humanity. I had not found anything being done which was likely to give children to women who were barren for physiological reasons; but I had seen ritual actions that were likely to evoke the power of love, which is not irrelevant to these matters. When the Moslem women in the Tekiya put out their arms to embrace the black stone and dropped their heads to kiss it, they made a gesture of the same nature, though not so absolute, as that which men and women make when they bend down to kiss the cloth which lies instead of Christ on the holy table at Easter. Such a gesture is an imitation by the body of the gesture made by the soul in loving. It says, 'I will pour myself in devotion to you, I will empty myself without hoping for return, and I can do this serenely, for I know that as I empty myself I shall be filled again.' Human beings cannot remind themselves too often that they are capable of performing this miracle, the existence of which cannot be proved by logic.

The women who lay in ritual sleep on the tomb of St George were working as fitly as the women in the Tekiya for the health of their souls. We prune our minds to fit them into the garden of ordinary life. We exclude from our consciousness all sorts of knowledge that we have acquired because it might distract us from the problems we must solve if we are to go on living, and it might even make us doubt whether it is prudent to live. But sometimes it is necessary for us to know where we are in eternity as well as in time, and we must lift this ban. Then we must let our full knowledge invade our minds, and let our memories of birth crawl like serpents from their cave and our foreknowledge of death spread its wide shadow. There is nothing shameful for women whose senses have been sharpened by the grief of barrenness to lie down on the tomb of one whose life was visible marvel and explore the invisible marvels of their own nature. Their ritual sleep was wholesome as common sleep.

But the rite of the Sheep's Field was purely shameful. It was a huge and dirty lie. There is a possibility that barrenness due to the mind could be aided by a rite that evoked love and broke down peevish desires to be separate and alone, or that animated a fatigued nature by refreshment from its hidden sources. But this could do nothing that it promised. Women do not get children by adding to the normal act of copulation the slaughter of a lamb, the breaking of a jar, the decapitation of a cock, the stretching of wool through blood and grease. If there was a woman whose womb could be unsealed by witnessing a petty and pointless act of violence, by seeing a jet of blood fall from a lamb's throat on a rock wet with stale and stinking blood, her fertility would be the reverse of motherhood, she would have children for the purpose of hating them.

The rite made its false claims not out of delusion: it was a conscious cheat. Those who had invented it and maintained it through the ages were actuated by a beastly retrogression, they wanted again to enjoy the dawn of nastiness as it had first broken over their infant minds. They wanted to put their hands on something weaker than themselves and prod its mechanism to funny tricks by the use of pain, to smash what was whole, to puddle in the warm stickiness of their own secretions. Hence the slaughter of the lambs and the cocks, the breaking of the jars, the mess of blood and grease. But the intelligence of man is sound enough to have noticed that if the fully grown try to go back to the infantile they cannot succeed, but must go on to imbecility and mania. Therefore those who wish to indulge in this make the huge pretension for it that it is a secret way of achieving what is good, and that there is a mysterious process at work in the world which has no relation to causality. This process is a penny-in-the-slot machine of idiot character. If one drops in a piece of suffering, a blessing pops out at once. If one squares death by offering him a sacrifice, one will be allowed some share in life for which one has hungered. Thus those who had a letch for violence could gratify it and at the same time gain authority over those who loved peace and life. It could be seen that the slaughterer of the lamb was very well pleased with his importance, and some of the Moslems round the rock smugly hastened to tell us that they had performed his office some time during the night. It was disgusting to think that they enjoyed any prestige, for though they were performing an action that was thousands of years old and sanctified by custom, there was about them a horrid air of whimsicality, of caprice, of instability. For all their pretensions they were doing what was not necessary. They had achieved unsurpassably what Monsieur André Gide licks his lips over, *l'acte gratuit*. This is the very converse of goodness, which must be stable, since it is a response to the fundamental needs of mankind, which themselves are stable.

I knew this rock well. I had lived under the shadow of it all my life. All our Western thought is founded on this repulsive pretence that pain is the proper price of any good thing. Here it could be seen how the meaning of the Crucifixion had been hidden from us, though it was written clear. A supremely good man was born on earth, a man who was without cruelty, who could have taught mankind to live in perpetual happiness; and because we are infatuated with this idea of sacrifice, of shedding innocent blood to secure innocent advantages, we found nothing better to do with this passport to deliverance than destroy him. There is that in the universe, half inside and half outside our minds, which is wholly adorable; and this it was that men killed when they crucified Jesus Christ. Our shame would be absolute, were it not that the crime we intended cannot in fact be committed. It is not possible to kill goodness. There is always more of it, it does not take flight from our accursed earth, it perpetually asks us to take what we need from it.

Of that lesson we had profited hardly at all, because resourcefulness rises from the rock like the stench of its blood. The cruel spirit which informed it saved itself by a ruse, a theological ruse. So successful has this ruse been that the rock disgusted me with the added loathsomeness of familiarity, as the drunkenness of a man known to be a habitual alcoholic is more offensive than the accidental excess of a temperate man. Its rite, under various disguises, had been recommended to me since my infancy by various religious bodies, by Roman Catholicism, by Anglicanism, by Methodism, by the Salvation Army. Since its earliest days Christianity has been compelled to seem its opposite. This stone, the knife, the filth, the blood, is what many people desire beyond anything else, and they fight to obtain it. There was an enemy of love and Christ called Saul of Tarsus who could not abide this demonstration by the cross that man was vile and cruelty the essence of his vileness, and for that reason persecuted Christians till his honesty could not tolerate his denial of the adorability of goodness and showed it to him under the seeming of a bright light. But the belief of his heart was in force and in pain, and his mind, which was very Jewish in its refusal to accept defeat, tinkered incessantly with the gospel till it found a way of making it appear as if cruelty was the way of salvation. He developed a theory of the Atonement which was pure nonsense yet had the power to convince, for it was spoken quickly in tones of genius to excited people who listened trustfully, knowing the innocence of Christ and assuming that everything said in his name was innocent also, and being tainted, as all human beings are, with the same love of blood as the speaker. This monstrous theory supposes that God was angry with man for his sins and that He wanted to punish him for these, not in any way that might lead to his reformation, but simply by inflicting pain on him; and that He allowed Christ to suffer this pain instead of man and thereafter was willing on certain terms to treat man as if he had not committed these sins. This theory flouts reason at all points, for it is not possible that a just God should forgive people who are wicked because another person who was good endured agony by being nailed to a cross.

There was a gap in the theory which could never be bridged, but those who loved cruelty tried from then on to bridge it. There were many lesser ones of this sort and one great one, Augustine, so curiously called a saint. Genius was his, and warm blood, but his heart was polluted like the rock. He loved love with the hopeless infatuation of one who, like King Lear, cannot love. His mother and he were like dam and cub in the strength of their natural relationship, but his appetite for nastiness made him sully it. Throughout their lives they achieved from time to time an extreme sweetness, but the putrescence gained, and at her death he felt an exaltation as mean as anything recorded in literature, because she died in Italy, far from her African home, and therefore could not be buried, as she had desired, beside her beloved husband. His relationship with God covered as wide a range. He wanted a supreme being sterilized of all that his genius recognized as foul, but he did not want him to be positively good. He hated all the milder aspects of virtue, he despised the spirit that lets all things flower according to their being, for he liked too well to draw the knife across the lamb's throat. In his desire to establish cruelty in a part of holiness he tried to find a logical basis for the abominable doctrine of St Paul, and he adopted a theory that the Devil had acquired a rightful power over man because of his sins, and lost it because he forfeited all rights by crucifying Christ, who was sinless. This went far to proving the universe to be as nonsensical as the devotees of the rock wished it to be. It presents us with a Devil who was apparently to a certain degree respectable, at least respectable enough to be allowed by God to exercise his legal rights in the universe, until he killed Christ. This robs the wickedness of man of its ultimate importance. His sins were evidently not so bad, just what you might expect from the subjects of a disorderly native prince. It was perhaps that which recommended the theory to Augustine, who knew he was wicked.

It was certainly that which recommended Augustine's theory to Martin Luther, who was not even like the rock, who was the rock, with the sullied grass, the cocks' heads, the grease, the stinking blood. He was the ugliest of the great, a hog magnified and with speech. His only virtue was the virtue of the wild boar; he was courageous. But all other merits he lacked, and strove to muddy life into a sty with his ill opinion of it. He howled against man's gift of reason, and in one of his sermons he cried out to his hearers to throw shit in her face, because she was the Devil's whore, rotten with itch and leprosy, who ought to be kept in the privy. He hated reason for a cause: because it exposed the idiocy of Augustine's theory of Atonement, which was dear to him in its bloody violence, which was dear to him because it substituted joy in murder for remorse at the murder of goodness. His honesty blurted out that there was no sense whatsoever in the idea of God's acceptance of Christ's death as a sacrifice for man, but all the same he smacked his lips over it, it was good, it was gorgeous, it was eternal life. Because of him Protestantism has bleated ever since of the blood of the lamb, though not more loudly than Roman Catholicism.

So there has been daily won a victory for evil, since so many of the pious give divine honours to the cruelty which Christ came to earth to expose. If God were angry with man and wanted to punish him, and then let him go scot-free because he derived such pleasure from the sufferings of Christ, then the men who inflicted these sufferings must be the instruments of our salvation, the procurers of God's pleasures; they are at least as high as the angels. The grinning and consequential man standing on the rock with a stained knife in his grubby hand is made a personage necessary to the spiritual world; and because cruelty was built into us in our mothers' wombs we are glad of this, while at the same time everything in us that approves of kindness and can love knows that it is an obscene lie. So it has happened that all people who have not been perverted by the West into caring for nothing but machine-made articles (among which a Church designed to be primarily a social organization can fairly be classed) have found Christianity a torturing irritation, since it offers both the good and the evil in us the most supreme satisfaction imaginable and threatens them with the most final frustration. We are continually told to range ourselves with both the crucified and the crucifiers, with innocence and guilt, with kind love and cruel hate. Our breasts echo for ever with the cries 'In murdering goodness we sinned' and 'By murdering goodness we were saved.' 'The lamb is innocent and must not be killed,' 'The dead lamb brings us salvation,' so we live in chaos. This state is the less likely to be relieved because those who defend the rock are too cunning to commit their case to terms that could be grasped and disputed. Though the doctrine of the Atonement profoundly affects most public and private devotions, it has never yet been defined in any creed or by any general Council of the Churches.

Nearly all writers dip their pens in inkwells tainted with this beastliness. Shakespeare was obsessed by it. He was fully aware of the horror of this rock, but he yielded to its authority. He believed that the rite was in accord with reality, which he thought to be perverse in character. He recognized the adorability of goodness, in its simplicity and in its finer shades, as in worsted kingliness or a magician's age. But there filters into his work from the depths of his nature a nostalgia for infantile nastiness, a love of groping for trout in the peculiar rivers of the body, a letch for cruelty which hardly took pleasure in it, but longed sickly for consummation with the disgusting and destructive but just moment, as martyrs long for their doom. He who perfectly understood the nature of love, who knew that 'love is not love which alters when it alteration finds, or bends with the remover to remove,' felt under an obligation to castrate it by smearing the sexual function which is the means of bringing together most lovers in the world, be they husbands and wives or parents and children. His respect for the rock forced him to write *King Lear* and take up all lambs of the herd one by one and draw his knife across their throats. All kinds of love are in that play presented as worthless: the love of parent for child, of child for parent, of married people and illicit lovers, all are impotent or bestial. But at the end the part of Shakespeare that was a grown man cries out that there is no health in the world save through love, that without it life is madness and death. It is not to the credit of mankind that the supreme work of art produced by Western civilization should do nothing more than embody obsession with this rock and revolt against it. Since we have travelled thus far from the speechless and thoughtless roots of our stock we should have travelled further. There must be something vile in us to make us linger, age after age, in this insanitary spot.

But some were not with us at the rock, but with the sunlight which the stench only so faintly disturbed, which shone inviolate above the mountains. That is the special value of Mozart. It is not that he was kind. When he wanted a lamb for food it had to die. But in all his music there is no phrase which consented to anything so lacking in precision as this ritual slaughter, so irrelevant to its professed purpose as this assault on infertility, nor does he ever concur in the belief that the disagreeable is somehow of magical efficacy. He believes that evil works nothing but mischief; otherwise it would not be evil. 'Psst! Psst!' says Leporello, beckoning the masked strangers in the garden, and bidding them to a ball; but since wickedness is the host it is no ball but an occasion for rape and bloodshed. After Don Juan is dead the characters of the play who are good, be it in solemnity or in lightness, gather together in a nightingale burst of song, because the departure of cruelty allows their goodness to act as it must according to its own sweet process. The same precision, the same refusal to be humbugged by the hypocritical claims of cruelty, account for the value of Jane Austen's work, which is so much greater than can be accounted for by its apparent content. But suavity of style is not the secret, for William Blake is rough. His rejection of the rock took another form, he searched his mind for belief in its fraud like a terrified woman feeling her breast for a cancer, he gave himself up to prophetic fury that his mind might find its way back to the undefiled sources of its knowledge of goodness. Here on the Sheep's Field it could be seen where the cleavage lies that can be apprehended to run through art and life: on one side are the people who are accomplices of the rock and on the other those who are its enemy. It appeared also where the cleavage lay in our human nature which makes us broken and futile. A part of us is enamoured of the rock and tells us that we should not reject it, that it is solemn and mystical and only the shallow deny the value of sacrifice. Because here a perfect myth had been found for a fundamental but foul disposition of the mind, we were all on an equality with the haggard and grimy peasant, his neckerchief loose about a goitre, who now slouched to the rock, the very man to attend a nocturnal rite late the next morning, and held up a twitching lamb to the fezed executioner, who was scrambling consequentially to the squalid summit.

Old Serbia

The Plain of Kossovo I

OUR ROAD FROM SKOPLJE TO THE KOSSOVO POLYE, THE
Field of the Blackbirds, took us towards grey hills patterned with
shadows blue as English bluebells by a valley that had the worn
look, the ageing air that comes on the southern landscape as soon
as the fruit blossom has passed. Soon Dragutin made us get out
because we had come to a famous well, and we found sitting by
the waters a couple of old Albanian Moslems, paupers in rags and
broken sandals, who were quietly merry as the morning. 'Good
day to you,' said Constantine. 'What are you doing here?' It was a
natural question, for this was far between villages, and they did not
look to be persons of independent means. 'I am doing nothing,' said
the older of the two. 'What, nothing?' 'Yes, nothing,' he said, his
grin gashing his beard widely. He had received moral instruction
somewhere, he had learned enough about the obligation of honest
toil to find a conscious joy in idleness. 'Shame on you!' mocked
Constantine. 'And your friend?' 'He has come to help me!' said
the Albanian; and over our glasses of stinging water, risen virile
from mountainy depths, we jeered at industry.

But back in the car Constantine slumped. It was as if he were
a very sick man, for he was sleepy, fretful, inferior to himself,
and quarrelsome. He could put nothing in a way that was not an
affront. Now he said, 'We will stop at Grachanitsa, the church I
told you of on the edge of Kossovo Plain, but I do not think you
will understand it, because it is very personal to us Serbs, and that
is something you foreigners can never grasp. It is too difficult for
you, we are too rough and too deep for your smoothness and your
shallowness. That is why most foreign books about us are insolently
wrong. In my department I see all books about us that are published
abroad, because I must censor them, and usually I am astonished
by their insolence, which for all the pretences made by Western
Europe and America to give our peoples culture is nothing more
than the insolence of a nasty peasant who has learned some trick
that lifts him up above the other peasants, who lends them money

at usury and then lifts his chin at their misery and says, "Peuh! What a stink!" but who is still ignorant like the worst of peasants. Did you read John Gunther's *Inside Europe*? Well, was it not a disgusting, a stupid book! How glad I was to forbid the sale of this imbecile book!'

'But it was not a bad book,' I objected. 'It was altogether bad,' said Constantine, 'it was ill-informed and what he did not know he could not guess.' 'Yes, I know some of it was not as good as the rest,' I said, 'but there were two things in it which were quite excellent: the descriptions of Dollfuss's death and the Reichstag trial. And in any case you should not have censored it.' 'And why not?' screamed Constantine. 'And why not?' 'Because,' I said, 'you know perfectly well that you could not censor *Inside Europe* except by applying standards so strict that they would prevent the publication of any sincere book on any subject.' 'You are wrong,' he shrieked, 'there is something your English brain does not know that our Serb blood is sure of, and that is that it is right to stamp on books written by such fools. Why should Western cretins drool their spittle on our sacred things?' He had, of course, censored *Inside Europe* in defiance of his own convictions just as Voltaire might, once in a while, have grimaced and put his liberal conscience to the door just for the sake of taking a holiday from his own nature. But Constantine was pretending to be somebody totally unlike himself, a stupid Prussian officer, a truculent Italian clerk, with whom he had so little in common that he could not persist in his imitation very long, and slumped into silence, his chin on his chest and his belly falling forward in a soft heap. He looked years older, and congested. It was as if in his abandonment to Gerda's nihilism he had withdrawn his consent to every integrating process, even to the circulation of his blood.

Nothing interested him on our journey. He did not leave the car with us when we got out to take some meadowsweet and wild roses, though it was his usual custom to follow us while we gathered flowers, relating to our bent behinds stories of his sexual or academic prowess. 'And when I closed my bedroom door that night,' we would hear as our fingers closed round the innocent stems, 'the wife of the Swiss minister jumped out of the wardrobe, quite naked,' or 'Do you understand truly the theory of prime numbers? It is something that throws a light on history. I will explain it to you, for I am a mathematician, I.' But now he sat in the car, neither asleep nor awake, but simply unhappy. We had to laugh alone when we were given a proof, more absolute than could be given by any homing bird, that the year had come to its kind ripeness. In a field outside one of the dullish Moslem villages which dappled these hillsides with poplars and minarets, we saw an old peasant look up into the sunshine and wipe the sweat from his brow, with the air of one observing clinical symptoms, and enact his verdict by changing from his winter to his summer clothes. No process could be simpler. He stepped out of a fine pair of those white serge trousers with allusive embroideries round the loins and the mysterious affixment to the hipbone, and he took up his hoe again. He was of the opinion that his shirt, which now showed a neat waist and a handsome gathered tail, and his under-pants made as good a summer suit as anybody needed, and he was right. But to the Western eye the publicity of the adjustment was very diverting. It was as if a stockbroker, talking to a client, should mark a patch of brightness on his office wall and should therefore strip off his coat and waistcoat and trousers, continuing his talk the while, serene in a common understanding that from now on all sane men faced a warmer world in their underclothes.

But Constantine came to life again when the car stopped under a little hill surmounted with a new white church. 'This is our church that we Serbs built for Kossovo,' he said; 'from there we will see the plain where the Turks defeated us and enslaved us, where after five hundred years of slavery we showed that we were not slaves.' He was red, he was passionate, he panted, he was as he was when he was happy. We followed a path to the church through the long grass, and as our steps brought us higher there spread before us a great plain. Dragutin clenched his fist and shouted down at the earth, where the dead Turks lay. To him the dead Christians were in Heaven or were ghosts, but not under the ground, not scattered lifeless bones; only the Turks perished thus utterly. Then we were stilled by the stillness of Kossovo. It is not one of the plains, like the *vega* of Granada or the English fens, that are flat as a floor, it lacks that sly look of geological aberration, of earth abandoning its essential irregularity. Its prototype is Salisbury Plain: the land lies loosely, like a sleeper, in a cradle of featureless hills. Not by any means is the ground level. There a shoulder rises, here a hand supports the sleeper's head. But it is obviously prostrate and passive, it has none of the active spirit which makes mountain and forest and the picturesque valley. It is active only as a sleeping body is, with that simplest residual activity, without which sleep would be death, without which the plain would be a desert: the grass pricks the sod, the fallow field changes its substances in biding its time, the green corn surpasses its greenness, but there is no excess beyond these simple functions.

It is the character of the skies that overarch plains to be not only wider than is common, but higher; and here one cloudy continent rode above another, under a vault visible yet of no colour except space. Here light lived. Its rays, brassy because it was nearly the summer, mild because it had been a bad spring, travelled slowly, high and low, discovering terraces of snow beyond the cradling hills on peaks of unseen mountains, the white blocks of a new settlement in a fold of falling fields, and the passage over downlands of a flock of sheep, cream-coloured and nigger-brown and slow-footed as stupidity. Those houses and those herds showed that there was here a world of human activity: thousands of men and women, even tens of thousands, lived and worked and sweated on Kossovo. But the plain absorbed them and nullified them by its own indifference, and there was shown before our eyes the first of all our disharmonies, the basis of our later tragedies: the division between man and nature. In childhood, when we fall on the ground we are disappointed that it is hard and hurts us. When we are older we expect a less obvious but perhaps more extravagant impossibility in demanding that there should be a correspondence between our lives and their setting; it seems to all women, and to many men, that destiny should at least once in their lives place them in a moonlit forest glade and send them love to match its beauty. In time we have to accept it that the ground does not care whether we break our noses on it, and that a moonlit forest glade is as often as not empty of anything but moonlight, and we solace ourselves with the love that is the fruit of sober judgment, and the flower of perfectly harmonious chance. We even forget what we were once foolish enough to desire. Then suddenly at some crisis of incongruity, when we see the site of a tragic historical event that ought to be blasted and is green and smiling, or pass a garden in full blossom when we are carrying our dead to burial, we recall our disappointment at this primary incongruity, and feel bitter desolation. The earth is not our mother's bosom. It shows us no special kindness. We cannot trust it to take sides with us. It makes us, its grass is our flesh, it lets us walk about on it, but this is all it will do for us; and since the earth is what is not us, and therefore a symbol of destiny and of God, we are alone and terrified.

Kossovo, more than any other historical site I know, arouses that desolation. It spreads peacefully into its vast, gentle distances, slow winds polishing it like a cloth passing over a mirror, turning the heads of the standing grain to the light. It has a look of innocence which is the extreme of guilt. For it is crowded with the dead, who died in more than their flesh, whose civilization was cast with them into their graves. It is more tragic even than its own legend, which with the dishonesty and obstinacy of a work of art commemorates one out of several battles of Kossovo. That battle which was fought under the leadership of Tsar Lazar in 1389, and placed the Serbs under the yoke of the Turks, was followed by three others of a major character, in which the Serbs stood up before the Turks and had their death demonstrated to them, the complete annihilation of their will established. Fourteen years later the son of Tsar Lazar fought here for the shrunken title of Serbian Despot against another Serb noble, George Brankovitch. They were competitive parasites of the Sultan's court and each led the half of a rent people. Definite victory was impossible, they both lived on in an undignified compromise; only Kossovo was the richer, and that by many graves. Forty-five years later the conditions of defeat had so thickened that, though there was another battle of Kossovo, the Serbs could not fight. They, who of all peoples feel the least reluctance to fighting, had to stand inactive on the field where it was natural they should determine their fate. Now another George Brankovitch, nephew of the first, was Despot of a diminished Serbia; he joined with the famous John Hunyadi, a Roumanian in the service of Hungary, and King Vladislav of Poland, and they formed a great expedition to recover Serbia and Bulgaria from the Turks. Bulgaria could not be saved, but Serbia came into full freedom. A solemn treaty was signed by all the belligerents, binding the Hungarians and the Poles to stay on their side of the Danube and the Sultan to stay on his, and giving George Brankovitch the whole of Serbia, as well as returning to him his two sons, who had been captured and blinded by the Turks. But as the Turks were then being attacked in Asia Minor it seemed to the Pope that this was the right time to drive them out of Europe, and he sent an army under the Cardinal Julian Cesarini to urge the Christian forces to take up arms again. When they protested that they had just signed a treaty pledging themselves to peace, the Cardinal told them that it is lawful for Christians to set aside and break an oath made with an infidel.

The peculiar flavour of the Western Church lies strong on the tongue in that declaration. George Brankovitch refused to join the Poles and Hungarians in availing himself of this licence to perfidy. It is easy to explain this by pointing out that he had done better out of the treaty than the other signatories; but the fact remains that, although such a ruling would have been a great advantage to the Christian subjects of Turkey, at no time during their enslavement did the Eastern Church encourage them to cast away their honour.

Therefore George Brankovitch stood by while the Catholic armies advanced on the Turks at Varna in Bulgaria, whose Sultan prayed as they came, 'O Christ, if thou art God, as they followers say, punish their perfidy.' His prayer was answered. Both the King of Hungary and the Cardinal fell on the field, with most of their soldiers. But the war dragged on with interruptions for another four years, and came to an end here on Kossovo, in a battle that lasted for three days and gave the plain about fifty thousand more dead. By this time the Serbs were demoralized by the division of the Christian world and by comradeship with their pagan enemies, and it is said that they waited on the hills around the plain till the battle ended and they could rob the dead.

So in the first battle of Kossovo the Serbs learned the meaning of defeat, not such defeat as forms a necessary proportion of all effort, for in that they had often been instructed during the course of their history, but of total defeat, annihilation of their corporate will and all their individual wills. The second battle of Kossovo taught them that one may live on such a low level of existence that even defeat cannot be achieved. The third taught them that even that level is not the lowest, and that there is a limbo for subject peoples where there is neither victory nor defeat but abortions which, had they come to birth, would have become such states. There was to be yet a fourth battle which was to prove still another horrible lesson. Very shortly after the third battle, in 1453 Byzantium fell; and the Turks were able to concentrate on the task of mastering the Balkans. The Serbs were constrained not to resist them by their fear of the Roman Catholic powers, who venomously loathed them and the Bulgarians for their fidelity to the Eastern Church and their liability to the Bogomil heresy. The night fell for four centuries, limbo became Hell, and manifested the anarchy that is Hell's essential character.

It happened that the Slavs who had become Janizaries, especially the Bosnian Serbs, who had been taken from their Christian mothers and trained to forswear Christ and live in the obedience and enforcement of the oppressive yet sluttish Ottoman law, had learned their lesson too well. When the Turks themselves became alarmed by the working of that law and attempted to reform it, the Janizaries rose against the reformation. But because they remembered they were Slavs in spite of all the efforts that had been made to force them to forget it, they felt that in resisting the Turks, even in defence of Turkish law, they were resisting those who had imposed that Turkish law on them in place of their Christian system. So when the rebellious Janizaries defeated the loyal Army of the Sultan in the fourth battle of Kossovo in 1831, and left countless Turkish dead on the field, they held that they had avenged the shame laid on the Christian Slavs in the first battle of Kossovo, although they themselves were Moslems. But their Christian fellow-Slavs gave them no support, for they regarded them simply as co-religionists of the Turkish oppressors and therefore as enemies. So the revolt of the Janizaries failed; and to add the last touch of confusion, they were finally defeated by a Turkish marshal who was neither Turk nor Moslem-born Slav, but a renegade Roman Catholic from Dalmatia. Here was illustrated what is often obscured by historians, that a people can be compelled by misfortune into an existence so confused that it is not life but sheer nonsense, the malignant nonsense of cancerous growth.

Kossovo speaks only of its defeats. It is true that they were nullified by the Serbs of Serbia, who snatched their own liberty from the Turks under the leadership of Karageorge and Milosh Obrenovitch in the early nineteenth century, and pressed on, against the hostility of the great powers, until they gave liberty to Old Serbia and Macedonia in the Balkan wars. But of this triumph Kossovo says nothing, for the battle which gave it to the Serbs in 1912 was fought not there but at Kumanovo, some miles to the south-east; and even after that it knew defeat again, for here the retreating Serbian Army was bombed by German aeroplanes as they fled towards the Albanian border, and though they pursued their enemies across it when they returned three years later it was without spectacular event. Here is the image of failure, so vast that it fills the eye as failure sometimes fills an individual life, an epoch.

The white church we found had been built to celebrate the recovery of the lost land, by a society of patriotic Serbian women. Inside it many plaques of thanksgiving, ardent beyond the habit of inscriptions, hung on the whitewashed walls, and outside it, darkened by its short noonday shadow, there lay the grave of this society's president who, her head-stone said, had worked all her life long to fire her countrymen with the ambition to free their enslaved brothers, and had expressed with her last breath the desire to be buried within sight of Kossovo. As we stood beside the cross two little boys came out of a white house lying under us on the Kossovo side of the hill, caught sight of us, and stalked us, as though it were we who were wild and shy, not they. They moved in circles about us through the long grass and paused at last about ten yards away, their thumbs in their mouths, their eyes like little dark tunnels down to their animal natures.

Constantine called out, 'Little ones! Little ones!' and charmed them to him, step by step; and when they were still some feet away they told him that the white house was an orphanage, founded by the same patriotic society, and that they were all alone there, because they were too young to go to school. It would not be in accordance with our Western ideas that two boys, hardly more than babies, should be left in an orphanage for a morning by themselves, or that they should be barefoot; but they looked quite uninstitutionalized and very healthy and serene. Very likely there was here a wise Slav disorder, as in the sanatorium in Croatia, that allowed human processes to develop according to their unpredictable design. When Constantine's enchantments had brought the children to his side, he asked them, 'Why was the orphanage built here?' and they answered him in a tender and infantile version of official oratory, touching as the flags and wreaths used for a patriotic celebration in a very little village. They spoke of the glorious ancient Serbian Empire, of its shameful destruction by the Turks at Kossovo, of the agonizing captivity that lasted five centuries, of the liberation offered through courage by the Serbian people, and the founding of Yugoslavia, that should be as glorious as ancient Serbia. 'And do you know,' asked Constantine, 'the songs that our people have sung about the terrible day of St. Vitus?' They began at once, with the inexhaustible, almost rank verbal memory of the Slav child:

> "Musitch Stephen his cool wine was drinking,
> In his palace, rich with purest silver,
> In his beautiful and lordly dwelling;
> And his servant Vaistina poured it,
> When of his cool wine he had drunk deeply,
> Then said Musitch Stephen to his servant:
> "Vaistina, thou my child beloved,
> I will lay me down a while to slumber.
> Drink some wine and eat some supper,
> Then walk before my lordly palace,
> Look upon the clear night sky and tell me,
> If the silver moon is sinking westward,
> If the morning star is shining eastward,
> If the time has come for us to travel
> To the fair and level Plain of Blackbirds."'

The little boys looked noble and devout as they recited. Here was the nationalism which the intellectuals of my age agreed to consider a vice and the origin of the world's misfortunes. I cannot imagine why. Every human being is of sublime value, because his experience, which must be in some measure unique, gives him a unique view of reality, and the sum of such views should go far to giving us the complete picture of reality, which the human race must attain if it is ever to comprehend its destiny. Therefore every human being must be encouraged to cultivate his consciousness to the fullest degree. It follows that every nation, being an association of human beings who have been drawn together by common experience, has also its unique view of reality, which must contribute to our deliverance, and should therefore be allowed a like encouragement to its consciousness. Let people, then, hold to their own language, their own customs, their own beliefs, even if this inconveniences the tourist. There is not the smallest reason for confounding nationalism, which is the desire of a people to be itself, with imperialism, which is the desire of a people to prevent other peoples from being themselves. Intense nationalist spirit is often, indeed, an effort by a people to rebuild its character when an imperialist power has worked hard to destroy it. Finnish nationalism, for example, is a blood transfusion given after the weakening wounds inflicted by Tsarist Russia, and it is accompanied by defensive but not aggressive feelings in relation to its neighbours. Here certainly I could look without any reservation on the scene, on the two little boys darkening their brows in imitation of the heroes as they spoke the stern verse, on Constantine, whose Jewish eyes were full of Serbian tears, on my husband, who bent over the children with the hieratic reverence Englishmen feel for boyhood that has put its neck under the yoke of discipline, on the green bed and stone cross of the happy grave, on the domes of the native church, and the hospitable farmlike orphanage. This was as unlikely to beget any ill as the wild roses and meadowsweets we had gathered by the road.

The scene was exquisite; but it was pitifully without weight, without mass, compared to the plain that spread for forty miles before us, thickened by tragedy. If a giant had taken Kossovo in his right hand and us and the church and the farmhouse and the grave in his left hand, his right hand must have fallen to his side because of the heaviness of the load, but it would have seemed to him that in his left hand there was nothing but a little dust. It is flattery of nature to say that it is indifferent to man. It grossly disfavours him in quantity and quality, providing more pain than pleasure, and making that more potent. The simplest and most dramatic example is found in our food: a good oyster cannot please the palate as acutely as a bad one can revolt it, and a good oyster cannot make

him who eats it live for ever though a bad one can make him dead for
ever. The agony of Kossovo could not be balanced by the joy that
was to be derived from it. The transports of the women who built
the church must dull themselves in continuance, and even if they
generated the steady delight of founding a new nation that itself was
dulled by the resistance offered to the will by material objects, and
by the conflict between different wills working to the same end,
which is often not less envenomed than the conflict between wills
working to different ends. But the agony of Kossovo must have
been purely itself, pain upon pain, newly born in acuteness for
each generation, throughout five centuries. The night of evil had
been supreme, it still was supreme on a quantitative basis.

Above the plain were the soft white castles of the clouds and
a blank blue wall behind them. Into this world I had been born,
and I must resign myself to it; I could not move myself to a
fortunate planet, where any rare tear was instantly dried by a
benediction. This is my glass, I must drink out of it. In my
anxiety to know what was in the glass, I wondered, 'The world
is tragic, but just how tragic? I wonder if it is finally so, if we
can ever counter the catastrophes to which we are liable and give
ourselves a workshop of serenity in which we can experiment
with that other way of life which is not tragedy, but which is
not comedy. Certainly not comedy, for that is merely life before
tragedy has fallen upon it, ridiculous as a clown on the films who
grins and capers without seeing that there is a policeman behind
him just about to bring down a club on his head. That other
way of life must transcend not only comedy but tragedy, must
refuse to be impressed by its grandiose quality and frustrate it at
every point.'

But I found my mind wandering from the subject, which was
surely the nature of tragedy and the points at which it attacked
man, to indulge in some of that optimism which serves us in the
West instead of fortitude. Life, I said to myself, was surely not as
tragic as all that, and perhaps the defeat of Kossovo had not been a
disaster of supreme magnitude. Perhaps the armies that had stood
up before the Turks had been a huddle of barbarians, impressive
only after the fashion of a pack of wolves, that in its dying presented
the world with only the uninteresting difference between a live
pack of wolves and a dead pack of wolves. That is a view held by
some historians, notably the person so unfortunately selected by
the editors of the *Cambridge Medieval History* to write the chapter
on the Serbian Empire; and it seems to receive some support
when one drives, as we did after we left the church, along

the fringes of the plain. The population of Old Serbia is sunk far deeper in misery than the Macedonians, and at a superficial glance they justify the poor opinion of the Christian rayahs held by nineteenth-century travellers. Their houses turn a dilapidated blankness on the village street; their clothes are often dirty and unornamented by a single stitch of embroidery; and they gape at the stranger with eyes empty of anything but a lethargic fear which is quite unapposite to the present, which is the residue of a deposit left by a past age, never yet drained off by the intelligence.

Actually I knew that there were many reasons why these women should be so, other than the predisposition of their stock. They were not a fair specimen of the Slav population as it had been at the time of the battle of Kossovo, for most of the noble families had died on the field, and the cream of what were left emigrated to Austrian territory within the next three hundred years. Such as were left suffered from all the disadvantages of Turkish rule without enjoying any of the advantages that had made the ruin of Macedonia so far from absolute. It had no rich capital like Bitolj, nor such trading centres as Skoplje, Veles, Tetovo, and Gostivar; and it had no picturesqueness to tempt wealthy Turks to build country houses. It was purely agricultural land. The Turks raped it of its crops and sent them back to Constantinople, and took the peasants' last farthings in taxes, and gave nothing in return. This plain might have blossomed like the rose with civilization and nothing would have remained. It was also probable, in view of the falsity of the face a house and a peasant turn on the world, that these women were not as they seemed. But for this moment I looked on them idiotically, as if I were Gerda, imputing to them worthlessness instead of difference; and I alleged to myself that probably nothing had fallen at Kossovo that was an irreparable loss, that perhaps tragedy draws blood but never lifeblood.

Grachanitsa I

But I could not keep that up for long. It happens that there stands on the plain of Kossovo, some miles south of the actual battle-field, a building which demonstrates what sort of civilization fell with the Serbs. It proves it as no nationalist rhetoric could hope to do, it leaves no room for differences of opinion, for it is a chunk of the Nemanyan Empire, irrefutable testimony to its quality. We drove along the straight road, through low-spirited villages, past herds and flocks, all of them ornery, plain ornery, and slouching peasants, so few that the land was almost empty as the sky; and we turned into a lane leading towards the hills, through fields whose crops were smothered by those aromatic flowers which are half-way to being scrub. I would fear to say that it was not rich ground, but it is being reclaimed after centuries of avid and ignorant farming, and the effect is destitution. There was no sufficiency anywhere save in the scented handsome sprawl of honeysuckle in the hedges. Then, across a field grey-green with the young maize, we saw a settlement of smallish farms lying among low trees, and in the midst of them a rose-red dome upheld by four lesser domes of the same warm and transparent colour. These made, as the dominant shape of a religious building should do, a reference to the reality which lies above the world of appearances, to the order which transcends the disorder of events.

Even from this distance it could be seen that Grachanitsa was as religious a building as Chartres Cathedral; though it made a simpler and smaller statement, the thought and feeling behind it were as complex, and the sublime subject matter was the same. But it was as if Chartres Cathedral should stand alone on a land that has been shorn of all that was France when it was built and has been France since then; with no Paris, no Sorbonne, no Académie Franéaise, in fact not a single modern representation of the culture that built the cathedral, and not a single trace within miles of the well-being that affords a physical basis for this culture, not a plump chicken, nor a pound of butter, nor a bottle of good wine, nor a comfortable mattress. Such spectacles are commonplace in Africa or Asia or America, which have their Pyramids and Angkor Vat and Inca memorials, but in Europe we are not accustomed to them. Our forms of historic tragedy have blotted a paragraph here and there, but they have rarely torn out the leaves of a whole volume, letting

846

only a coloured frontispiece remain to tease us. Of Grachanitsa, however, catastrophe has left us nothing but Grachanitsa.

At the moment when we reached the church its ruin of surroundings was emphasized by attempts to repair it. Grachanitsa lies in a bare enclosure shaded by a few trees, pitifully different from the gardens that surround the mosques of its conquerors, with their fountains and conduited waters and marble seats. It was now stacked with heaps of masonry, and on the further side a half-finished building stood among its scaffolding; and on benches in the shadow of the church twenty or thirty young soldiers sat at a meal, while an officer stood beside them, talking to a tall white-bearded priest and a man in townish clothes. They turned to look at us, and the man in townish clothes clapped his hands and ran towards us, crying, 'Constantine! Constantine!' 'You see, he knows me, all people know me,' said Constantine, as he always did in such circumstances, but without his usual vivacity. Formerly he said it as if he could remember the exact taste of the pleasure he had shared with his friend; but it was now as if he could think of it only as a payment from a fortune he had exhausted. 'He is a very well-known architect from Belgrade,' he explained. 'I know all such people. No doubt he is in charge of the new building, whatever it is.'

That this was so the architect explained, clinging happily to Constantine's coat lapels. He was putting up a new guest-house, which was needed because the monastery was so miserably poor and wanted a new opportunity to raise funds. Tens of thousands of pilgrims come here every year on St. Vitus's Day, the anniversary of the battle of Kossovo. There could be, of course, no question of housing all of them. These pilgrims, who would be half rosy with Bank-Holidayness and half agonized by the contemplation of the national tragedy, would continue to sleep on the summer-baked soil of the fields, as they had always done. The plan was to catch the few pounds now spent by the richer peasants at the inn at Prishtina, which is the nearest town. The architect went on, speaking French for our benefit, 'And it is the greatest joy to be here, for I have some little things to do also for the marvel, the pearl, the church itself. Look at her!

'It has been a wonderful thing for me to work here, because in Belgrade one forgets what one's people is, what paprika we really are. Look at this old monk here. You know, when I first came here, I had some hope of persuading the Abbot and the monks and their Bishop to let me take off the porch, for I knew that if they consented the Government would permit it. So I told them what a shame it was not to have Grachanitsa in its beauty as it was when King Milutin founded it, but they would not listen to me, and perhaps they had a little of the right on their side, for indeed the porch is historically interesting. It was built when the Turks in theory prohibited all building of Christian churches or repairing of them, and the reason it could be done is romantic. A member of the Sokolovitch family who had been taken by the Turks when a child to be a Janizary had become the Grand Vizier, and he used his position to protect all Serbs, and in particular to grant any favour asked him by his brother, who saw a priest and whom he had appointed Patriarch of Petch. But I am an architect and not a historian, and I became very angry when the monks would not grant me my wish. I turned my back on them and walked out of the room where we were, and I came out here and sat on the stone seat that runs along the wall of the church, fuming and kicking the pebbles in front of me. Presently this old one with the white beard came out and told me that they felt I had better know at once that if I came by night and did what I wanted to the porch they would get me excommunicated. The brave old one, he belongs to the days of comitadji and smuggled rifles and bombs and night raids, and that is the way he thought life was conducted, particularly by people who are angry. And indeed that is a way not inappropriate to this place, for it is fierce, very fierce, as you will see when you go inside. There you will see, if you have eyes in your head, that we were not barbarians, yet very fierce.'

He halted us again as we crossed the dust towards the church. 'No, certainly we were not barbarians,' he said. 'Look, look at her. Nothing about her is accidental. She is built not out of simplicity but out of the extremest sophistication. She is full of tricks, so elaborate that I can hardly explain them to those who are not trained architects. The towers supporting those cupolas are pulled out of their proper axes by somebody who knows—and it is unbelievable what theory and practice one would have to have mastered before one could know it—that thus there could be achieved an effect of airy lightness. Ah, but what this builder knew. Think of it, there is water, and much water, under this ground. At one point it lies within three feet of the walls. But he was calm, he was sure of his knowledge. I would not dare to build a building of such a size and importance so near water. He dared, and he was right in his daring, for after six hundred years the church is lying level as she was built, and she is not an inch nearer the water. Such things barbarians cannot do at all, such things hardly any of the cultured races have been able to do.' There was evidence of the unfortunate position of the Balkans in his realization that we had probably doubted the value of the culture which Kossovo had destroyed. 'But you must go inside. The interior of Grachanitsa tells you all about the people who built her.'

That was true; and what it told us was, to our surprise, not unfamiliar. From the immense height of the cupolas light descends on three naves, divided by gigantesquely sturdy columns, and arrives there multicoloured, dyed by the frescoes which cover every inch of the walls. There is here a sense of colossal strength, of animal vigour, of lust so lusty that it can sup off high pleasures as well as low, and likes crimson on its eye as well as wine on its tongue, and a godhead as well as a mistress. In fact, here is something very like the spirit of the late Tudor age; and this is the kind of church that the architects of Hampton Court might have built if the Gothic obsession had not laid its hand on their end of Europe. This was a startling correspondence, because the Serbian king who built Grachanitsa some seventy years before the battle of Kossovo closely resembled our Henry VIII.

This was King Milutin. In the twelfth century the Nemanyas, a family of chieftains who lived in a petty fortress on the Montenegrin border near the Adriatic coastline, produced a genius in the person of St Sava and a man of great talent in his brother, King Stephen the First-crowned, who together founded a stable Christian Serbian state, which their descendants expanded north towards the Danube, east towards the Vardar river, and south into Byzantine territory. When the dynasty had been under way about a hundred and fifty years Milutin came to the throne, and in himself and his royal functions his likeness to Henry VIII was very strong.

He worked marvels for his country, but was untender to many of his subjects. He hungered hotly for women, but was cold as ice when he discarded them or used them as political instruments. He was ardently devout, but used his religion as a counter in his international relationships without showing a sign of scruple. There is a robustness in him that charms from the yonder side of the grave, but without doubt his vitals were eaten by the worm of melancholy. His picture is among the frescoes here. He stands, deeply bearded, in the costume worn by Serbian royalty, which is clearly imitated from the Byzantine mode: a stiff tunic of rich material studded with jewels, which disregards the frailty of the enclosed flesh and constrains it to magnificence. That costume powerfully recalls the later Tudor portraits, the gorgeous robes that held together the grossness of Henry VIII and the brain-raddled emaciation of Elizabeth and presented them as massive monarchs. Such vestments speak of a world founded on the idea of status, which regarded a king as the beloved deputy of God, not because he was any particular sort of man, but because it was considered obvious that if he were crowned a king he would try to act like a beloved deputy of God, since society had agreed that was how a king should act. There stands beside him, equally sumptuous, his wife Simonis, the daughter of the Byzantine Emperor Andronicus II. She was Milutin's fourth wife. He had had to work up to her, earning the right through a long life to avenge an early disappointment.

Of that disappointment we read in the writings of a contemporary who was on the side of those who inflicted it. Pachymeres, the Byzantine historian, relates that the Byzantine Emperor Michael Palaeologus wished for an alliance with King Stephen Urosh of Serbia, and to that end offered his second daughter, Anna, as wife to King Stephen's second son, who was this same Milutin. Michael's wife, who was not only Empress but a great lady by birth, had a poor opinion of this proposal, and before the bride and her train started she sent some officials and a bishop as scouts to see if the Serbian court was fit for her daughter. Their adventures were sad. They were shocked by what seemed to them the poverty of the land; and for some reason this invariably happened in the Middle Ages when anybody visited any country other than his own, and Byzantines were likely to receive this unfavourable impression with peculiar poignancy. There was an authentic reason for this which held good over a long period. For hundreds of years their standard of living was higher than in most other countries, so much higher that when one of their ladies went to Venice to be the wife of the Doge Selvio in the eleventh century, the luxury of her habits, which included eating with a gold fork and wearing gloves, led her to be regarded as fit for Hell. But later, when this superiority was nothing like so marked, the Byzantines grew soft and insular and complaining, like a certain type of well-to-do English person who grumbles at French coffee, at American trains, at German bedclothes, to a degree far beyond what is justified by the amount of irritation these can cause in the sane. The Byzantine emissaries evidently belonged to this class, for they reported that the Serbians subsisted solely on what they brought down hunting and what they stole; but it is known that at that time they conducted a lively trade in timber and livestock and wheat and oil, that there were several rich mines, and that the organization of artisans set up by the Romans still flourished.

The insularity of these Byzantines was further alarmed when they came on a manifestation of the West with which they were unfamiliar. King Stephen Urosh was married to a French princess, Hélène of Anjou, who was a Roman Catholic zealot of an austere type. She is said to have been an admirable woman of great benevolence and intelligence, who did much excellent work in restoring the lands which had been laid waste by the Mongols, but she practised that extreme type of Catholic asceticism which is the root of Puritanism. Under her influence her elder son, Dragutin, who was a cripple, formed a habit of sleeping in a grave lined with thorns and sharp flints. Her husband, although he remained within the Orthodox Church, was governed by her ideas. When the officials and the Bishop arrived at his palace he received them coldly, and on hearing that they were part of Princess Anna's train and that many more were following, he said sourly that he was sorry to hear it, for he and his family were not accustomed to such luxury. Then in a spirit with which we are all familiar, particularly if we were young before the war, he took them to see the wife of his elder son Dragutin, who was the daughter of the King of Hungary. She was plainly dressed and was spinning wool. 'Now that,' said King Stephen, 'is the sort of wife that we like here.' The touch can be recognized by those of us who were brought up on relays of princesses who were all but dropping dead under the continuous effort of public simplicity, who wore shirt-blouses unusual for gauntness, who had no fires in their bedrooms, who went to bed so early that, even allowing for the early hour at which they rose, their slumbers must have been inordinate.

But the Byzantines did not understand. Leaving a bad impression behind them by their obvious perturbation, they rode back hastily and stopped the Princess at Ochrid. Not certain what to do, whether to take her straight back to Constantinople or wait for orders or let her go on and be recalled, they hung about the district till there arrived a Serbian ambassador named in the chronicles George, simple George. He seems to have been a person of great resource. He had plainly been sent to discourage the expedition from proceeding, since the Serbian court had liked the Byzantine emissaries as little as they had liked it. He began by telling them that on the way he had been robbed, and they naturally asked themselves what mercy they as foreigners could expect from robbers who did not spare notables of their own country. George also started a conversation in ambiguous terms which led them to question him sharply as to whether the conditions of the marriage contract to be signed between Michael Palæologus and Stephen Urosh were likely to be faithfully observed. He answered with transparent evasiveness. And in the night the Byzantine emissaries' horses were stolen. They found the local police unhelpful in the search for them, though ready enough to provide extremely inferior substitutes. Princess Anna and her train left in haste for home.

This incident cannot have pleased Milutin, though he probably liked the bit about the horses. He had a marked distaste for his family's ideas. Simplicity he abhorred, and throughout his life he showed that Roman Catholicism was to him simply a means of winning the support of a man called the Pope who exercised an enviable amount of power. He worked to become inarguably great, in terms that would be understood across a continent, that would be understood even by gorgeous Byzantium. There was a certain amount of preliminary waiting to be done, while his family life broke into curious blooms. His pious elder brother Dragutin rebelled against his father King Stephen; with the help of his brother-in-law, King Ladislas IV of Hungary, beat him thoroughly in a great battle in Herzegovina, and seized the throne for himself. He was so completely under his Roman Catholic mother's influence that it cannot be doubted she was in sympathy with his revolt, which they both probably justified by Stephen Urosh's fidelity to the Orthodox Church, although King Ladislas, a notorious scoundrel descended from an unlovable Asiatic tribe, was an odd ally in a Holy War. When Dragutin had won he threw his father into prison and proceeded to manoeuvre his country towards the abandonment of the Orthodox Church and conversion to Roman Catholicism. These plots were detected and resented by his people, and after he and King Ladislas had made an unsuccessful attempt on Byzantine territory, for which he had to make amends by the surrender of a large tract of Serbian land, he abdicated in favour of Milutin. He then settled in Bosnia, which his Hungarian wife had brought him in her dowry, became a Roman Catholic, and asked the Pope to send him a mission of Franciscan friars to convert the Bogomil heretics and the members of the Orthodox Church within his territory. Thus there was initiated the period of savage religious persecution which made the distracted Bosnians prefer Islam to Roman Catholicism, and enabled the Turk to entrench himself in a key position in South-East Europe. This was a truly lamentable rascal.

When Milutin ascended the throne he felt under no necessity to set his father free. He, a Lear who really had something to worry about, died in an Albanian prison a year later. Thereafter Serbia prospered steadily, for no other apparent reason than that Milutin was a fortunate ruler, like a garden whose owner has the 'green finger.' The mines gave up their riches, wine and wheat and oil and livestock flowed out of the country in a fat river of well-being. Abroad, he carried on a continuous policy of expansion at his neighbour's weakest points. He ate southwards into the disordered Byzantine Empire, his first marriage helping him. He had married the daughter of Duke John of Neopatras, the most powerful of the despots who were setting up for themselves here and there on the Greek islands in defiance of Constantinople. Then Byzantium sent the Tartars against Milutin, and on the plea of consolidating his position in the West he sent Duke John's daughter packing, quite in the manner of Henry VIII, and married Elizabeth, the sister of Dragutin's wife and his old ally, the Asiatic King Ladislas of Hungary. But this new marriage was remarkable for the number of ways in which it was bound to displease people. The Roman Catholics outside and inside the Serbian Empire were scandalized, not only because Milutin was divorced but because the bride was a nun. The members of the Orthodox Church were equally scandalized because she was the sister of Milutin's brother's wife, thus falling within the prohibited degrees. She was also unpopular with Milutin's party because she was Hungarian, and the alliance between Dragutin and her brother had meant a defeat for Serbia and the loss of territory. It is impossible to believe that this marriage can have secured more support for him than it lost, and that the motive was not passion. One must compare it to Henry's impolitic and impassioned marriage with Anne Boleyn. It resembled it too in brevity. Before long Milutin dismissed her and married Anna Terteri, the daughter of George Terteri, a fierce and able Emperor of Bulgaria, who was part Slav, part Asiatic. East and West found it not at all impossible to meet in South-East Europe after the barbarian invasions.

But soon Anna also was dismissed. Under Milutin's government Serbia had become so rich and his disingenuous statesmanship so notoriously successful that the Byzantine Empire regarded its power with alarm. But the Turks, massing decade by decade in Asia Minor, were a graver danger. So the Emperor Andronicus II, who had succeeded his father Michael Palaeologus, signed a treaty of peace with Milutin, and offered to seal it with the hand of his widowed sister Eudocia. This offer could not have been made unless Milutin had composed a masterly fantasia on legalist themes comparable to Henry VIII's divorce of Katherine of Aragon. On the face of it Milutin could not marry anybody, because the canon law of the Orthodox Church definitely forbids fourth marriages. But Milutin overcame that difficulty. He now claimed that his first divorce had been illegal. In support of this he brought it forward that the Orthodox Church officials would never permit the name of his second queen to be mentioned in the liturgy, though the real reason for this had been that she was connected to him within the prohibited degrees. This pretence that his first divorce had been invalid meant that not only his second but his third wife had never been really married to him, and that their children were all bastards. That did not distress him, for though he had two sons who were affected by this decision, a mere heir was not what he wanted. He wanted an heir who should have a title through himself to the Serbian crown and through his mother to one of the Byzantine crowns. Also there was at last to be won revenge for the sneers of Michael Palaeologus's eunuchs, sent to see if he were a fit bridegroom for Princess Anna. The precise moment had arrived when he could pursue these ends because his first wife, the very first of all, had died; and although the Orthodox Church looks on the remarriage of widows and widowers hardly more favourably than if they had been parted from their spouses by divorce, now that he had succeeded in wiping out his second and third marriages, the one he contemplated counted as only his second, and he was free to make it after performing a slight penance.

The Emperor's sister Eudocia, however, refused this opportunity. She put in the alternative pleas that she dearly loved the memory of her husband and would not for the world marry again, and that when she married again she wanted a more respectable bridegroom than Milutin. For public opinion was profoundly shocked by his matrimonial casuistries. It is to be noted, however, that there is nothing in Milutin's reign comparable to the beheading of Anne Boleyn and Catherine Howard. In certain respects Milutin was far more civilized than Henry VIII, though he lived a hundred and fifty years earlier in a country that had been Christianized three hundred years later. Few would care to say that Henry VIII might not have forgotten the duties of filial piety if he had had an energetic mother who led a campaign against all his divorces, and never ceased to act as a Roman Catholic propagandist in both his own realm and neighbouring territories. But although Hélène of Anjou denounced all Milutin's marriages but the first, and not only supported her Roman Catholic son in Bosnia on the western frontier of Serbia, but tried to convert the Emperor of Bulgaria on its east, she outlived Milutin. We know also what happened to Sir Thomas More; better luck attended the Archbishop Jacob, who was fearless in his opposition to Milutin's tortuous matrimonial policy, yet lost neither his life nor his archiepiscopate. Still, sufficient unto the day was Milutin's barbarity. It was in sorrow and shame that the Emperor Andronicus resolved to buy Serbian adherence at a higher price than he had meant to pay. Since his sister Eudocia refused to be sacrificed he had to offer up his daughter Simonis, who was only six years old.

Their services are insufficiently recognized, those girl children who held together the fabric of history by leaving their nurseries and going into far lands to experience the pains of rape and miscarriage, among strangers talking unknown tongues and practising unhomely customs. The practice has not been so long in desuetude that we can despise it as a remote barbarity; it was thought a pity that the Belgian Princess who married the Crown Prince Rudolph of Habsburg had not shown the signs of womanhood at the time fixed for her wedding, but the ceremony was not for that reason postponed. Nor is it necessary, in order to feel its horror, to exaggerate the infamy of early sexual activity; it is sheer humbug to pretend that a girl of twelve who is married to a kindly young bridegroom is in worse case than a woman in her forties, of the kind that would like to marry, who is not married. If child marriage were as fearful as the modern world pretends, the white race would be extinct by now. Erasmus declared in a sermon that, though it was usual for little girls of ten to marry and straightway have children, he himself thought it too young; and our own Henry VII was born of a thirteen-year-old mother who lived to be a vigorous woman with scholarly interests.

But the export trade in these little princesses was indubitably and totally repulsive. For a child-wife to be happy she must have a gentle husband of her own kith, and familiar faces round her when she comes to childbirth. But these royal children were sent out into strange lands, not to see their kinsfolk again for years and perhaps for ever, to be handed over to men who would not have been able to compel such precious gifts if they had not proved themselves bloody in mind and deed. Often such marriages marked the signature of peace between powers that had been savagely at war, so that little girls were sent to the beds of enemies who had been the Bluebeards of their nursery tales. Every child in the Byzantine Empire in the thirteenth century must have shuddered at nights to think of the Tartars, the little yellow men that passed over the land like living flames from hell. But when Michael Palaeologus needed the support of the Tartars against the Bulgars, he sent superb presents to their chief, Prince Chalaii. There was chosen as ambassador the priest and Abbot of the monastery of Christ Ruler of All, who took with him, among much else, a portable altar, screened with magnificent curtains and embellished with images of the saints and with a superbly worked cross, and furnished with costly chalices and plates for the celebration of the mysteries; and also an illegitimate daughter of the Emperor called Euphrosyne who had been promised to the Tartar chief as his bride. She was well under ten years of age. When the train arrived at the South Russian camp of the Tartars it was found that Prince Chalaii was dead, so his son Nogai married her instead. The bridegroom looked curiously at the pearls on the Byzantine bonnets of her suite and guessed them to be charms against thunder. Nothing is known of Euphrosyne's later life save that one of her sons was strangled in some convulsion of Bulgarian politics. Michael Palaeologus had another illegitimate daughter, Marya, whom he sent even further afield on the same sort of errand. She went to marry the Khan of Tartary who lived at Baghdad, a grandson of Genghis Khan. It is to be remembered that these Asian invaders were as shocking to that age as they are to this, for in spite of the greater social violence of the Middle Ages there was a stricter chivalry observed in war. No prisoner was put to death or held to ransom unless he was royal or noble, captured common soldiers were disarmed and turned loose, and there was no killing save in actual battle. A society which held this code would plainly be appalled as we are by the Tartars' massacre of millions and their destruction of all property and disregard for all human rights in the territories they ravaged. It is not to be believed that Euphrosyne and Marya were unafraid, either as children or as grown women.

So Simonis, for a little girl born to a lofty place in the hierarchy of Byzantium, was not faring so badly; but she fared ill enough. A historian of her day has described the manner of her going out to her martyrdom. It was at the beginning of Lent that the Emperor Andronicus left Constantinople to take her to Milutin. There had been a long and cruel winter which had killed many trees and plants. The land was still under snow and the rivers were frozen. The imperial train travelled slowly towards Salonika, halting sometimes to attend to local matters of state. One night they stayed at the monastery where the Patriarch had his residence, and in the morning all attended Mass. Afterwards the Patriarch tried to rebuke the Emperor for the scandal of the marriage and asked if he might talk to Simonis about it. But Andronicus, with the curtness which is the weak man's substitute for strength, told him they must be on their way, asked him to give himself and his daughter the benediction, and set out on the northward journey through the frozen country. Later he wrote to the Patriarch and told him that he would not take. Communion from his hands at Easter, according to custom. The task must be deputed to another priest. But at the same time he sent him the present of a thousand crowns which it was his habit to send him at that season.

His heart must have been heavy as he rode away from the monastery, for he knew well that the Patriarch was right. And the little girl was very dear to him, for she had been born after he had been greatly grieved by the loss of several other daughters in their infancy. Her name recorded his concern for her, since it was given her by reason of a magical device he had practised lest he lose her like her sisters. When she was born twelve candles of equal size and weight were lit before the images of the Twelve Apostles, and while these were burning prayers were said for the child, and she was put under the protection of the saint whose candle lasted longest. It was St. Simon who preserved her life, for the curious end that at the age of six she should be handed over to a bridegroom some forty years her senior who was, by consummating their marriage too soon, to render her barren. Yet Andronicus cannot be blamed. Over the sea, in Asia Minor, there were massing Turks, and more Turks, and yet more Turks, surpassing the Mongols in dreadfulness because of the reinforcement of their ferocity by persistence, in their stabilization of massacre by settlement. There was nothing a Christian king could do but swallow the vices of other Christian kings if they were possible allies in the defence of Europe against the Ottoman invaders.

At a gorgeous festival in Salonika the child and Milutin were married by the Archbishop of Ochrid; and hidden behind the crowds and the banners and the trumpeters and the processions of soldiers and eunuchs a second sombre and infestive ceremony took place. Two people were handed over to the Emperor Andronicus as some compensation for the loss of his daughter. One was a Byzantine deserter who had of late very successfully led King Milutin's troops against certain towns on the fringe of the Emperor's territory: Milutin had his Wolsey. The other was the daughter of the Bulgarian Emperor Terteri, till lately Milutin's wife. She was to be filed for reference with Andronicus, to be brought out or forgotten as political expediency was served. Hardly less than the bride she proved to what a limited degree it is possible, without falling into the most savage irony, to describe women as the protected sex. It is said that Milutin showed so little compunction in discarding her because her father had lately been driven from the Bulgarian throne: but he had been succeeded by her brother. For women, however, blood is constantly as thin as water, and nobody seems to have anticipated that her family would come to her defence.

Later Simonis was to face for some time the destiny of her predecessor. She was to survive Milutin, as Catherine Parr survived Henry VIII; but both were to have moments when it seemed that they too were going down into the abyss that suddenly fissured the uxorious ground on which they had seemed secure. Time brought certainty that Simonis could never bear Milutin an heir to the Byzantine throne; it also brought evidence that her father, the Emperor Andronicus, was an incompetent ruler who year by year became a less valuable ally. So Milutin entered into negotiations with Charles de Valois, titular Emperor of the Latin Empire and brother of Philip the Fair, with the purpose of forming an alliance to depose Andronicus. As a necessary prelude Milutin had to take steps towards being converted and converting his country to Roman Catholicism, and to that end entered upon a long correspondence with the Pope; and he also proposed marriage to a relative, and possibly any relative, of Charles de Valois. The project failed, because Charles lost interest. Had it succeeded Simonis would have been sent home to her father's court, which would probably itself have been removed to exile, to be despised as a failure as diplomat and breeder; and this disgrace would have befallen her because the hateful old man who had married her had abandoned himself to the Roman Catholic Church, which she, like every Byzantine since the sack of Constantinople by the Crusaders in 1204, regarded as a band of criminal enemies. Simonis had always loathed Serbia, and it is no wonder that she attempted to escape. When her mother died she took the body home to Constantinople and refused to return, and Milutin, to whom her flight must have recalled the contemptuous withdrawal of Michael Palaeologus's ambassadors in his youth, forced her back by threats of military action and would not listen to the plea which she reiterated through the years, that he should allow her to become a nun. In the routine of daily life he appears to have treated her kindly, and even with devotion. But it is no wonder that she leaves the same ugly mark on the fabric of Serbian history as Mary Tudor on our English record. She presents the same spectacle of piteous martyrdom not flowering into sanctity but withering into peevishness and hate. A fresco here at Grachanitsa shows her being crowned by an angel, tense as a cat under an undesired caress, full of that lack of peace which passes all understanding, recognizable in the shrew and the prisoner. She left behind her an undying legend of hatred and malice. Any Serbian peasant will tell one that Queen Simonis was an evil woman though he may know nothing else about her. The name 'Bloody Mary' has a similar independent existence in the English popular mind.

It is probable that Simonis caused this ill fame by the part she played in alienating her husband from his son Stephen. In the popular calendar of the old Serbian saints and kings which was reprinted from ancient sources for the first time about a hundred years ago, it is definitely stated that that was her offence. The story as it is told there cannot be true, for it represents her as trying to oust Stephen from his position as heir to the throne, and replace him by a son of her own, whereas she had no son, and not until she was manifestly barren did Milutin acknowledge Stephen as his heir. But the outline of the story seems to be correct. This Stephen was probably the son of Milutin's second wife, Elizabeth of Hungary, the nun of Asiatic descent. When he was quite young he had seen his mother displaced by the daughter of George Terteri the Bulgarian Emperor, but he himself remained at court and did valorous work for the state. He went as hostage to Nogai, the Prince of the Tartars, who had married the little Byzantine Euphrosyne, and he remained there in that dangerous capacity for some years. When he returned he was given as bride the daughter of Smilatz, a Bulgarian noble who for some years was the emperor, like many of his fellow-countrymen, for the Bulgarian throne was then as often and diversely occupied as the last chair in musical chairs. Stephen was also given a part of his father's kingdom as his own principality.

Then civil war broke out between Milutin and Stephen. It is possible that the son rebelled against the father, for there was a party in the state which thought that Milutin showed unpatriotic weakness in his relations with the Byzantine Empire, and it would have supported Stephen. But in a solemn document connected with the foundation of a monastery Stephen accused Simonis of having lied about him to his father; and it is significant that the campaign began by an invasion of Stephen's principality by Milutin. If this first guilt lies on Simonis, then later and blacker guilt lies on her too. For at the behest of his Byzantine advisers Milutin ordered his son to be banished to Constantinople, and to be blinded before he went. This was not a Serbian punishment; there the code punished criminals either by simple banishment or by the confiscation of their goods. But the Byzantines used mutilation of one sort and another as a penalty for many crimes, and blindness was often inflicted on persons of high position who might be dangerous to the state if left in possession of all their faculties. So Stephen, with his son Dushan and his daughter Dushitza, was taken by guards from his father's palace, and borne along the road to Constantinople. Before they left Serbian territory, at that same Sheep's Field where I saw

the slaughter of the lamb at the rock, the guards halted and put
out his eyes with red-hot irons. I do not know why they chose
that particular spot, but tradition is certain that they did. The
legend runs that that night St. Nicholas came to him in a dream
and said, 'Fear not, thine eyes are in my hand.' In fact, as quite
often happened when the men who used the irons were merciful
or clumsy or bribed, the sight had not been destroyed. But Stephen
said nothing.

At Constantinople the Emperor Andronicus received him with a
kindness hard to explain, save that to such a gentle temperament as
his to do a gracious act in this bloodthirsty age must have been like
an hour of rest under a shady tree. Stephen was comfortably lodged
in the Monastery of Christ Ruler of All, where he sat in affected
blindness, facing the sunshine as if it were the night for more
than five years. Such virtuosic performances of fearful cunning
did the Tudors inspire in the flesh of their flesh; so did Mary
Tudor hold her breath to keep it while her father lived, so did
Elizabeth when she was Mary Tudor's prisoner. At last Stephen
dared tell Andronicus that he could see; and Andronicus bade him
continue to bandage his eyes and to tell no one else.

The legend says that shortly afterwards Andronicus sent a
mission to Milutin to consider common measures of defence
against the Turks, and that he added to the train the Abbot
of the Monastery of Christ Ruler of All, with instructions that
he should find a chance to speak well of Stephen to his father.
It is certainly true that two great Serbian churchmen, the scholar
Daniel and the statesman Nicodemus, worked on Milutin year after
year till he was reconciled to his son. We get here a hint regarding
the nature of Simonis: her father Andronicus befriended her enemy
Stephen, and though she was devout the ecclesiastics of her Church
were not on her side. At last, thanks to these intercessions, Milutin
asked Andronicus to send his son back to him. So Stephen travelled
home with his little Dushan—his daughter had died during his
captivity—and was taken to his father's palace. There he was
led to the feet of his father, and he kneeled down and clasped
his stiff, jewelled robes, and cried out that whatever his father
said he had done he had indeed done, and had long repented of
it. Then his father bowed down his bearded bluffness to him and
raised him up, and gave him the kiss of forgiveness. But Stephen
did not unloose the bandage over his eyes. When Milutin gave him
another principality in place of the one he had lost, and bade him
go to it and leave his son Dushan at court to be reared as a prince,
he went blindfold to claim his possessions. A year or two later nobles

came and told him Milutin was dead. But Stephen did not put aside
the fiction of his sightlessness till he knew that his father was not
only dead but buried. So would a child of Henry VIII have acted,
had his father formed the intention to blind him and not succeeded
at the first doing.

All this story is implicit in Grachanitsa, in the lavished treasure
of its colours and the vigorous fertility of its form. 'But,' a Western
reader may object, 'it is a story of barbarism, it shows that it is
perfectly correct to say that nothing worth grieving over perished
at Kossovo.' That judgment applies standards that have never been
valid save in the reign of Queen Victoria, which must now be
recognized as an oasis in the moral desert of ordinary time. If
the amount of violence habitual to society is admitted it can be
seen that the reign of Milutin was the great age that came before
the greater age, as Henry VIII's morning came before the noon of
England which is called Elizabethan. Milutin was a true king. He
tilted his land towards the sun, wherever that might be in its course
across the heavens. This can never be done without negotiation, the
spirit must deny its appetite for principle. This is more of a sacrifice
than would appear, for all men have a letch to live by principle; the
good man would live by virtue, the bad man would live by vice, but
both alike want a fixed rule for their happiness. The ruler, however,
must have none. He must ask himself of every act the opportunist
question, whether it tilts his land towards the sun or the shadow,
and abide by the answer. This obligation prevents him from being
a bad or a good man, but it makes the people feel for him as if he
were a loving father.

Hence such a king brings glory and confusion to his country.
Conduct breaks its established bounds and covers the whole gamut
of conceivable action, not because of laxity, but because of a spirit
of inquiry. The king is bewildered by the effects of his own deeds,
which work well on the bodies and minds of his subjects, although
they are contrary to the accepted moral code. He imagines that he
must have discovered a new principle of morality, and feels about
for it by a number of experimental acts, of a kind not previously
sanctioned or even anticipated. His subjects share his sense of
triumph and bewilderment, knowing him to be right when he could
be proven wrong by all the authority they know. So they too give all
events their chance to happen, and since their land is tilted towards
the sun all seeds planted in the soil come to a prodigious growth.

Such a crescent age can be distinguished from decadence by its
discussion of fundamentals. The people that rots declares with
every breath that all is already known; the people that is young

falls into the other error of declaring that nothing is yet discovered. There is a testing of the capacity of women's bodies for pleasure and pain, which might be pronounced simple voluptuousness, were it not for the simultaneous exploration of their minds and respect for their wills shown in the art of the time. There are excesses of loyalty and treachery which might be put down as mere animal reactions, were it not for the speculative inquiries into the bases of faith and conduct sometimes conceived in a head that was to fall for treason to the axe, sometimes written in the hand that had signed the headsman's warrant. Such an age is moral, not because it conforms to a moral code but because it is in search for one.

Doubtless Milutin was a murderer and a lecher, as red-fanged a husband and father as our Henry VIII; but like him he made war here and treaties there as it profited his country, nourished commerce, and built higher the fortress of the law. This last achievement was neither safe nor simple. He was surrounded by nobles who wore magnificently furred and jewelled garments made from the costliest stuffs sent out by Greece and Italy and Flanders, and practised an etiquette based on the exalted ceremonial of Byzantium, but for all that were apt to fall into common banditry when away from court. Milutin gentled them, diverted their ferocity to the service of the state, and opposed their lawlessness by an increasing elaboration of the law. Here Serbia never took its inspiration from Byzantium. It drew on the juristic achievements of the kingdoms of the North, of Poland, Hungary, and Bohemia, and even borrowed here and there from the codes, which were not so simple as might be supposed, of the Mongol invaders. One sign of the Northern influence was the establishment of trial by jury, which under Milutin appeared and developed. We can see him dealing with a specifically Macedonian problem in arranging for the representation of the various races of the district on these juries.

In religion also he had renounced all animal simplicity, no matter what his sword arm and his loins might prefer. Though the Kingdom of Heaven will have to be broadminded indeed to receive him, he might even be called an adept in the Christian faith. With a dualism more often found in the realm of sexual relations, he constantly considered the advisability of betraying the Orthodox Church by capitulation to the Papacy, though he was loyal to it in his soul. His age found proof of his loyalty in his charity, which was indeed impressive; he maintained an army of what were then called lepers, which probably included some victims of true leprosy, but which would consist for the most part of those suffering from skin diseases and those appalling ulcerations due to the Puritan theory, still active and working incalculable harm in the Balkans, that to drive out an infection of the skin it is proper to apply a fiercely irritant ointment or lotion. But these good works may have been what Americans compactly call fire insurance, or even a mechanical continuance of the routine set up by his pious mother. His participation in the life of the Church, however, admits of no such reading. He was certainly not moved by fear of ecclesiastical power, for he never hesitated to defy it when it was a question of policy, of tilting his land towards the sun. Throughout his reign he ignored the hostility between the Orthodox Church and the Papacy by permitting six Roman Catholic sees in his kingdom. It is more likely that, after the strange fashion of Henry VIII, he believed. Both of them, longing to be free for all possible courses of action, might have prayed, 'Lord, I believe, help Thou my belief.'

That Milutin was a believer is proved by the fiercely, passionately—it might almost be said unnecessarily—religious quality of the churches he built. Grachanitsa speaks first of all regarding the union of church and state. Its architect saw in his mind's eye, when there was but the bare site, the Godhead shining from the secret darkness behind the iconostasis; and he saw, advancing towards the iconostasis to draw power from the hidden Godhead, to derive authority for their rank, Milutin and Simonis and their courtiers, dressed in glowing purple, girt with belts of gold studded with pearls and precious stones, multicoloured as flowers of the field. He permitted earthly glory to state its case, to establish its value; but he demonstrated the supremacy of the Godhead's glory by a paradox of forms which were solid as the rock, yet light as the spread wings of a bird. It would be improbable that a society, particularly a small and coherent society, should cause such a church to be built and should afterwards frequent it, without participating in the passion which had engendered it and which it engendered; and its records prove that many among Milutin's courtiers became so enamoured of the hidden Godhead that they could no longer bear to be divided from it by the iconostasis. The Serbian aristocracy included, as well as many sheep-stealers, many saints. Young men fled from the court to become hermits and monks, taking irrevocable vows far stricter than those imposed in the Roman Catholic Church, in such numbers that dangerous gaps began to appear in the governing class; and a law was passed which forbade a religious order to accept any novice, male or female, save with the consent of a bishop.

In the church the ardour of these young men becomes comprehensible. About us were the thick pillars, cold with their great mass, so like virgin rock that we might have been standing deep under the earth, among the sources of rivers. Above us the light, dripping down through the narrow windows of the cupolas from the simple unmeaning amplitude of the sky, lay on the frescoes, and revealed an age of perception so delicate, of speculation so profound, that it is almost outside our Western understanding. They do not represent the perfect classical Byzantine art as it was seen in its two great periods, the fourth to the sixth and the ninth to the twelfth centuries. It is not classical in spirit: it does not celebrate the completely comprehended discoveries which a civilization has achieved by mastering all available information about its environment. But before classicism there must come a preparatory phase of romanticism, in which the age feels its way towards such discoveries, by formulating all conceivable theories and fantasies, to the end that those which are not valid can be distinguished from those that are; and to such an experimental period, based on the remains of a substantial classicism, belong these frescoes. When Grachanitsa was built, Byzantium had already lost the firm and massive character of supremacy: too many of its forces were diverted by apprehension of the Turks. The spirit of the Empire had therefore found several provincial lodgments, in such places as Salonika, Trebizond, Mistra, and Serbia, among populations too different and too distant to be able to carry on the Byzantine tradition without adapting it to their alien natures. Hence Serbo-Byzantine art is a fusion of classicism and romanticism and of two racial spirits, unlike in age, intensity, and experience. It is therefore not a unified and completely satisfying art: but it presents many beauties that have never been surpassed by later ages.

There is in these frescoes, as in the parent works of Byzantium, the height of accomplishment in technique and of ambition in content. The Mother of God prays, her lifted hands far apart, in the fashion of those born not far from Asia; and her nature is as prodigious as might be expected from the mother of a god, the destiny which perplexes her is as amazing as we know it to have been. Two women meet, and a strong wind blows their red and blue cloaks about them. It is the Visitation, and the wind is the Will of God, blowing them to marvellous fruitfulness. An angel stands before the young Mary and gives her a sharp military command; she shrinks back, not in refusal, but because she realizes more fully than he does how the fulfilment of that order must affect destiny. This version of the Annunciation has an originality, what our grandfathers would have called piquancy, which is noticeable in others among these frescoes; for nothing here is not profoundly considered, and as the likeness of men lies on the surface and their uniqueness in their depths, this makes for unpredictable vision. Here and there this originality was exploited by the romantic element in this art till it substituted strangeness for beauty, and instead of making a revelation started a debate. It was so with the fresco that made my husband say, 'Look, here is something extraordinary. Do you remember at Neresi the fresco of a woman washing the Infant Christ, which looked like a Blake illustration to *The Mental Traveller*? Well, here is another fresco that looks like a Blake illustration to *Urizen* or *Los*.'

That was true, if one could imagine a Blake from whom there had been removed that discordant element which obliged him to see the naked body as an unharmonized assembly of muscles and begin all the prophetic books, and indeed interpenetrate them, with terrific groaning family rows among the supernatural beings. This fresco takes the breath away by the unanticipated beauty of the represented natural forms; it says, 'This is how you would see if you were not as bad as blind.' Against a background of great architectural magnificence, such as one sees in the works of the early Italians, a supernatural youth stands naked on a high and narrow altar, an old man is prostrated in adoring shame before him, and a bishop stands a little way off, worshipping in less humble ecstasy. The nakedness of the youth is depicted with extreme solemnity, as if the human body were the copy of a divine image, and whosoever could completely realize it could completely realize the form of God. The garments of the old man are a thin clothing for his limbs, his limbs are a thin clothing for his spirit's turmoil. The Bishop's cloak, a superb example of that early adventure in abstract art, the play that the Byzantine artists loved to make with the crosses on ecclesiastical garments, wraps an impressive man in greater impressiveness. The relations of these figures and their background are so proper that when we left the church we could not remember whether it was vast or minute, whether it covered half the chapel wall or only a fraction of it. Yet it lacked the effect of sufficiently great art. It raised the question—What are these people, and what are they doing? This would be asked by any spectator, however well he were acquainted with the subject, which is, in fact, an episode in the life of St. Peter of Alexandria, a martyr in the persecutions of Diocletian: Christ appeared to him in nakedness, to foretell that his garment, the Church, was to be reft from him by the Arian heresy. It remained true, after that historical fact was known, that these three people's strange demonstrations of their being, the opinions they are expressing on divinity and humanity and the fusion of these in ecclesiastical authority, required an amplification which can only be made in language. This new and experimental age had not discovered the limits of each art, it had not learned that painting must not touch a subject on which literature has still an essential word to say.

This resemblance of Serbo-Byzantine art to the work of Blake, which seems to me entirely mysterious, not to be explained by any conceivable theory, has nothing to do with romanticism; for it is strongly apparent in the most classical fresco in Grachanitsa. This depicts a mystic, and both the Orthodox Church and William Blake knew very well what mysticism was. The Orthodox Church had drawn its knowledge direct from Christ and the Apostles and had developed it in the monasteries of Mount Athos; and Blake was one of the long line of mystics which England finds it so much easier to produce outside the Church than inside. This fresco shows Elijah sitting in one of those caves to which El Greco has accustomed us, an enclosing womb of rock. Beyond it are signs of a forest that makes its own night in the day; and at its mouth are two highly stylized little trees, symbols of barrenness. The old man's clenched right hand supports his bearded chin; his head is thrown back in an ecstasy of thought; his left hand grips his bony knee. He is wrapped in a sheepskin, his tired feet are bare. 'This is a study of what our people alone know,' said Constantine, 'this is mysticism without suffering.'

In that he named a distinction between the modern Western world and this Byzantine world, which is at bottom a distinction between poverty and wealth. The West imagines a hermit in the desert as inconvenienced by lack of material objects. He is always assumed to have so few ideas about the spiritual world that he has difficulty in keeping his mind on them, and therefore has to regard the mere exclusion of physical comfort as a positive victory which has constantly to be rewon. This actually was the state of many of the Western mystics. St Jerome shows in his letters that his animal preoccupations were always bursting into the sparsely populated area of his spiritual life; and St Augustine describes in his *Confessions* how the sight of a lizard catching flies or a spider entangling them in his web was enough to distract him from contemplation. But in this fresco of Elijah and in another which shows St John, wild-eyed with more wisdom than a man can carry, there is depicted the mystic who went into the desert because his head was so full of ideas about the spiritual world that everyday talk was in his ears as a barrel-organ playing outside a concert-hall is to a musician, the mystic who does not want to eat or drink or sleep with women because that is to take time off from the ecstatic pleasure of pursuing the ramifications of good and evil through his bosom and through the universe. There is a raven alighting in Elijah's cave, food in its beak; he will hardly thank it. If a naked woman appeared before him she would be not a temptation but an offence, offending as a person in a library who begins chatting to a student who has found a long-sought reference a few minutes before closing time. Life is not long enough for these men to enjoy the richness of their own perceptions, to transmute them into wisdom.

Their wealth is past our computation. Our cup has not been empty, but it was never full like those in this world, at a spot where Asia met Europe, at a time when the governing civilization had known success as well as failure, and there were these new Slav races to give the sensibility and vigour of their youth to exploiting this inherited treasure of experience. Across one of the walls of Grachanitsa is shown the Falling Asleep of the Virgin Mary, the state which preceded her Assumption, a subject often treated by the Byzantines. There is no man living today who, exploring his mind in the light of that idea, could draw out so much.

In the foreground of the fresco is the Virgin lying on her bier. By the lax yet immutable line is rendered the marvel of death, the death which is more than the mere perishing of consciousness, which can strike where there is no consciousness and annul a tree, a flower, an ear of corn. Above her bier there shines a star of light; within it stands Christ, taking into his arms his mother's soul in the likeness of a swaddled child. Their haloes make a peaceful pattern, the stamp of a super-imperial power, within the angles of the star. About them throngs a crowd of apostles and disciples, come hastily from the next world or from distant lands to attend the Virgin's death, wearing their haloes as bubbling yet serene spheres. On the edge of the crowd stand some bishops in their cross-covered mantles, rock-like with the endurance of the Church, which cannot be perturbed by the most lacerating grief, and still others, also in flowing garments but with bodies liquid with grief, and others, also in flowing garments but with bodies tautened by effort, low under the weight of the bier. One astonished man is attached to it by both arms; he is a Jew of the party that killed Christ, who has tried to upset the bier, and will be glued to it until an angel cuts off his hands with a sword. The background is full of angels as the Eastern Church loved to conceive them, ethereal messengers who are perpetually irradiated by the divine beauty and communicate its laws to flesh-bound man, who embody, in fact, a dream of perfect vision and unfrustrated will, unhampered by the human handicaps

of incomplete information and clumsy faculties. Without a taint
of labour but with immense force they throw open the doors of
Heaven, and light blazes on its threshold, a light inhabited by
welcoming saints.

The huge imaginative space occupied by this small fresco is
washed by two swinging tides. There is a wave of such sincere and
childish grief as children feel when their mothers die, that breaks
and falls and ebbs; there is a rising sea of exaltation in the Son who
can work all magic and cancel this death or any other, making glory
and movement where stillness and the end seemed to be ineluctable.
The sides of the fresco are filled in with buildings, distorted with the
most superb audacity in order to comply with the general pattern,
yet solid and realistic in effect; we are amazed, as we all so often are
during our lives, that our most prodigious experiences take place in
the setting of the everyday world, that the same scenery should be
used for the pantomime and the tragedy. Behind these buildings
there is a firmament which evokes another recurrent amazement.
It is the most astonishing of all the things which happen to us that
anything should happen at all. It is incredible that there should
be men and women, mothers and sons, biers and buildings, grief
and joy; it would seem so much more probable that the universe
should have as its sole packing empty nothingness. Existence in
itself, taken at its least miraculous, is a miracle.

But this fresco, though it is inspired by these ideas and com-
municates them, is pure painting; it essays no task proper to
another art. These ideas manifest themselves because they were
part of the intellectual and spiritual wealth which the painter had
inherited from Byzantium, and he could engage in only the most
superficial activities without being reminded of them. But he was
wholly loyal to his art. He restricted himself to dealing with certain
problems of form and colour, but such was his command over his
technique that these restrictions gave him as much liberty as most
men's talents and allotment of time are likely to need. He knew
how to put circle by straight line and straight line by circle, and
pattern by pattern within an enfolding pattern, in a design which
by a certain angularity never consented to renounce its nature,
always refused to pretend to be a plain copy of material objects;
he knew how to exploit the Near Eastern palette of strong colours
which have had their strength eroded by stronger sunlight to pale
virile essences, or obscured in the labyrinths of Byzantine palaces
and only half revived by the glow from torches and candelabra. It
is a convention of form and colour which we of the West know
through its use by El Greco, and which we are tempted to mistake

for his self-made fortune, if we do not know the treasure house of tradition where he found it. In Grachanitsa, where the painting of these frescoes and the architecture of the church illustrate two arts proceeding from the same late Byzantine culture, we can see how inexhaustible were the treasures of this tradition. Here artists knew the supremest wealth their kind can know; they were rich in creation and they worked for an audience rich in perception. These people were born into a kingdom which was as kingdoms of earth should be, yielding good grain and good meat and good wine; and they had had enough of everything for long enough to forget starvation and outgrow excess. Before their eyes was a kingdom of the mind, founded by another people, which, like all kingdoms of the mind, had never been completed, but was unique in beauty. Well nourished and full of power, the Serbs went forth to know the new pleasures of art and thought, and to complete this culture with a richness that should match the richness of its first intention.

And when we went out of the church there was nothing. Defeat had taken all. Across a dusty yard which had once been a garden, soldiers wheeled barrows full of stones, not to rear again the vanished palaces, but to put up a hostel to divert pence from peasants that might otherwise be spent at a poor inn. On the footboard of our car Dragutin sat smoking, and by him there stood a dull-eyed boy, wearing an unbuttoned shirt of stained linen, patched breeches, and broken sandals. A sore on his lip was smeared with sky-blue ointment. 'Go now! Go now!' Dragutin said to him, and crushed his cigarette under-foot. 'Look, he is foolish. He knows you are going on to the Trepcha mines, because most English people who come to Grachanitsa are on their way to Trepcha, or have been there. So he wants you to give him a letter to the manager, the great Gospodin Mac. But I ask you, what would they want with the likes of this poor little one? For everything there is *fino, fino, brlo fino*, and they can have anyone they like to work for them, for they pay well and are just people, all dukes.' The boy said, 'There is nothing for me to do here. I want to work in the mines. Lady, gentlemen, there is nothing at all for me to do here, I want to go to the mines.'

Outside the walls of the compound rose the shabby, empty hills which in Milutin's time had been covered with villages. They receded into distances that were truly vast, for a traveller could penetrate them for many miles before he came on life that was gentle, where the meals were full and delicate, and there was clerkly knowledge. Yet when Grachanitsa was built the people on these plains and hills had eaten game and fine fattened meats off gold and silver and pewter, and the noble men and women, of whom there were a great number, closely kind to the peasantry, spoke Greek as well as Serbian. But because the Christians had lost the battle of Kossovo all this life had perished. Only there remained the pious gravity of the soldiers, which is something the West does not know. An English soldier is more cynical than an English civilian; but when the Serbian puts on uniform he becomes quiet with a deep unformulated faith, which is perhaps a memory of a Cæsaropapist empire whose emperor was the Vicar of Christ. Also there was in Dragutin a kind of lordliness that might have been an inheritance from a nobility which, because it was half peasant, did not lose its force when its possessions were rapt from it. Nothing else was left on this scene of what had once been there; the residue was pitifully thin, thin as a shadow cast by a clouded sun. The boy shifted his weight from one leg to the other, and said, 'There is nothing here for me to do.'

Prishtina

'This is Prishtina,' said Constantine. Prishtina was one of the capitals of the Serbian monarchs; for they had a peripatetic court to cope with the immensity of their new country, as was the custom in early Hungary and Germany, and held it now at Skoplje, now at Tetovo, now here, now in some northern town nearer the Danube. We blinked at a dull and dusty little village. 'Here we must have lunch,' continued Constantine, 'for it will be too late when we get to Trepcha. You can throw away your flowers,' he added, with the melancholy and unaggressive malice of an invalid, 'they are all dead.' We sat down at a table outside a hotel in the principal square. Near us a horse, angular as a Euclidean diagram, seemed to be holding up and to be held up by a greenish cab. Rickety little wooden shops, like hencoops on an ill-found small-holding, leaned up against each other, proffering at their oblique doors and in their tiny windows the smallest and most ingenuous specimens conceivable of the goods it was their business to sell.

A waiter took our order. Because the Turks were in the Balkans, and where Turks were there were coffee-houses, the smallest town here-abouts is familiar with the waiter, who in Western countries is the sign of a sophisticated centre. There came to stand beside us the hotel-keeper, very complacent about his position. Around us sat men in Western clothes more fantastic than any peasant costume could be, because they and their tailors had never seen a suit till they were grown men. It did not take us long to order lunch, for the bill of fare was short. 'Chicken and rice,' the waiter said, and the hotel-keeper echoed plumply, 'Chicken and rice.' He bent down, and shifted the tablecloth so that there fell at my place a particularly fine wine-stain, large and of a decorative shape, which the sunlight of some days had mellowed to a delicate mauve. With such an air, on days when I have been looking my best or have been companioned by the great, the *maîtres d'hôtel* of famous restaurants have greeted me with gardenias.

'When you go back to England,' said Constantine sourly, 'you will despise us for this, and say that we are all like pigs, and you will forget that we have had no advantages like you in your country who have always been rich.' 'Nonsense,' I said, 'I know quite well that this means nothing more than that people hereabouts have not yet heard about the convention that tablecloths should be clean.

They know in most places that the world has made up its mind that bedclothes must not be dirty, they have learned it only too well. In a hotel at Nish I once spent a most wretched night, coughing and choking myself awake every time I fell asleep, because the sheets had been boiled in a powerful disinfectant. It was like going to bed in a bottle of smelling salts. Those people will be far cleaner than the English once they begin.'

'There is one thing, I notice,' said my husband, 'and that is that whether Prishtina is clean or dirty, and in spite of the fact that it is extremely poor, I think poorer than any other town that we have visited—though not of course poorer than some of the villages—the people are not downcast. The hotel-keeper is very proud of being what he is and where he is. He does not dream of apologizing for his surroundings, as I have known hotel-keepers do in places that struck me as simple and beautiful. And the people who go by look very cheerful, though their faces are lined and their bodies marrowless and bent.' 'It is because they were worse before,' said Constantine. 'This district was the worst of any place in the Christian provinces of Turkey, because there was nothing here but the simplest agriculture, there were neither urban centres of trade and industry, nor even any luxury crops like tobacco. They raised nothing here but grain and animals.' 'In fact,' said my husband, 'they raised the most necessary things there are, therefore they were desperately poor. You need not trouble to tell us that. It is so in our country also, and indeed all over the world. That is perhaps the fault for which we are going to be punished.'

'It is perhaps the fault for which Byzantium was punished,' I said; 'the two classes, the "powerful" and the "poor," fought hard from the ninth century. The small landowners and the free peasants were so constantly harried by invasion and civil war that they bartered their liberty in return for the protection of the great nobles, who took advantage of the position to absorb the small landowners' estates and to make serfs of the free peasants. At first the monarchy fought these great nobles, and even appeared to have vanquished them. Feudalism, the exploitation of a country by its large landowners, could not exist in a declared theocracy, which implied the conception of divinely impartial justice for all individuals and every class. But when the Latins invaded the Byzantine Empire they brought with them the feudal system which was established in their own countries, and it could not be driven out with them, because the Byzantine nobles, like all the rich, would rather choke than not have their mouths full, and applauded the idea of any extension of their wealth and their power, however dangerous. Therefore Byzantine society became inconsistent. Its claim to theocracy was no longer a holy myth, but a glutton's lie.

'Yes,' I continued, delighted to speak on a subject of which my husband knew less than I did, 'that sowed the seed of ruin in the state. The poor were thereafter so poor that the aggressive among them became mercenary soldiers with no loyalty save to the nobles who paid them. I fancy that the centre of power was shifting towards Serbia in these last days because the peasant, though he was nearly everywhere bound to his land and forbidden to sell it, had his definite legal rights on which the nobles were not allowed to encroach, and he could very easily, if he showed ability in managing his land and in his general conduct, join the ranks of the lesser nobility. One got, in fact, an expanding country that gave its citizens no reason to foment civil disorder and every reason to resist invasion. Had it not been for the Turks, Byzantine civilization could have retreated here and known a second flowering in the Serbian Empire, just as a considerable part of our European civilization has retreated to America and lives there in universities and art galleries and concert-rooms and laboratories planned on an ampler scale than we can afford.'

'What is this?' asked my husband. This was no rhetorical question. He really wanted to know. 'It is your chicken and rice,' said the waiter. 'Yes, it is your chicken and rice,' chirruped the hotel-keeper. The dish regarded as a whole was not unpalatable, for the rice was well cooked; with some good bread, butter, sheep's cheese, white wine, and cherries, we did not do so badly. But the bird itself was a ghastly prodigy, lean and twisted in its leanness, like one of El Greco's fasting saints. In these parts, because the poverty of the land forbids the peasants to fatten their stock for more than a few weeks, one often eats very young meat, the stuff the germ plasm puts out into the world however its adult transmitter has been nourished, part of the continuous belt of animal life. The lamb and the sucking-pig are made on such a scale that their birth-right of flesh amounts to something, but on the small and complicated bone structure of a bird it is hardly more than a flavour. This being the only kind of poultry that the hotel-keeper knew, he beamed at us as we worried the carcass. A plump chicken that was easy to eat would have seemed to him wrong in the same way as a golf-course with no hazards.

'It does not matter at all, my dear,' said my husband. 'I have really done very well.' But the chicken had perhaps some part in making him say, 'Perhaps you are right in thinking that Serbia could have carried on the work of Byzantium, but I doubt it. I seem to remember that there were Byzantine writers who recorded their impressions of visits to Serbia with positive disgust at its barbarity. There was, I think, a writer called Gregoras.' 'There was indeed,' I replied, 'but he was an ass.' That was apt to be the character of Byzantine writers. There could be no effective literature, because there was no integrated language. Three kinds of Greek were known in Byzantium. There was first the childish and degenerate Greek spoken by the poor, and secondly the supple and developed Greek used by the wealthy, and there was a vast difference between these two languages because there was a wide gulf between these two classes. There was also classical Greek which all educated people had to learn; and the professional man of letters felt that to keep up his dignity he must either write this third form of language or the wealthy man's Greek distorted to resemble it as much as possible. That is to say he wrote as a conscious snob and dilettante, which is never a good prescription; and Gregoras brought to the task a fatuity which we can recognize in its full distastefulness, because it flourishes unchanged today.

He wrote with that verbosity which results not from exuberance but from destitution. 'The sun had crossed half our meridian,' he writes somewhere, 'it was now on its way to hide itself and was descending *as it does every day*, towards the horizon.' Through millions of such phrases there emerges the horrid fact that he exactly resembled the more tiresome type of well-to-do Englishman. He wrote a letter to a friend about his visit on a diplomatic mission to Serbia at the end of the thirteenth century which has been widely quoted by historians, particularly by those who are anti-Slav; and in this the resemblance is stark. This expedition which, as he put it, 'comprised a sevenfold decade of man and beast,' began badly by starting at night, for no respectable reason, and blundering along a path by a river through a forest, where they became embroiled with a number of armed men whom they assumed to be bandits, but who turned out to be a frontier police maintained by the Serbian Empire. There is something very English in the circumstance that none of the party knew more than a few words of Serbian, although for a hundred years it had been of vital importance to Byzantium to have good commercial and diplomatic relations with Serbia. When they got to the Serbian court at Skoplje, Gregoras and his friends had no eyes for anything native to the country, for they were so enormously impressed by the Serbian King Stephen's mother-in-law, who had been married to the Byzantine Emperor John Palaeologus and had recently been bereaved of her husband. He himself took enormous snob-pleasure in her grief which took the form of magnificent purple Gummidgery, and felt flattered at being allowed to watch her apostrophizing her husband as 'Oh, thou heir to numerous Emperors, who wert adorned with all the virtues,' while tearing at her cheeks till her nails were red with blood.

The insufficiently diplomatic mission clustered round her for ten days, comforting her for her loss and for bearing it in his savage country. The Serbian King, they whispered, was not showing nearly enough respect to the Queen Mother in the arrangements he was making for her return to Constantinople, but what could one expect? Monkeys, they tartly agreed, must act like monkeys and ants like ants, and neither can be expected to behave like eagles and lions. In a typical sentence Gregoras says, 'He was truly a sage who first conceived in his mind, and expressed it in his words, whether he was Thales of Mileto or Plato son of Aristo, or both, the second having borrowed from the first, that he was grateful from the bottom of his heart because he had been born a Greek and not a barbarian.' Really, he titters, when he and his party remembered how things were done in Constantinople, they felt as if here in Serbia they had fallen among beetles that were decked out with necklaces and bracelets.

That touches a chord familiar to those of us who are acquainted with the Transatlantic situation: 'My dear, it was too awful, seeing all those wonderful jewels and marvellous clothes worn by these dreadfully vulgar people.' It unfortunately happens that, though many nice little boys and girls die when young, the nasty child who spoils the Christmas party by jeering at the presents on the tree always grows up; and if he is a European he is certain, though not so certain as he would have been a hundred years ago, to despise the United States. Such as he affect to hate a new and expanding society for its ostentation and vulgarity, but the truth is that they can tolerate social ritual only when it has crystallized into an opaque form which conceals its inner meaning. Hospitality that is still determined by generosity and wealth that enjoys its own good fortune disturb them by recalling fundamental realities which their effeteness would prefer to forget. To this class Gregoras clearly belonged; and just as nothing that could be said against America by an English dowager duchess who had not done so well as she had hoped out of her lectures on her herb garden could avail against the known handsomeness of the continent, so Gregoras's letter cannot prove its point against the genius of Grachanitsa.

'But tell me,' said my husband, 'which King Stephen was it who had the Byzantine mother-in-law? For I thought that the Stephen who was Milutin's son and was blinded by him and succeeded him had married a Bulgarian princess.' But this was one of the occasions when life falls into a pattern, when the design repeats itself, Stephen did not come easily to his crown. In order to inherit it he had been obliged to keep up his pretence that he was blind until his father was dead, and therefore quite a number of people believed that he would be unable to defend it. His brother or half-brother, Constantine, who like himself had been bastardized by Milutin's annulment of his earlier marriages when he married Simonis, and his cousin Vladislav, son of that crippled King Dragutin who had abdicated and become the Catholic King of Bosnia, both tried to snatch his throne. Vladislav he merely exiled to Hungary, but Constantine he had nailed to a cross and then sawn asunder. This was not an uncommon form of punishment in the fourteenth century, and Stephen, though humane, was no more than a man of his time. Then, and not until then, was he sure of his kingdom and free to live according to his own nature.

But immediately Stephen became a faithful copy of his father, who had been his enemy and had been thought his antithesis. At the first possible moment he initiated just such overtures to the Papacy as Milutin had made in the earlier part of his reign, even going so far as receiving a Papal Legate to discuss the terms on which the Serbian Empire was to be handed over to Roman Catholicism. He had no need to imitate his father in divorce, for his first wife had died, but he attempted to follow him in matrimonial opportunism, for he tried to marry Blanche, the daughter of Philip of Taranto, a member of the house of Anjou exercising titular suzerainty over most of Greece and Albania, in order to ally himself with the Catholic Latin powers who were threatening Orthodox Byzantium. This was perfidy more monstrous than Milutin's, for it was the great Archbishop Nicodemus who had saved Stephen from exile by persuading his father to recall him and who had secured him his throne by throwing the influence of the Church against Constantine and Vladislav. It was also exceedingly imprudent, for the Serbs were fully as devoted to Orthodoxy as they had been in the previous reign, and the Papacy had lost much of its influence by leaving Rome for Avignon. When after five years he abandoned this policy it was only to imitate another of Milutin's mistakes, for he then married a Byzantine princess. It is true that his bride, Marya Palaeologus, was a less sinister character than Simonis, but the marriage resembled its earlier prototype in two respects. It was unpopular with the Serbian nationalist party, who wanted the Byzantines to be united with them by military force rather than by family relations; and it sowed trouble between the King and his heir.

Life is most apt to repeat a design and fall into a pattern when it is weak and diseased. When it is powerful and healthy it is always unpredictable. This means that timid people refuse to let it take its course and insist on provoking events with which they are already familiar, preferring the known evil to the unknown. Some of the repetition on which Stephen insisted added to the power and the glory of Serbia, for what he imitated was his father's strength. He followed him in church-building; Dechani, the great monastery at Petch we were going to visit after we had seen Kossovo and the Trepcha mines, was his foundation. He followed him in military triumph; there was a new Bulgarian Tsar, Michael, who found the Byzantine Empire quite ready to combine with him against Serbia, in spite of the marital alliance made through Marya Palaeologus, and this invasion Stephen brilliantly defeated in a decisive battle at Kustendil, which was then known as Velbuzhd. But the weakness that made him an imitator made his imitations of strength of no avail.

Milutin had raged against his son, blinded and exiled him, pardoned him and kept him impotent after the reconciliation, because he was the stronger of the two. Even had Stephen had the power to revolt against him, his political wisdom had created a people so contented that they would never have considered supporting the son against the father. Milutin's genius guaranteed him the right to sit in his throne till natural death removed him. But when Stephen raged against his son he invited a different destiny, for his son was a greater man than himself or Milutin, and against this menacing and prodigious heir he had built no bulwark of a people's loyalty. He had indeed greatly alarmed and irritated the nobles by failing to consolidate his victory over Bulgaria by statesman-like action and leaving it a resentful and armed autonomous state. His son set himself at the head of the malcontents, conquered his father, and imprisoned him in a castle to the north of Kossovo. Then he had himself crowned king by the great scholar and statesman, Archbishop Daniel. It was necessary that this should be done soon, while his hands were still clean, since Daniel was incorruptible; for two months later, with his connivance if not by his actual orders, Stephen was strangled in prison.

Thus dreadfully was it announced that this family of amazing genius, which had now been reinforced with Byzantine and French and Bulgarian and Asiatic blood of proven worth, had reached its moment of divine positiveness. The seed that had travelled from loin to loin of the Nemanyas, driving them from the Adriatic swamp of their beginnings to glory and torture and art and crime and civilization, had at last found its proper instrument. This son of Stephen was also called Stephen. To distinguish them the father is called Stephen Dechanski, from the great monastery he founded, and the son is called Stephen Dushan. There is a dispute about the meaning of the word *dushan*. It might be a term of endearment, a diminutive of *dusha*, the soul; but some have tried to derive it from the verb *dushiti*, to strangle, and seen in it a reference to his father's fate. But plainly the first is the proper root. He was probably called that in childhood, for his sister was called Dushitza; and Slavs would not find it incongruous to give a national hero such a tender name. It is, on the other hand, unlikely that they should go about calling him 'the strangler,' for if he had been that once he could be it again. It is as improbable that Queen Elizabeth's courtiers should have gone about speaking of her not as Gloriana but by some name alluding to the axe that put an end to Raleigh and Essex and Mary. The analogy must suggest itself, for, even as Milutin was Serbia's Henry VIII, so Stephen Dushan was its Elizabeth.

Stephen Dechanski came between him and his grandfather Milutin, as Edward and Mary came between Henry VIII and Elizabeth: fragile creatures not insulated from the lightning that played round their families and wilted by it, not inspired. But Stephen Dushan could grasp any thunderbolt, perhaps because, like Elizabeth, he needed all arms, being wholly surrounded by enemies and in mortal fear. In a few years he made himself the most powerful monarch in the fourteenth century, and if he had not he would have become a vassal. On his east was Bulgaria, which his father had left only half pacified; on his west was Catholic Bosnia, always plotting with the Papacy to attack Orthodox Serbia; on his north was Hungary, as always suicidally eager to attack its neighbours when they were attacked by Asiatic invaders; on his south was the Byzantine Empire, which was ready to fight him but quite unable to fight the Turks as they swept on towards Europe. To confront all these enemies he must be more than a king, he must be an emperor, and unconquered at that. It was so with Elizabeth. If she were not to be Gloriana of a supreme England her head must be on the block and her country the wash-pot of France or Spain.

Stephen Dushan dealt first of all with Bulgaria; he threatened it with arms and then married the Tsar's sister Helen. It is typical of this perplexing age that this woman, who must have been handed over to her husband like so much merchandise, who had every reason to be timid and cultivate no art but the smile that melts the jailer, became a figure of commanding ability. She was her husband's constant companion and adviser, and impressed foreign diplomats by her sense and courage both before and after his death. Next he led a campaign against Byzantium, conquering a large part of Macedonia and besieging Salonika. That he could not follow up to its full conclusion, for he was stabbed in the back by the King of Hungary and had to hurry northward to repel an invasion. But his successes had already been sufficient to enable him to impose a treaty on the Byzantines which was likely to make them respect him in future. In the north he defeated the King of Hungary and seized a considerable slice of his territory. Later he drove the house of Anjou out of its possessions in Greece and Albania, which improved his strategical position in relation to Byzantium.

All these were affairs of arms; but he worked by diplomacy also. He stretched across his troublesome Catholic neighbours in Bosnia and shook hands with the Republic of Venice, which was inclined to regard him with sympathy, since it was at war with his own enemy, Hungary, over Dalmatia. It is needless to say that he found Venice, as always, selfish and short-sighted and anti-Slav, and to protect his interests he had to practise the cunctatory, teasing guile that we take as characteristic of Queen Elizabeth. Sometimes we recognize in him, as well, her secret, mystifying grin by which she so often infuriated foreign diplomats. Once he wrote to Venice begging to be allowed shelter there if his country should be overrun with enemies. That has been regarded by some historians, who have not taken the precaution of examining its date, as evidence of the insecurity of his reign. But it was written nine years after his accession to the throne, when he had just defeated the Angevins and had every reason to feel pleased with himself. 'What a business it is to treat with a woman,' complained one of Elizabeth's Spanish ambassadors, 'who must have a hundred thousand devils in her body, notwithstanding that she is for ever telling me that she yearns to be a nun and to pass her time praying.'

That tale Stephen Dushan also could tell. He had a prolonged correspondence with the Popes Clement VI and Innocent VI which he must have carried on in a spirit of pure cynicism, for the Papacy had been at Avignon for thirty years or so and was now simply an instrument of French foreign policy, and far too heavily involved with Hungarian interests to be able to promise much to Serbia.

But he affected to be anxious for conversion, though when the Pope dispatched precise instructions as to how this might be arranged he was apt to assume a glassy blankness, as if he had hardly understood what all these letters were about. In fact he was a devoted member of the Orthodox Church, though his relations with it were curious. It did not forgive him then or afterwards for the murder of his father. Though the Nemanyan kings were described by the astonishing term 'born in sainthood' because they were descended from St. Simeon, and both Milutin and Stephen Dechanski were revered as saints, there was no nonsense about canonizing Stephen Dushan. But like his father and grandfather he took no important step without consulting the great Archbishop Daniel; and as time went on he became actively interested in the organization of the Church, for legal and political reasons.

The path of his ambitions lay southwards. He meant to win one of the multiple crowns of Byzantium; the Empire was distraught by civil war and he knew he could seize it and rule it. That alone would have prevented his adherence to the Roman Catholic Church, for it was not thinkable that Byzantium could be ruled by anyone not Orthodox. But there was also a technical problem to be solved. Only a patriarch could crown an emperor and it was quite obvious that the Ocumenical Patriarch, who was a fierce partisan of the existing imperial families, would never consent to crown a Serb conqueror. So Stephen Dushan convoked a Great Council of Serb and Bulgarian ecclesiastics at Skoplje and induced them to raise the Serbian Archbishopric of Petch to a Patriarchate. Less than a month later the newly appointed Patriarch crowned Stephen Dushan Emperor and Autocrat of the Serbs and the Byzantines, the Bulgarians and Albanians, his wife an empress, and their son a king. This amounted to the schismatic foundation of a new nationalist church, but the situation was treated with great calm, so different are the tempers of the Roman Catholic and the Orthodox faiths. Ultimately the Ocumenical Patriarch anathematized the Emperor, the new Patriarch, the whole Serbian Church, and the whole Serbian nation, but not for nearly seven years, and then for reasons that were largely political. Meanwhile Stephen Dushan behaved handsomely to such remnants of the purely Byzantine Church as were incorporated in his expanding territories, not only confirming but increasing the privileges of the See of Ochrid. He was an extremely tolerant ruler, and it was definitely his policy to let conquered territories inhabited by non-Serbian populations retain all their accustomed forms of government.

This theory broke down, however, when he took Thessaly from

the Empire. There he found that the Byzantine clergy were urging their congregations to revolt, and he had to supplant them by Serbians. This was undoubtedly an interference with the soul of a people, but it can at least be argued that he was constrained by necessity. When Mussolini prevents the Slovenes from using their own language in their churches and their schools and their homes, it cannot be urged in his excuse that if they were not part of Italy they would be part of a neighbouring disorder which would be fatal to Italian peace, for if they were on the other side of his frontier they would be incorporated in the unaggressive and civilized state of Yugoslavia. But in the days of Stephen Dushan, the Byzantine Empire was a masterless land, where weeds grew that spread to all neighbouring fields and smothered all profitable crops. We know its state from the unimpeachable evidence of one who recorded that state without shame, since he himself was responsible for it and thought that all he did was good; we have the memoirs of John Cantacuzenus, the Byzantine usurper.

That detestable man was one of those men who are the price a civilization pays in its decay for the achievements of its prime. In Byzantium, as in many other societies, government was reserved to the hereditarily favoured and to the lucky, who were immediately taken into the bosom of the hereditarily favoured as soon as their luck had declared itself, since the rich are apt to believe riches are a mark of divine favours. A closed and self-satisfied group, they were able to develop the technique of government to a point very near perfection, and to realize its full potentialities by exchanging the information which came to their hands through their monopoly of power. Thus they secured more and more successes for their country and for themselves, until they became in their own eyes magicians who could not know failure. In the end they came to regard national prosperity as a secretion of their class, which it could produce for ever provided it led a healthy life and was allowed to practise its traditional activities; and this was a fantasy so delicious that they could not bear to be awakened from it even when it conflicted with their own interests. We English are familiar with such bemusement. Many of our manufacturers refuse to alter their methods by which they established their wealth in the nineteenth century, although it is written in their balance-sheets that they are losing the twentieth-century market; and our diplomats have for long behaved as if British sovereignty were guaranteed simply by the mode of living habitual in legations and embassies.

There comes a time in the history of every country when even its most subdued and credulous children see through the fantasy of its governors, usually for the reason that it is threatened by famine and danger, and its governors exaggerate that fantasy to an insulating madness rather than face reality. Cantacuzenus was the sign that the Byzantine Empire had come to such a pass. It was, of course, doomed. Destruction by the Turks awaited it, but it had already been destroyed by the merciless West: by the greed of Venice and Genoa and Pisa, which had demanded murderously exorbitant trade agreements from it in return for help against the marauding Latins; by the intrigues of the Papacy, which always hated the Orthodox Church more bitterly than Islam; by the foreign mercenaries who bound themselves to fight against the Turks and turned in treachery against their employer. There is, indeed, no end to the crimes committed against Byzantium by the other and supposedly more civilized side of Europe; and while it worked slowly Asia worked faster. Quite soon the Turks had eaten into Byzantine territory over in Asia Minor, and this was of the gravest importance, for from those districts the Empire had drawn most of her sailors and soldiers. There was nothing the Byzantines could have done save resign themselves to partnership with Serbia and Bulgaria, who were of the same religion and related in culture. This could have been arranged without the embarrassment of a confessed capitulation, through the institution of the multiple crowns. There was no limit to the number of Byzantine emperors which could coexist, and at one time there had been five. One only of these exercised the imperial power, and the others were sleeping partners, ready to act in a consultative capacity or as successors. In Serbia this custom had already been adopted and several Nemanyan kings had crowned their sons as secondary kings with special rights over a part of the country. It should have been easy to make an arrangement which would have united the Orthodox Balkan peoples under two or three emperors, particularly as by now the Byzantine population was largely Slav. That, however, was not the will of John Cantacuzenus.

He was the heir to one of the great fortunes which shamefully existed in this shattered state, and he was the Great Domestic, which is to say the military commander-in-chief of the Emperor Andronicus II. His disintegrating influence was first made manifest when the Emperor disinherited his grandson, Andronicus the Younger, after he had pushed generally unsatisfactory conduct to a climax by employing some archers to hide outside his mistress's door and assassinate a visitor of whom he was jealous. As the dead man proved to be his brother, and his father, who was an invalid, died of shock on hearing of the tragedy, the old Emperor's action was explicable enough. But so violent were the times that some of the nobles thought it unreasonable and refused to accept the Emperor's nomination of another grandson as his heir. This preposterous movement was supported by John Cantacuzenus, who thereupon led the country into seven years of civil war. He left an extremely detailed autobiography to tell us why and how he did it, which is a disgusting work. It resembles that mixture of white of egg and sugar used instead of pure cream by some pastrycooks: endless pleas of self-justification make the page unnaturally white, it is sickly with a smug sense of good form, it is slimy for lack of principle and recognition of reality. There could be no more convincing proof that in certain periods a conservative class can be more disruptive than any revolutionary horde.

Unquestionably Cantacuzenus was a man of great ability. Byzantine administration had developed a tradition of efficiency and the Army was the most highly organized that Europe was to see till modern times, so a successful commander-in-chief was likely to be a brilliant man by any standards. He prided himself on his powers of negotiation, no doubt with reason, for Byzantine diplomacy was extremely accomplished. But negotiation is an art safely to be practised only in the years of plenty, when there is a surplus which can be comfortably haggled over by the parties involved. In gaunter times a country must lay down the conditions necessary for its own preservation, and annihilate those that will not concede them. Cantacuzenus, however, was constitutionally unable to see that Byzantium could ever not be at its zenith, and with the utmost recklessness he encouraged the difference between the Emperor and his grandson, in the hope that his skill would arrange a compromise between them. That hope was more than gratified. During the seven years of civil war he thus precipitated, he was able to present three most ably framed treaties for the signatures of the disputants as they stood bloodstained in their ravaged country. Cantacuzenus was a surgeon to Byzantium, and the operation was always successful, but the patient always died.

At length his fellow-countrymen began to notice something about him. They showed an extreme reluctance to suffer him in any position of power, and they manifested it in an unmistakable manner when the younger Andronicus died and left him guardian of his twelve-year-old son, John. Cantacuzenus could not understand their ingratitude. He knew that he had ability of a sort that had in the past rendered Byzantium many services, and the exemption of his class from all criticism prevented him from

realizing that the technical accomplishment of diplomacy is not
the same thing as statesmanship. With sublime dignity and the
full authority of a conscience that his autobiography brings to the
reader's eye in the likeness of an immense and tasteless building,
he started the civil war again by crowning himself Emperor and
claiming the executive power from the child Emperor John and
his mother, Anne of Savoy. There followed thirteen years of
the most painful disorder, which Cantacuzenus saw as a series
of triumphs for his own dexterity, as indeed they were if they
were considered individually, without regard to their cumulative
effect in murdering the Byzantine Empire.

During this time Cantacuzenus turned constantly to neighbouring states for aid, and conducted his negotiations with them on
the highest imaginable plane of tact and discretion. These greatly
expedited the collapse of civilization in South-East Europe, for
his neighbours required order in Byzantium for the sake of the
common front they had to form against the Turks, and they
could not be certain whether this could better be guaranteed by
Cantacuzenus or by the Empress Anne, and they too vacillated and
added to the confusion. Later, he gave a disastrous exhibition of
his virtuosic talents in his achievement of an alliance with Orkhan,
the chief of the Ottoman Turks. Nothing could have been more
expert. But it brought the Turks to Europe in numbers that made
it impossible ever to expel them again; and when he gave his
daughter in marriage to Orkhan he weakened the clear picture
of the antithesis between the Christian Byzantines and the Islamic
Turks which should have been preserved at all costs in the minds
of his own people and the West.

Finally Cantacuzenus set the seal on his adept and imbecile
achievements by ingeniously making peace with the Emperor
John, who was now a young man, on condition that there were two
emperors and three empresses—himself, young John, his mother
Anne of Savoy, Cantacuzenus's wife and his daughter, whom he
had induced young John to marry—and that he himself reserved
the right to be sole ruler for the next ten years. It was certainly a
masterpiece of diplomacy to get this agreement signed, but he must
have been powerfully aided by the exhaustion he had brought on
his country. Civil war had so depredated the state that even the
court, which had not long before amazed the world, was stripped
of its gold and jewels. At the wedding feast of the Emperor John
and Cantacuzenus's daughter, royalty and nobles alike adorned
themselves with gilt leather and coloured glass, and the toasts were
drunk from tin and lead.

But the defence of humanity against its Cantacuzenuses is its quick resilience. As soon as the truce between the two combatants had given the country a breathing-space, the young John rebelled and brought in Genoese help, and was supported by most of his subjects. Cantacuzenus's response was to make his son Matthew emperor in John's stead; he knew that what the country really needed was one more of a family who knew how to do things. At this point the Byzantines at last lost patience. They turned on him as one man and ran him into a monastery. In the most graceful fashion imaginable he accepted the situation, took his vows, and, since his attentions had been insufficiently appreciated here on earth, transferred them with unabated self-confidence to the next world. He spent the many remaining years of his life in fomenting the spiritual equivalent of civil war by writing ingenious treatises against Jews and Mohammedans. It was characteristic of him that first he ably invited the Turks to Europe, where they had no business to be, and then as ably assailed them for the ideas which they had every right to hold.

This conservative politician, shining smooth, smooth as water as it slips over the lip of a precipice, came to Prishtina at a time when he should have been doubtful about his fate, being a new-fledged and not popularly acclaimed usurper; and indeed he was diffident as a Member of Parliament who for the sake of holding office has just crossed the floor of the House. He perhaps never knew a deeper diffidence. The town he entered, the town in which Constantine and my husband and I were lunching, was then very proud. It was built of wood, which some historians have mentioned as proof that it was primitive; but the Slav, like the Scandinavian, always builds in timber when he can, and the Mediterranean habit of using stone was determined by the lack of forest and the abundance of quarries in the south. Between the wooden houses the Serbian nobles and their ladies rode out to meet him, themselves handsome in red cloaks lined with fur and embroidered in gold, and their horses as handsome with silver trappings, often brought from Venice. They were not greatly divided by their Slavdom from their visitor. Many of them spoke Greek, and to Stephen Dushan it was as a second mother-tongue, since he had lived in Constantinople from his eighth to his fifteenth year; and the protocol of the court was definitely Byzantine, which pleased Cantacuzenus very much.

It was the Serb custom, he tells us, that when an eminent foreigner came to visit their King they both descended from their horses and the foreigner kissed his host on his face and breast. But Stephen Dushan ordered that when Cantacuzenus came he was to be greeted as he would have been within his own Empire; so all the nobles dismounted as soon as they saw him in the distance and when he approached them they stepped forward to kiss his knee where it was crooked against the saddle. Then he was taken to the palace, and was received very graciously by the Emperor and Empress, and when it was time for banqueting he was taken into a great hall and set at a table in a chair higher than Stephen Dushan's own. Byzantine though he was, this banquet impressed him. The nobles and their ladies wore their ceremonial costume of green or yellow tunics, studded with diamonds and precious stones and the cut gems of ancient Greece, and belted with silver and gold. Then men carried magnificent daggers and wore jewelled rings and bracelets and crosses suspended from the neck, and the women were crowned with intricately wrought diadems of gold and silver, from which fine chains ran down to take part of the weight of their immense and gorgeous earrings. To the music of flutes they drank great quantities of mead and wine, and ate game and venison and fish which had come in snow from the Danube, with many kinds of vegetables and fruits and sheep's milk and honey; and there was also about the table the orchestral murmur of a great cosmopolitan court. Many Italians and Spanish and Asiatics had come to Serbia to seek their fortune, and Stephen Dushan had for his personal guard a company of German soldiers, in imitation of the Byzantine Emperor's famous Varangian guard of Scandinavians and English. But Cantacuzenus was not more impressed by the wealth and cosmopolitan quality of the court than by its fine and formal manners. He was hardly ever suffered, he says, to remain alone in his tent. Nearly every day Stephen Dushan sent a deputation of the most distinguished old nobles and the most charming young pages, to beg him to come to the palace and give the court more of his delightful company; and when Cantacuzenus obeyed the summons Stephen Dushan would come to meet his guest at the door of his great apartment, and sometimes even at the place where he dismounted.

When enough time had passed to satisfy the convention that there was nothing behind the visit save pure sociability, Stephen Dushan asked Cantacuzenus whether he had come to ask any favour of him, and expressed the hope that if this were so he would be able to accede. Cantacuzenus answered by a reference to the myth of the gods gone avisiting, and said that he had come to gain Stephen Dushan's friendship, since the wise esteemed nothing so highly as a faithful friend. But he went on to admit that he sought his host's aid in restoring order to the Byzantine

Empire. He added that if Stephen Dushan did not want to help
him he would like to be told so at once, in order that he could
look for other means of salvation; and one perceives in his account
of his own conversation how clever a performing flea he was. He
made his appeal in terms that enmeshed Stephen Dushan by the
twin assumptions that they were gentlemen talking together, and
that the one who altered the tone of the conversation from the
tenor determined by himself would prove himself no gentleman,
and by a strong hint that if help were refused the refusal would
be taken as proceeding from impotence.

This last suggestion Stephen Dushan, whose security depended
largely on his prestige, could not let pass. He had soldiers
enough to give Cantacuzenus all the help he needed, he said,
if Cantacuzenus proved that he really wanted it. Cantacuzenus
expressed wonder at the phrase. What proof could be necessary?
Stephen Dushan replied that he could believe in Cantacuzenus's
desire for help if he handed over to the Serbian crown all
the towns of Thrace: that is to say, on the Greek seaboard
east of Salonika. It was in fact not an exorbitant demand. The
inhabitants of the Byzantine Empire were by this time mostly
Slav and not Greek, so there was no racial reason why the
Serbs and Bulgars and Byzantines should not coalesce, and it
was imperative that the territory should fall under the shield of
a strong government. Often aggressors have justified their thefts
on such grounds, but here in South-East Europe, in the middle
of the fourteenth century, they happened to be valid. Ungoverned
towns on the seaboard meant a door unlocked to the robbers from
the Catholic West.

Cantacuzenus answered Stephen Dushan very much as an
English diplomat of the worst old type might speak to an American
who was being tiresome about the debt settlement. The theme
of gentlemanliness was recapitulated with frosty delicacy. 'You
speak very reasonably,' he told him, 'concerning the reward
you want; for there is no wise man who does not expect a
return when he goes to trouble and expense. So, if your instinct
does not tell you that you ought to help me as an act of grace,
you are right to ask me to buy your assistance. But if I buy
it and pay for it, I shall be under no obligation to you, for
who pays for what he buys feels under no obligation to the
seller. But if you help me out of generous friendship, and out
of ambition of a sort honourable to a sovereign, it will be a
glory to you to have taken up arms for such noble motives, and
not from greed, as low natures would. Moreover,' he added, 'if

you have me as a friend while I enjoy the imperial power, you will possess all that I possess, since everything is shared among friends, as the philosophers say.' He had made perfect use of his technique; he was now to show his perfect blindness to reality. 'If your offer of help is conditional on the surrender of the towns you claimed, say so frankly,' he ended coldly, 'so that I can make other arrangements. For I swear to you that I will never surrender a single town; but I will guard them all as I have guarded my own children.' They were not his children; they could not be guarded so long as he pretended they were.

Stephen Dushan then fell into a transport of rage, which must have been impressive enough. Foreigners who visited his court describe him as 'the tallest of all men of his time,' and a fresco portrait shows him sinewy, with black eyes burning over high cheek-bones. There was reason in his rage against Cantacuzenus, for the usurper was in his weakness a threat to the peace of the whole Balkan world. But Stephen Dushan was calmed by his wife, the Empress Helen, and he consented to summon the Diet of twenty-four of his most important nobles and discuss the issue with them. There an important part was played by Helen, in a fashion illustrating the ambivalence with which men regard women. They love them and they hate them; they pamper them and ill-treat them; and women are at once slaves and freer than men. In medieval Serbia women must have been chattels, for their evidence was not accepted in the law courts; and such a rule always implies that no woman is sufficiently assured of protection by society to risk giving evidence that has not been dictated to her by some man. Yet the Empress Helen was able to rise in the Diet and make a long speech urging a rejection or at least a modification of her husband's policy, in terms which suggest that she was accustomed to using her mind vigorously and without fear.

This speech was extremely able. She affirmed that the Serbs were under no obligation to consider Cantacuzenus's interests before their own, but warned them to judge carefully what was best for them. In cryptic phrases, which we now know to have referred to an offer made by Anne of Savoy to hand over an immense slice of Byzantine territory in return for Cantacuzenus alive or dead, she repudiated the possibility of harming their guest. That, she said, would be a crime displeasing to men and odious to God. She believed that they should aid Cantacuzenus; for he had in the past proved himself an able governor, and if he regained imperial power might be a dangerous enemy. She suggested that the price they should ask of him for their aid should be not new towns but recognition of their claim to the towns which they and their ancestors had already taken from the Byzantines. With shrewdness greater than was recognized by Cantacuzenus, she pointed out that he would probably accept these conditions since the loss of these towns brought no personal disgrace on him.

The Empress convinced both the Diet and her husband. Stephen Dushan made a speech and thanked her for her care for his people, and then went to Cantacuzenus and said, smiling, 'You have won, you have persuaded us to undertake all sorts of hardships and trials for your sake.' When Cantacuzenus heard Helen's proposals he accepted them eagerly and sat down happily to turn out more of his exquisitely accomplished paperwork. But his fortune was crumbling so fast that the basis of the treaty altered between its drafting and its signing. A military adventurer who was straddling the border between Serbia and Byzantium, acknowledging the allegiance of now one and now the other according to their fortunes, took another Byzantine town and hastened to drop it into Stephen Dushan's lap. It was an ill omen. The fellow was an infallible barometer, and since it was his opinion that Cantacuzenus meant nothing, that probably was his real value, and alliance with him was of no service to Serbia. But Stephen Dushan went on with the treaty, insisting merely that the town should be added to the list of his possessions and the adventurer should be declared his subject, though Cantacuzenus fought hard to keep them under his impotence. Then the twenty-four members of the Diet were called together and told, by an admirable form of parliamentary procedure which has been insufficiently imitated, that since they had decided that military aid should be given to Cantacuzenus they must now provide it, and twenty of them were sent off at the head of troops with orders to obey their new general in all things. They must have left Stephen Dushan reflecting, as Elizabeth was so often forced to do, that no man has any reliable ally save in his own right hand.

Eight years later Cantacuzenus and Stephen Dushan met again: a long way from Prishtina, outside Salonika. By this time Cantacuzenus was far advanced in his competent and complacent pursuit of destruction, and Stephen Dushan had pushed out his strength to north, south, east, and west, gathering to himself mastery of the Balkans. He had made Skoplje a great city, and there he had been crowned one Easter Sunday Emperor and Autocrat of the Serbs and Byzantines, the Bulgars and the Albanians. His upbringing in Constantinople had always profoundly influenced the etiquette of his palace, and now he lived in an exact imitation of the Byzantine court; he had assumed the tiara and used the double eagle as his emblem, and his officials were called by the names borne by their originals in Byzantium, Sebastocrator and Grand Logothete, Grand Domestic and Sacellary. The imitation went deeper than nomenclature. He was not, of course, wholly free from care. When Cantacuzenus, in a last ill-considered effort to reclaim territory which he could not hold, had marched against him he had found it far from child's-play to repel the attack, for his Catholic enemies had stabbed him in the back on the Bosnian frontier. But he was magnificent, imperially magnificent. The land he stood on as he faced Cantacuzenus was to its further distances his, or about to become his, drawn to him by the magnetism of his true power, which all others lacked.

He had first to resist Cantacuzenus's reproaches of perfidy. Like Elizabeth he awoke in his enemies an indignant sense that they had had to deal with an infinity of cunning and trickery; but any animal will run like a fox if it is hunted like a fox. Unquestionably he had broken treaties he had made with Cantacuzenus, but the alteration in the two men's statuses must have made it difficult to observe them. It would be hard to execute a document signed by a living man and a phantom. The further rights and wrongs of this dispute cannot be judged, for at this stage of his memoirs Cantacuzenus had arrived at a decision, not unfamiliar in autobiography, that he could only be fair to himself by lying. But he tells us something of Stephen Dushan which we can believe because it is not credible. It struck the unimaginative Cantacuzenus as so odd that he put it down in the hope of discrediting his successful rival. He says that in the midst of their open conference, in the hearing of all the Byzantines and Serbs, Stephen Dushan suddenly confessed that he was very greatly frightened of Cantacuzenus and his forces. Yes, he said, he feared them horribly. If the thought of them came to him as he slept, he woke in a sweat; if it came to him before he slept, he stayed awake all night. This was a surprising note; and it was struck again later in the conversation. Cantacuzenus asked him how he had come to lower himself by paying a certain state visit to Venice and making obeisances to the republic unsuitable in the ruler of a kingdom so much more mighty and extensive; and he answered that he was well aware how much beneath his dignity his bearing had been, but fear had compelled him. He added that, considering what fear was, he wondered it had made him do nothing baser. Cantacuzenus naïvely said to himself that evidently he and the whole world had been acting on far too elevated a conception of Stephen Dushan's character, and forthwith demanded from him the return of all the Byzantine territory he had conquered.

Stephen Dushan was amazed by the suggestion. He had merely been discussing the nature of fear and the occasional sick fancies to which he, like all born of woman, was subject; he had not had the slightest intention of acting weakly. It is as if a Dostoievsky character came marching to us through Cæsar's *De Bello Gallico*. There could be no more curious proof of the identity of the Slav character through the ages, for he was plainly giving rein to the desire that governs the Slav of today, the desire to know the whole. Finding himself at the extremity of a condition, he leaned out of his destiny towards its opposite, trying to understand that also. Had he been defeated and hopeless, he would have talked of triumph till his hearers would have wondered at his boasting. So it was natural for him to explore his potentialities for terror, since, though danger still threatened him, it seemed that he had found a formula for its control.

The core of his power was his great strength, which enabled him to support the delicacy of his Slav mind. He was apparently a man of the explosive but easy temper which goes with perfect health and exceptional vitality. A glimpse of his habitual being is given in that part of the *Acts of the Saints* which deals with St Peter Thomas, a curiously stupid and tactless person who was very unsuitably employed as a Papal Legate. He was sent to the Serbian court to labour for its conversion, but for some mysterious reason refused to make the usual obeisance on being received by the Emperor. Not unnaturally Stephen Dushan was carried away by rage, and he forbade the Roman Catholics about the court to attend a Mass at which the Legate was to officiate on the following day, on pain of having their eyes put out. St Peter Thomas interpreted this to mean that he ran the risk of being killed, though blinding, which was a recognized penalty borrowed by the Serbs from the Byzantines, never entailed death. But he went ahead and celebrated the Mass, which was attended by many of the German guards and other Catholic courtiers. It was a singularly graceless act on their part, for there was complete religious freedom in the Serbian Empire, and they could have attended any Mass save that celebrated by the priest who had insulted their Emperor. But when Stephen Dushan sent for them, and they told him they were prepared to lose their lives as well as their eyes for their faith, he was shaken by sudden laughter and let them go unpunished as a reward for their spirit; and he treated St Peter Thomas for the rest of his stay with a special courtesy.

There shines through the story a reluctance to waste time on hatred and compulsion which is characteristic of Stephen Dushan. That may seem an odd testimonial to give a parricide; yet even that vast initial crime has aspects that warn us not to judge it as if it were a piece of our age. When Stephen Dushan murdered his father he neither killed nor imprisoned nor even exiled his stepmother. Six years afterwards he married her to the despot John Oliver and gave her a large dowry, including the Sheep's Field and the town of Veles; and documents in which he called her his 'well-beloved mother' show that in the meantime she had been a respected figure at his court. We ask ourselves in vain how it can have been done, how the persons involved found it possible to go on breathing when they were in the same room, so great their reciprocity of fear and shame. But the situation is not shocking compared with Tudor practice, for Lady Jane Grey might well have sighed for some Nemanyan tolerance; and any comparison with the practice of modern times, though it would have been to our advantage thirty years ago, becomes less so with the dawning of each day. It cannot be doubted that if Stephen Dushan failed to achieve the millennium it was not because he lacked the appetite for it. Like most of us, he would have used the means if he had known what they were.

He liked life to take its own course. There was nothing totalitarian or xenophobic about his regime. His people showed a reluctance to trade in towns and work in mines, preferring, very reasonably, to farm their fat lands. Their sovereign let them have their way, and brought in Venetians and Ragusans as traders and Saxons as miners, and treated them well. We know exactly how his mind ran on these and many other matters, for he left behind him a legal code comprising nearly two hundred articles. This is a very creditable achievement, which brought up to date the laws made by the earlier kings of the Nemanyan dynasty and was in sum a nicely balanced fusion of Northern jurisprudence and the Byzantine system laid down by Justinian. It coped in an agreeable and ingenious spirit with the needs of a social structure not at all to be despised even in comparison with the West.

There, at this time, the land was divided among great feudal lords who ruled over innumerable serfs; but here in Serbia there were very few serfs, so few that they formed the smallest class in the community, and there was a large class of small free landowners. There was a National Diet which met to discuss such important matters as the succession to the throne or the outbreak of civil war, and this consisted of the sovereigns, their administrators, the great and small nobility, and the higher clergy; it was some smaller form of this, designed to act in emergencies that met to discuss whether John Cantacuzenus should receive Serbian aid. All local government was in the hands of the whole free community, and so was all justice, save for the special cases that were reserved for royal jurisdiction, such as high treason, murder, and highway robbery. This means that the people as a whole could deal with matters that they all understood, while the matters that were outside common knowledge were settled for them by their sovereign and selected members of their own kind; for there were no closed classes, and both the clergy and the nobility were constantly recruited from the peasantry.

Against the military difficulties that constantly beset Stephen Dushan there could be counted the security of this possession: a country rich in contented people, in silver and gold, in grain and cattle, in oil and wine, and in the two traditions, one Byzantine and mellow, one Slav and nascent, which inclined its heart towards civilization. Here was plenty, and a plentiful spirit: with a gesture that recalls our own Tudor age, when a gentleman leaving his country house for some months would leave orders that all visitors should be well entertained in his absence, Stephen Dushan ordered that all foreign envoys travelling through the land should be given all the meat and drink they desired at the imperial expense. As he pressed southward into Byzantine territory he restored to it elements necessary to civilized life which it had almost forgotten. He was not in need of money, so he did not need to rob his new subjects after the fashion of participants in the Civil War; he taxed them less, repaired gaps in their strongholds, and lent them Serbian soldiers as police. He also practised the principle of toleration, which was very dear to the Byzantine population; it must be remembered that the Orthodox crowd of Constantinople rushed without hesitation to defend the Saracen merchants' mosque when it was attacked by the fanatic Latin knights. There could be no complete application of this principle, and Stephen Dushan certainly appointed Serbian governors to rule over his new territories, as well as Serbian ecclesiastics when the local priests were irreconcilable; but he left the indigenous social and political systems just as he found them, and there was no economic discrimination against the conquered.

It was as if there were falling down the map from the Serbian Empire an ooze of honey, runnels of wine. They must drip across

Byzantium, they must spread all over the country to the sea, to the Bosporus. To all men's minds it became possible that some day Stephen Dushan might come to Constantinople and that he might be Emperor not only of the Byzantines but of Byzantium, seated at its centre in the palace that had known Constantine the Great and Justinian. There are many reasons why he should not have succeeded in this enterprise. It would have been hard to capture Constantinople without a fleet, and Stephen Dushan could neither develop maritime power nor persuade the short-sighted Republic of Venice to enter into an alliance with him for the sake of his aid against the Turks. But there were many reasons why he should not have been able to found the Empire that he did; the cards stacked against him by his neighbours on every frontier made any further extension of territory seem impracticable. But even so the end of our Queen Elizabeth's reign could not have been foretold at its beginning. It is chiefly Russian nineteenth-century historians, pro-Bulgar and anti-Serb, who allege that Stephen Dushan could not have reached Constantinople. His own age, and those who lived within recollection of its glory, believed him capable of that journey, and more. He would have found it a poor place; it had been stripped of its wealth by the civil wars, its population had been wasted by the first onslaughts of the plague, its valuable harbour was in the hands of loutish Italians who seized its commerce and insulted those they had robbed. Those who knew him trusted him to restore its splendour, which would have been to perform a miracle. He might have achieved deeds more miraculous still. He might have saved Europe from the Turks; he must, in any case, have held them in check and given Europe a longer time to arm herself. It might have been that Hungary need never have had her hundred and fifty years of Turkish tyranny, and Vienna need never have been besieged, and then that abomination of abominations, the Austro-Hungarian Empire, need never have been founded. Our night would have been less black, and our glory far more glorious.

But Stephen Dushan died. In the forty-ninth year of his life, at a village so obscure that it is not now to be identified, he died, in great pain, as if he had been poisoned. Because of his death many disagreeable things happened. For example, we sat in Prishtina, our elbows on a tablecloth stained brown and puce, with chicken drumsticks on our plates meagre as sparrow-bones, and there came towards us a man and a woman; and the woman was carrying on her back the better part of a plough. Here, where women had worn diadems of gold and silver, and the Empress had spoken her fine mind before the respect of the Diet, where the worth of womanhood had been so generally conceded that a painter could treat it passionately in his frescoes and assume the sympathy of his audience, this woman had walked a great distance by the side of her husband, bearing a heavy burden, while he went free.

It could be seen that they had made a long journey, for their sandals and woollen stockings were white with dust, and though she was of my own sturdy pack-horse build, a blue shadow of fatigue lay across her mouth. Her husband went up to the hotel-keeper, who was leaning against the door, and had a long talk with him, while she stood and looked at us. She could not sit down because of the long iron blade that was bound to her back and ran from above her head down to her knees. It was apparent that neither she nor her husband felt any embarrassment at the sight they presented. They had smug and serious faces, and would not, I think, have done anything that was not approved by the community; indeed, when he tied the ploughshare to her they were both automatically carrying out a custom which nobody in their world had ever criticized, without any intention of unkindness on the one side or resentment on the other. It was not as if she were a middle-aged woman against whom her husband might have turned as she had lost her sexual value, for she was in her early twenties, and showed a certain handsomeness; and there looked to be a steady though dull good-humour between them.

It may be said that if that were so, that if she and her husband were contented and the community were not shocked, there was no reason for strangers to become excited. In Prishtina it could be seen that this was not true. Any area of unrestricted masculinism, where the women are made to do all the work and are refused the right to use their wills, is in fact disgusting, not so much because of the effect on the women, who are always taught something by the work they do, but because of the nullification of the men. This Kossovo peasant was strong and upstanding, but he had the pulpy look of a eunuch, and this was not unnatural, for he had resigned from the sphere of effort. He had expected the woman to do everything, to produce the next generation and to do all the work for this one; he had left not enough of the task for himself. Though the woman was not so null, she had a displeasing air of essential slovenliness which cancelled the superficial neatness of her black dress and orange kerchief. She had grown careless of her womb. She had forgotten that she must use herself delicately, not out of pride or cowardice, but because her body was an instrument of the race. Life, that should have proceeded from these people, running ahead to conquer the next stage of time, dragged behind them like a shadow cast on mud. Yet people here had once known all that we know, and more, but the knowledge had died after the death of Stephen Dushan, it had been slain on the field of Kossovo.

The pair moved off into the sunlight, high-coloured and well-fleshed, hollow with stupidity. I went upstairs to the lavatory. Open doors in the corridor showed me bedrooms monastic in cleanliness and austerity, with iron bedsteads, flimsy washstands and enamelled ewers and basins, and bare boards scrubbed white by the secret process the gipsies use. In one room a kilted Albanian lay on the bed, staring at the ceiling and counting on his fingers. The lavatory was of the old Turkish kind: that is to say, it was a small room paved with stone, with a round hole in the floor near one wall, and a tap not far away. The whole floor was wet. Everybody who used the place must go out with shoes stained with urine. It was an unlovable apartment. The dark hole in the floor, and something hieratic in the proportions of the place, made it seem as if dung, having been expelled by man, had set itself up as a new and hostile and magically powerful element that could cover the whole earth with dark ooze and sickly humidity. There came on me the panic that bad sanitation can sometimes arouse even in the most hardened travellers. I felt as if the place were soiling me with filth which I would never be able to wash off because it was stronger in its essence than mere mild soap and water.

I went downstairs and said to my husband, who was standing outside the hotel looking at a piece of orange cloth, 'In Byzantine Constantinople there was an abundant water supply, and we know from the charters of the hospitals that they had elaborate bathrooms and lavatories.' He answered, 'My poor dear, I was afraid it would be like that. But look at this. I went over to the shops to see if I could buy you a local handkerchief, but this is all they use.' It was a square of poorly woven cloth with a machine-stitched hem; at eight-inch intervals there were knotted through the hem wispy skeins of four or five orange threads, about three inches long, which were as poor attempts at decoration as have ever been made. 'They say one can buy good embroideries in the town, there is a well-known woman who sells them,' said my husband, 'but this is what most of the women wear. They are the plainest things we have found anywhere. They say the people here are so poor they have no wool to spare to make things for themselves, they have lost the habit of ornament.'

Plain of Kossovo II

As we got into the automobile Constantine made a face at some scented rags of meadowsweet, a few rose-petals, that had fallen from the dead flowers I had thrown away before lunch. 'That I cannot understand,' he said, 'that you pretend to love beautiful things, and yet you pick flowers though you know they must wither and die, and will have to be thrown away.' 'Why not?' I asked. 'There were hundreds of others where these grew, so nobody would miss them, and we all enjoyed them for two or three hours.' He shrugged his shoulders and said, 'Oh, well, if that is your point of view, it is your point of view.' Then, huddling down in his place, he threw back his head and sat with his eyes shut and a contemptuous smile on his lips. 'You are very different from my wife,' he said. 'She is a mystic, she would rather dance round a wayside flower than pluck it. But that you would not understand, for you English are not tender.' My baser part silently remarked that Gerda could not have danced round a wayside flower without inflicting the most untender damage on the surrounding growth. I thought also of her hatred of the gipsy boys and girls who were like flowers. 'She is as tender as the Turks were,' I said to myself, 'the Turks who loved nature, who slaughtered humankind'; and we sat dumb as the road rose out of the trench where Prishtina lies, looking back at the new whitewashed Government buildings that protrude square as a set chin among the shapeless lumber of the old town, or forward to the dark green of the plains. The close opaque texture of the grass gave them an artificial look, as if they had been prepared for a special purpose, like our race-tracks and golf-courses, or that mound at Silbury which our prehistoric ancestors put to some unknown use.

I tried to deny its flat, monotonous boast of irreparable damage done to our kind. I pretended that perhaps very little had been destroyed here, since if Slav culture had been a reality the Serbian Empire would not have fallen to pieces in the thirty-four years between the death of Stephen Dushan and the battle of Kossovo. That is the opinion of the anti-Serb historians; they point out that within a short time his Empire had dissolved into its constituent parts, so that the Turks were faced not by a united people, but by a loose federation of feudal barons and their followers. But as I resorted to repeating it I knew it was nonsense. England might

897

have passed into a disabling period of faction fights if Elizabeth had died at forty-eight instead of seventy; and there were many reasons why Serbia was specially liable to such disorders.

One proceeded from a genetic fatality that has been largely responsible for the unstable character of civilization. Stephen Dushan had forgotten, as great men sometimes do, a son that was a faint echo of his father's genius; of a like rarity and fineness but without the needed volume and force. Though Stephen Urosh was only nineteen when he came to the throne, his limitations had already been recognized. It seems certain that his able mother, the Empress Helen, did not want him to assume power. For a time she transacted the imperial business herself, even to commanding the armies in the field, and even after she had retired to the cloister as the nun Elizabeth she continued to administer a certain amount of territory. Eight years after Stephen Dushan's death the Byzantine Emperor John became anxious for an alliance with Serbia against the Turks, and sent his Patriarch to take the necessary preliminary step of arranging for the repeal of the excommunication he had pronounced against the Serbian Church. It was to the Empress in her convent that the mission addressed itself. It is typical of the fitful and distracted spirit of the age that when this mission was aborted by the death of the Patriarch on the road, no step was taken to send out another.

A further reason for the collapse of Serbia was a calamity which ravaged the country shortly after Stephen Dushan's death and would have shaken the authority of any successor, no matter however able. It is described as a famine which killed many men; and it can be identified as an attack of the form of plague then devouring the population of Constantinople. Such an epidemic left vast areas of farm-lands undercultivated, destroyed centres of craftsmanship, and annihilated foreign trade. This catastrophe must have affected the Empire, which by this time had enjoyed the happiest expansion for three-quarters of a century, as the slump of 1929 affected the United States. In those days, when economic theory had hardly begun to be formulated and was wholly beyond the comprehension of ordinary man, material discontents often expressed themselves in theological or dynastic disputes quite irrelevant to the hardships experienced.

The Byzantines of that age vented their misery in the controversy of the Zealots; but the Serbs were artists rather than intellectuals, and they preferred to dispute about the seen. They therefore wrangled about their rulers. It would have been far better if they had discussed whether the divine light of the Transfiguration could have been apprehended by the corporeal eye, for that could only have gratified the vanity of the unseen powers, and Serbia had to be very careful of disturbing the seen powers. For it was still creating its nobility, that is to say its administrative class, by means which demanded an acknowledged authority. We realize this in learning that when a noble was given a military or civil charge he was given by the sovereign arms and a war-horse; and when he died these or new ones had to be handed back to the sovereign, who decided whether to return them to a son of the dead man or to confer them on another family. This required a monarch of almost ecclesiastical authority whose will was sacred law. If he vacillated in the many decisions of a like personal nature which he had to make, a crowd of feudal barons would press in on him, disputing his title to domination and then claiming it for themselves. It has always been the special tragedy of Slav communities that at any moment of crisis they can furnish not too few but far too many men capable of taking charge of affairs.

In the first few years of Stephen Urosh's reign there were quite a number of aspirants to his power. There was his mother; his father's brother Simeon, and his son-in-law; two brothers, Uglyesha and Vukashin, formerly his cupbearer and marshal, who rebelled against him and stole large portions of his land; and there were several lesser chieftains, including some vigorous personalities who fell on Bulgaria and partitioned it. For some time before the battle of Kossovo all these rivals had been obscured. Stephen Urosh was driven into exile and murdered, and presently the fame of his gentleness made the faithful speak of miracles at his tomb. It was of him that the Russian monk had said to us at the monastery of Yazak in the Frushka Gora, 'No, there is nothing interesting here, only the body of a Serbian emperor.' Vukashin and Uglyesha were killed leading their armies against the Turks, Vukashin at the hand of a treacherous servant. Of the others those who were not obliterated by natural death or military failure were outshone by two princes of conspicuous ability.

One was Tvrtko, King of Bosnia, an offshoot of the Nemanya family, who had seized a great part of Dalmatian and Serbian territory; the other was Prince Lazar, the same Lazar whose brown defeated hand I touched at Vrdnik, who was lord of the northern and eastern Serbian lands. Tvrtko had shown signs of military genius and Lazar could claim at least a high degree of military efficiency. In the pact they signed for the sake of maintaining Slav unity against the Turks they showed considerable statesmanship. The quality of these two men suggests that the decadence of the Serbian Empire after the death of Stephen Dushan was only the trough that follows a great wave, and that a wave as great might have succeeded it. The historians, in trying to prove that Balkan Christian civilization was already self-doomed before its destruction, are moved by a snobbish and pusillanimous desire not to speak ill of the Old Squire, destiny. It is probable that the battle of Kossovo deducted as much from civilization as the sum of England after the Tudor age.

It was a painful thought, implying that the world we have embarked on is a leaky ship and may not keep afloat. I did not want to get out of the automobile when Constantine said, 'See, now we must walk and I will show you all things of our tragedy.' But when I stood on the road I felt nothing. I saw before me simply green downs like those that lie along some Wiltshire valleys, and a high silver sky which took all foreignness from the scene, since it made the snow ranges on the horizon look like shining bars of cloud; some winding roads and lanes, and some scattered buildings. Nothing that had happened here was present to me. At Grachanitsa I had seen medieval Serbia in its living guise as the visitor may see the Tudors at Hampton Court or Frederick the Great at Potsdam; but the armies that had waited here on the eve of St Vitus's Day in 1389 were not even ghosts to me, they were words out of a book. Nothing could be more agreeable than to be so exempt. I remembered how I had dreaded the first anniversary of the most disagreeable event that had ever befallen me, and how I had awakened on the day and felt nothing, absolutely nothing. I walked away from the automobile towards a tuft of pinkish-purple flowers that grew about a hundred yards away, enjoying the cool, freely flowing air of the uplands, and I did not turn round when Constantine called to me. But Dragutin ran after me, and said slowly, in order that I might understand, 'Like a child, like a child.' He put his hand flat two or three feet above the ground, and with the other pointed to Constantine. 'Like a child he is, but he has a bad wife. Come to the hill, it is very interesting. Do not mind him.'

'No, no, it is not that,' I said, but I could not explain, so I followed him across the grass, and we joined my husband and Constantine, who were on a path running up a little hill, on the top of which was a whitewashed hexagonal building, surmounted by a grey-blue metallic dome. Around it the turf was pierced here and there with the white toppling poles of Moslem tombs, and there were some wild rose bushes and a fruit tree, hung with brown wreaths of dead blossom. Out of the folds of what had seemed an empty landscape there emerged suddenly a number of people who converged on us just as we reached the building. There was a veiled woman, her black cotton garments made a strange ghostly colour by the heavy summer dust, gliding along with a baby in her arms and two little children at her heels, exhibiting a dark and slippery and un-individualized fecundity like caviare. There was a lean and wildish-looking man with a shepherd's staff, his cheeks so hollow that one might have thought he usually wore false teeth and had taken them out, were it not that his belly was as concave. There was a Christian girl of about fourteen who had better been veiled, for her face showed a fixed and empty stare of hunger, of appetite so completely starved that it was ignorant of its own object. She wore a skirt that was a straight piece of cloth gathered along one selvedge to form a waistband so that it stood out round her knees like a coarse version of the ballerina's toutou. There were several boys, all wearing the fez, all bandy. The veiled woman slipped with her children into the shabby porch of the octagonal building, and Constantine explained sententiously, 'This is a holy place for them,' and indeed she had the air of being on some errand which at once satisfied the motor impulses and the sense of duty, like shopping or calling, but more so, which Moslem women bring to their religious exercise. The man with the shepherd's staff stared at Dragutin with the admiration due to a very handsome man. The children held out to us bunches of flowers with an almost aristocratic lack of insistence, and Constantine said, 'These are the famous poppies of Kossovo that grow nowhere else, they are supposed to have sprung from the blood of the slaughtered Serbs. Later the whole plain is red with them, but as you see it is too early for them, these are only buds.' They were a very beautiful kind of wild peony, with golden centres and pink stamens. My husband bought some from the girl and Dragutin bought some from the boys; he was behaving at Kossovo as he behaved at springs and in churches, with a mystical and soldierly excitement, like one who salutes the sacred spectre of valour.

Constantine began to tell us how the troops had been marshalled for the battle. Here Prince Lazar had had his tent, there the Turks had waited. 'But no!' interrupted Dragutin. He was shouting slowly and without rage, as he did when moved by patriotic fervour. 'How could they wait in the North-West! Not here, but there were they, the dogs! And there, over there, Vuk Brankovitch should have come in with his troops but turned away and left the battle-field!' 'Vuk Brankovitch,' said Constantine, 'is the Judas of our story. He was the specially beloved brother-in-law of the Prince Lazar, and he is supposed to have sold himself to the Turks and to have led his army off the battle-field at a crucial moment, thus exposing

Lazar's flank. But now historians do not think there was any treachery, though it seems likely that one of the Serbian princes did not receive a message in time telling him to go forward to Lazar's support, and so failed him. But we all know that it was not treachery that lost us Kossovo, it is that we were all divided among ourselves.' 'Yes,' said Dragutin, 'it is so in our songs, that we were betrayed by Brankovitch, but we know that it was not so, that we lost the battle because we were not of one mind.' 'How do you mean you know it?' I asked. 'Do you mean you learned it at school?' 'No,' he said, 'we know it before we go to school. It is something our people remember.' I was again checked by the curious honesty of the Slav mind, by its refusal to dress up its inconsistencies and make them superficially acceptable to the rationalist censor. They had evolved a myth which accounted for their defeat by treachery within their own ranks and thereby took the sting out of it, just as the Germans did after the war; but they did not suppress the critical part of their mind when it pointed out to them that this myth was merely a myth. With an inconsistency that was not dangerous because it was admitted, they let their myth and the criticism of it coexist in their minds.

Constantine and Dragutin waved their arms at the downland, and still I saw nothing. I turned aside and looked at the white building behind us and I said, 'What is this place? Can we go in?' 'Certainly, certainly,' said Constantine, 'it is very interesting; this is the mausoleum of Gazi Mestan, a Turkish standard-bearer who was killed in the battle and was buried where he lay.' 'Yes,' shouted Dragutin, 'many of us fell at Kossovo, but, praise be to God, so did many of them.' As we went into the wooden porch, the veiled woman and her children padded past us. We found ourselves in a room which, though light and clean, had that look of having been long disused by any normal forces which one expects to be completed by stuffed animals; but there was nothing there except two coffins of the Moslem type, with a gabled top, higher at the head than the heels. They were covered with worn green baize, and hung with cheap pieces of stuff, some clumsily embroidered, others printed. On the walls were a few framed scraps of Turkish calligraphy, a copy of a Sultan's seal, and some picture postcards. A man came towards us, smiling sweetly and indecisively. He wore a faded fez and neat but threadbare Western clothes, and his whole appearance made a wistful allusion to a state better than his own; I have seen his like in England, walking through November rain in a summer suit and a straw hat, still mildly cheerful. He told us of the fame and gallantry of Gazi Mestan in a set speech, unnaturally uttered from some brain-cell petrified by memory. 'And you? Who are you?' said Constantine. 'I am the descendant of Gazi Mestan's servant,' the man answered, 'the descendant in the sixteenth generation. My forefather was by him as he fell, he closed his dead master's eyes for him, he preserved his body and guarded it after it had been placed in this tomb. So have we all guarded him.'

A weak-eyed boy ran into the room and took his stand beside the man, who laid an arm about his shoulder. 'My brother,' he said tenderly, and laid his face against the boy's fine lank hair. They looked incredibly fragile. If one had tapped them with a pebble on the paperthin temples they would have dropped to the ground, still faintly smiling; the bare ankle-bones showing between the boy's brown shoes and frayed trouser-hems were so prominent that the skin stretched across them was bright red. 'What do these people live on?' I asked. 'Doubtless they receive gifts, this is a kind of shrine,' said Constantine, 'and there would probably be an allowance from the Vakuf, the Moslem religious endowment fund. In any case they can do nothing else, this is the family's destiny and it is a distinction.' 'But they are not like human beings at all,' I said, 'they are to human beings what a ship inside a glass bottle is to a real boat.' I saw before me what an empire which spreads beyond its legitimate boundaries must do to its subjects. It cannot spread its own life over the conquered areas, for life cannot travel too far from its source, and it blights the life that is native to those parts. Therefore it imprisons all its subjects in a stale conservatism, in a seedy gentility that celebrates past achievements over and over again. It could be seen what these people had been. With better bones, with more flesh, with unatrophied wills, they would have been Turks as they were in the great days of the past, or as they are in the Ataturk's Turkey, robust and gracious. But there they were sweet-sour phantoms, human wine gone to vinegar.

Outside we found Dragutin lying on the ground, the girl and the boys about him and a field mouse curled in his hand. 'You do not want to go inside?' asked Constantine. 'No,' he said. 'That a Turk was alive and is dead is good news. But this one has been dead so long that the news is a bit stale. Hola!' he roared, and opened his hand and the field mouse made a brown streak for safety. 'Now I am to take you to the tomb of the Sultan Murad,' he said, standing up, 'but thank God we stop at a Christian monument first.' It was some miles down the main road, a very plain cross set back in a fenced garden where irises and lupins and the first roses grew with an astounding profusion. It could be understood that Kossovo had really been fertile, that it had once supported many fat villages. The two soldiers who were guarding the monument came down to the gate to meet us, two boys in their earliest twenties, short and sturdy and luminous with health, their skins rose under bronze, their black eyes shining deep and their black hair shining shallow.

When I admired the garden one of them fell back and picked some flowers for me from a bed, not in the main avenue, lest the general effect should be spoiled, and Constantine said to the other one, 'You are a Serb from the North, aren't you?' He answered smiling, 'Yes, I am from the North, I am from the same town as you, I am from Shabats.' 'What!' exclaimed Constantine, looking like a baby that has seen its bottle. 'Do you know me?' 'Which of us in Shabats does not know the great poet who sprang from our town?' replied the soldier; and I liked the people of Shabats, for I could see from his face that they knew the best as well as the worst of Constantine, and revered him as well as mocked him. 'But tell me,' interrupted Dragutin, 'is that other one not a Croat?' 'Yes,' he said, 'he is from Karlovats.' 'Is it not hard to be here all day with a Croat?' 'No, indeed,' said the soldier, 'it is most surprising how pleasant he is; he is my true friend, and he is a good soldier; I never would have believed it.' 'You don't say so!' said Dragutin. 'I tell you,' said Constantine, 'there are many good Croats, and we Serbs must make friends with them.' 'So,' said Dragutin.

We were silent for a time at the foot of the memorial which bore the appalling words, 'To the heroes who fell for the honest cross, freedom, and the right of the people, 1389–1912, erected by the people of Prishtina.' It made the head ache with its attempt to commemorate people who were utterly outside the scope of memory; slaves born of slaves, who made their gesture of revolt and died, isolated by their slavery from the weakest, furthest light and warmth of fame. When we turned our faces to the garden again, we found the other soldier standing beside us, holding out a bouquet that was like a bouquet on a fire-screen made for a court, that had form and a tune of colour. All Slavs, except those who become florists, have a natural genius for arranging flowers. After I had thanked him, Dragutin said, 'Hey, Croat! You're a brave fellow. How do you like us Serbs?' 'Very well, very well!' he answered smiling. 'Everybody is kind to me here, and I had thought you were my enemies.' '*Eyah!*' said Dragutin, twisting the lobe of the boy's ear, 'We'll kill you all some day.' The boy wriggled and laughed, and they all talked till we turned to go, and Dragutin gave the boy a great smack on the back, saying, 'Well, you two, if you come to Skoplje, you'll find me at the Ban's garage, and maybe there'll be some paprikasch for you. You're what Yugoslavia needs.' On this little ledge they met and clung together, on this cross-wide space from which the dark grasses of Kossovo had been driven back, they who had been born under different flags and had to beat down a wall of lies before they could smile at each other.

If the battle of Kossovo was invisible to me it was because it had happened too completely. It was because the field of Kossovo had wholly swallowed up the men who had awaited destiny in their embroidered tents, because it had become sodden with their blood and now was a bog, and when things fell on it they were for ever lost. Constantine said, 'Now I am taking you to the mausoleum of the Sultan Murad, who was commanding the Turkish forces and was killed the night before the battle by a Serb called Milosh Obilitch, who had been suspected of treachery by our people and wished to clear his name.' The Sultan Murad, or Amurath, was the son of Orkhan the Victorious and a Greek girl raped from her bridegroom's arms, whom the Turks called Nilufer, the Lotus Flower, and his records suggest an immoral attempt to create the kind of character admired by morality, for an astounding cruelty seems to have been introduced as an alloy to harden the soft gold of his voluptuous delight in all exercises of the mind and body. 'His mausoleum,' said Constantine, 'was built where he fell.'

A track led from the road across the opaque and lustreless pastureland characteristic of this place, to what looked like a deserted farmhouse. As we came to the gate in the farm paddock it was as it had been at the tomb of Gazi Mestan: the bare countryside exhaled people. They came to meet us at the gate, they whipped round the corners of the paddock, men in Western clothes who had the look of Leicester Square or Place Pigalle touts, not that they knew much or perhaps anything of infamy. The resemblance lay in their terrible desire to sell what they had, which since they had nothing caused them to make piteous claims to the possession of special knowledge, the power to perform unusual services. Their bare feet, treading softly on rag-bound leather sandals, pattered before us, beside us, behind us, as we followed a stone path across a grassy quadrangle. A house looked down on us, its broken windows stuffed with newspaper, its wall eczematous where the plaster lacked.

Through another gateway we came on a poor and dusty garden where the mausoleum stood. A fountain splashed from a wall, and there was nothing else pleasant there. The door of the mausoleum was peculiarly hideous; it was of coarse wood, painted chocolate-colour, and panes of cheap glass, all the wrong shape.

Public libraries and halls in small provincial towns in England sometimes have such doors. Beyond was a rough lawn, cropped by a a few miserable sheep, which was edged with some flowers and set with two or three Moslem graves which were of the handsome sort, having a slab as well as a column at the top and bottom, but were riven across by time and neglect. On the grass sat some veiled women picnicking among their pretty, sore-eyed children, with the infinitely touching sociability of Moslem women, which reticently reveals a brave and frustrated appetite for pleasure, doling itself out crumbs and making them do. On a fence made of small sticks, defending a young tree from the sheep, hung a line of many-coloured rags, just recognizably garments that had been washed very clean. At least one of these women lived in a cottage so far from all other water that it was worth her while to bring her washing to the fountain; yet on these bare downs it could be seen there was no cottage for a mile or two.

We drew near to the hideous door of the mausoleum, and it was opened by an old man whom we knew to be an *imam*, a priest, only from the twist of white cloth about his fez; not in his manner was there any sign of sacred authority. He greeted us blearily and without pride, and we followed him, our touts padding behind us, into the presence of the Sultan Murad. The walls of his last lodging were distempered in drab and ornamented with abstract designs in chocolate, grey, and bottle-green, such as Western plumbers and decorators loved to create in the latter half of the last century, and its windows were curtained with the intensely vulgar dark green printed velvet used in wagons-lits. In a sloping gabled coffin such as sheltered Gazi Mestan, but covered with velvet and votive offerings of stuffs by some halfpence costlier, lay Murad. His turban hung from a wooden pole at the head of the coffin, a dusty wisp. The priest turned blindish eyes on Constantine and told him something; after the telling his fishlike mouth forgot to close. 'This old one is relating that only the Sultan's entrails are here,' said Constantine, 'the rest of him was taken away to Broussa in Turkey, but I do not know when.' Even the most rational person might have expected that the priest would have shown some slight regret that this shrine held the entrails of the Sultan and not his heart or his head. But in the pale luminousness of his eyes and the void of his open mouth there was seated the most perfect indifference.

Two of the touts padded past us and sank mumbling into the prostration of a Moslem prayer, in the hope that we might gape and tip. It is impossible to have visited Sarajevo or Bitolj or even Skoplje, without learning that the Turks were in a real sense magnificent, that there was much of that in them which brings man off his four feet into erectness, that they knew well that running waters, the shade of trees, a white minaret the more in a town, brocade and fine manners, have a usefulness greater than use, even to the most soldierly of men. They were truly aristocratic, they had prised up the clamp of necessity that fixes man with his belly close to the earth. Therefore it was painful to see these Turks to whom two full meals in succession were more remote objects of lust than the most fantastic luxuries had been to their forefathers, to whom rags and a dusty compound represented a unique refreshment. These mock devotions were disgusting not because they were prostitutions of a gallant religion, since that represented an invincible tendency of mankind, but because they were inspired by the hope of dinars far too few for any purchase worth making. I turned away; and the tail of my eye caught the touts in a furtive movement betraying an absolute bankruptcy of the vital forces, an inability to make an effort except when financed by some expectation for that specific purpose. Once they saw they had not interested us they stopped their prostrations in mid-air, wearily straightened themselves, and shuffled after us into the paddock.

'It is silly to bring foreigners to see these old Turkish things,' said Dragutin to Constantine. 'Everything Turkish is now rotten and stinks like a dunghill. Look at these creatures that are more like rotten marrows than men, they ought to be in mausoleums themselves, their mothers must have been dead for years before they were born.' His animal lack of pity was the more terrible because it was not even faintly malicious. We hurried out of the paddock, some of the touts gaining on us and pattering ahead, looking back at us with their terrible inexorbitant expectancy. One could easily have become cruel to them. Beyond the gate Constantine led us along the plasterless walls till he found the spot where, it is said, the man who murdered Murad was put to death. 'His name,' he said, 'was Milosh Obilitch; but to tell you the truth it was not. It was Kobilitch, which means Brood-mare, for in those days our people, even in the nobility, did not have surnames but only Christian names and nicknames. But in the eighteenth century when all the world became refined it seemed to us that it was shameful to have a hero that was called Broodmare, so we dropped the K, and poor Milosh was left with a name that meant nothing at all and was never his. What he would have minded worse was that many people nowadays say we should not honour him at all, because he gained the Sultan's presence by a trick, by saying that he was a deserter and wished to join his enemies. He felt, and patriots still feel, that he had to clear his name in the eyes of his people from the suspicion of being a traitor, and that he had bought the right to play that trick on the Turks because he gave them his life in return.'

'It is strange,' I said, 'that the Turks were not disorganized by the murder of their Sultan.' 'Nothing could have disorganized them,' said Constantine, 'they were superb, they had *superbia*, they were all as Mohammed would have had them, they were soldiers ready to submit to all discipline because they believed that they had been enlisted by God, who at the end of the world would be with them as their general.' 'Our Sir Charles Eliot,' I said, 'wrote of them that "The Sultan may be a Roman Emperor, but every Turk is a Roman citizen with a profound self-respect and a sense not only of his duties, but what is due to him."' As I spoke I noticed that my husband was no longer walking beside me, and, as wives do, I looked round to see what the creature might be doing. He was some paces behind us, giving some dinars to the touts, who were taking them with a gentle, measured thankfulness, unabject in spite of their suppliance, which proved that what Eliot had said of them had once been true, though the total situation showed it to be now false. They stopped following us after that, and remained staring mildly after us, boneless as flames, their pale faces and dusty clothes dingy in the sunlight. They stood wide, wide apart on the dark grass of Kossovo, for their flesh was too poor to feel the fleshy desire to draw together. A people that extends its empire too far from its base commits the sin of Onan and spills its seed upon the ground.

We had not been driving very long when the road ran through a grove, and Dragutin brought the automobile to a halt. 'Here we will eat,' he said, holding the door open. 'What do you mean?' asked Constantine. 'Well, did you people not bring bread and wine and eggs from Skoplje?' asked Dragutin. 'This is the best place to eat them, and it is high time too, for it is very late and the English are accustomed to meals at regular hours. So get you out and eat.' 'No, no,' said Constantine, taking out his watch and shaking his head, 'we must push on to Kossovska Mitrovitsa, and it may be dark before we get there.' 'What are you talking about?' said Dragutin. 'It is about three in the afternoon, this is May, and Kossovska Mitrovitsa is not two hours away. Step quickly, you must get out.' He did not speak out of insolence, but in recognition that Constantine had suffered some sort of disintegrating change during the last few days, and that his judgment was not now to be trusted. Constantine looked at him in unresentful curiosity, as if to say, 'Am I as bad as that?' and obeyed. Dragutin put out the rugs and the food on the grass and said, 'There now, you can have fifteen minutes,' and walked up and down the road in front of us, eating an apple. He called to me, 'You don't much like being here.' 'No,' I said, 'it's too sad. And just now I have been thinking of the Vrdnik monastery in the Frushka Gora, where I saw the body of the Prince Lazar and touched his hand.' 'Ah, yes, the poor saint,' said Dragutin, 'they cut off his head because our Milosh Obilitch had killed their Sultan, though doubtless they would have done it anyway. They were wolves, it was their nature to shed gentler blood. Well, it could not be helped. We were not of one mind.'

He took another mouthful of apple and munched himself down the road, and I said to Constantine, 'It is strange, he does not blame the nobles for quarrelling among themselves.' Constantine said thoughtfully. 'No, but I do not think that is what he means.' 'But he says, "We were not of one mind," he has said it twice today, and in all the history books it is said that the Slavs were beaten at Kossovo because the various princes quarrelled among themselves. What else can he mean?' 'It is true that our people always say that we were beaten because we were not of one mind, and it is true that there were many Slav princes before Kossovo, and that they all quarrelled, but I do not think that the phrase has any connexion with that fact,' said Constantine. 'I think the phrase means that each individual Slav was divided in his attitude to the Turk, and it makes an allusion to our famous poem about the grey falcon.' 'I have never heard of it,' I answered. Constantine stood up and called to Dragutin, who was now munching his way back to us, 'Think of it, she had never heard of our poem about the grey falcon!' 'Shame!' cried Dragutin, spitting out some pips, and they began chanting together:

'*Poletio soko titsa siva,*
Od svetinye, od Yerusalima,
I on nosi titsu lastavitsu. . . .'

'I will translate it for you,' said Constantine. 'In your language I cannot make it as beautiful as it is, but you will see that at any rate it is not like any other poem, it is peculiar to us. . . .

There flies a grey bird, a falcon,
From Jerusalem the holy,
And in his beak he bears a swallow.

That is no falcon, no grey bird,
But it is the Saint Elijah.
He carries no swallow,

But a book from the Mother of God.
He comes to the Tsar at Kossovo,
He lays the book on the Tsar's knees.
This book without like told the Tsar:
'Tsar Lazar, of honourable stock,
Of what kind will you have your kingdom?
Do you want a heavenly kingdom?
Do you want an earthly kingdom?
If you want an earthly kingdom?
Saddle your horses, tighten your horses' girths,
Gird on your swords,
Then put an end to the Turkish attacks!
And drive out every Turkish soldier.
But if you want a heavenly kingdom
Build you a church on Kossovo;
Build it not with a floor of marble
But lay down silk and scarlet on the ground,
Give the Eucharist and battle orders to your soldiers,
For all your soldiers shall be destroyed,
And you, prince, you shall be destroyed with them.'

When the Tsar read the words,
The Tsar pondered, and he pondered thus:
'Dear God, where are these things, and how are they!
What kingdom shall I choose?
Shall I choose a heavenly kingdom?
Shall I choose an earthly kingdom?
If I choose an earthly kingdom,
An earthly kingdom lasts only a little time,
But a heavenly kingdom will last for eternity and its centuries.'

The Tsar chose a heavenly kingdom,
And not an earthly kingdom,
He built a church on Kossovo.
He built it not with floor of marble
But laid down silk and scarlet on the ground.
There he summoned the Serbian Patriarch
And twelve great bishops.
Then he gave his soldiers the Eucharist and their battle orders.
In the same hour as the Prince gave orders to his soldiers
The Turks attacked Kossovo.

There follows,' said Constantine, 'a long passage, very muddled, about how gallantly the Tsar fought and how at the end it looked as if they were to win, but Vuk Brankovitch betrayed them, so they were beaten. And it goes on:

Then the Turks overwhelmed Lazar,
And the Tsar Lazar was destroyed,
And his army was destroyed with him,
Of seven and seventy thousand soldiers.

All was holy, all was honourable
And the goodness of God was fulfilled.'

I said, 'So that was what happened, Lazar was a member of the
Peace Pledge Union.' Through a long field of rye on the crest of
a hill before me, a wind ran like the tremor that shuddered over
my skin and through my blood. Peeling the shell from an egg, I
walked away from the others, but I knew that the poem referred to
something true and disagreeable in my own life. 'Lazar was wrong,'
I said to myself, 'he saved his soul and there followed five hundred
years when no man on these plains, nor anywhere else in Europe for
hundreds of miles in any direction, was allowed to keep his soul. He
should have chosen damnation for their sake. No, what am I saying?
I am putting the state above the individual, and I believe that there
are certain ultimate human rights that must have precedence over
all others. What I mean is rather that I do not believe in the thesis
of the poem. I do not believe that any man can procure his own
salvation by refusing to save millions of people from miserable
slavery. That it was a question of fighting does not matter, because
in actual fact fighting is not much more disgusting, though probably
slightly so, than many things people have to do in order that the race
may triumph over certain assaults. To protect us from germs many
people have to perform exceedingly distasteful tasks in connexion
with sewage, and to open to the community its full economic
resources sailors and miners have to suffer great discomfort and
danger. But indeed this poem shows that the pacifist attitude does
not depend on the horrors of warfare, for it never mentions them.
It goes straight to the heart of the matter and betrays that what the
pacifist really wants is to be defeated. Prince Lazar and his troops
were to take the Eucharist and they were to be destroyed by the
Turks and then they would be saved. There is not a word about
avoiding bloodshed. On the contrary, it is taken for granted that
he fought as well as he could, and killed every Turk within reach.
The important thing is not that he should be innocent, but that he
should be defeated.'

I realized fully why this poem had stirred me. When I had stood
by the tomb in the monastery at Vrdnik in the Frushka Gora and
touched Prince Lazar's mummied hand, I had been well aware that
he was of a pattern familiar to me, that he was one of that company

loving honour and freedom and harmony, which in our day includes Herbert Fisher and Lord Cecil and Professor Gilbert Murray. Such people I have always followed, for I know that they are right, and my reason acknowledges that by their rule and by their rule only can a growing and incorrupt happiness be established on earth. But when all times have given birth to such good men and such as myself who follow them, why has this happiness not long been accomplished? Why is there still poverty, when we are ready for handsomeness? Why is there carelessness for the future of children? Why is there oppression of women by men? Why is there harshness of race towards race? I know the answer. I had known the answer for long, but it had taken this poem to make my mind admit that I knew it.

It is revealed at all meetings addressed or attended by the lesser of those who care for the freedom and the well-being of others, which often exhale a strange sense of danger. Meetings of the opposite party, of those who desire others to be enslaved for their benefit or to preserve iniquitous social institutions because of the profit they derive from them, offer the simple repulsiveness of greed and stupidity, but not this sense of danger. It is evoked in many ways: by the clothes worn by the women among the speakers and the audiences, which are of a sort not to be accounted for by poverty and by overwork, since they are not specially cheap and must indeed require a special effort to find, so far do they depart from the normal. They can serve no purpose save to alienate public opinion; and it is sad that they should not do all that they can to secure the respect of the community when they are trying to revise communal beliefs. It appears possible that they do not really want to succeed in that attempt; and that suspicion is often aroused by the quality of the speakers' voices and the response of their audiences. The speakers use all accents of sincerity and sweetness, and they continuously praise virtue; but they never speak as if power would be theirs tomorrow and they would use it for virtuous action. And their audiences also do not seem to regard themselves as predestined to rule; they clap as if in defiance, and laugh at their enemies behind their hands, with the shrill laughter of children. They want to be right, not to do right. They feel no obligation to be part of the main tide of life, and if that meant any degree of pollution they would prefer to divert themselves from it and form a standing pool of purity. In fact, they want to receive the Eucharist, be beaten by the Turks, and then go to Heaven.

By that they prove themselves inferior to their opponents, who do not want to separate themselves from the main channel of life, who believe quite simply that aggression and tyranny are the best methods of guaranteeing the future of man and therefore accept the responsibility of applying them. The friends of liberty have indeed no ground whatsoever for regarding themselves as in any way superior to their opponents, since they are in effect on their side in wishing defeat and not victory for their own principles. Not one of them, even the greatest, has ever been a Cæsar as well as his kind self; and until there is a kind Cæsar every child of woman is born in peril. I looked into my own heart and I knew that I was not innocent. Often I wonder whether I would be able to suffer for my principles if the need came, and it strikes me as a matter of the highest importance. That should not be so. I should ask myself with far greater urgency whether I have done everything possible to carry those principles into effect, and how I can attain power to make them absolutely victorious. But those questions I put only with my mind. They do not excite my guts, which wait anxiously while I ponder my gift for martyrdom.

'If this be so,' I said to myself, 'if it be a law that those who are born into the world with a preference for the agreeable over the disagreeable are born also with an impulse towards defeat, then the whole world is a vast Kossovo, an abominable blood-logged plain, where people who love go out to fight people who hate, and betray their cause to their enemies, so that loving is persecuted for immense tracts of history, far longer than its little periods of victory.' I began to weep, for the leftwing people among whom I had lived all my life had in their attitude to foreign politics achieved such a betrayal. They were always right, they never imposed their rightness. 'If this disposition to be at once Christ and Judas is inborn,' I thought, 'we might as well die, and the sooner the better, for the defeat is painful after the lovely promise.' I turned my back on the plains, not to see the sodden grass, not to think of the woman stupid under her ploughshare in Prishtina, the weak-eyed loving brothers embracing feebly in the standard-bearer's mausoleum, the pale touts falsely and hungrily genuflecting about the Sultan's coffin, not to imagine the lost glory of the Christian Slavs, the glory, different but equal and equally lost, of the Ottoman Turks. Even when I saw none of these things with the eye of the body or the mind I felt despair, and I began to run, to be more quickly with my companions.

The party I had left had now been joined by a fourth, an old Albanian wearing the white skullcap which is as the fez to the Moslems of that people. He had been invited to share our food, and he was sitting on the ground with his back to me. When I drew nearer he turned about to greet me with the smiling social grace peculiar to Albanians, and I saw that in his arms there was lying a black lamb such as I had seen sacrificed at the rock of the Sheep's Field; and the meaning of Kossovo was plain.

The black lamb and the grey falcon had worked together here. In this crime, as in nearly all historic crimes and most personal crimes, they had been accomplices. This I had learned in Yugoslavia, which writes obscure things plain, which furnishes symbols for what the intellect has not yet formulated. On the Sheep's Field I had seen sacrifice in its filth and falsehood, and in its astonishing power over the imagination. There I had learned how infinitely disgusting in its practice was the belief that by shedding the blood of an animal one will be granted increase; that by making a gift to death one will receive a gift of life. There I had recognized that this belief was a vital part of me, because it was dear to the primitive mind, since it provided an easy answer to various perplexities, and the primitive mind is the foundation on which the modern mind is built. This belief is not only hideous in itself: it pollutes the works of love. It has laboured for annulment of the meaning of Christianity, by insinuating itself into the Church and putting forward, by loose cries and the drunkenness of ecstasy, a doctrine of the Atonement too absurd to be set down in writing. By that doctrine it is pretended that Christ came to earth to cook up a senseless and ugly magic rite, to buy with his pain an unrelated good, and it is concealed from us that his death convicted us of sin, that it proved our kind to be so cruel that when goodness itself appeared amongst us we could find nothing better to do with it than kill it. And I had felt, as I walked away from the rock with Militsa and Mehmed, that if I thought longer about the sacrifice I should learn something more, of a nature discreditable to myself.

Now that I saw the lamb thrusting out the forceless little black hammer of its muzzle from the flimsy haven of the old man's wasted arms, I could not push the realization away from me very much longer. None of us, my kind as little as any others, could resist the temptation of accepting this sacrifice as a valid symbol. We believed in our heart of hearts that life was simply this and nothing more, a man cutting the throat of a lamb on a rock to please God and obtain happiness; and when our intelligence told us that the man was performing a disgusting and meaningless act, our response was not to dismiss the idea as a nightmare, but to say, 'Since it is wrong to be the priest and sacrifice the lamb, I will be the lamb and be sacrificed by the priest.' We thereby set up a principle that doom was honourable for innocent things, and conceded that if we spoke of kindliness and recommended peace it was fitting that afterwards the knife should be passed across our throats. Therefore it happened again and again that when we fought well for a reasonable cause and were in sight of victory, we were filled with a sense that we were not acting according to the divine protocol, and turned away and sought defeat, thus betraying those who had trusted us to win them kindliness and peace.

Thus it was that the Slavs were defeated by the Turks on the field of Kossovo. They knew that Christianity was better for man than Islam, because it denounced the prime human fault, cruelty, which the military mind of Mohammed had not even identified, and they knew also that their essential achievements in conduct and art would be trodden down into the mud if they were vanquished. Therefore, because of the power of the rock over their minds, they could not go forward to victory. They knew that in this matter they were virtuous, therefore it was fitting that they should die. In that belief they betrayed all the virtuous who came after them, for five hundred years. And I had sinned in the same way, I and my kind, the liberals of Western Europe. We had regarded ourselves as far holier than our tory opponents because we had exchanged the role of priest for the role of lamb, and therefore we forgot that we were not performing the chief moral obligation of humanity, which is to protect the works of love. We have done nothing to save our people, who have some little freedom and therefore some power to make their souls, from the trampling hate of the other peoples that are without the faculty for freedom and desire to root out the soul like a weed. It is possible that we have betrayed life and love for more than five hundred years on a field wider than Kossovo, as wide as Europe. As I perceived it I felt again that imbecile anxiety concerning my own behaviour in such a crisis, which is a matter of only the slightest importance. What mattered was that I had not served life faithfully, that I had been too anxious for a fictitious personal salvation, and imbecile enough to conceive that I might secure it by hanging round a stinking rock where a man with dirty hands shed blood for no reason.

'Is this not a lovely old Albanian man?' asked Constantine. Indeed he was; and he was the lovelier because he was smiling, and the smile of an Albanian is cool and refreshing as a bite out of a watermelon, their light eyes shine, their white teeth gleam.

Also this old man's skin was white and transparent, like a very thin cloud. 'I think he is very good,' said Constantine, 'and he is certainly very pathetic, for he has guessed we are going to the Trepcha mines and he wants us to get a job for his grandson, who, he says, is a clever boy. I wonder if we could not do something about it.' Constantine was always at his happiest when he was being kind, and this opportunity for benevolence made his eye shine brighter than we had seen it for many a day; but the cheek below was pouched and raddled like a weeping woman's. Perhaps he had been weeping. The grey falcon had visited him also. He had bared his throat to Gerda's knife, he had offered his loving heart to the service of hate, in order that he might be defeated and innocent.

'Naturally,' said Dragutin, speaking broken German so that the old man should not understand, 'this one must be something of a villain, since he is an Albanian. The Albanians, having the blood-feud and being brigands and renouncers of Christ, are great villains. But this one is poor and very old, and whatever harm he does he cannot do for much longer, so let us do what we can for him.' He shuddered, then laid his open hand on his chest and breathed deeply, as if he had thought of old age and was restoring himself by savouring his own health and strength. It would have been possible to take him as an image of primitive simplicity had he not, only a little time before, recited this subtle and complicated poem about the grey falcon, and had not that poem survived simply because his people were able to appreciate it. This is the Slav mystery: that the Slav, who seems wholly a man of action, is aware of the interior life, of the springs of action, as only the intellectuals of other races are. It is possible that a Slav Cæsar might be moved in crises by a purity of metaphysical motive hardly to be conceived elsewhere, save among priests and philosophers. Perhaps Stephen Dushan was not only influenced by thoughts of innocence and guilt, as all great statesmen are, but was governed by them almost to the exclusion of simpler and more material considerations. Perhaps he died in his prime as many die, because he wished for death; because this image of bloody sacrifice which obsesses us all had made him see shame in the triumph which seemed his destiny. He stood at his doorway in the Balkan mountains and looked on the gold and ivory and marble of Constantinople, on its crosses and its domes and the ships in its harbours, and he knew that he was as God to these things, for they would cease to be, unless he retained them as clear thoughts in his mind. He feared to have that creative power, he stepped back from the light of his doorway, he retreated into the blameless world of the shadows; and Constantinople faded like a breath on a windowpane.

'Yugoslavia is always telling me about one death or another,' I said to myself, 'the death of Franz Ferdinand, the death of Alexander Obrenovitch and Draga, the death of Prince Michael, the death of Prince Lazar, the death of Stephen Dushan. Yet this country is full of life. I feel that we Westerners should come here to learn to live. But perhaps we are ignorant about life in the West because we avoid thinking about death. One could not study geography if one concentrated on the land and turned one's attention away from the sea.' Then I cried out, for I had forgotten the black lamb, and it had stretched out its neck and laid its cold twitching muzzle against my bare forearm. All the men laughed at me, though the Albanian was careful to keep a central core of courtesy in his laughter. I returned their laughter, but I was frightened. I did not trust anybody in this group, least of all myself, to cast off this infatuation with sacrifice which had caused Kossovo, which, if it were not checked would abort all human increase.

Kossovska Mitrovitsa I

The town lay on the limits of the plain, at the threshold of the warm, broken Serbian country that reminds Somerset men of Somerset and Scots of the Lowlands, a little town, a standard town, with barracks on a hill, some minarets, the main body of its houses round the bend in the river; some exquisite old Turkish houses, with their beautifully proportioned upper stories and intricately carved lattices, notably in the street where we found our hotel. 'Go in, go in,' said Dragutin impatiently, 'do not look at the rat warrens left by the abominable, look rather at this hotel, which has been built since the mines at Trepcha were opened, and is *fino, fino*.' Certainly the large café we entered was very clean and proud and well found, and entirely lacked the Balkan touch: that is to say, nothing in the place looked as if it had been brought from somewhere else and adapted to its present purposes by a preoccupied intellectual. But the people who were sitting there were Balkan enough. Four men were playing cards with their hats on, and a young priest was circling round them with a glass of tea in his hand, looking at their cards. He was supremely beautiful; his long hair and beard were wavy and blue-black, his eyes were immense and gentian-blue. At the sight of one man's hand he flung back his head, cried out something mocking, sat down, and sipped his tea between gusts of silent laughter. 'From his accent I think he is Russian,' said Constantine; and indeed he had the spiral and ethereal air, as of one formed from smoke-wreaths, which I had noticed in some of the Russian priests and monks I had met in Yugoslavia. 'Yes, he is a Russian,' said the waiter; 'there are people of all nations working in the Trepcha mines, and among them are many Russians, and this is the son of one amongst them.'

'Now I have engaged our rooms,' said my husband, 'I must go and telephone to the people at the mines, to see if it will be convenient for them to let us go up and see them now.' 'Certainly, certainly,' said Constantine, 'I will tell the waiter to show you the telephone and get you the number.' But when my husband came and told us, 'It is all right, they sound very nice people, very Scotch, and they say they will be very delighted to see us, and that we are to come up at once,' Constantine said with a sad smile, 'I hope that you did not frighten your friends by telling them that you were bringing me with you, for I am going to excuse myself.' 'But why?' exclaimed my husband. 'They sounded as if they would really be so pleased to see you, it was not merely a matter of politeness. And I am sure you will be interested to visit the mine.' Constantine shook his head and continued to smile. 'I do not think they will really be very disappointed if I do not come with you,' he said. 'I understand the English too well to believe that. I think you and your friends will be happier if you are all English together and you can say what you really think of my country.' He said it with Gerda's accent. 'And as for seeing the mine, I am a writer and I do not really need to visit a mine to know what it is like.' He added, that I might not fail to note that he had let fly at me, 'I am not a journalist, me. I am a poet.'

He was depriving himself horribly. If he had come with us there would have been new people to impress and charm; and his mind, which was actually not at all autokinetic, but which, like a New Zealand geyser, let loose its fountains only when some solid object had been dropped into it, would have been inspired to its best by the spectacle of anything so remote from his experience as a mine. But it was no use arguing. One by one he was closing the shutters of all his windows. We sat for a moment in silence drinking our coffee. A waiter came in with a plate of sweet cakes, slices of the Dobosh and Sacher Torten that in the Balkans mean sophistication and pride and contact with the West, and put it down by the card-players. The young priest took one and began to circle round the players again, eating it upwards instead of downwards, pressing it against the roof of his mouth with his tongue, as the bears in the zoo do when they are given a spoonful of honey. The upper half of the tall café windows nearly touched the projecting first floor of a Turkish house opposite. Two bare hands gripped the top of the lattice; we were being watched by a hidden face.

Dragutin walked through the café and Constantine called out, 'Are you ready to take them to the mines in a minute or two?' He answered, 'Yes, indeed. I have put my head in a basin of cold water, and I am just as fresh as if I had just left Skoplje. And if I had not I should still be ready to go to the mines, for that place up there is *fino, fino*. There would I live if I were not the Ban's chauffeur, and I say it seriously.'

Before Dragutin shut the automobile door on us, he cried again, '*Fino, fino!*' and waved his arm in promise that we were going to drive to Paradise. 'I wonder what it is that Dragutin considers *fino, fino*,' said my husband, 'I fear it may be something quite terrible in concrete.' Looking out of the window, I said, 'There are an extraordinary number of shops, and they sell excellent things, really quite excellent fruit.' 'I see that everybody moves quickly and lightly,' said my husband. 'This little place has a pride, as if it were somewhere like Bitolj.' The road took us out of Kossovska Mitrovitsa, into a valley, hugging the base of steep hills covered with dwarf beechwoods and winding with the willow-hung course of a river, and brought us soon to a succession of prodigies alien from the idyllic character of the countryside, which suggested the more delicate type of folk-song, just a little more robust than the written lyric. There was a multiplication of railway tracks by the river-bank; and then there was a low hill, not a mound but a hill, square-cut and the colour of death. 'That is waste from the mines,' said my husband; 'nothing can ever be done with it, nothing will ever grow on it.' Then came a group of pale corrugated buildings, fantastic according to the whimsey of engineering, straddling high on stilts here, there dropping long galleries from third floor to ground like iron necks that want to drink, or lifting little tanks that stand on thin legs among the roofs like storks. 'This is an immense place,' said my husband happily. Then the river regained its peace and ran among its water-meadows again, and the road forsook it and swung up the southern incline of a steep hill. '*Fino, fino!*' cried Dragutin, waving at the hillside; and he was perfectly right. The upper half of the hillside was unreclaimed from wild nature and wild history; above beechwoods and thickets, a slope of long grass harlequined with flowers ran up to a pinched peak confused with the ruins of a castle. This was lovely enough, but not so lovely as what lay below. The lower half of the hillside was entirely covered with villas of the Golder's Green sort, standing in little gardens; and it was indeed *fino, fino*. I would not have thought so before I went to the Balkans, but now I knew it.

'I never realized before,' said my husband, 'that a garden is a political thing.' For weeks past we have never seen a country house which was not planned on the definite understanding that the people living in it were bound to be frightened most of the time, and for very good reason. Unless houses were in the centre of a town they turned blank sides to the road, and surrounded themselves with high walls, to halt the attack of the Turkish soldier, the brigand, or the tax-collector. But here we saw windowed walls freely exposed to the four quarters, their irises and their roses and green peas and runner beans left unguarded before every eye. Here nobody's grandmother had been raped and hamstrung, nobody's grandfather had had his entire crop stolen by brigands and been marched off by the disappointed tax-collectors to do a season's forced labour for the Pasha and never been seen again. Some of the windows were brightly giving back the westering sun, and it seemed like a blast blown by a jolly trumpeter who had never known despair. 'These houses belong to the chiefs,' said Dragutin, 'but the men also have beautiful homes. Look down in the valley! But let us go on, for the Gospodin Mac's home is at the very top, and it's the most beautiful of all!' Thus we ascended to heights superior to Golder's Green, to Chislehurst, to very Heaven, which is indeed what Chislehurst is, can one but see it for a second brushed clear of that dust which settles on institutions, not when they are disused but when they have been so long in use that they are taken for granted.

There was a gravel sweep, and beds of standard roses on each side of the front door, and Dorothy Perkins all over the white rough-cast walls, and a perambulator on the porch. An Aberdeen terrier waddled out to meet us, and we acclaimed him, since not for weeks had we heard a country dog bark so comfortably, with so palpable a mere feint of exasperation. But this dog had known no graver incident in its life than a moment's uncertainty about the verdict of the judges at Crufts'; he did not come of a line of dogs trained to take food only from their master's hands lest his enemies should poison them. Within the villa there was English chintz, fatly upholstered armchairs and sofas, polished floors, and, as so often in an English home, a Scottish family. There was the Gospodin Mac, a Scotsman of the toughly delicate type, whose sharp features and corded neck and lean body looked as if the east winds that had blown on him in his childhood had twisted and wrung every part of him save the head and the heart. His wife was a sample of the other Scotland, the abundant Scotland, the one country which knows how to make its cakes rich enough, that scorns the superficial voluptuousness of icing and cream fillings and achieves the sober luxury of shortbread and Scotch bun. She was strongly built; Ayrshire-born, she used the deep soft speech of the Western Lowlands; and she moved slowly and confidently, as those do, no doubt, who work in the Mint. For she too had behind her a store of wealth, in her mother wit and powers of observation, her invincible curiosity, and her unalterably high standards. There was a married daughter, who wrung my heart without knowing it by her resemblance to the dearest friend of my schooldays, whose angular grace and fine cheek-bones and clear colouring and sweet voice she had borrowed without the slightest excuse of a blood tie. These people instantly entranced us. I hung round them shamelessly, like a hungry dog at a larder door. We stayed with them too long that day, for we accepted when we were asked to supper, and did not go back to the hotel afterwards as soon as we should. Indeed, whenever I found myself in their presence I stayed with them exactly as long as I could, because they knew all sorts of things that I and my friends do not know, they were all sorts of things that I and my friends are not.

'Neither this nor any of the mines we own in Yugoslavia is being worked for the first time. First the Greeks worked them, and then the Romans; then in the Middle Ages the Serbs brought in the Saxons to work them. Then under the Turks the work stopped, stopped dead, for five centuries, until we started it again. And the funny thing is that you can tell each period by its style, without looking at its age. The Greeks had great fancy, they seem to have been wonderful at guessing where the stuff was likely to be and finding the most ingenious way of getting at it. But their construction was only fairish. The Romans don't seem to have had such good ideas but they were grand on construction. They always made a lovely job of the building. And the Saxons just came along nicely, without adding anything, but following on well. And we're using a lot of it just as it was. I never go by the stone seat where the Roman sentinel sat, without giving it a pat, and wondering too. For just by that seat there's a bit of construction that none of us can understand. There's a long piece of tunnelling, too small for even a child to crawl through, running from one full-sized gallery to another, and no way of getting from one to the other that I can see. We've all puzzled our heads over it, and not one of us can work out an explanation. But sometimes that happens, you find workings in old mines that are incomprehensible to the finest engineers.' It was disconcerting, this emergence of mystery, constant character of human activities, in anything so concrete as mining.

There was an offer to take us up to the mine next day, which I accepted so eagerly that the Gospodin Mac brought forward his immensely thick eyebrows and made his terms plain. 'I said *up to* the mine, not *down* the mine, mind you.' My husband and I smiled at one another, for I have a terror of going below the earth, which has kept me out of London and New York subways for twenty years; but I said, 'Is it so dangerous, then?' But it was not a matter of danger; it was the men's feelings that had to be considered. 'They believe that if women come down the mine there is bound to be an accident. Now will you explain me that? They had just that same belief out in the mines where we were in South America, and they have it in mines all over the world. But elsewhere than here you have miners whose families have been working below surface for generations and who have worked in different countries. It's natural they should have developed their superstitions and then pooled them with the miners of these other countries. But the people here haven't worked in a mine for five hundred years; in fact I don't think these people have ever worked in mines, because under the Serbian Empire it was Saxons and Saxons only who were miners. The foreign miners who taught these chaps their mining work can't have given them these ideas, for they couldn't speak Serbian enough for general conversation, indeed they have to teach them largely by the look-see method. Well, how does it happen that miners here now hold, and hold passionately, as if they had held them for generations, exactly the same superstitions that miners hold all over the world? I wish somebody would explain me that.' His daughter said, 'And there's no use arguing with them over this superstition, for whenever Dad's insisted on letting a woman go down the mine there's been an accident just afterwards.' 'A serious one?' The Gospodin Mac shrugged his shoulders. We paused, confronted for a moment by the suspicion that the universe was idiotic; or that man was idiotic, made idiotic to the point of suicide, which would make his unconscious self pull down a prop and let blackness devour him, rather than that his libel on the female of his kind should be proved untrue.

The women talked too, always well, always of known things. They spoke of the people in the town. Yes, there were still some Turkish families who had not gone back to Turkey, who were indeed too wealthy to abandon their interests here. There was one family which Mrs Mac knew quite well, who still kept a nice house outside the town. There were some fine sons, but they were all at odds, all pulled apart because they wanted to fit in with Yugoslavian life but had their family pride and tradition keeping them to Mohammedanism, which made them aliens in their own country. One had recently consented to obey his parents and marry the daughter of a merchant in Bitolj, in order to cement some business alliance. 'But the boys here get used to seeing the girls that work in our offices down at the mill,' said Mrs Mac, 'and right smart they are; indeed, I think the White Russians almost overdo it.' The girl from Bitolj did not satisfy these standards, and it was the habit of the young husband to get drunk every now and then and go with his wife to some public place and twitch off her veil and cry, 'Look at the dreary piece I've been given!' But he always woke up afterwards a good Turk, and suffered agonies of repentance for his outbreak, so he had the worst of both worlds.

'Most of the Moslems we have working for us are Albanians,' said the Gospodin Mac, 'and everybody likes the Albanians.' That is universally said: the enmity the Turks fostered between the Albanians and all the other Slav races is being allayed simply by Albanian charm. They began to talk of their old gardener, an Albanian Moslem, whom they had loved dearly, and who was now desperately ill of an internal disease. 'I doubt his wife's any great help to him,' said Mrs Mac. 'It's a funny thing, these Moslem women aren't so domesticated as you would think. They say they don't take any pleasure in cooking, and that if they're by themselves they just live on black coffee, drinking it all the day through. I don't think they know how to make their men comfortable. But the people round here were in a terrible state until the mine started. Lots of them had no notion of cooking. They'd bake a kind of unleavened bread in the ashes and that's all they'd do; and in the time when the gourds are in they'd mix up some gourds and dough and bake it into the most awful mash you ever saw, just like the dog's dinner. Meat they'd never see from one year to another, so they just lived on this mess.'

It is written in the history books that three hundred years after Kossovo the Serbs of this district tried to find a remedy for their misery by emigration. They had never been subdued and had spent those intervening centuries in perpetual revolt, but after they had aided the Austrians in their attacks on the Ottoman Empire in the latter half of the seventeenth century and had seen the Westerners, with all their advantages, fail, they lost heart. Then came the time that is written of again and again, when the Patriarch Arsenius III accepted the Austrian Emperor Leopold's offer to receive hospitably all Serbians migrating into his territory, and he marched at the head of thirty-seven thousand Serbian families across the waste lands of the Slavs into Hungary in 1690. That is what is set out in the history books. But of course it is not the whole truth. Nothing is written of the people who did not join in the trek, for of course not all of them did. When Caulaincourt passed across Russia at the side of Napoleon they found that none of the towns which had been evacuated were quite empty. In each of them were '*Quelques malheureux de la dernière classe du peuple,*' '*quelques vieils hommes et femmes de la dernière classe.*' It would be so here. There would be some people who would not join in the emigration because their extreme misfortune made them unacceptable even by their own unfortunate community: the old, the sick, the criminal, women without men, victims of odd obligations, those on whom the enemy had some hold. They stayed behind, and the generations after them forgot. Forgot everything, even how to cook. So what they ate looked like the dog's dinner. History came up in its real colours, blown on by this woman's breath.

We said good-night and stood in the porch under the Dorothy
Perkins roses waiting for Dragutin. In the valley below a dog
howled, and howled again: a bore of a dog that had never been told
about climax. 'Confound that dog,' said Gospodin Mac, 'that's the
one that keeps me from sleeping. We must see about that tomorrow;
this is the third night that it's been giving us a concert.' 'It's the
German's dog,' said his daughter. 'Do you have many Germans
working here?' asked my husband. 'Only the one that takes care
of the rope-way,' said the Gospodin Mac. 'Well, if you have to
have a rope-way, you have to have Germans,' said my husband.
'I don't think I like that, the way that all the decent funiculars in
the world are made by a German company.' 'I don't like it myself,'
said the Gospodin Mac, 'but we console ourselves with thinking that
they won't make a funicular except with English steel rope.' His
happy knowledge of material objects made me think of two lines
of a poem taught me in my childhood, which had always till now
seemed ironic:

> 'The world is so full of a number of things,
> I'm sure we should all be as happy as kings.'

The night wind blew through the women's thin dresses, and
I murmured apologetically, 'That chauffeur is a very long time
in coming.' Then we heard through the darkness the voice of
Dragutin making his farewells to the butler and the cook at the
kitchen door, slow and deep-chested and rhetorical, and he came
striding along with primitive but superb panache: so might a subject
of Stephen Dushan's have borne himself, sure that at any moment
now he might receive the horse and armour which would make him
a noble. With a new breadth of style, he drove us down the hillside,
where naked lights over gateways carved out of the blackness a white
cell of garden that would be for ever England as far as Carter's seeds
could help it, along the dark highway, through the sleeping town,
to the hotel, which was oddly at this late hour a square of light. The
café was still half full of people. It had the same air as all places
where Slavs sit up at night: it was as if time had precipitated itself
in the artificial light and hung there suspended, brooding before
it again committed itself to the curious course of life. 'You are up
late,' my husband said to the proprietor. He answered, 'It is the
White Russians from the mines, they never want to go to bed.'
And indeed it could be seen that it was so, for these people had
the Russian quality which, not the same as merit, nor even beauty,
makes them a point of departure for the imagination, that special
quality which makes any actor or actress with Terry or Barrymore

blood light up a stage, whether he or she can act or not. 'I do not complain,' said the proprietor, 'it means money. We had no money till the mines opened, but now it comes in, more and more every day. God be thanked!' he said.

We were in a town drenched with a rising tide, but the tide had not yet risen so far as one might suppose. That we learned next morning as we went about making purchases before they came to take us up to the mines. This was an island: parts of it were even now *incommunicado*, not having had whispered to them the words we all know. We realized this when a photographer from whom we had bought some films halted us at the show-case outside his shop, saying, 'Look! Of these I am unusually proud!' He spoke of several pictures representing a middle-aged woman, wearing the full trousers and embroidered jacket of an odalisque, and offering the spectator a cup of coffee with a leer which indicated that it was a symbol for the joys of the harem. The portraits were in fact not unattractive. It is true that she was plump as an elephant, but she was so beautiful that the resemblance only served to explain what it is that male elephants feel about female elephants. 'Very nice,' said my husband, 'who is she?' 'The wife of the general in command of our garrison,' said the photographer. It was as if a show-case in Aldershot High Street should be filled with portraits of the wife of the general in command of the district, clad in the coquetry and localized plumage of Mistinguett.

But we spoke no more of her, for my husband had caught sight of another photograph, set just below these portraits, which were so exuberant in the literal sense of the word. It strangely contrasted with them. Four astonished mourners presented to the street a lidless coffin, in which there lay a bearded man with closed eyes, death collecting visibly in the hollows of his cheeks. About the coffin stood some children, wild-eyed with grief, and a woman putting her hand to a forehead blank with distraction. 'My God, who was that?' my husband asked. 'It is our late Mayor,' said the photographer. 'He was a very good man.' 'Was he assassinated, or was it an accident?' asked my husband. 'Who? The Mayor?' said the photographer. 'No, no, it was remarkable how everybody liked him. He died of something wrong with his stomach.' 'Then what is this scene?' 'It is just his funeral.' 'But look!' I said, pulling at my husband's sleeve, for I had found yet a third indication of a life different from ours. It was the photograph of a young black-haired man wearing the kind of face which Slavs assume when they intend to look romantic, which all Russian ballet-dancers use when they are teetering for balance: it resembles a sad spoon. The portrait showed his nude torso to the waist; and between his mammary glands, which were a shocking waste, a chain suspended that most innocent exemplar of jewellery, a heart-shaped pendant with a seed pearl in its centre. 'Who is this young man?' asked my husband. 'He is a lieutenant in the garrison here,' replied the photographer, wholly without embarrassment. 'He is a funny fellow, always coming to be photographed, always in fancy dress, sometimes in woman's clothes.' 'Are there many such young men here?' asked my husband. 'He is the only one,' said the photographer.

At our hotel a car waited to take us up to the mines and Constantine sat dunking a roll in his coffee. 'Good-morning!' we called, and he answered us civilly, but with a look of condemnation checked only by the painful exercise of courtesy. It was apparent that we were committing the same crime as those who are not sea-sick when others are. 'Will you be ready soon?' we asked. His forehead contracted in agony. It was apparent that we spoke too loud. 'Ready for what?' he asked. 'To go up to the mines,' I said, 'it will all be very interesting, and you'll like the manager, he is a most wonderful person.' Constantine laughed silently into the distance. It was apparent that we had shown gross insensitiveness. 'No, I do not think I would like the manager,' he said. 'I have read of such people in Dickens, and I think we are of quite different sorts.' 'Oh! Come on!' we pleaded, but he raised his eyebrows and pulled his mouth down and looked down at the tablecloth, slowly shaking his head. 'No,' he said, 'where men claw at the sides of the noble mountains, for the sake of money, mere money, there I would be quite out of place. But you go,' he said kindly, 'you go. I shall not blame you. We cannot all feel the same repugnances. Go up there and be happy. And I will get Dragutin to drive me to some place where the mountains have not been violated. And there I will be at peace, and I will remember that I am a poet, and I will be very happy. Happier than I think you could understand.' We murmured and left him, not because we were angered by him, for we were not. Both of us loved him, and he was at this moment most piteous, for his floridity was purplish and the whites of his eyes were dun. But it was as physically exhausting to talk to him when he was fixed in this preverse attitude as it would be to talk to a contortionist whose mouth spoke out of the shadow under his crooked knee.

The chauffeur who had come to take us to the mines was the personal chauffeur of the Gospodin Mac; and it appeared that there are some who are heroes to their valets. 'Does he hope we will repeat all this to his employer?' my husband wondered; but answered himself, 'No, he is too noble a creature and anyway he conceives his relationship with the Gospodin Mac as already ideal.' We went out of the town and received proof that we were indeed in the South, where the land burns in summertime like the human skin; a bridge joined brown land to brown land, and in a brown river there swam brown youths. In a valley where still browner babies kicked and squealed among bulrushes in a shallow stream, there marched over the mountainside the pylons of a rope-way, with here and there a carrier riding down from the mines to the mill. Thereafter there was a group of gay new houses up on the hills, and the chauffeur halted us. 'Our workmen live there,' he said, and we responded that they were very beautiful; and so they were, they had the same lyrical quality as some modern French industrial garden cities, such as those on the Seine near Caudebec where the hydroplanes are made. 'Some of the houses you will see later on are built by the company, and they are magnificent,' continued the chauffeur, 'but these are built by the workmen themselves, and they are fine enough. They also have the wonderful thing that the Gospodin Mac has brought to our country. They also have the septic tank.' He turned towards us passionately. 'Is it not a most wonderful thing, the septic tank? All this filth that gushes out'—his arms drew on the sky an image of the impurity that floods the universe, not to be beaten back by the spirit, only to be conquered by the talisman of the Gospodin Mac—'turned into water, clear water!' His hands fluttered, saluting salvation. 'Many centuries after my master is dead,' he cried, 'he will be honoured because he brought us the septic tank.' The primal idea of sanitation surprised us by its angelic appearance. Yet the memory of the obscure apartment at Prishtina, with the age-old coat of slime on its floor, made it not so surprising.

I would never have known the mine-head for what it was. It looked like a railway station, standing under a scar in the wooded hills at the valley-head, with a goods tram loaded with lumps of ore, the colour of ageing and desperate silver, puffing away from it. In what looked like a waiting-room, and was a kind of office, we found two young Englishmen wearing overalls and carrying electric torches, who paused to tell us before they went off to take baths that they had just been down the mine with the Gospodin Mac, and that he had come up first and would be with us as soon as he had bathed and dressed. They were admirable young men, neatly shaped by their profession, like well-sharpened pencils. Not theirs the long points of the artists and scientists, which are as like as not to break and necessitate a fresh use of the knife; not theirs the bluntness of those who know no craft. They were just right. As they went I looked at the map of the mine that was hanging on the wall and said, 'I cannot understand the name of this place—Stan Trg. Trg I know to be market, but what is Stan? It does not seem like a Serbian word at all.' 'Neither it is,' said one of the Englishmen, 'it is simply a mistake. Somebody copied the name wrongly when the mine was started, and nobody about the place knew enough Serbian to correct it. But it ought to be Stari.' They left us marvelling at the impersonality of the governing demon of mining, which goes into a country of which it knows nothing, not so much of its language as the word which means 'old,' and digs down into its vitals for its secret wealth.

By daylight the Gospodin Mac's wind-bitten fragility looked even frailer than on the night before, his strength more apostolic in its meek sternness. We walked out of the office with him and the drivers of some passing ox-carts turned their heads to look at us, strangers partaking in the local glory. Each of them was enough to ravish the heart of woman, for they wore the Lika cap. This is the most attractive form of headgear ever designed for men. It is a round black cap with a red edge to it, and a bunch of fine black braid falling to the left shoulder where it gives any man an air of gallantry and amusing faithlessness. By itself it would explain why Lord Byron loved the Near East. 'But Lika is far away,' I said. It is on the Karst, on the limestone behind the Dalmatian coast, to be reached from Kossovo only through Montenegro or by by-ways in the Bosnian hills. 'We are full of those chaps,' said Gospodin Mac, 'the Government sends batches of them down here to work for us, from the villages up there on the mountains, where they can never make a decent living, because there's literally no land, just pocketfuls of earth in the rock. We have all sorts of people here, you know. It's a fine mix-up of races and religions. We have the Catholic Croats from Croatia, Catholic Croats from Dalmatia, the local Orthodox Serbs who were here when we came, the Orthodox Serbs from Serbia who are quite different, some Orthodox Serbs from Montenegro, who are quite different again, the local Albanians, who are some of them Moslems and some of them Catholic and a few of them Orthodox, some White Russians in the offices and in the mill, and us Scotch and English and Americans. Yes, they get on well now. At first it wasn't good. Sometimes it was very bad indeed. We had a Croat foreman who engaged the hands, and there was a devil of a row about him with the Serbs, they swore he was favouring the Croats. But he was a good man, and I thought there was nothing in it, and I wouldn't fire him. So one day the poor fellow was sitting in his office and a Serb workman who had had too much to drink came in and shot him dead.

It was a terrible business. But we caught the murderer, though he had gone up into the hills, and he was sent down for a long sentence, and that got us all on a stage further. They saw that the old days were over, and that you didn't pay for a life with a life, but with a life in a prison. That they don't like so much, and they began to see things differently.' 'Had the Croat foreman been favouring the Croats?' I asked, and when he did not answer but talked of something else, I asked him again at his first pause: I never learned better when I was a child, though they often tried to teach me. 'We have a Croat now in much the same position, and no man could be fairer,' was his answer, and I fell behind, staring in the dust while the two men talked mineral technicalities. 'I *thought* there was nothing in it. . . . We have a Croat now who . . .' I saw him sitting alone in an office, turning over a dead man's papers, growing suddenly white and pinched round the nostrils as he recognized some obstacle to order which had taken the mean advantage of being ideological and not metallurgical, of not being amenable to treatment on sound mining principles.

A winding road took us up a steep hill through a garden city of white houses and pink roofs, set about with orchards. It was exactly like such places in the West and totally different. With us they mean an attempt to mitigate a victory of darkness over decent earth; but here it meant that the decent earth had for the first time in centuries known other than darkness. With us industrial workers appear as victims of a social system that has prevented them from enjoying the relatively agreeable existence of a free peasant or an artisan, and has condemned them to a standard of comfort far below that enjoyed by other classes who do easier work or none at all. That view was moonshine here. For five centuries no way of living had been within reach of these people which could be considered as a preferable alternative; this was not so in Macedonia and not so in Serbia, but it was true of this particular area. For five centuries there had been no class in this community which enjoyed such a high standard of comfort, and there still is none; the functionaries and Army officers are far more pinched for means. In the porches of these little houses women were sitting as the blessed in Paradise, with the reinforced satisfaction of those who have known a previous inferiority. Their children, playing among the flowers, turned on us eyes that, whether black or that profound yet light Slav blue, seemed to lack something and be the better for it; and we realized how many of the children we had seen lately had been solemnized by the knowledge of hunger and peril. 'Running water in every house,' murmured the Gospodin Mac, 'and they keep them like new pins.' We passed through this ordinary yet authentic Eden, and came to a canteen where the unmarried workers eat their midday meal. There cooks stood smiling with the special pride of those who practise mysteries not only beneficent but novel, beside cauldrons where bean soup bubbled brown and sooty black, and lamb chops simmered in gravy peat-red with paprika. I know of at least one English public school where the food is not so good. There was no mistake about it, here mechanical civilization was enticing. This modern industrial unit pleased like a paper transparency held against light, for the double reason that it was a superb specimen of its kind, and that there was behind it the vacuum of Turkish misrule.

It was as touching as the glow of contentment in the eyes of the foreign immigrants in the United States during the good old days before 1929, who were entranced to find themselves where there was an abundance of food, no matter what the weather might be, warm and cheap clothing, comfortable footwear, water-tight housing, and, not easily to be acquired but within the possibility of acquirement as never in Polish Galicia or Portugal, radios, refrigerators, and automobiles. They had not realized that in this new industralized world there are seasons other than those determined by the course of the sun, which are both crueller and longer; and that the urban versions of blizzard and drought are more terrible because they must be suffered in an absolute destitution, unknown to communities where each owns or has the right of access to at least a strip of land, and where all are joined by ties of blood or friendship cultivated through generations. The process had been slower in our own country, but I had seen its last lamentable phase. The English manufacturers of the nineteenth century had appeared as redeemers to the downtrodden agricultural labourers who were dying rather than living under a land system which would have shocked the Balkans, and who found food and warmth such as they had never known in the towns of Lancashire and Yorkshire and the Midlands; but they have no such reputations among the vast unhappy army of the unemployed. My instinct therefore was to warn the miners who were coming in at the door, grinning with happy appetite, 'Do not be deceived. Whom you suppose to be your benefactor is in fact your enemy, and will enslave you and take from your children what you never lost even under the Turk, the right to work.'

They would have answered, 'What, we are to count as an enemy one who gave us food for our bellies and clothes for our back, and a reasonable chance of dying in our beds? If you ask that, then you can never have known hunger and cold and fear.' And they would have been right. It is a monstrous piece of bogus liberalism to deny that industrialism has done much for the highest interests of humanity by raising the standard of living. It is as foolish as to deny the harm it has done them by not raising it enough, by poisoning the skies and fields with cheap cities, and taking away the will of its employees by keeping them in political and economic subjection. I was at fault in assuming that because English and American industry had proved unable to maintain its workers as it had at first promised, that must be so in Yugoslavia. The slow decline of prosperity in England was due to the shrinkage of markets, caused largely by the increasing capacity of the Orient to produce its own requirements, to the defects of the upper-class education which put all industrial undertakings with the promise of stability into the hands of heirs incapable of adapting themselves to altered conditions, and to overconservative banking. The quick decline of prosperity in America was due to industrialists who had lost sight of the existing limitations of consumption, and to reckless banking. In both England and America the ultimate blame lay, of course, deeper than this: in the insistence of the richer classes in keeping too large a proportion of the profits of industry, and all its control, in their own hands. This meant that it was exploited for the benefit of their immediate needs and not with regard to its perpetuation. That deepest factor of all was present in the Yugoslavian situation. These miners were working for the share-holders, whose interests came first. But the mine had been started after the war, when European aspirations had become more modest, by Anglo-American financiers of the more stable sort, who had never suffered from the gambling fever that swept Wall Street and the Middle West. It was probably under cautious and disillusioned management, and was certainly staffed by men who had no hopes of rising to permanent grandeur in a Scotch baronial mansion with twenty-five bedrooms, all kept up by grinding the faces of the poor. It might well be that the industrial unit would last so long as there was metal to be fetched out of the ground, prudently and patiently.

Was there, one wondered, unity among these workers? Were the English and Americans, who formed the high command of the mines, as it were, sensible of the necessity to make this enterprise an instrument of life instead of death? That depended on what mining engineers were like, which was a matter wholly veiled from me. I knew that the one beside me was fully aware of the issues within his control.

The Gospodin Mac was pointing to a hillside that showed the particular charm of Serbian scenery, the upland lawn among woodlands, proper place for nymphs to dance, and he was saying, 'That's our land too. And I was sorry to buy it, though it's as well for us to have as much land as we can round here. There was a piece down on the other side of the valley that we couldn't snap up in time, and some blackguards started a red-light district there that's the source of almost all the trouble we have with the men. But this land up here I was sorry to buy, because the Albanian who owned it hadn't wanted to move out of it, and he was a really decent old man. He came to me and he said, "Here you'd better have my land. It's no use to me any more. My women can't walk about unveiled on the place, and we can't live the same sort of life we used to before you came. So give me some money for it and we'll go down and live in the town." And mind you, I think the family had been there for ever. We gave him two thousand pounds for the place and every step of the transaction was a pleasure, he was so honest and polite, and he knew perfectly well we were being fair with him, and he would have cut off his hand rather than not be fair with us. I often grieve that we should have put an end to the way he and his family were living, for it was producing fine people. Every now and again he comes in for advice, because he trusts us, but I don't know that there's much of his two thousand left. It's not easy to find investments in this country that give as good return as land, and it's not easy to live a life in a little town that's as good as life in your own place up in the hills. There's no sense trying to fool oneself, not every change is for the better.' That is the sort of ancient wisdom modern man must have.

He added, 'But anyway I've a soft spot for the Albanians. We all like them. And it's not just because they knuckle down to us. They've got plenty of spirit. They're good trade unionists. When we had a wages dispute some time ago the Albanians stood firmer than anybody, and I admired them for it. Afterwards the Government sent a commission down to inquire into the causes of the strike, and they hinted to me they thought it a pity we employed so many Albanians, but I wasn't having any. I said straight out we employed them because we found them decent, hard-working fellows, and we'd go on employing them. But that's something that's getting better. The Serb administrators all get to like the Albanians and less and less make a distinction between them and their own people. This country's getting over its past nicely.' We paused to take breath on a steep turn in the road, and looked down on the workmen's canteen. My husband asked me, 'Did you see the two men who just went into the building? No? Well, I thought one of them was Dragutin.' 'It could not have been,' I said confidently, 'he is taking Constantine somewhere up into the mountains.' At the thought of Constantine both of us felt guilty, as if we had failed in charity by being happy away from him, with this whole and untroubled man.

But this man was a genius: the unique exception that not only fails to prove the rule, but leaves it in doubt what the rule may be. Nor could one judge anything from Gospodin Mac's predecessor, Mr Cunningham, whom we found higher up in the road, a broad grizzled Scotsman standing in his garden with a monk, both intent on a beehive. It seemed that bee-keeping was his hobby, and he spent much of his time teaching people of the district to make and use modern hives instead of the primitive sort which have to be broken every time a comb is removed; and this was of special interest to the poorer monasteries, which could not afford to buy sugar. When the monk had left us we walked among Mr Cunningham's flowers, which were magically not desiccated by the South, which grew as if the earth were cooled by the Highland air that had nourished his accent. I said to him, 'What columbines! They look like living things that might fly away at any minute,' and he answered, 'Ay, you know they call them the fairy flowers.' His Scottish *r*'s roared past me like the March wind in Princes Street. 'Fehrrry flowerrrs. . . .' Presently Mr Cunningham said, 'I'll be telling Sasha to send a bottle of absinthe up to the mess for our cocktails, if the company is as partial to it as I am,' and he called to the house, 'Sasha! Sasha!' He explained to us, 'Sasha's our factotum here; he's a great character. Lord knows what would happen to us all if Sasha wasn't here to look after us.' When Sasha came out into the garden this conversation followed the pattern so often to be remarked in countries where people of a mechanized Western race live among people of a more primitive race whom they have dominated. The Scotsman opened the conversation in the peremptory tones of a nurse speaking to a child, and the Serb answered like a child who accepts the authority of a nurse, but made a further remark in which he in his turn spoke like the nurse, and was answered by the Scotsman as if he were the child. It is thus that an English officer in India talks with his Hindu batman, it is thus that a Southerner talks with his coloured butler, it is thus that a Canadian holiday-maker talks with his Indian guide, should they be intelligent people. Only stupidity fails to recognize that each of the parties in such a relationship has command of a store of information almost wholly forbidden to the other; so that each, in the other's sphere, is helpless and astray unless his host is generous. That recognition was fully present in the Scotsman's voice. His climate-toughened shrewdness made him sensitive to the problems of his profession, the nature of ore and its hiding-places under the earth. It made him wise also about bees, flowers, and men, and not to be deflected from his wisdom by vanity. He could not have borne to sacrifice his just perception of Sasha in order to exaggerate his sense of superiority to Sasha. Such men favour the growth of civilization.

But the ordinary run of mining engineers might not be of the same breed as their leaders. There was this inveterate disposition to care only for their hard inorganic quarry, and to leave the state of living men which was the mine's matrix unnoticed and uncomprehended, which had been responsible for the naming of a Serbian mine with the gibberish of 'Stan Trg,' which had been a characteristic of those who had worked here before them, in the days anterior to the Turkish night. On a plateau by this hillside road stood the ruins of a chapel where the Saxon miners, brought here by the medieval Serbian kings, had worshipped according to their faith. Those Saxons were not Serbs, nor Saxons either, but simply miners. They formed a state within the state. The Serbian laws did not bind them; they were subject to the code, which was not borrowed from Saxony, but was simply and purely of the mines. It was not, as might have been suspected, a permit to laxity, extorted by those who rendered essential services to an expanding state; it was a juristic provision for the miner's mystery, to use that admirable English word meaning all information relating to the theory and practice of a craft, which we borrowed from the Old French *mestier*, and by carelessness amounting to genius confused in spelling with the word we derive from the Greek for occult. It made that craft an iron-bound dedication: a man found damaging a mine was hung by a rope downwards in the pitshaft, and the rope was cut. For their Catholic worship these separate people had taken a church such as was built by the natives of this soil, a Byzantine church planned for the Orthodox rite, and had brought a German artist to paint it with frescoes. Centuries after, now that its vaults were broken and its frescoes washed pale by rain and sun, it was apparent that something had happened which had left this not a true growth of the genius of the land. These were true internationalists, disregarding the nation's peculiar soul.

So, too, were the young men we met in the mess at the top of the road. They were mining engineers, without any doubt. Other things they might be, sons and lovers, husbands and fathers, saints and sinners, philosophers and natural men; but each of them, picked up between divine finger and thumb, and asked by the thunder who he was, would have answered, 'I am a mining engineer.' Their preoccupation with their calling was so great that it excluded any dangerously excessive intensification of itself. A mining engineer must keep fit; he must not be irritable and he must be able to bear up under physical strain. Therefore they played tennis, they read a bit, they took photographs, they learned languages; and they faced life with smooth brows and not a paunch among them. And they presented, as a shining tiled wall, this detachment from the life around them.

There was one Serbian among them, a doctor, a jolly soul with reddish hair and a face that had begun to wrinkle not because he was older than his age but because he still loved to laugh like a child. When we said we had been in Bitolj he told me he was a native of that city, and we talked for a little about the place, its mosques, its lovely girls, its acacias, and the rich civilization that lay under its surface. It was his belief that the town, though so much poorer than it was when it was the capital of Macedonia, was still enormously rich. 'Many, many of the women that shuffle about the little shops by the river in the morning, in their cotton wrappers,' he said, 'have more gold round their necks and their wrists than five hundred Viennese ladies who wear silk dresses ever see in their lives. I tell you the city is full of gold, is stuffed and crammed with gold.' He spoke, too, with Balkan gusto of a perilous childhood. 'My father was a schoolmaster,' he said, 'he was the head teacher of the first Serbian school that was ever in Bitolj. The Bulgarians had their schools and the Greeks had their schools, but we Serbs had none. So my father, who was a Serb from the Shumadiya, came down and taught his own people. So my mother was always very nervous, for of course any day he might have been killed, whether by the Turks or the Bulgars or the Greeks, she did not know.' 'But why should he be killed because he was a schoolmaster?' asked some of the engineers. 'And why was Bitolj such a rich city?' They knew nothing of the tradition of the Turkey in Europe which had shaped the land in which they lived.

They were ignorant too of something which was more recent, and had been commemorated in print, for even the English to read. I said to the doctor, 'And what happened to you during the war?' and he answered, clapping his hand over his laughing mouth, 'You will never guess! Do you know, I went with the retreating Serbian Army through the Albanian mountains down to the sea. You see, I should have gone with my mother and my brother and sisters in the refugee train to Salonika, but I was sent with a message to an old grand-uncle of mine in another part of the town, and on the way home I began to worry about a little boy I liked very much, so I went to see what he was going to do, and by the time I realized I could not find him I was too late to catch the train. So I joined some soldiers whom I saw walking in the street, and I went off with them to Ochrid, and away into the Albanian mountains. And, do you know, it was not so terrible. Yes, all you have heard is true. There was snow and ice, and very little to eat, and the Albanians sniped at us from the rocks. But I felt very grown-up, and all Serb boys want to be grown-up and to fight, and the soldiers made a great pet of me. When we got up into the mountains, they took a coat off a dead soldier and put it on me, and of course it was far too big for me, it came right down to my feet, so they called me "General Longcoat." They were really very kind to me; when there was any food I always got the first of it. So, when we got to Corfu and they found my family was at Salonika, and sent me off to find them, I really was not so pleased. Think of being told to go to bed when you had been through all that!'

It was as astonishing as if one day a fellow-guest announced that he had been to Moscow and back with Napoleon; but it was not less astonishing that most of the Englishmen who were listening had never heard of the retreat through Albania, and not one of them had ever heard the folk-song which commemorates that agony: '*Tamo Daleko, Daleko od mora. Tamo ye selo, Tamo ye Serbiya.*' Yonder, far yonder, far from the sea, is my village, my Serbia! It meant that they could not know Yugoslavia; or rather that they could not synthesize all the valuable information they held regarding her into any valid picture of her. It seemed to follow from this that they were a danger to the state, because they would not be controlled by regard for her interests of which they were ignorant. Such would have been the opinion of Brigham Young, who was one of the few really great statesmen of the nineteenth century. He always regarded as enemies of the state the prospectors and miners who came to Utah in search of her mineral wealth. They were not part of his people, and therefore would not serve its interests. That was his theory; but in this mess-room above the mines of Stan Trg it emerged that there was nothing in it so far as this part of the world was concerned.

These men were not free to turn against their fellows. A force bound them. They fell to recounting tales of their beginnings; all, it seemed, had gone into strange lands as youths, it might almost be said as children, and had been assailed by climates that were torturing misconducts of the sun and snows, and events that were monstrous births that should have been kept in bottles in the Surgeons' Hall of circumstance. They had, however, not been perturbed. They had been, and were still, sustained by a code. They believed . . . what did they believe? That one must be clean in body; that one must not tell lies, or suffer lies to be told to one; that one must do whatever work one was paid for doing, and do it well; and that one must not cause pain in other people, and must let them make their own souls as far as possible. This is the ethical tradition built into the English and American mind by Protestantism, and it is easy to deride it. There is indeed positive need that it should be derided, since it is an insufficient prop, and worse, for people who are prosperous; it is to them actually a prescription for ruin. Any Englishman of the upper bourgeoisie and the classes above it finds no difficulty about being clean; he can persuade himself that what he says is true, and can compel his economic inferiors to tell him the truth; he has probably chosen work that makes no great demands on his powers; and the duty to leave others in peace may be construed as permission to indulge in the pleasures of indifference. But this same code, applied by such as these mining engineers, was a discipline that can even become an instruction in mysticism. To be clean in lands where nature intends one to be sweaty and unkempt; to tell the truth and exact it in circumstances so difficult that cautiousness cries out to let all be glossed over; to do work well, far away from criticism, and in fatigue of the flesh and spirit; to respect the rights of alien people, who are uncomprehended and therefore terrible: this rule makes no man an enemy of the state. There are, of course, mining engineers who follow this discipline imperfectly or not at all. But since these in this mess were chosen by the Gospodin Mac, who was himself that discipline made visible, they were not of that sort. Though the West has again and again infected the Balkans with corruption, it seemed probable that this contact was innocent.

In the afternoon we drove away from the mines, down the valley to the town and the pale sprawling buildings where the ore was milled; about us conveyor belts went on their endless journeys to nowhere and puffs of smoke at escape-valves registered the culmination of a process which, so far as I, with my mechanical incompetence, was concerned, had never begun.

'It is no use whatsoever for you to explain these things to me,' I told the Gospodin Mac; 'to me it is all magic and nothing but magic.' 'It is funny you should say that just here,' he answered, 'for that's exactly what these particular machines are to me, and to everybody else in the outfit.' We were standing among a number of tanks, all filled with a seething solution of ore, but each bubbling in a different tempo and stained to a different shade of grey. 'These machines are the most valuable we have,' he continued. 'They're the last word. They're wizards. In each bath the ore throws off one of its constituents, either silver or magnesium or sulphur or whatever, so that by the time it's got through this room all the goodness has been taken out of it and we've just to collect the various minerals from the baths. But I can't understand the theory on which these machines work, nor does anybody else here that I know of. I don't mean that we can't mend them when they break down. We can, just as you could correct the faults of grammar in a book of mining, though you wouldn't be able to make the sense of the book. But the principle of the things is far beyond me. The chaps who brought them over from America understood them all right, and they stayed here for a bit. But the machines were their life-work, they'd specialized on those lines, and we're general-purposes fellows who have to get on with the business of running the mine.' 'Do you mean that in mining also there is too much to be known?' I asked. 'Much too much,' he said, 'for any one man.' There is no escape from mystery. It is the character of our being.

But this man was not perturbed. We stood on the bridge that crossed the railway line, running from the mill to the high-road. On our left was the rope-way, striding across the hills up to the high mines; on our right was the steep wooded peak, crowned with the fortress. The afternoon was golden on these heights, but the Gospodin Mac looked before him at the square-cut hill of waste which in the sunshine was the colour of something deader than death, of death without the hope of wholesome putrefaction and dissolution. 'That worries me a lot,' he murmured. 'So far as we can see, nothing will ever grow on that, not to the end of time. Well, it's an eye-sore. And this was a bonny place before we started on it.' On the line below us a dozen men were digging a pit, Albanian Moslems in their white fezes and linen tight-waisted shirts and trousers. I levelled my camera on them, and one looked up and saw me. Instantly he was transformed, and so, the instant after, was the whole group. Gallantry ran through their bodies, turning their heads to a provocative angle, setting their hands on their hips; their eyes and teeth flashed through the distance. Perhaps they could not see that I was no longer young, or perhaps their romanticism forbade them to notice it, so that they could go through the day with the idea that they had attracted the admiration of a beautiful Englishwoman.

The Gospodin Mac brooded over them as over his children. 'I tell you they're fine, these Albanians,' he said. 'And I think this lot have got over the blood-feud. That's the curse of Albanian life. But they say they're dropping it. It stands to reason they will. Give a man a decent job and a house and a garden he likes, and he'll think twice about trapesing off to kill the uncle of a man who killed his second cousin, particularly if he knows he'll go to jail. That blood-feud, you know, it made everything impossible. When the Yugoslavs took over this country after the war, it was hard to get the roads safe for travelling. Under the Turks, people simply did not travel, unless they were rich enough to have an armed escort or unless they had to for some reason. There were whole villages up in the hills where every single family was in the brigandage business. You couldn't blame them. They'd been pushed into it. Maybe they'd fallen foul of the authorities at some time and got driven on to the land that can't be cultivated. Or maybe there'd been a strong character born who'd turned the whole lot of them wrong. Anyway they used to sweep down on the roads round here and rob and murder. It had to be stopped. And the only way the gendarmes could stop it was by going up into these villages and killing every man, woman, and child. Mind you, nothing less would do. If they'd let one child get away, as soon as it had grown up it would have had to carry on the blood-feud against the gendarmes, or the people who were supposed to be responsible for the gendarmes' attack. And that was a cruel hard thing, not only on the villagers but on the gendarmes, who are usually very decent fellows; and it was hard on the whole people. It lowered their standards. If you made the gendarmes as tough as that they were as tough with everybody. But settling down, it was just a phase. . . .'

So it went on, this living exposition of the trials of a state engaged in resurrection, and therefore ravaged by the pangs of both death and birth.

When we went back to the hotel we were still glowing with satisfied listening, and we hushed each other as we caught sight of Constantine, sitting florid and miserable in the café, alone among the White Russians, a newspaper spread out on the table before him. 'May we sit down with you and have coffee?' I said timidly. 'Certainly, certainly,' he replied, but once we were seated, imposed on us hurt and smiling silence. My husband cleared his throat and asked, 'Did you have a good day in the mountains?' 'I did not go. I did not care to go.' Constantine answered shortly, and the silence fell again. At last he asked, 'And you, I suppose you have had a charming day with your friends in the mines?' With an air of guilt, we admitted that we had. 'I am very glad,' he said, 'I am exceedingly glad, for maybe it will not always be so happy for you and your countrymen up at the mines.' He tapped on the newspaper that lay before him. 'It is all written here.' 'What is it?' asked my husband. 'An attack on the

British company's title to the mine?' Constantine grimly nodded his head. 'Yes. The concession was given as a reward to one of our great statesmen, and his son sold it. But he was perhaps not very clever; and all the world knows that to do business with the English one must be very clever indeed, perhaps more than clever.' He raised his eyebrows and shrugged. 'So perhaps a wrong was done, and perhaps it will be righted.' 'But the deal cannot have been crooked,' said my husband. 'I know the chairman of the company and what is more important I know his reputation in England and America, and the reputation of the company and its associates, and that's not how they behave. Besides, it would have meant taking an immense risk. The company put a million pounds of their money into the mine before they got a penny out. If they did that on a property out of which they might be kicked at any moment because they had stolen it, they wouldn't come out of it so well.'

Constantine shrugged again. 'You are a city man,' he said, 'a man of the city of London. No doubt all your countrymen do looks well to you. But we are a simpler people. We see things from a different angle, and perhaps on what we see we shall some day act.' A silence fell. We sadly drank our coffee and would have risen to go had not a young man, dressed rather in the style of a French romantic poet in the nineteenth century, paused before our table. 'Good evening, Monsieur Constantine,' he said in French, giving us a side-way look, 'Monsieur Constantine, who was a poet, who is a Government servant.' We saw that here also there were young intellectuals, as there had been in Belgrade and in Sarajevo and in Zagreb, who could not forgive Constantine for having left the opposition, who said of him quite unfairly, 'Just for a handful of silver he left us, just for a ribbon to stick in his coat.' 'Good evening,' said Constantine, and he explained to us, 'This is a young writer who works by day in the laboratories at the mine. I know him well. All people are my friends everywhere.' The young man continued, 'Why are you sitting with that abominable rag in front of you? You know that it is full of the most abominable lies. These people at the mines are part of the filthy capitalist system, but they are as good as they can be in that condition. And it is all nonsense, it is galimatias, it is *Quatsch*, about the title to the mine. You know all that quite well, and you know that these papers are financed by German money, simply so that the Nazis can get their claws into our country. But you and your accursed pack of gangsters in Belgrade, you let the blackguards bring out these lying papers and threaten one of the few decent institutions in our unhappy country.' 'We do not,' cried Constantine, 'we suppress them as soon as we find out they are being published! Again and again the miserable things appear, and always we send out our forces after them and we destroy them, we stamp them into the dirt as they deserve!' He looked miserably round at us, realizing as he spoke that he had contradicted himself; and he was now so disintegrated that he could not take any of the obvious ways out of the situation, he could not laugh at himself or pretend, as his talent for sleight of mind would have enabled him to do better than most men, that there was some subtle consistency behind his apparent inconsistency. There was nothing for us to do but rise and say good-night.

Kossovska Mitrovitsa II

We stayed another day in the town, but we never got Constantine near the Gospodin Mac, whom he would have been bound to like and to love, both because of his connoisseurship of greatness, and because of their common love for Yugoslavia. So that afternoon, while the Gospodin Mac and my husband indulged in some last orgies of technicalities in the mill, I sat alone with Mrs Mac on the terraces of her garden, overlooking the hills and the valley where the river ran, reflecting willows, between the sweet green pastures. I was a child who had been left alone with a honeypot, for this woman, like so many Scotswomen, had all the essential gifts of the novelist. She had been long an exile, and was homesick: half her talk made a palimpsest of the scene before us, overlaying old Serbia with Ayrshire, coloured as it lives. Touch by touch she built up a picture, harsh and honest like the portraits Degas painted in his youth, of the terrific ceremony that was performed every time her mother, a widow in the Scotland of forty years ago, arrayed herself in her weeds to leave her house: I saw and smelt again the thick black blistered crape, and felt the cutting edge of the starched white collar, and was awed and perplexed by the drugged and thickened expression, characteristic of widows in those days, which suggested that their state had about it some joyless and degrading satisfaction. Soberly but with the feeling she described flowing as fresh through her words as when it had first gushed from her eyes and heart, she told how the character of her youth had been changed, to something precious but less gay than youth should be, by her long engagement to Gospodin Mac, who was then seeking his fortune abroad, and who had been too unsure of himself to make their betrothal more than a matter of murmured vows. All her spring days had been clouded by heartache: 'It's not good, running for the post, year after year.' Often she had felt that people thought her dull and a failure, and she had longed to tell her secret; but that would have been to tempt the gods by speaking of what she desired to happen as if it were already happening. Her story had the depth and vigour of early Scots poetry, of William Dunbar and Douglas's *Æneid*.

This woman, with her masterly power of observation, with her inflexible standards, had been married nearly thirty years to the Gospodin Mac, and marriage is not so much a mystery as a microscope; but he had survived all her scrutiny, he had passed

943

all her tests. Now he was the test she applied to life. She spoke constantly of Dad. 'You see that big square white building at the foot of the hill facing this one? That's the school the company gave the district. They were delighted with it and there was a tremendous to-do when the foundation stone was laid. And will you believe it? There was a priest, and we thought he had just come to say a prayer and give the place his blessing, but suddenly they upped with a lamb and he cut the throat of the poor wee thing all over the foundation stone. That's nothing to do with Christianity, I thought. But it's their own place. That's what Dad always says. It's their own place. They must do things their own way. They're funny, mind you. They built the school too big. That's one of their weaknesses. They build everything too big. They're building a town hall down in Mitrovitsa. You'd think the place must be the size of Glasgow to look at it. But Dad says it's no use raging at them for it. Just reckon with it on your side, and see that when they get in trouble on their side that they understand just how they caused themselves the trouble.'

She knitted a row or two of a jumper, and laid it by to say, 'It's time Dad retired. We've lived long enough abroad. We were twenty years and more out in South America. Both the children were born out there. Then we came back, and we had taken a house in Scotland, and they asked Dad to come out and have a look at this mine. They'd got the concession, you see, and they couldn't find the right way of tackling it. So Dad came out and he saw that they had to go after the ore in a roundabout way, that they'd never get it by going any of the ways that looked direct. And then it fascinated Dad, the whole problem of the place, all the labour being different sorts of people and all wanting to cut each other's throats. So I had to sell the furniture I'd just bought and the house, and come out here. And it's been a great piece of work for him. But now it's time both of us went home. We need a rest.' She ran a knitting needle reflectively through her hair.

'It's difficult, you know, retiring now. Because there aren't the middle-aged men to take over the responsible jobs. There's plenty of good youngsters, but not men of forty to fifty. They're the ones that got killed in the war. So it's a temptation to the old ones to wait on till the youngsters get a bit older. And Dad's got together a nice crowd here. He's got the right spirit. You see it's difficult here, they've got to be good in the mines and good with the people. There has to be a clear understanding about that in this sort of country. Dad always says to everybody who comes out here to the mines, "Now, you've got to be polite to the Yugoslavs, for it's their country, and we're only guests here." But some of them don't take the hint,

particularly if they've been nobodies at home. They look to lord
it over the Slavs here then. Sooner or later we get to hear of it if
they do. The Yugoslavs only report it if one of our people is rude
to an officer. The Army is sacred to them, you know. I do believe
it's more sacred than the Church is at home for we don't think it's
so terrible to laugh at a minister. But anyway it comes out one way
or another. I caught a common wee body making a face after I had
taken a doctor's wife from Belgrade round the bridge club when
she thought I'd turned my back, and we watched the husband and
found he was just the same. So they found themselves in the train
for London before they knew where they were.'

She drew her hand across her forehead and down till her chin was
cupped in it and then sighed into the palm, looking downward: the
most Scots of gestures. 'But it's terrible here in some ways! The
way they treat the women! And the law's behind them, mind you!'
She shuddered, and told a story of a cultivated Bosnian woman,
a graduate of Belgrade and Vienna universities, who had come to
the mines to work as a chemist, had married a Serbian mining
engineer, and been left a widow after some years; and had found
herself visited by his peasant family, who seized all her furniture
and every penny of the dead man's savings, as the inheritance laws
of the country permitted them to do, and made the startling demand
that she should return with them and marry his brother. She spoke
as one who had savoured the full horror of the subjection of women,
as it is when it is actually practised and not merely dreamed about
in a voluptuous reverie: a plundering, a mutilation, an insult to the
womb and life, an invocation to mud and death. It was evident that,
like all people who have lived long in exile, she sometimes felt that
everything peculiar to the strange place where she found herself was
a spreading sore, bubo of a plague that will infect and kill if there is
not instant flight to the aseptic. But she was disciplined. She knew
what shadowed her for the mere shadow that it was. After she had
shuddered she instantly grew stable. She turned her head, which
was lioness-massive, towards the green and red hills, the willowed
stream in the valleys, and said she loved them all.

At half-past four we were to go down the hill to the tennis courts;
for it was a saint's day that was a public holiday, and the whole
mining staff was to be there, because a famous professional player
had come down for the day from Belgrade. First we had to perform
some of those trivial domestic rites which are delicious to women
like myself, who have had to work at a specialized task all their lives.
Mrs Mac's knitting had to be rolled up and her work-basket set in
order. She moved with a slowness that was a sign of richness; cream

does not pour quickly. We had to persuade the Aberdeen terrier to be shut in the house lest he should follow us. It seemed that the creature who had been sitting at my feet so gravely all afternoon, putting himself in just the right position to be scratched under the left ear, was the victim of an intemperate passion for balls. It was like hearing that a good sound Hegelian philosopher was given to drink. 'Well, we'll away!' sighed Mrs Mac. We passed down a path through an orchard, round a curve to the tennis ground. It was superbly placed. Beyond the courts rose the peaked hill crowned with ruins, creamy with wild flowers that grew strong among the bushes.

The game had already begun, and it had fallen, as games between professionals and true amateurs are apt to do, into the pattern of a dance. The Serb professional sent the ball first into the left-hand corner of the court, and the English amateur returned it; then the Serb professional sent it into the right-hand corner of the court, and the English amateur returned it. Then the ball fell just over the net, and stayed there. Though the professional had not to exert himself to impose this pattern on the game he was nevertheless still working out a problem: how to economize his expenditure of effort to the minimum degree. He had succeeded so far that he never needed to hurry, he was always moving slowly to where the ball was going to be. It would have been entertaining to watch him had not the spectators been as remarkable on precisely the same count of graceful economy. An audience proves its discipline by its capacity for stillness. Those who have never practised continuous application to an exacting process cannot settle down to simple watching; they must chew gum, they must dig the peel off their oranges, they must shift from foot to foot, from buttock to buttock. But the people round this tennis court were calm and true in their attention. Their eyes and chins smiled neatly from left to right and from right to left, no further than was necessary to follow the ball, and their lips were quiet mouths, their fingers quiet hands, their bodies closely furled.

There were present most of the men who worked at the mines and mills at other than manual labour, and two sorts of women: their wives, and the women who were themselves working here, as secretaries and scientific workers and household administrators. Sight could not tell one the difference between the two sorts. They were alike curled and shining about the head, for here, as everywhere in Yugoslavia which has seen the glint of money, the women are at least as well coiffed as they are in Vienna, and their clothes were discreet yet gay. Many were beautiful. There was one

White Russian, always to be remembered: an office worker, whose face was clear-cut and cold yet tender, whose figure was armoured with elegance yet fluid with a grace wilder than ordinary motion. There was a Montenegrin girl, handsome as a hero, born to live under black heights crowned with snow, under skies where eagles circle. There were Englishwomen, to go with gardens. But even these highly individualized women were, like the men who sat with them, rubbed down by the pressure of a common purpose to what was not uniformity so much as unanimity. The mine shaped them. They worked in the interest of the maintenance of themselves and their kind, as peasants do, though modern industry was their medium; and they had joined to their educated brilliance the sacred grimness of the peasant that will not be vanquished by his environment. Here, certainly, Yugoslavia might take the gifts of the West without fearing that they were poisoned, and might learn a formula for prosperity that would let it exploit its economic resources without danger to its human resources.

The slanting sunshine of late afternoon emphasized with bright light and black shadows the sugar-loaf sharpness of the peaked hill above us, the fishbone fineness of the ruins on its summit. Some cattle wandered up there among the burning bushes, incandescent like pious beasts that had received their reward here on earth and been transfigured; it could be seen that some purple flowers as well as white grew among the long grasses. There stood at my side the Gospodin Mac: he and my husband had just arrived, hot but contented, from their tour of the miracles in the mill. 'I see you're having a good look at our castle,' he said. 'I suppose you know that's where Stephen Dushan strangled his father, Stephen Dechanski.' I exclaimed, 'But I thought that happened at Zvechan, not at Trepcha.' He answered, 'But this is not Trepcha. Trepcha is the valley-head where the mine is, down here we are at Zvechan.' I said, 'I wish I could go up and look at it,' but the woman beside me objected, 'There is nothing to be seen now, only some broken walls. And you could not go up in those shoes, there are snakes up there.'

That there should be snakes in the castle of Zvechan was most fitting. The event which had come to pass on that cone had not been compact; it had dragged along its deadly length. There were the years when Stephen Dechanski and his father Milutin had hated one another, when the son had, like a hunted beast, imitated the stillness of a stone, that he might not be struck dead. There were the years when Stephen Dechanski might have lived according to his nature, Milutin being dead, but instead provoked a repetition of his earlier peril by the offence he offered to a son, of whom nothing was more certain than that he was the most dangerous of all his stock. Again he imitated the stillness of a stone, but not in order that he might escape destruction. Here on this bronze crest he had lain quiet in order to be the doomed mark of the sweeping sword, wielded by an executioner whom he had begotten by his flesh and instructed by his policy. Destiny is another name for humanity's half-hearted yet persistent search for death. Again and again peoples have had the chance to live and show what would happen if human life were irrigated by continual happiness; and they have preferred to blow up the canals and perish of drought. They listen to the evil counsel of the grey falcon. They let their throats be cut as if they were black lambs. The mystery of Kossovo was behind this hill. It is behind all our lives.

It was behind this community. It was childish to suppose that these people of the mine could offer a formula for the future well-being of the South Slavs; or even for themselves. It was not childish to regard them and their effect on their surroundings as wholly admirable. But this was only a clearing in the jungle hewn by pioneers whom some peculiar genetic excellence, some inspiring oddity of environment, had made superior to their fellows. These people could not save South-Eastern Europe, because they could not save England: which, indeed, would certainly not save them, if their existence was at stake. These people stood for life; it is impossible to maintain that a large part of England does not stand for death. The men and women of Trepcha were not of the highest social or economic importance in their origins. None, I imagine, had had a duke for a father or was heir to a million. They came from homes where there was upheld a tradition of comfort and fine manners, but where there was no chance to enjoy either unless each generation worked. They therefore knew better than those above them, as a paid athlete earning his keep by daily performance realizes more intensely than any amateur that he must not poison his strength by alcohol or unwholesome food, that it is good for a man to be temperate and precise and to respect the quality of others. But the people who determine the fate of England have not learned that lesson; for we are still governed by our great houses.

There is no sense in a house of extravagant size, unless it is the seat of a small court such as all forces in European history have combined to eliminate, or the home of a devotee inspired by passionate charity to feed and house all comers. Yet the pride of those who occupy such 'places' is quantitative. They exult in the number and magnitude of their rooms, the extent of their gardens and glass-houses and stables, the troops of their servants and grooms and gardeners. It is rarely the harmonious proportions of their homes that please them, and there indeed lies their true destruction. For they have lost their taste, which left them during the nineteenth century, and has scarcely been recovered save by those separated from their own class by some barrier such as exceptional gifts, physical weakness, or homosexuality. The proof is written on their walls by their family portraits; beside their Holbeins and Van Dycks, their Gainsboroughs and Reynoldses and Lawrences, hang their Dicksees and Millais' and Herkomers, Sargents and Laszlos and Birleys. The eye has lost its acuteness because the well-being of the whole organism does not depend on sight or any other of its senses. These people would eat well, if they were blind and deaf and dumb, because the Industrial Revolution and colonial expansion had in the past combined to drop food into their mouths.

Having lost their taste, they lost their souls. For they could no longer base their standards on quality, and so developed their pride in quantity. But a quantity of possessions, on the scale that they have learned to enjoy them, can only be the massed result of past achievements. They cannot have any relation to present achievement. Therefore these people turn away from life. The best of them escape into concentration on the craft knowledge of certain pursuits, such as horsemanship and shooting and fishing, which does not give them the general good sense that often follows from the practice of a craft, because of the insane emotional exaltation engendered by their sense of superiority to those who, by reason of intellectual preoccupations or economic insufficiency, are unwilling to exchange all other interests for these exercises. It cannot be conceived, if the proposition is examined coldly, that a conservative society, which behaves as if hunting were as sacred as the practice of religion, does not make each of its members a fool for life. Those who preserve enough mental vigour to make their mark in public life sit on the benches of Parliament with a majesty related to some other period in our history; and their contact with the present is the reading of memoranda prepared by experts, whom they are apt to distrust because of their different social origins. They have certain principles to which they are ponderously loyal; they protect mass accumulations of past effort and deny the claims of the present. They would not lift a finger to defend the Gospodin Mac and his officers. They would not understand the beauty and ingenuity of their work at Trepcha, because it was not hunting and shooting, because it was modern. They would become moderately excited about it as a source of dividends, but they would let international politics take a direction perilous to the maintenance of the mine, because they were still in the nineteenth century and could not believe that English authority was not absolute the whole world over, and English capital inviolably safe. This governing class meant death for England, however well scattered Englishmen might serve life; and therefore English example could not mean salvation for Yugoslavia.

I said to the Gospodin Mac, 'Are the Foreign Office and the Legation people interested in you?' He answered, 'Not in the least. Though I've often thought they might be. After all we're an important British influence in the Balkans. But they've never even told me what to do in case of war. I should ask them more insistently, I suppose. But you know what these diplomats are, they're bored with you, and you get bored with them.' There is nothing more to the discredit of the great house than the tendency of its children to fret for their homes in the Foreign Legations. Social extremes meet in exile. The average English diplomat *en poste* anywhere but the great familiar capitals, in Paris, Berlin, Rome, or Vienna, reacts exactly like a young woman who has given up duty at the haberdashery counter to marry a young man in a Continental branch of a bacon firm. There is the same frenzied interest in clothes, and the same resentful indifference to the exotic surroundings. This is not an aristocratic attitude, but the great house no longer produces aristocrats but only the privileged.

Their privileges are enormous, and they afford ill examples for the ambitions of other classes. Their wealth fascinates and impresses the rest of society because it is inherited. To be fortunate from the womb, to be so fortunate that we can outstrip the curse of Adam all the way from the cradle to the grave, this is the fate we would have chosen for ourselves in our childhood; and therefore it is what we would desire for our children, since when we think of them we are all childish. We look at the great house, with its obvious foundation of secular wealth, and we regard it as evidence that our hopes can be gratified; and thus thrift, that most innocent of virtues, which is rediscovered every time a child puts by a sweet for tomorrow, is enlarged and degraded into that swollen monster of insensate expectation, the desire to invest savings in return for enormous and eternal dividends.

We have no basis for our hopes in practice or theory. The wealth that sustains the great house was usually made by ancestors who had the luck to seize land or mineral rights or a monopoly of trade in the days before society had learned to protect itself from exploitation, or to discover some means of cheapening articles for which there is a widespread and permanent demand. The first form of luck cannot be enjoyed in the present stabilized world, and the second occurs more and more rarely in our highly competitive industrial system. Nor can it be believed that ordinary savings are so scarce that borrowers need pay a very high and perpetual rate of interest on them. But the whole of our economic structure is based on that pretence, and a millstone of greed is tied round the neck of every industrial enterprise, calculated to be just as heavy as its power can bear without collapse. Even here at Trepcha the dividends that were paid out to the shareholders must have been a handicap on the mine's social value. It was true that a million pounds had been put into the mine before it yielded its ore, but the price which is paid for all such advances is altogether excessive. Much went to the distant dividend-drawer, who cared not a hoot for the miners or for Yugoslavia but he, poor dog, helpless as anyone else in this chaotic world, was facing enormous political risks, and might presently draw no dividends at all. International finance is not so Machiavellian as the simpler forms of Socialist and Fascist propaganda pretend. Its fault is probably that it pulls too few strings rather than too many, and it can no longer be counted as among the major causes of war. But it is like a learned but deaf and prejudiced judge sitting on the bench as a trial raising tremendous issues of personal destiny and juristic principle. Sometimes it hears and is wise. Sometimes it babbles.

These people of the Trepcha mines were not wholly innocent; for the England which was inferior to them nevertheless existed by their consent. It is probable that the Gospodin Mac was an old-fashioned Scottish liberal, reared in reverence for Mr Gladstone, and it is certain that he was a radical in spirit; again and again he betrayed his sense that the spirit of society was not loyal to the creative spirit that expressed itself in sound mining and sound administration. His wife would have witnessed a revolution, had it been the right one, with the sturdy approval of a housewife who sees a sluttish neighbour at last tackling her spring cleaning. But most of the others who sat round the tennis court would, I think, have been fiercely conservative. They would have leaped to the defence of the forces which were working for their destruction; they would at least have excused, if they would not have totally exonerated, any governor who murdered those revolutionaries who were seeking to come to their relief. Everywhere such men as these, men of definite and distinguished action, tend to vote for the maintenance of the great house. They cannot give any close intellectual justification for their feelings. Plainly they are obeying their instincts; and instincts, it is proverbial, are sound. But that is a self-flattering lie we humans tell ourselves, which was disproved by the peak above us, goal of Stephen Dechanski's indeflectable instinct for death.

My husband said, 'It is time that we must go,' and we began our farewells. I felt real sorrow that I should probably never see these people again, and as I left I turned to a group of men and women whom I had not met and said, 'Good-bye,' although I knew it was an action appropriate to a royal person leaving a bazaar, because I wanted to look squarely at their pleasantness. But in the very intensity of my admiration for them I realized how impotent the West was to help the rest of the world; for it produces individuals so entirely excellent, so single-minded and honest and fastidious, that a paradisal society should long ago have established itself, had not there been within them a dark force impelling them to trace with their actions, so delicate and graceful when considered separately, a hideous and gloomy pattern. Here, through the genius of the Gospodin Mac, that force had been so far as possible frustrated, and the Western virtues showed themselves in their purity. But this was a purely local exorcism. The West, as I thought of it extending thousands of miles beyond the setting sun, was astonishing in its corruption, in its desire for death, and in its complacency towards its disease.

Only in Macedonia, it seemed to me, had I seen mankind medicining its corruption, trying to raise up its love of life so that it might contend with its love of death and defend the kingdom of human affairs from a government that should extend only over the grave. I remembered how Bishop Nikolai had seemed to wrestle with this desire to die as if he were throwing a steer, though his columnar body had stood stock-still in his rich robes. I remembered how the monks of Sveti Naum had held up an enticing symbol of life to those who had lost their taste for it. I remembered with hope that we were going that evening to Petch, and would the next day visit the great monastery which Stephen had founded at Dechani, for it is a seminary for the training of monks, and there it would be made plain whether these achievements in Macedonia were the works of individual genius, or whether the Orthodox Church were in possession of wisdom which it could impart to all its children; if that were so, then even the mediocre could perform such feats, and the preference for life could be established everywhere. We were standing at the gate now: Dragutin was waiting for us beside the automobile, his hand to his forehead, looking as if he had brought our gold-harnessed horses to the tent of Tsar Lazar. The Gospodin Mac said, 'You'll like Dechani, it's a beautiful place up there in the mountains, it's like a Highland glen,' and his wife said, 'I hope you'll not be shown round by that wee monk with the awful galoshes.' At last we slid down the hillside that was like Golder's Green, that was like Chislehurst, that was truly very Heaven, and the dark, proliferating complexity of Slavonic life again absorbed us.

Petch I

When we got back to the hotel Constantine was walking up and down in a frenzy of impatience, holding his watch in his hand. That fretfulness which we had begun to notice as part of the disintegration that Gerda had worked upon him now took the form of a continual allegation that everybody but himself was either too late or too early for every event in the daily routine. If he saw people drinking coffee it seemed to him that they might have done it with propriety an hour earlier or an hour later, but not then. Now we had come back to the hotel twenty minutes before the time set for our departure for Petch, but it was to him as if we were very late, so late that we would have to put off the journey till the next morning. As we got out of the car he ran towards us, waving his watch and crying out reproaches, but Dragutin jumped out and faced him with the detached malevolent intensity and cold health of the snake. It was day by day more apparent that he was repelled by Constantine's sick state and would have liked to chase him away from us. Though we could not understand what he said to him, we felt the chill of its insolence, and there was suddenly a muffled quality about Constantine, as if he had slipped on a padded garment to protect himself. I wondered if there had been a scene between the two of which I knew nothing. But Constantine only said, 'Well, you know we must not start too late, for until a short time ago this road was the most dangerous in Yugoslavia.' 'But it is so no longer,' said Dragutin, and began to load the car with our luggage.

They began to wrangle on the point again, when we had travelled some distance from the town and were passing through low hills covered with scrub-oak, now ruddy with the early sunset. Where the road cut across a twisting valley we saw a car drawn up by the roadside and a man standing on a raised hillock, his head bent towards the west. We slowed down and saw that he was crossing himself, and we stopped dead. 'When he has finished I will ask him why he is praying here,' said Dragutin; 'perhaps it is a holy place where some Turkish beg was killed.' When the man stepped down from the hillock he shouted to him, 'Why are you praying, friend?' The man came up to our car and answered, 'Because I am glad to be alive. But are you not English? Listen how well I speak English! My friends in England laugh at me and say I speak so well that I speak Scotch. For all the war I was at school at Aberdeen. And afterwards I came back here, and because of my good education I became a dealer in factory-made clothes and that is why I am praying here now. For very often I had to make this journey from Kossovska Mitrovitsa to Petch, and because of the brigands I was always very frightened, particularly just at this spot, for they used to come down this valley and lay a tree-trunk across the road. I used to think of my dear wife and my little children, and pray to God for protection, and now that there is no more danger I am thanking him for giving it to me. But since you come from England I would like very much to talk to you. Are you going to Petch? Are you staying there long? Ah, well, then I shall see you, but now I must hurry, for I must go to supper with a friend of mine who has a farm outside the town.' 'You see,' said Constantine, as he left us in dust, 'he said the road was dangerous.' 'He said it had been dangerous,' Dragutin corrected him, 'and he showed by his action he believed it was so no longer. I believe in God as much as anybody, but on a road where I thought there were still brigands I would not leave my car and stand beside it praying, I would pray as I drove, and so would any sane man.'

The brigands who had operated on this road were by way of being political insurgents. They were Albanians claiming to represent the element which had been dispossessed by the redistribution of land made by the Yugoslavian Government after the war. All over the Balkans there is an association between highway robbery and revolutionary idealism which the Westerner finds disconcerting, but which is an inevitable consequence of the Turkish conquest. This crystallized the conditions of the fourteenth century; and in the Middle Ages anybody who stepped out of the niche into which he was born had no other resource but banditry, as he could neither move to another district nor change his trade. If a peasant excited the displeasure of authority by standing up for the rights of his kind, he had to make himself scarce and thereafter live in cover of the forests and make forays on rich travellers, alike under the Nemanyas and under the Turks. Hence the Balkan peoples are not, to this day, initially shocked by a rebel who professes political idealism though he habitually loots and murders, though sooner or later they become irritated by the practical results of this application of medieval theory to modern conditions. The weak point in the programme is the present lack of rich travellers. A Robin Hood working on the road between Petch and Kossovska Mitrovitsa would earn a few good meals in spring and autumn and none at all in summer and winter. So he would have to fall back either on robbery from travellers of inconsiderable means, or regular exactions from the local peasants: that is to say, he would become a pest to the very class

which he claimed to be championing. This is the real reason why
I.M.R.O., the Internal Macedonian Revolutionary Organization,
perished; and these Albanians could not surmount the difficulty,
particularly after the Trepcha mines brought money to the district.
The peasants became so anxious to get on with their lives and enjoy
their share of this new prosperity that, actively or passively, they
were all on the side of the gendarmes. But even so the business
of exterminating these bandits must have been formidable. To the
right of this road runs a wall of mountains, fissured with deep
wooded glens, and to the left lies a flat plain, green and sweet and
fertile as our Vale of Pewsey. The loot was as tempting as the cover
was kind.

'Look, there is Tserna Gora, there is Montenegro,' said
Constantine; and it was so. The country, the fact of it, the
essence of it, not just a part of it, was before our eyes. A wall
of mountains ran south from Kossovska Mitrovitsa, another wall
ran north to meet it from the misty limits of the plain, but they
stopped short of meeting; and above the gap was a still higher
wall, a black cliff-face, half as tall as the sky. That was Tserna
Gora, Monte Negro, which may fairly be translated as the Black
Mountain, but meant nothing of the sort when the name was given,
for then it meant the mountain of Strashimir Ivo the Black, that is
to say the outlaw, a Serbian chief who fled there half a century after
Kossovo and established a Christian principality. The Turks did
not follow him, not for a couple of centuries. They sat on the plain
and looked up at this colossal fortress, this geological engineering
feat that brings rock as it is seen only deep below earth in caverns
and abysms and hangs it in an area that had seemed reserved for
clouds.

About the mouth of this gap were scattered agreeable foothills,
on which we discerned as we grew nearer the mosques and cubes
of a city. The buildings glimmered blue-white about us as we drove
into an evening iced and shadowed by the precipice at the end of the
gorge, but still light enough to disclose the tottering and dilapidated
charm of Petch. It is not unlike a Swiss town, for a river rushes
beside the high-street, bringing the cold breath of the glacier with
it, and as the light fails the mountains seem to draw closer; but the
place knows nothing so solid as a chalet. Nobody can imagine how
insubstantial an inhabited building can be till he has visited Petch.
Most of the houses we passed, and nearly all the shops, could be
knocked down in half an hour by any able-bodied person with a
small pick, and quite a number could be razed to the ground. Many
are made of thin planks and petrol tins, and such as had essayed

the use of plaster had been stricken with a kind of architectural mange.

We went up the high-street, which was very broad, with a breadth that was the more remarkable because the shops and inns on each side were so low and rickety. A stream ran down one side of it, one of those channelled by the Turks to take the drainage. It was the hour of the corso, and a crowd of people, mostly very tall, were shuffling up and down, their passionate faces and fantastic dresses shot with two aspects, both equally passionate and fantastic, by the conflicting lights of the dusk and the white downpour from the electric standards. There was contrapuntal sense of movement, for there was the leisurely shuffle of the crowd, the quick ripple of the stream in the roadway, and the leaping and dancing of the river which could be seen through the gaps in the houses, driving over a wide bed of shingle among poplars and willows. Yet I was reminded of a ghost town I once visited in Colorado, where a ribbon of untrodden dust led between windowless frame houses to an abandoned mine.

The hotel received us into a vast eccentric bosom. It was built round a restaurant, a strange irregular quadrilateral apartment, with a gallery and a line of super-Corinthian pillars marching across it, all painted a hot dull maroon. It was yet another specimen of the innate architecture of the Balkans, which seems to have been run up without a pattern by somebody who had never seen a building of the type he was constructing. In this restaurant a few people in Western clothes, probably functionaries, sat about at the tables, attended by several waiters; all, because of the vastness of the room, in which the beams of the electric light wandered loosely and ineffectively, seemed to be featureless. We went upstairs and traversed passages that were true to the Petch fashion for insubstantiality. When the floor creaked underfoot it was making no idle complaint, it had indeed suffered an injury.

The manager flung open the door of a bedroom and we looked in on an ebony-haired young officer, his olive-green coat tapering exquisitely to a dandyish waist, who was standing at an iron table and washing his hands in an enamel basin with bright pink soap. The scent of the soap was so powerful, so catastrophically floral, that we remained in a still and startled semicircle, looking down at the magical lather. It was as if one had opened a door and found a man taking a white rabbit out of a tophat. It was the manager who first recovered his self-possession. 'It seems the room is occupied,' he explained to us. Reluctantly we retired, our eyes on the extraordinary soap. 'But the officer is going quite soon,' he said, when we were out on the landing. 'If you will sit down here you will not have long to wait.' 'Have you not other rooms?' asked my husband severely, in German. 'Yes,' the manager answered, 'but there is something special about this room and the next; I have often remarked it. I would like you to have them.' 'And I?' said Constantine. 'Do I also have to wait?' 'Yes,' said the manager, 'there is another officer in yours. I do not know why they have not gone. They said they would be gone at half-past five. But of course they are both young, and when one is young one often does not know how the time is passing. You will find these comfortable chairs.'

About that he was wrong. They were cane chairs with large holes in the seats. But it was not disagreeable to occupy them, for they were set beside a table where a chambermaid was ironing a pile of sheets, and she was a very agreeable person. She was a Hungarian, not very young or pretty, but she had a jolly, monkeyish face, with russet cheeks and shining brown eyes, which she twisted into amusing grimaces. The sheets were very coarse, so that to iron them required a real muscular effort, and every time she responded to the strain with a delicious expression, a blend of ascetic voluptuousness and self-mockery. It was quite pleasant sitting there in the warm dusk. The sheets smelt like toasted tea-cakes. I nearly went to sleep several times, but I was awakened because the doors of a cupboard just beside me kept on bursting open for no other cause but sheer flimsiness, sheer inability to stay put together another instant, disclosing a number of unidentifiable objects wrapped in brown paper. I remembered a Russian novel I had once reviewed in which the description of a bedroom had ended with the sentence, 'And under the bed there was an enormous enema.'

At last the officers clattered down the passage, and we took over their rooms. Ours was still tenanted by the scent of the pink soap, the spectre of an unthinkably lush and oleaginous summer. We changed our clothes, and just as we were ready Constantine knocked on the door and came in looking very pleased and happy. 'That little Hungarian chambermaid,' he announced, 'she is perhaps not so good as she might be, or perhaps she is a little better. I have told her I want a hot, hot bath, because I have a little fever and I want to sweat, and she says to me, "Yes, you will have a hot, hot bath, myself I will make it very hot, but who will give you the massage afterwards? Is it myself also?" Ah, it is so with all our chambermaids, they are very naughty, but very good also, you saw how she worked.' He turned his back on us to straighten his tie among the delirious reflections of the extravagantly framed mirror, with a sudden revival of the gallant spirit of self-parody that had so often enchanted us, when we had first travelled with him; and all three of us laughed. But I noticed that the back of his neck was fiery red, and I said, 'But what about this fever? Constantine, are you really ill?' He whirled about and answered, 'It is from my hand.' We stared at it in horror: the whole hand between the knuckles and the wrist was scarlet and pulpy. 'But what happened?' 'Just this morning as we got up from breakfast,' said Constantine, 'I was stung by a great ferocious insect with huge wings. It was either a wasp or a hornet. But you did not notice.'

We both hung about him and made penitent and sympathetic murmurs, and suddenly we were friends as we had been at the beginning. He was to us as our child and a great man, and we were to him as his father and mother and his pupils, and there was no barrier between us and our words. But soon his face grew vacant, as if he were listening to a distant voice, and then hardened. He said, 'Yes, I feel very ill, but you need not bother, I will come downstairs, and though I will not be able to eat one mouthful, I will sit with you when we have dinner, and afterwards I will take you a walk round the town.' 'You will do nothing of the sort,' said my husband, 'you will go to bed and have some dinner sent up to you.' 'No,' said Constantine. 'I know your habits very well now. The walk round the town after dinner, you would feel terribly if you missed it. And I know what you English are.' My husband said suddenly a short word which has so rarely been spoken in my presence that I wonder how it is I understand it, and taking Constantine's arm in his led him from the room. When he came back, he said, 'Forgive me, my dear. But I thought this situation could only be handled by the natural man. And do not worry. He was quite happy to be sent to bed.'

We dined in the restaurant of the principal hotel and there we ate excellent trout, but not until after an immense delay. The apartment was so large that as soon as a waiter took an order he broke into a trot towards the kitchen; and I have no doubt that the kitchen was also vast, and that the cooks had to stop their work every now and then to re-build a wall or re-lay a floor. We passed the time in spelling out the news in the Belgrade newspapers which were constantly brought in by little dark boys of distinguished appearance in very ragged clothes, and in talking to a young man who came up to us and asked in German if he could be of any help to us, since we were strangers. He told us he was a Croat lawyer, come to be clerk of the local law court, and he gave a very pleasant impression of youthful simplicity and courtesy, of a real knightliness. He left us when our trout was brought, and as soon as we had finished it we had another visitor. A dark full-bodied man, more smartly dressed than anybody else in the restaurant, had been watching us from a near-by table for some time and now came up to us. He said to my husband, 'Good evening. It is interesting to meet a German so far from home.' 'I am not a German,' said my husband, 'I am English.'

The dark man looked at his reply as if it might be picked up, carried away, dropped down, buried, or accorded any treatment except belief. 'Yet you speak German like a German,' he said. 'That is because I spent some years as a boy in Hamburg,' answered my husband, 'and I have spent much of my life doing business with Germans.' The dark man said nothing to distract us from his disbelief, and my husband said testily, 'And you? You are a German; what are you doing here?' 'Oh, I am not a German!' exclaimed the dark man with an air of surprise. 'Yet you speak like a German,' said my husband. 'That is because I am a Dane,' said the dark man. After an instant he appeared to become intensely irritated with my husband's face, which is long and intelligent, and he left us with a curt farewell. 'He does not believe me when I say I am English,' commented my husband, 'but he is infuriated when I do not believe him when he says, "I am a Dane." He feels I am not playing the game. That means that he is a German.' 'Could he possibly be a Dane?' 'Not possibly,' said my husband; 'he does not even speak with a North German accent. That man has spoken Berliner German from his infancy.'

At that point Dragutin, who had been sitting on the other side of the room, came up to say good-night to us. We gathered that he was telling us that Petch was very depressing after Trepcha, and that he had never seen anything more wonderful than the house and works he had seen at Goru. After he had gone it struck me that Goru is not the name of a place but a word meaning 'up in the mountain.' He had, in fact, been to the mine-head. 'This is too frightful!' I said. 'Do you remember when I thought I saw Dragutin at that canteen just before we had lunch in the mess? Well, I did! He must have got a friend to take him up there!' 'What is so frightful about that?' asked my husband. 'It means,' I answered, 'that he went off and left Constantine, probably without asking permission, so that instead of Constantine going off for a solitary drive and feeling superior to us and all the people at the mines, because he was a poet and acting poetically, he had to sit in the hotel feeling left out and despised.' 'My God, I believe you're right!' exclaimed my husband. We gazed at each other in real horror. 'I do not think Dragutin would deliberately disobey Constantine,' he said, 'I think he simply forgot him. He knows quite well that Constantine is not a whole man, and that he has been in some way destroyed, and he fears an infection. Now I understand another cause for anti-Semitism; many primitive peoples must receive their first intimation of the toxic quality of thought from Jews. They know only the fortifying idea of religion; they see in Jews the effect of the tormenting and disintegrating ideas of scepticism. Dragutin sees a man made as miserable as sickness, as poverty, as disgrace could make him, by an idea which is so mighty that it can exercise this power even though it was let loose on him by a woman. No wonder he is appalled. Well, let us go and get some sleep.'

So we climbed the creaking staircase and came to our room, passing the little Hungarian chambermaid as she burrowed among candles in a store cupboard, still busy; and we slept well, though once I woke and turned on the light and watched a frieze of five mice pass along the skirting. In the morning as many beetles watched me as I dried after my antique bath. But all was clean, aseptically clean; and for the explanation there was the chambermaid down on her knees, her right hand swishing the suds across the flimsy floor, her head rolling from side to side and a tune coming in a half hum, half whistle, through her teeth. We bade her good-morning and told her she worked too hard for a pretty girl, and she looked up laughing, and from a plank in front of her broke off a huge splinter like a piece of toast. 'Yes,' said Constantine, who just then came out of his room, 'she is a good girl, and she has great sensibility. Last night she came into my room and she said so kindly, "Ah, I would so like to be with you, for there is something about you very sweet, and you are far more cultured than most men who come to this hotel, but I see you are too ill, and so I will bring you a little orange drink instead." '

We went down and had our breakfast outside the principal hotel, and sat over our coffee for an unnecessary length of time, enchanted by the scene. The most enchanting element in it was a number of pretty little girls with dark hair sun-bleached on the surface, and fair delicate bronze skins, who darted about in most beautiful costumes, consisting of fitted jackets and loose trousers gathered at the ankles, cut out of brilliant curtain material with an extreme sense of elegance that was not of an Oriental sort. The effect is too feminist. The little girl is set apart as a little girl, as a possible object for poetical feeling, but her will is respected, she can run and jump as she likes. We ceased to look at them only to wonder about several cheap cars waiting in front of the hotel, which as we breakfasted filled up with people apparently strangers to each other, who all held lemons in their hands and looked exceedingly apprehensive. 'They fear to be sick,' explained Constantine, 'and it is to prevent it that they are going to suck lemons. They are going to travel through Montenegro, to Kolashin or Tsetinye or Podgoritsa or Nikshitch, and they must go by motor bus or by car, since there is no railway in all Montenegro, it is too mountainous.' And looking up the road at the walls of rock which barred the way, that seemed obvious. Nothing but a Simplon tunnel that took a whole day to pass could meet the case. 'The poor passengers,' continued Constantine, 'they have reason for fearing to be sick, and even to die. For the Montenegrins are a race of heroes, but since the Turks have gone they have nothing to be heroic about, and so they are heroic with their motor cars. A Montenegrin chauffeur looks on his car as a Cossack or a cowboy looks on a horse, he wishes to do tricks with it that show his skill and courage, and he is proud of the wounds he gets in an accident as if they were scars of battle. It is a superb point of view, but not for the passenger. One cannot work out a formula, not in philosophy, not in aesthetics, not in religion, not in nothing that would make it good for the passengers. Yet there have to be passengers for there to be a chauffeur. It is a very grave disharmony.'

There came to our table at that moment a lean and hard-bitten and harassed man in uniform, who introduced himself as the Chief of Police at Petch. He spoke American English, for he had been in the Middle West nearly twenty years, and he was consumed by that emotion so socially disruptive, so critical of all our sentimental pretences, that it has no name: the opposite of nostalgia, a sick distaste for the fatherland. 'All here is as strange to me as it is to you,' he complained. 'They asked me to come back from the United States and become Chief of Police, and because I was for Yugoslavia I obeyed, but I made a mistake. There is too much to do. These folks here won't act right unless you make 'em, and to make 'em you have to know every one of them by sight. Will you believe that I have to come down every evening and watch the corso, just to see how they all act and get in my mind who's who? Can you imagine folks acting that way in the States?' There are nearly fourteen thousand inhabitants of Petch; in the plain which stretches from Petch south to Prizren, a matter of fifty-five miles or so, there were in Turkish days a steady six hundred assassinations a year; I found some pathos in the lot of a gentleman who was trying to induce by individual attention such a large number of people, who had been shaped by such a tradition, to behave like good Babbitts. My husband said, 'But many of your charges look very charming,' and I added, 'The little girls are really lovely.' The Chief of Police said in astonishment, 'Do you really think so?' 'But certainly,' we said. 'Oh, no, you are mistaken!' he exclaimed. 'But we have seen the most exquisite little girls,' I began, but Constantine interrupted me. 'The Chief of Police,' he explained, 'is a Montenegrin, and he is trying to tell you, if you would only let him, that only up there behind that wall at the end of the street in Montenegro are people really charming and little girls really lovely.' 'Well, I doubt if a man not fortified by such beliefs would accept such a post,' said my husband. I asked, after the Chief of Police had made exactly the speech that Constantine had anticipated, 'But are not the people influenced a great deal by the monks at the Patriarchate church and the Dechani monastery?' He looked at me in bewilderment. 'Influenced? But in what way?' 'Why, for good,' I stammered; 'the monks, you know.' He continued to look at me in perplexity, but just then a gendarme came in and, after saluting, whispered in his ear; and he jumped up and left us in the manner of a mother who has just heard that two of her children have been fighting and have hurt themselves.

'It is hotter than it has been,' I said, as we drove out of the town, along the road towards Montenegro, on our way to the Patriarchate church of Petch, which is nearly as famous as the monastery of Dechani.

It was a very pleasant drive, with the houses thinning and showing us the rich pastures that ran up to the wooded foothills, and the brilliant river that dashed down from the gorge. 'I do not think that it is hot at all,' said Constantine. 'But the sun is strong,' I said. 'I find it very weak,' said Constantine. 'Oh, no!' I exclaimed. 'This morning at eight the stockings that I washed last night and hung at the window were quite dry.' I realized that I had spoken foolishly even before he had sneered, 'You have proof for everything.' His face was heavy and swollen, half with fever, half with the desire to hurt. Gerda had convinced him that being a Jew he was worthless, and he wanted to establish that everybody else she despised was worthless too, so that we could crash down together to common annihilation under her blond, blind will. The three of us kept silent till we came to the Patriarchate, which lies in a walled compound among the foothills at the opening of the gorge, low by the river under the wooded cliffs.

Through an archway we entered what seemed a decent little country estate, with proper outbuildings and a trim wood-stack, a kitchen garden as neat as a new pin, and an orchard with its trunks new-washed against blight. A very old monk, lean and brown as a tree-trunk, smiled at us but did not answer what Constantine said, and led us along an avenue to a round fountain shaded by some trees. We thought he was deaf, but he was a Russian who had never learned any Serbian during his seventeen years of exile here. While he fetched the Abbot from his house, there appeared at our elbows Dragutin, to enforce the observance of his special rite and see that we drank from the fountain. It cured all ills, he said, and bestowed also the blessing of Christ. He had brought tumblers from the automobile, so that we could drink in comfort, and indeed it was delicious beyond the nature of water.

When I had finished drinking, I looked round with satisfaction. This was a fat little estate: the buildings were not only new, they were well kept, and on the finely tilled terraces behind the guest-house there were trim beehives of modern pattern, and the stone runner that took the fountain's overflow to a stream was weedless. I remembered the account of the Patriarchate in that valuable book, *Travels in the Slavonic Provinces of Turkey-in-Europe*, by Miss Muir Mackenzie and Miss Irby, so penetrating in its view of the Balkans that, though it was written seventy-six years ago, it still answers some questions that the modern tourist will find unanswered anywhere else. These two ladies arrived here with a guard of Moslem Albanian soldiers, with the intention of staying the night, and found terrified monks who, with an inhospitability most uncharacteristic of the Slav or the Orthodox Church, made every effort to turn them away. The ladies, who were, like so many Victorian women outside fiction, models of courage and good sense, turned their guards out of the room and talked to the monks privately, and found that the poor wretches had had all their food seized by a passing troop of Moslem Albanians, and were terrified lest the new invaders should punish them for their empty cupboards. When the ladies met the situation by sending their guards not only out of the room but out of the monastery, there was still some delay before they could get to bed, since the relative flea population of the different rooms had to be considered, and empty windows had to be fitted with glazed frames, which were not brought out till the soldiers had gone. It is a very strong compact of medieval discomfort and medieval insecurity. Nothing could be more remote from the present atmosphere which could be best expressed by the Scottish word 'douce.' Yes, we were standing in as douce a wee policy as could be wished.

The Abbot still did not come. We passed some time looking at the carvings on the fountain, which had an extremely primitive air yet in one panel represented a man carrying a fairly modern rifle, but Constantine grew nervous and restless and we took him off to look at the church. It lay on our right, among some walnuts and mulberries and pines, the green ground rising steep behind it. 'I have a prejudice against this church,' said my husband, as we went towards it, 'because a French author wrote of it, "*Elle a la couleur tendre de la chair des blondes.*" ' I said, in some bewilderment, 'This is even more than I should have asked of you, my dear.' 'I felt strongly,' he explained, 'that he should not have followed that sentence with his next, "*Elle est bâtie de gros blocs rectangulaires, irréguliers.*" The picture one is left with is hardly pleasing.' But indeed what was in the French author's mind was very apparent. The church is actually the colour of a fair woman's skin, where it gets some weathering but not much, say in the throat or just above the wrist; and in form it is a many-breasted Diana of Ephesus. It is an assembly of three small churches lying side by side, each with a cupola and a rounded apse, and all its masses are maternally curved. It seemed very fitting that there should come out of the porch a company of matrons in whom age had destroyed all that is evanescent in womanhood, all that is peculiar to the period of mating and child-bearing, yet who might have served gloriously as types of their sex because what was left was so plainly dedicated to all its essential purposes, the continuity of life and its harmony. They were slender and erect, like the old women of Ochrid, but lacked that aristocratic and even luxurious air which was natural enough in a town with its Byzantine past; they might have been Romans when Rome was still a sturdy republic. All of them were old enough to remember the bad days in Petch when the Turks had so encouraged the Albanian Moslems to ill-treat their Christian fellow-Slavs that at every Serb funeral the corpse was pelted with stones and filth; but they carried themselves with the most untroubled dignity. It came back to me that Miss Muir Mackenzie and Miss Irby had been immensely impressed by a woman of Petch called Katerina Simitch, a childless widow who carried on a Christian school for girls, with a courage that never broke before the persistent hostility of the Moslems. She was a nun solely because the status was useful to her in her nationalist work; the Englishwomen's descriptions of her evoke the calm and wise personality of a great statesman. Yet it is safe to say that she took her vows without impiety, for in those days Christianity and Slav nationalism must have seemed, even to the most spiritual, almost one and the same. These women who were coming out of the church would certainly be kin to Katerina Simitch's pupils, and some might even be of her blood. If she had seen them she would have felt pride. She would have taken for granted their quiet fierceness and their fleet dignity for it was hers also, and she could not have conceived Slav women otherwise; but she would have recognized a sign of new times, and rejoiced at it, in the white sleeves which were disclosed by their black cloth boleros. They were made of the striped silk which is woven in the district; in Katerina's day only a few Christian women could afford to buy it, or even to make it, since the mulberry leaves for the silkworms cost more than Christians could afford.

We went into the porch, which formed a long hall outside the three churches. There were two more old women sitting and talking thoughtfully on a stone bench that ran round the wall, one holding a branch cut from a walnut tree. Their ease, and a proud and hospitable gesture that this woman made with her walnut branch when she saw we were visitors come to admire, recalled the history of these churches.

The first had been built in the early thirteenth century by a Patriarch named Arsenius, by order of St Sava, who felt that the seat of the Serbian archiepiscopate, Zhitcha, was dangerously exposed to Hungarian invasion from the West and Tartar invasion from the East, and told him to find a safer shelter for it in the South. Here the growing Serbian civilization had the centre of its spiritual life, and when Stephen Dushan was obliged to detach his Church from the domination of Constantinople this became the seat of the Patriarchate. It was to meet the needs of this increasing importance that two other churches were joined to it in the following hundred years. When the Turks came the independence of the Serbian Church was destroyed, and for a time the Christian Slavs were again subject to Constantinople. But in the sixteenth century there took place the drama of the Sokolovitch brothers, which we had already heard of at Grachanitsa, to which their complicity had added the great porch. One, known as Mehmed, was taken by the Turks as a child and reared as a Janizary, and had risen to be Grand Vizier, in which office he restored the Serbian National Church and made his brother, the monk Macarius, Patriarch of Petch with many privileges. It would be interesting to know how seriously the state of such a renegade as Mehmed was regarded: whether time and repetition rubbed down the crime till it was accepted as a legitimate ruse of Christian self-preservation, or whether it preserved its primal horror. Through this porch Macarius must have walked many thousand times, and either he was not glad, not sorry, child of a twilit age, where faith was grey with incrustations of compromise, or he believed that his brother must burn in Hell, and must have been sorely perturbed to consider that he could not give the saving bread and wine to his people had not his brother chosen damnation. But there exists no record of these people's interior lives. As yet humanity has chronicled little more than its simpler and more agreeable experiences.

In any case Macarius carried on his work efficiently; and he was succeeded by a number of able patriarchs until the Great Trek to the Danube in 1690, when the Patriarchate was transferred to its present seat at Karlovats, which we had visited among its lilacs from Belgrade. But that did not mean that the building was ever wholly abandoned. There was always some ecclesiastical activity here, even in the darkest days of the Turkish subjection during the nineteenth and early twentieth centuries. This continuity of Christian worship resulted, as it often does, in destruction of the most valuable part of the Christian heritage. St Mark's would be far more beautiful if Venice had not been prosperous enough to alter and adorn it for some hundreds of years after it had attained its perfection; and here in the three churches of Petch the most exquisite Serbo-Byzantine frescoes were covered over during recent times with pious trivialities paid for by peasants who wanted to mark their appreciation of the comfort they had received there throughout the long ages of their servitude. These are now, as at Neresi, being removed from the walls, so that one may see the old beside the new, and learn again the paradox by which the greatest tragic art has been produced. In the happy Austria of the eighteenth and early nineteenth centuries Mozart and Beethoven both looked into the dark springs of human destiny; in the petty and sordid Austria of the late nineteenth and early twentieth centuries, which every day carried the plot for the doom of itself and Europe a stage further, there was heard the clear ripple of the waltz and the operetta. Here at every ragged edge that joins the frescoes which were divided by from three to four hundred years it is shown that the free and fortunate subjects of the Nemanyas could bear to contemplate the mystery of pain, while the downtrodden Christian rayahs asked only to think of favour and of prettiness. The contrast was at its most positive where a charming fresco, visibly affected by what I have called the Turkish Regency style, depicting some bland and chic angels having a party at a table obviously arranged by someone with a modish sense of fun, before a window hung with coquettish muslin curtains, was being hewn asunder and flaked off to bring to light an enormous and merciless presentation of the relationship between man and his mother.

All these early frescoes, though they range in date over two hundred years and show marked variations in style, are alike in being merciless. Here the angels sweep down like furies, the Holy

Ghost is seen as a bird of prey, and at the Transfiguration the multitude is aghast, as well it might be at that demonstration that man is wholly deceived by the material world, and there is another one beyond for him to master. In the dome of one of the three churches there is a Christ Ruler of All, dressed in an amber robe and crowned with a golden halo against a silver background, confined by a whirlwind of angels, which puts before the eye, as some great music has put before the ear, the ecstasy of pain that comes from great gifts, great power, great responsibility. Sometimes this central core of harshness is disguised by the most delicious grace. One fresco represents the Mother of God feeding the infant Jesus at her breast while three women adore him and two angels stand in waiting, which recalls a Duccio or a Giunta Pisano, but shows an even greater refinement, an ethereal force very rarely present in Italian painting. It is as if the artist was working in a world where grossness and feebleness were almost unknown, or at least under the ban of the common consciousness. But even here there is a lack of mercy. The infant Jesus is not so much a baby as a reduced adult, a miscroscopic sage and ruler, and he is sucking his mother's nipple with mature unsmiling greed, as if he meant to take the last drop and give her no payment of gratitude, although her body is a soft mass about him, protecting him as the pulp of a ripe fruit about its kernel. The resemblance between the Nemanyan and the Tudor ages is strong. So did the Elizabethan poets know that though Elizabeth was Gloriana and England glorious, God is not kind to man, not here on earth.

But the most merciless of all these frescoes was the Virgin and Child that stared out through the angels' tea-party. This is terrible, with a terror that makes the efforts at realism of later artists such as Rouault seem the fee-fo-fum of a child playing at ogres in the nursery. A vast Virgin is massive as a mother must seem to the child she picks up in her arms and carries where he has not wished to go, that is, unfairly massive; and she grips him with fingers of masonic strength, which are as ten towers, ten lighthouses, affixed to her huge palm. Her features are as gigantesquely marked as all adults' must seem to a baby's hand, and she appears unreasonably stern, as those yet unacquainted with the dangers of this world must consider their mothers. The love and kindness published on her huge face is as a huge army entrenched about its object. At her bosom the Christ child is poised like a tiny fettered athlete, his muscular legs bared by runners' shorts, his glittering enraged face proclaiming revolt against this imprisoning benevolence and shining with the intention of flight to a remote and glorious goal which is his secret.

A mind unaware of timidity had considered those questions, 'Who is my brother or my brethren?' and 'Woman, what have I to do with thee?' and had taken into account certain agonizing arguments he had heard in the world about him.

They were still, it seemed, being carried on. Constantine turned his back on the fresco and took two letters out of his pockets, which he had already told us in the automobile he had received from Gerda and his mother that morning. He opened them both, stared at them in turn, and seemed to grow hot though the shadow of the church was cool about us. 'You are worried,' I said. 'Why do you not leave us and go straight home to Belgrade?' He answered in a whining tone, 'But if I go home I will only have to take round a French woman journalist who is coming early next week to write about us barbarians. I do not like these political Frenchwomen, they are all the same; they are all like Geneviève Tabouis and Andrée Viollis, they drag round the world and disapprove of all that real men do.' He looked up at the tremendous Virgin, his upper lip lifting from his teeth in a sneer; his eyes left her and stared apprehensively into space. 'I have other ideas what women should do,' he said weakly, as if he were very tired. We turned away and looked at other frescoes and the great marble tombs of the patriarchs, but he followed us restlessly, and we went out of the church.

Outside I saw a monk, whom I knew to be the Abbot because he wore the broad scarlet sash of his office, standing under a very twisted old nut tree, talking to the old women who had passed us as we went into the church. Now that I saw them from a distance I noted, what I had not seen before, since my eyes had been fixed on their magnetic faces and their snowy sun-bright sleeves, that they wore not skirts but trousers of dark flowered material, gathered at the ankle into a black braided cuff, which seemed incongruous garments on women who might very well have been heads of colleges. They were speaking to the Abbot with a charming reverence which was due partly to their sense of his priesthood and partly to his special suitability for it; for they were looking at him with calm and chaste approbation of his extreme good looks. He was a tall man with a clear white skin and a dark wavy beard, like one of the Assyrians in the British Museum; everything about him spoke of quiet strength and good health. He must have pleased them by the proof he gave that their darling care, the race, was still sound. There was standing a little distance off a monk of very different appearance. He was extremely short and so round-shouldered that he was nearly hunchbacked, and his long hair and beard shone chorus-girl golden. The Abbot looked up and saw me coming out of the church with my husband and Constantine just behind me, and with a curious combination of a welcoming smile and an embarrassed gesture he moved towards us, joined by the small blond monk. He was glad to see us; he was a Serb from Serbia and knew Constantine's name, and in any case he came of good Orthodox stock with its tradition of hospitality; yet he was not at ease. After he had greeted us he introduced the short blond monk, saying, 'This is a brother from the monastery at Dechani who came over to help me at a special service we had this morning. I am afraid he will have to go at once, if he is to catch his motor bus back.'

But the little creature pressed forward and with the pinched and dwarfish vivacity of a pantomime child shook his finger at us, crying, in a peculiar German, 'I know what you are thinking about me!' It was an intensely embarrassing remark coming from one so physically odd, but at once he continued, with a great deal of trilling laughter, 'You are thinking, "How fair he is! How can he be so fair, being a Yugoslavian? He is fair as a German!" ' We had, of course, been thinking nothing of the sort, for a number of Slavs, particularly Bosnians, are fairer than Germans, are as fair as Scandinavians. All that had struck us about his hair was the peculiar harshness of its colour. 'I will explain the mystery to you,' he tittered. 'I am a Croat, yes, I am a Croat from Zagreb. But my mother, my beloved and saintly mother, she was a true German born in Austria, and she it was who gave me my golden hair!' His little fists swept forward the curls that hung down his back so that they covered his eyes and became tangled in his beard. 'Always when I was a child people stopped in the street and said, "Who is this child that is fair like an angel, that looks like a real German child?" and my mother would say, "It is a German child, and yet it is not a German child." '

The creature reeled about in paroxysms of laughter, and the Abbot said, 'If you do not hurry you will miss the motor bus.' 'Yes, yes,' the little creature cried, 'I must not do that, for I receive all the distinguished visitors who come to Dechani. I speak to them my mother-tongue, the beautiful German. This afternoon I must receive an Italian general, and his wife who is a princess; tomorrow morning I must receive a professor who is at the head of the greatest university in France. They will have to be shown round by me, for the other monks do not know German, it is only I who speak German.' 'The motor bus,' said the Abbot. 'Oh, isn't it a shame that I must go! Well, good-bye, good-bye, good-bye!' He ran away from us with tiny twinkling steps, smiling at us over his shoulder and undulating his outstretched arm, like an old-fashioned fairy queen quitting the stage of a pantomime.

The Abbot took off his tall hat, blew into it, replaced it, and evidently felt much better. It was an odd gesture, but we all knew what he was feeling and sympathized. He had suffered acutely from this bizarre interlude, because, as we were to find out later on, he was primarily a country gentleman. That was why he had been made the Abbot here. It was his duty to restore the estate of the Patriarchate to order and productivity, so that the Christians of Petch might see how their God wished them to live in fair weather, when martyrdom was no longer required from them. In this he was succeeding admirably, for the monastery had that look of agrarian piety to be seen in many French and some English farms and market gardens. I do not think that the frescoes meant very much to him, but he spoke with great pleasure of the two visits that Bernard Berenson and Gabriel Millet had made for the purpose of examining them. He had his full measure of the countryman's feeling for craftsmanship, and he could see that these people knew their jobs. Also, he explained with enthusiasm that he had derived great enjoyment from the handsomeness of Mr Berenson and his personal exquisiteness. 'He is like a prince!' he said. 'With his white hair, and his fine hands, and his slender body, and all his clothes so neat and clean, he is like someone from a great court. I hope that there are many pictures of him all over England and America.'

He took us up to his parlour, which was sweet and clean, and we drank good coffee and ate crystalline spoonfuls of quince jam, while he talked of his work and the place. Yes, it was beautiful, though in winter the winds came down the gorge from Montenegro very bitterly, and there was a great deal of snow. The land was very good, though this monastery was far from being rich like Dechani, and he found the people who worked for it very pleasant indeed, particularly the Albanians. We noted again the liking that most Serbs now feel for the Albanians, who during the Turkish occupation were their most constant tormentors. His congregations, he went on to say, were very good and pious, and came many miles to the services. Yet the Abbot's large handsomeness, which should have been as placid as cream, was dimmed by a cloud of perplexity and exasperation immediately he had given us an assurance of his satisfaction with the district. His dark brows drew together under his clear fleshy forehead, and his eyes, luminous as a peat stream, seemed to see something not very far off and not entirely gratifying, perhaps the main street of Petch as it would appear to eyes for whom nothing in it had the charm of unfamiliarity, a track, too wide for any traffic that could conceivably pass this way, with telegraph posts marching along it in full futility, bringing no useful messages to the town.

We should have gone to Dechani that afternoon, but at lunch it was plain that Constantine's fever had come back to him, so he telephoned to the Abbot and arranged that we should go the next morning instead. We sent Constantine to bed and tried to sleep a little ourselves, for we were both deadly tired. But I found it difficult to rest, because whenever my mind was not preoccupied by some new sight it was invaded by the recollection of some of the tremendous events which had been shown or explained to me during the last two months: the struggle of the Croat soul between its Slav self and its Western education, the outlawry of the Dalmatian Uskoks, the martyrdoms of Franz Ferdinand and Sophie Chotek and Princip and Chabrinovitch, the conflict between the Obrenovitches and the Karageorgevitches, the magical practices of Macedonian Christianity, the rites of St George's Eve, the glory of Grachanitsa and the self-slaughter of Kossovo, the noble effort of Trepcha, and the nihilism of Gerda, with its demand that all these efforts of the human spirit should be set aside and that all the forces of the universe should be directed to the purpose of cramming her with whatever material belonged to others. When at last I slept a dream distressed me by its proof that the thing which stung Constantine's hand was his wife. She did not want him to write any more poetry, because he was a Jew like Heine.

My husband was awakened by the scamper of mice among our shoes, so we gave up and went for a walk on the hills overlooking the Patriarchate on the other side of the river, among budding woods and through meadows tangled with pale-purple and blue flowers. We met a good-looking young man who was stripped to the waist and carried a bright-blue shirt and wet bathing dress. He looked at us very hard and then turned back, and asked if he might walk with us and show us one of the hermits' caves which are so numerous in this district that they gave the town its name; for *Petch* is an old word for cave. He spoke a didactic kind of English which he said he had learned in America as a child, during a visit to an uncle, but which had the hollow ring of the propagandist printed word. 'You may wonder why I approached you when my torso is nude,' he said, 'but I did so in full confidence for I am sure that you are people who have swept all unwholesome prejudices out of your minds, and are open-minded and receptive to such healthful ideas as sun-bathing.' 'How did you know that?' asked my husband. 'I watched you last night as you had dinner outside the hotel,' answered the young man, 'and I am sure of it.' 'But what did we do as we dined that convinced you we're in favour of sun-bathing?' pursued my husband. 'You are very polite to your wife,' said the young man; 'it is evident that you have conquered your animal instinct to oppress the female and have accepted intellectually and emotionally the point of view that by child-bearing she contributes as much to the state as the male by his characteristic activities. You talk together very intently also, so it is evident that you have raised her to your intellectual level. Yesterday I went back to my house and made my wife come out and look at you as an example, for she is of these parts, and she is not always sure that she ought to be advanced. She is dragged down by her early surroundings. But she is very beautiful and very good, and there is something special about her which would be difficult to describe. But besides your attitude to each other, you have the appearance of cultured people. I am sure you read many books. What sort of books do you prefer and why?'

Towards such people who ask such questions my husband feels as a shepherd towards lambs. He does not ask himself whether he would not rather be thinking his own thoughts or spending the time with companions more like himself, he wholly abandons himself to the feeling that there is a breed valuable to the community and that he must cherish every member of it. He talked with the boy about books as we strolled along the hillside under green firwoods so high that the spring had only lately reached them, through the flowery pastures, past a ruined house where snakes slid among rank hemlocks and hellebores, to the visibly icy reservoirs where the boy had been bathing, and up a grassy slope to the cavern. It still glowed faintly with holy pictures painted by a medieval hermit, and it resounded with cries that might have been thought to proceed from a spirit in travail, had not the angular behind and bell-rope tail of some form of cattle been visible in its depths. On the grass near by, in the shadow cast by an acacia tree, sat an old Albanian, his bright eyes and smile fresh as a bubbling spring. We felt that he would have been sure to pick the best place for a rest, so we sat ourselves down beside him.

The young man exchanged jokes with him; and one was so funny that the young man rolled over and over on the ground, but he remembered to pick himself up and say, in a superior manner, 'The Albanians are a people of great mother-wit, but they are not at all advanced,' and started talking about books again. His special interests were economics and political theory, and he called himself a Communist, but he had in fact a far more intelligent interest in Marxism than most Yugoslavs who claim that name. They are for the most part simply exponents of the age-long opposition between the country and the towns and have much more sympathy with William Morris than with Marx, but this young man had read *Das Kapital* with a mind of good tough critical fibre. My husband repeated to him some of the most amusing passages out of H. W. B. Joseph's book on the Marxian theory of value, and in spite of his faith he laughed aloud and rolled over on his back just as he had done at the Albanian's jokes. 'Who is the man that wrote that book?' he asked. 'He must have a wonderful mind, though of course essentially frivolous. Do you know him?' 'He has one of the finest minds in the world,' said my husband, 'and he was my philosophy tutor at Oxford.' 'Oh, what I could do,' cried the boy, 'if I had the advantages you have had!' He sat up and held his chin in his hands and looked sulkily down the valley, and then a light stirred in his eyes and he turned to my husband. 'I heard them say in the town that you came from Kossovska Mitrovitsa and that you were great friends with the people at the Trepcha mines. Could you not give me a letter to the Gospodin Mac asking him to give me work? For there is nothing here for me to do. I help my father in the hotel he keeps, but there is not enough work for the two of us, and I am too good for the work there is, I could do much better. Sometimes I weep, because Petch has nothing for me to do.'

On our way down to dinner we went into Constantine's room to see how he was faring with his fever, and on the landing we saw that the chambermaid was ironing her pile of sheets as she had been doing the night before, but this time she was quietly weeping. I said to Constantine, 'Your little admirer is crying her eyes out, have you been cruel to her?' He answered, 'No, she has told me what grieves her and it is something more important than me. She came in here to bring me an orangeade and she sat on my bed and she said, "I should be happy, for they pay me well here. They know well that the hotel is falling to pieces and that if I were not here to scrub the floors and keep the mattresses clean we would be overrun with mice and beetles and bugs. But sometimes I cannot bear life." I said to her, "What is it you cannot bear, my little one?" and she answered, "It is death. It makes me so angry. Three days ago a man died here, he was a very rich man and he held high office in the town. When the Prime Minister came here he was among those who received him, and he wore a tall hat such as the gentlemen wear in Budapest. I knew him well, and he was a proud and powerful man, with many things passing through his head. And three days ago he died, and yesterday they carried his coffin through the streets, and he was nothing, just a body that would soon begin to stink and would be just dirt, just filth!" And then she began to cry, so I said, "Did you love him, my little one?" and she answered, "No, not at all, but it makes me so angry that death can do such a thing, that one day there can be a man, full of importance, and the next day there is nothing. It should not be so. Oh, I felt so furious, I wanted to fight death and kill him." And she sat there and wept, and I think she was speaking the truth. I think she had not loved this man but was only enraged at the idea of death, for she wept like a woman who has been insulted, not like a woman who has been hurt. Then she said, "I must iron my sheets," and she beat my pillow, and she went from me.' When we went out on to the landing she had left her task for a moment, and a guttering candle, standing on the rucked ironing-blanket between a pile of rough sheets and smooth ones, cast tremendous shadows on the walls and ceiling as we passed.

As we sat down in the restaurant there came to our table the traveller in ready-made clothing we had seen praying on the road near Kossovska Mitrovitsa, who was so civil that we asked him to dine with us. He accepted our invitation with alacrity because he longed to speak of the abode of joy, a blend of Venice in Carnival time and the New Jerusalem, to which his memory had transformed Aberdeen. But there was some other alchemic agent beside his memory; there were personalities at work which had softened the gaunt handsomeness of that town and injected blandness into the veins of my maternal country to mix with its grim vigour. For he spoke of many people he had met in Great Britain with tenderness, particularly of one woman whom he proved by his story to be remarkable. She had organized the scheme for placing the Serbian refugee boys in English and Scottish homes and schools and had travelled perpetually to see how they were getting on; and later she had astonished them by her interest in them as individuals. 'She was like a *baba*, like a grandmother,' he said, 'but many people are fond of children, and young people, it is like being fond of dogs or horses. It is what happens afterwards that matters. And do you know, last year, she came out here. She said she was getting very old and might die before long, and she wanted to see what had happened to her boys. So she travelled all over the country seeking us out, and when we had done well she was so pleased. She came to my house and had tea with my wife and saw my children, and she sat and nodded her head and said, "This is very good, this is very good indeed. It couldn't be better. I shall often think about this when I get home." She had really liked us boys, for ourselves, not because we were boys. That I think very nice.' And indeed we thought it a paradisal action, full of promise that earth need not always be what it is.

'I shall always be glad that I was in England,' he went on, 'for I learned to do things neatly and in order and at a definite time, which we do not do here, and this has made me successful in business. Not very successful, I am not an eagle; but I have all I want and much more than I expected as a child, and I can keep my wife well and give her a nice home, and my children are strong and well-educated. But I am glad I came back to Yugoslavia, for it is a most beautiful country.' He asked us if we had visited many of the monasteries, and was sorry that we had not visited more in Serbia proper, in the valleys south of Belgrade, but glad that we had seen Sveti Naum and the Frushka Gora. 'How do you know the monasteries so well?' asked my husband. 'You cannot take much time off to look at them while you are travelling in your business.' 'Then I have no time at all,' he replied, 'but I belong to a society in Belgrade, and every time there is a holiday such as Easter or Whitsuntide we members hire motor charabancs and we drive off with our wives and children to some monastery and stay there two or three days. It is an excellent way of spending a holiday, for it keeps us close to the Church, even when we do not like what the patriarchs do, and forget to go to services in Belgrade, and it reminds us of our national history, and the places are always exceedingly beautiful, and there are many good monks whom it is pleasant to meet.' I tried to imagine Canterbury or Gloucester invaded by a Bank Holiday crowd, who picnicked all over the Close and sang and danced and drank, and occasionally rushed into the cathedral and joined heartily in the service and rushed out when they felt like it, and freely and familiarly conversed with the Dean and Chapter. The imagination cannot contrive such a picture. The Anglican Church has bought decorum at such a great price that it is indelicate to imagine her deprived of her purchase. 'I am glad,' continued our friend, 'that you are to see Dechani. It is one of the most beautiful monasteries. My friends and I spent last Easter there and we were amazed by its richness. It gives some idea of what our land must have been like in the days of the Nemanyas.' 'Has Dechani much influence on this town?' I asked. 'It does not seem so,' answered the traveller; 'this is a miserable town, not because the people here are not good, for the Serbs of Petch have always been remarkable for character and intelligence, but because nothing ever happens here. They say that dinars amounting to two or three thousand pounds a month are paid into the town as war pensions and gratuities, and the people live chiefly on that. It is a subsidy of a little over two pounds a year per head. You see, under the Turks it was a frontier town, and that meant a lot of money, both in the employment of troops and in selling the troops goods and in smuggling; and the people had a great interest in maintaining their faith against persecution. But now they need a new thing.'

He excused himself early, for he had to start driving south the next morning shortly after dawn; but he did not go till he had performed a service for us in the way of some supplies from a chemist. He was an altogether admirable person, but his place was almost at once taken by a person whom we found less admirable, the Dane who spoke German like a German. 'Good evening,' he said. 'I suppose you will be going to Tsetinye tomorrow?' 'No,' said my husband. 'But what are you doing here so long?' demanded the Dane. 'We are tourists,' said my husband. 'But there is nothing here to keep a tourist longer than one day!' exclaimed the Dane in a tone of exasperation. 'We have not yet seen Dechani,' said my husband. 'But you should have seen Dechani in the morning, and the Patriarchate in the afternoon!' the Dane said in a very loud and threatening voice. 'What are you doing here in Petch?' asked my husband. The Dane clearly thought this an impertinent question. 'I am a traveller in agricultural machinery,' he answered coldly, as if to tell us to mind our own business. 'I suppose you will be here for weeks,' said my husband. 'Why do you say weeks?' asked the Dane. 'Well, would you rather I said days, months, or years?' replied my husband. In open ill-humour the Dane went back to his own table and studied a German newspaper.

Petch II

The next morning we spoke of this suspicious person to Constantine, as we breakfasted outside the hotel. 'Certainly he will be a German agent,' he said. 'That is the second we have come across, for I am sure the little one in knickerbockers at Sveti Naum was a German agent also. But I cannot think what can be going to happen here, for this is not an important place. In Macedonia the Germans make much trouble with the Bulgarians, and it is worth their while, but here there are only Albanians, and it is worth nobody's while to stir them up.' The day was hotter and there had been no rain for days; a wind came down from the wall of rock at the end of the gorge, stabbed us with unexpected chill, and blew into our teeth, into our eyes, a film of warm dust from the high-street. The slight discomfort aroused in Constantine his chronic malaise, and he turned to us with a gorgon smile. 'Yes, the Germans are terrible people,' he sneered, 'they employ secret agents to serve their interests abroad. I suppose the English never did so, not in Russia, not in India.' 'Of course we use secret agents like every other power,' said my husband, 'and sometimes we use them justifiably and sometimes unjustifiably, which again can be said of any other power. What is interesting us is not the fact that this man is a secret agent, but that he practises his art with so little discretion that we have only to describe his proceedings for you to be quite sure that he is a secret agent.' 'Yes,' squealed Constantine, clenching his fists, 'the English are always cold and dignified and they are never ridiculous, and the Germans are clowns and make fools of themselves, but there is a mystery there, and what is behind it may not mean that the English are saved and the Germans damned.' His voice sounded charlatanish and bewildered; he was using the spiritual vocabulary of the Slav, who is preoccupied with the ideas of failure and humiliation, to justify his allegiance to Gerda, who had no sympathy with them and would have regarded his interest in them as proof of his Slav inferiority, and as he spoke his taste exposed to him his own falsity, though he persisted in it.

But once we had started on our way to Dechani Constantine became himself again, for the road was beautiful. I have said that Petch stands where a wall of mountains running from the north just fails to meet a wall of mountains running from the south. The road from Kossovska Mitrovitsa to Petch lies under the mountains that

come from the north; the road from Petch to Dechani lies under
the mountains that come from the south, and passes country that is
better watered and shadowed, and is therefore green with a fertility
that seems to well up from deep wet roots. Forests are thick on the
hillside, tall trees hold up handsome densities of foliage, and on
the left of the road stretches the plain we had seen on our way
from Kossovska Mitrovitsa, that is rich and damp as the Vale of
Pewsey. In its fat fields parties of labourers worked in close-set
teams, looking like a *corps de ballet* in their white pleated skirts,
and in the villages women stately as the queens in their frescoes
gossiped round the fountains. But the houses we passed told an
appalling story. The narrow windows were set high, so that they
could be shot from and not into, and the walls were pock-marked
with bullets. I remembered having read that on this road there
stand two houses, side by side, which in 1909 were the subject of
an imbecile tragedy. In that year a man living in one slew four men of
the family living in the other. He had to flee. That is natural enough.
What was not natural, what was as artificial a constriction of human
nature as any abuse of Western civilization, was that thirteen other
men belonging to his family, who had nothing whatsoever to do with
the crime, were obliged to flee. Had they not done so, the institution
of the blood-feud, which flourished unchecked under Turkish rule,
would have involved them in a welter of butchery, in which all
must have acquired the guilt of murder and would themselves have
been murdered. In 1919, under Yugoslavian rule, the criminal
was arrested, and his innocent relatives, with the consent of the
inhabitants of the other house, who were equally anxious to be
relieved from the blood-feud, were able to return home.

Order is something. I thought so again when we passed through
a grove of trees which the Turks, in their great love for any
beauty that did not involve careful maintenance, had chosen for
a graveyard. It must have been at this grove that the downtrodden
monks of Dechani had waited when Miss Muir Mackenzie and
Miss Irby came to visit them on their way from the Patriarchate
more than seventy years ago, that they might beg the ladies not to
bring their Turkish military guard to the monastery, as they were
worn out with defending their treasures and the sanctity of their
altar. Miss Mackenzie and Miss Irby had had to act with great
decisiveness, even scribbling notes to demonstrate their command
over the magical art of writing, before they could rid themselves
of the soldiers, who had evidently promised themselves great sport
at the monastery. Now the grove was empty save for an Albanian
shepherd-boy, pretty as a girl, who sat playing on a pipe, while his

flock nibbled among the tree-trunks and the marble stumps of the tombs, dappled like them with sunshine and shadow.

We were at Dechani. Across a wide neatness of farmland we looked into a glen of the Highland sort, with a background of mountain falling back from mountain to show snow peaks that must have been many miles distant, far beyond the Albanian frontier. The nearer hills were emerald on their lower slopes and above that shrill green, where there were beeches and limes; and where there were pines they were feathered with blackness. At the mouth of the glen was the white oblong of the monastery. It was larger than any other we had seen, and even from this distance it could be seen that it was a rarity, a jewel. As we drew nearer to it down a by-road we could see that it could never be spoiled, and also that it was as near to being spoiled at this moment as it could ever be. For it was covered with scaffolding and surrounded with the potent and infective disorder that builders, by a malign kind of compensation, diffuse round what they repair. But when we had crossed the ramp of planks that was now the only entrance to the monastery, and picked our way among the trenches and heaps of rubble in the courtyard, it was fully apparent that what we had come to see was a pearl of architecture. It has the unity of a pearl, its living texture, and even its tint, for it is built of blocks of white, grey, and rose marble, which merge in the eye to a soft pale glow.

It happens, however, that I have no great taste for pearls; and I did not like Dechani. It represents an inspired moment in that phase of Christian architecture when Armenian influence fused with the Byzantine and Lombard schools; and many French churches demonstrate what virtue can be in that conjunction. But with the religious tolerance characteristic of the Nemanyas Stephen Dechanski had employed a Roman Catholic architect, a Franciscan friar, to build this, his chief, and, indeed, his only remarkable foundation; and this contact with the Western Church has introjected an element into Dechani which strikes an eye accustomed, as mine was by this time, to the Byzantine standard, as soft and impure. In the Roman Catholic faith it often appears that the partitions between the different kinds of human activity have been broken down, and that the worshippers often bring to religion desires which could be properly satisfied only in the sphere of sex or by the exercise of power or the enjoyment of respect. Hence the Church may often, through its art or ritual or dogma, speak of voluptuousness or pomp or respectability; and it seemed to me that Dechani spoke of all three. Grachanitsa was built for people who never thought of sex when they came to church, since they had already judged its claims in relation to society and had settled them, who had been assigned their places in the social structure and had play for their powers within those limits, and who knew that if they were to earn the respect of their fellows they must be good soldiers or scholars or craftsmen. But Dechani might have been built for people who were repressed and sentimentally lecherous, who were acquiring a nihilist standard of ability and a negative standard of virtue because an honoured place in the community could be bought simply by the continued possession of material goods. It is exquisite, but it is unaustere and complacent.

At this moment, in any case, it was hard to give it its due of admiration, although its perfection could not be disguised by the scaffolding. The trenches and rubble-heaps among which we walked had a look of more than necessary disorder, as if nobody had tried to mitigate it out of pride in the place; and there had come to stare at us several young monks, students in the theological college, who were as unkempt as they were uncouth. Their clothes were dirty and neglected. The cassock of one had no buttons at the chest, and the gap showed an equally buttonless shirt, from which there projected a bunch of matted and lustreless hair. Nobody can blame a monk if the intensity of his religious life leaves him no attention to spare for his body. But the lax faces of these young men, which were spongy with boredom, showed that their untidiness was due to no such preoccupation. Simply they had been removed from the discipline of their peasant homes and no other discipline had been imposed on them. But they were silent as they dragged after us, and we were getting on with our inspection of the outside of the church, until there suddenly ran out on us from behind a corner the golden-haired little monk we had seen at the Patriarchate the day before.

'Do you remember meeting me yesterday?' he cried, clapping his hands and making movements which, though contracted and not particularly agile, nevertheless indicated a feeling for ballet-dancing. 'I am the monk who you thought must be a German because I am so fair, and I told you that I am a German and not a German! Well, here I am. I told you that I receive all visitors because I alone know German, the other monks know none.' He kept on talking in the same strain of racial and personal coquetry, while we irritably tried to go on looking at the church, until an older monk, a man of dignity and fine manners, came out and wearily rebuked him. He had, it seemed, been sent out to bid us to come at once to lunch, since the Abbot had to start on a journey early in the afternoon and could not wait. The golden-haired monk said immediately, 'That is what I have been trying to tell them, but none of them understands German very well.' We went into the monastery buildings which formed three sides of the courtyard, and were taken to a dining-room where the Abbot, a middle-aged man with black hair and a multivermiform beard of tight, black, corkscrew curls, sat at a table with four or five monks. He greeted us in fluent but not very good French, and proposed the health of our English King in a glass of rakia. When we had swallowed it and my husband had made a short and suitable speech, he proposed the health of our Queen; and before the meal began we had to toast most of the royal family. Fortunately, he had not yet learned of the existence of Princess Margaret Rose.

The occasion was not without liveliness. The Abbot was far from unintelligent; as well as his fair French he spoke Russian, Greek, and Turkish, and he talked with some vivacity. All the monks, except for one of Oriental appearance, across whose yellow face there passed no shade of expression, hung on his words and sometimes threw in laughing remarks. These last phrases would have been used if this had been a meal in a girls' boarding-school, but they were not therefore inappropriate. This establishment might easily have been named St. Hilda's or St. Winifred's. The most talkative monk, who was plump and dark and intense in manner, closely resembled many an art mistress. In spite of this light-hearted and quite innocent atmosphere the meal was not altogether agreeable. It was served on a cloth filthier than I have ever seen in any Balkan inn, and it was gross in quantity and quality. Since it was Friday this was a fast; and for that reason we were given barley soup, a stew of butter beans, a purée of potatoes with onion sauce, a very greasy stew of sardines and spinach, and a mess of rice cooked with fried potatoes. Of each dish we were given enough for a whole meal, and each was cooked without skill. The wild disregard of this menu for the digestive weaknesses of mankind reminded me of St. Augustine's monastic friends, mentioned in *The City of God*, who were able to produce an effect of singing by unusual means.

But there was here a lack of perception about other things than food. The Abbot politely mentioned Miss Muir Mackenzie and Miss Irby and their account of their visit to Dechani, and we tried to return the courtesy by speaking of other foreigners who had come to the monastery in the last few years. Constantine had sent many on their way from Belgrade, and I too knew several. We found that not one had made the slightest impression on the Abbot. He did not remember a single one of them. Nothing about any of them, no matter of what nationality or rank or profession, had excited his interest. He had forgotten the British Minister, a distinguished French diplomat who is also a man of letters, and an American scholar and an Italian philosopher, both eminent. At first we thought that these people had visited the convent before he had assumed office, but on examination of the dates we found it was not so. It may be objected that there was no reason why the head of a great religious institution should be interested in casual foreign tourists, but one of the personalities he had ignored was a Dutch artist who was also a mystic and a devout member of the Eastern Church.

The truth was, we discovered as the meal went on, that nothing in the West had any meaning for him; and, by an unfortunate historical accident, nothing had any meaning anywhere else either. His face was turned, as his repertory of languages suggested, towards the East, which was natural enough in an Orthodox priest who had taken orders before the Balkan wars, when his home was Turkish territory and the ally who promised to alter this was Tsarist Russia, and the new Turkey had no desire to be seen by him. He was therefore left isolated in a provinciality that would have been tolerable only if it had been transformed by spiritual genius. But of that there was no trace whatsoever. He spoke of the plot which Stoyadinovitch had made to placate Italy and the Croatian priests by a Concordat which gave the Roman Catholic Church an unfair advantage over the Orthodox Church; and he used just such words as might have come to any politician, untempered by charity or resignation. He spoke of the Montenegrins who worked on the monastery farmlands and lived in the neighbourhood with an unrestrained hostility very different from the discretion usually observed by priests in this country laid waste by racial enmities. There was no attempt in anything he said to improve upon the natural man or his natural state; and the effect was of a chattering lethargy, fatiguing to the ear, alarming to the heart.

'It is very interesting,' said Constantine; 'the man with the yellow face who is so silent and does not laugh, he is the son of a Turk and a Serbian woman. His mother seemed very happy with his father, and she grieved very much when he died, and then she and her son lived very happily. But when she came to die she had a long illness and often did not know what she spoke, and then he found out that it had always been a horrible grief to her that he and his father had not been Christians, so he promised her that he would become a monk, and she died happy.' There was no difficulty in understanding why he did not laugh. It would be a mystery past comprehending why one's best-beloved should have known no peace till she had condemned one to sit in this little room, listening to littleness.

But the church remained, and we went back to it as soon as the Abbot left. Its interior was far more beautiful than the exterior, for here the Serbian genius had not commissioned an alien to make it a masterpiece but had worked according to its own nature. Though the church had been built by Stephen Dechanski, it was given its frescoes and its furnishments by his son Stephen Dushan; and these bore further witness to the resemblance between his reign and the Elizabethan age. In each there was a coincidence between national expansion and a flowering of creative art. The flesh and the spirit waxed in a common beauty. There were several royal portraits, radiant with a Tudor positiveness, notably one of Stephen Dushan himself, which showed a tall, hale man of whom it could well be believed that, as his chroniclers tell, he was sometimes shaken by tremendous laughter. It is easy to imagine that his people thought of him as Elizabethans thought of Elizabeth, as a fountain of plenty, irrigating his land with richness. The astonishing degree of that plenty, the quality of that richness, was by an odd paradox supremely illustrated by a fresco depicting a martyrdom. An executioner waits ready to decapitate St. Barbara, his feet in dancing stance, his long fingers trying his sword edge. On his head is a high yellow hat, not lower than a couple of feet; his mantle is rose his tunic green. His victim bows before him, a rose-and-gold mantle swathing her blue robe. She too has assumed a dancing stance, for they are performing the well-known dance and counter-dance of sadist and masochist. This fresco proceeds from an intense experience of luxury. The painter has seen many kinds of textiles dipped in many dyes; he formed part of a society which treated even its most sinister functionaries honourably, so sure was it of its own honour; his kind had outstripped necessity and had therefore full leisure to examine their uncomprehended hearts.

But I could not look at these frescoes as I wished, for there was running and jumping around me the little golden-haired monk, who was talking insistently and, as time went on, impertinently and angrily. As soon as we had come in, Constantine, who was genuinely impassioned for the history and historical monuments of Serbia, had taken us to see the coffin lying on the marble tomb before the iconostasis which holds the masked and silk-shrouded body of Stephen Dechanski, and the other relics of the church, but now the tiresome little creature wanted to show them to me all over again. I looked round for Constantine and my husband, but they were out of sight. When I started to look for them the little creature ran in front of me, so I decided to wait where I was till they returned. I had therefore to look for a second time at the giant candle which was given to the monastery by the widow of the Tsar Lazar who was killed at Kossovo, with the direction that it should be lit only when that defeat was avenged, and which was duly lit by King Peter Karageorgevitch in 1913. But my eyes ranged round me to such wonders as an astonishing fresco which showed the martyred St. George, a beautiful creature bearing the signs of all mundane distinction who neither moves nor speaks because he is the victim of a murderous death, and two bishops and a fury-like angel, who lean over and, by a miraculous power impersonal and unloving as the force of a magnet, raise him back to life. 'You are not listening!' cried the little creature. 'Why will you not listen to me?' 'I am listening,' I said.

But he knew I was not. He had been telling me a story about his brother, which apparently made some claim on my sympathies, and had I been listening I would have been sure to make certain responses. 'I am afraid I do not understand German,' I pleaded. 'You understand it well enough,' he replied, 'it is simply that you are not attending; I will say it all over again.' I saw my husband come back into the church and I walked towards him, clapping my hands over my ears, mocked as I went by glimpses of magnificence, here a superb group of lions fighting with sphinxes, there an Annunciation that annihilates time by showing a rooftree throw the shadow of a cross between the Virgin and the angel, which I should not see again perhaps for years and could not look at under these conditions. When I reached my husband I forgot why I had come to him, for my eyes followed his to the chandelier above us, which was one of the glorious kind to be found in all Byzantine churches from the beginning. There is one in St. Sophia, and in every church on Mount Athos. Chains drop from the drum of the central dome and support a horizontal ring of metal links, closely set with candles and ornamented with icons. These links are very loosely joined, for at a certain point in the great nocturnal services the chandelier is set slowly swinging, and this covers the whole church with a shifting pattern of light and shadow, which is regarded as a symbol of the dance of the angels and saints before the heavenly throne. 'What sound, sober work, what sound, sober taste!' sighed my husband. The golden-haired monk pressed in on us, scolding and complaining, and I cried out, 'What can we do to get rid of him?' My husband said to him severely, in German, 'What is all this yammering about?' The little creature fell silent, looked down at his slippers, and cried out, 'Oh, dear, I must go and put on my galoshes!' As we watched him run away, my husband said, 'Here is Constantine, I must ask him to stop this.' But as Constantine came towards us he pointed over his shoulder, and again we forgot our irritation, this time out of interest in the party which one of the older monks was leading into the church.

There were two men, three women, one holding a baby in a wicker cradle, two little boys. They were Albanian Moslems. The men wore the white skullcaps that are to them as the fez to other Moslems, and their characteristic white serge trousers, braided with black about the loins and ankles, and clinging miraculously to the hip-bone. The little boys wore tiny skullcaps, tiny braided trousers. The women were veiled and wore floppy white dresses that fell in deep, limp frills like old-fashioned lampshades. In the tall multi-coloured square of painted walls, among the shafts of yellow light that drove down from the high windows, they looked pale and dusty like moths. The priest spoke to the men and they took off their white skullcaps and saw to it that the boys did likewise. He spoke to the women and they took off the veils slowly and clumsily, perhaps because they were reluctant to break a lifelong pious custom, but also for the reason that one strand of Islamic custom (though not all) seems to insist on lack of fleetness and grace as part of the feminine ideal. But their faces bore the slight lubricious smile of those who perform a forbidden action, and this expression seemed particularly ghastly and frivolous because one of the women revealed the livid skin and preoccupied stare of the typical cancer patient. 'It is their Friday,' whispered Constantine, 'that is the Moslem's holy day, it is to them as Sunday is to us. And they bring their sick to be cured by our Christian saints. See what they do.' They made their way to the tomb of Stephen Dechanski and stood there in a hushed fluttered group, summoning up their intention.

The priest withdrew from them and came over to us, murmuring with a smile, 'They have worked out this ritual themselves; it is entirely their own idea, we have nothing to do with it.' First the cradle was set down on the floor and the child taken out of it; its cry expressed the accumulated griefs and the final weakness of a nonagenarian; its mother pressed its face against the coffin-lid and then knelt down beside the tomb while one of the men knelt at the end. Trembling, she held the wailing baby under the tomb and the man took it from her and passed it round the end back to her. Three times the baby was passed under the tomb and back again. By this tenuous contact with the man whose father had burnt out his eyes, who had killed his brother and who had been killed by his son, it was presumed that the baby would now enjoy physical health. Then it was put back in its cradle, and one of the little boys kissed the tomb and crawled under it three times. After that the woman with the livid skin and the stare slowly performed the ritual, so stiffly and mechanically that it was as if her own malady were hypnotizing her from within. The third time she could not pass under the tomb by her own volition. She had to be dragged out by the two men. Even if the ritual were effective she had come too late; it was no longer for her to say if she would dispense with her malady or not, it was now for her malady to decide when it would dispense with her. The two men got her on to her feet, and they became again a huddled, over-awed group. Softly they padded across the church towards the porch. One of the women and two of the men looked up at the frescoes with the conscious calm of tourists who in a tropical island see the natives practising what in their country of origin would be considered indecent exposure: Islam forbids the representation of living creatures. We followed them to the archway and watched them in the sunshine among the trenches and the rubble-heaps, reassuming their veils and their skullcaps.

At Sveti Naum they had told me that the Moslems brought them their lunatics to be cured, but I had never seen it for myself. Of course this was not an actual flouting of the theory of Islam. We remember only that Mohammed bade his followers strike off the heads of all misbelievers; we forget that in the Koran he alluded to Christ with deep respect, and held that Adam, Noah, Abraham, Moses, Christ, and himself were God's best-beloved. These Moslems had been brought here by several motives. First, and most piteous, they had already cried to their own God and found Him indifferent. Also this was a place of great past and present prestige. Before Dechani was a monastery it was a palace of the Nemanyas; though most of it was destroyed by the Turks after Kossovo an indestructibly solid kitchen still survives. The memory of its grandeur would certainly have still lingered in this country where a century seems less than a decade elsewhere; and that the monks who a generation ago lived here in poverty and fear should now be among the rulers of the land, while the Sultan and his pashas had been driven out, must have given the ignorant a sense of phœnix-like resurgence, triumphant over death. But whatever the motives of the people were, the visit itself made a painful impression, because they were getting so little good from it. This crawling under Stephen Dechanski's tomb was not a vicious ritual, but it was idiotic. It was a plain piece of infantilism, purely regressive. The human being pretended it was a child again by going down on its hands and knees, and by crawling under a symbol of authority enacted a fantasy of flight from responsibility, of return to dependence. That was all these people got from a visit to this church which on its walls bore such strong and subtle evidence of the support that Christianity can give to the tortured human animal. On the dome, and again behind the altar, was Christ Pantocrator, the Ruler of All: that magnificent conception of man which shows him worn with care, utterly defeated by necessity, utterly triumphant because he continues to exist under the defeat and exercise his will. On the wall the Mother of God holds up her thin and loving hands in prayer; the folds of her gown are cut from the very stuff of religion, for in their long fall they make an image of endurance, continuance. She too is utterly defeated, she too is utterly triumphant in her refusal to abandon under that defeat her preference for love. People who grasped those conceptions would for ever know some measure of comfort. I think that they, as well as Aberdeen, accounted for the peculiar sweetness and serenity of our friend the seller of ready-made clothing. But there seemed to be no force working in the life of the monastery which would make these conceptions clear to those who were not prepared for them by their own tradition. No one could have entered Sveti Naum, not the wildest mountain Moslem, without receiving some intimation of what its founders and those who lived under their influence had believed about life. But though there were several monks here at Dechani who looked as if they were wise and would have transmitted wisdom, they all wore an air of helplessness and frustration.

'I am taking your husband to look at some carving on the outer wall,' said Constantine. 'Will you come?' But I stayed where I was among the frescoes, which the afternoon light was now irradiating and showing more and more manifestly superb as pure painting, quite apart from their revelation of the sensibility of a demonic people. Suddenly the little golden-haired monk was back at my side. I had thought that he had said he was going away to put on his galoshes as a pretext for escaping from my husband, but he had actually changed into curious flapping footwear of blue cloth. I heard again Mrs Mac's words, 'I hope you'll not be shown round by that wee monk with the awful galoshes.' Apparently such imbecile scenes were the usual lot of the visitors to Dechani. 'You must give me your passport,' he said. 'But why?' I asked. 'It is a rule,' he said, 'that everybody who comes to the monastery must give me his passport.' 'But we are not staying here.' I objected. 'We are going back to Petch quite soon, before evening.' 'That does not matter,' said the little creature, 'everybody who comes here, even for a few moments, must give me his passport.' This was, of course, perfect nonsense. 'Give it to me, give it to me,' he clamoured. I knew well that if I handed it over to him I would never see it again. He would probably take it away, tear it up, and come back saying that he had never had it. 'I am sorry,' I said, 'I haven't got it with me. We all left ours at the hotel at Petch.' His face screwed up in anger. 'But I know you have got it!' he insisted. 'I saw it inside your bag when you took out your handkerchief! Give it to me at once!' I made a ridiculous flight out of the church and, since I could not see my husband and Constantine anywhere, began to run round it in search of them, jumping over the trenches and rubble-heaps. Round the first corner I found them talking to one of the older and more dignified monks. The little monk, who was scrambling and jabbering at my heels, came to a sudden halt and scuttled away, crying over his shoulder, 'I am looking for the Hungarian count I have to show round the monastery. I cannot think what has happened to him.'

I said angrily, 'It really is not fair to have this disgusting little pest running about this lovely place, preventing people from looking at it.' Though I spoke English the monk had caught my meaning, and, looking distressed and embarrassed, he suggested that we go down to the stream which runs through the farmlands a short distance from the monastery and drink from a famous healing spring that rises on its bank. We followed him down a steep path through an orchard, and met three Moslem women, coming up, leading a pack-horse. They asked breathlessly, their black veils shaking and twitching with their agitation, 'May we go into the church?' and the monk answered, 'Yes, but you must leave the horse outside.' The stream ran shining in and out of the shadows cast by poplars and oaks, willows and acacias; like the quite distinct river which runs through Petch, it is called the Clean One. From the bridge we looked on a far panorama of operatic picturesqueness, a nearer composition of water-meadows and woodlands that was limpid and lovely as ideal flute-music. The only touches in the scene not exquisitely fresh were the filthy black coats of the young theological students who stood about and gaped at us.

As we sipped the spring water we found pleasure in watching some young Albanians who were kneeling between the willows on the river's brink and were bathing their faces and heads. It is a salient difference between the Serbs and Albanians that, whereas a Serb boy baby looks definitely and truculently male as soon as it is out of its mother's arms, the sex of many Albanians is not outwardly determined until they are in their late teens, and these

boys, who were perhaps thirteen to seventeen, might have been
so many Rosalinds. They had long lashes, bright lips, bloomy
skins, and a nymph-like fluency of movement. I said, 'Why are
they bathing their faces and heads like that? It is not so very hot.'
The monk answered, 'It is a ceremony of purification which they
have invented themselves. They like to come up to the church every
Friday, and always they come here first and wash as you see them
doing now. We never ask them to do it, they do it of their own
accord. I suppose that they feel guilty, for they are not like the
Turks, who have always been heathen. They were Christians when
this monastery was built, in the fourteenth century, and I think they
know they should be as they were then, and should come back to
us.' I thought to myself, 'But the trouble is that you too are not as
you were in the fourteenth century, and that there is not so much
as there ought to be for them to come back to. This reconquered
country is like a chalice waiting to be filled, and it seems to me that
the wine is lacking.'

At that moment an elbow was thrust into my side, and the
little golden-haired monk forced himself between Constantine and
myself. He waved a disparaging hand at the landscape and cried,
'I too have made sacrifices for my religion. For this have I left all
the pleasures of city life. *Hierfür hab' ich das schönste Stadtleben
aufgegeben.*' Constantine turned on him with a shout of rage, and
the other monk flung out an arm at him and told him to go away.
Tossing his head defiantly, like a character in an old-fashioned book
about schoolgirls, he scampered away and ran up the steep path
through the orchard, sometimes pausing because he had lost one or
other of his galoshes. The Albanian boys tilted up the lovely ovals
of their faces towards the bridge, the unkempt students gathered
closer and stared harder, while Constantine kept on shouting. 'For
a Croat, and a Schwab Croat at that, to speak so of one of our holiest
Serbian places!' he ended, and the monk shrugged his shoulders
wearily.

'Let us go away,' I said, 'let us go away at once.' As we passed
through the quadrangle the church was glowing more brightly than
a pearl, like a lily in strong sunlight, in spite of all the scaffolding and
hugger-mugger. 'Do you want to go in again?' asked Constantine.
'Not at all,' I said. 'I only want to walk for a little in the woods
outside.' When we had said good-bye to the monk and given him
some money for the church, we went out to the road and found
Dragutin standing beside the automobile with his arms folded,
while the little golden-haired monk skipped round him. 'Yes,'
he was crying, 'and that is not the end of the famous folk who

are proud to be our guests! For today we have had great news, we have heard that next Whitsuntide we will have the great honour of entertaining at Dechani Herr Hitler and General Göring!' 'Drive us a short way down the road,' said Constantine; 'the Gospodja does not want to stay here any longer, she would rather walk in the woods.' 'I don't wonder,' said Dragutin; 'this isn't my idea of a holy place. If this little one had a dancing bear I'd think we were in the gipsy quarter.'

We found a path through very still and fragrant pinewoods, leading to a holiday camp for children, not yet opened for the summer, and we sat down on one of the seats. Soon Constantine fell into a doze, and I went for a stroll among the trees, and came back with a handful of peppermint. My husband too was asleep now, and I sat down between the two men till they wakened. When Constantine opened his eyes he asked, 'What are those things on your lap? I like those dark-green leaves, and those sad, middle-aged mauve flowers. Peppermint, you say? But what have they to do with peppermint? Do they smell like it?' 'No,' I said, 'it is peppermint itself.' 'What are you telling me!' he exclaimed. 'I am like a little one who has thought all his life that babies came in the doctor's bag and is suddenly told the truth by a cruel schoolmaster. Always I have thought that peppermint came simply from a shop, or at furthest a jar in a shop, and now you tell me brutally that it grows out of the earth, in my own land, in woods such as I have seen all my life.' I crushed a piece and held it under his nose. 'Hey, it is truly peppermint,' he cried ecstatically, for he loved pungent scents and flavours. But suddenly his expression changed from a grin of delight to a rictus of horror. He pushed my hand away and groaned. It was as if he suddenly rebelled against the intensity of sensation, as if he loathed the acute quality of experience. 'I am very ill,' he sighed. 'I am in great pain. And there is nothing whatsoever the matter with me,' he added, more faintly still.

My husband and I put our arms round him because we were afraid he would fall off the bench. He remained with his eyes closed for a moment, then said, 'I am quite all right. It is the sting on my hand that has given me fever. That is all.' 'No,' I said, 'there is more than that the matter with you. You are very tired.' I paused, at a loss for words. I did not know how to say that he was dying of being a Jew in a world where there were certain ideas to which some new star was lending a strange strength. But my husband said, 'Dear Constantine, you know you are tired to death. Why do you not go straight away back to Belgrade and let us find our way over Montenegro to Kotor? You think we are English and stupid, but not a dog could lose its way from here to Dubrovnik.' 'How bored you are with me,' said Constantine. 'I have seen that coming for a long time.' 'Dear Constantine, that is not true,' I said. 'We could not have had a more wonderful companion,' said my husband. 'Is it so?' asked Constantine very earnestly. We patted his hand, but he looked away as if he found our reassurance not so interesting as he had expected. 'I will come with you,' he said. 'Montenegro is a very interesting country and nobody can explain it to you so well as myself. Now, let us sit here and enjoy the calm. Breathe, breathe deep! This is the sweetest air, such as you have not in England.'

When we returned to Petch Constantine went to bed at once, and we sat for a time drinking plum brandy outside the hotel, watching the corso. 'Our relations with Constantine are painful but very interesting,' I said; 'it is as if we had ceased to be people, and had become figures in a poet's dream.' 'I cannot help feeling,' said my husband, 'that there are more restful ways of taking a holiday than becoming characters in the second part of *Faust*.' Before us streamed the mountain people, large-boned and majestic, and always tragic when old; the trim functionaries moving whippily, as if they were determined to dodge out of the path of destiny likely to work such a change on them between youth and age; lads ranged in groups yet loosely, like skeins of wool, as they do in the distressed areas of our own country; grave and pallid little boys circled between the tables selling newspapers and picture postcards, gay little girls ran through the crowd in their enchanting costumes of flowered tight jackets and loose trousers.

Suddenly we were jerked out of our contented drowsiness. Two lads were talking at the edge of the stream that runs down the roadway; they drew apart, one struck the other on the chest, not violently, but with an intention of insult; before he had well delivered the blow its answer came to him. He was struck with a force that had at least thought of murder. His body pivoted on one heel and fell obliquely, with the arms wind-milling, into the middle of the stream. As he scrambled out of the water a silence fell on the whole street. Not a shocked silence; simply the silence of a circus audience watching the acrobats as they hang impaled on the climax of their great trick. Maybe many of the audience thought that the old days had come back when men were allowed to be men and have their excitements. But the silence was broken. A sword rattled. It had not been drawn, it had got caught in the legs of a chair. The Chief of Police had risen from his table in the café, with a look of extreme exasperation on his hard-bitten face, and was hurrying across the street to the two lads. He boxed the ears of the one who was standing on the edge of the stream; the other he helped out of the water, and then cuffed him with just as little tenderness. Then he stood over them and scolded them in the very pose of a nursemaid. The corso shuffled on again, the newsboys once more shouted '*Pravda!*' and '*Politika!*' Doubtless many hearts were the heavier as they realized, as they must have done many times, that the old days were over.

We strolled along the main street, passing some bright caves in the dim simplicity of the low buildings, where the functionaries and their wives could buy Kolynos and Listerine, Coty powders and Lenthéric lip-sticks. At length we came to a point in the road which we had remarked on our way to the Patriarchate, where objects not in themselves remarkable, a disused mosque of no great architectural distinction, a square Turkish tower two or three hundred years old, a patch of grass and some trees, and a gravelled open space, were set at angles which gave them a mysterious and exciting value. We stood for a while and enjoyed its challenge to the imagination. Twilight was falling. The brilliant sky was bluish and white, lit with stars that minute by minute grew more immense. The mountains were the colour and texture of lamp-black and the woods on the foothills looked liquid as green water. Beside the mosque a puddle lay pure white. We heard a drumming, throbbing sound, and thought that the mosque could not be disused as we were told, since surely this was the chanting of a service. But when we drew near the mosque the droning grew fainter, and bats flew straight out of the walls, and our search for the sound led us to round the open space to a little cottage with a garden where somebody was giving a party and entertaining his guests with very old records played on a very old gramophone. It must have been a very small party, for it was the smallest of cottages. I do not think there can have been more than two or three guests; but there were the solemn, self-consciously orgiastic noises of a Slav party.

As we looked and listened there was a scuffle behind us, and a tug at my coat. One of the little girls in flowered jacket and trousers was there behind me, panting through her laughter, '*Parlez-vous français, madame?*' The golden patina on her sun-bleached brown hair shone like a halo through the half-light. Softly shrieking with laughter, hampered and delayed by laughter, she fled back to a group of shadows that was hiding at a corner of the Turkish tower and now scattered, laughing as she had laughed, into the dusk. Though we called her she would not come; but it did not matter, for she had no more need than a kingfisher to break her flight to prove her loveliness. The town seemed the quieter for this sudden unfolding and furling of wings in its stillness. We turned at random down a street, where white houses showed blank and secretive faces, and were defended by a broad stream that flowed between them and the roadway. We did not hear a human sound until we met a Turk, wearing a red-and-white turban of archaic fashion, and carrying two amphoræ; as he passed us his spectacles flashed at us but he went on talking contentiously to himself. I said to my husband, 'Miss Kemp says in her book, *The Healing Ritual*, that she met a young man here who studied occultism and had in his home two hundred ancient manuscripts and books dealing with the art.' 'If one lived in Petch one would do queer things,' said my husband; 'its dignified decay makes me feel like a fly walking over velvet.'

At last we heard voices. On a bridge leading over the stream from a house stood a young girl in a white blouse and black skirt, holding a lantern with one hand while her other arm was laid about the shoulders of four young children as they all looked earnestly along the street. 'They are coming!' cried a little boy at the sight of us. 'No, they are not!' jeered the others. 'These people are not they! Do you not know them better than that?' That broke the tensity of the children's interest, and they ran back into the house, but the young girl continued to look down the street, even when a glance had told her that we had come to a stop in front of her, startled out of our good manners by her incomparable beauty. The slight change of expression by which she rebuked our impudence was neither excessive nor complaisant; she was noble in her manners as well as her appearance. I thought it probable that she too was of the strain that had produced the great Katerina Simitch, or at least her followers, and I hoped that the visitors she awaited would bring her some food for her splendid appetites, some opportunity to coerce life into a superior phase by an act of courage. But, if they came on such an annunciatory errand, I could not think that they would belong to the same organization that had fostered the genius of Katerina Simitch: I could not think that they would be sent out by the local church. The Abbot of the Patriarchate was performing his pious and non-mystical function to perfection; when this girl was older his monastery would be a refuge and a refreshment to her. But there was no force here to tell her youth, as the Church had told Katerina Simitch when she needed the lesson, how to take the Kingdom of Heaven by storm. I looked nervously over my shoulder lest I should see the only emissary of the faith that was likely to appear in this place at this hour, since he was likely to appear anywhere at any hour. I could well imagine him caponing

and curveting down the twilit street, coquetting with his shadow,
while his blond curls swung.

The starlight waxed stronger, and colour drained out of the
world. The stream in its deep channel glittered like a black snake;
the houses were pale as chalk, as a ghost, as a skeleton. I might
be wrong; I would be able to check it when I got back to the
high-street, where Petch was sitting down for its evening meal,
for this was Friday, and a fast-day. When we got back to our
hotel and sat down in the restaurant, I said to my husband, 'Eat
what you like, I want to make an experiment.' I asked the waiter
what I could eat, and he mentioned dish after dish containing meat
or eggs or butter, or fish cooked in butter, or cheese or milk, and
all these things are forbidden by the Orthodox Church on fast-days.
'These will not do,' I said; 'though I am a foreigner I want to keep
the fast. Have you no dish that fulfils the condition? Haven't you
any beans, or fish fried in oil or boiled in water?' 'No,' he said.
'Is that because this is the evening meal?' I asked. 'Perhaps at
midday you had such dishes.' 'No,' he said, 'we are never asked
for them.' I said, 'Very well, then, I must eat somewhere else.'
My husband by this time had become interested in the test I was
applying. We went up and down the high-street from inn to inn,
and they were all full of people eating their evening meal, none of
whom was fasting. This was a strange sign in a town which lies in
the shadow of Dechani, which for centuries lived not only in a state
of ecstatic faith, but by it; for man loves his little abstinences, and
he does not abandon the obscure pleasure of fasting until he actually
wishes to dissociate himself from the belief which is its apparent
justification. If the West had failed to provide Yugoslavia with a
formula for happiness, it could not be pretended that the failure of
new things did not matter, because there were old things here which
were all the country needed. In parts of the country these old things
are as valuable as they ever were, as they have ever been. In other
parts they are not valid. The people will no longer accept them as
currency; and here, since no new currency has been minted there
is bankruptcy. As we went back to the restaurant the wind came
down from the gorge ice-cold, and like a battering-ram; there was a
sound of splintering wood and the crash of sheet-iron. A small shop
had come to pieces.

Montenegro

Montenegro

ROAD

I WOKE EARLY. BECAUSE OF MY INQUIRY INTO THE STATE
of religion in Petch, I had had to dine on sardines, dry bread, red
wine, and black coffee, and the diet had not suited me. I crept out of
my room and along the groaning, grumbling corridors and down into
the street, and took a cab out to the Patriarchate, because I wanted to
have another look at the huge Madonna and her tiny rebellious and
athletic Christ-child. The Albanian cab-driver brought a friend with
him on the box, who also, he said, wished to enjoy the opportunity of
conversation with me, so I spread out my dictionary on my knee and
did what I could for them. The cab-driver was a sombrely handsome
young man of a type familiar in the Balkans; his friend was a natural
comedian, a Robin Goodfellow, with straight red hair long about his
shoulders, a crowing voice, and stiff, signalling hands. They were
Roman Catholics, but I found they knew nothing of the sayings or
doings of Pope Pius X, and most of their Western co-religionists
would have found them not altogether congenial. The driver was
single, but Robin Goodfellow had married a girl of fourteen seven
years ago and had six children. They were resentful against the
Government and expressed the desire and even an intention to
murder as many of its officials as possible, but their chief grievance
seemed nothing more than the price of sugar. This is indeed high,
owing to the state monopoly, but not so high as to justify this extreme
ferocity. They were very much interested in all sweet things, and had
heard about the superiority of English and Swiss chocolate, so I had to
talk with the pedantry of a wine connoisseur about Peters and Tobler
and Nestlé, Cadbury and Rowntree and Fry. Jam and spices they
wanted to learn about also; but I failed to surmount the difficulty
of describing curry in an imperfectly mastered language. They asked
me how old I was, what my husband did, and why he had not come
out with me. When I said he was still asleep they suggested to each
other, not facetiously, but as realists in a world of men, that he had
as like as not been drunk the night before.

999

The garden of the Patriarchate was golden-green in the slanting
early sunlight, the church was honey-coloured and filled with the
honey of the Abbot's voice. Among the chief glories of the Orthodox
Church are the number of priests who can sing and speak as the
mouthpieces of a god should do. I had come in for the end of a
service which had been attended by two middle-aged men, who
bore themselves like devotees of unusual fervour, some young
women with their children, and a number of the straight-backed
old ladies in trousers whom I had noticed here before. When the
service was over I had half an hour with the frescoes, which were
now still lovelier than I had thought them. The morning light,
striking the windows of the dome at right angles, was deflected
into the softest possible radiance as it poured down into the church,
and under it the paintings gave up their full gentleness, the elegance
and spring-like freshness that made them kin to much early Italian
art. I looked not so long at the terrible Mother and Child as at the
scenes which showed the Christian legend taking place in a country
that I had thought to be ancient Tuscany, that I now knew to have
wider frontiers. Then I went out into the sunlight, warm enough
now to draw the scent out of the walnut trees and the pines, and I
took a last draught of the healing water from the fountain before I
went to say good-bye to the priest, who was drinking his morning
coffee at a table under the trees. I stood beside him for a minute
before he noticed me, for his Albanian servant and an old labourer
had laid down before him a plant with fleshy leaves and stem that
had been trampled and broken, and he was staring at it, with his
elbows on the table and his coffee-cup held in his hands. I think they
were debating what animal had been that way. Their deliberation
had an air of essential virtue. By such carefulness life survives.

On the way home the cab-driver and his friend inquired what
countries I had visited, and which I liked best. I said I had been
to the United States and every country in Europe except Russia,
Roumania, Poland, and Portugal; and that I liked Yugoslavia, the
United States, France, and Finland best of all. They cried out at
the name of France. The French they could not abide. They had
fought against them in the Great War, they said, and they were glad
of it. They liked, they said, the Germans and the Bulgarians, and
they hated the Serbs. They both agreed that they would thoroughly
enjoy another war if only it would give them the chance of shooting
a lot of Serbs. They help up their left arms and looked along them
and twitched their right thumbs against their left elbows and said
'Boom! Boom! A Serb is dead!' I said, 'But what have you against
the Serbs?' They said, 'After the war they ill-treated us and took

our land from us.' There was some justification for this, I knew. The district of Petch was handed over to an old man who had been King Peter's Master of the Horse, and he appears, like our own followers of the Belvoir and the Quorn, to have offered conclusive proof of the powerfully degenerative effect of equine society on the intellect. 'But now what do they do to you?' I asked. They shrugged and grumbled. 'We live so poor,' they said; 'in Albania our brothers live far better than we do.' It was as pathetic as the belief of the Bulgarian schoolboy in Bitolj that Bulgaria was a richer country than Yugoslavia; for everybody who comes out of Albania into Yugoslavia is amazed at the difference, which is all in Yugoslavia's favour, of the standard of living.

When they left me at my hotel, I gave the driver a good tip, and he thanked me in a phrase so remarkable that I made him repeat it several times. But it was true; he had really said, 'I am glad of this money, for tomorrow I am going to Paris to be married.' It sounded such a *Sketch* and *Tatler* thing to do that, though by this time I was exhausted by the strain of picking a conversation piecemeal out of a dictionary, I made him explain it. The explanation gave me fresh evidence of the capacity of France to assimilate strange stuff and make it her own. 'You must know,' he said, 'that I am not only the driver of this cab, I own it.' 'He is Rothschild!' shrieked Robin Goodfellow, poking him in the ribs, 'he owns a dozen cabs.' He owned in fact eight. They took the visitors to Dechani, and anyway no woman of property went about Petch on foot except to the market. When he had bought the eighth he had written to his aunt, who had married the Italian proprietor of a small hotel in Paris, and asked her to find him a wife. She had found him the photographs of several candidates in the Albanian colony of Paris, which was small but prosperous, and he had chosen one to whom he was to be married in five days' time. In a missionary spirit I said, 'Is your aunt happy in Paris?' 'Yes,' he said, 'she and her husband made a lot of money, and they say they are very free there.' 'And the Albanians who live there, are they happy?' 'Yes,' he answered, 'they are all doing well.' 'But don't you think maybe that means the French are good enough people?' I said. But it was not a point that was likely to convince people who had been brought up to regard as normal a state where different races grew up in conditions decided by a distant ruler. To them the idea of a country being directly governed by its inhabitants is one of abnormal compactness, like a hermaphrodite.

I went up to our bedroom and found my husband locking his suitcase. On the middle of my bed there had been built with offensive ingenuity a little cairn of the things I had forgotten to pack in mine. 'They are all things,' I pointed out, 'that I would not mind losing.' 'Packing,' said my husband, 'belongs to a different category from criticism.' The little Hungarian chambermaid popped her head inside the door, and we tipped her fifty dinars, which is four and twopence, and she thought it so handsome that she kissed my hand furiously. 'That is a good little one,' said Constantine, as he went downstairs to breakfast; 'this morning she helped me to pack and she said to me, "I tell you, I would have liked to be with you, you are so charming, so very cultured, it might even have been that you would have quoted select passages of poetry to me. So I have been to you every night when I had finished my work, but each time you had fever, you were red as a lobster, so I saw it was not written in the stars that we should be together." '

We had our breakfast outside the large restaurant, and presently Constantine left us to say good-bye to the Chief of Police, who was giving some advice to a man standing with two pack-horses in the middle of the road, and we were joined by the Danish seller of agricultural machinery, who regarded us with a benevolence that was galling. We had the impression that he had just received information that we were completely harmless and unimportant, and that in any case even if we had some grain of significance we were leaving, so it did not matter. 'You are going, *hein?*' he said. 'Over the mountains to Kolashin and then to Tsetinye? And up the coast to Split, and then to Budapest, and home, very nice, very nice.' 'How kind of you to be so interested in our itinerary as to find out what it is,' said my husband. 'Oh, the people here talk, you know,' said the alleged Dane. 'I should think it more likely that they read,' said my husband darkly. There fell a silence, which I weakly broke by saying to him, 'Look, do you see that young man walking along carrying that black portfolio? Bow to him, he has greeted us. It is the clerk of the court, who so kindly offered to show us the sights of the town the first night we got here.' The alleged Dane burst into laughter. 'That young *Lümmel*! He was fool enough to tell me what he earns. Think of it, he is a university graduate, and he makes each week twelve marks—one of your pounds! Here they're a starveling lot.' 'Yes, it's a pity they're so poor,' said my husband. 'For they are such nice people,' said I. 'You waste your pity,' said the alleged Dane, in sudden and brutal passion; 'these are Slavs, they have no right to anything, they are as sheep, as cattle, as swine.'

The hotel tried to overcharge us, but its experience of the world was so small that its efforts were scarcely perceptible. However,

Constantine and Dragutin were very indignant, and we did not get clear of the dispute until ten minutes past seven. Then we started off for the gorge, for Tserna Gora. 'Now we will climb like eagles!' cried Dragutin. 'And there,' he said, as we passed a grassy patch under the willows on the river's bank on the way to the Patriarchate, 'is where I have slept each night since we came to Petch. These accursed thieves at the hotel tried to charge me, a chauffeur, for my room at the same rate as you people, and though I knew you would have paid, I would not have it so, and I came out here and flung myself down, and it was no sacrifice, for I slept like a king.'

We left the bosomy domes of the Patriarchate behind us, and we went into the Rugovo gorge, which would at any time be superb, and was now a pageant of the sterner beauties possible in nature and man. It was over the rocks at the mouth of this gorge that the retreating Serbian Army of 1915 pushed its guns lest the Austrians and Bulgarians should make use of them, and walked on into ice and famine; and the scenery is appropriate to that drama. Its sheer precipices and fretted peaks show the iron constitution our planet hides under its grass and flowers; and down the road there were swinging in majestic rhythm men and women who showed the core of hardness humanity keeps under its soft wrapping of flesh. They were going down to the market at Petch, and most were on foot; before nightfall they would return to their homes. And they were coming from villages five, ten, and even fifteen miles up the gorge. In fact, they were going to walk ten to thirty miles in the day, the latter half of the journey up a steep mountain road. It seemed so Herculean a trip that we got Constantine to question two typical wayfarers, an Albanian wearing a white turban with its ends brought across his throat, to hide one of the goitres which are so common in the mountains, and his wife, a raw-boned woman wearing a black dress which oddly broke into a flounce just above her knees, with something of a Cretan air. Yes, they came from that village up there, about a mile away on the hillside, and they would walk to Petch and back by nightfall. There was no question of riding their pack-pony for it was loaded now with what they were going to sell, which was wool, and on the return journey it would be loaded with what they were going to buy, which would probably be wood, if the price were right; in any case I doubt if it could have carried their pylon-like forms. Their leathery faces slowly split into enormous grins as they grasped our astonishment. All these people on the road were very deliberate and stiff and emphatic in their movements and their speech, like frescoes come to life. One woman, who was sitting in a cart with her young child under her blue mantle, resembled exactly one of the Madonnas of Dechani, twisted by the strain put upon her endurance by her love. Again it seemed that Byzantine art is not so much stylized as we believe, and that it may be a more or less naturalist representation of a highly stylized life.

The gorge widened to a valley where snow mountains looked down on beechwoods, widened and steepened to another Switzerland; and so it might be, and may yet become. The grass grows short and thick as gourmand cows would have it. Here there might be cheese and tinned milk and milk chocolate, if the population could but afford to buy good cows and knew how to keep them. In Stephen Dushan's time fat flocks and herds were driven up here every summer, but under the Turks such luxurious husbandry was forgotten among Christians, and only a few nomads cared for pastures in such a disputed district as the frontier between Montenegro and Albania. Even those had their movements circumscribed by the definition of the Yugoslavian frontier, for some of them had their winter pastures in territory that was assigned to Greece and to Albania, hence they could no longer pass from one to the other. Also there might be practised a moderate form of mountaineering, for there is some excellent rock-climbing and some eternal snow; but the tradition of guides and chalets has yet to be created. There are as good as Swiss flowers. Where the road mounted to the pass it hairpinned across a slope too high for trees, which was clouded purple with crocuses, golden with kingcups. On the razor-edge of the pass we looked, as one may often do in Switzerland, backward and forward at two worlds. Behind us the mountains stretched to a warm horizon, themselves not utterly cold, as if the low hills and plains beyond exhaled a rich, thawing breath from their fertility. Before us the mountains and valleys fused into a land cooler than all others, as a statue is cooler than a living body. It is not, as the school books have it, that Montenegro is barren: that is a delusion of those who see it only from the sea. Its inland half, if it has little for the plough, has many woods and pastures. But they are held in a cup of rock, they are insulated from the common tide of warmth that suffuses the rest of earth. What the cup holds is pure. In summer, they say, there is here pure heat; in autumn pure ripeness; in winter pure cold. Now, in this late springtime it was pure freshness, the undiluted essence of what that season brings the world to renew its youth.

'At this pass was the old Turkish frontier,' said Constantine. 'And is no more, and is no more, thank God,' said Dragutin. Down below, at the end of a valley bright with the thin green flames of beechwoods and clouds of flowers, we came on a poorish village and halted at the inn. 'Now I must ask the way to Lake Plav,' said Constantine, 'for you should certainly see Lake Plav. Did you ever hear of it?' I knew the name. An unfortunate *contretemps* occurred here during the Balkan War. When Montenegro captured the village of Plav from the Turks in 1912, they were greatly aided by a local Moslem priest, who joined the Orthodox Church and was appointed a major in the Montenegrin Army. His first action when left unsupervised was to hold a court-martial on his former congregation and to shoot all those who refused to be baptized. They numbered, it is said, five hundred. The incident has the terrible quality of juvenile crime. Little Willie was told to be a good boy and keep his baby from crying, and it was precisely because he wanted to be a good boy that he held a pillow over baby's face. I had thought of the place where this happened as a circle of mud huts in a hollow of gleaming stones below vertical mountains. But two or three miles over a bumpy road took us to a place that was a perfect and rounded image of pleasure. A circle of water lay in a square of emerald marshland, fringed with whitish reeds, and framed by hills patterned with green grass and crimson earth, with a sheer wall of snow mountains behind them. The glowing hills and the shining peaks were exactly mirrored in the lake, and received the embellishment of a heavenly bloom peculiar to its waters. We sat down on a stone dike, shaded by a thorn which the winds had whipped into the form of a modest Chinese lady. Below us a man was cutting turf at the lake edge, and loading it on a bright-blue cart drawn by a grey pony; he was as graceful as if he had never known fatigue in his life, and his white shirt, kilt, and trousers and black bolero were white as snow and black as coal against the emerald marsh. This was as good a place as can be, if beauty is of any good. 'Lake Plav,' said Constantine, 'means blue lake. *Plav* is a strange word. It means blue or fair-haired. All that is beautiful without being sombre.'

Back at the inn, we had an early lunch in distasteful surroundings. A dog that had lost a paw limped about our feet; it was still, they said, wonderful at rabbiting, and it looked up at us with the cold eye and the snarl of one who lives in pain and by wile. As we ate, a motor bus which had left Tsetinye at dawn arrived and disgorged a load of pallid people, holding the battered yellow hemispheres of sucked lemons and making no effort to conceal that they had found the remedy against sickness not wholly satisfactory. One demonstrated that in her case it had been completely ineffectual. 'There is everything here that Aldous Huxley could desire,' said my husband; and it was true, for in the inn garden on the other side of the road was a little building like a summer-house, poised high on piles over a stream, which we were forced to believe was a sanitary installation of too simple a kind. But squalor is not a Montenegrin characteristic. If the country has a blatant fault, it is a chilling blankness. The typical house stands high-shouldered on a small base under a steeply raked roof tiled with what looks like slate but is pine; its face is singularly inexpressive. It is often isolated, for as this land was not occupied by the Turks there was not the same necessity to huddle together for protection from armed raiders; but even when such houses are gathered together in villages they never warm into welcoming sociability. Andriyevitsa, a village of fifteen hundred inhabitants, which we came to after ten miles' drive through olive groves and plum orchards, is well set on a ledge above a river with heaths and pinewoods about it, and has a handsome main street planted with great trees and lined with substantial stone houses, which are ornamented with fine balconies, an architectural feature which marks that one has crossed the cultural watershed and has come down on the side of Dalmatia and Venice and the West, for the Oriental cares little for them. In spite of these advantages its effect on the stranger is cold and dreary. It is as if the genius of the place lacked emotional and intellectual pigmentation. And that effect is intensified by the terrible purity of Montenegrin good looks. The beauty of both the men and the women is beyond what legend paints it; because legends desire to please, and this perfection demonstrates that there can be too much of a good thing. They are fabulous non-monsters. Such symmetry of feature and figure, such lustre of hair and eye and skin and teeth, such unerring grace, chokes the eye with cream.

Outside the village of Andriyevitsa, on a glassy plateau high above a river, was a kind of park which contained a new white church built in the Byzantine style and a war memorial consisting of a black marble needle marked in white letters with a prodigious number of names. We went to see what this might be, and a young man who had been asleep in the long grass beside the memorial rose up in such white immobile handsomeness as Disraeli would have ascribed to a duke, and told us that it commemorated the members of the Vasoyevitch tribe who had fallen in the wars. The Serbs who took refuge here after Kossovo split up into tribes, each with its own chief, very much after the order of our Scottish clans, and the Vasoyevitches were among the most powerful. All four sides of the needle were covered with names; there must have been seven or eight hundred of them. I exclaimed aloud when I saw that the inscription gave the dates of the war as 1912–21, but of course it is true that this country was continually under arms for nine years. First they joined with the Serbs in the Balkan wars, but when the Turks were beaten they had to continue a local war with the Albanians until the Great War came, and then the Austrians attacked them; and the peace brought them none, for they fought against the Serbs in protest against their incorporation in Yugoslavia. As we stood there we were joined by an elderly woman, poorly dressed but quite as aristocratic-looking as the young man; and they acted as our host and hostess in a tour of interesting graves. Two generals belonging to the tribe were buried in the park; and over the road, in the open heathland, lay two tribesmen who had been hanged on this spot by the Austrians, and not far off two other members of an earlier generation who had been imprudent enough to demand a liberal constitution from King Nicholas.

The air we breathed was pine-scented and rarefied by height; the moorland and mountain and waters about us enjoyed their elemental innocence; these marvellously beautiful people, placid as prize animals, showed us the tombs of their butchered kin. I remembered that this country, with greater certainty than any other country that I could think of, might attribute its survival to one single event, and that that event was loathsome in character. For three hundred years after Kossovo the Montenegrins fought against the Turks with unremitting courage, and vanquished them again and again. But when the Turks were outside Vienna in 1683 and then were driven out of Hungary they turned their full attention to this enemy who was weaker and nearer home. They marched through the mountains, guided by Montenegrins who had adopted the Islamic faith, and they occupied Tsetinye. Thereafter it seemed that the last Christian Slav stronghold must fall, largely because there were so many of the renegades. Two-thirds of the Albanian people had been converted during the seventeenth century, and it looked as if their example had corrupted their neighbours. In 1702 a bishop was kidnapped by the Turks when he was on his way home from the consecration of a new church and he was held to ransom. The ruler of Montenegro, Daniel Nyegosh, saw that his people must strike then or perish. It is told in one of the national ballads that he called a meeting of the tribes and bade them go forth on Christmas Eve and offer every Montenegrin Mohammedan the choice between baptism and death. Five brothers named Martinovitch alone obeyed him, and though the ballad assumes that they themselves executed the plan, it is obvious that they must have used the whole of their tribe. 'The time fixed for the holy vigil is at hand; the brothers

Martinovitch light their holy tapers, pray earnestly to the new-born God, drink each a cup of wine to the glory of Christ. Seizing their consecrated maces, they set out in the dark.'

I am on the side of the brothers Martinovitch. Having seen what Turkish conquest meant to the Slav, it is certain they were justified in their crime. A man is not a man if he will not save his seed. But the destiny is abhorrent that compelled the brothers, who may be assumed to have been of flawless and inhuman beauty, like the Montenegrins of today, to go out into the night and murder the renegades, who also would be beautiful. 'Please give me some brandy,' I said to my husband, 'I feel rather ill.' But when he poured it out of his flask it was not what I wanted. I would have preferred a drink that was enormously strong, that would instantly have clouded my consciousness, that would have smelt of nothing, like vodka. The bouquet of brandy recalls the pageant of the earth, the lovely and logical process of flower and fruit that causes man, with his leaning towards argument by analogy, to harbour such excessive hopes concerning his own life. It is a subtlety, and up here subtleties seemed doomed. As we drove out of the heathland into greener country, where there were farms that were astonishingly trim, considering they had to stand on end, we passed churches that had neither within nor without the faintest air of mysticism. They might have been town-halls, or even, in some cases, blockhouses.

That was natural enough, for in Montenegro church and state were till recently not merely welded but identical. In the sixteenth century the last king of the line of John Tserno, John the Outlaw, after whom the land was named Tserna Gora, abdicated and went to live in Venice; and before he left he called an assembly of the people and transferred his authority to the Bishop of Tsetinye, who was the head of the Montenegrin Church. Even so the Emperor Constantine the Great, on leaving Rome to found Constantinople, transferred his authority to the Pope, and thus gave the Papacy its claim to temporal power. Thus it happened that until 1851, when Danilo II fell in love with a pretty girl and changed the constitution so that he could marry her and transmit his royalty to their children, Montenegro was governed by a succession of prince-bishops who passed their power from uncle to nephew. The Church was, therefore, the Government, and its buildings were therefore adapted to the state's chief function, which was to resist the Turk: not here could goodness be adored and its indestructibility be recognized in ecstasy. The first and real need was an altar where the Martinovitch brothers could take a stirrup-cup before they set out on their pious errand, their truly pious errand, swinging their consecrated maces. Christianity was still an inspiration, and one that had proven its worth, but, like Montenegrin houses and good looks, it was too simple, too stark, so full of one perfect thing that it was as good as empty.

'Have the Montenegrins not made enormous sacrifices to preserve their independence?' I asked Constantine, and he answered, 'Greater than you can believe. They have sacrificed almost everything except their heroism. They are nothing but heroes. If they eat or sleep it is so that they shall wake up heroes. If they marry it is so that they should beget little heroes, who would not trouble to come out of their mothers' wombs were they not certain that they would grow up in heroism. They are as like the people of Homer as any race now living: they are brave, and beautiful, and vainglorious. A soldier must be vainglorious. He must go into the battle believing that he is so wonderful a human being that God could not let it be that the lesser men in front of him should kill him. And since the men in front of them were Turks who were often really prodigious fighters, there was no end to the fairy-tales that the Montenegrins had to tell to themselves about themselves. You get it in the two classic stories that are always told about these people. One is really true; it was a thing noticed in the Balkan wars. You know that when soldiers drill they have to number off—'One, two, one, two.' In the Montenegrin Army it could not be done. No man was willing to be second, so the first man said, 'One,' and the second said, 'I-am-beside-him,' very quickly. The other may be true, but perhaps only in the spirit. It is said that a traveller said to a Montenegrin, 'How many of your people are there?' and he answered, 'With Russia, one hundred and eighty millions,' and the traveller, knowing there were not two hundred thousand of them, said, 'Yes, but how many without the Russians?' and the Montenegrin answered, 'We will never desert the Russians.' And it was not a joke, for the vainglory of these people was necessary to them lest they should be conquered in battle.

'This vainglory will not permit them to have any other characteristics, except a little cunning that is quite simple, like the cunning of the Homeric heroes, for to be perfectly and absolutely vainglorious you must hold back from all activity, because you dare not ever fail at anything. So the Montenegrins are not really interested in any kind of work, and that makes it very difficult to fit them into the modern state of Yugoslavia. For in earlier centuries they lived by fighting, which always included a lot of looting, and by foreign subsidies, which were freely given, as this state was an important strategic point on the Adriatic coast; and in the late nineteenth and twentieth centuries they lived very much on these subsidies, particularly from Russia. And now all that is over, and they must earn their livings, and they do not want to do anything at all, for even farming used to be done chiefly by their women, since they always were at war or resting between wars, and no work interests them. No child here says, "I would like to be a builder, or a doctor, or a carpenter," though some want to be chauffeurs because to them it is still a daring and romantic occupation. So they pester the Government with demands for posts as functionaries and for pensions, which are of a terrible simplicity, for there is no need for so many functionaries, and if there were these people could not perform their functions, and God Himself, if He had a knife at His throat, could not invent a reason why they should all have pensions. This is hard on a poor country like Yugoslavia, and this is not an easy matter to settle by patience and patriotism, as many things can be settled in Bosnia and Old Serbia and Macedonia, because the Montenegrins are empty-headed except for their wild and unthinking heroism, which is to say they are often like madmen. I tell it you, this country is a sacrifice to itself of itself, and there is nothing left.'

There is no way out of the soul's dilemma. Those displeased by the rite on the Sheep's Field, who would be neither the priest nor the black lamb, who would be neither converted to Islam nor defeated on Kossovo plain, are forced to fight the priest. Since we must live in the same world as those we fight, this means sharing this upland bleakness, furnished too simply with its bloodstained monolith. 'Whoso liveth by the sword shall die by the sword' is only half the damnatory sentence passed on mankind by war; the other half reads, 'Whoso refuseth to die by the sword shall live by the sword.' Montenegro was something like a prison. Though it was airy as Heaven, instead of airless, like other prisons, it was stony like a cell, and it reeked of heroism as strongly as institutions reek of disinfectant; and the straitened inhabitants were sealed up in space with the ideas of slaughter and triumph as convicts are in their confinement with guilt and punishment. If one shut the eyes and thought of any pleasantness but the most elemental, any enjoyment that helped the mind further on its task of exploring the universe, one had to say on opening them, 'It is not here, nothing but the root of it is here.'

So it seemed. Then the road looped round the mountainside to a steeper mountain, and wound up to yet another pass, so high that as we rose the noontide sky showed pale above the distant peaks, though it was deeply blue above us. The country, which here is highly variable, changed its character again; it was Buckinghamshire on this cool northward slope, so tall the beeches, so dense the woods they drove to the skyline, so gardenish the grass. Up and up we drove until we had to stop, to cool the engine. We none of us regretted it, for there were many gentians on the banks beside the road, and below us the woods lay like bonfires of green flame on the mild rolling turf, and further the distant infinity of mountains was blue as wild hyacinths. We sat there so long that a woman we had passed on a lower curve of the road overtook us, halted in her trudging, came up to the car, and laid her arm along the frame of the open window, looking round at us all. Her face had once been perfect but was no longer so, and was the better for it. 'Good morning,' she said to Constantine, 'who are you?' 'I am Constantine,' he said. 'I am from Shabats and I am a poet.' 'And who are you?' she asked my husband and me. 'They are English,' said Constantine. 'Because they are great fighters, and they love nature,' she said. 'How do you know they are like that?' asked Constantine. She lifted her arm from the window, took a ball of fine white wool and knitting-needless from her other hand, and set to work again, as if sensing from his question an indication that the conversation might not be of the first order and she might as well get on with her material duties. 'Oh, everybody knows that,' she answered absently. 'And you,' said Constantine, 'who are you? Are you a native of this place?' 'No,' she said, 'I live here now, but I was born by Durmitor.' Durmitor is the great snow mountain, with a black lake at its foot, on the northern side of Montenegro. 'Who brought you here?' asked Constantine.

She laughed a little, lifted her ball of wool to her mouth, sucked the thin thread between her lips, and stood rocking herself, her eyebrows arching in misery. 'It is a long story. I am sixty now,' she said. 'Before the war I was married over there, by Durmitor. I had a husband whom I liked very much, and I had two children, a son and a daughter. In 1914 my husband was killed by the Austrians. Not in battle. They took him out of our house and shot him. My son went off and was a soldier and was killed, and my daughter and I were sent to a camp. There she died. In the camp it was terrible, many people died. At the end of the war I came out and I was alone. So I married a man twenty years older than myself. I did not like him as I liked my first husband, but he was very kind to me, and I had two children of his. But they both died, as was natural, for he was too old, and I was too old, and also I was weak from the camp. And now my husband is eighty, and he has lost his wits, and he is not kind to me any more. He is angry with everybody; he sits in his house and rages, and I cannot do anything right for him. So I have nothing.' 'Are you poor?' asked Constantine. 'Not at all,' she said. 'My husband's son by his first wife is a judge in Old Serbia, and he sends me three hundred dinars a month to hire a man to work our land, so we want nothing. Oh, that is all right, but the rest is so wrong.' 'Oh, sister, sister,' said Constantine, 'this is very hard.' 'Yes, it's hard,' she said. 'And can we do nothing for you,' asked Constantine, 'for we feel very friendly towards you? Can we not give you a lift to where you are going?' 'That you cannot do, though you mean so kindly,' she said, 'for I am not going anywhere. I am walking about to try to understand why all this has happened. If I had to live, why should my life have been like this? If I walk about up here where it is very high and grand it seems to me I am nearer to understanding it.' She put the ball of wool to her forehead and rubbed it backwards and forwards, while her eyes filled with painful speculation. 'Good-bye,' she said, with distracted courtesy, as she moved away, 'good-bye.'

This woman was of no importance. It is doubtful whether, walk as she would on these heights, she would arrive at any conclusion that was of value even to herself. She was, however, the answer to my doubts. She took her destiny not as the beasts take it, nor as the plants and trees; she not only suffered it, she examined it. As the sword swept down on her through the darkness she threw out her hand and caught the blade as it fell, not caring if she cut her fingers so long as she could question its substance, where it had been forged, and who was the wielder. She wanted to understand the secret which Gerda denied, the mystery of process. I knew that art and science were the instruments of this desire, and this was their sole justification, though in the Western world where I lived I had seen art debauched to ornament and science prostituted to the multiplication of gadgets. I knew that they were descended from man's primitive necessities, that the cave man who had to hunt the aurochs drew him on the rock-face that he might better understand the aurochs and have fuller fortune in hunting and was the ancestor of all artists, that the nomad who had to watch the length of shadows to know when he should move his herd to the summer pasture was the ancestor of all scientists. But I did not know these things thoroughly with my bowels as well as my mind. I knew them now, when I saw the desire for understanding move this woman. It might have been far otherwise with her, for she had been confined by her people's past and present to a kind of destiny that might have stunned its victims into an inability to examine it. Nevertheless she desired neither peace nor gold, but simply knowledge of what her life might mean. The instrument used by the hunter and the nomad was not too blunt to turn to finer uses; it was not dismayed by complexity, and it could regard the more stupendous aurochs that range within the mind and measure the diffuse shadows cast by history. And what was more, the human will did not forget its appetite for using it.

I remembered what Denis Saurat had said about Militsa: 'If there are but twenty people like her scattered between here and China, civilization will survive.' If during the next million generations there is but one human being born in every generation who will not cease to inquire into the nature of his fate, even while it strips and bludgeons him, some day we shall read the riddle of our universe. We shall discover what work we have been called to do, and why we cannot do it. If a mine fails to profit by its riches and a church wastes the treasure of its altar, we shall know the cause: we shall find out why we draw the knife across the throat of the black lamb or take its place on the offensive rock, and why we let the grey falcon nest in our bosom, though it buries its beak in our veins. We shall put our own madness in irons. Then, having defeated our own enmity, we shall be able to face the destiny forced on us by nature, and war with that. And what does that mean? What name is behind nature, what name but one name? Then there will be the wrestling match that is worth the prize, then defeat will be eternal glory, then there can be no issue but magnificence. That contest may endure a million, million years, seeing the might of the combatants. And after that, what then? Could the mind twitch away the black curtain behind the stars, it might be dazzled by a brightness brighter than the stars, which might be the battle-field for another splendid conflict as yet not to be conceived. It was towards this splendour that the woman was leading, as we passed her later, leaving the road and treading a path over the turf among gentians which she did not see. 'Good-bye!' Dragutin cried to her. 'Good-bye, Mother!'

Kolashin

Save for a peppering of graves by the roadside, this might have been a better Lake District, a lovelier Coniston. About four in the afternoon we came on the town, which was of the prim and stony Montenegrin pattern, lying on a plain surrounded by shapely hills feathered with delicate woodland, and which greeted us with an inn terrible in its cleanliness, and awe-inspiring in its landlady. She was one of those widows whose majesty makes their husbands seem specially dead. Her large Elgin Marble head bore a crown of lustrous black plaits, and was veiled by a black lace mantilla; her full black gown draped a massive and dignified body which it was impossible to imagine as divided into limbs in the usual manner. While we drank some coffee in the dining-room she bent over us, directing the immense lamps of her eyes on Constantine, and addressed us for some stately moments. I asked in amazement, 'Is she reciting an ode of welcome?' 'Not at all,' said Constantine, 'she is telling me that the house is in great disorder because she is having a bathroom and a water-closet put in, but that they will not be ready for ten days, so that in the meantime you will have to wash in a tin basin and use the earth-closet at the end of the garden.'

'But surely,' I interrupted, after a minute or so, 'she is speaking in Alexandrines.' 'No, in blank verse,' said Constantine, 'there are ten lambs and not twelve in each of her sentences. All Montenegrins speak so when they are at all formal, which is to say when there is any but their family listening. Listen, she is going on to tell us that our Prime Minister, Mr Stoyadinovitch, always stays here, and it is true, for this is his constituency. You will find that she says it all in blank verse.' And so she did. I had been misled into thinking that the measure was Alexandrine because of the singing sweet yet faintly nasal quality of her speech, which recalled a poetry matinée at the Comédie Française. Serbo-Croat is, of course, a language that falls very easily into verse, and until recently was encouraged to do so on occasions at all exalted above the ordinary: when the great American foreign correspondent, Stephen Bonsal, first came to the Balkans in the early nineties he was enchanted to hear the Serbian Minister of Finance introducing his budget in the form of a long poem in blank verse. The logic is obvious. A free people who could make their lives as dignified as they could would naturally choose to speak in verse rather than in prose, as one would choose to wear silk rather than linen. There is, of course, a flaw in the logic, because there are many occasions on which linen and prose are more convenient to wear than silk and verse.

There called on us presently the Chief of Police, who invited us to come with him to see a lake that was fifteen miles or so away. I looked at him with respect, as at a Wild Western sheriff, for Kolashin is no tender district. Its original name was Kol i shen, which, tortuously enough, is the Albanian for St Nicholas. Though it was a Serb settlement in the days of the medieval Serbian Empire, it was later invaded by Catholic Albanians, and in time became a fortified Turkish outpost. During the eighteenth century it happened here, as in many other parts of Montenegro, that the Albanians merged with the Serbs, adopting their language and the Orthodox Faith. Those Albanians who did not do so often joined with the Albanians on Turkish territory to attack the Christianized Albanians. As a climax in 1858 the members of several tribes in the neighbourhood attacked the town and destroyed all the inhabitants who had kept their Albanian identity or who were Moslem. Thereafter there was a kind of surly peace in the district, but it developed a spirit of resistance, of independence, tending towards pure negativism, which made them bitterly resentful after the war when Montenegro was amalgamated with Yugoslavia.

This disaffection had quieted down, for here there were certainly no signs of resentment at the Government automobile as there were in the Macedonian districts where there were unpacified Bulgarians, but it was improbable that it had yet become the bride of quietness. And indeed nothing in the appearance of the Chief of Police suggested that he would have been there if it had. He had a face so tough and imperturbable that one could have played darts on it. But his manners were excellent, and it was with real courtliness that he led us out to the local automobile which we were to use for going to the lake, since ours was too heavy for the road. Like all Montenegrin automobiles, it was a debauched piece of ironmongery. This idyllic country, fresh under every dawn as Nausicaa going down to bathe with her maidens, unmarred by a railway system and possessing no modern nor indeed even medieval town, which is but pastures and woodlands and mountains and primitive villages, set on earth sweet as new bread taken from the oven, is defiled by the presence on its roads of twisted and pointless wrecks of automobiles, which might have been salvaged from Slough dump, driven by lads who have an air of enacting a heroic fantasy. One such, pale and statuesque, with self-consciously dilated nostrils, stood beside this black and crooked carcass.

In the gold of the late afternoon we drove beside a clear brawling river, over a cultivated plain into a valley that was like Coniston Crag, recollected in a dream under an opiate which let the mind stretch a point in favour of loveliness rather than probability. We passed into a beechwood and ran on out of shadow lit by the silver trunks and sunlight stained green, till we were halted by the strange lateral summer of an uprooted tree. My husband and I walked off first with the chauffeur as guide, and Dragutin lingered behind us, looking for animals, catching us up sometimes to show us an emerald beetle or some such creature. Well behind us came Constantine and the Chief of Police, who, like the Chief of Police at Petch, had an air of being a harassed governess in charge of backward and undisciplined children, and was taking the chance to pour out his grievances. After a mile or so the chauffeur told us we must leave the road and take a short cut up the hillside. We turned and saw Dragutin on his knees beside a tangle of tree roots, casting a spell on some form of life, and called to him, pointing upwards to our new path. We found the climb very pleasant, following the soft track through the beechmast under the flaming green roof of tree-tops, for we had had little opportunity of late to take any real exercise. Once I looked back and could not see Dragutin anywhere, so I came to a halt, and heard some shouting down below. It occurred to me that we might have come the wrong way and that the others might be trying to recall us, so I asked the chauffeur, 'Is this really the path?' He replied, 'Yes,' very emphatically, so we shouted to give the others our direction, and pushed on. The path now swung from side to side to avoid some steep stone bluffs, and for a time I was preoccupied in keeping my footing on it. Then I paused to look back. Even now there was nobody in sight. I shouted and no answer came.

Though the tree-tops above us were still catching the sun all the woods below us were in shadow. The sun was setting. I looked at my watch and said to my husband, 'Do you know we have been climbing for half an hour? This cannot be right.' But he learned his climbing in Switzerland, and is indoctrinated with the necessity for trusting the guide. 'The lad lives here,' he said, 'he must know the way.' I asked again, 'Are you sure this is the path?' He answered strangely, looking back as if a danger were pursuing us up the hillside, but impatiently waved us up the path. We worked on for another five minutes up a patch of hillside so steep that I had to plod along with my knees bent and my head down. When I straightened myself my eyes fell on the chauffeur standing some distance ahead with his back to us, and his hand raised on a level with his head and pressed flat against a tree-trunk. This meaningless attitude somehow expressed a definite meaning. I knew that he was lost. I cried out, 'Let us go down again!' but he turned on me a face dark with sullen terror, and at once ran away among the thickets and the tree-trunks.

In a second he was lost to me, for the whole wood was in shadow. I turned and shouted into the darkening valley below me, and there was no reply. My husband was standing a little way off, and I went to him, and put my arm in his, saying, 'Where on earth has that wretched boy gone?' He answered, 'I think there is a woodcutter's hut in the hollow over there, he has probably gone to see if there is anybody there who knows the way. It will be all right.' Just then the chauffeur came back, hurrying so much that he often stumbled, and behind him were two men and a boy in wild white clothes, who were crying out to him in tones of warning and anguish. I could not find any satisfying interpretation of the scene. For a minute it passed through my mind that we had been led into a camp of brigands who would hold us for ransom, but this seemed an unlikely enterprise, since the Chief of Police was one of the party. And it was away from these people that the chauffeur led us when, scrambling up from a fall and brushing the beechmast off his clothes, he stood up before us and panted, with the sweat running down his brow, 'This way! This way!' I looked round to see what danger could be threatening us from the quarter he wanted us to flee, thinking of landslides and forest fires, but there was not a grain of earth shifting on the hill, and the air smelt of nothing but evening.

'Here!' said the chauffeur. 'Here!' He had brought us, with the two men and the boy in white clothes at our heels, to the top of a cliff, where stunted trees leaned into an abyss they veiled with their foliage. 'Where?' He pointed at a track down the face of the cliff which was no more than a mere slippery edge, pressed two or three inches out of the level by a geological fault. I said, 'We cannot go down here in a failing light.' The chauffeur was moved to agony by my hesitation. 'You must go! You must go!' he groaned. 'He must think we are in some danger,' I said to my husband, 'but what is it?' 'I have no idea,' he said. I looked back at the people in white clothes, meaning to ask their advice, and I found the two men stiffened in attitudes of horror and despair, while the boy, who alone of his straight-nosed people had a nose snub as if it had been pressed against something for most of his life, had come forward as if following his own goggling gaze. 'Look!' I cried to my husband, and he turned and saw them also. But he speaks even less Serbian than I do, which is to say he speaks no Serbian at all. So it was I who had to say to the chauffeur, 'We will not go by that path. Take us back to the Chief of Police.' But he answered through his set teeth, 'You must go here! Come, come!'

His resolution weakened mine; but I turned to look at the people in white clothes, and found that the relief they were showing was so great that our refusal to go down the cliff must have had some enormous implications for them, as enormous, say, as the difference between us alive and us dead. I said again, 'Take us back to the Chief of Police!' But his face grew desperate, and he stepped towards me as if he were going to lay hands on me. I realized that I must act as if I were more dangerous than the unknown object of his fear. It had to be a dramatic performance, for I keep no fury in stock, rage makes me silent. I thought of Charlotte Brontë's description of Rachel in *Villette* and, modelling myself on those lines, I waved my arms at the chauffeur and shrieked, 'To the Chief of Police! Down the hill! To the Chief of Police!' He gaped, recoiled, and ran helter-skelter down the hill through the trees, looking back at me and crying, with conciliatory gestures, 'Yes, this is the road!' The breaking of a branch on our left turned our heads that way, and we saw that the snub-nosed boy belonging to the wood-cutters was running down the hill along a course parallel to our track, but about thirty yards away, keeping his face turned towards us as though we were a great wonder and he could not bear to lose sight of us for a second. The chauffeur came to a halt, for the reason that I was out of breath and had not made a minatory sound for some time; he folded his arms and looked sullen. But from the valley below we heard an outburst of panic-stricken shouting and the thin drill of a police whistle. We were at the top of the line of stony bluffs, and I had no idea of the way down. I could think of no more Serbian words, so I began to shriek in the rhythm of the Valkyries, and the chauffeur dived forward again.

When we met they were all white-faced, Constantine and the Chief of Police and Dragutin. 'But what have you been doing?' screamed Constantine. 'Why did you not come back? We have been yelling and yelling and blowing the whistle till we have broken our hearts!' 'Where did you take them?' the Chief of Police shouted at the chauffeur. 'He took us,' I said, 'to the top of the hill, and then he wanted us to go down a track across the face of a cliff.' The Chief of Police threw up his hands. 'That track!'

he cried. The chauffeur, who had thrown his head back and was looking very noble, said something, and Constantine cried, 'But he says that he did not want to take you anywhere, that you insisted on climbing the hill, and that he did not ask you to go down the cliff, but it was your idea.' I exclaimed, 'But what an astonishing liar!' but my husband said, 'Wait a minute, there is something here we do not understand. We may be doing the lad an injustice. You see, up on the hill he began to look disturbed, and my wife asked him if he had lost his way. Then he seemed definitely distressed, and we gathered he was afraid of something. When he wanted us to go down the cliff path, it was as if it was necessary we should do so, as if——' 'Yes, it was necessary,' screamed Constantine, 'for a Montenegrin!' He repeated to the others what my husband had said, and they made signs of impatience and scorn, the Chief of Police holding his head and groaning, Dragutin spitting between his feet.

'These Montenegrins,' hissed Constantine, 'you have not listened to what I have told you about them. I say they are all heroes, they are boastful imbeciles, like the Homeric heroes, and this little *espèce de héros* could not bear to admit to you and to us that he had lost his way and had guided you all wrong. So you had to go down the face of a cliff, you had perhaps to die, in order to show that after all he was right, there was a way.' He shook his clenched fists in the chauffeur's face, shouting, 'How dared you take them that dangerous way?' He shook back his longish hair and replied haughtily, 'The way was not dangerous.' 'That it was,' piped a voice behind. The woodcutter's boy had silently joined us in the dusk. 'We told him how dangerous it was. I cannot go that path, even I in my bare feet, and the lady and gentleman would slip at once in their shoes. Indeed nobody goes that path. It has not been safe for years, and since the great storm last winter trees and lumps of rock fall away from the cliff all the time. My father and my uncles never work under it if they can help.' Shuddering, I said, 'It cannot be so bad. After all, if we had died, he would have been killed too.' 'Do you think that would matter to a Montenegrin?' spluttered Constantine.

A silence fell. The three men looked murderously at the chauffeur. His head went higher and a white tooth bit into his lower lip. The woodcutter's boy, regarding him with a territorial malice that thoroughly enjoyed what evils might befall the inhabitant of another village, drew closer to see the fun. 'And now could we possibly see the lake?' suggested my husband. Constantine and the Chief of Police looked at him as if he were interrupting a trial or a church service. 'It is, after all, what we came here for,' insisted my husband, and they gave in to him, because they were not sure whether he was being quite idiotic, so idiotic that it was useless trying to act reasonably in his neighbourhood, or whether he was practising some last exotic refinement of gentlemanliness. We caught the lake in its last moment of beauty before the dusk took away its colour; beechwoods drooped over a mirror, and behind them pinewoods mounted black over castellated peaks. The trouble was that we could none of us see it, though we sat down on a bench facing it. I was violently shaken by the realization that my husband and I had just escaped being dashed to pieces in order that a young man whom we had never seen till then should not have to admit that he had lost his way. Constantine and the Chief of Police were shaking with rage, Dragutin was uneasy as a child who is obliged to be present at another's punishment, the chauffeur leaned against a tree-trunk, his chin up and his arms folded.

Constantine burst out, 'You see how stubborn they are! They are heroes, they must always go on, they cannot go back, not even if it is merely an evening promenade that is in question, and going on means that you must die! How are we to change them into reasonable men, men of our times, if we are not to beat and beat and beat them?' 'Well, if they had not been like this they would not have kept off the Turk so successfully,' said my husband. 'Yes, but if what was good has been done must it be to do for ever and ever?' asked Constantine angrily. 'I have in my time done many things that were excessively brave, in North Bosnia during the war I have cut myself out of a valley through the bodies of many soldiers with my bayonet, in Bulgaria after the peace I have saved my troops by seizing a railway train in *manu militari*. Must I then always be killing people by my bayonet, must I every day seize a railway train, because it was good that I did so once?' The Chief of Police and he then carried on a passionate exchange of complaining undertones, until the chauffeur cleared his throat and made a remark with an air of sense and dignity, in correct blank verse metre, and they both broke out into angry shouts. 'He is saying such fatuities,' cried Constantine; 'he is saying that you wanted to go to the edge of the cliff to look at the view.' 'Nevertheless,' said my husband, 'I think that the person concerned in this incident for whom I feel the least affection is the woodcutter's boy. Look, he is watching us from under that elder tree on the left.' 'What have you against the little one?' asked Constantine. 'I feel so strongly,' said my husband, 'that if we had gone over the cliff he would have been the first, by quite a long way, to find our bodies.'

When we returned to the inn I was very tired, for it was now thirteen hours since I had risen to go to the Patriarchate at Petch, and I thought I would not be able to eat any dinner. But I ate a great deal, for the stately landlady brought us rich bean soup, and some home-cured raw ham, and a dish of lamb roasted with herbs, and a pile of little cakes, made in the Turkish fashion, of pounded fruit and nuts pressed between two layers of pastry, very well made indeed. There was also some good wine from the southern slope of Montenegro. Dragutin was eating at a table in the opposite corner of the dining-room from ours, and we and he raised our glasses and drank to the health of the widow, who stood in the centre of the room, responding with unexpected animation by contralto cluckings and coy agitations of her black draperies; it was as if we had pleased a rookery.

All was drowsy and agreeable, when the door opened, or rather was thrown open with considerable panache, and the chauffeur came in, very pale. We all fell still and watched him as he came across to our table and halted. 'What is it? What is it?' asked Constantine, and the boy set out on a speech, all in blank verse. Constantine shot out of his chair, he beat the table with his fist, he screamed at the boy, and Dragutin stood up, uttering cries of derision and rage. 'Will you believe it?' Constantine explained when he had gone, 'He does not come to say he is sorry, he is still trying to prove that it was not a fault to take you to that cliff where you might have been dashed to a thousand pieces.' He shuddered and took a deep draught from his glass, wincing at what he saw at the bottom of it. Then his face was shadowed by sinister recollection, by caution, by malice. He remembered that we were English, that we were liberals, that we liked him; and the disposition he had made of his soul required that he should be loyal only to those who were German, who were Nazi, who despised him. He snarled, 'See what trouble you have caused by always being so independent! You two must always do the thing that is extra! If you had kept by the Chief of Police and myself we would have had none of this trouble!' There was nothing for us to say, the charge was so unjust, for we had been sent ahead with the chauffeur as our guide. When Constantine saw that we were not going to answer he looked at Dragutin and repeated what he had said in Serbian. But Dragutin also said nothing.

The widow grew sensible of a change in the atmosphere and began moving about the room on petty errands, tweaking a curtain straight, taking away an empty salt-cellar. My husband put a match to a cigar and said over the flame, 'I do not know why I have never asked you this before, Constantine, for it has often come into my mind. Did you ever pass through a phase in your youth when it seemed to you that no writer existed except Dostoievsky?' The sneer, the look of self-dedication to death vanished from Constantine's face. He said, 'For two years it was so with me. But indeed it was more than so, for I felt that I myself did not exist save as a part of Dostoievsky's mind. I would ask myself, whenever I was at a new thing, "Who are you now? Are you Stavrogin or Shatov? Are you Karamazinov or Alyosha?" ' He set about defining the revelation that Dostoievsky had made to all of us, talking as brilliantly and nobly as I had ever heard him. 'Turgeniev is greater than he, the critics say, and they are right, but if we had not been saved from the pit by Dostoievsky we would not be here to read Turgeniev. . . .'

Nevertheless I shook with a chill that even his recovered fire could not exorcize. The chauffeur had been willing to cast away his life on the hills, and ours also, in order that he should not be thought foolish enough not to know a certain path; Constantine was willing to cast away his self-respect, and indeed all he cared for, art and philosophy and his country's life, for a cause as frivolous: he wished to win the good opinion of those who had given him a sense of their social superiority by pointing out that Berlin was a richer city than Belgrade. So one could not say of the chauffeur, 'He has erred out of curable ignorance,' because Constantine, who was one of the most gifted and learned men in Europe, surpassed him in guilt, and one could not say of Constantine, 'He would not plan his self-destruction had he not overstrained our human equipment,' because the chauffeur had committed the same offense in a state of simplicity. The woman we had met walking on the mountains that afternoon seemed not such a consoling portent as I had thought her. On the great mountains she was so small; against the black universal mass of our insanity her desire for understanding seemed so weak a weapon. Therefore I shuddered, and could take no pleasure in the genius of my friend, nor in my husband's kindness to my friend. I was glad when the widow rose from her seat by the hearth, and, to let us know that hours were getting late for Kolashin, gave us a message which I think Constantine failed to translate with his usual felicity. For I am almost sure that she said she was anxious to do everything she could for us, and that we had better use the earth-closet while the lantern in the garden was still alight; but Constantine announced, 'The widow says she will give you her all, and hopes you will go to the closet before you have an accident.'

Podgoritsa

We left the inn early, taking all the remaining little cakes the widow could give us, and travelled for some miles further through the beechwoods and streams of this sensuous version of the Lake District. Then we crossed a pass into the traditional Montenegro, the land which defies cultivation so that no peasantry could live there were its breast not bound with oak and triple bronze. It is an astonishing country, even to those who know the bleakness of Switzerland and Scotland and the Rockies. There one sees often enough trees growing askew from the interstices of a hillside paved with rocky slabs; but here it is as if a volcanic eruption had been arrested just at the moment when it was about to send the whole countryside flying into the air. The hillside bulges outwards, and slabs and trees jut out at frantic angles to a surface itself at a frantic angle. The inhabitants of such a fractured and anfractuous landscape are obliged to alter some of the activities that might be thought to be unalterably the same all the world over. There could be no such thing as strolling a few hundred yards from one point to another; the distance could be covered only by jumping, striding, and climbing, unless a track were made.

But the next pass brought us to a district even wilder and less easily habitable. It could not be accurately called barren, for there was a certain amount of very rich earth to be seen; but again it had suffered an internal assault that had sent it spinning. We have all seen houses so ruined that only part of the ground-floor walls were left standing, to define rooms that were now plots where grass and weeds and flowers grew more lush than in the wilderness outside. Here it is as if the whole mountainside for twenty miles around were covered with such houses, but the walls were of lilac-blue rock and no mason had built them. If the plots they defined were more than a few yards across crops grew there, or stunted trees, for we were drawing nearer the Adriatic, where timber is precious. But if these plots were small or inaccessible they flamed with flowers, with thickets of tall iris and torches of broom, rising out of the blanched hellebore. It was a hungry scene, yet it offered distractions to hunger.

As we came down towards the lowlands and the distant sea we ran within sight of a canyon, cut by a river that flowed a dull bright-green, clear and yet snake-like, over sand and pebbles.

This colour delights the Yugoslavs very much. It is mentioned in the folk-songs of the district, and all sorts of people, from Militsa to an assistant in a Belgrade shoe-shop, had said to me, 'You are going to Montenegro? Then you must look long at the water of the Moracha, which runs through Podgoritsa, for it is very beautiful.' Beyond the canyon were low mountains ruled into natural terraces so level that the artificial terraces on the fertile land at their base seemed faultily ruled. Then the distance flattened out into plains, and before we got to them we halted for a minute or two to hang over a bridge that spanned a river sent down from the mountains to join the Moracha. 'This bridge,' said Constantine, 'was fought over again and again by the Turks and the Montenegrins, again and again it has run with blood. For this is the key position to these fertile flatlands, which are the best part of the Zeta, which was Turkish until the Montenegrins took it from them once and for all in 1876.' 'They are good lands,' said Dragutin, rubbing his stomach; 'now others as well as the Turk can eat.' 'God, why do you speak of eating when we are out here in the country!' exclaimed Constantine. 'Drive us at once to Podgoritsa.'

We travelled fast beside the river in the canyon, which runs all the way into the town without losing the integrity of its strange and brilliant colour, and soon we were eating trout in the dining-room of the principal hotel. We had not wasted one moment looking at the sights of Podgoritsa, for too evidently it has none. There are hardly any relics of the Turkish occupation; and as a modern town it lacks charm. It is solid, for it used to be the second town of Montenegro, and it is now the administrative capital of the district, but it is built without eloquence. Stone, which everywhere else imposes a certain rhetoric on those who build with it, can do nothing against the limitations of the Montenegrin genius, and expresses nothing but forthrightness and resistance. But there was an immense amount of human sightseeing to be done here, even in this dining-room.

As soon as we sat down, a plump elderly man, with hair artlessly dyed an incredible piano-black, rushed across the dining-room and embraced Constantine. 'What are you doing so far from Belgrade?' he cried. 'And you? I did not know you could breathe outside the Café Moscow,' cried Constantine. A beautiful young man, who was sitting at the next table and had been staring at a letter instead of eating his trout, looked up at these metropolitan greetings, seemed to recognize both parties, and broke into bitter silent laughter. Fiercely he folded up the letter, put it into his pocket, and started on his fish. The fat man explained that he was in Podgoritsa rehearsing the local repertory company in one of his dramas. 'And a very fine job they are making of it too,' waving his hand in a courtly gesture; and we saw that the players were all around us, eating trout. The men sat at one table: a couple of spaniel-eyed juveniles, the *père noble* with a toupee that rode higher and higher as he laid down the law with a wagging forefinger, and the funny man, who had the anxious face of a concerned mother and a shelving belly. The leading lady ate alone. Though she was not young she was very handsome and she had authentic glamour. That is not to say that she resembled Miss Marlene Dietrich, and announced herself poisoned by special self-generated sexual toxins, affecting the face like the heavier sorts of beer. It is to say that while she was well equipped for love and sensible of its claims, she would be far more difficult for a lover to subjugate than the most frigid spinster. For it was inconceivable that the love of a man could ever matter to her so much as the approval of an audience. No lover, therefore, could ever feel sure of her, even after he had physically possessed her; she would leave any Romeo to play Juliet. And every man could promise himself the triumph of breaking down her preoccupation and making himself more precious to her than applause.

She could not have been more attractive as she sat there, doubly dazzling with the radiance of a Slav blonde and the maquillage of her profession, which seemed to proclaim her as more accessible than other women and actually proved her less; for the black on her lashes was designed to convince not a lover within kissing distance but the man at the back of the gallery, and her complexion did not aim at freshness but at transporting into ordinary life the climate of the footlights. How little she and her kind represented pure passivity was shown by two older actresses at another table, who illustrated another phase of their being. Both were elderly, one had been very beautiful; about them was neither embitterment nor despair, only the cynicism of old foxes that had evaded the hunters a thousand times and found their holes in time. Their value, real or imagined, in the world of art had given them a refuge from all the common ills of life, had given them the power to tell any person who tried to humiliate or disappoint them that it was not to be done, that they could only be hurt by unknown people, sitting in rows. As I watched them, one said to the other, 'My dear! What can you expect from such people!' Her darkened eyebrows went up, her rouged lips went down at the corners, her fine wrist turned and showed a safety-pin where a button should have been at her cuff. The sight evoked the disorder I knew would be characteristic of the rooms of all these three women, of all women like them in every country, which would proceed not so much from slovenliness as from defiance of all conventions touching on regularity, and from refusal to spend one drop of nervous force anywhere but on the stage. I put down my knife and fork and clapped my hands, for I had thought of something pleasant that I could say to Constantine about the Germans.

It took him and his friend some time to part. The spectacle of their prolonged conversation made the young man at the next table take out the letter he had put in his pocket and tear it to pieces. It was typewritten and no doubt administrated a rebuff to some notable literary ambition; and no doubt that was a real tragedy, for there is an astonishing amount of ability in these small Slav towns. In another Montenegrin town, Nikshitch, there is published a brilliant satirical journal. At last Constantine sat down with us, smiling and panting, 'You see, I have friends everywhere!' and I said, 'Listen, Constantine, I have just thought of something that proves you right and me wrong!' 'Aha, such news I love to hear,' he cried, beaming and falling on his fish. 'I have sometimes spoken ill of Goethe in your presence,' I said, 'and I take it all back. There is one thing he did perfectly, and he did it for all time. I remembered it as soon as I saw your friend's company waiting around him. Nobody can see actresses in any country, neither a touring company waiting at an English railway junction, nor Comédie Française *pensionnaires* rehearsing in a Roman arena, nor stars lunching at the Algonquin in New York, without thinking of one thing, and one thing only!'

'And that is?' asked Constantine. '*Wilhelm Meister's Apprenticeship!*' I said. 'Yes,' said Constantine. 'Yes, indeed,' I said happily. 'Do you not remember the wonderful description of the untidiness of the lovely Mariana's bedroom? He has a superb image for the theatrical make-up and costumes that lay about, as different from what they were in use as the glittering skin of a fish cast aside by the cook in a kitchen. He catalogues the other oddments in her room, the plays and pincushions and hairpins and sheet-music and artificial flowers, as all united by a common element, an amalgam of powder and dust. And he describes how young Wilhelm, used to the order of his bourgeois home, was at first shocked when he had to lift aside his mistress's bodice before he could open the harpsichord, and had to find another place for her gown if he wanted a seat, but later came to find a special charm in this chaotic housewifery.' 'Yes, yes,' said Constantine.

'What, do you not like *Wilhelm Meister?*' I asked, for he spoke a little coldly. 'Oh, yes, very much,' he said. But his eyes stared over my right shoulder, returned to me, examined me without much interest, then sought space again. 'He does not believe me,' I thought penitently. 'I have convinced him too well that I don't like Goethe.' So I continued aloud, 'I am sure that if you went home with the leading lady over there you would find that her room was just like Mariana's and that she herself was like Mariana and Philina, and perhaps even the serious Aurelia.' 'Yes, yes,' said Constantine, 'I think you are right.' But his voice was distant as his eyes. 'It is no use,' I thought, 'he believes I cannot really be fair to anything German. And it is he who is not being fair to me, for I can see beauty there as everywhere else.' I saw the Germany which was the setting for Mariana and Philina and Aurelia, the neo-classical villas with their creamy white stucco pilasters and pediments, the lilacs and chestnuts, the fountains and the statuary that was none the worse for being none too good; and I was about to tell Constantine how much I liked that scene when my husband asked, 'Constantine, why are you looking so hard at those people?'

I turned, and saw that while I had been looking at an antique Germany, Constantine had been looking in the opposite direction at the actual Germany. At a round table behind me sat eight people, four men in open shirts and leather shorts, four women in dirndlish cotton dresses, all very fair and much overweight. 'They look very harmless,' I said. 'You have not found the right word,' answered Constantine, 'for the oldest and tallest of the men is Altdorff, the chief German agent in Yugoslavia.' 'Well, surely he is being very harmless at the moment,' I said; 'he is evidently just having an outing with his friends.' Constantine did not answer for a minute. Then he burst out, 'I am not sure. I think he is doing more than having a *Bummel* with these pieces of raw meat. I believe there must be something with Albania. Why was that little one with the knickerbockers whom the monk did not trust waiting at Sveti Naum, which is the Albanian frontier? Why was there that fool who said he was a Dane at Petch, which is also on the Albanian frontier? Why is this Altdorff here in Podgoritsa, which again is on the Albanian frontier? It is certain that there is trouble to come in Albania, that the Italians are to do something frightful to the Albanians, and their friends the Germans, who do not so greatly love them, wait outside to see how it goes. I do not think you English know anything about Albania. For it is nearly Italian, they have their officials there, they control the whole country; some day they will have their army there too, and it will be as a pistol pointed at Yugoslavia.' He shuddered violently and said, '*Ils avancent toujours.*' He spoke as a Serb, as a Jew, as an inheritor of the French tradition.

Beams of sunshine, dancing with motes, struck the unstained wooden floor, the stiff coarse tablecloths, the emphasized faces and gestures of the players, who were so little confident in their natural endowment that they had brightened all that was bright and darkened all that was dark with cosmetics, who paid their kind the lovely tribute of living for their applause, the featureless, stockish spies, who were contented with their mission, who cared nothing for good opinion. There was a strong smell of fish, for all of us were eating trout. Constantine said, in a faltering voice, 'My friend who is here rehearsing his play is not a true writer. He is a very rich man who would give his all to be a writer. But his plays are very, very bad, because he does not write them. He is a shrewd man of much appetite, he likes to eat and drink and to be with women, and he has so made himself much experience, and he is intelligent enough to understand what he does. But when he picks up a pen it is not himself who guides it, it is some little woman whom he has swallowed when he was yawning with his great mouth, and who now lives somewhere in him, say in his kidney, and chooses the time when he picks up a pen to have things her way. For his plays are so small, and so *fade*, and so weak, they are just what a nun would write for her *pensionnaires*.'

Lake Scutari

For an hour that afternoon we sat on a bouldered hillside, tufted with great blue flowers and peppermint, looking down on the plains about Podgoritsa which were cut into sections, slender as cake-slices in a genteel household, and tidily planted with maize and tobacco, apple orchards, fig trees, and full-foliaged mulberry trees. A puff of dust travelling rapidly along a straight road cut through this neatness showed that my husband had left his hat in the inn at Podgoritsa and that Dragutin had gone back to fetch it. It was warm now, with a clear blue sky overhead and some white mists lying like scarves on the plain. On a little knob of rock above us a white cloud stood like a toy. I strolled about picking flowers within earshot of the two men. 'There is no equivalent in English,' I heard my husband say, 'for the French word *banaliser*.' 'That shows an insensitiveness,' said Constantine, 'for banalization is one of the most important processes in life. There are two sorts of banalization, the sort that comes from below, and the sort that comes from above. The first I have recognized when I have been successful. For I have sometimes been successful, more successful than anyone else in Yugoslavia. I have written plays which were so popular that people were crushed to death going into the theatre every night. I have written novels of which nobody in Belgrade has not talked of nothing else. In those days the papers sent many reporters to interview me, and I noticed always that they would take out of my remarks all that is characteristic of me, all that had made my plays and books successful. Often I have wished to ask, "But why do you think your editors sent you to interview me if it were not for that little thing I have which you have so cleverly removed from what I say? Do you not understand that it is precisely because I have that way of thinking and writing which is not yours that I am a favourite writer and you are a reporter?" But I did not, of course. That is why folly is immortal; wise men are too busy to correct fools.

'Then, when I found I could not write fast enough to keep my wife and children, and I became a Government official, I learned of the other kind of banalization. For I had to write speeches for our Ministers, and I wrote them speeches which were not only good but magnificent, as nobody else in the world could have written them, great in themselves, very great, and always wonderfully appropriate to the occasion when they must be given. And to my stupefaction the Ministers altered them, every one they altered, just in the same way as the reporters altered what I said to them. They banalized them. When the speeches left my pen, they were wise and memorable and persuasive. When the Ministers delivered them, they were not as sensible as any grocer in a quiet little town, they must be forgotten one minute after they were heard, they would make nobody not change no opinion. Yet this kind of banalization was not the same as the reporter's kind, though it looked the same. For that meant poverty and obscurity, this meant wealth and glory. It was something absolutely necessary to being a Minister. For sometimes a Minister came who did not alter my speeches, and who spoke them so that his audiences cheered again and again and said they would die for him; and always he fell and was disgraced. Now, that I cannot understand, that the way to be poor and the way to be rich should be the same. But here I am very comfortable, for there is nothing but the rocks and the sun.'

Dragutin was a long time away; and when he came back he was as pleased as a doctor who finds that a patient he suspected of anaemia has enough red corpuscles. 'There's still a lot of life in that town,' he said, and with gusto showed us how a lawless Podgoritsan had attracted his attention by winking and folded back his jacket to show pockets stuffed with cigarettes that had never paid duty to the internal revenue. 'Take one,' said Dragutin, 'they're good. Oh, they're not done, down there, by any means. But, *houp la!* If you're to have a good look at Lake Scutari we must start now.' We mounted to regions of rock washed by rain and baked by sun to surgical cleanliness. At a great cement cistern we stopped to take water for the engine and look at some girls who were sitting near by round the great trunk of a plane tree, their black and white sheep standing in the shadow. On this side of Montenegro the women have lost their Byzantine tensity and are Du Maurier duchesses, with the same numismatic profiles and uptilted, humourless dignity, and the same underlying simplicity and amiability and resolution in good behaviour. These girls needed only tie-backs and tennis rackets and little boys in sailor suits to be as familiar as any old volume in *Punch*.

'Is it not one of the world's wonders?' asked Dragutin, when a few more turns of the road took us to a view of Lake Scutari; and indeed it was among landscapes what dragons are among beasts. Through a deep fiord, a thousand feet or so below us, a river flowed into the lake, slowly and without confusion of the two substances, as water from a dripping tap might seep into a cask of molasses.

For this lake is not water, it is mud. It was green as a horse-pond on an English common, but the substance was not so liquid. It was nearly solid; the reflections it bears were not superficial images which a breeze will confuse and annul, but photographs imposed on a sensitive jelly. The forms that were photographed followed a strictly geometric pattern. The fiord described a curve, and between its green margins the river dragged the slow snake of its trail in the same curve. The rocky world that framed the lake was hewn into triangles, great and small. The higher peaks lifted acute apices, the low hills and islands lay squat under obtuser apices. Under each of these triangles, except the high peaks, was the inverted triangle of its image, more solid, more dogged, more of a fact than reflections commonly are, because they were registered on this viscid medium. The archipelago at the mouth of the fiord looked like a fleet of overloaded ships, becalmed in a Sargasso sea; the light shone back from the lake between them a white opaque haze, as if it could not rise freely into the upper air. In this landscape there had happened to matter what happens to time when, as they say, it stands still. Mobility was not. There was this grey rock, its dwarf trees and bushes growing so low among the boulders that they were as if nailed to the mountainside; and there was this greenish jelly in which rivers and reflections and even light itself foundered and were fixed. It would have been appropriate to come on this inspissation through tropical heat, but as we looked down on it we were blown on by the freshest sort of airs, winds from the sea and the peaks. Here nature was at its most unnatural; and the scale of the scene, which was immense, as much as the eye could see from a great height, made this prodigiousness alarming. It was as if one learned that nightmares might fill not only a troubled hour after midnight but the whole of the night and the day, that a historical epoch might hold horror and nothing else. Yet it was beautiful, so beautiful that the appalled sight could not have enough of it.

'There is a child looking at us from behind those boulders,' said my husband. 'Say nothing and she may come nearer,' said Constantine, 'but we must be very cautious, here even the little ones are shy and proud.' It was ten minutes before the little girl came from cover, and then she had been joined by a friend. 'Good day, little ones,' called Constantine. 'Please, can you tell me if that island with the two peaks is Vranina?' They would not be discourteous. They came to us, though reluctantly. Perhaps they were ten years old, and they were clad in homespun linen frocks, multi-coloured woollen stockings, and sandals with upturned toes. They carried long withies, and below them their black and dust-coloured sheep spread in a munching fan over the mountainside. One was fair and the other dark, with the fine hair about the brows and temples sunburned to honey colour. Both were beautiful, with a thorough and careful beauty that attended to everything, making marvels of such matters as the arch of the eyebrows and the indentation of the upper lip. Both were sublimely dignified. Neither their features nor their limbs sprawled. They were as proud as good people would choose to be in the sight of strangers, revealing nothing ungentle and nothing too tender.

It could be seen that they were amused by the sight of Constantine. They thought that this little fat man with the animal muzzle and the tight black curls was a great joke. But they showed it not by sneering or by any breach of courtesy, but by grave fascinated smiles. They were as little princesses, trained never to fall from graciousness. A boy pushed up the hillside and stood beside them, indubitably a little prince. Another princess came, another prince. The five stood in a line of loveliness, and Constantine sat himself down on a boulder, and set himself to display the tried and potent magic he stored under those black curls, with spreading hands, pouting lips, rolling eyes, and voice that lifted and paused before the crises so that the hearers squeaked the delivering syllable. So, centuries before, one of his blood may have enchanted the market-place of ancient Asian towns. Soon the children were asking him breathless questions, sometimes they were choking with excited laughter, sometimes they made him go back and alter what he had said, because it had offended some fairy-tale convention.

I have no idea what story he told them. Usually he translated to us what passed in his wayside conversations, but this time he was too happy and spoke to us only twice. Once he spun round on his boulder and said, 'They have a name for each of their sheep, very fanciful names.' Then later, when another princess had scrambled up the path and joined the circle at his feet, a little girl who held her chin as if she stood before many judges, all despised, he greeted her, and told us: 'This is very interesting. Her name is Gordan, which is as if you should call a child Proud. There must be some story there, for her parents to have called their child that name.' As he spoke the children watched as if they understood, nodding faintly, their eyes bright with intelligence and hooded with restraint. Plainly they admired their companion's distinction, whatever it was, and could have told the story behind her name, but would not talk of such things to strangers. So they put aside their gravity before it settled on them and clamoured to Constantine that he should go on with his story.

But the fair little princess who had been the first to come up the hillside did not give him her full attention, though at first she had been the most eager listener. She looked across at my husband and myself every now and then, with increasing uneasiness. We were not being honoured as guests should be. She tried to remedy this by giving us a sweet personal smile; but her conscience told her that this was not enough and would not let her settle down to listen. So she went down the hillside to a patch of flowers and began picking us a proper ceremonial nosegay, of the prescribed size and variety. This was a great sacrifice, and sometimes it was too much. She would catch a burst of laughter from the circle she had left, and she would run back and join the listeners for a moment or two. But her eyes would fall on us again, and she would pick herself up and go back to her task. When she had the nosegay she thought correct, she brought it to me at a leisured pace, curtsied, and kissed my hand. For a minute I could not bear to let her go; I put my arm round her shoulders, for to have this exquisite creature of remote and superior race so close was such luck as having a butterfly alight on one's fingers. She bore my touch with good manners, smiling straight into my eyes and giving my husband also his share of greeting, but the minute I let her go she was back in a flash at the circle round Constantine.

I went to the automobile and fetched the cakes I had brought from Kolashin, and found Dragutin sitting on the automobile trying to teach a tortoise he had just picked up on the road to lick a piece of chocolate. 'Why always grass, grass, grass?' he was asking. I took the cakes over to Constantine, and put them under his nose so as not to interrupt him; and instantly they became part of his story. His eyes did not fall from the far towers and domes he was describing, his voice did not sink from the great billows which were washing heroes and giants and emperors' daughters to this mountainside. With a wizard's gesture he called the fair princess to him and handed her the cakes, bidding her give one to each of the children. 'Now all of you kneel!' he ordered. They went down on their knees. 'Now the first bite!' They all obeyed him. 'Now the second! Now the third!'

He had told them, I think, that these were magic cakes, and that the first three bites would exempt them from some ill fortune or guarantee them some virtue, and they half disbelieved and wholly believed him. They gurgled with laughter as they ate, but between bites they eyed the cakes very solemnly; however, their tongues, which knew nothing about magic, but recognized good rich pastry when they met it, shot out and licked in the crumbs, and it was taste which dominated them in the end. They sat back on their little haunches, and slowly and delicately finished the last morsels while Constantine silently watched them, his elbow on his knee, his chin on his hand. Behind their loveliness the long high vista of Lake Scutari, with its grey pyramids of rock mounting towards the noon of the sky though ooze-bound in the adhesiveness of green jelly, was earth's self-drawn ideogram, expressing its monstrosity.

Tsetinye I

Underneath the mountainside a town slept beside a river which was a mirror of woodlands. It was called by its name, Riyeka, which is to say, river: or, in full, Riyeka Tcherniyevitsa, the river of the Tchernivitches, the tribe inhabiting this slope of the Montenegrin fastness. While Dragutin sought some petrol we sat under the trees on the embankment, looking about us at an unbelievable prettiness. There was an old and asymmetrical bridge of enchanting camber; along our side of the river lay rowing-boats curved like bows; on the opposite bank blossoming trees stood above their reflections. Behind us was a line of sober stone houses with handsome people sitting at open doors. In the nearest house three middle-aged women and an old one were superb. We were to notice then and later that the female Montenegrin is better to look at as a little girl or as an ageing woman than in the period of her sexual attractiveness, for then she presents a disconcerting blankness. Her face is like a niche designed for a statue it does not hold. Perhaps this is because there is part of a mature woman's nature which must be filled by sexual love or a sublimation of it, or be sensibly empty, and the male Montenegrin has kept his liberty only by maintaining a continuous masculinist frenzy which prevents him from loving women or letting them forget lack of love in thought and work. This leaves the female Montenegrin no worse off than many women in the industrialized West whose men are bled white by invisible enemies more dangerous than the Turks, but her tragedy is made more dramatic by her marked physical appropriateness to love.

'God be thanked,' said Dragutin, 'I have found petrol. We can be in Tsetinye in half an hour, for it is only sixteen kilometres straight up that mountainside.' But when we went to tell Constantine he was not pleased. He had fallen in with three old men who at first had taken him for an ordinary tourist and had grumbled, 'This is a ruined town; all is falling into decay, we are all poor as dogs and Belgrade does nothing for us,' but became more cheerful when he retorted, 'Well do I know why this town is ruined, and there is nothing Belgrade can do about it, nor should, you wicked old men. For if you were rich before the war it was only because this was a frontier town, and you were all smugglers. Yes, all of you offended against the law, and I do not know that I could bring myself to speak to such people were it not that I come from Shabats, from Shabats

on the river Sava, that used to be on the Serbian frontier, and there
we all of us smuggled from the day we were born, and I would like
to know whether you are as clever as me at packing tobacco into a
shoe.' By now the four of them were old cronies, and Constantine
turned a desolate face on us. 'We cannot yet go to Tsetinye,' he
said. 'I must take you across the bridge, for you must see Lake
Scutari from the other side, and also you must see the ruins of
the monastery of Obod, where the first Slav printing-press was
installed in the fifteenth century, and was destroyed by the Turks,
who destroyed all, in the sixteenth century. Many religious books
were published there. That, very certainly you must see.' In the
automobile he groaned, 'Up there in Tsetinye, Sava Militchevitch,
my official, is waiting for me; up there it will be the world, it will
be like Belgrade.'

After we had crossed the bridge we heard no more of the
monastery of Obod, and we wandered among pleasantness of a
sort I had never imagined, never heard described. Beyond the
bridge the river widened out into a curd of yellow water-lilies,
edged with a streak of mirror at each bank, in which willow
trees, standing above their exact reflections, amazed us by their
shrill green and cat-o'-thousand-tails form; they were like static
fireworks. Handsome boys in uniform from a naval station rowed
about, their arched boats cutting the golden cream of waterlilies
with the action of an icebreaker. Beyond the river mouth Lake
Scutari was more solid still than it had been in the fiord on the other
side, and more bewildering: beneath hills covered with delicious
woodland, emerald water-meadows met at an invisible line of
marshes apparently only a shade less firm than themselves, which
were impressed with a heavy and faulty image of the woodlands,
like an unsuccessful colour photograph. About such shining viscous
lochs we followed wandering lanes that took us past a quarry choked
with honeysuckle; a quince orchard rising in terrace upon terrace
of coarse clean blossom; a farmhouse with closed shutters of ardent
blue, standing in lands trim as a stage, yet desolate and unpeopled
as if they were tilled by phantoms. From that silence we looked
up at a mountainside which from here was a sheer grey wall
surmounted with a parapet of snow, flushed now from the west;
there Constantine had told his tale and given the cakes to the little
princes and princesses, who would still be keeping their sheep
among the scrub, for their day is long. 'Time to go up to Tsetinye,'
said Dragutin. 'Yes, yes,' said Constantine sadly; but he recovered
his spirits on the way back to Riyeka when he started playing with
the automobile radio and tuned in to Milan, for that station was

broadcasting a particularly palpitant opera, and he discovered that if he turned it on at the right moments it was an effective substitute for a hooter. Astonished peasants taking home their calves or their pack-horses were hurled out of our way by soprano invocations of *amore* which were cut off before the obvious tryst could be kept with the tenor. 'For this,' said Constantine unjustly, 'has Italian music been made.'

We climbed the sheer mountainside and dropped over the crest, and found Tsetinye. It lies in a stony crater like a town set inside the brainpan of an enormous skull. Its square stone houses, laid out in broad streets, are typically Montenegrin in a Puritanism that suffers no decoration save an occasional great tree; and all its horizons are edged with a breaking wave of rock, which at this hour was the colour of chill itself. A division of the Sokols, the Hawks, the patriotic gymnastic societies, was holding a congress here, and as we entered this town that looked like a Golgotha we heard the sound of several bands and had to drive slowly through crowds of beautiful young men and women in various kinds of peasant dress and uniform. For some time we could not reach the front door of our hotel because the people standing in front of it had suddenly taken it into their heads to form a great circle and dance the kolo. A moon, caught in the foliage of a great tree behind them, shone back from the windows of a large house beside the hotel, giving it an air of being no sort of habitation for the living. 'That,' said Constantine, 'was the boarding school for young ladies which was financed by the Tsarina of Russia.' There the little dears of Dalmatia and Croatia and Bosnia, imported here to be imbued with the principles of absolutism, learned to read Stepniak and Kropotkin and Gorki. I was receiving a last demonstration of the Balkan habit of making life fully visible, of gathering up diffused events into an apprehensible symbol. The bleached town, set on aridity, was the scene of innumerable futilities committed by Imperial Russia. The moon had continued to shine on it, the people had continued to dance.

After the Montenegrin vespers, when the Martinovitch brothers had purged their people of the spreading Moslem taint, Peter the Great conceived an admiration for these people. He had an eye for the quality of the South Slavs, it was to Kotor he had sent a party of his young nobles to learn seamanship. He treated Montenegro with special favour, proclaiming the Prince-Bishop Danilo as his ally 'to conquer the Turk and glorify the Slav faith and name,' and sending him money and gifts calculated to foster the Orthodox religion, such as missals, vestments, and icons. This tradition was maintained by his successors until it was interrupted by a priggish and doctrinaire attitude of bureaucrats towards a people fighting for its life in primitive conditions. In 1760 a Russian envoy was sent to inquire into the disposition the then Prince-Bishop Sava was making of the subsidy. This envoy was scandalized when he found that the Prince-Bishop was using his nephew, Bishop Vasili, an able politician, to dole out the money to the different tribes in such a way as to cement their loyalty to the central government; the loyal were rewarded, the troublesome had to go without. The Russian bureaucrat had an idea that the money ought to have been distributed equally among the tribes in the name of Russia, and he coldly withdrew, leaving out of account the excellent resistance the Montenegrins were making against the Turks, and advised the Empress to send them no more subsidies or gifts. Vasili went to St. Petersburg to beg for a reversal of the decision, and there he died. He was taken ill and had not a penny for his ordinary necessities or medical attention. Because he was a Bishop the Russians gave him a gorgeous funeral in St. Alexander Nevsky.

As the Russian Government had thus destroyed the mechanism by which order was maintained, the country was plunged into riot, which the Prince-Bishop Sava could not control now that he had lost Vasili. The day was saved by the emergence of a new and gifted leader, a monk named Stephen the Little, who claimed that he was Tsar Peter III, Catherine the Great's husband, although that sad nonentity had been safely murdered by Orloff some years before. It is difficult to suppose that Stephen the Little's claim was believed in by the people who accepted it in anything like the strict sense of the word 'believe.' A monk cannot well appear in a monastery from nowhere, and indeed it is said that many recognized him as a member of a well-known Dalmatian family. Like many impostors he probably put forward his story as a symbolic expression of his inborn right to power, and though his followers would have denied that they regarded it in such a light, they showed very clearly that they were not going to abandon him if it were proved untrue.

Stephen the Little very soon showed unusual ability by restoring order among the tribes and bringing them into a united front against the Turks. But Catherine the Great was inspired to send a suite of thirty officers under Prince Dolgoruki to Montenegro on the double and inharmonious mission of denouncing Stephen the Little as a fraud and enlisting Montenegrin volunteers to fight against the Turks with the Russian Army. They had an unenjoyable visit. When they arrived to stay with the Prince-Bishop they were appalled by the amount of rakia they were expected to drink with the monks, and by the irregularity and frugality of the meals. Then the heads of the tribes came to pay their respects, and when they were all assembled they were joined by Stephen the Little and an enthusiastic band of followers. It should be understood that Stephen the Little must have realized that Prince Dolgoruki would denounce him if he presented himself. When the denunciation was made the Montenegrins refused to shoot Stephen the Little, as the Russians suggested, but they consented to imprison him, and locked him up in a room above the quarters occupied by Prince Dolgoruki.

The troubles of the mission then began. During the next few days the Turkish forces made preparations for a fresh attack, and the Patriarch of Petch and one of his Bishops arrived at Tsetinye to beg for help against tyranny in their district; and spies came in with the news that the Turks had been delighted by the imprisonment of Stephen the Little. The Montenegrins then gathered round and pointed out how regrettable it was that they now had a Prince-Bishop, a visiting Patriarch and Bishop, a Russian prince and thirty Russian officers, and no leader. They went on to point out that Prince Dolgoruki had allowed them to imprison Stephen the Little in a room above his own, and that this was a proof that he knew the monk was of a rank superior to his own.

Incredible as it may seem, this remark has been recorded by historian after historian as a sign of Montenegrin simplicity and ignorance. Actually this was a convention respected both at Versailles and at the court of the Romanoffs. For this reason the rooms above the suites of the French King and the Tsar always were left vacant. Prince Dolgoruki and his thirty officers then hastily fled down the face of Mount Lovchen to Kotor, and sailed away, leaving Stephen to share power over Montenegro with the Prince-Bishop for the next eight years, till 1774. He might have reigned much longer, for he was an excellent governor, teaching the tribes to respect life and property as never before, had he not been murdered by a barber who was sent to his monastery by the Pasha of Scutari. This crime looks as if it could be counted against the Turks, but the Pashalik of Scutari was a hereditary office held by a family of renegade Serbs; and it cannot even be counted against Islam, for the records of the Venetian Inquisition candidly disclose that the Inquisition sent a certain count to Montenegro with instructions to kill Stephen the Little and equipped him with a bottle of poison.

The order created by this great impostor survived him. The country was still well disciplined when the Prince-Bishop Sava died in 1782 and it was taken over by his brilliant nephew, Prince-Bishop

Peter I. This man was almost as much of a prodigy as Stephen the Little, for he was as fine a soldier and as dexterous in the political work of civilizing and unifying the tribes, and he had a legal mind of a high order; he codified the law and inaugurated a judicial system. He had also the advantage of longevity, which made him able to carry his ideas into effect during a reign of forty-eight years, and win one of his most spectacular victories against the Turks at the age of seventy-three. He appealed powerfully to the imaginative mind of the Tsar Alexander I, who subsidized him handsomely in return for the use of his troops. They must have been the most disconcerting allies. There exists the horrified testimony of a Russian naval officer, who had fought beside them, a Monsieur Broniewsky. 'When, at the attack of Clobuk, a little detachment of our troops was obliged to retreat, one of our officers, a man of stout habit, no longer young'—one sees him as a subsidiary character in *Evgenye Onegin*—'fell to the ground from exhaustion. A Montenegrin perceived it and ran immediately to him and drew his yataghan, saying, "You are very brave, and must wish that I should cut off your head rather than that you should fall into the hands of the enemy. So say a prayer and make the sign of the cross." '

I could understand the feelings of that officer after we had spent the evening with Constantine's friend, Sava Militchevitch, who came out and claimed us, as we stood watching the kolo sway and pause and beat out a rhythm and pause again, dusted like the ground it danced on with the fine white powder of the moonlight. Sava was cast in the handsome Montenegrin mould, and his character was plainly as noble as his appearance, but I could not dismiss a suspicion that in certain circumstances he might invite me to say a prayer and make the sign of the cross in order that he might cut my head off, and that he would be inspired by such exalted sentiments it would be unthinkable to resist them. Over dinner he conversed in French and Italian, and revealed himself as spiritual brother to the nicest kind of don; he would have fitted very well into Oxford or Princeton. But he was heroic, he was classical. He offered to step into our modern and minor world, since he knew we were at ease there, but his heart was hardly able to carry his offer.

This attitude was pervasive; it touched the whole of life, yet sprang strong and undeflected from the small confines of his people's customs. It appeared at once when he handed us our mail, and I found in my packet a letter from my mother-in-law over which I groaned, for the reason that her handwriting has every good quality except legibility. Sava was visibly shocked, and was not really soothed when I explained that I was groaning because of my impatience to read the letter which was sure to be sensible and humorous. He would have liked it better if I had begun my married life by extravagant rites of prostration before my mother-in-law which would have taught me to regard her as a representative of Demeter and to take what she gave me in the way of handwriting or anything else. Later, when he heard that I had received the Order of St Sava for lecturing in Yugoslavia, he said to my husband, 'And you, did you not get anything? Here in Montenegro we men would not be content if our wives were given something and we did not have it too.' Though he laughed at himself, it was obvious that he felt that there was really something a little ridiculous about a husband whose wife had a distinction he had not, even if his own distinctions were far greater. A man should have everything, because he is a hero, because he is half divine in his courage, and because there must be a predestined attraction between him and the fruits of the earth if his lot is not to be intolerably uncertain. The theory would be invalidated if women were allowed to draw to themselves a single fruit, for though women may be heroic it is only as amateurs, they are never dedicated, full-time professionals. But as compensation the bountiful male will accord the female the last degree of respect and protection, and Sava spoke of the Montenegrin women as if they were so many saints, for all of whom and each of whom he would have given his life.

This was not merely talk. It could be taken for granted that this man had no timidity, as it can be taken for granted that most of us Westerners have much of it. This, of course, was not to the point, for what women want is not individual protection but a high standard of civil order, and the two things are not completely harmonious. That we realized when my husband asked whether Montenegrin peasant costume, with its wealth of gold and silver and silk braid, was expensive, and Sava told him that it represented a heavy tax on a poverty-stricken people, for the suit alone cost thirty pounds, and there were many accessories, including a rifle. 'Does one have to take out a licence to carry a rifle?' asked my husband. 'Yes,' answered Sava, 'of course one has to take out a licence if one is going to carry a rifle, as in any other civilized state, but not if one is wearing our national costume.' 'Surely that defeats the whole idea of a gun licence,' said my husband. 'But we are a military people,' said Sava, 'how could we have a national costume that did not include a rifle?'

Among my husband's mail was a telegram asking him to be in Budapest three days earlier than we had planned, and we were discussing the changes this involved when Constantine suddenly said, 'Is that not the German Minister from Albania sitting over there?' 'Yes,' said Sava, 'he arrived this afternoon.' 'Why is that?' asked Constantine. 'I have no idea,' said Sava, 'perhaps he is on his way home for a holiday.' 'Has anything happened in Albania?' asked Constantine. 'I haven't heard so,' said Sava, 'and certainly there is nothing in the papers.' 'But there must be something happening in Albania!' exclaimed Constantine, and he pushed his plate away from him, and held his forehead between his hands. He told Sava about the German agents we had seen at Sveti Naum and Petch and Podgoritsa, and Sava groaned. 'I cannot believe that has happened to the Italians, whom I learned to love when I was a student in Rome. That they should do such things, and that they should be in league with the Germans, that is an offence against nature.'

They sat in uneasy silence for an instant and Constantine said, 'You do not see anybody else here who has come from Albania?' Sava looked round the room and shook his head. 'Then you must ask the German Minister what has happened,' said Constantine. 'That I cannot do!' exclaimed Sava indignantly. 'You can do it very easily,' said Constantine; 'you are an official here, you can easily present yourself to him and ask if there is anything you can do for him. And then, quite easily, as you turn away, you can say, "By the way, there are rumours that there is"—oh, anything will do!—"a revolution in Albania."' 'No, that I cannot do,' said Sava. 'But why not?' asked Constantine. 'He might refuse to tell me,' said Sava. 'And what would that matter?' said Constantine, growing red. 'Then we are no worse off than we were before.' 'And I,' said Sava, growing white, 'am I not worse off, if I ask a man a question and he humiliates me by not answering?' 'No, you are not, not by a dinar,' said Constantine. The two men glared at each other, and Constantine gave a shrug of resignation. 'Very well, we shall not know till tomorrow what it is, this threat to our country,' he said, and we fell to talking of our plans for the next day. We resolved to see what we could of Tsetinye in the morning, go down for lunch and a bathe at the sea-coast town of Budva below us, catch a boat at Kotor in the afternoon, and land at Dubrovnik late at night.

That night I said to my husband, 'How strange it was to see those two men each thinking that if everybody behaved like the other the world would simply have to stop.' 'Yes,' said my husband, 'Sava Militchevitch thought that if men went about unarmed, putting themselves at a disadvantage before strangers, they would never be able to defend themselves. Constantine thought that if men did not use all means to discover what their enemies were doing they would never be able to defend themselves. Dignity was everything to the one, understanding was everything to the other.' Five minutes after his voice spoke out of the darkness again, very sleepily now, 'Sava's attitude reminded me of something that happened on the mountainside when we were leaving those children. I do not think you saw this, you were too busy trying to convince Dragutin that the tortoise's bowels would immediately act if it was carried in an automobile. By the way, what curious things you know. What happened was that Constantine gave the remaining cakes to the little fair princess and told her to distribute them among the other children. But there were six children and only four cakes. They would have to be divided, and that entailed an admission that they wanted those cakes, that they would care if the division was unequal. To have one's mouth water for pastry, to feel like crying if one does not get it: these are not the grand classical emotions. So the little princess took the cakes and set them aside till we should be gone.' Later he spoke again. 'It is such a pity you do not read Greek.' 'I am too old for that now,' I said, 'but why does that distress you at this moment?' 'The little princess's action,' he said, and then stopped for drowsiness, but pushed himself on to finish, 'the little princess's action when she put away the cakes was lovely not only for what it meant but for what it was. Exactly similar movements must have been made a million million million times since the world began, yet the thrust of her arm seemed absolutely fresh. Well, it is so in the *Iliad*. When one reads of a man drawing a bow or raising a shield it is as if the dew of the world's morning lay undisturbed on what he did. The primal stuff of humanity is very attractive.'

Tsetinye II

In the morning Tsetinye seemed even stranger than it had the night before. What earth lies round the town is richly fertile, and nourishes tall trees, green grass, and upstanding crops under the abundant rainfall. But there is hardly any earth, the fields are tiny, and all the rest of the countryside is porous rock that holds water no better than a sieve. It lies bone-dry not only under the sunshine but under the rain. A matching peculiarity of its inhabitants is their inability to accept this landscape although they are native to it. Few of them have travelled, but they all know that there is something unusual in the elevation and the bleakness of Montenegro. There still stands in the town the old Episcopal Palace, which is probably unique among the episcopal palaces of the world in being known to the population only as 'Billiards'; this was because in the eighteen-thirties the Prince-Bishop Peter II had had a billiard-table brought up the mule track from Kotor, and it was a great wonder. In a room attached to this palace some Italian prisoners of war made a giant relief map under the direction of the Austrian Staff geographers, which Sava Militchevitch showed to us with a sense of the prodigiousness of its frenetic contours that would have been more natural in an English Fenlander. This surprise the Montenegrins constantly express concerning Montenegro suggests that they have retained a traditional memory of their homes on the plains and valleys of the Serbian Empire.

Beside the Billiards is the monastery of Tsetinye, a fifteenth-century building to which restoration in the late seventeenth century had given the sturdy look characteristic of Montenegrin ecclesiastical architecture. On a rock above it were the ruins of a round tower, which I recognized as the occasion of the distress felt by an Englishman named Sir Gardner Wilkinson when he came here to visit the Prince-Bishop Peter II. When Peter I, the great law-giver, died in 1830 after a reign of forty-eight years, he was succeeded by one of the most interesting monarchs who ever occupied a European throne. He had been educated in this monastery at Tsetinye, then at the monastery of Savina down on the Adriatic shore, where Alexander of Yugoslavia tolled his own passing bell when he was on his way to his assassination at Marseille, and later he was tutored by a Serbian poet named Milutinovitch. It is part of the common babble of historians that

Orthodox monasteries were dens of ignorance, superstition, and debauchery, and that the Serbs were a nation of pig-drivers. Peter II spoke German, French, Latin, and Russian, and learned the literatures of each language; he was an admirable administrator and jurist; he was a student of philosophy, and was deeply instructed in mysticism; he wrote, among much other verse, *The Discovery of the Microcosm*, which is one of the great metaphysical poems of the world. At this time the English throne was occupied by King William IV. Peter II left his country only once, to be ordained as Bishop and accepted as an ally in St Petersburg. But he often received foreign visitors, who were immensely impressed by his picturesque appearance. He was marvellously beautiful, in a style more delicate than is common among Montenegrins, with long black hair and black beard and a pale face; his voice was noticeably sweet; he was six foot eight inches in height. He wore a red fez, which was the habit of all his people in those days, a scarlet pelisse bordered with fur, a white coat, full blue breeches, a scarlet sash bristling with weapons, white stockings, and Turkish slippers. He also, very oddly, wore a flowing black tie, after the fashion of the French Romantic poets, by whom he was greatly influenced, and black kid gloves.

The foreign visitor whom he would have most liked to entertain was Lamartine, for whose works he felt a passionate admiration. But he had to put up with less illustrious guests, who, when they were British, usually displayed the utmost courage in reaching their destination, but lacked both the intelligence and the information to discover anything of interest when they got there. In *Blackwood's Magazine* for January 1845, beside a review of Monsieur Alexandre Dumas's new success, *The Three Musketeers*, an English officer and his wife record a visit they paid to the Prince-Bishop when he was commanding his army on the islands beyond Riyeka on Lake Scutari. Their journey must really have been terrifying; but the Montenegrins, who were such thoroughly professional soldiers, albeit of a specialized sort, that they could not practice any other profession, struck them as 'amateur soldiers,' and they suspected that Peter II was only waiting till he had saved enough of his apanage to run away to some more civilized country. Sir Gardner Wilkinson was better than this, but he must have been irritating enough to his host. He thoroughly appreciated Peter II's gifts from his favourite trick of shooting a lemon thrown into the air by one of his attendants ('a singular accomplishment for a Bishop,' he thought) to his administrative ability; but he was scandalized by this round tower beside the monastery of Tsetinye, because it was stuck with the heads of Turks fixed on stakes and surrounded by a welter of skulls.

'The face of one young man,' wrote Sir Gardner, 'was remarkable; and the contraction of the upper lip, exposing a row of white teeth, conveyed an expression of horror, which seemed to show that he had suffered much, either from fright or pain, at the moment of death.' The sight distressed him enormously; and indeed it was a terrible proof of the demoralization wrought by the presence of the Turks in Europe. He remonstrated with Peter II, who wearily told him that nothing could be done. If the Montenegrins ceased to pay out the Turks in their own coin, the Turks would think they were weakening and would invade them. He might also have pointed out that the Montenegrins were constantly obliged to cut off the heads of their fellow-countrymen who were wounded on the field of battle lest the Turks should find them alive and torture and mutilate them; and that they could hardly be blamed if they did to the Turks what the Turks had often forced them to do to their own kind.

Sir Gardner, deeply shocked, went off to Herzegovina and, when calling on the Vizier of Mostar in his palace, was still more shocked to find beside it a round tower which was stuck with the heads of Montenegrins. He tried remonstrances there also, but the Vizier said he could do nothing, since the Montenegrins were so extraordinarily cruel to the poor Turks, who never did anybody any harm. Sir Gardner then proposed that he should declare a truce and hold a conference with Peter II, but the Vizier declined on the ground that all members of the Orthodox Church were cheats; however, he promised that if Montenegrins would stop cutting off the Turks' heads then the Turks would stop cutting off the Montenegrins' heads. This convinced Sir Gardner, who wrote to poor Peter II telling him that the Vizier was a very nice man and was anxious to arrive at a humanitarian agreement regarding this abuse. Peter II cannot have engaged in this correspondence with any zest, for he could not hope that a family should twice have such a success as his uncle Peter I had enjoyed, when Napoleon's Marshal Marmont had rebuked him on the same subject and he had replied, 'It is surprising that you should find this practice shocking, since you French cut off the heads of your King and Queen.' He contented himself in replying that the Vizier of Mostar was in fact not a very nice man and was unlikely to be moved by humanitarian considerations, since he was notorious for his cruelties and had often impaled living men. There was no remedy, he said, but to drive the Turks out of Europe.

Peter II died at forty-seven, an absurdly early age for a Montenegrin to die a natural death. But he was phthisical, perhaps for literary reasons. For his tutor, the Serbian poet Milutinovitch, had lived in Germany and had been profoundly affected by the Romantics. From them he had acquired a belief in the elevating influence of storms, and he had been in the habit of taking his infatuated pupil during his delicate adolescent years across the mountains in drenching rain and storm, in order to bring him into relation with the Sublime. In any case, poor Peter II must have been fatigued by his destiny. It cannot be easy to be a beautiful giant, with a poetic genius of the Miltonic sort and a nature saintly in its sweetness, and to be obliged to live as chief of a nation of noble savages forced to wrangle barbarously for every sippet of civilization, with a moral enigma gnawing at the roots of both his religion and his national faith. If civilization were worth fighting for, why was the Western civilized world so indifferent to the tragedy of his people and so friendly to their oppressors?

It is not surprising that with Peter II the reigning dynasty lost the full force of its moral passion. Since the great Prince-Bishop Danilo I, who had sent the Martinovitch brothers out on their terrible errand, his office had been hereditary, descending from an uncle to a nephew, or some member of the same family whom he adopted as his nephew, all parties taking monastic vows. Peter's nephew, Prince Danilo, refused the latter condition, for he had arranged to marry a beautiful and well-educated Dalmatian Serb, but he quite rightly thought himself a proper governor for the people. So he changed the constitution and gave all ecclesiastical power to the Metropolitan of Tsetinye and all the secular power to himself as a hereditary absolute prince. Thereupon he brought upon himself a long nightmare by his courageous and far-seeing conduct of foreign affairs. He supported Prince Alexander Karageorgevitch of Serbia—Karageorge's mild son who came to the throne after Milosh and Michael Obrenovitch had been driven out of the country—in his policy of neutrality, of evasive refusals to be entangled in the intrigues of the great powers. This was not easy; neither he nor Alexander Karageorgevitch could resist foreign attempts to drag them into war against their own interests without exposing themselves to humiliations which their subjects bitterly resented.

Danilo would not give Russia aid against Turkey in the Crimean War, because he feared that if he did the Turks would launch a more serious attack on Montenegro than ever before. Since his subjects loved Russia, this left him in the position of a ship's captain with a mutinous crew. But equally he would not be the creature of Austria, who in revenge continually plotted against him. In 1858 his policy seemed to have failed, for the Turks, unmindful of the benefits of Montenegrin neutrality in the Crimean War, attacked his country; but Danilo, who had been training his country on Western lines, smashed the invading army to pieces at the battle of Grahovo. The next year he lost his Serbian collaborator and got a better one; Alexander Karageorgevitch was deposed, and after Milosh Obrenovitch had filled his place for a little he was succeeded by his son Michael, now recognizably a genius. There is no knowing what the two brilliant men might have done for the South Slav people, had not both of them been destroyed by assassins.

In the summer of 1861 Prince Danilo's wife, the Dalmatian Darinka, was ordered sea-bathing by her doctor, and went down to spend some time at Kotor. Her husband insisted on going with her, though his counsellors warned him that his safety on Austrian soil could not be guaranteed. On fine evenings the society of Kotor used to gather in a little public garden on the seashore where a band played, and the Princess liked to frequent these minuscule entertainments, and then be rowed back to her villa. One night Danilo was handing his wife into the boat when a shot rang out and he fell dead. A Montenegrin had fired a pistol into his back. 'The murderer,' said Sava, who was leading us through the wide, unsecretive, banal streets of Tsetinye towards its centre, 'was a man whose wife had been seduced by Prince Danilo.'

'Surely not,' said my husband, very firmly. 'Why do you think that?' said Sava in surprise. 'Have you heard otherwise?' 'No,' said my husband, 'but I have never been in a country where every point was so thoroughly overlooked. Prince Danilo could not have taken this woman to the woods round Kolashin, for in his reign that was perpetually the scene of military activities. He certainly could not have seen her clandestinely in Tsetinye, which I suppose had a population of something like four or five thousand inhabitants, all with their attention fixed on the Prince. Every ledge in the valleys is as exposed as the shelf of a china cupboard. I should think that the only spots in Montenegro where a man and a woman could meet unobserved would be at the extreme tops of the mountains, which I understand are covered with snow and ice in the winter-time and infested with snakes in summer-time.

An obscure peasant might surmount these difficulties, but not a prince.'

'Nevertheless,' said Sava coldly, 'it is known that it was so. The wife of this man had been expelled by her tribe, and we know now that it was for that reason.' 'Was that,' said my husband, 'what you did to unfaithful wives in Montenegro?' 'Yes, indeed,' said Sava with solemn gust. 'We drove, and still drive, them out of their homes.' We had observed him to be one of the kindest people in the world in all his human relations, adored by his relatives and his secretary and his servant. 'And in early times, she would have been stoned.' 'That I find very curious,' said my husband, 'for it was really a terrible punishment to turn a woman loose in this country, where every plot of earth is accounted for, and every human being has a niche. It is like turning Hagar into the desert. And I would have thought there was no need for such harshness here, since your women are obviously of a type that feels no impulse towards looseness. They would find unchastity far more of a strain and effort than chastity.' My husband said this without guile, but he had faced our host with a disagreeable dilemma. For Sava wanted at one and the same time to agree with him that Montenegrin women were innately and unalterably pure, and to maintain that Montenegrins were performing a sacred duty by protecting their hearthstones from a possible taint.

His handsome face clouded, he went on to other things. 'It is interesting,' he said, 'to know how carefully this man prepared his vengeance. For he left Montenegro, he went to the Greek islands and earned his living as a fisherman, and then came back to Kotor; and as all the Greek sailors spoke of him as one of themselves nobody there realized he was a Montenegrin, so he was able quite easily to approach Prince Danilo when the day came.' 'That is very strange,' said my husband, who sometimes resembles a dog which has become quite certain that there is something buried beneath a rosebed, 'for surely if a Montenegrin believed that his ruler had seduced his wife he could have shot him anywhere except actually in Tsetinye, and gone scot-free.' To this Sava answered nothing, and we found afterwards that we had touched on a dubious point in his national history. There had been at this time a group of Montenegrin exiles who had revolted against Danilo's imposition on the tribes of a new legal code, very harsh on brigandage and the bloodfeud, and had taken refuge in Zara, the capital of Austrian Dalmatia. It is certain that the assassin belonged to their party. They existed on pensions paid them by the Austrian Government, and Danilo had refused submission to Austria; and it is to be remembered that seven years later Prince Michael of Serbia, who had also earned Austrian disfavour, fell as the result of what was most improbably said to be a Karageorgevitch plot. It is to avoid distressing speculations that Montenegrins prefer to tell this story, implausible as the plot of an opera, about a wronged husband wandering round the Greek islands for years in preparation for a revenge he could have executed on his doorstep.

In this tragedy can be seen the touch that the great powers were to lay on the Balkans from the middle of the nineteenth century: which can be rightly termed corruption, which was bad when it plunged a knife in a good man's back, which was worse when it changed warrior peasants dowered with rather more of the medieval virtues than the medieval vices into panders who procured their own people for their Western paymasters. That depraving process is commemorated in a big bare villa that still stands in Tsetinye, alarming in the contrast of its mean yet grandiose design to the stately and severe and ramshackle houses with their pine shingles which are characteristic of Montenegro, for nothing could be more alarming than the attempt of a primitive society to adapt itself to the standards of another society so far advanced as to be decadent. This was the palace of Nicholas, the last ruler of Montenegro before its absorption, who was first its Prince and then its self-elevated King. He was Danilo's nephew, the son of his brother Mirko, a man with a fine reputation as a general and an unpleasant one as a miser; he inherited the throne because Danilo's only child was a daughter. In him there survived a great deal of the family ability and not a particle of its moral passion. He was that most disagreeable and embarrassing kind of eccentric, he was a conscious buffoon. He liked to behave so grotesquely that he compelled people to laugh at him, and then he laughed at them behind his hand for having been so easy to deceive so that there was no good feeling anywhere, only jeers and sniggers.

Nicholas was a man of culture. He was educated in Paris and spoke French, German, Italian, Russian, and some English; and he had considerable literary talent. He was so good a soldier that though the Turks took advantage of the consternation caused by Danilo's death to seize much of the most fertile land in his kingdom, he had driven them out and acquired a great deal of Turkish territory by the time he had been twenty years on the throne, and at the end of the Balkan wars had doubled the size of his kingdom. He was also a skilful politician, who could not only steer his people through most difficult transitional periods but hold his own with European statesmen such as Disraeli and Gladstone. But to have his ignoble joke at the expense of Europe he assumed the role of boastful and cunning and unscrupulous peasant. He pretended to a boorish simplicity which was immeasurably inferior to the general manners of his subjects and an unnatural decline from the famous charm of his grand-uncle Peter II. He also affected to approach diplomacy in the spirit of a farmer playing off the cattle dealers one against the other at a market. It was as if his conscience made him want to sacrifice by indecorous outward behaviour the public respect he knew he deserved to forfeit for his secret relations with the great powers.

These relations were revolting. He lived, and lived well, on subsidies from Turkey, Austria, Italy, and Russia. With a leer he proclaimed, '*Ich bin ein alter Fechter.*' *Fechter* means 'fighter' but is old-fashioned German slang for 'borrower.' But his subjects, cut to the bone by their poverty, never profited; and he sucked out of them what marrow he could get. When there was a famine and Russia sent him gifts of grain for his starving people, he did not distribute it amongst them, he sold it to such as could buy. When he took the Albanian town of Scutari in 1913, after twenty thousand of his soldiers had poured out their lives before it in a seven months' siege, he surrendered it again, after he had had time to make a fortune by speculating on the Viennese bourse in the light of his foreknowledge. After putting himself up to auction by the great powers, he came to the conclusion that the financial inducements offered by Austria were the most satisfactory, and in her service he sterilized his people. Though he had been educated abroad, and his family had always been conscious of the value of foreign travel, he refused passports to all but a few privileged families. As far as was possible he kept his subjects as mindless fighting-cocks, troops that could be promised to one power if there was a chance of screwing up another power to a bigger subsidy. So completely did he demoralize them that when they conquered Petch and Prizren and Dyakovitsa in the Balkan wars they were quite unable to administer them. There simply were not enough literate men in Montenegro. Yet enough foreign money had poured into the country to give every man and woman a good schooling. It is peculiarly ironical that Nicholas was noble and romantic in appearance, and looked like the genial father of his people. In the stationers' shops in most Southern Adriatic towns there can still be bought postcards showing King Nicholas with his stately Queen on his arm, walking like Jupiter and Juno through the garlanded streets, with the Montenegrin men in their white full-skirted coats and the women in their black boleros and white robes bowing and curtsying like submissive children.

His reign mounted to peak upon peak of treachery. In 1914, when he had been fifty-three years on the throne, he telegraphed to Belgrade as soon as the war had broken out, and promised King Peter Karageorgevitch that he and his subjects would stand by Serbia till death. When the Serbian and Montenegrin troops jointly invaded Bosnia, they were more successful than they had hoped, and soon were sweeping down on Sarajevo. Just when it seemed inevitable that the town must fall into their hands Nicholas withdrew his army without notice, and the Serbians were obliged to retreat. In the following year when the Serbian armies had to abandon their country and make their way to the sea across the mountains a royal order was issued to the Montenegrin Army and police commanding them to prevent the population giving or selling any food to the starving soldiers. In January 1916 Mount Lovchen was handed over to the Austrians by Nicholas's son, Prince Peter, and his father manoeuvred his own army, which numbered fifty thousand troops, into a position where they were bound to be seized by the Austrians, and himself left his country. Relations had gone wrong between himself and the Austrians, but he had betrayed his soldiers to them all the same, because he was afraid that if they escaped to Corfu like the Serbs they would dethrone him. He then fled to France, and was allowed to remain there by the authorities, more because they wanted to keep an eye on him than for any other reason; and Montenegro was overrun by the Austrians, who brought death and famine and misery to every crevice of it. When it was proposed that it should be revictualled on the same system as Belgium, Nicholas objected. 'Let them wait,' he said, 'and when the moment comes for my return, I will go back with large supplies and be most popular.' It was at this time that the woman we met on the hillside was in a concentration camp watching her daughter die.

We had arranged to meet Constantine outside the palace, but he was not here; and it was most unpleasant to wait for him by this commemoration of a uniquely ugly node in Slav history, when it was probable that he was late because he was trying to find out the news from Albania, which also was probably not a fair word spoken by destiny. 'Come across the road,' said Sava, 'and see the house where Alexander of Yugoslavia was born.' It is a roomy building, which is something less harsh and strained than most Montenegrin houses. Perhaps it was inspired by a recollection of the easier Serbian farmhouses that look out on long grass and not an infinity of rock, for it was built by Peter Karageorgevitch before he was King of Serbia, when he came here in 1883 to organize the Montenegrin Army. It happened that Nicholas had married a very beautiful woman, member of a tribe famous for its intelligence and pride; and her brother, Vukotitch, was much beloved in Montenegro for his public spirit and financial integrity. By his wife Nicholas had several beautiful daughters whom he planted all over Europe to suit his foreign policy. One became the Queen of Italy, and led a distressing life. Because this goddess, accustomed to the classically beautiful costume of her nation, looked awkward in hats the size of tea-trays and dresses that cut her in two with high petersham belts, she was regarded as inherently barbarian and vulgar. Another one was married to an Austrian aristocrat, two to Russian Grand Dukes, and there was one, Zorka, who was given to Peter Karageorgevitch, for no more amiable reason than to weaken the prestige of the Obrenovitches and thus cause trouble in Serbia.

He built this house for her, just over the way from her father's palace. It is now the club for the garrison officers; and Serb and Croat boys, solemn with Slav militarism, pressed against the wall so that we could climb the stairs and see the room where Princess Zorka, hardly older than themselves, had borne her children and had died. It was a long, low room with three windows looking on the foliage of the trees which line this cul-de-sac of perished royalty. So long as it was summer and the leaves hid the palace anybody in this room might think that they were in the country. It can be imagined that a woman with a good husband, as Peter certainly was in his sober and grizzled way, might enjoy lying here, suffering birth pains cancelled by their usefulness; and it is even a little terrifying to compute how much she gained by dying young.

Of the five children she bore in this room three survived. The eldest, George, has sat in darkness these many years. Yelena married the Grand Duke Constantine, and saw him murdered by the Bolsheviks, fell out with her family, and is an exile. Alexander of Yugoslavia was murdered at Marseille. Those tragedies, however, she could have perhaps supported. On the wall hang photographs of her which show the heroic mould. She would have found it more difficult to endure the petty nastiness that emanated from her father, such as the bomb scandal of 1907. By that time her husband Peter Karageorgevitch had come to the Serbian throne, had made a success of his kingdom, and had therefore become the object of Nicholas's envy. This fitted in well with Austrian plans; for Austria intended to annex Bosnia and Herzegovina before many more years had passed, and would be able to do that with a free hand were Europe persuaded that Belgrade was a centre of crime and corruption, quite unfit to be trusted with fresh territory. Also she wanted to deprive Serbia of a possible useful ally by weakening the brotherly love felt for her by the Montenegrin common people. It happened therefore that Nicholas announced himself to be the victim of a bomb conspiracy.

The bombs certainly existed. They were sent in ordinary portmanteaux to two different frontier stations where, as even the naïvest conspirator might have foreseen, they were discovered by the customs officials. Their whereabouts had been reported by a person called Nastitch, which is an appropriate name for an unpleasant Slav. This creature gives terrible evidence of the degradation that had been wrought in such inhabitants of the Balkans as were not heroes by their dependency on the great powers. His grandfather had spied on his fellow-Serbs for the Turks; his father had spied on his fellow-Serbs and Croats for the Austro-Hungarian Government of Bosnia; he himself spied on his fellow-Serbs, Croats, and Montenegrins first for the Bosnian Government then for the Austrian Foreign Office. The most respectable action ascribed to him was the theft of a pair of opera-glasses in the Vienna Opera House. He was concerned in the notorious Zagreb high-treason trial; there he furnished Professor Friedjung, the anti-Slav Austrian historian, with evidence which the Professor, being an honest man, later found himself obliged to denounce as forgeries. He was responsible for a great many other cases, particularly in Sarajevo, which meant imprisonment and death for Slavs of high character. It was this Nastitch who discovered that bombs were being sent to a body of disloyal Montenegrins, who meant to use them for blowing up King Nicholas and his palace, by his grandson, Prince George of Serbia, Peter Karageorgevitch's elder son. This was, of course, flagrant nonsense. Prince George was already recognized by his family as eccentric and was strictly supervised, and just at this time his sister, Yelena, to whom he was greatly devoted, was staying with her grandfather. But the conspiracy served its purpose. It added to the ill-fame of Belgrade and the Karageorgevitches, and made Austria a more generous paymaster; also it enabled Nicholas to murder a number of Montenegrins and to imprison many more. Two of them had lain in the graves we saw by the roadside outside Andriyevitsa.

We left this modest and tragic house and walked up and down the blanched street outside the palace, the stench of nineteenth-century Europe strong in our nostrils. It was the gangrened corpse of Austria that had infected Montenegro; and it appeared that Montenegro had taken its revenge on another member of the imperial breed. 'It is strange to think that out of our palace, which I must own is not very big or very grand, came the ruin of Russia. Did you not know? King Nicholas's eldest daughter, Militsa, became the wife of the Grand Duke Peter, and as she got older she became very much interested in the *coulisses* of religion, any monk or priest who pretended to have something new in the way of visions and miracles. Because of this known taste of hers somebody brought her Rasputin, and it was she and her sister, the Grand Duchess Anastasia, who took him to the Tsarina. This is particularly strange, because our women are usually very sensible. But let us go into the palace; it is a museum now, and though there is nothing there of any importance it is at least one way of spending the time that we are obliged to spend waiting for Monsieur Constantine.'

It was certainly a distraction, but, like all this hour, most mortuary. For immediately we entered the palace we were reminded of the dissolution of yet a third empire, not by a stench, a ghostly echo of idiocy, but by a fragrance. It happens that the system of provinces or banovinas which King Alexander devised put Tsetinye under the central control of Sarajevo, where the Moslem political party has great influence; and so it happens that the State Museum of Montenegro, which is chiefly occupied by the records of five centuries of warfare against the Turks, is under the care of a Turk who follows his faith and wears the fez. He is not a Bosnian Moslem, but a true Ottoman Turk. This is taken ill by many Montenegrins, as an affront to their past; but it is objectionable on quite another score. A Turkish gentleman is not a trophy that should be exhibited in public. Far more merciful would it be to keep up the old local custom and prick the round tower on the hill above the monastery with a few Moslem heads on stakes.

Superficially all was well with him; plump and dimpled, he conducted us round the museum in a spirit of pure and unaggressive courtesy, talking that Oriental French which is as sweet as rose-leaf jam. But all his movements showed a perfect adaptation to a system that was not there, that did not exist either to be served by him or to reward him. The palace dining-room now houses Nicholas's collection of Oriental and Occidental arms, which is extremely extensive, for the reason that the trade route from Dubrovnik to Constantinople passed through Montenegro, and Montenegrins often chose to take their fee for services rendered to travellers in the shape of a formidable new weapon. Now feeling the temper of a yataghan, now demonstrating the primitive yet ingenious loading device of an early rifle, the fezzed curator moved along these arms with a pride and leisured delight in a mastered technique which was exquisitely relevant to a particular phase in individualistic warfare, when a man had to rely on his horse, his smith, and his courage. Since the phase was over it was relevant to nothing, absolutely nothing.

It would be easy to dispute that, to argue that since an aviator has to rely on his plane, his mechanic, and his courage there were some bridges between that age and today. But no part of the aviator's life is leisured, he knows nothing of the Turkish counterpoise between fanaticism and relaxation, between sluttishness and elegance. An air marshal grown old would have no sort of resemblance to a pasha rounding to the hour of his assumption to Mohammed's Paradise. There would be more in the Westerner's face, and less. There was no end to the evidence that the Turk's spiritual universe had perished. At his elbow, as he caressed a sword-blade, was a death mask taken from a pasha's head that had come to Montenegro without his body. It looked strangely un-Asiatic; if I had been told that it represented Louis Napoleon I would have believed it; and indeed this pasha had been no Turk but a Pole, moved to fight for Turkey for no other reason than that she was the enemy of Poland's oppressor, Russia. In the old days the Turks had delighted, and been inspired by that delight to create one of the best secret services the world has ever seen, in order to turn to their own advantage the mutual hatreds of the Christians, which always seemed to them ridiculous because there ran through them the silly gold thread of a desire for peace, a preference for harmony. But now if such a secret service still existed, it would have found Christian hatreds of a different and coarser sort, not so easily to be exploited by cynicism because they were cynical themselves, and the authority to which it reported would be irritating in its indifference to finesse, its concentration on economic and financial matters far beneath the dignity of a people which scorned commerce.

The curator was as heart-rending a spectacle when he took us upstairs to what had been the private apartments of the royal family, period pieces enchanting in themselves but misleading to the historian; for I am told by a servant who had worked

in the palace that it presented a very different appearance when
the King lived there, that most of his household goods were sent
away when he left, and that much of the furniture we saw were
presents for foreign royalties which he had never used. But as it
is, it presents some delicious moments. Vast polar bear rugs lie
on the floor of a drawing-room decorated in an ingenuous shade
of blue, and embroidered chairs reiterate the letter N, which
stood for Nicholas as well as Napoleon, and on the walls hang,
indubitably genuine, the portraits of the family and their royal
contemporaries, mostly photographs faded to the palest possible
brown, the colour of chicken broth, or pictures in which the artists
had attempted to render with photographic accuracy the textiles in
which their sitters were arrayed, particularly if they were shiny. It
was on this unpromising material that the curator brought to bear
his Turkish sensuousness, which is so simple that it appears to us
perverse.

'*Regardez la pluche!*' he said before the pictures, making no
secret of it that his mouth was watering. '*Le satin! La fourrure! Les
bel-les fem-mes!*' And before the faded photographs he mouthed
the titles, '*Son altesse le Prince, sa majesté la Reine Impératrice,*'
and made each of them a sultan or a sultana, reclining on silken
cushions under golden domes. Being Western and therefore
obsessed with the secondary meaning, we wondered, 'What
dreams have these substances and ranks evoked in this Turk
that he is so enraptured?' But we were wrong. He was enraptured
simply because plush has a deep pile, because satin gives back the
light, because fur is soft and warm, because jewels flash coloured
fires, because beautiful women are beautiful and women, and it
is better to be a prince or an empress than to be a slave; and it
was proof of his amiability that he was putting forth a special
effort to feel such raptures in this room, because it had once
been dedicated to pomp and elegance, although the dedication
had not been very successful. But here he was showing himself
true to his race, for Turks will gather in any little coffee-house
that claims neighbourhood to some natural beauty, say a grove
or a cascade, be it the very meanest of its sort, a few leggy trees
or a trickle of water, and they will deliberately fall into a mood
of delight over the alleged pleasantness. It would be detestable to
find one's people abandoning such a talent and striving like the
mad weak Westerners to investigate and analyse, to follow a trial
that can lead to all sorts of unpleasantness such as mental exertion.
There was some heroism in continuing to practise this talent, even
though the portraits which could now be its only objects were alike

in ghostliness, whether they were faded photographs or too highly coloured pictures.

There were other visitors to the museum, so presently Sava and my husband and I found ourselves alone in a little room that had been the boudoir of one of the princesses. It was furnished chiefly with an ornate upright piano and a tapestry picture of Verdi wearing white spats, and it looked on the palace gardens, which are now a public park but were nevertheless being used at the moment as a drying-ground for somebody's sheets. I found myself thinking of the thousands of men with fezes and women with veils that I had seen in the streets of Sarajevo, turning away in desolation because the representatives of the New Turkey had looked on them coldly and had told them that the old Turkey, which had been their mother, was dead and buried. I asked Sava, 'Is that man not very unhappy now that the old Turkey has gone?' 'Yes, indeed,' answered Sava, 'and that was very noticeable when a party of Turkish journalists visited us recently. This poor fellow looked forward to their coming with the greatest expectations, for the Moslems here never realize, you know, how completely they have been cut off by the Turks of Turkey. They like to think it is the Yugoslavian Government which prevents them from communicating with their co-religionists. So for days before this poor fellow talked of nothing else, and made endless plans for welcoming them. But when they arrived here they were not at all keen to come and see him out of his turn, and he had already been awaiting them for some hours when they arrived. It was obvious that the sight of them was a shock to him, for our Moslems cannot realize that the Turks of Turkey dress like Christians; and then when he had made his little speech to them they did not answer at once, but first said, "We think it a pity you wear a fez. The Ataturk does not wish us to wear fezes and it is he we follow nowadays." But when they had got over that point he took them to see the collection, and began to show them the plaster cast of the Pasha's head, as something that should make them feel very sorry, because the poor man had been a good servant to the Sultan and to Mohammed, and the Montenegrins cut off his head and brought it here, and took this mask of it so that they might gloat over it. But the Turkish journalists would hear nothing of that; they said, "We will rather not think of such things. He was one of our soldiers and his head was cut off. But it was we who brought into Europe the sort of civilization that cuts off heads, and the Ataturk has taught us not to be proud of it." The visit here was not a success, and the poor curator thought it was not a successful banquet that we gave that night to the Turkish journalists in the hotel here. For we have a delicious kind of raw ham here in Montenegro and they ate a great deal of it. That the curator could not bear to see. He is a very pious Moslem, and not only does he put down his rug and pray at all the prescribed times, but he observes all prohibitions, so you can imagine what it was for him to see the Turks eating pig, the most unclean of all unclean things according to the Prophet. Nor does he drink wine, and these journalists drank much rakia. But he is a very polite man, he rose and said that he must go home because he was feeling ill; and they were polite also, for they said that they regretted it and hoped he would soon be better. And, indeed, their hopes were needed, for he looked like a sick man for days.'

I pressed my face against the window-pane. In the gardens below a woman knelt beside the sheets and fingered them to see if they were still wet; she must have put them out at dawn if she expected them to be dry by now. Behind two romping children lagged a sad-faced girl, probably a German or an Italian governess. It would be better to be a drudge or an exile than to suffer what this Turk was suffering: to find suddenly that the beliefs which one had learned from one's parents and at school, and which had been the basis of all one's dealings with one's fellow-men, had been abandoned by everybody except oneself. That must be a beggary as bad as lack of bread, for it would take away one's appetite, since to live out tomorrow would be a puzzle without an answer. I told myself, 'This must always happen if a national faith is not valid. Of course the Turkish faith was not valid. Ferocity and voluptuousness, though they travel with superior companions, with courage and beauty, are apparently insufficient. Death must be allowed to carry out the dead, and if a civilization cannot stand it must fall.'

After a moment when I believed I was thinking of nothing, only watching the woman pick up her sheets and the girl call her pupils and heavily quicken her steps when they paid no heed, my heart turned over. I must, in fact, have been thinking of many things, all of them disagreeable. I said to myself, 'My civilization must not die. It need not die. My national faith is valid, as the Ottoman faith was not. I know that the English are as unhealthy as lepers compared with perfect health. They do not give themselves up to feeling or to work as they should, they lack readiness to sacrifice their individual rights for the sake of the corporate good, they do not bid the right welcome to the other man's soul. But they are on the side of life, they love justice, they hate violence, and they respect the truth. It is not always so when they deal with India or

Burma; but that is not their fault, it is the fault of Empire, which makes a man own things outside his power to control. But among themselves, in dealing with things within their reach, they have learned some part of the Christian lesson that it is our disposition to crucify what is good, and that we must therefore circumvent our barbarity. This measure of wisdom makes it right that my civilization should not perish.'

Sava said to me, 'Over there is a coach-house which I would like you to notice. For years it was crammed with trunks containing valuable articles of clothing and jewellery, the personal property of Nicholas and his family, who left them behind in the haste of their flight to Scutari. Poor as our people are, and accustomed to looting as an actual part of military technique, nobody touched these things. They thought it beneath their dignity to take what had belonged to their unworthy king.' It was an impressive story, but his tone and his profile evoked the monotonous white colonnade of Montenegrin heroism, its tedious temple of victory. I felt a distaste I had better stop feeling, if I were not to find myself in the same plight as the Turk. If I wanted my civilization to survive under attack—and I would have learned from this journey that it was going to be attacked, even had I started in ignorance—I had to be willing to fight for it. This necessity did not lessen because fighting meant the sacrifice of most of the subtle variations that it has been the happy business of the intellect to impose on the instinctive life. I had to be willing to fight for it even though my own cause could not fail to be repulsive to me, since the essence of civilization was disinclination for violence, and when I defended it habit would make me fear that I was betraying it.

'But surely, surely,' said Sava, 'Constantine must have got here by now.' And when we got downstairs there was the automobile with Dragutin at the wheel and Constantine inside, ominously in the same attitude, each with his arms folded and his chin sunk on his chest. 'Dear God,' said Sava, under his breath, 'what has this madman from Belgrade been doing now?' My husband went forward and asked Constantine, 'Have you found out what has been happening in Albania?' 'No,' said Constantine, 'I got through to Belgrade and talked to my ministry and they knew nothing.' 'That conversation has taken a long time,' said Sava. Constantine shot off his seat like a jack-in-the-box. 'It has not! It did not take twenty minutes; no, it took not fifteen minutes! I wonder at you that you compromise our telephone system before foreigners! But since then I had much to do. Much to do,' he repeated with a murderous look at Dragutin's shoulders. 'Listen,' said Dragutin, 'only listen. There is no petrol in Tsetinye. None at all. It is because of the Sokol Congress yesterday. But I have enough petrol to take us up Mount Lovchen, and down to Kotor and Budva, where I can get as much more as I want. But we must not think of that. Oh, no! Instead we must go to every bug-ridden inn and every hencoop that calls itself a garage, and beg them for whatever horse's water they may have chanced to catch in a petrol-tin, until we have enough to go down to the sea and back. So the morning has gone.' 'He does not understand,' said Constantine haughtily. 'I have much experience of travel, I know all roads in Yugoslavia, and in Switzerland and France. I have driven very much also, and I will always take what petrol is necessary to go and come, because I know.'

I knew that as he spoke his own words sounded infinitely foolish to him, and that he had driven about Tsetinye because he wanted to strike out at something, no matter what, and nothing but Dragutin's will presented itself. 'But certainly there would have been petrol at Kotor or Budva,' said Sava. He also was on edge, and he felt a desire to hurt and insult one of the Serb officials who represented the Yugoslavian authority which had been imposed on Montenegro. 'So you say,' said Constantine, 'but how do you know? I tell you, I have vast experience of travel, and I am not so sure.' They repeated slight variations on these remarks several times, and there seemed no reason why the conversation should ever stop, so I said, 'And now are we going straight to Mount Lovchen?' This distraction was not so successful as I had hoped. For Sava looked along the road and said in a voice sharp as broken glass with anger, 'Look what has happened while you have been running round and round Tsetinye because you think there is no petrol on the Adriatic.'

The amphitheatre of rock which encloses the town was now surmounted by a high parapet of fog. 'Now,' said Sava, very straightnosed, 'they will never see the view from Mount Lovchen, which is the most beautiful in the world, which is something you have not got anything like in Serbia. Now they will never see the tomb of the poet Prince-Bishop Peter. Now they will never see Nyegush, which is the cradle of our royal dynasty.' 'That may be,' said my husband, 'but it will not be because we are late in starting, for that mist has been there all morning.' Sava looked at him distrustfully; but he was such an intellectual that it was easy to persuade him. 'I am sure of it,' continued my husband, 'for I noticed it when I was shaving in front of my window at seven.' When Dragutin gathered from the others what he was saying he looked at him with no sort of doubt at all. Later he told me it was a pity that my husband was a banker and that I wrote books, for we could have done very well at selling things. 'And now,' said my husband, 'let Dragutin drive wherever the mist is thinnest and we will see what we can.'

Budva

We stood on a mountainside in a circular cell which held ourselves, Constantine and Sava, an obelisk, and a curved balustrade. This cell was cut out of a dense fog by some magic and arbitrary force which permitted everything within five feet of the spectator to be clearly seen and nothing whatsoever beyond. The automobile on the road was a shadow hardly to be identified save when Dragutin impatiently tooted on the horn. Some time before, Sava had sadly told us, 'I can assure you that the view from this obelisk is usually very fine, very fine indeed,' and there had followed between him and Constantine one of those conversations which came so easily to those two, without any visible exit.

'I tell you,' said Constantine, 'that we should go straight down to the sea. I know very well all that is to do with mist. I lived a very long time in Geneva, and I have often observed the mists that come down the Rhone Valley, and I know that when the mist is so it does not lift. It would be quite useless to take them up to Mount Lovchen. They would see nothing, nothing at all.' 'But what has Switzerland to do with Montenegro?' asked Sava. 'Switzerland is a country far north of this, and in the centre of the Continent. The conditions are not at all the same. It is here as it is in the Abruzzi, which I know very well, and it is perfectly possible that such a mist as this might lift at any moment, and then they would see what is really the finest sight in the whole of Yugoslavia.' 'But it is no use going up to the mountain, they would see nothing, nothing at all,' said Constantine; 'this is something I understand, for in Switzerland it is not as you think, the mists which come down the Rhone Valley are like all mists, by them you can exactly judge all mists, and I tell you I have studied them for years and years.' 'But they should take every chance of seeing the view from Lovchen for there is nothing more beautiful,' said Sava. 'I must point out that the conditions here would naturally be more like those in Italy than those in Switzerland, and there such a mist as this would lift.' As they spoke Constantine seemed to get shorter and shorter, and Sava taller and taller.

My husband and I moved away, and after a few steps we stood alone in our own cell. 'We are perhaps characters in Ethel Smyth's *The Wreckers*,' he said. 'Or we are travelling on the old Underground as it used to be when I was a child,' I said, 'in which case we will end up by visiting Whiteley's Menagerie.' There sounded above us a soft clop-clop of hooves, Dragutin's horn tooted, there was a scurry and an admonishing cry, and there suddenly strode into visibility a peasant and a pack-horse loaded with wood, which were accompanied by a cloud of fragrance. 'Look,' said my husband, 'he is carrying a huge bunch of narcissus!' So we followed him a little way down the road, as far as would make it certain that Sava and Constantine should not hear my bad Serbian, and then greeted him and asked him to sell us some. He answered, 'That I will be glad to do, but I cannot give you all, for I must take some home to my little boy.' He was a giant with slaughter written on his brows, and it might have been supposed that his child would have played only with hand grenades.

We were standing in great contentment, each with a nose in a handful of cool flowers, when we heard cries of agitation above us. 'Holla! Holla!' shouted Constantine, and broke off to exclaim, 'Ah, but those two will for ever be doing something extra!' We sent out reassuring calls, and went towards them with some reluctance, for as soon as our friends were satisfied of our safety, they continued to compare Switzerland and the Abruzzi. But they stopped when they saw the narcissus. 'Where did you get them?' laughed Constantine, anxious to be mystified. 'It is not what I supposed about English bankers, that if you let one wander off in a fog on a barren mountainside he would come back with his hands full of flowers.' 'It is the banker's wife,' said Sava. The compliment was not completely filled in, but the handsome intention was obvious. 'Fancy talking so much that you didn't smell that narcissus going by,' jeered Dragutin. 'I sniffed in all I could, it was as good as incense in church. And now look over your shoulders! Don't start talking again and miss that!'

There had appeared in the mist below us a silver shape, which might have been a scythe held in an invisible hand only a few yards away, or a vast and unnaturally tilted crescent moon. As we stared it grew greater, it could be recognized as the curved surf of a bay. We exclaimed in wonder, for we had all thought that what we saw was hanging high above the horizon. It faded and was lost, but in another place there appeared a medallion of blue sea stamped with a couchant island, which also defined itself and vanished, and elsewhere we saw the proud nose of a terraced cape dropping to the sun's sparkling wake. Then the wall closed and we were in our cell again. 'Hey, what's the use of stopping up here?' cried Dragutin. 'Jump in! Jump in! There's a fine day down there at Budva! Come along now, or we'll have no time for a swim before lunch!' We drove down the road into a theatrical brightness of sunshine.

Beside the road was a gendarmerie that the Austrians had not quite finished building in 1914; through its sashless windows glittered the diamond waves. Below us we could see Budva, a walled town on a round peninsula, a little white tortoise against the blue sea. Golden broom made the sunshine more dazzling, streaming its whips from every crevice where the hoe had not harried it out of existence; for now we were back in an area of cultivation such as we had not seen for many days, of fertility such as made even the fields round Podgoritsa seem haggard in their handsomeness. Here were vineyards and olive groves strong as wine and dense as oil in their abundance, here were terraces insolent with their crop of springing wheat. Dalmatia is not in fact very rich land, even here in the South; but we were looking at it with eyes conditioned by Macedonia and Montenegro, which found a certain grossness in the spectacle of fields completely covered with earth, and that probably to a depth of several inches. The sea also astonished us by its tokens of freedom and wealth. Far out a steamer was less visible than the straight line of its smoke, nearer a yacht lounged like a lazy albatross beside the glassy image of the island, some smaller boats took white sails out on the further crinkled waters. There were many people who did not have to keep their noses to the grindstone lest they should starve, who could travel for pleasure, there were some who could afford to buy expensive objects, costing more than many meals, and to have many of their kind to wait on them and render all sorts of services that are not strictly necessary, to build them boats, to row them about. In Serbia and Macedonia we had forgotten that there were such.

The Turks ruined the Balkans, with a ruin so great that it has not yet been repaired and may prove irreparable. Budva is one of the smaller Dalmatian towns, for it lay too far south and was too much exposed to naval attack to be valuable to Venice; yet we felt it very rich, curiously unassailed, very stable. There was a market, held where there have been markets, archaeologists believe, ever since this was a Greek colony. Under the lovely landward walls of the city, which are flecked with magenta wallflowers, two lines of tables are set in the shade of tall twisted plane trees, and peasants sit before them on low stone benches, in the black costumes of the country. Among these people I walked in rapture. They were poor and their wares would have been considered pitiful in any Western market; but they were not stringy with real physiological lack, none sat with only a little heap of beans before him.

The sight of such plenty, purely relative though it was, exhilarated us all. We hurried under the Lion of St Mark that held its open book over the city gateway, and took too few moments to admire the neat Chinese-box perfection of the town, which offered in a few yards a ninth-century church, shaped grimly by that fierce early piety, a garden wall hung with a fleece of red roses, stone steps sweeping from the shadow of a great plane tree up to the sunlit heights of a Venetian fortress. For we all dispersed to buy objects we hardly needed, for sheer joy in what seemed to us almost unrestricted merchandise. When we met again outside the shops my husband said, 'Look, my dear, I have bought you a silver buckle of Albanian workmanship,' and I said, 'Look I have bought us all bathing dresses,' and Constantine said, 'Look, I have bought these two Turkish daggers for my little son, and the man has said he will make them blunt for me while we have lunch,' and Dragutin said, 'Look, I have bought a pair of silk stockings for my wife.' And Sava came towards us, through the city gate, saying, 'At the hotel over there I have ordered red mullet and palatschinken for lunch, and we will have it on the terrace among the roses, but you must hurry, you must hurry! You will not have time to bathe and have lunch and catch your boat at Kotor if you do not hurry!' Yet we felt as if the world were bare and empty.

Over the mountains in Macedonia there had been nothing: nothing visible. But there had been the vast invisible treasure left by Byzantium, which had been put out to usury during the captivity of the Slavs, which is now great enough to finance explorations of the spirit not to be considered in poorer countries. It was as if we had lost a large sum of capital, as if we must look forward to a future full of mean economies.

As we walked to the bathing-beach we paused from time to time to look back at the exquisite profile of Budva, the island lying complacent in the bay beyond, the fastness of Montenegro, which ran up half the sky behind them. On the beach about thirty people, grown-ups and children, were being gently happy, without much noise, splashing in the water or lying on the sand, showing a nakedness not beautiful but clean and sturdy. A girl gave us towels and tickets for bathing-boxes, and said wickedly, 'So many men and only one woman. I would like to know how that gets itself done,' and all my companions laughed gallantly, as if they were indeed with me for some romantic reason. As we came out of the boxes the hot sand burned our feet, and the people lying on their spread towels smiled at us lazily and not unkindly as we hopped down to the sea. There came no shock as we went in, for the water was hardly water, being fused with sunshine. It worked its progressive magic on us, delighting the skin, then the blood, then the muscles.

We took it according to our natures: Sava and my husband struck out to sea with the deliberate stateliness of trained athletes, while Constantine pulled himself through the water like a strong dog, and Dragutin, revelling in the buoyancy of the sea compared to the rivers where he usually bathed, was rolling over and over on the surface.

'Just to be alive is good,' I said to my husband, as we stood outside the box squeezing the water out of our bathing-dresses. 'Just to be alive,' he said. Constantine came out of his box, pulling down his tie like a dandy, and said, 'Now do I feel an upright man. I know I am only a clean man, but I feel I am also upright.' A passing child tripped over his foot, and he steadied it by putting his hand behind its neck. It thanked him in a strange sing-song. 'The little one is a Czech,' said Constantine, his eyes following it benignly. 'Most of the visitors here are Czechs,' said Sava, 'and we find them very quiet, honest people. It is only the poorer kind that come here, tradesmen and clerks, for there is no big modern hotel, but they could not be better behaved.' 'Yes, the Czechs are good,' said Constantine, 'we Yugoslavs laugh at them, but they are very good, and they are our brothers.' The two men, nodding in agreement, looked round at the brown and wholesome people, who had by now all come out of the water and were lying still and relaxed under the thumb of the noon. Dragutin burst out of his box, slapping himself on the chest. 'Now I feel like a hero!' he said. 'Show me a Turk, show me a Croat, show me a Swab!'

As we made our way back to the town Sava said, 'Now you have seen what the Adriatic is like in summer, I hope you will come back another year and will enjoy yourselves as much as your King Edward (for I do not know how you stand in this matter and whether you prefer to call him that or the Duke of Windsor) did when he came here on his yacht. It was to me that it fell to make the arrangements for his stay here, since my district extends to Dubrovnik, and I must tell you that I could not have had a pleasanter duty. I found him most sympathetic. I have never had to look after any ruler, or indeed any public character, who was so anxious to be considerate.' He told us how the Duke had taken pains to find out whether his presence at a garden-restaurant meant that the police forbade people to dance, and how he had moved his yacht from an anchorage because the occupants of a villa near the landing-stage were inconvenienced by the crowds that waited for him. This was Sava's form of homage to the day, to the bathe. He said nothing about his bodily sensations, for that was contrary to the reticence which is part of the heroic Montenegrin role; but to show that he was finding life agreeable he was relating agreeable anecdotes, and he thought an anecdote would be specially agreeable to us if it concerned our royal family.

We sat down at our table on the balcony. Roses grew about the wooden pillars, among the napkins were scattered pink geraniums, smelling of earth. For aperitif we drank a wine of the country like a light port, but running thinner over the tongue. Sava's reminiscences took a melancholy turn which were entirely sincere, yet at the same time artistic, a phrase in a minor key that gave an appropriate end to the melody. 'But he could not be king,' he said firmly; 'he was a most admirable prince, but it was not right he should be king. That we all realized one night at Dubrovnik. When he was at table it happened that a telegram was delivered to him which was not for him but for his secretary. It was hard for us to believe our eyes when we saw him look at the telegram and toss it down the table to the secretary. Do you understand? He did not give it to the waiter, he tossed it to his secretary—so.' At the end of the gesture he shook his head sadly and finished his glass. 'No, he could not have been king.'

Under my clothes my skin still kept the joy given by the salt water, the freshness had not left my blood. They brought a great platter of picturesque fish and another kind of wine. A wind blew fragrance from the roses, and brought six white sails scudding towards the town from the open sea. Constantine, who was sitting next me, stood up. 'But what is this?' he cried. 'Look at those automobiles!' Not far from the city gate is an open space shaded with palm trees, where automobiles can be parked, and when we had left our own there it had been alone. Now there were six or seven with it, all of makes more costly than one would have expected to see at Budva. 'Look, every one of them has its little flag! They are all diplomatic automobiles. Certainly they cannot have come from the Legations at Belgrade. There is only one place they can have come from, and that is Tirana, that is Albania. I wish very much that we knew what it is with Albania.' We stopped eating and sat with our eyes fixed on the enamelwork and chromium that gleamed darkly in the shadow of the palms, the little twitching flags. 'Must it be something important?' I asked reluctantly. 'Certainly, it must be something very important!' exclaimed Constantine. 'The diplomats have not all come out of Albania merely to swim on the *plage* at Budva! They came into Yugoslavia so that they can telephone and telegraph to their

Governments without the Albanians' knowing what they say. I am afraid it is bad, very bad, with Albania, for it cannot be good, since Italy has her foot in there.'

Sava said, 'It is again as it was in the time of the Turks.' 'How can we find out what it is?' mourned Constantine, and added bitterly, 'If I were an official here I would have known long ago, I would have known as soon as it happened.' Sava marmoreally gave answer, 'But I am not in the police,' and there might have been an acrimonious exchange had not Constantine cried, 'Ah, now I can find out! You see that young man over there, on the other side of the road? I know him well. I tell you I have many friends and they are everywhere, and he is from Albania, this little one. Stephanopoli! Holla, Stephanopoli! He is a Greek, and it was in Athens that I have been with him, and he knows all languages, so he works in one of the Legations at Tirana. Holla, Stephanopoli! Ah, he heard me!' 'The whole of Dalmatia must have done that,' said Sava.

Monsieur Stephanopoli, waving to show that he was pleased to see Constantine, but not smiling, came towards us and halted under the balcony, bowing formally. No, he could not lunch with us. Since he found himself at Budva he must pay a call on a cousin of his who was married to the Mayor. He was a spruce young man, with a felt hat perched at a proper angle on his crenellated hair and a well-cut lounge suit, and it seemed strange that he should show the face that, as the picture papers and news reels have taught us, the inhabitants of regions long vexed by ungenial history wear in times of crisis. It is above all weary; such a look might come to an often beaten drunkard's wife when she hears staggering footsteps coming to her door. Constantine stopped speaking French and barked out inquiries in that angular tongue, modern Greek. The young man answered in short grumbling sentences, growing sullen-eyed and pinched about the nostrils. His lower lip protruding, he took out a pocket-comb and passed it through his crenellated hair while Constantine cried, 'I told you it was bad with Albania. It is very bad. It is a massacre. The officials all are bought by Italian money, and they have taken the four hundred young men who were most likely to give Italy trouble when she takes the country, and they have pretended it is a Communist rising, and they have killed them all. It is all nasty, so nasty, and it will not stop till the end.'

Epilogue

Epilogue

THAT WAS THE END OF OUR EASTER JOURNEY. WE SAID goodbye to Constantine at Kotor and caught our great white shining boat, and before we slept laid eyes again on Dubrovnik, which was complete beyond the habit of real cities against the whitish darkness of the starry June night, complete as a city on a coin. In the morning the Dalmatian coast slid by us, naked as a quarry, until at dusk we came to Sushak, the port where we had started. The next day we travelled back towards Zagreb through mountains which had seemed, when we saw them last, to be incapable of knowing anything but winter, to be committed to snow, but were now lion-coloured and so parched that it seemed inconceivable they should know any hour but noon, any season but summer. Now, as then, nothing human dared to be abroad. In valleys so archetypal of desolation that the memory stirred with forgotten Biblical names, and muttered of Horeb and Baca, scarlet flowers and colourless boulders wavered in the glassy, heat-demented air, and there was no more actual movement anywhere. The high pastures and the pine-forests of the Croatian uplands, where girls with coloured head kerchiefs kept their cows and woodcutters in round caps swung their axes, were a relief not only to the eyes but to the lungs and the muscles.

Three or four hours short of Zagreb, we left the train and spent a day at the Plitvitse Lakes, the most laughing and light-minded of natural prodigies. Here the creative spirit is as far from the normal as at Niagara or the Grand Canyon or the Matterhorn; but it is untouched by the tragic or by terror, it is dedicated solely to gaiety and loveliness. Sixteen lakes, some large, some small, lie among lawns and wooded hills, joined by glittering and musical waterfalls that are sometimes spiral staircases and sometimes amphitheatres and sometimes chutes, but are always ingeniously pretty, without a trace of the majestic. It is rare to find great beauty on this plane; Mozart put the finest metal of his genius into Susanna, who is nevertheless a soubrette, but there are few analogies in any art. Here, for a morning and an afternoon, we walked between the green shades of the woodlands, where light was ambient, and the light of the waters which rose clear through the green shadows, and we talked of Constantine. This place was in a sense his discovery. He had gone to it as a boy, when it was still in Austria and unvisited because it lay in the territory of the barbarous Slavs, and he had often celebrated it in his work. Some of his phrases came back to our memories and made us miserable by their aptness, for we both loved him, and now he was utterly lost to us.

There was embarrassment and uneasiness in our grief. For we could not have been more finally divided if there had been between us a bitter personal dispute in which all three had behaved as badly as possible. Yet there was nothing of the sort, merely impersonal differences. We were English, Constantine was a Slav Jew with a German wife. But we had grown up in a world which told us that to transcend such differences and to insist that intercourse should depend on the recognition of individuality was the mark of a civilized person, so we felt that we had been childish and ill-bred in permitting the estrangement to declare itself. This, however, we knew to be nonsense. The truth was worse than this. The past had bade us overlook racial and national differences because they had then no significance to compare with that which must follow from the clash between one man's good faith and another's roguery; for all Europeans were agreed in their ideal of a moral society. Since then the world had altered. Now different races and nationalities cherish different ideals of society that stink in each other's nostrils with an offensiveness beyond the power of any but the most monstrous private deed. My husband and I thought Gerda's black was white, she thought our white was black; Constantine's eyes were as ours, but his heart was with Gerda, and he could not compel her as the clever should compel the stupid, for he felt himself weak, being of a stateless and persecuted people. That the subject of our difference was political and not sexual or financial made it less and not more reparable.

Late in the afternoon, as we drank coffee and ate bread and cherry jam on our balcony, the light grew steely, the great lake below us blackened, a searching cyclonic wind tossed every single tree-top in the forests to a green twisting peak. The scene was suddenly hidden by curtains of shrieking rain. 'Our thunderstorms are very fine,' said the waiter in dreamy pride, 'and they usually last for three days.' He was surprised that we ordered an automobile to take us to the station. In the remoter parts of Europe one is always coming on vestiges of antique literary movements, and this waiter belonged to the romantic epoch, though he was actually quite a young man. It seemed to him proper, since we were persons of some means and education, that we should follow the style of the lovers in *The Sorrows of Werther*, who at the sound of thunder fell into each other's arms, trembling with sensibility and murmuring the name of the German poet who had written an ode to a storm: Klopstock, it unfortunately was. Three days of thunderstorm, to people with luggage like ours, should have been like a Bayreuth Festival.

A quick train took us to Zagreb by nightfall. In the restaurant of the large modern hotel near the station we felt again, though more intensely, that resentment at being glutted with material goods and at the same time deprived of certain more important essentials which had come on us before the comparative abundance of the Budva shops. There were countless dishes on the menu, but the people around us were colourless and inexpressive. Their clothes did not tell us where they came from or what they were, and their vivacity fell short of explaining its causes to the onlooker. Here, we thought as we lay ungratefully in our comfortable beds, the life of the soul would not, as in the other Slav lands, take forms visible to the corporeal eye. In this the morning proved us wrong. It was to be written before us, in letters as large as Zagreb, that here also, as at the Plitvitse Lakes, romanticism still lingered, but took a less innocent form than a swoon beneath a thunderstorm.

The town we at first imagined to be simply on holiday, as Roman Catholic towns so often are, for most of the shops were shut and many people were sitting on the benches in the public gardens. But soon we were perplexed by an incongruity. It was apparent that this was no festival but a day of mourning, for there hung from many windows the long narrow black flags which all over the Balkans mark a bereaved household. Yet it was pleasure that the people seemed to be expecting. They were looking sly as if they knew someone meant to take it from them, but they were certain of enjoying it in the end. We forgot all this when we came to the market-place, for whatever was afoot in the town the peasant from the country cared more about selling his goods, and the stalls were out and the umbrellas up round the statue of Yellatchitch. Again it was startling to see peasants with such large stores in their possession: though when we had bought a sackful of lustrous and luscious black cherries for a penny or two and an elaborately embroidered tablecloth for a few shillings and remembered that these people had to buy a certain amount of manufactured goods, such as boots, farm tools, and kitchen-ware, it was apparent that to them this plenty must be a mockery of itself. Without anything like Italian or German importunity but with a sober thoroughness, the people were showing us what they had to sell, when a babble sounded and they looked over their shoulders. A crowd was pouring down the steps that fall from the cathedral square to the corner of the market-place. The woman who had spread out some tray-cloths in front of us compressed her lips and folded up her goods, then turned about and began to take down the umbrella that sheltered her stall. The spring was stiff and her fingers crooked on it as she said wearily, 'It is the funeral of the three Croats who were killed by the Serbs at the Song Festival at Senj. There will be a riot, you had better go.'

Six months later, in London, I learned what had really happened at Senj, from an English girl who had actually seen the shooting. She had been motoring from Zagreb to Dubrovnik, and a collision with a cart had meant she had to stay at Senj for forty-eight hours while the local garage carried out repairs. On the second day of her sojourn the town was given over to a Congress of Croatian and Dalmatian Choral Societies. Often, on the Continent, clubs that are ostensibly dedicated to simple and straightforward pastimes have a covert political purpose. In Poland, for example, table-tennis associations were often foci of Jewish liberalism; and in Croatia and Dalmatia people apparently only sing part-songs if they are convinced Separatists and followers of the dead Raditch and the living Matchek. There were a great many of these part-singers here. They flocked in from earliest dawn in such numbers that the peace of the town was shattered, though some extra gendarmes had been imported during the previous night. Throughout the day, which was very hot, there was much singing, and towards evening there was much drinking, liberating the political sentiments as well as the voices of the choristers. By dusk the gendarmes, who had been jeered at and baited since morning, were trying to impose order on narrow streets packed with crowds roaring seditious songs, through which horse-carts and automobiles which were taking home members of the remoter societies could hardly force a way. At one cross-roads a gendarme was running up and down among the pedestrians in a vain attempt to clear a way for a charabanc full of choristers; both the people in the street and in the charabanc were shouting taunts and insults at him. Suddenly there was the sound of an explosion. The gendarme believed that he had been fired at by the people in the charabanc, and that was the first impression of the English girl, who was standing a few yards away from him. Actually a small automobile, hidden from them by the charabanc, had suffered a tire-burst. But the gendarme, hot, tired, exasperated, and frightened, spent no time in investigation. He shot back at the charabanc and killed five young men.

The Croat leaders, who are not naïve, cannot have believed that the Yugoslav Government wanted a gendarme to pick off five Croats of no particular importance in circumstances which admitted of no concealment and were bound to provoke far-reaching resentment. But they were not moved by this consideration to allay the passions of their followers. These now poured down the steps and spread all over the market-place, entirely surrounding the peasants who, with increasing gloom and haste, were dismantling their stalls and gathering their wares into heaps. 'You should have gone,' said the woman who had been selling us linen, 'the gendarmes are here, and there may be shooting.' From the side of the market-place opposite the steps there were advancing some twenty gendarmes, holding their rifles ready for use. At the sight of them the crowd, which numbered at least a thousand, stopped singing. Then, in one corner, several young men in succession shouted anti-Serb, pro-Croat slogans, and the people round them raised fierce cheers. At that the gendarmes began to charge them, not savagely, but as if to get the demonstrators moving, and immediately the crowd in front of them fell silent, while those behind them broke into louder slogans, fiercer cheers. The gendarmes stopped, wavered, spun about, and charged the new storm-center. As soon as they were under way the second group of patriots became quiet and submissive, drawing back timidly, while the first group raised shouts and cheers that were warcries, that incited to bloodshed, and made a threatening rush at the gendarmes' back. The wretched creatures wheeled round again, and the whole market-place burst into hoots and whistles.

This demonstration must have been rehearsed as carefully as an American football game; and indeed, in spite of its mournful cause, it was a game to those who took part in it. The glee that the city had been promising itself since morning shone undisguised from their faces, and if there had been any in the Cathedral who had remembered to grieve for the dead youths, there were none here. All were lost in the intoxication of their sport, in defiance of the claims of pity and not less of self-preservation, for it was as dangerous as any on earth. They were wrestling with their natural friends, their fellow-Slavs, while their natural foes, the Germans and Austrians, the Italians and the Hungarians, stood round them in a circle, waiting for the first sign of collapse that would make it safe to fall on them and strip them and slay them.

Adequate reinforcements arrived for the gendarmes, the crowd melted, the peasants sighed and set about putting up their stalls again and displaying their wares. We finished our transaction with the linen-seller, but she would not discuss what had been happening round us. 'It's politics, all politics,' she said, 'no sensible person talks about politics.' But the man at the next stall we stopped by, who sold leather-work, was eager to tell us that two 'of us Croats' had been murdered by Serb gendarmes in cold blood. He spoke with a peculiar whining drawl, complaining and yet exultant, but his eyes remained cheerful, and he must have taken little interest in the affair not to have discovered that more than two were being buried. 'Let us go to the University,' I said, 'there we will find Valetta, and he will tell us what all this is about.' We went through narrow streets where some shopkeepers were putting up their shutters and others were taking them down, all with a look of furtive glee, and the long black flags were flapping from every second house, and we found the open space round the University given up to a static kind of riot. Gendarmes were standing on the steps in front of locked doors, while a number of young men walked up and down before the building, sometimes breaking into mocking cheers and shouting slogans.

'Will you be good enough to explain to us what all this is about?' asked my husband, addressing a little man in a mustard-coloured suit who was standing at a street corner. He was one of those individuals to be seen in the larger towns of the Balkans, or in Scandinavia, or in any country with a predominantly peasant population, who, though poor almost to the point of beggary, and driven to the most menial occupations, are sustained in happy gentility by their possession of Western clothes and urban status. 'I am delighted to be of service to strangers of quality,' he answered, in old-fashioned and flowery German. 'What has happened here is that the students were anxious to make a demonstration about the massacre of Senj, and the authorities will not have it, so they have closed the University.' 'And what was the massacre of Senj?' asked my husband. 'Why,' said the little man, falling into the same complaining and exultant whine, 'Serb gendarmes down there at a Senj Festival killed some of us Croats for no reason, with dum-dum bullets.' Without strength or skill or land, he would not have lasted out a single winter under a Nazi regime. He could only hope to survive in just such a loose and unspecialized economy as this Yugoslavian state, against which, in obedience to a political habit as mechanical and irrationalized as a facial twitch, he was complacently rebelling. Just then my eye was caught by two large, loosely formed spheres in neutral colours, one blackish grey, the other brownish black. These were the behinds of two peasant women who were employed by the municipalities to weed the flower-beds at the corners of the square. They were being idiots, private persons in the same sense as the nurse in my London nursing-home, who was unable to imagine why the assassination of King Alexander should perturb anybody but his personal friends. They were paid to pull up weeds, and they wanted the money, so they continued to pull them up, even when the students raised a shout and brought some gendarmes down on them not fifteen yards away. As I looked at those devoted behinds, bobbing up and down over their exemplary task, and the smug face of the automatic rebel, I thanked God for the idiocy of women, which must in many parts of the world have been the sole defender of life against the lunacy of men.

On our way back to the hotel we saw a dozen gendarmes slinking back into a police station, turning their faces away from a booing crowd. They looked very frightened men, and that is not to say that they were cowards. They were well aware that a Croat need pay no higher price than three years' imprisonment for killing a Serb gendarme and had been known to get off with eighteen months. And they must have been well aware also that there was hardly a soul in the city, save the Serb population, who here are wholly disregarded, to feel one movement of goodwill or pity for them. Before we left Zagreb we spoke of the demonstrations to several people, in the shops, at our hotel, and at the railway station, and all save one, who was not a Croat but a Slovene, expressed a loathing for Yugoslavia, and for all the instruments of its being. In every case the reason for that loathing was candidly exposed as dislike for the inferior Oriental civilization of the Serb, the South Slav. The Croats' place, it was felt, was with the West: which implied, with what remained of the Austro-Hungarian Empire. We were to find out just how reciprocal that feeling was on the next stage of our journey.

After midday we took the train to Budapest, and all the hot afternoon we travelled through fields that were purple and white and rose with flowers, or smouldered brass-coloured with ripening grain. In winter the mud of the Central European plains makes them seem, to the urban visitor, the very essence of the negative; in summer their fertility, which has nothing of vegetable innocence about it, which is charged with a sense of abandonment and gratification, make them as positive as any mountain range. Then the darkness came, and with it the lights of Budapest. They dazzled us. In no Balkan towns are there such lights, nor is there any such hotel as the Dunapalota, with its polished floors of costly woods, its thick carpets and its tapestries, its lavishness of finely woven and extravagantly washed linen on the tables, on the waiters' bosoms, in the bathrooms, and on the beds. Nor in any Balkan town are there shops such as lined the streets we walked in the next morning, shops stuffed with goods, all new and fresh, none mildewed or faded, of many different patterns, far beyond the requirements of strict necessity. 'Are there so many kinds of shoes?' I marvelled, before a window that was itself a marvel, with its width of plate-glass. 'And why did you break your journey at Zagreb?' asked our friends in Budapest. 'There is nothing there.'

In a sense it was true. The lights of Zagreb are hardly lights, compared with the staring brilliance of Budapest. And we could not explain the sense in which it was not true, for here there was no such pursuit of ideas through the vaults and corridors of the mind as was the custom at Zagreb. In no café in Budapest were we invited to discuss the greatness of Vaughan the Silurist, or the nature of the spirit. The conversation here was preoccupied exactly to the degree and to the intensity which it had been when I had last visited it in 1924, with the need for the territory lost to Hungary by the Treaty of Trianon. There had been sold everywhere in those days a map, inscribed with the words '*Nem, nem soba,*' which is Magyar for 'No, no never again,' and showing the country in a black ring of the lands that were formerly hers and were now joined to Czechoslovakia, Roumania, Yugoslavia, and Austria. It was still being sold, and it appeared to be a complete map of the Hungarian mind. The hairdresser at the Dunapalota talked Irredentist propaganda to me from the first moment that my head came out of the suds till the last moment before it went under the dryer, not as if he were a fanatic, for he seemed of comfortable temperament, but as if he knew nothing else to talk about. The only new element that had succeeded in surviving alongside this preoccupation was pride in the growing intimacy with Italy. Our friends boasted of the splendid reception that Budapest had given to King Victor Emmanuel a week or two before, and even offered to take us to see news films of the processions.

This was as near national imbecility as may be; it exceeded the folly of the Croats. These people were attending to none of their internal problems, though they had an unreformed land system which prevented the peasant from feeling full loyalty to the state, and their financial policy had committed them to a degree of industrialization incompatible with their limited markets. The areas they desired to reclaim were by a substantial majority not Hungarian by blood, and had always loathed them and their rule; so the reclamation would confront them with grave administrative difficulties. And the sole hope of maintaining Hungarian independence lay in continuance of the dispensation set up by the peace treaties. If the state of Europe were such that Czechoslovakia, Roumania, and Yugoslavia could be dismembered, then Hungary could be annihilated. She has no military or strategic or political advantage that she could use as a bargaining point; she would be ground to powder between the upper and the nether millstones of Germany and Italy. Though she would probably be given her lost territories as a bribe to expedite her submission, they would be of no use to her. They served her interests formerly only because Austria was anxious to build up a solid Dual Monarchy to counterbalance the Hohenzollern Germany on the one hand and Russia on the other, and irrigated Hungary with an artificial prosperity. Germany and Italy would have no such reason for pampering her; they would steal her grain and cattle, partition her, flood her with traders and colonists, attack her language, attempt to destroy her identity.

'We cannot think,' said our friends to us, as we sat drinking apricot brandy in rooms glorious with Gobelin tapestries and Aubusson carpets, 'why you English do not support our revisionist programme more strongly. After all, we Hungarians are so like the English, our lives are governed by the same conception of "the gentleman." ' Had they not better, we suggested, get on good terms with their Balkan neighbours and join them in preparation against the evil day? They thought not. How could they ever be on good terms with those neighbours, they demanded, isolated in their obsession as goldfish in a bowl, until the stolen lands had been restored? And of the evil day they would not think. A young man paused in playing the piano to say languidly, 'If it should come to a war against *Nazismus* it will be very unpleasant, for one will not know on which side one should fight.' Astonished, we asked him what he meant. 'Well,' he explained airily, as if he spoke of something that was going to happen only in a play or a novel, 'it will be a war between *Nazismus* and *Kommunismus*, and the one is as bad as the other.' That there were other ideas which humanity might consider it worth while to defend could quite easily be forgotten in this country, on whose heart was written the not subtle, not complicated text, '*Nem, nem soha.*' But the cause of our astonishment was not that forgetfulness. This young man was a Jew, and we would have supposed that he would lie in no doubt as to whether he would fight for or against the Nazis, if only because the Nazis themselves would have felt no doubts on the subject. 'Yes,' said an Englishman who had long lived in Budapest, 'the Jews here are all like that. The tide of anti-Semitism is rising around them. Not a single Jew was asked to any of the parties given for the King of Italy. Yet they seem quite unresentful against the Germans, who called that tune, or the Italians, who are keeping it up.'

But they were not unresentful against the Slavs. Jews and Gentiles alike were puzzled and irritated because we had spent so long in Yugoslavia. 'But what do you find to do there?' they asked. 'You found it beautiful? Yes, I suppose it is, but then the people are such barbarians, the life is so savage, it is like going among animals.' People who, I must own, seemed not greatly superior to me in refinement, described how they had been unable to enjoy the scenery and architecture of Dalmatia because of the revolting manners of the inhabitants. Remembering the Professor at Split, the man with the port-wine stain at Hvar, the Cardinal and his family at Korchula, I thought they had been singularly unfortunate or were insanely delicate. I heard again the legend that the whole of Trogir, not only a small stone relief of a lion, had been destroyed by Yugoslav vandals. I heard many anecdotes: one related to an expedition of steamer tourists from Kotor up to Tsetinye which was marred because a doctor, accustomed, it was said by way of explanation, to live in Africa, had struck, though only lightly, a Montenegrin chauffeur. On hearing of this event, I closed my eyes as if some heavy explosion were about to take place in the room. But turning the subject to Croatia had not at all the effect that would have been hoped for in Zagreb. 'But the Croats are so stupid!' said our Budapest friends, their voices rising in the squeak of laughter that comes with memory of a joke learned from Nanny in the nursery. It appeared that in the old Austro-Hungarian Empire the Croats were as the Wise Men of Gotham, as the natives of silly Suffolk, as the men of Pudsey seem to the men of Leeds. I think that is the only part they have ever played in the Habsburg cosmos.

The Croats looked to the German-speaking world and had received nothing but a sense that sweet and decorous it is to hate all their brother Slavs. The Hungarians looked to the German-speaking world and had received nothing but a sense that sweet and decorous it is to despise all others than oneself, and to seize whatever these despised others might think to be their own. This destructive education had imposed itself even on the Jews, who once were a great creative people, who are now the greatest interpreters of modern European creativeness. What was in them had been emptied out and spilt on the earth. There was not even left to them the necessary fear that should leap up in a man's breast to defend it from his enemy's sword. And it was not any post-war exhaustion, nor any perplexity caused by the world slump, that had depleted them. Long before the war, the Jewish 'revolver journalists' were notorious. They sat at Zemun, on the Hungarian-Serbian frontier, and sent back to Budapest and Vienna wholly unreliable and desperately venomous dispatches representing Belgrade as a nest of anti-Habsburg conspiracies. It is often alleged in defence of these international saboteurs that they were moved by respectable racial motives: the anti-Semitic policy of Russia had inspired them with a desire to take vengeance on all Slavs. Unfortunately for this apology they had fulfilled their mischievous function with equal ardour during the years when Serbia and Russia were enemies. They were acting not as Jews, but as Germanized Jews.

It is as if a fountain of negativism plays in the centre of Europe, killing all living things within the reach of its spray. This lethal action is not to be conceived as a Teuton reaction to the Slav. It knows no such racial limitation. Life, under any label, is the enemy. That was to be demonstrated to me in Vienna by a golden-haired girl who presented herself one evening at my hotel on what I found an embarrassing errand. I found her in our sitting-room after an unpleasant incident. We had lunched with a friend out at his house beyond Baden-bei-Wien, and we had been driven there by the chauffeur who always served us during our visits, a thick-set man in his early thirties, with yellow hair and blue eyes that looked blind, like Gerda's. On our journey home there had been a sudden thunderstorm, and to avoid the height of its violence we drew up at a wayside inn. The three of us sat and drank beer in the well-scrubbed little saloon, and presently there came up, as could have been foretold, the subject of Vienna's economic distress and political unrest. The chauffeur, his voice falling into the whine that can be heard in Austria whenever it has to be recognized that loaves do not grow on trees, said, 'It is terrible for us Viennese, terrible. And we are all so disappointed, for we had hoped that things would be better. Did I not drive for Major Fey in the February Revolution, because I thought that it was going to put an end to talk, and that Major Fey and his party were really going to do something, but here we are, it is just the same as ever.' I groaned aloud.

That February Revolution of 1934 lives in popular memory for its malevolent destruction of the Karl-Marx-Hof and other blocks of apartment houses; but worse than that was its nihilism. A group of people with no economic or political ideas had believed that they could magically induce prosperity simply by destroying another group of people whom they believed, not wholly with foundation, to have such ideas. They had no other programme. Schuschnigg, who was their nominee, stood for absolutely nothing, for no principle, for no theory, even for no opinion, except the rejection of everyone else's opinions. I had been for the last few weeks with people so poor that the chauffeur's food and clothes would have represented an extreme of luxury that they could never hope to enjoy if they worked for fifty years. They could outbid him on his own excuse, and their history showed, when it had brought them a ruler of spurious royalty, that the springs of ferocity were high in them. But they would not have gone out and destroyed a number of their brothers in the cause of pure nothingness. 'To put an end to talk . . . really going to do something . . .' The peasants on the Black Mountains of Skoplje, the Bulgarian pastrycooks at Ochrid, the innkeeper's son at Petch, the old woman walking on the road over the Montenegrin mountains, none of them was involved in arguments so void of content that such phrases would have come to them. As the chauffeur looked at us, wondering at our sudden silence, his gaze was astonishing in its blindish quality. It was as if there were a stupidity behind the retina which admitted only light, which excluded all else that man usually learns by seeing.

In my sitting-room I found the golden-haired girl, with a letter from a Viennese friend of mine who coaches university students in English, saying that this was one of his favourite pupils and that she had chosen my works as the subject of her thesis. I was naturally appalled. I explained that I was a writer wholly unsuitable for her purpose: that the bulk of my writing was scattered through American and English periodicals; that I had never used my writing to make a continuous disclosure of my own personality to others, but to discover for my own edification what I knew about various subjects which I found to be important to me; and that in consequence I had written a novel about London to find out why I loved it, a life of St. Augustine to find out why every phrase I read of his sounds in my ears like the sentence of my doom and the doom of my age, and a novel about rich people to find out why they seemed to me as dangerous as wild boars and pythons, and that consideration of these might severally play a part in theses on London or St. Augustine or the rich, but could not fuse to make a picture of a writer, since the interstices were too wide.

To my annoyance the golden-haired girl treated this explanation as a proof of modesty, which it was not, and I saw something inexorable in her intensity, which I could not regard as proof of my importance, in view of the determination of every German university student to find a subject for his thesis which nobody has treated before. I remembered how one such student had gained his doctorate by a thesis on Mealy Potatoes, a Drury Lane dancer, mentioned on one single occasion by Dickens, whose identity he had tracked through London parish registers, and how he had been surpassed by a successor whose effort was entitled '*Die Schwester von Mealy Potatoes.*' The golden-haired girl belonged to this inexorable tradition, and my uneasiness did not prevent her from putting to me a long list of questions. But my answers soon made her even more uneasy than I was. She wanted to pigeon-hole me into a recognized school, and demanded to know what writers had influenced me. It disconcerted her when I reported that as a young person I had tried to write like Mark Twain, that he still seemed to me more fortunate than the princes of the earth in his invariably happy relations with his medium. 'But is not Mark Twain an American?' she asked doubtfully. 'And a humorous writer?' It was instantly clear to me, as it would have been to any writer, that literature was a closed territory to her and that she would never be able to read a single book. In spite of my glowering she continued, but we found no common ground in the discussion of any of my preferences, even when she accepted them as legitimate.

Presently she said, 'I have enough about English writers now,' looking at her notes with some sullenness, as if she foresaw trouble before her in pushing my mind, which appeared to have lost its label, into the proper pigeon-hole. 'Tell me,' she asked, 'about the European writers that have influenced you.' 'There was Dumas first of all,' I said, 'whose *Three Musketeers*, whose *Count of Monte Cristo*, taught one in the nursery what romance was, how adventure could prove that what looks to be the close-knit fabric of life is in fact elastic. Then in one's early teens there was Ibsen, who corrected the chief flaw in English literature, which is a failure to recognize the dynamism of ideas. The intellectual world is largely of English creation, yet our authors write of ideas as if they were things to pick and choose, even though the choice might be pushed to the extremity of martyrdom, as if they could be left alone, as if they came into play only as they were picked and chosen. But that ideas are the symbols of relationships among real forces that make people late for breakfast, that take away their breakfast, that make them beat each other across the breakfast-table, is something which the English do not like to realize. Lazy, bone-lazy, they wish to believe that life is lived simply by living.

'Yes,' I continued, glowing with interest in my theme, though my listener was not, 'Ibsen converted me to the belief that it is ideas which make the world go round. But as I grew older I began to realize that Ibsen cried out for ideas for the same reason that men call out for water, because he had not got any. He was a moralist for an extremely simple sort, who had heard, but only as a child might hear the murmur of a shell, the voice of the philosophical ocean. *Brand* is not a play about religion, it is a crude presentation of the ascetic impulse. *The Doll's House* is not a play about the emancipation of women—indeed none of the fundamental issues of that movement are touched—but a naïve and sturdy suggestion that in the scales of justice perhaps mean integrity may weigh less than loving fraud. But with my appetite for ideas whetted by Ibsen I turned back to the literature of my own country, which was then claiming to satisfy it. For this was the time of Galsworthy, Wells, Shaw—'

'Ah, Show, Show,' cried the golden-haired girl, pronouncing it to rhyme with 'cow.' 'Shaw,' I said irritably. 'Yes, Show, Show,' she went on, 'we have not talked of him. I suppose you admire him greatly.' 'Not very much,' I said. 'How is that possible?' she asked. 'Here we think him your greatest writer, next to Shakespeare and Oscar Wilde.' 'Next to Oscar Wilde, perhaps, but not to Shakespeare,' I snapped; 'and now that I re-read him I cannot find traces of any ideas at all. Wells at least had an idea that people would have ideas if they were taught by other people who had some, and was also almost as sublime a controversialist as Voltaire when he met with an irrational fool, but Shaw stands for nothing but a socialism which has nothing to it except a belief that it would be a nicer world if everybody were all clean and well fed, which is based on no analysis of man and depends on no theory of the state, and an entirely platitudinous denunciation of hypocrisy, which nowhere rises to the level of *Tartuffe*. Of course our country has produced better than Shaw and I found them later, but they are not easy to find, for there is a lack of continuity about our literature. A man starts up in isolation, inspired by an idiosyncratic passion to write about a certain subject, but rarely inspired to read what other people have written about it. That is why French literature is of such service to the mind, since each writer is fully aware of his own culture, and knows when he takes part in an argument precisely to what stage his predecessors have brought it.'

'But what is this you are saying about French literature?' interrupted the golden-haired girl. I repeated it, and she exclaimed in amazement, 'French literature! But surely all French literature is trivial and artificial?' 'Trivial and artificial!' I echoed. 'Abélard! Ronsard! Joachim du Bellay! Montaigne! Rabelais! Racine! Pascal! La Fontaine! Voltaire! La Rochefoucauld! Balzac! Baudelaire! Victor Hugo! Benjamin Constant! Proust! And Diderot—did you never read *Le Neveu de Rameau?*' 'I do not read French,' she said; 'hardly any of us learn French. But surely all these people put together do not equal Goethe?' I grieved, for it seemed to me that any one of them had as much to say as Goethe, whose philosophy, indeed, boils down to the opinion, 'Ain't Nature grand?' I said, 'It is a pity you cannot read Montaigne; he also thought much about nature, though he thought of it not as grand, but as inevitable.' She looked at me as if she thought that was no very great discovery to have made, and I looked back at her, wondering what words would convey to her the virtue that lies in the full acceptance of destiny, realizing that my words would convey it to her better than Montaigne's. For there was as yet nothing in her which could appreciate what he meant when he said that nothing in the life of Alexander the Great was so humble and mortal as his whimsical fancy for deification, and that it was no use thinking to leave our humanity behind, for if we walked on stilts we still had to walk on our legs, and there was no way of sitting on the most elevated throne save on the bottom. I found myself smiling as I remembered how he adds, inconsequently and yet with the most apposite wisdom, that for old people life need not be so realistically conceived, '*Or, la vieillesse a un peu besoin d'être traitée plus tendrement.*'

Though I was completely preoccupied as I stared at her face, my eyes eventually pressed some information about it on my mind. I realized that her brows and her cheekbones were cast in a mould that had become very familiar to me in the past few months, and that she was fair not negatively, like a Nordic woman, but after the fashion of the golden exceptions to the dark races, as if she had been loaded with rich gold pigment. A suspicion made me look at her visiting-card, which I had been twisting between my fingers, and I exclaimed, 'But you are not an Austrian! You have a Slav name!' She answered, 'I have lived in Vienna nearly all my life,' but I did not notice her tone and objected, 'All the same you must be Slav by birth.' Miserably, shifting in her chair, with the demeanour of a justly accused thief, she said, 'Yes! Both my parents are Croats.' I was embarrassed by her manner and said, 'Well, I suppose you speak Serbo-Croat as well as German and English, and that is another language for your studies.' She answered passionately, 'No, indeed, I speak not a word of Serbo-Croat. How should I? I am Viennese, I have lived here nearly all my life, I have not been to Croatia since I was grown up, except for a few days in Zagreb.' 'And did you not find the people there very clever?' I asked. 'I did not speak to them,' she cried scornfully. 'I thought it a horrible little town, so provincial.' 'Are you not at all proud of having Slav blood in you?' I exclaimed. 'Why should I be? What is there to be proud about in being a Slav?' she asked blankly.

Such is the influence that Central Europe exerts on its surroundings. It cut off this girl from pride in her own race, which would have been a pity had her race had much less to be proud of than the superb achievement of defending European civilization from extinction by the Turks. It cut her off from enlightenment by that French culture which has the advantage over all others of having begun earlier, branching straight from the Roman stem, and having developed most continuously. What it offered her instead was sparse, was recent. It might fairly be defined as Frederick the Great and Goethe. In music it might have offered enough to compensate for all its other lacks, but it had annulled the harmonies of Bach and Beethoven, Mozart and Haydn, by its preference for the false genius, Wagner. It had left this girl flimsy as a jerry-built house with no foundation deeper than the nineteenth century, when loyalty to her Slav blood and adherence to the main current of European culture would have made her heiress to the immense fortune left by the Western and Eastern Roman Empires. Not only Constantine, but this girl and her family, and many others like them, had made this curious choice. Nothing is less true than that men are greedy. Some prefer poverty to wealth, and some even go so far as to prefer death to life. That I was to learn when I returned to England.

This return meant, for me, going into retreat. Nothing in my life had affected me more deeply than this journey through Yugoslavia. This was in part because there is a coincidence between the natural forms and colours of the western and southern parts of Yugoslavia and the innate forms and colours of my imagination. Macedonia is the country I have always seen between sleeping and waking; from childhood, when I was weary of the place where I was, I wished it would turn into a town like Yaitse or Mostar, Bitolj or Ochrid. But my journey moved me also because it was like picking up a strand of wool that would lead me out of a labyrinth in which, to my surprise, I had found myself immured. It might be that when I followed the thread to its end I would find myself faced by locked gates, and that this labyrinth was my sole portion on this earth. But at least I now knew its twists and turns, and what corridor led into what vaulted chamber, and nothing in my life before I went to Yugoslavia had even made plain these mysteries. This experience made me say to myself, 'If a Roman woman had, some years before the sack of Rome, realized why it was going to be sacked and what motives inspired the barbarians and what the Romans, and had written down all she knew and felt about it, the record would have been of value to historians. My situation, though probably not so fatal, is as interesting.' Without doubt it was my duty to keep a record of it.

So I resolved to put on paper what a typical Englishwoman felt and thought in the late nineteen-thirties when, already convinced of the inevitability of the second Anglo-German war, she had been able to follow the dark waters of that event back to its source. That committed me to what was in effect some years of a retreat spent among fundamentals. I was obliged to write a long and complicated history, and to swell that with an account of myself and the people who went with me on my travels, since it was my aim to show the past side by side with the present it created. And while I grappled with the mass of my material during several years, it imposed certain ideas on me.

I became newly doubtful of empires. Since childhood I had been consciously and unconsciously debating their value, because I was born a citizen of one of the greatest empires the world has ever seen, and grew up as its exasperated critic. Never at any time was I fool enough to condemn man for conceiving the imperial theory, or to deny that it had often proved magnificent in practice. In the days when there were striking inequalities among the peoples of the earth, when some were still ignorant of agriculture and the complex process that lies behind the apparent simplicity of nomadism, and were therefore outrageously predatory in their hunger, when some were still candid in their enjoyment of murder, those further advanced must have found the necessity to protect their goods and their lives turn insensibly into a habit of conquest. In those times, also, it could well be that barbarians might possess a metal or a plant for which more cultured peoples had invented a beneficial use, and might refuse them access to it from sheer sullenness; and then, should one hold a communist theory of life and believe that all things are for all people, an attempt to break down that refusal must be approved. It is true that long ago it became untrue that peoples presented any serious damage because of backwardness; the threat of savagery has for long lain in technical achievement. For many centuries, too, a war waged by the civilized for access to materials unused by their primitive owners has failed to remain absolutely justifiable for long, since the inequality between the parties involved tempted the stronger to abuse. But if these moral sanctions for imperialism could not be claimed without hypocrisy in its later stages, they then acquired the value of all hypocritical pretences, which is to give a good example. The theory of the British Empire that it existed to bring order into the disordered parts of the earth was more than half humbug, but it inspired to action those in whose love of action there was nothing humbugging. These fought plagues and flood and drought and famine on behalf of the subject races, and instituted law courts where justice, if not actually blind when governors and governed came into conflict, was as a general rule blindfolded. These services might be conceived—though probably nothing could be more irritating to those who were its objects—as chivalrous acts, and those who performed them as *veray parfit gentil* knights. This had the wholly satisfactory result that the common people, proud of their empire and its builders, adopted the standpoint of chivalry.

One evening in London forty years ago, my mother came into my nursery and, all glowing, described how she had been coming home from a tea-party in the central district when she had seen a crowd standing in front of an hotel, obstinately cheering some curtained windows. So long and loudly did they cheer that at last the curtains were drawn, and some bearded men, wooden-faced with bewilderment, bowed out of the brightness into this curious night. They were the Boer generals, come to sign peace after their defeat in the South African War. This scene might be regarded as the apotheosis of complacency, were it not that the spirit which informed it resulted a few years later in the grant to South Africa of a constitution handsomer than vanquished had ever received from victors, and a quarter of a century later in the enactment of the Statute of Westminster, which gave most of the British dependencies the fullest measure of self-government ever conceived possible within an imperial framework. This is a fairer tale than is written on most of history's pages; and since the English enjoy few moral and intellectual advantages over other races, it is unlikely that they alone should be prompted to excellence by the idea of Empire.

But I saw in British imperialism room for roguery and stupidity as well as magnificence. A conquered people is a helpless people; and if they are of different physical type and another culture from their conquerors they cannot avail themselves of anything like the protection which would otherwise be given them by the current conceptions of justice and humanity. Carlyle, who said he loved God but really worshipped Timurlane, put the economic consequences of this situation in a nutshell when he wrote, in a pamphlet called *The Nigger Question*, that 'it is the law of our nature' that the black man 'who will not work according to what ability the gods have given him' shall not have 'the smallest right to eat pumpkin or to any fraction of land that will grow pumpkin, however plentiful such land may be,' but he has 'an indisputable and perpetual *right* to be compelled, by the real proprietors of said land, to do competent work for his living': that is, to work for the white owners of the West Indian sugar plantations. This attitude is even more dangerous than it appears, for if a man has power to make another man work for him against his will, he certainly has power to determine the conditions of this work; and unless he is a man of the rarest integrity he will see that these conditions keep him rich and his servants amenable. Capitalism at its greediest is thus given its head, and labour is kept brutish, so the general level of civilization and culture sinks. This must be the tendency of Empire, in so far as it is founded on the occupation of countries settled by another race, and time has not medicined it as might be hoped. Carlyle wrote of a rebellion in Jamaica in 1865; because of another rebellion a commission was appointed to inquire into the condition of West Indian labour in 1937.

There is also the difficulty, which did much to wreck Rome, of accepting the services of men fitted to govern the wild periphery of Empire without making them persons of influence at its core, where another sort of governor is needed. Soldiers and administrators, who are without limit in patience and understanding when they are dealing with those whom they regard as children, whether these be their subordinates in a service or members of another race, have no time and no bent for learning the different method appropriate to dealing with those who are their equals in race and before the law. It therefore seems to them that the first thing to do before society can be put on a proper basis is to exaggerate all social inequalities, and to this end, which may be wholly irrelevant to the actual social problems confronting them or to the tradition of their people's culture, they will sacrifice all other considerations. Thus it was that the later Roman emperors destroyed the structure built up by the old Romans, which gave the citizen considerable freedom in exchange for his submission to the essential discipline of the state, until they themselves felt wholly alien from Rome, and visited the city only for a few days of their reign, or perhaps not at all. Thus it is that 'Poona,' which is the name of a city in the Bombay presidency, is used, half in jest and wholly in earnest, to convey a reactionary strain in politics which could not be associated with the name of any English district.

In contemplating Yugoslavia these disadvantages of Empire are manifest. I can think of no more striking relic of a crime than the despoilment of Macedonia and Old Serbia, where the Turks for five hundred and fifty years robbed the native population till they got them down to a point beyond which the process could not be carried any further without danger of leaving no victims to be robbed in the future. The poverty of all Bosnians and Herzegovinians, except the Moslems and the Jews, is as ghastly an indictment of both the Turks and their successors, the Austrians. Dalmatia was picked clean by Venice. Croatia has been held back from prosperity by Hungarian control in countless ways that have left it half an age behind its Western neighbours in material prosperity. Never in the Balkans has Empire meant trusteeship. At least, there are such trustees, but they end in jail. The South Slavs have also suffered extremely from the inability of empires to produce men who are able both to conquer territory and to administer it. This does not apply to the portions that belonged to Austria and Venice, for these powers never conquered them and acquired them by the easier method of huckstering diplomacy; but it is the keynote of the Turkish symphony. In Sir Charles Eliot's profound book, *Turkey in Europe*, he says of the Turks that if 'they quoted from the Bible instead of the Koran, no words would better characterise their manner of life than "Here have we no continuing city,"' and describes a room in a Turkish house as 'generally scrupulously clean, but bare and unfurnished,' to such a degree that a European would be bound to believe that 'a party of travellers have occupied an old barn and said, "Let us make the place clean enough to live in; it's no use taking any more trouble about it. We shall probably be off again in a week."' Nothing could be more proper than this disregard for comfort, this refusal to relax, so long as these men were conquerors in the act of extending and confirming their conquests. But in the administrators of a vast territory this meant sluttish disorder, poverty, disease, and ignorance. It meant, above all, that the tax-collector milked the lands each year as if this were to be his last extortion before they were abandoned by an army that must always press forward. Here and there individual Slavs were saved by the only foreign missionary which has ever benefited the Balkans: the Oriental love of pleasure. Here and there Turks pleased their sensuousness by surrounding themselves with poplar groves, fountains, and prosperous Christian neighbours who also learned to be sensuous. Dalmatia derived an exceptional benefit from that Frenchman of unappreciated excellence, Marmont; he too spread about him his sensuousness as oil upon troubled waters. But he was overruled by his master Napoleon, who proved the rule and could not keep in peace what he had gained in war.

The contemplation of Yugoslavia suggests other, and catastrophic, aspects of Empire. Certain doubts as to the efficacy of the imperial system as an aid to civilization past any exceeding primitive phase had arisen in my mind when I was writing an essay on the life of St. Augustine. Africa, it had seemed to me, would have been considerably happier if Balbus had never built a wall. Those doubts were immensely reinforced by my Yugoslavian researches. The Dalmatian coast is one side of a coffin. Within lies dead Illyria: a great kingdom which was slain by the Roman Empire in the name of a civilizing mission. The Illyrians were drunken, the Romans said priggishly, not knowing what Suetonius was going to do with their own fair fame; they were pirates, they could not maintain safety on their high-roads. But if a bandit robbed and murdered a family and afterwards declared them to be of such disgusting character that he had fulfilled a public duty in annihilating them, we should hesitate to believe him, particularly if there were any evidence to the contrary. Here there was much. Illyria held up its head among the Eastern powers whom Rome never equalled in subtlety or splendour; Alexander the Great, beside whom any Roman shows as mediocre, was three parts Illyrian; and after the Illyrians had been conquered they produced many men who, intervening in Roman affairs, dwarfed all their contemporaries of Italian birth. It is therefore not possible to believe the Roman version.

Checked by the clock, the conquest of Illyria cannot be justified. It took two hundred and fifty years of open warfare, followed by fifty years of rebellion and pacification, to procure a peace that lasted only a hundred years. But this peace was maintained only by gifted Illyrians who were obliged to take over the management of the decrepit imperial machine and were therefore exercising their ability under a handicap to which they might not have been subjected in a free Illyria. Moreover, even their gifts were rendered unavailing by a catastrophe directly due to Empire. The barbarian invasions which brought the empire to a standstill and sank much of European civilization without trace, swept westwards over the continent at the pace of a flame. This might not have been so if they had encountered the close-knit opposition of states whose political administration corresponded with their racial and economic frontiers. But all such states had been destroyed by Rome. In their place had been established a flabby federation of peoples, long demoralized by subordination to an alien control itself rendered highly inefficient by political and economic and military misfortunes. The Mongols had only to touch such peoples to knock them over.

This is a hypothesis and no more; but its probability can be judged by our knowledge of Africa, with its much more documented history. Rome destroyed Punic civilization because it had not yet arrived at the conception of trade and could not understand that a rival might also be a customer, and because it wanted North Africa as its granary. It gave as bad an account of this victim as of Illyria, and not more credibly. For here, too, the vanquished race took over the victors' business. The Illyrian line of Roman emperors known as the *Restitutores Mundi* were remarkable; but the African Fathers preserved the Christian Church with the salt of genius when it might have perished with the rest of society, and thus it secured the continuity of Western culture. Through the greatest of the African Christians, St. Augustine, we know how it was with these gifted people and their fertile land when the barbarians came. North Africa had not been allowed to lead its own economic life, and had been organized as a cell in the Roman Empire; when its host fell into bankruptcy it was itself infected with financial decay. Property became useless owing to the intolerable burden of imperial taxation, and the Church was embarrassed by the number of estates handed over to it by owners incapable of bearing their responsibility. Many of the artisans and labourers were so poor that they ran mad and joined bands of wandering sectaries who combined religious frenzy with suicidal mania. The news of this collapse travelled southwards, and tribesmen crept up from the dark heart of the continent to gnaw at the edge of civilization, immensely aided by the circumstance that the empire was then split by a feud between a spindling emperor and his domineering sister, which split again into an intricate series of feuds between several military factions. The Governor of North Africa, an unhappy man named Boniface, of whom we know a great deal, was unable to find out to what authority he owed his fealty. He was thus forced into the position of a rebel, and two Roman armies had been sent against him when the Vandals launched their attack on the bedevilled provinces. There, with the help of the many elements which were distracted by misgovernment, they established easily enough the state of ruin which has persisted in these parts, save for a brief period of Islamic culture, throughout the subsequent fifteen hundred years. Thus the idea of Empire is rendered suspect on the territory where it seems to have most justified itself. In modern Africa the phrase 'the white man's burden' is far from being ironical: countless Europeans have given their lives to save Africans from such ills as sleeping sickness and the slave-trade. But it is dubious whether this missionary service would ever have been required if spontaneous African culture had not been hamstrung by the Roman Empire.

It is possible that Rome destroyed far more human achievement than she ever fostered. By Byzantium the Balkans were given much, but that was only when the Western Empire had fallen upon difficult days, when aggression was a half-forgotten dream, so unremitting was the need for defence. It is certain that the Balkans lost more from contact with all modern empires than they ever gained. They belonged to the sphere of tragedy, and Empire cannot understand the tragic. Great Britain was useless to them, except for Mr. Gladstone, who would have been shocked if he had known the truth about the Christian rebels, who therefore pretended they were other than they were, and who by that hypocrisy served the truth; and except for certain noble women, such as Miss Irby, who travelled with her friend, Miss Muir Mackenzie, all through Macedonia when this was a dangerous enterprise, told the truth about Turkish maladministration, and afterwards started a school for Christians in Sarajevo where fortitude was among the subjects taught. But Englishmen have usually been foolish about the Peninsula, being imbued with the imperialist idea that it is good to have and therefore apt to draw the false conclusion that those who have not are not good. The nineteenth-century English traveller tended to form an unfavourable opinion of the Christian subjects of the Ottoman Empire on the grounds that they were dirty and illiterate and grasping (as poor people, oddly enough, often are) and cringing and inhospitable and ill-mannered (as frightened people, oddly enough, often are). He condemned them as he condemned the inhabitants of the new industrial hells in Lancashire and Yorkshire, who insisted on smelling offensively, drinking gin to excess, and being rough and rude. Even as he felt glad when these unfortunate fellow-countrymen of his were the objects of missionary efforts by philanthropists drawn from the upper and middle classes, he felt glad because these Christian

Slavs were in the custody of the Turks, who were exquisite in their personal habits, cultivated, generous, dignified, hospitable, and extremely polite. His gladness felt a cold check when the Turkish Empire collapsed. Philanthropists should not go bankrupt. But in the twentieth century his grandsons transferred their enthusiasm to the Russian and Austrian Empires, and regretted that one or the other was not custodian of the Balkans. Even after the war, which showed both these great powers soft as rotten apples, and the Serbs as strong in the saving of European civilization, many Englishmen lamented that the Balkan peoples were not under the tutelage of the charming, cultured Austrians.

How strange a dream it was, it is, that the Southern Slavs should be reared to civilization by Russia! The Old Russia was not even a true empire, she was not even a modern state, she was rather a symbol of immense spiritual value but of little material efficacy, by which millions of people, scattered over vast and alienating territories, and bruised beyond belief by past defeat, were able to believe that they were taking part in the drama by which man shall discover the meaning of his extraordinary destiny. Nothing had ever enabled these people to recover from the disorganization inflicted on them by the Mongol tribe known as the Golden Horde, who occupied their country for nearly two hundred years, and cut them off from the Byzantine Empire in its paradoxical apotheosis, when it was a dying and a fecundating power. During this long night the land fell into confusion, and though there have emerged from it some colossal geniuses, compact of fire and smoke, to prove the value of the stock, few of them have had the appropriate quality of nursemaids. There could have been nothing more fantastic than the idea of handing over the wretched victims of the Turks, who needed above all else tranquillity and order and their own way, to the care of the Russians, who themselves had been plunged by Asiatic influence into a permanent and impassioned state of simultaneous anarchy and absolutism: nothing, save the idea of handing them over to the Austrian Empire.

It is difficult to write the plain truth about the Austrian Empire as any historian not a Roman Catholic propagandist knows it. The lilacs and chestnuts of Vienna, the gilded staircases and crystal chandeliers of its baroque palaces, its divine musicians, great and little, have confused the judgement of the world; but a defence of the Japanese Empire which relied largely on its cherry blossoms and pagodas and the prints of Hiroshige would not convince. It is delightful to drink the *heuriger* wine in the gardens of Grinzing, but all the same Mr. Gladstone was not speaking intemperately when he said that he knew nothing good of Austria. It represented just as much of the German people as could be organized into unity. The rest of them were too quarrelsome and unaware of any reason to prefer harmony to disharmony to sink their local differences, and it is probable that the Austrians would have remained in the same state had it not been for the threat of Turkish invasion. They were witless and careless to a degree that can be judged by their tolerance of the Habsburgs as their rulers, century after century.

This family, from the unlucky day in 1273 when the College of Electors chose Rudolf of Habsburg to be King of the Romans, on account of his mediocrity, till the abdication of Charles II, in 1918, produced no genius, only two rulers of ability in Charles V and Maria Theresa, countless dullards, and not a few imbeciles and lunatics. While they were responsible for Germany they lost it Switzerland and plunged it into the misery, from which it has never wholly recovered, of the Thirty Years War; they brought on Spain a ruin that seems likely to endure for all time; they made their names spell infamy in the Netherlands. If in Austria they appeared to have been successful in driving back the Turks, it is because they had developed a certain technical ability in the course of generations spent in organizing failures and afterwards retaining their thrones, and were thus able to procure foreign generals, such as Eugène of Savoy and John Sobieski, to lead foreign troops against the invaders. Their actions were again and again horrible: the campaign by which the Emperor Ferdinand converted his largely Protestant dominions to solid Roman Catholicism was one of the most hideous in history. The very beauty of Vienna was a testimony of the gulf between the rulers and their people. For Austria is not naturally rich; too much of it is mountainous, and too much is agricultural land ill served by communications. It could afford these baroque palaces only by the most merciless exploitation of its peasants and artisans. To do the Habsburgs justice, they made no hypocritical pretence that they paid any undue regard to the interests of their people. 'He may be a patriot for Austria,' the Emperor Franz Josef cynically inquired concerning a politician who had been recommended to him as a possible Minister on the ground of his patriotism, 'but is he a patriot for me?'

The Habsburgs and their people alike were at their worst in their relations with the alien races of their empire. Austria annexed Hungary after the Turks had been driven out, and never learned either to work in amity with it or to coerce it. It lost its Italian possessions by sheer brutality and administrative incompetence.

And it was still entirely uncritical of a twofold passion that had raged in the German bosom since earliest times. 'The Slavs,' the Saxons were informed by a manifesto of their princes and bishops in the eleventh century, 'are an abominable people, but their land is very rich in flesh, honey, grain, and herds, and it abounds in all crops when it is cultivated, so that none can be compared to it. So say they who know. Thus, you can both save your souls and acquire the best of land to live in.' Eight hundred years later, Bismarck, when he was revising the Treaty of Berlin, was seized with fury at the sight of one clause, and ran his pencil through it again and again, because it safeguarded the rights of the Kutzo-Vlachs, an inoffensive people whom he falsely believed to be Slav; he then continued to draft the treaty to the end of delivering the Balkans up to the hungry maw of the Austrian people.

This was the most persistent, the most vivid strain in the German character. It reconciled the German Austrians to admitting the Hungarians to equality within the empire by the Dual Monarchy, for the Hungarians also hated the Slavs and would not forget to use their independent power in harrying the Croats and Serbs within their borders. 'You look after your barbarians,' the Hungarian statesman, Andrassy, assured the Austrian Chancellor, Beust, 'and we will look after ours.' A great part of Austrian internal political life was given to naïve assertions of the German Austrian's inalienable right to enjoy every sort of favouritism at the expense of his Slav fellow-subjects. When it was ordained that German civil servants working in Czech districts must learn Czech, thus putting them on a parity with Czech civil servants, who were obliged to know German, all German Austrians revolted and their representatives obstructed all parliamentary business till the ordinances were withdrawn. This is the only positive feature in the political life of nineteenth-century Vienna. That age was not noble anywhere, since then the ignorance of townsmen, who must inevitably be very ignorant unless they are very learned, lay as a thickening shadow on human thought, but in Vienna it was even less noble than in the rest of Europe. There was manifest a clericalism that was seven-eighths political obscurantism of a childish type; the class greed of a bureaucracy far too numerous for the country's resources; a liberalism that represented nothing more than the opposition of the industrialists and bankers and lawyers to the landowners; and a Christian Socialism which was anti-Semitic and dedicated to the protection of the *Spiessbürger*, the mediocrity who despises the working man but has not the wit to attach himself to the more fortunate classes, and cries out to be hoisted up into a position of privilege by party action. This latter was Nazism without that audacity which is its only handsome attribute. The automatism with which the Habsburgs carried on their inherited tradition of external order made them control this movement so that it never had a leader more objectionable than the famous Mayor of Vienna, Dr Karl Lueger, who, though he was barren of any ideas save hatred and greed, acted within the limits to which the bourgeoisie then confined themselves. But the dynamic force of that and all other Viennese movements was loathing of the Slavs.

So much I had read in books. But in Yugoslavia I saw with my own eyes the German hatred of the Slavs: as a scar on the Slav peoples, in the chattering distraction of Croatia, and the lacerated moral beauty of Bosnia; as an abscess on a German soul, when Gerda looked on the seven thousand French graves at Bitolj and wounded a husband who had treated her with infinite tenderness by saying sourly, 'To think of all those people giving their lives for a lot of Slavs'; as a womb swollen with murder, in the German war memorial at Bitolj. For the first time I knew the quality of the parties to this feud. I saw the solemn and magnificent embroideries of the Slav peasant women and knew what degeneration of skill and taste was represented by the bright little flowers and hearts on the Austrian belts that the skiers like to bring back from St. Anton. I saw the Serbs, who make more sombre expeditions than open-air meals at little restaurants in the Wienerwald, who go in pilgrimage to the Frushka Gora and see defeat itself in the person of the Tsar Lazar, laid in a golden shroud: it is headless, as defeat should be, since it is a frustration of personality, but its hands are preserved, as is fitting, for it is the hand that is the sign of humanity, that distinguishes man from all other animals, and it is conflict with defeat that divides human beings from the natural world. I saw the Serbs, to whom the subjects of the Habsburgs could certainly teach nothing. Twice the Serbs drove their would-be teachers out of Serbia, and being vanquished the third time, not so much by arms as by sickness and famine, fled through icy mountains to the sea, rested for a little space, then fought them a fourth time, and were victorious. Such is not the proper relationship between pupil and professor. I saw in Yugoslavia many people such as the mother of the idiot child at the tomb of Sveti Naum who said to us, 'I don't know what to say to God about this, there's so much to say, I don't know where to begin, it's such a strange thing to have happened,' and the old woman who walked on the mountain road in Montenegro, asking the skies, 'If I had to live, why should my life have been like this?' There were others, such as Militsa, who is a poet and a scholar and a woman of the world, yet recognizably the sister of these women, to prove that they were not merely exhibiting a pristine excellence preserved by the lack of use, that their subtlety was no superficial bloom which would be brushed away by their first contact with modern civilization, that their stuff was of the sort that can achieve what is most cause for pride among human achievement. I knew that few Austrians had shown the degree of sensibility that would enable them to instruct such people, and that it would not have mattered if there had been few or many of them, for they would have recognized that people like these have no need to be instructed by other human beings, but can learn for themselves.

I said to myself quite often, as I wrestled with the material of this book, that now what was well would at last happen. For the old Turkey had gone and its successor had no interest in Empire, and Russia was a Union of Soviet Republics, and the Habsburgs were fallen; and the treaties of Versailles and Trianon and St. Germain had set the small peoples free. Freedom was for these people an ecstasy. That I knew to be true, for I had seen it with my own eyes. Finland, Estonia, Latvia, Czechoslovakia, and Yugoslavia, they were all like young men stretching themselves at the open window in the early morning after long sleep. To eat in a public place in these countries, to walk in their public gardens, was to fill the nostrils with the smell of happiness. Nothing so fair has happened in all history as this liberation of peoples who, during centuries of oppression, had never forgotten their own souls, and by long brooding on their national lives had changed them from transitory experience to lasting and inspiring works of art. It is not even imaginable what they would have achieved, had they been given time to acquire the technique of self-government, for though there are free peoples, and these have contributed largely to civilization, they have been free because they were fortunate, and have not, like the Slavs and the Finns and the Balts, learned that wisdom which 'is sold in the desolate market where none comes to buy, And in the withered fields where the farmer ploughs for bread in vain.'

It surprised me that many Englishmen and Americans, who professed to be benevolently concerned with the future of man, were not in the least exalted by this prospect. The left wing, especially, was sharply critical of the new states and all that they did. This was inconsistent in those who believed, often to a point far beyond the practical, that the individual must be free to determine his own destiny, and it was partly due to a theory, so absurd that not even its direct opposite has any chance of being true, that nationalism is always anti-democratic and aggressive, and that internationalism is always liberal and pacific. Yet nationalism is simply the determination of a people to cultivate its own soul, to follow the customs bequeathed to it by its ancestors, to develop its traditions according to its own instincts. It is the national equivalent of the individual's determination not to be a slave. The fulfilment of both those determinations is essentially a part of the left programme. But the liberation of an individual or a people may lead to all sorts of different consequences, according to their different natures. The nationalisms of Hungary and Ireland have always been intense, but Hungary has always been industrially ambitious and resolute both in maintaining a feudal land system and in oppressing the aliens within her frontiers while Ireland, though she desires to annihilate Ulster, wishes to be a peasant state with industries well within manageable proportions. It was extremely probable that all the countries liberated by the peace treaties would tend to be liberal, since their populations had long been in active revolt against the absolutism of Russia, Turkey, and Austria-Hungary, and indeed, considering the difficult conditions they had inherited, their practice kept close to liberalism. Nevertheless the left wing regarded these new states with the utmost suspicion, and if they visited them immediately allied themselves with the opposition parties, even if these were extremely reactionary. Thus I was often surprised, when I spoke of Yugoslavia to Bloomsbury intellectuals, themselves free-thinking and Marxist, to find them expressing the warmest sympathy with the Catholic Croats, even those of a far more reactionary cast than Matchek's followers.

Any discussion of these points was complicated by the tendency of these intellectuals to use the words 'nationalism' and 'imperialism' as if they meant the same thing. It is fair to say that three out of four times that English and American authors write of French nationalism they are thinking of French imperialism; these are two distinct strands in the life of France. Napoleon was a French imperialist, but he was completely detached from French nationalism, which was natural enough, as he was not a Frenchman; and Charles Péguy was the flower of French nationalism, but was actively hostile to French imperialism. But not all talk on this subject rose even to the high level of this confusion. As the state of Europe grew worse innumerable people, most of them Americans sighed, 'Ah, it's the fault of these small nations,' and had not the faintest idea what they meant when they said it.

They cannot have thought it was really the small nations that were shaking the mailed fist, and indeed when they were pressed they fell back on allegations that the small nations had impeded the free flow of European trade by the tariff barriers within which they enclosed themselves. But the Scandinavian and Baltic countries offered no ground whatsoever for this justification, and if the Balkan countries had never formed a Danubian federation, it was because Italy, with the intention of keeping these countries weak so that it might some day seize them, saw to it at conference after conference that they were forbidden to form any such association.

All this campaign against the small new states was inchoate, and uninformed to a point well below the general level of the people who took part in it. They must have had some prejudice against them; and this I found astonishing, for if there is an assurance in the Europe of our day that sometimes life goes well, a promise that some day it may go better, it is offered by these countries. I cannot but think it exhilarating, from the point of view of both the Turks and the Slavs, that the Turkish tax-collector no longer beggars the peasants on the Skoplje hills and plains for the benefit of a pasha whom the Turkish peasant also had no cause to love, and this was but one example of the supersession of the disagreeable by what was at least more agreeable, which I assumed was desired by all reasonable human beings. But I remembered, and both the art of the Byzantine frescoes and the speculation that underlies all but the most trivial of Slav conversations confirm my remembrance, that human beings are not reasonable, and do not to any decisive degree prefer the agreeable to the disagreeable. Only part of us is sane: only part of us loves pleasure and the longer day of happiness, wants to live to our nineties and die in peace, in a house that we built, that shall shelter those who come after us. The other half of us is nearly mad. It prefers the disagreeable to the agreeable, loves pain and its darker night despair, and wants to die in a catastrophe that will set back life to its beginnings and leave nothing of our house save its blackened foundations. Our bright natures fight in us with this yeasty darkness, and neither part is commonly quite victorious, for we are divided against ourselves and will not let either part be destroyed. This fight can be observed constantly in our personal lives. There is nothing rarer than a man who can be trusted never to throw away happiness, however eagerly he sometimes grasps it. In history we are as frequently interested in our own doom. Sometimes we search for peace, sometimes we make an effort to find convenient frontiers and a proper fulfilment for racial destinies; but sometimes we insist on war, sometimes we stamp into the dust the only foundations on which we can support our national lives. We ignore this suicidal strain in history because we are consistently bad artists when we paint ourselves, we prettify our wills and pretend they are not parti-coloured before the Lord. We pretend that the Thirty Years War disappointed the hope of those who engineered it because it brought famine to Central Europe, famine so extreme that whole villages were given over to silence and the spreading weed, so extreme that bands of desperate men waylaid travellers and ate their flesh. Yet perhaps these engineers of war did not like villages, and felt queasy at the thought of a society enjoying wholesome meals. It seems that, choked with our victory in the last war, we now have an appetite for defeat. The new states were full of life, Yugoslavia shook its clenched fists and swore it meant to live. Therefore England and America and France turned away, for what lived disgusted them; they wanted a blanched world, without blood, given over to defeat.

They would not interfere, therefore, with the marginal activity that ran parallel to the continuous national effort which I was chronicling. From time to time out of the text there emerged little black figures which postured on the white paper beside it, achieved a group which was magical, an incantation to death, and ran back again into the text, which carried on its story of the main and legitimate historical process.

Till then there had been a certain detachment between these irregular abandonments of the legal process and the large movement of history. The black little figures rushed out of the text and made their magic mark in the margin and disappeared; and the stout column of the text continued as before, only betraying by a later variation from the expected that the magic had been efficacious. The development of the nineteenth century was certainly affected to a slight degree, almost invisible save to the specialist eye, by the assassination of Prince Danilo of Montenegro, and to a more marked degree by the assassination of Prince Michael of Serbia; and when Alexander and Draga were murdered and Peter Karageorgevitch came to the throne, the map of Europe seemed to have been repainted in brighter and more discordant colours. But Danilo's death did not make my great-grandmother cry; I doubt if my grandfather was ever reminded by discomfort that Prince Michael of Serbia had left this earth; I did not eat different food or wear different clothes because of Alexander and Draga, or think different thoughts. The *attentat* at Sarajevo had a totally different effect. Its magical operation on the text was immediate. I and nearly all women in Europe wept times without number, said again and

again, 'Ah, that is because of the war,' and learned to eat against
hunger, to dress for warmth, to think not for amusement but to find
the clue out of the maze. We were marked by an impersonal event
as deeply as by any of the classic stages of the personal life. And
after the darkness of the contending armies cleared from Europe
it could be seen that the map had been painted yet once more, in
colours still more brilliant, which were also harmonious.

It might have been that the eye of the future should see Europe
for some space of time as a pale West like a fading fresco painted
by genius, a troubled and writhing German people, a barricaded
and preoccupied Russia, and a chaplet of shining small countries,
delighting in life as intense as human society has ever known. But
there was an intractable element that would not be satisfied with
this dispensation.

The Sarajevo *attentat* represented three of the dominant factors in
history. Princip was inspired by nationalism; the Austrian officers
who let Princip have his way were imperialists; the parties to the
other *attentat*, which was not committed because Princip forestalled
it, were children of 'Apis,' lovers of slaughter for its own sake. But
there was one important factor in modern times which had no share
in the *attentat*, and no part in the satisfaction that followed the
peace, though it had had no part in the satisfaction that preceded
it—the mindless, traditionless, possessionless section of the urban
proletariat which had sent Luccheni as its representative to murder
the Empress Elizabeth of Austria, but which, largely owing to the
site of the crime, had no say in the murder of Franz Ferdinand.
Its interests were therefore not specifically raised by the war that
ensued, and they were curiously neglected after it. The new age
was eager for reforms and was not niggardly in paying for them,
but it made no drastic reorganization of the social system. This was
partly due to the supineness of the left wing. They are the proper
people to make any revolution; it is their trade. But they were too
busy discussing the distant Bolshevist experiment in Russia to have
the time or energy to work out their local salvation. This gave the
revolutionaries of the right wing their chance.

Mindless, traditionless, possessionless, Mussolini came to power.
Italy was predestined to be the first country in the world to hand
its destiny over to a member of this class, for though France had
a large urban population it had an inveterate tendency not to be
mindless. Great Britain had strong traditions, and the United States
had possessions, while Italy had many peasants who had been
industrialized for a generation or so without becoming cultured,
had lost the tradition of its small states without acquiring a new

national one, and was very poor. Mussolini was its predestined leader, for while he had not sufficient intelligence to lift him out of this class, he had not too little to acquire some knowledge of the theory and practice of social revolution from an apprenticeship to the left. If he had achieved his rulership in times of peace he would have sought to commit some act of violence that would provoke a war; since his hour came when the whole world was sick with a surfeit of armies that programme was manifestly ill timed, so he had to find some method of applying violence to peace-time. He retrieved, whether from the half-comprehended talk of a clever comrade or by skimming a volume in the threepenny box outside the bookshop, the Code of Diocletian; and being either unaware or careless that Diocletian had perished of despair in his palace at Split, because he had failed to check the descent of ruin on the Roman earth, he enforced that Code on his country. This was a comical venture. For Diocletian had some excuse for seeking to stabilize by edict the institutions of an empire that had lasted for over a thousand years, but it was imbecile to attempt to fix the forms of a country that had been unified for less than a century and was deeply involved in a world economic system which was no older than the industrial revolution.

Mussolini, indeed, rested his case for the revival of the Code on nothing so acceptable to the high faculties of man as its capacity to further well-being. He recommended it because it had to be applied by violence, which he alleged to be the highest thing in life. But in peace the opportunities for violence are limited and not remunerative. He had to resort to war. He had taught his followers to enjoy the taste of assault, and he had to satisfy this appetite by promising them the wide mass murder of a European conflict; he had raised their material standards by lavish expenditure on social services the state could not afford, and he had to placate their new greed by promising them sea-power like Britain's and an empire in Asia and Africa. The first step towards any of these ends was the destruction of Yugoslavia. Its Dalmatian coast was necessary if he were to have command of the Adriatic; through its hinterland ran the high-road to Asia. But he lacked the heart for fair fighting. Traditionless, he had not learned what all but the most primitive communities have learned, that it is better for both parties to a conflict if there is no treachery on either side. He therefore strove to win his battle beforehand by fomenting revolution among Yugoslavian nationals in Croatia and Macedonia. But there he made an error. Belonging to the bored and under-employed urban class which is always glad of the excitement of a street fight, he could not understand that peasants quickly tire of guerrilla bands trailing backwards and forwards over their lands, interrupting work vitally necessary to a good harvest. So he looked north, to Austria.

Vienna still stands. That is to say, it is as it was. A great town engenders its tradition, which cannot be destroyed, because it is sown through the brains and loins of all men born within it or under its shadow, and because it determines the form of local customs and thus for ever afterwards constrains those who enter it from other parts to its way of living. So it was with Constantinople, which was made by the Byzantines in the image of their magnificent dreams, which imposed those dreams on the Turks, of wholly alien natural genius, who drove out the Byzantines. So it is with Vienna.

That city seemed at first to accept the destiny it had thrust on itself by its provocation of war. Henceforth it had to be poor; for it had always been that by nature. Only the merciless exploitation of its peasants and its Slav subjects had enabled it to support the extravagance of its aristocracy, the solid comfort of its bourgeoisie. But in its diminishment it might have known an age as great as its own eighteenth century had it reconciled itself to being a small town without vainglory but glorious in its university and its opera, its baroque palaces and art galleries, its lilacs and chestnuts, its abundance of Jewish genius. It could not, however, check the tradition which had struck its roots deeper and deeper during the nineteenth century, which was growing rankly among the ruins of Vienna and was even spreading rankly through another soil.

For this tradition had found its perfect instrument in Adolf Hitler. It must always be remembered that Hitler is not a German but an Austrian, and nothing he has brought to post-war Germany had not its existence in pre-war Austria. There is nothing original in his demonic fancies save their intensity. He is a man of the same class as Luccheni and Mussolini, a recruit to the hopeless and helpless urban proletariat; and like them he is mindless and possessionless, and, so far as the human tradition goes, traditionless. He did not know why the difficult and sometimes dangerous process of thinking is held in esteem; he did not know that fourteen hundred years before an emperor had proclaimed that a ruler 'must be not only glorified with arms, but also armed with laws,' and that all communities have been forced to hold that opinion or perish; he had not an inkling that it is actually healthy for the human race to prefer what is agreeable to what is disagreeable. He was a poor craftsman, with no pride in his craft, which was natural enough in the child of one of those parasites on our social system, a douanier. But what he had heard in his childhood lingered in his ears. His father's native village was only a few miles from the family estate of Schönerer, who founded the Pan-German movement that swept Vienna at the end of the last century, and there is nothing in *Mein Kampf* which was not in Schöonerer's programme. There is the same racial pride, the same anti-Semitism, the same hatred of the Slavs, the same hostility to the Church. Schönerer's movement was, however, stultified by his determination to find his followers among the educated classes. There was a hair-splitting tendency in those who had been exposed to culture which rendered them unable to admire the simplicity and strength of this platform, in which every plank was cut from hatred or vanity. Two leaders, neither of them peasants or workmen, both bureaucrats, recognized that the only hope for their faith lay in spreading it among the Caliban class of urban workers who were outside the trade unions. They started a German Socialist Workers' party, almost indistinguishable in programme from the Nazi party, which held three seats in the Austrian Parliament of 1911. Hitler is simply an exporter of Austrian goods, which he sells with an energy due to the dynamic passion for blood which is his special idiosyncrasy. For the pleasure he takes in murder is so great that 'Apis' now seems a moderate man who sometimes stamped his foot when annoyed.

Hitler, however, was working out his destiny in Germany, and there was no such dramatic figure in Vienna, but only the old actors conscientiously performing the same comedy on the themes of extravagance and *Schlamperei*. The financiers and industrialists acted their parts with such zest that they not only brought down their own house on their heads: they shattered the economic structure of the whole world. The collapse of the Credit Anstalt in 1931 caused the German crisis which perpetuated the world slump of 1929. These proceedings were unchecked by the political forces of the town, which was as frivolous and factious as it had ever been. The left wing produced some devoted and even saintly trade unionists and too many adherents to the type of international socialism which unfits its disciples for dealing with local problems. All alike were feckless and unaware that when a socialist-elected authority spends money as if socialism were already established, although it is not yet strong enough to overthrow capitalism, it provokes a formidable reaction. The right wing was what might have been expected from a community which was still capable of looking over its teacups and saying to a foreign visitor, 'Can you tell me if Mr So-and-so belongs to the first or second rank of English society?' The only hope for Austrian independence lay in comradeship with the Danubian states, who might have formed with her a solid block of defiant young nations, ready to face the rising forces of Nazism and Fascism, with their backs against an even more defiant Russia and Turkey. But Austria was still sneering at all peoples to her east, still vaunting herself as 'the frontier of Europe.' She looked west for her salvation, and when, like the rest of the world, she tumbled into the pit of the slump, she conceived a sick fancy that all her troubles would be ended if she were joined in a customs union with Germany. This, with a good sense that has been more than justified by the subsequent course of history, was forbidden by the powers as a threat to European peace; but in any case it was useless as a prescription for Austria's economic malady, for Germany was as sick as she was, and two states which are bankrupt for precisely similar reasons are not more solvent than one. Some of the right-wing politicians were aware of this, but there was nothing shrewd in their awareness. They were determined to keep their independence, yet fomented this desire for union with imperialist and internationalist Nazism, or else inspired their followers with an equally suicidal enthusiasm for imperialist and internationalist Fascism. To these insane impulses they sacrificed everything: honour, decency, humanity, and that other thing which a man sacrifices when he fails in these qualities towards the people of his own blood. The smoke curled up from a peculiar offering of this sort in February 1934.

One of the most typical features of post-war Vienna were the working-class tenements, built by the Government of Vienna, which was as far left as the National Government was right. These large buildings presented a modern and rationalist appeal to visitors who were already seduced by the lilacs and chestnuts of the Viennese gardens; and anywhere the sceptic who looks a housing scheme in the mouth is sure to be denounced as a hard-hearted wretch who grudges poor children a decent home. But the truth is that these tenements were a shocking extravagance for a ruined city. For they were not needed. Though the Vienna of the Habsburgs had been disfigured by abominable slums, the shrinkage in the population made it unnecessary for the poor to inhabit them any longer. They had simply to move up into the accommodation their former masters had vacated. There were acres of villas built, and well built, for the bourgeoisie and upper classes, which now stood in neglected gardens, either unoccupied or occupied by owners who had to starve to pay the taxes. These villas could easily have been subdivided and the gardens cut up into allotments for the new tenants. But instead they were left to decay, and the Town Council of this distressed and dwindling city spent over fourteen million pounds in building sixty thousand flats in the form of isolated blocks containing anything up to seventeen hundred families. A state still carrying on under the capitalist system should not have diverted so large a sum from industry in so short a time: the unemployment rate mounted in direct ratio to these lofty buildings. It is, moreover, extremely doubtful whether families should be encouraged to live in apartments if there is enough ground in the neighbourhood to permit them roomier accommodation with gardens; and these apartments were extremely small. Though there was no measure in the fascination they exercised on foreigners they were in point of fact inferior to many similar working-class tenements in Holland and Scandinavia; and though they were infinitely superior to most English pre-war dwellings of the kind, they fell below the standards applied to our housing schemes during the last twenty-five years.

It is said that the motives which inspired the Viennese municipal authorities to build these blocks were not simple. To be accepted as a tenant the citizen had to satisfy certain tests which in fact guaranteed him as a Social Democrat; if he followed a trade he had to be a trade unionist. Thus these apartments put solid blocks of Socialist voters into various districts that might otherwise have returned right-wing representatives. If this be true, then the Karl-Marx-Hof and the Goethe-Hof rival the Tower of Babel in architectural irony. For in February 1934 there was again an abandonment of the slow legitimate process of civilized existence, a resort to action too swift and too immediate in its logic to be the work of wisdom. Again black figures run out of the text of history and inscribe a magic character in the margin. The Austrian Chancellor, Dollfuss, was a fervent Catholic, Austrian nationalist, and agrarian protectionist, and he hated the atheism, the imperialism, and the economic programme of Hitler. He therefore secretly called on Mussolini for aid, and became virtually an instrument of Italian policy. So too did Prince Starhemberg, a wealthy aristocrat, who had been an early accomplice of Hitler, had turned against him, and was now head of a semi-fascist armed band called the *Heimwehr* or the Home Guard, which was supporting Dollfuss. In January 1934 it looked as if Dollfuss and Starhemberg were about to be forced by difficult internal conditions to come to a working agreement with the Social Democrats; and indeed the left government then holding office in France had extracted from them definite promises that they should do so. But in the middle of January Mussolini sent a message to Dollfuss to say that the Social Democrats must not be

conciliated but destroyed. It unluckily happened that on February
the seventh the French Government fell, after the disastrous battle
of the Place de la Concorde which revealed to the world the strength
of fascist influence in France; and Dollfuss was quick to read the
lesson. On February eleventh his Vice-Chancellor, Major Fey, and
Prince Starhemberg went out into Vienna and led the police and
the *Heimwehr* in a systematic battue of the Social Democrats. They
had very little difficulty in finding their victims as so many of them
were residents in these huge blocks of flats. These they surrounded,
bombarded, and cleared of their inhabitants. Civil war can keep
secret its casualties, and it has never been ascertained how many
of these luckless tenants were killed, imprisoned, or turned loose
homeless and destitute; but such victims must have numbered
many thousands. It was at this holocaust that my chauffeur with the
blindish blue eyes had assisted, by driving Major Fey about from
massacre to massacre, because he thought it was time somebody did
something.

This murder marked a new phase in the genius of murder which
has shaped our recent history. It was, of course, not novel in a
sense. It bore the familiar thumb-print of its prime mover. Like
the degradation of Croatia and Macedonia, it was utterly pointless.
It could serve no possible purpose, for had Mussolini marched
into Austria it would have been the armies of other countries, not
the unhappy tenants of the Karl-Marx-Hof and the Goethe-Hof,
who would have resisted him. And the crime is also reminiscent
of others committed by Austrians in its cold inhumanity. After the
Mayerling tragedy the uncles of Marie Vetsera were summoned
by night to the hunting-lodge, confronted with a laundry basket
containing the naked body of their niece, were given her clothes
and told to dress her, and were made to drive ten miles with her
corpse propped up between them to the cemetery where she was
to be furtively buried. In order to keep her on the seat it was
necessary to use an umbrella as a splint for her spine and neck.
None of the court officials found this service too repulsive to exact
from these unhappy young men. The callousness of the funeral
arrangements for the murdered Archduke Franz Ferdinand and
his wife twenty-five years later showed that this was no passing
phase of barbarity, and twenty years later these February massacres were to prove the truth of the saying, 'Like master, like man.'
The chauffeur's behaviour can be judged only if one imagines a
Cockney taxi-man cheerfully spending some days driving about a
ruffian who was making it his business to assault by bombardment
and machine-gun the tenants of all London County Council flats,

men, women, and children alike. It must further be imagined that this Cockney taxi-driver would be actuated not by indignation over any definite wrong or passion for any cause, but simply by a vague hope that times might be better; and that he was not maddened by poverty, being well fed and well clothed, and able to rely on an amplitude of social services in any emergency.

But the crime was, in one sense, terrible in its novelty. The people who assassinated Prince Danilo of Montenegro and Prince Michael of Serbia were individuals holding certain ideas who wanted to kill nationalists. The man who assassinated the Empress Elizabeth was not an individual, he was a representative of the undifferentiated human mass, who killed an individual, who was the representative of the class which he held responsible for allowing that portion of humanity to lose its differentiation and sink back into the mass. The people who assassinated Alexander and Draga Obrenovitch were for the most part individuals who were nationalist and objected to individualists who should have been nationalist but had been corrupted by an alien imperialism, and for the lesser part individuals who enjoyed murder. The murder of Franz Ferdinand was as pure a case as could be imagined of a nationalist individual murdering an imperialist individual. But these February butcheries represented mass murdering mass. Mussolini was destroying people of his own sort, not for any motive that could actuate an individual with a mind, with traditions and with an interest in maintaining stable conditions, but out of some elementary reaction such as might make an embryo kick in the womb. For the first time in the modern age the individual had been squeezed out of history. He was neither the subject nor the object of a crucial action which was to affect the destiny of many millions. This meant that henceforth events must take a violent and unreasonable course; embryos cannot control a complicated world made by adults. It meant also that existence must decline from what ease and dignity it had attained to a hitherto unknown level of pain and humiliation: adults cannot be happily governed by embryos.

The first result of the Viennese massacres was the famous Nazi 'Blood Bath' of June the thirtieth, 1934. Till now murder had played a minor part in Hitler's programme; his mainstay was a combination of torture and imprisonment, and he had only occasionally resorted to the assassination of some specially dangerous personality. But Vienna suggested to him that perhaps, if one were sufficiently powerful, one could murder people, even a lot of people, with impunity. He acted on that suggestion by killing without trial and without warning about twelve hundred

people, many of whom loved and trusted him, during the course
of a single night. He thus at one and the same time fed his appetite
for murder, and enacted a fantasy that all of us have played with
in our infancy. Few children have not lain in their cots like
little Timurlanes and prayed that in the night all the unkind
and difficult world might be swept away, so that in the morning
they might have a new Daddy and Mummy and Nurse, a new
kindergarten. With such baby ferocity Hitler included among his
victims the manager and two head waiters of the Munich restaurant
which he and his party had frequented in earlier days. This too
was murder of the mass by the mass; but here subject was so
identical with object that this murder was no more true murder
than masturbation is sexual intercourse. Many of those slaughtered
were so conscious of their unchangeable identity with the Nazis
that they assumed themselves to be victims of an anti-Nazi rising
and died crying, '*Heil*, Hitler!' However, Hitler's enjoyment of the
experience, such as it was, led him to venture on the more mature
form of indulgence before another month was past. On July the
twenty-fifth he arranged for a Nazi uprising in Vienna, which had
for its main purpose the assassination of Dollfuss. For this victim
nobody need shed a tear. He had acquiesced, if indeed he had not
actively collaborated, in the slaughter of his fellow-countrymen at
Mussolini's behest. But the murder was disgusting enough without
the element of personal pity being involved, both in the barbarity
which left Dollfuss to lie in his blood for hours, vainly asking
for a priest and a doctor, and the gross cowardice which sent
the conspirators scampering in every direction before they had
time to realize their further plans. These, however, were bound
in any case to be abortive. They could not lead to the annexation
of Austria by Germany, because, as must have been foreseen by any
sane observer, the first rumour of the uprising brought Mussolini's
troops up in force to the Brenner Pass between Italy and Austria.
Whether the Blood Bath of June the thirtieth served any purpose
is impossible to say, for civil war keeps its own secrets, and
many of the victims were so wholly submerged in the Nazi
party that they were unknown to any human being outside it;
but the murder of Dollfuss was astonishing as an example of the
pointlessness characteristic of historical events determined by the
dictators.

There was a little over two months' respite. All the world over
nothing much is done during August, and on the Mediterranean
coast this lassitude continues throughout September. But in October work began again in earnest. On the ninth of that month there

was committed at Marseille that crime which for so long preoccupied and perplexed me, the assassination of King Alexander of
Yugoslavia. It seems to me that I have explained this crime by
the material I collected on my Yugoslavian journey. He was killed
because the Balkan peoples had long ago been defeated by the
Turks, who like all imperialists found government nothing near
so easy as conquest, so that the misgoverned Peninsula became
the object of concupiscence in the neighbouring empires; and
these, sitting round like wolves on their haunches in expectation
of the hour when the Turks would have to hobble away and
leave their booty undefended, never forgave the Balkan peoples,
because in that hour, an ancient dream being strong in them, they
rose and claimed their own. These wolves longed to undo that
hour, recover the lost booty, and revenge themselves for their
time of disappointment in the sweetness, still sweeter than theft,
of butchery. Therefore they had to kill Alexander, who was the
Balkan spirit incarnate, who was terrible as all Balkan peoples are,
because he had twice risen from the dead, he had broken the tomb
of Kossovo, and after the Austrians had stamped down the earth
over him he had kicked it away and stood upright. There can be
nothing more abhorrent to murderers than a murdered man who
will not stay dead, who rises stiffly up into the light, dust on his
eyelashes, and in his eyes the new advantage of the wisdom he has
learned among the dark foundations of our life, during his death.

He had to die. So the material I had collected proved beyond
doubt. Yet as I sat at my desk and worked through the years, both
my material and the events that closed in on Europe more darkly
day by day suggested that perhaps Alexander died the particular
death that came to him on that particular day, for no other reason
than that if two embryos were partners in a game of bridge they
would be apt to trump each other's aces. Mussolini and Hitler were
bound to join in an alliance of negativism against the positivism of
the rest of the world; yet for a time they vied with each other
in futile murder. Mussolini killed the Viennese Social Democrats
in February; Hitler killed his comrades in June and, flown with
his success, got Dollfuss in July; Mussolini, not to be outdone,
brought down his man in October. The murder of Alexander
was an idea that had its roots deep in history; but perhaps it was
dragged across the threshold of the world of fact simply by this
spirit of competition in crime. This very pointlessness gave the
crime a terrifying point. The representatives of life without mind,
that is without memory or will, had killed the representative of
life that had raised itself from death by letting five hundred years

deposit no dust of forgetfulness, by resolving that though the heart were transfixed by the sword it should persist in beating.

History, it appeared, could be like the delirium of a madman, at once meaningless and yet charged with a dreadful meaning; and there existed a new agent to face this character of our age and intensify it. The kind of urban population which Mussolini and Hitler represented had been drawn away from the countryside to work on the production and distribution of machinery and manufactured goods; and this mechanical effort had given us the aeroplane. It was the dictators' perfect tool. For by raining bombs on the great cities it could gratify the desire of the mass to murder the mass; and by that same act it would destroy the political and economic centres of ancient states with pasts that told a long continuous story, and thus make an assault on mind, tradition, and what makes the settled hearth. Such warfare must mean ruin for all, for mass was nearly balanced by mass, and because it would be beyond the power of the world to rebuild what it had taken centuries and unclouded faith in destiny to build, save in an equal number of centuries and by an equal poetical achievement of the soul. But experience of this would not avail to stop these wars, for this was the gibbering phase of our human cycle, and defeat and extinction would be as eagerly pursued as victory. This I could deduce from the facts I was working on, and it was confirmed by the newspapers every day I wrote. These recorded the advance of a state of universal and imbecile war and worse beside. For they recorded the rehearsal of such a conflict, carried on openly and unimpeded by Germany and Italy on Spanish soil, while the powers it threatened, though still splendid with inherited strength, sat by in cataleptic quiet.

In the country it sometimes happens that the sleeper awakes to an unaccustomed stillness. It is as if silence stretched for miles above him, miles around him; and daybreak does not bring the usual sounds. He goes to his window and finds that the world is under snow. White the lawn, white the trees, white the fields beyond, black the frozen water on the path. No birds and beasts are abroad, and no labourer comes out to work. Nothing is heard but the singing of the blood in the ears, and in a pure light forms stand forth in their purity. The air, too, is cleansed by cold and is like absolution in the nostrils. Such sounds as there are, as the cry of a wild swan, such motions as there are, as the lope of a grey squirrel over the roadway, are more than they would be in a less lustrated world. That day, that week, the next week, the snowfall is an austere and invigorating delight, but if month passes month, and the snow still lies and the waters are still black, life is threatened. Such snows and ice are well on the heights which are frequented only for adventure, but ill on the lowlands where the human process is carried on. The cattle cannot drink when the springs are frozen at their sources, the sheep cannot find the hidden grass, seed cannot be sown in the adamantine earth, the fruit trees cannot put forth their buds. If the snow does not melt and the waters flow, beauty becomes a steely bondage and then a doom, by which all animals must die, and man among them. We tell ourselves, when the whiteness lasts too long, that all seasons have their term and that the spring has always come in time; and so it happened this year and last year. But it may not happen so next year. Winter has often made this visit that far outstays safety and consumes leaf and flower and fruit and loin. Snow has covered first threshold, then windows, then chimneys, of many an upland farm, enclosing at the last a silence that does not thaw in the spring sunshine. Sometimes fields and orchards that had not been thought to lie too high have been burned by cold as by fire, and those who tended them have gone down starving to the plain. And there was once an Ice Age.

In England there was such a stillness, such a white winter of the spirit, and such a prolongation of it that death was threatened. It would have been expected, with fascist Italy and Nazi Germany crying out to kill, and England being what they both needed to kill, that there would be much bustling to and from on the building of defences, that there would be shouts of warning, proclamations, calls to arms, debates on strategy. But there was silence, and no movement. It was as though a pall of nullity covered all the land, as if the springs of the national will were locked fast in frost. Certainly some people cried out in fear and anger against the dictators, but they were drawn from those who had detached themselves from the main body of Englishmen, some because they were better, some because they were worse. But the main body itself lay in an inertia in which, at first, there was reason for hope. For before England could attain mastery over her time she had to suffer a profound alteration from her bustling polychrome Victorian self, which was infinitely credulous regarding her own wisdom, that would assume, at a moment's notice and without the slightest reflection, the responsibility of determining the destiny of the most remote and alien people, whose material and spiritual circumstances were completely unknown to her. She needed to learn that action is not everything, that contemplation is necessary for the discovery of the way and for the refinement of the will.

She needed to be still for a time and surrender herself to the mystical knowledge which cannot give instruction while logic, with its louder voice, holds the floor. It was good that she should lie under quiescence as under snow, that there should be no coming and going, that the air should be cleansed by scepticism, and that only the simplest and most fundamental activities should be carried on, to reveal the essential qualities which had been forgotten in the more crowded days. There could have been no greater misfortune for England than that the period of inactivity which was super-intended by Lord Baldwin should have so perfectly resembled in outward appearances that period which would have been a necessary preliminary to her regeneration. For it might have been that a party which belonged to the past was confessing its inability to cope with the present, and was waiting to yield stoically and without fruitless struggles to the new and appropriate forces.

But the quietness lasted too long. The new forces did not emerge. The obsolete party did not mean to yield power. On the contrary, it gripped the nation's throat with a tenacity that was terrifying, because it pertained to another realm than life. For the grip of a living man must relax if he grow tired; it is only ghostly hands that, without term, can continue to clench. But these were not honest ghosts, for had they been such they would have re-enacted the pomp of Elizabeth's power; even if the dust lay thick on the national stage, they would have repeated the imperturbable insolence of Victoria, even if the words came hollow from the fleshless thorax. They were, however, as much strangers to all tradition of English pride as though they were alien in blood. Mussolini and Hitler threw courtesy away and yelled at our statesmen as waiters in a cheap foreign restaurant might yell at kitchen boys. Their peoples accepted from them, almost without dissent, a gospel which was in essence a call to the destruction of the British Empire and its regeneration in a baser form, and that this word was to be made flesh, and that bleeding and lacerated flesh, was proved by the tearing up of treaties and the re-creation of forbidden armies. The prospect was unprecedented in its horror, because the mindless, traditionless, possessionless urban proletariat was delighted by the prospect of making air-warfare. In Germany and Italy the people as a whole licked their lips over the promise of air warfare that was held out to them by their leaders. But the governors of England hardly stirred. Their faces were bland bags. They gave no orders for our defence. Although not one sane man in the continent of Europe but knew that soon England would be bombed from the air, we built no planes.

The farmer's family, when the snow rises above the threshold and above the windows and still does not thaw, must have felt as we did. Violence is the more terrible when it comes softly, when there is no sound but the throbbing of the alarmed blood in the ears. But our woe was worse than would be known by the victims of a natural catastrophe, for it was not nature that was handing us over to death, but people of our own blood, people of a class whom we looked on with a filial trust. We knew that they would bully us out of claiming our full adult privileges when we came of age, we knew that they would make us pay them too much of our weekly wages as a return for providing us with a home, but we trusted them to act in any last resort as our loyal parents, who would fight to the death in the defence of their young. But here came death, and they did not defend us. Rather was it that they had taken away our weapons and bound our arms to our sides and opened the door to our enemies, saying, 'Yes, we have them ready for you, we have trussed them up for killing, you will have no trouble with them.'

Many of us thought then that our governors were consciously betraying us because they wished to establish a totalitarian system in this country, and were eager to co-operate with Nazi Germany and fascist Italy in the enslavement of Europe. Indeed thus alone could there be explained the British policy of 'non-intervention' in the Spanish Civil War, which was in fact a furtive discouragement of any action, however licit, that might have aided the survival of an independent and friendly Spain, and a furtive encouragement of all actions, however illegal, that enabled our natural enemies the Germans and Italians to establish themselves on both flanks of our natural allies the French. To some small degree the allegation of treachery was valid. The coarser kinds of rogue love money, and the City therefore must inevitably hold a high proportion of them; and these were solidly pro-Nazi and profascist. Finance certainly threw some considerable influence on the side of complete surrender to Germany, on condition that the wealth of England be allowed to remain in the same hands as before. There were also certain influences in the Foreign Office which were against the defence of England. The British Minister to a certain Danubian country never ceased throughout his tenure of office to carry on fervent propaganda in favour of the Nazi plan for dismembering this country; and an attaché at a certain important Central European Legation made a point of intercepting visitors and urging on them the manifest superiority of the German people to all others, the wrongs it had suffered from the Peace Treaty, and the necessity for showing penitence by giving the Nazis all they demanded. But these were as much exceptions to the general mood as was a desire to arm against the dictators. The governors of England have proved beyond doubt their innocence of that particular crime. If they had wished to establish fascism they would certainly have attempted a *coup d'état* in the days of shame and bewilderment that followed Munich. But from that action, as indeed from all others, they refrained.

Now it was plain that it was not sleep which made the earth so still; it was death. As extreme cold can burn like fire, so an unmeasured peace was stamping out life after the fashion of war. Presently war itself would come, but it would destroy only what had already been destroyed. Our houses would fall on our broken bodies; but it was long since our hearthstones had been warm, and our bodies were as destitute of will as corpses. Under an empty sky lay an empty England. There is a pretence that this was not so, that Munich was not negative but positive, that Neville Chamberlain signed the treaty because he knew his country to be unprepared for war and therefore wanted to gain time for rearmament. If this were true it would still not acquit him of blame, since he had been a member of the Government which was responsible for the lack of arms; but it is a lie. He and his colleagues made no use of the respite to defend their people. Here and there individuals who individually loved life worked frantically in the Army, in the Navy, in the Air Force, in the factories; but the mass of England was still inert. Our governors stood beside us as we lay bound and helpless at their feet, smiling drunkenly without the reasonable excuse of consumed alcohol, while the strange treacherous spirit which possessed them continued to issue invitations to our enemies, saying, 'Come quickly and finish them now, they can do nothing against you.'

I, like all my kind, who could read and write and had travelled, was astonished. But as I looked round on this desolate historical landscape, which was desert beyond my gloomiest anticipation of where my ill fortune might bring me, it was not unfamiliar. 'I have been here before,' I said; and that was true, for I had stood on the plain of Kossovo. I had walked on the battle-field where Christian rulers, faced with those who desired to destroy their seed and their faith and their culture, resigned themselves without need to defeat, not from cowardice, not from treachery, but in obedience to some serene appetite of the soul, which felt fully sanctified in demanding its gratification. The difference between Kossovo in 1389 and England in 1939 lay in time and place and not in the events experienced, which resembled each other even in details of which we of the later catastrophe think as peculiar to our nightmare. There was in both the strange element of a gratuitous submission to a new menace of a technical sort. Even as the Nazis threatened us by their ardently prepared Air Force, so the Turks subdued the Balkan peoples by their ferocious and ingenious use of cavalry; and even as the English, though they made good guns and planes and were good artillerymen and aviators, built up no defences against attack from the air, so the Balkan peoples, though they had horses and a fine tradition of horsemanship and a long acquaintance with Turkish methods of warfare, gathered together no appropriate counter-forces. There was in both the same vertiginous spectacle of a steep gradient slanting from unchallenged supremacy down to abjection; the great Serbian Emperor Stephen Dushan, who was the most powerful monarch in the Europe of his time, died only thirty-four years before Kossovo, Munich was only thirty-seven years after the funeral of Queen Victoria.

Defeat, moreover, must mean to England the same squalor that it had meant to Serbia. Five centuries hence gentleness would be forgotten by our people; loutish men would bind ploughshares to their women's backs and walk beside them unashamed, we would grow careless of our dung, ornament and the use of foreign tongues and the discoveries made by the past genius of our race would be phantoms that sometimes troubled the memory; and over the land would lie the foul jetsam left by the receding tide of a conquering race. In a *Denkmal* erected to a German aviator the descendant of his sergeant in the sixteenth generation, a wasted man called Hans with folds of skin instead of rolls of fat at the back of his neck, would show a coffin under a rotting swastika flag, and would praise the dead in a set, half-comprehended speech, and point at faded photographs on the peeling wall, naming the thin one Göring and the fat one Goebbels; and about the tomb of a murdered *Gauleiter* women wearing lank blonde plaits, listless with lack of possessions, would picnic among the long grasses in some last recollection of the Strength Through Joy movement, and their men would raise flimsy arms in the Hitler salute, should a tourist come by, otherwise saving the effort. In the towns homeless children, children of homeless children, themselves of like parentage, would slip into eating-houses and grovel on the dirty floor for cigarette-butts dropped by diners reared in a society for long ignorant of the nice. That is defeat, when a people's economy and culture is destroyed by an invader; that is conquest, that is what happens when a people travels too far from the base where it has struck its roots.

It seemed that there was no help for us; for the Government was contriving our defeat, was beyond reason and beyond pity, caught up in a painful, brooding exaltation, like the Tsar Lazar.

> There flies a grey bird, a falcon,
> From Jerusalem the holy,
> And in his beak he bears a swallow.

> That is no falcon, no grey bird,
> But it is the Saint Elijah,
> He carries no swallow,
> But a book from the Mother of God,
> He comes to the Tsar at Kossovo,
> He lays the book on the Tsar's knees.
> This book without like told the Tsar:
> 'Tsar Lazar, of honourable stock,
> Of what kind will you have your kingdom?
> Do you want a heavenly kingdom?
> Do you want an earthly kingdom?
> If you want an earthly kingdom,
> Saddle your horses, tighten your horses' girths,
> Gird on your swords,
> Then put an end to the Turkish attacks,
> And drive out every Turkish soldier.
> But if you want a heavenly kingdom
> Build you a church on Kossovo;
> Build it not with a floor of marble
> But lay down silk and scarlet on the ground,
> Give the Eucharist and battle orders to your soldiers,
> For all your soldiers shall be destroyed,
> And you, prince, you shall be destroyed with them.'

> When the Tsar read the words,
> The Tsar pondered, and he pondered thus:
> 'Dear God, where are these things, and how are they?
> What kingdom shall I choose?
> Shall I choose a heavenly kingdom?
> Shall I choose an earthly kingdom?
> If I choose an earthly kingdom,
> An earthly kingdom lasts only a little time,
> But a heavenly kingdom will last for eternity and its centuries.'

So the Tsar chose a heavenly kingdom and the ruin of all his people.

> Then the Turks overwhelmed Lazar,
> And the Tsar Lazar was destroyed,
> And his army was destroyed with him,

Of seven and seventy thousand soldiers.

All was holy and honourable,
And the goodness of God was fulfilled.

So it had been at Kossovo, and so it was in England. Quite without
irony it could be said that in Mr Neville Chamberlain's Cabinet
and in Whitehall all was holy and honourable. These men were
not actuated by cowardice. When they were forced by the invasion of Poland to declare war on Germany they did not flinch,
though they knew better than anyone the hideous degree of our
defencelessness. They were not betraying their country either for
bribes or out of loyalty to fascism. It is true that one at least of the
men chiefly responsible for the lethargic conduct of the war under
the Chamberlain administration was a venal character with dubious associates in Germany; but treachery is alert and quickwitted
and expectant of gain, whereas the mood of our governors was
drowsy and hallucinated and, as in the case of communicants,
already satisfied before the time of their satisfaction, because it
was mystical. When Mr Chamberlain spoke at Birmingham after
the German annexation of Czechoslovakia in March 1939 his voice
carried over the radio a curious double counterpoint. There was
one theme which expressed the anger of a vain man who finds
he has been tricked, and there was another, the main theme,
the profounder theme, which solemnly received the certainty of
doom and salvation. 'We shall fight,' came the sharp and shallow
note of resentment against Hitler; 'we shall fight,' sounded the
cavernous secret thought, 'and no doubt we shall be defeated, and
the goodness of God shall be fulfilled.' Again the grey falcon had
flown from Jerusalem, and it was to be with the English as it was
with the Christian Slavs; the nation was to have its throat cut as
if it were a black lamb in the arms of a pagan priest. We were
back at the rock. We were in the power of the abominable fantasy
which pretends that bloodshed is peculiarly pleasing to God, and
that an act of cruelty to a helpless victim brings down favour and
happiness on earth. We, like the Slavs of Kossovo, had come to a
stage when that fantasy becomes a compulsion to suicide. For we
had developed enough sensibility to know that to be cruel is vile,
and therefore we could not wish to be the priest whose knife made
the blood spurt from the black lamb's throat; and since we still
believed the blood sacrifice to be necessary we were left with no
choice, if we desired a part in the service of the good, but to be
the black lamb.

We had been glutted for centuries with wealth and power, and in the worst war the world had yet seen we had gained a glorious victory which inflicted much pain on the defeated. The sense of guilt which is born in every man, and is willing to operate without reasonable cause, had here abundant food, and for long we had been sick with masochism. This could be seen in the strange propaganda against the Treaty of Versailles which was carried on year in year out by ordinary English people, who had never read a line of it and perhaps not even known anybody that had, who had never visited the Continent, and were not receiving instructions from any political party. These people utterly ignored the work the peace treaties had done in liberating the smaller nations, monstrously exaggerated the hardships inflicted by their economic clauses, which, indeed, for the most part were completely inoperative, and, what was most remarkable, seemed utterly ungrateful for the clauses which aimed at making it impossible for Germany to repeat her attack on England and France. They had lost all sense that it is sometimes necessary to fight for one's life; and many children born in the decade after the Great War can never have heard a word from their parents and teachers which suggested that their country had or could have been actuated by any motive except stupid and credulous jingoism in taking up arms in 1914. The idea of self-preservation was as jealously hidden from the young as the facts of sex had been in earlier ages. Thus England, not a perverse left-wing England that cared not what price it paid so long as it brought down the established order of society in ruins, but conservative, mediocre England, put itself in a position of insecurity unique in history by raising a generation of young men to whom the idea of defending their nation was repugnant not so much by reason of the danger involved (though indeed they were now often instructed in fear as in other times boys had been instructed in courage) as because they could not believe it would in any circumstances be necessary. Since every day Germany and Italy were formulating in more definite and vehement terms that they meant to vanquish and annihilate England, it was amazing that it should have been possible to enclose them in the magic sphere of this illusion. It would, of course, be comprehensible had they been drugged by sensual indulgence or grown careless of honour; but never had the mass of the people been more sober, and law-abiding, and restrained, never had they been so anxious for honourable dealings between class and class and between nation and nation. The fault was not decadence but the desire for holiness, the belief in sacrifice, and a willingness to serve as the butchered victim acceptable to God.

This I could read in the pages of my own book if I spread out the newspaper beside it; and it seemed to me I must be fantasticating history, so inveterate is our modern disposition to pretend that public actions must be inspired by simple and superficial motives. We all admit that when we see a man in the street and say, 'That is John Jones, he is an umbrella manufacturer, he is going to his works in Acton,' we are not really describing him, we are simply putting into currency a number of facts about him which the community will find useful in their dealings with him. An adequate account of him must be as the map of a jungle, in which there range many beasts, some benign, some abhorrent. It is the special greatness of Shakespeare that he demonstrated the complexity of the individual; after *Hamlet* and *Othello* and *King Lear* it could not be pretended that man was an animal who pursues pleasure and avoids pain. But of nations that pretence is still made. It is assumed that if a nation goes to war, it must have a reasonable motive, based on material calculations, and must desire to be victorious. It is not conceded that a nation should, like Hamlet, say that in its heart there was a kind of fighting that would not let it sleep, or, like Othello and King Lear, hatchet its universe to ruin.

But, as I wrote the last part of this book, France proved, in a tragedy that ranks as supreme in history as *Hamlet* and *Othello* and *King Lear* rank in art, that a nation can be under the same necessity as an individual of tracing out a destiny which strikes it as beautiful, even if it involves self-destruction; and the idea of this destiny, the theme of this poem which was inscribed not on paper but on life, was the theme of Kossovo, of the rock. Where England had one reason to know that Germany meant to attack her, France had ten reasons to tell her that her danger was imminent and extreme. Yet she was even more supine than England. Indeed, the wheel turned full circle, and she sprang to her feet and ran about opening all gates to her enemies, crying out that they must be welcomed, since defence was impossible and unwise. Every class had its reason for wanting to submit, which was always nonsensical. Rich men alleged that they wished to collaborate with the Nazis in order to keep their wealth, though the racial theory of Hitlerism made it obvious that Nazi conquerors of France would have no interest in protecting French Nazis, simply because they were not German. Roman Catholic reactionaries longed for Hitler to come and destroy the free thinking democrats they loathed, forgetting that the child of the *Los von Rom* movement was unlikely to treat their own faith with any special tenderness. The *Front Populaire* workmen in the towns shrugged their shoulders and contended that under the Nazis they would be no worse off than they were already, although all their German analogues were in concentration camps. The governing classes, though apparently active as ants, had no relation whatsoever with reality, even by means of the ideas which had engendered the parties to which they belonged. Charles Péguy once remarked that '*l'intérêt, la question, l'essentiel est que dans chaque ordre, dans chaque système, la mystique ne soit point dévorée par la politique à laquelle elle a donné naissance.*' That catastrophe was accomplished in the perspiring and meaningless political life of Paris. All these people achieved unity in their common preparation of the altar on which they were to offer themselves as a sacrifice. For, almost without dissent from a single group, they diverted the money that should have been spent on tanks and aeroplanes and poured it into the Maginot Line, which could not fulfil any defensive purpose since it was unfinished and could be outflanked. Lest this should not be enough, an immense army of traitors sprang up to meet the Germans as soon as they crossed the frontier and handed over fortress and bridgehead, railway and canal. Neither in them, nor in the fugitives who choked the roads and prevented the loyal French forces from resisting the invaders, was there any sense of shame. There could be no cause of shame in a nation that found itself consummating the martyrdom to which it had dedicated itself. Lest the world should miss the significance of this solemn and exultant surrender, two soldiers of the sacred French Army once led by Joan of Arc, two soldiers who had not been careless of glory in their prime, Marshal Pétain and General Weygand, announced it in voices which age paradoxically yet appropriately caused to resemble the bleating of young lambs. France, they said, was corrupt and must be regenerated by defeat. It is hard to guess what this could mean save that they were governed by the myth of Kossovo, of the rock. There was nothing Christian in such speeches. Long ago the Church had declared that its altar required nothing but 'the reasonable and unbloody sacrifice' of the bread and the wine. This was the propaganda of black magic, of paganism.

Now we in England stood alone. Now we, who had been unchallenged masters of the world, were poor and beset like the South Slavs. The brightness of an exceptional summer was about us, and we believed that this would immediately be blotted out by an eternal night. But the experience was not so disagreeable as might be supposed, for we had lost our desire to die without defending ourselves, and it was that, not danger, which was horrifying. The most terrible death is subject to the same limitations as the most beautiful girl, it can only give what it has got. But voluntarily to play a part in an act of cruelty, to subscribe to a theory of the universe which supposes a God capable of showering down blessings in return for meaningless bloodshed, that is to initiate a process of degradation which is infinite, because it is imaginary and not confined within the limits of reality. From that hell we were suddenly liberated, by forces which it is hard to name. Perhaps the Germans, by the nastiness of their campaigns, acquainted us beyond all possible doubt with the squalor of this rite in which we were about to be involved. Perhaps there is a balance in our souls which is hung truly between life and death, and rights itself if it swings over too far in the direction of death. Such an equipoise can be noted in Shakespeare's *King Lear*, which above all other works of art illuminates the sacrificial myth: he set out to prove that the case for cruelty is unanswerable, because kindness, even when it comes to its fine flower in love, is only a cloak for ravening and treachery, and at the end cries out that love is the only true jewel in the universe, that if we have not found it yet we must go on mining for it till we find it. So we go deep into the darkness and recoil to light in the supreme work of our English literature, and that was our course in the supreme crisis of our history. We offered up to death all our achievement, all that was ours down to our physical existence, and over-night we took that offer back. The instrument of our suicidal impetus, Neville Chamberlain, who had seemed as firmly entrenched in our Government as sugar in the kidneys of a diabetic patient, all at once was gone. We had sloughed our John Cantacuzenus. Now we were led by Winston Churchill, who cannot be imagined as wanting to die, though he would die if a more liberal allowance of life would be released by his death, if it were the necessary price to pay for the survival of his country. Thereafter all was easier.

Certainly it was easier. It was good to take up one's courage again, which had been laid aside so long, and feel how comfortably it fitted into the hand. But it has not been easy. How could it be anything but agony! All that time, when poor France broke and ran, we looked into the face of destiny and it was made of steel. It seemed that we might be treated like the French, like the people in the Low Countries, like the Czechs, like the Poles. And when our fear made that allusion it turned us cold, for the Czechs and the Poles need have suffered nothing if we had not been weak and mad with this strange folly of cringing to our executioners. Never to the end of our days shall we be clean of that stain. Often, when I have thought of invasion, or when a bomb has dropped near by, I have prayed, 'Let me behave like a Serb,' but I have known afterwards that I had no right to utter such a prayer, for the Slavs are brothers, and there is no absolution for the sins we have committed against the Slavs through our ineptitude. Thus we were without even the support of innocence when we went to our windows and saw London burn; and those who see the city where they were born in flames find to their own astonishment that the sight touches deep sources of pain that will not listen to reason, the same that grieve so wildly when one's own kin die. We may recognize that the streets that are burned are mean and may be replaced by better, but it is of no avail to point out to a son weeping for his mother that she was old and plain.

This has seemed to me at times an unendurably horrible book to have to write, with its record of pain and violence and bloodshed, carried on for so long by such diverse peoples; and perhaps the most horrible thing about it is that, in order to carry out my intention and show the past in relation to the present it begot, I have to end it while there rages round me vileness equal to that which I describe. Now all Europe suffers as the Slavs, under enemies harder to conquer than the Turks. It might be held that there is no ground for hope anywhere save the possibility that man will over-reach himself in his assault on his own kind and so become extinct. This may happen, and may be no occasion for tears. A world where there is no solid ground, only blood and mud poached to an ooze by the perpetual tramping back and forth of Judases seducing one another in an unending cycle of treacheries, of executioners who say chop-chop and hear it said in their own ears before they have time to clean the axe: who would prefer this to a world at peace under the snow of universal death?

Yet I believe that that choice does not have to be made. If human beings were to continue to be what they are, to act as they have acted in the phases of history covered by this book, then it would be good for all of us to die. But there is hope that man may change, for two factors work on him that might disinfect him. One is art. These days have given us a chance to test the artistic process, and judge whether it is a tool that does honest work or whether it simply makes toys for the childish. Now there is fear to distract us, now there is desolation to put up a counter-argument to any argument. We start a gramophone record, and from it there radiates the small white star of light that is, say, '*Deh vieni, non tardar*,' the song of Susanna as she waits in the garden for the happy night to fall, at the end of *The Marriage of Figaro*. There bursts across the whole sky above, there bursts across the earth below, the huge red star of light that is a high-explosive bomb. Surely the huge red star will consume the small white star. But it is not so. On the contrary, the huge red star withers at once. The bowels writhe to perceive it, but they immediately unknot, and the attention dismisses it, unless it is accompanied by some fantastic circumstance, a comic spatchcocking of victims against a wall, a Versaillesque ascension of the prodigious waters of a main. But the attention does not relinquish the small white star of the song, which is correct, permanent, important. 'Yes,' we say in our beings, heart and mind and muscles fused in listening, 'this is what matters.' 'What matters?' echoes the astonished reason. 'Can you say that a bomb which might have blown you to smithereens matters less than a song supposed to be sung by a lady's maid, who, however, never existed, when waiting for the embraces of a valet, who, also, never existed?' 'Yes,' we reply. For those of us who before the war loved pictures, music, and good writing find that in these days their delights are intensified. I remember wondering, when I sat in the restaurant on the Frushka Gora and a Mozart symphony poured out through the radio, whether there was anything at all in the lovely promise that seemed to be given by the music, or whether it simply happened that the composer had imitated in a melody the tones of a human voice speaking out of tender and protective love. Now it seems to me that I can only have felt the doubt because I did not then know the ultimate insecurity which comes from a threat not merely to one's individual existence but to the life of one's people. I now find it most natural that the Dalmatians, in peril like our own, built churches and palaces, deliberations in stone on the nature of piety and pleasure, under the seaward slopes of hills that were heavy on their crests with Turkish fortresses, and desolate to landward with the ruins of annihilated Bosnia. I find it most natural that the Macedonian peasants should embroider their dresses, that they should dance and sing. For, of course, art gives us hope that history may change its spots and man become honourable. What is art? It is not decoration. It is the re-living of experience. The artist says, 'I will make that event happen again, altering its shape, which was disfigured by its contacts with other events, so that its true significance is revealed'; and his audience says, 'We will let that event happen again by looking at this man's picture or house, listening to his music or reading his book.' It must not be copied, it must be remembered, it must be lived again, passed through those parts of the mind which are actively engaged in life, which bleed when they are wounded and give forth the bland emulsions of joy, while at the same time it is being examined by those parts of the mind which stand apart from life. At the end of this process the roots of experience are traced; the alchemy by which they make a flower of joy or pain is, so far as is possible to our brutishness, detected. What is understood is mastered. If art could investigate all experiences then man would understand the whole of life, and could control his destiny. This is a force that could destroy the myth of the rock itself, and will, no doubt, a thousand years hence. No wonder we reach out to lay hold on such a force when we are beset with disgusting dangers.

But such deliverance will not come soon, for art is a most uncertain instrument. In writing this book I have been struck again and again by the refusal of destiny to let man see what is happening to him, its mean delight in strewing his path with red herrings. Within these pages a prime minister falls dead, crying out his belief that he has been killed by order of a king who is shortly to fall dead, crying out in his belief that he has been killed by order of that same prime minister; whereas they had both been killed by order of a body composed of two parties of men who could not guess at each other's motives, so much opposed were they in character. This might be taken as a type of any complex historical event. And if people are severed one from another by misapprehensions of fact and temperamental differences, so are they alien from reality by confusions connected with the instruments which are all they have to guide them to it. The mind is its own enemy, that fights itself with the innumerable pliant and ineluctable arms of the octopus. The myth of the rock entangles itself with the Christian legend, so that religion at once urges mankind to go on all fours and to stand up facing the light. Art cannot talk plain sense, it must sometimes speak what sounds at first like nonsense, though it is actually supersense. But there is much nonsense about full of folly packed so tight that it has assumed the density of wisdom. The figure standing on the balcony of the little house outside Bitolj, announcing with his arms that he was about to proclaim deliverance to the plains and mountains, was a scarecrow stored from the weather till it was time to put him out among the fruiting vines. Perhaps half the total artistic activity of man has been counterfeit. The few guides that man has been allowed to help him on his way out of the darkness come to him surrounded by traitors, dressed in their guise, indistinguishable. It is not possible to exaggerate the difficulty of man's lot. Therefore no page in history, not even the bloodiest recorded in this volume, should be contemned.

It would be small blame to any man if he had turned his back on his goal and lived like the beasts, not seeking to know. But there is a gene in him that will not be deflected. On the Montenegrin mountains the old woman walked, making the true demand of art, 'Let me understand what my life means.' All had failed her: first, centuries before she was born, and miles outside the orbit of her physical life, the larger group, the Eastern Roman Empire and the Slav states which were dispersed at Kossovo; then later the Austro-Hungarian Empire, and the Montenegrin state; and lastly, the old man sitting at her hearth. But, unpredictably, her seeking spirit did not tire. And in that word, unpredictably, rings our other cause for hope. History, like the human loins, does not breed true. Honour does not always beget honour, crime and genius spring up where no one looked for them. In this volume the most terrible part of all is played by that section of the proletariat which, since the Industrial Revolution, an insane social economy has sent trooping from the country into the towns, to do work that teaches them little, in conditions that make it difficult for them to attach themselves to the existing urban culture. In Italy and Germany and Austria this class fell into the extreme destitution and degradation represented by Mussolini and Hitler, and in France its inertia did much to promote the state of political banditry which led to the tragedy of 1940. In England it was controlled by a national tradition, which transcends the traditions of town and country, and by this was kept from the shame which comes of ignorance and good and evil. It seemed certain that it would prove its worth and change its circumstances by rebellion against the economic injustice which made it what it was, and in that rebellion, and probably not before, it would achieve its splendours. It and its forefathers had furnished the bulk of the individual deeds that in sum made up the heroism of our armies and navies, the fisheries and merchant fleets and mines. But the order of events never hinted that it was reserved for them to create a new form of heroism and perfect it in the same hour that they conceived it.

With my own eyes I witnessed that attainment. While France was falling, and after she had fallen, my husband and I went every evening to walk for an hour in the rose-garden in Regent's Park. Under the unstained heaven of that perfect summer, curiously starred with the silver elephantines of the balloon barrage, the people sat on the seats among the roses, reading the papers or looking straight in front of them, their faces white. Some of them walked among the rose-beds, with a special earnestness looking down on the bright flowers and inhaling the scent, as if to say, 'That is what roses are like, that is how they smell. We must remember that, down in the darkness.' There is a lake beside the rose-garden, in which there is a little island, where dwarf and alpine plants are cultivated among rocks. Across the Chinese bridge that joins it to the mainland there slowly moved a procession, as grave in their intention to see the gay fragilities between the stones as if they were going to a lying-in-state. The English, as the old woman on the Montenegrin mountains had said, love nature. Most of these people believed, and rightly, that they were presently to be subjected to a form of attack more horrible than had ever before been directed against the common man. Let nobody belittle them by pretending they were fearless. Not being as the ox and the ass, they were horribly afraid. But their pale lips did not part to say the words that would have given them security and dishonour.

What they foresaw befell them. No kind hand stretched down from the sky to reward them for their gallantry and keep them safe. Instead bombs dropped; many were maimed and killed, and made homeless, and all knew the humiliating pain of fear. Then they began to laugh. Among the roses, when safety was theirs for a word, they had not even smiled. Now, though their knees knocked together, though their eyes were glassy with horror, they joked from sunset, when the sirens unfurled their long flag of sound, till dawn, when the light showed them the annihilation of dear and familiar things. But they were not merely stoical. They worked, they fought like soldiers, but without the least intoxication that comes of joy in killing, for they could only defend themselves, they could not in any way attack their assailants. In this sobriety, men and women went out and dug among the ruins for the injured while bombs were still falling, and they turned on fire, which it is our nature to flee, and fought it at close range, night after night, week after week, month after month. There have been heroes on the plains of Troy, on the Elizabethan seas, on the fields of Flanders, in the Albanian mountains that go down to the sea, but none of them was more heroic than these.

It could not have been predicted that aerial warfare, the weapon of the undifferentiated mass against the undifferentiated mass, should utterly defeat its users by transforming those who suffer it to the most glorious of individuals. This sly and exalted achievement of history at one stroke regenerated the town-dweller, who had fallen into a position as immoral as that of any prince by being able to vote for wars which had to be waged not by him but by professional soldiers, and lent him the innocence of the front-line soldier; it gave a promise that life can transcend itself, that we are not bound to repeat a limited pattern. This promise was fulfilled during the following year on the other side of Europe by the people whose destiny has been described in this volume. The closing months of 1940 saw the Continent sink into a state of degradation not paralleled in any other age. I could not now tell the golden-haired girl in Vienna so confidently that her ignorance of French had cost her the knowledge of a great culture and civilization, since she could answer the longest list of names which I could give her with the single word, 'Pétain.' In Scandinavia, in the Low Countries, and in Czechoslovakia men who had yesterday enjoyed freedom and dignity were dumb beasts of burden, to be hit in the mouth by German soldiers if they showed any recollection of their former state; and the continuing martyrdom of Poland was a warning against the sin of saying nay to evil. There was only one hopeful sign in the whole of Europe, and that was the resistance of Greece to the Italian invasion which began in October 1940. It was of course obvious that the Greeks need not fear the Italian forces. In the last war the Balkan forces had been very fond of a certain riddle: 'What is it that has feathers but is not a bird, that runs very fast but is not a hare, that carries a gun but is not a soldier?' The answer was a *bersagliero*. But the Greeks knew well they would not be allowed to enjoy their inevitable victory, for the Germans could not afford to let their ally lose, and indeed would prefer to intervene in this area, lest there should be any misunderstanding as to who was going to own it after the war. That the Greeks fought on in spite of this knowledge has been ascribed by some to their descent from ancient Greece, but it is part of the Balkan story. The blood of the modern Greeks is strongly laced with the Slav strain and the petticoated evzones who dealt with the Italians were predominantly Albanians.

During the early months of 1941 it became obvious that Hitler's intervention was to be expected soon; the British had been too successful against the Italians in North Africa. He found the stage prepared for him. Roumania had long ago been seduced. King Carol, who at the beginning of the war had shown a desire to align himself with the democratic powers, had gradually given way to Axis pressure; but he had been asked to prostitute his country to a degree beyond his tolerance, and in September 1940 he abdicated and crossed the frontier. He left his throne to his young son Michael, a lad of eighteen in whom the faults of a deplorable dynasty had been exaggerated by an ill-judged education, who thereafter governed under the control of a Nazi military and civil garrison and certain Roumanian traitors. The oilfields and mines were handed over to German use on German-dictated terms, foodstuffs were put on the trains to Germany until the land groaned with hunger, the army was put under German tutelage, ferocious punishments were inflicted by Roumanian courts on their own nationals who had dared to protest against this ruin of their people. In February 1941 the British Minister at Bucharest asked for his passports on the ground that Roumania had become a German dependency. Those who regard fascism as a natural and healthy development of the modern state, spoiled by some flaws but on the whole an advance in the direction of law, should note the depravation that this transformation had brought with it. Roumania had always, in spite of the gifts of its people, been noted for disorder and corruption; but its past now seemed a golden age. The arrival of the German Nazis meant privilege and protection for the Roumanian Nazis, the Iron Guard, who were a set of cut-throats and racketeers, long the terror of all decent people who were trying to earn an honest living. The situation was worsened because some of the Iron Guards were less rogues than others, and these, when they saw that the Germans had come not as brothers but as alien robbers, broke into surreptitious revolt. The country is now distracted by the worst kind of gang warfare.

Meanwhile Bulgaria was suffering a similar abasement. Whatever the royal family had done to preserve the country, it could do no more. All through the early months of 1941 thousands upon thousands of Germans entered the country as tourists; the Prime Minister announced in Parliament that Bulgaria could achieve its destiny only by harnessing itself to the Axis powers, and all the airfields and ports were in German hands. Here, too, the extension of German influence meant a retrogression from the native standards of civilization. The invading Nazis worked in collaboration with the criminals who had formed I.M.R.O. after it had been corrupted by Italian money: and these gunmen and blackmailers, white-slavers and drug pedlars, whom the joint action of King Boris and King Alexander Karageorgevitch had driven back into the rat-holes where they belonged, came out again and jostled off the streets the normal Bulgarian men and women, who, till the rise of Hitler, had been living in greater serenity than their kind had known for a thousand years. By the month of March there were half a million Germans in Bulgaria, and every trace of honourable and independent national life had been suppressed.

Now the position of Yugoslavia was desperate. It was now wholly encircled by the Axis powers and their victims; for Hungary, still grumbling and mumbling, '*Nem, nem soha,*' had become a vassal as pitiable as France. No aid could reach her from the allies; Greece would not let the R.A.F. use its airfields as bases for an attack on the gathering forces in Bulgaria, on the ground, for which some pro-German influence may have been responsible, that it was at war with Italy and not with Germany. It seemed certain that Yugoslavia could refuse nothing required of it by Hitler. No country that had laid down its arms, no country that had failed to take up arms, had a better excuse for capitulation. When Hitler demanded that the Yugoslavian Government send Ministers to Vienna in order to sign a pact which would make their country subordinate to the Axis powers, it seemed that resistance was impossible.

Yugoslavia was not in an entirely happy position to meet this crisis. It had partially solved one of its major problems in 1939, by giving home rule to a new province of Croatia which included most of Dalmatia, Herzegovina, and Slavonia. This new Croatia had been moderately successful; it had chosen its government from the Peasants' Party founded by Raditch and now led by Matchek, and this had pleased the peasants by agrarian reform on mildly socialist lines, but at the same time had alienated Zagreb and the bigger towns. The crisis which brought about the Croatian agreement had also led to the dismissal of Dr Stoyadinovitch, who had become a more and more enthusiastic admirer of Hitler, and showed signs of wishing to make himself a *Führer*. But his path was beset by difficulties; when he followed the customary technique of his kind and transported gangs of young men round the country so that they might attend the meetings he addressed and chant '*Vodyu! Vodyu! Vodyu!*' (Leader! Leader! Leader!) the local audiences joined in with gusto; but gradually they altered the rhythm, and by the end the halls used to ring with the chorus, '*Dyavod! Dyavod! Dyavod!*' (Devil! Devil! Devil!) He belonged to that pathetic order of minor historical characters who say, 'Evil, be thou my good,' but receive from evil only a tart toss of the head, since Mephistopheles makes it a rule to put back all Fausts under a certain size. It was unfortunate that his successor as Premier, Tsvetkovitch, was only another specimen of the same kind, another representative of the Belgrade clique of financial adventures and place-hunters. But his was a milder case. Rather had he said, 'Good, be thou my evil,' and prayed to be delivered from temptation. He was fortified but little by Matchek, who became Vice-Premier, and brought to the task too few and too simple ideas, and still less by his Minister of Foreign Affairs, a professional diplomat named Tsintsar-Markovitch. This man had never been accredited to London or Paris or Washington, and he had for long represented his country in Berlin. There he had learned to regard the Balkans as comically backward and the Germans as the proper rulers of the world. It is also to be noted that he was the nephew of that General Tsintsar-Markovitch who was shot on the same night as King Alexander Obrenovitch and Queen Draga. This may have induced in him a certain preference for taking the safer road.

These Ministers conducted a more or less dignified Government during the first eighteen months of the war, in close co-operation with the Regent, Prince Paul. This co-operation was the object of much suspicion throughout the country. All those who were in no position to judge, all the peasants and the intellectuals, particularly in the provincial towns, were convinced that he was pro-Axis and was only waiting to hand over his people to Hitler; but those who really knew him believed him to be inspired by British sympathies. Certain English diplomatic representatives in Belgrade held this opinion very strongly, and seemed to be confirmed by certain actions of the Government. When Dr Stoyadinovitch's pro-Nazi propaganda became too blatant he was interned in a small Serbian village. But for the most part the Government trod the familiar path of appeasement, with the familiar results. It fell into economic serfdom. It sent its agricultural produce to Germany in the quantities demanded, even when the 1940 harvest failed, and there was not enough for the home market. By January 1941 bread prices had risen by 157 per cent over the 1939 standard. In return Germany sent Yugoslavia such manufactured goods of which she happened to have a surplus, irrespective of whether they were welcome or not, and it altered the rate of exchange in its favour. But there were signs that not only in the economic sphere was German influence paramount. The Minister of War, General Neditch, looked over his shoulder at Roumania and came to the conclusion that if Yugoslavia were not to suffer the same fate it had better go to the assistance of Greece and drive the Italians out of Albania before Hitler could send his armies into the Peninsula. He was at once dismissed and replaced by a pro-Axis general. As time went on, and the situation developed according to General Neditch's apprehension, the Government refused to take any precautionary steps. They would not, even secretly, hold any conversations with the British or Greeks.

It could not be doubted, therefore, that the Yugoslav Government would accept Hitler's invitation to Vienna, and there would jump through any hoop held up to them. Immediately before, it is true, it had made a gesture of independence by deporting Dr Stoyadinovitch and putting him in the hands of the British authorities in Greece; but this was an astute move which at once removed him from the possibility of injury at the hands of anti-Nazi Yugoslavs, and placated them. On March the twenty-fifth Tsvetkovitch and Tsintsar-Markovitch toed the line and took the train for Vienna. There Ribbentrop received them in the Belvedere, the superb baroque palace which was built for Prince Eugéne of Savoy and was the home of Franz Ferdinand and Sophie Chotek, which looks over the lawns and fountains of its terraced gardens to the spires and domes of the city which has added so much beauty to art and so much infamy to life. In these high rooms, which are full of a cold secondary brightness reflected from ancient gilded mirrors and immemorially polished floors, the Yugoslav Ministers were asked to sign the familiar Tripartite Pact by which every country devoured by the Axis binds itself not to lift a finger against its devourer. They were also asked to pledge themselves not to permit in their territories any activity directed against the Axis, and to bring their national economy into harmony with the New Economic Order of the Reich. This would mean, as it had meant to all the other subjugated countries, enslavement of the national mind, starvation of the national body. There was also imposed on Yugoslavia an ignominy peculiar to the moment. The pact bound it to permit the passage of German war-material on the railways to Greece; and it was not to retain the right of inspection of such traffic. This meant that troops also would probably be carried. Thus Yugoslavia was forced to help Germany to knife in the back a Balkan brother, her kin by blood and tradition.

In order that the Ministers might be able to put up some sort of defence when they went home, the Germans inserted clauses which guaranteed the existing frontiers of Yugoslavia and promised it an outlet on the Ægean Sea. But this was a grimace, which popped the tongue out of the leering mouth, for Germany had already promised the Bulgarians substantial slices of Yugoslavia, and some of these actually barred the way to the Ægean Sea. The same spirit which had invented these clauses must have smiled to see that when Tsvetkovitch and Tsintsar-Markovitch signed this degrading pact they were watched by Count Ciano and the Japanese Ambassador. The presence of Count Ciano committed several offences against delicacy. The blood of King Alexander and of many Yugoslav peasants and policemen was on his hands;

at a moment when his people had made themselves the laughing-stock of the world by their poor performance on the battle-field it was not fitting that he should gloat over the abasement of a people who had never failed in courage and had been defeated only by the defection of other and stronger powers; and he was grinning at shame and ruin inflicted by one who was preparing to shame and ruin his own Italian compatriots. The presence of the Japanese Ambassador violated a more fundamental standard. Although the Germans have pondered so long on the problems of race, they had not realized that it is never right for a white man to behold the humiliation of a black or yellow man, never right for a black or yellow man to behold the humiliation of a white man. When Hitler received Tsvetkovitch and Tsintsar-Markovitch after the ceremony he presided over such a situation as is dear to his heart. No concession to human dignity had been made. As the Ministers went back to Belgrade that night they must have had one consolation, and one consolation only. Henceforth their people might live in slavery, but they would live. No Yugoslav need die before the term of his natural life.

But Yugoslavs did not want the life thus bought for them. With their subtlety they saw it for what it was, with their simplicity they spat on the hands which offered it. For many days, ever since it was first whispered that Yugoslavia was to be asked to submit to the yoke of Germany, the whole country had been declaring that it would prefer resistance and death. There was no class that did not make its protest. Although the Army had been peppered with pro-Axis generals the officers grimly demanded that they should be allowed to fight alongside the Greeks. The intellectuals who did not use the same spectacles as the army now saw eye to eye with them. Four Cabinet Ministers resigned, and Tsvetkovitch found it hard to replace them. Many civil servants resigned their posts, from the Governors of Croatia and the Vardar province, down to humble folk who when they left their offices walked out into starvation. The priests and monks of the Orthodox Church preached to their congregations that they must not let the Government sign them away to an alien domination which cared nothing for good and evil, and would not allow the Slav soul its own method of doing the will of God; and the Patriarch Gavrilo went to Prince Paul and bade him not misuse the power of the Regency to destroy the state which had been left in his care. But fiercest of all were the peasants. Everywhere they crowded into the towns and villages to cry out against the shame that the Government was forcing on them.

When it became known that the Prime Minister and the Minister of Foreign Affairs had been to Vienna and had signed the pact, the passion of the people blazed up into a steady flame. Now the police would no longer use their weapons against the demonstrators or arrest them, and the Army was so disaffected that all troops, including officers, had been confined to barracks. The whole country demanded that the pact must not be ratified, and that arms must be taken up against the Germans. It must be realized that this demand was not made by people who were ignorant of what modern warfare means. Many of those who were most insistent in their call for action were middle-aged and elderly people who had known in the last war what it was to be wounded and hungry and homeless. Moreover they had all followed the news and were well aware of what aerial bombardment had done to London and Rotterdam and Berlin; and some of them remembered the first use of aeroplanes in warfare, when the Serbian fugitives were bombed as they fled across Kossovo. It must also be realized that these people knew quite well that if they made war against Germany they would certainly be defeated. There were a few communist boys and girls who, not realizing that Stalin was still as devoted a practitioner of the policy of appeasement as Neville Chamberlain, believed that if they stood up against Hitler Russia would put out its strong arm and protect them. But for the rest no Yugoslav was under the delusion that his small and ill-equipped and encircled army had any chance of victory against the immense mechanized forces of Germany. He was also well aware of the kind of vengeance that Hitler would take on a people who combined the offences of being Slav and having resisted him. He knew very well that he must soon be in the hands of the same sort of jailers that had taken care of Princip and Chabrinovitch.

To Prince Paul, who was essentially though accidentally not a Serb, the aspirations of his people must have seemed inconveniently extraordinary and extraordinarily inconvenient. He dealt with the situation in his own way. He welcomed the returning Prime Minister and Minister of Foreign Affairs at a suburban station of Belgrade, telegraphed a message of thanks to Hitler, sending him 'good wishes for the further prosperity of the great German people,' and later took train for Slovenia, where he had a villa near Bled. Some thought he meant to decamp over the frontier into Austria, but this is improbable, for he left his wife and children in Belgrade. Merely he wanted to rest, to pretend that nothing was happening. While he was travelling through this country, in which he had never struck root, though he had no other, in which, with his facile but uncreative artistic temperament, he had been a kind of gipsy, Belgrade woke again from the sleep in which she had spent the last few years and was possessed by the genius of her history, harsh, potent, realistic, demonic, furtive, and nocturnal. Late on the night of March the twenty-sixth, the wife of General Dushan Simovitch, Chief of the Air Force, was puzzled because he was so wide awake. He expressed the opinion that perhaps he had drunk too much coffee. At half-past two in the morning he was still awake, and showed no surprise when there was a knock at his front door. 'What does all this mean?' she asked. 'Only,' said the General, 'that there has broken out a revolution, and I am the leader of it.' She answered, in a wifely spirit, 'Nonsense, it's no use telling me that you are the leader of a revolution!'

Her incredulity was not unnatural. General Simovitch, who was fifty-eight years old, had never been a fire-eater. He had not been one of the regicides, and he had not belonged to the Black Hand. In appearance he is like many Yugoslav officers: he is tall and spare, but his thick neck would take a deal of breaking; he has a pouched, deliberate, humorous eye, and a weatherbeaten skin. He was admitted to be a brilliant soldier and was an acknowl-edged authority on tactics; but he had five times been dismissed from important posts for reasons that were both creditable and, under his handling, amusing. The first of these famous disputes concerned two students of a military college whom he ploughed in an examination although they were relatives of an influential politician; the later ones concerned more serious matters. In such controversies he showed to advantage, for he was possessed of a subtle wit that could express itself in simple terms, and with apparent artlessness, in the half-smiling grumble of the old soldier, could pin down a character or a situation with a phrase that the most lapidary author could only envy. This felicity was supported not only by considerable intellectual gifts but by the kind of sturdy character that comes of an honourable family and national tradi-tion. He was descended from a Herzegovinian who had fled to Serbia at the time of the revolt against the Pashas, and had become a true man of the Shumadiya, fighting for national independence under Karageorge and Milosh Obrenovitch and begetting sons that took his place in later wars. What General Simovitch liked best in the world was his little country property outside Belgrade, but he was not averse from power.

Because of this man's instructions stealthy figures, murmuring passwords, had slipped through the shadows of the city all night long, effecting certain changes. But this was not as other nights that Belgrade had known, for there was but little bloodshed, and that through accident. Picked Air Force troops, joined by three out of the four battalions of the Royal Guards, and by other army units and many of the police, seized the important Government buildings. Most of them were surrendered without a blow by guardians who had received warning, but it unfortunately happened that the message sent to the police in charge of the radio had gone astray, and they attacked the party who came to take it over from them in the belief that they were Germans in disguise. Nowhere else was there any loss of life. Tsvetkovitch and Tsintsar-Markovitch were awakened out of their sleep, which was probably not very deep, and were courteously put under arrest. A message was handed into Prince Paul's sleeping coupé to ask him to return. He reluctantly broke his journey at Zagreb and, after a visit to the Governor of Croatia, took a train back to Belgrade. Meanwhile General Simovitch had been to Dedinye to tell the young King that he must assume power at once, instead of waiting for his eighteenth birthday in September. There he was setting foot on the most dangerous ground in the area of the revolution. But he gave orders to the Royal Guards who surrounded the Palace not to fire on the Royal Guards inside the Palace, who had, owing to certain timid or alien influences, not joined in the *coup d'état;* and as the King had given these men orders not to fire on the troops outside, the entry took place without incident.

The boy in the Palace had spent a day of solitary but intense excitement. On the previous evening the court officials, who had been dropping certain hints for some time past, had made the quite definite statement that his people had turned against him and that unless he locked himself in the Palace he would be assassinated. On the whole the boy was convinced by this story. He had been taken from school to attend the funeral of his murdered father when he was only twelve years old, and he knew the history of his country, so it seemed to him not improbable. He took two pistols out of a cupboard where he had hidden them and carried them about with him all day, in order that he might not have to meet his fate in a passive way. From his father he had inherited a stiff and reticent kind of physical courage, and that was not the only characteristic he owed to his family and his Serb blood. Like a creature of the wild, he was leery of traps. He did not commit himself entirely to his court. He had been educated, according to the democratic tradition of the Karageorgevitches, in the company of half a dozen boys of representative Serbian parentage, with whom he had to learn his lessons and play games on equal terms; and these boys were accustomed to ring him up at Dedinye on a private line. Some time before the King had contrived to get the telephone company to put in a new private line without the knowledge of his entourage, and he had entrusted the number to one of these friends, a boy named Kostitch. All the morning of March the twenty-sixth the King sat in his room not daring to make a call, but waiting to snatch at any incoming message. At noon Kostitch rang him up, and the King asked him if it were true that his people wanted to kill him. His friend answered that nothing could be less true, that it was Prince Paul and the Government that were hated, and that soon a revolutionary force would come to the Palace and set him free to rule over them in the moment of their rising against Germany. After this whispered announcement that he was to be asked to lead his country into disaster and could only look forward to death or imprisonment or exile, the young King was at ease. But the news that the people outside his Palace were his friends meant that those around him were his enemies, and he continued to carry his pistols. They were under his pillow when he was awakened to see General Simovitch.

At eight o'clock in the morning the exhilarated boy drove in radiant sunshine through Belgrade, which rejoiced as if he were returning from victory instead of being about to lead them to defeat. From the city Palace he issued a proclamation declaring that he was about to assume royal power, that the Army and the Navy had put themselves at his disposal, and appealing to the Croats and Slovenes and Serbs to stand firm round the throne. The crowd that gathered in the street to see him show himself on the balcony gave rapturous cheers and crossed the town to the Palace of the Patriarch, and the Patriarch Gavrilo came out and offered up thanks that the dynasty had put forth a King to protect the honour of the Serbian people when it seemed about to perish. Perhaps his tongue slipped, but he spoke the truth: this was indeed a drama played by the Serbian rather than by the Yugoslav people. The *coup d'état* was planned and executed by men of the Shumadiya, of the same stock as Karageorge and Milosh Obrenovitch. But during the day a Cabinet was formed which included representatives of all the three peoples, and all shades of opinion among them. This added to the joy of the people, when evening came and the lists of the new Ministers were posted on the walls, for they had regarded national unity as a poet might regard a poem he had never been able to finish. 'Whatever happens after this,' an old man said, 'nothing better could have happened, at last we are all together.' The only conspicuous figure who did not act according to the grand style of the occasion was Dr. Matchek. He had not felt any great revulsion against the signing of the pact with the Axis, though Hitler had cruelly mistreated some of the Croats he had found in Vienna, and he had not been one of the Ministers who had resigned in protest; and when it appeared that General Simovitch's Government contained some Serbs who had opposed Croat autonomy, Dr. Matchek felt doubtful about the possibility of collaborating with them, although that problem had been virtually settled two years before and was not likely to be reopened. Ultimately he abandoned this attitude, and became once more Vice-Premier, but not till several days later. History has made lawyers of the Croats, soldiers and poets of the Serbs. It is an unhappy divergence.

During the day public opinion hardened against Prince Paul. State papers were studied, officials interrogated, suspicions followed to their sources. It turned out that the peasants and provincial intellectuals, who had no means whatsoever of knowing what was going on in Prince Paul's head, had been right about his attitude; and the experts who had intimate knowledge of him were wrong. He had for some time been pro-Axis. His lack of resistance to Nazi claims was not only due to the feeling, which any scrupulous person in his position must have shared, that a Regent had not the same right as a reigning monarch to pledge his country to an expensive policy; nor was it due to the lack of respect he had naturally enough felt for Chamberlain's England and distrust of it as an ally. It was the result of a genuine admiration for Hitler's personality and a desire that Yugoslavia should throw in its lot with the winning side. So strongly had he held this view that he was actually responsible for the pro-Axis actions of those whom observers had believed to be far more Nazi than himself. Tsvetkovitch himself, cynical professional politician though he was, had not been the cynic of this crisis. He had presented to Prince Paul an admirable memorandum on the invitation to Vienna, which pointed out that no matter how Yugoslavia might act it was faced with material doom. If it resisted the German demands, the country would be over-run by German soldiers and officials, and its fields and mines and forests would be raided, and national life would be at an end; and if it yielded to the German demands, precisely the same would happen. There was little difference in hunger and oppression between Holland and Roumania, Belgium and Bulgaria. There was, of course, the very great difference that in the case of resistance innumerable Yugoslavs would meet death or injury under aerial bombardment and in warfare with invading troops. But this was not the ultimate consideration. For some day the rule of Hitler must pass; it could not endure for ever. Then, if Yugoslavia had moved against him with pride and courage, those that conquered him would have to admit it as comrade and grant it full right to exist in whatever new order of Europe might be instituted. But if Yugoslavs behaved like cowards, no one would respect them, not even themselves, and they would remain abased for ever. Therefore Tsvetkovitch desired Prince Paul to give the Government permission to refuse Germany's demands. This is a characteristically Serbian point of view, and is based on their experience of Turkish conquest, and their emergence from it. But Prince Paul was not sympathetic and persuaded Tsvetkovitch to act against his judgement and make the journey of humiliation to Vienna. Because such hidden dramas as these were now made plain, there grew in Belgrade during the day the fear that, since Prince Paul had not been so passive as people had supposed, he might be much more active, and that he might call on certain corrupted elements in the country and declare a state of civil war in Germany's interest. Many people, particularly in the Army, believed that for the sake of security he ought to be shot.

At seven o'clock in the evening General Simovitch went to the station to meet the train that was bringing Prince Paul back from Zagreb. He had given orders that another train was to be ready to proceed to the Greek frontier. When Prince Paul arrived the General drove with him to the War Office, one of the largest buildings in the administrative quarter on the east side of the city, so often denounced by travellers for its tastelessness and mediocrity. When they went into the hall of the War Office the General said, 'We must take the lift up to the first floor,' but before they could get into the lift an officer stepped forward and told Prince Paul, 'No, you must go by the staircase.' The words must have sounded like a knell in his ear, so terrible have these spare and dedicated men become in those hours when the subjects of their dedication have seemed to them to have forgotten the terms of their common hieratic faith. With a self-conscious smile Prince Paul murmured, 'Your chief tells me to go by the lift, and you tell me to go by the staircase. Which of you am I to obey?' 'It is better that you should go by the staircase,' said the officer, and General Simovitch told the Prince that perhaps they had better go that way. His kind of Serb knows his people's temper as a peasant knows the weather. But it was not, as Prince Paul must have feared, violence that was awaiting him. The staircase was broad and high; and on every step stood two officers, one on each side, who said, as Prince Paul passed between them, 'Long live the King!' These lines of men, holy and fierce like angry angels in their hatred of the ruler who had conspired against their death and salvation, transformed this commonplace feature of a building, quite undistinguishable from a thousand others in the minor capital cities of the world; and now it resembled such emblematic architecture as fills the distances of those Serbo-Byzantine frescoes, which convert the false rounded shapes seen in our weak corporeal eyes into the angular likeness of reality. The presence of Prince Paul on this scene was a profound incongruity, for though he was a lover of painting he had never appreciated these frescoes. To make a complex subject easier for the connoisseur and the art dealer, Byzantine art has been very elaborately graded, largely by experts who have never seen most of the surviving specimens, and the Serbian school, along with others which are difficult of access, has been marked low. It was a consideration which, for all his sincere aesthetic feeling, would have affected him. In the small room to which he was taken at the top of the stairs he made no difficulty about signing the deed of abdication which was presented to him; and when General Simovitch said, 'And now I await your orders,' he asked only to be allowed to leave the country. The next day the train which had been made ready took him and his family to Greece. He stayed for a short time in Athens, and later went to Kenya.

Once that faint alien personality had gone the scene closed up behind him and became wholly Serbian, wholly a fresco of the Nemanyan age. At Dedinye the Patriarch administered the oath of accession to the young King in the presence of the new Cabinet, and afterwards they attended a thanksgiving Mass at the Cathedral. Peter Karageorgevitch II stood rigid in his kingliness, as the earlier dynasty in their jewelled tunics and colossal diadems; the soldiers stood firm about him, content because his majesty made visible before their eyes the state, the life of their people; the priests and monks of the Orthodox Church, like those who had worn the white cloaks marked with black crosses in old time, completed the scene with their assertion that salvation and damnation are real things, and inflict the extreme of bliss and the extreme of woe; and the women who beheld them grieved like the Mother of God on the walls of Dechani and Grachanitsa, amazed at the bitter taste of tragedy, but not spitting it out because it was the sacramental food which goodness was dispensing in that hour. For a time the scene was still as a fresco. Germany asked the new Government for a ratification of the pact signed at the Belvedere Palace, and received a refusal, combined with the assurance that Yugoslavia was willing to be neutral and favour none of the belligerent powers. This reply was followed by a stunned pause. Then a familiar sound was heard from the German broadcasting stations. They broke into squawking complaints that in the streets of Yugoslavian towns inoffensive Germans had been set upon and beaten, and German shops had been looted, and that in the German settlements in Slovenia and by the Danube villages had been wiped out and farms burned. These announcements were given out in the tones of a hysterical woman accusing a man she had never seen of having raped her, whooping and lickerish and lying. The Consul-General of Lyublyana performed what was probably the most heroic act ascribed to any German since the Nazi domination. Knowing himself henceforward the victim of an ineluctable vengeance, he issued a statement branding all allegations of the mishandling of German minorities in Slovenia as totally untrue, and thanking the Yugoslav Government and people for the kindness and loyalty they had shown to their 'Swabs' when they might well have turned against them. But the matter of veracity was, of course, beside the point. The radio campaign was simply a warning to Europe that yet another innocent people was about to perish.

Why did the Yugoslavs choose to perish? It must be reiterated that it was their choice, made out of full knowledge. On none of them did their fate steal unawares. Their leader, General Simovitch, knew that he could lead his army only to defeat which could not long be delayed. When he had been Chief of Staff some years before he had worked out a scheme of national defence, perfectly adapted to this crisis, which provided against attack from any quarter by concentrating the reserve armies in the central districts and building radial roads as lines of communication. But his successor pigeon-holed this scheme and by a disposition of his own had drawn a cordon of troops all round the country, with a terrible gap on the Bulgarian frontier, from which, he had too optimistically conceived, no attack was now likely to come. In existing conditions this disposition meant that the German mechanized forces would pour into the country from every direction, would simultaneously pierce the front at a number of places, and would be able to cut off and surround the several defending armies. The situation was perfectly understood by all military ranks, and the vast crowds who thronged the churches and took communion showed that the civilian population were not behind them in understanding. This determination to resist oppression and bleed for it rather than submit and be safe cannot be explained, any more than the resolution of the English towndweller, by fearlessness. These people, being artists, knew death for what it is. The young soldiers who talked with Dragutin on the slopes of Kaimakshalan knew that the ghosts around them whimpered, '*Yao, matke!* Alas, Mother!' and could not overpass the bitterness that had befallen them on the battle-field. My friend Militsa has a most delicate mind, most delicate flesh, and both would flinch before the spreading chill of the grave. Nor were they governed by the myth of the rock, they did not desire defeat as a coin to buy salvation off an idiot god, they did not offer themselves up as black lambs to an unsacred priest. The appetite for death that comes on all human beings when they have enjoyed the fullness of life, because we as yet know only the swing of the pendulum and not the motion of growth, had in the Yugoslavs been glutted by Kossovo and the Turkish conquest. This was a state and a people that, above all others, wanted to live.

Yet in this hour the Yugoslavs often repeated the poem of the Tsar Lazar and the grey falcon, which above all other works of art celebrated this appetite for sacrificial self-immolation. 'All was holy, all was honourable,' they quoted, looking down from the tall tower of prescience on the field of their coming fate, 'and the goodness of God was fulfilled.' It was factually inappropriate. In the Yugoslavia of 1941 there was no one who would have bought his personal salvation by consenting to the subjugation of his people, and no one who would not have preferred to be victorious over the Nazis if that had been possible. It was their resistance, not their defeat, which appeared to them as the sacred element in their ordeal. Yet the poem sounded in their ears as a prophecy fulfilled in their action, a blessing given across the ages by omniscience perfectly aware of what it was blessing behind the curve of time, and indeed none who loved them could read it now without a piercing sense of appositeness. It applies; and the secret of its application lies in the complex nature of all profound works of art. An artist is goaded into creation on this level by his need to resolve some important conflict, to find out where the truth lies among divergent opinions on a vital issue. His work, therefore, is often a palimpsest on which are superimposed several incompatible views about his subject; and it may be that which is expressed with the greatest intensity, which his deeper nature finds the truest, is not that which has determined the narrative form he has given to it. The poem of the Tsar Lazar and the grey falcon tells a story which celebrates the death-wish; but its hidden meaning pulses with life.

'An earthly kingdom lasts only a little time,
But a heavenly kingdom will last for eternity and its centuries.'

Goodness is adorable, and it is immortal. When it is trodden down into the earth it springs up again, and human beings scrabble in the dust to find the first green seedling of its return. The stock cannot survive save by the mutual kindness of men and women, of old and young, of state and individual. Hatred comes before love, and gives the hater strange and delicious pleasures, but its works are short-lived; the head is cut from the body before the time of natural death, the lie is told to frustrate the other rogue's plan before it comes to fruit. Sooner or later society tires of making a mosaic of these evil fragments; and even if the rule of hatred lasts some centuries it occupies no place in real time, it is a hiatus in reality, and not the vastest material thefts, not world-wide raids on mines and granaries, can give it substance. The Yugoslavs, who have often been constrained to sin by history, are nevertheless well aware of the difference between good and evil. They know that a state which recognizes the obligation of justice and mercy, that is to say a state which forbids its citizens to indulge in the grosser forms of hatred and gives them the opportunity to live according to love, has more chance to survive in the world than a state based on the scurrying processes of murder and rapine; and they know too that if a state based on love bows to the will of a state based on hatred without making the uttermost resistance it passes into the category of the other in the real world. Therefore they chose that Yugoslavia should be destroyed rather than submit to Germany and be secure, and made that choice for love of life, and not love of death.

At dawn on April the sixth German planes raided Belgrade and continued the attack for four days. Germany had not made a declaration of war, and Belgrade had been proclaimed an open town. Eight hundred planes flew low over the city and methodically destroyed the Palace, the university, the hospitals, the churches, the schools, and most of the dwelling-houses. Twenty-four thousand corpses were taken away to the cemeteries, and many others lie buried under the ruins. On April the seventh the German Foreign Office announced that their troops had penetrated twenty miles over the frontier. Thereafter all happened as had been foretold. Invading troops encircled the country. From everywhere came the Germans and the Austrians, their age-old hatred of the Slav now perfectly equipped with the mechanical means of expression. The Italians shamelessly appeared in Dalmatia and Croatia, where by themselves they had never dared to go. In Budapest, four months after Hungary had signed a pact of eternal friendship with Yugoslavia, Count Teleki committed suicide from shame because his Cabinet was ready to give Germany permission to send its troops over Hungarian railways and use Hungarian airports; and now these procurers sent their own troops over the border towards the Danube. The eastern frontier was crossed by the German mechanized forces which Bulgaria had long been nourishing, who brought with them not only the Bulgarian Army but the worst of I.M.R.O. These invaders cut off and cut to pieces the defending forces. On the eighteenth of April the German Government made an announcement that the Yugoslav Army had capitulated, but this was not true. It was given out only in order that the Germans should have an excuse to shoot all surrendering Yugoslavs instead of taking them prisoner. The Yugoslav Army never capitulated, although it was destroyed; and the last remnants of it are still fighting, hidden in the mountains and forests.

Thereafter it was as if drops of black, foul-smelling oil were rolling down the map of Yugoslavia. The Italians were given control of Dalmatia, and as they desire comfortable possession of the Adriatic ports they have ruled without excessive inhumanity save to certain individuals. But in Croatia they are doing what the Germans have done in Roumania and Bulgaria; they have depraved the native standard of order by putting the criminal classes in power over the ordinary decent men and women. The post of Prime Minister, that is to say absolute ruler under Nazi control, has been given to Ante Pavelitch, the organizer of Croat terrorism who had conducted the training camps for assassins in Italy and Hungary, who was responsible for the deaths of countless people in bomb explosions and train wrecks, who personally accompanied the murderers of King Alexander of Yugoslavia to France, supplying them with weapons and giving them instructions, and for this was condemned to death in his absence by the French courts. This sordid specimen of the professional revolutionist is now ruling over the gentle intellectuals of Zagreb, the worshippers at Shestine, the doctors in the sanatorium. In Bosnia, Sarajevo and other towns have been laid waste from the air; and there all members of the Orthodox Church, all Jews, and all gipsies wear on their arms a common badge of disgrace, and may not travel in public vehicles. Conditions here are bad, but they are worse in Serbia, which Hitler rightly recognizes as the well-spring of South Slav resistance. There large numbers of men and boys over ten have been sent to concentration camps in Roumania and elsewhere, and there is in practice a policy of extermination such as has been directed against the Poles. In Macedonia all Serbs who have settled there during the last twenty-five years have been forced to abandon their property and return penniless to wander in the devastated area in the North. Large districts have been handed over to occupation by I.M.R.O. under its most merciless leader, Ivan Mihailov, and there has been such pillage and massacre that numbers of peasants have fled to the mountains. Many priests and monks have been killed. The mixed population of such towns as Skoplje has irritated the racial purism of the Germans; a number of Turkish Moslems have been executed. This land was already the nonpareil of suffering, but it is now transcending its own experience.

A part of the Yugoslav Army retreated through the mountain passes into Greece, and there fought a rear-guard action beside the British, and of these some soldiers made their way across the Mediterranean to Egypt; some sailors and fishermen escaped by sea; and some civilians reached Turkey, and others, incredibly enough, emerged at Lisbon. The Government sent King Peter out of Belgrade at the beginning of the air-raids, to stay at the monastery of Ostrog, a bleak pigeon-hole in a Montenegrin cliff. They chose this place because it is only a few miles from Nikshitch, which possesses an airfield. When it was seen that defeat was coming very soon, the royal party was told to go to the airfield and wait for a plane to pick them up and take them to Yanina in Greece, which was still in British hands. They sat for some time in Nikshitch, which is a pleasant little stone town set among mulberry trees on a fertile plateau encircled by bare mountains; but the plane did not come, and it was found impossible to communicate with any other Yugoslavian airfield. The Germans had now seized them all. There was nothing to do but take one of the planes which was already on the airfield; and these were all Italian Marchettis. If they took one of these, they would inevitably be attacked by any British plane or anti-aircraft battery which saw them approaching; and it would be impossible to send a message to Yanina by radio lest it should be intercepted by the Germans. They sent a plane ahead of them, but had to start without knowing whether it had got through. The journey was made safely, but only owing to a singular piece of good fortune. As the plane came to Yanina, a swarm of fighters rose up around it, and the pilot, in an effort to convey that this was not an enemy craft, dropped some signals at random. It happened that the British authorities had sent them a message, which they had not received, telling them to declare their identity by dropping almost exactly the combination of signals which the pilot had picked by chance.

From Yanina the King flew to Jerusalem, whence the falcon had flown to Kossovo with the message from the Mother of God. There he was joined by General Simovitch and some of his Ministers, who also had flown from Nikshitch. Two others were shot down during their flight; and some, including Matchek, were trapped in their homes and are in prison. Later the King and his Ministers flew out of Asia across Africa to Lisbon, and then to London, where they now await peace and the reconstitution of their state. They have come to the West not as unfortunate petitioners but as benefactors; for the resistance they had made against Germany had given Great Britain a valuable respite. The Germans, it is now known, had meant to use their forces in Bulgaria not against Yugoslavia but against Turkey, as a preliminary step to an attack on Russia. This step should have been taken in March, to coincide with the *coup d'état* of Raschid Ali in Iraq and the German penetration of Syria, and Russia should have been attacked in May by an enemy which already held the subjugated Near East. But the unexpected resistance of Yugoslavia diverted the German forces in Bulgaria from East to West, and prolonged the German advance through Greece until the *coup d'état* in Iraq had been suppressed and the English preparations for the invasion of Syria were well under way. Thus the attack on Russia was postponed for a month, and then had to be a frontal attack, delivered without the advantages Germany would have derived from the subjugation of the Near East. The South Slavs had achieved another stage in their paradoxical destiny. They who were among the last to accept Christianity are the last to preserve it in the morning strength of its magic. They who were among the last to achieve order and gentleness are the last legatees of the Byzantine Empire in its law and magnificence. In this war, as in the one before it, they have made out of their defeats great victories, which have preserved the powerful empires that were their allies from the shame of becoming weak like themselves. Now, in this hour when their King is in exile and their hearths are defiled by swine, their state seems as a rock in a shifting world; and all over Europe the sorrowful find comfort in thinking on their history, though it passes from woe to woe. For the news that Hitler had been defied by Yugoslavia travelled like sunshine over the countries which he had devoured and humiliated, promising spring. In Marseille some people picked flowers from their gardens and others ordered wreaths from the florists, and they carried them down to the Cannebière. The police guessed what they meant to do, and would not let them go along the street. But there were trams passing by, and they boarded them. The tramdrivers drove very slowly, and the people were able to throw down their flowers on the spot where King Alexander of Yugoslavia had been killed.

Bibliography

Bibliographical Note

I do not propose to give a complete list of the sources I have consulted for the purposes of these volumes, for two reasons.

One is the consideration of space. So many issues are raised by any study of the Balkans that the student has to cast his nets far and wide. To gain any insight into the South Slav mind it is necessary to have a clear picture of both the Byzantine Empire and its legacy to the modern world. I have therefore consulted Gibbon, Bury, Norman Baynes, G. P. Baker, C. Chapman, Stephen Runciman, Diehl, Schlumberger, Iorga, and others, for enlightenment on the first of these subjects, and Dean Stanley, Neale, Adeney, Hore, Harnack, R. Janin, d'Herbigny, Battifol, Salaville, Arsenev, Berdyaev, Darzad, and others, for enlightenment on the other. But many of these writers deal with material only indirectly connected with the Balkans, and the citation of them would confuse and irritate any reader who tried too quickly to trace the connection. To take but one example, I have found Mr L. G. Browne's *The Eclipse of Christianity in Asia* invaluable; but only because his exposition of how Christianity was forgotten in Asia opened my eyes to the process by which it was preserved in the Balkans. In the same way, I have found that nearly all books I have read about the Austrian or Ottoman Empire have proved useful; but a list of them would not disclose the reason why. I have also hesitated to burden these pages with references that would be at once unimportant and obvious. There are a few paragraphs in this book which refer to Mithraism; the authorities to which I referred were, inevitably, Cumont, and the *Cambridge Ancient History*. In such cases, where few would want to follow such a by-path, and full directions could be found in any library catalogue, I have let the matter go.

The other reason for curtailing the list is the peculiar character of the literature which deals with the Balkans. A large proportion of it is propaganda bought and paid for by the great powers. An even larger proportion represents a sour controversy between birds of two different feathers, persons who do not like oppression and cruelty and persons who do, both content to beat their wings in the empyrean of ignorance. I have deliberately omitted from this book all but the briefest mention of the battle over the 'Eastern question' which raged in nineteenth-century England. I have wanted to give a picture of the reality of South Slav life; and the picture of Turkey in Europe given by the English controversialists was usually entirely subjective. It is to be hoped that some expert historian will at some future date deal with this curious example of the difficulty humanity experiences in acquiring information about itself. When whole periods have been seduced into such fantasies, it is only to be expected that individual authors have succumbed.

Hence there are a number of books I have consulted which I have omitted from my bibliography because I could not conscientiously mention them without comment so adverse as to be libellous. Under this head falls the work of a writer universally recognized as an authority on the Balkans. I trust that the publication of this book still leaves me in a position to say that a major inaccuracy on every page seems to me too many; and besides inaccuracies that spring from a desire to exalt one Balkan race above another this author commits many which are due simply to disregard for fact. It is hard to forgive a writer who includes in the same volume a panegyric on a certain eighteenth-century Balkan ruler and a polemic against him, written under the delusion that he was two different persons. There are several other authors whom I have rejected on similar counts.

Other writers I have rejected, who, though not so inaccurate by nature, repeat inaccuracies which have been invented by others for political motives. There is, for example, a persistent legend that the Sarajevo *attentat* was planned and executed with the connivance of the Russian General Staff, through the instrumentality of 'Apis' and the Russian Military Attaché in Belgrade, General Artamanoff. This Russian complicity is alleged in Herr In der Mauer's *Die Jugoslavie einst und jetzt* (Johannes Günther Verlag, Leipzig und Wien, 1936); and Mr M. W. Fodor, the respected Hungarian writer, in *South of Hitler* (Allen & Unwin, 1938) states, 'With the cognisance of the Russian General Staff (with whom Dombrievitch was in contact through the medium of the Russian Military Attaché, General Artamanoff) the murder of the Archduke was carried out on June 28, 1914.' I have asked Mr Fodor for the evidence for his statement, but he only replied that 'these facts were generally known.' But no eye witness has come forward and no document has ever been found that bears out this theory; and I understand that the Bolsheviks, with a free run of the relevant archives, have never discovered an atom of evidence in support of it. The time element, as Professor Seton-Watson has pointed out in his *Sarajevo*, makes it highly improbable. I leave readers to judge if the Russian General Staff, or 'Apis,' when attempting to involve the Russian General Staff in a European war, would have relied on the naïve group of conspirators Mr Stephen Graham has described with such admirable accuracy in *St. Vitus' Day*. But nonsense like this Russian legend is scattered through a great many books, particularly if the writer is of Austrian or German origin. A conspicuous recent example is Otto Strasser's *A History of My Own Times*, all of whose references to Balkan history are wildly inaccurate. A particularly absurd passage accuses on the most grotesque grounds the late Svetozar Privitchevitch of complicity in the Sarajevo *attentat*. Professor Gilbert Murray or Mr Justice Frankfurter would not be a less likely criminal.

The following works are those which I think the reader will find the most directly relevant among those I have consulted for the purposes of this work:

The History of the Decline and Fall of the Roman Empire by E. Gibbon. London, 1896.

The History of the Roman Empire (1893)
The History of the Later Roman Empire (1889) ⎱ by J. B. Bury
The History of the Eastern Roman Empire (1912) ⎰
Cambridge Ancient History, Volume XII

Les Invasions Barbares by Ferdinand Lot. Payot, 1937. (An exposition of highly important material, absolutely necessary to the understanding of modern European history.)

History of the Byzantine Empire by A. A. Vasilev. University of Wisconsin, 1928. (This is faintly tinted with a Russian pro-Bulgarian bias, which, with Slav persistence, is brought to bear on events now remote by centuries.)

Histoire de Constantinople jusqu'à la fin de l'empire, Tr. sur les Originals grecs de Monsieur Cousin. (4 vols.) 1672–4. (It is time some British scholar imitated this enterprise, which is an extraordinary feat. It translates the histories of Agathias, Anna Comnena, Cantacuzenus, Ducas, Leo, Menander, St Nicephorus, Nicephorus Bryennius, Nicetas, Pachymeres, Procopius, Theophylactus Simocatta.)

Byzantine Civilisation by Steven Runciman. Arnold, 1933; Longmans, 1933. (An admirable study.)

The Byzantine Achievement by Robert Byron. Routledge, 1929; Knopf, 1929. (The author, whose death by enemy action all his friends and readers must deplore, wrote this when he was under twenty-five, and it is a remarkable effort. It forms a wholesome corrective to the nonsense that used to be talked about the decadence of Byzantium.)

La Civilisation serbe au moyen âge by Konstantin Jirechek, tr. 1920. (A brief work of the greatest importance.)

Geschichte der Serbei by Konstantin Jirechek. Gotha, 1911–18

Christianity in the Balkans by M. Spinka. The American Society of Church History, 1933. (This is a work of considerable historical importance, covering ground till now neglected.)

Cambridge Medieval History, Vol. IV. (Very poor. Although it was planned by Professor Bury, the level of the whole volume is disappointing. But it gathers the facts, or rather approximations of the facts, in a single volume, and can be used as a basis for further study.)

The Servian People by Prince and Princess Lazarovitch Hrbelianovitch. T. Werner Laurie, 1914. (This book is artless in appearance, but is actually extremely able.)

History of Serbia by H. W. Temperley. G. Bell, 1917. (A very useful book.)

Serbia by L. F. Waring. Home University Library, 1917

Serbia of the Serbians by Cheddo Miyatovitch. Pitman, 1915

History of Servia and the Servian Revolution by Leopold von Ranke, Tr. Mrs A. Kerr.

The Lives of the Serbian Saints by Voyeslav Yanitch and C. Patrick Hankey. Macmillan, New York, 1921

Kossovo; a translation of the heroic songs of the Serbs by Helen Rootham. Blackwell, 1920

The Ballads of Marko Kralyevitch by D. H. Lowe. Cambridge University Press, 1922

Yugoslav Popular Ballads by Dragutin Subotitch. Cambridge University

Press, 1932

L'Histoire de Dalmatie by L. de Voinovitch (–1918). Hachette, 1934. (A brilliant study.)

Dalmatia, the Quarnero and Istria, with Cettinje and the Isle of Grado by Sir T. G. Jackson. Oxford, 1887. (A classic work to be read by everyone about to visit Dalmatia, both for its historical and its architectural studies.)

Mémoires du duc de Raguse (le maréchal Marmont).

Geschichte von Venedig: I.*Band bis zum Tode Enrico Dandalos*, Gotha, 1905; II.*Band, Die Blüte bis 1516*, Gotha, 1920; III.*Band, der Niedergang*, Stuttgart, 1934, by H. Kretschmayr.

Travels in Dalmatia and Montenegro; History of Dalmatia by Sir Gardner Wilkinson, 1848

Architecture of Diocletian's Palace at Spalato by Robert Adam

Through Bosnia and Herzegovina on Foot during the Insurrection, 1875, with Historical Review of Bosnia, etc., 1876 by Sir Arthur Evans. Longman

Travels in the Slavonic Provinces of Turkey in Europe by Miss Muir Mackenzie and Miss Irby. Bell & Daldy, 1867 (This is an admirable work, indispensable to the student of the Balkans.)

Turkey in Europe by Sir Charles Eliot under the pseudonym 'Odysseus.' (A key work. Sir Charles Eliot was one of the finest minds of his time, and a writer of beautiful and restrained prose. It must, however, be remembered that at the end of his life he became a Buddhist, and an inability to appreciate the Christian contribution to civilisation affects his view of the Turkish invasion.)

Sarajevo by R. W. Seton-Watson. Hutchinson, 1927. (An admirable work, which ought to be read by those who have swallowed whole Professor B. Sidney Fay's *Origins of the World War*. Macmillan, 1928; revised 1931. Professor Fay's bias can be judged by the fact that he contributed a preface to the English edition of *Apis und Este*, the first novel of Bruno Brehm's venomous anti-Slav trilogy.)

L'Attentat de Sarajevo by Albert Mousset. Payot, 1930 (The report of the trial.)

St. Vitus' Day by Stephen Graham. Benn, 1930; Appleton, 1931. (An account, fictional in appearance, but faithful to fact, of the Sarajevo conspirators.)

La Serbie d'hier et de demain by N. Stoyanovitch, 1917

La Crise bosniaque (1908–9), 2 vols., by M. Nintchitch. Alfred Costes, 1937

The Annexation of Bosnia by Bernadotte Schmitt. Cambridge, 1937

The Great Powers and the Balkans (1875–78) by M. D. Stoyanovitch. Cambridge University Press, 1938

A Royal Tragedy by Cheddo Miyatovitch

The Southern Slav Question and the Hapsburg Monarchy by R. W. Seton-Watson, 1911

The Hapsburg Monarchy by H. Wickham Steed. Constable, 1913

The Reign of the Emperor Franz Josef by Karl Tschuppik. G. Bell, 1930.

(Published in America as *Francis Joseph I; the Downfall of an Empire* by Karl Tschuppik. Harcourt, 1930.)

Letzte Jahrzehnte einer Grossmacht by R. Sieghart, 1932

Aus Meiner Dienstzeit by Field-Marshal Conrad von Hötzendorf

Franz Ferdinand, Erzherzog by T. von Sosnosky, 1920

Das Ende der Dynastie Obrenovitch by P. F. Bresnitz, 1899. (Written by a rogue called Georgevitch, who was at one time Prime Minister of Serbia. A fascinating piece of scoundrelism.)

The Servian Tragedy, with impressions of Macedonia by Herbert Vivian, 1904

Macedonia, Its Races and Their Future by H. N. Brailsford, 1906

The Serbs, Guardians of the Gates by R. G. Laffan. Oxford, 1918

The Birth of Yugoslavia by Henry Baerlein. Parsons, 1922

Alexander of Yugoslavia by Stephen Graham. Cassell, 1938; Yale University Press, 1939

The Native's Return by Louis Adamic. Gollancz, 1934; Harper, 1934. (A study by a Slovene who had emigrated to America. It is written from the Communist point of view of that date, and is lively and interesting, particularly in passages that relate to Slovenia. But the picture of the country as a whole is over-simplified, and, oddly enough, although strongly pro-Croat greatly irritated the Croats by what they thought to be its expatriate, non-Slav attitude.)

Balkan Holiday by David Footman. Heinemann, 1935; Ryerson Press, 1935. (This is an entertaining travel book, designed to amuse, but it is full of knowledge and good sense.)

L'Itinéraire de Yougoslavie by A. T'Serstevens. Grasset, 1938

Profane Pilgrimage by L. Fielding Edwards. Duckworth, 1938

A Wayfarer in Yugoslavia by L. Fielding Edwards. Methuen, 1939; McBride, 1939

Undeclared War by Elizabeth Wiskemann. Constable, 1939. (A very able presentation of the situation of Yugoslavia immediately before the war.)

Living Space by Stoyan Pribitchevitch. Heinemann, 1940. (Published in America as *World without End* by P. B. Stoyan [Stoyan Pribitchevitch]. Reynal, 1939.) (One of the most useful books written in late years. It is a survey of the Balkans, with particular reference to the Yugoslavs, by a young Liberal, the son of Svetozar Pribitchevitch, whom King Alexander drove into exile.)

The Soul of Yugoslavia by H. D. Harrison. Hodder & Stoughton, 1941. (I include this because it is a work full of information by a reliable journalist who was a resident for some years in Belgrade, but it appeared too late for me to consult it.)

Much of the material for this book I have derived from conversations with individual Yugoslavs, either during this journey or during a later and longer visit. Some of these conversations I have reproduced, and some I have not, either because the information imparted was of more interest than the way it was imparted, or for reasons of discretion. I would, for example, like to reproduce the testimony of the officer to whom Tankositch said, at a time when it cannot have seemed specially advisable to make that statement, 'We told nobody about the young men from Sarajevo, nobody at all'; but he detested the deed, and would greatly have disliked his involuntary association with it to be disclosed. I have therefore allowed his information to colour my views without defining it. But I had hoped to acknowledge the help of all these friends. This is, however, not possible at present. All the people I mention in this book are now either dead or living in a state of misery as yet impossible for us to the West to imagine. Not one of them, except Gerda and the yellow-haired monk in Dechani, can have escaped. If I were to name any of my friends this might add a last extravagance to their sufferings.

I would like to express my gratitude for help in the preparation of this book to His Excellence, the Yugoslav Minister, Dr Soubbotich, and his wife, Dr Anna Soubbotich; to Dr Dragutin Subotitch of the School of Slavonic Studies; to Miss Vera Javarek; to Mrs Catherine Brown—a very heavy debt, this; to Miss Elizabeth Wiskemann; to Mr Jan Boissevain; Mr David Footman; to Mr Peter Brown; to Mrs Rudoi; and to Greta Wood. I cannot find the words to convey what I owe to Margaret Hodges, who has typed most of the manuscript, read the proofs, and enabled me to get the book to the press in spite of the distraction caused by a long and incapacitating illness.

As for my husband, Henry Andrews, it is true that whatever is best in this book is his, and that during the years of its writing he never flagged in his desire to relieve me of all the drudgery he could take on his shoulders. The maps and photographs have been his special care. But most of all I thank him for the patience with which he watched me as I engaged on what seemed till very recently the curiously gratuitous labour of taking an inventory of a foreign country. It took great faith, for which I am most grateful.

Index